INTRODUCTION TO SOCIOLOGY

SIXTH EDITION

Anthony Giddens
LONDON SCHOOL OF ECONOMICS

Mitchell Duneier
CITY UNIVERSITY OF NEW YORK
GRADUATE CENTER

PRINCETON UNIVERSITY

Richard P. Appelbaum
UNIVERSITY OF CALIFORNIA,
SANTA BARBARA

Editor: Karl Bakeman
E-media editor: Denise Shanks
Project editor: Lory A. Frenkel
Photo research: Stephanie Romeo
Page layout: Brad Walrod/High Text Graphics, Inc.
Composition: GGS Book Services, Atlantic Highlands
Manufacturing: The Courier Companies—Kendallville
Book design: Rubina Yeh
Production manager: Benjamin Reynolds
Editorial assistant: Rebecca Arata

Library of Congress Cataloging-in-Publication Data

Giddens, Anthony.
    Introduction to sociology / Anthony Giddens, Mitchell Duneier, Richard P. Appelbaum.—6th ed.
        p. cm.
    Includes bibliographical references.
    ISBN-13: 978-0-393-92921-8 (pbk.)
    ISBN-10: 0-393-92921-3 (pbk.)
    1. Sociology.   I. Duneier, Mitchell.   II. Appelbaum, Richard P.   III. Title.

HM585.G53 2007
301—dc22   2006046883

W. W. Norton & Company, Inc., 500 Fifth Avenue, New York, N.Y. 10110 www.wwnorton.com

W. W. Norton & Company Ltd., Castle House, 75/76 Wells Street, London W1T 3QT

1 2 3 4 5 6 7 8 9 0

W. W. Norton & Company has been independent since its founding in 1923, when William Warder Norton and Mary D. Herter Norton first published lectures delivered at the People's Institute, the adult education division of New York City's Cooper Union. The Nortons soon expanded their program beyond the Institute, publishing books by celebrated academics from America and abroad. By mid-century, the two major pillars of Norton's publishing program—trade books and college texts—were firmly established. In the 1950s, the Norton family transferred control of the company to its employees, and today—with a staff of four hundred and a comparable number of trade, college, and professional titles published each year—W. W. Norton & Company stands as the largest and oldest publishing house owned wholly by its employees.

INTRODUCTION TO
SOCIOLOGY

SIXTH EDITION

W. W. Norton & Company, Inc.
New York • London

CONTENTS

Part Two: The Individual and Society 53

Chapter 6: Groups, Networks, and Organizations 139

Chapter 7: Conformity, Deviance, and Crime 177

Part Three: Structures of Power 213

Chapter 8: Stratification, Class, and Inequality 215

Chapter 9: Global Inequality 259

Chapter 10: Gender Inequality 291

Chapter 11: Ethnicity and Race 329

Chapter 12: Aging 367

Chapter 13: Government, Political Power, and Social Movements 391

Part Four: Social Institutions 435

Part Five: Social Change in the Modern World 575

This book was written in the belief that sociology has a key role to play in modern intellectual culture and a central place within the social sciences. Our aim has been to write a book that combines some originality with an analysis of the basic issues that interest sociologists today. In some places, we attempt to bring the reader into a subject through the use of ethnographies written for this book. The book does not try to introduce overly sophisticated notions; nevertheless, ideas and findings drawn from the cutting edge of the discipline are incorporated throughout. We hope it is not a partisan treatment; we endeavored to cover the major perspectives in sociology and the major findings of contemporary American research in an evenhanded, although not indiscriminate, way.

Major Themes

The book is constructed around a number of basic themes, each of which helps give the work a distinctive character. The newest theme is *public sociology,* reflected in a series of boxes inspired by the 2004 annual meeting of the American Sociological Association. At this meeting, Michael Burawoy's path-breaking presidential address called for the discipline to draw on the insights and methods of sociology to involve ordinary people in studying and solving the social problems that afflict them. The book features twenty boxes that profile sociologists engaged in public sociology in diverse arenas—for example, Columbia sociology professor Diane Vaughan's influential research on the *Challenger* shuttle disaster, which helped shape subsequent governmental investigations; Douglas Massey's testimony before the U.S. Congress on immigration policy, and William Bielby's path-breaking testimony as an expert witness in gender discrimination cases. These boxes do not simply celebrate public sociology, rather they seek to give students a nuanced sense of the benefits and burdens of the position of the discipline in the public realm. It is certainly our hope that the Public Sociology boxes will inspire students to draw on their sociological imaginations to become more publicly involved and will provide some useful ideas for instructors who wish to generate class projects that directly engage students in the real world. In his speech, Burawoy also emphasized that public sociology cannot exist without a professional sociology that develops a body of theoretical knowledge and empirical findings. The central task of the book is to explain what the discipline of sociology has to offer along these lines.

A second theme of the book is that of the *world in change.* Sociology was born of the transformations that wrenched the industrializing social order of the West away from the ways of life characteristic of earlier societies. The world created by these changes is the primary object of concern of sociological analysis. The pace of social change has continued to accelerate, and it is possible that we stand on the threshold of transitions as significant as those that occurred in the late eighteenth and nineteenth centuries. Sociology has prime responsibility for charting the transformations of the past and for grasping the major lines of development taking place today.

Another fundamental theme of the book is the *globalizing of social life.* For far too long, sociology has been dominated by the view that societies can be studied as independent entities. But even in the past, societies never really existed in isolation. In current times, we can see a clear acceleration in processes of global integration. This is obvious, for example, in the expansion of international trade across the world. The emphasis on globalization also connects closely with the weight given to the interdependence of the industrialized and developing worlds today.

The book also focuses on the importance of *comparative* study. Sociology cannot be taught solely by understanding the institutions of any one particular society. Although we have slanted the discussion toward the United States, we have also balanced it with a rich variety of materials drawn from other cultures. These include research carried out in other Western countries as well as in Russia and eastern European societies, which are currently undergoing substantial changes. The book also includes much more material on developing countries than has been usual in introductory texts. In addition, we strongly emphasize the relationship between sociology and anthropology, whose concerns overlap comprehensively. Given the close connections that now mesh societies across the world, and the virtual disappearance of traditional social systems, sociology and anthropology have increasingly become indistinguishable.

A fifth theme is the necessity of taking a *historical approach* to sociology. This involves more than just filling in the historical context within which events occur. One of the most important developments in sociology over the past few years has been an increasing emphasis on historical analysis. This should be understood not solely as applying a sociological outlook to the past but as a way of contributing to our understanding of institutions in the present. Recent work in historical sociology is discussed throughout the text and provides a framework for the interpretations offered in the chapters.

Throughout the text, particular attention is given to *issues of gender*. The study of gender is ordinarily regarded as a specific field within sociology as a whole—and this volume contains a chapter that specifically explores thinking and research on the subject (Chapter 10). However, questions about gender relations are so fundamental to sociological analysis that they cannot simply be considered a subdivision. Thus many chapters contain sections concerned with issues of gender.

A seventh theme is the *micro and macro link*. At many points in the book, we show that interaction in micro-level contexts affects larger social processes and that such macro-level processes influence our day-to-day lives. We emphasize that one can better understand a social situation by analyzing it at both the micro and macro levels.

The final major theme is the relation between the *social* and the *personal*. Sociological thinking is a vital help to self-understanding, which in turn can be focused back on an improved understanding of the social world. Studying sociology should be a liberating experience: The field enlarges our sympathies and imagination, opens up new perspectives on the sources of our own behavior, and creates an awareness of cultural settings different from our own. Insofar as sociological ideas challenge dogma, teach appreciation of cultural variety, and allow us insight into the working of social institutions, the practice of sociology enhances the possibilities of human freedom.

All of the chapters in the book have been updated and revised to reflect the most recent available data. In addition, four chapters have received special attention: Chapter 8 ("Stratification, Class, and Inequality") now begins with research on peer group competition, status groups, and consumerism among high school students. It includes new material on executive pay, the working poor and poverty, and the most recent trends in inequality in the United States. Chapter 15 ("Families and Intimate Relationships") includes significant new material on the role of the family in maintaining and perpetuating social inequality in the United States, a new extended discussion of recent research on why many poor women have children without getting married, and a discussion of recent literature on divorce. Chapter 19 ("Urbanization, Population, and the Environment") now begins with a new section on Hurricane Katrina, which culminates in a new extended section on the history and meaning of ghettos. Chapter 20 ("Globalization in a Changing World") has been largely rewritten and now includes substantial discussions of why some societies thrive while others fail. The relative importance of environment, culture, technology (including the most recent breakthroughs in nanotechnology), the modern state, and religion in social change are also thoroughly examined. Finally, the debate over whether globalization is novel or not is revisited and updated.

Organization

There is little abstract discussion of basic sociological concepts at the beginning of this book. Instead, concepts are explained when they are introduced in the relevant chapters, and we have sought to illustrate them by means of concrete examples. Although these examples are usually taken from sociological research, we have also used material from other sources (such as newspaper articles). We have tried to keep the writing style as simple and direct as possible, while endeavoring to make the book lively and full of surprises.

The chapters follow a sequence designed to help achieve a progressive mastery of the different fields of sociology, but we have taken care to ensure that the book can be used flexibly and is easy to adapt to the needs of individual courses. Chapters can be deleted or studied in a different order without much loss. Each has been written as a fairly autonomous unit, with cross-referencing to other chapters at relevant points.

Study Aids

The pedagogy in this book has been completely reconfigured for the Sixth Edition to facilitate critical thinking and reinforce important concepts. Each chapter begins with a chapter organizer, which highlights the learning objectives of each section and allows students to preview that chapter's discussion. This edition of *Introduction to Sociology* includes significantly expanded chapter review material, including keyword and concept-review questions and data exercises linking material in the text to real-world data on the Web.

Another helpful aid is the use of a globe icon to indicate examples of the changing world, the globalization process, or comparisons of U.S. society with other societies. Social change, the globalization of social life, and comparative analysis are all important themes of this text. The icon alerts readers to discussions of these themes.

Further Research: Reading and Libraries

Libraries contain abundant sources of information that can be used to follow up or expand on issues discussed here. References are given throughout the text and are listed fully in the bibliography at the end. We have also included a short appendix that provides a guide to library resources and how to use them.

Acknowledgments

During the writing of all six editions of this book, many individuals offered comments and advice on particular chapters and, in some cases, large parts of the text. They helped us see issues in a different light, clarified some difficult points, and allowed us to take advantage of their specialist knowledge in their respective fields. We are deeply indebted to them. Special thanks go to Nick Ehrman for researching and writing fifteen outstanding new boxes on public sociology; Joe Conti, who worked assiduously to help us update data throughout the book, and contributed significantly to the editing process; and Todd Beer for his terrific work drafting questions for each of the book's figures.

William Danaher, College of Charleston
Lynda Dickinson, University of Colorado–Colorado Springs
Dennis Downey, University of Utah
Leslie Gates, SUNY–Binghamton
Bonita Harold, University of Arkansas
Rudolph Harris, Des Moines Area Community College
Hua-Lun Huang, University of Louisiana–Lafayette
Kristin Marsh, University of Mary Washington
Richard Miller, Missouri Southern State University
Paul Min, Texas A&M University
Rekha Mirchandani, Bowling Green State University
Adam Rafalovich, Texas Tech University
Lesley Williams Reid, Georgia State University
Robyn Rodriguez, Rutgers, The State University of New Jersey
Hasan Shahpari, Villanova University
William Snizek, Virginia Tech
Teresa Sobieszczyk, University of Montana
Terrence Jonathan Stewart, Charles Stewart Mott Community College
Joyce Tang, Queens College
John Toth, Hendrix College
Mary Paula Walsh, Montgomery College
Stephani Williams, Arizona State University
Rowan Wolf, Portland Community College

We would like to thank the numerous readers of the text who have written with comments, criticisms, and suggestions for improvements. We have adopted many of their recommendations in this new edition.

We have many others to thank as well. We are especially grateful to Candace Levy, who did a marvelous job of copyediting the book and offered numerous suggestions for alterations and improvements that have contributed in important ways to the final form of the volume. We are also extremely grateful to project editor Lory Frenkel, production manager Ben Reynolds, and editorial assistant Rebecca Arata for managing the myriad details involved in producing this book. Denise Shanks, our electronic media editor, deserves special thanks for creating the elegant new website to accompany the book. Finally, Stephanie Romeo showed unusual flair and originality in the selections made for illustrating the book.

We are also grateful to our editors at Norton, Steve Dunn, Melea Seward, and Karl Bakeman, who have made many direct contributions to the various chapters, and have ensured that we have made reference to the very latest research. We would also like to register our thanks to a number of graduate students whose contributions have proved invaluable: Deborah Carr, Wendy Carter, Neil Gross, Blackhawk Hancock, Paul LePore, Alair MacLean, Ann Meier, Susan Munkres, Josh Rossol, Sharmila Rudrappa, Christopher Wildeman, David Yamane and Katherina Zippel.

PART ONE

THE STUDY
OF SOCIOLOGY

We live in a world today that is increasingly more complex. Why are the conditions of our lives so different from those of earlier times? How will our lives change in the future? These are the types of questions that lead us to the study of sociology. Throughout your reading of this text, you will encounter examples from different people's lives that will help us answer these important questions.

In Chapter 1, we begin to explore the scope of sociology and learn what sort of insights the field can bring to our lives. Among these insights are the development of a global perspective and an understanding of social change. Sociology is not a subject with a body of theories everyone agrees on. As in any complex field, the questions we raise allow for different answers. In this chapter, we compare and contrast differing theoretical traditions.

Chapter 2 is an exploration of the tools of the trade and how sociologists set about doing research. A number of basic methods of investigation are available to help us find out what is going on in the social world. We must be sure that the information on which sociological reasoning is based is as reliable and accurate as possible. The chapter examines the problems encountered when gathering such information and indicates how they are best dealt with.

Developing a Sociological Perspective

Learn what sociology covers as a field and how everyday topics like love and romance are shaped by social and historical forces.

Recognize that sociology is more than just acquiring knowledge; it also involves developing a sociological imagination. Learn that studying sociology leads us to see that we construct society through our actions and are constructed by it. Understand that two of the most important components of the sociological imagination are developing a global perspective and understanding social change.

The Development of Sociological Thinking

Learn how sociology originated and how it developed. Think about the theoretical issues that frame the study of sociology. Be able to name some of the leading social theorists and the concepts they contributed to the study of sociology. Learn the different theoretical approaches modern sociologists bring to the field.

Is Sociology a Science?

Learn how sociology is similar to and different from natural sciences.

How Can Sociology Help Us in Our Lives?

See the practical implications that sociology has for our lives.

CHAPTER ONE

WHAT IS SOCIOLOGY?

from the tragic terrorist attacks on the World Trade Center and the Pentagon to the mass murder at Columbine High School in Littleton, Colorado, the world today is intensely worrying, but full of the most extraordinary promise for the future. It is a world awash with change, marked by deep conflicts, tensions, and social divisions as well as by the destructive onslaught of modern technology on the natural environment. Yet we have possibilities of controlling our destiny and shaping our lives for the better that would have been unimaginable to earlier generations.

How did this world come about? Why are our conditions of life so different from those of our parents and grandparents? What directions will change take in the future? These questions are the prime concern of sociology, a field of study that consequently has a fundamental role to play in modern intellectual life.

Sociology is the scientific study of human social life, groups, and societies. It is a dazzling and compelling enterprise because its subject matter is our own behavior as social beings. The scope of sociological study is extremely wide, ranging from the analysis of passing encounters between individuals on the sidewalk to the investigation of global social processes such as the rise of Islamic fundamentalism. A brief example will provide an initial taste of the nature and objectives of sociology.

Have you ever been in love? Almost certainly you have. Most people who are in their teens or older know what being in love is like. Love and romance provide, for many of us, some of the most intense feelings we ever experience. Why do people fall in love? The answer at first sight seems obvious. Love expresses a mutual physical and personal attachment two individuals feel for one another. These days, we might be skeptical of the idea that love is "forever"; but falling in love, we tend to think, is an experience arising from universal human emotions. It seems natural for a couple who fall in love to want personal and sexual fulfillment in their relationship, perhaps in the form of marriage.

Yet this situation, which seems so self-evident to us today, is in fact very unusual. Falling in love is *not* an experience most people across the world have—and where it does happen, it is rarely thought of as having any connection to marriage. The idea of romantic love did not become widespread until fairly recently in our society and has never even existed in most other cultures.

Only in modern times have love and sexuality come to be seen as closely connected. In the Middle Ages and for centuries afterward, men and women married mainly to keep property in the hands of the family or to raise children to work the family farm. Once married, they may have become close companions; this happened after marriage, however, rather than before. People sometimes had sexual affairs outside marriage, but these inspired few of the emotions we associate with love. Romantic love was regarded at best as a weakness and at worst as a kind of sickness.

Romantic love first made its appearance in courtly circles as a characteristic of extramarital sexual adventures indulged in by members of the aristocracy. Until about two centuries ago, it was wholly confined to such circles and kept specifically separate from marriage. Relations between husband and wife among aristocratic groups were often cool and distant—certainly compared to our expectations of marriage today. The wealthy lived in large houses, each spouse having his or her own bedroom and servants; they may rarely have seen each other in private. Sexual compatibility was a matter of chance and was not considered relevant to marriage. Among both rich and poor, the decision of whom to marry was made by family and kin, not by the individuals concerned, who had little or no say in the matter.

This remains true in many non-Western countries today. In Afghanistan under the rule of the Taliban, where Islam underwent a major revival and became the basis of an important political movement, men were prohibited from speaking to women they were not related or married to, and marriages were arranged by parents. If a girl and boy were seen by authorities to be speaking with one another, they would be whipped so severely that one or both of them could be left seriously injured, if not dead. The ruling Taliban government saw romantic love as deeply offensive, so much so that one of its first acts as a new power in 1996 was to outlaw music and films.

Like many in the non-Western world, the ruling Taliban believed Afghanistan was being inundated by Hollywood movies and American rock music and videos, filled as they are with sexual images. Osama bin Laden launched his terrorist attacks against the United States from Afghanistan, and the rhetoric of his followers has partly been aimed at criticizing such kinds of Western influences.

It is not only in those sections of the world where Islamic fundamentalism has taken root that romantic love is considered unnatural. In India, for example, the vast majority of marriages are arranged by parents or other relatives. The opinions of prospective marriage partners are quite often—but by no means always—taken into account. A study of marriage in Kerala, a state in India, showed that just over half the young people thought that meeting the prospective spouse before marriage was relevant to marital happiness. Among parents, only 1 percent was willing to let their children choose their own marriage partners. Romantic love is recognized to exist there, but it is equated with temporary infatuation or actually seen as a barrier to a happy marriage.

Neither romantic love, then, nor its association with marriage can be understood as a natural feature of human life. Rather, such love has been shaped by broad social and historical influences. These are the influences sociologists study.

Most of us see the world in terms of the familiar features of our own lives. Sociology demonstrates the need to take a much broader view of why we are as we are and why we act as we do. It teaches us that what we regard as inevitable, good, or true may not be such and that the "natural" in our life is strongly influenced by historical and social forces. Understanding the subtle yet complex and profound ways in which our individual lives reflect the contexts of our social experience is basic to the sociological outlook.

Developing a Sociological Perspective

In the aftermath of the attack by suicide terrorists on the World Trade Center and the Pentagon on September 11, 2001, many Americans asked themselves how such an event could have occurred and why anyone would want to carry it out. You undoubtedly encountered many explanations for this event in the mass media, and some of the inescapable ones were sociological. The war that America and its allies have had to fight has not been merely against the country of Afghanistan, whose former Taliban government supported the terrorists. The war is also against groups, networks, and organizations that stretch around the world. A key sociological question has to do with how human beings coordinate their activities in groups, networks, and organizations. To understand how the World Trade Center and Pentagon attacks were possible, many analysts have focused on understanding the kinds of coordinated activity that culminated in the attack of September 11. Over time, they came to see that events of September 11 did not occur through the efforts of a loose network or group but were carried out by a single hierarchical organization whose leaders planned the attack, coordinated all the activities, and received financial support from Osama bin Laden.

One of the things we have seen in discussions of the September 11 attacks is that our lives are connected to other societies that extend around the world. The people who worked in the World Trade Center did not imagine that their lives had very much to do with events being coordinated in Afghanistan. They also might not have imagined that their lives would come to an end due to large-scale global processes that have drawn different societies into interrelation with one another. The world in which we live today makes us much more *interdependent* with others, even with those thousands of miles away, than people have ever been previously.

Likewise, in the aftermath of the 1999 mass murder at Columbine High School in Littleton, Colorado, many Americans asked themselves how and why two high school students could murder thirteen of their classmates and teachers and then take their own lives. One explanation focused on the social cliques at Columbine High, which divided into "jocks," "preps," "geeks," "goths," and other groups. It was well known that the two murderers, part of a group called the "Trenchcoat Mafia," were teased and embarrassed by their classmates, especially the jocks. It was also reported that the two teens were obsessed with the video game *Doom,* in which each player tries to make the most kills. Many saw this as the embodiment of American culture's glorification of violence. The police also investigated how the two killers procured the guns and bombs used in the massacre. Many commentators denounced the easy availability of these weapons in American society. Others saw the tragedy as a symbol of the emptiness of suburban life, where young people have few public places to go to socialize with others.

While explanations like these focus on the social causes of violence in the United States, sociology can provide an even deeper understanding of events such as mass murder. Sociology shows us the need to look beyond the surface of people's actions and study the social context to understand what happened. Sociology can also teach us to try to identify general patterns of behavior in particular individuals and to be systematic in explaining the social influences on these behavioral patterns (Berger, 1963). A sociologist must look at a wide array of evidence before accepting any single explanation. Thus a sociologist studying the Columbine High killings might study

In an image from airport surveillance tape, two men identified by authorities as suspected hijackers Mohammed Atta (*right*) and Abdulaziz Alomari (*center*) pass through airport security on September 11, 2001, at Portland International Jetport in Maine. The two men took a commuter flight to Boston before boarding American Airlines Flight 11, which was one of four jetliners hijacked on September 11 and one of two that were crashed into New York's World Trade Center.

other mass murders and look to see if there was a pattern in the group characteristics—such as social class, race, gender, age, or cultural background—of the murderers and victims. This might lead a sociologist to ask why mass murders like the one at Columbine High seem to be mostly the doing of young, middle-class, white men and then explain why this is the case (Patterson, 1999). In other words, a sociologist would not simply ask "What led these two students at Columbine High to commit mass murder?" but also "What social factors explain why mass murders have occurred in the United States?"

Another question sociologists ask is, "What holds society together?" When you think of it, the very existence of an orderly society is remarkable. Take as an example the use of anthrax to kill innocent citizens in the United States. Isn't it amazing how rarely such terrorism has been attempted in the United States? The existence of order in the country is something we have long taken for granted. When you think of it, though, living is partly an act of faith that order will be maintained from minute to minute in skyscrapers and on sidewalks and everywhere in between. It is the faith that incidents such as the bioterrorism of sending anthrax through the mail, or the September 11 attacks, or the acts of the Trenchcoat Mafia will be few. But though we must take this order for granted to live our lives, sociologists seek to understand how such order comes about. For the sociologist who wants to know how society is possible in the first place, the interesting question is not merely why someone sends anthrax through the mail or why someone shoots up a high school. It is, more important, why such acts happen so infrequently. Why are so many willing to

Three businessmen relax and chat over coffee. A group of workers on a hashish plantation smoke hash during a break. In both instances, the socially acceptable consumption of a drug serves as an occasion to socialize.

work together to maintain the social order? And isn't it unsettling that in a society where so many work to maintain this order, just nineteen hijackers or two high school students are capable of doing so much harm?

Learning to think sociologically—looking, in other words, at the broader view—means cultivating the imagination. As sociologists, we need to imagine, for example, what the experience of sex and marriage is like for people—the majority of humankind until recently—to whom ideals of romantic love appear alien or even absurd. Or we need to imagine what life was like for the victims and the murderers in the September 11 terrorist attacks and at Columbine High. Studying sociology *cannot* be just a routine process of acquiring knowledge. A sociologist is someone who is able to break free from the immediacy of personal circumstances and put things in a wider context. His or her work depends on what the American sociologist C. Wright Mills (1959b), in a famous phrase, called the **sociological imagination**.

The sociological imagination requires us, above all, to *"think ourselves away" from the familiar routines of our daily lives to look at them anew.* Consider the simple act of drinking a cup of coffee. What could we find to say, from a sociological point of view, about such an apparently uninteresting piece of behavior? An enormous amount. We could point out first of all that coffee is not just a refreshment. It possesses *symbolic value* as part of our day-to-day social activities (see "Globalization and Everyday Life: The Sociology of Coffee"). Often the ritual associated with coffee drinking is much more important than the act of consuming the drink itself. Two people who arrange to meet for coffee are probably more interested in getting together and chatting than in what they actually drink. Drinking and eating in all societies, in fact, provide occasions for social interaction and the enactment of rituals—and these offer a rich subject matter for sociological study.

Second, coffee is a *drug* containing caffeine, which has a stimulating effect on the brain. Coffee addicts are not regarded by most people in Western culture as drug users. Like alcohol, coffee is a socially acceptable drug, whereas marijuana, for instance, is not. Yet there are societies that tolerate the consumption of marijuana or even cocaine but frown on both coffee and alcohol. Sociologists are interested in why these contrasts exist.

Third, an individual who drinks a cup of coffee is caught up in a complicated set of *social and economic relationships* stretching across the world. The production, transport, and distribution of coffee require continuous transactions between people thousands of miles away from the coffee drinker. Studying such global transactions is an important task of sociology because many aspects of our lives are now affected by worldwide social influences and communications.

Finally, the act of sipping a cup of coffee presumes a whole process of *past social and economic development.* Along with other now-familiar items of Western diets—like tea, bananas, potatoes, and white sugar—coffee began to be widely consumed only in the late 1800s. Although the drink originated in the Middle East, its mass consumption dates from the period of Western colonial expansion about a century and a half ago. Virtually all the coffee we drink in Western countries today comes from areas (South America and Africa) that were colonized by Europeans; it is in no sense a "natural" part of the Western diet.

Studying Sociology

As individuals, we all know a great deal about ourselves and about the societies in which we live. We tend to think we have a good understanding of why we act as we do, without needing sociologists to tell us! And to some degree this is true. We do many of the things in our day-to-day lives because we understand the social requirements involved. Yet there are definite boundaries to such self-knowledge, and it is one of the main tasks of sociology to show us what these are.

The sociological imagination allows us to see that many events that seem to concern only the individual actually reflect larger social issues. Divorce, for instance, may be a very difficult process for someone who goes through it—what Mills calls a personal trouble. But divorce, he points out, is also a public issue in a society like the present-day United States, where over half of all marriages break up within ten years. Unemployment, to take another example, may be a personal tragedy for someone thrown out of a job and unable to find another. Yet it is much more than only a matter for private despair when millions of people in a society are in the same situation: It is a public issue expressing large social trends.

Try applying this sort of outlook to your own life. It isn't necessary to think of only troubling events. Consider, for instance, why you are turning the pages of this book at all—why you have decided to study sociology. You might be a reluctant sociology student, taking the course just to fulfill a requirement. Or you might be enthusiastic to find out more about the subject. Whatever your motivations, you are likely to have a good deal in common, without necessarily knowing it, with others studying sociology. Your private decision reflects your position in the wider society.

Do the following characteristics apply to you? Are you young? White? From a professional or white-collar background? Have you done, or do you still do, some part-time work to boost your income? Do you want to find a good job when you leave school but are not especially dedicated to studying? Do you not really know what sociology is but think it has something to do with how people behave in groups? More than three quarters of you will answer yes to all these questions. College students are not typical of the population as a whole but tend to be drawn from more privileged backgrounds. And their attitudes usually reflect those held by friends and acquaintances. The social backgrounds from which we come have a great deal to do with what kinds of decisions we think appropriate.

But suppose you answered no to one or more of these questions. You might come from a minority-group background or one of poverty. You may be someone in midlife or older. If so, however, further conclusions probably follow. You will likely have had to struggle to get where you are; you might have had to overcome hostile reactions from friends and others when you told them you were intending to go to college; or you might be combining school with full-time parenthood and/or work.

Although we are all influenced by the social contexts in which we find ourselves, none of us is simply *determined* in his or her behavior by those contexts. We possess, and create, our own individuality. It is the business of sociology to investigate the connections between *what society makes of us and what we make of ourselves.* Our activities both structure—give shape to—the social world around us and at the same time are structured *by* that social world.

The concept of **social structure** is an important one in sociology. It refers to the fact that the social contexts of our lives do not just consist of random assortments of events or actions but are structured, or *patterned,* in distinct ways. There are regularities in the ways we behave and in the relationships we have with one another. But social structure is not like a physical structure, such as a building, which exists independently of human actions. Human societies are always in the process of **structuration.** They are reconstructed at every moment by the very "building blocks" that compose them—human beings like you and me.

As an example, consider again the case of coffee. A cup of coffee does not automatically arrive in your hands. You choose, for example, to go to a particular café, whether to drink your coffee black or light, and so forth. As you make these decisions, along with millions of other people, you shape the market for coffee and affect the lives of coffee producers living perhaps thousands of miles away on the other side of the world.

"How would you like me to answer that question? As a member of my ethnic group, educational class, income group, or religious category?"

The Sociology of Coffee

The world drinks about 2.25 billion cups [of coffee] per day—the United States alone drinks one fifth of this. Coffee drinking is a cultural fixture that says as much about us as it does about the bean itself. Basically a habit forming stimulant, coffee is nonetheless associated with relaxation and sociability. In a society that combines buzzing overstimulation with soul-aching meaninglessness, coffee and its associated rituals are, for many of us, the lubricants that make it possible to go on.

Perhaps for this reason coffee occupies a distinctive niche in our cultural landscape. Along with alcohol, it is the only beverage to engender public houses devoted to its consumption. *** Uniquely, though, coffee is welcome in almost any situation, from the car to the boardroom, from the breakfast table to the public park, alone or in company of any kind. Since its adoption as a beverage, coffee has been offered as an antipode to alcohol—more so even than abstinence, perhaps in recognition of a human need for joyfully mood-altering substances and the convivial social interactions that go along with them.

Only a handful of consumer goods has fueled the passions of the public as much as coffee. *** [C]offee has inspired impassioned struggles on the battlefields of economics, human rights, politics, and religion, since its use first spread. Coffee

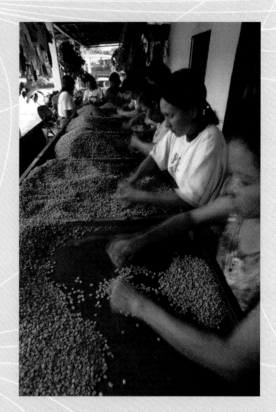

Developing a Global Perspective

As we just saw in our discussions of the terrorist attacks and of the sociological dimensions of drinking a cup of coffee, all our local actions—the ways in which we relate to one another in face-to-face contexts—form part of larger social settings that extend around the globe. These connections between the *local* and the *global* are quite new in human history. They have accelerated over the past thirty or forty years as a result of the dramatic advances in communications, information technology, and transportation. The development of jet planes; large, speedy container ships; and other means of fast travel has meant that people and goods can be continuously transported across the world. And our worldwide system of satellite communication, established only some thirty years ago, has made it possible for people to get in touch with each other instantaneously.

American society is influenced every moment of the day by **globalization,** the growth of world interdependence, a social phenomenon that will be discussed throughout this book. Globalization should not be thought of simply as the development of worldwide networks—social and economic systems that are remote from our individual concerns. It is a local phenomenon, too. For example, only a few years ago, when they dined out, most Americans were faced with a limited choice. In many U.S. towns and cities today, a single street might feature Italian, Chinese, Japanese, Thai, French, and other types of restaurants next door to each other. In turn, the dietary decisions we make are consequential for food producers who might live on the other side of the world. Another everyday aspect of global-may be a drink for sharing, but as a commodity it invites protectionism, oppression, and destruction. Its steamy past implicates the otherwise noble bean in early colonialism, various revolutions, the emergence of the bourgeoisie, international development, technological hubris, crushing global debt, and more. These forces, in turn, have shaped the way coffee has been incorporated into our culture and economy. Colonialism, for example, served as the primary reason for and vehicle of coffee's expansion throughout the globe; colonial powers dictated where coffee went and where it did not and established trading relationships that continue to this day.

The story of coffee also reveals how (and why) we interact with a plethora of other commodities, legal or not. Surprising similarities exist, for example, between coffee's early history and the current controversy over marijuana. Today's national debate over the merits of marijuana, although young by comparison, is the modern version of the strife surrounding coffee in other ages. The social acceptability of each has been affected by religious and political opinion, conflicting health claims, institutionalized cultural norms, and the monied interests of government and private industry. The evolution of coffee's social acceptability highlights the delicate dance of interests and "truths" that governs the ways in which we structure our societies.

Coffee is consumed with great fervor in rich countries such as the United States yet is grown with few exceptions in the poorest parts of the globe. In fact, it is the second most valuable item of legal international trade (after petroleum), and the largest food import of the United States by value. It is the principal source of foreign exchange for dozens of countries around

the world. The coffee in your cup is an immediate, tangible connection with the rural poor in some of the most destitute parts of the planet. It is a physical link across space and cultures from one end of the human experience to the other.

The coffee trading system that has evolved to bring all this about is an intricate knot of economics, politics, and sheer power—a bizarre arena trod *** by some of the world's largest transnational corporations, by enormous governments, and by vast trading cartels. The trip coffee takes from the crop to your cup turns out not to be so straightforward after all, but rather a turbulent and unpredictable ride through the waves and eddies of international commodity dynamics, where the product itself becomes secondary to the wash of money and power.

SOURCE: Gregory Dicum and Nina Luttinger, *The Coffee Book: Anatomy of an Industry from Crop to the Last Drop* (New York: The New Press, 1999), pp. ix–xi. Used with permission.

ization can be found in your closet and drawers. If you take a look at the labels of your clothes and see the many various countries in which they were manufactured, then you are experiencing globalization firsthand.

Do college students today have a global perspective? By at least one measure, the answer is yes. Furthermore, their activist values suggest that many students also possess a sociological imagination. According to an annual survey of more than 281,064 first-year college students, a record 47.5 percent of all students who entered U.S. colleges in 2001 reported that they had "participated in organized demonstrations" concerned with social, political, and economic issues during the previous year. This was the highest percentage since the University of California, Los Angeles (UCLA) survey began asking the question in 1966 (Sax et al. 2001). This upsurge in

activist values suggests that many entering college students possess a sociological imagination: They recognize that their private lives are shaped by larger social forces, and they are seeking to do something about it. The demonstrations these students participated in were concerned with a wide range of issues, including the growing power of global institutions such as the World Trade Organization and the World Bank, the production of clothing in overseas sweatshops, global warming, environmental destruction, and the right of workers to be paid a living wage (Meatto 2000). Concern with these issues reflects an awareness that globalization has a direct effect on our daily, private lives. As University of California, Berkeley student Joanna Evelan said at one anti-sweatshop rally, "We want to raise awareness among students that they wear Cal clothes from manufacturers that are socially responsible."

Columbine High School Shootings

It is the perfect suburban shrine, sprawling, growing without boundaries and taking on a life of its own.

The Columbine High School memorial is piled under tents and draped along fences. It crawls up and over hills in Clement Park, interrupted by parking lots filled with news media trucks, satellite dishes and the other trappings of the communications machine.

After days of rain, the mud is trying to win, though straw and bark chips have been spread on the ground.

The memorial has become a place where there is little sense of place. It is a color-drenched sea of teddy bears, flowers, butterfly balloons, poetry and paper chains in a neighborhood of gray and beige houses.

From a distance, the memorial looks like a fair.

People wander around the site, some with video cameras recording every bit of the experience, others handing out flowers to those who visit empty handed. You can hear the tears. One woman seemed to recoil when approached to take a bouquet. The young woman toting an armload of wrapped blossoms reassured her: "No, it's free."

That sense of material culture and its effect on attitudes toward the mystery of death are part of what emerges from the experience of the shrine. So does the tension on the hill where 15 crosses have been hoisted, a provocative act in all definitions of the word.

"Sleep baby sleep" was one of the first phrases scrawled on 13 of those crosses, but "hate breeds hate" was the message on the two erected for the young men who died at their own hand. "How can anyone forgive you?" someone has written on those two crosses. "I forgive you" is below, over and over. On the cross carrying Dylan Klebold's picture: "No one is to blame";

on the side of the cross carrying Eric Harris' picture: "You died over a year ago . . . and no one noticed."

On student Steven Curnow's cross, someone has scrawled, "Although I never met you, when you died, I died." At the foot of Rachel Scott's cross is a book about the Holocaust, *The Rescuers.*

Other mementos are spontaneous and heartbreaking; after all, each new loss brings back the memory of each past loss. The note attached to a fuzzy stuffed bunny, with pink bows around its ears, says: "My daughter died on Aug. 10, 1987. Her name was Heather and she was 19 years old. Her animals have been a great source of comfort to me and I hope that they will comfort you also. Be at peace."

John Tomlin's brown truck has become a parking lot shrine—Colorado tag 93922RS. There is a letter jacket with the notation: "To all the people of CHS. You are all creations of God. You are beautiful people."

Questions

- What can you learn about our society from the shrine?
- What religious, cultural, political, and social messages can you detect from the photographs and the article?
- What do people gain from public displays of grief?
- One of the crosses bore the inscription, "Although I never met you, when you died, I died." In our society, do we feel this kind of empathy only when we witness death? How does the presence of death change or intensify our emotions and alter our actions?

Growing daily, flowers crushed and decaying, the memorial at Columbine is a signal of a shifting cultural approach to death and how people participate in their society, says an American studies professor immersed in researching shrines, memorials and grieving.

"Spontaneous eruption" is how Erika Doss [a professor at the University of Colorado] describes the wave of memorials springing up across America, from the gifts left at the Vietnam Veterans Memorial in Washington, D.C., to the fence at the site of the Oklahoma City bombing.

SOURCE: Mary Voelz Chandler, "Heartbreak, Mystery Shroud Shrine," *Rocky Mountain News,* May 2, 1999, denver.rockymountain news.com/shooting/0502shr51.shtml (accessed spring 2006). Used with permission.

Developing a global perspective has great importance for sociology. A global perspective not only allows us to become more aware of the ways that we are connected to people in other societies but also makes us more aware of the many problems the world faces at the beginning of the twenty-first century. The global perspective opens our eyes to the fact that our interdependence with other societies means that our actions have consequences for others and that the world's problems have consequences for us.

Understanding Social Change

The changes in human ways of life in the last two hundred years, such as globalization, have been far reaching. We have become accustomed, for example, to the fact that most of the population does not work on the land and lives in towns and cities rather than in small rural communities. But this was *never* the case until the middle of the nineteenth century. For virtually all of human history, the vast majority of people had to produce their own food and shelter and lived in tiny groups or in small village communities. Even at the height of the most developed traditional civilizations—such as ancient Rome or traditional China—less than 10 percent of the population lived in urban areas; everyone else was engaged in food production in a rural setting. Today, in most of the industrialized societies, these proportions have become almost completely reversed. Quite often, more than 90 percent of the people live in urban areas, and only 2 to 3 percent of the population work in agricultural production. Yet, with changing conditions of economic activity central to the processes of globalization, the developing world is urbanizing rapidly as well. By 2030, about 61 percent of the world population is expected to live in urban areas and in more developed regions; 82 percent will live in urban areas (United Nations 2004).

It is not only the environment surrounding our lives that has changed; these transformations have radically altered, and continue to alter, the most personal and intimate side of our daily existence. To extend a previous example, the spread of ideals of romantic love was strongly conditioned by the transition from a rural to an urban, industrialized society. As people moved into urban areas and began to work in industrial production, marriage was no longer prompted mainly by economic motives—by the need to control the inheritance of land and to work the land as a family unit. "Arranged" marriages—fixed through the negotiations of parents and relatives—became less and less common. Individuals increasingly began to initiate marriage relationships on the basis of emotional attraction and to seek personal fulfillment. The idea of falling in love as a basis for contracting a marriage tie was formed in this context.

Sociology had its beginnings in the attempts of thinkers to understand the initial effect of these transformations that accompanied industrialization in the West. Our world today is radically different from that of former ages; it is the task of sociology to help us understand this world and what future it is likely to hold for us.

The Development of Sociological Thinking

When they first start studying sociology, many students are puzzled by the diversity of approaches they encounter. Sociology has never been a discipline with a body of ideas that everyone accepts as valid. Sociologists often quarrel among themselves about how to go about studying human behavior and how research results might best be interpreted. Why should this be so? Why can't sociologists agree with one another more consistently, as natural scientists seem able to do? The answer is bound up with the very nature of the field itself. Sociology is about our own lives and our own behavior, and studying ourselves is the most complex and difficult endeavor we can undertake.

Theories and Theoretical Approaches

Trying to understand something as complex as the effect of industrialization on society raises the importance of theory to sociology. Factual research shows *how* things occur. Yet sociology does not just consist of collecting facts, however important and interesting they may be. We also want to know *why* things happen, and to do so we have to learn to construct explanatory theories. For instance we know that industrialization has had a major influence on the emergence of modern societies. But what are the origins and preconditions of industrialization? Why do we find differences among societies in their industrialization processes? Why is industrialization associated with changes in ways of criminal punishment or in family and marriage systems? To respond to such questions, we have to develop theoretical thinking.

A **theory** involves constructing abstract interpretations that can be used to explain a wide variety of situations. A theory about industrialization, for example, would be concerned with identifying the main features that processes of industrial development share in common and would try to show which of these are most important in explaining such development. Of course, factual research and theories can never be completely separated. We can develop valid theoretical approaches only if we are able to test them out by means of factual research.

We need theories to help us make sense of facts. Contrary to popular assertion, facts do not speak for themselves. Many sociologists work primarily on factual research; but unless they are guided by some knowledge of theory, their work is unlikely to explain the complexity of modern societies. This is true even of research carried out with strictly practical objectives.

"Practical people" tend to be suspicious of theorists and may like to see themselves as too down to earth to need to pay attention to more abstract ideas, yet all practical decisions have some theoretical assumptions lying behind them. A manager of a business, for example, might have scant regard for theory. Nonetheless, every approach to business activity involves theoretical assumptions, even if they often remain unstated. Thus the manager might assume that employees are motivated to work hard mainly for money—the level of wages they receive. This is not only a theoretical interpretation of human behavior but is also a mistaken one, as research in industrial sociology tends to demonstrate.

Without a **theoretical approach**, we would not know what to look for in beginning a study or in interpreting the results of research. However, the illumination of factual evidence is not the only reason for the prime position of theory in sociology. Theoretical thinking must respond to general problems posed by the study of human social life, including issues that are philosophical in nature. Deciding to what extent sociology should be modeled on the natural sciences is a question that does not yield easy solutions. This question has been handled in different ways in the various theoretical approaches that have sprung up in the discipline.

Early Theorists

We human beings have always been curious about the sources of our own behavior, but for thousands of years our attempts to understand ourselves relied on ways of thinking passed down from generation to generation, often expressed in religious terms. (For example, before the rise of modern science, many people believed that natural events such as earthquakes were caused by gods or spirits.) Although writers from earlier periods provided insights into human behavior and society, the systematic study of society is a relatively recent development whose beginnings date back to the late 1700s and early 1800s. The background to the origins of sociology was the series of sweeping changes ushered in by the French Revolution of 1789 and the emergence of the Industrial Revolution in Europe. The shattering of traditional ways of life wrought by these changes resulted in the attempts of thinkers to develop a new understanding of both the social and natural worlds.

Auguste Comte (1798–1857).

A key development was the use of science instead of religion to understand the world. The types of questions these nineteenth-century thinkers sought to answer—What is human nature? Why is society structured like it is? How and why do societies change?—are the same questions sociologists try to answer today. Our modern world is radically different from that of the past; it is sociology's task to help us understand this world and what the future is likely to hold.

AUGUSTE COMTE

There were many contributors to early sociological thinking. Particular prominence, however, is usually given to the French author Auguste Comte (1798–1857), if only because he invented the word *sociology*. Comte originally used the term *social physics*, but some of his intellectual rivals at the time were also making use of that term. Comte wanted to distinguish his own views from theirs, so he introduced *sociology* to describe the subject he wished to establish.

Comte believed that this new field could produce a knowledge of society based on scientific evidence. He regarded sociology as the last science to be developed—following physics, chemistry, and biology—but as the most significant and complex of all the sciences. Sociology, he believed, should contribute to the welfare of humanity by using science to understand and therefore predict and control human behavior. In the later part of his career, Comte drew up ambitious plans for the reconstruction of French society in particular and for human societies in general, based on scientific knowledge.

ÉMILE DURKHEIM

The works of another French writer, Émile Durkheim (1858–1917), have had a much more lasting effect on modern sociology than those of Comte. Although he drew on aspects of Comte's

Émile Durkheim
(1858–1917).

work, Durkheim thought that many of his predecessor's ideas were too speculative and vague and that Comte had not successfully carried out his program—to establish sociology on a scientific basis. To become scientific, according to Durkheim, sociology must study **social facts,** aspects of social life that shape our actions as individuals, such as the state of the economy or the influence of religion. Durkheim believed that we must study social life with the same objectivity as scientists study the natural world. His famous first principle of sociology was "Study social facts as *things!*" By this he meant that social life can be analyzed as rigorously as objects or events in nature.

Like a biologist studying the human body, Durkheim saw society as a set of independent parts, each of which could be studied separately. A body consists of various specialized parts (such as the brain, heart, lungs, liver, and so forth), each of which contributes to sustaining the continuing life of the organism. These necessarily work in harmony with one another; if they do not, the life of the organism is under threat. So it is, according to Durkheim, with society. For a society to have a continuing existence over time, its specialized institutions (such as the political system, the religion, the family, and the educational system) must work in harmony with each other and function as an integrated whole. Durkheim referred to this social cohesion as **organic solidarity**. He argued that the continuation of a society thus depends on cooperation, which in turn presumes a general consensus, or agreement, among its members over basic values and customs.

Another major theme pursued by Durkheim, and by many others since, is that the societies of which we are members exert **social constraint** over our actions. Durkheim argued that society has primacy over the individual person. Society is far more than the sum of individual acts; when we analyze social structures, we are studying characteristics that have a "firmness" or "solidity" comparable to those of structures in the physical world. Think of a person standing in a room that has several doors. The structure of the room constrains the range of her or his possible activities. The position of the walls and the doors, for example, defines the routes of exit and entry. Social structure, according to Durkheim, constrains our activities in a parallel way, setting limits on what we can do as individuals. It is "external" to us, just as the walls of the room are.

Like the other major founders of sociology, Durkheim was preoccupied with the changes transforming society in his own lifetime. His analysis of social change was based on the development of the **division of labor** (the growth of complex distinctions among different occupations). Durkheim argued that the division of labor gradually replaced religion as the basis of social cohesion and provided organic solidarity to modern societies. He argued that as the division of labor expands, people become more and more dependent on each other, because each person needs goods and services that those in other occupations supply. Another of Durkheim's (1966; orig. 1897) most famous studies was concerned with the analysis of suicide. Suicide seems to be a purely personal act, the outcome of extreme personal unhappiness. Durkheim showed, however, that social factors exert a fundamental influence on suicidal behavior—**anomie,** a feeling of aimlessness or despair provoked by modern social life being one of these influences. Suicide rates show regular patterns from year to year, he argued, and these patterns must be explained sociologically. Many objections can be raised against Durkheim's study, but it remains a classic work whose relevance to sociology today is by no means exhausted. According to Durkheim, processes of change in the modern world are so rapid and intense that they give rise to major social difficulties, which he linked to anomie. Traditional moral controls and standards, which used to be supplied by religion, are largely broken down by modern social development, and this leaves many individuals in modern societies feeling that their daily lives lack meaning. Later in his life, Durkheim came to be especially concerned with the role of religion in social life. In his study of religious beliefs, practices, and rituals—*The Elementary Forms of the Religious Life* (1965; orig. 1912)—he focused particularly on the importance of religion in maintaining moral order in society.

KARL MARX

The ideas of Karl Marx (1818–1883) contrast sharply with those of Comte and Durkheim; however, Marx also sought to explain the changes in society that took place over the time of the Industrial Revolution. When he was a young man, his political activities brought him into conflict with the German authorities; after a brief stay in France, he settled permanently in exile in Britain. His writings covered a diversity of areas. Even his sternest critics regard his work as important for the development of sociology. Much of his writing concentrates on economic issues, but because he was always concerned with

Karl Marx
(1818–1883).

connecting economic problems to social institutions, his work was, and is, rich in sociological insights.

Marx's viewpoint was founded on what he called the **materialist conception of history.** According to this view, it is not the ideas or values human beings hold that are the main sources of social change, as Durkheim claimed. Rather, social change is prompted primarily by economic influences. The conflicts between classes—the rich versus the poor—provide the motivation for historical development. In Marx's words, "All human history thus far is the history of class struggles."

Though he wrote about various phases of history, Marx concentrated on change in modern times. For him, the most important changes were bound up with the development of capitalism. **Capitalism** is a system of production that contrasts radically with previous economic systems in history, involving as it does the production of goods and services sold to a wide range of consumers. Those who own capital—or factories, machines, and large sums of money—form a ruling class. The mass of the population make up a class of wage workers, or a working class, who do not own the means of their livelihood but must find employment provided by the owners of capital. Capitalism is thus a class system in which conflict between classes is a commonplace occurrence because it is in the interests of the ruling class to exploit the working class and in the interests of the workers to seek to overcome that exploitation.

According to Marx, in the future capitalism will be supplanted by a society in which there are no classes—no divisions between rich and poor. He didn't mean by this that all inequalities between individuals will disappear. Rather, societies will no longer be split into a small class that monopolizes economic and political power and the large mass of people who benefit little from the wealth their work creates. The economic system will come under communal ownership, and a more equal society than we know at present will be established.

Marx's work had a far-reaching effect on the twentieth-century world. Until recently, before the fall of Soviet commu-

nism, more than a third of the earth's population lived in societies whose governments claimed to derive their inspiration from Marx's ideas. In addition, many sociologists have been influenced by Marx's ideas about class divisions.

MAX WEBER

Like Marx, Max Weber (pronounced "Vaber," 1864–1920) cannot be labeled simply a sociologist; his interests and concerns ranged across many areas. Born in Germany, where he spent most of his academic career, Weber was an individual of wide learning. His writings covered the fields of economics, law, philosophy, and comparative history as well as sociology, and much of his work was also concerned with the development of modern capitalism. Like other thinkers of his time, Weber sought to understand social change. He was influenced by Marx but was also strongly critical of some of Marx's major views. He rejected the materialist conception of history and saw class conflict as less significant than did Marx. In Weber's view, economic factors are important but ideas and values have just as much effect on social change.

Some of Weber's most influential writings were concerned with analyzing the distinctiveness of Western society compared with other major civilizations. He studied the religions of China, India, and the Near East and, in the course of these researches, made major contributions to the sociology of religion. Comparing the leading religious systems in China and India with those of the West, Weber concluded that certain aspects of Christian beliefs strongly influenced the rise of capitalism. He argued that the capitalist outlook of Western societies did not emerge, as Marx supposed, only from economic changes. In Weber's view, cultural ideas and values help shape society and affect our individual actions.

One of the most persistent concerns of Weber's work was the study of bureaucracy. A **bureaucracy** is a large organization that is divided into jobs based on specific functions and staffed by officials ranked according to a hierarchy. Industrial

Max Weber
(1864–1920).

TABLE 1.1

Interpreting Modern Development

DURKHEIM
1. The main dynamic of modern development is the **division of labor** as a basis for social cohesion and **organic solidarity.**
2. Durkheim believed that sociology must study **social facts** as things, just as science would analyze the natural world. His study of suicide led him to stress the important influence of social factors, qualities of a society external to the individual, on a person's actions. Durkheim argued that society exerts **social constraint** over our actions.

MARX
1. The main dynamic of modern development is the expansion of **capitalism.** Rather than being cohesive, society is divided by class differences.
2. Marx believed that we must study the divisions within a society that are derived from the economic inequalities of capitalism.

WEBER
1. The main dynamic of modern development is the **rationalization** of social and economic life.
2. Weber focused on why Western societies developed so differently from other societies. He also emphasized the importance of cultural ideas and values on social change.

firms, government organizations, hospitals, and schools are all examples of bureaucracies. Weber believed the advance of bureaucracy to be an inevitable feature of our era. Bureaucracy makes it possible for these large organizations to run efficiently, but at the same time it poses problems for effective democratic participation in modern societies. Bureaucracy involves the rule of experts, whose decisions are made without much consultation with those whose lives are affected by them.

Weber's contributions range over many other areas, including the study of the development of cities, systems of law, types of economy, and the nature of classes. He also produced a range of writings concerned with the overall character of sociology itself. Weber was more cautious than either Durkheim or Marx in proclaiming sociology to be a science. According to Weber, it is misleading to imagine that we can study people using the same procedures that are applied to investigate the physical world. Humans are thinking, reasoning beings; we attach meaning and significance to most of what we do, and any discipline that deals with human behavior must acknowledge this.

Neglected Founders

Although Comte, Durkheim, Marx, and Weber are, without doubt, foundational figures in sociology, other important thinkers from the same period made contributions that must also be taken into account. Sociology, like many academic fields, has not always lived up to its ideal of acknowledging the importance of every thinker whose work has intrinsic merit. Very few women or members of racial minorities were given the opportunity to become professional sociologists during the "classical" period of the late nineteenth and early twentieth centuries. In addition, the few that were given the opportunity to do sociological research of lasting importance have frequently been neglected by the field. These individuals deserve the attention of sociologists today.

HARRIET MARTINEAU

Harriet Martineau (1802–1876) was born and educated in England. She has been called the "first woman sociologist"; but, like Marx and Weber, she cannot be thought of simply as a sociologist. She was the author of more than fifty books as well as numerous essays. Martineau is now credited with introducing sociology to England through her translation of Comte's founding treatise of the field, *Positive Philosophy* (Rossi, 1973). In addition, Martineau conducted a firsthand systematic study of American society during her extensive travels throughout the United States in the 1830s, which is the subject of her book *Society in America* (1962; orig. 1837). Martineau is significant to

Harriet Martineau
(1802–1876).

W. E. B. Du Bois
(1868–1963).

sociologists today for several reasons. First, she argued that when one studies a society, one must focus on all its aspects, including key political, religious, and social institutions. Second, she insisted that an analysis of a society must include an understanding of women's lives. Third, she was the first to turn a sociological eye on previously ignored issues, including marriage, children, domestic and religious life, and race relations. As Martineau (1962; orig. 1837) once wrote, "The nursery, the boudoir, and the kitchen are all excellent schools in which to learn the morals and manners of a people." Finally, she argued that sociologists should do more than just observe, they should also act in ways to benefit a society. As a result, Martineau was an active proponent of both women's rights and the emancipation of slaves.

W. E. B. DU BOIS

W. E. B. Du Bois (1868–1963) was the first African American to earn a doctorate at Harvard University. Du Bois's contributions to sociology were many. Perhaps most important is the concept of "double consciousness," which is a way of talking about identity through the lens of the particular experiences of African Americans. Du Bois (1903) argued that American society let African Americans see themselves only through the eyes of others: "It is a particular sensation, this double consciousness, this sense of always looking at one's soul by the tape of a world that looks on in amused contempt and pity. One ever feels his two-ness—an American, a Negro, two souls, two thoughts, two unreconciled strivings, two warring ideals in one dark body, whose dogged strength alone keeps it from being torn asunder." He made a persuasive claim that one's sense of self and one's identity are greatly influenced by historical experiences and social circumstances—in the case of African Americans, the effect of slavery and, after emancipation, segregation and prejudice. Throughout his career, Du Bois focused on race relations in the United States; as he said in an often repeated

quote, "the problem of the twentieth century is the problem of the color line" (Du Bois, 1903). His influence on sociology today is evidenced by continued interest in the questions that he raised, particularly his concern that sociology must explain "the contact of diverse races of men" (Du Bois, 1903). Du Bois was also the first social researcher to trace the problems faced by African Americans to their social and economic underpinnings, a connection that most sociologists now widely accept. Finally, Du Bois became known for connecting social analysis to social reform. He was one of the founding members of the National Association for the Advancement of Colored People (NAACP) and a long-time advocate for the collective struggle of African Americans. Later in his life, Du Bois became disenchanted by the lack of progress in American race relations and moved to the African nation of Ghana, where he died in 1963.

Understanding the Modern World: The Sociological Debate

From Marx's time to the present day, many sociological debates have centered on the ideas that Marx set out about the influence of economics on the development of modern societies. According to Marx, as was mentioned earlier, modern societies are *capitalistic*—the driving impulse behind social change in the modern era is to be found in the pressure toward constant economic transformation produced by the spread of capitalist production. Capitalism is a vastly more dynamic economic system than any other that preceded it in history. Capitalists compete with each other to sell their goods to consumers; and to survive in a competitive market, firms have to produce their wares as cheaply and efficiently as possible. This leads to constant technological innovation, because increasing the effectiveness of the technology used in a particular production process is one way in which companies can secure an edge over their rivals.

There are also strong incentives to seek out new markets in which to sell goods, acquire cheap raw materials, and make use of cheap labor power. Capitalism, therefore, according to Marx, is a restlessly expanding system, pushing outward across the world. This is how Marx explains the global spread of Western industry.

Marx's interpretation of the influence of capitalism has found many supporters. Subsequent Marxist authors have considerably refined Marx's own portrayal. On the other hand, numerous critics have set out to rebut Marx's view, offering alternative analyses of the influences shaping the modern world. Virtually everyone accepts that capitalism *has* played a major part in creating the world in which we live today. But other sociologists have argued both that Marx exaggerated the effect of purely *economic* factors in producing change and that capitalism is *less central* to modern social development than he claimed. Most of these writers have also been skeptical of Marx's belief that a socialist system would eventually replace capitalism.

One of Marx's earliest and most acute critics was Max Weber. Weber's writings, in fact, have been described as involving a lifelong struggle with "the ghost of Marx"—with the intellectual legacy that Marx left. The alternative position that Weber worked out remains important today. According to Weber, noneconomic factors have played the key role in modern social development. Weber's celebrated and much discussed work *The Protestant Ethic and the Spirit of Capitalism* (1977; orig. 1904) proposes that religious values—especially those associated with Puritanism—were of fundamental importance in creating a capitalistic outlook. This outlook did not emerge, as Marx supposed, only from economic changes.

Weber's understanding of the nature of modern societies, and the reasons for the spread of Western ways of life across the world, also contrasts substantially with that of Marx. According to Weber, capitalism—a distinct way of organizing economic enterprise—is one among other major factors shaping social development in the modern period. Underlying capitalistic mechanisms, and in some ways more fundamental than them, is the effect of *science* and *bureaucracy*. Science has shaped modern technology and will presumably continue to do so in any future society, whether socialist or capitalist. Bureaucracy is the only way of organizing large numbers of people effectively and therefore inevitably expands with economic and political growth. The development of science, modern technology, and bureaucracy are examples of a general social process that Weber refers to collectively as **rationalization.** Rationalization means the organization of social, economic, and cultural life according to principles of efficiency, on the basis of technical knowledge.

Which interpretation of modern societies, that deriving from Marx or that coming from Weber, is correct? Again, scholars are divided on the issue. It must be remembered that within each camp there are variations, so not every theorist will agree with all the points of one interpretation. The contrasts between these two standpoints inform many areas of sociology.

Modern Theoretical Approaches

Although the origins of sociology were mainly European, over the last century the subject has become firmly established worldwide, and some of the most important developments have taken place in the United States. The following sections explore these developments.

SYMBOLIC INTERACTIONISM

The work of George Herbert Mead (1863–1931), a philosopher teaching at the University of Chicago, had an important influence on the development of sociological thought, in particular through a perspective called **symbolic interactionism.** Mead placed particular importance on the study of *language* in analyzing the social world. According to him, language allows us to become self-conscious beings—aware of our own individuality. The key element in this process is the **symbol,** something that *stands for* something else. For example, the word *tree* is a symbol by means of which we represent the object tree. Once we have mastered such a concept, Mead argued, we can think of a tree even if none is visible; we have learned to think of the object symbolically. Symbolic thought frees us from being limited in our experience to what we actually see, hear, or feel.

Unlike animals, according to Mead, human beings live in a richly symbolic universe. This applies even to our very sense of self. Each of us is a self-conscious being because we learn to look at ourselves as if from the outside—we see ourselves as others see us. When a child begins to use *I* to refer to that object (herself) whom others call "you," she is exhibiting the beginnings of self-consciousness.

George Herbert Mead (1863–1931).

Virtually all interactions between individuals, symbolic interactionists say, involve an exchange of symbols. When we interact with others, we constantly look for clues to what type of behavior is appropriate in the context and how to interpret what others are up to. Symbolic interactionism directs our attention to the detail of interpersonal interaction and how that detail is used to make sense of what others say and do. For instance, suppose two people are out on a date for the first time. Each is likely to spend a good part of the evening sizing the other up and assessing how the relationship is likely to develop, if at all. Neither wishes to be seen doing this too openly, although each recognizes that it is going on. Both individuals are careful about their own behavior, being anxious to present themselves in a favorable light; but, knowing this, both are likely to be looking for aspects of the other's behavior that would reveal his or her true opinions. A complex and subtle process of symbolic interpretation shapes the interaction between the two.

FUNCTIONALISM

Symbolic interactionism is open to the criticism that it concentrates too much on things that are small in scope. Symbolic interactionists have found difficulty in dealing with larger-scale structures and processes—the very things that a rival tradition of thought, **functionalism,** tends to emphasize. Functionalist thinking in sociology was originally pioneered by Comte, who saw it as closely bound up with his overall view of the field.

To study the *function* of a social activity is to analyze the contribution that that activity makes to the continuation of the society as a whole. The best way to understand this idea is by analogy to the human body, a comparison Comte, Durkheim, and other functionalist authors made. To study an organ such as the heart, we need to show how it relates to other parts of the body. When we learn how the heart pumps blood around the body, we then understand that the heart plays a vital role in the continuation of the life of the organism. Similarly, analyzing the function of some aspect of society, such as religion, means showing the part it plays in the continued existence and health of a society. Functionalism emphasizes the importance of *moral consensus* in maintaining order and stability in society. Moral consensus exists when most people in a society share the same values. Functionalists regard order and balance as the normal state of society—this social equilibrium is grounded in the existence of a moral consensus among the members of society. According to Durkheim, for instance, religion reaffirms people's adherence to core social values, thereby contributing to the maintenance of social cohesion.

Functionalism became prominent in sociology through the writings of Talcott Parsons and Robert K. Merton, each of whom saw functionalist analysis as providing the key to the development of sociological theory and research. Merton's version of functionalism has been particularly influential.

Robert K. Merton (1910–2003).

Merton distinguished between manifest and latent functions. **Manifest functions** are those known to, and intended by, the participants in a specific type of social activity. **Latent functions** are consequences of that activity of which participants are unaware. To illustrate this distinction, Merton used the example of a rain dance performed by the Hopi Tribe of Arizona and New Mexico. The Hopi believe that the ceremony will bring the rain they need for their crops (manifest function). This is why they organize and participate in it. But using Durkheim's theory of religion, Merton argued that the rain dance also has the effect of promoting the cohesion of the Hopi society (latent function). A major part of sociological explanation, according to Merton, consists in uncovering the latent functions of social activities and institutions.

Merton also distinguished between functions and dysfunctions. To look for the dysfunctional aspects of social behavior means focusing on features of social life that challenge the existing order of things. For example, it is mistaken to suppose that religion is always functional—that it contributes only to social cohesion. When two groups support different religions or even different versions of the same religion, the result can be major social conflicts, causing widespread social disruption. Thus wars have often been fought between religious communities—as can be seen in the struggles between Protestants and Catholics in European history.

For a long while, functionalist thought was probably the leading theoretical tradition in sociology, particularly in the United States. In recent years, its popularity has declined as its limitations have become apparent. Although this was not true of Merton, many functionalist thinkers (Parsons is an example) unduly stressed factors leading to social cohesion at the expense of those producing division and conflict. In addition, it has seemed to many critics that functional analysis attributes to societies qualities they do not have. Functionalists often wrote as though societies had "needs" and "purposes," even though these concepts make sense only when applied to

FIGURE 1.1

Theoretical Approaches in Sociology

The solid lines *indicate direct influence; the* dotted line, *an indirect connection. Mead is not indebted to Weber, but Weber's views—stressing the meaningful, purposive nature of human action—have affinities with the themes of symbolic interactionism.*

Auguste Comte (1798–1857)

Karl Marx (1818–1883)

Max Weber (1864–1920)

Émile Durkheim (1858–1917)

George Herbert Mead (1863–1931)

FUNCTIONALISM **MARXISM** **SYMBOLIC INTERACTIONISM**

Why doesn't Weber follow Marx in sociological lineage? Name two influential founders of sociology who are not listed in this figure. What are the different areas of emphasis for functionalism and symbolic interactionism? Name two other sociologists who would be in line with Durkheim and who helped bring functionalist theory to prominence.

individual human beings. Figure 1.1 shows how functionalism relates to other theoretical approaches in sociology.

MARXISM AND CLASS CONFLICT

Functionalism and symbolic interactionism are not the only modern theoretical traditions of importance in sociology. A further influential approach is **Marxism.** Marxists, of course, all trace their views back in some way to the writings of Karl Marx. But numerous interpretations of Marx's major ideas are possible, and there are today schools of Marxist thought that take very different theoretical positions.

In all of its versions, Marxism differs from non-Marxist traditions of sociology in that its authors see it as a combination of sociological analysis and political reform. Marxism is supposed to generate a program of radical political change. Moreover, Marxists lay more emphasis on conflict, class divisions, power, and ideology than many non-Marxist sociologists, especially most of those influenced by functionalism. The concept of

power—and a closely associated notion, that of **ideology**—is of great importance to Marxist sociologists and to sociology in general. By *power* is meant the capability of individuals or groups to make their own concerns or interests count, even when others resist. Power sometimes involves the direct use of force but is almost always accompanied by the development of ideas (ideologies), which are used to *justify* the actions of the powerful. Power, ideology, and conflict are always closely connected. Many conflicts are *about* power because of the rewards it can bring. Those who hold most power may depend mainly on the influence of ideology to retain their dominance but are usually able also to use force if necessary.

FEMINISM AND FEMINIST THEORY

Feminist theory is one of the most prominent areas of contemporary sociology. This is a notable development because issues of gender are scarcely central in the work of the major figures who established the discipline. Sociologists did not add the study of women and gender inequality to their concerns without a pitched battle. The success of feminism's entry into sociology required a fundamental shift in the discipline's approach.

Many feminist theorists brought their experiences in the women's movement of the 1960s and 1970s to their work as sociologists. Like Marxism, feminism makes a link between sociological theory and political reform. Many feminist sociologists have been advocates for political and social action to remedy the inequalities between women and men in both the public and the private spheres.

Feminist sociologists argue that women's lives and experiences are central to the study of society. Sociology, like most academic disciplines, has presumed a male point of view. Driven by a concern with women's subordination in American society, feminist sociologists highlight gender relations and gender inequality as important determinants of social life in terms of both social interaction and social institutions such as the family, the workplace, and the educational system. Feminist theory emphasizes that gendered patterns and gendered inequalities are not natural, but socially constructed. (We will cover this point in more detail in Chapter 10.)

Today, feminist sociology is characterized by a focus on the intersection of gender, race, and class. A feminist approach to the study of inequality has influenced new fields of study, like men's studies, sexuality studies, and gay and lesbian studies.

RATIONAL CHOICE THEORY

The sociologist Max Weber had a very interesting way of dividing up the actions of human beings. He thought that all behavior could be divided into four categories: (1) behavior that is oriented toward higher values, such as politics; (2) behavior that is oriented toward habit, such as walking to school on a path you have taken before; (3) behavior that is oriented toward affect (emotions), such as falling in love; and (4) behavior that is oriented toward self-interest, such as making money. Behavior that falls into the last of these categories is often called "instrumental" or "rational action." In recent years, many sociologists have come to follow an approach that focuses on the last of these categories. This has led numerous scholars to ask under what conditions the behavior of human beings can be said to be rational responses to opportunities and constraints.

The **rational choice approach** to human behavior posits that if you could have only a single variable to explain society, self-interest would be the best one to work with. A person who believes in this approach might even try to use it to explain things that seem irrational. One popular rational choice theory sees decisions to marry as maximizing self-interest in a marriage market. This theory has been used to explain why marriage has declined the most in poor African American communities where rates of employment have been low. The explanation is that it is not in the self-interest of women to marry men who cannot support them (Wilson 1987). Such an explanation goes against other, competing explanations suggesting that poor African Americans don't marry because they don't share mainstream values. The rational choice argument is that this decline in marriage has little to do with values and much to do with self-interest under existing conditions. According to this theory, if employment rates for black men changed, so too would the number of "eligible" men and the desire of women to marry them.

Rational choice theorists tend to believe that there are few irrational mysteries in life. One of the few some note is love, which they define as the irrational act of substituting another person's self-interest for one's own (Becker 1991). But with such a definition, it is quite difficult to distinguish among basic altruism, friendship, and romantic love. Indeed, although a rational choice approach is often quite useful, there are some aspects of life that it would have trouble explaining. Consider, for example, an angry driver who tries to teach a lesson to other offending drivers by, for instance, tailgating a tailgater. Self-interest does not make this action sensible. Even if the lesson is well learned, the "teacher" is unlikely to personally reap the benefits of the student's progress (Katz 1999).

POSTMODERN THEORY

Advocates of the idea of **postmodernism** claim that the classic social thinkers took their inspiration from the idea that history has a shape—it "goes somewhere" and leads to progress—and that now this notion has collapsed. There are no longer any "grand narratives," or metanarratives—overall conceptions of history or society—that make any sense (Lyo-

New York's Times Square serves as the backdrop for live television programs such as MTV's *TRL: Total Request Live* and ESPN's *SportsCenter*. Covered with advertisements and constantly in flux, it epitomizes Baudrillard's theories of postmodern society.

tard 1985). Not only is there no general notion of progress that can be defended but there is no such thing as history. The postmodern world is not destined, as Marx hoped, to be a socialist one. Instead, it is one dominated by the new media, which "take us out" of our past. Postmodern society is highly pluralistic and diverse. In countless films, videos, TV programs, and Web sites, images circulate around the world. We come into contact with many ideas and values, but these have little connection with the history of the areas in which we live or indeed with our own personal histories. Everything seems constantly in flux. As one group of authors expressed things:

> Our world is being remade. Mass production, the mass consumer, the big city, big-brother state, the sprawling housing estate, and the nation-state are in decline: flexibility, diversity, differentiation, and mobility, communication, decentralization and internationalization are in the ascendant. In the process our own identities, our sense of self, our own subjectivities are being transformed. We are in transition to a new era (Hall et al. 1988).

One of the important theorists of postmodernity is the French author Jean Baudrillard, who believes that the electronic media have destroyed our relationship to our past and created a chaotic, empty world. Baudrillard was strongly influenced by Marxism in his early years. However, he argues, the spread of electronic communication and the mass media have reversed the Marxist theorem that economic forces shape society. Instead, social life is influenced above all by signs and images.

In a media-dominated age, Baudrillard says, meaning is created by the flow of images, as in TV programs. Much of our

LIB

For Public Sociology

On a Sunday evening in August 2004, Professor Michael Burawoy stood before more than five thousand of his colleagues at the American Sociological Association (ASA) conference to declare his vision for the future of *public sociology*. In attendance were not just professional sociologists but authors, activists, students, and journalists from both the United States and abroad. The ASA conference, held in downtown San Francisco, was the most heavily attended in years. Reflecting on Burawoy's speech, a reporter from London's *Guardian* (2004) newspaper would conclude that "something big is stirring in US academic life."

Titled "For Public Sociology," Burawoy's address sought to reawaken and celebrate the moral commitments of sociologists by connecting them to public engagement. Rather than stay isolated within the ivory tower, Burawoy (2004) called for "a sociology that seeks to bring sociology to publics beyond the academy, promoting dialogue about issues that affect the fate of society." Envisioning a collaborative relationship between sociologists and multiple publics, he described a future in which critical, policy, and public engagements would strengthen not just the profession but the fabric of civil society itself.

Founded as an academic discipline around a hundred years ago, sociology originally aspired to be "an angel of history" that sought order and justice in a rapidly changing world. Industrial transformations during the late nineteenth and early twentieth centuries had produced social dislocations on an unprecedented scale, inspiring scholars such as Karl Marx,

Michael Burawoy

Max Weber, Emile Durkheim W. E. B. Du Bois, and Jane Addams to "salvage the promise of progress" from the forces that helped the few at the expense of the many. Although sociology by the mid-1900s was becoming more scientifically rigorous, this shift failed to keep alive sociology's "original passion for social justice, economic equality, human rights, sustainable environment, [and] political freedom" (Burawoy 2004). By becoming a profession, sociology was in danger of losing its soul.

world has become a sort of make-believe universe in which we are responding to media images rather than to real persons or places. Thus, when Diana, Princess of Wales, died in 1997, there was an enormous outpouring of grief, not only in Britain but all over the world. Yet were people mourning a real person? Baudrillard would say not. Diana existed for most people only through the media. Her death was more like an event in a soap opera than a real event in the way in which people experienced it. Baudrillard (1983) speaks of "the dissolution of life into TV."

Theoretical Thinking in Sociology

So far in this chapter we have been concerned with theoretical approaches, which refer to broad, overall orientations to the subject matter of sociology. However, we can draw a distinction between theoretical approaches and theories. Theories are more narrowly focused and represent attempts to explain particular social conditions or types of event. They are usually formed as part of the process of research and in turn suggest problems to which research investigations should be devoted.

"What would happen," Burawoy (2004) asks, "if, rather than repressing the moral moment of sociology, we were to give it room to breath, recognize it rather than silence it, reflect on it rather than repress it? Would it enhance the legitimacy of sociology, or end its credibility?" These are critical questions with no easy answers; but if Burawoy is right, an active moral engagement with the publics beyond the classroom need not come at the expense of scientific integrity. Although some may disagree, providing the public with knowledge of *what is* while encouraging what *ought to be* allows public sociologists to reconnect with the moral impulses at the heart of the discipline.

Although sociology as a discipline has always been concerned with public issues, the resurgence of public sociology in recent years reflects a growing discomfort with levels of inequality in American society and throughout the world. In the face of "state despotism and market tyranny," public sociology is for Burawoy (2004) a way to regenerate the discipline's moral fiber. Whereas economics is mainly concerned with the virtues of the free market, and political science with political order and the state, the study of sociology "coincides with humanity's interest in opposing the erosion of civil liberties, the violation of human rights, the degradation of the environment, the impoverishment of working classes, the spread of disease, the exclusion of ever greater numbers from the means of their existence, and deepening inequalities—all forces that threaten the viability and resilience of civil society at home and abroad" (Burawoy et al. 2004). The role of *sociology* is to connect the burdens that people privately endure with the historical and contemporary conditions shaping the lives of hundreds, thousands, perhaps millions of people like them. The role of *public sociology* is to go a step further, to spark dialogue within and between multiple publics outside of academic classrooms by demonstrating how the sociological imagination can help us all better understand the world around us.

Burawoy's extensive fieldwork in eastern Europe, Africa, Russia, and America provides a view of that world from the bottom up. Inspired during the 1960s by prerevolutionary movements in the United States, Burawoy ventured to Zambia to study the integration of black and white workers as an employee at the Anglo American Mining Corporation. His book *The Colour of Class* (1972) documented how ideas about race allowed whites to be promoted over Zambian managers, providing a controversial reality check for the newly independent African state. His subsequent fieldwork at a Chicago machine shop (documented in *Manufacturing Consent*, 1979), the Lenin Steel Works in Hungary (described in *The Politics of Production*, 1985), and more recently at the Polar Furniture Enterprise in Syktyvkar, Russia, has allowed Burawoy to link personal experiences on the shop floor to patterns of class formation, cooperation, and dissent across settings (Byles 2001).

That "the world" is actually made up of multiple publics presents multiple opportunities for public sociology to thrive. Traditional routes of engagement have included authoring newspaper editorials, appearing on radio broadcasts, and testifying before government agencies (such as the local city council or the U.S. Congress). But public sociology also includes working in the trenches of civil society with publics such as labor movements, neighborhood associations, immigrant rights groups, and human rights organizations. Many of the categories that we now take for granted—women, gays, inner-city youth, people with AIDS—are themselves the social products of political actions taken by individuals, sociologists among them, who came together in moral opposition to the oppression of human beings in a country (and, increasingly, a world) dedicated to principles of equality and justice. Both of these forms of public sociology—the traditional and the organic—help "to make visible the invisible, to make the private public" (Burawoy 2004) and, in so doing, reaffirm the value of sociology in the conduct and creation of public life.

An example would be Durkheim's theory of suicide, referred to earlier in this chapter.

Innumerable theories have been developed in the many different areas of research in which sociologists work. Sometimes theories are very precisely set out and are even occasionally expressed in mathematical form—although this is more common in other social sciences (especially economics) than in sociology.

Some theories are also much more encompassing than others. Opinions vary about whether it is desirable or useful for sociologists to concern themselves with very wide-ranging theoretical endeavors. Robert K. Merton (1957), for example, argues forcefully that sociologists should concentrate their attention on what he calls *theories of the middle range*. Rather than attempting to create grand theoretical schemes (in the manner of Marx, for instance), we should be concerned with developing more modest theories.

Middle-range theories are specific enough to be tested directly by empirical research, yet sufficiently general to cover a range of different phenomena. A case in point is the theory of *relative deprivation*. This theory holds that how people evaluate their circumstances depends on whom they compare themselves to. Thus feelings of deprivation do not conform directly to the level of material poverty individuals experience. A family living in a small home in a poor area, where everyone is in more or less similar circumstances, is likely to feel less deprived than a family living in a similar house in a neighborhood where the majority of the other homes are much larger and the other people more affluent.

It is indeed true that the more wide ranging and ambitious a theory is, the more difficult it is to test empirically. Yet there seems no obvious reason that theoretical thinking in sociology should be confined to the "middle range."

Assessing theories, and especially theoretical approaches, in sociology is a challenging and formidable task. Theoretical debates are by definition more abstract than controversies of a more empirical kind. The fact that there is not a single theoretical approach that dominates the whole of sociology might seem to be a sign of weakness in the subject. But this is not the case at all: The jostling of rival theoretical approaches and theories is an expression of the vitality of the sociological enterprise. In studying human beings—ourselves—theoretical variety rescues us from dogma. Human behavior is complicated and many sided, and it is very unlikely that a single theoretical perspective could cover all of its aspects. Diversity in theoretical thinking provides a rich source of ideas that can be drawn on in research and stimulates the imaginative capacities so essential to progress in sociological work.

Levels of Analysis: Microsociology and Macrosociology

One important distinction among the different theoretical perspectives we have discussed in this chapter involves the level of analysis each is directed at. The study of everyday behavior in situations of face-to-face interaction is usually called **microsociology**. **Macrosociology** is the analysis of large-scale social systems, like the political system or the economic order. It also includes the analysis of long-term processes of change, such as the development of industrialism. At first glance, it might seem as though micro analysis and macro analysis were distinct from one another. In fact, the two are closely connected (Giddens 1984; Knorr-Cetina and Cicourel 1981).

Macro analysis is essential if we are to understand the institutional background of daily life. The ways in which people live their everyday lives are greatly affected by the broader institutional framework, as is obvious when the daily cycle of activities of a culture such as that of the medieval period is compared with life in an industrialized urban environment. In modern societies, as has been pointed out, we are constantly in contact with strangers. This contact may be indirect and impersonal. However, no matter how many indirect or electronic relations we enter into today, even in the most complex societies, the presence of other people remains crucial. While we may choose just to send an acquaintance an e-mail message on the Internet, we can also choose to fly thousands of miles to spend the weekend with a friend.

Micro studies are in turn necessary for illuminating broad institutional patterns. Face-to-face interaction is clearly the main basis of all forms of social organization, no matter how large scale. Suppose we are studying a business corporation. We could understand much about its activities simply by looking at face-to-face behavior. We could analyze, for example, the interaction of directors in the boardroom, people working in the various offices, or the workers on the factory floor. We would not build up a picture of the whole corporation in this way because some of its business is transacted through printed materials, letters, the telephone, and computers. Yet we could certainly contribute significantly to understanding how the organization works.

In later chapters, we will see further examples of how interaction in micro contexts affects larger social processes and how macro systems in turn influence more confined settings of social life.

Is Sociology a Science?

Durkheim, Marx, and the other founders of sociology thought of the discipline as a science. But can we really study human social life in a scientific way? To answer this question, we must first understand what the word means. What is science?

Science is the use of *systematic methods of empirical investigation, the analysis of data, theoretical thinking, and the logical assessment of arguments* to develop a body of knowledge about a particular subject matter. Sociology is a scientific endeavor, according to this definition. It involves systematic methods of empirical investigation, the analysis of data, and the assessment of theories in the light of evidence and logical argument.

Studying human beings, however, is different from observing events in the physical world, and sociology shouldn't be seen as directly equivalent to a natural science. Unlike objects in nature, humans are self-aware beings who confer sense and purpose on what they do. We can't even describe social life accurately unless we first grasp the concepts that people apply in their behavior. For instance, to describe a death as a suicide means knowing what the person in question was intending when he died. Suicide can occur only when an individual has self-destruction actively in mind. If he accidentally steps in front of a car and is killed, he cannot be said to have committed suicide.

The fact that we cannot study human beings in exactly the same way as objects in nature is in some ways an advantage to sociology. Sociological researchers profit from being able to pose questions directly to those they study—other human beings. In other respects, sociology creates difficulties not encountered in the natural sciences. People who are aware that their activities are being scrutinized frequently will not behave in the same way as they do normally. They may consciously or unconsciously portray themselves in a way that differs from their usual attitudes. They may even try to "assist" the researcher by giving the responses they believe he or she wants.

Is Sociology Merely a Restatement of the Obvious?

Because sociologists study things that you have some personal experience with, you will sometimes wonder if what this subject has to teach you is merely "a painful elaboration of the obvious" (Wright 2000). Is sociology merely the restatement, in more abstract jargon, of things we already know? Is it simply the tedious definition of social phenomena with which we are already familiar? Sociology at its worst can be all of these things, but it is never appropriate to judge any discipline by what its worst practitioners do. In fact, good sociology either sharpens our understanding of the obvious (Berger 1963), or it completely transforms our common sense. In either event, good sociology is neither tedious nor a restatement of the obvious. In this text, we will sometimes begin with definitions of things that you may already understand. It is necessary for any academic discipline to define its terms. But when, for example, we define a family as a unit of people who are related to one another, we do so not as an endpoint but instead as a beginning. We know that you may not need a sociology text to tell you the definition of a family, yet we also know that if we do not begin by defining our terms, we cannot move forward to sharper levels of understanding later on. Good sociology never defines terms as an end in itself.

How Can Sociology Help Us in Our Lives?

Sociology has several practical implications for our lives, as C. Wright Mills emphasized when developing his idea of the sociological imagination.

Awareness of Cultural Differences

First, sociology allows us to see the social world from many perspectives. Quite often, if we properly understand how others live, we also acquire a better understanding of what their problems are. Practical policies that are not based on an informed awareness of the ways of life of people they affect have little chance of success. Thus a white social worker operating in an African American community won't gain the confidence of its members without developing a sensitivity to the differences in social experience that often separate white and black in the United States.

Assessing the Effects of Policies

Second, sociological research provides practical help in assessing the results of policy initiatives. A program of practical reform may simply fail to achieve what its designers sought or may produce unintended consequences of an unfortunate kind. For instance, in the years after World War II, large public-housing blocks were built in city centers in many countries. These were planned to provide high standards of accommodation for low-income groups from slum areas and offered shopping amenities and other civic services close at hand. However, research later showed that many people who had moved from their previous dwellings to large apartment blocks felt isolated and unhappy. High-rise apartment blocks and shopping malls in poorer areas often became dilapidated and provided breeding grounds for muggings and other violent crimes.

Self-Enlightenment

Third, and in some ways most important, sociology can provide us with self-enlightenment—increased self-understanding. The more we know about why we act as we do and about the overall workings of our society, the more likely we are to be able to influence our own futures. We should not see sociology as assisting only policy makers—that is, powerful groups—in making informed decisions. Those in power cannot be assumed always to consider the interests of the less powerful or underprivileged in the policies they pursue. Self-enlightened groups can often benefit from sociological research by using the information gleaned to respond in an effective way to government policies or form policy initiatives of their own. Self-help groups such as Alcoholics Anonymous (AA) and social movements like the environmental movement are examples of social groups that have directly sought to bring about practical reforms, with some degree of success.

The Sociologist's Role in Society

Finally, it should be mentioned that many sociologists concern themselves directly with practical matters as professionals. People trained in sociology are to be found as industrial consultants, urban planners, social workers, and personnel managers as well as in many other jobs. An understanding of society can also help one in careers in law, journalism, business, and medicine.

Those who study sociology frequently develop a social conscience. Should sociologists themselves actively advocate and agitate for programs of reform or social change? Some argue that sociology can preserve its intellectual independence only if sociologists are studiously neutral in moral and political controversies. Yet are scholars who remain aloof from current debates necessarily more impartial in their assessment of sociological issues than others? There is often a connection between studying sociology and the prompting of social conscience. No sociologically sophisticated person can be unaware of the inequalities that exist in the world today, the lack of social justice in many social situations, and the deprivations suffered by millions of people. It would be strange if sociologists did not take sides on practical issues, and it would be illogical to try to ban them from drawing on their expertise in so doing.

In this chapter, we have seen that sociology is a discipline in which we often set aside our personal view of the world to look more carefully at the influences that shape our lives and those of others. Sociology emerged as a distinct intellectual endeavor with the development of modern societies, and the study of such societies remains its principal concern. But sociologists are also preoccupied with a broad range of issues about the nature of social interaction and human societies in general.

Sociology isn't just an abstract intellectual field but has major practical implications for people's lives. Learning to become a sociologist shouldn't be a dull academic endeavor! The best way to make sure it doesn't become so is to approach the subject in an imaginative way and to relate sociological ideas and findings to situations in your own life.

Study Outline

www.wwnorton.com/giddens

Developing a Sociological Perspective

- *Sociology* can be identified as the systematic study of human societies giving special emphasis to modern, industrialized systems. The subject came into being as an attempt to understand the far-reaching changes that have occurred in human societies over the past two to three centuries.
- Major social changes have also occurred in the most intimate and personal characteristics of people's lives. The development of romantic love as a basis for marriage is an example of this.
- The practice of sociology involves the ability to think imaginatively and to detach oneself as far as possible from preconceived ideas about social relationships.

Modern Theoretical Approaches

- A diversity of theoretical approaches is found in sociology. The reason for this is not particularly puzzling. Theoretical disputes are difficult to resolve even in the natural sciences, and in sociology we face special difficulties because of the complex problems involved in subjecting our own behavior to study.
- Important figures in the early development of sociological theory include Auguste Comte (1798–1857), Émile Durkheim (1858–1917), Karl Marx (1818–1883), and Max Weber (1864–1920). Many of their ideas remain important in sociology today.
- The main theoretical approaches in sociology are *symbolic interactionism, functionalism, Marxism, feminism, rational choice approach,* and *postmodernism.* To some extent, these approaches complement each other. However, there are also major contrasts among them, which influence the ways in which theoretical issues are handled by authors following different approaches.

Levels of Analysis

- The study of face-to-face interaction is usually called *microsociology*—in contrast to *macrosociology,* which studies larger groups, institutions, and social systems. Micro and macro analyses are in fact very closely related and each complements the other.

How Can Sociology Help Us in Our Lives?

- Sociology is a *science* in that it involves systematic methods of investigation and the evaluation of theories in the light of evidence and logical argument. But it cannot be modeled directly on the natural sciences, because studying human behavior is in fundamental ways different from studying the world of nature.

- Sociology is a subject with important practical implications. Sociology can contribute to social criticism and practical social reform in several ways. First, the improved understanding of a given set of social circumstances often gives us a better chance of controlling them. Second, sociology provides the means of increasing our cultural sensitivities, allowing policies to be based on an awareness of divergent cultural values. Third, we can investigate the consequences (intended and unintended) of the adoption of particular policy programs. Finally, and perhaps most important, sociology provides self-enlightenment, offering groups and individuals an increased opportunity to alter the conditions of their own lives.

Key Concepts

anomie (p. 14)
bureaucracy (p. 15)
capitalism (p. 15)
division of labor (p. 14)
feminist theory (p. 20)
functionalism (p. 19)
globalization (p. 8)
ideology (p. 20)
latent functions (p. 19)
macrosociology (p. 24)
manifest functions (p. 19)
Marxism (p. 20)
materialist conception of history (p. 15)
microsociology (p. 24)
organic solidarity (p. 14)
postmodernism (p. 21)
power (p. 20)
rational choice approach (p. 21)
rationalization (p. 18)
science (p. 24)
social constraint (p. 14)
social facts (p. 14)
social structure (p. 7)
sociological imagination (p. 6)
sociology (p. 3)
structuration (p. 7)
symbol (p. 18)
symbolic interactionism (p. 18)
theoretical approach (p. 13)
theory (p. 12)

Review Questions

1. What is the definition of sociology?
   a. Sociology is the study of individuals.
   b. Sociology is the study of group interaction, from the family to the system of nation.
   c. Sociology is the study of human social life, groups, and societies, focusing on the modern world.
   d. Sociology is a branch of the social reform movement. It is dedicated to providing a scientific underpinning for the liberal and social democratic political agendas.
2. What is the sociological imagination?
   a. It is the ability to "think ourselves away" from the familiar routines of our daily lives to look at them anew.
   b. It is the study of the way private troubles aggregate into public issues.
   c. It is the worldview of Karl Marx.
   d. It is the application of liberal and socialist political values to social scientific inquiry.
3. What is the definition of *functionalism?*
   a. It is the study of the function of a social activity to determine the contribution that the activity makes to society as a whole.
   b. It is the study of the way people function in groups.
   c. It is the study of the way social institutions reproduce social systems.
   d. It was the conservative response to the social reform movement.
4. Structuration is considered to be a double process because
   a. social structure patterns human activity and is created by it.
   b. human societies are complex and often contradictory.
   c. human beings operate in both a personal and a social sphere.
   d. social structures are both biological and social.
5. Why is Weber's study *The Protestant Ethic and the Spirit of Capitalism* important to sociology?
   a. It showed that capitalism is the only major factor of social development in the modern period.
   b. It was the first major study validating Marx's materialist conception of history.
   c. It demonstrated the importance of ideas, such as religious values, in creating a capitalistic outlook.
   d. It created the sociology of religion.
6. Sociology can be considered a science because it
   a. uses systematic methods to study a phenomenon.
   b. uses systematic methods of theoretical thinking.
   c. involves the logical assessment of arguments.
   d. All of the above.
7. Who developed the idea of symbolic interactionism in human social life?
   a. Émile Durkheim
   b. Karl Marx
   c. Max Weber
   d. George Herbert Mead
8. According to Karl Marx, the most important changes that occurred in the modern period were tied to the development of
   a. democracy.
   b. socialism.
   c. historical materialism.
   d. capitalism.

9. Why is Émile Durkheim's study of suicide important to sociology?

a. It introduced Durkheim's concept of social facts.

b. It showed that suicide, seemingly the most individual of acts, is socially influenced. Suicide rates vary according to the social cohesion of groups.

c. It showed that the meaning of suicide varies across social groups. It is not the same for Catholics as it is for Protestants.

d. It started the field known as the sociology of death.

10. Which of the following is true about good sociology?

a. It is merely a restatement of the obvious.

b. It reinforces our common sense.

c. It sharpens our understanding of the obvious.

d. It defines sociological terms only for the purpose of defining.

Thinking Sociologically Exercises

1. Healthy older Americans often encounter exclusionary treatment when younger people assume that they are feeble-minded and thus overlook them for jobs they are fully capable of doing. How would each of the popular theoretical perspectives presented in Chapter 1—functionalism, conflict theory, and symbolic interactionism—explain the dynamics of prejudice against the elderly?

2. The text discusses the sociology of coffee, suggesting that the consumption of coffee is more than a simple product designed to quench a person's thirst and to help fend off drowsiness. Mention and adequately discuss **five** sociological features of coffee that clearly show its "sociological" nature.

Data Exercises

www.wwnorton.com/giddens
Keyword: Data1

In this chapter you read about some of the early sociological theorists who made important contributions to the development of sociology as a social science and to our understanding of human behavior. The first data exercise will allow you to become more familiar with the important social theorists in this field and to get some practice using your sociological imagination. After completing this exercise you will understand how broader social forces shape individual experiences.

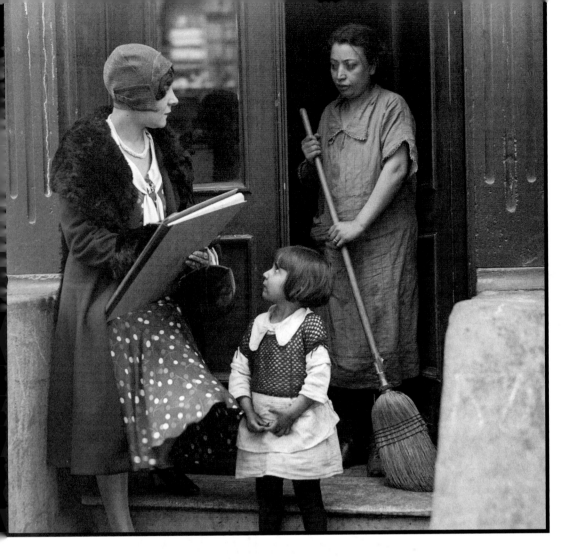

Sociological Questions

Be able to name the different types of questions sociologists try to answer in their research—factual, theoretical, comparative, and developmental.

The Research Process

Learn the steps of the research process and be able to complete the process yourself.

Understanding Cause and Effect

Be able to differentiate between causation and correlation.

Research Methods

Familiarize yourself with all the different methods available to sociological research and know the advantages and disadvantages of each.

Research in the Real World: Methods, Problems, and Pitfalls

See how research methods were combined in a real study and recognize the problems the researcher faced.

CHAPTER TWO

ASKING AND ANSWERING SOCIOLOGICAL QUESTIONS

toward the end of a working day, the public restroom of a particular St. Louis park is suddenly busier than one might expect. One man walks in clad in a gray suit; another has on a baseball cap, tennis shoes, shorts, and a T-shirt; a third is wearing the mechanic's uniform from the gas station where he has fixed cars all day. What are these men doing here? Surely there are more convenient places to use a restroom. Is there some common interest besides the restroom itself that brings them to this place?

Believe it or not, none of these men has come to the public toilet for the official use to which a toilet is usually put. Instead, they are searching for "instant sex." Many men—married and unmarried, those with straight identities and those whose self-image is as gay men—seek sex with people they do not know. They are hoping to experience sexual excitement, but they want to avoid involvement. They don't want any commitments that extend beyond the particular encounters they will have in this public bathroom.

Until the 1970s, the phenomenon of impersonal sex persisted as a widespread but rarely studied form of human interaction. In the gay community, such public bathrooms were called "tearooms." Laud Humphreys, a sociologist, went to these public restrooms to be part of these scenes and then conducted surveys of the participants. He wrote about them in his book *Tearoom Trade* (1970). On the basis of his research in the tearooms, Humphreys was able to cast a new light on the struggles of men who were forced to keep their sexual proclivities secret. He showed that many men who

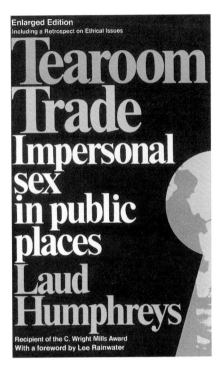

Laud Humphreys's groundbreaking study of anonymous gay sex in public bathrooms led to a deeper understanding of the consequences of the social stigma and legal persecution associated with gay lifestyles.

otherwise live "normal" lives—the people next door—find ways to engage in embarrassing behaviors that will not harm their careers or family lives. Humphreys's research was conducted more than three decades ago, when the stigma was associated with gay and lesbian identities was much greater than today and when police were vigilant in enforcing laws against such behavior. Many lives were ruined in the process of harsh enforcement.

Why Hang Out in Public Bathrooms?

Humphreys spent an extended period of time in such public bathrooms because an excellent way to understand social processes is to participate in and observe them. He also conducted survey interviews that enabled him to gather more information than he would have obtained by simply observing the bathrooms. Humphreys's research opened a window on an aspect of life that many people would be shocked to know existed at all and that certainly needed to be understood at a deeper level. His work was based on systematic research, but it also carried a note of passion.

Humphreys argued that persecution against gay lifestyles leads men to live anguished existences in which they must re-

sort to extreme secrecy and often dangerous activities. His study was conducted before the onset of AIDS; such activity would be much more dangerous today. He argued that tolerance for a gay subculture would put gays in a position in which they could provide one another with self-esteem, mutual support, and relief from torment.

Sociological Questions

The bathrooms under study in *Tearoom Trade* are perfect examples of phenomena that are subjects of many of the kinds of questions that sociologists ask. For example, in looking at the surprising uses to which bathrooms are put, Humphreys was asking how society works in ways that are different from the official versions of how it should work and how what we take to be natural—a public bathroom—is actually *socially constructed,* depending on how it is used.

It is also interesting to note that elements of modern theoretical approaches can help us understand the issues addressed by Humphreys's study. A *rational choice* approach would ask: How is this behavior in the tearooms a rational response to opportunities and constraints? The answer is that the men who go to the tearooms have few other ways to fulfill their needs, so they must engage in behavior with intense risks. An *interactionist* might ask: How does this behavior take place through processes of interaction? What kinds of interactions take place? Humphreys found that people who go into the tearooms learn from others to be silent. This is a response to the demand for privacy without involvement. Another finding is that men who go into the restroom and do not respond to initial sexual advances will not be approached any further. Each party must cooperate to make a sexual situation occur. A *functionalist* approach might ask: What contribution does the tearoom make to the continuation of society as a whole? The answer is that it provides an outlet for sexual activity that, when carried out in secret, enables the participants and other members of society to carry on as "normal" people in their everyday lives without challenging the accepted order of things. A *Marxist* approach might ask: Is thinking about economic class relations apparent in the tearooms? Humphreys found that the impersonal sex of the tearooms had a democratic quality. Men of all social classes and races would come together in these places for sexual contact, a finding that has been verified by a study of Times Square in New York City (Delany 1999). Finally, a *feminist* approach might ask: How can women's lives be considered in this study of an all-male group? This approach was not dominant at the time Humphreys conducted his study, but a feminist today would ask how women—

perhaps wives who know nothing about the activity of their male partners—are affected by this secret behavior in the tearooms.

It has been thirty years since *Tearoom Trade* was published, and in the interim society has become more tolerant of gay identities and gay sex. After the publication of his important book, Humphreys became part of the political movement—the gay rights movement—that made this change possible. He used his findings to convince courts and police to ease up on prosecuting men for engaging in gay sex so as to alleviate the damaging side effects of covert sexual activity.

It is the business of sociological research in general to go beyond surface-level understandings of ordinary life, as Humphreys did. Good research should help us understand our social lives in a new way. It should take us by surprise, in the questions that it asks and in the findings it comes up with. The issues that concern sociologists, in both their theorizing and their research, are often similar to those that worry other people. But the results of such research frequently run counter to our commonsense beliefs.

What are the circumstances in which racial or sexual minorities live? How can mass starvation exist in a world that is far wealthier than it has ever been before? What effects will the increasing use of the Internet have on our lives? Is the family beginning to disintegrate as an institution? Sociologists try to provide answers to these and many other questions. Their findings are by no means conclusive. Nevertheless, it is always the aim of sociological theorizing and research to break away from the speculative manner in which the ordinary person usually considers such questions. Good sociological work tries to make the questions as precise as possible and seeks to gather factual evidence before coming to conclusions. To achieve these aims, we must know the most useful **research methods** to apply in a given study and how to best analyze the results.

Some of the questions that sociologists ask in their research studies are largely **factual questions,** or empirical questions. For example, many aspects of sexual behavior, such as the aspects Humphreys studied, need direct and systematic sociological investigation. Thus we might ask: What kinds of occupations and domestic arrangements are most common among men who go to the tearooms? What proportion of tearoom participants are caught by the police? Factual questions of this kind are often difficult to answer. Official statistics on tearooms would not exist. Even official statistics on crime are of dubious value in revealing the real level of criminal activity. Researchers who have studied crime levels have found that only about one half of all serious crimes are reported to the police.

Factual information about one society, of course, will not always tell us whether we are dealing with an unusual case or a general set of influences. Sociologists often want to ask **comparative questions,** relating one social context within a society to another or contrasting examples drawn from different societies. There are significant differences, for example, between the social and legal systems of the United States and of Canada. A typical comparative question might be, How much do patterns of criminal behavior and law enforcement vary between the two countries?

In sociology, we need not only to look at existing societies in relation to one another but also to compare their present and past. The questions sociologists ask in this case are **developmental questions.** To understand the nature of the modern world, we have to look at previous forms of society and study the main direction that processes of change have taken. Thus we can investigate, for example, how the first prisons originated and what they are like today.

Factual investigations—or what sociologists usually prefer to call **empirical investigations**—concern how things occur. Yet sociology does not consist of just collecting facts, however important and interesting they may be. We always need to interpret what facts mean, and to do so we must learn to pose **theoretical questions.** Many sociologists work primarily on empirical questions; but unless they are guided in research by some knowledge of theory, their work is unlikely to be illuminating (Table 2.1).

At the same time, sociologists strive not to attain theoretical knowledge for its own sake. A standard view is that although values should not be permitted to bias conclusions, social research should be relevant to real-world concerns. In this chapter, we look further into such issues by asking whether it is possible to produce objective knowledge. First, we examine the stages involved in sociological research. We then compare the most widely used research methods as we consider some actual investigations. As we shall see, there are often significant differences between the way research should ideally be carried out and real-world studies.

The Research Process

Let's first look at the stages normally involved in research work. The research process takes in a number of distinct steps, leading from when the investigation is begun to the time its findings are published or made available in written form.

Defining the Research Problem

All research starts from a research problem. This is sometimes an area of factual ignorance: We may simply wish to improve

TABLE 2.1

A Sociologist's Line of Questioning

Factual question	What happened?	During the 1980s, there was an increase in the proportion of women in their thirties bearing children for the first time.
Comparative question	Did this happen everywhere?	Was this a global phenomenon? Or did it occur just in the United States or only in a certain region of the United States?
Developmental question	Has this happened over time?	What have been the patterns of childbearing over time?
Theoretical question	What underlies this phenomenon?	Why are more women now waiting until their thirties to bear children? What factors should we look at to explain this change?

our knowledge about certain institutions, social processes, or cultures. A researcher might set out to answer such questions as What proportion of the population holds strong religious beliefs? Are people today really disaffected with "big government"? How far does the economic position of women lag behind that of men?

The best sociological research, however, begins with problems that are also puzzles. A puzzle is not just a lack of information, but a *gap in our understanding.* Much of the skill in producing worthwhile sociological research consists in correctly identifying puzzles.

Rather than simply answering the question, What is going on here?, puzzle-solving research tries to contribute to our understanding of *why* events happen as they do. Thus we might ask, Why are patterns of religious belief changing? What accounts for the decline in the proportions of the population voting in presidential elections in recent years? Why are women poorly represented in high-status jobs?

No piece of research stands alone. Research problems come up as part of ongoing work; one research project may easily lead to another because it raises issues the researcher had not previously considered. A sociologist may discover puzzles by reading the work of other researchers in books and professional journals or by being aware of specific trends in society. For example, over recent years, an increasing number of programs for treating the mentally ill encourage such individuals to live in the community rather than being confined to asylums. Sociologists might be prompted to ask, What has given rise to this shift in attitude toward the mentally ill? What are the

likely consequences both for the patients themselves and for the rest of the community?

Reviewing the Evidence

Once the problem is identified, the next step taken in the research process is usually to review the available evidence in the field; it might be that previous research has already satisfactorily clarified the problem. If not, the sociologist will need to sift through whatever related research does exist to see how useful it is for his or her purpose. Have previous researchers spotted the same puzzle? How have they tried to resolve it? What aspects of the problem has their research left unanalyzed? Drawing on others' ideas helps the sociologist clarify the issues that might be raised and the methods that might be used in the research.

Making the Problem Precise

A third stage involves working out a clear formulation of the research problem. If relevant literature already exists, the researcher might return from the library with a good notion of how to approach the problem. Hunches about the nature of the problem can sometimes be turned into definite **hypotheses**—educated guesses about what is going on—at this stage. If the research is to be effective, a hypothesis must

In looking at this painting by Brueghel, we can observe the number of people, what each is doing, the style of the buildings, or the colors the painter chose. But without the title, *Netherlandish Proverbs,* these facts tell us nothing about the picture's meaning. In the same way, sociologists need theory as a context for their observations.

be formulated in such a way that the factual material gathered will provide evidence either supporting or disproving it.

Working Out a Design

The researcher must then decide just *how* the research materials are to be collected. A range of different research methods exists, and which one the researcher chooses depends on the overall objectives of the study as well as the aspects of behavior to be analyzed. For some purposes, a survey (in which questionnaires are normally used) might be suitable. In other circumstances, interviews or an observational study such as that carried out by Laud Humphreys might be appropriate. We shall learn more about various research methods later.

Carrying Out the Research

At the point of actually proceeding with the research, unforeseen practical difficulties can easily crop up. It might prove impossible to contact some of those to whom questionnaires are to be sent or those whom the researcher wishes to interview. A business firm or government agency may be unwilling to let the researcher carry out the work planned. Difficulties such as these could potentially bias the result of the study and give him or her a false interpretation. For example, if the researcher is studying how business corporations have complied with affir-

mative action programs for women, then companies that have not complied might not want to be studied. The findings could be biased as a result.

Interpreting the Results

Once the material has been gathered to be analyzed, the researcher's troubles are not over—they may be just beginning! Working out the implications of the data collected and relating these back to the research problem are rarely easy. Although it may be possible to reach a clear answer to the initial questions, many investigations are in the end less than fully conclusive.

Reporting the Findings

The research report, usually published as a journal article or book, provides an account of the nature of the research and seeks to justify whatever conclusions are drawn. In Humphreys's case, this report was the book *Tearoom Trade.* This is a final stage only in terms of the individual research project. Most reports indicate questions that remain unanswered and suggest further research that might profitably be conducted. All individual research investigations are part of the continuing process of research taking place within the sociological community. Other scholars have built on Humphreys's research findings.

Reality Intrudes!

The preceding sequence of steps is a simplified version of what happens in actual research projects (Figure 2.1). In real sociological research, these stages rarely succeed each other so neatly, and there is almost always a certain amount of sheer muddling through. The difference is a bit like that between the recipes outlined in a cookbook and the actual process of preparing a meal. Experienced cooks often don't work from recipes at all, yet they might cook better than those who do. Following fixed schemes can be unduly restricting; much outstanding sociological research could not in fact be fitted rigidly into this sequence, although most of the steps would be there.

Understanding Cause and Effect

One of the main problems to be tackled in research methodology is the analysis of cause and effect. A **causal relationship** between two events or situations is an association in which one event or situation produces another. If the parking brake is released in an automobile pointing down a hill, the car will roll down the incline, gathering speed progressively as it does so. Taking the brake off *caused* this to happen; the reasons for this can readily be understood by reference to the physical principles involved. Like natural science, sociology depends on the assumption that all events have causes. Social life is not a random array of occurrences, happening without rhyme or reason. One of the main tasks of sociological research—in combination with theoretical thinking—is to identify causes and effects.

Causation and Correlation

Causation cannot be directly inferred from **correlation.** Correlation means the existence of a regular relationship between two sets of occurrences or variables. A **variable** is any dimension along which individuals or groups vary. Age, differences in income, crime rates, and social-class differences are among the many variables sociologists study. When two variables are found to be closely correlated, it might seem as if one must have caused the other; however, such is often not the case. There are many correlations without any causal relationship between the variables. For example, over the period since World War II, a strong correlation can be found between a decline in pipe smoking and a decrease in the number of people who regularly go to the movies. Clearly one change does not

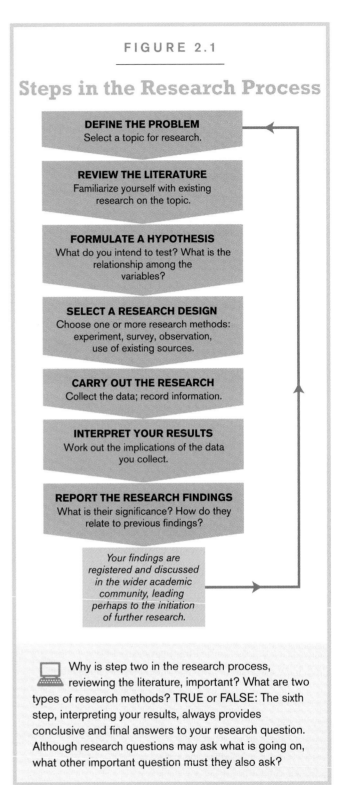

FIGURE 2.1

Steps in the Research Process

DEFINE THE PROBLEM
Select a topic for research.

REVIEW THE LITERATURE
Familiarize yourself with existing research on the topic.

FORMULATE A HYPOTHESIS
What do you intend to test? What is the relationship among the variables?

SELECT A RESEARCH DESIGN
Choose one or more research methods: experiment, survey, observation, use of existing sources.

CARRY OUT THE RESEARCH
Collect the data; record information.

INTERPRET YOUR RESULTS
Work out the implications of the data you collect.

REPORT THE RESEARCH FINDINGS
What is their significance? How do they relate to previous findings?

Your findings are registered and discussed in the wider academic community, leading perhaps to the initiation of further research.

Why is step two in the research process, reviewing the literature, important? What are two types of research methods? TRUE or FALSE: The sixth step, interpreting your results, always provides conclusive and final answers to your research question. Although research questions may ask what is going on, what other important question must they also ask?

cause the other, and we would find it difficult to discover even a remote causal connection between them.

There are many instances, however, in which it is not so obvious that an observed correlation does not imply a causal relationship. Such correlations are traps for the unwary and easily lead to questionable or false conclusions. In his classic work *Suicide,* Émile Durkheim (1966; orig. 1897) found a correlation between rates of suicide and the seasons of the year. In the societies Durkheim studied, levels of suicide increased progressively from January to around June or July. From that time onward they declined through the end of the year. It might be supposed that this demonstrates that temperature or climatic change is causally related to the propensity of individuals to kill themselves. Perhaps as temperatures increase, people become more impulsive and hotheaded? However, the causal relation here has nothing directly to do with temperature or climate at all. In spring and summer most people engage in a more intensive social life than they do in winter. Individuals who are isolated or unhappy tend to experience an intensification of these feelings as the activity level of other people rises. Hence they are likely to experience acute suicidal tendencies more in spring and summer than in autumn and winter, when the pace of social activity slackens. We always have to be on our guard both in assessing whether correlation involves causation and in deciding in which direction causal relations run.

CAUSAL MECHANISM

Working out causal connections involved in correlations is often a difficult process. There is a strong correlation, for instance, between level of educational achievement and occupational success in modern societies. The better the grades an individual gets in school, the better paying the job he or she is likely to get. What explains this correlation? Research tends to show that it is not mainly school experience itself; levels of school attainment are influenced much more by the type of home from which the person comes. Children from better-off homes, whose parents take a strong interest in their learning skills and where books are abundant, are more likely to do well than those coming from homes where these qualities are lacking. The causal mechanisms here are the attitudes of parents toward their children, together with the facilities for learning that a home provides.

Causal connections in sociology should not be understood in too mechanical a way. The attitudes people have and their subjective reasons for acting as they do are causal factors in relationships among variables in social life.

CONTROLS

In assessing the cause or causes that explain a correlation, we need to distinguish independent variables from dependent variables. An **independent variable** is one that produces an effect on another variable. The variable affected is the **dependent variable.** In the example just mentioned, academic achieve-ment is the independent variable and occupational income, the dependent variable. The distinction refers to the direction of the causal relation we are investigating. The same factor may be an independent variable in one study and a dependent variable in another. It all depends on what causal processes are being analyzed. If we were looking at the effects of differences in occupational income on lifestyles, occupational income would then be the independent variable rather than the dependent one.

To find out whether a correlation between variables is a causal connection we use **controls,** which means we hold some variables constant to look at the effects of others. By doing this, we are able to judge among explanations of observed correlations, separating causal from noncausal relationships. For example, researchers studying child development have claimed that there is a causal connection between maternal deprivation in infancy and serious personality problems in adulthood. (*Maternal deprivation* means that an infant is separated from his mother for a long period—several months or more—during the early years of his life.) How might we test whether there really is a causal relationship between maternal deprivation and later personality disorders? We would do so by trying to control, or "screen out," other possible influences that might explain the correlation.

One source of maternal deprivation is the admission of a child to a hospital for a lengthy period, during which he is separated from his parents. Is it attachment to the mother, however, that really matters? Perhaps if a child receives love and attention from *other* people during infancy, he might subsequently be a stable person. To investigate these possible causal connections, we would have to compare cases in which children were deprived of regular care from anyone with other instances in which children were separated from their mothers but received love and care from someone else. If the first group developed severe personality difficulties but the second group did not, we would suspect that regular care from *someone* in infancy is what matters, regardless of whether or not it is the mother. (In fact, children do seem to prosper normally as long as they have a loving, stable relationship with someone looking after them; this person does not have to be the mother herself.)

IDENTIFYING CAUSES

A large number of possible causes could be invoked to explain any given correlation. How can we ever be sure that we have covered them all? The answer is that we cannot be sure. We would never be able to carry out and interpret the results of a piece of sociological research satisfactorily if we were compelled to test for the possible influence of every causal factor we could imagine as potentially relevant. Identifying causal relationships is normally guided by previous research into the area in question. If we do not have some reasonable idea beforehand of the causal mechanisms involved in a correlation we would probably find it very difficult to discover what the real causal connections are. We would not know what to test *for*.

A good example of how difficult it is to be sure of the causal relations involved in a correlation is given by the long history of studies of smoking and lung cancer. Research has consistently demonstrated a strong correlation between the two. Smokers are more likely to contract lung cancer than nonsmokers, and very heavy smokers are more likely to do so than light smokers. The correlation can also be expressed the other way around. A high proportion of those who have lung cancer are smokers or have smoked for long periods in their past. So many studies have confirmed these correlations that it is generally accepted that a causal link is involved, but the exact causal mechanisms are thus far largely unknown.

However much correlational work is done on any issue, there always remains some doubt about possible causal relationships. Other interpretations of the correlation are possible. It has been proposed, for instance, that people who are predisposed to get lung cancer are also predisposed to smoke. In this view it is not smoking that causes lung cancer but rather some built-in biological disposition to smoking and cancer.

Research Methods

Let's now look at the various research methods sociologists commonly employ in their work (Table 2.2).

Ethnography

Humphreys used **ethnography** (or firsthand studies of people, using **participant observation** or interviewing) as his main research method. Here, the investigator hangs out or works or lives with a group, organization, or community and perhaps takes a direct part in its activities. An ethnographer cannot usually just be present in the group she studies, but must explain and justify her presence to its members. She must gain the cooperation of the community and sustain it over a period of time, if any worthwhile results are to be achieved.

For a long while, it was usual for research based on participant observation to exclude any account of the hazards or problems that had to be overcome, but more recently the published reminiscences and diaries of field workers have been more open about them. Frequently, field workers must cope with feelings of loneliness—it isn't easy to fit into a social context or community where you don't really belong. The researcher may be constantly frustrated because the members of the group refuse to talk frankly about themselves; direct queries may be welcomed in some contexts but meet with a chilly silence in others. Some types of fieldwork may even be physically dangerous; for instance, a researcher studying a delinquent gang might be seen as a police informer or might become unwittingly embroiled in conflicts with rival gangs.

In traditional works of ethnography, accounts were presented without very much information about the observer. This was because it was believed that ethnographers could present objective pictures of the things they studied. More recently, ethnographers have increasingly tended to talk about themselves and the nature of their connection to the people under study. Sometimes, for example, it might be a matter of trying to consider how one's race, class, or gender affected the work or how the power differences between observer and observed distorted the dialogue between them.

ADVANTAGES AND LIMITATIONS OF FIELDWORK

Where it is successful, ethnography provides information on the behavior of people in groups, organizations, and communities and how those people understand their own behavior. Once we see how things look from inside a given group, we are likely to develop a better understanding not only of that group, but of social processes that transcend the situation under study.

But fieldwork also has major limitations. Only fairly small groups or communities can be studied. And much depends on the skill of the researcher in gaining the confidence of the individuals involved; without this skill, the research is unlikely to get off the ground at all. The reverse is also possible. A researcher could begin to identify so closely with the group that he becomes too much of an "insider" and loses the perspective of an outside observer. Or a researcher may interpret the situation he is studying and reach conclusions that are more about his own effects on the situation than he or his readers ever realize.

Surveys

Interpreting field studies usually involves problems of generalization. Because only a small number of people are under study, we cannot be sure that what is found in one context will apply in other situations as well or even that two different researchers would come to the same conclusions when studying the same group. This is usually less of a problem in survey research. In a **survey,** questionnaires are either sent or administered directly in interviews to a selected group of people—sometimes as many as several thousand. This group of people

TABLE 2.2

Three of the Main Methods Used in Sociological Research

RESEARCH METHOD	STRENGTHS	LIMITATIONS
Ethnography	Usually generates richer and more in-depth information than other methods.	Can be used to study only relatively small groups or communities.
	Ethnography can provide a broader understanding of social processes.	Findings might apply only to groups or communities studied; not easy to generalize on the basis of a single fieldwork study.
Surveys	Make possible the efficient collection of data on large numbers of individuals.	Material gathered may be superficial; if questionnaire is highly standardized, important differences among respondents' viewpoints may be glossed over.
	Allow for precise comparisons to be made among the answers of respondents.	Responses may be what people profess to believe rather than what they actually believe.
Experiments	Influence of specific variables can be controlled by the investigator.	Many aspects of social life cannot be brought into the laboratory.
	Are usually easier for subsequent researchers to repeat.	Responses of those studied may be affected by the experimental situation.

is referred to by sociologists as a **population.** Fieldwork is best suited for in-depth studies of small slices of social life; survey research tends to produce information that is less detailed but that can usually be applied over a broad area.

STANDARDIZED AND OPEN-ENDED QUESTIONNAIRES

Two sorts of questionnaires are used in surveys. Some contain a standardized, or fixed-choice, set of questions, to which only a fixed range of responses is possible—for instance, *Yes, No, Don't know* or *Very likely, Likely, Unlikely, Very unlikely.* Such surveys have the advantage that responses are easy to compare and count up, because only a small number of categories are involved. On the other hand, because they do not allow for subtleties of opinion or verbal expression, the information they yield is likely to be restricted in scope, if not misleading.

Other questionnaires are open ended: respondents have more opportunity to express their views in their own words; they are not limited to making fixed-choice responses. Open-ended questionnaires typically provide more detailed informa-

tion than standardized ones. The researcher can follow up answers to probe more deeply into what the respondent thinks. On the other hand, the lack of standardization means that responses may be more difficult to compare statistically.

Questionnaire items are normally listed so that a team of interviewers can ask the questions and record responses in the same predetermined order. All the items must be readily understandable to interviewers and interviewees alike. In the large national surveys undertaken regularly by government agencies and research organizations, interviews are carried out more or less simultaneously across the whole country. Those who conduct the interviews and those who analyze the results could not do their work effectively if they constantly had to be checking with each other about ambiguities in the questions or answers.

Questionnaires should also take into consideration the characteristics of respondents. Will they see the point the researcher has in mind in asking a particular question? Have they enough information to answer usefully? Will they answer at all? The terms of a questionnaire might be unfamiliar to the respondents. For instance, the question "What is your marital status?" might baffle some people. It would be more appropriate to ask, "Are you single, married, separated, or divorced?" Most surveys are preceded by pilot studies in order to pick up problems not anticipated by the investigator. A **pilot study** is a trial run in which a questionnaire is completed by just a few people. Any difficulties can then be ironed out before the main survey is done.

SAMPLING

Often sociologists are interested in the characteristics of large numbers of individuals—for example, the political attitudes of the American population as a whole. It would be impossible to study all these people directly, so in such situations researchers engage in **sampling**—they concentrate on a **sample,** or small proportion of the overall group. One can usually be confident that results from a population sample, as long as the sample was properly chosen, can be generalized to the total population. Studies of only two to three thousand voters, for instance, can give a very accurate indication of the attitudes and voting intentions of the entire population. But to achieve such accuracy, the sample must be a **representative sample:** The group of individuals studied must be typical of the population as a whole. Sampling is more complex than it might seem, and statisticians have developed rules for working out the correct size and nature of samples.

A particularly important procedure used to ensure that a sample is representative is **random sampling,** in which a sample is chosen so that every member of the population has the same probability of being included. The most sophisticated way of obtaining a random sample is to give each member of the population a number and then use a computer to generate a random list, from which the sample is derived—for instance, by picking every tenth number.

"THE PEOPLE'S CHOICE"

One of the most famous early examples of survey research was "The People's Choice" a study carried out by Paul Lazarsfeld and a number of colleagues about half a century ago (Lazarsfeld, et al. 1948). This study, which investigated the voting intentions of residents of Erie County, Ohio, during the 1940 campaign for the U.S. presidency, pioneered several of the main techniques of survey research in use to this day. To probe a little more deeply than a single questionnaire would do, the investigators interviewed each member of a sample of voters on seven separate occasions. The aim was to trace and understand the reasons for changes in voting attitudes.

The research was set up with a number of definite hypotheses in view. One was that relationships and events close to voters in a community influence voting intentions more than distant world affairs, and the findings on the whole confirmed this. The researchers developed sophisticated measurement techniques for analyzing political attitudes; yet their work also made significant contributions to theoretical thinking. Among the concepts they helped introduce were those of "opinion leaders" and the "two-step flow of communication." The study showed that some individuals—opinion leaders—tend to shape the political opinions of those around them. People's views are not formed in a direct fashion, but in a two-step process. In the first step, opinion leaders react to political events; in the second step, those leaders influence people around them—relatives, friends, and colleagues. The views expressed by opinion leaders, filtered through personal relationships, then influence the responses of other individuals toward political issues of the day.

ADVANTAGES AND DISADVANTAGES OF SURVEYS

Surveys are widely used in sociological research for several reasons. Questionnaire responses can be more easily quantified and analyzed than material generated by most other research methods; large numbers of people can be studied; and, given sufficient funds, researchers can employ an agency specializing in survey work to collect the responses. The scientific method is the model for this kind of research, as surveys give researchers a statistical measure of what they are studying.

However, many sociologists are critical of the survey method. They argue that an appearance of precision can be given to findings whose accuracy may be dubious, given the relatively shallow nature of most survey responses. Levels of nonresponse are sometimes high, especially when questionnaires are sent and returned through the mail. It is not uncommon for studies to be published based on results derived from little over half of those in a sample, although normally an effort is made to recontact nonrespondents or to substitute other people. Little is known about those who choose not to respond to surveys or refuse to be interviewed, but survey research is often experienced as intrusive and time consuming.

Experiments

An **experiment** can be defined as an attempt to test a hypothesis under highly controlled conditions established by an investigator. Experiments are often used in the natural sciences, as they offer major advantages over other research proce-

and the level of tension so high that the experiment had to be called off at an early stage. The results, however, were important. Zimbardo concluded that behavior in prisons is more influenced by the nature of the prison situation itself than by the individual characteristics of those involved.

Life Histories

In contrast to experiments, **life histories** belong purely to sociology and the other social sciences; they have no place in natural science. Life histories consist of biographical material assembled about particular individuals—usually as recalled by the individuals themselves. Other procedures of research don't usually yield as much information as the life-history method does about the development of beliefs and attitudes over time. Life-historical studies rarely rely wholly on people's memories, however. Normally, sources such as letters, contemporary reports, and newspaper descriptions are used to expand on and check the validity of the information individuals provide. Sociologists' views differ on the value of life histories: Some feel they are too unreliable to provide useful information, but others believe they offer sources of insight that few other research methods can match.

Life histories have been successfully employed in studies of major importance. A celebrated early study was *The Polish Peasant in Europe and America,* by W. I. Thomas and Florian Znaniecki (1966), the five volumes of which were first published between 1918 and 1920. Thomas and Znaniecki were able to provide a more sensitive and subtle account of the experience of migration than would have been possible without the interviews, letters, and newspaper articles they collected.

Comparative Research

Each of the research methods just described is often applied in a comparative context. **Comparative research** is of central importance in sociology because making comparisons allows us to clarify what is going on in a particular area of research. Let's take the American rate of divorce—the number of divorces granted each year—as an example. Divorce rates rose rapidly in the United States after World War II, reaching a peak in the early 1980s. Current trends suggest that as many as one in five couples marrying today will divorce—a statistic that expresses profound changes taking place in the area of sexual relations and family life (U.S. Bureau of the Census 2005). Do these changes reflect specific features of American society? We can find out by comparing divorce rates in the United States with those of other countries. Such a comparison reveals that although the U.S. rate is higher than that of

In Philip Zimbardo's make-believe jail, tension between students playing guards and students playing prisoners became dangerously real. From his experiment Zimbardo concluded that behavior in prisons is influenced more by the nature of the prison itself than the individual characteristics of those involved.

dures. In an experimental situation, the researcher directly controls the circumstances being studied. As compared with the natural sciences, the scope for experimentation in sociology is quite restricted. We can bring only small groups of individuals into a laboratory setting, and in such experiments, people know that they are being studied and may behave unnaturally.

Nevertheless, experimental methods can occasionally be applied in a helpful way in sociology. An example is the ingenious experiment carried out by Philip Zimbardo (1992), who set up a make-believe jail, randomly assigning some student volunteers to the role of guards and other volunteers to the role of prisoners. His aim was to see how far playing these different parts led to changes in attitude and behavior. The results shocked the investigators. Students who played at being guards quickly assumed an authoritarian manner; they displayed real hostility toward the prisoners, ordering them around and verbally abusing and bullying them. The prisoners, by contrast, showed a mixture of apathy and rebelliousness—a response often noted among inmates in real prisons. These effects were so marked

Studying the Homeless

Since the 1980s, there has been a remarkable growth in the number of homeless people in the United States. But how big is the problem? How can we know whom to count as homeless? These are questions that social scientists have sought to answer, often coming up with dramatically different results.

Until the mid-1980s, the conventional wisdom was that there were over one million homeless people, but the statistics were essentially undocumented. Why was it so difficult to know? The reason is that it is difficult to count people living in bus stations, subways, abandoned buildings, doorways, or Dumpsters. In the absence of hard data, politicians relied on estimates provided by "homeless activists." For instance, one prominent activist, Mitch Snyder, told Ted Koppel in a 1984 episode of ABC's *Nightline* that the number was between two and three million. When asked where his numbers came from, he responded, "We got on the phone, we made a lot of calls, we talked to a lot of people, and we said, 'Okay, here are some numbers.'"

In his 1994 book *The Homeless,* the sociologist Christopher Jencks stressed how important it is to look at hard data based on documented research instead of political numbers chosen to have the maximum effect on government policy. Jencks's research strategy was to assess carefully data and research collected by other social scientists or government agencies and come up with a more precise definition and count of the homeless. His definition excluded a number of people generally counted as homeless, such a those living in welfare hotels at the expense of social welfare programs, and therefore produced a number far smaller than the rough guesses of journalists and activists.

immediate concerns? What do they do with their limited possessions? Why do they think they are homeless?

The differences between Jencks's and Liebow's studies illustrate the differences between quantitative and qualitative research and between macrosociology and microsociology. By carefully scrutinizing the known data on the homeless, Jencks contributed a better knowledge of the extent of homelessness. By learning more about the day-to-day experiences of being homeless, Liebow contributed a better understanding of the everyday life conditions of the homeless. Both are crucial for coming to grips with the problem and developing more informed welfare policies.

The sociologist Elliot Liebow studied homelessness entirely differently and wrote about it in his book *Tell Them Who I Am* (1993). Liebow went out on the streets of Washington, D.C., and observed homelessness firsthand. He befriended the homeless women he was studying, volunteered to work in shelters, and helped them get along with their lives. Some would argue that in doing so, Liebow breached the rules of research discussed in this chapter, allowing himself to identify too closely with the group he was studying. But Liebow was able to learn something about homelessness that other research failed to illuminate: What do homeless people do all day? What are their most

Questions

- What are the benefits of a quantitative method of talking about homelessness or about any social problem? What are the disadvantages of this method?
- How and why is it advantageous for sociologists to distance themselves from their subjects? How can identifying with one's subject help one's research?

most other Western societies, the overall trends are similar. Virtually all Western countries have experienced steadily climbing divorce rates over the past half century.

Historical Analysis

As was mentioned in Chapter 1, a historical perspective is often essential in sociological research. For we frequently need a *time perspective* to make sense of the material we collect about a particular problem.

Sociologists commonly want to investigate past events directly. Some periods of history can be studied in a direct way, when survivors are still alive—such as in the case of the Holocaust in Europe during World War II. Research in **oral history** means interviewing people about events they witnessed at some point earlier in their lives. This kind of research work, obviously, can stretch at the most only some sixty or seventy years back in time. For historical research on an earlier period, sociologists depend on the use of documents and written records, often contained in the special collections of libraries or the National Archives.

An interesting example of the use of historical documents is sociologist Anthony Ashworth's (1980) study of trench warfare during World War I. Ashworth was concerned with analyzing what life was like for men who had to endure being under constant fire, crammed in close proximity for weeks on end. He drew on a diversity of documentary sources: official histories of the war, including those written about different military divisions and battalions; official publications of the time; the notes and records kept informally by individual soldiers; and personal accounts of war experiences. By drawing on such a variety of sources, Ashworth was able to develop a rich and detailed description of life in the trenches. He discovered that most soldiers formed their own ideas about how often they intended to engage in combat with the enemy and often effectively ignored the commands of their officers. For example, on Christmas Day, German and Allied soldiers suspended hostilities, and in one place the two sides even staged an informal soccer match.

Combining Comparative and Historical Research

Ashworth's research concentrated on a relatively short time period. As an example of a study that investigated a much longer one and that also applied comparative research in a historical context, we can take Theda Skocpol's *States and Social Revolutions* (1979), one of the best-known studies of social change. Skocpol set herself an ambitious task: to produce a theory of the origins and nature of revolution grounded in detailed empirical study. She looked at processes of revolution in three different historical contexts: the 1789 revolution in France, the 1917 revolution in Russia (which brought the communists to power and established the Soviet Union, which was eventually dissolved in 1989), and the revolution of 1949 in China (which created communist China).

By analyzing a variety of documentary sources, Skocpol was able to develop a powerful explanation of revolutionary change, one that emphasized the underlying social structural conditions. She showed that social revolutions are largely the result of unintended consequences. Before the Russian Revolution, for instance, various political groups were trying to overthrow the preexisting regime, but none of these—including the Bolsheviks (communists), who eventually came to power—anticipated the revolution that occurred. A series of clashes and confrontations gave rise to a process of social transformation that was much more radical than anyone had foreseen.

Research in the Real World: Methods, Problems, and Pitfalls

All research methods, as was stressed earlier, have their advantages and limitations. Hence it is common to combine several methods in a single piece of research, using each to supplement and check on the others in a process known as **triangulation.** We can see the value of combining methods—and, more generally, the problems and pitfalls of real sociological research—by looking once again at Humphreys's *Tearoom Trade.*

One of the questions that Humphreys wanted to answer was: What kinds of men came to the tearooms? But it was very hard for him to find this out because all he could really do in the bathrooms was observe. The norm of silence in the restrooms made it difficult to ask any questions or even to talk. Plus, it would have been very odd if he had begun to ask personal questions of people who basically wanted to be anonymous.

Humphreys's solution was to try to find out more about the men in the tearooms using survey methods. Standing by the door of the restrooms, he would write down the license plate numbers of people who pulled up to the parking lot and then went into the restrooms for the purpose of engaging in sexual

Statistical Terms

Research in sociology often makes use of statistical techniques in the analysis of findings. Some are highly sophisticated and complex, but those most often used are easy to understand. The most common are **measures of central tendency** (ways of calculating averages) and **correlation coefficients** (measures of the degree to which one variable relates consistently to another).

There are three methods of calculating averages, each of which has certain advantages and shortcomings. Take as an example the amount of personal wealth (including all assets such as houses, cars, bank accounts, and investments) owned by thirteen individuals. Suppose the thirteen own the following amounts:

1	$ 0	8	$ 80,000
2	$ 5,000	9	$ 100,000
3	$10,000	10	$ 150,000
4	$20,000	11	$ 200,000
5	$40,000	12	$ 400,000
6	$40,000	13	$10,000,000
7	$40,000		

The **mean** corresponds to the average, arrived at by adding together the personal wealth of all the people and dividing the result by the number of people in the sample (13). The total is $11,085,000; dividing this by 13, we calculate the mean to be $852,692.31. The mean is often a useful calculation because it is based on the whole range of data provided. However, it can be misleading when one or a small number of cases are very different from the majority. In this example, the mean is not in fact an appropriate measure of central tendency, because the presence of one very large figure, $10,000,000, skews the picture. One might get the impression when using the mean to summarize these data that most of the people own far more than they actually do.

In such instances, one of two other measures may be used. The **mode** is the figure that occurs most frequently in a given set of data. In our example, it is $40,000. The problem with the mode is that it doesn't take into account the *overall distribution* of the data—that is, the range of figures covered. The most frequently occurring case in a set of figures is not necessarily representative of the distribution as a whole and thus may not be a useful average. In this example, $40,000 is too close to the lower end of the figures.

The third measure is the **median,** which is the middle of any set of figures; here, this would be the seventh figure, again $40,000. Our sample inclues an odd number of figures, 13. If there had been an even number—for instance, 12—the median would be calculated by taking the mean of the two middle cases, figures 6 and 7. Like the mode, the median gives no indication of the actual *range* of the data measured.

Sometimes a researcher will use more than one measure of central tendency to avoid giving a deceptive picture of the average. More often, he will calculate the **standard deviation** for the data in question. This is a way of calculating the **degree of dispersal,** or the range, of a set of figures—which in this case goes from 0 to $10,000,000.

Correlation coefficients offer a useful way of expressing how closely connected two (or more) variables are. When two variables correlate completely, we can speak of a perfect positive correlation, expressed as 1.0. When no relation is found between two variables—they have no consistent connection at all—the coefficient is 0. A perfect negative correlation, expressed as −1.0, exists when two variables are in a completely inverse relation to one another. Perfect correlations are never found in the social sciences. Correlations of the order of 0.6 or more, whether positive or negative, are usually regarded as indicating a strong degree of connection between whatever variables are being analyzed. Positive correlations on this level might be found between, say, social class background and voting behavior.

relations. He then gave those license plate numbers to a friend who worked at the Department of Motor Vehicles, securing the addresses of the men.

Months later, Washington University in St. Louis was conducting a door-to-door survey of sexual habits. Humphreys asked the principal investigators in that survey if he could add the names and addresses of his sample of tearoom partici-

pants. Humphreys then disguised himself as one of the investigators and went to interview these men at their homes, supposedly just to ask only the survey questions but actually to also learn more about their social backgrounds and lives. He found that most of these men were married and otherwise led very conventional lives. He often interviewed wives and other family members as well.

Reading a Table

You will often come across tables in reading sociological literature. They sometimes look complex but are easy to decipher if you follow the few basic steps listed here; with practice, these will become automatic. (See Table 2.3 as an example.) Do not succumb to the temptation to skip over tables; they contain information in concentrated form, which can be read more quickly than would be possible if the same material were expressed in words. By becoming skilled in the interpretation of tables, you will also be able to check how justified the conclusions a writer draws actually are.

1. Read the title in full. Tables frequently have longish titles, which represent an attempt by the researcher to state accurately the nature of the information conveyed. The title of Table 2.3 gives first the *subject* of the data, second the fact that the table provides material for comparison, and third the fact that data are given only for a limited number of countries.

2. Look for explanatory comments, or *notes,* about the data. A footnote to Table 2.3 linked to the main column heading indicates that the data cover only licensed cars. This is important, because in some countries the proportion of vehicles properly licensed may be lower than in others. Footnotes may say how the material was collected or why it is displayed in a particular way. If the data have not been gathered by the researcher but are based on findings originally reported elsewhere, a source will be included. The source sometimes gives you some insight into how reliable the information is likely to be as well as tells you where to find the original data. In Table 2.3, the source note makes clear that the data have been taken from more than one source.

3. Read the *headings* along the top and left-hand side of the table. (Sometimes tables are arranged with "headings" at the foot rather than the top.) These tell you what type of information is contained in each row and column. In reading the table, keep in mind each set of headings as you scan the figures. In our example, the headings on the left name the countries involved, while those at the top refer to the levels of car ownership and the years for which numbers apply.

4. Identify the units used; the figures in the body of the table may represent cases, percentages, averages, or other measures. Sometimes it may be helpful to convert the figures to a form more useful to you: If percentages are not provided, for example, it may be worth calculating them.

5. Consider the conclusions that might be reached from the information in the table. Most tables are discussed by the author, and what he or she has to say should of course be borne in mind. But you should also ask what further issues or questions could be suggested by the data.

TABLE 2.3

Automobile Ownership:
Comparisons of Several Selected Countries

Several interesting trends can be seen from the figures in this table. First, the level of car ownership varies considerably among different countries. The number of cars per 1,000 people is more than six times greater in the United States than in Brazil, for example. Second, there is a clear connection between car ownership ratios as a rough indicator of differences in prosperity. Third, in all the countries represented, the rate of car ownership increased between 1971 and 2002, but in some the rate of increase was higher than others—probably indicating differences in the degree to which countries have successfully generated economic growth or are catching up.

COUNTRY	NUMBER OF CARS PER 1,000 OF THE ADULT POPULATION[a]							
	1971	1981	1984	1989	1993	1996	2001	2002
Brazil	12	78	84	98	96	79	95	116
Chile	19	45	56	67	94	110	133	NA
Ireland	141	202	226	228	290	307	442	445
France	261	348	360	574	503	524	584	592
Greece	30	94	116	150	271	312	428	450
Italy	210	322	359	424	586	674	638	655
Japan	100	209	207	286	506	552	577	581
Sweden	291	348	445	445	445	450	497	500
United Kingdom	224	317	343	366	386	399	554	551
United States	448	536	540	607	747	767	785	789
West Germany[b]	247	385	312	479	470	528	583	588
China	NA	NA	NA	5[c]	6	8	12[d]	16

[a] Includes all licensed cars.

[b] Germany as a whole after 1989.

[c] Data for 1990.

[d] Data for 2000.

NA, not applicable.

SOURCES: Baltic 21 Secretariat, "Passenger Car Density," www.baltic21.org/reports/indicators/re08.htm (accessed spring 2006); International Bank for Reconstruction and Development, World Bank, "World Development Indicators 1999"; International Monetary Fund, World Economic Lookout, 2005, www.imf.org/external/pubs/ft/weo/2005/01/pdf/chapter4.pdf (accessed spring 2006); International Road Federation, *United Nations Annual Bulletin of Transport Statistics,* cited in *Social Trends* (London, HMSO, 1987), p. 68; Organization for Economic Co-operation and Development, *Factbook: Economic, Environmental, and Social Statistics,* 2005, www.oecd.org/site/0,2865,en_21571361_34374092_1_1_1_1,00.html (accessed spring 2006); Statistical Office of the European Communities, *Basic Statistics of the Community* (Luxembourg: European Union, 1991); *The Economist, Pocket World in Figures,* 1996; Toyota Corporation, www.toyota.co.jp/en/pdf/toyota_world/Chap7.pdf; United Nations Economic Commission for Europe, "Ireland," www.unece.org/stats/trend/irl.pdf (accessed spring 2006); World Bank, "World Development Indicators, 2005."

The Sociological Imagination

In the decades following World War II, C. Wright Mills used his sociological imagination to explore the most pressing public issues of his time. Mills was formally affiliated with the Columbia University department of sociology, but refused to confine his critiques of stratification systems, the cold war, and U.S. Latin American foreign policy to the narrow halls of academia. At the time, sociology as a discipline was in the process of becoming a more professional science, mainly by refining theory through the collection and statistical analysis of empirical data. Although he was a professional sociologist by training, Mills resisted the pressure to conform to what his colleagues were doing and the subjects they chose to study. Although he paid a price for this resistance (and perhaps because of it), Mills is remembered today as the most inspiring and courageous American public sociologist of the past fifty years.

Mills was preoccupied with how the experiences of private individuals are formed by the historical conditions in which they live. He wrote, "Men make their own history...but they do not make it under the conditions of their own choice" (Mills 2000, orig. 1959). These conditions affect life chances; and despite a strong American cultural belief in free will, Mills believed that people are not completely autonomous actors capable of determining their own fate. His famous trilogy of books—*The New Men of Power* (1948), *White Collar* (1951), and *The Power Elite* (1956a)—extends this theme to investigate how power has become consolidated in the hands of business, political, and military leaders in modern American society. His words remain eerily relevant today: "The more we understand

C. Wright Mills

what is happening in the world, the more frustrated we often become, for our knowledge leads to feelings of powerlessness. We feel that we are living in a world in which the citizen has become a mere spectator or a forced actor, and that our personal experience is politically useless and our political will a minor illusion" (Mills 2000, orig. 1959).

Mills was not, however, simply a pessimist bent on criticizing the world for its shortcomings. The fact that individual lives are constrained by social forces makes concerted social action all the more important. He sincerely believed in the

Human Subjects and Ethical Problems

All research concerned with human beings can pose ethical dilemmas. A key question that sociologists agree must be asked is whether the research poses risks to the subjects that are greater than the risks they face in their everyday lives.

In writing *Tearoom Trade,* Humphreys said he was less than truthful to those whose behavior he was studying. He said he didn't reveal his identity as a sociologist when ob-

serving the tearoom. People who came into the tearoom assumed he was there for the same reasons they were and that his presence could be accepted at face value. While he did not tell any direct lies while observing the tearoom, he also did not reveal the real reason for his presence there. Was this particular aspect of his behavior ethical? The answer is that, on balance, this particular aspect of his study did not put any of his subjects at risk. On the basis of what he observed in the tearoom, Humphreys did not collect information about the participants that would have identified power of the sociological imagination to connect "personal troubles into public issues, and public issues into the terms of their human meaning" (Mills 2000, orig. 1959). As an exercise in using your sociological imagination, take educational performance as an example. Pretend that you are a teacher; during your first year of teaching you encounter among your twenty-seven students a twelve-year-old boy named Jonathan who reads below grade level. Some might guess that Jonathan's predicament rests in individual explanations of underperformance—he may have a learning disability or perhaps he hasn't applied himself in his schoolwork and should be held personally responsible.

On the other hand, what if you then learned that 70 percent of your students were reading below grade level? The sociological imagination requires a shift in perspective; we may want to ask different types of questions about the forces that effect the lives of students at school. Perhaps these students are members of a historically underprivileged community and have been attending school in substandard buildings. Perhaps they have grown up in a community characterized by high rates of poverty, violence, social disorder, and an absence of professional role models. Perhaps English is not their native language and they have fallen behind in their reading curricula as they worked to acquire a second language. Looking through a sociological lens, educational failure is a complex phenomenon involving a combination of multiple factors, some of which Jonathan may be capable of overcoming and some of which may remain beyond his control. For Mills, the sociological imagination is not just about asking certain types of questions but having the ability to shift from one perspective to another and back again, having "the capacity to range from the most impersonal and remote transformations to the most intimate features of the human self—and to see the relations between the two" (Mills 2000, orig. 1959).

As a writer, speaker, and countercultural icon, Mills used his public role to shed light on the social forces that governed people's lives, connect those forces to people's personal experiences, and advocate collective action as a means of protecting democracy from the reign of powerful elites. As his career progressed, Mills increasingly relished this role. In the final two years of his life, Mills became a well-known public figure. His *Listen, Yankee* appeared on the cover of *Harper's* magazine, and his "Letter to the New Left" inspired writings (such as the Port Huron Statement) that helped launch the civil rights movement. To reach a broad audience, Mills rid himself of "crippling academic prose" to develop an "intelligible way of communicating" to nonspecialized publics (Gitlin, 2000). Unlike many of his colleagues, Mills believed that social science had a role to play in politics. By generating public discussion of issues rather than ingesting them whole as delivered by politicians, Mills (echoing Max Weber) believed that social scientists had an obligation to help repair damage done to democracy by the bureaucratization of the economy and the state. Mills was prophetic in recognizing the limits of both Marxism and liberalism to address the problems of developing countries; in his final years he began to focus attention on forms of international inequality that persist today.

If a passionate commitment to public sociology gave C. Wright Mills meaning in his professional life, it may also have helped hasten his untimely death. In December 1960, as Mills was preparing to debate foreign policy expert A. A. Berle Jr. on network television, he collapsed from a heart attack. In under fifteen months he was dead. Mills was only forty-five years old. He had produced an impressive body of work in a career that spanned just over a decade, and he relentlessly attacked "irresponsibility organized in high places," which he believed caused "those on the bottom—the forced actors who take the consequences—[to go] without leaders, without ideas of opposition" (Mills 2000, orig. 1959). Mills was not only a force of opposition but a renegade leader who committed his considerable intellectual energy to the hope that democratic engagement would one day be revived.

them. What he knew about them was similar to what all the other people in the tearoom knew. In this way, his presence did not subject them to any more risk than they already encountered in their everyday lives. At the same time, had Humphreys been completely frank at every stage, the research might not have gotten as far as it did. Indeed, some of the most valuable data that have been collected by sociologists could have never been gathered if the researcher had first explained the project to each person encountered in the research process.

If this were the only dilemma posed by Humphreys's research project, it would not stand out as a notable problem in the ethics of social research. What raised more eyebrows was that Humphreys wrote down the license plate numbers of the people who came into the tearooms, obtained their home addresses from a friend who worked at the Department of Motor Vehicles, and visited their homes in the guise of conducting a neutral survey. Even though Humphreys did not reveal to the men's families anything about their activities in the tearooms, and even though he took great pains to keep the data confidential, the knowledge he gained could have been damaging. Because the activity he was documenting was illegal, police officers might have demanded that he release information about the identities of the subjects. It is also possible that a less skilled investigator could have slipped up when interviewing the subjects' families or that Humphreys could have lost his notes, which could then have been found later by someone else. Considering the number of things that could go wrong in the research process, researchers do not consider projects of this kind to be legitimate.

Humphreys was one of the first sociologists to study the lives of gay men. His account was a humane treatment that went well beyond the existing stock of knowledge on sexual communities. Although none of his research subjects actually suffered as a result of his book, Humphreys himself later agreed with his critics on the key ethical controversy. He said that were he to do the study again, he would not trace license plates or go to people's homes. Instead, after gathering his data in the public tearooms, he might try to get to know a subset of the people well enough to inform them of his goals for the study and then ask them to talk about the significance of these activities in their lives.

In recent years, the federal government has become increasingly strict with universities that make use of government grant money for research purposes. The National Science Foundation and the National Institutes of Health have strict requirements outlining how human subjects must be treated. In response to these requirements, American universities now routinely review all research that involves human subjects. The result of these review procedures has been both positive and negative. On the one hand, researchers are more aware of ethical considerations than ever before. On the other hand, many sociologists are finding it increasingly difficult to get their work done when institutional review boards required them to secure informed consent from their research subjects before they are able to establish a rapport with the subjects. There will likely never be easy solutions to problems of this kind.

The Influence of Sociology

Sociological research is rarely of interest only to the intellectual community of sociologists. Its results are often disseminated throughout society. Sociology, it must be emphasized, is not just the *study* of modern societies; it is a significant element *in the continuing life* of those societies. Take the transformations occurring in the United States in marriage, sexuality, and the family. Few people living in a modern society do not have some knowledge of these changes, as a result of the filtering down of sociological research. Our thinking and behavior are affected by sociological knowledge in complex and often subtle ways, thus reshaping the very field of sociological investigation. A way of describing this phenomenon, using the technical concepts of sociology, is to say that sociology stands in a reflexive relation to the human beings whose behavior is studied. **Reflexivity** describes the interchange between sociological research and human behavior. We should not be surprised that sociological findings often correlate closely with common sense. The reason is not simply that sociology comes up with findings we knew already; it is rather that sociological research continually influences what our common-sense knowledge of society actually *is*.

Study Outline

www.wwnorton.com/giddens

The Research Process

- Sociologists investigate social life by posing distinct questions and trying to find the answers to these by systematic research. These questions may be *factual, comparative, developmental,* or *theoretical.*
- All research begins from a *research problem,* which interests or puzzles the investigator. Research problems may be suggested by gaps in the existing literature, theoretical debates, or practical issues in the social world. There are a number of clear steps in the development of research strategies—although these are rarely followed exactly in actual research.

Understanding Cause and Effect

- A *causal relationship* between two events or situations is one in which one event or situation brings about the other. This is more problematic than it seems at first. *Causation* must be distinguished from *correlation,* which refers to the existence of a regular relationship between two *variables.* A variable can be differences in age, income, crime rates, and so on. We need to also distinguish *independent variables* from *dependent variables.* An independent variable is a variable that produces an effect on another. Sociologists often use *controls* to ascertain a causal relationship.

Research Methods

- In fieldwork, or *participant observation,* the researcher spends lengthy periods of time with a group or community being studied. A second method, *survey research,* involves sending or administering questionnaires to samples of a larger *population.* Documentary research uses printed materials, from archives or other resources, as a source for information. Other research methods include *experiments,* the use of *life histories,* historical analysis, and *comparative research.*

- Each of these various methods of research has its limitations. For this reason, researchers will often combine two or more methods in their work, each being used to check or supplement the material obtained from the others. This process is called *triangulation.*

The Influence of Sociology

- Sociological research often poses ethical dilemmas. These may arise either where deception is practiced against those who are the subjects of the research, or where the publication of research findings might adversely affect the feelings or lives of those studied. There is no entirely satisfactory way to deal with these issues, but all researchers have to be sensitive to the dilemmas they pose.

Key Concepts

causal relationship (p. 36)
causation (p. 36)
comparative questions (p. 33)
comparative research (p. 41)
controls (p. 37)
correlation (p. 36)
correlation coefficients (p. 45)
degree of dispersal (p. 45)
dependent variable (p. 37)
developmental questions (p. 33)
empirical investigations (p. 33)
ethnography (p. 38)
experiment (p. 40)
factual questions (p. 33)
hypotheses (p. 34)
independent variable (p. 37)
life histories (p. 41)
mean (p. 45)
measures of central tendency (p. 45)
median (p. 45)
mode (p. 45)
oral history (p. 44)
participant observation (p. 38)
pilot study (p. 40)
population (p. 39)

random sampling (p. 40)
reflexivity (p. 50)
representative sample (p. 40)
research methods (p. 33)
sample (p. 40)
sampling (p. 40)
standard deviation (p. 45)
survey (p. 38)
theoretical questions (p. 33)
triangulation (p. 44)
variable (p. 36)

Review Questions

1. The order of the stages of the sociological research process is
   a. defining the problem, making the problem precise, reviewing the evidence, working out a design, carrying out research, interpreting the results, and reporting the findings.
   b. defining the problem, reviewing the evidence, making the problem precise, working out a design, carrying out research, interpreting the results, and reporting the findings.
   c. defining the problem, reviewing the evidence, making the problem precise, working out a design, interpreting the results, carrying out research, and reporting the findings.
   d. making the problem precise, defining the problem, reviewing the evidence, working out a design, carrying out research, interpreting the results, and reporting the findings.

2. What is the standard deviation?
   a. a measure of the degree of concentration around the arithmetic mean
   b. a measure of the degree of dispersal, or range, of a set of figures
   c. the median divided by the mode
   d. the degree of variation in respect of group norms

3. What are the main steps that must be taken to administer a social survey?
   a. making the problem precise enough to study, deciding whether to use fixed-choice or open-ended questions, and generating a representative sample
   b. doing a pilot study, generating a representative sample of respondents, and calculating correlation coefficients
   c. deciding whether to use fixed-choice or open-ended questions, doing a pilot study, and generating a representative sample of respondents
   d. generating a representative sample of respondents, calculating correlation coefficients, and writing up the study

4. What are the main limitations of using documents in sociological research?
   a. They may be partial and difficult to interpret.
   b. They are not as useful as interviews with those who wrote them.

c. They are quickly outdated by subsequent events.

d. They do not lend themselves to statistical analysis.

5. Which type of sociological method is exemplified by Thomas and Znaniecki's *Polish Peasant in Europe and America* (1966)?

   a. life histories

   b. oral history

   c. historical analysis

   d. comparative analysis

6. What does it mean to say that, unlike the natural sciences, sociology stands in reflexive relationship to its subject of study?

   a. The findings of sociology can reflect the behavior of those studied.

   b. The findings of sociology can be understood by those studied, whereas the findings of the natural sciences cannot.

   c. The findings of sociology can affect the behavior of those studied and influence our collective understanding of what society actually is.

   d. The findings of sociology are the subject of public debate, whereas those of the natural sciences are not.

7. All research begins with

   a. a hypothesis.

   b. conclusions.

   c. the research design.

   d. a research problem.

8. The process in which researchers often combine two or more methods in their work, each being used to check or supplement the material obtained from the others, is called

   a. sampling.

   b. correlation.

   c. triangulation.

   d. control.

9. How does the text suggest sociologists can conduct good sociological research?

   a. By working in teams, sociologists are less likely to let personal bias influence their research.

   b. By asking subjects numerous questions, including trick questions, sociologists can make sure a subject is telling the truth.

   c. There is no standard for conducting sociological research.

   d. The best results can be obtained by making the questions posed as precise as possible and by gathering factual evidence before making a conclusion.

10. Which of the following research methods tests a hypothesis in a highly controlled environment?

    a. experiment

    b. survey

    c. life history

    d. participant observation

Thinking Sociologically Exercises

1. Let's suppose the dropout rate in your local high school increased dramatically. Faced with such a serious problem, the board offers you a $500,000 grant to do a study to explain the sudden increase. Following the recommended study procedures outlined in the text, explain how you would go about doing your research. What might be some of the hypotheses to test in your study? How would you prove or disprove them?

2. Explain in some detail the advantages and disadvantages of doing documentary research. What will it yield that will be better than experimentation, surveys, and ethnographic field work? What are its limitations compared with those approaches?

Data Exercises

www.wwnorton.com/giddens
Keyword: Data2

Now that you have read about the research process in sociology, it is time to gain some experience of your own. This Data Exercise is an opportunity for you to apply the sociological perspective as you analyze data and draw conclusions about Americans' attitudes toward abortion.

PART TWO

THE INDIVIDUAL AND SOCIETY

We start our exploration of sociology by looking at the connections between individual development and culture and by analyzing types of society from the past and present. Our personalities and outlooks are strongly influenced by the culture and society in which each of us exists. However, we actively re-create and reshape the cultural and social contexts in which our activities occur.

In Chapter 3, we examine the unity and diversity of human culture. We consider how human beings resemble and differ from animals and analyze the range of variations among human cultures.

Chapter 4 discusses socialization, concentrating on how the human infant develops into a social being. Socialization continues through the life span, so studying it also means analyzing the relationships among young, middle-aged, and older people.

In Chapter 5, we discuss how people interact in everyday life. We look at the mechanisms individuals use to interpret what others say and do. The study of social interaction can tell us a great deal about the larger social environment in which we live.

In Chapter 6, we study social groups, networks, and organizations and how individuals interact in various settings. Chapter 7 moves on to look at deviance and crime. We can learn much about the way a population behaves by studying people whose behavior deviates from generally accepted patterns.

The Sociological Study of Culture

Know what culture consists of and recognize how it differs from society.

The Development of Human Culture

Begin to understand how both biological and cultural factors influence our behavior. Learn the ideas of sociobiology and how others have tried to refute them by emphasizing cultural differences.

Disappearing World: Premodern Societies and Their Fate

Learn how societies have changed over time.

Societies in the Modern World

Recognize the factors that changed premodern societies, particularly how industrialization and colonialism influenced global development. Know the differences among the First World, the Second World, and the developing world (Third World) and how they came about.

The Effect of Globalization

Recognize the effect of globalization on your life and the lives of people around the world. Think about the effect of a growing global culture.

CHAPTER THREE

CULTURE AND SOCIETY

n the last decade of the twentieth century the French president Jacques Chirac was visiting France's new National Library, where he reportedly viewed for the first time a computer mouse. Chirac expressed wonderment at the new technology (Cairncross 1997). The United States at that time ranked first among major countries in terms of Internet servers; France was not even among the top twenty-five (Starrs 1997).

France is no less modern than the United States. Why was it so reluctant to come online? Could it be that in 1997, as today, the Internet was dominated by the United States and was thus a powerful source for spreading American culture, along with the English language?

The unofficial language of the Internet is English, yet this is changing fast. In 2000, nearly half of all Internet users worldwide were American (Nua.com 2000). Today, just over 20 percent of world Internet users are American (Internet World Stats 2005a). The Chinese are also going online in increasingly large numbers, with more than 100 million Internet users in 2005—nearly 460 percent more than in 2000 (China Internet Network Information Center 2005; Magnier 2005). One study (published in French) concluded that 82 percent of all Web sites are in English—even though 94 percent of the world's population speaks some other language (Internet Society [ISOC] 1997; Wallraff 2000) and only about 30 percent of Internet users are native English speakers (Internet World Stats 2005b). The French are especially sensitive about the threat of American culture and the English language to their way of life. The French government spends $100 million a year promoting the country's language and culture (Jones 1998) and has actively sought to curb the "invasion" of English words such as *software* and *computer*. Many French people resent what they call American "cultural imperialism," seen as a form of conquest—one of values and attitudes—and including such unwelcome imports as McDonald's restaurants. McDonald's, their high golden arches a visible symbol of American cultural domination, have even been attacked and burned down in France.

France is not alone in resisting the inroads of American culture. In Germany, for example, the Club for the Preservation of the German Language was founded to combat, in the words of its founder, "the colonization of German by English" (quoted in Jones, 1998). As American culture spreads around the world through film, television, and now the Internet, many people fear the erosion of their own cultures—even as they tune in to *The Simpsons*, sip Coke or Pepsi, and download music from the Web. Is modern technology an irresistable force that will eventually press the world's diverse cultures into a single mold? Or will it permit local cultures to flourish? These are some of the questions we explore in this chapter.

First, however, we look at what culture is and its role in encouraging conformity to shared ways of thinking and acting. We then consider the early development of human culture, emphasizing features that distinguish human behavior from that of other species. After assessing the role of biology in shaping human behavior, we examine the different aspects of culture that make it essential for human society. This leads to a discussion of cultural diversity, examining not only the cultural variations across different societies but also the cultural variations within a society such as the United States.

Cultural variations among human beings are linked to differing types of society, and we compare and contrast the main forms of society found in history. The point of doing this is to closely tie together the two aspects of human social existence—the different cultural values and products that human beings have developed and the contrasting types of society in which such cultural development has occurred. Too often, culture is discussed separately from society as though the two were disconnected, whereas in fact, as we've already emphasized, they are closely meshed. Throughout the chapter, we concentrate on how social change has affected cultural development. One instance of this is the effect of technology and globalization on the many cultures of the world, a topic we explore in the conclusion to this chapter.

The Sociological Study of Culture

The sociological study of culture began with Durkheim in the nineteenth century and soon became the basis of *anthropology,* a social science specifically focused on the study of cultural differences and similarities among the world's many peoples. The work of early sociologists and anthropologists was strongly biased toward the beliefs and values of highly educated Europeans. These early social scientists assumed that "primitive" cultures were inferior, lagging far behind modern European "civilization." However, two destructive world wars, fought largely between European countries that claimed to be the most "civilized" cultures on earth, helped discredit that belief. Sociologists and anthropologists now recognize that there are many different cultures, each with its own distinctive characteristics. The task of social science is to understand this cultural diversity, which is best done by avoiding value judgments.

What Is Culture?

Culture consists of the values the members of a given group hold, the languages they speak, the symbols they revere, the norms they follow, and the material goods they create, from tools to clothing. Some elements of culture, especially the beliefs and expectations people have about each other and the world they inhabit, are a component of all social relations. **Values** are abstract ideals. For example, monogamy—being faithful to a single marriage partner—is a prominent value in most Western societies. In other cultures, on the other hand, a person may be permitted to have several wives or husbands simultaneously. **Norms** are definite principles or rules people are expected to observe; they represent the dos and don'ts of social life. Norms of behavior in marriage include, for example, how husbands and wives are supposed to behave toward their in-laws. In some societies, they are expected to develop a close relationship with their spose's parents; in others, they keep a clear distance from each other.

Norms, like the values they reflect, vary widely across cultures. Among most Americans, for example, one norm calls for direct eye contact between people engaged in conversation; completely averting one's eyes is usually interpreted as a sign of weakness or rudeness. Yet, among the Navajo, a cultural norm calls for averting one's eyes as a sign of respect. Direct eye contact, particularly between strangers, is seen as violating a norm of politeness and consequently as insulting. When a Navajo and a Western tourist encounter one another for the first time, the Navajo's cultural norm calls for averting the eyes, while the tourist's cultural norm calls for direct eye contact. The result is likely to be a misunderstanding: The Navajo may see the tourist as rude and vulgar, while the tourist may see the Navajo as disrespectful or deceptive. Such cultural misunderstandings may lead to unfair generalizations and stereotypes and even promote outright hostility. Values and norms work together to shape how members of a culture behave within their surroundings. For example, in cultures that value learning highly, cultural norms would encourage students to devote great energy to studying and would support parents in making sacrifices for children's education. In a culture that places great value on hospitality, cultural norms might guide expectations about gift giving or about the social behaviors of both guests and hosts.

Finally, **material goods** refer to the physical objects that a society creates, which influence the ways in which people live. They include the goods we consume, from the clothes we wear to the cars we drive to the houses we live in; the tools and technologies we use to make those goods, from sewing machines to computerized factories; and the towns and cities that we build as places in which to live and work. A central aspect of a society's material culture is technology.

Today material culture is rapidly becoming globalized, thanks in large part to modern information technology such as the computer and the Internet. As noted at the beginning of this chapter, the United States has been in the forefront of this technological revolution, although most other industrial countries are rapidly catching up. In fact, it no longer makes sense to speak of an exclusively "U.S. technology" any more than it makes sense to speak of a U.S. car. The "world car," with parts manufactured across the planet in a global assembly line, embodies technology developed in Japan, the United States, and Europe. Automobiles have increasingly come to resemble each other, so that it is difficult to distinguish a car made in Japan from one made in Detroit. Another example of the globalization of material culture is the way classrooms the world over have increasingly come to resemble each other, as have department stores, and the fact that McDonald's restaurants are now found on nearly every continent.

When we use the term *culture* in ordinary daily conversation, we often think of the higher things of the mind—art, literature, music, dance. As sociologists employ it, the concept includes these activities but also far more. Culture refers to the ways of life of the individual members or groups within a society: how they dress, their marriage customs and family life, their patterns of work, their religious ceremonies, and their leisure pursuits. The concept also covers the goods they create and the goods that become meaningful for them—bows and arrows, plows, factories and machines, computers, books, dwellings. We should think of culture as a "design for living" or "tool kit" of practices, knowledge, and symbols acquired—as we shall see later—through learning rather than by instinct (Kluckhohn 1949; Swidler 1986).

How might we describe American culture? It involves, first, a particular range of values shared by many, if not all, Americans—such as the belief in the merits of individual achievement or in equality of opportunity. Second, these values are connected to specific norms: For example, it is usually expected that people will work hard to achieve occupational suc-

cess (Bellah et al. 1985; Parsons 1964). Third, it involves the use of material artifacts created mostly through modern industrial technology, such as cars, mass-produced food, clothing, and so forth.

Values and norms vary enormously across cultures. Some cultures value individualism highly, whereas others place great emphasis on shared needs. A simple example makes this clear. Most pupils in the United States would be outraged to find another student cheating on an examination. In the United States, copying from someone else's paper goes against core values of individual achievement, equality of opportunity, hard work, and respect for the rules. Russian students, however, might be puzzled by this sense of outrage among their American peers. Helping each other pass an examination reflects the value Russians place on equality and on collective problem solving in the face of authority. Think of your own reaction to this example. What does it say about the values of your society?

Even within one society or community, values may conflict: Some groups or individuals might value traditional religious beliefs, whereas others might favor progress and science. Some people might prefer material comfort and success, whereas others might favor simplicity and a quiet life. In our changing age—filled with the global movement of people, ideas, goods, and information—it is not surprising that we encounter instances of cultural values in conflict. Sociological research suggests that such conflicts foster a sense of frustration and isolation in American society (Bellah et al. 1985).

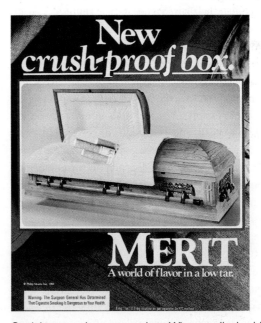

Social norms change over time. When medical evidence linked smoking with serious health problems, a strong social norm in the United States favoring smoking turned toward a strong antismoking social norm.

Norms, like the values they reflect, also change over time. Beginning in 1964, with the U.S. Surgeon General's report "Smoking and Health," which reported definitive medical evidence linking smoking with a large number of serious health problems, the U.S. government waged a highly effective campaign to discourage people from smoking. A strong social norm favoring smoking—once associated with independence, sex appeal, and glamour—has increasingly given way to an equally strong antismoking social norm that depicts smoking as unhealthful, unattractive, and selfish. Today, the percentage of American adults who smoke is only 23 percent (National Center for Health Statistics 2004), half the rate of 1964, when the Surgeon General's Report was issued.

Many norms that people now take for granted in their personal lives—such as premarital sexual relations and unmarried couples' living together—contradict commonly held values even from only several decades ago. The values that guide our intimate relationships have evolved gradually and naturally over a period of many years. But what about instances in which cultural norms and behaviors are altered in a deliberate way?

In January 2000, a Japanese government commission published a report that outlined the main goals for Japan in the twenty-first century. In the face of economic recession, rising crime rates, and high unemployment, the commission was established by the prime minister and given the task of charting a new course for the country in the coming decades. The commission's main findings surprised many people: It found that Japanese citizens need to loosen their hold on some of their core values if their country is to address its current social ills successfully. The commission first concluded that the Japanese culture places too much value on conformity and equality and then called for action to reduce the excessive degree of homogeneity and uniformity in society. The commission pointed to some basic facets of Japanese life that reflect this conformity: For example, almost all schoolchildren in Japan wear identical dark-blue uniforms that mask signs of individuality, and employees generally stay late at the office even if they don't need to because of an unspoken rule that proscribes leaving early. These values, the commission concluded, were preventing Japanese people from embracing notions of individual achievement that would be essential in the coming years. Cultural norms and values are deeply embedded, and it is too early to say whether a government mandate will succeed in altering traditional Japanese values. Yet a common Japanese expression—"the nail that sticks up must be hammered down"—suggests that it may take some time and effort before the Japanese cultural values of conformity and self-effacement are weakened.

Many of our everyday behaviors and habits are grounded in cultural norms. As we shall see in Chapter 5, movements,

The uniforms worn by these Tokyo schoolboys reflect the traditional Japanese value of conformity. A government commission proposed that holding on to such traditional values would prevent the Japanese people from aiming for the individual goals they believe will be necessary for success in the twenty-first century.

gestures, and expressions are strongly influenced by cultural factors. A clear example of this can be seen in the way people smile—particularly in public contexts—across different cultures.

Among the Inuit (Eskimos) of Greenland, for example, one does not find the strong tradition of public smiling that exists in many areas of western Europe and North America. This does not mean that the Inuit are cold or unfriendly; it is simply not their common practice to smile at or exchange pleasantries with strangers. As the service industry has expanded in Greenland in recent years, however, some employers have made efforts to instill smiling as a cultural value in the belief that smiling and expressing "polite" attitudes toward customers are essential to competitive business practices. Clients who are met with smiles and told to "Have a nice day" are more likely to become repeat customers. In many supermarkets in Greenland, shop assistants are now shown training videos on friendly service techniques; the staff at some have even been sent abroad on training courses. The opening of fast-food restaurants like McDonald's in Greenland has introduced Western-style service approaches for the first time. McDonald's employees have been taught to greet customers, introduce themselves, and smile frequently. Initially these requirements were met with some discomfort by staff who found the style insincere and artificial. Over time, however, the idea of public smiling—at least in the workplace—has become more accepted.

Culture and Society

"Culture" can be distinguished from "society," but these notions are closely connected. A **society** is a *system of interrelationships* that connects individuals together. No culture could exist without a society; and equally, no society could exist without culture. Without culture, we would not be human at all, in the sense in which we usually understand that term. We would have no language in which to express ourselves and no sense of self-consciousness; our ability to think or reason would be severely limited.

Culture also serves as a society's glue, because culture is an important source of conformity, providing ready-made ways of thinking and acting for its members. For example, when you say that you subscribe to a particular value, such as formal learning, you are probably voicing the beliefs of your family members, friends, teachers, or others who are significant in your life. When you choose a word to describe some personal experience, that word acquires its meaning in a language you learned from others. When you buy a seemingly unique article of clothing to express your individuality, that garment was very

likely created by the design department of a global manufacturer that carefully studied the current tastes of consumers and then ordered the mass production of your "unique" garment. When you listen to music, it is most likely the same kind of music that your friends listen to.

Cultures differ, however, in how much they value conformity. Research based on surveys of more than 100,000 adults in over sixty countries shows that Japanese culture lies at one extreme in terms of valuing conformity (Hofstede 1997), while at the other extreme lies American culture, one of the least conformist, ranking among the world's highest in cherishing individualism. Americans pride themselves on their independence of spirit, represented by the lone bald eagle, the U.S. national symbol. The assertion "that government is best which governs least" and Hollywood's version of the maverick lawman reinforce as positive the image of the person standing alone, revered and emulated for his independence and individuality.

American high school and college students often see themselves as especially nonconformist. Like the body piercers of today, the hippies of the 1960s and the punks of the 1980s all sported distinctive clothing styles, haircuts, and other forms of bodily adornment. Yet how individualistic are they? Are young people with dyed hair or nose rings or studs in their tongues or tattoos really acting independently? Or are their styles perhaps as much the uniforms of their group as are navy

Members of a 1960s commune pose together for a group portrait (*left*). Punks gather on the street in 1989 (*right*). Though their distinctive styles set them apart from mainstream society, these people are not as nonconformist as they may think they are. Both the hippies and the punks pictured here conform to the norms of their respective social groups.

The Amish and Cell Phones

Amish settlements have become a cliché for refusing technology. Tens of thousands of people wear identical, plain, homemade clothing, cultivate their rich fields with horse-drawn machinery, and live in houses lacking that basic modern spirit called electricity. But the Amish do use such 20th-century consumer technologies as disposable diapers, in-line skates, and gas barbecue grills. Some might call this combination paradoxical, even contradictory. But it could also be called sophisticated, because the Amish have an elaborate system by which they evaluate the tools they use; their tentative, at times reluctant use of technology is more complex than a simple rejection or a whole-hearted embrace. What if modern Americans could possibly agree upon criteria for acceptance, as the Amish have? Might we find better ways to wield technological power, other than simply unleashing it and seeing what happens? What can we learn from a culture that habitually negotiates the rules for new tools?

Last summer, armed with these questions and in the company of an acquaintance with Amish contacts, I traveled around the countryside of Lancaster County, Pennsylvania. *** At one farm we passed, a woman was sitting a hundred yards from her house on the edge of a kitchen garden. She wore the traditional garb of the conservative Old Order—a long, unadorned dress sheathed by an apron, her hair covered by a prayer bonnet. She was sitting in the middle of the garden, alone, the very image of technology-free simplicity. But she was holding her hand up to her ear. She appeared to be intent on something, strangely engaged.

"Whenever you see an Amish woman sitting in the field like that," my guide said, "she's probably talking on a cell phone."

"It's a controversy in the making," he continued. A rather large one, it turns out—yet part of the continuum of determining whether a particular technology belongs in Amish life. They've adopted horses, kerosene lamps, and propane refrigerators; should they add cell phones?

Collective negotiations over the use of telephones have ignited intense controversies in the Amish community since the beginning of the 20th century. In fact, a dispute over the role of the phone was the principal issue behind the 1920s division of the Amish church, wherein one-fifth of the membership broke away to form their own church.

Eventually, certain Amish communities accepted the telephone for its aid in summoning doctors and veterinarians, and in calling suppliers. But even these Amish did not allow the telephone into the home. Rather, they required that phones be used communally. Typically, a neighborhood of two or three extended families shares a telephone housed in a wooden shanty, located either at the intersection of several fields or at the end of a common lane. These structures look like small bus shelters or privies; indeed, some phones are in outhouses. Sometimes the telephone shanties have answering machines in them. (After all, who wants to wait in the privy on the off chance someone will call?)

The first Amish person I contacted, I reached by answering machine. He was a woodworker who, unlike some of his brethren, occasionally talked to outsiders. I left a message on his phone, which I later learned was located in a shanty in his neighbor's pasture. The next day the man, whom I'll call Amos, returned my call. We agreed to meet at his farmstead a few days later.

I couldn't help thinking it was awfully complicated to have a phone you used only for calling back—from a booth in a meadow. Why not make life easier and just put one in the house?

"What would that lead to?" another Amish man asked me. "We don't want to be the kind of people who will interrupt a conversation at home to answer a telephone. It's not just how you use the technology that concerns us. We're also concerned about what kind of person you become when you use it."

***

I asked another Amish workshop owner whom I'll call Caleb what he thought about technology. He pulled some papers out of a file cabinet, handed them to me, and said, "I share some of this fellow's opinions," pointing to a magazine interview with virtual reality pioneer Jaron Lanier. Asked for an opinion he shared with the dreadlocked-and-dashikied Jaron, he replied, "I agree with his statement that you can't design foolproof machines, because fools are so clever."

Caleb also discussed the Amish resistance to becoming "modern." They're not worried about becoming people without religion or people who use lots of technology, he explained; rather, the Amish fear assimilating the far more dangerous ideas that "progress" and new technologies are usually beneficial, that individuality is a precious value, that the goal of life is to "get ahead." This mind-set, not specific technologies, is what the Amish most object to.

"The thing I noticed about the telephone is the way it invades who you are," Caleb said. "We're all losing who we are because of the telephone and other machines—not just the Amish."

***

Donald Kraybill, who is also provost of Messiah College, on the outskirts of Amish country, believes taboos about telephones are "a symbolic way of keeping the technology at a distance and making it your servant, rather than the other way around."

***

It's a pretty safe prediction that when the bishops get around to their formal ruling, cell phones will not be deemed appropriate for personal use. In the 1910s, when the telephone was only beginning

to change the world at large, the Old Order Amish recognized that the caller at the other end of the line was an interloper, someone who presumed to take precedence over the family's normal, sacred communications. Keeping the telephone in an unheated shanty in a field, or even an outhouse, was keeping the phone in its proper place.

*** I appreciate the deliberation put into their decision. In fact, similar reflection might highlight conflicts between our own practices and values. How often do we interrupt a conversation with someone who is physically present in order to answer the telephone? Is the family meal enhanced by a beeper? Who exactly is benefiting from call waiting? Is automated voicemail a dark hint about the way our institutions value human time and life? Can pagers and cell phones that vibrate instead of ring solve the problem? Does the enjoyment of virtual communities by growing numbers of people enhance or erode citizen participation in the civic life of geographic communities?

***

I never expected the Amish to provide precise philosophical yardsticks that could guide the use of technological power. What drew me in was their long conversation with their tools. We technology-enmeshed "English" don't have much of this sort of discussion. And yet we'll need many such conversations, because a modern heterogeneous society is going to have different values, different trade-offs, and different discourses. It's time we start talking about the most important influence on our lives today.

I came away from my journey with a question to contribute to these conversations: If we decided that community came first, how would we use our tools differently?

SOURCE: Howard Rheingold, "Look Who's Talking," *Wired* 7.01 (Jan. 1999).

Questions

- Do you think cell phones have drastically changed life in Amish communities?
- Why do the Amish believe that telephones change the people that use them?
- How could the use of cellular technology make people more isolated?

blue suits or basic black among conservative businesspeople? There is an aspect of conformity to their behavior—conformity to their own group.

Because some degree of conformity to norms is necessary for any society to exist, one of the key challenges for all cultures is to instill in people a willingness to conform. This is accomplished in two ways (Parsons 1964). First, members of all cultures learn the norms of their culture. While this occurs throughout one's life, the most crucial learning occurs during childhood, and parents play a key role. When learning is successful, the norms are so thoroughly ingrained that they become unquestioned ways of thinking and acting; they come to appear "normal." (Note the similarity between the words *norm* and *normal*.) Chapter 4 covers the important topic of learning social norms, also known as "socialization."

When the learning of social norms falls short of what is deemed desirable by a society—that is, when a person fails to adequately conform to a culture's norms—a second way of instilling cultural conformity comes into play: *social control*. Social control often involves punishing rule breaking. Punishment includes such informal behavior as rebuking friends for minor breaches of etiquette, gossiping behind their backs, or ostracizing them from the group. Official, formal forms of discipline might range from parking tickets to imprisonment (Foucault 1979). Émile Durkheim, one of the founders of sociology (introduced in Chapter 1), argued that punishment serves not only to help guarantee conformity among those who would violate a culture's norms and values but also to vividly remind others what the norms and values are.

Culture and Change: A "Cultural Turn" in Sociology?

Because of the power of culture in our lives, it is easy to assume that culture determines everything about us, that we are so thoroughly shaped by a more or less uniform culture from the day we are born until the day we die that we never escape its influence. In fact, that is how most sociologists thought about culture until recently, if they thought about culture at all (DiMaggio 1997). Most sociologists simply took for granted the importance of culture, without stopping to study seriously how culture works in daily life.

Today, a growing number of sociologists are studying culture, once primarily the domain of anthropologists. The phrase **cultural turn** is often used to describe sociology's recent emphasis on the importance of understanding the role of culture in daily life. One result has been to challenge the assumption that culture blindly determines our values and behaviors. Instead, the sociologist Ann Swidler (1986) has charac-

terized culture as a "tool kit" from which people can select different understandings and behaviors, enabling them to choose among different courses of action rather than constraining them to conform to a single one. Thus some people can choose to dye their hair and wear nose rings and adorn their bodies with tattoos but still accept their parents' traditional ideas about sexual restraint. Because people participate in many different (and often conflicting) cultures, the tool kit can be quite large and its contents varied (Bourdieu 1990; Sewell 1992; Tilly 1992).

Our cultural tool kits include a variety of "scripts" that we can draw on to shape our beliefs, values, and actions. Like the written script of a stage play, cultural scripts help determine our actions as well as our words. As actors in real life, however, we are not bound by a single script but are able to choose the scripts we want to follow as well as to improvise along the way. The more appropriate the script to a particular set of circumstances, the more likely we will be to follow it—and recall events that conform to it long after they have occurred (D'Andrade 1995; DiMaggio 1997). For example, imagine that you are a woman walking alone in an unfamiliar city late at night and suddenly encounter a male stranger who begins to cross the street, stating as he approaches, "Excuse me, but may I ask you a question?" Your choice of cultural script will shape how you respond to this situation. A popular cultural script—honed by film and television entertainment, reality TV, and politicians—is to fear such encounters, especially if you are female (Glassner 1999). As a result, instead of hearing him out, you quickly turn and head for the safety of a nearby all-night restaurant. Later, when retelling the story, you might recall the stranger as taller and more dangerous than he was—perhaps even that he was brandishing a weapon—traits consistent with American cultural scripts about such encounters.

On the other hand, imagine that you are the male in this brief encounter—perhaps an out-of-town businessman trying to find your hotel in an unfamiliar neighborhood. You see a woman walking on the other side of the street, and as you cross to ask directions, she immediately turns and disappears into a restaurant. Your experience of this encounter would be very different from that of the woman: You are concerned about the late hour, worried about being lost, and stunned by her sudden actions. Perhaps when you return home you will describe this event as evidence that people in this city are cold and indifferent to strangers, if not downright unfriendly.

The cultural turn calls on sociologists to examine the many meanings of such behavior to better understand the ways people interpret their social worlds and thereby choose appropriate courses of action. In studying this case, sociologists would go beyond merely reporting the circumstances of the late-night encounter. Instead, they would attempt to understand the different cultural scripts each person was following and why he or she might have chosen those scripts. How did physical appearance influence their different experiences? What words, if any, were spoken, and what meanings did they convey? What did the two people's "body language" communicate? Sociologists would also be interested in examining alternating scripts that might have been available and how these scripts could have altered the experience of each participant. For example, the woman might have chosen the script of "good Samaritan," viewing the approaching stranger as potentially in need of assistance and thereby offering to lend a helping hand. Or the stranger might have recognized that a lone woman might feel threatened by the situation and instead chosen a less confrontational, more empathetic script—perhaps remaining on his side of the street and beginning his sentence with a soft-spoken, "Excuse me, can you please tell me the way to my hotel? I seem to be lost."

The cultural turn in sociology reveals that there is no single "reality" to social encounters and that there are multiple cultural scripts that can be applied and followed in any one situation. The challenge of sociology is to seek to understand people's differing realities, the various scripts that they follow, and the reasons they choose one set of scripts over another (Bonnell and Hunt 1999; Chaney 1994; Glassner 1999; Hays 2000; Long 1997; Seidman 1997b; Sewell 1999; Smith and West 2000; Swidler 2001).

The Development of Human Culture

Human culture and human biology are closely intertwined. Understanding how culture is related to the physical evolution of the human species can help us better understand the central role that culture plays in shaping our lives.

Early Human Culture: Adaptation to Physical Environment

Given the archaeological evidence, as well as knowledge of the close similarities in blood chemistry and genetics between chimpanzees and humans, scientists believe that the first humans evolved from apelike creatures on the African continent some four million years ago. The first evidence of human-like culture dates back only two million years. In these early cultures, early humans fashioned stone tools, derived sustenance by hunting animals and gathering nuts and berries, harnessed the use of fire, and established a highly cooperative way of life.

Because early humans planned their hunts, they must also have had some ability for abstract thought.

Culture enabled early humans to compensate for their physical limitations, such as lack of claws, sharp teeth, and running speed, relative to other animals (Deacon 1998). In particular, culture freed humans from dependence on the instinctual and genetically determined set of responses to the environment characteristic of other species. The larger, more complex human brain permitted a greater degree of adaptive learning in dealing with major environmental changes such as the Ice Age. For example, humans figured out how to build fires and sew clothing for warmth. Through greater flexibility, humans were able to survive unpredictable challenges in their surroundings and shape the world with their ideas and their tools. In a mere instant of geological time, we became the dominant species on the planet.

Yet early humans were closely tied to their physical environment because they still lacked the technological ability to modify their immediate surroundings significantly (Bennett 1976; Harris 1975, 1978, 1980). Their ability to secure food and make clothing and shelter depended largely on the physical resources that were close at hand. Cultures in different environments varied widely as a result of adaptations by which people fashioned their cultures to be suitable to specific geographic and climatic conditions. For example, the cultures developed by desert dwellers, where water and food were scarce, differed significantly from the cultures that developed in rain forests, where such natural resources abounded. Similarly, people who lived in the frozen Arctic created cultures that varied greatly from those that evolved in more temperate climates. Human inventiveness spawned a rich tapestry of cultures around the world. As you will see at the conclusion of this chapter, however, modern technology and other forces of globalization pose both challenges and opportunities for future global cultural diversity.

Nature or Nurture?

Because humans evolved as a part of the world of nature, it would seem logical to assume that human thinking and behavior are the result of biology and evolution. In fact, one of the oldest controversies in the social sciences is the "nature/nurture" debate: Are we shaped by our biology or are we products of learning through life's experiences—that is, of nurture? Biologists and some psychologists emphasize biological factors in explaining human thinking and behavior. It is not surprising that sociologists stress the role of learning and culture. They are also likely to argue that because human beings are capable of making conscious choices, neither biology nor culture wholly determines human behavior.

The Sociology of Body Image

Victoria Pitts studies the human body. She is not a medical doctor. She is not a surgeon. She is not a nutritionist or a physical therapist or an exercise guru. Pitts is a sociologist who studies the ways that we see and shape and mold our bodies in response to prevailing cultural standards. Although we may act as individual people, our actions are also responses to social messages. Currently, our culture views the body as something changeable, a pliable product under our control rather than a fixed entity that we are stuck with forever. Such messages are so strong we can hear them ringing in our ears. Although in different tones, they speak strongly to both men and women. We should lose weight. We should exercise regularly. We should tone our figures, lift weights, and buy supplements to look and feel healthy. We should search the Internet for health information; take action to prevent diseases; and take prescriptions to help us sleep, concentrate, or have sex. We should manage our appearance and health as well as create our personal style. Those messages are so prevalent they have come to resemble common sense. But they also create intense pressure to conform to social standards of beauty and, regardless of our choice of clothing or tattoo or hairstyle, to express our identities through our physical appearance.

"Consumer culture is obsessively body-oriented, and the media industries continue to capitalize on our fascination with both beautiful and anomalous bodies," says Pitts (2004). "Politically, the body continues to be a site of contest: cloning, genetic screening, [in vitro fertilization] treatments, abortion, contraception, drug use, sex work, pornography, body modifi-

Victoria Pitts

cation practices, and performance art . . . all raise important issues about the ownership and regulation of the body and body technologies. It now seems that embodiment is a site for a great deal of the 'action' in contemporary cultures."

Nowhere is that action more bizarre and spectacular than those practicing *body modification* (BM), a form of self-expression popularized in San Francisco in the 1990s. BM includes not only tattoos and body piercings but also scarifica-

The nature/nurture debate has raged for more than a century, opinion swinging first one way and then the other. For example, in the 1930s and 1940s, many social scientists tended to focus on biological factors, with some researchers seeking (unsuccessfully), for example, to prove that a person's physique determined his or her personality. In the 1960s and 1970s, scholars in different fields emphasized culture. For example, social psychologists argued that even the most severe forms of mental illness were the result of the labels that society attaches to unusual behavior rather than of biochemical processes

(Scheff 1966). Today, partly because of new understandings in genetics and brain neurophysiology, the pendulum is again swinging toward the side of biology.

The resurgence of biological explanations for human behavior began in 1975 when the evolutionary biologist Edward O. Wilson of Harvard University published *Sociobiology: The New Synthesis.* The term **sociobiology** refers to the application of biological principles to explain the social activities of animals, including human beings. Using studies of insects and other social creatures, Wilson argued that genes influence not tion, which is accomplished by cutting repeatedly with a scalpel or a cauterizing tool, and strike branding, which is akin to cattle branding. After cleaning the area and stenciling on the design, an artist begins cutting or burning the skin until the right depth is reached. "It can take 15 minutes, but I've also done pieces that took eight hours over two days," said Ryan Ouellette, a body-modification artist in Nashua, New Hampshire (quoted in Guynup 2004). Subdermal implants are a more shocking form of BM in which foreign objects are surgically implanted beneath the skin to create a raised or textured appearance. Now that tattoos, once symbolized a refusal to conform to standard expectations of appearance, have become more mainstream, perhaps even normal, those seeking to make defiant statements through body practices are increasingly turning to body modification to express themselves in unique and shocking ways.

Although body modification may appear disturbing, the practice does not mean that individuals themselves are disturbed. Predominantly a middle-class, educated, and sane group, body modifiers are consciously choosing to contradict and subvert the cultural sensibilities in which they feel trapped.

"Until recently, body modifiers were perceived as sick people in need of psychiatric, not sociological, attention," says Pitts, who was awarded an Advancement of the Discipline Award from the American Sociological Association in 2002. Her first application to study the topic as a graduate student was met with rejection. The official report stated plainly that these people need to be studied by mental health professionals, not sociologists. But Pitts (2004) believes this interpretation is wrong: "It suggests both that the only healthy body is an unmarked one, and also that the surface body is a place where the 'truth' of an individual's depth psyche is revealed." Feminists have also been quick to reject body modification as a sign of internalized oppression or a form of self-hatred, creating intellectual land mines that Pitts has been able to avoid largely by using her sociological imagination. Indeed, many so-

ciologists are now taking the view that the body is a "deeply meaningful space where sociality, culture and history are inscribed, reflected or produced" (Pitts 2004). Rather than seeing body modification as pathological, scholars are instead asking why individuals are moved to engage in particular body projects and how those projects create and respond to social forces regulating what we should and should not do to our own bodies.

One of Pitts's most difficult experiences as a public sociologist involved a court case in Vancouver, British Columbia, in which she was asked to testify as an expert witness. A young man who had performed scarification on the arm of his girlfriend had been charged with felony sexual assault after her parents discovered the marks and contacted police. Pitts felt conflicted about participating. She has never intended to glorify body modification as a cultural practice as much as she has tried to understand it sociologically. At the same time, it became clear to her that the young man would have difficulty getting a fair hearing if a sociological perspective on the cultures and subcultures of body modification was absent from the proceedings. Pitts decided to participate. The young man claimed in his trial that marking his girlfriend's arms was not in any way sexually abusive. It was perhaps foolish and extreme, but it was an attempt to express their identities as individuals and as a couple.

This book consistently forces you to wrestle with the theme of *social change*. Cultural norms of the body and how we assert our own identity within those norms are determined by a complex interaction of personal motives and the time and place in which we live. We all respond to cultural pressures. And the way we respond is conditioned by pressures largely beyond our control. But by keying our attention to some of the most dramatic body projects occurring worldwide (her new work is on the rise of cosmetic surgery), Pitts helps us realize that by developing an understanding of "deviant" bodies, we arrive at a better understanding of ourselves.

only physical traits but behavior as well. For instance, some species of animals engage in elaborate courtship rituals, whereby sexual union and reproduction are achieved. Human courtship and sexual behavior, according to sociobiologists, generally involve similar rituals, based also on inborn characteristics. In most species, to take a second example, males are larger and more aggressive than females and tend to dominate the "weaker sex." Some suggest that genetic factors explain why, in all human societies that we know of, men tend to hold positions of greater authority than women.

One way in which sociobiologists have tried to illuminate the relations between the sexes is by means of the idea of "reproductive strategy." A reproductive strategy is a pattern of behavior, arrived at through evolutionary selection, that favors the chances of survival of offspring. The female body has a larger investment in its reproductive cells than the male—a fertilized human egg takes nine months to develop. Thus according to sociobiologists, women will not squander that investment and are not driven to have sexual relations with many partners; their overriding aim is the care and protection of children. Men, on the other hand, tend toward promiscuity. Their wish to have sex with many partners is sound strategy from the point of view of the species; to carry out their mission, which is to maximize the possibility of impregnation, they move from one partner to the next. In this way, it has been suggested, we can explain differences in sexual behavior and attitudes between men and women.

Sociobiologists do not argue that our genes determine 100 percent of our behavior. For example, they note that, depending on the circumstances, men can choose to act in nonaggressive ways. Yet even though this argument would seem to open up the field of sociobiology to culture as an additional explanatory factor in describing human behavior, social scientists have roundly condemned sociobiology for claiming that a propensity for particular behaviors such as violence, is somehow "genetically programmed" into our brains ("Seville Statement on Violence" 1990).

How Nature and Nurture Interact

Most sociologists today would acknowledge a role for nature in determining attitudes and behavior, but with strong qualifications. For example, no one questions that newborn babies come into the world with certain basic human reflexes, such as the automatic ability to "root" for the mother's nipple without being taught to do so. There is also evidence that babies are born with the ability to recognize faces: Babies a few minutes old turn their heads in response to patterns that resemble human faces but not in response to other patterns (Cosmides and Tooby 1997; Johnson and Morton 1991). But it is a large leap to conclude that because babies are born with basic reflexes, the behavior of adults is governed by **instincts,** inborn, biologically fixed patterns of action found in all cultures.

Sociologists no longer pose the question as one of nature *or* nurture. Instead they ask how nature and nurture interact to produce human behavior. But their main concern is with how our different ways of thinking and acting are learned in interactions with family, friends, schools, television, and every other facet of the social environment. For example, sociologists argue that it's not some inborn biological disposition that makes American males feel attracted to a *particular* type of woman. Rather it is the exposure they've had throughout their lives to tens of thousands of magazine ads, TV commercials, and film stars that emphasize specific cultural standards of female beauty. Any American male who is at all uncertain about just what constitutes an "attractive" woman need only reach into his cultural tool kit and pull out the latest *Sports Illustrated* swimsuit issue for an answer.

Early child rearing is especially relevant to this kind of learning. Human babies have a large brain, requiring birth relatively early in their fetal development, before their heads have grown too large to pass through the birth canal. As a result, human babies are totally unequipped for survival on their own, compared with the young of other species, and must spend a number of years in the care of adults. This need, in turn, fosters a lengthy period of learning, during which the child is taught its society's culture.

Because humans think and act in so many different ways, sociologists do not believe that "biology is destiny." If biology were all-important, we would expect all cultures to be highly similar, if not identical. Yet this is hardly the case. For example, pork is forbidden to religious Jews and Muslims, but it is a dietary staple in China. Americans are likely to greet one another with a casual "How are you?" On the other hand, the Yanomamö, a tribe that lives in the rain forests of Venezuela and Brazil, greet each other with an exchange of gifts and would find the casual American greeting an insult.

This is not to say that human cultures have nothing in common. Surveys of thousands of different cultures have concluded that all known human cultures have such common characteristics as language, forms of emotional expression, rules that tell adults how to raise children or engage in sexual behavior, and even standards of beauty (Brown 1991). But there is enormous variety in exactly *how* these common characteristics play themselves out.

All cultures provide for childhood socialization, but what and how children are taught vary greatly from culture to culture. An American child learns the multiplication tables from a classroom teacher, whereas a child born in the forests of Borneo learns to hunt with older members of the tribe. All cultures have standards of beauty and ornamentation, but what is regarded as beautiful in one culture may be seen as ugly in another (Elias 1987; Elias and Dunning 1987; Foucault 1988). The half-starved body of a typical *Vogue* model or the bulked-up body of a weight lifter would be regarded as grossly unattractive to the Borneo forest dweller.

Cultural Diversity

The study of cultural differences highlights the importance of cultural learning as an influence on our behavior. However, not only do cultural beliefs vary across cultures but human behavior and practices also vary widely from culture to culture and often contrast radically with what people from Western societies consider "normal." For example, in the modern West, we regard the deliberate killing of infants or young children as one of the worst of all crimes. Yet in traditional Chinese culture, female children were sometimes strangled at birth because a daughter was regarded as a liability rather than an asset to the family. In the West, we eat oysters but we do not eat kittens or puppies, both of which are regarded as delicacies in some parts of the world. Jews and Muslims don't eat pork, whereas Hindus eat pork but avoid beef. Westerners regard kissing as a normal part of sexual behavior, but in other cultures the practice is either unknown or regarded as disgusting. All these different kinds of behavior are aspects of broad cultural differences that distinguish societies from one another.

SUBCULTURES

Small societies tend to be culturally uniform, but industrialized societies are themselves culturally diverse or multicultural, involving numerous different **subcultures.** As you will discover in the discussion of global migration in Chapter 11, processes such as slavery, colonialism, war, migration, and contemporary globalization have led to populations dispersing across borders and settling in new areas. This, in turn, has led to the emergence of societies that are cultural composites, meaning that the population is made up of a number of groups from diverse cultural and linguistic backgrounds. In modern cities, for example, many subcultural communities live side by side. For example, over ninety different cultural groups can be found in New York City today.

Subcultures do not refer only to people from different cultural backgrounds or those who speak different languages within a larger society. They concern any segments of the population that are distinguishable from the rest of society by their cultural patterns. Subcultures are very broad in scope and might include Goths, computer hackers, hippies, Rastafarians, and fans of hip-hop. Some people might identify themselves clearly with a particular subculture, whereas others might move fluidly among a number of different ones.

Culture plays an important role in perpetuating the values and norms of a society, yet it also offers important opportunities for creativity and change. Subcultures and countercultures—groups that largely reject the prevailing values and norms of society—can promote views that represent alternatives to the dominant culture. Social movements or groups of people sharing common lifestyles are powerful forces of change within societies. In this way, subcultures allow freedom for people to express and act on their opinions, hopes, and beliefs.

U.S. schoolchildren are frequently taught that the United States is a vast melting pot, into which various subcultures are assimilated. **Assimilation** is the process by which different cultures are absorbed into a single mainstream culture. Although it is true that virtually all peoples living in the United States take on many common cultural characteristics, many groups strive to retain some subcultural identity. In fact, iden-

tification based on race or country of origin in the United States persists and even grows, particularly among African Americans and immigrants from Asia, Mexico, and Latin America (Totti 1987).

Given the immense cultural diversity and number of subcultures in the United States, a more appropriate metaphor than the assimilationist melting pot might be the culturally diverse salad bowl, in which all the various ingredients, though mixed together, retain some of their original flavor and integrity, contributing to the richness of the salad as a whole. This viewpoint, termed **multiculturalism,** calls for respecting cultural diversity and promoting equality of different cultures. Adherents to multiculturalism acknowledge that certain central cultural values are shared by most people in a society but also that certain important differences deserve to be preserved (Anzaldua 1990).

Young people also have their own subcultures in many modern industrial nations. Examples of youth subcultures can be found in college dorms or neighborhoods near major universities, with pop music blaring from seemingly every window late into the night. Youth subcultures typically revolve around particular musical preferences (for example, hip-hop, techno, heavy metal, reggae) and somewhat distinctive style of dress, language (especially slang), and behavior. Like all subcultures, however, they still accept most of the norms and values of the dominant culture.

Consider the patchwork that is hip-hop. Although it emerged as a subculture in the Bronx, New York, in the mid-1970s, hip-hop owes much of its original identity to Jamaica. The first important hip-hop DJ, Kool Herc, was a Jamaican immigrant, and rapping, or rhythmic talk, derives from the Jamaican disc jockey tradition of "toasting": chanting stories into microphones over records. From these origins, hip-hop gradually spread across the world. Its story is a contemporary lesson in the fluidity of contemporary cultural identity. The music is built around beats often taken from other records. But in "sampling" from recordings, hip-hop artists often do something considerably more significant. They and their fans sample identities, taking on the characteristics of subcultures that can be considerably foreign to them.

Hip-hop's reach has widened over time. Rappers from Queens and Long Island—like Run-D.M.C., LL Cool J, and Public Enemy—recorded some of the first great hip-hop albums. By the end of the 1980s, the music had a national presence in the United States, as Los Angeles artists like N.W.A. and Ice-T developed gangsta rap, which soon had outposts in Oakland, New Orleans, Houston, and elsewhere. White rappers like Kid Rock and Eminem, belatedly following in the footsteps of the Beastie Boys, pioneered a rap–rock synthesis, and a Filipino American crew known as the Invisible Skratch Piklz revolutionized turntable techniques. Hip-hop became a global form,

The origins of hip-hop culture can be traced back to DJ Kool Herc, who brought the Jamaican disc jockey tradition of "toasting" to New York in the mid-1970s.

with British trip-hop artists like Tricky, French rappers like MC Solaar, and record spinners like Japan's DJ Krush.

The sampled beats of hip-hop can contain nearly anything. In "I'll Be Missing You," for example, Puff Daddy (Sean "Puffy" Combs), a master at finding unlikely sources of inspiration, liberally drew from the middle-of-the-road, Top 40 Police song "Every Breath You Take" to mourn the slain rapper Notorious B.I.G. The secret is transformation: A portion of an earlier song, recast to fit a new context, can take on an entirely different meaning while still retaining just enough of its former essence to create a complicated and richly meaningful finished product. In many ways, hip-hop is a music of echoes: rappers revisiting the funk music and "blaxploitation" films of the 1970s (black action movies, often criticized for glorifying violence and presenting blacks in negative stereotypes); suburban fans romanticizing inner-city street styles.

These borrowings have often proved controversial. The militant politics of Public Enemy, for example, were in many ways sampled from the Black Panther revolutionaries of the 1960s. The outrage stirred by Eminem's offensive language about women and gay people owes much to the fact that this rapper is white and blond and raps in a style that is easy to follow for those unfamiliar with street slang. Hip-hop is the soundtrack to an emerging global culture that treats the looks, sounds, and byways of particular subcultures, or particular moments in time, as raw material for the creation of new styles.

What does hip-hop tell us about cultural diversity? On the one hand, its history of incorporating an ever-wider circle of influences and participants demonstrates that what is "normal" in one community can quickly be adopted and become normal in another community far away, through the dissemination of ideas and styles and so on through records and other forms of media. On the other hand, the controversies that hip-hop has generated suggest that these cultural crossings are marked by a great deal of uncertainty, misperception, and fear. Finally, hip-hop's evolution suggests that even in a global culture, subcultural distinctions retain an important aura of authenticity. Even today, hip-hop remains stamped with the mark of its origins in social realities that most Americans would prefer not to contemplate.

Subcultures also take shape around different types of work often associated with unique cultural features. Long-distance truckers, coal miners, Wall Street stockbrokers, computer programmers, professional athletes, corporate lawyers, and artists, for example, form subcultures that differ by the degree of importance they attach to such values as physical strength, bravery, shrewdness, speed, knowledge, material wealth, and creativity. However, they seldom stray far from the dominant culture. For example, even professional thieves who make their living engaging in such illegal activities as robbing banks, burglarizing grocery stores, or passing bad checks, share most of the values of U.S. society. Professional thieves often marry and raise children. Like most Americans, they want to make it by accumulating wealth, power, and prestige. They eat with knives and forks, drive on the right side of the road, and try to avoid trouble as much as possible. Indeed, the subculture of thieves comprises people who believe in *almost* all of the values and norms of U.S. society (Chambliss 1988).

CULTURAL IDENTITY AND ETHNOCENTRISM

Every culture displays its own unique patterns of behavior, which seem alien to people from other cultural backgrounds. If you have traveled abroad, you are probably familiar with the sensation that can result when you find yourself in a new culture. Aspects of daily life that you unconsciously take for granted in your own culture may not be part of everyday life in other parts of the world. Even in countries that share the same language, you might find their everyday habits, customs, and behaviors to be quite different. The expression *culture shock* is an apt one! Often people feel disoriented when they become immersed in a new culture. This is because they have lost the familiar reference points that help them understand the world around them and have not yet learned how to navigate in the new culture.

As an example of the uniqueness of each culture's patterns of behavior, we can take the Nacirema, a group described by Horace Miner. Miner concentrated his attention on the strange and exotic body rituals in which the Nacirema engage. His discussion is worth quoting at length:

> The fundamental belief underlying the whole system appears to be that the human body is ugly and that its natural tendency is to debility and disease. Incarcerated in

Eminem represents one aspect of the widening appeal of hip-hop across cultural lines, arguably for better and for worse.

such a body, man's only hope is to avert these characteristics through the use of the powerful influences of ritual and ceremony. Every household has one or more shrines devoted to this purpose. . . . The focal point of the shrine is a box or chest which is built into the wall. In the chest are kept the many charms and magical potions without which no native believes he could live. These preparations are secured from a variety of specialized practitioners. The most powerful of these are the medicine men, whose assistance must be rewarded with substantial gifts. However, the medicine men do not provide the curative potions for their clients, but decide what the ingredients should be and then write them down in an ancient and secret language. This writing is understood only by the medicine man and by the herbalists who, for another gift, provide the required charm. . . .

The Nacirema have an almost pathological horror of and fascination with the mouth, the condition of which is believed to have a supernatural influence on all social relationships. Were it not for the rituals of the mouth, they believe that their teeth would fall out, their gums bleed, their jaws shrink, their friends desert them, and their lovers reject them. They also believe that a strong relationship exists between oral and moral characteristics. For example, there is a ritual ablution of the

mouth for children which is supposed to improve their moral fibre.

The daily body ritual performed by everyone includes a mouth-rite. Despite the fact that these people are so punctilious about care of the mouth, this rite involves a practice which strikes the uninitiated stranger as revolting. . . . [T]he ritual consists of inserting a small bundle of hog hairs into the mouth, along with certain magical powders, and then moving the bundle in a highly formalized series of gestures. (Miner 1956)

Who are the Nacirema, and in which part of the world do they live? You can answer these questions for yourself as well as identify the body ritual described, simply by spelling *Nacirema* backward. The Nacirema, in other words, are Americans (and other Westerners), and the ritual described is the brushing of teeth. Almost any familiar activity will seem strange if described out of context. Western cleanliness rituals are no more or less bizarre than the customs of some Pacific groups who knock out their front teeth to beautify themselves or of certain South American tribal groups who place discs inside their lips to make them protrude, believing that this enhances their attractiveness.

We cannot understand these practices and beliefs separately from the wider cultures of which they are a part. A culture must be studied in terms of its own meanings and values—a key presupposition of sociology. Sociologists endeavor as far as possible to avoid **ethnocentrism,** which is judging other cultures in terms of the standards of one's own. Because human cultures vary so widely, it is not surprising that people belonging to one culture frequently find it difficult to sympathize with the ideas or behavior of those from a different culture. In studying and practicing sociology, we must remove our own cultural blinders to see the ways of life of different peoples in an unbiased light. The practice of judging a society by its own standards is called **cultural relativism.**

Applying cultural relativism—that is, suspending your own deeply held cultural beliefs and examining a situation according to the standards of another culture—can be fraught with uncertainty and challenge. Not only can it be hard to see things from a completely different point of view but sometimes troubling questions are raised. Does cultural relativism mean that all customs and behaviors are equally legitimate? Are there any universal standards to which all humans should adhere? Consider, for example, the ritual acts of what opponents have called "genital mutilation" practiced in some societies. Numerous young girls in certain African, Asian, and Middle Eastern cultures undergo clitoridectomies. This is a painful cultural ritual in which the clitoris and sometimes all or part of the vaginal labia of young girls are removed with a knife or a sharpened stone and the two sides of the vulva are partly

Reggae Music

When those knowledgeable about popular music listen to a song, they can often pick out the stylistic influences that helped shape it. Each musical style, after all, represents a unique way of combining rhythm, melody, harmony, and lyrics. And though it doesn't take a genius to notice the differences among grunge, hard rock, techno, and hip-hop, musicians often combine a

number of styles in composing songs. Identifying the components of these combinations can be difficult. But for sociologists of culture, the effort is often rewarding. Different musical styles tend to emerge from different social groups, and studying how styles combine and fuse is a good way to chart the cultural contacts between groups.

Some sociologists of culture have turned their attention to reggae music because it exemplifies the process whereby contacts between social groups result in the creation of new musical forms. Reggae's roots can be traced to West Africa. In the seventeenth century, large numbers of West Africans were enslaved by the British and brought by ship to work in the sugarcane fields of the West Indies. Although the British attempted to prevent slaves from playing traditional African music, for fear it would serve as a rallying cry to revolt, the slaves managed to keep alive the tradition of African drumming, sometimes by integrating it with the European musical styles imposed by the slave owners. In Jamaica, the drumming of one group of slaves, the Burru, was openly tolerated by slaveholders because it helped meter the pace of work. Slavery was fi-

sewn together as a means of controlling sexual activity and increasing the sexual pleasure of the man.

In cultures where clitoridectomies have been practiced for generations, they are regarded as normal, even expected practice. A study of two thousand men and women in two Nigerian communities found that nine out of ten women interviewed had undergone clitoridectomies in childhood and that the large majority favored the procedure for their own daughters, primarily for cultural reasons. Yet a significant minority believed that the practice should be stopped (Ebomoyi 1987). Clitoridectomies are regarded with abhorrence by most people from other cultures and by a growing number of women in the cultures where they are practiced (El Dareer 1982; Johnson-Odim 1991; Lightfoot-Klein 1989). These differences in views can result in a clash of cultural values, especially when people from cultures where clitoridectomies are common migrate to countries where the practice is actually illegal.

France is an example. France has a large North African im-

migrant population, in which many African mothers arrange for traditional clitoridectomies to be performed on their daughters. Some of these women have been tried and convicted under French law for mutilating their daughters. These African mothers have argued that they were only engaging in the same cultural practice that their own mothers had performed on them, that their grandmothers had performed on their mothers, and so on. They complain that the French are ethnocentric, judging traditional African rituals by French customs. Feminists from Africa and the Middle East, while themselves strongly opposed to clitoridectomies, have been critical of Europeans and Americans who sensationalize the practice by calling it "backward" or "primitive," without seeking any understanding of the cultural and economic circumstances that sustain it (Accad 1991; Johnson-Odim 1991; Mohanty 1991). In this instance, globalization has led to a fundamental clash of cultural norms and values that has forced members of both cultures to confront some of their most deeply held beliefs. The

"Rastafarians." The Rastafarian cult soon merged with the Burru, and Rastafarian music came to combine Burru styles of drumming with biblical themes of oppression and liberation. In the 1950s, West Indian musicians began mixing Rastafarian rhythms and lyrics with elements of American jazz and black rhythm and blues. These combinations eventually developed into ska music and then, in the late 1960s, into reggae, with its relatively slow beat, its emphasis on the bass, and its stories of urban deprivation and of the power of collective social consciousness. Many reggae artists, such as Bob Marley, became commercial successes and by the 1970s, people the world over were listening to reggae music. In the 1980s, reggae was first fused with hip-hop (or rap) to produce new sounds, as can be heard today in the dance hall music of the Jamaican rapper Sean Paul.

The history of reggae is thus the history of contact among different social groups and of the meanings—political, spiritual, and personal—that those groups expressed through their music. Globalization has intensified these contacts. It is now possible for a young musician in Scandinavia, for example, to grow up listening to music produced by men and women in the ghettos of Los Angeles and to be deeply influenced as well by, say, a mariachi performance broadcast live via satellite from Mexico City. If the number of contacts among groups is an important determinant of the pace of musical evolution, we can predict that a veritable profusion of new styles will flourish in the coming years as the process of globalization continues to unfold.

nally abolished in Jamaica in 1834, but the tradition of Burru drumming continued, even as many Burru men migrated from rural areas to the slums of Kingston.

It was in these slums that a new religious cult began to emerge—one that would prove crucial for the development of reggae. In 1930, a man who took the title Haile Selassie ("Power of the Trinity") was crowned emperor of the African country of Ethiopia. While opponents of European colonialism throughout the world cheered his accession to the throne, a number of people in the West Indies came to believe that Haile Selassie was a god, sent to earth to lead the oppressed of Africa to freedom. Haile Selassie's original name was Ras Tafari Makonnen, and the West Indians who worshiped him called themselves

role of the sociologist is to avoid knee-jerk responses and to examine complex questions carefully from as many different angles as possible.

Cultural Universals

Amid the diversity of human behavior, there are some common features. When these are found in virtually all societies, they are called **cultural universals.** For example, there is no known culture without a grammatically complex **language.** All cultures possess some recognizable form of family system, in which there are values and norms associated with the care of the children. The institution of **marriage** is a cultural universal, as are religious rituals and property rights. All cultures also practice some form of incest prohibition—the banning of sexual relations between close relatives, such as father and daughter, mother and son, or brother and sister. A variety of

other cultural universals have been identified by anthropologists, including art, dancing, bodily adornment, games, gift giving, joking, and rules of hygiene.

Yet there are variations within each category. Consider, for example, the prohibition against incest. Most often, incest is regarded as sexual relations between members of the immediate family; but among some peoples, it includes cousins, and in some instances all people bearing the same family name. There have also been societies in which a small proportion of the population have been permitted to engage in incestuous practices. This was the case, for instance, within the ruling class of ancient Egypt, when brothers and sisters were permitted to have sex with each other.

Among the cultural characteristics shared by all societies, two stand out in particular. All cultures incorporate ways of expressing meaning and communication, and all depend on material means of production. In all cultures, *language* is the primary vehicle of meaning and communication. It is not the only such vehicle, however. Material culture itself carries meanings, as we shall show in what follows.

LANGUAGE

Language is one of the best examples for demonstrating both the unity and the diversity of human culture, because there are no cultures without language, yet there are thousands of different languages spoken in the world. Anyone who has visited a foreign country armed with only a dictionary knows how difficult it is either to understand anything or to be understood. Although languages that have similar origins have words in common with one another—as do, for example, German with English—most of the world's major language groups have no words in common at all.

Language is involved in virtually all of our activities. In the form of ordinary talk or speech, it is the means by which we organize most of what we do. (We will discuss the importance of talk and conversation in social life at some length in Chapter 5.) However, language is involved not just in mundane, everyday activities but also in ceremony, religion, poetry, and many other spheres. One of the most distinctive features of human language is that it allows us to extend vastly the scope of our thought and experience. Using language, we can convey information about events remote in time or space and can discuss things we have never seen. We can develop abstract concepts, tell stories, and make jokes.

In the 1930s, the anthropological linguist Edward Sapir and his student Benjamin Lee Whorf advanced the **linguistic relativity hypothesis,** which argues that the language we use influences our perceptions of the world. That is because we are much more likely to be aware of things in the world if we have words for them (Haugen 1977; Malotki 1983; Witkowski and Brown 1982). Expert skiers or snowboarders, for example, uses terms such as *black ice, corn, powder,* and *packed powder* to describe different snow and ice conditions. Such terms enable them to more readily perceive potentially life-threatening situations that would escape the notice of a novice. In a sense, then, experienced winter athletes have a different perception of the world—or at least, a different perception of the alpine slopes—than do novices.

Language also helps give permanence to a culture and an identity to a people. Language outlives any particular speaker or writer, affording a sense of history and cultural continuity, a feeling of who we are. In the beginning of this chapter, we argued that the English language is becoming increasingly global in its use, as a primary language of both business and the Internet. One of the central paradoxes of our time is that despite this globalization of the English language, local attachments to language persist, often out of cultural pride. For example, the

Protesting against the English-only initiative in Colorado, parents and students voice their opposition to Amendment 31, which would have changed the state constitution in 2002 to require schools to replace bilingual education with intensive English-immersion programs. Voters did not ratify the bill.

French-speaking residents of the Canadian province of Quebec are so passionate about their linguistic heritage that they often refuse to speak English, the dominant language of Canada, and periodically seek political independence from the rest of Canada. Minority languages are sometimes even outlawed by the majority government: Turkey restricts the use of the Kurdish language spoken by one of its minority populations, and the "English-only" movement in the United States seeks to restrict the language of education and government to English, even though numerous other languages are spoken throughout the country.

Languages—indeed, all symbols—are representations of reality. The symbols we use may signify things we imagine, such as mathematical formulas or fictitious creatures, or they may represent (that is, "re-present," or make present again in our minds) things initially experienced through our senses. Human behavior is oriented toward the symbols we use to represent "reality," rather than toward the reality itself—and these symbols are determined within a particular culture. Because symbols are representations, their cultural meanings must be interpreted when they are used. When you see a four-footed furry animal, for example, you must determine which cultural symbol to attach to it. Do you decide to call it a dog, a wolf, or something else? If you determine it is a dog, what cultural meaning does that convey? In American culture, dogs are typically regarded as household pets and lavished with affection. In Guatemalan Indian culture, on the other hand, dogs are more likely to be seen as watchdogs or scavengers and treated with an indifference that might strike many Americans as bordering on cruelty. Among the Akha of northern Thailand, dogs are seen as food and treated accordingly. The diversity of cultural meanings attached to the word *dog* thus requires an act

Regensburg Cathedral, built in the Middle Ages, stands at the center of Regensburg, Germany, and towers over the city, symbolizing the central role Christianity played in medieval European life.

Before the terrorist attacks of September 11, 2001, the World Trade Center dominated the New York City skyline. Today, the buildings of lower Manhattan's financial district still stand significantly taller than those in other areas of the city. Commerce and business occupy the symbolic center of contemporary American culture.

of interpretation. In this way, human beings are freed, in a sense, from being directly tied to the physical world around us. For example, whereas a cat instinctively recoils when a dog appears, the response of human beings is not so inflexible. Humans, depending on their culture, will have different interpretations, seeing the dog as a neighbor's household pet, a wild dog scrounging for food, or tonight's meal.

SPEECH AND WRITING

All societies use speech as a vehicle of language. However, there are other ways of "carrying," or expressing, language—most notably, writing. The invention of writing marked a major transition in human history. Writing first began as the drawing up of lists. Marks would be made on wood, clay, or stone to keep records about significant events, objects, or people. For example, a mark, or sometimes a picture, might be drawn to represent each tract of land possessed by a particular family or set of families (Gelb 1952). Writing began as a means of storing information and as such was closely linked to the administrative needs of the early civilizations. A society that possesses writing can locate itself in time and space. Documents can be accumulated that record the past, and information can be gathered about present-day events and activities.

Writing is not just the transfer of speech to paper or some other durable material. It is a phenomenon of interest in its own right. Written documents or *texts* have qualities in some ways quite distinct from the spoken word. The effect of speech is always by definition limited to the particular contexts in which words are uttered. Ideas and experiences can be passed down through generations in cultures without writing, but only

if they are regularly repeated and passed on by word of mouth. Texts, on the other hand, can endure for thousands of years, and through them those from past ages can in a certain sense address us directly. This is, of course, why documentary research is so important to historians. Through interpreting the texts that are left behind by past generations, historians can reconstruct what their lives were like.

SEMIOTICS AND MATERIAL CULTURE

The symbols expressed in speech and writing are the chief ways in which cultural meanings are formed and expressed. But they are not the only ways. Both material objects and aspects of behavior can be used to generate meanings. A **signifier** is any vehicle of meaning—any set of elements used to communicate. The sounds made in speech are signifiers, as are the marks made on paper or other materials in writing. Other signifiers, however, include dress, pictures or visual signs, modes of eating, forms of building or architecture, and many other material features of culture (Hawkes 1977). Styles of dress, for example, normally help signify differences between the sexes. In our culture, at least until relatively recently, women used to wear skirts and men pants. In other cultures, this is reversed: women wear pants and men skirts (Leach 1976).

Semiotics—the analysis of nonverbal cultural meanings—opens up a fascinating field for both sociology and anthropology. Semiotic analysis can be very useful in comparing one culture with another. Semiotics allows us to contrast the ways in which different cultures are structured by looking at the cultural meanings of symbols. For example, the buildings in cities are not simply places in which people live and work. They often have a symbolic character. In traditional cities, the main temple or church was usually placed on high ground in or near the city center. It symbolized the all-powerful influence that religion was supposed to have over the lives of the people. In modern societies, by contrast, the skyscrapers of big business often occupy that symbolic position.

Of course, material culture is not simply symbolic but is also vital for catering to physical needs—in the tools or technology used to acquire food, make weaponry, construct dwellings, and so forth. We have to study both the practical and the symbolic aspects of material culture to understand it completely.

Culture and Social Development

Cultural traits are closely related to overall patterns in the development of society. The level of material culture reached in a given society influences, although by no means completely determines, other aspects of cultural development. This is easy to see, for example, in the level of technology. Many aspects of culture characteristic of our lives today—cars, telephones, computers, running water, electric light—depend on technological innovations that have been made only very recently in human history.

The same is true at earlier phases of social development. Before the invention of the smelting of metal, for example, goods had to be made of organic or naturally occurring materials like wood or stone—a basic limitation on the artifacts that could be constructed. Variations in material culture provide the main means of distinguishing different forms of human society, but other factors are also influential. Writing is an example. As has been mentioned, not all human cultures have possessed writing—in fact, for most of human history, writing was unknown. The development of writing altered the scope of human cultural potentialities, making different forms of social organization possible from those that had previously existed.

We now turn to analyzing the main types of society that existed in the past and that are still found in the world today. In the present day, we are accustomed to societies that contain many millions of people, many of them living crowded together in urban areas. But for most of human history, the earth was much less densely populated than it is now, and it is only over the past hundred years or so that any societies have existed in which the majority of the population were city dwellers. To understand the forms of society that existed before modern industrialism, we have to call on the historical dimension of the sociological imagination.

Disappearing World: Premodern Societies and Their Fate

The explorers, traders, and missionaries sent out during Europe's great age of discovery met with many different peoples. As the anthropologist Marvin Harris wrote in his work *Cannibals and Kings* (1978):

> In some regions—Australia, the Arctic, the southern tips of South America and Africa—they found groups still living much like Europe's own long-forgotten stone age ancestors: bands of twenty or thirty people, sprinkled across vast territories, constantly on the move, living entirely by hunting animals and collecting wild plants. These hunter-collectors appeared to be members of a rare and endangered species. In other regions—the forests of eastern North America, the jungles of South America, and East Asia—they found denser populations, inhabiting more or less permanent villages, based on farming and consisting of perhaps one or two large communal structures, but here too the weapons and tools were relics of prehistory. . . .
>
> Elsewhere, of course, the explorers encountered fully developed states and empires, headed by despots and ruling classes, and defended by standing armies. It was these great empires, with their cities, monuments, palaces, temples and treasures, that had lured all the Marco Polos and Columbuses across the oceans and deserts in the first place. There was China—the greatest empire in the world, a vast, sophisticated realm whose leaders scorned the "red-faced barbarians," supplicants from puny kingdoms beyond the pale of the civilised world. And there was India—a land where cows were venerated and the unequal burdens of life were apportioned according to what each soul had merited in its previous incarnation. And then there were the native American states and empires, worlds unto themselves, each with its distinctive arts and religions: the Incas, with their great stone fortresses, suspension bridges, overworked granaries, and state-controlled economy; and the Aztecs, with their bloodthirsty gods fed from human hearts and their incessant search for fresh sacrifices.

This seemingly unlimited variety of premodern societies can actually be grouped into three main categories, each of which is referred to in Harris's description: hunters and gatherers (Harris's "hunter-collectors"), larger agrarian or pastoral societies (involving agriculture or the tending of domesticated animals), and nonindustrial civilizations or traditional states. We shall look at the main characteristics of these societies in turn (Table 3.1).

The Earliest Societies: Hunters and Gatherers

For all but a tiny part of our existence on this planet, human beings have lived in **hunting and gathering societies,** small groups or tribes often numbering no more than thirty or forty people. Hunters and gatherers gain their livelihood from hunting, fishing, and gathering edible plants growing in the wild. Hunting and gathering cultures continue to exist in some parts of the world, such as in a few arid parts of Africa and the jungles of Brazil and New Guinea. Most such cultures, however, have been destroyed or absorbed by the spread of Western culture, and those that remain are unlikely to stay intact for much longer. Currently, less than a quarter of a million people in the world support themselves through hunting and gathering—only 0.001 percent of the world's population (Global Map 3.1).

Compared with larger societies—particularly modern societies, such as the United States—little inequality was found in most hunting and gathering groups. The material goods they needed were limited to weapons for hunting, tools for digging and building, traps, and cooking utensils. Thus there was little difference among members of the society in the number or kinds of material possessions—there were no divisions of rich and

---

TABLE 3.1

Types of Human Society

TYPE	PERIOD OF EXISTENCE	CHARACTERISTICS
Hunting and gathering societies	50,000 B.C.E. to the present. Now on the verge of complete disappearance.	Consist of small numbers of people gaining their livelihood from hunting, fishing, and the gathering of edible plants. Few inequalities. Differences of rank limited by age and gender.
Agrarian societies	12,000 B.C.E. to the present. Most are now part of larger political entities and are losing their distinct identity.	Based on small rural communities, without towns or cities. Livelihood gained through agriculture, often supplemented by hunting and gathering. Stronger inequalities than among hunters and gatherers. Ruled by chiefs.
Pastoral societies	12,000 B.C.E. to the present. Today mostly part of larger states; their traditional ways of life are being undermined.	Size ranges from a few hundred people to many thousands. Depend on the tending of domesticated animals for their subsistence. Marked by distinct inequalities. Ruled by chiefs or warrior kings.
Traditional societies or civilizations	6000 B.C.E. to the nineteenth century. All traditional states have disappeared.	Very large in size, some numbering millions of people (though small compared with larger industrialized societies). Some cities exist, in which trade and manufacture are concentrated. Based largely on agriculture. Major inequalities exist among different classes. Distinct apparatus of government headed by a king or emperor.

The Decline of Hunting and Gathering Societies

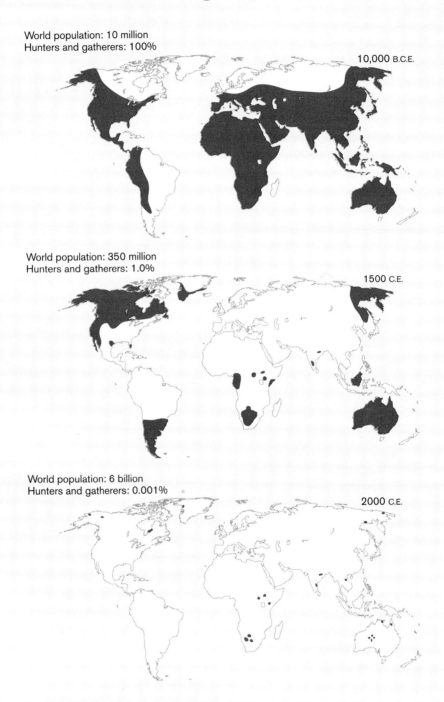

World population: 10 million
Hunters and gatherers: 100%

10,000 B.C.E.

World population: 350 million
Hunters and gatherers: 1.0%

1500 C.E.

World population: 6 billion
Hunters and gatherers: 0.001%

2000 C.E.

SOURCE: Richard B. Lee and Irven De Vore, eds., *Man the Hunter* (Chicago: Aldine Press, 1968), updated by authors.

poor. Differences of position or rank tended to be limited to age and gender; men were almost always the hunters, while women gathered wild crops, cooked, and brought up the children.

The "elders"—the oldest and most experienced men in the community—usually had an important say in major decisions affecting the group. But just as there was little variation in wealth among members, differences of power were much less than in larger types of society. Hunting and gathering societies were usually participatory rather than competitive: all adult male members tended to assemble together when important decisions were to be made or crises were faced.

Hunters and gatherers moved about a good deal but not in a completely erratic way. They had fixed territories, around which they migrated regularly from year to year. Because they were without animal or mechanical means of transport, they could take few goods or possessions with them. Many hunting and gathering communities did not have a stable membership; people often moved between different camps, or groups split up and joined others within the same overall territory.

Hunters and gatherers had little interest in developing material wealth beyond what was needed for their basic wants. Their main concerns were with religious values and ritual activities. Members participated regularly in elaborate ceremonials and often spent a great deal of time preparing the dress, masks, paintings, or other sacred objects used in such rituals.

Hunters and gatherers are not merely primitive peoples whose ways of life no longer hold any interest for us. Studying their cultures allows us to see more clearly that some of our institutions are far from being natural features of human life. We shouldn't idealize the circumstances in which hunters and gatherers lived; but the lack of major inequalities of wealth and power and the emphasis on cooperation rather than competition are instructive reminders that the world created by modern industrial civilization is not necessarily to be equated with progress.

Pastoral and Agrarian Societies

About fifteen thousand years ago, some hunting and gathering groups turned to the raising of domesticated animals and the cultivation of fixed plots of land as their means of livelihood. **Pastoral societies** relied mainly on domesticated livestock, whereas **agrarian societies** grew crops (practiced agriculture). Some societies had mixed pastoral and agrarian economies.

Depending on the environment in which they lived, pastoralists reared animals such as cattle, sheep, goats, camels, or horses. Some pastoral societies still exist in the modern world, concentrated especially in areas of Africa, the Middle East, and Central Asia. They are usually found in regions of dense grasslands or in deserts or mountains. Such regions are not amenable to fruitful agriculture but may support livestock.

At some point, hunting and gathering groups began to sow their own crops rather than simply collect those growing in the wild. This practice first developed as what is usually called *horticulture,* in which small gardens were cultivated by the use of simple hoes or digging instruments. Like pastoralism, horticulture provided for a more reliable supply of food than was possible from hunting and gathering and therefore could support larger communities. Because they were not on the move, people whose livelihood was horticulture could develop larger stocks of material possessions than people in either hunting and gathering or pastoral communities. Some peoples in the world still rely primarily on horticulture for their livelihood (Table 3.2).

TABLE 3.2

Some Agrarian Societies Still Remain

COUNTRY	PERCENT OF WORKFORCE IN AGRICULTURE
Nepal	92.9
Rwanda	90.2
Ethiopia	82.0
Uganda	79.6
China	66.0
Bangladesh	54.7
INDUSTRIALIZED SOCIETIES DIFFER	
Japan	3.8
Australia	4.5
Germany	2.4
Canada	2.3
United States	2.0
United Kingdom	1.8

SOURCE: Earth Trends, "Agriculture Inputs, 2003," earthtrends.wri.org/pdf_library/data_tables/agr2_2003.pdf (accessed fall 2005).

Traditional Societies or Civilizations

From about 6000 B.C.E. onward, we find evidence of societies larger than any that existed before and that contrast in distinct ways with earlier types. These societies were based on the development of cities, led to pronounced inequalities of wealth and power, and were ruled by kings or emperors. Because writing was used and science and art flourished, they are often called *civilizations*.

The earliest civilizations developed in the Middle East, usually in fertile river areas (Global Map 3.2). The Chinese Empire originated in about 1800 B.C.E., at which time powerful states were also in existence in what are now India and Pakistan. By the fifteenth century, a number of large civilizations also existed in Mexico and Latin America, such as the Aztecs of the Mexican peninsula and the Incas of Peru.

Most traditional (premodern) civilizations were also empires: They achieved their size through the conquest and incorporation of other peoples (Kautsky 1982). This was true, for instance, of traditional Rome and China. At its height, in the first century C.E., the Roman Empire stretched from Britain in northwest Europe to beyond the Middle East. The Chinese Empire, which lasted for more than two thousand years, up to the threshold of the twentieth century, covered most of the massive region of eastern Asia now occupied by modern China.

Societies in the Modern World

What happened to destroy the forms of society that dominated the whole of history up to two centuries ago? The answer, in a word, is **industrialization**—the emergence of machine production, based on the use of inanimate power resources (such as steam or electricity). The industrialized, or modern, societies differ in several key respects from any previous type of social order, and their development has had consequences stretching far beyond their European origins (Table 3.3).

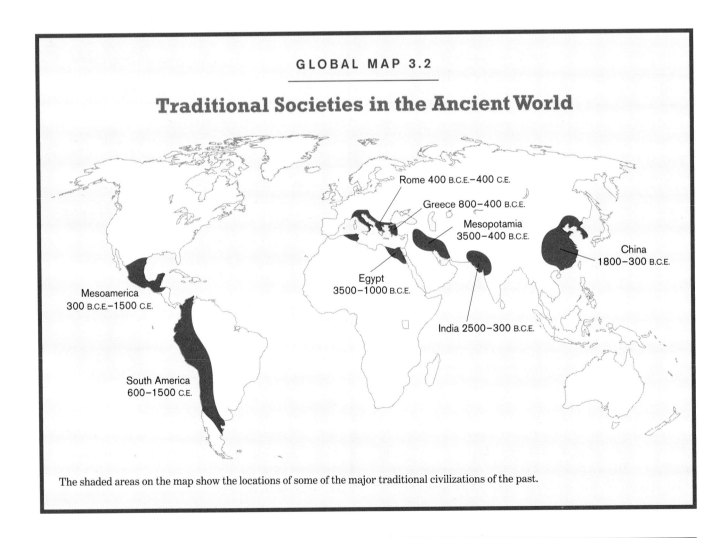

GLOBAL MAP 3.2

Traditional Societies in the Ancient World

Rome 400 B.C.E.–400 C.E.

Greece 800–400 B.C.E.

Mesopotamia 3500–400 B.C.E.

China 1800–300 B.C.E.

Egypt 3500–1000 B.C.E.

Mesoamerica 300 B.C.E.–1500 C.E.

India 2500–300 B.C.E.

South America 600–1500 C.E.

The shaded areas on the map show the locations of some of the major traditional civilizations of the past.

TABLE 3.3

Societies in the Modern World

TYPE	PERIOD OF EXISTENCE	CHARACTERISTICS
Industrialized "First World" societies	Eighteenth century to the present.	Based on industrial production and generally free enterprise. Majority of the population lives in towns and cities; a few live in rural areas and engage in agricultural pursuits. Major class inequalities, though less pronounced than in traditional states. Distinct political communities or nation-states, including the nations of the West, Japan, Australia, and New Zealand.
Communist "Second World" societies	Early twentieth century (following the Russian Revolution of 1917) to early 1990s.	Based on industry, but the economic system is centrally planned. Minority of the population works in agriculture; most live in the towns and cities. Major class inequalities persist. Distinct political communities or nation-states—until 1989, included the Soviet Union and Eastern Europe; but social and political changes began to transform their planned economies in free-enterprise economic systems.
Developing "Third World" societies	Eighteenth century (mostly as colonized areas) to the present.	Based on agricultural production, some of which is sold on world markets; some have free-enterprise systems, others are centrally planned. Majority of the population works in agriculture, using traditional methods of production. Most people live in poverty. Distinct political communities or nation-states, including China, India, and most African and South American nations.
Newly industrializing economies	1970s to the present.	Former developing societies now based on industrial production and generally free enterprise. Majority of the population lives in towns and cities; a few pursue agricultural production for their livelihood. Some have major class inequalities, more pronounced than in industrialized societies. Average per capita income considerably less than in industrialized societies, with the exception of Singapore; includes Hong Kong, South Korea, Singapore, Taiwan, Brazil, and Mexico.

The Industrialized Societies

Industrialization originated in eighteenth-century Britain as a result of the Industrial Revolution, a complex set of technological changes that affected the means by which people gained their livelihood. These changes included the invention of new machines (such as the spinning jenny for creating yarn), the harnessing of power resources (especially water and steam) for production, and the use of science to improve production methods. Because discoveries and inventions in one field lead to more in others, the pace of technological innovation in **industrialized societies** is extremely rapid compared with that of traditional social systems.

In even the most advanced of traditional civilizations, most people were engaged in working on the land. The relatively low level of technological development did not permit more than a small minority to be freed from the chores of agricultural production. By contrast, a prime feature of industrialized societies today is that the large majority of the employed population work in factories, offices, or shops rather than in agriculture. And over 90 percent of people live in towns and cities, where most jobs are to be found and new job opportunities are created. The largest cities are vastly greater in size than the urban settlements found in traditional civilizations. In the cities, social life becomes more impersonal and anonymous than before, and many of our day-to-day encounters are with strangers rather than with individuals known to us. Large-scale organizations, such as business corporations or government agencies, come to influence the lives of virtually everyone.

A further feature of modern societies concerns their political systems, which are more developed and intensive than forms of government in traditional states. In traditional civilizations, the political authorities (monarchs and emperors) had little direct influence on the customs and habits of most of their subjects, who lived in fairly self-contained local villages. With industrialization, transportation and communications became much more rapid, making for a more integrated "national" community.

The industrialized societies were the first nation-states to come into existence. **Nation-states** are political communities with clearly delimited borders dividing them from each other, rather than the vague frontier areas that used to separate traditional states. Nation-state governments have extensive powers over many aspects of citizens' lives, framing laws that apply to all those living within their borders. The United States is a nation-state, as are virtually all other societies in the world today.

The application of industrial technology has been by no means limited to peaceful processes of economic development. From the earliest phases of industrialization, modern production processes have been put to military use, and this has radically altered ways of waging war, creating weaponry and modes of military organization much more advanced than those of nonindustrial cultures. Together, superior economic strength, political cohesion, and military superiority account for the seemingly irresistible spread of Western ways of life across the world over the past two centuries.

Global Development

From the seventeenth to the early twentieth centuries, the Western countries established colonies in numerous areas previously occupied by traditional societies, using their superior military strength where necessary. Although virtually all these colonies have now attained their independence, the process of **colonialism** was central to shaping the social map of the globe as we know it today. In some regions, such as North America, Australia, and New Zealand, which were only thinly populated by hunting and gathering or pastoral communities, Europeans became the majority population. In other areas, including much of Asia, Africa, and South America, the local populations remained in the majority.

Societies of the first of these two types, including the United States, have become industrialized. Those in the second category are mostly at a much lower level of industrial development and are often referred to as less developed societies, or the **developing world.** Such societies include China, India, most of the African countries (such as Nigeria, Ghana, and Algeria), and those in South America (such as Brazil, Peru, and Venezuela). Because many of these societies are situated south of the United States and Europe, they are sometimes referred to collectively as the South, which is contrasted to the wealthier, industrialized North.

You may often hear developing countries referred to as part of the Third World. The term **Third World** was originally part of a contrast drawn between three main types of society found in the early twentieth century. **First World** countries were (and are) the industrialized states of Europe, the United States, Canada, Australasia (Australia, New Zealand, and Melanesia), South Africa, and Japan. Nearly all First World societies have multiparty, parliamentary systems of government. **Second World** societies meant the communist countries of what was then the Soviet Union (USSR) and Eastern Europe, including for example Czechoslovakia, Poland, East Germany, and Hungary. Second World societies were centrally planned economies, which allowed little role for private property or competitive economic enterprise. They were also one-party states: The Communist party dominated both the political and economic systems. For some seventy-five years, world history was affected by a global rivalry between the Soviet Union and Eastern European countries on the one hand and the capitalistic societies of the West and Japan on the other. Today that rivalry is over. With the ending of the cold war and the disintegration of communism in the former USSR and Eastern Europe, the Second World has effectively disappeared.

Even though the three worlds distinction is still often used in sociology textbooks, today it has outlived whatever usefulness it might have once had as a way of describing the countries of the world. For one thing, the Second World of socialist and communist countries no longer exists, and even exceptions such as China are rapidly adopting capitalist economies. More important, the ranking of First, Second, and Third Worlds reflects a value judgment, in which "first" means "best" and "third" means "worst," and is therefore best avoided.

The Developing World

The large majority of less developed societies are in areas that underwent colonial rule in Asia, Africa, and South America. A few colonized areas gained independence early, such as Haiti, which became the first autonomous black republic in January 1804. The Spanish colonies in South America acquired their freedom in 1810, while Brazil broke away from Portuguese rule in 1822.

Some countries that were never ruled from Europe were nonetheless strongly influenced by colonial relationships, the most notable example being China. By force of arms, China was compelled from the seventeenth century on to enter into trading agreements with European powers, by which the Europeans were allocated the government of certain areas, including major seaports. Hong Kong was the last of these. Most nations in the developing world have become independent states only since World War II—often following bloody anti-colonial struggles. Examples include India, which shortly after achieving self-rule split into India and Pakistan, a range of other Asian countries (like Myanmar, Malaysia, and Singapore), and countries in Africa (such as Kenya, Nigeria, the Democratic Republic of Congo, Tanzania, and Algeria).

Although they may include peoples living in traditional fashion, developing countries are very different from earlier forms of traditional society. Their political systems are modeled on systems first established in the societies of the West—that is to say, they are nation-states. Most of the population still live in rural areas, but many of these societies are experiencing a rapid process of city development. Although agriculture remains the main economic activity, crops are now often produced for sale in world markets rather than for local consumption. Developing countries are not merely societies that have "lagged behind" the more industrialized areas. They have been in large part created by contact with Western industrialism, which has undermined the earlier, more traditional systems that were in place there.

Conditions in the more impoverished of these societies have deteriorated rather than improved over the past few years. There are nearly 1.1 billion people living on less than $1 per day and an additional 1.5 billion people live on less than $2 per day (United Nations Development Program [UNDP] 2005). Together, nearly 40 percent of the world's population face the reality of extreme poverty on a daily basis. Some third of the world's poor live in South Asia, in countries such as India, Myanmar, and Cambodia. China, on the other hand has made great strides, reducing by half the number of people living in poverty since 1990. About half (46.4 percent) are concentrated in Africa, where the impoverished population has grown by 100 million people since 1990 (UNDP 2005). A substantial proportion, however, live on the doorstep of the United States—in Central and South America (Global Map 3.3).

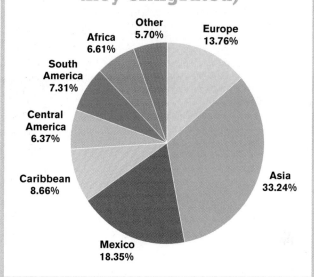

FIGURE 3.1

Immigrants to the United States, 2004 (by region from which they emigrated)

- Other 5.70%
- Africa 6.61%
- South America 7.31%
- Central America 6.37%
- Caribbean 8.66%
- Mexico 18.35%
- Europe 13.76%
- Asia 33.24%

Together, what two areas accounted for over 50 percent of the immigration to the United States? How does the percentage of immigrants from Mexico compare to that of the rest of Central and South America? According to the reading, almost half of those living in poverty in the United States immigrated from what region of the world? How does the most recent wave of immigration to the United States differ from previous generations?

SOURCE: Department of Homeland Security, "Yearbook of Immigration Statistics, 2004," uscis.gov/graphics/shared/statistics/yearbook/YrBk04Im.htm (accessed fall 2005).

Once more, the existence of global poverty shouldn't be seen as remote from the concerns of Americans. Whereas in previous generations the bulk of immigrants into the United States came from the European countries, most now come from poor, developing societies (Figure 3.1). Recent years have seen waves of Hispanic immigrants, nearly all from Latin America. Some U.S. cities near the entry points of much of this immigration, such as Los Angeles and Miami, are bursting with new immigrants and also maintain trading connections with developing countries.

In most developing societies, poverty tends to be at its

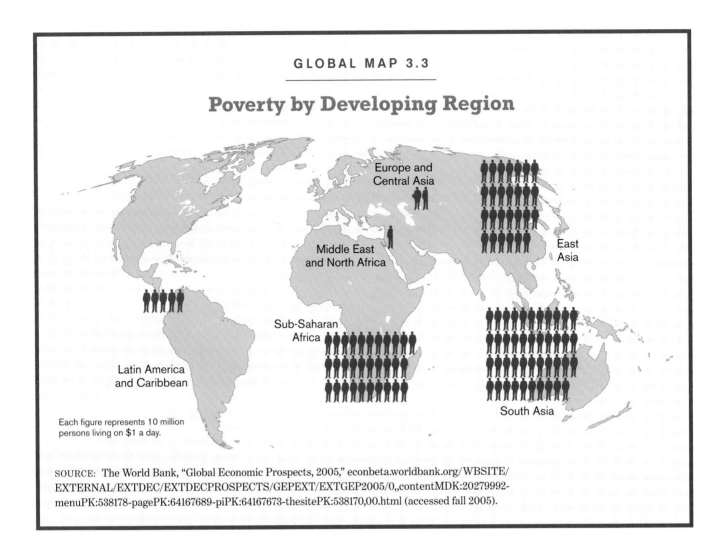

GLOBAL MAP 3.3

Poverty by Developing Region

Europe and Central Asia

Middle East and North Africa

East Asia

Sub-Saharan Africa

Latin America and Caribbean

South Asia

Each figure represents 10 million persons living on $1 a day.

SOURCE: The World Bank, "Global Economic Prospects, 2005," econbeta.worldbank.org/WBSITE/ EXTERNAL/EXTDEC/EXTDECPROSPECTS/GEPEXT/EXTGEP2005/0,,contentMDK:20279992- menuPK:538178-pagePK:64167689-piPK:64167673-thesitePK:538170,00.html (accessed fall 2005).

worst in rural areas. Malnutrition, lack of education, low life expectancy, and substandard housing are generally most severe in the countryside. Many of the poor are to be found in areas where arable land is scarce, agricultural productivity low, and drought or floods common. Women are usually more disadvantaged than men. They encounter cultural, social, and economic problems that even the most underprivileged men do not. For instance, they often work longer hours and, when they are paid at all, earn lower wages. (See Chapter 10 for a lengthier discussion of gender inequality.)

The poor in developing countries live in conditions almost unimaginable to Americans. Many have no permanent dwellings apart from shelters made of cartons or loose pieces of wood. Most have no running water, sewer systems, or electricity. Nonetheless, millions of poor people also live in the United States, and there are connections between poverty in America and global poverty. Almost half of the people living in poverty in the United States immigrated from the global South. This is true of the descendants of the black slaves brought over by force centuries ago; and it is true of more re-

cent, and willing, immigrants who have arrived from Latin America, Asia, and elsewhere.

The Newly Industrializing Economies

Although the majority of developing countries lag well behind societies of the West, some have now successfully embarked on a process of industrialization. These are sometimes referred to as **newly industrializing economies** (NIEs), and they include Brazil, Mexico, Hong Kong, South Korea, Singapore, and Taiwan. The rates of economic growth of the most successful NIEs, such as those in East Asia, are several times those of the Western industrial economies. No developing country figured among the top thirty exporters in the world in 1968, but twenty-five years later South Korea was in the top fifteen.

The East Asian NIEs have shown the most sustained levels of economic prosperity. They are investing abroad as well as promoting growth at home. South Korea's production of steel has doubled in the last decade, and its shipbuilding and electronics industries are among the world's leaders. Singapore is becoming the major financial and commercial center of Southeast Asia. Taiwan is an important presence in the manufacturing and electronics industries. All these changes in the NIEs have directly affected the United States, whose share of global steel production, for example, has dropped significantly since the 1970s.

The Effect of Globalization

In Chapter 1 it was pointed out that the chief focus of sociology has historically been the study of the industrialized societies. As sociologists, can we thus safely ignore the developing world, leaving this as the domain of anthropology? We certainly cannot. The industrialized and the developing societies have developed in *interconnection* with one another and are today more closely related than ever before. Those of us living in the industrialized societies depend on many raw materials and manufactured products coming from developing countries to sustain our lives. Conversely, the economies of most developing states depend on trading networks that bind them to the industrialized countries. We can fully understand the industrialized order only against the backdrop of societies in the developing world—in which, in fact, by far the greater proportion of the world's population lives.

Take a close look at the array of products on display the next time you walk into a local shop or supermarket. The diversity of goods we in the West have come to take for granted as available for anyone with the money to buy them depends on amazingly complex economic connections stretching across

Two African American children play near their home and an open sewer. This poverty-stricken area of Tunica, Mississippi, is sometimes referred to as "Sugarditch."

the world. The store products have been made in, or use ingredients or parts from, a hundred different countries. These parts must be regularly transported across the globe, and constant flows of information are necessary to coordinate the millions of daily transactions.

As the world rapidly moves toward a single, unified economy, businesses and people move about the globe in increasing numbers in search of new markets and economic opportunities. As a result, the cultural map of the world changes: Networks of peoples span national borders and even continents, providing cultural connections between their birthplaces and their adoptive countries (Appadurai 1986). A handful of languages come to dominate, and in some cases replace, the thousands of different languages that were once spoken on the planet.

It is increasingly impossible for cultures to exist as islands. There are few, if any, places on earth so remote as to escape radio, television, air travel—and the throngs of tourists they bring—or the computer. A generation ago, there were still tribes whose way of life was completely untouched by the rest of the world. Today, these peoples use machetes and other tools made in the United States or Japan, wear T-shirts and shorts manufactured in garment factories in the Dominican Republic or Guatemala, and take medicine manufactured in Germany or Switzerland to combat diseases contracted through contact with outsiders. These people also have their stories broadcast to people around the world through satellite television and the Internet. Within a generation or two at the most, all the world's once-isolated cultures will be touched and transformed by global culture, despite their persistent efforts to preserve their age-old ways of life.

The forces that produce a global culture are discussed throughout this book. These include:

- Television, which brings U.S. culture (through networks and shows such as MTV and *The Simpsons*) into homes throughout the world daily and which adapts other cultural products for the U.S. audience (the Swedish *Expedition: Robinson* spawned *Big Brother* and *Survivor*)
- The emergence of a unified global economy, with business whose factories, management structures, and markets often span continents and countries
- "Global citizens," such as managers of large corporations, who may spend as much time crisscrossing the globe as they do at home, who identify with a global, cosmopolitan culture rather than with their own nation's
- A host of international organizations—including United Nations agencies, regional trade and mutual defense associations, multinational banks and other global financial institutions, international labor and health organizations, and global tariff and trade agreements—which are creating a global political, legal, and military framework

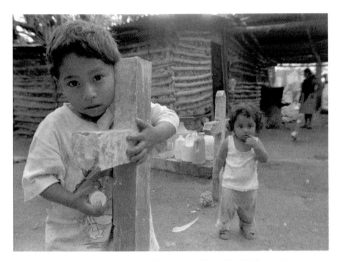

Due to extreme poverty and the lack of land in El Salvador, many Salvadorans are forced to make their homes in public cemeteries.

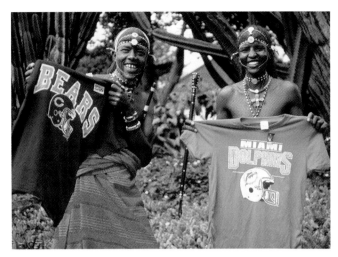

Two Masai natives proudly display T-shirts bearing the logos of American football teams. There is almost no place on earth untouched by the globalization of culture.

- Electronic communications (telephone, fax, e-mail, the Internet and the World Wide Web), which make instantaneous communication with almost any part of the planet an integral part of daily life in the business world

Does the Internet Promote a Global Culture?

Many believe that the rapid growth of the Internet around the world will hasten the spread of a global culture—one resembling the cultures of Europe and North America, currently home to nearly three quarters of all Internet users (Global Map 3.4). Belief in such values as equality between men and women, the right to speak freely, democratic participation in government, and the pursuit of pleasure through consumption are readily diffused throughout the world over the Internet. Moreover, Internet technology itself would seem to foster such values: Global communication, seemingly unlimited (and uncensored) information, and instant gratification are all characteristics of the new technology.

Yet it may be premature to conclude that the Internet will sweep aside traditional cultures, replacing them with radically new cultural values. As the Internet spreads around the world, evidence shows that it is in many ways compatible with traditional cultural values as well, perhaps even a means of strengthening them.

Consider, for example, the Middle Eastern country of Kuwait, a traditional Islamic culture that has recently experienced strong American and European influences. Kuwait, an oil-rich country on the Persian Gulf, has one of the highest average per-person incomes in the world. The government pro-

vides free public education through the university level, resulting in high rates of literacy and education for both men and women. Kuwaiti television frequently carries National Football League (NFL) games and other U.S. programming, although broadcasts are regularly interrupted for the traditional Muslim calls to prayer. Half of Kuwait's approximately two million people are under twenty-five years old; and like their youthful counterparts in Europe and North America, many surf the Internet for new ideas, information, and consumer products.

Although Kuwait is in many respects a modern country, Kuwait law treats men and women differently. Legally, women have equal access to education and employment, yet they are barred from voting or running for political office. Cultural norms treating men and women differently are almost as strong: Women are generally expected to wear traditional clothing that leaves only the face and hands visible and are forbidden to leave home at night or be seen in public at any time with a man who is not a spouse or relative.

Deborah Wheeler (1998) spent a year studying the effect of the Internet on Kuwaiti culture. The Internet is increasingly popular in Kuwait; half of all Internet users in Middle Eastern Arab countries live in this tiny country. Kuwaiti newspapers frequently carry stories about the Internet and the Web, and Kuwait University was the first university in the Arab world to hook its students up to the Internet.

Wheeler reports that Kuwait teenagers are flocking to Internet cafés, where they spend most of their time in chat rooms or visiting pornographic sites—two activities strongly frowned on by traditional Islamic culture. According to Wheeler (1998),

Many young people told me of encounters they were having with the opposite sex in cyberspace. There are even

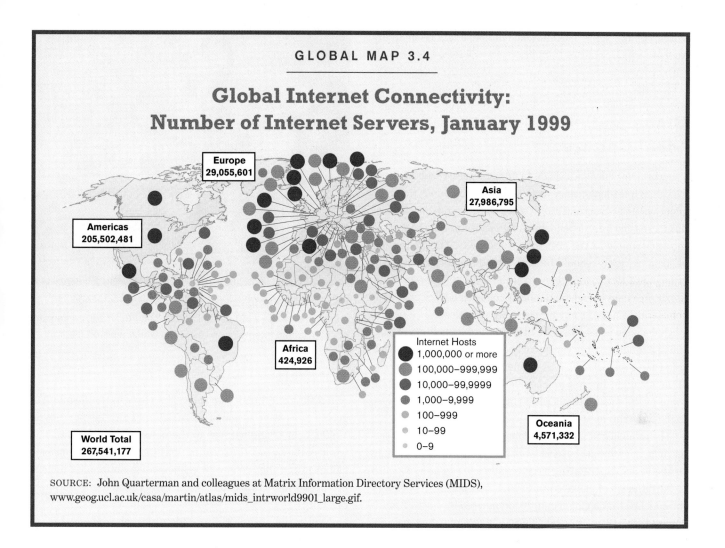

GLOBAL MAP 3.4

Global Internet Connectivity: Number of Internet Servers, January 1999

Europe
29,055,601

Asia
27,986,795

Americas
205,502,481

Africa
424,926

Internet Hosts
● 1,000,000 or more
● 100,000–999,999
● 10,000–99,9999
● 1,000–9,999
● 100–999
● 10–99
● 0–9

Oceania
4,571,332

World Total
267,541,177

SOURCE: John Quarterman and colleagues at Matrix Information Directory Services (MIDS), www.geog.ucl.ac.uk/casa/martin/atlas/mids_intrworld9901_large.gif.

keyboard symbols for kisses (*), kisses on the lips (:*), and embarrassed giggles (LOL)—all those interactions and reactions that make courtship exciting and, in this case, safe.

The new communications technologies are clearly enabling men and women to talk with each other, in a society in which such communications outside of marriage are extremely limited. Wheeler also notes that ironically men and women are segregated in the Internet cafés. Furthermore, she finds that Kuwaitis are extremely reluctant to voice strong opinions or political views online. With the exception of discussing conservative Islamic religious beliefs, which are freely disseminated over the Internet, Kuwaitis are remarkably inhibited online. Wheeler (1998) attributes this to the cultural belief that giving out too much information about oneself is dangerous:

In Kuwait, information is more of a potential threat than a means for individual empowerment. It is a weapon to use against your enemies, a tool for keeping

conformity, or a reinforcement of regulations of daily life. . . . Kuwait's transition to the information age is influenced by these attitudes and the desire to keep one's reputation protected. This keeps the Internet from registering significant political and social impacts, except for the rise in Kuwaiti Islamist discourses on the Internet. . . . In Kuwait, there is an ethos that states that having and/or pronouncing a political opinion publicly is bad. No one wants to talk on the record or to be quoted. The idea makes people scared or nervous. Only those who are elite feel they can speak freely and openly.

Wheeler concludes that Kuwaiti culture, which is hundreds of years old, is not likely to be easily transformed by simple exposure to different beliefs and values on the Internet. The fact that a few young people are participating in global chat rooms does not mean that Kuwaiti culture is adopting the sexual attitudes of the United States or even the form of everyday relations found between men and women in the West. The culture that eventually emerges as a result of the new technologies will not be the same as American culture; it will be uniquely Kuwaiti.

Globalization and Local Cultures

The world has become a single *social system* as a result of growing ties of interdependence, both social and economic, that now affect virtually everyone. But it would be a mistake to think of this increasing interdependence, or globalization, of the world's societies simply as the growth of world unity. The globalizing of social relations should be understood primarily as the reordering of *time and distance* in social life. Our lives, in other words, are increasingly and quickly influenced by events happening far removed from our everyday activities.

Globalizing processes have brought many benefits to Americans: a much greater variety of goods and foodstuffs is available than ever before. At the same time, the fact that we are all now caught up in a much wider world has helped create some of the most serious problems American society faces, such as the threat of terrorism.

The influence of a growing global culture has provoked numerous reactions at the local level. Many local cultures remain strong or are experiencing a rejuvenation, partly as a response to the diffusion of global culture. Such a response grows out of the concern that a global culture, dominated by North American and European cultural values, will corrupt the local culture. For example, the Taliban, an Islamic movement that controlled most of Afghanistan, sought to impose traditional, tribal values throughout the country. Through its governmental "Ministry for Ordering What Is Right and Forbidding What Is Wrong," the Taliban banned music, closed movie theaters, abolished the use of alcohol, and required men to grow full beards. Women were ordered to cover their entire bodies with *burkas,* tentlike garments with a woven screen over the eyes, out of which to see. They were forbidden to work outside their homes or even to be seen in public with men who were not their spouses or relations. Violations of these rules were severely punished, sometimes by death. The rise of the Taliban can be understood at least partly as a rejection of the spread of Western culture.

The resurgence of local cultures is sometimes seen throughout the world in the rise of **nationalism,** a sense of identification with one's people that is expressed through a common set of strongly held beliefs. Sometimes these include the belief that the people of a particular nation have historical or God-given rights that supersede those of other people. Nationalism can be strongly political, involving attempts to assert the power of a nation based on a shared ethnic or racial identity over people

Using the Internet to connect with the world around them is common among young people across cultures. Here, an Iranian girl at a Tehran Internet café reads the latest news on the Iraq crisis.

of a different ethnicity or race. The strife in the former Yugoslavia, as well as parts of Africa and the former Soviet Union, bear tragic witness to the power of nationalism. The world of the twenty-first century may well witness responses to globalization that celebrate ethnocentric nationalist beliefs, promoting intolerance and hatred rather than a celebration of diversity.

New nationalisms, cultural identities, and religious practices are constantly being forged throughout the world. When you socialize with students from the same cultural background or celebrate traditional holidays with your friends and family, you are sustaining your culture. The very technology that helps foster globalization also supports local cultures: The Internet enables you to communicate with others who share your cultural identity, even when they are dispersed around the world. American students who share a passion for a particular type of music can stay up all night in Internet chat rooms with like-minded people: if you are studying abroad you can stay connected with communities back home by logging on to the Web site of your hometown newspaper (Wallraff 2000). A casual search of the Web reveals thousands of pages devoted to different cultures and subcultures.

Although sociologists do not yet fully understand these processes, they often conclude that despite the powerful forces of globalization operating in the world today, local cultures remain strong and indeed flourish. But is it still too soon to tell whether and how globalization will transform our world, whether it will result in the homogenization of the world's diverse cultures, the flourishing of many individual cultures, or both.

Study Outline

www.wwnorton.com/giddens

The Concepts of Culture

- *Culture* consists of the *values* held by a given group, the *norms* they follow, and the *material goods* they create.

Culture and Change

- In recent years the sociology of culture has attracted renewed interest, a phenomenon known as the *cultural turn*. Attention is being given both to culture as a set of scripts we draw on to shape our beliefs, values, and actions and to the many different meanings of cultural symbols.

The Development of Human Culture

- Human cultures have evolved over thousands of years and reflect both human biology and the physical environment in which the cultures emerged. A defining feature of humankind is its inventiveness in creating new forms of culture.

How Nature and Nurture Interact

- Most sociologists do not deny that biology plays a role in shaping human behavior, especially through the interaction between biology and culture. Sociologists' main concern, however, is with how behavior is learned from the individual's interaction with society.
- Forms of behavior found in all, or virtually all, cultures are called *cultural universals. Language,* the prohibition against incest, institutions of *marriage,* the family, religion, and property are the main types of cultural universals—but within these general categories there are many variations in values and modes of behavior between different societies.
- We live in a world of symbols, or representations, and one of our most important forms of symbolization is language. The *linguistic relativity hypothesis* argues that language influences perception. Language is also an important source of cultural continuity, and the members of a culture are often passionate about their linguistic heritage.
- *Cultural diversity* is a chief aspect of modern culture, and in the United States it is seen in the large number of vibrant *subcultures* as well as in the existence of countercultures. Although some people feel that different subcultures should be *assimilated* into a single mainstream culture, others argue in favor of *multiculturalism.*
- Sociologists try to avoid *ethnocentrism* and instead adopt a stance of *cultural relativism,* attempting to understand a society relative to its own cultural norms and values.

Premodern Societies

- Several types of premodern society can be distinguished. In *hunting and gathering societies,* people do not grow crops or keep livestock but gain their livelihood from gathering plants and hunting animals. *Pastoral societies* are those that raise domesticated animals as their major source of subsistence. *Agrarian societies* depend on the cultivation of fixed plots of land. Larger, more developed, urban societies form traditional states or civilizations.

Societies in the Modern World

- The development of industrialized societies and the expansion of the West led to the conquest of many parts of the world through the process of *colonialism,* which radically changed long-established social systems and cultures.
- In industrialized societies, industrial production (whose techniques are also used in the production of food) is the main basis of the economy. Industrialized countries include the nations of the West, plus Japan, Australia, and New Zealand. They now include those industrialized societies ruled by communist governments. The *developing world,* in which most of the world's population live, is almost all formerly colonized areas. The majority of the population works in agricultural production, some of which is geared to world markets.

The Effect of Globalization

- The increase in global communications and economic interdependence represents more than simply the growth of world unity. Time and distance are being reorganized in ways that bring us all closer together, but even as globalization threatens to make all cultures seem alike, local cultural identifications are resurging around the world. This is seen in the rise of *nationalism,* which can result in ethnic conflict as well as ethnic pride.

Key Concepts

agrarian societies (p. 77)
assimilation (p. 67)
colonialism (p. 80)
cultural relativism (p. 69)
cultural turn (p. 62)
cultural universals (p. 71)
culture (p. 56)
developing world (p. 80)
ethnocentrism (p. 69)
First World (p. 80)
hunting and gathering societies (p. 75)
industrialization (p. 78)
industrialized societies (p. 79)
instincts (p. 66)

Review Questions

1. What are values?
   a. Values are those ideas that a culture holds in the highest esteem. They give people a purpose in life.
   b. Values are abstract ideals—for example, in most Western societies, monogamy is considered a virtue. In other cultures, a person may be permitted to have several wives or husbands simultaneously.
   c. Values are lists of dos and don'ts that regulate everyday behavior.
   d. Values depend on the development of a money economy and systems of credit.

2. What is a signifier?
   a. A signifier is the name given to the meaning of a spoken or written word.
   b. A signifier is any vehicle of meaning, such as speech, writing, dress, and buildings.
   c. A signifier is the meaning of a symbol.
   d. A signifier is an electronic sign.

3. Using one's own cultural values to judge another culture is called
   a. ethnocentrism.
   b. cultural relativism.
   c. cultural turn.
   d. cultural universals.

4. What is culture?
   a. Culture consists of the values, norms, and material goods of a people. Culture can be described as a "design for living."

   b. Culture is the sum total of a society's artistic expression—all the novels, poems, dance, theater, museums, and so on.
   c. Culture is the material apparatus of everyday life—the chairs, tables, cooking utensils, clothes, shoes, and coats that we use in our daily round.
   d. Culture consists of the values and norms of a society, its founding myths and ideals, and its beliefs about the kinds of conduct appropriate in everyday life.

5. What was the basis for the rise of modern societies?
   a. the fall of the Roman Empire
   b. the Renaissance
   c. the Industrial Revolution
   d. the cold war

6. Which of the following is not a cultural universal?
   a. the prohibition against incest
   b. some form of religion
   c. a concept of property
   d. the idea of adolescence

7. What was colonialism?
   a. The creation by the European powers of a network of colonies in ports of call along their trade routes.
   b. The military conquest of African peoples by Europeans.
   c. The process by which industrial powers incorporated regions rich in natural resources into their economic and political systems.
   d. The effect of trade with foreign empires on the economies of the European powers.

8. What is the position of sociologists on the debate of nature vs. nurture?
   a. Sociologists believe that biology is destiny.
   b. Sociologists ask how nature and nurture interact to produce human behavior.
   c. No sociologists today acknowledge a role for nature.
   d. Sociologists do not have a position.

9. Which of the following statements is true about developing countries?
   a. About one quarter of the world's population lives in developing countries.
   b. Very few of them are formerly colonized areas.
   c. The majority of the population works in manufacturing and service sectors.
   d. Some agricultural production in developing countries is geared to world markets.

10. Subcultures are
    a. abstract ideals, such as American ideals of liberty and justice.
    b. systems of relationships that connect individuals who share the same culture.
    c. smaller segments of society distinguished by unique patterns of behavior.
    d. populations made up of a number of groups from diverse cultural, ethnic, and linguistic backgrounds.

Thinking Sociologically Exercises

1. Mention at least two cultural traits that you would claim are universals; mention two others you would claim are culturally specific traits. Use case study materials from different societies you are familiar with to show the differences between universal and specific cultural traits. Are the cultural universals you have discussed derivatives of human instincts? Explain your answer fully.

2. What does it mean to be ethnocentric? How is ethnocentrism dangerous in conducting social research? How is ethnocentrism problematic among nonresearchers in their everyday lives?

Data Exercises

www.wwnorton.com/giddens
Keyword: Data3

Are you among the millions of Americans whose families have arrived in the United States in the past twenty-five years? Or have you noticed that your community, school, church, or workplace has become more diverse? In the data exercise for Chapter 3 you will learn more about the patterns of immigration to the United States, both historically and currently; how Americans feel about recent immigration; and how your own community has changed as a result of immigration.

Culture, Society, and Child Socialization

Learn about socialization (including gender socialization) and know the most important agencies of socialization.

Socialization through the Life Course

Learn the various stages of the life course and see the similarities and differences among different cultures.

CHAPTER FOUR

SOCIALIZATION AND THE LIFE CYCLE

a t the start of J. K. Rowling's first Harry Potter adventure, *Harry Potter and the Sorcerer's Stone,* the shrewd wizard Albus Dumbledore leaves Harry, a newly orphaned infant, at the doorstep of his nonmagician (or "Muggle") uncle and aunt's house. Harry has already shown himself to have unique powers, but Dumbledore is concerned that if left in the wizarding world, Harry won't mature healthily. "It would be enough to turn any boy's head," he says. "Famous before he can walk and talk! Famous for something he won't even remember. Can't you see how much better off he'll be, growing up away from all that until he's ready to take it?" (Rowling 1998).

The Harry Potter novels, each of which follows Harry through a single year of his life, are based on the premise that there is no adventure greater than that of growing up. Although Harry attends the Hogwarts School of Witchcraft and Wizardry, it's still a school, because everyone, even a young wizard with limitless power, needs help developing a set of values. We all pass through important life stages: the passage from childhood to adolescence and then to adulthood. So, for example, as the Harry Potter series progresses, Harry feels the onset of sexual urges, to which he responds with an entirely common awkwardness. Because sports are an important place for many children to learn about camaraderie and ambition, Harry plays the wizard sport Quidditch. Rowling loves to use the paranormal to help us see the enchanting complexities behind the fundamentals of everyday life. In her universe, owls unerringly deliver letters; is this really any stranger than the postal system or e-mail? The function of all classic children's stories is to make the process of growing up more understandable, whether they're set in a fairy-tale universe, our own world, or—as with the innovation of the Harry Potter series—both.

Socialization is the process whereby the helpless infant gradually becomes a self-aware, knowledgeable person, skilled in the ways of the culture into which he or she was born. Socialization among the young allows for the more general phenomenon of **social reproduction**—the process whereby societies have structural continuity over time. During the course of socialization, especially in the early years of life, children learn the ways of their elders, thereby perpetuating their values, norms, and social practices. All societies have characteristics that endure over long stretches of time, even though their members change as individuals are born and die. American society, for example, has many distinctive social and cultural characteristics that have persisted for generations—such as the fact that English is the main language spoken.

Socialization connects the different generations to one another (Turnbull 1983). The birth of a child alters the lives of those who are responsible for its upbringing—who themselves therefore undergo new learning experiences. Parenting usually ties the activities of adults to children for the remainder of their lives. Older people still remain parents when they become grandparents, of course, thus forging another set of relationships connecting the different generations with each other. Although the process of cultural learning is much more intense in infancy and early childhood than later, learning and adjustment go on through the whole life cycle.

In the sections to follow, we continue the theme of nature interacting with nurture, introduced in the previous chapter. We will first analyze the development of the human individual from infancy to early childhood, identifying the main stages of change involved. Different writers have put forward a number of theoretical interpretations about how and why children develop as they do, and we describe and compare these, including theories that explain how we develop gender identities. Finally, we move on to discuss the main groups and social contexts that influence socialization during the various phases of individuals' lives.

Culture, Society, and Child Socialization

"Unsocialized" Children

What would children be like if, in some way or another, they were raised without the influence of human adults? Obviously no humane person could bring up a child away from social in-

fluence. There are, however, a number of much-discussed cases of children who have spent their early years away from normal human contact.

THE "WILD BOY OF AVEYRON"

On January 9, 1800, a strange creature emerged from the woods near the village of Saint-Serin in southern France. In spite of walking erect, he looked more animal than human, although he was soon identified as a boy of about eleven or twelve. He spoke only in shrill, strange-sounding cries. The boy apparently had no sense of personal hygiene and relieved himself where and when he chose. He was brought to the attention of the local police and taken to a nearby orphanage. In the beginning he tried constantly to escape and was only recaptured with some difficulty. He refused to tolerate wearing clothes, tearing them off as soon as they were put on him. No parents ever came forward to claim him.

The child was subjected to a thorough medical examination, which turned up no major physical abnormalities. On being shown a mirror, he seemingly saw an image, but did not recognize himself. On one occasion, he tried to reach through the mirror to seize a potato he saw in it. (The potato in fact was being held behind his head.) After several attempts, without turning his head, he took the potato by reaching back over his shoulder. A priest who was observing the boy from day to day and who described this incident, wrote: "All these little details, and many others we could add prove that this child is not totally without intelligence, reflection, and reasoning power. However, we are obliged to say that, in every case not concerned with his natural needs or satisfying his appetite, one can perceive in him only animal behavior. If he has sensations, they give birth to no idea. He cannot even compare them with one another. One would think that there is no connection between his soul or mind and his body" (quoted in Shattuck 1980; see also Lane 1976).

Later the boy was moved to Paris and a systematic attempt was made to change him "from beast to human." The endeavor was only partly successful. He was toilet trained, accepted wearing clothes, and learned to dress himself. Yet he was uninterested in toys or games and was never able to learn or speak more than a few words. So far as anyone could tell, on the basis of detailed descriptions of his behavior and reactions, this was not because he was mentally retarded. He seemed either unwilling or unable to master human speech fully. He made little further progress and died in 1828.

GENIE

It cannot be proved how long the wild boy of Aveyron lived on his own in the woods or whether or not he suffered from some congenital defect that made it impossible for him to develop like a normal human being. However, more recent examples reinforce some of the observations made about his behavior. One case is provided by the life of Genie, a California girl who was locked in a room when she was about one and a half until she was over thirteen (Curtiss 1977). Genie's father kept his wife, who was going blind, more or less completely confined to the house. The main connection between the family and the outside world was through a teenage son, who attended school and did the shopping.

Genie had a hip defect from birth that prevented her from walking properly. Her father frequently beat her. When Genie was twenty months old, her father apparently decided she was retarded and put her away in a closed room with the curtains drawn and the door shut. She stayed there for the next eleven years, seeing the other members of the family only when they came to feed her. Genie had not been toilet trained and spent part of her time harnessed, naked, to a toddler's potty chair. Sometimes at night she was removed, only to be put into another restraining garment, a sleeping bag within which her arms were imprisoned. Tied up in this way, she was also enclosed in an infant's crib with wire-mesh sides and a mesh cover overhead. Somehow, in these appalling circumstances she endured the hours, days, and years of her life. She had almost no opportunity to overhear any conversation between others in the house. If she attempted to make a noise, or to attract attention, her father would beat her. Her father never spoke to her, but instead made barking, animal-like sounds if she did anything to annoy him. She had no proper toys or other objects with which to occupy her time.

In 1970, the mother escaped from the house, taking Genie with her. The condition of the girl came to the notice of a social worker, and she was placed in the rehabilitation ward of a children's hospital. When she was first admitted to the hospital, she could not stand erect; could not run, jump, or climb; and was only able to walk in a shuffling, clumsy fashion. She was described by a psychiatrist as "unsocialized, primitive, hardly human." Once in a rehabilitation ward, however, Genie made fairly rapid progress. She learned to eat quite normally, was toilet trained, and tolerated being dressed like other children. Yet she was silent almost all of the time, except when she laughed, her laugh being high-pitched and unreal. She masturbated constantly in public situations, refusing to abandon the habit. Later she lived as a foster child in the home of one of the doctors from the hospital. She gradually came to develop a fairly wide vocabulary and could make a limited number of basic utterances, but her mastery of language never progressed beyond that of a three- or four-year-old.

Genie's behavior was studied intensively and she was given a variety of tests over a period of some seven years. These seemed to indicate that she was not retarded, nor did she suf-

This is the only photograph of Genie to appear in the press on her discovery in 1970. Having been deprived of almost all human contact for the first thirteen years of her life, Genie provided some sense of what an unsocialized child would be like.

fer from any other congenital defects. What seems to have happened to Genie, as to the wild boy of Aveyron, is that by the time she came into close human contact, she had grown beyond the age at which children readily accomplish the learning of language and other human skills. There is probably a "critical period" for the learning of language and other complex achievements, after which it is too late to master them fully. The wild boy and Genie provide some sense of what an unsocialized child would be like. Each retained many "nonhuman" responses. Yet, in spite of the deprivations they suffered, neither displayed any lasting viciousness. They responded quickly to others who treated them sympathetically and were able to acquire a certain minimum level of ordinary human capabilities.

Of course, we have to be cautious about interpreting cases of this sort. In each of these examples it is possible that there was a mental abnormality that remained undiagnosed. Alternatively, the experiences to which the children were subjected may have inflicted psychological damage that prevented them from gaining the skills most children acquire at a much earlier age. Yet there is sufficient similarity between these two case histories, and others that have been recorded, to suggest how limited our faculties would be in the absence of an extended period of early socialization.

Theories of Child Development

One of the most distinctive features of human beings, compared with other animals, is that humans are *self-aware*. How should we understand the emergence of a sense of self—the awareness that the individual has a distinct identity separate from others? During the first months of life, the infant possesses little or no understanding of differences between human beings and material objects in the environment, and has no awareness of self. Children do not begin to use concepts such as *I, me,* and *you* until the age of two or after. Only gradually do they then come to understand that others have distinct identities, consciousness, and needs separate from their own.

The problem of the emergence of self is much debated and is viewed rather differently in contrasting theoretical perspectives. To some extent, this is because the most prominent theories about child development emphasize different aspects of socialization. The American philosopher and sociologist George Herbert Mead gives attention mainly to how children learn to use the concepts of *I* and *me*. Jean Piaget, the Swiss student of child behavior, worked on many aspects of child development, but his best-known writings concern **cognition**—the ways in which children learn to *think* about themselves and their environment.

G. H. MEAD AND THE DEVELOPMENT OF SELF

Because Mead's ideas form the main basis of a general tradition of theoretical thinking, *symbolic interactionism,* they have had a very broad impact in sociology. Symbolic interactionism emphasizes that interaction between human beings takes place through symbols and the interpretation of meanings (see Chapter 1). But in addition, Mead's work provides an account of the main phases of child development, giving particular attention to the emergence of a sense of self.

According to Mead, infants and young children first of all develop as social beings by imitating the actions of those around them. Play is one way in which this takes place, and in their play small children often imitate what adults do. A small child will make mud pies, having seen an adult cooking, or dig with a spoon, having observed someone gardening. Children's play evolves from simple imitation to more complicated games in which a child of four or five years old will act out an adult role. Mead called this "taking the role of the other"—learning what it is like to be in the shoes of another person. It is only at this stage that children acquire a developed sense of self. Children achieve an understanding of themselves as separate agents—as a "me"—by seeing themselves through the eyes of others.

Using their toy wheelbarrows to help their father with the gardening, these boys are, according to Mead, "taking on the role of the other" and achieving an understanding of themselves as separate social agents.

We achieve self-awareness, according to Mead, when we learn to distinguish the *me* from the *I*. The *I* is the unsocialized infant, a bundle of spontaneous wants and desires. The *me,* as Mead used the term, is the **social self.** Individuals develop **self-consciousness,** Mead argued, by coming to see themselves as others see them. A further stage of child development, according to Mead, occurs when the child is about eight or nine years old. This is the age at which children tend to take part in organized games, rather than unsystematic play. It is at this period that children begin to understand the overall *values* and *morality* according to which social life is conducted. To learn organized games, children must understand the rules of play and notions of fairness and equal participation. Children at this stage learn to grasp what Mead termed the **generalized other**—the general values and moral rules of the culture in which they are developing.

JEAN PIAGET AND THE STAGES OF COGNITIVE DEVELOPMENT

Piaget placed great emphasis on the child's active capability to make sense of the world. Children do not passively soak up information, but instead select and interpret what they see, hear, and feel in the world around them. Piaget described several distinct stages of cognitive development during which children learn to think about themselves and their environment. Each stage involves the acquisition of new skills and depends on the successful completion of the preceding one.

Piaget called the first stage, which lasts from birth up to about age two, the **sensorimotor stage,** because infants learn mainly by touching objects, manipulating them, and physically exploring their environment. Until about age four months or so, infants cannot differentiate themselves from their environment. For example, a child will not realize that her own movements cause the sides of her crib to rattle. Objects are not differentiated from persons, and the infant is unaware that anything exists outside her range of vision. Infants gradually learn to distinguish people from objects, coming to see that both have an existence independent of their immediate perceptions. The main accomplishment of this stage is that by its close children understand their environment to have distinct and stable properties.

The next phase, called the **preoperational stage,** is the one to which Piaget devoted the bulk of his research. This stage lasts from age two to seven. During this time, children acquire a mastery of language and become able to use words to represent objects and images in a symbolic fashion. A four-year-old might use a sweeping hand, for example, to represent the concept *airplane.* Piaget termed the stage "preoperational" because children are not yet able to use their developing mental capabilities systematically. Children in this stage are **egocentric.** As Piaget used it, this concept does not refer to selfishness but to the tendency of the child to interpret the world exclusively in terms of his own position. A child during this period does not understand, for instance, that others see objects from a different perspective from his own. Holding a book upright, the child may ask about a picture in it, not realizing that the other person sitting opposite can see only the back of the book.

Children at the preoperational stage are not able to hold connected conversations with another. In egocentric speech, what each child says is more or less unrelated to what the other speaker said. Children talk together, but not *to* one another in the same sense as adults. During this phase of development, children have no general understanding of categories of thought that adults tend to take for granted: concepts such as causality, speed, weight, or number. Even if the child sees water poured from a tall, thin container into a shorter, wider one, she will not understand that the volume of water remains the same—and conclude rather that there is less water because the water level is lower.

A third period, the **concrete operational stage,** lasts from age seven to eleven. During this phase, children master abstract, logical notions. They are able to handle ideas such as causality without much difficulty. A child at this stage of development will recognize the false reasoning involved in the idea that the wide container holds less water than the thin, narrow one, even though the water levels are different. The becomes capable of carrying out the mathematical operations of multiplying, dividing, and subtracting. Children by this stage are much less egocentric. In the preoperational stage, if a girl is asked, "How many sisters do you have?" she may correctly answer, "One." But if asked, "How many sisters does your sister have?" she will probably answer, "None," because she cannot see herself from the point of view of her sister. The concrete operational child is able to answer such a question with ease.

The years from eleven to fifteen cover what Piaget called the **formal operational stage.** During adolescence, the developing child becomes able to grasp highly abstract and hypothetical ideas. When faced with a problem, children at this stage are able to review all the possible ways of solving it and go through them theoretically to reach a solution. The young person at the formal operational stage is able to understand why some questions are trick ones. To the question, "What creatures are both poodles and dogs?" the individual might not be able to give the correct reply but will understand why the answer "poodles" is right and appreciate the humor in it.

According to Piaget, the first three stages of development are universal; but not all adults reach the formal operational stage. The development of formal operational thought depends in part on processes of schooling. Adults of limited educational attainment tend to continue to think in more concrete terms and retain large traces of egocentrism.

Agents of Socialization

Sociologists often speak of socialization as occurring in two broad phases, involving a number of different agents of socialization. **Agents of socialization** are groups or social contexts in which significant processes of socialization occur. Primary socialization occurs in infancy and childhood and is the most intense period of cultural learning. It is the time when children learn language and basic behavioral patterns that form the foundation for later learning. The family is the main agent of socialization during this phase. Secondary socialization takes place later in childhood and into maturity. In this phase, other agents of socialization take over some of the responsibility from the family. Schools, peer groups, organizations, the media, and eventually the workplace become socializing forces for individuals. Social interactions in these contexts help people learn the values, norms, and beliefs that make up the patterns of their culture.

THE FAMILY

Because family systems vary widely, the range of family contacts that the infant experiences is by no means standard across cultures. The mother everywhere is normally the most important individual in the child's early life, but the nature of the relationships established between mothers and their children is influenced by the form and regularity of their contact.

This is, in turn, conditioned by the character of family institutions and their relation to other groups in society.

In modern societies, most early socialization occurs within a small-scale family context. The majority of American children spend their early years within a domestic unit containing mother, father, and perhaps one or two other children. In many other cultures, by contrast, aunts, uncles, and grandparents are often part of a single household and serve as caretakers even for very young infants. Yet even within American society there are many variations in the nature of family contexts. Some children are brought up in single-parent households; some are cared for by two mothering and fathering agents (divorced parents and stepparents). A high proportion of women with families are now employed outside the home and return to their paid work relatively soon after the births of their children. In spite of these variations, the family normally remains the major agency of socialization from infancy to adolescence and beyond—in a sequence of development connecting the generations.

Families have varying "locations" within the overall institutions of a society. In most traditional societies, the family into which a person was born largely determined the individual's social position for the rest of his or her life. In modern societies, social position is not inherited at birth in this way, yet the region and social class of the family into which an individual is born affects patterns of socialization quite distinctly. Children pick up ways of behavior characteristic of their parents or others in their neighborhood or community.

Varying patterns of child rearing and discipline, together with contrasting values and expectations, are found in different sectors of large-scale societies. It is easy to understand the influence of different types of family background if we think of what life is like, say, for a child growing up in a poor black family living in a run-down city neighborhood compared to one born into an affluent white family living in an all-white suburb (Kohn 1977).

Of course, few if any children simply take over unquestioningly the outlook of their parents. This is especially true in the modern world, in which change is so pervasive. Moreover, the very existence of a range of socializing agents in modern societies leads to many divergences between the outlooks of children, adolescents, and the parental generation.

SCHOOLS

Another important socializing agency is the school. Schooling is a formal process: Students pursue a definite curriculum of subjects. Yet schools are agents of socialization in more subtle respects. Children are expected to be quiet in class, be punctual at lessons, and observe rules of school discipline. They are required to accept and respond to the authority of the teaching staff. Reactions of teachers also affect the expectations children have of themselves. These expectations in turn become linked to their job experience when they leave school. Peer groups are often formed at school, and the system of keeping children in classes according to age reinforces their influence.

PEER RELATIONSHIPS

Another socializing agency is the **peer group.** Peer groups consist of children of a similar age. In some cultures, particularly small traditional societies, peer groups are formalized as **age-grades** (normally confined to males). There are often specific ceremonies or rites that mark the transition of men from one age-grade to another. Those within a particular age-grade generally maintain close and friendly connections throughout their lives. A typical set of age-grades consists of childhood, junior warriorhood, senior warriorhood, junior elderhood, and senior elderhood. Men move through these grades not as individuals, but as whole groups.

The family's importance in socialization is obvious, because the experience of the infant and young child is shaped more or less exclusively within it. It is less apparent, especially to those of us living in Western societies, how significant peer groups are. Yet even without formal age-grades, children over the age of four or five usually spend a great deal of time in the company of friends the same age. Given the high proportion of women now in the workforce whose young children play together in day-care centers, peer relations are even more important today than before (Corsaro 1997; Harris 1998).

In her book *Gender Play* (1993), Barrie Thorne, a sociologist now at the University of California, Berkeley, looked at socialization in this way. As others had before her, she wanted to understand how children come to know what it means to be male and female (you will learn three classic theories of gender socialization later in this chapter). Rather than seeing children as passively learning the meaning of gender from their parents and teachers, she looked at the way in which children actively create and re-create the meaning of gender in their interactions with each other. The social activities that schoolchildren do together can be as important as other agents for their socialization.

Thorne spent two years observing fourth and fifth graders at two schools in Michigan and California, sitting in the classroom with them and observing their activities outside the classroom. She watched games—such as "chase and kiss," "cooties," and "goin' with"—and teasing to learn how children construct and experience gender meanings in the classroom and on the playground.

Thorne found that peer groups have a great influence on gender socialization, particularly as children talk about their changing bodies, a subject of great fascination. The social context created by these children determined whether a child's bodily change was experienced with embarrassment or worn with pride. As Thorne (1993) observed, "If the most popular women started menstruating or wearing bras (even if they didn't need to), then other girls wanted these changes too. But if the popular didn't wear bras and hadn't . . . gotten their periods, then these developments were viewed as less desirable."

Thorne's research is a powerful reminder that children are social actors who help create their social world and influence their own socialization. Still, the effect of societal and cultural influences is tremendous because the activities that children pursue and the values they hold are determined by influences such as their families and the media.

Peer relations are likely to have a significant effect beyond childhood and adolescence. Informal groups of people of similar ages, at work and in other situations, are usually of enduring importance in shaping individuals' attitudes and behavior.

THE MASS MEDIA

Newspapers, periodicals, and journals flourished in the West from the early 1800s onward, but they were confined to a fairly small readership. It was not until a century later that such printed materials became part of the daily experience of millions of people, influencing their attitudes and opinions. The spread of **mass media** involving printed documents was soon accompanied by electronic communication—radio, television, audio recordings, and videos. American children spend the equivalent of almost a hundred schooldays per year watching television.

Much research has been done to assess the effects of television programs on the audiences they reach, particularly children. Perhaps the most commonly researched topic is the effect of television on propensities to crime and violence.

The most extensive studies are those carried out by George Gerbner and his collaborators, who have analyzed samples of prime-time and weekend daytime TV for all the major American networks each year since 1967. The number and frequency of violent acts and episodes are charted for a range of programs. Violence is defined as physical force directed against the self or others, in which physical harm or death occurs. Television drama emerges as highly violent in character. On average, 80 percent of programs contain violence, with a rate of 7.5 violent episodes per hour. Children's programs show even higher levels of violence, although killing is less commonly portrayed. Cartoons depict the highest number of violent acts and episodes of any type of television program (Gerbner et al. 1985).

In general, research on the effects of television on audiences has tended to treat children as passive and undiscriminating in their reactions to what they see. Robert Hodge and David Tripp (1986) emphasize that children's responses to TV involve interpreting, or reading, what they see, not just registering the

Video games have become a key part of the culture and experience of childhood today. Studies have indicated that playing video games might have a positive effect on children's social and intellectual development.

content of programs. They suggest that most research has not taken account of the complexity of children's mental processes. TV watching, even of trivial programs, is not an inherently low-level intellectual activity; children read programs by relating them to other systems of meaning in their everyday lives. According to Hodge and Tripp, it is not the violence alone that has effects on behavior but rather the general framework of attitudes within which it is both presented and read.

In recent years home video games have come into widespread use. In his book *Video Kids* (1991), Eugene Provenzo analyzes the effect of Nintendo. There are currently some nineteen million Nintendo, Sony, and Sega games in the United States, and many more in other countries. Nearly all are owned and operated by children. Social codes and traditions have developed based on the games and their characters. Of the thirty best-selling toys in the United States in 1990, twenty-five were either video games or video equipment. The games are often directly linked to the characters or stories in films and TV programs; in turn, television programming has been based on Nintendo games. Video games, Provenzo concludes, have become a key part of the culture and experience of childhood today.

But is this effect a negative one? It is doubtful that a child's involvement with Nintendo harms her achievement at school. The effects of video games are likely to be governed by other influences on school performance. In other words, when strong pressures deflect students from an interest in their schoolwork, absorption with TV or video pursuits will tend to reinforce these attitudes. Video games and TV then can become a refuge from a disliked school environment.

But it is also possible that video games can act to develop skills that might be relevant both to formal education and to

Video Game Violence a "Risk Factor" for Children

He beat her once, he beat her twice, he beat her until she turned to pulp.

The 3-D sequence of a prostitute being bludgeoned drew a collective "Oh" from parents who came Wednesday to the Community Campus in Portsmouth [New Hampshire] for a workshop on violent video games and their effect on children.

"It won't create a generation of school shooters—thank God, it's not that powerful—but it does create a culture of disrespect," said Douglas Gentile, who runs the Media Research Lab at Iowa State University and was invited by Planned Parenthood of Northern New England and Families First to share his findings.

His research shows a link between violent video games and aggression in children, a correlation he said is so strong not even second-hand smoke and lung cancer can compare.

"The best way to talk about media is to talk about it as a risk factor, just like health issues," he said. "What's the chance of me having a heart attack in 40 years? Well, you'll have to look at my family history, cholesterol, smoking. . . . Some people can smoke their whole lives and not get cancer, but it doesn't mean it didn't have an effect."

Combined with lax parenting, negligence, and drug use, playing violent video games adds, according to Gentile, another ingredient to a potentially explosive mix. But even children who have no predisposition for hostility are more likely to get into physical fights if they play violent video games, he said.

His study of 607 eighth- and ninth-graders found 38 percent of the children with "low hostility" who played violent video games got into fights, compared to only 4 percent of those who did not play at all. And the more they played the more violent they wanted the game to be.

As games have evolved from the likes of *Death Race* in 1976, in which players earned points by mowing down pedestrians,

they are now sophisticated 3-D productions and, according to Gentile, even better teachers of violence.

"You shoot and shoot and shoot and shoot. Then you start over and do it all over again."

Overall, he said, violent video games and media violence contribute to a culture that teachers around the country have become quite familiar with: pushing and shoving in the corridors, verbal aggression, disrespect and impolite behavior.

Leaders of the American Medical Association, the American Academy of Pediatrics, the American Psychological Association, and the American Academy of Child and Adolescent Psychiatry also believe in the link, citing 3,500 studies during a Congressional Public Health Summit a few years ago.

But the Entertainment Software Association, along with some scientists, beg to differ.

"There are no studies that show a causal effect," said Carolyn Rauch, senior vice president of ESA. "Even the weakest links have serious methodological defects. It's totally subjective. Video games are today's rock n' roll in the '60s. Older people want to believe it's bad, but they don't understand it."

On the association's Web site, several studies are quoted, from the Australian government to the Surgeon General to the Health and Human Services of Washington State, calling evidence of a correlation "ambiguous" or "lacking consensus" at best.

Karen Sternheimer, sociologist at the University of Southern California and author of *It's Not the Media: The Truth About Pop Culture's Influence on Children* [2003], said many studies use contrived definitions of aggression to prove their point.

For example, she said some measured the trait by how much a player of violent video games would fine his opponent in Monopoly, how loudly he would blow a horn or how fast he could read a list of aggressive words.

"It's important to critically evaluate media content, but it's not a good way to solve social problems. I've no problem with saying 'This is offensive' at the same time as it's a giant leap from offensive to a major cause of social problems."

The Entertainment Software Rating Board has rated games for more than 10 years and, in 2003, placed 85 percent of all games sold in the categories of "E" for everyone or "T" for teens.

Gentile—who knows he has no fans in the industry—said the ratings represent a double standard by the gaming companies. Why rate something that they claim has no effect? he asked.

In a phone interview, the ESA's Rauch answered that, "It's just like in movies and music. Some content is not appropriate for children. It provides guidance to parents on what's in the games."

The image of the bloody prostitute discussed at the Portsmouth workshop comes from the best-selling game, *Grand Theft Auto: San Andreas,* rated M (Mature 17+) for its "blood and gore, intense violence, strong sexual content and use of drugs." Often used as an example of the "worst of the worst" by researchers like Gentile, it is still immensely popular among game players well below 17 years old.

Oblivious to its content, Marie Cowgill of Portsmouth bought the game for her 13-year-old son, but discovered their computer was too small to handle it. Now they have upgraded the computer but the game is still sitting on a shelf, and that is where the Cowgills are determined to keep it.

"I'll never let my son play it," said Cowgill, who attended the workshop. "My husband found out what it was about and we could say no."

Involved parents who check and enforce the ratings of their children's games do them a big favor, according to Gentile. His figures show children on average spend 38 hours in front of a screen a week, but only a total of 3 hours of active time with their parents.

"Limiting the amount and content appear to act as a protective factor," he said. "Parents who watch violence with their children and explain it to them seem to have a mitigating ef-

fect. If not, the negative effect is enhanced. You can watch the most heinous thing as long as you talk about it and make them think through it and explain that the script is not there because it mirrors reality."

Patricia Hughes of Stratham was intrigued by the idea.

"It supported my belief that communication is the key. I'm very outspoken and if my kid is involved, I'll say something," said Hughes, a mother of three who has outlawed the TV-program *SpongeBob* [*Square Pants*] in her household because she does not like "his attitude or mouth."

"You have to communicate your values," she said. "It's the simplest thing."

Gentile does not want to ban violent video games but said the responsibility of protecting the children is threefold: Gaming companies should make the ratings clearly visible, retailers should enforce the ratings, and parents should limit content and amount of gameplay.

"I'm a strong First Amendment proponent and companies should produce whatever they want and adults should be able to consume whatever they want," said Gentile. "They know the risks and are willing to take it."

Judy Eitler, guidance counselor at Stratham Memorial School, said she would like Gentile to speak to students, staff and teachers in SAU 16.

"There are many, many video games here and many concerned parents," she said. "Parents are looking for advice, direction and guidance. They wonder how much is too much."

SOURCE: Ulrika G. Gerth, "Video Game Violence a 'Risk Factor' for Children," *Foster's Daily Democrat,* January 16, 2005.

Questions

- According to Gentile, how do video games affect children?
- How are some of the studies that evaluate video games' influence on socialization problematic?
- Based on your reading in the chapter, what other influences might socialize children to act aggressively?

wider participation in a society that depends increasingly on electronic communication. The sound and look of video games has been a major influence on the development of rave music, rockers like Trent Reznor of Nine Inch Nails, and even films like *The Matrix, Tomb Raider,* and *Final Fantasy.* According to media scholar Marsha Kinder (1991), her son Victor's adeptness at Nintendo transferred fruitfully to other spheres. For example, the better he became at video games, the more interested and skillful he was at drawing cartoons. Patricia Greenfield (1993) has argued that "video games are the first example of a computer technology that is having a socializing effect on the next generation on a mass scale, and even on a world-wide basis."

The mass media are an important influence on socialization, in all forms of society. There are few societies in current times, even among the more traditional cultures, that remain completely untouched by the media. Electronic communication is accessible even to those who are unable to read and write; and in the most impoverished parts of the world, it is common to find people owning radios and television sets.

WORK

Work is in all cultures an important setting within which socialization processes operate, although it is only in industrial societies that large numbers of people go "out to work"—that is, go each day to places of work separate from the home. In traditional communities many people farmed the land close to where they lived or had workshops in their dwellings. Work in such communities was not so clearly distinct from other activities as it is for most members of the workforce in the modern West. In the industrialized countries, going out to work for the first time ordinarily marks a much greater transition in an individual's life than entering work in traditional societies. The work environment often poses unfamiliar demands, perhaps calling for major adjustments in the person's outlook or behavior.

Social Roles

Through the process of socialization, individuals learn about **social roles**—socially defined expectations that a person in a given social position follows. The social role of doctor, for example, encompasses a set of behaviors that should be enacted by all individual doctors, regardless of their personal opinions or outlooks. Because all doctors share this role, it is possible to speak in general terms about the professional role behavior of doctors, irrespective of the specific individuals who occupy that position.

Some sociologists, particularly those associated with the functionalist school, regard social roles as fixed and relatively unchanging parts of a society's culture. They are taken as social facts. According to such a view, individuals learn the expectations that surround social positions in their particular culture and perform those roles largely as they have been defined. Social roles do not involve negotiation or creativity. Rather, they are prescriptive in containing and directing an individual's behavior. Through socialization, individuals internalize social roles and learn how to carry them out.

This view, however, is mistaken. It suggests that individuals simply take on roles rather than creating or negotiating them. In fact, socialization is a process in which humans can exercise agency; they are not simply passive subjects waiting to be instructed or programmed. Individuals come to understand and assume social roles through an ongoing process of social interaction.

Identity

The cultural settings in which we are born and come to maturity influence our behavior, but that does not mean that humans are robbed of individuality or free will. It might seem as though we are merely stamped into preset molds that society has prepared for us, and some sociologists do tend to write about socialization as though this were the case. But such a view is fundamentally flawed. The fact that from birth to death we are involved in interaction with others certainly conditions our personalities, the values we hold, and the behavior we engage in. Yet socialization is also at the origin of our very individuality and freedom. In the course of socialization each of us develops a sense of identity and the capacity for independent thought and action.

The concept of *identity* in sociology is a multifaceted one and can be approached in a number of ways. Broadly speaking, **identity** relates to the understandings people hold about who they are and what is meaningful to them. These understandings are formed in relation to certain attributes that take priority over other sources of meaning. Some of the main sources of identity include gender, sexual orientation, nationality or ethnicity, and social class. There are two types of identity often spoken of by sociologists: social identity and self-identity (or personal identity). These forms of identity are analytically distinct but are closely related to one another. **Social identity** refers to the characteristics that other people attribute to an individual. These can be seen as markers that indicate who, in a basic sense, that individual is. At the same time, they place that individual in relation to other individuals who share the same attributes. Examples of social identities might include student, mother, lawyer, Catholic, homeless, Asian, dyslexic, and married. Many individuals have social identities comprising more than one attribute. A person could simultaneously be a mother, an engineer, a Muslim, and a city council member. Multiple social identities reflect the many dimensions of people's lives. Although this plurality of social identities can be a potential source of conflict for people, most individuals organize meaning and experience in their lives around a primary identity that is fairly continuous across time and place.

Social identities therefore involve a collective dimension. They mark ways that individuals are the same as others. Shared identities—predicated on a set of common goals, values, or experiences—can form an important base for social movements. Feminists, environmentalists, labor unionists, and supporters of religious fundamentalist and/or nationalist movements are all examples of cases in which a shared social identity is drawn on as a powerful source of personal meaning or self-worth.

If social identities mark ways in which individuals are the same as others, **self-identity** (or personal identity) sets us apart as distinct individuals. Self-identity refers to the process of self-development through which we formulate a unique sense of ourselves and our relationship to the world around us. The notion of self-identity draws heavily on the work of symbolic interactionists. It is the individual's constant negotiation with the outside world that helps create and shape his or her sense of self. The process of interaction between self and society helps link an individual's personal and public worlds. Though the cultural and social environment is a factor in shaping self-identity, individual agency and choice are of central importance.

Tracing the changes in self-identity from traditional to modern societies, we can see a shift away from the fixed, inherited factors that previously guided identity formation. If at one time people's identities were largely informed by their membership in broad social groups, bound by class or nationality, they are now more multifaceted and less stable. The processes of urban growth, industrialization, and the breakdown of earlier social formations have weakened the effect of inherited rules and conventions. Individuals have become more socially and geographically mobile. This has freed people from the tightly knit, relatively homogeneous communities of the past in which patterns were passed down in a fixed way across generations. It has created the space for other sources of personal meaning, such as gender and sexual orientation, to play a greater role in people's sense of identity.

In today's world, we have unprecedented opportunities to make ourselves and to create our own identities. We are our own best resources in defining who we are, where we have come from, and where we are going. Now that the traditional signposts of identity have become less essential, the social world confronts us with a dizzying array of choices about who to be, how to live, and what to do, without offering much guidance about which selections to make. The decisions we make in

People often exhibit multiple social identities simultaneously, sometimes seemingly conflicting ones. Focusing on her primary identity as a medical professional in this context, a male patient at King Fahd Military Medical Complex in Saudi Arabia allows a doctor who is also a Muslim woman to examine him.

our everyday lives—about what to wear, how to behave, and how to spend our time—help make us who we are. The modern world forces us to find ourselves. Through our capacity as self-conscious, self-aware human beings, we constantly create and re-create our identities.

Gender Socialization

Agents of socialization play an important role in how children learn **gender roles.** Let's now turn to the study of **gender socialization,** the learning of gender roles through social factors such as the family and the media.

REACTIONS OF PARENTS AND ADULTS

Many studies have been carried out on the degree to which gender differences are the result of social influences. Studies of mother–infant interaction show differences in the treatment of boys and girls even when parents believe their reactions to both are the same. Adults asked to assess the personality of a baby give different answers according to whether or not they believe the child to be a girl or a boy. In one experiment, five young mothers were observed in interaction with a six-month-old called Beth. They tended to smile at her often and offer her dolls to play with. She was seen as "sweet," having a "soft cry." The reaction of a second group of mothers to a child the same age, named Adam, was noticeably different. The baby was likely to be offered a train or other "male" toys to play with. Beth and Adam were actually the same child, dressed in different clothes (Will et al. 1976).

Women Reinventing Their Lives

On the first page of this chapter you read a quote inspired by J. K. Rowling, author and creator of Harry Potter: "There is no adventure greater than that of growing up." Sociologist Deborah Carr believes that nowadays that adventure extends well beyond our childhood years and into adulthood and old age. "Think about how much things have changed," she says, "especially for women." Throughout much of the twentieth century, after high school most middle-class women were expected to settle down with a husband, bear children, and embrace a life of motherhood. A career was a man's pursuit. For him, changing jobs was often a sign that he couldn't hold down a stable position. Families would live for decades in one community, and gender expectations in American culture were relatively clear. "In middle age especially, women are now in a process of reinventing their lives."

Times have changed. Carr has spent years studying these changes and how they influence the choices people make about their lives. Take the issue of women's work. In 1947 less than one third of women worked outside the home, a portion that doubled to almost 60 percent by the year 2000. What was a comparatively rare phenomenon at the middle of the twentieth century had become the norm just fifty years later (National Bureau of Economic Research [NBER] 2002). Not only are women working more but they are also delaying marriage, living longer, graduating college in unprecedented numbers, and having fewer children on average than they did in 1950. In other words, women are living very different lives from the ones their own mothers did just a generation ago.

As gender roles continue to blur, Carr's research has focused on the choices women make during a period she calls the "new mid-life." For many women, this is not an end but a time for new beginnings. More and more, women are feeling

Deborah Carr

empowered to exit stale marriages, start their own businesses, learn from their daughters, and pick up new hobbies. For a 2005 cover story in *Time* magazine titled "A Female Mid-Life Crisis?" Carr was asked to weigh in on the issue. "How are they [women] going to spend the second half of their life?" she asks, rhetorically. "They know they're going to have lots of healthy years, so I think it's a period of making choices to live out one's dreams that got put on the shelf during younger years" (quoted in Gibbs 2005).

Part of Carr's challenge as a public sociologist is to translate private troubles into public issues—to point out to individual women that they are not alone. This process of reinvention can be painful and emotionally complicated. Without the benefit of a road map or a script, "women are always questioning if what they're feeling is OK." Whereas psychologists may focus on the individual or couple when finding solutions to marital woes (for example, "Tell your husband to pick up his socks") the task for sociologists is to simultaneously balance two levels—the micro and the macro. For example, there are currently forty-three million American women aged forty to sixty passing through middle-age, and many of them are probably confronting similar feelings of excitement, confusion, and regret.

In a study, titled "My Daughter Has a Career; I Just Raised Babies," Carr (2004) describes the tension that can come between mothers and daughters growing up in different eras. For women who came of age in the 1950s and 1960s, maintaining a sense of self-worth in the midst of changing cultural norms can be very difficult. Having grown up amid considerable pressure to have children and ignore professional pursuits, many women in Carr's study watched with mixed feelings as their daughters took on new challenges: On the one hand, the pursuit of education and professional esteem was a sign of progress and liberation; but on the other hand, daughters experienced considerable difficulty balancing work and family life. In commentary that still rings true today, Carr (2004) describes the effects of cultural shifts over the past few decades.

> Social changes since the late 1960s have created a new normative context in which women and men are expected to be both successful workers and involved parents. Given this shift, midlife women who complied with the mid-twentieth century expectation that they should stay home with their children (rather than work for pay outside the home) may suffer regret or self-criticism, especially if they use the contemporary cultural ideal as the standard for evaluating their past decisions and experiences.

During periods of substantial social change, the definition of a "good mother" also changes, making it difficult for people to make important choices without questioning the roads not taken.

By connecting these individual-level anxieties to massive social shifts, Carr's research often sparks conversations outside of the university. Her studies have been covered a wide variety of news publications, including the *Chicago Tribune, Christian Science Monitor, Glamour,* the *Los Angeles Times,* the *New York Times, Newsweek* magazine, the *Philadelphia Inquirer, USA Today,* and the *Wall Street Journal.* Many of the reporters who call her for interviews are themselves young professional women, eager to share their own stories with Carr as they sort out the mixed messages they receive from generations past and present.

Although her interactions with the public may be numerous and frequent, Carr remains realistic about the effect she has as a public sociologist. "We all suffer from information overload," she says, commenting on the constant stream of information coming at us by way of the television, newspapers, magazines, the Internet and the radio. "The average person doesn't know what to believe anymore. Every day it's a new finding, and it's tough for people—laypersons or policy makers—to make heads or tails about what they hear." Among the millions of lines and quotes and pages printed every day in America, do the words of a sociologist stand out?

Every once in a while, they do. Carr often receives letters from complete strangers who connect personally to her perspectives and opinions. "I read what you said in *Good Housekeeping* magazine about losing a spouse and I was wondering if . . ." or "My daughter and I were reading about your study in *USA Today* and wanted to thank you for . . ." Sometimes the letters are much more personal. Carr recalls receiving a handwritten note from a woman "in middle America" who was going through a difficult divorce. The woman had come across a magazine article describing one of Carr's studies called "Back to School: Men's and Women's College Enrollment at Midlife" (2000) and wanted to use Carr's findings as evidence in court. In making financial arrangements for the impending divorce, her husband refused to help pay for her to go back to college. "You're too old to go back to school," she remembers him saying. But after reading Carr's work, the woman copied the findings and "marched back into court and showed them to the judge," hoping he would recognize the legitimacy of her plans for reinvention. Carr never heard back from the woman, but learned a valuable lesson from her experience with divorce. "As sociologists, we must never forget that the data points in our surveys are actually real people."

GENDER LEARNING

Gender learning by infants is almost certainly unconscious. Before a child can accurately label itself as either a boy or a girl, it receives a range of preverbal cues. For instance, male and female adults usually handle infants differently. The cosmetics women use contain scents different from those the baby might learn to associate with males. Systematic differences in dress, hairstyle, and so on provide visual cues for the infant in the learning process. By age two, children have a partial understanding of what gender is. They know whether they are boys or girls, and they can usually categorize others accurately. Not until five or six, however, does a child know that a person's sex does not change, that everyone has gender, and that sex differences between girls and boys are anatomically based.

The toys, picture books, and television programs with which young children come into contact all tend to emphasize differences between male and female attributes. Toy stores and mail-order catalogs usually categorize their products by gender. Even some toys that seem neutral in terms of gender are not so in practice. For example, toy kittens and rabbits are recommended for girls, whereas lions and tigers are seen as more appropriate for boys.

Vanda Lucia Zammuner (1986) studied the toy preferences of children aged between seven and ten in Italy and Holland. Children's attitudes toward a variety of toys were analyzed; stereotypically masculine and feminine toys as well as toys presumed not to be gender typed were included. Both the children and their parents were asked to assess which toys were suitable for boys and which for girls. There was close agreement between the adults and the children. On average, the Italian children chose gender-differentiated toys to play with more often than the Dutch children—a finding that conformed to expectations because Italian culture tends to hold a more traditional view of gender divisions than

Toys play a major role in children's gender learning, as they often emphasize the difference between male and female attributes.

does Dutch society. As in other studies, girls from both societies chose gender-neutral or boys' toys to play with far more than boys chose girls' toys.

STORYBOOKS AND TELEVISION

In the 1970s, Lenore Weitzman and her colleagues (1972) carried out an analysis of gender roles in some of the most widely used preschool children's books and found several clear differences in gender roles. Males played a much larger part in the stories and pictures than females, outnumbering females by a ratio of 11 to 1. When animals with gender identities were included, the ratio was 95 to 1. The activities of males and females also differed. The males engaged in adventurous pursuits and outdoor activities demanding independence and strength. When girls did appear, they were portrayed as passive and confined mostly to indoor activities. Girls cooked and cleaned for the males or awaited their return. Much the same was true of the adult men and women represented in the storybooks. Women who were not wives and mothers were imaginary creatures like witches or fairy godmothers. There was not a single woman in all the books analyzed who held an occupation outside the home. By contrast, the men were depicted as fighters, policemen, judges, kings, and so forth.

More recent research suggests that things have changed somewhat but that the large bulk of children's literature remains much the same (Davies 1991). Fairy tales, for example, embody traditional attitudes toward gender and toward the sorts of aims and ambitions girls and boys are expected to have. In versions of fairy tales from several centuries ago, the idea that "some day my prince will come" usually implied that a girl from a poor family might dream of wealth and fortune. Today that notion has become more closely tied to the ideals of romantic love. Some feminists have tried to rewrite some of the most celebrated fairy tales, reversing their usual emphases: "I really didn't notice that he had a funny nose. And he certainly looked better all dressed up in fancy clothes. He's not nearly as attractive as he seemed the other night. So I think I'll just pretend that this glass slipper feels too tight" (Viorst 1986). Like this version of "Cinderella," however, these rewrites are found mainly in books directed to adult audiences and have hardly affected the tales told in innumerable children's books.

Although there are some notable exceptions, analyses of television programs designed for children conform to the findings about children's books. Studies of the most frequently watched cartoons show that most of the leading figures are male and that males dominate the active pursuits. Similar images are found in the commercials that appear throughout the programs.

THE DIFFICULTY OF NONSEXIST CHILD REARING

June Statham (1986) studied the experiences of a group of parents committed to nonsexist child rearing. Thirty adults in eighteen families were involved in the research, which included children aged six months to twelve years. The parents were of middle-class background, mostly involved in academic work as teachers or professors. Statham found that most of the parents did not simply try to modify traditional gender roles by seeking to make girls more like boys, but wanted to foster new combinations of the feminine and masculine. They wished boys to be more sensitive to others' feelings and capable of expressing warmth, while girls were encouraged to seek opportunities for learning and self-advancement. All the parents found existing patterns of gender learning difficult to combat. They were reasonably successful at persuading the children to play with nongender-typed toys, but even this proved more difficult than many of them had expected. One mother commented to the researcher:

> If you walk into a toy shop, it's full of war toys for boys and domestic toys for girls, and it sums up society the way it is. This is the way children are being socialized: it's all right for boys to be taught to kill and hurt, and I think it's terrible, it makes me feel sick. I try not to go into toy shops, I feel so angry. (Statham 1986)

Practically all the children in fact possessed, and played with, gender-typed toys, given to them by relatives.

There are now some storybooks available with strong independent girls as the main characters, but few depict boys in nontraditional roles. A mother of a five-year-old boy told of her son's reaction when she reversed the sexes of the characters in a story she read to him:

> In fact he was a bit upset when I went through a book which has a boy and a girl in very traditional roles, and changed all the he's to she's and she's to he's. When I first started doing that, he was inclined to say "you don't like boys, you only like girls." I had to explain that that wasn't true at all, it's just that there's not enough written about girls. (Statham 1986)

Clearly, gender socialization is very powerful, and challenges to it can be upsetting. Once a gender is "assigned," society expects individuals to act like females and males. It is in the practices of everyday life that these expectations are fulfilled and reproduced (Bourdieu 1990; Lorber 1994).

Gender-typed toys are ubiquitous, making it difficult to raise children in a truly nonsexist environment. Barbie, one of the most popular and widely recognized girl toys, has been influencing children's ideas about what it means to act female for fifty years.

The Debate about Gender Socialization

FREUD'S THEORY

Perhaps the most influential—and controversial—theory of the emergence of gender identity is that of Sigmund Freud. According to Freud, the learning of gender differences in infants and young children is centered on the possession or absence of the penis. "I have a penis" is equivalent to "I am a boy," while "I am a girl" is equivalent to "I lack a penis." Freud is careful to say that it is not just the anatomical distinctions that matter here; the possession or absence of the penis is symbolic of masculinity and femininity.

At around age four or five, the theory goes, a boy feels threatened by the discipline and autonomy his father demands of him, fantasizing that the father wishes to remove his penis. Partly consciously, but mostly on an unconscious level, the boy recognizes the father as a rival for the affections of his mother. In repressing erotic feelings toward the mother and accepting the father as a superior being, the boy identifies with the father and becomes aware of his male identity. The boy gives up his love for his mother out of an unconscious fear of castration by his father. Girls, on the other hand, supposedly suffer from "penis envy" because they do not possess the visible organ that distinguishes boys. The mother becomes devalued in the little girl's eyes, because she is also seen to lack a penis and to be unable to provide one. When the girl identifies with the mother, she takes over the submissive attitude involved in the recognition of being "second best."

Once this phase is over, the child has learned to repress his erotic feelings. The period from about five years old to puberty, according to Freud, is one of latency—sexual activities tend to be suspended until the biological changes involved in puberty reactivate erotic desires in a direct way. The latency period, covering the early and middle years of school, is the time at which same-sex peer groups are most important in the child's life.

Major objections have been raised against Freud's views, particularly by feminists, but also by many other authors (Coward 1984; Mitchell 1975). First, Freud seems to identify gender identity too closely with genital awareness; other, more subtle factors are surely involved. Second, the theory seems to depend on the notion that the penis is superior to the vagina, which is thought of as just a lack of the male organ. Yet why shouldn't the female genitals be considered superior to those of the male? Third, Freud treats the father as the primary disciplining agent, whereas in many cultures the mother plays the more significant part in the imposition of discipline. Fourth, Freud believes that gender learning is concentrated at age four or five. Most later authors have emphasized the importance of earlier learning, beginning in infancy.

CHODOROW'S THEORY

Although many writers have made use of Freud's approach in studying gender development, they have usually modified it in major respects. An important example is the sociologist Nancy Chodorow (1978, 1988). Chodorow argues that learning to feel male or female derives from the infant's attachment to his parents from an early age. She places much more emphasis than Freud does on the importance of the mother rather than the father. Children tend to become emotionally involved with the mother because she is easily the most dominant influence in their early lives. At some point this attachment has to be broken in order for the child to achieve a separate sense of self— the child is required to become less closely dependent.

Chodorow argues that the breaking process occurs in a different way for boys and girls. Girls remain closer to the mother—able, for example, to go on hugging and kissing her and imitating what she does. Because there is no sharp break from the mother, the girl, and later the adult woman, develops a sense of self that is more continuous with other people. Her identity is more likely to be merged with or depend on another's: first her mother, later a man. In Chodorow's view, this

Nancy Chodorow argues that boys are socialized to be less attached to or dependent on their parents at an earlier age than girls. Girls are able to remain close to their mother, which in Chodorow's view encourages characteristics like sensitivity and compassion. In contrast, boys define their masculinity by rejecting behaviors they consider "feminine" and are less skilled in relating closely to others.

tends to produce characteristics of sensitivity and emotional compassion in women.

Boys gain a sense of self via a more radical rejection of their original closeness to the mother, forging their understanding of masculinity from what is not feminine. They learn not to be sissies or mama's boys. As a result, boys are relatively unskilled in relating closely to others; they develop more analytical ways of looking at the world. They take a more active view of their lives, emphasizing achievement, but they have repressed their ability to understand their own feelings and those of others.

To some extent, Chodorow reverses Freud's emphasis. Masculinity, rather than femininity, is defined by a loss, the forfeiting of continued close attachment to the mother. Male identity is formed through separation; thus men later in life unconsciously feel that their identity is endangered if they become involved in close emotional relationships with others. Women, on the other hand, feel that the absence of a close relation to another person threatens their self-esteem. These patterns are passed on from generation to generation, because of the primary role women play in the early socialization of children. Women express and define themselves mainly in terms of relationships. Men have repressed these needs and adopt a more manipulative stance toward the world.

Chodorow's work has met with various criticisms. Janet Sayers (1986), for example, has suggested that Chodorow does not explain the struggle of women, particularly in current times, to become autonomous, independent beings. Women (and men), she points out, are more contradictory in their psychological makeup than Chodorow's theory suggests. Femininity may conceal feelings of aggressiveness or assertiveness, which are revealed only obliquely or in certain contexts (Brennan 1988). Chodorow has also been criticized for her narrow conception of the family, one based on a white, middle-class model. What happens, for example, in one-parent households or, as in many Chicano communities, in families in which children are cared for by more than one adult (Segura and Pierce 1993)?

These criticisms don't undermine Chodorow's ideas, which remain important. They teach us a good deal about the nature of femininity, and they help us understand the origins of what has been called "male inexpressiveness"—the difficulty men have in revealing their feelings to others (Balswick 1983).

GILLIGAN'S THEORY

Carol Gilligan (1982) has further developed Chodorow's analysis. Her work concentrates on the images adult women and men have of themselves and their attainments. Women, she agrees with Chodorow, define themselves in terms of personal relationships and judge their achievements by reference to the ability to care for others. Women's place in the lives of men is traditionally that of caretaker and helpmate. But the qualities developed in these tasks are frequently devalued by men, who see their own emphasis on individual achievement as the only form of success. Concern with relationships on the part of women appears to them as a weakness rather than as the strength that in fact it is.

Gilligan carried out intensive interviews with about two hundred American women and men of varying ages and social backgrounds. She asked all of the interviewees a range of questions concerning their moral outlook and conceptions of self. Consistent differences emerged between the views of the women and the men. For instance, the interviewees were asked, "What does it mean to say something is morally right or wrong?" Whereas the men tended to respond to this question by mentioning abstract ideals of duty, justice, and individual freedom, the women persistently raised the theme of helping others. Thus a female college student answered the question in the following way:

> "It [morality] has to do with responsibilities and obligations and values, mainly values. . . . In my life situation I relate morality with interpersonal relationships that have to do with respect for the other person and myself." The interviewer then asked: "Why respect other people?" receiving the answer, "Because they have a consciousness or feelings that can be hurt, an awareness that can be hurt." (Gilligan 1982)

The women were more tentative in their moral judgments than the men, seeing possible contradictions between following a strict moral code and avoiding harming others. Gilligan suggests that this outlook reflects the traditional situation of women, anchored in caring relationships, rather than the outward-looking attitudes of men. Women have in the past deferred to the judgments of men, while being aware that they have qualities that most men lack. Their views of themselves are based on successfully fulfilling the needs of others, rather than on pride in individual achievement (Gilligan 1982).

Socialization through the Life Course

The various transitions through which individuals pass during their lives seem at first sight to be biologically fixed—from childhood to adulthood and eventually to death. But the stages of the human **life course** are social as well as biological in nature. They are influenced by cultural differences and by the material circumstances of people's lives in given types of society. For example, in the modern West, death is usually thought of in relation to old age, because most people enjoy a life span

Duccio da Buoninsegna's *Madonna and Child,* painted in the thirteenth century, depicts the infant Jesus with a mature face. Until recently, children in Western society were viewed as little adults.

Japanese and American Teenagers

Studies comparing socialization in a variety of cultural settings show some interesting contrasts. For example, the idea of the teen years as an extended period of transition between childhood and adulthood emerged in America before it did in Japan. In fact, the Japanese term *cheenayja* is an adaptation of the American *teenager*. In premodern Japan, the movement from childhood to adulthood occurred in an instant, because it happened as part of an age-grade system (one that included girls). A child would become an adult when he or she participated in a special rite. Japanese boys became adults at some point between the age of eleven and sixteen, depending on their social rank. The parallel ceremony at which girls were recognized as women was the *kami* age, the age at which they began to wear their hair up rather than down.

Just as in most other nonmodern societies, including those of medieval Europe, young people in Japan knew who they would be and what they would be doing when they became adults. The teenage years weren't a time to experiment. Japanese children were schooled to follow closely the ways of their parents, to whom they owed strict obedience; family norms emphasizing the duties of children toward their parents were very strong.

Such norms have endured to the present day, but they have also come under strain with the high pace of industrial devel-

opment in contemporary Japan. So are Japanese teenagers now just like American ones? Merry White, a sociologist at Boston University, attempted to answer this question. White (1993) interviewed one hundred teens in each culture over a period of three years, trying to gain an in-depth view of their attitudes toward sexuality, school, friendship, and parents. She found big differences between the Japanese and the American teenagers but also came up with unexpected conclusions about both. In neither culture are most teenagers the rebels she expected to find. Instead, she found a fairly high degree of confor-

of seventy years or more. In traditional societies of the past, however, more people died in younger age groups than survived to old age.

Childhood

To people living in modern societies, childhood is a clear and distinct stage of life. Children are distinct from babies or toddlers; childhood intervenes between infancy and the teen years. Yet the concept of childhood, like so many other aspects of social life today, has come into being only over the past two or three centuries. In earlier societies, the young moved directly from a lengthy infancy into working roles within the community. The French historian Philippe Ariès (1965) has argued that *childhood,* conceived of as a separate

phase of development, did not exist in medieval times. In the paintings of medieval Europe, children are portrayed as little adults, with mature faces and the same style of dress as their elders. Children took part in the same work and play activities as adults, rather than in the childhood games we now take for granted.

Right up to the twentieth century, in the United States and most other Western countries, children were put to work at what now seems a very early age. There are countries in the world today, in fact, where young children are engaged in full-time work, sometimes in physically demanding circumstances (for example, in coal mines). The ideas that children have distinctive rights and that the use of child labor is morally repugnant are quite recent developments.

Because of the long period of childhood that we recognize today, societies now are in some respects more child centered mity to wider cultural ideas and an expressed respect for parents in both countries.

What the adults say of their teenage offspring in Japan and the United States is much the same: "Why don't you listen more to what I say?" "When I was your age . . ." The Japanese and American teens also echo each other in some ways: "Do you like me?" "What should I aim for in my life?" "We're cool, but they aren't." Pop music, films, and videos figure large in the experience of both—as does at least a surface sexual knowledgeability, because from an early age in both cultures sexual information, including warnings about sexual disease, is widespread.

The Japanese teenagers, however, come out well ahead of the Americans in terms of school achievements: 95 percent of Japanese teenagers reach a level in academic tests met by only the top 5 percent of young Americans. And although both express respect for parents, the Japanese teenagers remain much closer to theirs than do most of the American teenagers.

The Japanese teenagers are certainly interested in sex but place it at the bottom of a list of priorities White presented them with; the Americans put it at the top. Teenagers in Japan are nonetheless very sexually active, probably even more so than their American counterparts. Two thirds of Japanese girls by age fifteen are sexually active. White reports that they are, by Western standards, amazingly forthcoming about their sexual fantasies and practices; nearly 90 percent of the Japanese girls reported that they masturbate twice or more a week.

The Japanese clearly separate three areas of sexuality that are more mixed up for the American teenagers: physical passion, socially approved pairing or marriage, and romantic fantasies. *Love marriages,* in which two people establish a rela-

tionship on the basis of emotional and sexual attraction, are now common in Japan. However, they are often the result of an initial introduction of suitable partners arranged by parents, followed by falling in love before marriage. Even the most sexually experienced young person in Japan may continue to prefer to have a mature adult arrange an appropriate marriage.

Japanese teenagers often stress that love should grow in marriage rather than being the basis of choosing a partner in the first place. The sexual activity of young girls tends to involve several older boys and not be bound up with dating. White quotes as typical of young, unmarried Japanese women a respondent who was in her early twenties when interviewed. She first had sexual intercourse at fifteen—like three quarters of her friends—and since had accumulated many "sex friends." These were not *boifurends* (boyfriends), a relationship that implies emotional attachment. She said, "I do it [have sex] because it is fun. However, marriage is a totally different story, you know. Marriage should be more realistic and practical" (White 1993).

than traditional ones. But a child-centered society, it must be emphasized, is not one in which all children experience love and care from parents or other adults. The physical and sexual abuse of children is a commonplace feature of family life in present-day society, although the full extent of such abuse has only recently come to light. Child abuse has clear connections with what seems to us today like the frequent mistreatment of children in premodern Europe.

It seems possible that as a result of changes currently occurring in modern societies, the separate character of childhood is diminishing once more. Some observers have suggested that children now grow up so fast that this is in fact the case. They point out that even small children may watch the same television programs as adults, thereby becoming much more familiar early on with the adult world than did preceding generations.

The Teenager

The idea of the teenager, so familiar to us today, also didn't exist until recently. The biological changes involved in puberty (the point at which a person becomes capable of adult sexual activity and reproduction) are universal. Yet in many cultures, these do not produce the degree of turmoil and uncertainty often found among young people in modern societies. In cultures that foster age-grades, for example, with distinct ceremonials that signal a person's transition to adulthood, the process of psychosexual development generally seems easier to negotiate. Adolescents in such societies have less to "unlearn" because the pace of change is slower. There is a time when children in Western societies are required to be children no longer: to put away their toys and break with childish pursuits. In traditional cultures, in which children are already

Before the twentieth century, young children in many Western countries were put to work at an early age. Some, like the coalmining boys above, were made to do dangerous or physically demanding work.

working alongside adults, this process of unlearning is normally much less jarring.

In Western societies, teenagers are betwixt and between: They often try to follow adult ways, but they are treated in law as children. They may wish to go to work, but they are constrained to stay in school. Teenagers in the West live in between childhood and adulthood, growing up in a society subject to continuous change.

Young Adulthood

Young adulthood seems increasingly to be a specific stage in personal and sexual development in modern societies (Goldscheider and Waite 1991). Particularly among more affluent groups, people in their early twenties are taking the time to travel and explore sexual, political, and religious affiliations. The importance of this postponement of the responsibilities of full adulthood is likely to grow, given the extended period of education many people now undergo.

Mature Adulthood

Most young adults in the West today can look forward to a life stretching right through to old age. In premodern times, few could anticipate such a future with much confidence. Death through sickness or injury was much more frequent among all age groups than it is today, and women in particular were at great risk because of the high rate of mortality in childbirth.

On the other hand, some of the strains we experience now were less pronounced in previous times. People usually maintained a closer connection with their parents and other kin than in today's more mobile populations, and the routines of work they followed were the same as those of their forebears.

In current times, major uncertainties must be resolved in marriage, family life, and other social contexts. We have to make our own lives more than people did in the past. The creation of sexual and marital ties, for instance, now depends on individual initiative and selection, rather than being fixed by parents. This represents greater freedom for the individual, but the responsibility can also impose difficulties.

Keeping a forward-looking outlook in middle age has taken on a particular importance in modern societies. Most people do not expect to be doing the same thing all their lives, as was the case for the majority in traditional cultures. Individuals who have spent their lives in one career may find the level they have reached in middle age unsatisfying and further opportunities blocked. Women who have spent their early adulthood raising a family and whose children have left home may feel themselves to be without any social value. The phenomenon of a midlife crisis is very real for many middle-aged people. A person may feel that she has thrown away the opportunities that life had to offer or that she will never attain goals cherished since childhood. Yet growing older need not lead to resignation or bleak despair; a release from childhood dreams can be liberating.

Old Age

In traditional societies, older people were normally accorded a great deal of respect. Among cultures that included age-

In traditional societies, older people are accorded a great deal of respect and play a major role in the community. The Tatas of Togo delegate an elder to greet a new chief.

grades, the elders usually had a major—often the final—say over matters of importance to the community. Within families, the authority of both men and women mostly increased with age. In industrialized societies, by contrast, older people tend to lack authority within both the family and the wider social community. Having retired from the labor force, they may be poorer than ever before in their lives. At the same time, there has been a great increase in the proportion of the population over age sixty-five. In 1900, only one in thirty people in the United States was over sixty-five; the proportion today is one in eight and will likely rise to one in five by the year 2030 (U.S. Bureau of the Census 1996a). The same trend is found in all the industrially advanced countries.

Transition to the age-grade of elder in a traditional culture often marked the pinnacle of the status an individual could achieve. In modern societies, retirement tends to bring the opposite consequences. No longer living with their children and often having retired from paid work, older people may find it difficult to make the final period of their life rewarding. It used to be thought that those who successfully cope with old age do so by turning to their inner resources, becoming less interested in the material rewards that social life has to offer. Although this may often be true, it seems likely that in a society in which many are physically healthy in old age, an outward-

In modern industrial societies, many elderly people face social alienation.

looking view will become more and more prevalent. Those in retirement might find renewal in what has been called the "third age," in which a new phase of education begins (see also Chapter 12 on lifelong learning).

Study Outline

www.wwnorton.com/giddens

Culture, Society, and Child Socialization

- *Socialization* is the process whereby, through contact with other human beings, the helpless infant gradually becomes a self-aware, knowledgeable human being, skilled in the ways of the given culture and environment.

Theories of Child Development

- According to G. H. Mead, the child achieves an understanding of being a separate agent by seeing how others behave toward him or her in social contexts. At a later stage, entering into organized games, learning the rules of play, the child comes to understand "the *generalized other*"—general values and cultural rules.
- Jean Piaget distinguishes several main stages in the development of the child's capability to make sense of the world. Each stage involves the acquisition of new cognitive skills and depends on the successful

completion of the preceding one. According to Piaget, these stages of cognitive development are universal features of socialization.

Agents of Socialization

- *Agents of socialization* are structured groups or contexts within which significant processes of socialization occur. In all cultures, the family is the principal socializing agency of the child during infancy. Other influences include *peer groups,* schools, and the *mass media.*
- Through the process of socialization and interaction with others, individuals learn about *social roles*—socially defined expectations that a person in a given social position will follow. One result of this process is the development of a *social identity,* the characteristics that other people attribute to an individual. If social identities mark ways in which individuals are the same as others, *self-identity* sets us apart as distinct individuals. The concept of self-identity, which draws on symbolic interactionism, refers to the process of self-development through which we formulate a unique sense of ourselves and our relationship to the world around us.
- The development of mass communications has enlarged the range of socializing agencies. The spread of mass printed media was later accompanied by the use of electronic communication. TV exerts a

particularly powerful influence, reaching people of all ages at regular intervals every day.

- *Gender socialization* begins virtually as soon as an infant is born. Even parents who believe they treat children equally tend to produce different responses to boys and girls. These differences are reinforced by many other cultural influences.

Socialization through the Life Cycle

- Socialization continues throughout the life cycle. At each distinct phase of life there are transitions to be made or crises to be overcome.

Key Concepts

age-grades (p. 96)
agents of socialization (p. 95)
cognition (p. 94)
concrete operational stage (p. 95)
egocentric (p. 95)
formal operational stage (p. 95)
gender roles (p. 101)
gender socialization (p. 101)
generalized other (p. 94)
identity (p. 100)
life course (p. 107)
mass media (p. 97)
peer group (p. 96)
preoperational stage (p. 95)
self-consciousness (p. 94)
self-identity (p. 101)
sensorimotor stage (p. 94)
social identity (p. 100)
socialization (p. 92)
social reproduction (p. 92)
social roles (p. 100)
social self (p. 94)

Review Questions

1. What are the main agents of socialization in contemporary society?
   a. Family, schools, the political system, the economic system, and the urban system
   b. Family, schools, peer groups, the mass media, and work
   c. movies, videos, computers, and the Internet
   d. newspapers, magazines, radio, and television

2. When does socialization end?
   a. at the beginning of adulthood
   b. during the midlife crisis
   c. on retirement
   d. socialization never ends because people are in a process of constant interaction.

3. What is the difference between the *I* and the *me*?
   a. the *I* is the unsocialized infant; the *me* is the social self.
   b. the *I* is the id; the *me* is the ego.
   c. the *I* is the private inner self; the *me* is the social self that others see.
   d. the *I* is the inner self who wants, wants, wants; the *me* is the inner self who works out what *I* actually needs.

4. What part do peer groups play in the gender socialization of children?
   a. None.
   b. A significant role. They help children judge the significance of ongoing changes to their bodies—for example, whether the first signs of puberty are treated as a matter of pride or embarrassment.
   c. A marginal role. Peer groups interpret only what parents and media are telling children.
   d. A dominating role. Only peer groups determine how children understand the significance of gender.

5. According to George Herbert Mead's theory of child development, what is the importance of playing organized games at the age of eight or nine?
   a. Children can have fun at an early age and then focus on succeeding at school and work later in life.
   b. Children begin to understand the overall values and morality according to which social life is conducted.
   c. Children learn to be competitive and see others as rivals.
   d. Children learn how to use a computer keyboard, an important skill throughout one's life.

6. In traditional versus modern societies, what is the most important difference regarding how the elderly are generally viewed?
   a. In traditional societies, elders had little authority in the family and community; in modern societies, elders have a great deal of authority.
   b. In traditional societies, elders had a great deal of authority in the family and community; in modern societies, elders have very little authority.
   c. In traditional societies, the concept of *elder* did not exist; in modern societies, people aspire to the age-grade elder.
   d. In traditional societies, elders were put to death; in modern societies, elders are put in old-age homes.

7. The learning of male or female roles takes place through a process called
   a. genderization.
   b. gender socialization.
   c. sexualization.
   d. sex role learning.

8. Groups or social contexts in which significant processes or socialization occur are called

a. context operations.

b. concrete operations.

c. sensorimotors.

d. agents of socialization.

9. Jean Piaget's theory of child development is based on

a. the stages of cognitive development.

b. the emergence of a sense of self, of self-awareness.

c. the importance of sociobiology.

d. all of the above.

10. Children learn the ways of their elders, thereby perpetuating the values, norms, and social practices of their culture. This process is known as

a. evolution.

b. social interaction.

c. socialization.

d. natural selection.

Thinking Sociologically Exercises

1. Concisely review how an individual becomes a social person according to each of the three leading theorists discussed in this chapter: G. H. Mead, Jean Piaget, and Sigmund Freud. Which of these three theories seems most appropriate and correct to you? Explain why.

2. Using alcoholic beverages is one of many things we do as a result of socialization. Suggest how the family, peers, schools, and mass media help establish the desire to consume alcoholic drinks. Of these influences, which force is the most persuasive? Explain.

Data Exercises

www.wwnorton.com/giddens
Keyword: Data4

In the data exercise for this chapter, you will once again use the General Social Survey data to explore the topic of socialization. Specifically, you will learn more about what behaviors Americans value and believe are important for a child to learn.

The Study of Daily Life

Familiarize yourself with the study of everyday life.

Nonverbal Communication

Know the various forms of nonverbal communication.

Social Rules and Talk

Learn the research process of ethnomethodology, the study of our conversations, and how we make sense of each other.

Face, Body, and Speech in Interaction

Recognize the different contexts of our social life and how they are used to convey or hide meaning. Also learn how our social actions are organized in time and space.

Interaction in Time and Space

Understand that interaction is situated, that it occurs in a particular place and for a particular length of time. See that the way we organize our social actions is not unique by learning how other cultures organize their social lives.

Linking Microsociology and Macrosociology

See how face-to-face interactions and broader features of society are closely related.

CHAPTER FIVE

SOCIAL INTERACTION AND EVERYDAY LIFE

eric Schmitz is a personal trainer and fitness director at the Santa Barbara Athletic Club (SBAC), an upscale health club. He has been employed at the gym since he graduated from the University of Wisconsin, Madison with a degree in Exercise physiology in 1987.

Schmitz knows hundreds of people who work out at the gym. Some of them he has worked with as fitness director as they were getting to know the machines in their early months there. He has met many others while teaching classes in spinning—a group cycling class. Others he came to know through casual contact because many of the same people work out at the same time every week.

The personal space is limited within a gym environment due to the proximity of the exercise equipment. For example, in the weight-training circuit at SBAC, one section contains a number of Cybex machines located closely together. Members must work out near each other, and their bodies constantly crisscross as they move through their workouts.

It is almost impossible for Schmitz to walk anywhere in this physical space without potentially making eye contact with someone he has at least met. He will greet certain of these patrons the first time he sees them in the day, but afterward it is usually understood that they will go about their own business without acknowledging one another in the way they did earlier.

When passersby quickly glance at each other and then look away again, they demonstrate what Erving Goffman (1967, 1971) calls the **civil inattention** we require of each other in many situations. Civil inattention is not the same as merely ignoring another person. Each individual

Walking along a crowded city street, one engages in civil inattention. Though the people in this photo can hear the phone conversations these men are having, they make no indication of their awareness.

indicates recognition of the other person's presence but avoids any gesture that might be taken as too intrusive. Can you think of examples of civil inattention in your own life? Perhaps when you are walking down the hall of a dormitory or trying to decide where to sit in the cafeteria or simply walking across campus? Civil inattention to others is something we engage in more or less unconsciously, but it is of fundamental importance to the existence of social life, which must proceed efficiently and, sometimes among total strangers, without fear. When civil inattention occurs among passing strangers, an individual implies to another person that she has no reason to suspect his intentions, be hostile to him, or in any other way specifically avoid him.

The best way to see the importance of this is by thinking of examples for which it doesn't apply. When a person stares fixedly at another, allowing her face openly to express a particular emotion, it is normally with a lover, family member, or close friend. Strangers or chance acquaintances, whether encountered on the street, at work, or at a party, virtually never hold the gaze of another in this way. To do so may be taken as an indication of hostile intent. It is only where two groups are strongly antagonistic to one another that strangers might indulge in such a practice. Thus when whites in the United States have been known in the past to give a "hate stare" to blacks walking past.

Even friends in close conversation need to be careful about how they look at one another. Each individual demonstrates attention and involvement in the conversation by regularly looking at the eyes of the other, but not staring into them. To look

too intently might be taken as a sign of mistrust about, or at least failure to understand, what the other is saying. Yet if each party does not engage the eyes of the other at all, he is likely to be thought evasive, shifty, or otherwise odd.

The Study of Daily Life

Why should we concern ourselves with such seemingly trivial aspects of social behavior? Passing someone on the street or exchanging a few words with a friend seem minor and uninteresting activities, things we do countless times a day without giving them any thought. In fact, the study of such apparently insignificant forms of **social interaction** is of major importance in sociology and, far from being uninteresting, is one of the most absorbing of all areas of sociological investigation. There are three reasons for this.

First, our day-to-day routines, with their almost constant interactions with others, give structure and form to what we do; we can learn a great deal about ourselves as social beings, and about social life itself, from studying them. Our lives are organized around the repetition of similar patterns of behavior from day to day, week to week, month to month, and year to year. Think of what you did yesterday, for example, and the day before that. If they were both weekdays, in all probability you got up at about the same time each day (an important routine in itself). You may have gone off to class fairly early in the morning, making a journey from home to school or college that you make virtually every weekday. You perhaps met some friends for lunch, returning to classes or private study in the afternoon. Later, you retraced your steps back home, possibly going out later in the evening with other friends.

Of course, the routines we follow from day to day are not identical, and our patterns of activity on weekends usually contrast with those on weekdays. And if we make a major change in our life, like leaving college to take up a job, alterations in our daily routines are usually necessary; but then we establish a new and fairly regular set of habits again.

Second, the study of everyday life reveals to us how humans can act creatively to shape reality. Although social behavior is guided to some extent by forces such as roles, norms, and shared expectations, individuals perceive reality differently according to their backgrounds, interests, and motivations. Because individuals are capable of creative action, they continuously shape reality through the decisions and actions they take. In other words, reality is not fixed or static—it is created through human interactions. This notion of the social construction of reality lies at the heart of the symbolic interactionist perspective introduced in Chapter 1.

Third, studying social interaction in everyday life sheds light on larger social systems and institutions. All large-scale social systems, in fact, depend on the patterns of social interaction we engage in daily. This is easy to demonstrate. Consider again the case of two strangers passing on the street. Such an event may seem to have little direct relevance to large-scale, more permanent forms of social organization. But when we take into account many such interactions, they are no longer irrelevant. In modern societies, most people live in towns and cities and constantly interact with others whom they do not know personally. Civil inattention is one among other mechanisms that give city life, with its bustling crowds and fleeting, impersonal contacts, the character it has.

In this chapter, we first learn about the nonverbal cues (facial expressions and bodily gestures) all of us use when interacting with each other. We then move on to analyze everyday speech—how we use language to communicate to others the meanings we wish to get across. Finally, we focus on the ways in which our lives are structured by daily routines, paying particular attention to how we coordinate our actions across space and time.

Nonverbal Communication

Social interaction requires numerous forms of **nonverbal communication**—the exchange of information and meaning through facial expressions, gestures, and movements of the body. Nonverbal communication is sometimes referred to as "body language," but this is misleading, because we characteristically use such nonverbal cues to eliminate or expand on what is said with words.

"Face," Gestures, and Emotion

One major aspect of nonverbal communication is the facial expression of emotion. Paul Ekman and his colleagues have developed what they call the Facial Action Coding System (FACS) for describing movements of the facial muscles that give rise to particular expressions (Ekman and Friesen 1978). By this means, they have tried to inject some precision into an area notoriously open to inconsistent or contradictory interpretations—for there is little agreement about how emotions are to be identified and classified. Charles Darwin, one of the originators of evolutionary theory, claimed that basic modes of emotional expression are the same in all human beings. Although some have disputed the claim, Ekman's research among people from widely different cultural backgrounds seems to confirm Darwin's view. Ekman and W. V. Friesen carried out a study of

Paul Ekman's photographs of facial expressions from a tribesman in an isolated community in New Guinea helped test the idea that basic modes of emotional expression are the same among all people. Here the instructions were to show how your face would look if you were a person in a story and (A) your friend had come and you were happy, (B) your child had died, (C) you were angry and about to fight, and (D) you saw a dead pig that had been lying there a long time.

an isolated community in New Guinea, whose members had previously had virtually no contact with outsiders. When they were shown pictures of facial expressions conveying six emotions (happiness, sadness, anger, disgust, fear, surprise), the New Guineans were able to identify these emotions.

According to Ekman, the results of his own and similar studies of different peoples support the view that the facial expression of emotion and its interpretation are innate in human beings. He acknowledges that his evidence does not conclusively demonstrate this, and it may be that widely shared cultural learning experiences are involved; however, his conclusions are supported by other types of research. I. Eibl-Eibesfeldt (1972) studied six children born deaf and blind to see how far their facial expressions were the same as those of sighted and hearing individuals in particular emotional situations. He found that the children smiled when engaged in obviously pleasurable activities, raised their eyebrows in surprise when sniffing at an object with an unaccustomed smell, and frowned when repeatedly offered a disliked object. Because the children could not have seen other people behaving in these ways, it seems that these responses must be innately determined.

Using the FACS, Ekman and Friesen identified a number of the discrete facial muscle actions in newborn infants that are also found in adult expressions of emotion. Infants seem, for example, to produce facial expressions similar to the adult expression of disgust (pursing the lips and frowning) in response to sour tastes. But although the facial expression of emotion seems to be partly innate, individual and cultural factors influence what exact form facial movements take and the contexts in which they are deemed appropriate. How people smile, for example, the precise movement of the lips and other facial muscles, and how fleeting the smile is all vary among cultures.

There are no gestures or bodily postures that have been shown to characterize all, or even most, cultures. In some societies, for instance, people nod when they mean no, the opposite of Anglo-American practice. Gestures Americans tend to use a great deal, such as pointing, seem not to exist among certain peoples (Bull 1983). Similarly, a straightened forefinger placed in the center of the cheek and rotated is used in parts of Italy as a gesture of praise but appears to be unknown elsewhere.

Like facial expressions, gestures and bodily posture are continually used to fill out utterances as well as to convey meanings when nothing is actually said. All three can be used to joke, show irony, or show skepticism. The nonverbal impressions that we convey inadvertently often indicate that what we say is not quite what we really mean. Blushing is perhaps the most obvious example, but innumerable other subtle indicators can be picked up by other people. Genuine facial expressions tend to evaporate after four or five seconds. A smile that lasts longer could indicate deceit. An expression of surprise that lasts too long may indicate deliberate sarcasm—to show that the individual is not in fact surprised after all.

Gender and Nonverbal Communication

Is there a gender dimension to everyday social interaction? There are reasons to believe there is. Because interactions are shaped by the larger social context, it is not surprising that both verbal and nonverbal communication may be perceived and expressed differently by men and women. Understandings of gender and gender roles are greatly influenced by social factors and are related broadly to issues of power and status in society. These dynamics are evident even in standard interactions in daily life. Take as an example one of the most common nonverbal expressions—eye contact. Individuals use eye contact in a wide variety of ways, often to catch someone's attention or to begin a social interaction. In societies where men on the whole dominate women in both public and private life,

Nonverbal cues, such as how we position ourselves in proximity to others, can expand on verbal communication. Above, the experience of flirtation is interpreted differently by the woman on the left, who angles herself demurely, and the man on the right, who more boldly occupies his seated space.

men may feel freer than women to make eye contact with strangers.

A particular form of eye contact—staring—illustrates the contrasts in meaning between men and women of identical forms of nonverbal communication. A man who stares at a woman can be seen as acting in a "natural" or "innocent" way; if the woman is uncomfortable, she can evade the gaze by looking away or choosing not to sustain the interaction. On the other hand, a woman who stares at a man is often regarded as behaving in a suggestive or sexually leading manner. Taken individually such cases may seem inconsequential; when viewed collectively they help reinforce patterns of gender inequality.

There are other gender differences in nonverbal communication as well. Studies have shown that men tend to sit in a more relaxed manner than do women. Men tend to lean back with their legs open, whereas women tend to have a more closed body position, sitting upright, with their hands in their lap and their legs crossed. Women also tend to stand closer to the person they are talking to than do men. Men also make physical contact with women during conversation far more often than the other way around (and women are expected to view this as normal). Studies have also shown that women tend to show their emotions more obviously (through facial expressions) and that they seek and break eye contact more often than men. Sociologists have argued that these seemingly small-scale micro-level interactions reinforce the wider macro-level inequality in our society. Men control more space when standing and sitting than do women because they tend to stand farther away from the person they are talking to and because they tend to sprawl when sitting; they demonstrate control through more frequent physical contact of women. Women, it has been argued, seek approval through eye contact and facial expression; and when men make eye contact a woman is more likely to look away than is another man. Thus, it is argued, micro-level studies of nonverbal forms of communication provide subtle cues that demonstrate men's power over women in wider society (Young 1990).

Social Rules and Talk

Although we routinely use nonverbal cues in our own behavior and in making sense of the behavior of others, much of our interaction is done through talk—casual verbal exchange—carried on in informal conversations with others. Sociologists have always accepted that language is fundamental to social life. However, an approach has been developed that is specifically concerned with how people use language in the ordinary contexts of everyday life.

Ethnomethodology is the study of the "ethnomethods"—the folk, or lay, methods—people use to *make sense* of what others do and particularly of what they say. We all apply these methods, normally without having to give any conscious attention to them. Often we can make sense of what is said in conversation only if we know the social context, which does not appear in the words themselves. Take the following conversation (Heritage 1985):

> **A:** *I have a fourteen-year-old son.*
>
> **B:** *Well, that's all right.*
>
> **A:** *I also have a dog.*
>
> **B:** *Oh, I'm sorry.*

What do you think is happening here? What is the relation between the speakers? What if you were told that this is a conversation between a prospective tenant and a landlord? The conversation then becomes sensible: Some landlords accept children but don't permit their tenants to keep pets. Yet if we don't know the social context, the responses of individual B seem to bear no relation to the statements of A. *Part* of the sense is in the words, and *part* is in the way in which the meaning emerges from the social context.

Shared Understandings

The most inconsequential forms of daily talk presume complicated, shared knowledge brought into play by those speaking. In fact, our small talk is so complex that it has so far proved impossible to program even the most sophisticated computers to converse with human beings. The words used in ordinary talk do not always have precise meanings, and we "fix" what we want to say through the unstated assumptions that back it up. If Maria asks Tom: "What did you do yesterday?" the words in the question themselves suggest no obvious answer. A day is a long time, and it would be logical for Tom to answer: "Well, at seven sixteen, I woke up. At seven eighteen, I got out of bed, went to the bathroom and started to brush my teeth. At seven nineteen, I turned on the shower. . . ." We understand the type of response the question calls for by knowing Maria, what sort of activities she and Tom consider relevant, and what Tom usually does on a particular day of the week, among other things.

Garfinkel's Experiments

The "background expectancies" with which we organize ordinary conversations were highlighted by some experiments Harold Garfinkel (1963) undertook with student volunteers. The students were asked to engage a friend or relative in conversation and to insist that casual remarks or general comments be actively pursued to make their meaning precise. If someone said, "Have a nice day," the student was to respond, "Nice in what sense, exactly?" "Which part of the day do you mean?" and so forth. One of the exchanges that resulted ran as follows. S is the friend; E, the student volunteer (Garfinkel 1963):

> **S:** *How are you?*
>
> **E:** *How am I in regard to what? My health, my finances, my school work, my peace of mind, my . . .*
>
> **S:** *(red in the face and suddenly out of control): Look! I was just trying to be polite. Frankly, I don't give a damn how you are.*

Why do people get so upset when apparently minor conventions of talk are not followed? The answer is that the stability and meaningfulness of our daily social lives depend on the sharing of unstated cultural assumptions about what is said and why. If we weren't able to take these for granted, meaningful communication would be impossible. Any question or contribution to a conversation would have to be followed by a massive "search procedure" of the sort Garfinkel's subjects were told to initiate, and interaction would simply break down. What seem at first sight to be unimportant conventions of talk, therefore, turn out to be fundamental to the very fabric of social life, which is why their breach is so serious.

Note that in everyday life, people on occasion deliberately feign ignorance of unstated knowledge. This may be done to

Interactional Vandalism: A Sociologist's Field Note

It is well known that streets and sidewalks are places where women are disadvantaged by public harassment. While the things we are witnessing are a case of the larger public harassments that occur between some people working the street and pedestrians of both genders, perhaps for women it is a problem in distinct ways. Keith is attempting to control the woman *as a woman*, knowing that even privileged women occupy vulnerable positions in public space. Like most males (black and white), he has been taught that to be a male is to possess this power, and he feels entitled to control her. I asked after his awareness of the dog's owner as a woman.

"So, you know the dog's name," I said after they left.

"Yeah."

"Do you know the woman's name?"

"No. I'd rather have the dog than her. You know why? Dog don't want nothing but a little attention. Give him some food. Take the fucker out for a walk. Let him watch TV with you, and it's cool. But she wants room and board, clothing, makeup, hairdos, fabulous dinners, and rent, plus they want a salary for giving you some pussy once in a while." ***

Out on Sixth Avenue one day, I ask Mudrick to tell me a little about his relationship to women on the street. Since most women ignore him, he says, he talks to all of them. That way he might get to have conversations with some of them.

Three white women in their twenties approach, and I am given a demonstration of his method. "Hi, ladies. How you-all feeling, ladies? You-all look very nice, you know. Have a nice day."

I have seen Mudrick engage in such behavior over and over again, but there is no doubt in my mind that this demonstration has been for me, a way of responding to the question I had just asked.

"Let me ask you a question, Mudrick. When you do that, explain to me the pleasure you get out of it."

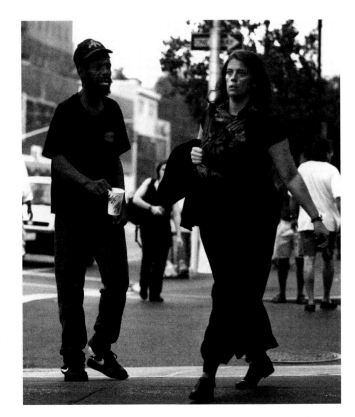

"I get a good kick out of it."

"Explain to me the kick you get out of it."

"It make me feel good and I try to make them happy, the things I say to them, you understand? The things I say, they can't accept. They gotta deal with it."

"What do you mean, 'They gotta deal with it?'"

"They *have* to deal with it. I say sweet things to a woman. Make her feel good. Like, You look nice. You look very nice. I'd like to be with you someday if I can. Try to make you happy.

Some womens treated so wrong they scared to talk to the right man. Men treat women *so* wrong. Women don't give a fuck about men. Now they go to women. They gets a woman to be their man. They turn into be a lesbian. Because they scared to mess with a man."

A woman walks by without acknowledging him, and Mudrick tells me that she must be a lesbian. He claims that the women he addresses never feel harassed, because he gives them respect, and he can tell from their smiles that they *like* the attention.

A white woman wearing sunglasses approaches with her friend.

"Hey, you, with the shades on. You look very nice."

"Thank you," she says.

"Your friend look nice, too."

"Thank you."

He tells me that the women never respond by turning away or looking angry.

"What's the worst things that women will do when you say that to them?"

"They can't do anything. Because, the words I say, they don't have any choice."

SOURCE: Reprinted from Mitchell Duneier, *Sidewalk* (New York: Farrar, Straus and Giroux, 1999), pp. 193–95, 210.

The author of this box, Mitchell Duneier, also co-authored this textbook. Duneier describes the behavior and lives of poor and sometimes homeless black men who work or beg in New York's Greenwich Village.

Questions

- In what ways do Mudrick and Keith take advantage of social convention and rules of politeness to interact with women?
- Why do you think these homeless men try to talk to women on the street, even though their remarks don't result in dates or even long conversations? What do they get out of it?
- Why are Mudrick's and Keith's questions and compliments to women a form of interactional vandalism?
- Why is the behavior of these men seen as different from the catcalls of construction workers or fraternity brothers?

rebuff the others, poke fun at them, cause embarrassment, or call attention to a double meaning in what was said. Consider, for example, this classic exchange between parent and teenager:

P: *Where are you going?*

T: *Out.*

P: *What are you going to do?*

T: *Nothing.*

The responses of the teenager are effectively the opposite of those of the volunteers in Garfinkel's experiments. Rather than pursuing inquiries where this is not normally done, the teenager declines to provide appropriate answers at all—essentially saying, "Mind your own business!"

The first question might elicit a different response from another person in another context:

A: *Where are you going?*

B: *I'm going quietly round the bend.*

B deliberately misreads A's question to ironically convey worry or frustration. Comedy and joking thrive on such deliberate misunderstandings of the unstated assumptions involved in talk. There is nothing threatening about this so long as the parties concerned recognize that the intent is to provoke laughter.

"Interactional Vandalism"

We have already seen that conversations are one of the main ways in which our daily lives are maintained in a stable and coherent manner. We feel most comfortable when the tacit conventions of small talk are adhered to; when they are breached, we can feel threatened, confused, and insecure. In most everyday talk, conversants are carefully attuned to the cues they get from others—such as changes in intonation, slight pauses, or gestures—to facilitate conversation smoothly. By being mutually aware, conversants "cooperate" in opening and closing interactions and in taking turns to speak. Interactions in which one party is conversationally "uncooperative," however, can give rise to tensions.

Garfinkel's students created tense situations by intentionally undermining conversational rules as part of a sociological experiment. But what about situations in the real world in which people make trouble through their conversational practices? One study investigated verbal interchanges between pedestrians and street people in New York City to understand why such interactions are often seen as problematic by passersby. The researchers used a technique called **conversation analysis** to compare a selection of street interchanges with samples of everyday talk. Conversation analysis is a methodology that examines all facets of a conversation for meaning—from the smallest filler words (such as "um" and "ah") to the precise timing of interchanges (including pauses, interruptions, and overlaps).

The study looked at interactions between black men—many of whom were homeless, alcoholic, or drug addicted—and white women who passed by them on the street. The men would often try to initiate conversations with passing women by calling out to them, paying them compliments, or asking them questions. But something "goes wrong" in these conversations, because the women rarely respond as they would in a normal interaction. Even though the men's comments are rarely hostile in tone, the women tend to quicken their step and stare fixedly ahead. The following shows attempts by Mudrick, a black man in his late fifties, to engage women in conversation (Duneier and Molotch 1999):

[Mudrick] begins this interaction as a white woman who looks about 25 approaches at a steady pace:
1. **Mudrick:** *I love you baby.*
She crosses her arms and quickens her walk, ignoring the comment.
2. **Mudrick:** *Marry me.*
Next, it is two white women, also probably in their mid-twenties:
3. **Mudrick:** *Hi girls, you all look very nice today. You have some money? Buy some books.*
They ignore him. Next, it is a young black woman.
4. **Mudrick:** *Hey pretty. Hey pretty.*
She keeps walking without acknowledging him.
5. **Mudrick:** *'Scuse me. 'Scuse me. I know you hear me.*
Then he addresses a white woman in her thirties.
6. **Mudrick:** *I'm watching you. You look nice, you know.*
She ignores him.

Negotiating smooth "openings" and "closings" to conversations is a fundamental requirement for urban civility. These crucial aspects of conversation were highly problematic between the men and the women. Where the women resisted the men's attempts at opening conversations; the men ignored the women's resistance and persisted. Similarly, if the men succeeded in opening a conversation, they often refused to respond to cues from the women to close the conversation once it had gotten under way (Duneier and Molotch 1999):

1. **Mudrick:** *Hey pretty.*
2. **Woman:** *Hi how you doin'.*
3. **Mudrick:** *You alright?*

4. **Mudrick:** *You look very nice you know. I like how you have your hair pinned.*
5. **Mudrick:** *You married?*
6. **Woman:** *Yeah.*
7. **Mudrick:** *Huh?*
8. **Woman:** *Yeah.*
9. **Mudrick:** *Where the rings at?*
10. **Woman:** *I have it home.*
11. **Mudrick:** *Y' have it home?*
12. **Woman:** *Yeah.*
13. **Mudrick:** *Can I get your name?*
14. **Mudrick:** *My name is Mudrick, what's yours?*

She does not answer and walks on.

In this instance, Mudrick made nine out of the fourteen utterances in the interaction to initiate the conversation and to elicit further responses from the woman. From the transcript alone, it is quite evident that the woman is not interested in talking, but when conversation analysis is applied to the tape recording, her reluctance becomes even clearer. The woman delays all of her responses—even when she does give them, while Mudrick replies immediately, his comments sometimes overlapping hers. Timing in conversations is a very precise indicator; delaying a response by even a fraction of a second is adequate in most everyday interactions to signal the desire to change the course of a conversation. By betraying these tacit rules of sociability, Mudrick was practicing conversation in a way that was "technically" rude. The woman, in return, was also technically rude in ignoring Mudrick's repeated attempts to engage her in talk. It is the technically rude nature of these street interchanges that make them problematic for passersby to handle. When standard cues for opening and closing conversations are not adhered to, individuals feel a sense of profound and inexplicable insecurity.

The term **interactional vandalism** describes cases like these in which a subordinate person breaks the tacit rules of everyday interaction that are of value to the more powerful. The men on the street often do conform to everyday forms of speech in their interactions with one another, local shopkeepers, the police, relatives, and acquaintances. But when they choose to, they subvert the tacit conventions for everyday talk in a way that leaves passersby disoriented. Even more than physical assaults or vulgar verbal abuse, interactional vandalism leaves victims unable to articulate what has happened.

This study of interactional vandalism provides another example of the two-way links between micro-level interactions and forces that operate on the macro level. To the men on the street, the white women who ignore their attempts at conversation appear distant, cold, and bereft of sympathy—legitimate "targets"

for such interactions. The women, meanwhile, may often take the men's behavior as proof that they are indeed dangerous and best avoided. Interactional vandalism is closely tied up with overarching class, gender, and racial structures. The fear and anxiety generated in such mundane interactions help constitute the outside statuses and forces that, in turn, influence the interactions themselves. Interactional vandalism is part of a self-reinforcing system of mutual suspicion and incivility.

Response Cries

Some kinds of utterances are not talk but consist of muttered exclamations, or what Goffman (1981) has called **response cries.** Consider Lucy, who exclaims, "Oops!" after knocking over a glass of water. "Oops!" seems to be merely an uninteresting reflex response to a mishap, rather like blinking your eye when a person moves a hand sharply toward your face. It is not a reflex, however, as shown by the fact that people do not usually make the exclamation when alone. "Oops!" is normally directed toward others present. The exclamation demonstrates to witnesses that the lapse is only minor and momentary, not something that should cast doubt on Lucy's command of her actions.

"Oops!" is used only in situations of minor failure, rather than in major accidents or calamities—which also demonstrates that the exclamation is part of our controlled management of the details of social life. Moreover, the word may be used by someone observing Lucy, rather than by Lucy herself, or it may be used to sound a warning to another. "Oops!" is normally a curt sound, but the "oo" may be prolonged in some situations. Thus someone might extend the sound to cover a critical moment in performing a task. For instance, a parent may utter an extended "Oops!" or "Oopsadaisy!" when playfully tossing a child in the air. The sound covers the brief phase when the child may feel a loss of control, reassuring him and probably at the same time developing his understanding of response cries.

This may all sound very contrived and exaggerated. Why bother to analyze such an inconsequential utterance in this detail? Surely we don't pay as much attention to what we say as this example suggests? Of course we don't—on a conscious level. The crucial point, however, is that we take for granted an immensely complicated, continuous control of our appearance and actions. In situations of interaction, we are never expected just to be present on the scene. Others expect, as we expect of them, that we will display what Goffman calls *controlled alertness.* A fundamental part of being human is continually demonstrating to others our competence in the routines of daily life.

Face, Body, and Speech in Interaction

Let us summarize at this point what we have learned so far. Everyday interaction depends on subtle relationships between what we convey with our faces and bodies and what we express in words. We use the facial expressions and bodily gestures of other people to fill in what they communicate verbally and to check if they are sincere in what they say. Mostly without realizing it, each of us keeps a tight and continuous control over facial expression, bodily posture, and movement in the course of our daily interaction with others.

Face, bodily management, and speech, then, are used to convey certain meanings and to hide others. We also organize our activities in the *contexts* of social life to achieve the same ends, as we shall now see.

"Hmmm... what shall I wear today...?"

Encounters

In many social situations, we engage in what Goffman calls **unfocused interaction** with others. Unfocused interaction takes place whenever individuals exhibit mutual awareness of one another's presence. This is usually the case anywhere large numbers of people are assembled together, as on a busy street, in a theater crowd, or at a party. When people are in the presence of others, even if they do not directly talk to them, they continually communicate nonverbally through their posture and facial and physical gestures.

Focused interaction occurs when individuals directly attend to what others say or do. Except when someone is standing alone, say at a party, all interaction involves both focused and unfocused exchanges. Goffman calls an instance of focused interaction an **encounter**, and much of our day-to-day life consists of encounters with other people—family, friends, colleagues—frequently occurring against the background of unfocused interaction with others present on the scene. Small talk, seminar discussions, games, and routine face-to-face contacts (with ticket clerks, waiters, shop assistants, and so forth) are all examples of encounters.

Encounters always need "openings," which indicate that civil inattention is being discarded. When strangers meet and begin to talk at a party, the moment of ceasing civil inattention is always risky because misunderstandings can easily occur about the nature of the encounter being established (Goffman 1971). Hence the making of eye contact may first be ambiguous and tentative. A person can then act as though she had made no direct move if the overture is not accepted. In focused interaction, each person communicates as much by facial

expression and gesture as by the words actually exchanged. Goffman distinguishes between the expressions individuals give and those they give off. The first are the words and facial expressions people use to produce certain impressions on others. The second are the clues that others may spot to check their sincerity or truthfulness. For instance, a restaurant owner listens with a polite smile to the statements of customers about how much they enjoyed their meals. At the same time, he is noting how pleased they seemed to be while eating the food, whether a lot was left over, and the tone of voice they use to express their satisfaction.

Impression Management

Goffman and other writers on social interaction often use notions from the theater in their analyses. The concept of social role, for example, originated in a theatrical setting. **Roles** are socially defined expectations that a person in a given **status** (or **social position**) follows. To be a teacher is to hold a specific position; the teacher's role consists of acting in specified ways toward her pupils. Goffman sees social life as though played out by actors on a stage—or on many stages because how we act depends on the roles we are playing at a particular time. People are sensitive to how they are seen by others and use many forms of **impression management** to compel others to react to them in the ways they wish. Although we may sometimes do this in a calculated way, usually it is among the things we do without conscious attention. When Philip attends a business meeting, he wears a suit and tie and is on his best behavior; that evening, when relaxing with friends at a football game, he wears jeans and a sweatshirt and tells a lot of jokes. This is impression management.

As we just noted, the social roles that we adopt depend highly on our social status. A person's social status can be different depending on the social context. For instance, as a "student" you have a certain status and are expected to act a certain way when you are around your professors. As a "son" or "daughter" you have a different status from a student, and society (especially your parents) has different expectations for you. Likewise, as a "friend" you have an entirely different position in the social order, and the roles you adopt would change accordingly. Obviously, a person has many statuses at the same time. Sociologists refer to the group of statuses that you occupy as a **status set**.

Sociologists also like to distinguish between ascribed status and achieved status. An **ascribed status** is one that you are assigned based on biological factors such as race, sex, or age. Thus your ascribed statuses could be "white," "female," and "teenager." An **achieved status** is one that is earned through your own effort. Your achieved statuses could be "high school graduate," "athlete," and "employee." Although we may like to believe that it is our achieved statuses that are most important, society may not agree. In any society, some statuses have priority over all other statuses and generally determine a person's overall position in society. Sociologists refer to this as a **master status** (Becker 1963; Hughes 1945). The most common master statuses are those based on gender and race. Sociologists have shown that, in an encounter, two of the first things that people notice about one another are gender and race (Omi and Winant 1994). As we shall see shortly, both race and gender strongly shape our social interactions.

FRONT AND BACK REGIONS

Much of social life, Goffman suggests, can be divided into front regions and back regions. **Front regions** are social occasions or encounters in which individuals act out formal roles; they are "onstage performances." Teamwork is often involved in creating front-region performances. Two prominent politicians in the same party may put on an elaborate show of unity and friendship before the television cameras, even though each privately detests the other. A wife and husband may take care to conceal their quarrels from their children, preserving a front of harmony, only to fight bitterly once the children are safely tucked in bed.

The **back regions** are where people assemble the props and prepare themselves for interaction in the more formal settings. Back regions resemble the backstage of a theater or the off-camera activities of filmmaking. When they are safely behind the scenes, people can relax and give vent to feelings and styles of behavior they keep in check when on front stage. Back regions permit

> profanity, open sexual remarks, elaborate griping . . . rough informal dress, "sloppy" sitting and standing posture, use of dialect or substandard speech, mumbling and shouting, playful aggressiveness and "kidding," inconsiderateness for the other in minor but potentially symbolic acts, minor self-involvement such as humming, whistling, chewing, nibbling, belching and flatulence. (Goffman 1973)

Thus a waitress may be the soul of quiet courtesy when serving a customer but become loud and aggressive once behind the swing doors of the kitchen. Probably few people would

These photos of Ozzy Osbourne provide a metaphorical depiction of front and back regions. Backstage, or in the back region, Osbourne discusses household chores in his kitchen with his wife. When he takes the stage, or begins his front region performance, however, he assumes the role of an aggressive, angry heavy metal star.

continue to patronize restaurants if they could see all that goes on in the kitchens.

ADOPTING ROLES: INTIMATE EXAMINATIONS

For an example of collaboration in impression management that also borrows from the theater, let's look at one particular study in some detail. James Henslin and Mae Biggs (1971, 1997) studied a specific, highly delicate type of encounter: a woman's visit to a gynecologist. At the time of the study, most pelvic examinations were carried out by male doctors, and hence the experience was (and sometimes still is) fraught with potential ambiguities and embarrassment for both parties. Men and women in the West are socialized to think of the genitals as the most private part of the body; and seeing, and particularly touching, the genitals of another person is ordinarily associated with intimate sexual encounters. Some women feel so worried by the prospect of a pelvic examination that they refuse to visit the doctor, male or female, even when they suspect there is a strong medical reason to do so.

Henslin and Biggs analyzed material collected by Biggs, a trained nurse, from a large number of gynecological examinations. They interpreted what they found as having several typical stages. Adopting a dramaturgical metaphor, they suggested that each phase can be treated as a distinct scene, in which the parts the actors play alter as the episode unfolds. In the prologue, the woman enters the waiting room preparing to assume the role of patient and temporarily discarding her outside identity. Called into the consulting room, she adopts the "patient" role, and the first scene opens. The doctor assumes a businesslike, professional manner and treats the patient as a proper and competent person, maintaining eye contact and listening politely to what she has to say. If he decides an examination is called for, he tells her so and leaves the room; scene one is over.

As he leaves, the nurse comes in. She is an important stagehand in the main scene shortly to begin. She soothes any worries that the patient might have, acting as both a confidante—knowing some of the "things women have to put up with"—and a collaborator in what is to follow. Crucial to the next scene, the nurse helps alter the patient from a person to a "nonperson" for the vital scene—which features a body, part of which is to be scrutinized, rather than a complete human being. In Henslin and Biggs's study, the nurse not only supervises the patient's undressing but takes over aspects that normally the patient would control. Thus she takes the patient's clothes and folds them. Most women wish their underwear to be out of sight when the doctor returns, and the nurse makes sure that this is so. She guides the patient to the examining table and covers most of her body with a sheet before the physician returns.

The central scene now opens, with the nurse as well as the doctor taking part. The presence of the nurse helps ensure that the interaction between the doctor and the patient is free of sexual overtones and provides a legal witness should the physician be charged with unprofessional conduct. The examination proceeds as though the personality of the patient were absent; the sheet across her separates the genital area from the rest of her body, and her position does not allow her to watch the examination itself. Save for any specific medical queries, the doctor ignores her, sitting on a low stool, out of her line of vision. The patient collaborates in becoming a temporary nonperson, not initiating conversation and keeping any movements to a minimum.

In the interval between this and the final scene, the nurse again plays the role of stagehand, helping the patient become a full person once more. After the doctor has left the room, the two may again engage in conversation, the patient expressing relief that the examination is over. Having dressed and regroomed herself, the patient is ready to face the concluding scene. The doctor reenters and, in discussing the results of the examination, again treats the patient as a complete and responsible person. Resuming his polite, professional manner, he conveys that his reactions to her are in no way altered by the intimate contact with her body. The epilogue is played out when she leaves the physician's office, taking up again her identity in the outside world. The patient and the doctor have thus collaborated in such a way as to manage the interaction and the impression each participant forms of the other.

Personal Space

There are cultural differences in the definition of **personal space**. In Western culture, people usually maintain a distance of at least three feet when engaged in focused interaction with others; when standing side by side, they may stand closer together. In the Middle East, people often stand closer to each other than is thought acceptable in the West. Westerners visiting that part of the world are likely to find themselves disconcerted by this unexpected physical proximity.

Edward T. Hall (1969, 1973), who has worked extensively on nonverbal communication, distinguishes four zones of personal space. Intimate distance, of up to one and a half feet, is reserved for very few social contacts. Only those involved in relationships in which regular bodily touching is permitted, such as lovers or parents and children, operate within this zone of private space. Personal distance, from one and a half to four feet, is the normal spacing for encounters with friends and close acquaintances. Some intimacy of contact is permitted,

Cultural differences frequently determine the acceptable boundaries of personal space. In the Middle East, for example, people frequently stand closer to each other than is common in the West.

but this tends to be strictly limited. Social distance, from four to twelve feet, is the zone usually maintained in formal settings such as interviews. The fourth zone is that of public distance, beyond twelve feet, preserved by those who are performing to an audience.

In ordinary interaction, the most fraught zones are those of intimate and personal distance. If these zones are invaded, people try to recapture their space. We may stare at the intruder as if to say, "Move away!" or elbow her aside. When people are forced into proximity closer than they deem desirable, they might create a kind of physical boundary: A reader at a crowded library desk might physically demarcate a private space by stacking books around its edges (Hall 1969, 1973).

Interaction in Time and Space

Understanding how activities are distributed in time and space is fundamental to analyzing encounters and to understanding social life in general. All interaction is situated—it occurs in a particular place and has a specific duration in time. Our actions over the course of a day tend to be "zoned" in time as well as in space. Thus, for example, most people spend a zone—say, from 9:00 A.M. to 5:00 P.M.—of their daily time working. Their weekly time is also zoned: They are likely to work on weekdays and spend weekends at home, altering the pattern of their ac-

tivities on the weekend days. As we move through the temporal zones of the day, we are also often moving across space as well: To get to work, we may take a bus from one area of a city to another or perhaps commute in from the suburbs. When we analyze the contexts of social interaction, therefore, it is often useful to look at people's movements across **time–space**.

The concept of **regionalization** will help us understand how social life is zoned in time–space. Take the example of a private house. A modern house is regionalized into rooms, hallways, and floors (if there is more than one story). These spaces are not just physically separate areas but are zoned in time as well. The living rooms and kitchen are used most in the daylight hours, the bedrooms at night. The interaction that occurs in these regions is bound by both spatial and temporal divisions. Some areas of the house form back regions, with "performances" taking place in the others. At times, the whole house can become a back region. Once again, this idea is beautifully captured by Goffman (1973):

> On a Sunday morning, a whole household can use the wall around its domestic establishment to conceal a relaxing slovenliness in dress and civil endeavor, extending to all rooms the informality that is usually restricted to kitchen and bedrooms. So, too, in American middle-class neighborhoods, on afternoons the line between children's playground and home may be defined as backstage by mothers, who pass along it wearing jeans, loafers, and a minimum of make-up. . . . And, of course, a region that is thoroughly established as a front region for the regular performance of a particular routine often functions as a back region before and after each performance, for at these times the permanent fixtures may undergo repairs, restoration, and rearrangement, or the performers may hold dress rehearsals. To see this we need only glance into a restaurant, or store, or home, a few minutes before these establishments are opened to us for the day.

Clock Time

In modern societies, the zoning of our activities is strongly influenced by **clock time**. Without clocks and the precise timing of activities, and thereby their coordination across space, industrialized societies could not exist (Mumford 1973). The measuring of time by clocks is today standardized across the globe, making possible the complex international transport systems and communications we now depend on. World standard time was first introduced in 1884 at a conference of nations held in Washington. The globe was then partitioned into twenty-four

International Tourism

Have you ever had a face-to-face conversation with someone from another country? Or connected to an overseas Web site? Have you ever traveled to another part of the world? If you answered yes to any of these questions, you have witnessed the effects of globalization on social interaction. Americans, of course, have always interacted with people from foreign lands if for no other reason than America itself is an ethnically and culturally diverse nation. At the same time, globalization—a relatively recent phenomenon—has changed both the frequency and the nature of interactions among people of different nations. The historical sociologist Charles Tilly (1995), in fact, defines globalization in terms of these changes. According to Tilly, "globalization means an increase in the geographic range of locally consequential social interactions." In other words, with globalization a greater proportion of our interactions come to involve, directly or indirectly, people from other countries.

What are the characteristics of social interactions that take place among individuals of different nations? Important contributions to the study of this problem have been made by those working in the area of the sociology of tourism. Sociologists of tourism note that globalization has greatly expanded the possibilities for international travel, both by encouraging an interest in other countries and by facilitating the move-

ment of tourists across international borders. As a result, more than forty-one million foreign tourists visited the United States in 2003, marking a decline in tourist visits after a significant increase in the 1990s. The decline in such travel to the United States is related to the international war on terrorism and the war in Iraq. These visitors pumped nearly $65 billion into the U.S. economy (World Tourism Organization 2004). On the other hand, Americans are traveling the world in record numbers.

time zones, each one hour apart, and an exact beginning of the universal day was fixed.

Fourteenth-century monasteries were the first organizations to try to schedule the activities of their inmates precisely across the day and week. Today, there is virtually no group or organization that does not do so—the greater the number of people and resources involved, the more precise the scheduling must be. Eviatar Zerubavel (1979, 1982) demonstrated this in his study of the temporal structure of a large modern hospital. A hospital must operate on a twenty-four-hour basis, and coordinating the staff and resources is a highly complex matter. For instance, the nurses work for one time period in ward A, another time period in ward B, and so on, and are also called on to alternate between day- and night-shift work. Nurses, doctors, and other staff, plus the resources they need, must be integrated together both in time and in space.

Social Life and the Ordering of Space and Time

The Internet is another example of how closely forms of social life are bound up with our control of space and time. The Internet makes it possible for us to interact with people we never see or meet, in any corner of the world. Such technological change rearranges space—we can interact with anyone without moving from our chair. It also alters our experience of time, because communication on the electronic highway is almost immediate. Until about fifty years ago, most communication across space required a duration of time. If you sent a letter to someone abroad, there was a time gap while the letter was carried, by ship, train, truck, or plane, to the person to whom it was written.

People still write letters by hand today, of course; but instantaneous communication has become basic to our social

High levels of international tourism, of course, translate into an increase in the number of face-to-face interactions between people of different countries. According to the British sociologist John Urry (1990), many of these interactions are shaped by the "tourist gaze," the expectation on the part of the tourist that he or she will have exotic experiences while traveling abroad. *Exotic experiences* are those that violate our everyday expectations about how social interaction and interaction with the physical environment are supposed to proceed. Americans traveling in England, for example, may delight in the fact that the British drive on the left-hand side of the road, although such behavior is disconcerting to American drivers. Our rules of the road are so ingrained that we experience systematic violations of those rules as strange, weird, and exotic. Yet, as tourists, we take pleasure in this strangeness. In a sense, it is what we have paid money to see—along with Big Ben and the Tower of London. Imagine how disappointed you would be if you traveled to a different country only to find that it was almost exactly the same as the city or town in which you grew up.

Yet most tourists do not want their experiences to be *too* exotic. One of the most popular destinations for young Americans in Paris, for example, is a McDonald's restaurant. Some come to see if there is any truth to the line from the movie *Pulp Fiction* that because the French use the metric system, McDonald's "quarter pounder with cheese" hamburgers are called "royales with cheese" (it is true, by the way). But many others come for the comfort of eating familiar food in a familiar setting. The contradictory demands for the exotic and the familiar are at the heart of the tourist gaze.

The tourist gaze may put strains on face-to-face interactions between tourists and locals. Locals who are part of the tourist industry may appreciate overseas travelers for the economic benefits they bring to the places they visit. Other locals may resent tourists for their demanding attitudes or for the overdevelopment that often occurs in popular tourist destinations. Tourists may interrogate locals about aspects of their everyday lives, such as their food, work, and recreational habits; they may do this either to enhance their understanding of other cultures or to judge negatively those who are different from themselves.

As tourism increases with the march of globalization, sociologists will have to watch carefully to see what dominant patterns of interaction emerge between tourists and locals, and to determine, among other things, whether these interactions tend to be friendly or antagonistic.

world. Our lives would be almost unimaginable without it. We are so used to being able to switch on the TV and watch the news or make a phone call or send an e-mail message to a friend in another state that it is hard for us to imagine what life would be like otherwise.

Everyday Life in Cultural and Historical Perspective

Some of the mechanisms of social interaction analyzed by Goffman, Garfinkel, and others seem to be universal. But much of Goffman's discussion of civil inattention and other kinds of interaction primarily concerns societies in which contact with strangers is commonplace. What about very small traditional societies, where there are no strangers and few settings in which more than a handful of people are together at any one time?

To see some of the contrasts between social interaction in modern and traditional societies, let's take as an example one of the least developed cultures in terms of technology remaining in the world: the !Kung (sometimes known as the Bushmen), who live in the Kalahari Desert area of Botswana and Namibia, in southern Africa (Lee 1968, 1969). (The exclamation mark refers to a click sound one makes before pronouncing the name.) Although their way of life is changing because of outside influences, their traditional patterns of social life are still evident.

The !Kung live in groups of some thirty or forty people, in temporary settlements near water holes. Food is scarce in their environment, and they must walk far and wide to find it.

Such roaming takes up most of the average day. Women and children often stay back in the camp, but equally often the whole group spends the day walking. Members of the community will sometimes fan out over an area of up to a hundred square miles in the course of a day, returning to the camp at night to eat and sleep. The men may be alone or in groups of two or three for much of the day. There is one period of the year, however, when the routines of their daily activities change: the winter rainy season, when water is abundant and food much easier to come by. The everyday life of the !Kung during this period is centered around ritual and ceremonial activities, the preparation for and enactment of which is very time consuming.

The members of most !Kung groups never see anyone they don't know reasonably well. Until contacts with the outside became more common in recent years, they had no word for "stranger." While the !Kung, particularly the males, may spend long periods of the day out of contact with others, in the community itself there is little opportunity for privacy. Families sleep in flimsy, open dwellings, with virtually all activities open to public view. No one has studied the !Kung with Goffman's observations on everyday life in mind, but it is easy to see that some aspects of his work have limited application to !Kung social life. There are few opportunities, for example, to create front and back regions. The closing off of different gatherings and encounters by the walls of rooms, separate buildings, and the various neighborhoods of cities common in modern societies are remote from the activities of the !Kung.

The Compulsion of Proximity

In modern societies, in complete contrast to the !Kung—as explored in the chapters that follow—we are constantly interacting with others whom we may never see or meet. Almost all of our everyday transactions, such as buying groceries or making a bank deposit, bring us into contact—but *indirect* contact—with people who may live thousands of miles away. The banking system, for example, is international. Any money you deposit is a small part of the financial investments the bank makes worldwide.

Some people are concerned that the rapid advances in communications technology such as e-mail, the Internet, and e-commerce will only increase this tendency toward indirect interactions. Our society is becoming "devoiced," some claim, as the capabilities of technology grow ever greater. According to this view, as the pace of life accelerates, people are increasingly isolating themselves; we now interact more with our televisions and computers than with our neighbors or members of the community.

Now that e-mail, instant messages, electronic discussion groups, and chat rooms have become facts of life for many people in industrialized countries, what is the nature of these interactions and what new complexities are emerging from them? One study conducted at Stanford University found that about 20 percent of Internet users use the medium to communicate with people that they do not know (Nie et al. 2004). At the same time, the study found that Internet use reduces face-to-face socializing, TV watching, and sleep. In another study of office workers conducted by Friedman and Currall in 1997, almost half of the respondents said that the Internet had replaced the need for face-to-face communication. A third of them admitted to using e-mail deliberately to avoid the need for direct communication. Others reported that the use of abusive or offensive e-mails within the workplace had resulted in the complete breakdown of some office relations. The substitution of e-mail for face-to-face communication in the office has led to a weakening of social ties and a disruption of techniques used in personal dialogue for avoiding conflict. As a result, online communication seems to allow more room for misinterpretation, confusion, and abuse than more traditional forms of communication (Friedman and Currall 2003).

> The problem lies in the nature of human communication. We think of it as a product of the mind, but it's done by bodies: faces move, voices intone, bodies sway, hands gesture. . . . On the Internet, the mind is present but the body is gone. Recipients get few clues to the personality and mood of the person, can only guess why messages are sent, what they mean, what responses to make. Trust is virtually out the window. It's a risky business. (Locke 2000)

Many Internet enthusiasts disagree. They argue that, far from being impersonal, online communication has many inherent advantages that cannot be claimed by more traditional forms of interaction such as the telephone and face-to-face meetings. The human voice, for example, may be far superior in terms of expressing emotion and subtleties of meaning, but it can also convey information about the speaker's age, gender, ethnicity, or social position—information that could be used to the speaker's disadvantage. Electronic communication, it is noted, masks all these identifying markers and ensures that attention focuses strictly on the content of the message. This can be a great advantage for women or other traditionally disadvantaged groups whose opinions are sometimes devalued in other settings (Pascoe 2000). Electronic interaction is often presented as liberating and empowering because people can create their own online identities and speak more freely than they would elsewhere.

The annual Group of 8 (G-8) summit, which brings together eight of the most powerful world leaders, is an example of what Molotch and Boden call the compulsion of proximity. Individuals prefer face-to-face interaction, because these situations provide richer information about how other people think or feel.

Who is right in this debate? How far can electronic communication substitute for face-to-face interaction? There is little question that new media forms are revolutionizing the way people communicate but even when it is more expedient to interact indirectly, humans still value direct contact—possibly even more highly than before. People in business, for instance, continue to attend meetings, sometimes flying halfway around the world to do so, when it would seem much simpler and more effective to transact business through a conference call or video link. Family members could arrange virtual reunions or holiday gatherings using electronic real-time communications, but we all recognize that they would lack the warmth and intimacy of face-to-face celebrations.

An explanation for this phenomenon comes from Deidre Boden and Harvey Molotch (1994), who have studied what they call the **compulsion of proximity**: the need of individuals to meet with one another in situations of *copresence*, or face-to-face interaction. People put themselves out to attend meetings, Boden and Molotch suggest, because situations of copresence, for reasons documented by Goffman in his studies of interaction, supply much richer information about how other people think and feel and about their sincerity than any form of electronic communication. Only by actually being in the presence of people who make decisions affecting us in important ways do we feel able to learn what is going on and confident that we can impress them with our own views and our own sincerity. "Copresence," Boden and Molotch (1994) say, "affects access to the body part that 'never lies,' the eyes—the 'windows on the soul.' Eye contact itself signals a degree of intimacy and trust; copresent interactants continuously monitor the subtle movements of this most subtle body part."

The Social Construction of Reality: The Sociological Debate

Within sociology, multiple theoretical frameworks are used to explain social reality. These theories differ in their explanations of social phenomena, yet they share the assumption that social reality exists independently of people's talking about it or living in it.

Not all sociologists share this assumption. The theoretical approach called **social constructionism** believes that what individuals and society perceive and understand as reality is itself a creation of the social interaction of individuals and groups. Trying to explain social reality, then, would be to overlook and to reify (regard as a given truth) the processes through which such reality is constructed. Therefore, social constructionists argue that sociologists need to document and analyze these processes and not simply the concept of social reality they give rise to.

In their 1966 classic, *The Social Construction of Reality*, the sociologists Peter Berger and Thomas Luckmann examine commonsense knowledge—those things that individuals take for granted as real. They emphasize that these "obvious" facts of social reality may differ among people from different cultures and even among different people within the same culture. The task becomes an analysis of the *processes* by which individuals come to perceive what is "real" to them as real (Berger and Luckmann 1966).

Social constructionists apply the ideas of Berger and Luckmann to the investigation of social phenomena to illuminate the ways in which members of society come to know and simultaneously create what is real. While social constructionists have examined such diverse topics as medicine and medical treatment, gender relations, and emotions, much of their work has focused on social problems, crime, and delinquency.

The work of Aaron Cicourel (1968) provides an example of social constructionist research in the area of juvenile delinquency. Within most of sociology, data regarding rates and cases of juvenile delinquency are taken as given (that is, real), and theories are created to explain the patterns observed in the data. For example, arrest and court data indicate that juveniles from single-parent families are more likely to commit delinquent acts than are juveniles from two-parent homes, thus sociologists develop explanations for this observed relationship: Perhaps children from single-parent homes have less supervision, or perhaps they lack appropriate role models.

By contrast, Cicourel observed the *processes* involved in the arrest and classification of juveniles suspected of delinquency—that is, he observed the creation of the "official" delinquency data. He discovered that police procedures in the handling of juveniles rely on commonsense understandings of what juvenile delinquents are really like.

"A Message from Bill Cosby"

Elijah Anderson, a professor at the University of Pennsylvania, has spent two decades studying inner-city Philadelphia and his insightful and provocative representations of ghetto life have extended far into the public realm. Anderson uses an ethnographic approach in his work, which means that he writes about the black community from firsthand experience. His findings are based on participant observation, interviewing, and socializing with residents of low-income communities. Through his work, he has developed as deep an understanding of these neighborhoods as any sociologist working today.

While vacationing with his family a few years ago, Anderson received a phone call from comedian Bill Cosby, who asked the professor if they could meet at a church in Newark, New Jersey, where Cosby had been invited to speak at a town hall meeting. Cosby had recently ignited an intense public debate by claiming that poor African Americans needed to take responsibility for their own problems. Blaming the problems of blacks on the street culture of the ghetto, Cosby implored African Americans to "hold up their end of the deal" (CNN 2004b). Many Americans believed that Cosby had hit the nail on the head, but Anderson, who had written a great deal about ghetto culture in the 1990s, held a different view.

Ever since the beginning of research on the American ghetto, scholars have observed that residents' basic values are the source of significant conflicts in ghetto neighborhoods. Such conflicts arise because people from many economic classes have been forced to live together due to racial discrimination. As a result, people who would not normally choose to be neighbors are thrown together in the same neighborhoods.

Elijah Anderson

Anderson has worked in the tradition of trying to understand these conflicts over basic values, and has noted that poor black communities are often divided between people who define themselves as "decent" and people who define themselves as "street."

Anderson's reference to "street" people and "decent" people is an attempt to show how the residents of these communities view themselves. This is very different from labeling some groups as "street" and others as "decent" and adopting those categories himself. The labels and categories are not his own, yet some people who read his work believe that Anderson himself supports the "decent" people. This may be the way Cosby had interpreted Anderson's work when he invited him to the church. Anderson knew that his subtle analysis of these prob-

For example, when juveniles from lower-class families were arrested, police were more likely to view their offenses as results of poor supervision or a lack of proper role models and would retain the juveniles in custody. Juveniles from upper-class homes, however, were more likely to be released to their parents' care, where police and parents believed the juvenile could receive proper discipline. Thus the practices of police

serve to formally assign the label of *juvenile delinquent* more often to youngsters from lower-class homes than to those from upper-class homes—even when the youths committed similar offenses. This assignment produces the very data which in turn confirm the relationships held by the commonsense views—for example, that juveniles from poor families are more likely to engage in delinquency. Cicourel's (1968) study shows that lems could become a basis for blaming the "street" for its own conditions, but rather than back away from a potentially difficult situation, he decided to embrace the opportunity to engage in a dialogue and accepted Cosby's invitation.

A recent spike in gang violence in Newark had resulted in the death of a local teenager, and caused both outrage and concern in the community. The mayor's office had responded by planning the town hall meeting at which Cosby would speak in addition to a panel of prominent local ministers, educators, physicians, political leaders, and Anderson.

Part of Anderson's work has focused on the ways that tense social interactions—the type that can quickly lead to violence—are the result of a complicated set of rules that govern how people on the street should act and react to one another. Anderson's *Code of the Street* (1999), explains that the issue of respect is critical for young people growing up in tough environments. "Hard won but easily lost," respect forms the foundation for the code of the street and must be constantly guarded. Anderson finds that gang members in particular are sensitive to advances and slights, which often serve as warnings of an impending confrontation. In places where the police provide only a limited form of personal protection, the code of the street dictates the rules for developing a reputation that can maintains an individual's personal safety. Small variations in hand gestures, eye contact, and conversational tone can make the difference between a handshake and a homicide. Even for kids growing up in so-called "decent" families, the code of the street must be learned to avoid conflict. What may appear as aggressive behavior to an outsider may actually be a set of facial, physical, and verbal expressions geared toward *avoiding* conflict. "To grow up in the streets you have to learn how to walk, how to talk, [and] how to deal with threats," Anderson says. Many people in the audience at the town meeting understood this from experience.

Sitting in the choir section of New Hope Baptist Church that night were members of the Crips and the Bloods, two Newark gangs that had recently come together to broker a cease-fire. The gang members listened with their heads down as the speakers, including Bill Cosby, told them they "should be ashamed" of themselves, and that instead of pulling the trigger, they should "get back in school" and try to live moral lives. Many people, including the majority of those in attendance that evening, believe that Cosby's earlier remarks were correct, that individuals need to make better choices and should be blamed for their actions when things go wrong. But Anderson believes it is also important to consider the conditions under which people make their choices. For those who grow up according to the code of the street, violating that code may actually be a dangerous move. For these kids, as with all kids, "choices" involve a balancing act between what we make of ourselves and what society makes of us.

When Anderson rose to speak that night, he recalled his working-class background and the feeling of stability that came along with his father's job at the Studebaker plant in South Bend, Ind., during the 1950s, '60s, and '70s. Starting about thirty years ago, however, such jobs began to disappear from inner-city neighborhoods as the economy changed. Employment became harder to find as industries left cities like Pittsburgh, Chicago, Cleveland, New York, Philadelphia, and Newark. Stable, well-paying jobs are scarce now, even for kids from "decent" families who have not succumbed to the temptations of street life. Middle-class families with the means to escape have moved out of these cities, leaving behind an isolated group of jobless and troubled residents. Increases in gang violence were directly associated with these changes.

Anderson believes that rather than casting blame, we need to "encourage young people to develop a positive sense of the future," since so much of the violence is really "a reflection of not feeling secure, [of] having short fuses and little patience." In his speech that night, Anderson took pains to explain that although conditions like job loss and family disruption do not excuse criminality, including drug dealing and violence, they may help us better understand why members of the Bloods and Crips may have joined gangs in the first place: to preserve a sense of community in the midst of communities that were falling apart.

through interacting with other people in society, we transform our commonsense notions of reality into independent, "objective" proof of their own validity.

Social constructionism is not without its critics. The sociologists Steve Woolgar and Dorothy Pawluch argue that social constructionists aim to show the subjective creation of social reality, yet in doing so selectively view certain features as objective and others as constructed. For example, in analyses examining which juveniles become labeled as delinquent, social constructionists often argue that the initial behaviors reported for the juveniles are identical; therefore, any differences between those juveniles labeled delinquent and those avoiding such a label must be due to the construction of the label *delinquent*. Critics argue that social constructionism

Immediate assumptions based on race, gender, economic status, and style of dress, among other signs and behavioral cues, affect the way strangers behave toward each other. Elijah Anderson's study of social interaction between strangers on urban streets showed a strong connection between such micro-level interactions and the creation of social order.

inconsistently presents the initial behaviors as objective, while arguing that the labeling process is subjective (Woolgar and Pawluch 1985).

Other sociologists have criticized social constructionism for its unwillingness to accept broader social forces as powerful influences on observable social outcomes. For example, some critics have argued that, although reality may be a constructed perpetuation of commonsense beliefs these beliefs themselves may be caused by existing social factors such as capitalism or patriarchy.

Ultimately, social constructionism offers a theoretical approach to understanding social reality that radically differs from most other sociological approaches. Rather than assuming that social reality objectively exists, social constructionists work to document and analyze the processes through which social reality is constructed, such that the construction then serves to confirm its own status as social reality.

Linking Microsociology and Macrosociology

As we saw in Chapter 1, *microsociology*, the study of everyday behavior in situations of face-to-face interaction, and *macro-*

sociology, the study of the broader features of society like class or gender hierarchies, are closely connected. We now examine social encounters on a crowded city sidewalk to illustrate this point.

Women and Men in Public

Take, for example, a situation that may seem micro on its face: A woman walking down the street is verbally harassed by a group of men. In a study published as *Passing By: Gender and Public Harassment*, Carol Brooks Gardner (1995) found that in various settings, most famously, the edges of construction sites, these types of unwanted interaction occur as something women frequently experience as abusive.

Although the harassment of a single woman might be analyzed in microsociological terms by looking at a single interaction, it is not fruitful to view it that simply. Such harassment is typical of street talk involving men and women who are strangers (Gardner 1995). And these kinds of interactions cannot be understood without also looking at the larger background of gender hierarchy in the United States. In this way we can see how microanalysis and macroanalysis are connected. For example, Gardner linked the harassment of women by men to the larger system of gender inequality, represented by male privilege in public spaces, women's physical vulnerability, and the omnipresent threat of rape.

Without making this link between microsociology and macrosociology, we can have only a limited understanding of these interactions. It might seem as though these types of interactions were isolated instances or that they could be eliminated by teaching people good manners. Understanding the link between micro and macro helps us see that to attack the problem at its root cause, one would need to focus on eliminating the forms of gender inequality that give rise to such interactions.

Blacks and Whites in Public

Have you ever crossed to the other side of the street when you felt threatened by someone behind you or someone coming toward you? One sociologist who tried to understand simple interactions of this kind is Elijah Anderson.

Anderson began by describing social interaction on the streets of two adjacent urban neighborhoods. In his book *Streetwise: Race, Class, and Change in an Urban Community* (1990), Anderson notes found that studying everyday life sheds light on how social order is created by the individual building blocks of infinite micro-level interactions. He was particularly interested in understanding interactions when at least one party was viewed as threatening. Anderson showed that the ways many blacks and whites interact on the streets of a northern city had a great deal to do with the structure of racial stereotypes, which is itself linked to the economic structure of society. In this way, he showed the link between micro interactions and the larger macro structures of society.

Anderson began by recalling Erving Goffman's description of how social roles and statuses come into existence in particular contexts or locations: "When an individual enters the presence of others, they commonly seek to acquire information about him or bring into play information already possessed. . . . Information about the individual helps to define the situation, enabling others to know in advance what he will expect of them and they may expect of him" (Anderson 1990).

Following Goffman's lead, Anderson asked, what types of behavioral cues and signs make up the vocabulary of public interaction? He concluded that

> skin color, gender, age, companions, clothing, jewelry, and the objects people carry help identify them, so that assumptions are formed and communication can occur. Movements (quick or slow, false or sincere, comprehensible or incomprehensible) further refine this public communication. Factors like time of day or an activity that "explains" a person's presence can also affect in what

way and how quickly the image of "stranger" is neutralized. If a stranger cannot pass inspection and be assessed as "safe," the image of predator may arise, and fellow pedestrians may try to maintain a distance consistent with that image. (Anderson 1990)

Anderson showed that the people most likely to pass inspection are those who do not fall into commonly accepted stereotypes of dangerous persons: "children readily pass inspection, while women and white men do so more slowly, black women, black men, and black male teenagers most slowly of all." In showing that interactional tensions derive from outside statuses such as race, class, and gender, Anderson shows that we cannot develop a full understanding of the situation by looking at the micro interactions themselves. This is how he makes the link between micro interactions and macro processes.

Anderson argues that people are streetwise when they develop skills such as "the art of avoidance" to deal with their felt vulnerability toward violence and crime. According to Anderson, whites who are not streetwise do not recognize the difference between different kinds of black men (e.g., middle-class youths vs. gang members). They may also not know how to alter the number of paces to walk behind a suspicious person or how to bypass bad blocks at various times of day.

Study Outline

www.wwnorton.com/giddens

Social Interaction

- Many apparently trivial aspects of our day-to-day behavior turn out on close examination to be both complex and important aspects of *social interaction*. An example is the gaze—looking at other people. In most interactions, eye contact is fairly fleeting. To stare at another person could be taken as a sign of hostility—or on some occasions, of love. The study of social interaction is a fundamental area in sociology, illuminating many aspects of social life.

Nonverbal Communication

- Many different expressions are conveyed by the human face. It is widely held that basic aspects of the facial expressions of emotion are innate. Cross-cultural studies demonstrate quite close similarities among members of different cultures both in facial expression and in the interpretation of emotions registered on the human face.

Ethnomethodology

- The study of ordinary talk and conversation has come to be called *ethnomethodology*, a term first coined by Harold Garfinkel. Ethnomethodology is the analysis of the ways in which we actively—although usually in a taken-for-granted way—make sense of what others mean by what they say and do.

Face, Body, and Speech in Interaction

- *Unfocused interaction* is the mutual awareness individuals have of one another in large gatherings when not directly in conversation together. *Focused interaction*, which can be divided up into distinct *encounters*, or episodes of interaction, is when two or more individuals are directly attending to what the other or others are saying and doing.
- Social interaction can often be illuminatingly studied by applying the dramaturgical model—studying social interaction as if those involved were actors on a stage, having a set and props. As in the theater, in the various contexts of social life there tend to be clear distinctions between *front regions* (the stage itself) and *back regions*,

where the actors prepare themselves for the performance and relax afterward.

Interaction in Time and Space

- All social interaction is situated in time and space. We can analyze how our daily lives are "zoned" in both time and space combined by looking at how activities occur during definite durations and at the same time involve spatial movement.
- Some mechanisms of social interaction may be universal, but many are not. The !Kung of southern Africa, for example, live in small mobile bands, in which there is little privacy and thus little opportunity to create front and back regions.

Indirect Interaction

- Modern societies are characterized largely by indirect interpersonal transactions (such as making bank deposits), which lack any copresence. This leads to what has been called the *compulsion of proximity*, the tendency to want to meet in person whenever possible, perhaps because this makes it easier to gather information about how others think and feel, and to accomplish *impression management*.

Key Concepts

achieved status (p. 125)
ascribed status (p. 125)
back regions (p. 125)
civil inattention (p. 115)
clock time (p. 127)
compulsion of proximity (p. 131)
conversation analysis (p. 122)
encounter (p. 124)
ethnomethodology (p. 119)
focused interaction (p. 124)
front regions (p. 125)
impression management (p. 124)
interactional vandalism (p. 123)
master status (p. 125)
nonverbal communication (p. 117)
personal space (p. 126)
regionalization (p. 127)
response cries (p. 123)
roles (p. 124)
social constructionism (p. 131)
social interaction (p. 116)
social position (p. 124)
status (p. 124)
status set (p. 125)
time–space (p. 127)
unfocused interaction (p. 124)

Review Questions

1. What is the difference between achieved status and ascribed status?
   a. There is no difference between achieved and ascribed status.
   b. Achieved status is a social standing that others accord to us on the basis of attributes we can change, whereas ascribed status is a social standing others accord to us on the basis of attributes we cannot change.
   c. Achieved status has to do with gender and ethnicity, whereas ascribed status has to do with social class.
   d. Achieved status is equivalent to economic status, whereas ascribed status is equivalent to cultural and political status.

2. What is the study of nonverbal communication?
   a. The study of the way people use tone of voice and pronunciation to convey the exact meaning of their words.
   b. The study of the use of dress, makeup, and jewelry to convey personal identity.
   c. The study of facial expressions, gestures, and body movements.
   d. The study of human interaction with such regular features of everyday life as pets and computers, which can communicate, but not verbally.

3. Ethnomethodology studies
   a. conversations in a café.
   b. casual greetings.
   c. response cries.
   d. all of the above.

4. Human beings have a "compulsion to proximity," or the need to
   a. use whatever electronic means are available to communicate.
   b. meet up with one another in situations of copresence.
   c. experience sexual intimacy.
   d. perceive themselves as discrete social units.

5. Which of the following is an example of impression management?
   a. A professor relaxes in the office after teaching.
   b. A physician listens to a patient before prescribing medicine.
   c. A candidate dresses appropriately for a job interview.
   d. A mother shops at a local grocery store.

6. If a waiter says, "Enjoy your meal" and you reply, "Enjoy in what sense, exactly?" then you have used one of
   a. Ekman's experiments in facial muscle analysis.
   b. Garfinkel's experiments in ethnomethodology.
   c. Goffman's experiments in conversational analysis.
   d. Goffman's experiments in social interactions.

7. According to Erving Goffman, if individuals at a large party exhibit mutual awareness of one another's presence, it is called
   a. mutual attraction.
   b. focused interaction.
   c. unfocused interaction.
   d. an encounter.

8. Men may feel more freedom than women in making eye contact with strangers in societies in which

a. women dominate men in both public and private life.

b. men dominate women in both public and private life.

c. women have the same status as men in both public and private life.

d. there are more men than women.

9. In a study by Ekman and Friesen, when members of an isolated New Guinea community were shown pictures of facial expressions conveying six emotions, they were able to identify

a. none of the six emotions.

b. all of the six emotions.

c. only half of the six emotions.

d. one emotion, happiness.

10. Which of the following concepts lies at the heart of the symbolic interactionist perspective?

a. inequality

b. division of labor

c. social construction of reality

d. social mobility and social stratification

Thinking Sociologically Exercises

1. Identify the important elements to the dramaturgical perspective. This chapter shows how the theory might be applied in the ministrations of the nurse to his or her patient.

Apply the theory similarly to account for a plumber's visit to a client's home. Are there any similarities? Explain.

2. Smoking cigarettes is a pervasive habit found in many parts of the world and a habit that could be explained by both microsociological and macrosociological forces. Give an example of each that would be relevant to explain the proliferation of smoking. How might your suggested micro- and macro-level analyses be linked?

Data Exercises

www.wwnorton.com/giddens
Keyword: Data5

This chapter highlights the structures and processes of everyday social interactions that have a significant influence on us, but are often overlooked. It is particularly difficult to accept the idea that social factors like class, race, and gender may affect our interactions with and perceptions of the world. The data exercise for this chapter focuses on how race shapes our understanding of reality.

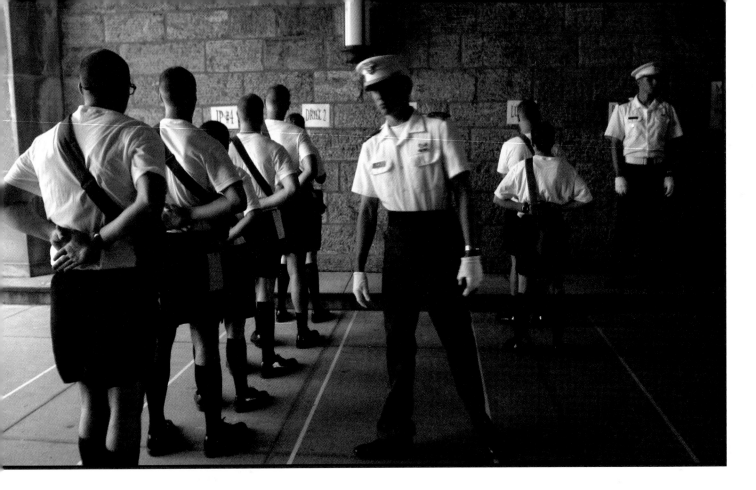

Social Groups

Learn the variety and characteristics of groups as well as the affect groups have on an individual's behavior.

Networks

Understand the importance of social networks and the advantages they confer on some people.

Organizations

Know how to define an organization and understand how organizations developed over the last two centuries.

Theories of Organizations

Learn Max Weber's theory of organizations and view of bureaucracy. Understand the importance of the physical setting of organizations and Michel Foucault's theory about surveillance.

Beyond Bureaucracy?

Familiarize yourself with some of the alternatives to bureaucracy that have developed in other societies or in recent times. Think about the influence of technology on how organizations operate.

Organizations That Span the World

See how organizations have become truly global in scale.

How Do Groups and Organizations Affect Your Life?

Learn how social capital enables people to accomplish their goals and expand their influence.

CHAPTER SIX

GROUPS, NETWORKS, AND ORGANIZATIONS

t he U.S. Military Academy—West Point—is very hard to get into. More than fifty thousand high school students open files at the academy, of which perhaps twelve thousand are sufficiently qualified to actually apply. Another four thousand are nominated by a congressional representative, a senator, or the White House. Yet among all of these, barely two thousand pass the physical fitness test, and only twelve hundred are finally admitted. Many of these are top students: Their "median grade point average is 3.5; 14 percent are Eagle Scouts, 20 percent are class presidents, 60 percent are varsity team captains" (Lipsky 2003a).

From "Reception Day" (R-Day), students' first day at West Point, the academy emphasizes conformiity to group norms. The first-year plebes, as they are called, say good-bye to their civilian life, giving up all aspects of their former identity to the army.

At R-Day you surrender your old self in stages. You've already left behind family and control over your environment. In the fluorescent Thayer hallways, you hand over your belongings, then file to the treasurers' office to give up your cash; any sum greater than forty dollars gets banked. . . . "No talking," cadre announce. "Do not move, do not smile. Hands will remain cupped at all times. You need to look at anything, look at my wall." Unless you had an unlucky home life, this is the first time anybody has spoken to you this way. The candidates are just blank eyes now, mouths so tight the lips appear to be hiding. . . . Now the army demands your clothing. In their dressing room, male candidates tuck on black gym shorts and white T-shirts with a speed that suggests graded events. "You *must* put on a jockstrap," a TAC-NCO commands. "Let's go—move with a purpose." . . . Then the academy takes custody of your actual skin. "If you have," the sergeant booms, "any tattoo, brand, or body piercing, regardless of whether it is visible while wearing a uniform, you must declare it at this time to the registration desk at my rear. . . ." Then the army takes your hair. . . . Every few minutes the guy working the push broom sweeps away what looks like a whole discarded wig. The barbers place bets on R-Day's yield. . . . Now you're shorn of everything. You look, act, dress like everyone beside you, maybe for the first time in your life. In five hours, West Point has reduced you to just the meat your parents made, topped by its frenetic, calculating brain. . . . The cadre introduces [you] to the basics of body language: how to stand, how to listen, how to respond with the grammar of obedience. (Lipsky 2003a)

David Lipsky, a writer for *Rolling Stone,* specialized in stories about youth culture—young people in colleges and universities, the media, TV actors, and movie stars. Then he was asked to write an article on the West Point class of 2002. Lipsky had been raised in a liberal family and held a dim view of the military profession. Although he initially was resistant to take the assignment, once the academy gave him unrestricted access to the cadets, he wound up staying the full four years. He wanted "to find out what kind of men and women would subject themselves to the intense discipline of West Point" (Lipsky 2003).

What he discovered was "a place where everyone tried their hardest. A place where everybody—or at least most people—looked out for each other. . . . Of all the young people I'd met, the West Point cadets—although they are grand, epic complainers—were the happiest" (Lipsky 2003a). Part of the reason, Lipsky concluded, was the military value system, one that emphasized self-sacrifice, discipline, honor, respect, and loyalty: "One of the efficient by-products of plebe-year stress is what's called *unit cohesion,* the bonds that cadets form. In battle, what often drives soldiers isn't simply courage but a complicated version of crisis loyalty, the desire not to let down their friends."

West Point cohesion is so strong that cadets seldom betray one another, even when they know that rules are being broken. According to one officer interviewed by Lipsky (2003a), "You see, for *honor* violations, your loyalty is to the organization . . . but for *regs* violations [such as drug use]—are you gonna turn your brother in? You're supposed to stick together and help each other out, not screw each other over."

Military discipline depends on such values as group loyalty and conformity. After all, some day a soldier's life may depend on such values. And the strict training regimen of military academies such as West Point is designed to foster these values—to create uniform ways of thinking and acting among young people raised in a culture that presumably emphasizes the very opposite. "We are a culture that stresses individually pleasing yourself. What surprised me, getting to know the officers and getting to know the cadets who love the army, is that often the best way to please yourself individually is to live that other way. We're group animals. There's a part of us that really responds to meeting challenges together" (Lipsky 2003b).

In this chapter we examine the ways in which all of us—not just cadets at West Point—are group animals. We all conform, at least to some degree, to groups. From small groups of friends to large organizations such as colleges and universities, we are all subject to the constraints and demands of group life. Indeed, through groups, we enjoy human culture; and to different degrees according to our backgrounds, we also benefit from freedoms and opportunities to pursue our chosen goals in life.

In this chapter you learn about different kinds of groups and their role in shaping your experiences. For example, you learn how group size affects your behavior in groups and about the nature of leadership. Special attention is given to sociological research into individual conformity to group norms, helping you understand how an institution such as West Point can produce highly disciplined officers who place the highest value on group loyalty out of a cross section of American teenagers. We will also examine the role played by organizations in American society, the major theories of modern organizations, and the ways in which organizations are changing in the modern world. The increased effect of technology on organizations and the prominence of the Internet in our group life is also explored. The chapter concludes with a consideration of the rising role of global organizations in the world today.

Social Groups

Nearly everything of importance in our lives occurs through some type of social group. You and your roommate make up a social group, as do the members of your introductory sociology class. A **social group** is a collection of people who share a common identity and regularly interact with one another on the basis of shared expectations concerning behavior. People who belong to the same social group identify with each other, expect each other to conform to certain ways of thinking and acting, and recognize the boundaries that separate them from other groups or people. In our need to congregate and belong, we have created a rich and varied group life that gives us our norms, practices, and values—our whole way of life.

Groups: Variety and Characteristics

We may sometimes feel as if we are alone, yet we seldom find ourselves far away from one kind of group or another. Every day nearly all of us move through various social situations, such as one involving an intimate two-person group or one within a large bureaucratic organization. We hang out with groups of friends, study with classmates, play team sports, and go online to find new friends or people who share our interests. Like people nearly everywhere, we are organizational addicts (Aldrich and Marsden 1988).

However, just because people find themselves in each other's company does not make them a social group. People milling around in crowds, waiting for a bus, or strolling on a beach are said to make up a social aggregate. A **social aggregate** is a simple collection of people who happen to be together in a particular place but do not significantly interact or identify with each other. The people waiting together at a bus station, for example, may be conscious of one another's presence, but they are unlikely to think of themselves as a "we"—the group waiting for the next bus to Poughkeepsie or Des Moines. By the same token, people may make up a **social category,** people sharing a common characteristic (such as gender or occupation) without necessarily interacting or identifying with one another. The sense of belonging to a common social group is missing.

IN-GROUPS AND OUT-GROUPS

The "sense of belonging" that characterizes social groups is sometimes strengthened by groups' scorning the members of other groups (Sartre 1965, orig. 1948). Creating a sense of belonging in this way is especially true of racist groups, which promote their identity as superior by hating "inferior" groups. Jews, Catholics, African Americans and other people of color, immigrants, and gay people are typically the targets of such hatred. This sense of group identity created through scorn is dramatically illustrated by the rantings on the former Web page of a racist skinhead group that called itself Combat 18 (1998): "We are the last of our warrior race, and it is our duty to fight for our people. The Jew will do everything to discredit us, but we hold that burning flame in our hearts that drove our ancestors to conquer whole continents."

Such proud, disdainful language illustrates the sociological distinction between in-groups and out-groups. **In-groups** are groups toward which one feels particular loyalty and respect— the groups that "we" belong to. **Out-groups,** on the other hand, are groups toward which one feels antagonism and contempt— "*those* people." Most people occasionally use in-group–out-group imagery to trumpet what they believe to be their group's strengths vis-à-vis some other group's presumed weaknesses. For example, members of a fraternity or a sorority may bolster their feelings of superiority—in academics, sports, or campus image—by ridiculing the members of a different house. Similarly, an ethnic group may prefer its sons and daughters to marry only within the group, a church often holds up its truths as the only ones, and immigrants—always outsiders upon arriving in a new country—are sometimes accused of ruining the country for "real" Americans.

PRIMARY AND SECONDARY GROUPS

Group life differs greatly in how intensely group members experience it. Beginning with the family—the first group to which most of us belong—many of the groups that shape our personalities and lives are those in which we experience strong emotional ties. This experience is common not only for families but also for groups of friends, including gangs and other peer groups, all of which are known as primary groups. **Primary groups** are usually small groups characterized by face-to-face interaction, intimacy, and a strong, enduring sense of commitment. In this type of group, there is also often an experience of unity, a merging of the self with the group into one personal "we." Individuals in these groups are also more likely to enjoy relationships for their own sake. Friends may ask you to take advantage of their offer of good theater seats or help writing a paper, but they will be hurt if they feel that that is all you want from them. The sociologist Charles Horton Cooley (1864–1929) termed such groups "primary" because he believed that they were the basic form of association, exerting a long-lasting influence on the development of our social selves (Cooley 1964; orig. 1902).

In contrast, **secondary groups** are large and impersonal and often involve fleeting relationships. Secondary groups seldom involve intense emotional ties, powerful commitments to the group itself, or an experience of unity. We rarely feel we can be ourselves in a secondary group; rather, we are often playing a particular role, such as employee or student. Cooley argued that people belong to primary groups mainly because such groups are inherently fulfilling, but people join secondary groups to achieve some specific goal: to earn a living, get a college degree, or compete in sports. Examples of secondary groups include business organizations, schools, work groups, athletic clubs, and governmental bodies. Secondary groups may of course become primary groups for some of their members. For example, when students taking a course begin to socialize after class, they create bonds of friendship that constitute a primary group.

For most of human history, nearly all interactions took place within primary groups. This pattern began to change with the emergence of larger, agrarian societies, which included such secondary groups as those based on governmental roles or occupation. Today most of our waking hours are spent within secondary groups, although primary groups remain a basic part of our lives.

Some early sociologists, such as Cooley, worried about a loss of intimacy as more and more interactions revolved around large impersonal organizations. However, what Cooley saw as the growing impersonality and anonymity of modern life may also offer an increasing tolerance of individual differences. Primary groups, which often enforce strict conformity to group standards (Durkheim 1964, orig. 1893; Simmel 1955), can be suffocating. Impersonal secondary groups are more likely than primary groups to be concerned with accomplishing a task rather than with enforcing conformity to group standards of behavior.

Advertising creates a set of imaginary reference groups meant to influence consumers' buying habits by presenting unlikely—often impossible—ideals to which consumers aspire.

REFERENCE GROUPS

We often judge ourselves by how we think we appear to others, which Cooley termed the "looking-glass self." Groups as well as individuals provide the standards by which we make self-evaluations. Robert K. Merton (1968, orig. 1938) elaborated on Cooley's concept by discussing reference groups as measures by which we evaluate ourselves. A **reference group** is a group that provides a standard for judging one's own attitudes or behaviors (see also Hyman and Singer 1968). The family is typically one of the more crucial reference groups in our lives, as are peer groups and co-workers. All these groups provide points of reference for standards or comparisons. However, you do not have to belong to a group for it to be your reference group. For example, regardless of his or her station in life, a person may identify with the wealth and power of *Fortune* 500 corporate executives, admire the contribution of Nobel Prize–winning scientists, or be captivated by the glitter of the lives of Hollywood stars. Although most of us seldom interact socially with such reference groups as these, we may take pride in identifying with them, glorify their accomplishments, and even imitate the ways of those people who do belong to them. This is why it is critical for children—minority children in particular, whose groups are often represented stereotypically in the media—to be exposed to reference groups that will shape their lives for the better.

The group to which you compare yourself may not necessarily make you feel better about yourself. An early major study of reference groups (Stouffer et al. 1949; see also Merton and Rossi 1968; orig. 1949) found that morale among American soldiers was not affected so much by the harshness of their experiences as by how they fared in comparison with other groups of soldiers. If soldiers felt they were relatively deprived in comparison with other soldiers, their morale would suffer, even if their actual living circumstances were not so bad.

Reference groups may be primary, such as the family, or secondary, such as a group of soldiers. They may even be fictional. One of the chief functions of advertising, for example, is to create a set of imaginary reference groups that will influence consumers' buying habits. For example, when lean female models with flawless complexions are shown in ads for cosmetics, the message to women is simple: "If you want to look as though you were part of an in-group of highly attractive, eternally youthful women, buy this product." In reality, of course, the models used in the ads seldom have the unblemished features depicted; instead, the ideal features are constructed through artful lighting, photographic techniques, and computer enhancement. Similarly, the happy-go-lucky, physically perfect young men and women seen sailing or playing volleyball or hang gliding in beer commercials have little to do with the reality of most of our lives—or, indeed, with the actual lives of the actors in those commercials. The message, however, is otherwise: "Drink this beer, and you will be viewed by others as a member of the carefree in-group depicted in this ad."

The Effects of Size

Another significant way in which groups differ has to do with their size. Sociological interest in group size can be traced to the German sociologist Georg Simmel (1858–1918), who studied and theorized about the effect of small groups on people's behavior. Since Simmel's time, small-group researchers have conducted a number of laboratory experiments to examine the effects of size on both the quality of interaction in the group and the effectiveness of the group in accomplishing certain tasks (Bales 1953, 1970; Hare et al. 1965; Homans 1950; Mills 1967).

DYADS

The simplest group, which Simmel (1955) called a **dyad,** consists of two people. Simmel reasoned that dyads, which involve both intimacy and conflict, are likely to be simultaneously intense and unstable. To survive, they require the full attention and cooperation of both parties. If one person withdraws from the dyad, it vanishes. Dyads are typically the source of our most elementary social bonds, often constituting the group in which we are most likely to share our deepest secrets. But dyads can be very fragile. That is why, Simmel believed, a variety of cultural and legal supports for marriage are found in societies in which marriage is regarded as an important source of social stability.

TRIADS

Adding a third person changes the group relationship. Simmel used the term **triad** to describe a group consisting of three people. Triads are apt to be more stable than dyads because the presence of a third person relieves some of the pressure on the other two members to always get along and energize the relationship. In a triad, one person can temporarily withdraw attention from the relationship without necessarily threatening it. In addition, if two of the members have a disagreement, the third can play the role of mediator, as when you try to patch up a falling-out between two of your friends.

On the other hand, however, alliances (sometimes termed coalitions) may form between two members of a triad, enabling them to gang up on the third and thereby destabilize the group. Alliances are most likely to form when no one member is clearly dominant and when all three members are competing for the same thing—for example, when three friends are given a pair of tickets to a concert and have to decide which two will get to go. The hit TV series *Survivor* provides many examples of alliance formation, as the program's characters forge special relationships with each other to avoid being eliminated in the weekly group vote.

In forming an alliance, a member is most likely to choose the weaker of the two other members as a partner, if there is one. In what has been termed *revolutionary coalitions,* the two weaker members form an alliance to overthrow the stronger one (Caplow 1956, 1959, 1969).

LARGER GROUPS

Going from a dyad to a triad illustrates an important sociological principle first identified by Simmel: As groups increase in size, their intensity decreases and their stability increases. There are, of course, exceptions to this principle, but in many cases, it is likely to apply. Increasing the size of a

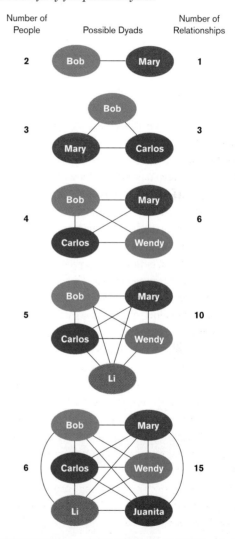

FIGURE 6.1

Dyads

The larger the number of people, the greater the possible number of relationships. Note that this figure illustrates only dyads; if triads and more complex coalitions were to be included, the numbers would be still greater (four people yield ten possibilities). Even a ten-person group can produce forty-five possible dyads!

Going from just three people to four increases the number of potential relationships by how many? Doubling the size of a group from three to six increases the number of potential relationships by how many? According to the reading, which types of groups are more stable, large or small? Why? Do large or small groups tend to be more exclusive? Why?

group tends to decrease its intensity of interaction, simply because a larger number of potential smaller group relationships exist as outlets for individuals who are not getting along with other members of the group. In a dyad, only a single relationship, that between two people, is possible; however, in a triad, three different two-person relationships can occur. Adding a fourth person leads to six possible combinations of two-person relationships, and this does not count the subgroups of more than two that could form. In a ten-person group, the number of possible two-person relationships explodes to forty-five! When one relationship doesn't work out to your liking, you can easily move on to another, as you probably often do at large parties.

At the same time, larger groups tend to be more stable than smaller ones because the withdrawal of some members does not threaten the group's survival. A marriage or love relationship falls apart if one person leaves, whereas an athletic team or drama club routinely survives—though it may sometimes temporarily suffer from—the loss of its graduating seniors.

Larger groups also tend to be more exclusive because it is easier for their members to limit their social relationships to the group itself and avoid relationships with nonmembers. This sense of being part of an in-group or clique is sometimes found in fraternities, sororities, and other campus organizations. Cliquishness is especially likely to occur when the group consists of members who are similar to each other in such social characteristics as age, gender, class, race, or ethnicity. People from rich families, for example, may be reluctant to fraternize with working-class groups, men may prefer to go to the basketball court with other men, and students who belong to a particular ethnic group (for example, African Americans, Latinos, or

Members of a large, exclusive group such as a fraternity or sorority develop a sense of being part of an in-group or clique. They may choose to limit their social relationships to the group itself.

Asian Americans) may seek out each other's company in the dormitory or cafeteria. Even so, groups do not always foster the restriction of relationships with outsiders. A group with a socially diverse membership is likely instead to foster a high degree of interaction with people outside the group (Blau 1977). For example, if your social group or club is made up of members from different social classes or ethnic groups, it is more likely that you will come to appreciate such social differences from firsthand experience and seek them out in other aspects of your life.

Beyond a certain size, perhaps a dozen people, groups tend to develop a formal structure. Formal leadership roles may arise, such as president or secretary, and official rules may be developed to govern what the group does. We discuss formal organizations later in this chapter.

Types of Leadership

A **leader** is a person who is able to influence the behavior of other members of a group. All groups tend to have leaders, even if the leader is not formally recognized as such. Some leaders are especially effective in motivating the members of their groups or organizations, inspiring them to achievements that might not ordinarily be accomplished. Such **transformational leaders** go beyond the merely routine, instilling in the members of their group a sense of mission or higher purpose and thereby changing the nature of the group itself (Burns 1978; Kanter 1983). These are the leaders who are seen as leaving their stamp on their organizations. They can also be a vital inspiration for social change in the world. For example, Nelson Mandela, the South African leader who spent twenty-seven years in prison after having been convicted of treason against the white-dominated South African society, nonetheless managed to build his African National Congress (ANC) political party into a multiracial force for change. Mandela's transformational leadership was so strong that, despite his long imprisonment, as soon as he was freed he assumed leadership of the ANC. After Mandela successfully led the ANC in overthrowing South Africa's system of apartheid, or racial segregation, he was elected president—leader—of the entire country.

Most leaders are not as visionary as Mandela, however. Leaders who simply get the job done are termed **transactional leaders.** These are leaders concerned with accomplishing the group's tasks, getting group members to do their jobs, and making certain that the group achieves its goals. Transactional leadership is routine leadership. For example, the teacher who simply gets through the lesson plan each day—rather than making the classroom a place where students explore new ways of thinking and behaving—is exercising transactional leadership.

Conformity

Not so long ago, the only part of the body that American teenage girls were likely to pierce was the ears—one hole per ear, enough to hold a single pair of earrings. For the vast majority of boys piercing was not an option at all. Today, earrings are common for many males—from teenage boys to male professional athletes, and a growing number of college students now proudly sport multiple earrings, navel rings, and even studs in their tongues. Pressures to conform to the latest styles are especially strong among teenagers and young adults, among whom the need for group acceptance is often acute.

While wearing navel rings or the latest style of jeans—or rigidly conforming to the military code of West Point—may seem relatively harmless, conformity to group pressure can lead to extremely destructive behavior, such as drug abuse or even murder. For this reason, sociologists and social psychologists have long sought to understand why most people tend to go along with others and under what circumstances they do not.

GOING ALONG WITH THE GROUP: ASCH'S RESEARCH

Some of the earliest studies of conformity to group pressures were conducted by psychologist Solomon Asch (1952) about fifty years ago. In one of his classic experiments, Asch asked individual subjects to decide which of three lines of different length most closely matched the length of a fourth line. The differences were obvious; subjects had no difficulty in making the correct match. Asch then arranged a version of the experiment in which the subjects were asked to make the matches in a group setting, with each person calling out the answer one at a time.

In this version of the experiment, all but one of the subjects were actually Asch's secret accomplices, and these accomplices all practiced a deception on that one subject. Each accomplice picked two lines that were clearly unequal in length as matches. The unwitting subject, one of the last to call out an answer, felt enormous group pressure to make the same error. Amazingly, one third of these subjects gave the same wrong answer as the others in the group at least half of the times the experiment was conducted. They sometimes stammered and fidgeted when doing so, but they nonetheless yielded to the unspoken pressure to conform to the group's decision. Asch's experiments clearly showed that many people

FIGURE 6.2

The Asch Task

In the Asch task, participants were shown a standard line (left) and then three comparison lines. Their task was simply to say which of the three lines matched the standard. When confederates gave false answers first, one third of participants conformed by giving the wrong answer.

What would cause someone to agree that the line on the left is actually the same length as line number 1? In the research, what portion of people were convinced by the group that two lines that were clearly different lengths were actually the same length? What can we conclude from Asch's experiment?

are willing to discount their own perceptions rather than buck a group consensus.

OBEDIENCE TO AUTHORITY: MILGRAM'S RESEARCH

Another classic study of conformity was Stanley Milgram's (1963) research. Milgram's work was intended to shed some light on what had happened in Nazi Germany during World War II. How could ordinary German citizens have gone along with—even participated in—the mass extermination of millions of Jews, Romanies (also known as Gypsies), homosexuals, intellectuals, and others who were judged to be inferior or undesirable by the Nazis?

Obedience is a kind of conformity. Milgram sought to find its limits, and his study produced a chilling answer. Milgram wanted to see how far a person would go when ordered by a scientist to give another person increasingly powerful electric shocks. He did so by setting up an experiment that he told the

(A) (B) (C)

(A) The Milgram experiment required participants to "shock" the confederate learner (seated). The research participant (left) helped apply the electrodes that would be used to shock the learner. (B) An obedient participant shocks the learner in the "touch" condition. More than half obeyed the experimenter in this condition. (C) After the experiment, all of the participants were introduced to the confederate learner so they could see he was not actually harmed.

subjects was about memorizing pairs of words. In reality, it was about obedience to authority.

The male subjects who volunteered for the study were supposedly randomly divided into "teachers" and "learners." In fact, the learners were actually Milgram's employees. The teacher was told to read pairs of words from a list that the learner was to memorize. Whenever the learner made a mistake, the teacher was to give him an electric shock by flipping a switch on a fake but official-looking machine. The control board on the machine indicated shock levels ranging from "15 volts—slight shock" to "450 volts—danger, severe shock." For each mistake, the voltage of the shock was to be increased, until it eventually reached the highest level. In reality, the learner, who was usually carefully concealed from the teacher by a screen, never received any electric shocks. Milgram's study would not be permitted today because its deception of subjects and potential for doing psychological harm would violate current university ethics standards.

As the experiment progressed, the learner began to scream out in pain for the teacher to stop delivering shocks. (His screams, increasingly louder as the voltage rose, had actually been prerecorded on a tape.) However, Milgram's assistant, who was administering the experiment, exercised his authority as a scientist and ordered the teacher to continue administering shocks if the teacher tried to quit. The assistant would say such things as, "the experiment requires that you continue," even when the learner could be heard protesting—even when he shrieked about his "bad heart."

The teacher was confronted with a major moral decision: Should he obey the scientist and go along with the experiment, even if it meant injuring another human being? Much to Milgram's surprise, over half the subjects in the study kept on administering electric shocks. They continued even until the maximum voltage was reached and the learner's screams had

subsided into an eerie silence as he presumably died of a heart attack. How could ordinary people so easily conform to orders that would turn them into possible accomplices to murder?

The answer, Milgram found, was deceptively simple. Although it is obvious that soldiers in military training, such as first-year plebes at West Point, will conform to orders given by someone in a position of power or authority, ordinary citizens will often do the same—even if those orders have horrible consequences. From this, we can learn something about Nazi atrocities during World War II, which were Milgram's original concern. Many ordinary Germans, who participated in the mass execution of Jews in Nazi concentration camps, did so on the grounds that they were just following orders. None of this is to say that Milgram's subjects were Nazis, yet his research has sobering implications for anyone who thinks that only "others" will always knuckle under to authority but "not me" (Zimbardo et al. 1977).

GROUPTHINK AND GROUP PRESSURES TO CONFORM: JANIS'S RESEARCH

Common sense tells us that "two minds are better than one." But sociological research has found that pressures to "go along with the crowd" sometime result in worse decisions, rather than creative new solutions to problems. You have probably had the experience of being in a group struggling with a difficult decision and feeling uneasy at voicing your opposition to an emerging consensus. Irving L. Janis (1972, 1989; Janis and Mann 1977) called this phenomenon **groupthink,** a process by which the members of a group ignore ways of thinking and plans of action that go against the group consensus. Not only does groupthink frequently embarrass potential dissenters into conforming but it can also produce a shift in perceptions so that alternative possibilities are ruled out without being seriously considered. Groupthink may facilitate reaching a quick consensus, but the consensus may also be ill chosen. It may even be downright stupid.

Janis engaged in historical research to see if groupthink had characterized U.S. foreign policy decisions. He examined several critical decisions, including that behind the infamous Bay of Pigs invasion of Cuba in 1961. John F. Kennedy, then the newly elected president, inherited a plan from the previous administration to help Cuban exiles liberate Cuba from the Communist government of Fidel Castro. The plan called for U.S. supplies and air cover to assist an invasion by an ill-prepared army of exiles at Cuba's Bay of Pigs. Although a number of Kennedy's top advisers were certain that the plan was fatally flawed, they refrained from bucking the emerging consensus to carry it out. As it happened, the invasion was a disaster. The army of exiles, after parachuting into a swamp nowhere near their intended drop zone, was immediately defeated, and Kennedy suffered a great deal of public embarrassment.

Kennedy's advisers were people of strong will and independent judgment who had been educated at elite universities. How could they have failed to adequately voice their concerns about the proposed invasion? Janis identified a number of possible reasons. For one, Kennedy's advisers were hesitant to disagree with the president lest they lose his favor. They also did not want to diminish group harmony in a crisis situation where teamwork was all-important. In addition, given the intense time pressure to act, they had little opportunity to consult outside experts who might have offered radically different perspectives. All these circumstances contributed to a single-minded pursuit of the president's initial ideas, rather than an effort to generate effective alternatives.

Although groupthink does not always shape decision making, it sometimes plays a major role. To avoid groupthink, the group must ensure the full and open expression of all opinions, even strong dissent.

Networks

"Who you know is often as important as what you know." This adage expresses the value of having "good connections." Sociologists refer to such connections as **networks**—all the direct and indirect connections that link a person or a group with other people or groups. Your personal networks thus include people you know directly (such as your friends) as well as people you know indirectly (such as your friends' friends). Personal networks often include people of similar race, class, ethnicity, and other types of social background, although there

are exceptions. For example, if you subscribe to an online mailing list, you are part of a network that consists of all the people on the list, who may be of different racial or ethnic backgrounds and genders. Because groups and organizations, such as sororities or religious groups, can also be networked—for example, all the chapters of Gamma Phi Beta or Hillel that the national organization comprises—belonging to such groups can greatly extend your reach and influence.

Social groups are an important source for acquiring networks; but not all networks are social groups. Many networks lack the shared expectations and common sense of identity that are the hallmark of social groups. For example, you are not likely to share a sense of identity with the subscribers to an online mailing list, nor will you probably even know the neighbors of most of your coworkers at the office, even though they would form part of your social network.

Networks serve us in many ways. Sociologist Mark Granovetter (1973) demonstrated that there can be enormous strength in weak ties, particularly among higher socioeconomic groups. Granovetter showed that upper-level professional and managerial employees are likely to hear about new jobs through connections such as distant relatives or remote acquaintances. Such weak ties can be of great benefit because relatives or acquaintances tend to have very different sets of connections than one's closer friends, whose social contacts are likely to be similar to one's own. Among lower socioeconomic groups, Granovetter argued, weak ties are not necessarily bridges to other networks and so do not really widen one's opportunities (see also Knoke 1990; Marsden and Lin 1982; Wellman et al. 1988). After graduation from college, you may rely on good grades and a strong résumé to find a job. But it may prove beneficial if it happens that your second cousin went to school with a top person in the organization in which you are seeking work.

Most people rely on their personal networks to gain advantages, but not everyone has equal access to powerful networks. Some sociologists argue, for example, that women's business and political networks are weaker than men's, so that women's power in these spheres is reduced (Brass 1985). The Bohemian Grove is a case in point. This is an annual summer political gathering that has been held on the Russian River, seventy miles north of San Francisco, since 1879. Its all-male membership includes Republican political leaders, the heads of major corporations, businessmen, and entertainers. The highly exclusive weekend includes horseback riding, meetings, entertainment, "lakeside talks," informal discussion groups—and some serious deal making. In 1999, the Bohemians included former president George H. W. Bush, then Texas governor (and later president) George W. Bush, former secretary of state Henry Kissinger, retired general Colin Powell (later secretary of state), and former Speaker of the House Newt Gingrich (Bohan 1999; Domhoff 1974).

In general, sociologists have found that when women look for work, their job market networks comprise fewer ties than do men's, meaning that women know fewer people in fewer occupations (Marsden 1987; Moore 1990). Meager networks tend to channel women into female-typical jobs, which usually offer less pay and fewer opportunities for advancement (Drentea 1998; Ross and Reskin 1992). Still, as more and more women move up into higher-level positions, the resulting networks can foster further advancement. One study found that women are more likely to be hired or promoted into job levels that already have a high proportion of women (Cohen et al. 1998).

Networks confer more than economic advantage. You are likely to rely on your networks for a broad range of contacts, from obtaining access to your congressperson or senator to finding a date for Saturday night. Similarly, when you visit another country to study a foreign language or see the Olympics, for example, your friends, school, or religious organization may steer you to their overseas connections, who can then help you find your way around in the unfamiliar environment. When you graduate from school, your alumni group can further extend your network of social support.

The Internet as Social Network

The advantages and potential reach of networks are evident in an increasingly productive means of networking, all but unknown ten years ago: the Internet. Internet use has exploded in recent years. Until the early 1990s, when the World Wide Web was developed, there were few Internet users out-

Launched in 2003, Myspace.com has over 85 million registered accounts and has become one of the most popular and controversial tools for building networks online. Purchased by Rupert Murdoch's News Corporation in 2005, the Web site allows members to post music, film clips, and other types of personal information to exchange with friends and acquaintances.

side of university and scientific communities. By 2005, however, an estimated 202.89 million Americans used the Internet (Internet World Stats 2005), and on any given day in the United States, 70 million people are online (Pew 2005). With such rapid communication and global reach, it is now possible to radically extend one's personal networks. The Internet is especially useful for networking with like-minded people on specific issues, such as politics, business, hobbies, and romance (Southwick 1996; Wellman et al. 1996). It also enables people who might otherwise lack contact with others to become part of global networks. For example, shut-ins can join chat rooms to share common interests, and people in small rural communities can now engage in distance learning through courses that are offered on the Web.

The Internet fosters the creation of new relationships, often without the emotional and social baggage or constraints that go along with face-to-face encounters. Although this might contribute to fleeting, impersonal relationships, it can also create opportunities for the expression of intimate feelings or discussion of topics that might be suppressed in ordinary face-to-face encounters. For example, chat rooms offer support for lesbians and gay men who can't find acceptance in their local communities. Similarly, some Web sites for teenagers provide answers to important questions on health and sexuality that teens may be shy about asking their parents. Internet communication is also effective in strengthening the bonds between friends and acquaintances who would otherwise seldom see each other (Wellman et al. 1996).

In the absence of the usual physical and social cues, such as skin color and residential address, people can get together electronically on the basis of shared interests rather than similar social characteristics. Such factors as social position, wealth, race, ethnicity, gender, and physical disability are less likely to cloud the social interaction (Coate 1994; Jones 1995; Kollock and Smith 1996). The Internet thus enables people to communicate first and then decide if the relationship is worth continuing in person. As a consequence, Internet-based social networks may be socially broader based than other networks (Wellman 1994). Whether this strengthens social diversity—or downgrades its importance—is a matter of debate.

The Internet can also enable people to join new organizations they otherwise might not have access to—for instance, professional groups, religious groups, and military academies such as West Point. The Internet has become increasingly instrumental in political action (Townsend 2002), demonstrated by MoveOn.org's fund-raising for the 2004 presidential election, and in the mobilization of protests, shown by the February 15, 2003, protest against the war in Iraq that drew eight million marchers into the streets of cities around the world (Ali 2003). Of course, there may be a downside to these opportunities, too, as in the case of hate groups, which use the Internet to recruit new members. These groups promote the scape-

FIGURE 6.3

Differences in Rates of Internet Access: Effects of Age, Education, Gender, Race, Ethnicity, and Income

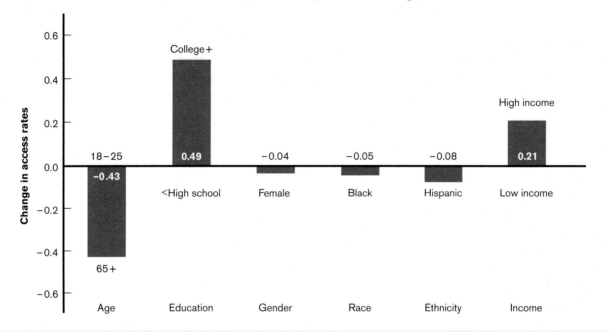

According to this figure what are the biggest factors affecting Internet usage? Who is more likely to have access to the Internet, an eighteen-year-old or a senior citizen? Do race, ethnicity, or gender differences affect who accesses the Internet? How does access to the Internet help people build networks?

SOURCE: Norman Nie and Lutz Ebring (2000) "Internet and Society–A Preliminary Report." Stanford Institute for the Quantitative Study of Society (SIQSS). www.stanford.edu/group/siqss/Press_Release/Preliminary_Report.pdf, accessed fall 2005. Data for chart was collected in December 1999.

goating of minorities in the hate literature that they transmit, and they encourage hate crimes. Some evidence indicates that hate groups concentrate on the Internet, where potential members and lone wolves who are attracted to racist notions but not fully committed to the hate movement can participate without exposing their identities (Intelligence Report 2001).

Another problem is that not everyone has equal access to the Internet. Though gender, racial, and class differences affect who is using the Internet and what they use it for, the most pronounced differences affecting Internet use are age and education (Nie and Ebring 2000). Still, within the span of a few years, Internet use has become much more widespread among all groups (Nielson Media Research 2001b, 2001c; Pew 2005). In the words of one recent study that tracked Internet use among different socioeconomic groups, "The Internet was, at first, an elitist country club reserved only for individuals with select financial abilities and technical skills. . . . Now, nearly every socioeconomic group is aggressively adopting the Web" (Nielsen Media Research 2001b).

Americans are by far the greatest Internet users in the world, although the rest of the world is rapidly coming on line. Besides in North America, Internet use is highest in Europe and East Asia, where the wealthiest countries are found. Some sociologists think that the Internet will eventually strengthen global ties, perhaps at the expense of local ones. Being able to connect with anyone in the world who shares similar interests may mean that one's own community becomes less important:

On-line relationships may be more stimulating than suburban neighborhoods and alienated offices. Even more than before, on the information highway each person is at the center of a unique personal community and work group. . . .Virtual communities are accelerating the ways in which people operate at the centers of partial, personal communities, switching rapidly and frequently between groups of ties. (Wellman et al. 1996)

The Internet may eventually lead to global communities based on shared interests, having the effect of diminishing local communities made up of families, neighbors, and friends. If this happens, will the ties that have bound people to locality throughout human history slowly disappear?

Organizations

People frequently band together to pursue activities that they could not otherwise readily accomplish by themselves. A principal means for accomplishing such cooperative actions is the **organization,** a group with an identifiable membership that engages in concerted collective actions to achieve a common purpose (Aldrich and Marsden 1988). An organization can be a small primary group, but it is more likely to be a larger, secondary one: Universities, religious bodies, and business corporations are all examples of organizations. Such organizations are a central feature of all societies, and their study is a core concern of sociology today.

Organizations tend to be highly formal in modern industrial and postindustrial societies. A **formal organization** is rationally designed to achieve its objectives, often by means of explicit rules, regulations, and procedures. The modern bureaucratic organization, discussed later in this chapter, is a prime example of a formal organization. As Max Weber (1979; orig. 1921) first recognized three quarters of a century ago, there has been a long-term trend in Europe and North America toward formal organizations. This rise of formality in organizations is in part the result of the fact that formality is often a requirement for legal standing. For a college or university to be legally accredited, for example, it must satisfy explicit written standards governing everything from grading policy to faculty performance to fire safety. Today, formal organizations are the dominant form of organization throughout the entire world.

Most social systems in the traditional world developed over lengthy periods as a result of custom and habit. Organizations, on the other hand, are mostly designed—established with definite aims in view and housed in buildings or physical settings specifically constructed to help realize those aims. The edifices in which hospitals, colleges, or business firms carry on their activities are mostly custom built.

In traditional societies, most people lived in small group settings. In a society such as traditional China, it was rare for members of a local village community ever to meet a national government official. National government edicts barely affected their lives.

In current times, organizations play a much more important part in our everyday lives than was ever true previously. Besides delivering us into this world, they also mark our progress through it and see us out of it when we die. Even before we are born, our mothers, and probably our fathers too, are involved in birthing classes, pregnancy checkups, and so forth, carried out within hospitals and other medical organizations. Every child born today is registered by government organizations, which collect information on us from birth to death. Most people today die in a hospital—not at home, as was once the case—and each death must be formally registered with the government too.

It is easy to see why organizations are so important to us today. In the premodern world, families, close relatives, and neighbors provided for most needs—food, the instruction of children, work, and leisure-time activities. In modern times, the mass of the population is much more *interdependent* than was ever the case before. Many of our requirements are supplied by people we never meet and who indeed might live many thousands of miles away. A substantial amount of coordination of activities and resources—which organizations provide—is needed in such circumstances.

The tremendous influence organizations have come to exert over our lives cannot be seen as wholly beneficial. Organizations often have the effect of taking things out of our own hands and putting them under the control of officials or experts over whom we have little influence. For instance, we are all *required* to do certain things the government tells us to do—pay taxes, abide by laws, go off to fight wars—or face punishment. As sources of social power, organizations can thus subject the individual to dictates she may be powerless to resist.

Theories of Organizations

Max Weber developed the first systematic interpretation of the rise of modern organizations. Organizations, he argued, are ways of coordinating the activities of human beings, or the goods they produce, in a stable way across space and time. Weber emphasized that the development of organizations depends on the control of information, and he stressed the central importance of writing in this process: An organization needs written rules for its functioning and files in which its "memory" is stored. Weber saw organizations as strongly hierarchical, with power tending to be concentrated at the top. Was Weber right? If he was, it matters a great deal to us all. For Weber detected a clash as well as a connection between modern organizations and democracy that he believed had far-reaching consequences for social life.

Bureaucracy

All large-scale organizations, according to Weber, tend to be bureaucratic in nature. The word *bureaucracy* was coined by Monsieur de Gournay in 1745, who added the word *bureau*, meaning both an office and a writing table, to *cracy*, a term derived from the Greek verb meaning "to rule." **Bureaucracy** is thus the rule of officials. The term was first applied only to government officials, but it gradually was extended to refer to large organizations in general.

From the beginning the concept was used in a disparaging way. De Gournay spoke of the developing power of officials as "an illness called bureaumania." The French novelist Honoré de Balzac saw bureaucracy as "the giant power wielded by pygmies." This sort of view has persisted into current times: Bureaucracy is frequently associated with red tape, inefficiency, and wastefulness. Other writers, however, have seen bureaucracy in a different light—as a model of carefulness, precision, and effective administration. Bureaucracy, they argue, is in fact the most efficient form of organization human beings have devised, because in bureaucracies all tasks are regulated by strict rules of procedure.

Weber's account of bureaucracy steers a way between these two extremes. A limited number of bureaucratic organizations, he pointed out, existed in the traditional civilizations. For example, a bureaucratic officialdom in imperial China was responsible for the overall affairs of government. But it is only in modern times that bureaucracies have developed fully.

According to Weber, the expansion of bureaucracy is inevitable in modern societies; bureaucratic authority is the only way of coping with the administrative requirements of large-scale social systems. However, Weber also believed bureaucracy exhibits a number of major failings, as we will see, which have important implications for the nature of modern social life.

To study the origins and nature of the expansion of bureaucratic organizations, Weber constructed an ideal type of bureaucracy. (*Ideal* here refers not to what is most desirable but to a pure form of bureaucratic organization. An **ideal type** is an abstract description constructed by accentuating certain features of real cases so as to pinpoint their most essential

Modern hospitals are complex organizations with impersonal structures and procedures—but they are designed for a very personal outcome.

characteristics.) Weber (1979, orig. 1921) listed several characteristics of the ideal type of bureaucracy:

1. **There is a clear-cut hierarchy of authority.** Tasks in the organization are distributed as "official duties." A bureaucracy looks like a pyramid, with the positions of highest authority at the top. There is a chain of command stretching from top to bottom, thus making coordinated decision making possible. Each higher office controls and supervises the one below it in the hierarchy.

2. **Written rules govern the conduct of officials at all levels of the organization.** This does not mean that bureaucratic duties are just a matter of routine. The higher the office, the more the rules tend to encompass a wide variety of cases and demand flexibility in their interpretation.

3. **Officials are full time and salaried.** Each job in the hierarchy has a definite and fixed salary attached to it. Individuals are expected to make a career within the organization. Promotion is possible on the basis of capability, seniority, or a mixture of the two.

4. **There is a separation between the tasks of an official within the organization and his life outside.** The home life of the official is distinct from his

activities in the workplace and is also physically separated from it.

5. **No members of the organization own the material resources with which they operate.** The development of bureaucracy, according to Weber, separates workers from the control of their means of production. In traditional communities, farmers and craft workers usually had control over their processes of production and owned the tools they used. In bureaucracies, officials do not own the offices they work in, the desks they sit at, or the office machinery they use.

Weber believed that the more an organization approaches the ideal type of bureaucracy, the more effective it will be in pursuing the objectives for which it was established. He often likened bureaucracies to sophisticated machines operating according to rational principles (see Chapter 1). Yet he recognized that bureaucracy could be inefficient and accepted that many bureaucratic jobs are dull, offering little opportunity for the exercise of creative capabilities. Although Weber feared that the rationalization of society could have negative consequences, he concluded that bureaucratic routine and the authority of officialdom over our lives are prices we pay for the technical effectiveness of bureaucratic organizations. Since Weber's time, the rationalization of society has become more widespread. Critics of this development who share Weber's initial concerns have questioned whether the efficiency of rational organizations comes at a price greater than Weber could have imagined. The most prominent of these critiques is known as "the McDonaldization of society," discussed later in this chapter.

FORMAL AND INFORMAL RELATIONS WITHIN BUREAUCRACIES

Weber's analysis of bureaucracy gave prime place to **formal relations** within organizations, the relations between people as stated in the rules of the organization. Weber had little to say about the informal connections and small-group relations that may exist in all organizations. But in bureaucracies, informal ways of doing things often allow for a flexibility that couldn't otherwise be achieved.

In a classic study, Peter Blau (1963) looked at **informal relations** in a government agency whose task was to investigate possible income-tax violations. Agents who came across problems they were unsure how to deal with were supposed to discuss them with their immediate supervisor; the rules of procedure stated that they should not consult colleagues working at the same level as themselves. Most officials were wary of approaching their supervisors, however, because they felt this

might suggest a lack of competence on their part and reduce their promotion chances. Hence they usually consulted one another, violating the official rules. This not only helped provide concrete advice but also reduced the anxieties involved in working alone. A cohesive set of loyalties of a primary group kind developed among those working at the same level. The problems these workers faced, Blau concludes, were probably coped with much more effectively as a result. The group was able to develop informal procedures allowing for more initiative and responsibility than was provided for by the formal rules of the organization.

Informal networks tend to develop at all levels of organizations. At the very top, personal ties and connections may be more important than the formal situations in which decisions are supposed to be made. For example, meetings of boards of directors and shareholders supposedly determine the policies of business corporations. In practice, a few members of the board often really run the corporation, making their decisions informally and expecting the rest of the board to approve them. Informal networks of this sort can also stretch across different corporations. Business leaders from different firms frequently consult one another in an informal way and may belong to the same clubs and leisure-time associations.

John Meyer and Brian Rowan (1977) argue that formal rules and procedures in organizations are usually quite distant from the practices actually adopted by the organizations' members. Formal rules, in their view, are often "myths" that people profess to follow but that have little substance in reality. The rules serve to legitimate—to justify—ways in which tasks are carried out, even while these ways may diverge greatly from how things are "supposed to be done" according to the rules.

Formal procedures, Meyer and Rowan point out, often have a ceremonial or ritual character. People will make a show of conforming to them to get on with their real work using other, more informal procedures. For example, rules governing ward procedure in a hospital help justify how nurses act toward patients in caring for them. Thus a nurse will faithfully fill in a patient's chart that hangs at the end of the bed but will check the patient's progress by means of other, informal criteria—how well the person is looking and whether he or she seems alert and lively. Rigorously keeping up the charts impresses the patients and keeps the doctors happy but is not always essential to the nurse's assessments.

Deciding how far informal procedures generally help or hinder the effectiveness of organizations is not a simple matter. Systems that resemble Weber's ideal type tend to give rise to a forest of unofficial ways of doing things. This is partly because the flexibility that is lacking ends up being achieved by unofficial tinkering with formal rules. For those in dull jobs, informal procedures often also help create a more satisfying work environment. Informal connections among officials in higher positions may be effective in ways that aid the organization as a whole. On the other hand, these officials may be more concerned about advancing or protecting their own interests than in furthering those of the overall organization.

THE DYSFUNCTIONS OF BUREAUCRACY

Robert Merton (1957), a functionalist scholar, examined Weber's bureaucratic ideal type and concluded that several elements inherent in bureaucracy could lead to harmful consequences for the smooth functioning of the bureaucracy itself. He referred to these as "dysfunctions of bureaucracy." First, Merton noted that bureaucrats are trained to rely strictly on written rules and procedures. They are not encouraged to be flexible, to use their own judgment in making decisions, or to seek creative solutions; bureaucracy is about managing cases according to a set of objective criteria. Merton feared that this rigidity could lead to *bureaucratic ritualism*, a situation in which the rules are upheld at any cost, even in cases where another solution might be a better one for the organization as a whole.

A second concern of Merton's is that adherence to the bureaucratic rules could eventually take precedence over the underlying organizational goals. Because so much emphasis is placed on the correct procedure, it is possible to lose sight of the big picture. A bureaucrat responsible for processing insurance claims, for example, might refuse to compensate a policyholder for legitimate damages, citing the absence of a form or a form being completed incorrectly. In other words, processing the claim correctly could come to take precedence over the needs of the client who has suffered a loss.

Merton foresaw the possibility of tension between the public and bureaucracy in such cases. This concern was not entirely misplaced. Most of us interact with large bureaucracies on a regular basis—from insurance companies to local government to the Internal Revenue Service (IRS). Not infrequently we encounter situations in which public servants and bureaucrats seem to be unconcerned with our needs. One of the major weaknesses of bureaucracy is the difficulty it has in addressing cases that need special treatment and consideration.

Organizations as Mechanistic and Organic Systems

Can bureaucratic procedures be applied effectively to all types of work? Some scholars have suggested that bureaucracy makes logical sense for carrying out routine tasks but that it can be problematic in contexts in which the demands of work change unpredictably. In their research on innovation and change in electronics companies, Tom Burns and G. M. Stalker (1994; orig. 1966) found that bureaucracies are of limited effectiveness in industries in which flexibility and being on the cutting edge are prime concerns.

Burns and Stalker distinguished between two types of organizations: *mechanistic* and *organic*. Mechanistic organizations are bureaucratic systems in which there is a hierarchical chain of command, with communication flowing vertically through clear channels. Each employee is responsible for a discrete task; once the task is completed, responsibility passes onto the next employee. Work within such a system is anonymous, with people at the top and those at the bottom rarely in communication with one another.

Organic organizations, by contrast, are characterized by a looser structure in which the overall goals of the organization take precedence over narrowly defined responsibilities. Communication flows and directives are more diffuse, moving along many trajectories, not simply vertical ones. Everyone involved in the organization is seen as possessing legitimate knowledge and input that can be drawn on in solving problems; decisions are not the exclusive domain of people at the top.

According to Burns and Stalker, organic organizations are much better equipped to handle the changing demands of an innovative market, such as telecommunications, computer software, or biotechnology. The more fluid internal structure means that they can respond more quickly and appropriately to shifts in the market and can come up with solutions more creatively and rapidly. Mechanistic organizations are better suited to more traditional, stable forms of production that are less susceptible to swings in the market. Although their study was first published in the 1960s, it is highly relevant to present-day discussions of organizational change. Burns and Stalker foreshadowed many of the issues that have taken center stage in recent debates over globalization, flexible specialization, and debureaucratization.

The Physical Setting of Organizations

Most modern organizations function in specially designed physical settings. A building that houses a particular organization possesses specific features relevant to the organization's activities, but it also shares important architectural characteristics with buildings of other organizations. The architecture of a hospital, for instance, differs in some respects from that of a business firm or a school. The hospital's separate wards, consulting rooms, operating rooms, and offices give the overall building a definite layout, whereas a school

The *Columbia* Shuttle Disaster: A Sociological Perspective

The tragic disintegration of the Space Shuttle *Columbia* on February 1, 2003 set me on an unexpected and remarkable eight-month journey in public sociology. In the hours after the accident, I was deluged with calls from the press. I had studied the causes of the 1986 *Challenger* disaster and written the book, *The Challenger Launch Decision: Risky Technology, Culture, and Deviance at NASA* (1996). I was defined as an expert the press could consult to give them bearings on this latest accident. Viewing this as both a teaching opportunity and professional responsibility, I tried to respond to everyone.

What I was teaching were the theoretical explanation and key concepts of the book, linking them to data about *Challenger* and *Columbia* as the changing press questions dictated. Because the investigation went on for months, these conversations became an ongoing exchange where the press brought me new information and I gave a sociological interpretation. I noticed that the concepts of the book—the normalization of deviance, institutional failure, organization culture, structure, missed signals—began appearing in print early in the investigation and continued, whether I was quoted or not.

The book also led to my association with the *Columbia* Accident Investigation Board. Two weeks after the accident, the publicity director at Chicago sent a copy of *The Challenger Launch Decision* to retired Admiral Harold Gehman, who headed the Board's investigation. ***

Diane Vaughan

The new centrality of sociological ideas and the connection with the *Challenger* accident were not lost on the media. In press conferences, Admiral Gehman stressed the importance of the social causes and used the book's central concepts. When he announced that I would testify before the Board in Houston, the field's leading journal, *Aviation Week and Space Technology,* headlined "*Columbia* Board Probes the Shuttle Pro-

may consist of classrooms, laboratories, and a gymnasium. Yet there is a general resemblance: Both are likely to contain hallways with doors leading off and to use standard decoration and furnishings throughout. Apart from the differing dress of the people moving through the corridors, the buildings in which modern organizations are usually housed have a definite sameness to them. And they often look similar from the outside as well as within their interiors. It would not be unusual to ask, on driving past a building, "Is that a school?" and receive the response, "No, it's a hospital." Although major in-

ternal modifications will be required, it can happen that a school takes over buildings that once housed a hospital.

MICHEL FOUCAULT'S THEORY OF ORGANIZATIONS: THE CONTROL OF TIME AND SPACE

Michel Foucault (1971; 1979) showed that the architecture of an organization is directly involved with its social makeup and system of authority. By studying the physical characteristics of gram's Sociology," while the *New York Times* ran "Echoes of *Challenger*." Unaware of the extent of the book's influence on the Board's thinking, however, I arrived in Houston in late April anxious about the public grilling to come.

But subsequent events showed me the Board was receptive to sociological analysis. I met separately with the Group 2 investigators assigned the decision making and organization chapters to discuss their data and analysis, then gave the Board a pre-testimony briefing, which turned into a three-hour conversation. My testimony covered the social causes of the *Challenger* accident, compared it to the *Columbia* incident, and identified systemic institutional failures common to both. The book's theory and concepts traveled farther as my testimony—like that of other witnesses—was shown live on NASA TV and videostreamed into television, radio, and press centers and the Internet.

***

So the Board's report gave equal weight to social causes of the accident—not only because the Admiral believed in the potential of sociology, but also because I, a sociologist, became part of this large team of Board and staff, working under deadline. Information and ideas flew fast and freely between people and chapters. Their extraordinary investigative effort, data, analysis, and insights were integrated into my chapter; sociological connections and concepts became integrated into theirs. ***

The Admiral kept the press informed of report changes, so prior to report publication, the *New York Times* announced the equal weight the report would give to technical and social causes, identifying me as the source of the Board's approach and author of Chapter 8. Upon the August 26 [2003] release, the language of sociology became commonplace in the press. The theory of the book traveled one more place that week. An [Associated Press] wire story, "NASA Finally Looks to Sociologist," revealed that NASA had invited me to headquarters to

talk with top officials, who had shifted from denial to acknowledge that the systemic institutional failures that led to *Challenger* also caused *Columbia*.

Never did I foresee the extent of my involvement or the impact that I ultimately had. *** The theory and concepts that explained *Challenger* were an analogical fit with the *Columbia* data and made sense of what happened for journalists and the Board. Analogy was the mechanism that enabled the theory and concepts of the book to travel. My book and university affiliation gave me the opportunity to engage in ongoing dialogic teaching—akin to daily grassroots activism—but with two tribunals of power with authoritative voice. Together, the press and the Board were a "polished machinery of dissemination," as Burawoy calls powerful advocacy groups, translating the ideas of the book into grist for critical public dialogue.

SOURCE: Diane Vaughan, "How Theory Travels: A Most Public Public Sociology," *Public Sociology in Action,* ASA Footnotes, Nov/Dec. 2003. www.asanet.org/footnotes/nov03/fn7.html last accessed April 24, 2006

DIANE VAUGHAN *teaches sociology at Boston College. Her other books are* Uncoupling: Turning Points in Intimate Relationships *(1986), and* Controlling Unlawful Organizational Behavior *(1983). Currently, she is writing about the uses of analogy in sociology and doing fieldwork on air traffic control.*

organizations, we can shed new light on the problems Weber analyzed. The offices Weber discussed abstractly are also architectural settings—rooms, separated by corridors. The buildings of large firms are sometimes actually constructed physically as a hierarchy, in which the more elevated one's position in the hierarchy of authority, the nearer to the top of the building one's office is; the phrase *the top floor* is sometimes used to mean those who hold ultimate power in the organization.

In many other ways, the geography of an organization will affect its functioning, especially in cases in which systems rely

heavily on informal relationships. Physical proximity makes forming primary groups easier, whereas physical distance can polarize groups, resulting in a "them" and "us" attitude between departments.

SURVEILLANCE IN ORGANIZATIONS

The arrangement of rooms, hallways, and open spaces in an organization's buildings can provide basic clues to how its system of authority operates. In some organizations, groups of people work collectively in open settings. Because of the dull, repetitive nature of certain kinds of industrial work, such as assembly-line production, regular supervision is needed to ensure that workers sustain the pace of labor. The same is often true of routine work carried out by telephone operators who respond to calls for information and who sit together where their activities are visible to their supervisors. Foucault laid great emphasis on how visibility, or lack of it, in the architectural settings of modern organizations influences and expresses patterns of authority. Their level of visibility determines how easily subordinates can be subject to what Foucault calls **surveillance,** the supervision of activities in organizations. In modern organizations, everyone, even in relatively high positions of authority, is subject to surveillance; but the lowlier a person is, the more his or her behavior tends to be closely scrutinized.

Surveillance takes two forms. One is the direct supervision of the work of subordinates by superiors. Consider the example of a school classroom. Pupils sit at tables or desks, usually arranged in rows, all in view of the teacher. Children are supposed to look alert or otherwise be absorbed in their work. Of course, how far this actually happens in practice depends on the abilities of the teacher and the inclinations of the children to conform to what is expected of them.

Workers on an assembly line build the circuit board and other computer devices that will become an electronic gambling machine for a Las Vegas casino. This arrangement allows for a high level of what Foucault calls *surveillance.*

The second type of surveillance is more subtle but equally important. It consists of keeping files, records, and case histories about people's work lives. Weber saw the importance of written records (nowadays often computerized) in modern organizations but did not fully explore how they can be used to regulate behavior. Employee records usually provide complete work histories, registering personal details and often giving character evaluations. Such records are used to monitor employees' behavior and assess recommendations for promotion. In many business firms, individuals at each level in the organization prepare annual reports on the performance of those in the levels just below them. School records and college transcripts are also used to monitor individuals' performance as they move through the organization. Records are kept on file for academic staff, too.

Organizations cannot operate effectively if employees' work is haphazard. In business firms, as Weber pointed out, people are expected to work regular hours. Activities must be consistently coordinated in time and space, something promoted both by the physical settings of organizations and by the precise scheduling of detailed timetables. **Timetables** regularize activities across time and space—in Foucault's words, they "efficiently distribute bodies" around the organization. Timetables are a condition of organizational discipline, because they slot the activities of large numbers of people together. If a university did not strictly observe a lecture timetable, for example, it would soon collapse into complete chaos. A timetable makes possible the intensive use of time and space: Each can be packed with many people and many activities.

UNDER SURVEILLANCE! THE PRISON

Foucault paid a great deal of attention to organizations, like prisons, in which individuals are physically separated for long periods from the outside world. In such organizations, people are incarcerated—kept hidden away—from the external social environment. A prison illustrates in clear detail the nature of surveillance because it seeks to maximize control over inmates' behavior. Foucault (1979) asks, "Is it surprising that prisons resemble factories, schools, barracks, hospitals, which all resemble prisons?"

According to Foucault, the modern prison has its origins in the Panopticon, an organization planned by the philosopher and social thinker Jeremy Bentham in the eighteenth century. "Panopticon" was the name Bentham gave to an ideal prison he designed, which he tried on various occasions to sell to the British government. The design was never fully implemented, but some of its main principles were incorporated into prisons built in the nineteenth century in the United States, Britain, and Europe. The Panopticon was circular in shape, with the cells built around the outside edge. In the center was an in-

Elevation, cross section, and plan of Jeremy Bentham's Panopticon, drawn in 1790.

spection tower. Two windows were placed in every cell, one facing the inspection tower and the other facing outside. The aim of the design was to make prisoners visible to guards at all times. The windows in the tower itself were equipped with venetian blinds, so that while the prison staff could keep the prisoners under constant observation, they themselves could be invisible.

THE LIMITS OF SURVEILLANCE

Foucault was right about prisons. Even today, most prisons look remarkably like the Panopticon. He was also right about the central role of surveillance in modern societies, an issue that has become even more important now because of the growing effect of information and communications technologies. We live in what some have called the **surveillance society** (Lyon 1994)—a society in which information about our lives is gathered by all types of organizations.

But Weber's and Foucault's argument that the most effective way to run an organization is to maximize surveillance—to have clear and consistent divisions of authority—is a mistake, at least if we apply it to business firms, which don't (as prisons do) exert total control over people's lives in closed settings.

Prisons are not a good model for organizations as a whole. Direct supervision may work tolerably well when the people involved, as in prisons, are basically hostile to those in authority over them and do not want to be where they are. But in organizations in which managers desire others to cooperate with them in reaching common goals, the situation is different. Too much direct supervision alienates employees, who feel they are denied any opportunities for involvement in the work they do (Grint 1991; Sabel 1982).

This is one main reason that organizations founded on the sorts of principles formulated by Weber and Foucault, such as large factories involving assembly-line production and rigid authority hierarchies, eventually ran into great difficulties. Workers weren't inclined to devote themselves to their work in such settings; continuous supervision was in fact *required* to get them to work reasonably hard at all, but it promoted resentment and antagonism (for further discussion, see Chapter 14).

People are also likely to resist high levels of surveillance in the second sense mentioned by Foucault, the collection of written information about them. That was in effect a principal cause for the breakdown of the Soviet-style communist societies. In those societies, people were spied on regularly either by the secret police or by others in the pay of the secret police—even relatives and neighbors. The government also kept detailed information on its citizenry to clamp down on possible opposition to their rule. The result was a form of society that was politically authoritarian and, toward the end, economically inefficient. The whole society did indeed come almost to resemble a gigantic prison, with all the discontents, conflicts, and modes of opposition prisons generate—and from which, in the end, the population broke free.

Bureaucracy and Democracy

Even in democracies like the United States, government organizations hold enormous amounts of information about us, from records of our dates of birth, schools attended, and jobs held to data on income used for tax collecting and information used for issuing drivers' licenses and allocating Social Security numbers. Because we don't have access to the files of most government agencies, such surveillance activities can infringe on the principle of democracy.

The diminishing of democracy with the advance of modern forms of organization was something that worried Weber a great deal (see also Chapter 13). What especially disturbed him was the prospect of rule by faceless bureaucrats. How can democracy be anything other than a meaningless slogan in the face of the increasing power bureaucratic organizations are wielding over us? After all, Weber reasoned, bureaucracies are necessarily specialized and hierarchical. Those near the bottom of the organization inevitably find themselves reduced to carrying out mundane tasks and have no power over what they do; power passes to those at the top. Weber's student Robert Michels (1967) invented a phrase, which has since become famous, to refer to this loss of power: In large-scale organizations, and more generally in a society dominated by organizations, he argued, there is an **iron law of oligarchy. Oligarchy** means rule by the few. According to Michels, the flow of power toward the top is simply an inevitable part of an increasingly bureaucratized world—hence the term *iron law*.

Was Michels right? It surely is correct to say that large-scale organizations involve the centralizing of power. Yet there is good reason to suppose that the "iron law of oligarchy" is not quite as hard and fast as Michels claimed. The connections between oligarchy and bureaucratic centralization are more ambiguous than he supposed.

We should recognize first of all that unequal power is not just a function of size. In modest-size groups there can be very marked differences of power. In a small business, for instance, in which the activities of employees are directly visible to the directors, much tighter control might be exerted than in offices in larger organizations. As organizations expand in size, power relationships often in fact become looser. Those at the middle and lower levels may have little influence over general policies forged at the top. On the other hand, because of the specialization and expertise involved in bureaucracy, people at the top also lose control over many administrative decisions, which are handled by those lower down.

In many modern organizations power is also quite often openly delegated downward from superiors to subordinates. In many large companies, corporate heads are so busy coordinating different departments, coping with crises, and analyzing budget and forecast figures that they have little time for original thinking. They hand over consideration of policy issues to others below them, whose task is to develop proposals about them. Many corporate leaders frankly admit that for the most part they simply accept the conclusions given to them.

Gender and Organizations

Until the late twentieth century, organizational studies did not devote very much attention to the question of gender. Weber's theory of bureaucracy and many of the influential responses to Weber that came in subsequent years were written by men and presumed a model of organizations that placed men squarely at the center. The rise of feminist scholarship in the 1970s, however, led to examinations of gender relations in all the main institutions in society, including organizations and bureaucracy. Feminist sociologists not only focused on the imbalance of gender roles within organizations but also explored the ways in which modern organizations themselves had developed in a specifically gendered way.

Feminists have argued that the emergence of the modern organization and the bureaucratic career depended on a particular gender configuration. They point to two main ways in which gender is embedded in the very structure of modern organizations. First, bureaucracies are characterized by occupational gender segregation. As women began to enter the labor market in greater numbers, they tended to be segregated into categories of occupations that were low paying and involved routine work. These positions were subordinate to those occupied by men and did not provide opportunities for women to be promoted. Women were used as a source of cheap, reliable labor but were not granted the same opportunities as men to build careers.

Second, the idea of a bureaucratic career was in fact a *male* career in which women played a crucial supporting role. In the workplace, women performed the routine tasks—as clerks, secretaries, and office managers—thereby freeing up men to advance their careers. Men could concentrate on obtaining promotions or landing big accounts because the female support staff handled much of the busywork. In the domestic sphere, women also supported the bureaucratic career by caring for the home, the children, and the man's day-to-day well-being. Women serviced the needs of the male bureaucrat by allowing him to work long hours, travel, and focus solely on his work without concern about personal or domestic issues.

As a result of these two tendencies, early feminist writers argued, modern organizations have developed as male-dominated preserves in which women are excluded from power, denied opportunities to advance their careers, and victimized on the basis of their gender through sexual harassment and discrimination.

Although most early feminist analysis focused on a common set of concerns—unequal pay, discrimination, and the male hold on power—there was no consensus about the best approach to take in working for women's equality. Two of the leading feminist works on women and organizations exemplified the split between liberal and radical feminist perspectives.

One was Rosabeth Moss Kanter's *Men and Women of the Corporation* (1977), one of the earliest examinations of women in bureaucratic settings. Kanter investigated the position of women in corporations and analyzed the ways in which they were excluded from gaining power. She focused on "male homosociability"—the way in which men successfully kept power within a closed circle and allowed access only to those who were part of the same in-group. Women and ethnic minorities were effectively denied opportunities for advancement and were shut out of the social networks and personal relationships that were crucial for promotions.

Although Kanter was critical of these gender imbalances within modern corporations, she was not entirely pessimistic about the future. In her eyes, the problem was one of *power*, not gender. Women were in a disadvantaged position, not because they were women per se, but because they did not wield sufficient power within organizations. As greater numbers of women came to assume powerful roles, according to Kanter, the imbalances would be swept away. Her analysis can be described as a liberal feminist approach because she is primarily concerned with equality of opportunity and ensuring that women are permitted to attain positions comparable with those of men.

The radical feminist approach, presented by Kathy Ferguson in *The Feminist Case against Bureaucracy* (1984), differs greatly from that of Kanter. Ferguson did not see the gender imbalance within organizations as something that could be resolved with the promotion of more women to positions of power. In Ferguson's view, modern organizations were fundamentally tainted by male values and patterns of domination. Women would always be relegated to subordinate roles within such structures, she argued. The only true solution was for women to build their own organizations on principles very different from those designed by and for men. Women, she argued, have the capacity to organize in a way that is more democratic, participatory, and cooperative than men, who are prone to authoritarian tactics, inflexible procedures, and an insensitive management style.

WOMEN IN MANAGEMENT

As women have entered professional occupations in greater numbers in recent decades, the debate over gender and organizations has taken new turns. Many scholars now see an opportunity to assess the effect of women leaders and managers on the organizations in which they work. Was Kanter correct when she predicted that gender imbalances would diminish as more women entered powerful positions? One of the most hotly contested questions today is whether women managers are making a difference in their organizations by introducing a "female" style of management into contexts that have long been dominated by male culture, values, and behavior.

Organizations of all types are confronted with the need to become more flexible, efficient, and competitive in today's global economy. This challenge is affecting organizations at all levels, from production processes and shop-floor relations to the use of technology and management practices. In recent years, many leadership qualities commonly associated with women have been held up as essential assets for organizations

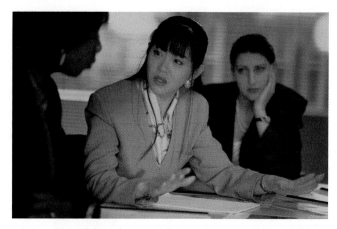

As women climb the corporate ladder, will they change the methods as well as the face of management or will they learn to manage like men?

attempting to become more flexible in their operations. Rather than relying on top-down, rigid management styles, organizations are encouraged to adopt policies that ensure employee commitment, collective enthusiasm for organizational goals, shared responsibility, and a focus on people. Communication, consensus, and teamwork are cited by management theorists as key approaches that will distinguish successful organizations in the new global age. These so-called soft management skills are ones traditionally associated with women.

Some writers claim that this shift toward a more "female" management style can already be felt. Women are attaining unprecedented influence at the top levels of power, they argue, and are doing so according to their own rules rather than adopting typically male management techniques (Rosener 1997). As the success of women's leadership is increasingly felt throughout the organizational world, some predict that a new way of thinking about management will emerge in which men will also adopt many of the techniques long favored by women, such as delegating responsibility, sharing information and resources, and collective goal setting.

Others do not subscribe to the view that women are successfully exercising a distinctly female brand of management. In *Managing Like a Man* (1998), Judy Wajcman takes issue with this approach on a number of grounds. First, she argues that the number of women who actually make it to the top levels of power is extremely limited. It is true, she says, that women are making substantial progress within the ranks of middle management; but despite their greater numbers in middle management, women are still largely prevented from accessing power at the highest levels. One out of thirteen senior executives (executive vice president or higher) are women. This is a dramatic increase from one in forty in 1995 (Epstein 2003). Even though women have increasingly made their way into the highest levels

More women are breaking into the upper reaches of corporate America . . .

Posts of executive vice president or higher held by women at the 500 largest companies

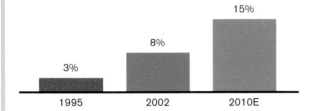

. . . *but the advances may be coming at a personal price.*

People earning more than $100,000 a year

What is the percentage increase in the number of women serving as executive vice president or higher between 1995 and 2002? How many women does the Bureau of Labor Statistics estimate will serve as executives in 2010? Why is it difficult for women to move into the highest ranks of organizations? Based on the figure, are female executives more likely to get divorced or never marry?

SOURCE: Gene Epstein, "More Women Advance but Sexism Persists," *Barron's*, 2003; available at www.collegejournal.com/successwork/workplacediversity/20030605-epstein.html, accessed spring 2006.

of business management this comes with costs, such as delaying or forgoing altogether having children or marital relationships (Figure 6.4). However, many of these positions held by women are "staff" positions or otherwise distanced from direct influence on profit margins. In *Fortune* 500 companies 90 percent of executive positions with direct influence on profit and loss were held by men (Epstein 2003). Men continue to receive

higher levels of pay for equivalent work and are employed in a broader spectrum of roles than are women, who tend to be clustered in fields such as human resources and marketing.

When women do reach top management positions, they tend to manage like men. Although great advances have been made since the 1980s in the areas of equal employment, sexual harassment policies, and overall consciousness about gender issues, Wajcman argues that organizational culture and management style remain overwhelmingly male. In her study of 324 senior-level managers in multinational corporations, she found that management techniques are dominated much more by the overall organizational culture than they are by the gender or personal style of individual managers. For women to get access to power and maintain their influence, they must adapt to the prevailing managerial style, which emphasizes aggressive leadership, tough tactics, and top-down decision making.

Wajcman argues forcefully that organizations are thoroughly gendered, in ways both obvious and subtle. The day-to-day organizational culture—including the way in which people talk to each other—is dominated by quick, competitive interactions. Despite a drop in overt sexual harassment—no longer tolerated in most organizations—more subtle sexualized relations remain prominent in the workplace and usually work to the disadvantage of women. Social networks and informal ties are the crucial elements behind job promotions and advancement, but these continue to be run in the style of an old-boys network. Many women find this realm alienating or uncomfortable, as one of Wajcman's (1998) respondents explained:

> You've got to be one of the boys. . . . I don't mind going down to the pub with the boys. . . . I don't get offended by the jokes . . . . [T]hat's how you get to the top . . . you start to see the breaks or where something's not going quite right and you make use of it . . . I personally don't like playing that game. It's not worth the hassle.

There is also reason to believe that it is difficult for women to break into traditional mentoring patterns in organizations. The model of mentoring has traditionally been the older man who takes on a young protégé in whom he sees traces of himself at a younger age. The mentor would work behind the scenes to advance the young employee's interests and to facilitate his future career moves. This dynamic is less easy to replicate between older male bosses and younger female employees, and there are not enough women in senior positions to serve as mentors to younger women. Among Wajcman's respondents, women were more likely than men to cite a lack of career guidance as a major barrier in their advancement.

Wajcman is skeptical about claims that a new age of flexible, decentralized organizations is upon us. Her findings reveal that traditional forms of authoritarian management are still firmly present. In her view, certain surface attributes of organizations may have been transformed, but the gendered nature of organizations—and the overwhelmingly dominant power of men within them—has not been challenged.

Beyond Bureaucracy?

For quite a long while in the development of Western societies, Weber's model, closely mirrored by that of Foucault, held good. In government, hospital administration, universities, and business organizations, bureaucracy seemed to be dominant. Even though, as Peter Blau showed, informal social groups always develop in bureaucratic settings and are in fact effective, it seemed as though the future might be just what Weber had anticipated: constantly increasing bureaucratization.

Bureaucracies still exist aplenty in the West, but Weber's idea that a clear hierarchy of authority, with power and knowledge concentrated at the top, is the only way to run a large organization is starting to look archaic. Numerous organizations are overhauling themselves to become less, rather than more, hierarchical.

In the 1960s, Burns and Stalker concluded that traditional bureaucratic structures can stifle innovation and creativity in cutting-edge industries; in today's electronic economy, few would dispute the importance of these findings. Departing from rigid vertical command structures, many organizations are turning to "horizontal," collaborative models to become more flexible and responsive to fluctuating markets. In this section we examine some of the main forces behind these shifts, including globalization and the growth of information technology, and consider some of the ways in which late modern organizations are reinventing themselves in the light of the changing circumstances.

Organizational Change: The Japanese Model

Many of the changes that can now be witnessed in organizations around the world were first pioneered in Japanese companies some decades ago. Although the Japanese economy has suffered recession in recent years, it was phenomenally successful during the 1980s. This economic success was often attributed to the distinctive characteristics of large Japanese corporations—which differed substantially from most business firms in the West (Vogel 1979). As we shall see, many of the unique organizational characteristics of Japanese corporations have been adapted and modified in other countries in recent years.

Japanese companies, especially in the 1980s and 1990s, diverged from the characteristics that Weber associated with bureaucracy in several ways:

1. **Bottom-up decision making.** The big Japanese corporations do not form a pyramid of authority as Weber portrayed it, with each level being responsible only to the one above. Rather, workers low down in the organization are consulted about policies being considered by management, and even the top executives regularly meet with them.

2. **Less specialization.** In Japanese organizations, employees specialize much less than their counterparts in the West. Take the case of Sugao, as described by William Ouchi (1982). Sugao is a university graduate who has just joined the Mitsubeni Bank in Tokyo. He will enter the firm in a management-training position, spending his first year learning generally how the various departments of the bank operate. He will then work in a local branch for a while as a teller and will subsequently be brought back to the bank's headquarters to learn commercial banking. Then he will move out to yet another branch dealing with loans. From there he is likely to return to headquarters to work in the personnel department. Ten years will have elapsed by this time, and Sugao will have reached the position of section chief.

   By the time Sugao reaches the peak of his career, some thirty years after beginning as a trainee, he will have mastered all the important tasks. In contrast, a typical American bank-management trainee of the same age will almost certainly specialize in one area of banking early on and stay in that specialty for the remainder of her working life.

3. **Job security.** The large corporations in Japan are committed to the long-term employment of those they hire; the employee is guaranteed a job. Pay and responsibility are geared to seniority—how many years a worker has been with the firm—rather than to a competitive struggle for promotion. This still remains a value, although it has weakened in recent years.

4. **Group orientation.** At all levels of the corporation, people are involved in small cooperative teams, or work groups. The groups, rather than individual members, are evaluated in terms of their performance. Unlike their Western counterparts, the *organization charts* of Japanese companies—maps of the authority system—show only groups, not individual positions. This is important because it contradicts the supposed *iron law of oligarchy*.

5. **Merging of work and private lives.** In Weber's depiction of bureaucracy, there is a clear division between the work of people within the organization and their activities outside. This is in fact true of most Western corporations, in which the relation between firm and employee is an economic one. Japanese corporations, by contrast, provide for many of their employees' needs, expecting in return a high level of loyalty to the firm. Japanese employees, from workers on the shop floor to top executives, often wear company uniforms. They may assemble to sing the company song each morning, and they regularly take part in leisure activities organized by the corporation on weekends. (A few Western corporations, like IBM and Apple, now also have company songs.) Workers receive material benefits from the company over and above their salaries. The electrical firm Hitachi, for example, studied by Ronald Dore (1980), provided housing for all unmarried workers and nearly half of its married male employees. Company loans were available for the education of children and to help with the cost of weddings and funerals.

Studies of Japanese-run plants in the United States and Britain indicate that bottom-up decision making does work outside Japan. Workers seem to respond positively to the greater level of involvement these plants provide (White and Trevor 1983). It seems reasonable to conclude, therefore, that the Japanese model does carry some lessons relevant to the Weberian conception of bureaucracy. Organizations that closely resemble Weber's ideal type are probably much less effective than they appear on paper, because they do not permit lower-level employees to develop a sense of control over, and involvement in, their work tasks.

Drawing on the example of Japanese corporations, Ouchi (1979, 1982) has argued that there are clear limits to the effectiveness of bureaucratic hierarchy, as emphasized by Weber. Overly bureaucratized organizations lead to internal failures of functioning because of their rigid, inflexible, and uninvolving nature. Forms of authority Ouchi calls *clans*—groups having close personal connections with one another—are more efficient than bureaucratic types of organization. The work groups in Japanese firms are one example, but clan-type systems often develop informally within Western organizations as well.

The Transformation of Management

Most of the components of the Japanese model just described come down to issues of management. Although it is impossible to ignore specific production-level practices developed by the Japanese, a large part of the Japanese approach focused on management–worker relations and ensured that employees at all levels felt a personal attachment to the company. The emphasis on teamwork, consensus-building approaches, and broad-based employee participation were in stark contrast to traditional Western forms of management that were more hierarchical and authoritarian.

In the 1980s, many Western organizations began to introduce new management techniques to boost productivity and competitiveness. Two popular branches of management theory—*human resource management* and the *corporate culture* approach—indicated that the Japanese model had not gone unnoticed in the West. **Human resource management** is a style of management that regards a company's workforce as vital to its economic competitiveness: If the employees are not completely dedicated to the firm and its product, the firm will never be a leader in its field. To generate employee enthusiasm and commitment, the entire organizational culture must be retooled so that workers feel they have an investment in the workplace and in the work process. According to human resource management theory, human resources issues should not be the exclusive domain of designated personnel officers but should instead be a top priority for all members of company management.

The second management trend—creating a distinctive **corporate culture**—is closely related to human resources management. To promote loyalty to the company and pride in its work, the company's management works with employees to build an organizational culture involving rituals, events, or traditions unique to that company alone. These cultural activities are designed to draw all members of the firm—from the most senior managers to the newest employee—together so that they make common cause with each other and strengthen group solidarity. Company picnics, casual Fridays (days on which employees can dress down), and company-sponsored community service projects are examples of techniques for building a corporate culture.

In recent years a number of Western companies have been founded according to the management principles described here. Rather than constructing themselves according to a traditional bureaucratic model, companies like the Saturn car company in the United States have organized themselves along these new managerial lines. At Saturn, for example, employees at all levels have the opportunity to spend time at positions in other areas of the company to gain a better sense of the operation of the firm as a whole. Shop-floor workers spend time with the marketing team, sharing insights into the way the vehicles are made. Sales staff rotate through the servicing department to become more aware of common maintenance problems that might concern prospective buyers. Representatives from both sales and the shop floor are involved in product design teams to discuss shortcomings that the management may not have been aware of in earlier models. A corporate culture focused on friendly and knowledgeable customer service unifies company employees and enhances the sense of company pride.

Technology and Modern Organizations

The development of **information technology**—computers and electronic communication media such as the Internet—is another factor currently influencing organizational structures (Attaran 2004; Bresnahan and Brynjolfsson 2002; Castells 2000, 2001; Kanter 1991; Kobrin 1997; Zuboff 1988). Anyone who draws money out of a bank or buys an airline ticket depends on a computer-based communications system. Because data can be processed instantaneously in any part of the world linked to such a system, there is no need for physical proximity between those involved. As a result, the introduction of new technology has allowed many companies to "reengineer" their organizational structure. The effect of these changes, while beneficial to organizational efficiency, can have both positive and negative consequences for the individuals within the organization.

For example, a particular company found the sales of some of its products falling and was faced with the need to reduce costs. The traditional route in such circumstances would be to lay off staff. But instead, the firm set up those who might have been laid off as independent consultants and established a computerized support network called Xanadu to provide basic office services to each of them working out of their homes. The company then bought back a substantial proportion of these former employees' working time for a number of years, but also left them free to use other time to work for different clients. The idea was that the new system would provide the corporation with access to the skills possessed by their former employees but at a cheaper rate because it no longer needed to provide office space or company benefits (pension, health insurance, and so on). The former employees, in their turn, had the opportunity to build up their own businesses. Initially, at least, the scheme seems to have worked well for both parties. In such a scheme, though, the burden is placed on the former employees because they have to match the loss of company benefits with their ability to attract new business clients.

This is just one example of how large organizations have become more decentralized as the more routine tasks disappear, reinforcing the tendency toward smaller, more flexible types of enterprises (Burris 1998). Another example of this process is the rise of telecommuting. A good deal of office work, for instance, can be carried out at home by telecommuters who use the Internet and other mobile technologies, such as cell phones, to do their work at home or somewhere other than their employer's primary office. Worldwide there are an estimated 137 million workers who telework (Telework Coalition 2004). According to the Telework Coalition, 44.4 million Americans telecommuted in 2004, which is approximately one fifth of the population of adult workers in the United States (Davis and Polonko 2001; Telework Coalition 2004). Of these, 21 percent worked at home, while the rest are about equally divided between working at special telework centers, satellite offices, or working while traveling (International Telework Association Council [ITAC] 2004). Telecommuters in the United States are typically males from the Northeast and West who have college degrees and work in professional or managerial positions (Davis and Polonko 2001). To reduce costs and increase productivity, several large firms in the United States and elsewhere have set up information networks connecting employees who work from home with the main office. For instance, in 2001 AT&T reported saving $65 million annually in increased productivity and $25 million annually in lower real estate costs (ITAC 2004). With the advent of high-speed Internet access, telecommuting has become even more efficient: ITAC estimated that upgrading the Internet service used by telecommuters to broadband could save employers as much as $5,000 per worker (Pratt 2003). In 2004, over eight million teleworkers working at home did so over broadband (Telework Coalition 2004).

One rationale for why telecommuting increases productivity is that it eliminates time spent by workers commuting to and from the office, permitting greater concentration of energy on work-related tasks. Hartig et al. (2003) found that telecommuters actually spend more time on paid work when working at home than their counterparts do while working in the office. However, there are repercussions from these new work arrangements. First, the employees lose the human side of work; computer terminals are not an attractive substitute for face-to-face interaction with colleagues and friends at work. The flexibility of telework creates new types of stress stemming from isolation, distraction, and conflicting demands of work and home responsibilities (Ammons and Markham 2004; Rhaguram and Wiesenfeld 2004). In addition, female telecommuters face more stress resulting from greater housework and child-care responsibilities (Ammons and Markham 2004; Olson 1989; Olson and Primps 1984). Nearly 59 percent of telecommuters say that they work longer hours because they are working at home, though employers view this increased productivity as a primary benefit of telecommuting (ITAC 2004). On the other hand, management cannot easily

The Computerization of the Workplace

For businesses competing in the global economy, investment in information technology—computer and communications equipment—is a necessity. Firms in the financial sector rely heavily on computers to engage in transactions in international financial markets; manufacturing firms depend on communications equipment to coordinate global production processes; and the customers of consumer services firms demand twenty-four-hour-a-day access to their accounts by telephone or the Internet. In short, information technology has become part of the basic infrastructure of business. In the service sector alone, businesses spent approximately $750 billion on information technology hardware between 1980 and 1990 (National Research Council 1994). This investment was a doubling of the amount spent per worker on technology and enabled firms to process vastly more transactions than they could in the past. Yet the investment in high-tech hardware did not pay off in terms of increased worker productivity until the late 1990s.

Although some of these technologies have made workers' lives easier, there is reason to worry that the new high-tech workplace may erode workers' power and rights. First, business reliance on information technology may undermine coalitions among workers. There is great demand today for employees with high-tech skills, whereas those who finish high school or college with few such skills find themselves eligible only for a limited number of positions. Increasingly, there are coming to be two "classes" of employees in firms: a privileged class with high-tech skills and another class relegated to lower-status work. But when employees negotiate with management over such issues as wages, hours, and benefits, employee unity is essential for securing concessions. Will high-tech workers side with lower-skilled employees in workplace disputes, or will they be more likely to side with management? The status of worker rights and benefits in the twenty-first century may well hinge on the answer to this question.

monitor the activities of employees not under direct supervision (Dimitrova 2003; Kling 1996). While this may create problems for employers, it allows employees greater flexibility in managing their nonwork roles, thus contributing to increased worker satisfaction (Davis and Polonko 2001). According to surveys by *Computer World* (2002) magazine, in the information technology field, workers perceive telecommuting as significant in determining the desirability of working for a particular company. Telecommuting also creates new possibilities for older and disabled workers to remain independent, productive, and socially connected (Bourma et al. 2004; Bricourt 2004).

The growth of telecommuting is effecting profound changes in many social realms. It is restructuring business management practices and authority hierarchies within businesses (Illegens and Verbeke 2004; Spinks and Wood 1996) as well as contributing to new trends in housing and residential development that prioritize spatial and technological requirements for telework in homes, which are built at increasing distances from city centers (Hartig et al. 2003). Finally, some have argued that telecommuting is contributing to a shift in the distribution of income toward the technologically literate while affecting marital and family relationships and altering demands for child care (Raines and Leathers 2001).

The experiences of telecommuters are reminders that negative consequences can result from the implementation of information technology to reorder organizations. Although computerization has resulted in a reduction in hierarchy, it has created a two-tiered occupational structure composed of technical "experts" and less-skilled production or clerical workers.

Second, in part because new communications technologies allow the branch offices and production facilities of multinational firms to communicate easily with each other, a higher proportion of manufactured goods is coming to be produced on a transnational basis—a situation that may make individual workers more easily replaceable. The former U.S. secretary of labor Robert Reich (1991) provides the following example of a global production process: "Precision ice-hockey equipment is designed in Sweden, financed in Canada, and assembled in Cleveland and Denmark for distribution in North America and Europe, respectively, out of alloys whose molecular structure was researched and patented in Delaware and fabricated in Japan. An advertising campaign is conceived in Britain; film footage is shot in Canada, dubbed in Britain, and edited in New York." Although high-tech, high-skilled workers will be needed to carry out many aspects of the production process, these skills may no longer give workers the same bargaining power vis-à-vis management that skilled craftsmanship carried with it in previous eras. Because the manufacturing process has been broken down into many small components, and because each of these components is carried out at a different production facility, the number of skills that any one worker must have is more limited than in previous eras, making it easier for companies to replace contentious workers. Communications technologies thus arguably further the process that the Marxist scholar Harry Braverman (1998) called "the deskilling of labor."

Third, the nature of workplace surveillance is likely to change substantially as information technology becomes even more important for business. Employers have always watched their employees closely, monitoring performance, seeking to improve efficiency, checking to make sure they do not steal.

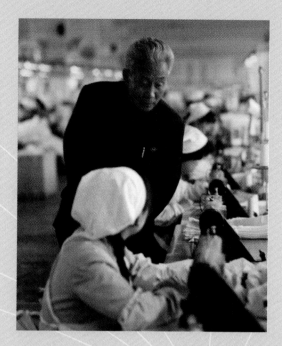

But as a greater proportion of work comes to be done by computer, the capacity of managers to scrutinize the behavior of their employees increases. Computerized performance evaluations, scrutiny of employee e-mail, and enhanced management access to personal employee information—such an Orwellian scenario becomes more likely as the role of information technology in the workplace expands.

Do you think these dangers are real, or is the effect of information technology on organizations essentially benign for employees? What steps, if any, do you think can be taken to counter these trends?

In these restructured organizations, jobs are redefined based more on technical skill than rank or position. For "expert" professionals, traditional bureaucratic constraints are relaxed to allow for creativity and flexibility, but other workers have limited autonomy (Burris 1993). Although professionals benefit more from this expanded autonomy, computerization makes production and service workers more visible and vulnerable to supervision (Wellman et al. 1996; Zuboff 1988). For instance, computerization allows organizations to carefully monitor employees' work patterns to the point at which they can count the number of seconds per phone call or keystrokes per minute, which in turn can lead to higher levels of stress for employees.

Granted, the computerization of the workplace does have some positive effects. It has made some mundane tasks associated with clerical jobs more interesting and flexible. It can also promote social networking (Wellman et al. 1996). For example, office computers can be used for recreation; private exchanges with other workers, friends, or family members; and work-related interaction. In some workplaces, computer-mediated communication can promote a more democratic type of workplace interaction. And, as in the case of telecommuting, computerization can contribute to greater flexibility for workers to manage both their personal and professional lives. But in the large majority of workplaces, computerization benefits the professionals who possess the knowledge and expertise about how to gain from it. It has not brought commensurate improvements in the career opportunities or salaries of the average worker (Kling 1996). As Foucault thought, in the new computerized workplace, knowledge and information are important sources of power and a means of controlling people.

Workplace Design

In the early nineteen-sixties, Jane Jacobs lived on Hudson Street, in Greenwich Village, near the intersection of Eighth Avenue and Bleecker Street. It was then, as now, a charming district of nineteenth-century tenements and town houses, bars and shops, laid out over an irregular grid, and Jacobs loved the neighborhood. In her 1961 masterpiece, "The Death and Life of Great American Cities," she rhapsodized about [the Village]. *** It was, she said, an urban ballet.

The miracle of Hudson Street, according to Jacobs, was created by the particular configuration of the streets and buildings of the neighborhood. Jacobs argued that when a neighborhood is oriented toward the street, when sidewalks are used for socializing and play and commerce, the users of that street are transformed by the resulting stimulation: they form relationships and casual contacts they would never have otherwise. The West Village, she pointed out, was blessed with a mixture of houses and apartments and shops and offices and industry, which meant that there were always people "outdoors on different schedules and *** in the place for different purposes." It had short blocks, and short blocks create the greatest variety in foot traffic. It had lots of old buildings, and old buildings have the low rents that permit individualized and creative uses. And, most of all, it had people, cheek by jowl, from every conceivable walk of life. Sparsely populated suburbs may look appealing, she said, but without an active sidewalk life, without the frequent, serendipitous interactions of many different people, "there is no public acquaintanceship, no

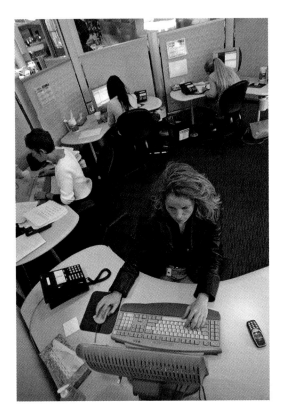

foundation of public trust, no cross-connections with the necessary people—and no practice or ease in applying the most ordinary techniques of city public life at lowly levels." ***

The parallels between neighborhoods and offices are striking. There was a time, for instance, when companies put their most valued employees in palatial offices, with potted plants in the corner, and secretaries out front, guarding access. Those offices were suburbs—gated communities, in fact—and many companies came to realize that if their best employees were isolated in suburbs they would be deprived of public acquaintanceship, the foundations of public trust, and cross-connections with the necessary people. In the eighties and early nineties, the fashion in corporate America was to follow what designers called "universal planning"—rows of identical cubicles, which resembled nothing so much as a Levittown. Today, universal planning has fallen out of favor, for the same reason that the postwar suburbs like Levittown did: to thrive, an office space must have a diversity of uses—it must have the workplace equivalent of houses and apartments and shops and industry. ***

The task of the office, then, is to invite a particular kind of social interatction—the casual, nonthreatening encounter that makes it easy for relative strangers to talk to each other. Offices need the sort of social milieu that Jane Jacobs found on the sidewalks of the West Village. "It is possible in a city street neighborhood to know all kinds of people without unwelcome entanglements, without boredom, necessity for excuses, explanations, fears of giving offense, embarrassments respecting impositions or commitments, and all such paraphernalia of obligations which can accompany less limited relationships," Jacobs wrote. If you substitute "office" for "city street neighborhood," that sentence becomes the perfect statement of what the modern employer wants from the workplace. ***

The point of the new offices is to compel us to behave and socialize in ways that we otherwise would not—to overcome our initial inclination to be office suburbanites. But, in all the studies of the new workplaces, the reservations that employees have about a more social environment tend to diminish once they try it. Human behavior, after all, is shaped by context, but how it is shaped—and whether we'll be happy with the result—we can understand only with experience. Jane Jacobs knew the virtues of the West Village because she lived there. What she couldn't know was that her ideas about community would ulti-

mately make more sense in the workplace. From time to time, social critics have bemoaned the falling rates of community participation in American life, but they have made the same mistake. The reason Americans are content to bowl alone (or, for that matter, not bowl at all) is that, increasingly, they receive all the social support they need—all the serendipitous interactions that serve to make them happy and productive—from nine to five.

SOURCE: Reprinted from Malcolm Gladwell, "Designs for Working," *New Yorker*, December 11, 2000.

Questions

- Why would it be in a company's interest to direct employees away from individual work and toward group interaction?
- This article describes a model for a white-collar office. Would the same kind of interaction and cooperative work be a productive model for blue-collar or unskilled labor also?
- Gladwell describes the old-fashioned office as a form of suburbia. Does the analogy hold? Why or why not?

Organizations as Networks

Traditionally, identifying the boundaries of organizations has been fairly straightforward. Organizations were generally located in defined physical spaces, such as an office building; a suite of rooms; or, in the case of a hospital or university, a whole campus. The mission or tasks an organization aimed to fulfill were also usually clear-cut. A central feature of bureaucracies, for example, was adherence to a defined set of responsibilities and procedures for carrying them out. Weber's view of bureaucracy was that of a self-contained unit that intersected with outside entities at limited and designated points.

We have already seen how the physical boundaries of organizations are being broken down by the capacity of new information technology to transcend countries and time zones. But the same process is also affecting the work that organizations do and the way in which it is coordinated. Many organizations no longer operate as independent units, as they once did. A growing number are finding that their operations run more effectively when they are linked into a web of complex relationships with other organizations and companies. No longer is there a clear dividing line between the organization and outside groups. Globalization, information technology, and trends in occupational patterns mean that organizational boundaries are more open and fluid than they once were.

In *The Rise of the Network Society* (1996), Manuel Castells argues that the "network enterprise" is the organizational form best suited to a global, informational economy. By this he means that it is increasingly impossible for organizations—be they large corporations or small businesses—to survive if they are not part of a network. What enables the process of networking to occur is the growth of information technology: Organizations around the world are able to locate each other, enter readily into contact, and coordinate joint activities through an electronic medium. Castells cites several examples of organizational networking and emphasizes that they have originated in diverse cultural and institutional contexts. According to Castells, however, they all represent "different dimensions of a fundamental process"—the disintegration of the traditional, rational bureaucracy.

An example of organizations as networks can be seen in the powerful strategic alliances formed between top companies. Increasingly the large corporation is less and less a big business and more an "enterprise web"—a central organization that links smaller firms together. IBM, for example, used to be a highly self-sufficient corporation, wary of partnerships with others. Yet in the 1980s and early 1990s, IBM joined with dozens of U.S.-based companies and more than eighty foreign-based firms to share strategic planning and cope with production problems.

Recent high-profile mergers among media and telecommunications companies have shown that even large and profitable corporations feel pressure to keep ahead of the rapidly changing market. The intentions of AOL, the popular online provider, and Time-Warner, the television and print media giant, in their merger proposals were to produce the world's largest corporation and link together the Internet and traditional media products. At a time when technological innovation is essential to remain competitive, it is difficult for even the leading firms to remain on top without drawing on the skills and resources of others. And as the financial difficulties of the AOL–Time-Warner merger show, technological innovation by itself cannot guarantee success.

Decentralization is another process that contributes to organizations functioning as networks. When change becomes both more profound and more rapid, highly centralized Weberian-style bureaucracies are too cumbersome and too entrenched in their established ways to cope. Stanley Davis (1988) argues that as business firms, and other organizations too, increasingly come to be networks, they go through a process of *decentralization* by which power and responsibility are devolved downward throughout the organization, rather than remaining concentrated at the top levels.

Networked organizations offer at least two advantages over more formal, bureaucratic ones: They can foster the flow of information, and they can enhance creativity. As you've already learned, bureaucratic hierarchy can impede the flow of information: One must go through the proper channels, fill out the right forms, and often avoid displeasing people in higher positions. These bureaucratic processes not only impede the sharing of information but also stifle creative problem solving. In networked organizations, by contrast, when a problem arises, instead of writing a memo to your boss and waiting for a reply before you act, you can simply pick up the phone or dash off an e-mail to the person who is responsible for working out a solution. As a result, members of networked organizations learn more easily from one another than do bureaucrats. It is therefore easier to solve routine problems and to foster more innovative solutions to all types of problems (Hamel 1991; Powell and Brantley 1992; Powell et al. 1996).

The "McDonaldization" of Society?

Not everyone agrees that our society and its organizations are moving away from the Weberian view of rigid, orderly bureaucracies. Some critics point out that a number of high-profile cases—such as the Saturn car corporation or Benetton—are seized on by the media and commentators, who in turn pronounce the birth of a trend that does not in fact exist. The idea that we are witnessing a process of debureaucratization, they argue, is overstated.

In a contribution to the debate over debureaucratization, George Ritzer (1993) developed a vivid metaphor to express his view of the transformations taking place in industrialized societies. He argues that although some tendencies toward debureaucratization have indeed emerged, on the whole what we are witnessing is the "McDonaldization" of society. According to Ritzer, McDonaldization is "the process by which the principles of the fast-food restaurants are coming to dominate more and more sectors of American society as well as the rest of the world." Ritzer uses the four guiding principles for McDonald's restaurants—efficiency, calculability, uniformity, and control through automation—to show that our society is becoming ever *more* rationalized with time.

If you have ever visited McDonald's restaurants in two different cities or countries, you will have noticed that there are very few differences between them. The interior decoration may vary slightly and the language spoken will most likely differ from country to country, but the layout, the menu, the procedure for ordering, the staff uniforms, the tables, the packaging, and the "service with a smile" are virtually identical. The McDonald's experience is designed to be the same whether you are in Bogota or Beijing. No matter where they are located, visitors to McDonald's know that they can expect quick service with a minimum of fuss and a standardized product that is reassuringly consistent. The McDonald's system is deliberately constructed to maximize efficiency and minimize human responsibility and involvement in the process. Except for certain key tasks such as taking orders and pushing the start and stop buttons on cooking equipment, the restaurants' functions are highly automated and largely run themselves.

Ritzer argues that society as a whole is moving toward this highly standardized and regulated model for getting things done. Many aspects of our daily lives, for example, now involve interactions with automated systems and computers instead of human beings. E-mail and voice mail are replacing letters and phone calls, e-commerce is threatening to overtake trips to the stores, bank machines outnumber bank tellers, and prepackaged meals provide a quicker option than cooking. If you have recently tried to call a large organization, such as an airline, you will know that it is almost impossible to speak to a human being. Automated touch-tone information services are designed to answer your requests; only in certain cases will you be connected to a live employee of the company. Computerized systems of all sorts are playing an ever greater role in our daily lives. Ritzer, like Weber before him, is fearful of the harmful effects of rationalization on the human spirit and creativity. He argues that McDonaldization is making social life more homogeneous, more rigid, and less personal.

Organizations That Span the World

For the first time in history, organizations have become truly global in scale. Information technologies have rendered national borders less meaningful because they can no longer contain key economic, cultural, and environmental activities. As a consequence, international organizations are expected to continue to grow in number and importance, providing a measure of predictability and stability in a world where nations are no longer the all-powerful actors they once were (Union of International Associations 1996–1997).

Sociologists therefore study international organizations to understand better how it is possible to create institutions that span national borders and what the effects of such institutions will be. Some sociologists even argue that global organizations will push the world's countries to become more and more alike (McNeely 1995; Scott and Meyer 1994; Thomas et al. 1987).

International organizations are not new, however. For example, organizations concerned with managing trade across borders have existed for centuries. The Hanseatic League, a business alliance among German merchants and cities, was one such organization, dominating trade in the North and Baltic Seas from the middle of the thirteenth century to the middle of the seventeenth century. But it was not until the creation of the short-lived League of Nations in 1919 that truly global organizations, with elaborate bureaucracies and member nations around the world, were formed. The United Nations, created in 1945, is perhaps the most prominent modern example of a global organization.

Sociologists divide international organizations into two principal types: *International governmental organizations* are composed of national governments, whereas *international non-governmental organizations* comprise private organizations. We will consider each of these separately.

International Governmental Organizations

The first type of global organization is the **international governmental organization (IGO),** which is established by treaties among governments for purposes of conducting business among the nations making up its membership. Such organizations emerge for reasons of national security (both the League of Nations and the United Nations were created after highly destructive world wars), the regulation of trade (for example, by the World Trade Organization), social welfare or human rights, or, increasingly, environmental protection.

Some of the most powerful IGOs today were created to unify national economies into large and powerful trading blocks. One of the most advanced IGOs is the European Union (EU), whose rules now govern twenty-five countries, mostly in western Europe. The EU was formed to create a single European economy, in which businesses could operate freely across borders in search of markets and labor and workers could move freely in search of jobs without having to go through customs or show passports at border crossings. EU members have common economic policies, and twelve of them even share a single currency (the euro). Thirteen additional countries, mostly of eastern Europe and representing 168 million people, have applied for membership, ten of which joined the EU in 2004 (Europa 2004). Not all Europeans welcome this development, however, because it means that member countries must surrender most of their economic decision making to the EU as a whole.

At the beginning of the twentieth century, there were only about three dozen IGOs in the world, although data for that time are sketchy. By 1981, when consistent reporting criteria were adopted, there were 1,039; by 1996, there were 1,830 (Union of International Associations 1996–1997). Today it is estimated that there are as many as 7,350 international governmental organizations (Union of International Organizations 2005).

IGOs can also wield considerable military power, provided that their member nations are willing to do so. The North Atlantic Treaty Organization (NATO) and the United Nations (UN), for example, used the full weight of their members' combined military might against Iraq during the Gulf War in 1991 and again in Kosovo, in the former Yugoslavia, in 1999. Yet, because nations ultimately control their own use of military force, there are limits to the authority of even the most powerful military IGOs, whose strength derives from the voluntary participation of their member nations. In the face of violent civil strife in Bosnia and the African countries of Somalia and Rwanda, for example, UN peacekeeping efforts have proved largely ineffective.

IGOs often tend to reflect inequalities in power among their member nations. For example, the UN Security Council, made up of fifteen member countries, is responsible for maintaining international peace and security and is therefore the most powerful organization within the UN. Its five permanent members are Britain, the United States, China, France, and Russia, giving these countries significant control over the council's ac-

tions. The remaining ten countries are elected by the UN General Assembly for two-year terms and thus have less ongoing power than the permanent members.

International Nongovernmental Organizations

The second type of global organization is the **international nongovernmental organization (INGO).** INGOs are established by agreements among the individuals or private organizations making up their membership. Examples include the International Planned Parenthood Federation, the International Sociological Association, the International Council of Women, and the environmental group Greenpeace. Like the number of IGOs, the number of INGOs has increased explosively in recent years—from fewer than two hundred near the beginning of the twentieth century to about fifteen thousand in the mid-1990s (Union of International Associations 1996–1997). There are an estimated 51,509 international nongovernmental organizations today (Union of International Organizations 2005).

In general, INGOs are primarily concerned with promoting the global interests of their members, largely through influencing the UN, other IGOs, or individual governments. They also engage in research and education and spread information by means of international conferences, meetings, and journals. INGOs have succeeded in shaping the policies of powerful nations.

One prominent (and highly successful) example of an INGO is the International Campaign to Ban Landmines (ICBL). The campaign, along with its founder Jody Williams, was awarded the Nobel Peace Prize in 1997 for its success in getting a majority of the world's countries to agree to a treaty banning the devastating use of land mines. The Nobel Prize committee commended the campaign for changing "a vision to a feasible reality," adding that "this work has grown into a convincing example of an effective policy for peace that could prove decisive in the international effort for disarmament" (ICBL 2001).

The ICBL is affiliated with over a thousand other INGOs in some sixty countries. Together they have focused public attention on the dangers posed to civilians of the more than one hundred million antipersonnel mines that are a deadly legacy of former wars fought in Europe, Asia, and Africa. These mines are unlike other weapons. They can remain active for decades after a war, terrorizing and trapping whole populations. In Cambodia, for example, fertile croplands have been mined, threatening with starvation farmers who are not willing to risk a misstep that could reduce them or their families to a shower of scraps. The campaign's efforts resulted in a treaty banning

Jody Williams, founder of the International Campaign to Ban Landmines, was awarded the Nobel Peace Prize in 1997 for her work and its eventual success in effecting the end of land-mine use by a majority of the world's countries.

the use, production, stockpiling, and transfer of antipersonnel land mines. The treaty, which became international law in March 1999, has been ratified by 147 countries. Five other countries are in the process of ratifying the agreement (ICBL 2005).

Although they are far more numerous than IGOs and have achieved some successes, INGOs have far less power because legal power (including enforcement) ultimately lies with governments. In the effort to ban land mines, for instance, although most of the major powers in the world signed the treaty, the United States, citing security concerns in Korea, refused, as did Russia. Some INGOs, like Amnesty International and Greenpeace, have nonetheless achieved considerable influence.

How Do Groups and Organizations Affect Your Life?

One of the principal reasons people join organizations is to gain connections and increase their influence. The time and energy invested in an organization can bring welcome returns. Parents who belong to the local Parent-Teacher Association (PTA), for example, are more likely to be able to influence school policy than those who do not belong. The members know whom to call, what to say, and how to exert pressure on school officials.

Sociologists call these fruits of organizational membership **social capital,** the social knowledge and connections that enable people to accomplish their goals and extend their influence (Coleman 1988, 1990; Loury 1987; Putnam 1993, 1995, 2000). Social capital includes useful social networks; a sense of mutual obligation and trustworthiness; an understanding of the norms that govern effective behavior; and, in general, other social resources that enable people to act effectively. College students often become active in the student government or the campus newspaper partly because they hope to learn social skills and make connections that will pay off when they graduate. They may get to interact with professors and administrators, who then will go to bat for them when they are looking for a job or applying to graduate school.

Differences in social capital mirror larger social inequalities. In general, for example, men have more capital than do women, whites more than nonwhites, the wealthy more than the poor. The Bohemian Grove you read about earlier, an important source of social capital for those who are invited to attend, is limited to wealthy, mainly white males. Attendance gives these men access to powerful social, political, and business resources, helping extend their wealth and influence. Differences in social capital can also be found among countries. According to the World Bank (2001), countries with high levels of social capital, where businesspeople can effectively develop the "networks of trust" that foster healthy economies, are more likely to experience economic growth. An example is the rapid growth experienced by many East Asian economies in the 1980s, a growth some sociologists have argued was fueled by strong business networks.

Robert Putnam (2000), a political scientist who has completed an extensive study of social capital in the United States, distinguishes two types of social capital: *bridging social capital,* which is outward looking and inclusive, and *bonding social capital,* which is inward looking and exclusive. Bridging social capital unifies people across social cleavages. The capacity to unify people can be seen in such examples as the civil rights movement, which brought blacks and whites together in the struggle for racial equality, and interfaith religious organizations. Bonding social capital reinforces exclusive identities and homogeneous groups; it can be found in ethnic fraternal organizations, church-based women's reading groups, and fashionable country clubs.

People who actively belong to organizations are more likely to feel connected; they feel engaged, able to somehow make a difference. From the standpoint of the larger society, social capital, the bridging form in particular, provides people with a feeling that they are part of a wider community, and one that includes people who are different from themselves. Democracy flourishes when social capital is strong. Indeed, cross-national survey evidence suggests that levels of civic engagement in the United States are among the highest in the world (Putnam 1993, 2000). But there is equally strong evidence that during the past quarter century, the ties of political involvement, club membership, and other forms of social and civic engagement that bind Americans to one another have significantly eroded. Could it be that democracy is eroding as a result?

Such declines in organizational membership, neighborliness, and trust in general have been paralleled by a decline in democratic participation. Voter turnout has dropped by 25 percent since the 1960s. In recent presidential elections, for example, the winning candidate (George H. W. Bush in 1988, Bill Clinton in 1992 and 1996, and George W. Bush in 2000 and 2004) received roughly only a quarter of the votes of all those who were eligible to cast a ballot. About half of the eligible voters did not bother to go to the polls. Even though the 2004 presidential election drew a record 122 million voters—the most ever in American history—these voters represent just over 60 percent of those eligible to vote (McDonald 2004). George W. Bush won just over 50 percent of the votes cast, meaning roughly 30 percent of the American electorate supported his Presidential bid. Similarly, attendance at public meetings concerning education or civic affairs has dropped sharply since the 1970s, and three out of four Americans today tell pollsters that they either "never" trust the government or do so only "sometimes" (Putnam 1995). Yet, after the terrorist attacks of September 11, 2001, researchers witnessed a resurgence of trust in government, with those saying that they trust the government "some of the time" doubling to nearly 60 percent (Pew 2002). Since then, trust has declined to 46 percent, but this is still significantly higher than in previous decades.

Even the recent increase in membership in organizations such as the Sierra Club, the National Organization for Women (NOW), and the American Association of Retired Persons (AARP, with thirty-five million members) is deceiving: The vast majority of these organizations' members simply pay their annual dues and receive a newsletter. Very few members actively participate, failing to develop the social capital Putnam regards as an important underpinning of democracy. Many of the most popular organizations today, such as twelve-step programs or weight-loss groups, emphasize personal growth and health rather than collective goals to benefit society as a whole.

There are undoubtedly many reasons for these declines. For one, women, who were traditionally active in voluntary organizations, are more likely to hold a job than ever before. For another, people are increasingly disillusioned with government and less likely to think that their vote counts. Furthermore, the flight to the suburbs increases commuting time, using up time and energy that might have been available for civic activities.

But the principal source of declining civic participation, according to Putnam is simple: television. The many hours Americans spend at home alone watching TV has replaced social engagement in the community.

Conclusion

You know better now how the groups and organizations you belong to exert an enormous influence over your life. They help determine whom you know and, in many ways, who you are. The primary groups of your earliest years were crucial in shaping your sense of self—a sense that changes very slowly thereafter. Throughout your life, groups are a wellspring of the norms and values that enable and enrich social life. At the same time, groups are also a source of nonconformist behavior: The rebel as much as the upright citizen is shaped by group membership.

Although groups remain central in our lives, group affiliation in the United States is rapidly changing. As you have seen in this chapter, conventional groups appear to be losing ground in our daily life. For example, today's college students are less likely to join civic groups and organizations—or even vote—than were their parents, a decline that may well signal a lower commitment to their communities. Some sociologists worry that this signals a weakening of society itself, which could bring about social instability.

As you have also seen, the global economy and information technology are redefining group life in ways that are now beginning to be felt. For instance, your parents are likely to spend much of their careers in a relative handful of long-lasting, bureaucratic organizations; you are much more likely to be part of a larger number of networked, "flexible" ones. Many of your group affiliations will be created through the Internet or through other forms of communication that today can barely be envisioned. It will become increasingly easy to connect with like-minded people anywhere on the planet, creating geographically dispersed groups that span the planet—and whose members may never meet each other face to face.

How will these trends affect the quality of your social relationships? For nearly all of human history, most people interacted exclusively with others who were close at hand. The Industrial Revolution, which facilitated the rise of large, impersonal bureaucracies where people knew one another poorly if at all, changed social interaction. Today, the information revolution is once again changing human interaction. Tomorrow's groups and organizations could provide a renewed sense of communication and social intimacy—or they could spell further isolation and social distance.

Study Outline

Social Groups

- *Social groups*, collections of people who share a sense of common identity and regularly interact with one another on the basis of shared expectations, shape nearly every experience in our lives. Among the types of social groups are *in-groups* and *out-groups, primary groups* and *secondary groups.*
- *Reference groups* provide standards by which we judge ourselves in terms of how we think we appear to others, what sociologist Charles Horton Cooley termed the "looking-glass self."
- Group size is an important factor in group dynamics. Although their intensity may diminish, larger groups tend to be more stable than smaller groups of two (*dyads*) or three (*triads*). Groups of more than a dozen or so people usually develop a formal structure.
- *Leaders* are able to influence the behavior of the other members of a group. The most common form of leadership is *transactional*—that is, routine leadership concerned with getting the job done. Less common is *transformational leadership*, which is concerned with changing the very nature of the group itself.
- Research indicates that people are highly conformist to group pressure. Many people will do what others tell them to do, even when the consequences could involve injury to others, as demonstrated by Stanley Milgram.
- *Networks* constitute a broad source of relationships, direct and indirect, including connections that may be extremely important in business and politics. Women, people of color, and lower-income people typically have less access to the most influential economic and political networks than do white males in American society.

Organizations

- All modern organizations are in some degree bureaucratic in nature. Bureaucracy is characterized by a clearly defined hierarchy of authority; written rules governing the conduct of officials (who work full time for a salary); and a separation between the tasks of the official within the organization and life outside it. Members of the organization do not own the material resources with which they operate. Max Weber argued that modern bureaucracy is a highly effective means of organizing large numbers of people, ensuring that decisions are made according to general criteria.
- Informal networks tend to develop at all levels both within and between organizations. The study of these informal ties is as important as the more formal characteristics on which Weber concentrated his attention.
- The physical settings of organizations strongly influence their social features. The architecture of modern organizations is closely connected to surveillance as a means of securing obedience to those in authority. *Surveillance* refers to the supervision of people's activities as well as to the keeping of files and records about them.

Theories of Organizations

- The work of Weber and Michels identifies a tension between bureaucracy and democracy. On the one hand, long-term processes of the centralization of decision making are associated with the development of modern societies. On the other hand, one of the main features of the past two centuries has been expanding pressures toward democracy. The trends conflict, with neither one in a position of dominance.

Gender and Organizations

- Modern organizations have evolved as gendered institutions. Women have traditionally been segregated into certain occupational categories that support the ability of men to advance their careers. In recent years, women have been entering professional and managerial positions in greater numbers, but some believe that women have to adopt a traditionally male management style to succeed at top levels.

Alternatives to Bureaucracy

- Large organizations have started to restructure themselves over recent years to become less bureaucratic and more flexible. Many Western firms have adopted aspects of Japanese management systems: more consultation of lower-level workers by managerial executives; pay and responsibility linked to seniority; and groups, rather than individuals, evaluated for their performance.
- New information technology is changing the way in which organizations work. Many tasks can now be completed electronically, a fact that allows organizations to transcend time and space. The physical boundaries of organizations are being eroded by the capabilities of new technology. Many organizations now work as loose networks, rather than as self-contained independent units.

Global Organizations

- Two important forms of global organization are *international governmental organizations (IGOs)* and *international nongovernmental organizations (INGOs)*. Both play an increasingly important role in the world today, and IGOs—particularly the United Nations—may become key organizational actors as the pace of globalization increases.

Social Capital

- *Social capital* refers to the knowledge and connections that enable people to cooperate with one another for mutual benefit and extend their influence. Some social scientists have argued that social capital has declined in the United States during the last quarter century, a process they worry indicates a decline in Americans' commitment to civic engagement.

Key Concepts

bureaucracy (p. 151)
corporate culture (p. 162)
dyad (p. 143)
formal organization (p. 150)
formal relations (p. 152)
groupthink (p. 146)
human resource management (p. 162)
ideal type (p. 151)
in-groups (p. 141)
informal relations (p. 152)
information technology (p. 163)
international governmental organization (IGO) (p. 169)
international nongovernmental organization (INGO) (p. 170)
iron law of oligarchy (p. 158)
leader (p. 144)
networks (p. 147)
oligarchy (p. 158)
organization (p. 150)
out-groups (p. 141)
primary groups (p. 141)
reference group (p. 142)
secondary groups (p. 141)
social aggregate (p. 141)
social capital (p. 171)
social category (p. 141)
social group (p. 140)
surveillance (p. 156)
surveillance society (p. 157)
timetables (p. 156)
transactional leaders (p. 144)
transformational leaders (p. 144)
triad (p. 143)

Review Questions

1. The term for the social knowledge and connections that enable people to accomplish their goals and extend their influence is
   a. cultural capital.
   b. political capital.
   c. social capital.
   d. economic capital.

2. Which kind of group provides standards by which we judge ourselves?
   a. in-group
   b. primary group
   c. out-group
   d. reference group

3. What is the derivation of the word *bureaucracy*?
   a. It was coined in 1910 by Max Weber: *bureau* means "writing table," and *cracy* is derived from the Greek verb "to know."
   b. It was coined in 1745 by Monsieur de Gournay: *bureau* means both "office" and "writing table," and *cracy* is derived from the Greek verb "to rule."
   c. It was coined in 1859 by Karl Marx: *bureau* means "house," and *cracy* is derived from the Greek verb "to control."
   d. It was coined in 1810 by Madame de Blancmange: *bureau* means "officer," and *cracy* is derived from the Greek verb "to exhibit signs of madness."

4. Which of the following scholars is concerned with the influence of cultural contexts on organizational forms?
   a. Henry Mintzberg
   b. Stuart Clegg
   c. George Ritzer
   d. Peter Blau

5. What is the difference between the way a new employee would be trained in a Western corporation (1) and the way he or she would be trained in a Japanese corporation (2)?
   a. In 1 employees are expected to acquire all relevant training themselves by investing in their own educations, whereas in 2 employees are expected to learn most of the skills relevant to their job through in-house training.
   b. In 1 the employee would spend up to a decade rotating among different branches and divisions and the head office, whereas in 2 the employee would specialize in the affairs of one department in one place from the very beginning.
   c. In 1 employees are expected to learn most of the skills relevant to their job through in-house training, whereas in 2 employees are expected to acquire all relevant training themselves by investing in their own educations.
   d. In 1 the employee would specialize in the affairs of one department in one place from the very beginning, whereas in 2 the employee would spend up to a decade rotating among different branches and divisions and the head office.

6. Transformational leaders are concerned with
   a. changing the very nature of a group.
   b. getting the job done.
   c. the well-being of group members.
   d. all of the above.

7. What is "bottom-up" decision making?
   a. The American system of letting the stock price and quarterly earnings dictate a firm's business strategy.
   b. A euphemism for paying attention to employees.
   c. The Japanese system of running large organizations with greater levels of participation from rank-and-file employees.
   d. A euphemism for the point at which the stock price has fallen so far that the directors have—metaphorically—put their heads between their knees.

8. Which of the following is *not* a characteristic of a primary group?
   a. members interacting on a face-to-face basis
   b. intimacy

c. members interacting to achieve a specific goal

d. a strong sense of bonding and commitment

9. International governmental organizations (IGOs) emerge for reasons of

   a. national security.

   b. the regulation of trade.

   c. social welfare of human rights.

   d. all of the above.

10. How do liberal feminists (early feminists) differ from radical feminists in their study of organizations?

    a. Liberal feminists and radical feminists do not differ in their study of organizations.

    b. Liberal feminists focus on unequal pay, discrimination, and the male hold on power.

    c. Radical feminists argue that women "serviced" the needs of the male bureaucrat by allowing him to work long hours, travel, and focus solely on his work without concern about personal or domestic issues.

    d. Liberal feminists maintain that to eliminate inequality in organizations women need to establish their own organizations on principles very different from those of men.

the addition of a child would alter the relationship between a husband and wife. Does the theory fit this situation?

2. The advent of computers and the computerization of the workplace may change our organizations and relationships with co-workers. Explain how you see modern organizations changing with the adaptation of newer information technologies.

Data Exercises

www.wwnorton.com/giddens
Keyword: Data6

After reading this chapter you can understand how important group memberships are to personal and social development. However, when individuals get involved in groups, society can also benefit, as the discussion of social capital and civic engagement demonstrates. In the data exercise for Chapter 6 you explore some of the current debate about this important issue.

Thinking Sociologically Exercises

1. According to George Simmel, what are the primary differences between dyads and triads? Explain, according to his theory, how

The Study of Deviant Behavior

Learn how we define deviance and how it is closely related to social power and social class. See the ways in which conformity is encouraged. Familiarize yourself with some traditional explanations for deviance and their limitations as theories.

Society and Crime: Sociological Theories

Know the leading sociological theories of crime and how each is useful in understanding deviance.

Crime and Crime Statistics

Recognize the helpfulness and limitations of crime statistics. Learn some important differences between men and women related to crime. Familiarize yourself with some of the varieties of crime. Think about the best solutions to reduce crime.

Victims and Perpetrators of Crime

Understand that some individuals or groups are more likely to commit or be the victims of crime.

Crime-Reduction Strategies

Consider the ways in which individuals and governments can address crime.

CHAPTER SEVEN

CONFORMITY, DEVIANCE, AND CRIME

illie was a street vendor who lived and worked on a street in New York City. He earned money by taking magazines out of recycled trash and reselling them to passersby. Willie lived on a corner for about six years, ever since he was released from serving a prison sentence for committing a robbery. During the early 1990s, he was one of approximately six hundred thousand people released from prison every year—about sixteen hundred per day (Mauer 2004).

In 2002, the number of prisoners held in federal, state, and county facilities exceeded two million people. One and a half million Americans were detained in prisons and jails for drug offenses, a threefold increase since 1980. This extreme focus on drug offenses has led the United States to become the world leader in this regard, surpassing Russia. The U.S. rate of incarceration is five to eight times higher than Canada and the countries of western Europe (Garland 2002).

This dramatic increase in incarceration has had a major effect on the African American and Latino populations in particular. According to Marc Mauer (2004), a leading student of incarceration, "In 1997, the state-wide population of Maryland, Illinois, North Carolina, South Carolina, and Louisiana was two thirds or more white, but prison growth since 1985 was 80% non-white. . . . In New York, where the state's adult minority population is less than 31.7%, nine out of ten new prisoners are from an ethnic or racial minority."

The effect of the criminal justice system is clear in the lives of people like Willie. While they are in prison, they are not part of the labor force, and thus a large amount of joblessness is not

FIGURE 7.1

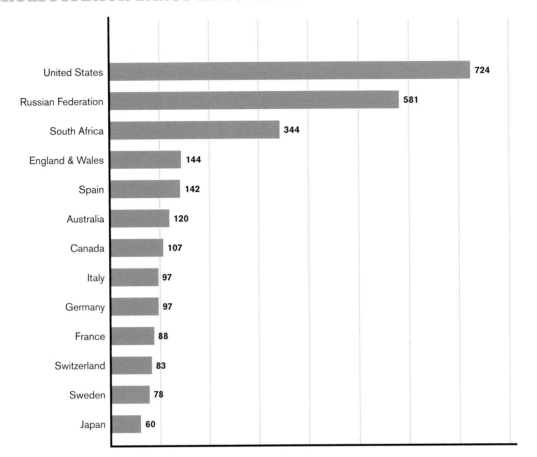

Incarceration Rates in Selected Industrialized Nations

Nation	Rate
United States	724
Russian Federation	581
South Africa	344
England & Wales	144
Spain	142
Australia	120
Canada	107
Italy	97
Germany	97
France	88
Switzerland	83
Sweden	78
Japan	60

Incarceration rate (number of people in prison per 100,000 population)

In Figure 7.1 the numbers corresponding to each nation represent what? How does the incarceration rate of the United States compare to that of England? How does the incarceration rate of Canada compare to that of Switzerland? In 2002, how many Americans were imprisoned for drug offenses? On average, how many people were released from prison each day in the 1990s?

SOURCE: International Centre for Prison Studies, "Prison Brief–Highest to Lowest Rates," October 12, 2005, www.kel.ac.uk/depsta/rel/icps/worldbrief/highest_to_lowest_rates.html (accessed spring 2006).

reflected in the rates of unemployment reported by the government. At the same time, incarceration also increases the long-term chances of unemployment for men like Willie once they are released from prison (Western and Beckett 1999).

Although the United States has imprisoned over two million people at the state and local level over the past few years, it has failed to make adequate preparations for their release (Gonnerman 2004). From prison, Willie went directly to the streets. He had nowhere to work and nowhere else to go. People he knew from prison were already living on a particular corner, and he heard he could find them there.

Willie is a man who many people would define as a deviant. We all know who deviants are, or so we tend to think. Deviants are those individuals who refuse to live by the rules that the majority of us follow. Sometimes they're violent criminals, drug addicts, or down-and-outs, who don't fit in with what most people would define as normal standards of acceptability. These are the cases that seem easy to identify. Yet things are not quite as they appear—a lesson sociology often teaches us, for it encourages us to look beyond the obvious. The notion of the deviant, as we shall see, is actually not an easy one to define.

We have learned in previous chapters that social life is governed by rules or norms. Our activities would collapse into chaos if we didn't stick to rules that define some kinds of behavior as proper in particular contexts and others as inappropriate. As we learned earlier in talking about the concept of culture, **norms** are definite principles or rules people are expected to observe; they represent the dos and don'ts of society. Orderly behavior on the highway, for example, would be impossible if U.S. drivers didn't observe the rule of driving on the right. No deviants here, you might think, except perhaps for the drunken or reckless driver. If you did think this, you would be incorrect. When we drive, most of us are not merely deviants but criminals. For most drivers regularly drive at well above the legal speed limits—assuming there isn't a police car in sight. In such cases, breaking the law is normal behavior!

We are all rule breakers as well as conformists. We are all also rule creators. Most American drivers may break the law on the freeways, but in fact they've evolved informal rules that are superimposed on the legal rules. When the legal speed limit on the highway is 65 mph, most drivers don't go above 75 or so, and they drive slower when driving through urban areas.

In most European countries, the legal speed limits are higher than in the United States—between 65 and 70 mph, depending on the country. Drivers there break the law most of the time just as they do in the United States, but their informal rules about proper driving produce higher speeds than in America. People regularly drive at 80–90 mph. Conventional rules about what is and isn't reckless driving also vary. Americans who drive in the south of Italy, for example, where drivers break other traffic rules as well, are apt to find the experience a hair-raising one.

When we begin the study of deviant behavior, we must consider which rules people are observing and which they are breaking. Nobody breaks *all* rules, just as no one conforms to all rules. Even an individual who might seem wholly outside the pale of respectable society, such as Willie, is likely to be following many rules of the groups and societies of which he is a member.

For example, when Willie would get enough money for a meal, he would go to a small Chinese restaurant around the corner from where he lived. There he would sit and eat his egg rolls, chow mein, and egg drop soup with the same manners as other diners. In this restaurant, he hardly appears as a deviant. When Willie is out on the street, he follows the rules of the other street vendors who subsist on the street. In the world of street vendors, he appears as a conformist most of the time. Indeed, some "de-

viant" groups such as the homeless h[...] havior for those who live among the[...] these informal codes of behavior m[...] from the group and be forced to g[...] Thus even "deviants" are conformi[...]

Willie's life is an example of wh[...] of people with drug convictions v[...] can criminal justice system. Bec[...] tle accommodation for people [...] prisoners are unable to find homes or jobs in the formal [...] omy. Working on the street is hardly a long-term solution for men like Willie, and after six years of "staying clean" on Sixth Avenue he was rearrested for another drug offense. This is very common: Almost two thirds of all reentering prisoners are likely to be rearrested within three years (Mauer 2004).

The Study of Deviant Behavior

The study of deviant behavior is one of the most intriguing yet complex areas of sociology. It teaches us that none of us is quite as normal as we might like to think. It also helps us see that people whose behavior might appear incomprehensible or alien can be seen as rational beings when we understand why they act as they do.

The study of deviance, like other fields of sociology, directs our attention to social *power*, as well as the influence of social class—the divisions between rich and poor. When we look at deviance from or conformity to social rules or norms, we always have to bear in mind the question, *Whose* rules? As we shall see, social norms are strongly influenced by divisions of power and class.

What Is Deviance?

Deviance may be defined as nonconformity to a given set of norms that are accepted by a significant number of people in a community or society. No society, as has already been stressed, can be divided up in a simple way between those who deviate from norms and those who conform to them. Most of us on some occasions transgress generally accepted rules of behavior.

The scope of the concept of deviance is very broad, as some examples will illustrate. Kevin Mitnick has been described as the "world's most celebrated computer hacker." It is probably fair to say that the thirty-six-year-old Californian is revered and despised in equal measure. To the world's estimated hundred

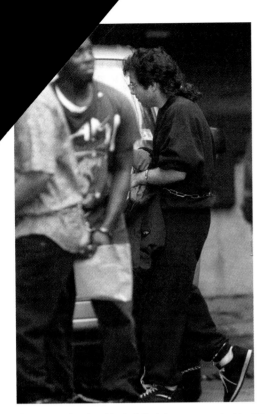

Computer hacker Kevin Mitnick was arrested in 1995 and later convicted of stealing millions of dollars worth of software from a number of technology companies. His release in 2000 was conditioned on the understanding that he would refrain from using computers or speaking publicly about technology issues.

thousand computer hackers, Mitnick is a pioneering genius whose five-year imprisonment in a U.S. penitentiary was unjust and unwarranted—concrete proof of how misunderstood computer hacking has become with the spread of information technology. To U.S. authorities and high-tech corporations—such as Sun Microsystems, Motorola, and Nokia—Mitnick is one of the world's most dangerous men. A recent survey by the U.S. Secret Service and Carnegie-Mellon University found that hackers are responsible for 40 percent of computer crime (E-Crime Watch 2004). Mitnick was captured by the FBI in 1995 and later convicted of downloading source codes and stealing software allegedly worth millions of dollars from these and other companies. As a condition of his release from prison in January 2000, Mitnick was forbidden to use computers or to speak publicly about technology issues.

Over the past decade or so, hackers have been gradually transformed from a little-noticed population of computer enthusiasts to a much-maligned group of deviants who are believed to threaten the very stability of the information age. The distributed denial of service (DDoS) attacks on prominent e-commerce Web sites that occurred in February 2000 provoked a type of "hacker hysteria" in the media, the corporate world, and among

international law-enforcement bodies. Some of the Internet's most heavily trafficked sites—such as Yahoo!, eBay, and Amazon.com—came to a standstill for hours as their servers were bombarded with millions of phony requests for information from computers around the world. Before anyone involved in the online raids was apprehended, fingers were pointed at computer hackers—portrayed as a shadowy population of socially maladjusted young people (mostly male) who avoid contact with human beings by creating alternative lives for themselves behind anonymous online user names.

Yet, according to Mitnick and others in the hacker community, such pathological depictions could not be further from the truth. "Hacker is a term of honor and respect," claimed Mitnick (2000) in an article written shortly after his release from prison. "It is a term that describes a skill, not an activity, in the same way that doctor describes a skill. It was used for decades to describe talented computer enthusiasts, people whose skill at using computers to solve technical problems and puzzles was—and is—respected and admired by others possessing similar technical skills." Hackers are quick to point out that most of their activities are not criminal. Rather, they are primarily interested in exploring the edges of computer technology, trying to uncover loopholes and to discover how far it is possible to penetrate into other computer systems. Once flaws have been discovered, the "hacker ethic" demands that the information be shared publicly. Many hackers have even served as consultants for large corporations and government agencies, helping them defend their systems against outside intrusion.

As another example, we might take the career of Ted Bundy. Bundy's way of life, on the face of things, conformed to the norms of behavior of a good citizen. He led what seemed not only a normal life but a most worthy one. For example, he played an active role in The Samaritans, an association that organizes a twenty-four-hour phone-in service for people who are distressed or suicidal. Yet Bundy also carried out a series of horrific murders. Before sentencing him to death, the judge at his trial praised Bundy for his abilities (he had prepared his own defense) but finished by noting what a waste he had made of his life. Bundy's career shows that a person can seem entirely normal while secretly engaging in acts of extreme deviance.

Deviance not only refers to individual behavior but also concerns the activities of groups. An illustration is the Heaven's Gate cult, a religious group whose beliefs and ways of life were different from those of the majority of Americans. The cult was established in the early 1970s when Marshall Herff Applewhite made his way around the West and Midwest of the United States preaching his beliefs, ultimately advertising on the Internet his belief that civilization was doomed and that the only way people could be saved was to kill themselves so their souls could be rescued by a UFO. On March 26, 1997, thirty-nine members of the cult followed his advice in a mass suicide at a wealthy estate in Rancho Santa Fe, California.

The Heaven's Gate cult represents an example of a **deviant subculture.** The members were able to survive fairly easily within the wider society, supporting themselves by running a Web site business and recruiting new members by sending e-mail messages to people they thought might be interested in their beliefs. They had plenty of money and lived together in an expensive home in a wealthy California suburb. Their position diverges from that of another deviant subculture that we discussed in the introduction to this chapter: the homeless.

Defining Deviance: The Sociological Debate

Many people take it for granted that a well-structured society is designed to prevent deviant behavior from occurring. But Émile Durkheim argued otherwise. He believed that deviance has an important part to play in a well-ordered society. Why did Durkheim think this? He said that by defining what is deviant, we become aware of what is not deviant and thereby become aware of the standards we share as members of a society. It is not necessarily the case, then, that we should aim to completely eliminate deviance. It is more likely that society needs to keep it within acceptable limits.

Seventy years after Durkheim's work appeared, the sociologist Kai Erikson published *Wayward Puritans*, a study of deviance in seventeenth-century New England. Erikson (1966) sought "to test [Durkheim's] notion that the number of deviant offenders a community can afford to recognize is likely to remain stable over time." His research led him to conclude that

a community's capacity for handling deviance, let us say, can be roughly estimated by counting its prison cells and hospital beds, its policemen and psychiatrists, its courts and clinics. . . . The agencies of control often seem to define their job as that of keeping deviance within bounds rather than obliterating it altogether.

Erikson advanced the hypothesis that societies need their quotas of deviance and that they function in such a way as to keep them intact.

What does a society do when the amount of deviant behavior gets out of hand? In a controversial 1993 article, "Defining Deviance Down," the former New York senator Daniel Patrick Moynihan argued that the levels of deviance in American society have increased beyond the point at which it can afford to recognize. As a result, we have been "redefining deviance so as to exempt much conduct previously stigmatized" and quietly

raising the "normal" [...]
by an earlier standard [...]

How has American [...]
that Moynihan gives is [...]
within the mental health p[...]
stead of being forced into [...]
treated with tranquilizers a[...]
ber of psychiatric patients i[...]
three thousand in 1955 to elev[...]

What happened to all of thos[...]
them are the homeless who toda[...]
"defining deviance down," people [...] re defined not as insane but as people [...] rdable housing. At the same time, the normal acceptable level of crime has risen. Moynihan points out that after the St. Valentine's Day massacre in 1929, in which seven gangsters were murdered, the nation was outraged. Today, violent gang murders are so common that there is hardly a reaction. Moynihan also sees the underreporting of crime as another form of normalizing it. As he concludes, "We are getting used to a lot of behavior that is not good for us."

Norms and Sanctions

We most often follow social norms because, as a result of socialization, we are used to doing so. Individuals become committed to social norms through interactions with people who obey the law. Through these interactions, we learn self-control. The more numerous these interactions, the fewer opportunities there are to deviate from conventional norms. And, over time, the longer that we interact in ways that are conventional, the more we have at stake in continuing to act in that way (Gottfredson and Hirschi 1990).

All social norms are accompanied by sanctions that promote conformity and protect against nonconformity. A **sanction** is any reaction from others to the behavior of an individual or group that is meant to ensure that the person or group complies with a given norm. Sanctions may be positive (the offering of rewards for conformity) or negative (punishment for behavior that does not conform). They can also be formal or informal. Formal sanctions are applied by a specific body of people or an agency to ensure that a particular set of norms is followed. Informal sanctions are less organized and more spontaneous reactions to nonconformity, such as when a student is teasingly accused by friends of working too hard or being a "nerd" if he or she decides to spend an evening studying rather than going to a party.

The main types of formal sanctions in modern societies are those represented by the courts and prisons. The police, of course, are the agency charged with bringing offenders to trial

Burning Man

Greetings from Burning Man

Stopped at the gas station for directions to the Burning Man Festival. Grizzled, portly Nevadan local growls: "If ya have to ask, you *don't belong* there!" ***

Burning Man is an art gig by tradition. Over the longer term it's evolved into something else; maybe something like a physical version of the Internet. The art here is like fan art. It's very throwaway, very appropriative, very cut-and-paste. The camp is like a giant swap meet where no one sells stuff, but people trade postures, clip art, and attitude. People come here in clumps: performance people, drumming enthusiasts, site-specific sculptors, sailplane people, ravers, journalists, cops. ***

I went to Burning Man. I took my kids. It's not scary, it's not pagan, it's not devilish or satanic. There's no public orgies, nobody gets branded or hit with whips. Hell, it's less pagan than the Shriners. It's just big happy crowds of harmless arty people expressing themselves and breaking a few pointless shibboleths that only serve to ulcerate young people anyway. There ought to be Burning Man festivals held downtown once a year in every major city in America. It would be good for us. We need it. In fact, until we can just relax every once in a while and learn how to do this properly, we're probably never gonna get well.

SOURCE: Bruce Sterling, "Greetings from Burning Man!" *Wired* 4.11 (November 1996). Sterling's article introduced Burning Man to the wider world, as he described his first trip to the Temporary Autonomous Zone. Since this article was written, attendance has ballooned to over thirty thousand people in 2004.

About a Man

I'm a Burner. I think we should have that straight from the outset.

I wasn't always a Burner. For several years after my first trip to Burning Man, I maintained a more or less objective viewpoint. Even when I went to the playa weeks before the event and helped construct various stages, roads and towers, I was half uncertain whether the event would survive its periodic attacks by the various governments that regulate its existence. There were times when I wasn't even sure it should survive.

Now I'm convinced the event should and will survive, although it may evolve. Actually, my theory is that the event must evolve or it will collapse under the weight of monotony.

This is a theory that won't be tested under any scientific rigor, but my belief is that this is the year that Burning Man grew up. It reached and probably slightly surpassed 30,000 attendees, the number that has often been bandied about by organizers as the end of population increase, the organizational endpoint of this party on the Black Rock Desert. If that's true, then this year was the first true representation of what the Burning Man Festival will be until the fire's put out. But I get ahead of myself. ***

Burning Man is a counterculture, anticonsumerism art event that happens up near Gerlach every Labor Day weekend. It attracts artists and people who like art. It doesn't generally attract the kind of artists who make paintings you'd hang on a wall in a museum. It attracts the kind of artists who build fanciful, thought-provoking and inspirational artifacts of steel and gas and light and wood. Especially wood.

Because wood burns.

The festival used to culminate with the burning of a large wood-and-neon man. Hence the name. ***

The event has been going since 1986, when founder Larry Harvey burned an effigy on Baker Beach in San Francisco. When the event got too large and attracted too much official attention, it moved to the Black Rock Desert playa, about 120 miles north of Reno, in 1990. In years past, local governments castigated event organizers for allowing too much freedom, too much nudity, too many drugs, too few rules. ***

Back in the day, local businesses accepted the participants' money, but behind their backs they'd often call participants hippies, druggies, weirdoes, freaks, pretty much anything except what they were: artists and tourists. But that was when the participants numbered in the thousands. Now the event is a financial windfall, bringing $10 million, according to some estimates, into the local economy every year. ***

The question of whether Burning Man will be able to attract 30,000 first- and second-timers will remain moot, as long as Larry Harvey and company can keep the themes and the art fresh. ***

Back in 1995, Harvey told me that his art, the thing that most interested him about Burning Man, was the movement of people, the art and science of how to motivate and control crowds. At the time, I didn't truly understand what he was talking about, but Saturday I think I did. It was beautiful and frightening and a hint of things to come. ***

I've seen more children and elderly people this year than I've seen in years past. Other people tell me I'm wrong, but if there are not more children, then the children that are here are being brought to more of the performances and are out riding their bikes and playing in community areas without adult supervision.

I think I understand the reason for this. In reaching maturity, Black Rock City became a safer city. I don't have a feeling for whether drug use has increased or decreased this year. I do feel that users are more discreet. I know drugs are there; I see people on drugs, and I hear people talk about having been on drugs, but nobody offers me cocaine or acid or mushrooms, and the smell of burning herb is infrequent. I've also heard many comments that the police presence has increased this year, but I don't really see evidence of that, either.

Anyway, this is a peaceful city by almost any definition. While bikes are stolen with frequency, apparently often by people who just want to get somewhere fast, who then abandon the bikes, there isn't the kind of violence you'd associate with a rock concert, street festival or classic-car event. ***

It's difficult to say where Burning Man will go from here. Recent published interviews with Larry Harvey have suggested that he will integrate this Burning Man with the other ones that happen around the world, bringing together a very large community of people who think life should mimic art, instead of the other way round. Maybe he'll be able to institute some political and social change. I wouldn't be surprised.

I don't know; my job won't change, and nearly every year I'll continue to write these essays. It's obvious why I do it— Burning Man is the largest cultural event held in this neck of the woods. More important, though, is why does anybody care to read this stuff? ***

The reason people want to read about Burning Man is because Burning Man matters.

At least it matters to us Burners. And there are a lot of us.

SOURCE: D. Brian Burghart, "About a Man," *Reno News and Review*, September 4, 2003.

Questions

- How is Burning Man an example of a subculture?
- Is the concept of "deviance" a meaningful way of understanding what is happening at the Burning Man Festival?
- How does the Burning Man Festival illustrate Durkheim's idea that deviance has an important part to play in a well-ordered society?

and possible imprisonment. **Laws** are norms defined by governments as principles that their citizens must follow; sanctions are used against people who do not conform to them. Where there are laws, there are also **crimes,** since crime can most simply be defined as any type of behavior that breaks a law.

It is important to recognize, however, that the law is only a guide to the kind of norms that exist in a society. Oftentimes, subcultures invent their own dos and don'ts. For example, the street people that Willie lives among have created their own norms for determining where each of them can set up the magazines that he sells on the sidewalk. Other homeless vendors don't set up in Willie's spot on the sidewalk because that would show "disrespect." This example further illustrates that even members of so-called deviant groups usually live in accordance with some norms. What makes them deviant subcultures is that these norms are at odds with the norms of the mainstream of society.

We shall now turn to the main sociological theories that have been developed to interpret and analyze deviance. In contrast to some areas of sociology, in which a theoretical perspective has emerged over time as preeminent, many theoretical strands remain relevant to the study of deviance. After a brief look at biological and psychological explanations, we shall turn to the four sociological approaches that have been influential within the sociology of deviance: *functionalist theories, interactionist theories, conflict theories*, and *control theories.*

The Biological View of Deviance

Some of the first attempts to explain crime were essentially biological in character. The Italian criminologist Cesare Lombroso, working in the 1870s, believed that criminal types could be identified by the shape of the skull. He accepted that social learning could influence the development of criminal behavior, but he regarded most criminals as biologically degenerate or defective. Lombroso's ideas became thoroughly discredited, but similar views have repeatedly been suggested. Another popular method of trying to demonstrate the influence of heredity on criminal tendencies was to study family trees. But this demonstrates virtually nothing about the influence of heredity, because it is impossible to disentangle inherited and environmental influences.

A later theory distinguished three main types of human physique and claimed that one type was directly associated with delinquency. Muscular, active types (mesomorphs), the theory went, are more likely to become delinquent than those of thin physique (ectomorphs) or more fleshy people (endomorphs) (Glueck and Glueck 1956; Sheldon et al. 1949). This research has also been widely criticized. Even if there were an overall relationship between body type and delinquency, this would show

nothing about the influence of heredity. People of the muscular type may be drawn toward criminal activities because these offer opportunities for the physical display of athleticism. Moreover, nearly all studies in this field have been restricted to delinquents in reform schools, and it may be that the tougher, athletic-looking delinquents are more liable to be sent to such schools than fragile-looking, skinny ones. Although older studies on the biological explanations of crime have been dismissed, more recent research has sought to rekindle the argument. In a study of New Zealand children, researchers sought to prove that childrens' propensity to aggression was linked to biological factors present at a child's birth (Moffitt 1996).

However, studies such as this only show that some individuals might be inclined toward irritability and aggressiveness, and this could be reflected in crimes of physical assault on others. Yet there is no decisive evidence that any traits of personality are inherited in this way, and even if they were, their connection to criminality would at most be only a distant one. In fact, the New Zealand study did not argue that there is a biological cause to crime but rather that biological factors, when combined with certain social factors such as one's home environment, could lead to social situations involving crime.

The Psychological View of Deviance

Like biological interpretations, psychological theories of crime associate criminality with particular types of personality. Some have suggested that in a minority of individuals, an amoral, or psychopathic, personality develops. **Psychopaths** are withdrawn, emotionless characters who delight in violence for its own sake.

Individuals with psychopathic traits do sometimes commit violent crimes, but there are major problems with the concept of the psychopath. It isn't at all clear that psychopathic traits are inevitably criminal. Nearly all studies of people said to possess these characteristics have been of convicted prisoners, and their personalities inevitably tend to be presented negatively. If we describe the same traits positively, the personality type sounds quite different, and there seems no reason why people of this sort should be inherently criminal. Should we be looking for psychopathic individuals for a research study, we might place the following ad:

ARE YOU ADVENTUROUS?

Researcher wishes to contact adventurous, carefree people who've led exciting, impulsive lives. If you're the kind of person who'd do almost anything for a dare, call 337-XXXX any time. (Widom and Newman 1985)

Such people might be explorers, spies, gamblers, or just bored with the routines of day-to-day life. They *might* be prepared to contemplate criminal adventures but could be just as likely to look for challenges in socially respectable ways.

Psychological theories of criminality can at best explain only some aspects of crime. Although some criminals may possess personality characteristics distinct from the remainder of the population, it is highly improbable that the majority of criminals do so. There are all kinds of crimes, and it is implausible to suppose that those who commit them share some specific psychological characteristics. Even if we confine ourselves to one category of crime, such as crimes of violence, different circumstances are involved. Some such crimes are carried out by lone individuals, whereas others are the work of organized groups. It is not likely that the psychological makeup of people who are loners will have much in common with the members of a close-knit gang. Even if consistent differences could be linked to forms of criminality, we still couldn't be sure which way the line of causality would run. It might be that becoming involved with criminal groups influences people's outlooks, rather than that the outlooks actually produce criminal behavior in the first place.

Both biological and psychological approaches to criminality presume that deviance is a sign of something "wrong" with the individual, rather than with society. They see crime as caused by factors outside an individual's control, embedded either in the body or the mind. Therefore, if scientific criminology could successfully identify the causes of crime, it would be possible to treat those causes. In this respect, both biological and psychological theories of crime are *positivist* in nature. As we learned in our discussion of Comte in Chapter 1, positivism is the belief that applying scientific methods to the study of the social world can reveal its basic truths. In the case of positivist criminology, this led to the belief that empirical research could pinpoint the causes of crime and in turn make recommendations about how to eradicate it.

Society and Crime: Sociological Theories

Early criminology came under great criticism from later generations of scholars. They argued that any satisfactory account of the nature of crime must be sociological, for what crime is depends on the social institutions of a society. One of the most important emphases of sociological thinking about crime is on the interconnections between conformity and deviance in different social contexts. Modern societies contain many different subcultures, and behavior that conforms to the norms of one particular subculture may be regarded as deviant outside it; for instance, there may be strong pressure on a member of a boys' gang to prove himself by stealing a car. Moreover, there are wide divergences of wealth and power in society that greatly influence opportunities open to different groups. Theft and burglary, not surprisingly, are carried out mainly by people from the poorer segments of the population; embezzling and tax evasion are by definition limited to persons in positions of some affluence.

Functionalist Theories

Functionalist theories see crime and deviance resulting from structural tensions and a lack of moral regulation within society. If the aspirations held by individuals and groups in society do not coincide with available rewards, this disparity between desires and fulfillment will be felt in the deviant motivations of some of its members.

CRIME AND ANOMIE: DURKHEIM AND MERTON

As we saw in Chapter 1, the notion of **anomie** was first introduced by Émile Durkheim, who suggested that in modern societies traditional norms and standards become undermined without being replaced by new ones. Anomie exists when there are no clear standards to guide behavior in a given area of social life. Under such circumstances, Durkheim believed, people feel disoriented and anxious; anomie is therefore one of the social factors influencing dispositions to suicide.

Durkheim saw crime and deviance as social facts; he believed both of them to be inevitable and necessary elements in modern societies. According to Durkheim, people in the modern age are less constrained than they were in traditional societies. Because there is more room for individual choice in the modern world, it is inevitable that there will be some nonconformity. Durkheim recognized that no society would ever be in complete consensus about the norms and values that govern it.

Deviance is also necessary for society, according to Durkheim; it fulfills two important functions. First, deviance has an *adaptive* function. By introducing new ideas and challenges into society, deviance is an innovative force. It brings about change. Second, deviance promotes *boundary maintenance* between "good" and "bad" behaviors in society. A criminal event can provoke a collective response that heightens group solidarity and clarifies social norms. For example, residents of a neighborhood facing a problem with drug dealers might join together in the aftermath of a drug-related shooting and commit themselves to maintaining the area as a drug-free zone.

Durkheim's ideas on crime and deviance were influential in shifting attention from individual explanations to social forces. His notion of anomie was drawn on by the American sociologist Robert K. Merton (1957), who constructed a highly influential theory of deviance that located the source of crime within the very structure of American society.

Merton modified the concept of anomie to refer to the strain put on individuals' behavior when accepted norms conflict with social reality. In American society—and to some degree in other industrial societies—generally held values emphasize material success, and the means of achieving success are supposed to be self-discipline and hard work. Accordingly, it is believed that people who really work hard can succeed no matter what their starting point in life. This idea is not in fact valid, because most of the disadvantaged are given only limited conventional opportunities for advancement or none at all. Yet those who do not "succeed" find themselves condemned for their apparent inability to make material progress. In this situation, there is great pressure to try to get ahead by any means, legitimate or illegitimate. According to Merton, then, deviance is a by-product of economic inequalities.

Merton identifies five possible reactions to the tensions between socially endorsed values and the limited means of achieving them. *Conformists* accept both generally held values and the conventional means of realizing them, whether or not they meet with success. The majority of the population fall into this category. *Innovators* continue to accept socially approved values but use illegitimate or illegal means to follow them. Criminals who acquire wealth through illegal activities exemplify this type.

Ritualists conform to socially accepted standards although they have lost sight of the values behind these standards. They follow rules for their own sake without a wider end in view, in a compulsive way. A ritualist would be someone who dedicates herself to a boring job, even though it has no career prospects and provides few rewards. *Retreatists* have abandoned the competitive outlook altogether, thus rejecting both the dominant values and the approved means of achieving them. An example would be the members of a self-supporting commune. Finally, *rebels* reject both the existing values and the means but wish actively to substitute new ones and reconstruct the social system. The members of radical political groups fall into this category.

Merton's writings addressed one of the main puzzles in the study of criminology: At a time when society as a whole is becoming more affluent, why do crime rates continue to rise? By emphasizing the contrast between rising aspirations and persistent inequalities, Merton points to a sense of relative deprivation as an important element in deviant behavior.

SUBCULTURAL EXPLANATIONS

Later researchers located deviance in terms of subcultural groups that adopt norms that encourage or reward criminal behavior. Like Merton, Albert Cohen saw the contradictions within American society as the main cause of crime. But while Merton emphasized individual deviant responses to the tension between values and means, Cohen saw the responses occurring collectively through subcultures. In *Delinquent Boys* (1955), Cohen argued that boys in the lower working class who are frustrated with their positions in life often join together in *delinquent subcultures*, such as gangs. These subcultures reject middle-class values and replace them with norms that celebrate defiance, such as delinquency and other acts of nonconformity.

Richard A. Cloward and Lloyd E. Ohlin (1960) agree with Cohen that most delinquent youths emerge from the lower working class. But they argued that such gangs arise in subcultural communities where the chances of achieving success legitimately are slim, such as among deprived ethnic minorities. Their work rightly emphasized connections between conformity and deviance: Lack of opportunity for success in the terms of the wider society is the main differentiating factor between those who engage in criminal behavior and those who do not.

Research by sociologists has examined the validity of claims that immediate material deprivation can lead people to commit crimes. A survey of homeless youth in Canada, for instance, shows a strong correlation between hunger, lack of shelter, and unemployment on the one hand, and theft, prostitution, and even violent crime on the other (Hagan and McCarthy 1992).

Functionalist theories rightly emphasize connections between conformity and deviance in different social contexts. We should be cautious, however, about the idea that people in poorer communities, like Willie, aspire to the same level of suc-

According to Durkheim, deviance has two important functions—it brings about change and it provokes a collective response that solidifies norms. For instance, these Pittsburgh neighbors joined together to form a neigborhood watch group to patrol the streets after an escalation in drug-related violence.

Members of a Los Angeles gang show off scars and tattoos. Are these men, like those in Cohen's *Delinquent Boys* (1955), replacing the values of the middle class with norms that express pride in defiance and nonconformity—in this case bullet and knife wounds?

cess as more affluent people. Most tend to adjust their aspirations to what they see as the reality of their situation. Merton, Cohen, and Cloward and Ohlin can all be criticized for presuming that middle-class values have been accepted throughout society. It would also be wrong to suppose that a mismatch of aspirations and opportunities is confined to the less privileged. There are pressures toward criminal activity among other groups too, as indicated by the so-called white-collar crimes of embezzlement, fraud, and tax evasion, which we will study later.

Interactionist Theories

Sociologists studying crime and deviance in the interactionist tradition focus on deviance as a socially constructed phenomenon. They reject the idea that there are types of conduct that are inherently "deviant." Rather, interactionists ask how behaviors initially come to be defined as deviant and why certain groups and not others are labeled as deviant.

LEARNED DEVIANCE: DIFFERENTIAL ASSOCIATION

One of the earliest writers to suggest that deviance is learned through interaction with others was Edwin H. Sutherland. In 1949, Sutherland advanced a notion that was to influence much of the later interactionist work: He linked crime to what he called **differential association.** The idea is very simple. In a society that contains a variety of subcultures, some social environments tend to encourage illegal activities, whereas others

do not. Individuals become delinquent through associating with people who are the carriers of criminal norms. For the most part, according to Sutherland, criminal behavior is learned within primary groups, particularly peer groups. This theory contrasts with the view that psychological differences separate criminals from other people; it sees criminal activities as learned in much the same way as law-abiding ones and as directed toward the same needs and values. Thieves try to make money just like people in orthodox jobs, but they choose illegal means of doing so.

Differential association can be used to assess Willie's life. Before Willie went to prison, he lived in Pennsylvania Station with a group of homeless men. From this group, he learned how to target and rob restaurant delivery boys, whom he learned were unlikely to report the crime to the police because many of them were illegal immigrants from Mexico and China. Willie would not have known these facts unless he had learned them from associating with others who were already the carriers of criminal norms.

LABELING THEORY

One of the most important interactionist approaches to the understanding of criminality is called **labeling theory**—although this term itself is a label for a cluster of related ideas rather than a unified view. Labeling theory originally came to be associated with Howard S. Becker's (1963) studies of marijuana smokers. In the early 1960s, marijuana use was a marginal activity carried on by subcultures rather than the lifestyle choice—that is, an activity accepted by many in the mainstream of society—it is today (Hathaway 1997). Becker found that becoming a marijuana smoker depended on one's acceptance into the subculture, close association with experienced users, and one's attitudes toward nonusers. Labeling theorists like Becker interpret deviance not as a set of characteristics of individuals or groups, but as a *process* of interaction between deviants and nondeviants. In other words, it is not the act of marijuana smoking that makes one a deviant, but the way others react to marijuana smoking that makes it deviant. In the view of labeling theorists, we must discover why some people become tagged with a "deviant" label in order to understand the nature of deviance itself.

People who represent the forces of law and order or are able to impose definitions of conventional morality on others do most of the labeling. The labels that create categories of deviance thus express the power structure of society. By and large, the rules in terms of which deviance is defined are framed by the wealthy for the poor, by men for women, by older people for younger people, and by ethnic majorities for minority groups. For example, many children wander into other people's gardens, steal fruit, or play truant. In an affluent neighborhood, these might be regarded by parents, teachers, and police alike as relatively innocent pastimes of childhood. In poor areas, they might be seen as evidence of tendencies toward juvenile delinquency.

Once a child is labeled a delinquent, he or she is stigmatized as a criminal and is likely to be considered untrustworthy by teachers and prospective employers. The child then relapses into further criminal behavior, widening the gulf with orthodox social conventions. Edwin Lemert (1972) called the initial act of transgression **primary deviation. Secondary deviation** occurs when the individual comes to accept the label and sees himself or herself as deviant. Other research has shown that how we think of ourselves and how we believe others perceive us influences our propensity for committing crime. One study examining self-appraisals of a random national sample of young men showed that such appraisals are strongly tied to levels of criminality (Matsueda 1992).

Take, for example, Luke, who smashes a shop window while spending a Saturday night out on the town with his friends. The act may perhaps be called the accidental result of overboisterous behavior, an excusable characteristic of young men. Luke might escape with a reprimand and a small fine. If he is from a respectable background, this is a likely result. And the smashing of the window stays at the level of primary deviance if the youth is seen as someone of good character who on this occasion became too rowdy. If, on the other hand, the police and courts hand out a suspended sentence and make Luke report to a social worker, the incident could become the first step on the road to secondary deviance. The process of "learning to be deviant" tends to be reinforced by the very organizations supposedly set up to correct deviant behavior—prisons and social agencies.

Labeling theory is important because it begins from the assumption that no act is intrinsically criminal. Definitions of criminality are established by the powerful through the formulation of laws and their interpretation by police, courts, and correctional institutions. Critics of labeling theory have sometimes argued that certain acts are consistently prohibited across virtually all cultures, such as murder, rape, and robbery. This view is surely incorrect; even within our own culture, killing is not always regarded as murder. In times of war, killing of the enemy is positively approved; and until recently, the laws in most U.S. states did not recognize sexual intercourse forced on a woman by her husband as rape.

We can more convincingly criticize labeling theory on other grounds. First, in emphasizing the active process of labeling, labeling theorists neglect the processes that *lead* to acts defined as deviant. For labeling certain activities as deviant is not completely arbitrary; differences in socialization, attitudes, and opportunities influence how far people engage in behavior likely to be labeled deviant. For instance, children from deprived backgrounds are on average more likely to steal from shops than are richer children. It is not the labeling that leads them to steal in the first place so much as the background from which they come.

Second, it is not clear whether labeling actually does have the effect of increasing deviant conduct. Delinquent behavior tends to increase after a conviction, but is this the result of the labeling itself? Other factors, such as increased interaction with other delinquents or learning about new criminal opportunities, may be involved.

Conflict Theory

Conflict theory draws on elements of Marxist thought to argue that deviance is deliberately chosen and often political in nature. Conflict theorists reject the idea that deviance is "determined" by factors such as biology, personality, anomie, social disorganization, and labels. Rather, they argue, individuals actively choose to engage in deviant behavior in response to the inequalities of the capitalist system. Thus members of countercultural groups regarded as deviant—such as supporters of the black power or gay liberation movements—are engaging in distinctly political acts that challenge the social order. Theorists of the **new criminology** frame their analysis of crime and deviance in terms of the structure of society and the preservation of power among the ruling class.

For example, they argue that laws are tools used by the powerful to maintain their own privileged positions. They reject the idea that laws are neutral and are applied evenly across the population. Instead, they claim that as inequalities increase between the ruling class and the working class, law becomes an ever more important instrument for the powerful to maintain order. This dynamic can be seen in the workings of the criminal justice system, which has become increasingly oppressive toward working-class offenders, or in tax legislation that disproportionately favors the wealthy. This power imbalance is not restricted to the creation of laws, however. The powerful also break laws, scholars argue, but are rarely caught. These crimes on the whole are much more significant than the everyday crime and delinquency that attracts the most attention. But fearful of the implications of pursuing white-collar criminals, law enforcement instead focuses its efforts on less powerful members of society, such as prostitutes, drug users, and petty thieves (Chambliss 1988; Pearce 1976).

These studies and others associated with the new criminology were important in widening the debate about crime and deviance to include questions of social justice, power, and politics. They emphasized that crime occurs at all levels of society and must be understood in the context of inequalities and competing interests among social groups.

Control Theory

Control theory posits that crime occurs as a result of an imbalance between impulses toward criminal activity and the social or physical controls that deter it. It is less interested in individuals' motivations for carrying out crimes; rather, it is assumed that people act rationally and that, given the opportunity, everyone would engage in deviant acts. Many types of crime, it is argued, are a result of "situational decisions"—a person sees an opportunity and is motivated to act.

One of the best-known control theorists, Travis Hirschi, has argues that humans are fundamentally selfish beings who make calculated decisions about whether to engage in criminal activity by weighing the potential benefits and risks of doing so. In *Causes of Delinquency* (1969), Hirschi claims that there are four types of bonds that link people to society and law-abiding behavior: attachment, commitment, involvement, and belief. When sufficiently strong, these elements help maintain social control and conformity by rendering people *unfree* to break rules. If these bonds with society are weak, however, delinquency and deviance may result. Hirschi's approach suggests that delinquents are often individuals whose low levels of self-control are a result of inadequate socialization at home or at school (Gottfredson and Hirschi 1990).

Some control theorists see the growth of crime as an outcome of the increasing number of opportunities and targets for crime in modern society. As the population grows more affluent and consumerism becomes more central to people's lives, goods such as televisions, video equipment, computers, cars, and designer clothing—favorite targets for thieves—are owned by more and more people. Residential homes are increasingly left empty during the daytime as more and more women take on employment outside the home. Motivated offenders interested in committing crimes can select from a broad range of suitable targets.

Responding to such shifts, many official approaches to crime prevention in recent years have focused on limiting the opportunities for crime to occur. Central to such policies is the idea of *target hardening*—making it more difficult for crimes to take place by intervening directly into potential crime situations. Control theorists argue that rather than changing the criminal, the best policy is to take practical measures to control the criminal's ability to commit crime.

Target-hardening techniques and zero-tolerance policing have gained favor among politicians in recent years and appear to have been successful in some contexts in curtailing crime. But criticisms of such an approach can also be made. Target-hardening and zero-tolerance policing do not address the underlying causes of crime but instead are aimed at protecting and defending certain elements of society from its reach. The growing popularity of private security services, car alarms, house alarms, guard dogs, and gated communities has led some people to believe that we are living in an armored society in which segments of the population feel compelled to defend themselves against others. This tendency is occurring not only in the United States, as the gap between the wealthiest and the most deprived widens, but is particularly marked in countries such as South Africa, Brazil, and those of the former Soviet Union, where a fortress mentality has emerged among the privileged.

There is another unintended consequence of such policies: As popular crime targets are hardened, patterns of crime may simply shift from one domain to another. Target-hardening and zero-tolerance approaches run the risk of displacing criminal offenses from better-protected areas into more vulnerable ones. Neighborhoods that are poor or lacking in social cohesion may well experience a growth in crime and delinquency as affluent regions increase their defenses.

THE THEORY OF BROKEN WINDOWS

Target hardening and zero-tolerance policing are based on a theory known as *broken windows* (Wilson and Kelling 1982). The theory is based on a study by the social psychologist Philip Zimbardo (1969), who abandoned cars without license plates and with their hoods up in two entirely different social settings, the wealthy community of Palo Alto, California, and a poor

In the early 1990s, New York City mayor Rudy Giuliani and police commissioner William Bratton applied the broken windows theory to New York's petty crime problem. They started producing "graffiti-proof" subway cars and the city's police force cracked down on vandals, public drinking, and jumping subway turnstiles. During the 1990s the crime rate in the city dropped to pre-1970s levels.

neighborhood in the Bronx, New York. In both places, both cars were vandalized once passersby, regardless of class or race, sensed that the cars were abandoned and that "no one cared." Extrapolating from this study, the authors of the broken windows theory argued that any sign of social disorder in a community, even the appearance of a broken window, encourages more serious crime to flourish. One unrepaired broken window is a sign that no one cares, so breaking more windows —that is, committing more serious crimes—is a rational response by criminals to this situation of social disorder. As a result, minor acts of deviance can lead to a spiral of crime and social decay.

In the late 1980s and 1990s, the broken windows theory served as the basis for new policing strategies that aggressively focused on minor crimes such as drinking or using drugs in public and traffic violations. Studies have shown that proactive policing directed at maintaining public order can have a positive effect on reducing more serious crimes, such as robbery (Sampson and Cohen 1988). However, one flaw of the broken windows theory is that the police are left to identify social disorder however they want. Without a systematic definition of disorder, the police are authorized to see almost anything as a sign of disorder and anyone as a threat. In fact, as crime rates fell throughout the 1990s, the number of complaints of police abuse and harassment went up, particularly by young, urban, black men who fit the "profile" of a potential criminal.

Linking Microsociology and Macrosociology: Saints and Roughnecks

The connections between the processes by which deviant behavior occurs and the larger class structure were noted by William Chambliss in a famous study, "The Saints and the Roughnecks" (1973). Chambliss studied two groups of delinquents in an American high school, one from upper-middle-class families ("the Saints") and the other from poor families ("the Roughnecks"). Although the Saints were constantly involved in petty crimes such as drinking, vandalism, truancy, and theft, none of their members was ever arrested. The Roughnecks were involved in similar criminal activities, yet they were constantly in trouble with the police. After Chambliss concluded that neither group was more delinquent than the other, he looked to other factors that could explain the different reaction of the police and the broader community to these two groups.

Chambliss found, for example, that the upper-class gang had automobiles and thus were able to remove themselves from the eyes of the community. The lower-class boys, through necessity, congregated in an area where everyone in the community frequently saw them. Chambliss concluded that differences of this sort indicated the class structure of American society, which gave certain wealthier groups advantages when it came to being labeled as deviant. For instance, the parents of the Saints saw their sons' crimes as harmless pranks, whereas the parents of the Roughnecks acquiesced to the police's labeling of their sons' behavior as criminal. The community as a whole also seemed to agree with these different labels.

These boys went on to have lives consistent with this labeling; the Saints lived conventional middle-class lives and the Roughnecks had continual problems with the law. As we saw earlier in the chapter, this outcome is linked to what Lemert called secondary deviance, because it is thought to result from the inability of a person to carry on as "normal" once he or she has been labeled as a deviant.

Chambliss's study is widely cited by sociologists for showing the connection between macrosociological factors such as social class and microsociological phenomena such as how people become labeled as deviant. This study provides an example of how difficult it is to isolate micro- and macro-level factors in the social construction of deviance.

Theoretical Conclusions

The contributions of the sociological theories of crime are twofold. First, these theories correctly emphasize the continuities between criminal and respectable behavior. The contexts in which particular types of activity are seen as criminal and punishable by law vary widely. Second, all agree that context is important in criminal activities. Whether someone engages in a criminal act or comes to be regarded as a criminal is influenced fundamentally by social learning and social surroundings.

In spite of its deficiencies, labeling theory is perhaps the most widely used approach to understanding crime and deviant behavior. This theory sensitizes us to the ways in which some activities come to be defined as punishable in law and the power relations that form such definitions, as well as to the circumstances in which particular individuals fall afoul of the law.

The way in which crime is understood directly affects the policies developed to combat it. For example, if crime is seen as the product of deprivation or social disorganization, policies might be aimed at reducing poverty and strengthening social services. If criminality is seen as voluntaristic, or freely chosen by individuals, attempts to counter it will take a different form. Now let's look directly at the nature of the criminal activities occurring in modern societies, paying particular attention to crime in the United States.

Crime and Crime Statistics

How dangerous *are* our streets compared with yesteryear? Is American society more violent than other societies? You should be able to use the sociological skills you have developed already to answer these questions.

In Chapter 2, for example, we learned something about how to interpret statistics. The statistics of crime are a constant focus of attention on television and in the newspapers. Most TV and newspaper reporting is based on official statistics on crime, collected by the police and published by the government. But many crimes are never reported to the police at all. Some criminologists think that about half of all serious crimes, such as robbery with violence, are not reported. The proportion of less serious crimes, especially small thefts, that don't come to the attention of the police is even higher. Since 1973, the Bureau of the Census has been interviewing households across the country to find out how many members were the victims of particular crimes over the previous six months. This procedure, called the National Crime Victimization Survey, has confirmed that the overall rate of crime is higher than the reported crime index. For instance, in 2004, only 50 percent of

violent crime was reported, including just 36 percent of rapes, 61 percent of robberies, 45 percent of simple assaults, and 53 percent of burglaries. Auto theft is the crime most frequently reported to the police (85 percent) (Catalano 2005).

Public concern in the United States tends to focus on crimes of violence—murder, assault, and rape—even though only 13.2 percent of all crimes are violent (Figure 7.2). In the United States, the most common victims of murder and other violent crimes (with the exception of rape) are young, poor, African American men living in the larger cities (Figure 7.3). The rate of murder among black male teenagers is particularly high, over five times the rate for their white counterparts, although this disparity has been declining in recent years. In general, whether indexed by police statistics or by the National Crime Victimization Survey, violent crime, burglary, and car theft are more common in cities than in the suburbs surrounding them, and they are more common in the suburbs than in smaller towns (Table 7.1).

In the 1990s, there was a drop in the overall crime rate throughout the United States to its lowest levels since 1973, when the victimization survey was first used. Rates of violent crime in particular dropped substantially: murders by 31 percent and robberies by 32 percent. There is no one prevailing explanation among sociologists for this decline, although many politicians would like to take credit for it. Aggressive new efforts by local police to stop the use of guns certainly contributed to the decrease in homicides, but other social factors were also at work. Foremost among these is related to the declining market for crack cocaine and the stigmatization of crack among young urban dwellers. Another factor was the booming economy of the 1990s, which provided job opportunities for those who may have been enticed to work in the drug trade (Butterfield 1998).

One reason often given for the relatively high rates of violent crime in the United States is the widespread availability of handguns and other firearms. This is relevant but does not provide a complete answer. Switzerland has very low rates of violent crime, yet firearms are easily accessible. All Swiss males are members of the citizen army and keep weapons in their homes, including rifles, revolvers, and sometimes other automatic weapons plus ammunition; nor are gun licenses difficult to obtain.

The most likely explanation for the high level of violent crime in the United States is a combination of the availability of firearms, the general influence of the frontier tradition, and the subcultures of violence in the large cities. Violence by frontiersmen and vigilantes is an honored part of American history. Some of the first established immigrant areas in the cities developed their own informal modes of neighborhood control, backed by violence or the threat of violence. Similarly, young

FIGURE 7.2

Crime Rates in the United States, 1985–2004

VIOLENT CRIMES*

PROPERTY CRIMES

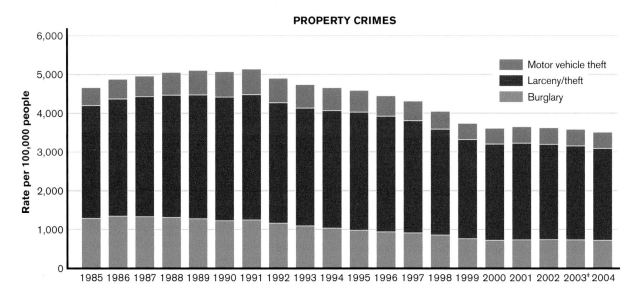

During what year were property crimes the highest? What was the approximate crime rate? What is the general trend of violent crime rates between 1985 and 2004? From 1985 through 2004, which is greater: the rate of reported violent crimes or the rate of reported property crimes? What percentage of all crimes are violent crimes? Why might the figures above not represent an accurate account of the number of violent and property crimes reported in the United States?

* Although arson data are included, sufficient data are not available to estimate totals for this offense.

† The murder and nonnegligent homicides that occurred as a result of the events of September 11, 2001, are not included in this table.

‡ The 2003 crime figures have been adjusted.

SOURCE: Federal Bureau of Investigation, Uniform Crime Report, 2005a, Table 1, www.fbi.gov/ucr/cius_04/offenses_reported/offense_tabulations/table_01=01a.html (accessed fall 2005).

people in African American and Hispanic communities today have developed subcultures of manliness and honor associated with rituals of violence, and some belong to gangs whose everyday life is one of drug dealing, territory protection, and violence.

A notable feature of most crimes of violence is their mundane character. Most assaults and homicides bear little resemblance to the murderous, random acts of gunmen or the carefully planned homicides given most prominence in the media. Murders generally happen in the context of family and other interpersonal relationships; the victim usually knows his or her murderer.

Victims and Perpetrators of Crime

Are some individuals or groups more likely to commit crimes or to become the victims of crime? Criminologists say yes—research and crime statistics show that crime and victimization are not randomly distributed among the population. Men are more likely than women, for example, to commit crimes; the young are more often involved in crime than older people.

The likelihood of someone becoming a victim of crime is closely linked to the area in which he or she lives. Areas suffering from greater material deprivation generally have higher crime rates. Individuals living in inner-city neighborhoods run a much greater risk of becoming victims of crime than do residents of more affluent suburban areas. That ethnic minorities are concentrated disproportionately in inner-city regions appears to be a significant factor in their higher rates of victimization.

Gender and Crime

Like other areas of sociology, criminological studies have traditionally ignored half the population. Feminists have been correct in criticizing criminology for being a male-dominated discipline in which women are largely invisible in both theoretical considerations and empirical studies. Since the 1970s, many important feminist works have drawn attention to the way in which criminal transgressions by women occur in different contexts from those by men and how women's experiences with the criminal justice system are influenced by certain gendered assumptions about appropriate male and female roles. Feminists have also played a critical role in highlighting the prevalence of violence against women, both at home and in public.

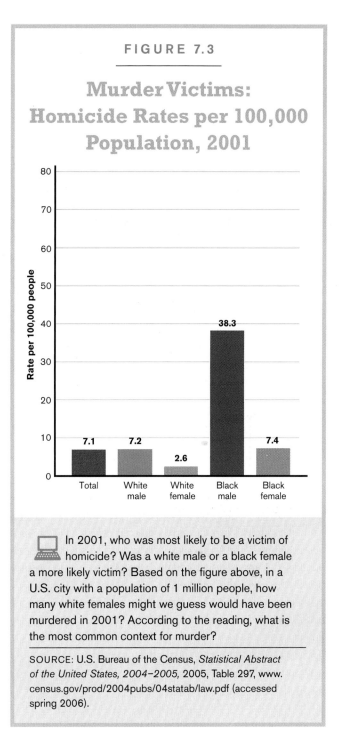

FIGURE 7.3

Murder Victims: Homicide Rates per 100,000 Population, 2001

In 2001, who was most likely to be a victim of homicide? Was a white male or a black female a more likely victim? Based on the figure above, in a U.S. city with a population of 1 million people, how many white females might we guess would have been murdered in 2001? According to the reading, what is the most common context for murder?

SOURCE: U.S. Bureau of the Census, *Statistical Abstract of the United States, 2004–2005*, 2005, Table 297, www.census.gov/prod/2004pubs/04statab/law.pdf (accessed spring 2006).

MALE AND FEMALE CRIME RATES

The statistics on gender and crime are startling. For example, of all crimes reported in 2004, an overwhelming 76.2 percent of arrestees were men (Table 7.2). There is also an enormous imbalance in the ratio of men to women in prison, not only in the United States but in all the industrialized countries. Women made up only 7.4 percent of the prison population in 2004.

TABLE 7.1

Crime Rates in Metropolitan vs. Rural Areas for 2002

TYPE OF CRIME	METROPOLITAN RATE (PER 100,000 POPULATION)	RURAL RATE
Violent crime	545.6	212.6
Murder	6.2	3.6
Forcible rape	33.8	23.8
Robbery	173.4	16.7
Assault	332.3	168.5
Property crime	3,863.5	1,696.1
Burglary	768.5	558.2
Larceny	2,596.4	1,005.0
Auto theft	498.6	132.8

SOURCE: U.S. Bureau of the Census 2002, Table 313.

There are also contrasts between the types of crimes men and women commit. The offenses of women rarely involve violence and are almost all small scale. Petty thefts like shoplifting and public order offenses such as public drunkenness and prostitution are typical female crimes.

Of course, it may be that the real gender difference in crime rates is less than the official statistics show. In the 1950s, Otto Pollak suggested as much, contending that certain crimes perpetrated by women tend to go unreported. He saw women's predominantly domestic role as providing them with the opportunity to commit crimes at home and in the private sphere. Pollak regarded women as naturally deceitful and highly skilled at covering up their crimes. He claimed this was grounded in biology, as women had learned to hide the pain and discomfort of menstruation from men and were also able to fake interest in sexual intercourse in a way that men could not! Pollak (1950) also argued that female offenders are treated more leniently because male police officers tend to adopt a "chivalrous" attitude toward them.

Pollak's portrayal of women as conniving and deceptive is based in groundless stereotypes, yet the suggestion that women are treated more leniently by the criminal justice system has prompted much debate and examination. The *chivalry thesis*

has been applied in two ways. First, it is possible that police and other officials may regard female offenders as less dangerous than men and let pass activities for which males would be arrested. Second, in sentencing for criminal offenses, women tend to be much less likely to be imprisoned than male offenders. A number of empirical studies have been undertaken to test the chivalry thesis, but the results remain inconclusive. One of the main difficulties is assessing the relative influence of gender compared to other factors such as age, class, and race. For example, it appears that older women offenders tend to be treated less aggressively than their male counterparts. Other studies have shown that black women receive worse treatment than white women at the hands of the police.

Another perspective, which has been adopted by feminists, examines how social understandings about femininity affect women's experiences in the criminal justice system. It has been argued that women are treated more harshly in cases in which they have allegedly deviated from the norms of female sexuality. For example, young girls who are perceived to be sexually promiscuous are more often taken into custody than boys. In such cases, women are seen as doubly deviant—not only have they broken the law but they have also flouted appropriate female behavior. In such cases, they are judged less on the nature of the offense and more on their deviant lifestyle choice. Thus a double standard exists within the criminal justice system: Where male aggression and violence is seen as a natural phenomenon, explanations for female offenses are sought in psychological imbalances (Heidensohn 1985).

In an effort to make female crime more visible, feminists have conducted a number of detailed investigations on female criminals—from girl gangs to female terrorists to women in prison. Such studies have shown that violence is not exclusively a characteristic of male criminality. Women are much less likely than men to participate in violent crime but are not always inhibited from taking part in violent episodes. Why, then, are female rates of criminality so much lower than those of men?

There is some evidence that female lawbreakers are quite often able to escape coming before the courts because they are able to persuade the police or other authorities to see their actions in a particular light. They invoke what has been called the *gender contract*—the implicit contract between men and women whereby to be a woman is to be erratic and impulsive on the one hand and in need of protection on the other (Worrall 1990).

Yet differential treatment could hardly account for the vast difference between male and female rates of crime. The reasons are almost certainly the same as those that explain gender differences in other spheres. Male crimes remain "male" because of differences in socialization and because men's activities and involvements are still more nondomestic than those of most women.

TABLE 7.2

Percentage of Crimes Committed by Men, 2004

CRIME	PERCENT MALE*
Total	**76.2**
Murder and nonnegligent manslaughter	88.4
Forcible rape	98.5
Robbery	89.0
Aggravated assault	79.3
Burglary	85.7
Larceny–theft	61.7
Motor vehicle theft	82.9
Arson	83.5

*Data represent arrests (not charges), estimated by the FBI.

SOURCE: Federal Bureau of Investigation, *Uniform Crime Report,* 2004, Table 42.

Ever since the late nineteenth century, criminologists have predicted that gender equality would reduce or eliminate the differences in criminality between men and women; but as yet, crime remains a gendered phenomenon. Whether the variations between female and male crime rates will one day disappear we still cannot say with any certainty.

CRIMES AGAINST WOMEN

There are certain categories of crime in which men are overwhelmingly the aggressors and women the victims. Domestic violence, sexual harassment, sexual assault, and rape are crimes in which males use their superior social or physical power against women. Although each of these has been practiced by women against men, they remain almost exclusively crimes carried out against women. It is estimated that one quarter of women are victims of violence at some point in their lives, but all women face the threat of such crimes either directly or indirectly.

For many years, these offenses were ignored by the criminal justice system; victims had to persevere tirelessly to gain legal recourse against an offender. Even today, the prosecution of crimes against women remains far from straightforward. Yet feminist criminology has done much to raise awareness of crimes against women and to integrate such offenses into main-

stream debates on crime. In this section we examine the crime of rape, leaving discussions of domestic violence and sexual harassment to other chapters (see Chapters 10 and 15).

The extent of rape is very difficult to assess with any accuracy. Only a small proportion of rapes actually come to the attention of the police and are recorded in the statistics. In 2004, 108,950 cases of rape or attempted rape and 95,420 cases of sexual assault were reported. Though from surveys of victims, we know that only about 36 percent of rapes are reported to the police (Bureau of Justice Statistics 2004a).

During the 1990s, there was an increase in the number of reported incidents in which the attacker was known to the victim: 62 percent of sexual assaults are committed by relatives, friends, former partners, or recent acquaintances—so-called date or acquaintance rapes. By 2004, this rate had risen to 67 percent (Bureau of Justice Statistics 2004a). It is estimated that half of all acquaintance rapes involve someone whom the victim has known for less than twenty-four hours. While the number of acquaintance rapes has risen, reported rapes involving strangers have dropped, accounting for 31 percent of all attacks in 2004 (Bureau of Justice Statistics 2004a).

There are many reasons that a woman might choose not to report sexual violence to the police. The majority of women who are raped either wish to put the incident out of their minds or are unwilling to participate in what can be a humiliating process of medical examination, police interrogation, and courtroom cross-examination. The legal process often takes a long time and can be intimidating. Courtroom procedure is public, and the victim must come face to face with the accused. Proof of penetration, the identity of the rapist, and the fact that the act occurred without the woman's consent all have to be forthcoming. A woman may feel that *she* is the one on trial, particularly if her own sexual history is examined publicly, as is often the case.

Over the last few years, women's groups have pressed for change in both legal and public thinking about rape. They have stressed that rape should not be seen as a sexual offense but as a type of violent crime. It is not just a physical attack but an assault on an individual's integrity and dignity. Rape is clearly related to the association of masculinity with power, dominance, and toughness. It is not for the most part the result of overwhelming sexual desire but of the ties between sexuality and feelings of power and superiority. The sexual act itself is less significant than the debasement of the woman (Estrich 1987). The campaign has had some real results in changing legislation, and rape is today generally recognized in law to be a specific type of criminal violence.

There is a sense in which all women are victims of rape. Women who have never been raped often experience anxieties similar to those who have. They may be afraid to go out alone at night, even on crowded streets, and may be almost equally fearful of being on their own in a house or apartment. Emphasizing the close connection between rape and orthodox male sexuality, Susan Brownmiller (1975) has argued that rape is part of a system of male intimidation that keeps all women in fear. Those who are not raped are affected by the anxieties thus provoked and by the need to be much more cautious in everyday aspects of life than men have to be.

Crimes against Gays and Lesbians

Feminists have pointed out that understandings of violence are highly gendered and are influenced by commonsense perceptions about risk and responsibility. Because women are generally seen as less able to defend themselves against violent attack, common sense holds that they should modify *their* behavior to reduce the risk of becoming a victim of violence. For example, not only should women avoid walking in unsafe neighborhoods alone and at night but they should be careful not to dress provocatively or to behave in a manner that could be misinterpreted. Women who fail to do so can be accused of "asking for trouble." In a court setting, their behavior can be taken as a mitigating factor in considering the perpetrator's act of violence (Dobash and Dobash 1992; Richardson and May 1999).

It has been suggested that a similar commonsense logic applies in the case of violent acts against gay men and lesbians. Victimization studies reveal that homosexuals experience a high incidence of violent crime and harassment. A national survey of over four thousand gay men and women found that in the previous five years, one third of gay men and one quarter of lesbians had been the victim of at least one violent attack. One third had experienced some form of harassment, including threats or vandalism. An overwhelming 75 percent had been verbally abused in public.

Because sexual minorities remain stigmatized and marginalized in many societies, there is a greater tendency for them to be treated as deserving of crime, rather than as innocent victims. Homosexual relationships are still seen as belonging to the private realm, whereas heterosexuality is the overwhelming norm in public spaces. Lesbians and gay men who deviate from this private–public contract by displaying their homosexual identities in public are often blamed for making themselves vulnerable to crime. There is a sense that introducing homosexuality into the public sphere represents a form of provocation.

This notion forms the basis of the "homosexual panic" legal defense that can be used in the legal system to reduce a charge of murder to that of manslaughter. The accused murderer can claim that an unwanted homosexual advance caused him or

Aaron McKinney, one of the men who killed Matthew Shepard, attempted to use the "homosexual panic" defense to reduce his sentence from murder to manslaughter, but the court disallowed it and he was convicted of first-degree felony murder.

her to lose control and to attack the victim. Such a defense was used unsuccessfully by a young man in the state of Wyoming in the murder trial of university student Matthew Shepard. The accused and two other men severely beat Shepard outside a bar before leaving him tied to a fence in the woods, in near-freezing temperatures. After eighteen hours he was found, and he died several days later. In cases like these, homophobic violence is taken as a justifiable response, and the essential personhood or right to life of the victim is discounted or denied. Crimes such as the murder of Matthew Shepard have led to calls by many social groups for the adoption of hate crime legislation to protect the human rights of groups who remain stigmatized in society.

Youth and Crime

Popular fear about crime centers on offenses such as theft, burglary, assault, and rape—street crimes that are largely seen as the domain of young working-class males. Media coverage of rising crime rates often focuses on moral breakdown among young people and highlights such issues as vandalism, school truancy, and drug use to illustrate the increasing permissiveness in society. This equation of youth with criminal activity is not a new one, according to some sociologists. Young people are often taken as an indicator of the health and welfare of society itself.

Official statistics about crime rates do reveal high rates of offense among young people. About 30 percent of all offenders arrested for criminal offenses in 2004 were under the age of twenty-one (Federal Bureau of Investigation 2005). For both males and females, the share of arrests by age peaks around age eighteen or nineteen and declines thereafter (Federal Bureau of Investigation 2005c). Yet we must approach assumptions about youth and crime with some caution. Moral panics about youth criminality may not accurately reflect social reality. An isolated event involving young people and crime can be transformed symbolically into a full-blown crisis of childhood, demanding tough law-and-order responses. The high-profile mass murder at Columbine High School is an example of how moral outrage can deflect attention from larger societal issues. Columbine was a watershed event in media portrayals of youth crime, and some have speculated that it led to copycat school killings in high schools in Arkansas, Kentucky, California, and elsewhere. Even though the number of murders committed on school grounds has been declining, attention to these mass murders has led many to think that all young children are potential violent threats. Although the perpetrators of the Columbine killings were labeled "monsters" and "animals," less attention was paid to how easily they were able to obtain the weapons they used to commit these murders.

Similar caution can be expressed about the popular view of drug use by teenagers. Every year, the Department of Health and Human Services conducts the National Survey of Drug Use and Health about the drug use habits of teens. In 2004 it surveyed nearly sixty-eight thousand noninstitutionalized individuals over the age of twelve and found that 42 percent of respondents between the ages of 12 and 17 had ever consumed alcohol and 34 percent had consumed alcohol in the last year. Similarly, about 12 percent had smoked a cigarette in the last month, while 30 percent had ever tried an illegal drug (U.S. Department of Health and Human Services 2005). Trends in drug use have shifted away from hard drugs such as heroin and toward combinations of substances such as amphetamines, prescription drugs like OxyContin, alcohol, and the drug ecstasy. Ecstasy in particular has become a "lifestyle" drug, associated with the rave and club subcultures, rather than the basis of an expensive, addictive habit. The war on drugs, some have argued, criminalizes large segments of the youth population who are generally law abiding (Muncie 1999).

What makes one drug a psychological tool and another a national menace? Ecstasy, the chemical compound methylenedioxymethamphetamine (MDMA), gives users a sustained feeling of pleasure by sending waves of the neurotransmitters serotonin and dopamine into the brain. In this regard, it is not dissimilar to antidepressants such as Prozac, which also influence the amount of serotonin that the brain produces. The use of both ecstasy and antidepressants by college students has risen dramatically in recent years, yet one is illegal and the other is a routinely prescribed medical option. Admittedly, the amphetamine-like and mildly hallucinogenic effects of ecstasy are considerably more dramatic and short-lived than the effects of Prozac. Long-term ecstasy use may cause brain damage. Nonetheless, MDMA was legal in the United States until 1985; because it has the effect of overcoming emotional inhibitions, some therapists used it on their patients in therapy sessions. More recently, MDMA has been used to treat rape victims in Spain, sufferers from post-traumatic stress disorder in Switzerland, and end-stage cancer patients in the United States.

The divergent ways in which ecstasy and Prozac have been viewed illustrate how deviant behavior is socially defined. From the perspective of lawmakers, MDMA became a dangerous drug as it morphed into ecstasy, now associated with youth culture, parties, and hedonism rather than medicine. Media coverage of ecstasy has also often been monolithic. It has become common for teen-oriented television shows such as *The O.C.* to do an ecstasy episode. Invariably, the protagonist taking ecstasy for the first time has a bad reaction and has to be rushed to the hospital. This is easier to portray than the more common experience: Ecstasy users find their early experiences with the drug to be blissful; problems occur over time, as the brain's receptivity to the drug diminishes.

Taking illegal drugs, like other forms of socially deviant behavior, is often defined in racial, class, and cultural terms; different drugs come to be associated with different groups and behaviors. When crack cocaine appeared in the 1980s, it was quickly defined by the media as the drug of choice for black, inner-city kids who listened to hip-hop. Perhaps as a result, jail sentences for crack possession were set at higher levels than sentences for possession of cocaine, which was associated more with white and suburban users. Ecstasy has, until recently, had similar white and middle- or upper-class associations.

Crimes of the Powerful

It is plain enough that there are connections between crime and poverty. But it would be a mistake to suppose that crime is concentrated among the poor. Crimes carried out by people in positions of power and wealth can have farther-reaching consequences than the often petty crimes of the poor.

The term **white-collar crime,** first introduced by Edwin Sutherland (1949), refers to crime typically carried out by people in the more affluent sectors of society. This category of criminal activity includes tax fraud, antitrust violations, illegal sales practices, securities and land fraud, embezzlement, the manufacture or sale of dangerous products, and illegal environmental pollution as well as straightforward theft. The distribution of white-collar crimes is even harder to measure than that of other types of crime; most do not appear in the official statistics at all.

Efforts made to detect white-collar crime are ordinarily limited, and it is only on rare occasions that those who are caught go to jail. Although the authorities regard white-collar crime in a more tolerant light than crimes of the less privileged, it has been calculated that the amount of money involved in white-collar crime in the United States is forty times greater than the amount involved in crimes against property, such as robberies, burglaries, larceny, forgeries, and car thefts (President's Commission on Organized Crime 1986). Some forms of white-collar crime, moreover, affect more people than lower-class criminality. An embezzler might rob thousands—or today, via computer fraud, millions—of people.

CORPORATE CRIME

Some criminologists have referred to **corporate crime** to describe the types of offenses that are committed by large corporations in society. Pollution, product mislabeling, and violations of health and safety regulations affect much larger numbers of people than does petty criminality. The increasing power and influence of large corporations and their rapidly growing global reach mean that our lives are touched by them in many ways. Corporations are involved in producing the cars we drive and the food we eat. They also have an enormous effect on the natural environment and financial markets, aspects of life that affect all of us.

Both quantitative and qualitative studies of corporate crime have concluded that a large number of corporations do not adhere to the legal regulations that apply to them (Slapper and Tombs 1999). Corporate crime is not confined to a few bad apples but is instead pervasive and widespread. Studies have revealed six types of violations linked to large corporations: *administrative* (paperwork or noncompliance), *environmental* (pollution, permits violations), *financial* (tax violations, illegal payments), *labor* (working conditions, hiring practices), *manufacturing* (product safety, labeling), and *unfair trade practices* (anticompetition, false advertising).

Sometimes there are obvious victims, as in environmental disasters such as the spill at the Bhopal chemical plant in India and the health dangers posed to women by silicone breast implants. The most famous recent case of white-collar crime with obvious victims was the Enron scandal. Enron grew to become America's seventh largest company in just fifteen years, but the company and its accountants lied about its profits and concealed its debts so they would not appear in the company accounts. The victims include pension holders, employees, and investors. Several executives, including Jeffrey Skilling and Kenneth Lay, were convicted of fraud and insider trading. Recently those injured in car crashes or relatives of those who were killed have called for the executives of car manufacturers to be brought to trial when the companies have shown negligence. But very often victims of corporate crime do not see themselves as such. This is because in "traditional" crimes the proximity between victim and offender is much closer—it is difficult not to realize that you have been mugged! In the case of corporate crime, greater distances in time and space mean that victims may not realize they have been victimized or may not know how to seek redress for the crime.

The effects of corporate crime are often experienced unevenly within society. Those who are disadvantaged by other types of socioeconomic inequalities tend to suffer disproportionately. For example, safety and health risks in the workplace tend to be concentrated most heavily in low-paying occupations. Many of the risks from health-care products and pharmaceuticals have had a greater effect on women than on men, as is the case with contraceptives and fertility treatments with harmful side effects (Slapper and Tombs 1999).

Violent aspects of corporate crime are less visible than in cases of homicide or assault, but they are just as real—and

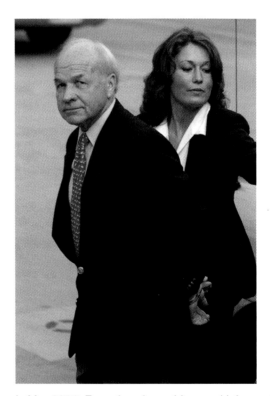

In May 2006, Enron founder and former chief executive Kenneth Lay was convicted of conspiracy and fraud. Lay died of heart disease in July 2006 before he could be sentenced.

may on occasion be much more serious in their consequences. For example, flouting regulations concerning the preparation of new drugs, safety in the workplace, or pollution may cause physical harm or death to large numbers of people. Deaths from hazards at work far outnumber murders, although precise statistics about job accidents are difficult to obtain. Of course, we cannot assume that all, or even the majority, of these deaths and injuries are the result of employer negligence in relation to safety factors for which they are legally liable. Nevertheless, there is some basis for supposing that many are due to the neglect of legally binding safety regulations by employers or managers.

Organized Crime

Organized crime refers to forms of activity that have some of the characteristics of orthodox business but that are illegal. Organized crime embraces illegal gambling, drug dealing, prostitution, large-scale theft, and protection rackets, among other activities. In *End of Millennium* (1998), Manuel Castells argues that the activities of organized crime groups are becoming increasingly international in scope. He notes that the coordination of criminal activities across borders—with the help of new information technologies—is becoming a central feature of the new global economy. Involved in activities ranging from the narcotics trade to counterfeiting to smuggling immigrants and human organs, organized crime groups are now operating in flexible international networks rather than within their own territorial realms.

According to Castells, criminal groups set up strategic alliances with each other. The international narcotics trade, weapons trafficking, the sale of nuclear material, and money laundering have all become linked across borders and crime groups. Criminal organizations tend to base their operations in "low-risk" countries where there are fewer threats to their activities. In recent years, the former Soviet Union has been one of the main points of convergence for international organized crime. The flexible nature of this networked crime makes it relatively easy for crime groups to evade the reach of law-enforcement initiatives. If one criminal safe haven becomes more risky, the organizational geometry can shift to form a new pattern.

The international nature of crime has been felt in the United States. Among the newest arrivals are criminals from the former Soviet Union. Some commentators believe that the new Russian mafia is the world's most dangerous organized crime syndicate. Russian criminal networks are deeply involved in money laundering, linking up their activities with Russia's largely unregulated banks. Some think the Russian groups may come to be the world's largest criminal networks. They have their basis in a mafia-riddled Russian state, where underworld protection is now routine for many businesses. The most worrying possibility is that Russia's new mobsters are smuggling nuclear materials on an international scale, materials taken from the old Soviet nuclear arsenal.

Despite numerous campaigns by the government and the police, the narcotics trade is one of the most rapidly expanding international criminal industries, having an annual growth rate of more than 10 percent in the 1980s and early 1990s and an extremely high level of profit. The United Nations Office on Drugs and Crime (2005) has estimated that in 2004 the global trade in illegal drugs was worth $322 billion—more than the global trade in coffee, grains, or meat. Heroin networks stretch across the Far East, particularly South Asia, and are also located in North Africa, the Middle East, and Latin America. Supply lines also pass through Vancouver and other parts of Canada, from where drugs are commonly supplied to the United States.

Cybercrime

Not only is international organized crime greatly facilitated by recent advances in information technology but it seems certain that the information and telecommunications revolution will change the face of crime in fundamental ways. Advances in technology have provided exciting new opportunities and benefits, but they also heighten vulnerability to crime. In 2005, a survey of computer security practitioners conducted by the FBI found that nearly 60 percent of companies have had unauthorized entry into their computer systems and that cybercrime cost over $130 million to American businesses (Computer Security Institute and Federal Bureau of Investigation 2005). Yet nearly 40 percent of security violations were not reported to the police out of fears that negative publicity would damage the stock price of the company or that competitors would steal valuable information. A similar survey of medium and large firms in the United Kingdom reported that 89 percent of respondents had experienced unauthorized access to their firm's computer networks and that computer crime cost those business over £2.4 billion in 2004 (National Hi Tech Crime Unit 2005).

There are indications that **cybercrime** is already on the rise. Internet-based fraud was the fastest growing category of crime in the United States in the late 1990s. From 1999 to 2000, losses from Internet fraud and forgery rose from $12 million to $117 million over the course of one year. The increase has been attributed to the growth in Internet-based crime.

The global reach of telecommunications crime poses particular challenges for law enforcement. Criminal acts perpe-

Drug Trafficking

How easy would it have been for you to purchase marijuana in high school? How easy would it be to do so today? Lamentable as it may seem to some, most young people in the United States have relatively easy access to illegal drugs. According to the National Survey on Drug Use and Health, nearly 11 percent of individuals between twelve and seventeen years old have used illegal drugs in the last month but less than 1 percent have tried heroin. Almost 53 percent of those between eighteen and twenty-five have tried marijuana at least once and nearly 2 percent have tried heroin (U.S. Department of Health and Human Services 2005).

What factors determine the availability of illegal drugs in your community? The level of police enforcement is important, of course, as is the extent of local demand. But no less important is the existence of networks of traffickers able to transport the drugs from the countries in which they are grown to your hometown. These networks have been able to flourish in part because of globalization.

While the cultivation of marijuana in the United States represents a major illicit industry, almost all of the world's coca

plants and opium poppies are grown in the developing world. The U.S. government spends billions of dollars each year to assist developing nations with eradication efforts and devotes significant resources to stopping the flow of drugs past U.S. borders. In 1995, the federal government spent more than $8.2 billion on the war on drugs; and between 1981 and 1996, it spent

trated in one country have the power to affect victims across the globe. This has troubling implications for detecting and prosecuting crimes. It becomes necessary for police from the countries involved to determine the jurisdiction in which the act occurred and to agree on extraditing the offenders and providing the necessary evidence for prosecution. Although police cooperation across national borders may improve with the growth of cybercrime, at present cybercriminals have a great deal of room to maneuver.

At a time when financial, commercial, and production systems in countries around the world are being integrated electronically, rising levels of Internet fraud and unauthorized electronic intrusions such as the DDoS attacks are serving as potent warnings of the vulnerability of existing computer security systems. From the FBI to the Japanese government's antihacker police force, governments are scrambling to contend with new and elusive forms of cross-national computer activity.

Crime-Reduction Strategies

Despite the misleading picture presented by official statistics, when they are taken together with data from victimization surveys it becomes clear that criminal offenses are assuming a more prominent role in society. Moreover, citizens *perceive* themselves to be at greater risk of falling victim to crime than in times past. Residents of inner-city areas have more reason to be concerned about crime than people living in other settings.

In the face of so many changes and uncertainties in the world around us, we are all engaged in a constant process of risk management. Crime is one of the most obvious risks that confront people in the late modern age. Yet it is not only individuals that have been caught up in risk management: Governments are now faced with societies that seem more dangerous a total of $65 billion (Bertram et al. 1996). By 2005, the federal budget for the war on drugs had climbed to $12.4 billion, but this figure excludes the costs of incarceration and military involvement (Office of National Drug Control Policy 2005). It also excludes funds spent to wage the war on drugs by state governments, which is estimated to be an additional $30 billion (Drug War Facts 2005). Despite this massive expenditure, there is little evidence that eradication or interdiction efforts have significantly decreased the supply of illegal drugs in the United States. Why have these efforts failed?

One answer is that the profit is simply too great. Farmers struggling to scratch out a living for themselves in Bolivia or Peru, members of the Colombian drug cartels, and low-level street dealers in the United States all receive substantial monetary rewards for their illegal activities. These rewards create a strong incentive to devise ways around antidrug efforts and to run the risk of getting caught.

Another answer—one discussed at a summit attended by leaders of the eight major industrial powers—is that drug traffickers have been able to take advantage of globalization. First, in their attempts to evade the authorities, traffickers make use of all the communications technologies that are available in a global age. As one commentator put it, drug traffickers "now use sophisticated technology, such as signal interceptors, to plot radar and avoid monitoring . . . [and] they can use faxes, computers and cellular phones to coordinate their activities and make their business run smoothly" (Chepesiuk 1998). Second, the globalization of the financial sector

has helped create an infrastructure in which large sums of money can be moved around the world electronically in a matter of seconds, making it relatively easy to "launder" drug money (i.e., to make it appear as if it came from a legitimate business venture). Third, recent changes in government policy designed to allow the freer flow of persons and legitimate goods across international borders have increased the opportunities for smuggling.

At the same time, globalization may create new opportunities for governments to work together to combat drug trafficking. Indeed, world leaders have called for greater international cooperation in narcotics enforcement, stressing the need for information sharing and coordinated enforcement efforts.

and uncertain than ever before. One of the central tasks of social policy in modern states has been controlling crime and delinquency. But if at one time government sought to guarantee security for its citizens, increasingly policies are aimed at managing insecurity.

Are Prisons the Answer?

"What are we going to do about these kids (monsters) who kill with guns??? Line them up against the wall and get a firing squad and pull, pull, pull. I am volunteering to pull, pull, pull" (anonymous letter received by a judge in Dade County, Florida).

This letter writer isn't alone. Although as measured by police statistics (problematic, as we have seen) rates of violent crime have declined since 1990, many people in the United States have started to view crime as their most serious social concern—more so than unemployment or the state of the econ-

omy (Lacayo 1994). Surveys show that Americans also favor tougher prison sentences for all but relatively minor crimes. The price of imprisonment, however, is enormous: It costs an average of $905,280 to keep a prisoner in the federal prison system for twenty years ($22,632 per inmate per year in 2001) (Stephen 2004). Moreover, even if the prison system were expanded, it wouldn't reduce the level of serious crime a great deal. Only about a fifth of all serious crimes result in an arrest—and this is of crimes known to the police, an underestimate of the true rate of crime. And no more than half of arrests for serious crimes result in a conviction. Even so, America's prisons are so overcrowded (Figure 7.4) that the average convict serves only a third of his or her sentence. The United States already locks up more people (nearly all men) per capita than any other country.

The United States has by far the most punitive justice system in the world. More than 2.1 million people are presently incarcerated in American prisons, with another 4.5 million

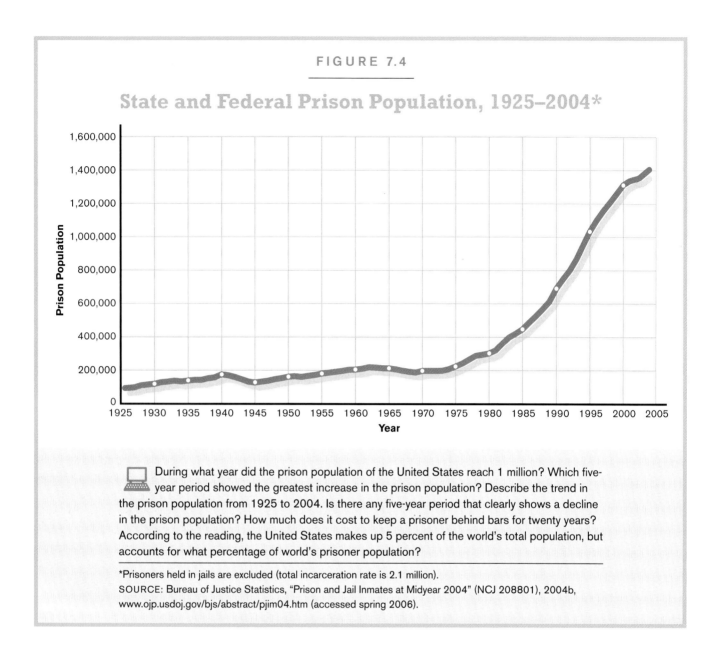

FIGURE 7.4

State and Federal Prison Population, 1925–2004*

During what year did the prison population of the United States reach 1 million? Which five-year period showed the greatest increase in the prison population? Describe the trend in the prison population from 1925 to 2004. Is there any five-year period that clearly shows a decline in the prison population? How much does it cost to keep a prisoner behind bars for twenty years? According to the reading, the United States makes up 5 percent of the world's total population, but accounts for what percentage of world's prisoner population?

*Prisoners held in jails are excluded (total incarceration rate is 2.1 million).
SOURCE: Bureau of Justice Statistics, "Prison and Jail Inmates at Midyear 2004" (NCJ 208801), 2004b, www.ojp.usdoj.gov/bjs/abstract/pjim04.htm (accessed spring 2006).

falling under the jurisdiction of the penal system (McDonough 2005; Slevin 2005). Although the United States makes up only 5 percent of the world's overall population, it accounts for 25 percent of the world's prisoners.

The American prison system employs more than 750,000 people (Slevin 2005) and costs nearly $60 billion annually to maintain (Bureau of Justice Statistics 2003b). It has also become partially privatized, with private companies now able to win government contracts to build and administer prisons to accommodate the growing inmate population. In 2004, almost 7 percent of the prison population were held in private facilities (Bureau of Justice Statistics 2004b). Critics charge that a "prison-industrial complex" has emerged: Large numbers of people—including bureaucrats, politicians, and prison employees—have

vested interests in the existence and further expansion of the prison system.

Support for *capital punishment* (the death penalty) is high in the United States. In 2005, approximately 74 percent of adults surveyed said that they believed in capital punishment; 23 percent opposed it (Gallup Organization 2005). This represents a significant shift from 1965, when 38 percent of those surveyed supported the death penalty and 47 percent were opposed. However, given the choice between the death penalty and life imprisonment, the share of those supporting the death penalty falls to 56 percent (Gallup Organization 2005). The number of individuals awaiting execution has climbed steadily since 1977, when the Supreme Court upheld state capital punishment laws. Since that time there have been 885 executions in the

United States (Bureau of Justice Statistics 2003a). Two thirds of these executions have taken place in five states: Texas (313), Virginia (89), Oklahoma (68), Missouri (61), and Florida (57). At the end of 2003, a total of 3,374 prisoners were held on death row (Bureau of Justice Statistics 2003a). Of these, 144 were new to death row in 2003 (Bureau of Justice Statistics 2003a), and all were convicted of murder. The group was 98.6 percent men, 56 percent white, and 42 percent black. In 2004, a total of 59 prisoners were executed in twelve states and all were men. Of these, 39 were white, 19 were black, and 1 was Asian (Bureau of Justice Statistics 2005).

In addition, more than one quarter of African American men are either in prison or under the control of the penal system. More than half (55 percent) of individuals in federal prisons in the United States are serving sentences for nonviolent drug-related crimes, while only 23 percent are serving time for a violent offense (The Sentencing Project 2004).

Although we might suppose that imprisoning large numbers of people or stiffening sentences would deter individuals from committing crimes, there is little evidence to support this. In fact, sociological studies have demonstrated that prisons can easily become schools for crime. Instead of preventing people from committing crimes, prisons often actually make them more hardened criminals. The more harsh and oppressive prison conditions are, the more likely inmates are to be brutalized by the experience. Yet if prisons were made into attractive and pleasant places to live, would they have a deterrent effect?

Although prisons do keep some dangerous men (and a tiny minority of dangerous women) off the streets, evidence suggests that we need to find other means to deter crime. Robert Gangi, director of the Correctional Association of New York, says that "building more prisons to address crime is like building more graveyards to address a fatal disease" (quoted in Molowe 1994). A sociological interpretation of crime makes clear that there are no quick fixes. The causes of crime, especially crimes of violence, are bound up with structural conditions of American society, including widespread poverty, the condition of the inner cities, and the deteriorating life circumstances of many young men.

The Mark of a Criminal Record

A recent experiment by sociologist Devah Pager (2003) showed the long-term consequences of prison on the lives of felons. Pager had pairs of young black and white men apply for real entry-level job openings throughout the city of Milwaukee. The applicant pairs were matched by appearance, interpersonal style, and—most important—by all job-related characteristics such as education level and prior work experience. In addition to varying the race of the applicant pairs, Pager also had applicants alternate presenting themselves to employers as having criminal records. One member of each of the applicant pairs would check the yes box on the applicant form in answer to the question, Have you ever been convicted of a crime? The pair alternated each week which young man would play the role of the ex-offender, to make sure that it was the criminal record—not the individual—that made a difference in employment outcomes.

The value of this experimental design is that it allows the sociologist to control for all the individual differences that may lead members of one group to be preferred to members of another. If whites, for example, on average have higher levels of education or more steady work experience than blacks, it's hard to determine whether race influences their employment opportunities or whether these other skill differences determine the results. The same problem applies to the question of how individuals with criminal records fare in the job market. Some would argue that a criminal record doesn't hold people back; instead, they might argue, it's the fact that people with criminal records don't work as hard as nonoffenders, or aren't as qualified for many jobs. The experiment allowed Pager to make the applicant pairs identical on all job-relevant characteristics so that she could know for sure that any differences she saw were the result of discrimination. It tested whether employers respond differently to otherwise equal candidates on the basis of race or criminal record alone.

Pager's study revealed some striking findings. To begin with, whites were much preferred over blacks, and nonoffenders were much preferred over ex-offenders. Whites with a felony conviction were half as likely to be considered by employers as equally qualified nonoffenders. For blacks the effects were even larger! Black ex-offenders were only one third as likely to receive a callback compared to nonoffenders. But most surprising was the comparison of these two effects: Blacks with *no criminal history* fared no better than did whites with a felony conviction! Essentially, these results suggest that being a black male in America today is about the same as being a convicted criminal, at least in the eyes of Milwaukee employers. For those who believe that race no longer represents a major barrier to opportunity, these results represent a powerful challenge. Being a black felon is a particularly tough obstacle to overcome.

Situational Crime Prevention

"Situational" crime prevention—such as target hardening and surveillance systems—has been a popular approach to managing the risk of crime. Such techniques are often favored by policy makers because they are relatively simple to introduce

When a Dissertation Makes a Difference

For Devah Pager, a young sociologist from Honolulu, "kulia i ka nu'u"—"to strive for the summit"—means to do research that can influence policy, a realistic quest for her if the last few years are any indication.

As a graduate student at the University of Wisconsin, she studied the difficulties of former prisoners trying to find work and, in the process, came up with a disturbing finding: It is easier for a white person with a felony conviction to get a job than for a black person whose record is clean.

Ms. Pager's study won the American Sociological Association's award for the best dissertation of the year in August [2003], prompting a *Wall Street Journal* columnist to write about it. Howard Dean repeated her main finding in stump speeches and interviews throughout his glory days as the front-runner.

Then, addressing the overall problem convicted felons have re-entering the job market, President Bush announced in the State of the Union message a $300 million program to provide mentoring and help them get work. Jim Towey, the director of the White House Office of Faith-Based and Community Initiatives, said that Ms. Pager's study was one of the many sources of information that helped shape the administration's four-year plan.

Ms. Pager, 32, is thrilled to see the issue receive national attention. More than half a million inmates will leave penal insti-

Devah Pager

tutions this year, and "the Administration is finally recognizing that the problems created by our incarceration policies can no longer be ignored," she said. Even if the promised amount is trivial, she said, the gesture is important symbolically.

Conversation with Ms. Pager flows easily. Over a plate of pancakes, she brushes aside a crush of thick loose auburn curls to punctuate less serious points with flashes of the wide, arresting smile her colleagues say is emblematic. She is known for her good nature and charismatic style, but it is her research that has made her one of the most promising young sociologists around.

alongside existing policing techniques, and they reassure citizens by giving the impression that decisive action against crime is being taken. Yet because such techniques do not engage with the underlying causes of crime—such as social inequalities, unemployment, and poverty—their greatest success lies in protecting certain segments of the population against crime and displacing delinquency into other realms.

One illustration of this dynamic can be seen in the physical *exclusion* of certain categories of people from common spaces in an attempt to reduce crime and the perceived risk of crime.

In response to feelings of insecurity among the population at large, public spaces in society—such as libraries, parks, and even street corners—are increasingly being transformed into "security bubbles." Risk-management practices such as police monitoring, private security teams, and surveillance systems are aimed at protecting the public against potential risks. In shopping malls, for example, security measures are becoming more prominent as part of a contractual bargain between businesses and consumers. To attract and maintain a customer base, businesses must ensure the safety and comfort of their

Initially Ms. Pager's interest was race, stirred by her move from Hawaii to Los Angeles to attend the University of California. "I was struck by the level of separation between racial groups on campus, throughout the city," she said. "Race seemed to define space. Hawaii, by contrast, has the highest rate of intermarriage in the country. Growing up, every other person, it seemed, was *hapa,* or half, the term used to describe someone multiracial or mixed." She added, "When you grow up with that being normal, everything else seems strange—and wrong."

She completed a master's degree at Stanford University and a second master's at the University of Cape Town in South Africa ***.

***

The interest in released prisoners arose while she was studying for her doctorate in Madison, Wisconsin. She *** volunteered for an organization that provides services and shelter to homeless men. There she met many black men with prison records. "It was a nice break to get out and do some direct service," she said. She spent time with the men *** and made herself available "as a resource, to allow them to unload." Those who had served jail time often talked about how it complicated the job search. "That was one of the first things that clued me into what an immutable barrier it was standing in their way," she said.

At about this time Human Rights Watch and the Sentencing Project reported that in seven states felony convictions had permanently disenfranchised one in four African American men. An innovative but difficult research plan began to take shape.

Both of her main advisers, Robert M. Hauser and Erik Olin Wright, tried to dissuade her, gently suggesting how hard it is for graduate students to obtain financial support, manage complicated field work and end up with meaningful results.

"She was undaunted," Mr. Wright said. "Her pluckiness is part of what makes her successful. She knew she could do it."

To isolate the effect of a criminal record on the job search, Ms. Pager sent pairs of young, well-groomed, well-spoken college men with identical resumes to apply for 350 advertised entry-level jobs in Milwaukee. The only difference was that one said he had served an 18-month prison sentence for cocaine possession. Two teams were black, two white.

*** For her black testers, the callback rate was 5 percent if they had a criminal record and 14 percent if they did not. For whites, it was 17 percent with a criminal record and 34 percent without.

"I expected there to be an effect of race, but I did not expect it to swamp the results as it did," Ms. Pager said. "It really was a surprise."

Jeff Manza, a colleague at Northwestern University, where she teaches, said, "Devah's work demonstrates in a new and convincing way the extent to which the 'second chance' that Bush talks about runs headlong into the realities of race and the fear of crime and criminals."

Similarly, Reginald Wilkinson, Ohio's top corrections official and the president of the Association of State Correctional Administrators, was impressed by her findings and methodology. "In my estimation, we can't eliminate the race question when we're talking about re-entry," he said. "I think what Professor Pager has done is raise consciousness about this."

***

Ms. Pager is replicating her research on a grander scale with one of the field's leading experts, Bruce Western of Princeton University ***.

The new study is another chance to further document the effects of race and imprisonment, another chance at "kulia i ka nu'u."

SOURCE: Brooke Kroeger, "When a Dissertation Makes a Difference," *New York Times,* March 20, 2004.

---

clients. Young people tend to be excluded from such spaces disproportionately because they are perceived as a greater threat to security because malls create "locations of trust" for consumers. Young people find that the public spaces open to them are shrinking.

Police forces have also been expanded in response to growing crime. When crime rates are on the rise, there is almost inevitably public clamor for putting more police on the street. Governments eager to appear decisive on crime tend to favor increasing the number and resources of the police in an at-

tempt to deter crime. The popularly held view of policing is that it is the cornerstone of maintaining law and order. But what is the role of the police in actually controlling crime? It is not clear that a greater number of police necessarily translates into lower crime rates. In the United States, official statistics on the violent crime rate and number of police cast doubt on the link between the two (Figure 7.5). This raises several puzzling questions. If increased policing does not prevent violent crime, why does the public demand a visible police presence? What role does policing play in our society?

FIGURE 7.5

Justice Employment and Crime Rates

Although the number of police steadily increased between 1982 and 2002, the crime rate dropped, increased, and dropped again during this period. Therefore, no causal link can be made between the number of police and the crime rate.

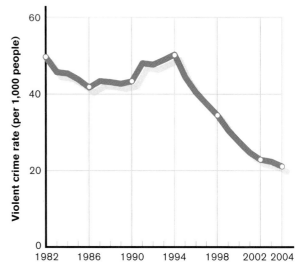

From 1986 to 1994 did the justice employment rate increase or decrease? During that same period, did the crime rate generally increase or decrease? Between 1982 and 1994, approximately how many additional justice employees (police, etc.) were added? What are the approximate crime rates in 1982 and 1994? According to the reading, the informational demands of what industry now directly shape the way in which police work?

SOURCE: Bureau of Justice Statistics, "Justice Expenditure and Employment Extracts, 2002," 2002c, Table 2, www.ojp.usdoj.gov/bjs/eande.htm#selected (accessed spring 2006) and Bureau of Justice Statistics, "National Crime Victimization Survey: Violent Crime Trends, 1973–2004," 2004d, www.ojp.usdoj.gov/bjs/glance/tables/viortrdtab.htm (accessed spring 2006).

Policing

Some sociologists and criminologists have suggested that visible policing techniques, such as patrolling the streets, are reassuring for the public. Such activities are consistent with the perception that the police are actively engaged in controlling crime, investigating offenses, and supporting the criminal justice system. But sociologists also suggest that we need to reassess the role of policing in the late modern age. Although maintaining law and order, interacting with citizens, and providing services are indeed part of a contemporary policing, they represent only a fraction of what the police actually do. Policing, sociologists argue, is now less about controlling crime and more about detecting and managing risks. Most of all, it is about communicating knowledge about risk to other institutions in society that demand that information (Ericson and Haggerty 1997).

According to this view, police are first and foremost "knowledge workers." By this sociologists mean that the vast majority of police time is spent on activities aimed at processing information, drafting reports, or communicating data. The "simple" case of an automobile accident in Ontario, Canada, illustrates this point. A police officer is called to the scene of an automobile accident involving two vehicles. No one has been killed, but there are minor injuries and one of the drivers is drunk. The investigation of the incident takes one hour; the drunk driver is criminally charged with the impaired operation of a motor vehicle causing bodily harm and with operating a motor vehicle with excess alcohol. The driver's license is automatically suspended for twelve hours.

Following this routine investigation, the officer spends three hours writing up sixteen separate reports documenting the incident. It is here that the role of police as brokers of information is clear:

- The *provincial motor registry* requires information about the location of the accident and the vehicles and people involved. This is used for risk profiling for use in accident prevention initiatives, traffic management, and resource allocation.
- The *automobile industry* needs to know about the vehicles involved in the accident to improve safety standards, to report back to regulatory agencies, and to provide safety information to consumer groups.
- The *insurance companies* involved need information about the accident to determine responsibility and to make awards in the case. They also require police information to develop their own statistical profiles of risk to set premiums and compensation levels for clients.
- The *public health system* requires details on the injuries involved and how they occurred. This knowledge is used for statistical profiles and to plan emergency service provision.
- The *criminal courts* require police information as material for the prosecution and as proof that the scene was properly investigated and evidence collected.
- The *police administration* itself requires reports on the incident for both internal records and national computer databases.

This example reveals how the police are a key node in a complicated information circuit of institutions that are all in the business of risk management. With the help of new forms of technology, police work is increasingly about "mapping" and predicting risk within the population.

The informational demands of other institutions, such as the insurance industry, now directly shape the way in which the police work. Police must gather and report information in a way that is compatible with the informational needs of outside agencies. Computerized systems and forms now define the way in which police report information. Rather than writing narrative accounts of incidents, police input the facts of a case into standardized forms by checking off boxes and choosing among available options. The information entered into such formats is used to categorize people and events as part of creating risk

profiles. But the closed-ended nature of such reporting formats influences what police observe and investigate, how they understand and interpret an incident, and the approach they take to resolving a problem.

This emphasis on information collection and processing can be alienating and frustrating for police. For many police officers, there is a distinction between real police work—such as investigating crimes—and the "donkey work" of reports and paper trails. Bureaucratic reporting procedures such as these are like a one-way mirror for many police officers who do not see the point of the extensive documentation that is required.

Crime and Community

Preventing crime and reducing fear of crime are both closely related to rebuilding strong communities. As we saw in our earlier discussions of the broken windows theory, one of the most significant innovations in criminology in recent years has been the discovery that the decay of day-to-day civility relates directly to criminality. For a long while attention was focused almost exclusively on serious crime—robbery, assault, and other violent crime. More minor crimes and forms of public disorder, however, tend to have a cumulative effect. When asked to describe their problems, residents of troubled neighborhoods mention abandoned cars, graffiti, prostitution, youth gangs, and similar phenomena.

People act on their anxieties about these issues: They leave the areas in question if they can, or they buy heavy locks for their doors and bars for their windows and abandon public places. Unchecked disorderly behavior signals to citizens that the area is unsafe. Fearful citizens stay off the streets, avoid certain neighborhoods, and curtail their normal activities and associations. As they withdraw physically, they also withdraw from roles of mutual support with fellow citizens, thereby relinquishing the social controls that formerly helped maintain civility within the community.

COMMUNITY POLICING

What should be done to combat this development? One idea that has grown in popularity in recent years is that the police should work closely with citizens to improve local community standards and civil behavior, using education, persuasion, and counseling instead of incarceration.

Community policing implies not only drawing in citizens themselves but changing the characteristic outlook of police forces. A renewed emphasis on crime prevention rather than law enforcement can go hand in hand with the reintegration of policing with the community. The isolation of the police from those they are supposed to serve often produces a siege mentality because the police have little regular contact with ordinary citizens.

In order to work, partnerships among government agencies, the criminal justice system, local associations, and community organizations have to be inclusive—all economic and ethnic groups must be involved (Kelling and Coles 1997). Government and business can act together to help repair urban decay. One model is the creation of business improvement districts providing tax breaks for corporations that participate in strategic planning and offer investment in designated areas. To be successful, such schemes demand a long-term commitment to social objectives.

Emphasizing these strategies does not mean denying the links between unemployment, poverty, and crime. Rather, the struggle against these social problems should be coordinated with community-based approaches to crime prevention. These approaches can in fact contribute directly and indirectly to furthering social justice. Where social order has decayed along with public services, other opportunities, such as new jobs, decline also. Improving the quality of life in a neighborhood can revive them.

SHAMING AS PUNISHMENT

The current emphasis on imprisonment as a means of deterring crime has a potentially crippling effect on the social ties within certain communities. In recent years, **shaming,** a form of punishing criminal and deviant behavior that attempts to maintain the ties of the offender to the community, has grown in popularity as an alternative to incarceration. According to some criminologists, the fear of being shamed within one's community is an important deterrent to crime. As a result, the public's formal disapproval could achieve the same deterrent effect as incarceration, without the high costs of building and maintaining prisons.

Criminologist John Braithwaite (1996) has suggested that shaming practices can take two forms: reintegrative shaming and stigmatizing shaming. Stigmatizing shaming is related to labeling theory, which we discussed earlier in the chapter, by which a criminal is labeled as a threat to society and is treated as an outcast. As a result, the labeling process and society's efforts to marginalize the individual reinforce that person's criminal conduct, perhaps leading to future criminal behavior and higher crime rates. The much different practice of reintegrative shaming works as follows. People central to the criminal's immediate community—such as family members, employers and co-workers, and friends—are brought into court to state their condemnation of the offender's behavior. At the same time, these people must accept responsibility for reintegrating the offender back into the community. The goal is to rebuild the social bonds of the individual to the community as a means of deterring future criminal conduct.

Japan, with one of the lowest crime rates in the world, has been quite successful in implementing this approach. The process is largely based on a voluntary network of over five hundred thousand local crime prevention associations dedicated to facilitating reintegration into the community and on a criminal justice system that is encouraged to be lenient for this purpose. As a result, in Japan only 5 percent of individuals convicted for a crime serve time in prison, compared to 30 percent in the United States. Though reintegrative shaming is not a standard practice in the American criminal justice system, it is a familiar practice in other social institutions such as the family. Think of a child who misbehaves. The parent may express disapproval of the child's behavior and try to make the child feel ashamed of her conduct, but the parent may also reassure the child that she is a loved member of the family.

Could reintegrative shaming succeed in the United States? In spite of the beliefs that these tactics are "soft" on crime, that Americans are too individualistic to participate in community-based policing, and that high-crime areas are less community oriented, community networks have been successful in working with the police in preventing crime. These social bonds could also be fostered to increase the power of shame and reintegrate offenders into local networks of community involvement.

Study Outline

www.wwnorton.com/giddens

Deviant Behavior

- Deviant behavior refers to actions that transgress commonly held norms. What is regarded as deviant can shift from time to time and place to place; normal behavior in one cultural setting may be labeled deviant in another.
- *Sanctions*, formal or informal, are applied by society to reinforce social norms. *Laws* are norms defined and enforced by governments; *crimes* are acts that are not permitted by those laws.

Biological and Psychological Theories of Crime and Deviance

- Biological and psychological theories have been developed claiming that crime and other forms of deviance are genetically determined, but these have been largely discredited. Sociologists argue that conformity and deviance intertwine in different social contexts. Divergencies of wealth and power in society strongly influence opportunities open to different groups of individuals and determine what kinds of activities are regarded as criminal. Criminal activities are learned in much the same way as are law-abiding ones and in general are directed toward the same needs and values.

Society and Crime: Sociological Theories

- Functionalist theories see crime and deviance as produced by structural tensions and a lack of moral regulation within society. Durkheim introduced the term *anomie* to refer to a feeling of anxiety and disorientation that comes with the breakdown of traditional life in modern society. Robert Merton extended the concept to include the strain felt by individuals whenever norms conflict with social reality. Subcultural explanations draw attention to groups, such as gangs, that reject mainstream values and replace them with norms celebrating defiance, delinquency, or nonconformity.
- *Interactionist theories* focus on deviance as a socially constructed phenomenon. Sutherland linked crime to *differential association*, the concept that individuals become delinquent through associating with people who are carriers of criminal norms. *Labeling theory*, a strain of interactionist theory that assumes that labeling someone as deviant will reinforce their deviant behavior, is important because it starts from the assumption that no act is intrinsically criminal (or normal). Labeling theorists are interested in how some behaviors come to be defined as deviant and why certain groups, but not others, are labeled as deviant.

- Conflict theories analyze crime and deviance in terms of the structure of society, competing interests between social groups, and the preservation of power among elites.
- *Control theories* posit that crime occurs when there are inadequate social or physical controls to deter it from happening. The growth of crime is linked to the growing number of opportunities and targets for crime in modern societies. The theory of broken windows suggests that there is a direct connection between the appearance of disorder and actual crime.

Gender and Crime

- Rates of criminality are much lower for women than for men, probably because of general socialization differences between men and women, and the greater involvement of men in nondomestic spheres. Unemployment and the crisis of masculinity have been linked to male crime rates. In some types of crimes, women are overwhelmingly the victims. Rape is almost certainly much more common than the official statistics reveal. There is a sense in which all women are victims of rape, since they have to take special precautions for their protection and live in fear of rape. Homosexual men and women experience high levels of criminal victimization and harassment, yet they are often seen as "deserving" of crime rather than innocent victims because of their marginalized position in society.

Types of Crime

- Popular fear about crime often focuses on street crimes—such as theft, burglary, and assault—that are largely the domain of young, working-class males. Official statistics reveal high rates of offense among young people, yet we should be wary of moral panics about youth crime. Much deviant behavior among youth, such as antisocial behavior and nonconformity, is not in fact criminal.
- *White-collar crime* and *corporate crime* refer to crimes carried out by those in the more affluent sectors of society. The consequences of such crime can be farther-reaching than the petty crimes of the poor, but there is less attention paid to them by law enforcement. *Organized crime* refers to institutionalized forms of criminal activity, in which many of the characteristics of orthodox organizations appear but the activities engaged in are systematically illegal. *Cybercrime* describes criminal activity that is carried out with the help of information technology, such as electronic money laundering and Internet fraud.

Crime, Deviance, and Social Order

- Prisons have developed partly to protect society and partly with the intention of reforming the criminal. Prisons do not seem to deter crime, and the degree to which they rehabilitate prisoners to face the outside world without relapsing into criminality is dubious. Alternatives to prison, such as community-based punishment, have been suggested.

Key Concepts

anomie (p. 185)
community policing (p. 207)
conflict theory (p. 188)
control theory (p. 189)
corporate crime (p. 198)
crimes (p. 184)
cybercrime (p. 199)
deviance (p. 179)
deviant subculture (p. 181)
differential association (p. 187)
labeling theory (p. 187)
laws (p. 184)
new criminology (p. 188)
norms (p. 179)
organized crime (p. 199)
primary deviation (p. 188)
psychopaths (p. 184)
sanction (p. 181)
secondary deviation (p. 188)
shaming (p. 208)
white-collar crime (p. 197)

Review Questions

1. What is deviance?
   a. A transgression of social norms that are accepted by most people in a community
   b. Breaking the law
   c. The kind of behavior engaged in by members of groups that have been marginalized by society
   d. None of the above
2. What is the theory of differential association?
   a. Individuals become delinquents by associating with those who are different from themselves.
   b. Individuals become delinquents by associating with carriers of criminal norms.
   c. Individuals become delinquents by associating with a range of deviant groups.
   d. Individuals become delinquents by associating with such aspects of aggressive male culture as professional wrestling and hunting clubs.

3. Compared with ordinary crimes against property (robberies, burglaries, larceny, etc.), the amount of money stolen in white-collar crime (tax fraud, insurance fraud, etc.) is
   a. about the same. Crimes against property cost the nation about as much as white-collar crime.
   b. less. White-collar crimes involve only one quarter of the money involved in crimes against property.
   c. more. White-collar crime involves perhaps forty times as much money as crimes against property.
   d. not really comparable. White-collar crimes such as embezzlement affect very few people.
4. Crime is sociological in nature because
   a. anomie is common in modern societies.
   b. the definition of crime depends on the social context.
   c. criminals are socialized into committing crimes.
   d. criminals tend to be psychopaths.
5. Why did Émile Durkheim think a certain amount of crime was functional for society?
   a. Because it gave a healthy release for male aggression.
   b. Because it highlighted the boundaries of social norms.
   c. Because it kept the police and court system active.
   d. Because the existence of crime makes law-abiding citizens more careful about protecting their property.
6. Why is the crime rate so much higher in the United States than in other industrialized countries?
   a. It isn't.
   b. Crime rates in most of America are close to the average for industrialized countries, but the U.S. average is pulled up by very high crime rates in New York City.
   c. It is caused by a combination of ready access to firearms, the influence of the frontier tradition, and the violent subculture of American cities.
   d. It comes from the fast pace of American life and our bad diet: the potent concoction of junk food packed with carbohydrates and artificial sweeteners, endless traffic congestion, and violent television shows make Americans more bad tempered and hostile to one another than people in other industrialized countries.
7. What is target hardening?
   a. A technique to make it more difficult for crimes to take place by intervening directly in potential crime situations
   b. Any small sign of social disorder that will encourage more serious crime
   c. A form of punishing criminal and deviant behavior that attempts to maintain the ties of the offender to the community
   d. A theory that posits that crime occurs as a result of an imbalance between impulses toward criminal activity and the social or physical controls that deter it
8. Howard S. Becker found a number of reasons to account for a person becoming a marijuana smoker. Which of the following is not a factor mentioned by Becker?
   a. Acceptance into the marijuana subcultures
   b. Close association with experienced users

c. Peer pressure

d. Attitudes toward nonusers

9. What is the attitude toward capital punishment in the United States over the past few decades?

a. More people are in favor of capital punishment.

b. Fewer people are in favor of capital punishment.

c. There has been no change in attitude toward capital punishment during the past few decades.

d. There is no clear trend in people's attitudes toward capital punishment.

10. What is the essence of labeling theory?

a. Deviance is defined through the process of interaction between deviants and nondeviants.

b. Deviance is in the eye of the officeholder.

c. One person's deviance is another's indulgence.

d. Deviants resist the labels they are given by law enforcement authorities.

Thinking Sociologically Exercises

1. Briefly summarize several leading theories explaining crime and deviance presented in this chapter: differential association, anomie, labeling, conflict, and control theories. Which theory appeals to you more than the others? Explain why.

2. Explain how differences in power and social influence can play a significant role in defining and sanctioning deviant behavior.

Data Exercises

www.wwnorton.com/giddens
Keyword: Data7

How much do you know about patterns of crime in your community, your state, or in the United States as a whole? What are your sources of information—personal experiences, the experiences of family or friends, or the media? In the data exercise for Chapter 7 you will have a chance to study state-level crime rates and the changes in the rate over time to gain a better understanding of what the patterns are like.

PART THREE

STRUCTURES OF POWER

Power is an ever-present phenomenon in social life. In all human groups, some individuals have more authority or influence than others, and groups themselves have varying degrees of power. Power and inequality tend to be closely linked. The powerful are able to accumulate valued resources, such as property and wealth; possession of such resources is in turn a means of generating more power.

In this part, we look at some of the main systems of power and inequality. Chapter 8 discusses stratification and class structure—the ways in which inequalities are distributed within societies. Chapter 9, on global inequality, builds on this and examines the ways in which inequalities are distributed across societies. Chapter 10 then analyzes the differences and inequalities between men and women and how these inequalities are tied to other forms of inequality based on class and race. Chapter 11, on race and ethnicity, examines the tensions and hostilities often found between people who are physically or culturally different from one another. Chapter 12, on aging, discusses the experience of growing old and analyzes the social problems resulting from this experience. Chapter 13 analyzes the state, political power, and social movements. Governments are specialists in power; they are the source of the directives that influence many of our daily activities. On the other hand, they are also the focus of resistance and rebellion, political action that can lead to far-reaching political and social change.

Systems of Stratification

Learn about social stratification and the importance of social background in an individual's chances for material success.

Classes in Western Societies Today

Know the class differences that exist in U.S. society, what they are influenced by, and how they are defined and determined.

Inequality in the United States: A Growing Gap between Rich and Poor

Recognize the many ways in which the gap between rich and poor has grown larger.

Social Mobility

Understand the dynamics of social mobility, and think about your own mobility.

Poverty in the United States

Learn about the conditions of poverty in the United States today, competing explanations for why it exists, and means for combating it.

Social Exclusion

Learn the processes by which people become marginalized in a society and the forms that it takes.

Theories of Stratification in Modern Societies

Become acquainted with the most influential theories of stratification—those of Karl Marx, Max Weber, and Erik Olin Wright.

Growing Inequality in the United States

Learn how changes in the American economy have led to growing inequalities since the 1970s.

CHAPTER EIGHT

STRATIFICATION, CLASS, AND INEQUALITY

ate and Ellen were joking with Robert about having found him a date for the dance. I did not catch the name of the girl they were making fun of, but they told him he could go with that "big, fat, blond girl." This inspired Robert to start making jokes about the trouble he would have wrapping his arms around the girl and to laugh about how she would roll over him. (Milner 2004)

This high school conversation was recorded as part of a study of teenage behavior by sociologist Murray Milner. Milner wanted to find out why American teenagers are so status conscious—why it is so important to look good and be popular that high school students routinely spend large amounts of money on clothing and other consumer goods, while ruthlessly putting down anyone who in their view doesn't make the grade.

Milner's book—*Freaks, Geeks, and Cool Kids*—is based on interviews with hundreds of college students about their high school experiences as well as detailed observations of a single high school over a three-year period. It sets out to answer some questions about behavior that have troubled American teenagers for a half century or more:

Why are many teenagers obsessed with who sits with them at lunch, the brand of clothes they wear, what parties they are invited to, the privacy of their bedrooms, who is dating or hooking up with whom, what is the latest popular music? Why have alcohol, drug use, and casual sex become so widespread? ... Why are teenagers frequently mean and even cruel to one another? Why do girls see one another as more petty and catty than the boys? (Milner 2004)

The answers, Milner argues, have to do with teenage power, or rather the lack of it. Teenagers have little economic or political power. Stuck somewhere between childhood and adulthood, they spend most of their days in class, where they have little influence over their lives. After school, their parents have the last say (or at least think they should). Teenagers respond by creating social worlds in which their ability to evaluate one another—usually by standards very different from those of their parents or teachers—provides them with a sense of power.

Milner calls such power "status power." Sociologists define **status** as the prestige that goes along with one's social position. Status power derives from the ability to increase one's own prestige, often at the expense of others. This ability depends in large part on the basis of one's social location, in this case, in the high school pecking order. Who you date is important, because the people you hang out with have a big influence on your social status. Putting others down helps make sure that the in-crowd is a small, exclusive club. Dressing like the in-crowd, or having the latest model cell phone, iPod, or other consumer gadget, is another important marker of status. In fact, consumerism in general is a key source of status power. As Milner (2004) notes: "consumerism in high schools is not only about clothes, but also a broader array of expensive items, such as the limousine to go to the prom or the hotel suite that is rented for the all-night party afterward, or where you will fly to for spring break."

The importance of teenage consumption is not lost to corporations, which target the high school market with a vengeance. Milner argues that, although many high schools may fail to fully achieve their educational goals, they most certainly teach a "desire to consume"—not through the formal curriculum, "but through the status concerns and peer groups that intensify during adolescence." This is a key feature of American consumer capitalism: producing lifelong consumers.

In this chapter we examine the relationships among social status, economic position, and inequality in society.

Sociologists speak of **social stratification** to describe such inequalities among individuals and groups within human societies. Often we think of stratification in terms of assets or property; but it can also occur on the basis of other attributes, such as gender, age, religious affiliation, or military rank. The three key aspects of social stratification are class, status, and power (Weber 1947). Although they frequently overlap, this is not always the case. The "rich and famous" often enjoy high status; their wealth often provides political influence and sometimes direct access to political power. Yet there are exceptions. Drug lords, for example, may be wealthy and powerful, yet they usually enjoy low status. On the other hand, when Mahatma Gandhi died in 1948, his total worldly possessions could be carried in his blanket. Although he chose to live in poverty, he enjoyed the highest status and power in India, having led his country to independence from Britain through nonviolent civil disobedience. In this chapter, we focus on stratification in terms of inequalities based on wealth and income, status, and power. In later chapters, we will look at the ways in which gender (Chapter 10), race and ethnicity (Chapter 11), and age (Chapter 12) all play a role in stratification.

Individuals and groups enjoy unequal access to rewards on the basis of their position within the stratification scheme. Thus stratification can most simply be defined as **structured inequalities** among different groupings of people. Sociologists believe that these inequalities are built into the system, rather than resulting from individual differences or chance occurrences, such as winning a lottery. It is useful to think of stratification like the geological layering of rock in the earth's surface. Societies can be seen as consisting of "strata" in a hierarchy, with the more favored at the top and the less privileged nearer the bottom.

We can speak of an American system of stratification because individuals' chances for material success are strongly influenced by their social background. We will study stratification and inequality in the United States later in the chapter, but first we need to analyze the different types of stratification that exist and have existed in the past.

Systems of Stratification

All socially stratified systems share three characteristics:

1. **The rankings apply to social categories of people who share a common characteristic without necessarily interacting or identifying with each other.** Women may be ranked differently from men, wealthy people differently from the poor. This does not mean that individuals from a particular category cannot change their rank; however, it does mean that the category continues to exist even if individuals move out of it and into another category.

2. **People's life experiences and opportunities depend heavily on how their social category is ranked.** Being male or female, black or white, upper class or working class makes a big difference in terms of your

life chances—often as big a difference as personal effort or good fortune (such as winning a lottery).

3. **The ranks of different social categories tend to change very slowly over time.** In U.S. society, for example, only in the last quarter century have women as a whole begun to achieve equality with men (see Chapter 10). Only in the past quarter century have significant numbers of African Americans begun to obtain economic and political equality with whites—even though slavery was abolished nearly a century and a half ago and discrimination outlawed in the 1950s and 1960s (see Chapter 11).

As you saw in Chapter 3, stratified societies have changed throughout human history. The earliest human societies, which were based on hunting and gathering, had very little social stratification—mainly because there was very little by way of wealth or other resources to be divided up. The development of agriculture produced considerably more wealth and, as a result, a great increase in stratification. Social stratification in agricultural societies increasingly came to resemble a pyramid, with a large number of people at the bottom and a successively smaller number of people as you move toward the top. Today, advanced industrial societies are extremely complex; their stratification is more likely to resemble a teardrop, with large number of people in the middle and lower-middle ranks (the so-called middle class), a slightly smaller number of people at the bottom, and very few people as one moves toward the top.

But before turning to stratification in modern societies, let's first review the three basic systems of stratification: slavery, caste, and class.

Slavery

Slavery is an extreme form of inequality, in which certain people are owned as property by others. The legal conditions of slave ownership have varied considerably among different societies. Sometimes slaves were deprived of almost all rights by law, as was the case on Southern plantations in the United States. In other societies, their position was more akin to that of servants. For example, in the ancient Greek city-state of Athens, some slaves occupied positions of great responsibility. They were excluded from political positions and from the military but were accepted in most other types of occupations. Some were literate and worked as government administrators; many were trained in craft skills. Even so, not all slaves could count on such a good fate. For the less fortunate, their days began and ended in hard labor in the mines.

Throughout history, slaves have often fought back against their subjection; the slave rebellions in the American South before the Civil War are one example. Because of such resistance, systems of slave labor have tended to be unstable. High productivity could be achieved only through constant supervision and brutal punishment. Slave-labor systems eventually broke down, partly because of the struggles they provoked and partly because economic or other incentives motivate people to produce more effectively than does direct compulsion. Slavery is simply not economically efficient. Moreover, from about the eighteenth century on, many people in Europe and America came to see slavery as morally wrong. Today, slavery is illegal in every country of the world, but it still exists in some places. Recent research has documented that people are taken by force and held against their will—from enslaved brick makers in Pakistan to sex slaves in Thailand to domestic slaves in France. Slavery remains a significant human rights violation in the world today (Bales 1999). It is estimated that in 2001 one million women and girls were forced or lured into prostitution and sold in the international sex trafficking business, which is valued at an estimated $7 billion a year (Hughes 2001).

Caste Systems

A **caste system** is a social system in which one's social status is bestowed for life. In **caste societies,** therefore, different social levels are closed, so that all individuals must remain at the social level of their birth throughout life. Everyone's social status is based on personal characteristics—such as perceived race or ethnicity (often based on such physical characteristics as skin color), parental religion, or parental caste—that are accidents of birth and are therefore believed to be unchangeable. A person is born into a caste and remains there for life. In a sense, caste societies can be seen as a special type of class society—in which class position is ascribed at birth, rather than achieved through personal accomplishment. They have typically been found in agricultural societies that have not yet developed industrial capitalist economies, such as South Africa before the end of white rule in 1992 or in rural India.

Before modern times, caste systems were found throughout the world. In Europe, for example, Jews were frequently treated as a separate caste, forced to live in restricted neighborhoods and barred from intermarrying (and in some instances even interacting) with non-Jews. The term *ghetto,* for example, is said to derive from the Venetian word for "foundry," the site of one of Europe's first official Jewish ghettos, established by the government of Venice in 1516. The term eventually came to refer to those sections of European towns in which Jews were legally compelled to live, long before it was used to describe minority neighborhoods in U.S. cities, with their castelike qualities of racial and ethnic segregation.

In caste systems, intimate contact with members of other castes is strongly discouraged. Such "purity" of a caste is often maintained by rules of **endogamy,** marriage within one's social group as required by custom or law.

CASTE IN INDIA AND SOUTH AFRICA

The few remaining caste systems in the world are being seriously challenged by globalization. The Indian caste system, for example, reflects Hindu religious beliefs and is more than two thousand years old. According to Hindu beliefs, there are four major castes, each roughly associated with broad occupational groupings. The four castes consist of the *Brahmins* (scholars and spiritual leaders) on top, followed by the *Ksyatriyas* (soldiers and rulers), the *Vaisyas* (farmers and merchants), and the *Shudras* (laborers and artisans). Beneath the four castes are those known as the "untouchables" or *Dalits* ("oppressed people"), who—as their name suggests—are to be avoided at all costs. Untouchables are limited to the worst jobs in society such as removing human waste, and they often resort to begging and searching in garbage for their food. In traditional areas of India, some members of higher castes still regard physical contact with untouchables to be so contaminating that mere touching requires

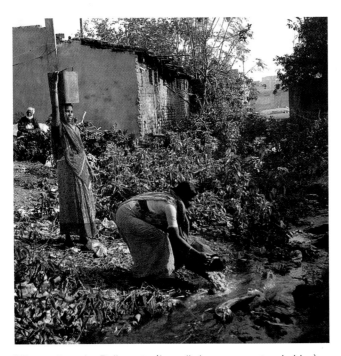

Women from the Dalit caste (formally known as untouchables) earn a living as sewage scavengers in the slums of Ranchi. They are paid between 30 and 100 rupees per house per month for retrieving human waste from residential dry latrines and emptying the buckets into nearby gutters and streams.

cleansing rituals. India made it illegal to discriminate on the basis of caste in 1949, but aspects of the caste system remain in full force today, particularly in rural areas.

As India's modern capitalist economy brings people of different castes together, whether it be in the same workplace, airplane, or restaurant, it is increasingly difficult to maintain the rigid barriers required to sustain the caste system. As more and more of India becomes affected by globalization, it seems reasonable to assume that its caste system will weaken still further.

Before its abolition in 1992, the South African caste system, termed *apartheid* (pronounced "a-PART-ide"; Afrikaans for "separateness"), rigidly separated black Africans, Indians, "colored" (people of mixed races), and Asians from whites. In this case, caste was based entirely on race. Whites, who made up only 15 percent of the total population, controlled virtually all of the country's wealth, owned most of the usable land, ran the principal businesses and industries, and had a monopoly on political power because blacks lacked the right to vote. Blacks —who made up three quarters of the population—were segregated into impoverished *bantustans* ("homelands") and were allowed out only to work for the white minority.

Apartheid, widespread discrimination, and oppression created intense conflict between the white minority and the black, mixed-race, and Asian majority. Decades of often violent struggle against apartheid finally proved successful in the 1990s. The most powerful black organization, the African National Congress (ANC), mobilized an economically devastating global boycott of South African businesses, forcing South Africa's white leaders to dismantle apartheid, which was abolished by popular vote among South African whites in 1992. In 1994, in the country's first ever multiracial elections, the black majority won control of the government, and Nelson Mandela—the black leader of the ANC, who had spent twenty-seven years imprisoned by the white government—was elected president.

CASTE IN THE UNITED STATES

In the South in United States before the Civil War, African Americans were officially members of a lower caste. As in South Africa, their caste was based on their race. Most African Americans were born as slaves and died as slaves. They were forbidden to marry across racial lines and were legally treated as the property of their white owners. Although the North's victory in the Civil War officially put an end to slavery in 1865, legal segregation of schools, restaurants, and public facilities maintained aspects of the caste system in many southern states for another century. The U.S. Supreme Court, in the landmark *Brown v. Board of Education* decision in 1954, ended legal segregation in public schools, and the Civil Rights Act of

1964 abolished discrimination on the basis of race. The treatment of African Americans as a separate caste is no longer legal in the United States, but it continues nonetheless in the form of discrimination and prejudice—for example, it was not until November 2000 that Alabama voters deleted a part of the state's constitution that prohibited interracial marriages. Studies show that when equally qualified black and white individuals apply for the same job, whites are much more likely than blacks to be hired (Bendick et al. 1993). Blacks are also more likely than whites to be turned down for bank loans for mortgages, automobile insurance, or small businesses (*Business Journal* 2000; Hamilton 2000).

Milner's study of high school status systems reveals its caste-like qualities. High school cliques are typically closed groups: you are either in or out, a distinction that is maintained through informal dress codes, dating patterns, and intense peer pressure. Much like the Indian caste system, students in the in-group avoid associating with lower-status students at all costs, except for purely practical purposes: "the beautiful cheerleader can work with a bright nerd on a class project, [just as] the Brahmin can supervise Untouchables working in the field . . . but when work is done, they go their separate ways" (Milner 2004). Group membership often reflects the accidents of birth: high schools are frequently stratified by race and ethnicity as well as by social class. The wealthiest students tend to hang out together, their status marked by patterns of consumption that other students can only envy: fancy cars, large homes, expensive vacations.

Class

The concept of **class** is most important for analyzing stratification in industrialized societies like the United States. Everyone has heard of class, but most people in everyday talk use the word in a vague way. As employed in sociology, the word has some precision.

A social class is a large group of people who occupy a similar economic position in the wider society. The concept of life chances, introduced by Max Weber, is the best way to understand what class means. Your **life chances** are the opportunities you have for achieving economic prosperity. A person from a humble background, for example, has less chance of ending up wealthy than someone from a more prosperous one. And the best chance an individual has of being wealthy is to start off as wealthy in the first place.

America, it is always said, is the land of opportunity. For some, this is so. There are many examples of people who have risen from lowly circumstances to positions of great wealth and power. And yet there are more cases of people who have

not, including a disproportionate share of women and members of minority groups. The idea of life chances is important because it emphasizes that although class is an important influence on what happens in our lives, it is not completely determining. Class divisions affect which neighborhoods we live in, what lifestyles we follow, and even which sexual or marriage partners we choose (Mare 1991; Massey 1996). Yet they don't fix people for life in specific social positions, as the older systems of stratification did. A person born into a caste position has no opportunity of escaping from it; the same isn't true of class.

Class systems differ from slavery and castes in four main respects:

1. **Class systems are fluid.** Unlike the other types of strata, classes are not established by legal or religious provisions. The boundaries between classes are never clear cut. There are no formal restrictions on intermarriage between people from different classes.

2. **Class positions are in some part achieved.** An individual's class is not simply assigned at birth, as is the case in the other types of stratification systems. Social mobility—movement upward and downward in the class structure—is more common than in the other types.

3. **Class is economically based.** Classes depend on economic differences between groups of individuals—inequalities in the possession of material resources. In the other types of stratification systems, noneconomic factors (such as race in the former South African caste system) are generally most important.

4. **Class systems are large scale and impersonal.** In the other types of stratification systems, inequalities are expressed primarily in personal relationships of duty or obligation—between slave and master or lower- and higher-caste individuals. Class systems, by contrast, operate mainly through large-scale, impersonal associations. For instance, one major basis of class differences concerns inequalities of pay and working conditions.

WILL CASTE GIVE WAY TO CLASS?

There is some evidence that globalization will hasten the end of legally sanctioned caste systems throughout the world. Most official caste systems have already given way to class-based ones in industrial capitalist societies; South Africa, mentioned earlier, is the most prominent recent example. Modern industrial production requires that people move about freely, work at whatever jobs they are suited or able to do, and change jobs frequently according to economic conditions. The rigid restrictions found in caste systems interfere with this necessary freedom. Furthermore, as the world increasingly becomes a single economic unit, castelike relationships will become more and more vulnerable to economic pressures. Nonetheless, elements of caste persist even in advanced industrial societies. For example, some Indian immigrants to the United States seek to arrange traditional marriages for their children along caste lines, and the relatively small number of intermarriages between blacks and whites in the United States suggests the strength of caste barriers.

And moving up in the American class structure, which according to popular belief is always possible with hard work and a little luck, in fact turns out to be rather difficult: As we will see later in this chapter, the social class into which one is born has a large effect on where one winds up later in life. While examples can always be found of Americans born to humble origins who rose to be come heads of major corporations, prominent politicians, or Supreme Court justices, these examples are not typical. The American class system, in other words, has castelike aspects. To the extent that inequality and poverty continue to increase in the coming years, the prospects of improving one's class position will likely diminish even further.

IS INEQUALITY DECLINING IN CLASS-BASED SOCIETIES?

There is some evidence that at least until recently, the class systems in mature capitalist societies became increasingly open to movement between classes, thereby reducing the level of inequality. In 1955, the Nobel Prize–winning economist Simon Kuznets proposed a hypothesis that has since been called the **Kuznets curve:** a formula showing that inequality increases during the early stages of capitalist development, then declines, and eventually stabilizes at a relatively low level (Figure 8.1). Studies of European countries, the United States, and Canada suggested that inequality peaked in these places before World War II, declined through the 1950s, and remained roughly the same through the 1970s (Berger 1986; Nielsen 1994). Lowered postwar inequality was due in part to economic expansion in industrial societies, which created opportunities for people at the bottom to move up, and because of government health insurance, welfare, and other programs aimed at reducing inequality. However, Kuznets's prediction may well turn out to apply only to a particular phase of economic growth in industrial societies. As you will see later in this chapter, as well as in Chapter 14 (where we discuss the changing nature of the American economy), during the past quarter century or so inequality has actually been increasing in the United States.

Classes in Western Societies Today

Let's begin our exploration of class differences in modern societies by looking at basic divisions of income, wealth, educational attainment, and occupational status within the population as a whole.

Income

Income refers to wages and salaries earned from paid occupations, plus unearned money from investments. One of the most significant changes occurring in Western countries over the past century has been the rising real income of the majority of the working population. (Real income is income excluding rises owing to inflation, to provide a fixed standard of comparison from year to year.) Blue-collar workers in Western societies now earn three to four times as much in real income as their counterparts at the turn of the century, even if their real income has dropped over the past twenty years. Gains for white-collar, managerial, and professional workers have been higher still. In terms of earnings per person (per capita) and the range of goods and services that can be purchased, the majority of the population today are vastly more affluent than any peoples have previously been in human history. One of the most important reasons for this growth is the increasing productivity—output per worker—that has been secured through technological development in industry. The volume of goods and services produced per worker has risen more or less continually since the 1900s.

Nevertheless, income distribution is quite unequal. In 2004, the top 5 percent of earners in the United States received 21.8 percent of total income; the highest 20 percent obtained 50.1 percent; and the bottom 20 percent received only 3.4 percent (Figure 8.2). Between 1977 and 2004, income inequality has increased dramatically. The average pretax earnings of the bottom 80 percent of people in the United States declined by 10.9 percent (U.S. Bureau of the Census 2005a). During the same period, the richest fifth saw their incomes grow by 13.8 percent before taxes, while the richest 5 percent of the population increased their share of all income by nearly 30 percent—and the tax burden on these people was lower in 2004 than it had been in 1977. For the top 1 percent of earners, incomes approximately doubled during the same period. And despite the growth of the economy and the creation of millions of new jobs, these trends continued throughout the 1990s and into the new century, leading some observers to deem the United States a "two-tiered society" (Freeman 1999).

FIGURE 8.1

The Kuznets Curve

The Kuznets curve, named for the Nobel Prize–winning economist who first advanced the idea in 1955, argues that inequality increases during early industrialization, then decreases during later industrialization, eventually stabilizing at low levels. There is some evidence that inequality may increase once again during the transition to postindustrial society.

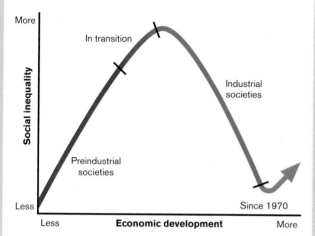

According to the reading, why does the Kuznets curve predict that social inequality will go down as nations transition from preindustrial societies to industrial societies? What actions can individual governments in industrial societies take that would lower the level of social inequality?

SOURCE: Francois Nielsen, "Income Inequality and Industrial Development: Dualism Revisited," *American Sociological Review* 59 (October 1994), pp. 654–677.

Wealth

Wealth refers to all assets individuals own: cash, savings and checking accounts, investments in stocks, bonds, real estate properties, and so on. Although most people earn their income from their work, the wealthy often derive the bulk of theirs from investments, some of them inherited. Some scholars argue that wealth—not income—is the real indicator of social class.

The best source of information about wealth comes from a national survey called the Survey of Consumer Finances, which is conducted every three years by the Governors of the Federal Reserve Bank. These data show that wealth is highly concentrated in the United States, with enormous differences according to income, age, and education. The wealthiest 10 percent of families in 2001, for example, had a median net worth of $833,600—105 times as much as the poorest 20 percent of families, whose median net worth was only $7,900 (Table 8.1, p. 223). Education also pays off in terms of wealth: The median net worth of college graduates is more than eight times greater than that of high school dropouts. Owning a home makes a great difference, since homes are the principal asset for most families: Homeowners' net worth is $171,700, compared with only $4,800 for renters. Finally, age matters also, at least to some extent: Net worth, like income, increases with age, although it peaks by age seventy-five, after which savings are likely to be used as income and thus depleted.

If one excludes the ownership of cars and homes—which for most people are not really sources of wealth that can be used to pay the bills or used to get richer—the difference in wealth between high-income families and everyone else is even more pronounced. Net financial assets are far lower for minority groups than whites (Oliver and Shapiro 1995). Between 1983 and 2000, the median net financial assets of white Americans nearly tripled, from $19,900 to $67,000 (Table 8.2, p. 224). African Americans, on average, began to accumulate net financial assets only in the 1990s; by 2000, the median net worth was $6,166. Households of Hispanic origin have only recently begun to realize this important source of wealth; their median financial net worth has grown dramatically from effectively zero in 1998 to surpass African Americans with a median net worth of $6,766 in 2000.

What are some of the reasons for the racial disparity in wealth? Is it simply that blacks have less money with which to purchase assets? To some degree, the answer is yes. The old adage "It takes money to make money" is a fact of life for those who start with little or no wealth. Because whites historically have enjoyed higher incomes and levels of wealth than blacks, whites are able to accrue even more wealth, which they then are able to pass on to their children (Conley 1999). In fact, economists estimate that more than half the wealth that one accumulates in a lifetime can be traced to a person's progenitors. But family advantages are not the only factors. Oliver and Shapiro (1995) argue that it is easier for whites to obtain assets, even when they have fewer resources than blacks, because discrimination plays a major role in the racial gap in home ownership. Blacks are rejected for mortgages 60 percent more often than whites, even when they have the same qualifications and creditworthiness. When blacks do receive mortgages, they are more likely to take "subprime" mortgage loans that charge on average 2 percent more in interest. These are mortgages offered in predominantly minority communities by smaller lenders, where the principal lenders are unwilling to make loans. On a $200,000 loan this would result in an additional

FIGURE 8.2

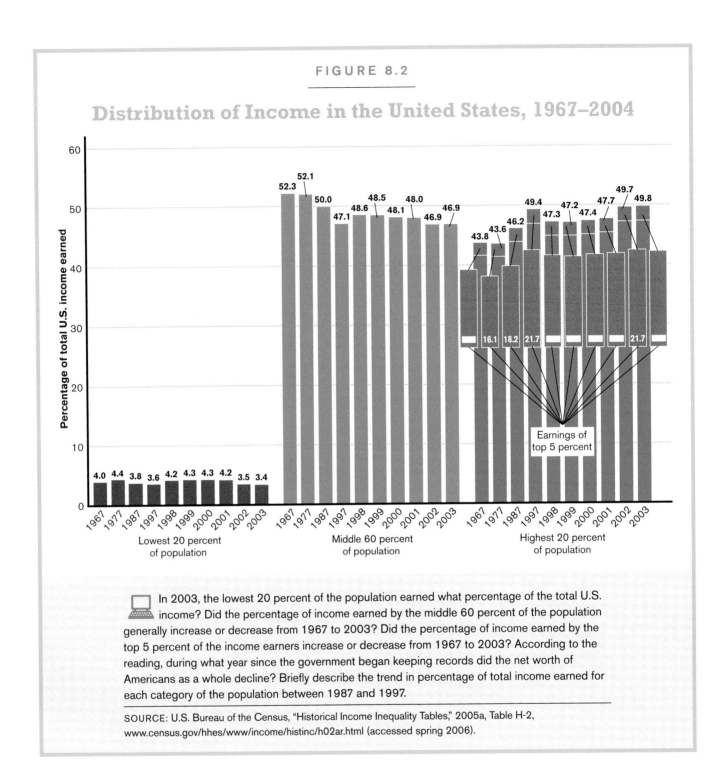

Distribution of Income in the United States, 1967–2004

In 2003, the lowest 20 percent of the population earned what percentage of the total U.S. income? Did the percentage of income earned by the middle 60 percent of the population generally increase or decrease from 1967 to 2003? Did the percentage of income earned by the top 5 percent of the income earners increase or decrease from 1967 to 2003? According to the reading, during what year since the government began keeping records did the net worth of Americans as a whole decline? Briefly describe the trend in percentage of total income earned for each category of the population between 1987 and 1997.

SOURCE: U.S. Bureau of the Census, "Historical Income Inequality Tables," 2005a, Table H-2, www.census.gov/hhes/www/income/histinc/h02ar.html (accessed spring 2006).

$3,000 in interest. In 2004, nearly 40 percent of blacks took out subprime loans, compared to 12 percent of whites. The research shows that subprime loans are offered by only a few lenders; but those lenders focus their business predominantly on minority communities, whereas the prime lenders are unable or unwilling to lend in those same communities (Avery and Canner 2005). These issues are particularly important because home ownership is the primary means of the accumulation of wealth for most American families.

In 1998, the wealthiest 1 percent of all Americans accounted for 38 percent of the nation's total net worth; the top 20 percent accounted for 83 percent of net worth. Of the top 20 percent, 95 percent were white, 4 percent were Asian, and 1 percent were black (Keister 2000). At the other end of

TABLE 8.1

Median Family Net Worth, by Percentile of Family Income, Age, and Housing Tenure, 2001

POPULATION	PERCENTAGE OF ALL U.S. FAMILIES	MEDIAN NET WORTH ($)
All families	100	86,100
Percentile of income		
Less than 20	20	7,900
20–39.9	20	37,200
40–59.9	20	62,500
60–79.9	20	141,500
80–89.9	10	263,100
90–100	10	833,600
Education of head of household		
No high school diploma	16	25,500
High school diploma	32	58,100
Some college	18	71,600
College degree	34	213,300
Age of head (years)		
Less than 35	23	11,600
35–44	22	77,600
45–54	21	132,000
55–64	13	181,500
65–74	11	176,300
75 or more	10	151,400
Housing status		
Owner	68	171,700
Renter or other	32	4,800
Percentile of net worth		
Less than 25	25	1,100
25–49.9	25	40,800
50–74.9	25	156,100
75–89.9	15	430,200
90–100	10	1,301,900

SOURCE: Aizorbe et al. 2003.

the scale, in 1998 the bottom 60 percent of Americans accounted for less than 5 percent of the country's total net worth (Wolff 2000). For this group, accumulating stocks or bonds in hopes of cashing them in someday to pay for their children's college educations is not even a fantasy. In fact, it is more likely that they owe far more than they own. In recent years, as credit has become more available, many Americans have gone increasingly into debt, using credit cards

TABLE 8.2

Median Financial Net Worth ($), 1983–2000: Whites, African Americans, and Latinos

RACE/ETHNICITY	1983	1989	1992	1995	1998	2000
White	19,900	26,900	21,900	19,300	37,600	67,000
African American	0	0	200	200	1,200	6,166
Latino	0	0	0	0	0	6,766

SOURCE: Hartman 2000; U.S. Bureau of the Census 2003a; Wolff 2000.

and refinancing their mortgages to pay for their lifestyles, rather than relying on their earnings. Today, there are 144 million credit card holders. The average amount owed on credit cards increased nearly fivefold between 1970 and 1998, to more than $4,000 (U.S. Federal Reserve Board 2000). During the following two years, credit card debt increased another 11 percent. Increased debt means less net worth, which for Americans as a whole declined in 2000 for the first time since the government began recording such figures in 1945 (Leonhardt 2001).

Today the average credit card balance that is carried from month to month is $7,519 (McGeehan et al. 2004). It is estimated that in 2002 credit card issuers made $2.5 billion in pretax profits. College students often live on credit; in 2004, the typical student owed nearly $2,200 on his or her credit card (Nellie Mae 2005). Seniors, whose income is often insufficient to make ends meet, have also fallen increasingly into debt; among sixty-five- to sixty-nine-year-olds, for example, credit card debt more than tripled between 1992 and 2001, to an average of nearly $6,000 (SeniorJournal.com 2004).

Wealth is highly unequal globally as well. The world's richest 500 individuals have a combined income greater than that of the poorest 416 million. The poorest 40 percent of the world's population—those living on less than $2 per day—account for only 5 percent of global income, but the richest 10 percent, who all live in high-income countries, account for 54 percent of global income (United Nations 2005). But even the poorest 10 percent of Americans are better off than two thirds of the world population (*The Guardian* 2002). We'll come back to this in Chapter 20.

Differences in wealth often take the form of differences in privilege, which in turn affects a person's life chances as much as income does. Members of Congress, high-level military officers at the Pentagon, and White House staff members do not have gargantuan salaries like the chief executive officers of corporations. What they do have, however, are privileges that translate into wealth. Members of Congress and White House staff members enjoy access to limousines and military aircraft, not to mention expense accounts that pay for many of their meals and hotel bills when they travel.

Education

Sociologists also believe that education, or the number of years of schooling a person has completed, is an important dimension of social stratification. The value of a college education has increased significantly in the past twenty years as a result of the increased demand for and wages paid to educated workers in the more computer- and information-based economy (Danziger and Gottschalk 1995). Education is one of the strongest predictors of one's occupation, income, and wealth later in life. As we will see later in this chapter, how much education one receives is often influenced by the social class of one's parents.

Racial differences in levels of education persist, and this explains in part why racial differences in income and wealth also persist. In 2004, of those eighteen and older, roughly 85 percent of whites and Asian Americans had completed high school, whereas only 80 percent of African Americans had a high school degree (U.S. Bureau of the Census 2004).

Occupation

Status refers to the prestige that goes along with one's social position. In the United States and other industrialized societies, occupation is an important indicator of one's social standing. Occupational status depends heavily on one's level of educational attainment. In fact, in studies in which people are asked to rate jobs in terms of how "prestigious" they are, the occupations that are ranked most highly are those requiring the most education (Treiman 1977). These studies use what is called the Standard International Occupational Prestige Scale. Research shows that physicians, college professors, lawyers, and dentists are at the top of the scale, whereas garbage collectors and gas station attendants are at the bottom. About at the middle are jobs such as registered nurse, computer programmer, and insurance sales representative. It is interesting that similar rankings occur regardless of who does the ranking and

in what country. Comparisons of status rankings across fifty-five countries show that there is a general agreement as to how high status an occupation is (Table 8.3).

Class and Lifestyle

In analyzing class location, sociologists have traditionally relied on conventional indicators such as market position, relations to the means of production, and occupation. Some recent authors, however, argue that we should evaluate individuals' class location not only, or even mainly, in terms of economics and employment but also in relation to cultural factors such as

TABLE 8.3

Occupational Prestige in the United States and Around the World

OCCUPATION	UNITED STATES	AVERAGE OF 55 COUNTRIES	OCCUPATION	UNITED STATES	AVERAGE OF 55 COUNTRIES
Supreme Court judge	85	82	Professional athlete	51	48
College president	82	86	Social worker	50	56
Physician	82	78	Electrician	49	44
College professor	78	78	Secretary	46	53
Lawyer	75	73	Real estate agent	44	49
Dentist	74	70	Farmer	44	47
Architect	71	72	Carpenter	43	37
Psychologist	71	66	Plumber	41	34
Airline pilot	70	66	Mail carrier	40	33
Electrical engineer	69	65	Jazz musician	37	38
Biologist	68	69	Bricklayer	36	34
Clergy	67	60	Barber	36	30
Sociologist	65	67	Truck driver	31	33
Accountant	65	55	Factory worker	29	29
Banker	63	67	Store sales clerk	27	34
High school teacher	63	64	Bartender	25	23
Registered nurse	62	54	Lives on public aid	25	16
Pharmacist	61	64	Cab driver	22	28
Veterinarian	60	61	Gas station attendant	22	25
Classical musician	59	56	Janitor	22	21
Police officer	59	40	Waiter or waitress	20	23
Actor or actress	55	52	Garbage collector	13	13
Athletic coach	53	50	Street sweeper	11	13
Journalist	52	55	Shoe shiner	9	12

SOURCE: Treiman 1997.

Income Inequality in the Global Economy

Although many economists, politicians, and businesspeople have sung the praises of globalization, there is reason to approach such claims cautiously. Globalization may well be increasing economic inequality in the world's advanced industrial societies. Even though the U.S. economy has been consistently growing since the end of the recession of 1982–1983, the gap between the wages of high-skilled and low-skilled workers has also been increasing. In 1979, college graduates taking entry-level positions earned on average 37 percent more than those without college degrees. By 2004, the differential had grown to 98 percent (U.S. Bureau of the Census 2005f). And although this growing "wage premium" has encouraged more Americans to go to college—such that nearly 32 percent of the American workforce had college degrees in 2003, compared with 18 percent in 1979 (*Business Week* 1997; U.S. Bureau of the Census 2005g)—it has also helped widen the gap between the wealthiest and the poorest workers. As an analyst for the U.S. Department of Labor (1997) put it, "it is by now almost a platitude . . .

lifestyle and consumption patterns. According to this approach, our current age is one in which symbols and markers related to *consumption* are playing an ever greater role in daily life. Individual identities are structured to a greater extent around *lifestyle choices*—such as how to dress, what to eat, how to care for one's body, and where to relax—and less around more traditional class indicators such as employment.

The French sociologist Pierre Bourdieu (1984) sees class groups as identifiable according to their varying levels of *cultural and economic capital*. Increasingly, individuals distinguish themselves from others not according to economic or occupational factors but on the basis of cultural tastes and leisure pursuits. They are aided in this process by the proliferation of "need merchants," the growing number of people involved in presenting and representing goods and services—either symbolic or actual—for consumption within the capitalist system. Advertisers, marketers, fashion designers, style consultants, interior designers, personal trainers, therapists, and Web page

designers, to name but a few, are all involved in influencing cultural tastes and promoting lifestyle choices among an ever widening community of consumers.

In general, it would be difficult to dispute that stratification within classes, as well as between classes, has come to depend not only on occupational differences but also on differences in consumption and lifestyle. This is borne out by looking at trends in society as a whole. The rapid expansion of the service economy and the entertainment and leisure industry, for example, reflects an increasing emphasis on consumption within industrialized countries. Modern societies have become consumer societies, geared to the acquisition of material goods. In some respects a consumer society is a "mass society," where class differences are to a degree overridden; thus people from different class backgrounds may all watch similar television programs or shop for clothing in the same mall stores. Yet class differences can also become *intensified* through variations in lifestyle and "taste" (Bourdieu 1984).

that wage inequality has increased quite sharply since the late 1970s, for both men and women."

Although few studies have directly implicated globalization as a cause of this growing inequality, there is reason to view it as an indirect causal factor. It is true that, whereas countries such as the United States, Canada, and the United Kingdom have witnessed a growth in earnings inequality since the late 1970s, countries like Germany, Japan, and France—which have, presumably, been equally affected by the forces of globalization—have seen either a decline or little change in inequality. At the same time, many of the factors that sociologists see as causes of inequality are clearly linked to globalization. First, in some cases, U.S. companies that manufacture in the United States lowered wages to compete with other U.S. firms that manufacture their products overseas, especially in the developing world. Second, globalization has encouraged immigration to the United States. Immigrants—many of whom are relegated to low-wage work—increase the competition for jobs among those in the low-wage labor pool, lowering wages somewhat in this segment of the labor market. Third, globalization has undermined the strength of U.S. labor unions. A number of studies have shown that when firms that used to do the bulk of their manufacturing in one region begin to spread their manufacturing base out across countries and continents, it becomes increasingly diffi-

cult for unions to organize workers and negotiate with management. But strong unions decrease earnings inequality through their commitment to raising wages.

Of course, globalization is not the only cause of inequality. Many researchers, for example, blame increasing inequality on the spectacular growth of high-tech industries, which employ mostly well-paid, white-collar workers and offer little in the way of traditional blue-collar employment. Still, it seems safe to conclude that globalization is not without its role in the growing stratification of American society.

While bearing these shifts in mind, however, it is impossible to ignore the critical role played by economic factors in the reproduction of social inequalities. For the most part, individuals experiencing extreme social and material deprivations are not doing so as part of a lifestyle choice. Rather, their circumstances are constrained by factors relating to the economic and occupational structure (Crompton 1998).

A Picture of the U.S. Class Structure

Although money clearly cannot buy everything, one's class position can make an enormous difference in terms of lifestyle. Most sociologists identify social classes in terms of wealth and income, noting how social class makes a difference in terms of consumption, education, health, and access to political power. The purpose of the following discussion is to describe broad

class differences in the United States. Bear in mind that there are no sharply defined boundaries between the classes.

THE UPPER CLASS

The **upper class** consists of the very wealthiest Americans—those households earning more than $157,185 or approximately 5 percent of all American households (U.S. Bureau of the Census 2005a). Most Americans in the upper class are wealthy but not superrich. They are likely to own a large suburban home as well as a town house or a vacation home, to drive expensive automobiles, to fly first class to vacations abroad, to educate their children in private schools and colleges, and to have their desires attended to by a staff of servants. Their wealth stems in large part from their substantial investments, from stocks and bonds to real estate. They are politically influential at the national, state, and local levels. The upper class does include the superwealthy as well—the heads of major

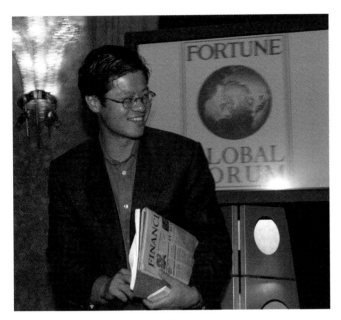
Jerry Yang, co-founder of Yahoo!, was part of the explosion of wealth associated with the dot-com information revolution.

corporations, people who have made large amounts of money through investments or real estate, those fortunate enough to have inherited great wealth from their parents, a few highly successful celebrities and professional athletes, and a handful of others.

At the very top of this group are the superrich, people who have accumulated vast fortunes permitting them to enjoy a lifestyle unimaginable to most Americans. The superrich are highly self-conscious of their unique and privileged social class position; some give generously to such worthy causes as the fine arts, hospitals, and charities. Their homes are often lavish and sometimes filled with collections of fine art. Their common class identity is strengthened by such things as being listed in the social register or having attended the same exclusive private secondary schools (to which they also send their children). They sit on the same corporate boards of directors and belong to the same private clubs. They contribute large sums of money to their favorite politicians and are likely to be on a first-name basis with members of Congress and perhaps even with the president (Domhoff 1998).

The turn of this century saw extraordinary opportunities for the accumulation of such wealth. Globalization is one reason. Those entrepreneurs who are able to invest globally often prosper, both by selling products to foreign consumers, and by making profits cheaply by using low-wage labor in developing countries. The information revolution is another reason for the accumulation of wealth. Before the dot-com bubble finally burst in 2001, young entrepreneurs with startup high-tech companies such as Yahoo! or eBay made legendary

fortunes. As a consequence, the number of superrich Americans has exploded in recent years. At the end of World War II, there were only 13,000 people worth $1 million or more in the United States. Today, there are nearly 7.5 *million* millionaires in the United States (Christie 2005), along with 346 *billionaires* (*Forbes* 2005). The 400 richest Americans are worth more than $1.1 *trillion* dollars—equal to almost one tenth the gross domestic product of the United States and only slightly less than the gross domestic product of China (*Forbes* 2005; Sklair 1999). There are billionaires outside the United States as well—345 of them. The collective net worth of the world's 691 billionaires was $2.2 trillion in 2005 (*Forbes* 2005), which was slightly more than the gross domestic product of France.

Unlike "old-money" families such as the Rockefellers or the Vanderbilts, who accumulated their wealth in earlier generations and thus are viewed as a sort of American aristocracy, this "new wealth" often consists of upstart entrepreneurs such as Microsoft's Bill Gates, whose net worth—estimated by *Forbes* (2005) at $51 billion—makes him the wealthiest individual in the world for the eleventh year in a row.

THE MIDDLE CLASS

When Americans are asked to identify their social class, the large majority claim to be middle class. The reason is partly the American cultural belief that the United States is relatively free of class distinctions. Few people want to be identified as being too rich or too poor. Most Americans seem to think that others are not very different from their immediate family, friends, and co-workers (Kelley and Evans 1995; Simpson et al. 1988; Vanneman and Cannon 1987). Many blue-collar workers, for example, prefer to think of themselves as middle class rather than working class (although sociologists would classify blue-collar workers as working class). Because people rarely interact with others outside of their social class, they tend to see themselves as like "most other people," who they then regard as being "middle class" (Kelley and Evans 1995).

The **middle class** is a catchall for a diverse group of occupations, lifestyles, and people who earn stable and sometimes substantial incomes at primarily white-collar jobs. It grew throughout much of the first three quarters of the twentieth century, then shrank during most of the last quarter century. During the late 1990s, however, economic growth halted this decline. Whether this trend will continue will depend on whether or not the economy expands or contracts during the next several years. Currently, the middle class includes slightly more than half of all American households. Although the middle class was once largely white, today it is increasingly diverse, both racially and culturally, including African Americans, Asian Americans, and Latinos.

The American middle class can be subdivided into two groups: the upper middle class and the lower middle class.

The Upper Middle Class The *upper middle class* consists of relatively high-income professionals (doctors and lawyers, engineers and professors), mid-level corporate managers, people who own or manage small businesses and retail shops, and even some large-farm owners. Household incomes in this group range from about $88,029 to perhaps $157,184. It includes approximately 15 percent of all American households (U.S. Bureau of the Census 2005b). Its members are likely to be college educated and many hold advanced degrees. Their children almost always receive a college education as well. Their jobs have historically been relatively secure as well as likely to provide them with retirement programs and health benefits. They own comfortable homes, often in the suburbs or in trendy downtown neighborhoods. They drive the more expensive late-model cars or sport-utility vehicles. They have some savings and investments. They are likely to be active in local politics and civic organizations.

The Lower Middle Class The *lower middle class* in the United States consists of trained office workers (for example, secretaries and bookkeepers), elementary and high school teachers, nurses, salespeople, police officers, firefighters, and others who provide skilled services. Often members of this group enjoy relatively high status; it is their relatively low income that determines their class position. Household incomes in this group, which includes about 40 percent of American households, range from about $34,738 to $88,028 (U.S. Bureau of the Census 2005b). They may own a modest house, although many live in rental units. Their automobiles may be late models, but they are not the more expensive varieties. Almost all have a high school education, and some have college degrees. They want their children to have a college education, although this will usually have to be paid for with the help of work-study programs and student loans. They are less likely to be politically active beyond exercising their right to vote.

THE WORKING CLASS

The **working class,** which makes up about 20 percent of all American households, includes primarily blue-collar and pink-collar laborers. Household incomes in this group range from perhaps $18,500 to $34,737 (U.S. Bureau of the Census 2005b), and at least two people in each household will usually have to work to make ends meet. Family income is just enough to pay the rent or the mortgage, to put food on the table, and perhaps to save for a summer vacation. The working class includes factory workers, mechanics, secretaries, office workers, sales clerks, restaurant and hotel workers, and others who earn a modest weekly paycheck at a job that involves little control over the size of their income or working conditions. As you will see later in this chapter, many blue-collar jobs in the United States are threatened by economic globalization, and so members of the working class today are likely to feel insecure about their own and their family's future.

The working class is racially and ethnically diverse. While older members of the working class may own a home that was bought a number of years ago, younger members are likely to rent. The home or apartment is likely to be in a lower-income suburb or a city neighborhood. The household car, a lower-priced model, is unlikely to be new. Children who graduate from high school are unlikely to go to college and will attempt to get a job immediately instead. Most members of the working class are not likely to be politically active even in their own community, although they may vote in some elections.

THE LOWER CLASS

The **lower class,** which makes up roughly 15 percent of American households, includes those who work part time or not at all; household income is typically lower than $18,499 (U.S. Bureau of the Census 2005b). Most lower-class individuals are found in cities, although some live in rural areas and earn a little money as farmers or part-time workers. Some manage to find employment in semiskilled or unskilled manufacturing or service jobs, ranging from making clothing in sweatshops to cleaning houses. Their jobs, when they can find them, are dead-end jobs, since years of work are unlikely to lead to promotion or substantially higher income. Their work is probably part time and highly unstable, without benefits such as medical insurance, disability, or social security. Even if they are fortunate enough to find a full-time job, there are no guarantees that it will be around next month or even next week. Many people in the lower class live in poverty. Very few own their own homes. Most of the lower class rent, and some are homeless. If they own a car at all, it is likely to be a used car. A higher percentage of the lower class is nonwhite than is true of other social classes. Its members do not participate in politics, and they seldom vote.

THE "UNDERCLASS"

In the lower class, some sociologists have recently identified a group they call the **underclass** because they are "beneath" the class system in that they lack access to the world of work and mainstream patterns of behavior. Located in the highest-poverty neighborhoods of the inner city, the underclass is sometimes called the "new urban poor."

The underclass includes many African Americans, who have been trapped for more than one generation in a cycle of poverty from which there is little possibility of escape (Wacquant 1993, 1996; Wacquant and Wilson 1993; Wilson 1996). These are the poorest of the poor. Their numbers have grown rapidly over the past quarter century and today include unskilled and unemployed men, young single mothers and their children on welfare, teenagers from welfare-dependent families, and many of the homeless. They live in poor neighborhoods troubled by drugs, teenage gangs, drive-by shootings, and high levels of violence. They are the truly disadvantaged, people with extremely difficult lives who have little realistic hope of ever making it out of poverty.

The emergence of an underclass of the new urban poor has been attributed to social forces that have come together during the past quarter century (Sawhill 1989; Wacquant 1993, 1996; Wilson 1996). First, economic globalization has led to unemployment among workers lacking education and skills, since many unskilled and semiskilled jobs have moved to low-wage countries. The threat of such job loss, in turn, has depressed wages in the remaining unskilled jobs. Because African Americans and recent immigrants from Latin America (and to some extent Asia) provide much of the unskilled labor in the United States, they are particularly disadvantaged in today's labor market. Furthermore, racial discrimination has made it especially difficult for minority groups to compete for the dwindling supply of unskilled jobs.

Second, government programs that once provided assistance for the poor were cut back sharply during the 1980s under the Reagan and elder Bush administrations, so that the poor were left with few resources to use to get ahead. These problems were compounded during the Clinton administration, whose welfare reforms severely restricted the length of time people could remain on welfare. This approach reduced the number of people on welfare, and the growing economy of the 1990s provided low-wage jobs for many welfare recipients. A sustained economic slowdown, however, could swell the ranks of the new urban poor, by leaving a growing number of people both jobless and without welfare benefits.

More recently, some sociologists have argued that members of the underclass perpetuate their own inequality because the difficult conditions they face have made them "ill suited to the requirements of the formally rational sector of the economy" (Wacquant 2002). Although these scholars see the sources of such behavior in the social structure, they believe the culture of the underclass has taken on a life of its own, serving as both cause and effect. Such claims have generated considerable controversy, inspiring a number of studies that have taken issue with these claims. Those who stand on the other side argue that although urban poverty is an immobile stratum, it is not simply a "defeated" and disconnected class, as theorists of the underclass believe. Thus studies of fast-food workers and homeless street vendors have argued that the separations between the urban poor and the rest of society are not as great as scholars of the underclass believe (Duneier 1999; Newman 2000).

Inequality in the United States: A Growing Gap Between Rich and Poor

The United States prides itself on being a nation of equals. Indeed, except for the Great Depression of the 1930s, inequality declined throughout much of the twentieth century, reaching its lowest levels during the 1960s and early 1970s. But during the past quarter century inequality has started to increase once again. The rich have gotten much, much richer. Middle-class incomes have stagnated. The poor have grown in number and are poorer than they have been since the 1960s. Currently, the gap between rich and poor in the United States is the largest since the Census Bureau started measuring it in 1947 (U.S. Bureau of the Census 2000b) and the largest in the industrial world (Figure 8.3). One statistical analysis of income and poverty among industrial nations found that the United States had the most unequal distribution of household income among all twenty-one industrial countries studied (Sweden had the most equal) (Smeeding 2000).

In 2004, the richest 20 percent of all U.S. households accounted for slightly more than half (51 percent) of all income generated in the United States (Figure 8.2, p. 222). Moreover, their share has steadily increased. Table 8.4 (p. 232) divides American households into five equal-size groups, based on household income in 2004. It also looks at the richest 5 percent of all households. The table compares the average after-tax income of each group in 2004 with the income each group would have had if its share of total income had remained the same as it was in 1974—that is, if inequality had not increased during the twenty-five year period. Three out of the five groups were worse off in 2004 than they would have been had inequality not increased; the range was between $1,000 and $2,000 poorer. The top 20 percent, on the other hand, was $35,114 richer; the top 5 percent, $87,338 richer.

Corporate Executives versus Their Workers

The earnings gap between top corporate officials and average working Americans has ballooned in recent years. According to

FIGURE 8.3

Income Inequality in Selected Industrialized Countries: Ratio of Richest 20 Percent to Poorest 20 Percent for 2002

In the 1990s, the richest fifth of all Americans were on average nine times richer than the poorest fifth, one of the highest ratios in the industrialized world. In Japan, at the other extreme, the ratio was about 3.4 to 1.

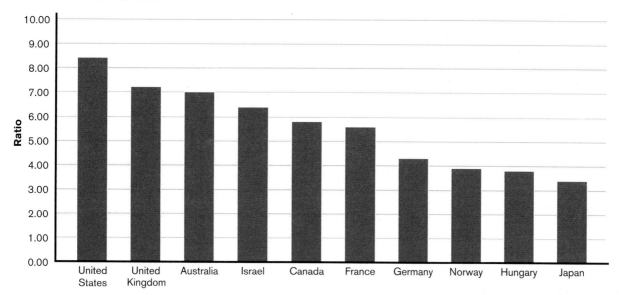

What is the ratio in this figure measuring? In Canada, how many times richer were the richest fifth of the population compared to the poorest fifth of the population? In Japan, the world's second largest economy, how did the ratio of income inequality compare to that of the United States? How much did the average CEO's pay grow between 1990 and 2004 compared to the increase in pay for a production worker? How did the Reagan, Bush, and Clinton administrations exacerbate the problems of the poor?

SOURCE: United Nations Development Programme, *Human Development Report, 2005,* 2005, Table 15, hdr.undp.org/reports/global/2005/ (accessed spring 2006).

Forbes magazine (2005), the average pay of the twenty-five best-paid chief executive officers (CEOs) in the United States was $67.3 million in 2005. The CEOs of the largest five hundred American corporations earned $5.1 billion in 2004, up 54 percent from 2003. The top earner was Terry S. Semel, CEO of Yahoo!, who took home $230.6 million, mostly in stocks in his company. For the entire group of highly paid CEOs, stock gains account for 53 percent of total compensation versus 39 percent just a year ago.

The average American blue-collar worker averaged $15.46 an hour in 2004, earning $32,156 for the entire year, assuming he or she labored for fifty-two weeks a year, forty hours a week (U.S. Bureau of Labor Statistics 2005). Sociologist William Domhoff (2005) estimates that between 1990 and 2004 CEO pay increased by 300 percent while production worker pay increased by only 4.5 percent. Yet, when inflation is taken into account, the purchasing power of the federal minimum wage actually declined by 6 percent in the same period.

The difference between executive and worker compensation is even more pronounced if one takes into account that U.S. firms today rely increasingly on workers in low-income

TABLE 8.4

How Has an Increase in Income Inequality Affected American Households during the Last 30 Years?

INCOME CATEGORY	ACTUAL 2004 MEAN INCOME ($)[a]	2004 INCOME IF INEQUALITY HAD NOT CHANGED FROM 1974 ($)[b]	DIFFERENCE: HOW MUCH POORER OR RICHER ($)
Lowest fifth	10,264	11,365	−1,101
Second fifth	26,241	28,247	−2,006
Middle fifth	44,455	45,521	−1,066
Fourth fifth	70,085	65,743	+4,342
Highest fifth	151,593	116,479	+35,114
Top 5 percent	264,387	177,049	+87,338

SOURCE: (a) U.S. Bureau of the Census, "Historical Income Inequality Tables," 2005a, Table H-3, www.census.gov/hhes/www/income/histinc/h03ar.html (accessed spring 2006); (b) calculations based on historical inflation rate change of 308.37 percent between January 1974 and December 2004, inflationdata.com/inflation/Inflation_Rate/InflationCalculator.asp (accessed spring 2006).

countries. To take one example, in 2004 H. Lee Scott Jr., the president and CEO of Wal-Mart, the world's largest corporation, took home some $5.3 million in compensation—$1.2 million in salary and $4.1 million in bonuses (and was also awarded stock options worth approximately $11.2 million) (TimesDispatch.com 2005). Virtually all of the thousands of factories that make products sold by Wal-Mart are in low-wage countries such as China, where workers are fortunate if they earn $3 a day. The wage gap between Scott's compensation and a Chinese factory worker is somewhere in the range of 6,500 to 1 (and if stock options are included, the gap widens to 21,000 to 1!).

Minorities versus White Americans

There are substantial differences in income based on race and ethnicity because minorities in the United States are more likely to hold the lowest-paying jobs. Black and Latino household income, for example, averages between two thirds and three quarters that of whites (Figure 8.4). For blacks, this is a slight improvement over previous years, as a growing number of blacks have gone to college and moved into middle-class occupations. For Latinos, however, the situation has worsened, as recent immigrants from rural areas in Mexico and Central

America find themselves working at low-wage jobs (U.S. Bureau of the Census 2001a).

Oliver and Shapiro (1995) found that the "wealth gap" between blacks and whites is even greater than the income gap. While blacks on average earned two thirds that of whites, their net worth was only one tenth as much. Moreover, these differences increased between 1967 and 1988. More recent data show that the wealth gap has decreased only slightly: In 2000, whites had a median net worth of $58,716, compared with $6,166 for blacks and $6,766 for Hispanics (U.S. Bureau of the Census 2003a). Oliver and Shapiro also found that when blacks attained educational or occupational levels comparable to whites, the wealth gap still did not disappear. For example, the net worth of college-educated blacks was only $17,000 in 1988, compared with nearly $75,000 for whites.

Oliver and Shapiro (1995) argue that blacks have encountered numerous barriers to acquiring wealth throughout American history, beginning with slavery and continuing to the present day. After the Civil War ended slavery in 1865, legal discrimination (such as mandatory segregation in the South or separate schools) tied the vast majority of blacks to the lowest rungs of the economic ladder, until racial discrimination was made illegal by the Civil Rights Act of 1964. Nonetheless, discrimination has remained, and although some blacks have moved into middle-class occupations, many have remained poor or in low-wage jobs where the opportunities for accumulating wealth are nonexistent. Among those who successfully started businesses, many found there were racial barriers to breaking into the more profitable white markets. In effect, many blacks have suffered from a vicious circle that prevents them from accumulating wealth. Less wealth means less social and cultural capital: fewer dollars to invest in schooling for one's children, a business, or the stock market—investments that in the long run would create greater wealth for future investments.

FIGURE 8.4

Black and Latino Household Income Compared to Whites'

Since the mid-1980s, the gap between black and white household income has narrowed, although blacks still earn, on average, only two thirds as much as whites earn. In 1972, the average black income was 57 percent of white income; by 2004, the gap had dropped slightly to 65 percent (the average household income in 2004 was $40,814 for blacks and $62,598 for whites). Latino households are today roughly the same relative to white households as they were in 1972: In that year Latino household income averaged 74 percent, whereas in 2004 they averaged 75 percent (the average household income in 2004 for Latinos was $45,871). While black households experienced steady gains over the period, Latino households experienced a worsening condition relative to white households until the 1990s. The economic growth at that time improved the relative situation of both blacks and Latinos, although some of these gains have been lost since 2000.

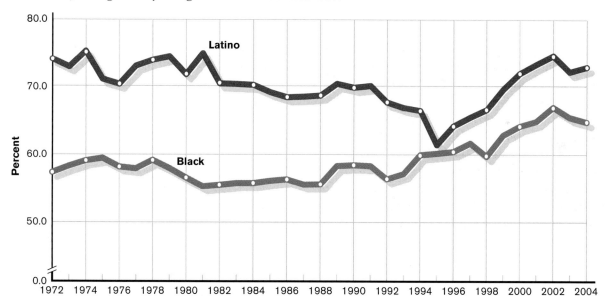

The figure above measures the income of Latinos and blacks compared to what? Between 1972 and 2004, approximately what gain in percentage did blacks achieve toward earning an equal income to that of whites? In 2000, how did the median *net worth* of whites compare to that of blacks and Latinos? From 1995 to 2004, how did the Latino gain in income compare to that of blacks? During what year did blacks' income clearly rise above 60 percent of whites' income?

SOURCE: U.S. Bureau of the Census, "Historical Income Tables–Households," 2005, Table H-9, www.census.gov/hhes/www/income/histinc/h09ar.html (accessed spring 2006); shares derived using data for all households in current dollars.

Single-Parent Families versus Married-Couple Families

Single-parent families are especially likely to have low incomes. Those headed by men earned only 70 percent as much as all married families in 2004, whereas those headed by women earned only 48 percent as much as all married families. Race and ethnicity also play a significant role: Black married-couple families earned 79 percent as much as white married-couple families, while Latino married-couple families earned only 68 percent as much. Finally, nonwhite families headed by single women are by far the worst off: Black female-headed families earned only about 37 percent as much as white married-couple families, while Latino female-headed families earned 40 percent as much as white married-couple families (U.S. Bureau of the Census 2005c).

Social Mobility

In studying stratification and inequality, we must consider not only the differences between economic positions but also what happens to the individuals who occupy them. **Social mobility** refers to the movement of individuals and groups between different class positions as a result of changes in occupation, wealth, or income.

There are two ways of studying social mobility. First, we can look at people's own careers—how far they move up or down the socioeconomic scale in the course of their working lives. This is called **intragenerational mobility.** Alternatively, we can analyze where children are on the scale compared with their parents or grandparents. Mobility across the generations is called **intergenerational mobility.** Sociologists have long studied both types of mobility, with increasingly sophisticated methods. Unfortunately, with the exception of some recent studies, much of this research has been limited to male mobility, particularly white males. We shall look at some of this research in the sections to follow.

Another important distinction sociologists make is between structural mobility and exchange mobility. If there were such a thing as a society with complete equality of opportunity—in which each person had the same chance of getting on in life as everyone else—there would be a great deal of downward as well as upward mobility. This is what is meant by **exchange mobility:** There is an exchange of positions, such that more talented people in each generation move up the economic hierarchy, while the less talented move down.

In practice, there is no society that even approaches full equality of opportunity; and most mobility, whether intragener-

ational or intergenerational, is **structural mobility,** upward mobility made possible by an expansion of better-paid occupations at the expense of more poorly paid ones. Most mobility in the United States since World War II has depended on continually increasing prosperity. Levels of downward mobility, therefore, have been historically low.

Intergenerational Mobility

Much of the research on intergenerational mobility has been at least implicitly motivated by the **industrialism hypothesis,** which says that societies become more open to movement between classes as they become more technologically advanced (Kerr et al. 1960). The hypothesis says that as societies become more industrial, workers increasingly get jobs because of *achievement,* or skill, rather than because of **ascription,** which refers to placement in a particular social status based on characteristics such as family of origin, race, and gender.

Some evidence supports the industrialism hypothesis. A review of mobility patterns in thirty-five countries finds a gradual increase in openness over time within all of the countries (Ganzeboom et al. 1989). However, much research contradicts the industrialism hypothesis. The earliest study of comparative mobility, by Pitirim Sorokin (1927), analyzed a wide range of societies, from traditional Rome and China to the United States. Sorokin concluded that opportunities for rapid ascent in the United States were more limited than American folklore suggested. The techniques he used to gather his data, however, were relatively primitive. Another classical study of social mobility was carried out by Seymour Lipset and Reinhard Bendix (1959). Their research—drawing on data from Britain, France, West Germany, Sweden, Switzerland, Japan, Denmark, Italy, and the United States—concentrated on the mobility of men from blue-collar to white-collar work. Contrary to the researchers' expectations, they also found no evidence that the United States was more open to social mobility than the European societies. They concluded that all of the countries were experiencing an expansion of white-collar jobs. This led to increased structural mobility, and an "upward surge of mobility." More recently, Robert Erikson and John Goldthorpe (1992) compared twelve European and three non-European industrialized nations. They found that most countries had similar patterns of intergenerational mobility. However, they also discovered significant variations: Sweden, for example, was found to be considerably more open to social mobility than the other Western countries. In contrast to the industrialism hypothesis, societies did not tend to get more open to movement between classes over time.

There are also big differences within societies—for example, differences in mobility between racial and ethnic groups (Featherman and Hauser 1978). The obvious comparison in the United States is between African Americans and whites. The black middle class is much smaller than the white middle class relative to the proportions of blacks and whites in the population as a whole. Someone born in a black inner-city ghetto has only a fraction of the chance of a person from a white background of obtaining a white-collar or professional job.

Research on intergenerational mobility has tended to find that children of parents who had low-status or high-status occupations are likely to work at occupations with similar status. Children of parents with middle-status occupations, such as crafts or service, tend to be relatively more mobile (Featherman and Hauser 1978; Grusky and Hauser 1984).

Intragenerational Mobility

Relatively less research has focused on intragenerational mobility. The work that has been done finds that earnings, status, and satisfaction increase most dramatically when workers are in their twenties, with more subtle increases later on (Spilerman 1977). Workers tend to be promoted twice: first by the time they are thirty-four and then again between their mid-thirties and early fifties (DiPrete and Soule 1988; Lashbrook 1996; Rosenbaum 1979).

The pattern for women is slightly different from that for men. Women are more likely to continue changing jobs after the early part of their careers than are men (DiPrete and Nonnemaker 1997). In addition, women workers have recently been affected by two historical trends: a decline in occupational gender segregation and increased labor force participation. This means that women are more likely now than they were in the 1950s to hold the same jobs as men (Goldin 1990). And many more women are working today than was the case in the 1950s (Quinn and Burkhauser 1994; Siegel 1993).

Opportunities for Mobility: Who Gets Ahead?

Why is it more difficult for someone from the "new urban poor" to become an upper-class professional? Many people in modern societies believe it is possible for anyone to reach the top through hard work and persistence. Why should it be difficult to do so? Sociologists have sought to answer these questions by trying to understand which social factors are most influential in determining an individual's status or position in society.

In a classic study of social mobility in the United States, the sociologists Peter Blau and Otis Dudley Duncan (1967) surveyed over twenty thousand men in order to assess intergener-

ational mobility. Blau and Duncan concluded that while there has been a great deal of **vertical mobility,** or movement along the socioeconomic scale, nearly all of it was between occupational positions quite close to one another. Long-range mobility —that is from working class to upper-middle class—was rare. Why? Blau and Duncan sought to answer this question by assessing the effect of social background in determining ultimate social status. They concluded that the key factor behind status was educational attainment. But a child's education is influenced by its family's social status; this, in turn, affects the child's social position later in life. The sociologists William Sewell and Robert Hauser (1980) later confirmed Blau and Duncan's conclusions. They added to the argument by claiming that the connection between family background and educational attainment occurs because parents, teachers, and friends influence the educational and career aspirations of the child and that these aspirations then become an important part of the status attainment process throughout the child's life. Sewell and Hauser sought to prove that social status was influenced by a pattern of related social influences going back to one's birth: Family background affects the child's aspirations, which in turn affect the child's educational attainment,

Demonstrators protest the Gap for exploiting low-wage workers in the Third World.

Bridging the Gap: Sociology and the *New York Times*

On Sunday morning of Labor Day weekend 2005, nearly two million copies of the *New York Times* were delivered to doorsteps around the country. Hurricane Katrina had on August 31 inflicted catastrophic damage on the central Gulf Coast, most notably by causing extensive flooding in New Orleans, Louisiana; and reporters like Jason DeParle (2005) were just beginning to make sense of the tragedy:

What a shocked world saw exposed in New Orleans last week wasn't just a broken levee. It was a cleavage of race and class, at once familiar and startlingly new, laid bare in a setting where they suddenly amounted to matters of life and death. Hydrology joined sociology throughout the story line, from the settling of the flood-prone city, where well-to-do white people lived on the high ground, to its frantic abandonment. No one was immune, of course. With 80 percent of the city under water, tragedy swallowed the privilege and poor, and traveled spread across racial lines. But the divides in the city were evident in things as simple as access to a car. The 35 percent of black households that didn't have one, compared with just 15 percent among whites.

On the same day, reporters were also grappling with inequality closer to home. With race and class debates already stirred into a frenzy by the hurricane, Sam Roberts (2005) broke news of rising inequality in Manhattan, home to the *New York Times* headquarters and over 1.6 million of the richest and poorest residents in America living side by side:

Andrew Beveridge

Trump Tower on Fifth Avenue is only about 60 blocks from the Wagner Houses in East Harlem, but they might as well be light years apart. They epitomize the highest- and lowest-earning census tracts in Manhattan, where the disparity between rich and poor is now greater than in any other county in the country. That finding, in an analysis conducted for the *New York Times,* dovetails with other new regional economic research. . . . The top fifth of earners in Manhattan now make 52 times what the lowest fifth make—$365,826 compared with $7,047— which is roughly comparable to the income disparity in Namibia. . . . Put another way, for every dollar made by households in the top fifth of Manhattan earners, households in the bottom fifth made about 2 cents.

which in turn affects the adult's later occupational prestige, and so on and so on.

The French sociologist Pierre Bourdieu (1984, 1988) has also been a major figure in examining the importance of family background to social status, but his emphasis is on the cultural advantages that parents can provide to their children. Bourdieu argues that among the factors responsible for social status the most important is the transmission of cultural capital.

Those who own economic capital often manage to pass much of it on to their children. The same is true, Bourdieu argues, of the cultural advantages that coming from a "good home" confers. These advantages stem partly from having greater economic capital, which succeeding generations inherit, thus perpetuating inequalities. As we have seen, wealthier families are able to afford to send their children to better schools, an economic advantage that benefits the children's social status

Much of what we read in newspapers consists of statistics—that 35 percent of black households in New Orleans didn't have a car compared to just 15 percent of white households, that the top 20 percent of incomes in New York City average $365,826 compared to only $7,047 for the bottom fifth. These statistics reveal important patterns about race and class in America and help us understand how power is concentrated in our society. But where do these statistics come from? Is there somewhere that reporters like DeParle and Roberts can go to find reliable statistics about class and inequality in America?

For the past thirteen years, they have gone to Andrew Beveridge, a professor of sociology at Queens College in New York City. Beveridge has a formal partnership with the *New York Times* to answer these questions and back them up with data. This partnership is a unique example of how a sociologist can help provide information to the public while framing that information in a sociological way. For example, in the days before and after Katrina hit the Gulf Coast, millions of viewers around the country watched local residents pack the roadways in an effort to escape the storm. Many suspected that those trapped behind lacked access to a car, but who knew for sure? Reporters and news anchors were scrambling to find out the real story. For the answer, they contacted Beveridge. On very short notice, he conducted and delivered a demographic analysis of the New Orleans area using U.S. Census data on car ownership. Within hours he had produced the first solid statistics on the issue and helped work with reporters to craft stories that explained to general readers how class inequality may have been what drove some to escape and others to drown.

Harlem lies 1,315 miles northeast of New Orleans on the island of Manhattan and houses many of New York's poorest residents living within walking distance of mansions (such as the Duke-Semans townhouse) which sell for up to $50 million. Manhattan is known to attract some of the most talented and driven professionals from around the world, so it is not surprising that levels of inequality exist in New York City. What is surprising is that those levels have increased dramatically over the past few decades. When Beveridge brought this to the at-tention of editors at the *Times,* they assigned reporters to the story immediately. Again using census data for his analysis, Beveridge showed that as of 2000, the top fifth of earners made fifty-two times what the lowest make in Manhattan. Ten years earlier, in 1990, the number for the top fifth was thirty-two times greater than the bottom fifth. In 1980, the difference was a factor of only twenty-one. Since the 1980s, "the gains are all going to the top," Beveridge said. "It's a massive class disparity" (Roberts 2005).

Beveridge uses his role as a public sociologist to help the general public understand tough issues like class in America. Americans can (and often do) change their class positions over time, which makes class a difficult thing to understand. For example, although we know that money matters in America, it's hard to draw lines that separate one class from another. This has led many academics to conclude that class distinctions do not exist in the United States like they do in other places. Beveridge has no patience for these dismissals. "People can talk about class all they want, but it's not until you see Katrina and these Manhattan statistics that you start to really understand what it's like to be left behind in America." Far from diminishing, "class has actually become more and more important" over the past three decades.

By emphasizing not only income but education, prestige, and wealth, Beveridge helps bring a sociological understanding to class analysis. He takes his partnership with the *Times* very seriously, viewing it as a way to bridge a gap between science and public understanding. That's why Beveridge was asked to join high-level editorial meetings to plan out a ten-part series titled "Class in America" during the summer of 2005. That's why Beveridge has been asked repeatedly to testify in court as an expert witness in neighborhood and community disputes. That's why, by 2005, Beveridge had authored more than fifty articles for Gotham Gazette, a non-profit Web site (www.gothamgazette.com) about the issues facing New York City, and contributed analyses for over forty *New York Times* articles over the past decade. By selecting and analyzing data he considers important to society, Beveridge not only influences newsmakers but helps create the news itself.

as adults. In addition to this material advantage, parents from the upper and middle classes are mostly highly educated themselves and tend to be more involved in their children's education—reading to them, helping with homework, purchasing books and learning materials, and encouraging their progress. Bourdieu notes that working-class parents are concerned about their children's education but lack the economic and cultural capital to make a difference. Bourdieu's study of French society confirmed his theory. He found that a majority of office professionals with high levels of educational attainment and income were from families of the "dominant class" in France. Likewise, office clerical workers often originated from the working classes.

The socioeconomic order in the United States is similar. Those who already hold positions of wealth and power have many chances to perpetuate their advantages and to pass them on to their offspring. They can make sure their children have the best available education, and this will often lead them into the best jobs. Most of those who reach the top had a head start; they came from professional or affluent backgrounds. Studies of people who have become wealthy show that hardly anyone begins with nothing. The large majority of people who have "made money" did so on the basis of inheriting or being given at least a modest amount initially—which they then used to make more. In American society, it's better to start at the top than at the bottom (Duncan et al. 1998; Jaher 1973; Rubinstein 1986).

Your Own Mobility Chances

Sometime in the next four years, you will graduate from college and be faced with the prospect of starting a new career. Do you have any idea what you will do? If you are like most of your classmates, you have no idea. Perhaps you will make a go of something that is interesting to you and start your own business. Or perhaps you will go to work for someone else and become interested in something you have never heard of, working your way up the hierarchy of an organization in a formal career. What implications might be drawn from mobility studies about the career opportunities you are faced with, as someone searching for a good job? Managerial and professional jobs may continue to expand relative to lower-level positions. Those who have done well in the educational system and earned a college degree are most likely to fill these openings and make a high income. Indeed, 60 percent of Americans in the top fifth of income earners graduated from college, whereas in the bottom fifth, just 6 percent hold a college degree (Cox and Alm 1999). Educational attainment seems to be the key variable for upward mobility in the United States (Hout 1988).

Research indicates, however, that the effect of education on your mobility chances has decreased somewhat (Hout 1988; Hout and Lucas 1996). Because you are a college student, chances are that one or both of your parents are college educated and middle class or above. Even if you earn a good income, you might not enjoy upward mobility. In addition, as a result of global economic competition, not nearly enough well-paid positions are open for all who wish to enter them, and some of you are bound to find that your careers do not match your expectations. Even if a higher proportion of jobs are created at managerial and professional levels than existed before, the overall number of jobs available in the future may not keep pace with the number of people with college degrees seeking work. One reason for this is the growing number of women entering the workforce. Another is the increasing use of information technology in production processes. Because computerized machinery can now handle tasks—even of a highly complicated kind—that once only humans could do, it is possible that many jobs will be eliminated in future years.

If you are a woman, although your chances of entering a good career are improving, you face certain obstacles to your progress. Male managers and employers still discriminate against female applicants, compared with males seeking the same positions. They do so at least partly because of their belief that women are not really interested in careers and are likely to leave the workforce to begin families. This latter factor substantially affects opportunities for women, who are often forced to choose between a career and having children. Men are rarely willing to share equal responsibility for domestic work and child care.

Downward Mobility

Although downward mobility is less common than upward mobility, about 20 percent of men in the United States are downwardly mobile intergenerationally, although most of this movement is short range. A person with **short-range downward mobility** moves from one job to another that is similar—for example, from a routine office job to semiskilled blue-collar work. Downward intragenerational mobility, also a common occurrence, is often associated with psychological problems and anxieties. Some people are simply unable to sustain the lifestyle into which they were born. But another source of downward mobility among individuals arises through no fault of their own. During the late 1980s and early 1990s, corporate America was flooded with instances in which middle-aged men lost their jobs because of company mergers or takeovers. These executives either had difficulty finding new jobs or could only find jobs that paid less than their previous jobs.

Many of the intragenerational downwardly mobile are women. It is still common for women to abandon promising careers on the birth of a child. After spending some years raising children, such women often return to the paid workforce at a level lower than when they left—for instance, in poorly paid, part-time work. (This situation is changing, although not as fast as might be hoped.)

Downward mobility is particularly common today among divorced or separated women with children. As an illustration, we might take the life of Sandra Bolton, described by John Schwarz and Thomas Volgy in their book *The Forgotten Americans* (1992). Sandra's fate belies the idea that people who work hard and follow the rules will be able to prosper. Sandra's husband had regularly assaulted her during the six years of their marriage, and child welfare officials considered him a threat to their two children. She divorced her husband after the Child Protective Services told her that the state would take her children if she didn't leave him.

Sandra receives no maintenance from her ex-husband, who, two weeks before the divorce was finalized, piled their furniture and valuables into a truck and drove away, not to be seen again. Whereas while married she sustained a moderately comfortable, middle-class way of life, Sandra now lives a hand-to-mouth existence. She tried to remain in college, supporting herself and her children by doing various menial jobs, but was unable to earn enough money to keep up.

A neighbor looked after her children while she took a full-time job as a secretary at a medical center. Taking courses at night and during the summers, she eventually completed a college degree. Although she applied at many places, she was not able to find a position paying more than her secretarial job. She took on a second job, as a checkout person in a supermarket, in the evenings just to make ends meet. "You try to do the responsible thing," she said, "and you're penalized, because the system we have right now doesn't provide you with a way to make it. I mean, I work so hard. There's only so much a person can do" (Schwarz and Volgy 1992). As a result of her divorce, Sandra sank from a life of some comfort to living in poverty. She is not alone.

Gender and Social Mobility

Although so much research into social mobility has focused on men, in recent years more attention has begun to be paid to patterns of mobility among women. At a time when girls are outperforming boys in school and females are outnumbering males in higher education, it is tempting to conclude that long-standing gender inequalities in society may be relaxing their hold. Has the occupational structure become more open to women, or are their mobility chances still guided largely by family and social background?

One study traced the lives of nine thousand people born during the same week in 1970 (Bynner et al. 1997). In the most recent survey of the respondents, at age twenty-six, it was found that for both men and women family background and class of origin remain powerful influences. The study concluded that the young people who were coping best with the transition to adulthood were those who had obtained a better education, postponed children and marriage, and had fathers in professional occupations. Individuals who had come from disadvantaged backgrounds had a greater tendency to remain there.

The study found that, on the whole, women today are experiencing much greater opportunity than did their counterparts in the previous generation. Middle-class women have benefited the most. They were just as likely as their male peers to go to college and to move into well-paid jobs on graduation. This trend toward greater equality was also reflected in women's heightened confidence and sense of self-esteem, compared with a similar cohort of women born just twelve years earlier.

Poverty in the United States

At the bottom of the class system in the United States are the millions of people who exist in conditions of poverty. Many do not maintain a proper diet and live in miserable conditions; their average life expectancy is lower than that of the majority of the population. In addition, the number of individuals and families who have become homeless has greatly increased over the past twenty years.

In defining poverty, a distinction is usually made between absolute and relative poverty. **Absolute poverty** means that a person or family simply can't get enough to eat. People living in absolute poverty are undernourished and, in situations of famine, may actually starve to death. Absolute poverty is common in the poorer developing countries.

In the industrial countries, **relative poverty** is essentially a measure of inequality. It means being poor compared with the standards of living of the majority. It is reasonable to call a person poor in the United States if he or she lacks the basic resources needed to maintain a decent standard of housing and healthy living conditions.

Measuring Poverty

When President Lyndon B. Johnson began his War on Poverty in 1964, around thirty-six million Americans lived in poverty. Within a decade, the number had dropped sharply, to around twenty-three million (Figure 8.5 shows changes in poverty rates since 1959). But then, beginning in the early 1970s, poverty again began to climb, peaking in 1993 at thirty-nine million people. Since that time, the number of poor has dropped but is on the increase again. In 2003, the number of people living in poverty stood at thirty-seven million, roughly 12.7 percent of the population, up from 12.5 percent a year before (DeNavas-Walt et al. 2005). Yet even this level of poverty greatly exceeds that of most other advanced industrial nations. In the mid-1990s, for example, when the U.S. poverty rate was around 14 percent, France's was 10 percent; Canada's and Germany's, 7 percent (Smeeding et al. 2000).

What does it mean to be poor in the world's richest nation? The U.S. government calculates the **poverty line** as an income

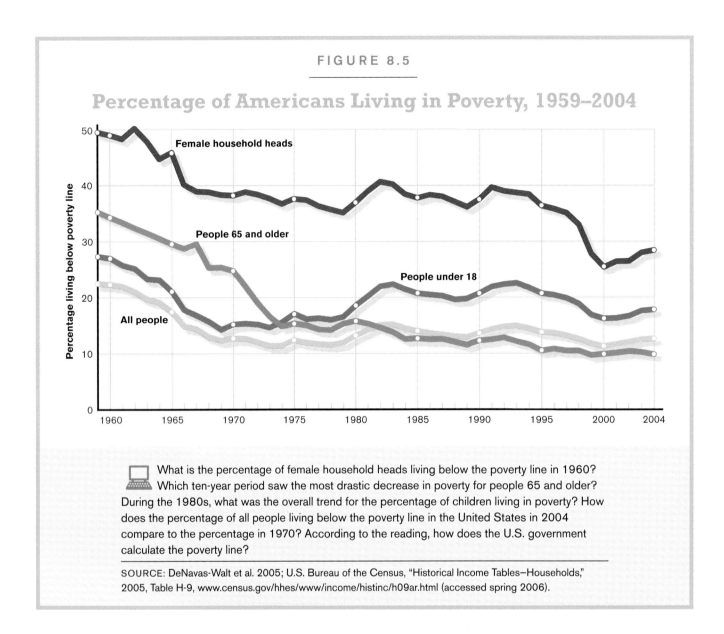

FIGURE 8.5

Percentage of Americans Living in Poverty, 1959–2004

Y-axis: Percentage living below poverty line

Female household heads

People 65 and older

People under 18

All people

What is the percentage of female household heads living below the poverty line in 1960? Which ten-year period saw the most drastic decrease in poverty for people 65 and older? During the 1980s, what was the overall trend for the percentage of children living in poverty? How does the percentage of all people living below the poverty line in the United States in 2004 compare to the percentage in 1970? According to the reading, how does the U.S. government calculate the poverty line?

SOURCE: DeNavas-Walt et al. 2005; U.S. Bureau of the Census, "Historical Income Tables–Households," 2005, Table H-9, www.census.gov/hhes/www/income/histinc/h09ar.html (accessed spring 2006).

equal to three times the cost of a nutritionally adequate diet—a strict no-frills budget that assumes a nutritionally adequate diet could be purchased in 1999 for only $3.86 per day for each member, along with about $7.72 on all other items (including rent and utilities, clothing, medical expenses, and transportation). For a family of four in 2002, that works out to an annual cash income of $19,350 (*Federal Register* 2005).

How realistic is this formula? Some critics believe it *over*estimates the amount of poverty. They point out that the current standard fails to take into account noncash forms of income available to the poor, such as food stamps, Medicare, Medicaid, and public housing subsidies as well as cash obtained from work at odd jobs that is concealed from the government. For example, one study looked at the poorest tenth of all families with children, comparing government survey data on their reported income with comparable data on their reported expenditures (Mayer and Jencks 1994). It found that these families actually spent twice as much, on average, as the income they reported to the government.

Other critics argue that the government's formula greatly *under*estimates the amount of poverty. They argue that to label a three-person family as "nonpoor" in 1999 because it earned more than $12,680 (less than $35 a day) is simply unrealistic. Some scholars point out that such figures are based on an assumption from a half century ago that an "average" family spends a third of its income on food, even though more recent studies show that the actual figure is closer to one sixth, and that as much as three quarters of a poor family's income may go to rent alone (Dolbeare 1995; Joint Center for Housing Studies 1994; Schwarz and Volgy 1992; Stone 1993). By this reasoning, food expenditures should be multiplied by at least 6, rather than 3, to yield the poverty level. Patricia Ruggles (1990, 1992), an adviser to the University of Wisconsin's Institute for Research on Poverty, estimates that this formula would effectively double the official number of Americans living in poverty. That would mean that in 2000, over 62 million people were living in poverty, or 22.6 percent—almost a quarter—of the population, instead of the official Census Bureau estimate for that year of 31.1 million people, or only 11.3 percent of the population.

The official U.S. poverty rate is the highest among the major advanced industrial nations, more than three times that of such European countries as Sweden or Norway (Smeeding et al. 2000). The largest concentrations of poverty in the United States are found in the South and the Southwest, in central cities, and in rural areas. Among the poor, 15.6 million Americans (or 5.4 percent of the country) live in extreme poverty: Their incomes are only *half* of the official poverty level, meaning that they live at near-starvation levels (DeNavas-Walt et al. 2005).

Who Are the Poor?

What do you think about poverty? Most Americans of all social classes think of the poor as people who are unemployed or on welfare. Americans also tend to display more negative attitudes toward welfare provisions and benefits than people in other Western countries. Surveys repeatedly show that the majority of Americans regard the poor as being responsible for their own poverty and are antagonistic to those who live on "government handouts." For example, a Gallup poll found that 55 percent of the public believed that lack of effort by the poor was the principal reason for poverty. Nearly two thirds believed that government assistance programs reduced incentives to work. A survey by National Public Radio in 2001 found similar results, but it is interesting that they discovered attitudes that blamed the poor for lack of motivation were even stronger among those that lived just above the poverty line. These views, however, are out of line with the realities of poverty. The poor are as diverse as other groups.

WORKING POOR

Many Americans are the **working poor**—that is, people who work but whose earnings are not high enough to lift them above poverty. The federal minimum wage, the legal floor for wages in the United States, was first set in 1938 at $0.25 an hour. Individual states can set higher minimum wages than the federal standard, and fifteen have chosen to do so; the highest is in the state of Washington, at $7.35 per hour. Although the federal minimum wage has increased over the years, since 1965

it has failed to keep up with inflation (Figure 8.6). As a result, in 2005 the U.S. minimum wage of $5.15 an hour resulted in a yearly income of only $10,300 for full-time workers—barely three quarters of poverty-level income ($14,494) for a single

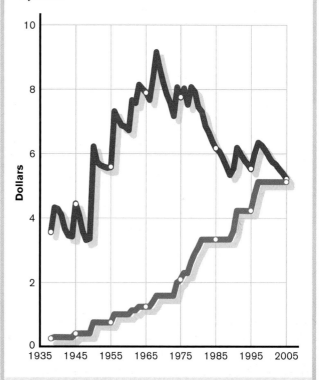

FIGURE 8.6

Changes in the Federal Minimum Wage, 1938–2005

The red line shows the federal minimum wage in each year, in "current" dollars—that is, dollars that are unadjusted for inflation. The blue line shows the same wage in "constant" 2005 dollars, thereby controlling for inflation.

What is the difference between the blue line and the red line? When did the minimum wage have the most value (based on its value adjusted for inflation)? Has the value of the minimum wage increased or decreased since the 1990s? Can a family earning minimum wage live above the poverty level? Why or why not?

SOURCE: U.S. Department of Labor, "History of Federal Minimum Wage Rates under the Fair Labor Standards Act, 1938–1996," n.d., www.dol.gov/esa/minwage/chart.htm (accessed spring 2006).

The Information Revolution and Inequality

What effect will the information revolution have on social inequality?

The answer in part depends on how well the American educational system responds to the challenge of preparing students for a high-technology world. A good education can pay off in the digital society. Although Bill Gates may be the world's richest college dropout (Gates left Harvard to found Microsoft), he is clearly the exception to the rule.

Recall what has happened to blue-collar factory work—the kinds of jobs that made possible a middle-class lifestyle throughout much of this century. As you have seen in this chapter, thanks to the information revolution, U.S. businesses today can relocate their manufacturing operations around the globe with the click of a mouse, filling out orders on their suppliers' Web pages almost as easily as consumers buy books on Amazon.com. Beginning in the late 1970s, U.S. firms began to take advantage of modern information technology to downsize, moving their production to low-wage countries. The result: stagnant or declining wages for much of the American working class. Inequality has increased for people whose skills limit them to blue-collar work.

College graduates today earn more than they did a decade ago—the higher the degree, the greater the gains. High school dropouts, on the other hand, earn less (Hout 1997). One U.S. Bureau of the Census (2004b) study found that, in 2003, men with a professional degree had a median income of $88,530, three times as much as men with only a high school diploma ($28,763). Employment in professional and service occupations are anticipated to grow the fastest between 2002 and 2012 (Hecker 2004). These occupational groups, which are at opposite ends of educational attainment and expected earnings, are anticipated to provide more than half of the total job growth in the near future. Over half of the thirty fastest growing occupations are health related, seven are computer related, and three are in education—all jobs that require advanced education. However, of the thirty *largest* growing occupations, those that will provide the most employment, only seven require a postsecondary education. Most new jobs will be in such occupations as nurses, teachers, salespersons, customer service representatives, food service, cashiers, janitors, managers, waitresses, nurses aides, and truck drivers.

How well are students today being educated for tomorrow's digital world? A recent U.S. Department of Education study (National Center for Education Statistics [NCES] 2000) gives mixed grades to public schools. The report, *Teachers' Tools for the 21st Century,* surveyed public school teachers in 1999, asking them about the technology that was available in their classrooms and how well prepared they were to use it. The good news was that virtually all of the teachers reported that their schools had computers connected to the Internet. Nearly all had at least one computer in their classroom, and two thirds of the classrooms were hooked up to the Internet as well. The bad news was that only half of the teachers used computers or the Internet to teach their students. Perhaps this was because only a third reported feeling prepared to use computers and the Internet in their classrooms.

Current patterns of computer use in public schools reinforce existing social stratification. For example, teachers in white middle-class schools were much more likely to use computers for Internet research than teachers in schools with large numbers of poor minority students. They were also less likely to report that outdated, unreliable computers were a barrier to their classroom instruction (NCES 2000). Poor inner-city schools, which often lack basic instructional materials such as textbooks, much less computers, are especially ill equipped to prepare their students.

There are some promising signs that the digital revolution may yet reach a broad cross section of American students. For example, Brown University, in conjunction with MCI World-Com, recently announced a small program to finance twenty college-community partnerships to help provide low-income children in inner-city schools and on Indian tribal reservations with science and technology training. The program would provide elementary school children and their families with help in buying computers, connecting to the Internet, and learning skills required to use them (Carnevale 2000). A growing number of American colleges and universities, as well as some private companies, are beginning to provide "virtual high schools" over the Internet, offering college prep and advanced placement courses to students in inner-city schools that traditionally lack such offerings (Carr 1999; Carr and Young 1999). The state of Maine recently approved a program to provide every seventh- and eighth-grade student with a laptop computer to be used throughout high school. Maine, which currently ranks thirty-seventh in the nation in per capita income, hopes that a high-tech future will reverse its economic fortunes (*Ellsworth American* 2001; Goldberg 2001).

It is still too early to give a final grade to American schools. The digital revolution is fairly recent, and schools and teachers are only beginning to catch up with it. It remains to be seen whether the new information technology ultimately reinforces existing social inequalities—or is used to overcome them.

Questions

- Describe how the advent of computers and the information technology industry could affect the kind of jobs available in the United States. How could the American occupational makeup change? How has it changed already?
- Can the use of computers in schools close the digital divide? Why or why not?
- How might the rise in high-tech jobs and the end of blue-collar jobs affect American society and lifestyle? Will society be increasingly stratified? How might it become more egalitarian?

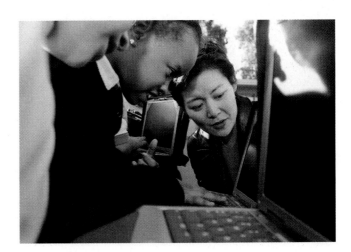

parent supporting two children (*Federal Register* 2005). About one third of those officially living in poverty are actually working. In 2003, there were an estimated 7.4 million working poor, or 5.4 percent of the population (U.S. Bureau of Labor Statistics 2005b). Of these working poor, 4.4 million usually worked full-time and another 2.5 million usually worked part-time. Most poor people, contrary to popular belief, don't receive welfare payments, because they earn too much to qualify for welfare. Only 5 percent of all low-income families with a full-time, full-year worker receive welfare benefits and over half rely on public health insurance rather than employer-sponsored insurance. The working poor are disproportionately non-white and immigrant (Urban Institute 2005).

Katherine Newman (2000) spent two years documenting the lives of three hundred low-wage workers and job seekers at fast-food restaurants in Harlem, a predominantly African American section of New York City. Her award-winning book *No Shame in My Game* found that the people interviewed were hard workers who valued their jobs, despite the low status associated with "slinging burgers." Moreover, Newman found that the working poor had to overcome enormous obstacles simply to survive: They typically lacked adequate educations, and some attended school while working; they had no health insurance to cover medical costs; and many were supporting families on poverty-level wages.

POVERTY, RACE, AND ETHNICITY

Poverty rates are much higher among most minority groups, even though more than two thirds of the poor are white. As Table 8.5 shows, blacks and Latinos continue to earn around two thirds of what whites earn in the United States while experiencing three times the poverty rate whites experience. This is because they often work at the lowest-paying jobs and because of racial discrimination. Asian Americans have the highest income of any group, but their poverty rate is almost one and a half times that of whites, reflecting the recent influx of relatively poor immigrant groups.

Latinos have somewhat higher incomes than blacks, although their poverty rate is comparable. Nonetheless, the number of blacks living in poverty has declined considerably in recent years. In 1959, 55.1 percent of blacks were living in poverty; by 2004 that figure had dropped to 24.7 percent. The recent high point for black poverty came during the recession of 1992, when 33.4 percent of the black population was poor. Since that time, the number of blacks in poverty has fallen by 2.5 million. This is mainly because the economic expansion of the 1990s created new job opportunities. A similar pattern is seen for Latinos: Poverty grew steadily between 1972 and 1994, peaking at 30.7 percent of the Latino population. By 2004, however, the poverty rate for Latinos had fallen to 21.9 percent (DeNavas-Walt et al. 2005).

THE FEMINIZATION OF POVERTY

Much of the growth in poverty is associated with the **feminization of poverty,** an increase in the proportion of the poor who are female. Growing rates of divorce, separation, and single-parent families have placed women at particular disadvantage because it is extremely difficult for unskilled or semiskilled, low-income, poorly educated women to raise children by themselves while they also hold down a job that could raise them out of poverty. As a result, in 2004 over one third (35.9 percent) of all single-parent families headed by women were poor,

---

TABLE 8.5

Median Income and Poverty Rates for Households in 2004, by Race and Ethnicity

	WHITE	ASIAN AMERICAN	LATINO	BLACK	TOTAL U.S.
Median income ($)[a]	46,697	57,475	34,241	30,268	44,389
Percentage of median income of whites	100.0	123.1	73.3	64.8	95.1
Poverty rate (%)[b]	10.8	9.8	21.9	24.7	12.7

SOURCE: (*a*) U.S. Bureau of the Census, "Historical Income Tables–Households," 2005, Table H-9, www.census.gov/hhes/www/income/histinc/h09ar.html (accessed spring 2006).; (*b*) DeNavas-Walt et al. 2005.

compared to only 5.5 percent of married couples with children (U.S. Bureau of the Census 2005d).

Households headed by single parents are much more likely to live in poverty than those headed by married couples, and the incidence of poverty is far higher if the single parent is a woman. The feminization of poverty is particularly acute among families headed by Latino women (Table 8.6). Although the rate declined by almost 30 percent since its peak in the mid-1980s (64 percent in 1985), 45.9 percent of all female-headed Latino families lived in poverty in 2004. An almost identical percentage (43.8 percent) of female-headed African American families also live in poverty; both considerably higher than either white (28.8 percent) or Asian (18.8 percent) female-headed households (U.S. Bureau of the Census 2005d).

A single woman attempting to raise children alone is caught in a vicious circle of hardship and poverty. If she does succeed in finding a job, she must find someone to take care of her children because she cannot afford to hire a baby-sitter or pay for day care. From her standpoint, she will take in more money if she accepts welfare payments from the government and tries to find illegal part-time jobs that pay cash not reported to the government rather than find a regular full-time job paying minimum wage. Even though welfare will not get her out of poverty, if she finds a regular job she will lose her welfare altogether. As a result, she and her family may even be worse off economically.

CHILDREN IN POVERTY

Given the high rates of poverty among families headed by single women, it follows that children are the principal victims of poverty in the United States. Child poverty rates (defined as poverty among people under eighteen) in the United States are by far the highest in the industrial world. Nonetheless, the child poverty rate has varied considerably over the last forty years, declining when the economy expands or the government increases spending on antipoverty programs and rising when the economy slows and government antipoverty spending falls. The child poverty rate declined from 27.3 percent of all children in 1959 to 14.4 percent in 1973—a period associated with both economic growth and the War on Poverty declared by the Johnson administration (1963–1969). During the late 1970s and 1980s, as economic growth slowed and cutbacks were made in government antipoverty programs, child poverty grew, exceeding 20 percent during much of the period. The economic expansion of the 1990s saw a drop in child poverty rates, and in 2002 the rate had fallen to 16.3 percent, a twenty-year low (U.S. Bureau of the Census 2003e). Yet, today child poverty rates are again on the increase, reaching 17.8 percent in 2004 (DeNavas-Walt et al. 2005).

The statistics are significantly higher for racial minorities and children of single mothers. Of those children under the age

---

TABLE 8.6

Families with Children: Percentage in Poverty, by Race and Ethnicity, Marital Status, and Sex of Head of Household, 2004

	MARRIED COUPLE	MALE HEAD	FEMALE HEAD
White	4.3	13.8	28.2
Black	9.2	25.3	43.8
Latino	17.9	20.5	45.9
Asian	6.4	16.5	18.8

SOURCE: U.S. Bureau of the Census, "Historical Poverty Tables," 2005d, Table 4, www.census.gov/hhes/www/poverty/histpov/hstpov4.html (accessed spring 2006).

---

of eighteen who were living in poverty in 2004, 10.5 percent were white, 33.6 percent were black, 10 percent were Asian, and 28.9 percent were Hispanic; furthermore, 28.4 percent lived with single mothers (DeNavas-Walt et al. 2005).

Child poverty is not due only to the state of the national economy or to government spending on antipoverty programs. As the statistics just given show, child poverty is most severe among children who live with single mothers. During the past forty years, the number of single-parent families headed by women more than doubled, contributing to the increase in child poverty.

Explaining Poverty: The Sociological Debate

Explanations of poverty can be grouped under two main headings: theories that see poor individuals as responsible for their own poverty and theories that view poverty as produced and reproduced by structural forces in society. These competing approaches are sometimes described as "blame the victim" and "blame the system" theories, respectively. We shall briefly examine each in turn.

There is a long history of attitudes that hold the poor responsible for their own disadvantaged positions. Early efforts to address the effects of poverty, such as the poorhouses of the nineteenth century, were grounded in a belief that poverty was the result of an inadequacy or pathology of individuals. The poor were seen as those who were unable—due to lack of skills, moral or physical weakness, absence of motivation, or below-average ability—to succeed in society. Social standing was taken as a reflection of a person's talent and effort; those who deserved to succeed did so, while others less capable were doomed to fail. The existence of winners and losers was regarded as a fact of life.

Such outlooks have enjoyed a renaissance, beginning in the 1970s and 1980s, as the political emphasis on entrepreneurship and individual ambition rewarded those who "succeeded" in society and held those who did not responsible for the circumstances in which they found themselves. Often explanations for poverty were sought in the lifestyles of poor people, along with the attitudes and outlooks they supposedly espoused. Oscar Lewis (1968) set forth one of the most influential of such theories, arguing that a **culture of poverty** exists among many poor people. According to Lewis, poverty is not a result of individual inadequacies but is a result of a larger social and cultural atmosphere into which poor children are socialized. The culture of poverty is transmitted across generations because young people from an early age see little point in aspiring to something more. Instead, they resign themselves fatalistically to a life of impoverishment.

The culture of poverty thesis has been taken further by the American sociologist Charles Murray (1984). According to Murray, individuals who are poor through "no fault of their own"—such as widows or widowers, orphans, or the disabled—fall into a different category from those who are part of the **dependency culture.** By this term, Murray refers to poor people who rely on government welfare provision rather than entering the labor market. He argues that the growth of the welfare state has created a subculture that undermines personal ambition and the capacity for self-help. Rather than orienting themselves toward the future and striving to achieve a better life, those dependent on welfare are content to accept handouts. Welfare, he argues, has eroded people's incentive to work.

Theories such as these seem to resonate among the U.S. population. Surveys have shown that the majority of Americans regard the poor as responsible for their own poverty and are suspicious of those who live "for free" on "government handouts." Many believe that people on welfare could find work if they were determined to do so. Yet, as we have seen, these views are out of line with the realities of poverty.

A second approach to explaining poverty emphasizes larger social processes that produce conditions of poverty that are difficult for individuals to overcome. According to such a view, structural forces within society—factors like class, gender, eth-

nicity, occupational position, education attainment, and so forth—shape the way in which resources are distributed (Wilson 1996). Writers who advocate structural explanations for poverty argue that the lack of ambition among the poor that is often taken for the dependency culture is in fact a *consequence* of their constrained situations, not a cause of it. Reducing poverty is not a matter of changing individual outlooks, they claim, but instead requires policy measures aimed at distributing income and resources more equally throughout society. Child-care subsidies, a minimum hourly wage, and guaranteed income levels for families are examples of policy measures that have sought to redress persistent social inequalities.

Both theories have enjoyed broad support, and we consistently encourage variations of each view in public debates about poverty. Critics of the culture of poverty view accuse its advocates of "individualizing" poverty and blaming the poor for circumstances largely beyond their control. They see the poor as victims, not as freeloaders who are abusing the system. Yet we should be cautious about accepting uncritically the arguments of those who see the causes of poverty as lying exclusively in the structure of society itself. Such an approach implies that the poor simply passively accept the difficult situations in which they find themselves.

Combating Poverty: Welfare Systems

Well-developed and systematically administered welfare programs, in conjunction with government policies that actively assist in keeping down unemployment, reduce poverty levels. But an economic and political price has to be paid for this. Such a society requires high levels of taxation; and the government bureaucracies needed to administer the complex welfare system tend to acquire considerable power, even though they are not democratically elected.

Being poor does not necessarily mean being *mired* in poverty. A substantial proportion of people in poverty at any one time have either enjoyed superior conditions of life previously or can be expected to climb out of poverty at some time in the future.

As we saw in the last section, critics of existing welfare institutions in the United States have argued that these produce "welfare dependency," meaning that people become dependent on the very programs that are supposed to allow them to forge an independent and meaningful life for themselves. They become not just materially dependent but psychologically dependent on the arrival of the welfare check. Instead of taking an active attitude toward their lives, they tend to adopt a resigned and passive one, looking to the welfare system to support them.

Others deny that such dependency is widespread. "Being on welfare" is commonly regarded as a source of shame, they say, and most people who are in such a position probably strive actively to escape from it as far as possible.

However widespread it may be, tackling welfare dependency has become a main target of attempts at reform of American welfare institutions. Among the most significant of such reforms have been welfare-to-work programs, whose driving force is to move recipients from public assistance into paid jobs. Daniel Friedlander and Gary Burtless (1994) studied four different government-initiated programs designed to encourage welfare recipients to find paid work. The programs were roughly similar. They provided financial benefits for welfare recipients who actively searched for jobs as well as guidance in job-hunting techniques and opportunities for education and training. The target populations were mainly single-parent family heads of households who were recipients of Aid to Families with Dependent Children, at the time, the largest cash welfare program in the country. Friedlander and Burtless found that the programs did achieve results. People involved in such programs were able either to enter employment or to start working sooner than others who didn't participate. In all four programs, the earnings produced were several times greater than the net cost of the program. The programs were least effective, however, in helping those who needed them the most—those who had been out of work for a lengthy period, the long-term unemployed.

In 1996, Congress enacted and President Bill Clinton signed a law to "end welfare as we know it." The resulting program, Temporary Assistance for Needy Families (TANF), required that welfare recipients begin work after receiving benefits for two years. Families were cut off entirely after a cumulative five years of assistance. Before this reform, there were no time limits or work requirements imposed by the federal government for welfare recipients, many of whom are single mothers.

Although welfare-to-work programs succeeded in reducing welfare claims from 5.1 million families to 2.7 million families in its first three years (Figure 8.7, p. 248), some statistics suggest that the outcomes are not entirely positive. Among those who had left welfare for work, only 61 percent had found jobs, 20 percent relied on help from family members or private charities, and about 19 percent had no work or source of independent income. Among those working, the average wage was $6.61 an hour. For about half of this group, this amounted to less than what they had received from the welfare system. Only 23 percent had health insurance through their employer. In Wisconsin, the state that was one of the first to introduce welfare-to-work programs, two thirds of former welfare recipients live below the poverty line. Most have difficulty finding enough money for food and other essentials (Loprest 1999).

Kathryn Edin and Laura Lein (1997) have shown that for low-income mothers, the costs of leaving welfare for work can outweigh the advantages. These mothers face expenses for food, rent, and other necessities that often exceed their income. Mothers who work must often pay for child care, so that their expenses surpass those of unemployed mothers. In addition, the jobs available to low-income mothers tend to be less stable and to pay less than welfare.

Because their expenses exceed their income, both working and welfare mothers must often find other sources of money. Mothers on welfare tend to rely on aid from charitable agencies or side work, which is likely to be unreported. (Reporting additional income can reduce or end welfare benefits.) Low-income working mothers also rely on support from people in their social networks, such as family members or boyfriends, to help pay the costs of daily life. Pointing to such findings, critics argue that the apparent success of the welfare-to-work initiatives in reducing the number of people on welfare conceals some troublesome patterns in the actual experiences of those who lose their welfare benefits. Moreover, even the most hopeful studies were conducted during a period of economic expansion. When growth slows—or declines—it will be increasingly difficult, if not impossible, for welfare recipients to find any jobs at all.

Social Exclusion

What are the social processes that lead to a large number of people's being marginalized in society? The idea of **social exclusion** refers to new sources of inequality—ways in which individuals may become cut off from involvement in the wider society. It is a broader concept than that of the underclass and has the advantage that it emphasizes *processes*—mechanisms of exclusion. For instance, people who live in a dilapidated housing project, with poor schools and few employment opportunities in the area, may effectively be denied opportunities for self-betterment that most people in society have. It is also different from poverty as such. It focuses attention on a broad range of factors that prevent individuals or groups from having opportunities that are open to the majority of the population. We have already encountered an important example of social exclusion in Milner's (2004) study of high school status systems. One way that teenagers mark themselves of as "superior" is by excluding others who they perceive as "inferior." High school students become well practiced in the art of exclusion long before they go on to college.

Social exclusion can take a number of forms, so that it may occur in isolated rural communities cut off from many services and opportunities or in inner-city neighborhoods marked by

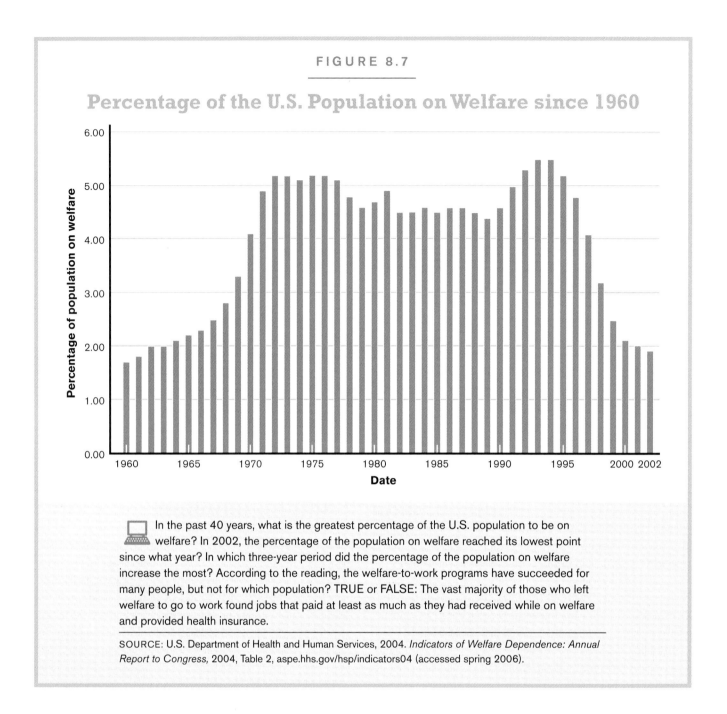

FIGURE 8.7

Percentage of the U.S. Population on Welfare since 1960

In the past 40 years, what is the greatest percentage of the U.S. population to be on welfare? In 2002, the percentage of the population on welfare reached its lowest point since what year? In which three-year period did the percentage of the population on welfare increase the most? According to the reading, the welfare-to-work programs have succeeded for many people, but not for which population? TRUE or FALSE: The vast majority of those who left welfare to go to work found jobs that paid at least as much as they had received while on welfare and provided health insurance.

SOURCE: U.S. Department of Health and Human Services, 2004. *Indicators of Welfare Dependence: Annual Report to Congress,* 2004, Table 2, aspe.hhs.gov/hsp/indicators04 (accessed spring 2006).

high crime rates and substandard housing. Exclusion and inclusion may be seen in economic terms, political terms, and social terms.

The concept of social exclusion raises the question of agency. After all, the word *exclusion* implies that someone or something is being shut out by another. Certainly in some instances, individuals are excluded through decisions that lie outside their own control. Banks might refuse to grant a current account or credit cards to individuals living in a certain ZIP code. Insurance companies might reject an application for a policy on the basis of an applicant's personal history and

background. An employee laid off later in life may be refused further jobs on the basis of his or her age.

But social exclusion not only is the result of people's being excluded but can also result from people excluding themselves from aspects of mainstream society. Individuals can choose to drop out of education, to turn down a job opportunity and become economically inactive, or to abstain from voting in political elections. In considering the phenomenon of social exclusion, we must once again be conscious of the interaction between human agency and responsibility on the one hand and the role of social forces in shaping people's circumstances on the other hand.

Forms of Social Exclusion

Sociologists have conducted research into the different ways in which individuals and communities experience exclusion. Investigations have focused on topics as diverse as housing, education, the labor market, crime, young people, and the elderly. We shall now look briefly at several examples of exclusion that have attracted attention in industrialized societies.

HOUSING AND NEIGHBORHOODS

The nature of social exclusion can be seen clearly within the housing sector. While many people in industrialized societies live in comfortable, spacious housing, others reside in dwellings that are overcrowded, inadequately heated, or structurally unsound. When entering the housing market, individuals are able to secure housing on the basis of their existing and projected resources. Thus a dual-income childless couple will have a greater chance of obtaining a mortgage for a home in an attractive area, whereas a household whose adults are unemployed or in low-paying jobs may be restricted to less desirable options in the rented or public-housing sector.

Stratification within the housing market occurs at both the household and the community level. Just as disadvantaged individuals are excluded from desirable housing options, whole communities can be excluded from opportunities and activities that are norms for the rest of society. Exclusion can take on a spatial dimension: Neighborhoods vary greatly in terms of safety, environmental conditions, and the availability of services and public facilities. For example, low-demand neighborhoods tend to have fewer basic services such as banks, grocery stores, and post offices than more desirable areas. Community spaces such as parks, playing fields, and libraries may also be limited. Yet people living in disadvantaged places often depend on what few facilities are available. Unlike residents of more affluent areas, they may not have access to transportation (or funds) that would allow them to shop and use services elsewhere.

In deprived communities, it can be difficult for people to overcome exclusion and to take steps to engage more fully in society. Social networks may be weak; this reduces the circulation of information about jobs, political activities, and community events. High unemployment and low income levels place strains on family life; crime and juvenile delinquency undermine the overall quality of life in the neighborhood. Low-demand housing areas often experience high household turnover rates as many residents seek to move on to more desirable housing, while new, disadvantaged entrants to the housing market continue to arrive. Finally, because most public schools in the United States are financed with property taxes, poor neighborhoods are likely to have underfunded schools, which lowers the quality of education available to poor children.

RURAL AREAS

Although much attention is paid to social exclusion in urban settings, people living in rural regions can also experience exclusion. Some social workers and caregivers believe that the challenges or exclusion in the countryside are as large, if not larger, than those in cities. In smaller villages and sparsely populated areas, access to goods, services, and facilities is not as extensive as in more settled areas. In most industrial societies, proximity to basic services such as doctors, post offices, schools, houses of worship, libraries, and government services is considered a necessity for leading an active, full, and healthy life. But rural residents often have limited access to such services and depend on the facilities available within their local community.

Access to transportation is one of the biggest factors affecting rural exclusion. If a household owns or has access to a car, it is easier to remain integrated in society. For example, family members can consider taking jobs in other towns, periodic shopping trips can be arranged to areas that have a larger selection of shops, and visits to friends or family in other areas can be organized more readily. Young people can be fetched home from parties. People who do not have access to a car, however, depend on public transportation, and in rural areas such services are limited in scope.

SOCIAL EXCLUSION AT THE TOP

The examples of exclusion that we have considered thus far all concern individuals or groups who, for whatever reason, are unable to participate fully in institutions and activities used by the majority of the population. Yet, not all cases of exclusion occur among those who are disadvantaged at the bottom of society. In recent years, new dynamics of "social exclusion at the top" have been emerging. This means that a minority of individuals at the very top of society can opt out of participation in mainstream institutions by merit of their affluence, influence, and connections.

Exclusion at the top can take a number of forms. The wealthy might retreat fully from the realm of public education and health care services, preferring to pay for private services and attention. Affluent residential communities—the so-called gated communities located behind tall walls and security checkpoints—are increasingly closed off from the rest of society. Tax payments and financial obligations can be drastically reduced through careful management and the help of private financial planners. Particularly in the United States, active political participation among the elite is often replaced by large donations to political candidates who are seen to represent their interests. In a number of ways, the very wealthy are able to escape from their social and financial responsibilities into a closed, private realm largely separate from the rest of society.

Just as social exclusion at the bottom undermines social solidarity and cohesion, exclusion at the top is similarly detrimental to an integrated society.

Crime and Social Exclusion

Some sociologists have argued that in industrialized societies such as the United States there are strong links between crime and social exclusion. There is a trend among late modern societies, they argue, away from inclusive goals (based on citizenship rights) and toward arrangements that accept and even promote the exclusion of some citizens (Young 1998, 1999). Crime rates may be reflecting the fact that a growing number of people do not feel valued by—or feel they have an investment in—the societies in which they live.

Elliott Currie is a sociologist who has investigated the connections between social exclusion and crime in the United States, particularly among young people. Currie (1998) argues that American society is a "natural laboratory" that is already demonstrating the "ominous underside" of market-driven social policy: rising poverty and homelessness, drug abuse, and violent crime. He notes that young people are increasingly growing up on their own without the guidance and support they need from the adult population. While faced by the seductive lure of the market and consumer goods, young people are also confronted by diminishing opportunities in the labor market to sustain a livelihood. This can result in a profound sense of relative deprivation and a willingness to turn to illegitimate means of sustaining a desired lifestyle.

According to Currie, there are several main links between crime and social exclusion. First, shifts in the labor market and government taxation and minimum wage policies have led to an enormous growth in both relative and absolute poverty within the American population. Second, this rise in social exclusion is felt in local communities, which suffer from a loss of stable livelihoods, transient populations, increasingly expensive housing, and a weakening of social cohesion. Third, economic deprivation and community fragmentation strain family life. Adults in many poor families are forced to take on multiple jobs to survive—a situation that produces perpetual stress, anxiety, and absence from home. The socialization and nurturing of children is, as a result, weakened; the overall "social impoverishment" of the community means that there is little opportunity for parents to turn to other families or relatives for support. Fourth, the state has rolled back many of the programs and public services that could reincorporate the socially excluded, such as early childhood intervention, child care, and mental health care.

Finally, the standards of economic status and consumption that are promoted within society cannot be met through legitimate means by the socially excluded population. According to Currie (1998), one of the most troublesome dimensions to this connection between social exclusion and crime is that legitimate channels are bypassed in favor of illegal ones. Crime is favored over alternative means, such as the political system or community organization.

THE HOMELESS

No discussion of social exclusion is complete without reference to the people who are traditionally seen as at the very bottom of the social hierarchy: the **homeless.** The growing problem of homelessness is one of the most distressing signs of changes in the American stratification system. The homeless are a common sight in nearly every U.S. city and town and are increasingly found in rural areas as well. Two generations ago, the homeless were mainly elderly, alcoholic men who were found on the skid rows of the largest metropolitan areas. Today they are primarily young single men, often of working age. The fastest-growing group of homeless, however, consists of families with children, who make up as much as 40 percent of those currently homeless (National Law Center on Homelessness and Poverty [NLCHP] 2004). Approximately 42 percent of those children are under the age of five. In 2004, the National Law Center on Homelessness and Poverty estimated that 41 percent of the homeless are single men and 14 percent are single females. Equal shares of the homeless population are black and white (40 percent), 11 percent are Hispanic, and 8 percent

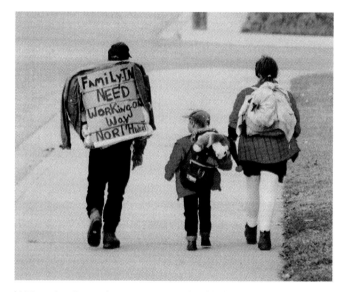

With a sign for assistance strapped to his back, Rick Cathy, his wife, and their five-year-old daughter make their way to Sacramento. The family, originally from Buffalo, New York, was on the road continuously for more than eighteen months after losing their home.

are Native American. Very few homeless are Latino or Asian American immigrants, possibly because these groups enjoy close-knit family and community ties that provide a measure of security against homelessness (Waxman and Hinderliter 1996). As many as 33 percent of homeless men are veterans, many of the Vietnam War (NLHCP 2004).

No one really knows how many homeless people there are because it is extremely difficult to count people who do not have a stable residence (Appelbaum 1990). Estimates of the number of homeless vary widely. The most recent estimate is that there are 462,000 homeless people in the United States on any given day, and that between 2.3 and 3.5 million adults and children experience a spell of homelessness at least once during a year (National Coalition for the Homeless 2005; Urban Institute 2000). One survey of twenty-five cities, conducted by the U.S. Conference of Mayors in 2001, found a 17 percent increase in the number of homeless families applying for help over the previous year (Bernstein 2001).

There are many reasons why people become homeless. One problem is that about two thirds report having a problem with alcohol at some point during their life, another two thirds report having a problem with drugs at some point, and nearly 60 percent have experienced a mental health problem (NLCHP 2004). One reason for the widespread incidence of such problems among the homeless is that many public mental hospitals have closed their doors. The number of beds in state mental hospitals has declined by as many as half a million since the early 1960s, leaving many mentally ill people with no institutional alternative to a life on the streets or in homeless shelters. Such problems are compounded by the fact that many homeless people lack family, relatives, or other social networks to provide support.

The rising cost of housing is another factor, particularly in light of the increased poverty noted elsewhere in this chapter. Declining incomes at the bottom, along with rising rents, create an affordability gap between the cost of housing and what poor people can pay in rents (Dreier and Appelbaum 1992). The median share of income that renters spend on rent is 29 percent. It is estimated that nearly one third of all households spend 30 percent or more of their incomes on housing and 13 percent spend 50 percent of their income on housing (Joint Center for Housing Studies 2005). The burden of paying rent is extremely difficult for low-income families whose heads work for minimum wage or slightly higher. Paying so much in terms of rent leaves them barely a paycheck away from a missed rental payment and eventual eviction (National Low Income Housing Coalition [NLIHC] 2000). The housing affordability gap has been worsened by the loss of government programs aimed at providing low-cost housing for the poor during the 1980s, which removed a crucial safety net just as poverty was increasing in the United States.

The sociological imagination enables us to understand how personal characteristics and larger social forces can combine to increase the risk of becoming homeless. Imagine two hard-working people with similar personal problems—for example, both struggle with alcoholism, depression, and family problems. One is an unskilled worker in a low-wage job, whereas the other is a doctor with a substantial income. Which one is more likely to become homeless?

The unskilled worker has little margin for mistakes, misfortunes, or economic changes that could threaten his or her job. During a time when American firms are moving their lowest-paying, least-skilled work overseas, the workers who hold such jobs are especially vulnerable to job loss and homelessness. A bout with too much drinking might be all that it takes to be thrown out of work. On the other hand, the doctor's job is unlikely to be threatened by globalization. Furthermore, he or she most likely has health insurance that covers counseling for personal problems and perhaps even costly treatment for alcoholism. There are likely other resources to fall back on as well: savings, investments, credit and loans, and friends and family who can afford to help out. This is not to say that only poor people run the risk of becoming homeless: If you have ever volunteered at a homeless shelter, you may have been surprised to encounter formerly middle-class families who "ran out of luck." But the people overwhelmingly at risk of becoming homeless are those who face a combination of low-paying jobs, poverty, and high housing costs along with a tangle of personal problems (Burt 1992).

Theories of Stratification in Modern Societies

So far, we have examined closely types of class division, inequality, social mobility, poverty, and social exclusion. In this section, we step back and look at some broad theories by which thinkers have attempted to *understand* stratification. The most influential theoretical approaches are those developed by Karl Marx and Max Weber. Most subsequent theories of stratification are heavily indebted to their ideas.

Marx: Means of Production and the Analysis of Class

For Marx, the term *class* refers to people who stand in a common relationship to the **means of production**—the means by which they gain a livelihood. In modern societies, the two main classes are those who own the means of production—industrialists, or **capitalists**—and those who earn their living by selling their labor to them, the working class. The relationship between classes, according to Marx, is an exploitative one. In the course of the working day, Marx reasoned, workers produce more than is actually needed by employers to repay the cost of hiring them. This **surplus value** is the source of profit, which capitalists are able to put to their own use. A group of workers in a clothing factory, say, might be able to produce a hundred suits a day. Selling half the suits provides enough income for the manufacturer to pay the workers' wages. Income from the sale of the remainder of the garments is taken as profit.

Marx (1977; orig. 1864) believed that the maturing of industrial capitalism would bring about an increasing gap between the wealth of the minority and the poverty of the mass of the population. In his view, the wages of the working class could never rise far above subsistence level, while wealth would pile up in the hands of those owning capital. In addition, laborers would daily face work that is physically wearing and mentally tedious, as is the situation in many factories. At the lowest levels of society, particularly among those frequently or permanently unemployed, there would develop an "accumulation of misery, agony of labor, slavery, ignorance, brutality, moral degradation."

Marx was right about the persistence of poverty in industrialized countries and in anticipating that large inequalities of wealth and income would continue. He was wrong in supposing that the income of most of the population would remain extremely low. Most people in Western countries today are much better off materially than were comparable groups in Marx's day.

Weber: Class and Status

There are two main differences between Weber's theory and that of Marx. First, according to Weber, class divisions derive not only from control or lack of control of the means of production but from economic differences that have nothing directly to do with property. Such resources include especially people's skills and credentials, or qualifications. Those in managerial or professional occupations earn more and enjoy more favorable conditions at work, for example, than people in blue-collar jobs. The qualifications they possess, such as degrees, diplomas, and the skills they have acquired, make them more "marketable" than others without such qualifications. At a lower level, among blue-collar workers, skilled craft workers are able to secure higher wages than the semiskilled or unskilled.

Second, Weber distinguished another aspect of stratification besides class, which he called "status." *Status* refers to differences between groups in the social honor, or prestige, they are accorded by others. Status distinctions can vary independent of class divisions. Social honor may be either positive or negative. For instance, doctors and lawyers have high prestige in American society. **Pariah groups,** on the other hand, are negatively privileged status groups, subject to discrimination that prevents them from taking advantage of opportunities open to others. The Jews were a pariah group in medieval Europe, banned from participating in certain occupations and from holding official positions.

Possession of wealth normally tends to confer high status, but there are exceptions to this principle. In Britain, for instance, individuals from aristocratic families continue to enjoy considerable social esteem even after their fortunes have been lost. Conversely, "new money" is often looked on with some scorn by the well-established wealthy.

Whereas class is an objective measure, status depends on people's subjective evaluations of social differences. Classes derive from the economic factors associated with property and earnings; status is governed by the varying lifestyles that groups follow.

Weber's writings on stratification are important because they show that other dimensions of stratification besides class strongly influence people's lives. Most sociologists hold that Weber's scheme offers a more flexible and sophisticated basis for analyzing stratification than that provided by Marx.

Davis and Moore: The Functions of Stratification

Kingsley Davis and Wilbert E. Moore (1945) provided a functionalist explanation of stratification, arguing that it has beneficial consequences for society. They claimed that certain positions or roles in society are functionally more important than others, such as brain surgeons, and these positions require special skills for their performance. However, only a limited number of individuals in any society have the talents or experience appropriate to these positions. To attract the most qualified people, rewards need to be offered, such as money, power, and prestige. Davis and Moore determined that since the benefits of different positions in any society must be unequal, then all societies must be stratified. They concluded that social stratification and social inequality are functional because they ensure that the most qualified people, attracted by the rewards bestowed by society, fill the roles that are most important to a smoothly functioning society.

Davis and Moore's theory suggests that a person's social position is based solely on his or her innate talents and efforts. It is not surprising that their theory has been met with criticism by other sociologists. For example, Melvin Tumin (1953) critiqued the theory for several reasons. First, he argued that the functional importance of a particular role is difficult to measure and that the rewards that a society bestows on those in "important" roles do not necessarily reflect their actual importance. For instance, who is more important to society, a lawyer or a schoolteacher? If, on average, a lawyer earns four or five times the amount that a schoolteacher does, does that accurately reflect his or her relative importance to society? Second, Tumin argued that Davis and Moore overlooked the ways in which stratification limits the discovery of talent in a society. As we have seen, the United States is not entirely a meritocratic society. Those at the top tend to have unequal access to economic and cultural resources, such as the highest quality education, which help the upper classes transmit their privileged status from one generation to the next. For those without access to these resources, even those with superior talents, social inequality serves as a barrier to reaching their full potential.

Erik Olin Wright: Contradictory Class Locations

The American sociologist Erik Olin Wright (1978, 1985, 1997) developed a theoretical position that owes much to Marx but also incorporates ideas from Weber. According to Wright, there are three dimensions of control over economic resources in modern capitalist production, and these allow us to identify the major classes that exist:

1. Control over investments or money capital
2. Control over the physical means of production (land or factories and offices)
3. Control over labor power

Those who belong to the capitalist class have control over each of these dimensions of the production system. Members of the working class have control over none of them. In between these two main classes, however, are the groups whose position is more ambiguous—the managers and white-collar workers mentioned earlier. These people are in what Wright calls **contradictory class locations,** because they are able to influence some aspects of production but are denied control over others. White-collar and professional employees, for example, have to contract their labor power to employers to make a living, in the same way as manual workers do. Yet at the same time they have a greater degree of control over the work setting than do most people in blue-collar jobs. Wright terms the class position of such workers "contradictory," because they are neither capitalists nor manual workers, yet share certain common features with each.

A large segment of the population—85 to 90 percent, according to Wright (1997)—falls into the category of those who are forced to sell their labor because they do not control the means of production. Yet within this population is a great deal of diversity, ranging from the traditional manual working class to white-collar workers. To differentiate class locations within this large population, Wright takes two factors into account: the relationship to authority and the possession of skills or expertise. First, Wright argues that many middle-class workers, such as managers and supervisors, enjoy *relationships toward authority* that are more privileged than those of the working class. Such individuals are called on by capitalists to assist in controlling the working class—for example, by monitoring an employee's work or by conducting personnel reviews and evaluations—and are rewarded for their "loyalty" by earning higher wages and receiving regular promotions. Yet, at the same time, these individuals remain under the control of the capitalist owners. In other words they are both exploiters and exploited.

The second factor that differentiates class locations within the middle classes is the *possession of skills and expertise.* According to Wright, middle-class employees possessing skills that are in demand in the labor market are able to exercise a specific form of power in the capitalist system. Given that their expertise is in short supply, they are able to earn a higher wage. The lucrative positions available to information technology specialists in the emerging knowledge economy illustrate this point. Moreover, Wright argues, because employees with knowledge and skills are more difficult to monitor and control, employers are obliged to secure their loyalty and cooperation by rewarding them accordingly.

Frank Parkin and Social Closure

Frank Parkin (1971, 1979), a British author, has proposed an approach drawing more heavily on Weber than on Marx. Parkin agrees with Marx, as Weber did, that ownership of property—the means of production—is the basic foundation of class structure. Property, however, according to Parkin, is only one form of social closure that can be monopolized by one group and used as a basis of power over others. We can define as **social closure** any process whereby groups try to maintain exclusive control over resources, limiting access to them. Besides property or wealth, most of the characteristics Weber associated with status differences, such as ethnic origin, language, or religion, may be used to create social closure.

Two types of processes are involved in social closure. The first type, *exclusion,* we have already discussed. It refers to strategies that groups adopt to separate outsiders from themselves, preventing them from having access to valued resources. As we have seen, high school students forcefully exclude others from their status groups (Milner 2004). An emphasis on credentials is one major way by which groups exclude others in order to hold on to their own power and privilege. In some U.S. school systems, for example, only those who have earned a secondary-school teaching certification in their subject, awarded by a school of education, are allowed to teach in the public schools.

The second type of processes involved in social closure, *usurpation*, refers to attempts by the less privileged to acquire resources previously monopolized by others—as when blacks struggle to achieve the rights of union membership.

The strategies of exclusion and usurpation may be used simultaneously in some circumstances. Labor unions, for instance, might engage in usurpatory activities against employers (going on strike to obtain a greater share of the resources or a position on the board of directors of a firm) but at the same time exclude ethnic minorities from membership. Parkin calls this dual closure. Here there is clearly a point of similarity between Wright and Parkin. Dual closure concerns much the same processes as those discussed by Wright with his concept of contradictory class locations. Both notions indicate that those in the middle of the stratification system in some part cast their eyes toward the top yet are also concerned with distinguishing themselves from others lower down.

Growing Inequality in the United States

Throughout this chapter, we have touched on the various ways in which changes in the American economy have affected social stratification, emphasizing the importance of both globalization and changes in information technology. We have pointed out that the global spread of an industrial capitalist economy, driven in part by the information revolution, has helped to break down closed caste systems around the world and replace them with more open class systems. The degree to which this process will result in greater equality in countries undergoing capitalist development will be explored in the next chapter.

What do these changes hold in store for you? On the one hand, new jobs are opening up, particularly in high-technology fields that require special training and skills and pay high wages. A flood of new products is flowing into the United States, many made with cheap labor that has lowered their costs. This has enabled consumers such as yourselves to buy everything from computers to automobiles at costs lower than you otherwise would have paid, thereby contributing to a rising standard of living.

But these benefits come with potentially significant costs. As you have read throughout this chapter, you live in a fast-paced world, in which you may find yourselves competing for jobs with workers in other countries who work for lower wages. This has already been the case for the manufacturing jobs that once provided the economic foundation for the working class and segments of the middle class. Companies that once produced in the United States—from automobiles to apparel to electronics—now use factories around the world, taking advantage of labor costs that are a fraction of those in the United States. Will the same hold true for other, more highly skilled jobs—jobs in the information economy itself? Many jobs that require the use of computers—from graphic design to software engineering—can be done by anyone with a high-speed computer connection, anywhere in the world. The global spread of dot-com companies will open up vastly expanded job opportunities for those with the necessary skills and training—but it will also open up equally expanded global competition for those jobs.

Partly as a result of these forces, inequality has increased in the United States since the early 1970s, resulting in a growing gap between rich and poor. The global economy has permitted the accumulation of vast fortunes at the same time that it has contributed to declining wages, economic hardship, and poverty in the United States. Homelessness is at least in part due to these processes, as is the emergence of an underclass of the new urban poor. Although the working class is especially vulnerable to these changes, the middle class is not exempt: A growing number of middle-class households experienced downward mobility from the late 1970s through the mid-1990s, until a decade of economic growth (now over) benefited all segments of American society. Although it is always hazardous to try to predict the future, global economic integration will likely continue to increase for the foreseeable future. How this will affect your jobs and careers—and stratification in the United States—is much more difficult to foresee.

The world today is undergoing a transformation as profound as the industrial revolution. The effect of that transformation will be felt well into the twenty-first century, touching our lives in every way. In the next chapter, we will further examine the effect of this transformation on stratification and inequality in other countries in the world, especially the poorer countries that have recently begun to industrialize.

Study Outline

Social Stratification

- *Social stratification* refers to the division of people socioeconomically into layers, or strata. When we talk of social stratification, we draw attention to the unequal positions occupied by individuals in society. In the larger traditional societies and in industrialized countries today there is stratification in terms of *wealth,* property, and access to material goods and cultural products.
- Three major types of stratification systems can be distinguished: *slavery, caste,* and *class.* Whereas the first two of these depend on legal or religiously sanctioned inequalities, class divisions are not "officially" recognized but stem from economic factors affecting the material circumstances of people's lives.

Class Systems

- Classes derive from inequalities in possession and control of material resources and access to educational and occupational opportunities. An individual's class position is at least in some part achieved, for it is not simply "given" from birth. Some recent authors have suggested that cultural factors such as lifestyle and consumption patterns are important influences on class position. According to such a view, individual identities are now more structured around lifestyle choices than they are around traditional class indicators such as occupation.
- Class is of major importance in industrialized societies, although there are many complexities in the class system within such societies. The main class divisions are between people in the *upper, middle,* and *lower working classes*, and the *underclass.*

Inequality in the United States

- Most people in modern societies are more affluent today than was the case several generations ago. Yet the distribution of *wealth* and *income* remains highly unequal. Between the early 1970s and the late 1990s, partly as a result of economic globalization, the gap between rich and poor grew. Incomes at the top increased sharply, while many ordinary workers and families saw their incomes drop as higher-wage manufacturing jobs moved offshore to low-wage countries.

Social Mobility

- In the study of *social mobility,* a distinction is made between *intragenerational* and *intergenerational mobility.* The first of these refers to movement up or down the social scale within an individual's working life. Intergenerational mobility is movement across the generations, as when the daughter or son from a blue-collar background becomes a professional. Social mobility is mostly of limited range. Most people remain close to the level of the family from

which they came, though the expansion of white-collar jobs in the last few decades has provided the opportunity for considerable short-range upward mobility.

Poverty

- Poverty remains widespread in the United States. Two methods of assessing poverty exist. One involves the notion of *absolute poverty*, which is a lack of the basic resources needed to maintain a healthy existence. *Relative poverty* involves assessing the gaps between the living conditions of some groups and those enjoyed by the majority of the population.
- Problems of declining income and poverty are especially pronounced among racial and ethnic minorities, families headed by single women, and persons lacking education. The *feminization of poverty* is especially strong among young, poorly educated women who are raising children on their own.

Social Exclusion

- Social exclusion refers to processes by which individuals may become cut off from full involvement in the wider society. People who are socially excluded, due to poor housing, inferior schools, or limited transportation, may be denied the opportunities for self-betterment that most people in society have. Homelessness is one of the most extreme forms of social exclusion. Homeless people lacking a permanent residence may be shut out of many everyday activities that most people take for granted.

Theories of Stratification

- The most prominent and influential theories of stratification are those developed by Marx and Weber. Marx placed the primary emphasis on class, which he saw as an objectively given characteristic of the economic structure of society. He saw a fundamental split between the owners of capital and the workers who do not own capital. Weber accepted a similar view, but distinguished another aspect of stratification, *status.* Status refers to the esteem, or "social honor," given to individuals or groups.

Key Concepts

absolute poverty (p. 239)
ascription (p. 234)
capitalists (p. 252)
caste societies (p. 217)
caste system (p. 217)
class (p. 219)
contradictory class locations (p. 253)
culture of poverty (p. 246)
dependency culture (p. 246)

Review Questions

1. What is the difference between income and wealth?
   a. Income is the wages and salaries that you earn; wealth is what you are worth if you sell everything you own.
   b. Income is salary; wealth is the interest that accrues on investments.
   c. Income is money in the bank; wealth is locked up in physical assets.
   d. Income and wealth are the same thing.

2. What is the basis of Karl Marx's theory of class?
   a. Class is a byproduct of the Industrial Revolution.
   b. Modern societies are divided into those who own the means of production and those who sell their labor.
   c. People with power will always use it to protect their material interests.
   d. Class is a transitory system of stratification between feudal estates and the classlessness of communist society.

3. Which of the following is *not* true about the effect of globalization in the United States?
   a. Some manufacturing jobs have been lost.
   b. You may be competing for jobs with someone from a less-developed country.
   c. Inequality has declined as a result of globalization.
   d. Those with high skill levels are likely to get high compensation.

4. According to William Sewell and Robert Hauser, how does family background influence one's educational attainment?
   a. Family background determines the type of school children attend.
   b. Family background is a good indicator of family income, which has a direct impact on the economic resources parents can provide for their children.
   c. Family background influences one's educational aspiration.
   d. Family background influences educational attainment through its cultural capital.

5. What is the difference between intragenerational mobility and intergenerational mobility?
   a. Intragenerational mobility is about matters of social status, whereas intergenerational mobility is about matters of social class.
   b. Intragenerational mobility is the comparison of parents' class position with those achieved by their children, whereas intergenerational mobility is a person's movement up or down the socioeconomic scale in his or her working life.
   c. Intragenerational mobility is a person's movement up or down the socioeconomic scale in his or her working life, whereas intergenerational mobility is the comparison of parents' class position with those achieved by their children.
   d. Intragenerational mobility is a comparison of the occupational achievement of siblings, whereas intergenerational mobility is a comparison of parents' occupational achievement and with that of their children.

6. The feminization of poverty is highest among
   a. Latino female-headed families.
   b. Asian American female-headed families.
   c. white female-headed families.
   d. all female-headed families.

7. Erik Olin Wright called the class positions of those who exploit and/or dominate but are also exploited and dominated
   a. dual closure points.
   b. contradictory class locations.
   c. pariah groups.
   d. the working class.

8. How does Murray explain the cause of the underclass in the inner cities?
   a. Murray maintains that racist barriers are the key to accounting for the urban underclass.
   b. Murray sees economic factors (class) as most important in accounting for the urban underclass.
   c. Murray argues that welfare dependence explains the existence of the urban underclass.
   d. All of the above.

9. What is the relationship between social exclusion and crime?

   a. Social exclusion reduces the crime rate.

   b. Social exclusion increases the crime rate.

   c. Social exclusion has no effect on the crime rate.

   d. No clear evidence is available.

10. Which of the following systems of stratification permits the least amount of mobility?

   a. caste

   b. class

   c. slavery

   d. clan

Thinking Sociologically Exercises

1. If you were doing your own study of status differences in your community, how would you measure people's social class? Base your answer on the textbook's discussion of these matters to explain why you would take the particular measurement approach you've chosen. What would be its value(s) and shortcoming compared with adopting alternative measurement procedures?

2. Using occupation and occupational change as your mobility criteria, view the social mobility within your family for three generations. As you discuss the differences in jobs among your grandfather, father, and yourself, apply all these terms correctly: *vertical* and *horizontal mobility, upward* and *downward mobility, intragenerational* and *intergenerational mobility*. Explain fully why you think people in your family have moved up, moved down, or remained at the same status level.

Data Exercises

www.wwnorton.com/giddens
Keyword: Data8

As you learned in Chapter 8, the stratification that exists among different groups of individuals is not only real but has important consequences. These structured inequalities influence opportunities for achieving economic prosperity, referred to as *life chances* by sociologists. The data exercise for Chapter 8 explores the differences in social class at the community level.

Global Inequality: Differences among Countries

Understand the systematic differences in wealth and power among countries.

Life in Rich and Poor Countries

Recognize the impact of different economic standards of living on people throughout the world.

Can Poor Countries Become Rich?

Analyze the success of the newly industrializing economies.

Theories of Global Inequality

Consider various theories explaining why some societies are wealthier than others, as well as how global inequality can be overcome.

Why Global Economic Inequality Matters to You

Learn how globalization might shape global inequality in the future.

CHAPTER NINE

GLOBAL INEQUALITY

t he past quarter century has seen the appearance of more global billionaires than ever before in history. In 2005, there were 691 billionaires worldwide—341 in the United States, 158 in Europe, 81 in South and East Asia, 16 in South America, 10 in Mexico, 17 in Canada, 26 in the Middle East, 6 in Australia, 27 in Russia, and 3 in Africa (*Forbes* 2005). Their combined assets in 2005 were estimated at $2.2 trillion—greater than the total gross national income of 169 countries (calculated from World Bank 2005). The success of America's high-technology economy, coupled with the financial crisis that struck Asia in the late 1990s, enabled the United States to lay claim to over half the world's billionaires.

As of 2005, the wealthiest person in the world was Microsoft Corporation's founder Bill Gates, with a net worth of $46.5 billion in that year—down from $63 billion in 2000, thanks to the decline in the stock market. Gates, whose fortune is based largely on ownership of his company's stock, would seem the personification of American entrepreneurialism: a computer nerd turned capitalist whose software provides the operating system for nearly all personal computers. During the late 1990s, Gates was the first person in history to have a net worth in excess of $100 billion. Shortly after achieving this mark, the lofty value of Microsoft's stock began to decline, leaving Gates's fortune greatly reduced but still sufficient to rank him number one in wealth in the world for eleven consecutive years.

Gates was followed by the financier Warren Buffett, at $44 billion. Buffett is an investor and CEO of Berkshire Hathway, Inc., which owns companies such as Geico Direct Auto Insurance,

Dairy Queen, and See's Candies. In 2003, Buffet became an adviser to California's governor, Arnold Schwarzenegger.

Next on the list is Lakshmi Mittal, with $25 billion. Mittal was born in India but resides in London and owns a strong majority of the world's largest steel conglomerate, Mittal Steel. The fourth richest person in the world is also Latin America's richest man. Carlos Slim Helu owns a diverse array of investments in retail, banking, and insurance but made his way to the top of the list based on his investment in two Mexican telecom companies as well as significant shares of American-based MCI, which was recently bought out by Verizon. Fifth on the list is Prince Alwaleed Bin Talal Alsaud of Saudi Arabia, whose investments have established his worth at $23.7 billion (*Forbes* 2005). Now this nephew of the king is transforming himself from businessman to activist, calling for a range of reforms in his country: elections, women's rights, and job creation. Among the twenty-five richest people, twelve were from the United States, seven were from Europe, one was from Hong Kong, one was from Russia, one was from Canada, one was from Saudi Arabia, and one was from Mexico. Both the Russian and Indian billionaires live in London (*Forbes* 2005). If Bill Gates typifies the American high-tech entrepreneur, Hong Kong's Li Ka-shing—who was number twenty-two on the list (down from nineteen a year before) and Asia's richest man—is the hero in a rags-to-riches story that characterizes the success of many Asian businessmen. Li (his surname) began his career by making plastic flowers; in 2005, his $13 billion in personal wealth derived from a wide range of real estate and other investments throughout Asia.

Globalization—the increased economic, political, and social interconnectedness of the world—has produced the opportunities for unthinkable wealth. Yet at the same time it has produced widespread poverty and suffering. Consider, for example, Wirat Tasago, a twenty-four-year-old garment worker in Bangkok, Thailand. Tasago—along with more than a million other Thai garment workers, most of whom are women—labors from 8 A.M. until about 11 P.M. six days a week, earning little more than $3 an hour working days that can last sixteen hours (Dahlburg 1995). Billions of workers such as Tasago are being drawn into the global labor force, many working in oppressive conditions that would be unacceptable, if not unimaginable, under U.S. labor laws. And these are the fortunate ones: Those who remain outside the global economy are frequently even worse off.

In the previous chapter, we examined the American class structure, noting vast differences among individuals' income, wealth, work, and quality of life. The same is true in the world as a whole: Just as we can speak of rich or poor individuals within a country, so we can talk about rich or poor countries in the world system. A country's position in the global economy affects how its people live, work, and even die. In this chapter,

we look closely at the systematic differences in wealth and power between countries in the late twentieth and early twenty-first centuries. We examine what differences in economic standards of living mean for people throughout the world. We then turn to the newly industrializing economies of the world to understand which countries are improving their fortunes and why. This will lead us to a discussion of different theories that attempt to explain why global inequality exists and what can be done about it. We conclude by speculating on the future of economic inequality in a global world.

Global Inequality: Differences among Countries

Global inequality refers to the systematic differences in wealth and power that exist among countries. These differences between countries exist alongside differences within countries: Even the wealthiest countries today have growing numbers of poor people, while less wealthy nations are producing many of the world's superrich. Sociology's challenge is not merely to identify all such differences but to explain why they occur—and how they might be overcome.

One simple way to classify countries in terms of global inequality is to compare the wealth produced by each country for its average citizen. This approach measures the value of a country's yearly output of goods and services produced by its total population and then divides that total by the number of people in the country. The resulting measure is termed the *per-person gross national income* (GNI), a measure of the country's yearly output of goods and services per person. The World Bank (2005), an international lending organization that provides loans for development projects in poorer countries, uses this measure to classify countries as high income (an annual 2004 per person GNI of $10,066 or more, in 2004 dollars), upper middle income ($3,256–10,065), lower middle income ($826–3,255), or low income (under $825). This system of classification will help us better understand why there are such vast differences in living standards between countries.

Figure 9.1 shows how the World Bank (2005) divides 208 countries' economies (such as the West Bank and Gaza, Taiwan, and Macau), containing over six billion people, into the three economic classes. The figure shows that although nearly 40 percent of the world's population lives in low-income countries, less than 16 percent lives in high-income countries. Bear in mind that this classification is based on *average* income for each country; it therefore masks income inequality *within* each

FIGURE 9.1

Population and Per Capita Income in Low-, Middle-, and High-Income Countries, 2004

Like most countries, the world as a whole is highly unequal. Nearly 40 percent (36.8 percent) of the people in the world live in low-income countries, whereas less than 16 percent (15.8 percent) live in high-income countries. The average income of people in high-income countries is 63 times that of people in low-income countries. The remainder of the world's population—about 47 percent—live in middle-income countries. According to the World Bank, the world has become considerably more "middle class" in recent years: In 1999, the World Bank reclassified China from low income to middle income, moving its 1.3 billion people (22 percent of the world's population) into the latter category. Although China's average income has risen to global middle-class standards, the large majority of China's people remain distinctly low income.

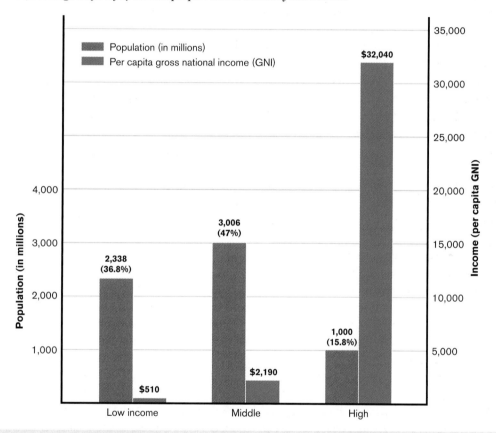

Low-income and middle-income nations comprise what percentage of the world's total population? What is the per capita gross national income in low-income countries? TRUE or FALSE: As demonstrated by the blue bars, most of the people in today's world live in high-income nations, while just a small percentage live in low-income nations. Explain. How many people live in low-income countries? This figure represents data from what year? According to the reading, how is the gross national income measured? The World Bank's decision to move which country from low income to middle income in 2000 greatly changes the percentage of the world they report as middle income?

SOURCE: World Bank, "World Development Indicators, 2005," 2005, devdata.worldbank.org/dataonline (accessed fall 2005).

country. Such differences can be significant, although we do not focus on them in this chapter. For example, the World Bank classifies India as a low-income country because its per-person GNI in 2004 was only $620. Yet, despite widespread poverty, India also boasts a large and growing middle class. China, on the other hand, was reclassified in 1999 from low to middle income because its per capita GNI in that year was $780 (at that time, the World Bank's lower limit for a lower-middle-income country was $736). Yet even though its average income grew to $1,290 in 2004, placing China squarely in the world's lower-middle-class status, it nonetheless has hundreds of millions of people living in poverty.

Comparing countries on the basis of economic output alone may be misleading, however, since gross national income includes only goods and services that are produced for cash sale. Many people in low-income countries are farmers or herders who produce for their own families or for barter, involving non-cash transactions. The value of their crops and animals is not taken into account in the statistics. Furthermore, economic output is not a country's whole story: Countries possess unique and widely differing languages and traditions. Poor countries are no less rich in history and culture than their wealthier neighbors, but the lives of their people are much harsher.

High-Income Countries

The *high-income countries* are generally those that were the first to industrialize, a process that began in England some two hundred fifty years ago and then spread to Europe, the United States, and Canada. About thirty years ago, Japan joined the ranks of high-income, industrialized nations, while Singapore, Hong Kong, and Taiwan moved into this category only within the last decade or so. The reasons for the success of these Asian latecomers to industrialization are much debated by sociologists and economists. We will look at these reasons later in the chapter.

High-income countries have 15.8 percent of the world's population, or just more than a billion people, yet they lay claim to just over 80 percent (80.3 percent) of the world's annual output of wealth (derived from World Bank 2005). Since then, the Russian economy has recovered somewhat, with foreign investment gradually increasing and the energy market booming. High-income countries offer decent housing, adequate food, drinkable water, and other comforts unknown in many parts of the world. Although these countries often have large numbers of poor people, most of their inhabitants enjoy a standard of living unimaginable by the majority of the world's people.

Middle-Income Countries

The *middle-income countries* are primarily found in East and Southeast Asia and also include the oil-rich countries of the Middle East and North Africa, the Americas (Mexico, Central America, Cuba and other countries in the Caribbean, and South America), and the once-communist republics that formerly made up the Soviet Union and its East European allies (Global Map 9.1). Most of these countries began to industrialize relatively late in the twentieth century and therefore are not yet as industrially developed (nor as wealthy) as the high-income countries. The countries that the Soviet Union once comprised, on the other hand, are highly industrialized, although their living standards have eroded during the past decade as a result of the collapse of communism and the move to capitalist economies. In Russia, for example, the wages of ordinary people dropped by nearly a third between 1998 and 1999, while retirement pensions dropped by nearly half: Millions of people, many of them elderly, suddenly found themselves destitute (Central Intelligence Agency [CIA] 2000). Since then, the Russian economy has recovered somewhat, with foreign investment gradually increasing and the energy market booming.

In 2004, middle-income countries included 47.4 percent of the world's population (3 billion people) but accounted for only 16.7 percent of the wealth produced in that year. Although many people in these countries are substantially better off than their neighbors in low-income countries, most do not enjoy anything resembling the standard of living common in high-income countries.

Low-Income Countries

Finally, the *low-income countries* include much of eastern, western, and sub-Saharan Africa; Vietnam, Cambodia, Indonesia, and a few other East Asian countries; India, Nepal, Bangladesh, and Pakistan in South Asia; eastern and central European countries such as Georgia and Ukraine; and Haiti and Nicaragua in the Western Hemisphere. These countries have mostly agricultural economies and are only recently beginning to industrialize. Scholars debate the reasons for their late industrialization and widespread poverty, as we will see later in this chapter.

In 2004, the low-income countries included over 37 percent of the world's population (2.3 billion people) yet produced only 3 percent of the world's yearly output of wealth (World Bank 2005). What is more, this inequality is increasing. Fertility is much higher in low-income countries than elsewhere, where large families provide additional farm labor or otherwise contribute to family income. (In wealthy industrial societies, where children are more likely to be in school than on the farm, the economic benefit of large families declines, so people tend to have fewer children.) Because of this, the populations of low-income countries (with the principal exception of India) grew 2.7 times as fast as those of high-income countries between 1990 and 2004 (Table 9.1).

In many of these low-income countries, people struggle with poverty, malnutrition, and even starvation. Most people live in rural areas, although this is rapidly changing: Hundreds of millions of people are moving to huge, densely populated cities, where they live either in dilapidated housing or on the open streets (see Chapter 19).

Growing Global Inequality: The Rich Get Richer, the Poor Get Poorer

During the last forty years, the overall standard of living in the world has slowly risen. The average global citizen is today better off than ever before (Table 9.2). Illiteracy is down, infant deaths and malnutrition are less common, people are living longer, average income is higher, and poverty is down. Because these figures are averages, however, they hide the substantial

---

TABLE 9.1

Differences in Fertility and Population Growth: Low-, Middle-, and High-Income Countries

	INCOME LEVEL			
	LOW	MIDDLE	HIGH	WORLD
Annual births per woman, 2003	3.64	2.12	1.72	2.59
Average yearly percent population growth, 1990–2004	2.04	1.12	.75	1.38

SOURCE: World Bank, "World Development Indicators, 2005," 2005.

TABLE 9.2

The Global Quality of Life Has Risen during the Past 40 Years

QUALITY OF LIFE INDICATORS	1967–1970	2002–2004
Percentage illiterate[a, b]	53	22
Average number of children per woman[a, c]	6	2.6
Mortality rate for children under five years (per 1,000 population)[d, e]	147	80
Infant mortality rate (per 1,000 births)[d, e]	96	54
Number of people suffering from malnutrition[a, f]	4 out of 10	1 out of 4
Life expectancy at birth[a, c]	50 years	67 years
Annual per person income (per capita GNI)[b, g]	$640	$6,280
Percent living on less than $1/day[a, b]	~ 50	~ 20

SOURCES: (a) Data for 1968, Salter 1998; (b) data for 2004, World Bank 2005; (c) data for 2003, World Bank 2005; (d) data for 1970, United Nations 2005; (e) data for 2003, United Nations 2005, (f) data for 2002, United Nations 2005; (g) data for 1967, World Bank 2005.

Rich and Poor Countries: The World by Income, 2005

*Like individuals in a country, the countries of the world as a whole can be seen as economically
stratified. In general, those countries that experienced industrialization the earliest are the richest,
while those that remain agricultural are the poorest. An enormous—and growing—gulf separates
the two groups.*

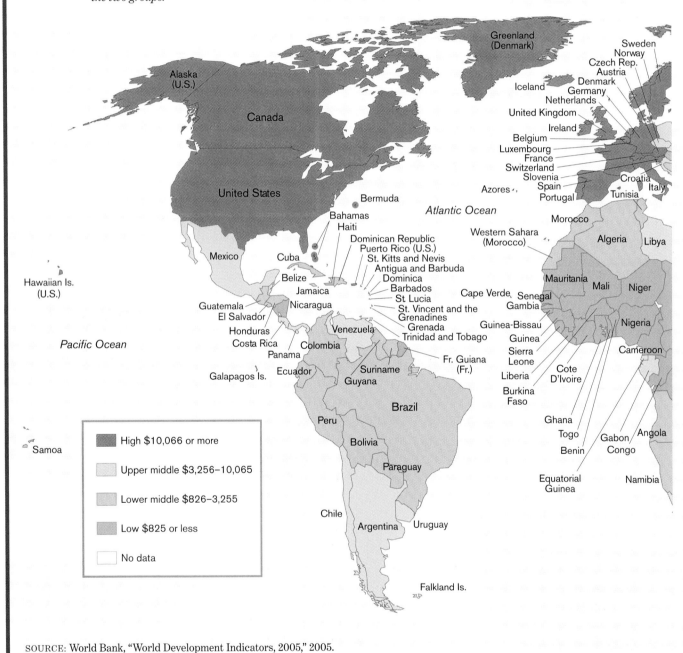

High $10,066 or more

Upper middle $3,256–10,065

Lower middle $826–3,255

Low $825 or less

No data

SOURCE: World Bank, "World Development Indicators, 2005," 2005.

Finland
Estonia
Latvia
Lithuania
Poland
Belarus
Slovakia
Hungary
Ukraine
Serbia & Montenegro
Bosnia/Herzegovina
Moldova
Romania
Georgia
Bulgaria
Macedonia
Turkey
Greece
Albania Cyprus
Lebanon
Libya
Egypt
Israel
Jordan
Chad
Eritrea
Sudan
Yemen
Cent.
African
Rep.
Ethiopia
Djibouti
Uganda
Democratic
Rep. of
Congo
Kenya
Rwanda
Tanzania
Burundi
Seychelles
Zambia
Madagascar
Botswana
Mauritius
Malawi
Mozambique
Zimbabwe
Swaziland
Lesotho
South Africa

Russia

Armenia
Azerbijan
Kazakhstan
Mongolia

Uzbekistan
Turkmenistan
Syria
Iraq
Iran
Tajikistan
Kyrgyzstan
Afghanistan
Bahrain
Qatar
Pakistan
Kuwait
Saudi
Arabia
U.A.E.
Oman
Somalia
Nepal
Bangladesh
India
Bhutan
Myanmar
Thailand
Cambodia
Sri Lanka
Maldives
Singapore

People's Republic of
China
N. Korea
S. Korea
Japan

Taiwan
Hong Kong
Macao
Laos
Vietnam
Brunei
Malaysia
Philippines

Indonesia
East Timor

Palau
Papua
New
Guinea

Mariana
Islands
(U.S.)
Guam (U.S.)
Federated
States of
Micronesia
Marshall
Islands
Nauru

Solomon Is.
Vanuatu
New
Caledonia
(Fr.)
Fiji

Australia

New
Zealand

NOTE: The map presents economies classified according to World Bank estimates of 2005 per capita GNI. Not shown on the map because of space constraints are French Polynesia (high income), American Samoa (upper middle income), Kiribati and Tonga (lower middle income), and Tuvalu (no data).

FIGURE 9.2

GNI per Person in Low-, Middle-, and High-Income Countries, 1984, 1994, and 2004

Despite overall growth in the global economy, the gap between rich and poor countries has not declined in recent years. Between 1984 and 2004, per-person GNI in low-income countries increased an average of 2.9 percent a year, far less than in high-income countries (6.5 percent). As a consequence, the average person in a high-income country earned roughly 63 times as much as the average person in a low-income country. Average per-person GNI in middle-income countries split the difference and increased by an average 4.3 percent.

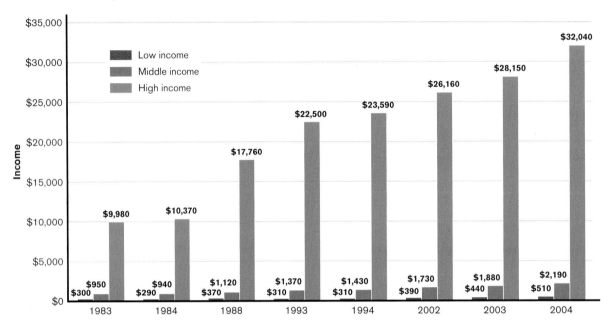

Between 1984 and 2004, what was the increase in GNI per person in low-income countries? Between 1984 and 2004 does GNI per person in high-income countries increase, decrease, or stay the same, and if so by how much? What does the figure indicate about the gap in GNI per capita between rich and poor countries? According to the reading, what is misrepresented by the reporting of global trends that include the average of all nations?

SOURCE: World Bank, "World Development Indicators, 2005," 2005.

differences among countries: Many of these gains have been in the high- and middle-income countries, while living standards in many of the poorest countries have declined. Overall, the gap between rich and poor countries has widened.

Between 1988 and 2004, average per-person GNI increased by 80.4 percent in high-income countries and 37.8 percent in low-income countries, widening the global gap between rich and poor (Figure 9.2). But most of the growth in low-income per capita income has been since 2000, when it was $380 per

person (it was $370 in 1988, declined to a low of $310 in 1993–1994, and then gradually increased back to 1970s levels of income per capita by 2000). But by 2004, per capita income in low-income countries had jumped to $510. Middle-income countries have grown steadily, nearly doubling in the twenty-year period between 1994 and 2004.

In 2004, the average person in a typical high-income country earned $32,040 (per capita GNI; Atlas method based on current U.S. dollars), 63 times as much as the $510 earned by his or her counterpart in a low-income country (World Bank 2005). This income gap has increased by 2 percent in two years. Some 2.5 billion people—about a quarter of the world's population—are estimated to live on less than $2 a day (United Nations 2005).

Life in Rich and Poor Countries

An enormous gulf in living standards separates most people in rich countries from their counterparts in poor ones (*Harvard Magazine* 2000). Wealth and poverty make life different in a host of ways. For instance, about one third of the world's poor are undernourished, and almost all are illiterate and lack access to even primary-school education. The world is no longer preponderantly rural. By 2007, over half of the world's population will live in urban areas. And by 2030, urban areas will house 82 percent of the world's population (United Nations 2004). More than 40 percent of all urban residents in developing countries live in slums (United Nations Food and Agriculture Organization [UN FAO] 2004). Many of the poor come from tribes or racial and ethnic groups that differ from the dominant groups of their countries, and their poverty is at least in part the result of discrimination (Narayan 1999).

Here we look at differences between high- and low-income countries in terms of health, starvation and famine, and education and literacy.

Health

People in high-income countries are far healthier than their counterparts in low-income countries. Low-income countries generally suffer from inadequate health facilities, and when they do have hospitals or clinics, these seldom serve the poorest people. People living in low-income countries also lack proper sanitation, drink polluted water, and run a much greater risk of contracting infectious diseases. They are more likely to suffer malnourishment, starvation, and famine. All of these factors contribute to physical weakness and poor health, making people in low-income countries susceptible to illness and disease. There is growing evidence that the high rates of HIV/AIDS infection found in many African countries are due in part to the weakened health of impoverished people (Stillwagon 2001).

Because of poor health conditions, people in low-income countries are more likely to die in infancy and less likely to live

---

TABLE 9.3

Differences in Infant Mortality and Life Expectancy: Low-, Middle-, and High-Income Countries, 2003

	INCOME LEVEL			
	LOW	MIDDLE	HIGH	WORLD
Infant mortality rate (per 1,000 live births)	79	32	5[a]	57
Life expectancy at birth (years)	58	70	78	67

[a]Data from 2002.

SOURCE: World Bank, "World Development Indicators, 2005," 2005.

---

to old age than people in high-income countries. Infants are eleven times more likely to die at birth in low-income countries than they are in high-income countries, and—if they survive birth—they are likely to live on average eighteen years fewer (Table 9.3). Children often die of illnesses that are readily treated in wealthier countries, such as measles or diarrhea. In some parts of the world, such as sub-Saharan Africa, a child is more likely to die before the age of five than to enter secondary school (World Bank 2005). Still, conditions have improved in low- and middle-income countries: Between 1980 and 2003, for example, the infant mortality rate dropped from 97 (per thousand live births) to 79 in low-income countries and from 60 to 32 in middle-income countries (World Bank 2005). AIDS, and growing poverty in some regions of the world, have contributed to the increase in infant mortality in the poorest countries in recent years.

During the past three decades, some improvements have occurred in most of the middle-income countries of the world and in some of the low-income countries as well. Throughout the world, infant mortality has been cut in half, and average life expectancy has increased by ten years or more because of the wider availability of modern medical technology, improved sanitation, and rising incomes.

Hunger Is a Global Problem

Hunger is a global problem, although it is disproportionately found in the poorest regions of the world. The world's great concentrations of hunger are in central and sub-Saharan Africa, followed by the Indian subcontinent. Although somewhat less widespread, significant amounts of hunger are also found in parts of Asia, Russia, and other republics of the former Soviet Union, South America, Central America, and Mexico. It is estimated that at any given time, 852 million people are hungry, 200 million of whom are children.

Legend:
- <2.5% Extremely low
- 2.5–4% Very low
- 5–19% Moderately low
- 20–34% Moderately high
- >35% Very high
- No data

SOURCE: UN FAO 2003.

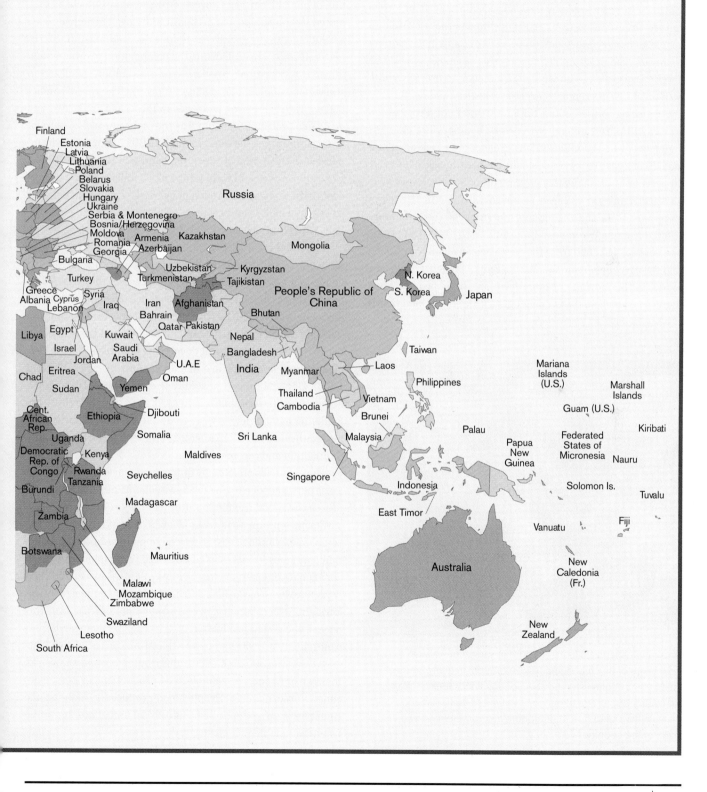

Finland
Estonia
Latvia
Lithuania
Poland
Belarus
Slovakia
Hungary
Ukraine
Serbia & Montenegro
Bosnia/Herzegovina
Moldova
Romania
Georgia
Bulgaria
Turkey
Greece
Albania
Lebanon
Libya
Israel
Jordan
Chad
Eritrea
Sudan
Cent.
African
Rep.
Uganda
Democratic
Rep. of
Congo
Burundi
Zambia
Botswana

Russia
Kazakhstan
Mongolia
Armenia
Azerbaijan
Uzbekistan
Kyrgyzstan
Turkmenistan
Tajikistan
People's Republic of China
N. Korea
S. Korea
Japan
Iran
Afghanistan
Syria
Cyprus
Iraq
Bahrain
Qatar
Pakistan
Bhutan
Nepal
Kuwait
Egypt
Saudi
Arabia
U.A.E
Oman
Yemen
Djibouti
Ethiopia
Somalia
Kenya
Rwanda
Tanzania
Seychelles
Madagascar
Mauritius
Malawi
Mozambique
Zimbabwe
Swaziland
Lesotho
South Africa

Bangladesh
India
Myanmar
Laos
Taiwan
Philippines
Thailand
Cambodia
Vietnam
Brunei
Sri Lanka
Maldives
Malaysia
Singapore
Indonesia
East Timor

Mariana
Islands
(U.S.)
Marshall
Islands
Guam (U.S.)
Kiribati
Palau
Papua
New
Guinea
Federated
States of
Micronesia
Nauru
Solomon Is.
Tuvalu
Vanuatu
Fiji
New
Caledonia
(Fr.)
Australia
New
Zealand

Hunger, Malnutrition, and Famine

Hunger, malnutrition, and famine are major global sources of poor health. These problems are nothing new. What seems to be new is their extent—the fact that so many people in the world today appear to be on the brink of starvation (Global Map 9.2). A recent study by the United Nations Food and Agriculture Organization (FAO; 2004) estimates that 852 million people go hungry every day, 95 percent of them in developing countries. The program defines "hunger" as a diet of 1,800 or fewer calories a day—an amount insufficient to provide adults with the nutrients required for active, healthy lives.

According to the United Nations World Food Programme (WFP; 2004), 200 million of the world's hungry are children under five, who are underweight because they lack adequate food. Every year 10.9 million children under the age of five die; 60 percent of those deaths are a result of hunger. Every year another 17 million children are born with low birth weight stemming from the inadequate nutrition of their mothers (United Nations World Food Programme [UN WFP] 2004). As one ten-year-old child from the west African country of Gabon told researchers from the World Bank, "When I leave for school in the mornings I don't have any breakfast. At noon there is no lunch, in the evening I get a little supper, and that is

An Afghan shepherd leads his herd in search of water in Kabul. Four years of harsh and successive drought in many areas of land-locked Afghanistan has caused the water level to drop drastically. Hundreds of people and tens of thousands of animals have died due to drought-related problems in various parts of the country.

not enough. So when I see another child eating, I watch him, and if he doesn't give me something I think I'm going to die of hunger" (Narayan 1999). Yet more than three quarters of all malnourished children under the age of five in the world's low- and middle-income countries live in countries that actually produce a food surplus (Lappe et al. 1998).

Most famine and hunger today are the result of a combination of natural and social forces. Drought alone affects an estimated 100 million people in the world today. In countries such as Sudan, Ethiopia, Eritrea, Indonesia, Afghanistan, Sierra Leone, Guinea, and Tajikistan, the combination of drought and internal warfare has wrecked food production, resulting in starvation and death for millions of people. The role of conflict and warfare in creating hunger is on the increase: Conflict and economic problems were cited as the main cause of 35 percent of food shortages between 1992 and 2003, compared with 15 percent in the period between 1986 and 1991 (UN FAO 2005a). In Latin America and the Caribbean, 53 million people (11 percent of the population) are malnourished—a number that rises to 180 million (33 percent) in sub-Saharan Africa and 525 million (17 percent) in Asia (UN WFP 2001).

The AIDS epidemic has also contributed to the problem of food shortages and hunger, killing many working-age adults. One recent study by the FAO (2001) predicts that HIV/AIDS-caused deaths in the ten African countries most afflicted by the epidemic will reduce the labor force by 26 percent by the year 2020. Of the estimated 40.3 million people worldwide infected with HIV, 95 percent live in developing countries, and 64 percent of new infections are in sub-Saharan Africa (UNAIDS 2005). Of the 3 million people that died from AIDS in 2004, about 500,000 were children. According to the FAO (2001), the epidemic can be devastating to nutrition, food security, and agricultural production, affecting "the entire society's ability to maintain and reproduce itself."

The countries affected by famine and starvation are for the most part too poor to pay for new technologies that would increase their food production. Nor can they afford to purchase sufficient food imports from elsewhere in the world. At the same time, paradoxically, as world hunger grows, food production continues to increase, often in the very countries experiencing hunger emergencies (UN FAO 2004). Between 1965 and 1999, for example, world production of grain doubled. Even allowing for the substantial world population increase over this period, the global production of grain per person was 15 percent higher in 1999 than it was thirty-four years earlier. This growth, however, is not evenly distributed around the world. In much of Africa, for example, food production per person declined in recent years. Surplus food produced in high-income countries such as the United States is seldom affordable to the countries that need it most.

Education and Literacy

Education and literacy are important routes to economic development. Here, again, lower-income countries are disadvantaged, because they can seldom afford high-quality public education systems. As a consequence, children in high-income countries are much more likely to get schooling than are children in low-income countries, and adults in high-income countries are much more likely to be able to read and write (Table 9.4). While virtually all high school–age males and females attend secondary school in high-income countries, in 2002 only 76 percent did so in middle-income countries and only 43 percent in low-income countries. In 2004, 28 percent of male adults and half of female adults in low-income countries were unable to read and write. One reason for these differences is a sizable gap in public expenditures on education: High-income countries spend a much larger percentage of their gross domestic product on education than do low-income countries (World Bank 2005).

Education is important for several reasons. First, as noted, education contributes to economic growth, since people with advanced schooling provide the skilled workers necessary for high-wage industries. Second, education offers the only hope for escaping from the cycle of harsh working conditions and poverty, because poorly educated people are condemned to low-wage, unskilled jobs. Finally, educated people are less likely to have large numbers of children, thus slowing the global population explosion that contributes to global poverty (see Chapter 19).

Can Poor Countries Become Rich?

As we saw in Chapter 3, by the mid-1970s a number of low-income countries in East Asia were undergoing a process of industrialization that appeared to threaten the global economic dominance of the United States and Europe (Amsden 1989). This process began with Japan in the 1950s but quickly extended to the **newly industrializing economies (NIEs)**—that is, the rapidly growing economies of the world, particularly in East Asia but also in Latin America. The East Asian NIEs included Hong Kong in the 1960s and Taiwan, South Korea, and Singapore in the 1970s and 1980s. Other Asian countries began to follow in the 1980s and the early 1990s, most notably China, but also Malaysia, Thailand, and Indonesia. Today, most are middle income, and some—such as Hong Kong, South Korea, Taiwan, and Singapore—have moved up to the high-income category.

TABLE 9.4

Differences in Education and Literacy: Low-, Middle-, and High-Income Countries

	INCOME LEVEL		
	LOW	MIDDLE	HIGH
School enrollment secondary (% gross), 2002	43	76	104
Public spending on education, total (% of GDP), 2002[a]	3	4	6
Literacy rate, adult male (% of males aged 15 and above), 2004	72	94	No data
Literacy rate, adult female (% of females aged 15 and above), 2004	50	87	No data

[a]Data for low-income countries from 2000. *GDP*, gross domestic product.

SOURCE: World Bank, "World Development Indicators, 2005," 2005.

The low- and middle-income economies of the East Asian region as a whole averaged 7.7 percent growth a year from 1980 to 1999, a rate that is extraordinary by world standards (World Bank 2000–2001). By 1999, the gross domestic product (GDP) per person in Singapore was virtually the same as that in the United States. China, the world's most populous country, has one of the most rapidly growing economies on the planet. At an average annual growth rate of 10 percent between 1980 and 1999, the Chinese economy more than doubled in size.

Economic growth in East Asia has not been without its costs. These have included the sometimes violent repression of labor and civil rights, terrible factory conditions, the exploitation of an increasingly female workforce, the exploitation of immigrant workers from impoverished neighboring countries, and widespread environmental degradation. Nonetheless, thanks to the sacrifices of past generations of workers, large numbers of people in these countries are prospering.

How do social scientists account for the rapid economic growth in the East Asian NIEs, especially from the mid-1970s through the mid-1990s? The answer to this question may hold some crucial lessons for those low-income countries elsewhere that hope to follow in the steps of the NIEs. Although the NIEs' success is partly due to historically unique factors, it is also the result of factors that could lead to a rethinking of the causes of global inequality. To understand the rapid development of this region, we need to view these countries both historically and within the context of the world economic system today (So and Chiu 1995).

The economic success of the East Asian NIEs can be attributed to a combination of factors. Some of these factors are historical, including those stemming from world political and economic shifts. Some are cultural. Still others have to do with the ways these countries pursued economic growth. Following are some of the factors that aided their success:

1. **Historically, Taiwan, South Korea, Hong Kong, and Singapore were once part of colonial situations that, while imposing many hardships, also helped pave the way for economic growth.** Taiwan and Korea were tied to the Japanese Empire; Hong Kong and Singapore were former British colonies. Japan eliminated large landowners who opposed industrialization, and both Britain and Japan encouraged industrial development, constructed roads and other transportation systems, and built relatively efficient governmental bureaucracies in these particular colonies. Britain also actively developed both Hong Kong and Singapore as trading centers (Cumings 1987; Gold 1986). Elsewhere in the world—for example, in Latin America and Africa—countries that are today poor did not fare so well in their dealings with richer, more powerful nations.

2. **The East Asian region benefited from a long period of world economic growth.** Between the 1950s and the mid-1970s, the growing economies of Europe and the United States provided a big market for the clothing, footwear, and electronics that were increasingly being made in East Asia, creating a window of opportunity for economic development. Furthermore, periodic economic slowdowns in the United States and Europe forced businesses to cut their labor costs and spurred the relocation of factories to low-wage East Asian countries (Henderson and Appelbaum 1992).

3. **Economic growth in this region took off at the high point of the cold war, when the United States and its allies, in erecting a defense against communist China, provided generous economic and military aid.** Direct aid and loans fueled investment in such new technologies as transistors, semiconductors, and other electronics, contributing to the development of local industries. Military assistance frequently favored strong (often military) governments that were willing to use repression to keep labor costs low (Amsden 1989; Castells 1992; Cumings 1987, 1997; Deyo 1987; Evans 1987; Haggard 1990; Henderson 1989; Mirza 1986).

4. **Some sociologists argue that the economic success of Japan and the East Asian NIEs is due in part to their cultural traditions, in particular, their shared Confucian philosophy.** Over a century ago, Max Weber (1977; orig. 1904) argued that the Protestant belief in thrift, frugality, and hard work partly explained the rise of capitalism in western Europe. Weber's argument has been applied to Asian economic history. Confucianism, it is argued, inculcates respect for one's elders and superiors, education, hard work, and proven accomplishments as the key to advancement as well as a willingness to sacrifice today to earn a greater reward tomorrow.

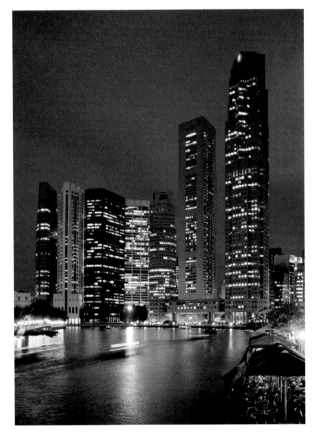

Singapore, along with Taiwan, South Korea, and Hong Kong, was transformed from a low-income country to a relatively prosperous, newly industrialized country.

As a result of these values, the Weberian argument goes, Asian workers and managers are highly loyal to their companies, submissive to authority, hardworking, and success oriented. Workers and capitalists alike are said to be frugal. Instead of living lavishly, they are likely to reinvest their wealth in further economic growth (Berger 1986; Berger and Hsiao 1998; Helm 1992; Redding 1990; Wong 1986)

This explanation has some merit, but it overlooks the fact that businesses are not always revered and respected in Asia. Students and workers throughout the East Asian NIEs have opposed business and governmental policies they felt to be unfair, often at the risk of imprisonment and sometimes even their lives (Deyo 1989; Ho 1990). Furthermore, such central Confucian cultural values as thrift appear to be on the decline in Japan and the NIEs, as young people—raised in the booming prosperity of recent years—increasingly value conspicuous consumption over austerity and investment (Helm 1992).

5. **Many of the East Asian governments followed strong policies that favored economic growth.** Their governments played active roles in keeping labor costs low, encouraged economic development through tax breaks and other economic policies and offered free public education.

Whether the growth of these economies will continue is unclear. In 1997–1998, a combination of poor investment decisions, corruption, and world economic conditions brought these countries' economic expansion to an abrupt halt. Their stock markets collapsed, their currencies fell, and the entire global economy was threatened. The experience of Hong Kong was typical: After thirty-seven years of continuous growth, the economy stalled, and its stock market lost more than half its value. Yet the "Asian meltdown," as the newspapers called it in early 1998, turned out to have been merely a blip in the region's growth. China in particular has been growing at a high rate, and is today the world's fourth largest economy.

Theories of Global Inequality

What causes global inequality? How can it be overcome? In this section we examine four different kinds of theories that have been advanced over the years to explain global inequality: market-oriented, dependency, world-systems, and state-centered theories. These theories each have strengths and weaknesses. One shortcoming of all of them is that they frequently give short shrift to the role of women in economic development. By putting the theories together, however, we should be able to answer a key question facing the 85 percent of the world's population living outside high-income countries: How can they move up in the world economy?

Market-Oriented Theories

In the 1960s, the most influential theories of global inequality advanced by American economists and sociologists were **market-oriented theories.** These theories assume that the best possible economic consequences will result if individuals are free—uninhibited by any form of governmental constraint—to make their own economic decisions. Unrestricted capitalism, if allowed to develop fully, is said to be the avenue to economic growth. Government bureaucracy should not dictate which goods to produce, what prices to charge, or how much workers should be paid. According to market-oriented theorists, governmental direction of the economies of low-income countries results only in blockages to economic development. In this view, local governments should get out of the way of development (Berger 1986; Ranis 1996; Ranis and Mahmood 1992; Rostow 1961; Warren 1980).

Market-oriented theories reflect the belief that "any country can make it if it does it 'our way' "—that is, like the United States and other similar high-income countries. These theories inspired U.S. government foreign-aid programs that attempted to spur economic development in low-income countries by providing money, expert advisers, and technology, paving the way for U.S. corporations to make investments in these countries.

One of the most influential early proponents of such theories was W. W. Rostow, an economic adviser to former U.S. president John F. Kennedy, whose ideas helped shape U.S. foreign policy toward Latin America during the 1960s. Rostow's explanation is one version of a market-oriented approach, termed "modernization theory." **Modernization theory** argues that low-income societies can develop economically only if they give up their traditional ways and adopt modern economic institutions, technologies, and cultural values that emphasize savings and productive investment.

According to Rostow (1961), the traditional cultural values and social institutions of low-income countries impede their economic effectiveness. For example, many people in low-income countries, in Rostow's view, lack a strong work ethic: They would sooner consume today than invest for the future. Large families are also seen as partly responsible for "economic backwardness," since a breadwinner with many mouths to feed can hardly be expected to save money for investment purposes.

What Can You Do about Child Labor?

Does child labor still exist in the world today? According to the United Nations International Labor Organization (ILO), more than 250 million boys and girls between the ages of five and fourteen are working in developing countries, about one out of every four children in the world. Some 50 to 60 million children between the ages of five and eleven work under hazardous conditions. Child labor is found throughout the developing world—in Asia (61 percent of the children are engaged in labor), Africa (32 percent), and Latin America (7 percent). They are forced to work because of a combination of family poverty, lack of education, and traditional indifference among some people in many countries to the plight of those who are poor or who are ethnic minorities (ILO 2000; UNICEF 2000).

Two thirds of working children labor in agriculture, with the rest in manufacturing, wholesale and retail trade, restaurants and hotels, and a variety of services such as working as servants in wealthy households. At best, these children work for long hours with little pay and are therefore unable to go to school and develop the skills that might eventually enable them to escape their lives of poverty. Many, however, work at hazardous and exploitative jobs under slavelike conditions, suffering a variety of illnesses and injuries. The ILO (2000) provides a grisly summary: "wounds, broken or complete loss of body parts, burns and skin diseases, eye and hearing impairment, respiratory and gastro-intestinal illnesses, fever, headaches from excessive heat in the fields or factories."

A United Nations (UNICEF 1997) report provides several examples:

In Malaysia, children may work up to 17-hour days on rubber plantations, exposed to insect and snake bites. In the United Republic of Tanzania, they pick coffee, inhaling pesticides. In Portugal, children as young as 12 are subject to the heavy labor and myriad dangers of the construction industry. In Morocco, they hunch at looms for long hours and little pay, knotting the strands of luxury carpets for export. In the United States, children are exploited in garment industry sweatshops. In the Philippines, young boys dive in dangerous conditions to help set nets for deep-sea fishing.

Conditions in many factories are horrible:

Dust from the chemical powders and strong vapors in both the storeroom and the boiler room were obvious. . . . We found 250 children, mostly below 10 years of age, working in a long hall filling in a slotted frame with sticks. Row upon row of children, some barely five years old, were involved in the work. (UNICEF 1997)

One form of child labor that is close to slavery is "bonded labor." In this system, children as young as eight or nine are pledged by their parents to factory owners in exchange for small loans. These children are paid so little that they never manage to reduce the debt, condemning them to a lifetime of bondage. One recent case of bonded labor that attracted international attention was that of Iqbal Masih, a Pakistani child who, at age four, was sold into slavery by his father to borrow six hundred rupees (roughly $16) for the wedding of his first-born son. For six years, Iqbal spent most of his time chained to a carpet-weaving loom, tying tiny knots for hours on end. After fleeing the factory at age ten, he began speaking to labor organizations and schools about his experience. Iqbal paid a bitter price for his outspokenness: At age thirteen, while riding his bicycle in his hometown, he was gunned down by agents believed to be working for the carpet industry (Free the Children 1998; India's Tiny Slaves 1998).

Abolishing exploitative child labor will require countries around the world to enact strong child-labor laws and be willing to enforce them. International organizations, such as the United Nations ILO, have outlined a set of standards for such laws to follow. In June 1999, the ILO adopted Convention 182, calling for the abolition of the "Worst Forms of Child Labor." These are defined as including

- all forms of slavery or practices similar to slavery, such as the sale and trafficking of children, debt bondage and serfdom, and forced or compulsory labor, including forced or compulsory recruitment of children for use in armed conflict
- the use, procuring, or offering of a child for prostitution, for the production of pornography, or for pornographic performances
- the use, procuring, or offering of a child for illicit activities, in particular for the production and trafficking of drugs as defined in the relevant international treaties; and
- work that, by its nature or the circumstances in which it is carried out, is likely to harm the health, safety, or morals of children.

Countries must also provide free public education and require that children attend school full time (UNICEF 2000). But at least part of the responsibility for solving the problem lies with the global corporations that manufacture goods using child labor—and, ultimately, with the consumers who buy those goods. Here are two things that you can do right now:

1. **Check the label.** Mind what you are buying. Begin by looking at the label. When you purchase clothing, rugs, and other textiles, the label will tell you where it was made, if unionized labor was used, and, in a few cases, whether it is certified to be "sweatshop free." Avoid buying garments made in countries with known human rights abuses, such as Myanmar (Burma). If the product has a label indicating

it was made with union labor, it is likely to be free from child labor. "Sweatshop free" labels, although still rare, are likely to become more common in coming years, as labor and consumer groups pressure the U.S. government to more closely monitor imported goods. In one well-publicized campaign that grew out of Iqbal's tragic experience, Indian human rights activists developed the "Rugmark" label, which certifies that the carpet is free of child labor. The U.S. Department of Labor is also working toward a way of certifying goods that are sold in the United States to be sweatshop free, although at this time there is no way to do so reliably: The millions of factories around the world involved in making consumer goods are too vast and dispersed to monitor.

2. **Join up.** Join (or start) an antisweatshop campaign at your own college or university. There is a national campaign, organized by United Students Against Sweatshops, to require schools to engage in "responsible purchasing" when they buy or sell clothing, athletic equipment, and other goods that carry the school logo. Schools are urged to sign agreements with all their vendors that require full disclosure of the names and locations of the factories where the goods are made, certifying that the goods are free from child labor and other forms of exploitation. School sales are a multibillion-dollar business, and if schools set a high standard, manufacturers will be forced to take notice.

In a global economy, you can choose what you buy, as well as influence others to make informed and ethical choices about the products they consume. Be a smart shopper—it can make a difference.

But to modernization theorists, the problems in low-income countries run even deeper. The cultures of such countries, according to the theory, tend to support "fatalism"—a value system that views hardship and suffering as the unavoidable plight of life. Acceptance of one's lot in life thus discourages people from working hard and being thrifty to overcome their fate. In this view, then, a country's poverty is due largely to the cultural failings of the people themselves. Such failings are reinforced by government policies that set wages and control prices and generally interfere in the operation of the economy. How can low-income countries break out of their poverty? Rostow viewed economic growth as going through several stages, which he likened to the journey of an airplane:

1. **Traditional stage.** This is the stage just described. It is characterized by low rates of savings, the supposed lack of a work ethic, and the so-called fatalistic value system. The airplane is not yet off the ground.

2. **Takeoff to economic growth.** The traditional stage, Rostow argued, can give way to a second one: economic takeoff. This occurs when poor countries begin to jettison their traditional values and institutions and start to save and invest money for the future. The role of wealthy countries, such as the United States, is to facilitate this growth. They can do this by financing birth-control programs or providing low-cost loans for electrification, road and airport construction, and starting new industries.

3. **Drive to technological maturity.** According to Rostow, with the help of money and advice from high-income countries, the airplane of economic growth would taxi down the runway, pick up speed, and become airborne. The country would then approach technological maturity. In the aeronautical metaphor, the plane would slowly climb to cruising altitude, improving its technology, reinvesting its recently acquired wealth in new industries, and adopting the institutions and values of the high-income countries.

4. **High mass consumption.** Finally, the country would reach the phase of high mass consumption. Now people are able to enjoy the fruits of their labor by achieving a high standard of living. The airplane (country) cruises along on automatic pilot, having entered the ranks of high-income countries.

Rostow's ideas remain influential. Indeed, the prevailing view among economists today, **neoliberalism,** argues that free-market forces, achieved by minimizing governmental restrictions on business, provide the only route to economic growth. Neoliberalism holds that global free trade will enable all countries of the world to prosper; eliminating governmental regulation is seen as necessary for economic growth to occur. Neoliberal economists therefore call for an end to restrictions on trade and often challenge minimum wage and other labor laws, as well as environmental restrictions on business.

Sociologists, on the other hand, focus on the cultural aspects of Rostow's theory: Whether and how certain beliefs and institutions hinder development (W. Davis 1987; So 1990). These include religious values, moral beliefs, belief in magic, and folk traditions and practices. Sociologists also examine other conditions that resist change, particularly the belief local cultures have that moral decay and social unrest accompany business and trade.

Dependency Theories

During the 1960s, a number of theorists questioned market-oriented explanations of global inequality such as modernization theory. Many of these critics were sociologists and economists from the low-income countries of Latin America and Africa who rejected the idea that their countries' economic underdevelopment was due to their own cultural or institutional faults. Instead, they build on the theories of Karl Marx, who argued that world capitalism would create a class of countries manipulated by more powerful countries just as capitalism within countries leads to the exploitation of workers. Adherents to **dependency theories** argue that the poverty of low-income countries stems from their exploitation by wealthy countries and the multinational corporations that are based in wealthy countries. In their view, global capitalism locked their countries into a downward spiral of exploitation and poverty.

According to dependency theories, this exploitation began with **colonialism,** a political-economic system under which powerful countries establish, for their own profit, rule over weaker peoples or countries. Powerful nations have colonized other countries usually to procure the raw materials needed for their factories and to control markets for the products manufactured in those factories. Under colonial rule, for example, the petroleum, copper, iron, and food products required by industrial economies are extracted from low-income countries by businesses based in high-income countries. Although colonialism typically involved European countries establishing colonies in North and South America, Africa, and Asia, some Asian countries (such as Japan) had colonies as well.

Even though colonialism ended throughout most of the world after World War II, the exploitation did not: Transnational corporations continued to reap enormous profits from their branches in low-income countries. According to dependency theory, these global companies, often with the support of the powerful banks and governments of rich countries, established factories in poor countries, using cheap labor and raw

Although Nigeria is the world's eighth largest producer of oil, the overwhelming majority of the profits generated in the energy trade go to oil companies and the military government, providing no benefit to the country's poverty-stricken inhabitants. These women are protesting Royal Dutch Shell's exploitation of Nigeria's oil and natural gas resources.

materials to maximize production costs without governmental interference. In turn, the low prices set for labor and raw materials prevented poor countries from accumulating the profit necessary to industrialize themselves. Local businesses that might compete with foreign corporations were prevented from doing so. In this view, poor countries are forced to borrow from rich countries, thus increasing their economic dependency.

Low-income countries are thus seen not as underdeveloped, but rather as misdeveloped (Amin 1974; Emmanuel 1972; Frank 1966, 1969a, 1969b, 1979; Prebisch 1967, 1971). With the exception of a handful of local politicians and businesspeople who serve the interests of the foreign corporations, people fall into poverty. Peasants are forced to choose between starvation and working at near-starvation wages on foreign-controlled plantations and in foreign-controlled mines and factories. Because dependency theorists believe that such exploitation has kept their countries from achieving economic growth, they typically call for revolutionary changes that would push foreign corporations out of their countries altogether (Frank 1966, 1969a, 1969b).

Whereas market-oriented theorists usually ignore political and military power, dependency theorists regard the exercise of power as central to enforcing unequal economic relationships. According to this theory, whenever local leaders question such unequal arrangements, their voices are quickly suppressed. Unionization is usually outlawed, and labor organizers are jailed and sometimes killed. When people elect a gov-

ernment opposing these policies, that government is likely to be overthrown by the country's military, often backed by the armed forces of the industrialized countries themselves. Dependency theorists point to many examples: the role of the CIA in overthrowing the Marxist governments of Guatemala in 1954 and Chile in 1973 and in undermining support for the leftist government in Nicaragua in the 1980s. In the view of dependency theory, global economic inequality is thus backed up by force: Economic elites in poor countries, backed by their counterparts in wealthy ones, use police and military power to keep the local population under control.

The Brazilian sociologist Enrique Fernando Cardoso, once a prominent dependency theorist, argued in the late 1970s that some degree of **dependent development** was nonetheless possible—that under certain circumstances, poor countries can still develop economically, although only in ways shaped by their reliance on the wealthier countries (Cardoso and Faletto 1979). In particular, the governments of these countries could play a key role in steering a course between dependency and development (Evans 1979). Today, as the immediate past president of Brazil, Cardoso has changed his thinking, calling for greater integration of Brazil into the global economy.

World-Systems Theory

During the last quarter century, sociologists have increasingly seen the world as a single (although often conflict-ridden) economic system. Although dependency theories hold that individual countries are economically tied to one another, **world-systems theory** argues that the world capitalist economic system is not merely a collection of independent countries engaged in diplomatic and economic relations with one another but rather must be understood as a single unit. The world-systems approach is most closely identified with the work of Immanuel Wallerstein and his colleagues. Wallerstein (1974a, 1974b, 1979, 1990, 1996a, 1996b) showed that capitalism has long existed as a global economic system, beginning with the extension of markets and trade in Europe in the fifteenth and sixteenth centuries (Hopkins and Wallerstein 1996). The world system is seen as comprising four overlapping elements (Chase-Dunn 1989):

- A world market for goods and labor
- The division of the population into different economic classes, particularly capitalists and workers
- An international system of formal and informal political relations among the most powerful countries, whose competition with one another helps shape the world economy
- The carving up of the world into three unequal economic zones, with the wealthier zones exploiting the poorer ones

World-systems theorists term these three economic zones *core, periphery,* and *semiperiphery.* All countries in the world system are said to fall into one of the three categories. **Core countries** are the most advanced industrial countries, taking the lion's share of profits in the world economic system. These include Japan, the United States, and the countries of western Europe. The **peripheral countries** comprise low-income, largely agricultural countries that are often manipulated by core countries for their own economic advantage. Examples of peripheral countries are found throughout Africa and to a lesser extent in Latin America and Asia. Natural resources, such as agricultural products, minerals, and other raw materials, flow from periphery to core—as do the profits. The core, in turn, sells finished goods to the periphery, also at a profit. World-systems theorists argue that core countries have made themselves wealthy with this unequal trade while limiting the economic development of peripheral countries. Finally, the **semiperipheral countries** occupy an intermediate position: These are semi-industrialized, middle-income countries that extract profits from the more peripheral countries and in turn yield profits to the core countries. Examples of semiperipheral countries include Mexico in North America; Brazil, Argentina, and Chile in South America; and the newly industrializing economies of East Asia. The semiperiphery, though to some degree controlled by the core, is thus also able to exploit the periphery. Moreover, the greater economic success of the semiperiphery holds out to the periphery the promise of similar development.

Although the world system tends to change very slowly, once-powerful countries eventually lose their economic power and others take their place. For example, some five centuries ago the Italian city-states of Venice and Genoa dominated the world capitalist economy. They were superseded by the Dutch, then the British, and currently the United States. Today, in the view of some world-systems theorists, American dominance is giving way to a more "multipolar" world where economic power will be shared among the United States, Europe, and Asia (Arrighi 1994).

An important offshoot of the world-systems approach is a concept that emphasizes the global nature of economic activities. **Global commodity chains** are worldwide networks of labor and production processes yielding a finished product. These networks consist of all pivotal production activities that form a tightly interlocked "chain" extending from the raw materials needed to create the product to its final consumer (Appelbaum and Christerson 1997; Gereffi 1995, 1996; Hopkins and Wallerstein 1996).

The commodity-chain approach argues that manufacturing is becoming increasingly globalized. Manufactures accounted for approximately three quarters of the world's total economic growth during the period 1990–1998. The sharpest growth has been among middle-income countries: Manufactures accounted for only 54 percent of these countries' exports in 1990, compared with 71 percent just eight years later. Yet the high rate of increase of manufactures as a share of world exports has since slowed; in 2002, 75 percent of world exports were manufactures (World Trade Organization [WTO] 2003b). China, which has moved from the ranks of low- to middle-income countries in part because of its role as an exporter of manufactured goods, partly accounts for this trend. Yet the most profitable activities in the commodity chain—engineering, design, and advertising—are likely to be found in the core countries, whereas the least profitable activities, such as factory production, usually are found in peripheral countries.

One illustration of the global commodity chain can be found in the manufacture of Barbie, the most profitable toy in history. The forty-something teenage doll sells at a rate of two per second, bringing the Los Angeles–based Mattel corporation well over a billion dollars in annual revenues. Although she sells mainly in the United States, Europe, and Japan, she can also be found in 140 countries around the world. She is a truly global citizen (Tempest 1996). Barbie is global not only in sales but in terms of her birthplace as well. Barbie was never made in the United States. The first doll was made in Japan in 1959, when that country was still recovering from World War II and wages were low. As wages rose in Japan, Barbie moved to other low-wage countries in Asia. Her multiple origins today tell us a great deal about the operation of global commodity chains.

Barbie is designed in the United States, where her marketing and advertising strategies are devised and where most of the profits are made. But the only physical aspect of Barbie that is "made in the U.S.A." is her cardboard packaging, along with some of the paints and oils that are used to decorate the doll.

Barbie's body and wardrobe span the globe in their origins:

- Barbie begins her life in Saudia Arabia, where oil is extracted and then refined into the ethylene that is used to create her plastic body.
- Taiwan's state-owned oil importer, the Chinese Petroleum Corporation, buys the ethylene and sells it to Taiwan's Formosa Plastic Corporation, the world's largest producer of polyvinyl chloride (PVC) plastics, which are used in toys. Formosa Plastics converts the ethylene into the PVC pellets that will be shaped to make Barbie's body.
- The pellets are then shipped to one of the four Asian factories that make Barbie—two in southern China, one in Indonesia, and one in Malaysia. The plastic-mold injection machines that shape her body, which are the most expensive part of Barbie's manufacture, are made in the United States and shipped to the factories.

- Once Barbie's body is molded, she gets her nylon hair from Japan. Her cotton dresses are made in China, with Chinese cotton—the only raw material in Barbie that actually comes from the country where most Barbies are made.
- Hong Kong plays a key role in the manufacturing process of the Chinese Barbies. Nearly all the material used in her manufacture is shipped into Hong Kong—one of the world's largest ports—and then trucked to the factories in China. The finished Barbies leave by the same route. Some twenty-three thousand trucks make the daily trip between Hong Kong and southern China's toy factories.

So where is Barbie actually from? The cardboard and cellophane box containing the My First Tea Party Barbie is labeled "Made in China," but as we have seen, almost none of the materials that go into making her actually originates in that country. For a $20 Barbie, China gets only about 70 cents, mainly in wages paid to the eleven thousand peasant women who assemble her in the two factories. Back in the United States, on the other hand, Mattel makes about $2 in profits.

What about the rest of the money that is made when Barbie is sold for $20? Only 65 cents is needed to cover the plastics, cloth, nylon, and other materials used in her manufacture. Most of the money goes to pay for machinery and equipment, transoceanic shipping and domestic trucking, advertising and merchandising, retail floor space—and, of course, the profits of Toys "R" Us and other retailers.

Although manufacturing in the global commodity chain typically takes place in peripheral countries, an exception to this trend has developed. Low-wage, low-profit factories known as sweatshops are today reappearing in core countries, sometimes for the first time in half a century or more. A sweatshop is a small factory that has numerous violations of wage, health, and safety laws. In New York City and Los Angeles, for example, more than a hundred thousand workers labor in tiny garment factories that make many of the brands of clothing you can buy in major department stores. Many laborers work for less than minimum wage, in buildings described by government officials as firetraps.

The private experience of these workers is shaped by larger social forces. First, garment workers in New York and Los Angeles are in direct competition with workers in the Caribbean and Mexico, where wages are a tenth as much as in the United States. If workers in New York and Los Angeles want to keep their jobs, they are often forced to settle for sweatshop wages and conditions. Otherwise, the work will be moved to another country. Second, most garment workers are immigrants, many lacking proper papers. If they complain about their working conditions, they will lose their jobs and possibly be deported.

The global economy has brought sweatshops back to the United States, a country where they were largely unknown for more than half a century. The global economy has also provided the immigrants to work in them.

Barbie, the quintessentially American doll, has never actually been produced in the United States. Since she was first made in Japan in 1959, rising wages in Asia have moved Barbie production from one low-wage country to another. The four factories that currently make Barbie are located in southern China, Indonesia, and Malaysia.

Women and Economic Development

Although the theories of economic development reviewed in this chapter largely ignore women, women in fact play a key role in the global economy (Blumberg 1995; Scott 1995). Even where women contributed to revolutionary social change—such as in Vietnam, where more than a quarter of a million female soldiers died on behalf of communism during the Vietnam War—their economic role has not been fully acknowledged (Tétreault 1994).

Today, women make up a major part of the workforce in the world's factories. Yet studies that stress cheap factory work in the global economy often fail to examine the central importance of women's labor. In export-processing zones throughout the world, young women assemble clothing, electronics, and other components into finished products for sale in Europe and North America. The jobs in these factories pay little and offer few opportunities for advancement. They are repetitive, monotonous, and frequently hazardous. These factories often employ women as young as fourteen or fifteen years old, who work long hours for low wages.

Women make up a large portion of the world's workforce for two very different sorts of reasons (Fernández Kelly 1987; Tiano

1994). First, many are compelled to work in factories by their husbands or parents who need additional income. Second, many women view these jobs—however unsatisfactory—as preferable to unpaid work at home, since wage earning provides them with a measure of economic stability and financial independence.

Women are often the most exploited of workers. Because they are seen as less likely to protest than men, from the standpoint of employers they are "ideal" workers who will take a lot of abuse. The following accounts are from four women who work in giant Mexican denim factories, where they sew stonewashed jeans for major U.S. manufacturers for forty-eight to sixty hours a week. They spoke to a U.S. human rights delegation under conditions of secrecy, fearful that they would lose their jobs for speaking out:

Cristina:

I've worked there for five years. I earn 280 pesos a week [U.S. $35]. I pay 72 pesos a week [U.S. $9] to get a ride to work. I'm never allowed to take a vacation. Monday through Friday, I work from 8:15 in the morning to 8:15 or 8:30 at night. I get one hour for lunch. Saturday I work from 8 A.M. to 4 or 5 P.M., with no break. I am very hungry by the time I leave work. I'm never paid anything extra if I work more hours.

Elena:

If there's something the matter with the stitching, we have to sew them by hand to fix them. So only when we finish with all the repairs can we leave. We can't leave earlier because they won't give us our IDs. If we get to work five minutes late, they deduct 10 pesos from our pay. Sometimes if we arrive late they won't let us into the factory until 9 A.M., and they deduct 30 or more pesos for this.

Carolina:

We don't have any safety equipment besides mouth covers and aprons; nothing for our hands or eyes, and there aren't any machine guards either. If we lose scissors or other equipment, they make us pay for it.

Luz:

Supervisors yelled at us and pressured us. Once a supervisor threw pants at me and yelled at me because the stitches weren't exactly the same on 30 pairs of pants. I had to re-do these pants before I left as punishment. . . . We had to contribute 3 pesos a month to buy soap, Pine Sol and Ajax to clean the bathroom. Then they assign us to take turns cleaning the bathroom after we've finished our work for the day, because there's no one who works there to clean the bathrooms. They don't have toilet paper in the bathrooms, we have to bring it from home. We're only supposed to go to the bathroom once a day. (National Interfaith Committee for Worker Justice [NICWJ] 1998)

It is important not only to recognize women's contribution to the global economy but to take steps to avoid their exploitation as well.

Questions

- The text calls women "often the most exploited of workers." At the same time, it mentions that women often choose to work outside the home. How can you reconcile these two seemingly contradictory remarks? What drives women to work in exploitative jobs?
- How can exploited workers get pay raises or increased benefits? What tactics might they use? What role does gender play in salary negotiations?
- Compare the photographs with the quotes from the workers. Do the words and the images create different impressions? How? Why?

State-Centered Theories

Some of the most recent explanations of successful economic development emphasize the role of state policy in promoting growth. Differing sharply from market-oriented theories, **state-centered theories** argue that appropriate government policies do not interfere with economic development but rather can play a key role in bringing it about. A large body of research now suggests that in some regions of the world, such as East Asia, successful economic development has been state led. Even the World Bank, long a strong proponent of free-market theories of development, has changed its thinking about the role of the state. In its 1997 report *The State in a Changing World,* the World Bank concludes that without an effective state, "sustainable development, both economic and social, is impossible."

Strong governments contributed in various ways to economic growth in the East Asian NIEs during the 1980s and 1990s (Amsden et al. 1994; Appelbaum and Henderson 1992; Cumings 1997; Evans 1995; World Bank 1997):

1. **East Asian governments have sometimes aggressively acted to ensure political stability, while keeping labor costs low.** They have accomplished this by acts of repression, such as outlawing trade unions, banning strikes, jailing labor leaders, and, in general, silencing the voices of workers. The governments of Taiwan, South Korea, and Singapore in particular have engaged in such practices.

2. **East Asian governments have frequently sought to steer economic development in desired directions.** For example, state agencies have often provided cheap loans and tax breaks to businesses that invest in industries favored by the government. Sometimes this strategy has backfired, resulting in bad loans held by the government (one of the causes of the region's economic problems during the late 1990s). Some governments have prevented businesses from investing their profits in other countries, forcing them to invest in economic growth at home. Sometimes governments have owned and therefore controlled key industries.

3. **East Asian governments have often been heavily involved in social programs such as low-cost housing and universal education.** The world's largest public housing systems (outside of socialist or formerly socialist countries) have been in Hong Kong and Singapore, where government subsidies keep rents extremely low. As a result, workers don't require high wages to pay for their housing, so they can compete better with American and European workers in the emerging global labor market. In Singapore, which has an extremely strong central government, well-funded public education and training help provide workers with the skills they need to compete effectively in the emerging global labor market. The Singaporean government also requires businesses and individual citizens alike to save a large percentage of their income for investment in future growth.

Evaluating Global Theories of Inequality

Each of these four sets of theories of global inequality just discussed has its strengths and weaknesses. Together they enable us to better understand the causes and cures for global inequality.

1. **Market-oriented theories** recommend the adoption of modern capitalist institutions to promote economic development, as the recent example of East Asia attests. They further argue that countries can develop economically only if they open their borders to trade, and they can cite evidence in support of this argument. But market-oriented theories also fail to take into account the various economic ties between poor countries and wealthy ones—ties that can impede economic growth under some conditions and enhance it under others. They tend to blame low-income countries themselves for their poverty rather than looking to the influence of outside factors, such as the business operations of more powerful nations. Market-oriented theories also ignore the ways government can work with the private sector to spur economic development. Finally, they fail to explain why some countries manage to take off economically while others remain grounded in poverty and underdevelopment.

2. **Dependency theories** address the market-oriented theories' neglect in considering poor countries' ties with wealthy countries by focusing on how wealthy nations have economically exploited poor ones. However, although dependency theories help account for much of the economic backwardness in Latin America and Africa, they are unable to explain the occasional success story among such low-income countries as Brazil, Argentina, and Mexico or the rapidly expanding economies of East Asia. In fact, some countries once in the low-income category have risen economically even in the presence of multinational corporations. Even some former colonies, such as Hong Kong and Singapore, both once dependent on Great Britain, count among the success stories.

3. **World-systems theory** seeks to overcome the short-comings of both market-oriented and dependency theories by analyzing the world economy as a whole. Rather than beginning with individual countries, world-systems theorists look at the complex global web of political and economic relationships that influence development and inequality in poor and rich nations alike. Within the world-systems framework, the concept of *global commodity chains* takes this notion one step further, focusing on global businesses and their activities rather than relationships between countries. World-systems theory is thus well suited to understanding the global economy at a time when businesses are increasingly free to set up operations anywhere, acquiring an economic importance that rivals that of many countries. Yet this is also a weakness of the commodity chains approach: It tends to emphasize the importance of business decisions over other factors, such as the role that both workers and governments play in shaping a country's economy (Amsden 1989; Cumings 1997; Deyo 1989; Evans 1995).

4. **State-centered theories** stress the governmental role in fostering economic growth. They thus offer a useful alternative to both the prevailing market-oriented theories, with their emphasis on states as economic hindrances, and dependency theories, which view states as allies of global business elites in exploiting poor countries. When combined with the other theories—particularly world-systems theory—state-centered theories can explain the radical changes now transforming the world economy.

Why Global Economic Inequality Matters to You

Today the social and economic forces leading to a single global capitalist economy appear to be irresistible. The principal challenge to this outcome—socialism—came to an end with the collapse of the Soviet Union in 1991. The largest remaining socialist country in the world today, the People's Republic of China, is rapidly adopting many capitalist economic institutions and is the fastest-growing economy in the world. It is too soon to tell how far the future leaders of China will move down the capitalist road. Will they eventually adopt a complete market-oriented economy or some combination of state controls and capitalist institutions? Yet most China experts agree on one thing: As China, with its 1.3 billion people, increasingly becomes a central participant in the world capitalist system, it will continue to have a major worldwide effect. China has an enormous workforce, much of which is well trained and educated and now receives extremely low wages—less than one twentieth as much as comparable U.S. workers. Such a workforce will be extremely competitive in a global economy and will force wages down from London to Los Angeles.

What does rapid globalization mean for the future of global inequality? No sociologist knows for certain, but many possible scenarios exist. In one, our world might be dominated by large, global corporations, with workers everywhere competing with one another at a global wage. Such a scenario might predict falling wages for large numbers of people in today's high-income countries and rising wages for a few in low-income countries. There might be a general leveling out of average income around the world, although at a level much lower than that currently enjoyed in the United States and other industrialized nations. In this scenario, the polarization between the haves and the have-nots within countries would grow, as the whole world would be increasingly divided into those who benefit from the global economy and those who do not. Such polarization could fuel conflict between ethnic groups and even nations, as those suffering from economic globalization would blame others for their plight (Hirst and Thompson 1992; Wagar 1992).

On the other hand, a global economy could mean greater opportunity for everyone, as the benefits of modern technology stimulate worldwide economic growth. According to this more optimistic scenario, the more successful East Asian NIEs, such as Hong Kong, Taiwan, South Korea, and Singapore, are only a sign of things to come. Other NIEs such as Malaysia and Thailand will soon follow, along with China, Indonesia, Vietnam, and other Asian countries. India, the world's second most populous country, already boasts a middle class of around 250 million people in 2004, about a quarter of its total population (although roughly the same number live in poverty) (*Time Asia* 2004).

A countervailing trend, however, is the technology gap that divides rich and poor countries, which today appears to be widening, making it even more difficult for poor countries to catch up. The global technology gap is a result of the disparity in wealth between nations, but it also reinforces those disparities, widening the gap between rich and poor countries. Poor countries cannot easily afford modern technology—yet, in the absence of modern technology, they face major barriers to overcoming poverty. They are caught in a vicious downward spiral from which it is difficult to escape.

Jeffrey Sachs (2002), director of the Center for International Development and professor of international trade at Harvard University, and a prominent adviser to many eastern European and developing countries, claims that the world is divided into three classes: technology innovators, technology adopters, and the technologically disconnected.

Sociology in South Africa

Public sociologists must balance a commitment to the university with a desire to work with groups beyond campus walls. When this tension is balanced well, public involvement enriches and sustains good academic research, provides a real-life context that improves teaching, and initiates a dialogue with wider publics about important issues in society. At other times, however, strong commitments to public sociology can have more serious consequences.

On January 8, 1978, Richard Turner, a lecturer at the University of Natal, South Africa, was killed by an assassin's bullet. Beginning in the 1960s, Turner had combined academic teachings with social activism designed to rally whites in South Africa to unite in opposition to the repressive Apartheid government, a regime based on the strict separation of the races. Because for years he had successfully translated black social and political unrest into a language embraced by progressive whites, Turner was viewed as a threat to the stability of the South African government. In addition to encouraging white students to get involved in black labor organizations and helping create the race-blind National Union of South African Students, Turner was a moving force behind the Institute for Industrial Education and the Durban strikes of 1973. In the years immediately before his assassination, Turner helped recruit and train labor organizers who would fight vigorously to dismantle the Apartheid regime and establish a comprehensive bill of rights for black workers.

Turner lived with his family in a modest suburban home outside the city of Durban. Shortly after midnight on January 8, a bullet entered the home through a downstairs window and struck Turner in the chest. His thirteen-year-old daughter, Jann, was awakened by the shooting and ran to her father's side. Minutes later, Turner died in his daughter's arms. After a

Richard Turner

brief police investigation turned up no clues, Professor Richard Turner's case was promptly closed.

Professor David Webster was a contemporary of Turner's in the anti-Apartheid struggle. Webster's dissertation on migrant workers exposed him to the methods used by business and government to exploit black workers. While living alongside his research subjects, Webster developed what would become a lifelong commitment to racial justice through political activism. As a professor at the University of Witwatersrand in Johannesburg, he frequently agitated government authorities by hosting "tea parties" at his home. Tea may have been served, but the purpose of each gathering was to mobilize support for the release of individuals who had been detained by the state.

To crack down on political dissent, the Apartheid government had begun to secretly imprison and detain those considered to be threats to state stability. Month after month, individuals would disappear from their homes. Frantic relatives had few places to turn for answers. Webster responded by organizing the Detainees' Parents' Support Committee

Technology innovators are those regions that provide nearly all of the world's technological inventions; they account for no more than 15 percent of the world's population. *Technology adopters* are those regions that are able to adopt technologies invented elsewhere, applying them to production and consumption; they account for 50 percent of the world's population. Finally, the *technologically disconnected* are those regions that neither innovate nor adopt technologies developed elsewhere; they account for 35 percent of the world's population. In fact, the Organization for Economic Cooperation and Development (2005) reports that over half of the patents issued worldwide were concentrated inside just ten regions within the most advanced industrial nations. Note that Sachs also speaks of regions rather than countries: In today's increasingly borderless

(DPSC), a support group for relatives of a rapidly growing list of detainees and banished people. While maintaining his academic responsibilities at the university, Webster helped relatives track down the whereabouts of loved ones who had disappeared.

"He wrote letters and documents chronicling and protesting against the conditions of repression. He did not keep quiet and was always there for detainees and their families. In this concrete sense he was a thorn in the flesh of the state—an obstacle to the success of their emergency strategy of removing activists from their society" (*Grassroots* 1989).

During the late 1980s, Webster began research in a remote part of KwaZulu-Natal province called Kosi Bay. He was especially interested in the psychological trauma experienced by detainees during interrogations by the state, and had started conducting extensive anthropology fieldwork to explore the issue. Kosi Bay happened to be close to the Tembe Elephant Park, which doubled as a secret training ground for government assassins during Apartheid. Eugene De Kock, the leader of the infamous "Vlakplaas" assassins brigade, was rumored to have trained his soldiers at Tembe. Although evidence remains unclear, some suspect that during his research Webster learned the truth behind the Tembe Elephant Park and became too curious.

On May 1, 1989, a man named Ferdi Barnard approached Webster outside his home in the city Johannesburg, just miles

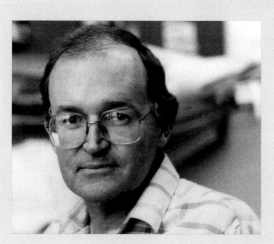

David Webster

from the university where he taught. Barnard was an employee of a covert Apartheid police force called the Civil Co-Operation Bureau that specialized in assassinations. After aiming his shotgun, Barnard fired at point blank range. Webster died immediately.

As followed Turner's death, the public outcry was emotional and sustained. Friends, family, and students of both professors demanded answers from government officials who for decades had systematically buried evidence of atrocities committed under their watch. No answers were forthcoming. An editorial published in the wake of Webster's death courageously stated that "the South African police have always denied allegations that they have been involved in political assassinations. Despite their denials, many serious questions remain unanswered. The most obvious is why have none of the killings been solved?" (*Grassroots* 1989).

It was not until 1998, four years after the rise of President Nelson Mandela and the establishment of democratic rule in South Africa, that Ferdi Barnard was convicted of Webster's murder. Barnard, who had received a bonus of 40,000 rand (approximately $8,000) for the killing, was sentenced to two life terms plus sixty-three years for atrocities committed under the Apartheid regime. As of 2006, the case of Richard Turner remains unsolved.

Jann Turner, Richard's daughter, is now forty-one years old, and she has spent her life trying to identify her father's killer. She recently paid a visit to Eugene De Kock, the former commander of the Vlakplaas who would likely have ordered her father's death. If he recalled the circumstances, he did not reveal them to Jann during their meeting. As she looked into his eyes and asked him questions, as she listened to his stories about nightmares and he listened to her own, Jann realized that her search was about something more. "I've spent years looking for my father's killer, for *the* killer," she writes in a journal she now keeps on the Web (www.jannturner.co.za). "Instead I found a killer—and for me this is about understanding"—a fitting reminder of the true purpose of public sociology: to connect public issues and private troubles in a way that leads, sometimes painfully, sometimes tragically, toward greater collective enlightenment.

world, technology use (or exclusion) does not always respect national frontiers. For example, Sachs (2002) notes that technologically disconnected regions include "southern Mexico and pockets of tropical Central America; the Andean countries; most of tropical Brazil; tropical sub-Saharan Africa; most of the former Soviet Union aside from the areas nearest to European and Asian markets; landlocked parts of Asia such as the

Ganges valley states of India; landlocked Laos and Cambodia; and the deep-interior states of China." These impoverished regions lack access to markets or major ocean trading routes. They are caught in what Sachs (2000) terms a "poverty trap," plagued by "tropical infectious disease, low agricultural productivity and environmental degradation—all requiring technological solutions beyond their means."

Innovation requires a critical mass of ideas and technology to become self-sustaining. That is why the technological innovation in the United States tends to be concentrated in regions rich in universities and high-tech firms: for example, California's Silicon Valley, which grew up around Stanford University and other educational and research institutions located south of San Francisco. Poor countries are ill equipped to develop such high-tech regions. In 2005, the U.S. Patent and Trademark Office issued 165,485 patents worldwide. Of these, 98 percent went to people living in high-income countries, with just over half (51.5 percent) going to inventors residing in the United States. Mainland China and India, which were the leading recipients of U.S. patents after the high-income countries and which have a combined population of nearly 2.4 billion people (nearly 40 percent of the world's population) accounted for less than 1 percent of patents granted in 2005. Most poor countries lack even a science adviser to their government. Moreover, these countries are too poor to import computers, cell phones, fax machines, computerized factory machinery, or other kinds of high technology. Nor can they afford to license technology from the foreign companies that hold the patents.

What can be done to overcome the technological abyss that divides rich and poor countries? Sachs calls on wealthy, high-technology countries to provide much greater financial and technical assistance to poor countries than they now do. For example, lethal infectious diseases such as malaria, measles, and diarrhea claim million of lives each year in poor countries. The modern medical technology necessary to eradicate these illnesses would cost only $10 billion a year—less than $15 from every person who lives in a high-income country, if the cost were shared equally.

Sachs urges the governments of wealthy countries, along with international lending institutions, to provide loans and grants for scientific and technological development. Sachs notes that very little money is available to support research and development in poor countries. The World Bank, a major source of funding for development projects in poor countries, spends only $60 million a year supporting tropical, agricultural, or health research and development. By way of comparison, Pfizer (2005)—the world's largest pharmaceutical corporation in terms of market share—spends 128 times that much ($7.7 billion in 2004) for research and development for its own products. Even universities in wealthy nations could play a role, establishing overseas research and training institutes that would foster collaborative research projects. From computers and the Internet to biotechnology, the wealth of nations increasingly depends on modern information technology. As long as major regions of the world remain technologically disconnected, it seems unlikely that global poverty will be eradicated.

In the most optimistic view, the republics of the former Soviet Union, as well as the formerly socialist countries of Eastern Europe, will eventually advance into the ranks of the high-income countries. Economic growth will spread to Latin America, Africa, and the rest of the world. Because capitalism requires that workers be mobile, the remaining caste societies around the world will be replaced by class-based societies. These societies will experience enhanced opportunities for upward mobility.

What is the future of global inequality? It is difficult to be entirely optimistic for now. Global economic growth has slowed, and many of the once promising economies of Asia now seem to be in trouble. The Russian economy, in its move from socialism to capitalism, has encountered many pitfalls, leaving many Russians much poorer than ever. It remains to be seen whether the countries of the world will learn from one another and work together to create better lives for their peoples. What is certain is that the past quarter century has witnessed a global economic transformation of unprecedented magnitude. The effects of this transformation in the next quarter century will leave few lives on the planet untouched.

Study Outline

www.wwnorton.com/giddens

Differences between Countries

- The countries of the world can be stratified according to their per-person gross national product. Forty percent of the world's population live in low-income countries, compared with only 16 percent in high-income countries.
- An estimated 1.3 billion people in the world, or nearly one in four people, live in poverty today, an increase since the early 1980s. Many are the victims of discrimination based on race, ethnicity, or tribal affiliation.
- In general, people in high-income countries enjoy a far higher standard of living than their counterparts in low-income countries. They are likely to have more food to eat, less likely to starve or suffer from malnutrition, and likely to live longer. They are far more likely to be literate and educated and therefore have higher-skilled, higher-paying jobs. Additionally, they are less likely to have large families, and their children are much less likely to die in infancy of malnutrition or childhood diseases.

Can Poor Countries Become Rich?

- Such newly industrializing economies as Hong Kong, Singapore, Taiwan, and South Korea have experienced explosive economic growth since the mid-1970s. This growth is due partly to historical circumstances; to a lesser degree to the cultural characteristics of these countries; and most important, to the central role played by their governments. Whether this growth will continue is now in question, given the economic difficulties some of these countries currently face.

Theories of Global Inequality

- *Market-oriented theories of global inequality,* such as *modernization theory,* claim that cultural and institutional barriers to development explain the poverty of low-income societies. In this view, to eliminate poverty, fatalistic attitudes must be overcome, government meddling in economic affairs ended, and a high rate of savings and investment encouraged.
- *Dependency theories* claim that global poverty is the result of the exploitation of poor countries by wealthy ones. *Dependent development theory* argues that even though the economic fate of poor countries is ultimately determined by wealthy ones, some development is possible within dependent capitalistic relations.
- *World-systems theory* argues that the capitalist world system as a whole—not just individual countries—must be understood if we hope to make sense of global inequality. World-systems theory focuses on the relationships of *core, peripheral,* and *semiperipheral countries* in the global economy; long-term trends in the global economy; and *global commodity chains* that erase national borders.
- *State-centered theories* emphasize the role that governments can play in fostering economic development. These theories draw on the experience of the rapidly growing East Asian newly industrializing economies as an example.

The Future of Global Inequality

- No one can say for sure whether global inequality will increase or decrease in the future. It is possible that some leveling out of wages will occur worldwide, as wages decline in wealthy countries and rise in poor countries. It is also possible that all countries will someday prosper as the result of a unified global economy.

Key Concepts

colonialism (p. 276)
core countries (p. 278)
dependent development (p. 277)

dependency theories (p. 276)
global commodity chains (p. 278)
global inequality (p. 260)
market-oriented theories (p. 273)
modernization theory (p. 273)
neoliberalism (p. 276)
newly industrializing economies (NIEs) (p. 271)
peripheral countries (p. 278)
semiperipheral countries (p. 278)
state-centered theories (p. 282)
world-systems theories (p. 277)

Review Questions

1. Which of the following is considered a high-income country?
   a. Singapore
   b. United States
   c. Taiwan
   d. All of the above
2. Most famine and hunger today are the result of
   a. natural and social forces.
   b. natural force only.
   c. social force only.
   d. wars.
3. Economic growth in East Asia has its costs. These include
   a. violent repression of labor and civil rights.
   b. terrible factory conditions.
   c. the exploitation of an increasingly female workforce.
   d. all of the above.
4. Which country has the highest rate of economic growth?
   a. United States
   b. Canada
   c. China
   d. Brazil
5. Which theory argues that the world capitalist economic system must be understood as a single unit, not in terms of individual countries?
   a. state-centered development theory
   b. modernization theory
   c. dependency theory
   d. world-systems theory
6. Which theory argues that the poverty of low-income countries stems from their exploitation by wealthy countries and the multinational corporations that are based in wealthy countries?
   a. state-centered development theory
   b. modernization theory
   c. dependency theory
   d. world-systems theory
7. Of the estimated twenty-six million people worldwide infected with HIV/AIDS, what percent live in developing countries?
   a. 5 percent
   b. 35 percent

c. 75 percent

d. 95 percent

8. What is the relationship between income and fertility at the national level?

a. positive

b. negative

c. no relationship

d. can be either positive or negative

9. What percent of the world's population lives in poverty?

a. about 75 percent

b. about 50 percent

c. about 25 percent

d. about 10 percent

10. _____ claims that cultural and institutional barriers to development explain the poverty of low-income societies.

a. Dependency development theory

b. Modernization theory

c. Dependency theory

d. World-systems theory

Thinking Sociologically Exercises

1. Concisely review the four theories offered in this chapter that explain why there are gaps between nations' economic developments and resulting global inequality: market-oriented theory, dependency theory, world-systems theory, and state-centered theories. Briefly discuss the distinctive characteristics of each theory and how each differs from the others. Which theory do you feel offers the most explanatory power to addressing economic developmental gaps?

2. This chapter states that global economic inequality has personal relevance and importance to people in advanced, affluent economies. Briefly review this argument. Explain carefully whether you were persuaded by it or not.

Data Exercises

www.wwnorton.com/giddens
Keyword: Data9

The nations of the world are not all equal when it comes to national wealth, but have you ever stopped to think about why such inequalities exist? Or what consequences these differences have in terms of patterns of consumption and social development? The data exercise for this chapter will give you an opportunity to learn more about global inequalities and to evaluate the different theoretical perspectives on global stratification.

Gender Differences: Nature versus Nurture

Think about whether differences between women and men are the result of biological differences or social and cultural influences.

Forms of Gender Inequality

Recognize that gender differences are a part of our social structure and create inequalities between women and men. Learn the forms these inequalities take, particularly in the workplace, the family, the educational system, the political system, and as violence against women.

Gender Inequality in Global Perspective

Understand the ways in which women around the world experience economic and political inequality.

Analyzing Gender Inequality

Think about various explanations for gender inequality and apply them to a real-life example. Learn some feminist theories about how to achieve gender equality.

Why Gender Inequality Matters

Learn how globalization has transformed ideas about women's rights.

CHAPTER TEN

GENDER INEQUALITY

round midnight one cold night in December, a little before the end of the second shift, Andrea Ellington is standing by the Coke machine in the workers' lounge, cleaning out her oversize pocketbook. She empties its contents, which begin with a gold plastic makeup bag, a wallet, and a bunch of monthly bills. "I gotta go wake my five-year-old daughter up at my mother's house," she says as she opens the makeup bag. "Then I go to the other baby-sitter and get my baby twins. Then I take them home and they've gotta go back to sleep, try to go back to sleep. By the time my daughter gets back to sleep, it's time for her to get back up again" (interview by the authors).

An African American woman of twenty-three, Andrea Ellington has three children to support on a low-rung clerical salary of $20,000 per year. She has been working at a Chicago law firm for four years; she had taken the job believing that with hard work, eventually she could advance enough to move her family out of public housing, her foremost goal.

Most of the five hundred or so employees in the law office where she works are not attorneys but "support staff," who work in one of many departments at the center of the floors, surrounded by plush attorneys' offices on the perimeter. The Network Center where she types is solely a nighttime word-processing department, with shifts from 4 P.M. to midnight and midnight to 8 A.M. The people who work as word processors are all women. They sit at computer terminals in one of four clusters separated by gray partitions. Almost all of these women who work at night are also rearing children during the day. Most live far from the law firm's gleaming downtown building.

Balancing the commitments of work and family is a challenge in terms of not only time but also money. Raising three children on her modest income, Andrea lives from paycheck to paycheck. She seeks out extra work to help her get by with her everyday responsibilities. As she says, working "overtime has helped me pay bills on time, buy clothes for my children, and buy food that I normally have had to wait until each paycheck to get." As a result of Andrea's persistence, her supervisor assigned her to work an extra eight hours of overtime per week, on Sundays. Andrea came to work for the first two Sundays and then began missing her weekend assignments when she couldn't find a baby-sitter for her three children. When her supervisor learned of the absences, she canceled the overtime.

Many people who encounter someone like Andrea Ellington might make certain assumptions about her life. They might assume, for example, that a disproportionate number of women become typists and word processors because it is natural for women to have certain kinds of occupations, including secretarial jobs. They might also assume that mothers should be responsible for taking care of children. Finally, they might assume that Andrea's poverty and low position in society are a result of her natural abilities. It is the job of sociology to analyze these assumptions and allow us to take a much wider view of our society and people like Andrea. Sociology allows us to understand why women are likely to work in low-paying clerical jobs, why women are likely to spend more time on child care, and why women on the whole are less powerful in society than men. Explaining the differences and inequalities between women and men in a society is now one of the most central topics in sociology.

In this chapter, we explore a sociological approach to gender differences and gender inequality. Gender is a way for society to divide people into two categories: "men" and "women." According to this socially created division, men and women have different identities and social roles. In other words, men and women are expected to think and act in certain different ways. Because in almost all societies, men's roles are valued more than are women's roles, gender also serves as a social status. Men and women are not only different but also unequal in terms of power, prestige, and wealth. Despite the advances that many women have made in the United States and other Western societies, this remains true today. Sociologists are interested in explaining not only how society differentiates between women and men but also how these differences serve as the basis for social inequalities (Chafetz 1990). Some sociologists are also concerned about the ways in which women can achieve positions of equality in society.

In this chapter, we first look at the origins of gender differences, assessing the debate over the role of biological versus social influences on the formation of gender roles. We also look to other cultures for evidence on this debate. We then review the various forms of gender inequality that exist in American society. In this section, we focus on the prominent social institutions of the workplace, the family, the educational system, and the political system. We also examine how women are so often the targets of sexual violence. Next, we examine how economic and political inequality affects women all over the world. We review the various forms of feminism and assess prospects for future change toward a gender equal society. We then analyze some theories of gender inequality and apply them to the circumstances of Andrea's life. We conclude the chapter by looking at the role of women around the world as we enter the twenty-first century.

Gender Differences: Nature versus Nurture

We begin by inquiring into the origins of the differences between boys and girls, men and women. The nature–nurture debate, noted earlier in Chapter 3, appears again with some force here. Scholars are divided about the degree to which inborn biological characteristics have an enduring effect on our gender identities as "feminine" or "masculine" and the social roles based on those identities. The debate is really about how much learning there is. No one any longer supposes that our behavior is instinctive in the sense in which the sexual activity of many lower animals—like the celebrated birds and bees—is instinctive. Some scholars, however, allow more prominence than others to social influences in analyzing gender differences.

Before we review these competing theories, we need to make an important distinction between sex and gender. While **sex** refers to physical differences of the body, **gender** concerns the psychological, social, and cultural differences between males and females. The distinction between sex and gender is fundamental, because many differences between males and females are not biological in origin.

The Role of Biology

How much are differences in the behavior of women and men the result of sex rather than gender? In other words, how much are they the result of biological differences? The opinions of researchers are divided. Some hold that innate differences of behavior between women and men appear in some form in all cultures and that the findings of sociobiology point strongly in this direction. Such researchers are likely to draw attention to the fact, for example, that in almost all cultures, men rather than women take part in hunting and warfare. Surely, they argue, this indicates that men possess biologically based tendencies toward aggression that women lack. In looking at the case of the word processors, they might point out that typing is a more passive occupation than being a bicycle messenger (an equivalent job category within the firm), which requires more physical strength and aggressiveness in traffic.

Most sociologists are unconvinced by these arguments. The level of aggressiveness of men, they say, varies widely among different cultures, and women are expected to be more passive or gentle in some cultures than in others (Elshtain 1981). Theories of "natural difference" are often grounded in data on animal behavior, critics point out, rather than in anthropological or historical evidence about human behavior, which reveals variation over time and place. In the majority of cultures, most women spend a significant part of their lives caring for children and therefore cannot readily take part in hunting or war.

Although the hypothesis that biological factors determine behavior patterns in men and women cannot be dismissed out of hand, nearly a century of research to identify the physiological origins of such an influence has been unsuccessful. There is no evidence of the mechanisms that would link such biological forces with the complex social behaviors exhibited by human men and women (Connell 1987). Theories that see individuals as complying with some kind of innate predisposition neglect the vital role of social interaction in shaping human behavior.

What does the evidence show? One possible source of information is the differences in hormonal makeup between the sexes. Some have claimed that the male sex hormone, testosterone, is associated with the male propensity to violence (Rutter and Giller 1984). Research has indicated, for instance, that if male monkeys are castrated at birth, they become less aggressive; conversely, female monkeys given testosterone will become more aggressive than normal females. However, it has also been found that providing monkeys with opportunities to dominate others actually increases the testosterone level. Aggressive behavior may thus affect the production of the hormone, rather than the hormone's causing increased aggression.

Another possible source of evidence is direct observations of animal behavior. Writers who connect male aggression with biological influences often stress male aggressiveness among the higher animals. If we look at the behavior of chimpanzees, they say, male animals are invariably more aggressive than females. Yet there are in fact large differences between types of animals. Among gibbons, for instance, there are few noticeable differences in aggression between the sexes. Moreover, many

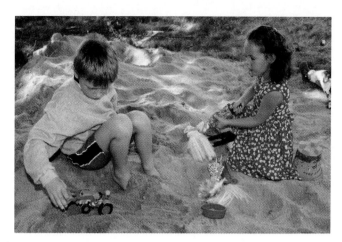

Many children's toys may promote gender stereotyping.

female apes or monkeys are highly aggressive in some situations, such as when their young are threatened.

Another source of information comes from the experience of identical twins. Identical twins derive from a single egg and have *exactly the same* genetic makeup. In one particular case, one of a pair of identical male twins was seriously injured while being circumcised, and the decision was made to reconstruct his genitals as a female. He was thereafter raised as a girl. The twins at six years old demonstrated typical male and female traits as found in Western culture. The little girl enjoyed playing with other girls, helped with the housework, and wanted to get married when she grew up. The boy preferred the company of other boys, his favorite toys were cars and trucks, and he wanted to become a firefighter or police officer.

For some time, this case was treated as a conclusive demonstration of the overriding influence of social learning on gender differences. However, when the girl was a teenager, she was interviewed during a television program, and the interview showed that she felt some unease about her gender identity, even perhaps that she was "really" a boy after all. She had by then learned of her unusual background, and this knowledge may very well have been responsible for this altered perception of herself (Ryan 1985).

Gender Socialization

Another route to take in understanding the origins of gender differences is the study of **gender socialization,** the learning of gender roles with the help of social agencies such as the family and the media (see also Chapter 4). Such an approach makes a distinction between biological sex and social gender—an infant is born with the first and develops the second. Through contact with various agencies of socialization, both primary and secondary, children gradually internalize the social norms and expectations that are seen to correspond with their sex. Gender differences are not biologically determined; they are culturally produced. According to this view, gender inequalities result because men and women are socialized into different roles.

Theories of gender socialization have been favored by functionalists, who see boys and girls as learning "sex roles" and the male and female identities—masculinity and femininity—that accompany them. They are guided in this process by positive and negative *sanctions*, socially applied forces that reward or restrain behavior. For example, a small boy could be positively sanctioned in his behavior ("What a brave boy you are!") or be the recipient of negative sanction ("Boys don't play with dolls"). These positive and negative reinforcements aid boys and girls in learning and conforming to expected sex roles. If an individual develops gender practices that do not correspond with his or her biological sex—that is, he or she is deviant—the explanation is seen to reside in inadequate or irregular socialization. According to this functionalist view, socializing agencies contribute to the maintenance of social order by overseeing the smooth gender socialization of new generations.

This rigid interpretation of sex roles and socialization has been criticized on a number of fronts. Many writers argue that gender socialization is not an inherently smooth process; different agencies such as the family, schools, and peer groups may be at odds with one another. Moreover, socialization theories ignore the ability of individuals to reject, or modify, the social expectations surrounding sex roles.

It is important to remember that humans are not passive objects or unquestioning recipients of gender programming, as some sociologists have suggested. People are active agents who create and modify roles for themselves. Although we should be skeptical of any wholesale adoption of the sex roles approach, many studies have shown that to some degree gender identities *are* a result of social influences.

To understand this argument, let's take a look at the following two scenes. Two newborn infants lie in the nursery of a hospital maternity ward. One, a male baby, is wrapped in a blue blanket, the other, a female, is in a pink blanket. Both babies are only a few hours old and are being seen by their grandparents for the first time. The conversation between one pair of grandparents runs along these lines:

Grandma A: *There he is—our first grandchild, and a boy.*

Grandpa A: *Hey, isn't he a hefty little fellow? Look at that fist he's making. He's going to be a regular little fighter, that guy is.* (Grandpa A smiles and throws out a boxing jab to his grandson.) *At-a-boy!*

Grandma A: *I think he looks like you. He has your strong chin. Oh, look, he's starting to cry.*

Grandpa A: *Yeah—just listen to that set of lungs. He's going to be some boy.*

Grandma A: *Poor thing—he's still crying.*

Grandpa A: *It's okay. It's good for him. He's exercising and it will develop his lungs.*

Grandma A: *Let's go and congratulate the parents. I know they're thrilled about little Fred. They wanted a boy first.*

Grandpa A: *Yeah, and they were sure it would be a boy too, what with all that kicking and thumping going on even before he got here.*

When they depart to congratulate the parents, the grandparents of the other child arrive. The dialogue between them goes like this:

Grandma B: *There she is . . . the only one with a pink bow taped to her head. Isn't she darling.*

Grandpa B: *Yeah—isn't she little. Look at how tiny her fingers are. Oh, look—she's trying to make a fist.*

Grandma B: *Isn't she sweet . . . you know, I think she looks a little like me.*

Grandpa B: *Yeah, she sorta does. She has your chin.*

Grandma B: *Oh, look, she's starting to cry.*

Grandpa B: *Maybe we better call the nurse to pick her up or change her or something.*

Grandma B: *Yes, let's. Poor little girl.* (To the baby) *There, there, we'll try to help you.*

Grandpa B: *Let's find the nurse. I don't like to see her cry . . .*

Grandma B: *Hmm. I wonder when they will have their next one. I know Fred would like a son, but little Fredericka is well and healthy. After all, that's what really matters.*

Grandpa B: *They're young yet. They have time for more kids. I'm thankful too that she's healthy.*

Grandma B: *I don't think they were surprised when it was a girl anyway . . . she was carrying so low.* (Walum 1977)

The contrast between the two sets of conversations sounds so exaggerated that it is tempting to think they were made up. In fact, they are composed of transcripts of actual dialogue recorded in a maternity ward. The very first question usually asked of a parent—in Western culture at least—is, "Is it a boy or a girl?" Our images of others are fundamentally structured around gender identity. In turn, social and cultural expectations for each gender create expectations about the roles and identities one should assume.

People create gender through social interactions with others, such as family members, friends, and colleagues. As we just saw, this process begins at birth when doctors, nurses, and family members—the first to see an infant—assign the person to a gender category on the basis of physical characteristics. Babies are immediately dressed in a way that marks the sex category: "parents don't want to be constantly asked if their child is a boy or a girl" (Lorber 1994). Once the child is marked as male or female, everyone who interacts with the child will treat it in accordance with its gender. They do so on the basis of the society's assumptions, which lead people to treat women and men differently, even as opposites (Renzetti and Curran 1995).

Clearly, gender socialization is very powerful, and challenges to it can be upsetting. Once a gender is "assigned," society expects individuals to act like "females" and "males." It is in the practices of everyday life that these expectations are fulfilled and reproduced (Bourdieu 1990; Lorber 1994).

The Social Construction of Gender

In recent years, socialization and gender role theories have been criticized by a growing number of sociologists. Rather than seeing sex as biologically determined and gender as culturally learned, they argue that we should view *both* sex and gender as socially constructed products. Not only is gender a purely social creation that lacks a fixed essence but the human body itself is subject to social forces that shape and alter it in various ways.

According to such a perspective, writers who focus on gender roles and role learning implicitly accept that there *is* a biological basis to gender differences. In the socialization approach, a biological distinction between the sexes provides a framework that becomes culturally elaborated in society itself. In contrast to this, theorists who believe in the **social construction of gender** reject all biological bases for gender differences. Gender identities emerge, they argue, in relation to perceived sex differences in society and in turn help shape those differences. For example, a society in which ideas of masculinity are characterized by physical strength and tough attitudes will encourage men to cultivate a specific body image and set of mannerisms. In other words, gender identities and sex differences are inextricably linked within individual human bodies (Butler 1989; Connell 1987; Scott and Morgan 1993).

Gender Identity in Everyday Life

Our conceptions of gender identity are formed so early in life that as adults we mainly take them for granted. Yet gender is

more than learning to act like a girl or boy. Gender differences are something we live with every day.

In other words, gender as a physical concept does not exist; we all, as some sociologists put it, "do gender" in our daily interactions with others (West and Zimmerman 1987). For instance, Jan Morris, the celebrated travel writer, used to be a man. As James Morris, she was a member of the British expedition, led by Sir Edmund Hillary, that successfully climbed Mount Everest. She was, in fact, a very "manly" man—a race

The top photo, dated November 30, 1952, shows George Jorgensen before his sex change. After he was discharged from the U.S. Army he traveled to Copenhagen, Denmark, where he had a sex-change operation. After the operation he changed his name to Christine. The bottom photo shows Christine Jorgensen, returning from a nightclub engagement in Cuba in 1953.

car driver and an athlete. Yet she had always felt herself to be a woman in a male body. So she underwent a sex-change operation and lived the rest of her life as a woman.

Jan Morris had to learn how to do gender when she discovered how differently she was expected to behave as a woman, rather than as a man. As she says, there is "no aspect of existence" that is not gendered. But she did not notice this until she changed her sex.

> It amuses me to consider, for instance, when I am taken out to lunch by one of my more urbane men friends, that not so many years ago th[e] waiter would have treated *me* as he is now treating *him*. Then he would have greeted me with respectful seriousness. Now he unfolds my napkin with a playful flourish, as if to humor me. Then he would have taken my order with grave concern, now he expects me to say something frivolous (and I do). (Morris 1974)

The subtle ways in which we do gender are so much a part of our lives that we don't notice them until they are missing or radically altered.

This differentiation between the roles and identities that society creates for men and women not only occurs in face-to-face interaction but is also part of society's institutions, such as the economy, the political system, the educational system, religions, and family forms. Because gender is so pervasive in structuring social life, gender statuses must be clearly differentiated if society is to function in an orderly manner. However, gender differentiation can also be the basis for inequalities between men and women (Lorber 1994; West and Fenstermaker 1995).

Findings from Other Cultures

If gender differences were mostly the result of biology, then we could expect that gender roles would not vary much from culture to culture. However, one set of findings that helps show gender roles are in fact socially constructed comes from anthropologists, who have studied gender in other times and cultures.

NEW GUINEA

In her classic New Guinea study, *Sex and Temperament in Three Primitive Societies*, Margaret Mead (1963) observed wide variability among gender role prescriptions—and such marked differences from those in the United States—that any claims to the universality of gender roles had to be rejected. Mead stud-

ied three separate tribes in New Guinea, which varied widely in their gender roles. In Arapesh society, both males and females generally had characteristics and behaviors that would typically be associated with the Western female role. Both sexes among the Arapesh were passive, gentle, unaggressive, and emotionally responsive to the needs of others. In contrast, Mead found that in another New Guinea group, the Mundugumor, both the males and females were characteristically aggressive, suspicious, and, from a Western observer's perspective, excessively cruel, especially toward children. In both cultures, however, men and women were expected to behave very similarly.

Mead then studied the Tchambuli tribe of New Guinea. The gender roles of the males and females were almost exactly reversed from the roles traditionally assigned to males and females in Western society. Mead (1972) reported in her autobiography that "among the Tchambuli the expected relations between men and women reversed those that are characteristic of our own culture. For it was Tchambuli women who were brisk and hearty, who managed the business affairs of life, and worked comfortably in large cooperative groups."

The children also exhibited these characteristics. Girls were considered the brightest and most competent and displayed "the most curiosity and the freest expression of intelligence." The Tchambuli boys "were already caught up in the rivalrous, catty, and individually competitive life of the men" (Mead 1972). Mead also reported that while the women managed the affairs of the family, the men were engaged differently: "Down by the lake shore in ceremonial houses the men carved and painted, gossiped and had temper tantrums, and played out their rivalries."

THE !KUNG

Another example can be found among the !Kung of the Kalahari Desert. Although "men hunt and women gather" in this society, a vast majority of its food comes from the gathering activities of women (Draper, quoted in Renzetti 2000). Indeed, !Kung women are respected for their specialized knowledge of the bush: "Successful gathering over the years requires the ability to discriminate among hundreds of edible and inedible species of plants at various stages in their life cycle" (Draper 1975). In addition, women return from their gathering expeditions armed not only with food for the community but also with valuable information for hunters. Draper (1975) noted that "women are skilled in reading the signs of the bush, and they take careful note of animal tracks, their age, and the direction of movement. . . . In general, the men take advantage of women's reconnaissance and query them routinely on the evidence of game movements, the location of water and the like."

Due to the nonconfrontational parenting practices of the !Kung, who oppose violent conflict and physical punishment, children learn that aggressive behavior will not be tolerated by either men or women. The !Kung do have specific sex roles, but it is very common for both men and women to engage in child care. Whereas in the United States it is still common for boys and girls to have very distinct upbringings, this is not true in the !Kung society (Draper, quoted in Renzetti 2000).

SUDHEST ISLAND

More recent anthropological evidence continues to contradict the idea that gender inequality is universal. The anthropologist Maria Lepowsky of the University of Wisconsin did ethnographic research with the people of Sudhest Island, two hundred miles south of Papua, New Guinea in the South Pacific. After living with them for two years, she concluded that the inhabitants of the island, the Vanatinai society, "offers any adult, regardless of sex or kin group, the opportunity of excelling at prestigious activities" (Lepowsky 1990, quoted in Renzetti 2000). Men even participate in child care. On the other hand, even here she did not find absolute equality: Women tend to sweep up pig excrement whereas men hunt wild boar.

MULTIPLE GENDERS

The understanding that only two genders (i.e., male and female) exist is not true among all societies. The Spaniards who came to both North and South America in the seventeenth century noticed men in the native tribes who had taken on the mannerisms of women, as well as women who occupied male roles. Indeed, many citizens of the United States who are intolerant of same-sex marriage are surprised to learn that Native Americans have a long tradition in which men enact female roles and women enact male roles and that allows same-sex marriage. This practice has now been documented by anthropologists in over 155 Native American tribes.

A person occupying an opposite gender role is called a *berdache*. But many scholars are unhappy with this term because its derivation does not come from the Native American cultures themselves (it derives from Persia), and some believe it has a negative connotation, not unlike *faggot*. Others argue that it is more often a substitute for lover or boyfriend (Roscoe 2000). In any event, some anthropologists have tried to replace *berdache* with "two-spirit." In fact, "two-spirit" has become a contemporary label used by Native Americans who are gay, lesbian, bisexual, and transgendered.

Berdaches are not the counterpart of transsexuals or transvestites in the United States, however. Roscoe (1991) studied

A *we'wha* (or *berdache*) of the Zuni people of New Mexico.

Zuni *berdaches* and noted that although *berdaches* technically do "cross-dress," their cross-dressing is routine, public, and without erotic motives. Moreover, *berdaches* are not necessarily homosexual; rather, some are heterosexual, some homosexual, and others sexually oriented toward other *berdaches*.

In one society, Roscoe found that both males and females have characteristics typically associated with the female role in the West. In another group, both males and females are aggressive. In both cultures, men and women are expected to behave similarly. These findings demonstrate that culture—not biology—is at the root of gender differences. There was a time in the development of feminist approaches when gender roles and gender socialization were the dominant concepts in understanding why women tended to cluster in particular occupations.

In more recent years, however, sociologists have noted that while society teaches people to assume certain "masculine" or "feminine" gender roles, such an approach does not tell us where these gender roles come from or how they can be changed. For this, we need to look at the way that gender is built into the institutions of society (Lorber 1994). For example, we need to know how the schools Andrea Ellington attended and the law firm she works in operate to establish "patterns of expectations" that lead people to assume certain roles (Lorber 1994).

The Political Work of Drag

Although many sociologists tend to focus on abstract concepts or faraway places, some scholars write about the issues and places that are part of their everyday lives—their own communities. Verta Taylor and Leila Rupp are two of the United States' leading scholars of gender and social movements. Their 2003 book *Drag Queens of the 801 Cabaret* is an example of how

sociological research can be used to illuminate the aspects of everyday community life that are usually taken for granted.

Taylor is chair of the department of sociology at the University of California, Santa Barbara (UCSB), and Rupp is chair of the Women's Studies Program; but when they are not occupied in Santa Barbara they live in Key West, Florida, where they have a second home. Key West is a small island city with diverse communities—Cuban, Bahamian, gay, hippie—and is a destination for many gay and lesbian tourists. Taylor and Rupp have been going there for over twenty years and know the town intimately.

One night they walked into the 801 Cabaret to see a new drag show, and they were utterly entranced with what was going on. They had seen men impersonating women in other drag shows, but these performers made no effort to pass as women. They spoke in their male voices, talked about tucking away their male genitals, and mimed sexual acts with various audience members. Through their performance, the drag queens were remolding and simultaneously creating new gender and sexual possibilities. Knowing that drag has a long history building gay communities and educating straight audiences about gay life and alternative gender forms, Taylor and Rupp saw this as a perfect research project.

To depict the social world of the 801 Cabaret, Taylor and Rupp used ethnographic methods. They spent three years attending the shows and hanging out behind the scenes. In the process, they developed a special rapport with the drag queens and got them to open up about all aspects of their lives. They also conducted focus groups with audience members to find out why all sorts of people—gay and straight, men and women, tourists and locals—come to the show and what they take away. The book is naturalistic ethnography because it shows the way people live in their natural setting. It teaches readers about the people behind a stereotype and humanizes them in the best traditions in careful ethnography.

In addition, Taylor and Rupp make an important argument about what the drag queens are doing. Not only are they dancing and entertaining but something more serious is taking place. The performers are doing political work because their shows solidify community among gay, lesbian, bisexual, and transgender audience members at the same time that they impart messages about the blurred boundaries between masculine and feminine and gay and straight to curious tourists who wander into the show.

How is work like this public sociology? Because it stimulates discussion about what it means to be a man or woman and what it means to be gay or straight in a number of different venues. People in Key West read the book, debating what was going on at the cabaret in the local papers. Across the country, scholars, journalists, and activists respond to the notion that drag performances can serve as an important tactic for gay and lesbian social movements.

After the book appeared, the two professors invited the drag queens to visit their classes at UCSB. Three of the girls performed in Taylor's introduction to sociology class, and for the last number, one of them stripped, leaving on only the wig and makeup. Karen Sikola, a student in the class, wrote the next day in the student paper, *The Nexus:* "When I first came to this school, I was under the impression that many of the students here were pretty closed minded. So I was nervous for the drag queens . . . when I heard they would be doing a special performance for the 800 or so Sociology 1 students. . . . My assumption was wrong. . . . The ladies put on an incredible show filled with entertainment as well as subtle political messages. The packed crowd ate it up. From the moment the three queens came out on the stage doing their rendition of En Vogue's 'Free Your Mind,' guys and girls alike were waving dollar bills in the air."

The UCSB student went on to write: "Here at UCSB, we are used to seeing tan, buff men and gorgeous blondes walking around campus. This time, we got both in one. It takes balls—pun definitely intended—to bare it all in front of a group of 18 to 22 year olds. I expected some people to walk out. No one did. . . . I just wanted to thank the drag queens for coming all the way from Key West and opening our hearts and minds. They are an inspiration to all to be confident in who you are. . . . I also want to thank Verta Taylor for believing we could handle such an event. I myself am thankful that my stereotypical impression of the students here has been challenged. And to the girls at the 801 Cabaret, you made my day."

The drag queens at the 801 Cabaret dressed Verta Taylor and Leila Rupp in drag so that they would understand how the audience objectifies their bodies.

Forms of Gender Inequality

Anthropologists and historians have found that most groups, collectives, and societies throughout history differentiate between women's and men's societal roles. Although there are considerable variations in the respective roles of women and men in different cultures, there are few instances of a society in which women are more powerful than men. Women everywhere are primarily concerned with child rearing and the maintenance of the home, while political and military activities tend to be resoundingly male. Nowhere in the world do men have primary responsibility for the rearing of children. Conversely, there are few if any cultures in which women are charged with the main responsibility for the herding of large animals, the hunting of large game, deep-sea fishing, or plow agriculture (Brown 1977). Just because women and men perform different tasks or have different responsibilities in societies does not necessarily mean that women are unequal to men. However, if the work and activities of women and men are valued differently, then the division of labor between them can become the basis for unequal gender relations. In modern societies, the division of labor between the sexes has become less clear cut than it was in premodern cultures, but men still outnumber women in all spheres of power and influence.

Male dominance in a society is usually referred to as **patriarchy.** Although men are favored in almost all of the world's societies, the degree of patriarchy varies. In the United States, women have made tremendous progress, but several forms of gender inequality still exist.

Sociologists define **gender inequality** as the difference in the status, power, and prestige women and men have in groups, collectives, and societies. In thinking about gender inequality between men and women, we can ask the following questions: Do women and men have equal access to valued societal resources—for example, food, money, power, and time? Second, do women and men have similar life options? Third, are women's and men's roles and activities valued similarly? We now turn to look at the various forms of gender inequality in the workplace, in the home, in education systems, and in politics, as well as in the violence practiced on women. As you read through this section, keep the above questions in mind.

Women and the Workplace

Rates of employment of women outside the home, for all classes, were quite low until well into the twentieth century. Even as late as 1910 in the United States, more than a third of gainfully employed women were maids or house servants. The female labor force consisted mainly of young, single women and children. When women or girls worked in factories or offices, employers often sent their wages straight home to their parents. When they married, they withdrew from the labor force.

Since then, women's participation in the paid labor force has risen more or less continuously, especially since the 1950s (Figure 10.1). In 2004, 60 percent of women age sixteen and older were in the labor force. In contrast, 38 percent of working-age women were in the labor force in 1960. An even greater change in the rate of labor force participation has occurred among married mothers of young children. In 1978, only 14 percent of married women with preschool-age children (under six years old) worked full time year round, yet this figure increased to 56.5 percent by 2004 (U.S. Bureau of Labor Statistics 2005a).

How can we explain this increase? One force behind women's increased entry into the labor force was the increase in demand, since 1940, for clerical and service workers like Andrea Ellington, as the U.S. economy expanded and changed (Oppenheimer 1970). From 1940 until the middle to late 1960s, labor force activity increased among women who were past their prime child-rearing years. During the 1970s and 1980s, as the marriage age rose, fertility declined, and women's educational attainment increased, the growth in labor force participation spread to younger women. Many women now postpone family formation to complete their education and establish themselves in the labor force. Despite family obligations, today a majority of women of all educational levels now work outside the home during their child-rearing years (Spain and Bianchi 1996).

Inequalities at Work

Until recently, women workers were overwhelmingly concentrated in routine, poorly paid occupations. The fate of the occupation of clerk (office worker) provides a good illustration. In 1850 in the United States, clerks held responsible positions, requiring accountancy skills and carrying managerial responsibilities; fewer than 1 percent were women. The twentieth century saw a general mechanization of office work (starting with the introduction of the typewriter in the late nineteenth century), accompanied by a marked downgrading of the status of clerk—together with a related occupation, secretary—into a routine, low-paid occupation. Women filled these occupations as the pay and prestige of such jobs declined. Today, most secretaries and clerks are women.

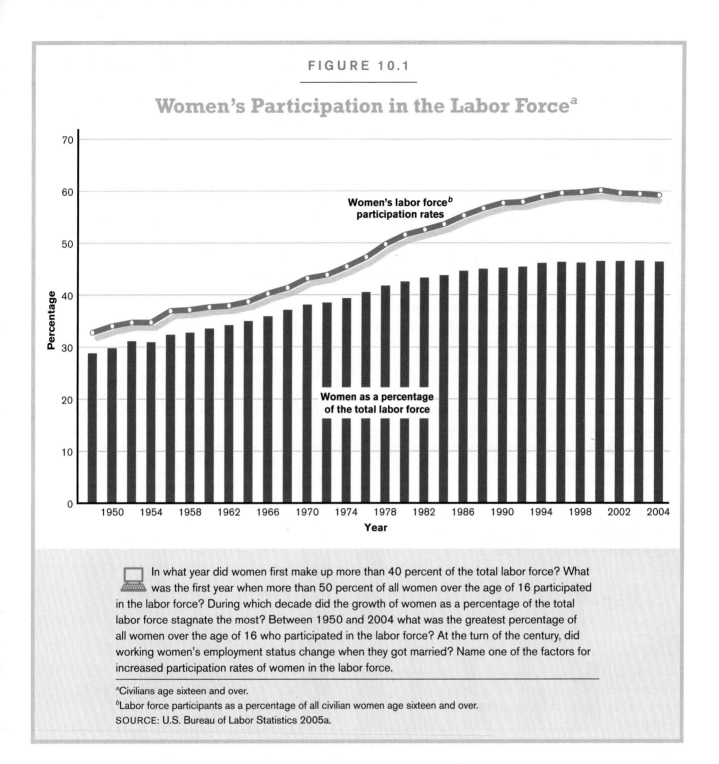

FIGURE 10.1

Women's Participation in the Labor Force[a]

> In what year did women first make up more than 40 percent of the total labor force? What was the first year when more than 50 percent of all women over the age of 16 participated in the labor force? During which decade did the growth of women as a percentage of the total labor force stagnate the most? Between 1950 and 2004 what was the greatest percentage of all women over the age of 16 who participated in the labor force? At the turn of the century, did working women's employment status change when they got married? Name one of the factors for increased participation rates of women in the labor force.

[a]Civilians age sixteen and over.
[b]Labor force participants as a percentage of all civilian women age sixteen and over.
SOURCE: U.S. Bureau of Labor Statistics 2005a.

Studies of particular types of occupations have shown how **gender typing** occurs in the workplace. Expanding areas of work of a lower-level kind, such as secretarial positions or retail sales, draw in a substantial proportion of women. These jobs are poorly paid and hold few career prospects. Men with good educational qualifications aspire to something higher, whereas others choose blue-collar work. Once an occupation has be-come gender typed—once it is seen as mainly a "woman's job"—inertia sets in. Job hierarchies are built around the assumption that men will occupy superior positions, while a stream of women will flow through subordinate jobs. Employers are guided in future hiring decisions by gender labels. And the very conditions of most female jobs lead to adaptive responses on the part of women—low job commitment, few career ambitions, high turnover, seeking alternative rewards in social relations—which fortify the image of women as suitable for only lower-level jobs (Lowe 1987).

These social conditions often tend to reinforce outlooks produced by early gender socialization. Women may grow up believing that they should put their husband's career before their own. (Men also are frequently brought up to believe the same thing.)

Women have recently made some inroads into occupations once defined as "men's jobs" (Figure 10.2). By the 1990s, women constituted a majority of workers in previously male-dominated professions such as accounting, journalism, psychology, public service, and bartending. In fields such as law, medicine, and engineering, their proportion has risen substantially since 1970.

In 2003, a woman was more likely to be in a managerial or professional job than a clerical or service position.

Another important economic trend since the 1970s has been the narrowing of the gender gap in earnings. Between 1970 and 2004, the ratio of women's to men's earnings among full-time, year-round workers increased from 62 to 80 percent (Table 10.1). Moreover, this ratio increased among all races and ethnic groups. During the 1980s, women's hourly wages as a percentage of men's increased from 64 to 71 percent, weekly earnings rose from 63 to 75 percent, and the ratio of annual earnings among all workers (not just those working full time) increased from 46 to 61 percent (Spain and Bianchi 1996; U.S. Bureau of Labor Statistics 2005b). Despite the lessening of the gender gap in pay, men still earn substantially more than women (Figure 10.3, p. 304). Several competing theories have been offered by economists and sociologists to explain this gap.

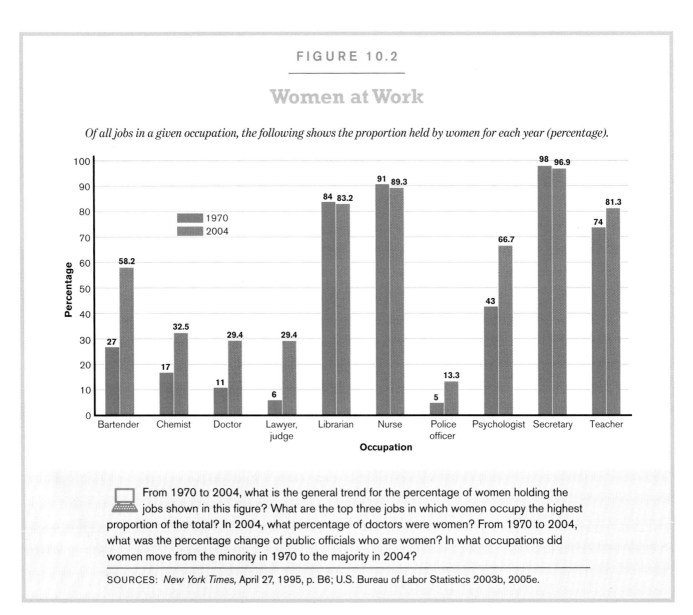

FIGURE 10.2

Women at Work

Of all jobs in a given occupation, the following shows the proportion held by women for each year (percentage).

From 1970 to 2004, what is the general trend for the percentage of women holding the jobs shown in this figure? What are the top three jobs in which women occupy the highest proportion of the total? In 2004, what percentage of doctors were women? From 1970 to 2004, what was the percentage change of public officials who are women? In what occupations did women move from the minority in 1970 to the majority in 2004?

SOURCES: *New York Times*, April 27, 1995, p. B6; U.S. Bureau of Labor Statistics 2003b, 2005e.

The Gender Pay Gap: The Sociological Debate

The "gender gap" in pay is a widely recognized fact. Even as recently as 2004, women who worked full-time year round (i.e., more than thirty-five hours per week for fifty-two weeks per year) earned only 80.4 percent as much as men. What could account for this discrepancy?

Sex segregation, or gender typing, is viewed by many sociologists as a cause of the gender gap in earnings. Sex segregation refers to the fact that men and women are concentrated in different occupations. For instance, in 1989, jobs that were over 80 percent female included secretary, child-care worker, hairdresser, cashier, bookkeeper, telephone operator, receptionist, typist, elementary school teacher, librarian, and nurse. Jobs that were over 80 percent male included doctor, lawyer, dentist, taxi driver, plumber, electrician, carpenter, firefighter, auto mechanic, machinist, and truck driver (Reskin and Padavic 1994).

In 1990, many women still worked in primarily female occupations. Of the 56 million women in the labor force in 1990, one third worked in just ten of the 503 detailed occupations recognized in the U.S. Census. These top ten occupations included secretary, elementary school teacher, cashier, registered nurse, bookkeeper, nurse's aide, and waitress. Men were more evenly distributed across the 503 census occupational groups; only 25 percent worked in the top ten occupations (versus 33 percent of women).

The reason that sex segregation is problematic is that the gender composition of a job is associated with the pay received for that job. This finding has emerged in numerous studies. An analysis of 1980 census data (England 1992) showed that both women and men are directly disadvantaged by employment in an occupation that is predominantly female. Even "after adjusting for cognitive, social, and physical skill demands, amenities, disamenities, demands for effort, and industrial and organization characteristics, jobs pay less if they contain a higher proportion of females" (England 1992).

Although an Equal Pay Act was established in 1963, it has done little to eradicate pay differences attributable to gender. The Equal Pay Act requires employers to provide equal pay to workers in the *same job*. Consequently, the gender gap in pay hasn't been remedied since the 1963 act because men and women often do not work at the same jobs. As long as employers segregate men and women into separate jobs, the best hope for narrowing the pay gap is to establish a pay-equity policy, meaning that pay policies remunerate workers on the basis of the worth of their work and not the sex, race, or other personal characteristics of the majority of workers in a job (Stryker 1996). Comparable-worth policies would be one such strategy.

TABLE 10.1

Women's Earnings Compared with Men's

Although the earnings gap between women and men is narrowing, it remains substantial. It is also significant that since the early 1990s, the gap has remained fairly constant. Analysts wonder whether this is temporary or permanent. The table shows what women earned for each dollar earned by men.

YEAR	EARNINGS RATIO
1970	.62
1980	.64
1990	.71
1991	.74
1992	.75
1993	.76
1994	.76
1995	.75
1996	.75
1997	.74
1998	.76
1999	.76
2000	.76
2001	.76
2002	.78
2003	.80
2004	.80

SOURCES: U.S. Bureau of Labor Statistics 2003d, 2004, 2005b.

However, economists and sociologists differ in their explanations of *how* occupational segregation leads to a gender gap in pay. Economists typically focus on the occupational choices women make, while sociologists tend to focus on the constraints women face. Specifically, many economists—as well as employers and public-policy makers—endorse a **human capital theory** explanation. Human capital theory, developed by Gary Becker (1964), argues that individuals make investments in their own "human capital" to increase their productivity and earnings. *Human capital* includes formal schooling, on-the-job training, and work experience. Those who invest more in their own human capital are considered more productive and consequently are paid higher wages.

This theory has been specifically applied to explain gender differences in earnings. Human capital theorists reason that

FIGURE 10.3

The Gender Pay Gap

This figure, in which weekly earnings are shown in constant 2000 dollars, illustrates what has been happening to the gender pay gap over time. After narrowing gradually for years, it widened a little after 1993, when men's inflation-adjusted earnings were increasing slightly and women's were not.

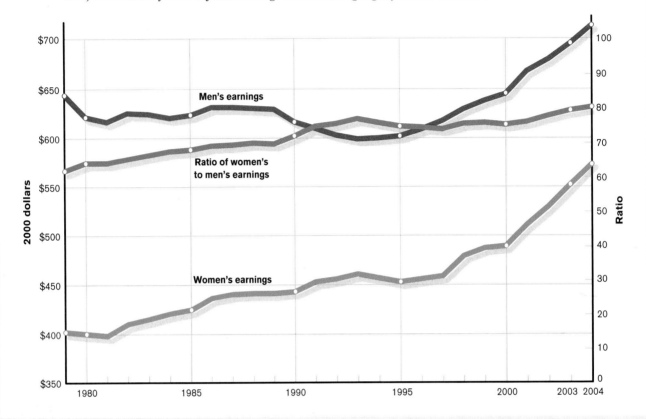

In 1980, what was the ratio of women's median weekly earnings to men's median weekly earnings? As we entered the twenty-first century, what was the dollar amount difference between men's median weekly earnings and women's median weekly earnings? Over the twenty-four-year period from 1980 to 2004, what was the change in the ratio of women's median weekly earning to men's median weekly earnings? What is "human capital"? What is the feminist critique of human capital theory? In what year did the ratio of women's median weekly earnings to men's median weekly earnings stop showing growth?

SOURCES: U.S. Bureau of Labor Statistics 2003c, 2004, 2005b.

women intentionally select occupations that are easy to move in and out of, while still providing moderately good incomes. Central to this argument is the assumption that women's primary allegiance is to home and family; thus they seek undemanding dead-end jobs that require little personal investment in training or skills acquisition so that they can better tend to their household responsibilities. When women leave the labor force to rear children, the skills they have deteriorate and they suffer a wage penalty when they reenter. Moreover, employers may also choose to "invest" less in women workers because they believe women will work less continuously than men and that consequently they will not realize the return on investment in women workers that they will in male workers.

Feminist sociologists critique human capital theory on several grounds. First, they dispute the claim that women freely "choose" certain occupations. The forces blocking women from freely choosing a career may be indirect or direct. For instance, childhood socialization promoting traditional gender roles often indirectly limits women's career choices; girls may choose occupations such as teaching or nursing, which are viewed as compatible with feminine traits such as warmth or nurturance. More direct obstacles to women's career choices come in the form of discriminatory bosses, co-workers, and customers. Workplace "gatekeepers" have been shown to prohibit women from entering certain occupations. For example, State Farm Insurance was successfully sued in 1992 for sex discrimination; the firm was forced to provide back pay to 814 women who were denied jobs as insurance agents because of their sex. Currently a class-action lawsuit about gender discrimination has been filed against Wal-Mart and is working its way through federal courts. On behalf of 1.6 million former and current female employees, the suit alleges that Wal-Mart discriminated against its female employees in making promotions, job assignments and pay decisions and that it retaliates against women who complain against such practices (Wal-Mart Class 2005).

Sociologists further argue that human capital theory neglects power differentials between men and women in the workplace and society. Numerous studies reveal that even when men and women are in the same job, men are paid more.

Women's work is devalued by society and by employers, and thus women are rewarded less for performing their work. Moreover, women's relative powerlessness prevents them from redefining the work they do as "skilled." As long as jobs predominantly filled by women, such as caring for children and the elderly, are viewed as "unskilled," wages in women's jobs will remain low.

These competing explanations have very different implications for the future. According to human capital theory, the gender gap in pay could disappear if women and men received equal amounts of education and workplace training and if they took equal responsibility for family commitments, such as child care. If feminist sociologists are correct in arguing that women's work is devalued, a drastic change in gender ideology must occur if men and women are to become equally rewarded for their participation in the workplace.

COMPARABLE WORTH

Comparable worth is a policy that compares pay levels of jobs held disproportionately by women with pay levels of jobs held disproportionately by men and tries to adjust pay so that the women and men who work in female-dominated jobs are not penalized. The policy presumes that jobs can be ranked objec-

tively according to skill, effort, responsibility, and working conditions. After such a ranking, pay is adjusted so that equivalently ranked male- and female-dominated jobs receive equivalent pay (Hartmann et al. 1985).

Although comparable worth policies may help reduce the gender gap in pay, only a handful of U.S. states have instituted comparable worth policies for public sector employees (Blum 1991). One reason that comparable worth policies have not been implemented is that they raise multiple technical, political, and economic issues. Perhaps most important is the issue of job evaluation, or the technical process that reduces male- and female-dominated jobs to an underlying common denominator of skill, effort, responsibility, and working conditions so they can be compared and ranked independent of the race and gender of job incumbents (Stryker 1996). Effective implementation requires that job evaluations be free from gender bias. However, substantial research shows that gender-neutral assessments of jobs and required job skills are very difficult. Once men and women know which jobs are predominantly male and which are predominantly female, they tend to attribute to them the job content that best fits with gender stereotypes (Steinberg 1990).

Opposition to comparable worth policies has been offered by both economists and feminists. Some economists worry that comparable worth is inflationary and will cause wage losses and unemployment for some (disproportionately women) because of benefits enacted for others. Feminists counter that comparable worth reinforces gender stereotyping rather than breaking down gender barriers at work (Blum 1991).

In 2004, a federal judge approved a class-action gender discrimination lawsuit against Wal-Mart in what has become one of the largest civil rights cases in U.S. history. From right: Betty Dukes, Patricia Surgenson, Stephanie Odle, and Christine Kwapnoski charge that Wal-Mart, including its Sam's Club division, systematically discriminates against its hourly and salaried female employees by denying them promotions and equal pay.

Whether or not comparable worth policies are enacted, the surrounding debates show that what jobs society values are determined not by their market or societal worth but by power relations (Blum 1991).

THE GLASS CEILING AND THE GLASS ESCALATOR

Although women are increasingly entering traditionally male jobs, their entry into such jobs may not necessarily be accompanied by increases in pay—and increases in occupational mobility—due to the **glass ceiling.** The glass ceiling is a promotion barrier that prevents a woman's upward mobility within an organization. The glass ceiling is particularly problematic for women who work in male-dominated occupations and the professions. Women's progress is blocked not by virtue of innate inability or lack of basic qualifications but by not having the sponsorship of well-placed, powerful senior colleagues to articulate their value to the organization or profession (Alvarez et al. 1996). As a result, women tend to progress into mid-level management positions, but they do not, in proportionate numbers, move beyond mid-management ranks.

One explanation for women's blocked mobility is based on gender stereotypes. Research shows that college-educated white males in professional jobs tend to identify potential leaders as people who are like themselves. Women are thus assessed negatively because they deviate from this norm or standard (Cleveland 1996).

What about men who work in female-dominated professions? Do they also face subtle obstacles to promotion? On the contrary, the sociologist Christine Williams (1992) has observed that a **glass escalator** pushes these men to the top of their corporate ladders. She found that employers singled out male workers in traditionally female jobs, such as nurse, librarian, elementary school teacher, and social worker, and promoted them to top administrative jobs in disproportionately high numbers. "Often, despite their intentions, they face invisible pressures to move up in their professions. Like being on a moving escalator, they have to work to stay in place," writes Williams (1992). These pressures may take positive forms, such as close mentoring and encouragement from supervisors or they may be the result of prejudicial attitudes of those outside the profession, such as clients who prefer to work with male rather than female executives. Some of the men in Williams's study faced unwelcome pressure to accept promotions, such as a male children's librarian who received negative evaluations for "not shooting high enough" in his career aspirations.

SEXUAL HARASSMENT IN THE WORKPLACE

Sexual harassment is unwanted or repeated sexual advances, remarks, or behavior that are offensive to the recipient and cause discomfort or interference with job performance. Power imbalances facilitate harassment; even though women can and do sexually harass subordinates, because men usually hold positions of authority, it is more common for men to harass women (Reskin and Padavic 1994).

The U.S. courts have identified two types of sexual harassment. One is the quid pro quo, in which a supervisor demands sexual acts from a worker as a job condition or promises work-related benefits in exchange for sexual acts. The other is the "hostile work environment," in which a pattern of sexual language, lewd posters, or sexual advances makes a worker so uncomfortable that it is difficult for her to do her job (Reskin and Padavic 1994).

Recognition of sexual harassment and women's willingness to report it have increased substantially since the testimony of Anita Hill to the Senate Judiciary Committee during the confirmation hearings for Clarence Thomas's 1991 nomination to the U.S. Supreme Court. Although Thomas was ultimately confirmed as a U.S. Supreme Court justice, Hill's recounting of his harassment raised public awareness of the seriousness of the problem and encouraged more women to report harassment incidents (Figure 10.4). In the first six months of 1992 alone, the number of workplace harassment complaints increased by

Sociologist Christine Williams asserts that men in female-dominated professions, such as this elementary school teacher, are routinely promoted to top administrative positions and face constant pressure to advance.

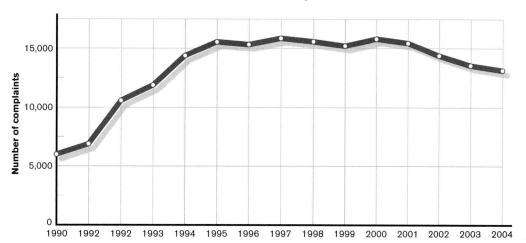

FIGURE 10.4

Increase in Sexual Harassment Complaints in the United States, 1990–2004

Why is 1992 listed twice? During what year did the number of sexual harassment complaints increase the most? During what year did the number of sexual harassment complaints in the United States begin to level off? What are two reasons that women may not report sexual harassment? What are two potential explanations for the decline in sexual harassment complaints since 2000?

SOURCE: U.S. Equal Employment Opportunity Commission, "Sexual Harassment Charges, EEOC & FEPAs combined: FY 1992–FY 2004."

more than 50 percent (Gross 1992). In 1992 overall, workers filed over ten thousand complaints of sexual harassment with the Equal Employment Opportunity Commission (Equal Employment Opportunity Commission [EEOC] 1993).

Despite this increased awareness, sociologists have observed that "the great majority of women who are abused by behavior that fits legal definitions of sexual harassment—and who are traumatized by the experience—do not label what has happened to them as sexual harassment" (Paludi and Barickman 1991).

Women's reluctance to report may be due to the following factors: (1) many still do not recognize that sexual harassment is an actionable offense; (2) victims may be reluctant to come forward with complaints, fearing that they will not be believed, that their charges will not be taken seriously, or that they will be subject to reprisals; (3) it may be difficult to differentiate between harassment and joking on the job (Giuffre and Williams 1994).

In 1998, the U.S. Supreme Court decided that the Civil Rights Act outlaws harassment between members of the same sex. The case involved a Louisiana man who was forced to quit

his job on an offshore oil rig because he had been repeatedly grabbed, ridiculed, and threatened by two male supervisors. Justice Antonin Scalia ruled neither "roughhousing" among men, nor "flirtations" between men and women, nor even some types of "verbal or physical harassment" is illegal. Nonetheless, he determined, when sexual harassment is so "severely hostile or abusive" that it prevents workers from doing their jobs, it violates the Civil Rights Act—regardless of whether the offender and the person who is harassed are of the same or the opposite sex (Savage 1998).

The Family and Gender Issues

BALANCING WORK AND CHILD CARE

One of the major factors affecting women's careers is the male perception that for female employees, work comes second to having children. One study carried out in Britain investigated the views of managers interviewing female applicants for positions as technical staff in the health services. The researchers found that the interviewers always asked the women about whether or not they had, or intended to have, children (this is now illegal in the United States). They virtually never followed this practice with male applicants. When asked why, two themes ran through their answers: Women with children may require extra time off for school holidays or if a child falls sick and the responsibility for child care is the mother's problem, not a parental one.

Some managers thought their questions indicated an attitude of "caring" toward female employees. But most saw such a line of questioning as part of their task in assessing how far a female applicant would prove a reliable colleague. Thus one manager remarked:

> It's a bit of a personal question, I appreciate that, but I think it's something that has to be considered. It's something that can't happen to a man really, but I suppose in a sense it's unfair—it's not equal opportunity because the man could never find himself having a family as such. (Homans 1987)

Although men cannot biologically "have a family" in the sense of bearing children, they can be fully involved in and responsible for child care. Such a possibility was not taken into account by any of the managers studied. The same attitudes were held about the promotion of women. Women were seen as likely to interrupt their careers to care for young children, no matter how senior a position they might have reached. The few women in this study who held senior management positions were all without children, and several of those who planned to have children in the future said they intended to leave their jobs and would perhaps retrain for other positions subsequently.

How should we interpret these findings? Are women's job opportunities hampered mainly by male prejudices? Some managers expressed the view that women with children should *not* work but should occupy themselves with child care and the home. Most, however, accepted the principle that women should have the same career opportunities as men. The bias in their attitudes had less to do with the workplace itself than with the domestic responsibilities of parenting. So long as most of the population take it for granted that parenting cannot be shared on an equal basis by both women and men, the problems facing women employees will persist. It will remain a fact of life, as one of the managers put it, that women are disadvantaged, compared with men, in their career opportunities.

In her book *Working Women Don't Have Wives* (1994), Terri Apter argues that women find themselves struggling with two contradictory forces. They want and need economic independence but at the same time want to be mothers to their chil-

Can men and women truly share equal responsibility for their children or will women always be regarded as the primary caretakers?

dren. Both goals are reasonable, but while men with wives who take prime responsibility for domestic work can achieve them, women cannot do likewise. Greater flexibility in working life is one partial solution. Much more difficult is getting men to alter their attitudes.

HOUSEWORK

Although there have been revolutionary changes in women's status in recent decades in the United States, including the entry of women into male-dominated professions, one area of work has lagged far behind: housework. Because of the increase of married women in the workforce and the resulting change in status, it was presumed that men would contribute more to housework. On the whole, this has not been the case. Although men now do more housework than they did in the 1970s (one to two hours more per week) and women do slightly less, the balance is still unequal (Shelton and John 1993). Sociologists calculate that working women perform fifteen more hours of housework per week than their husbands, in effect a "second shift" of work (Hochschild 1989; Shelton 1992). The United Nations (2003) estimates that women in the United States work 6 percent more than men, a majority of which is spent in non-market activities. These figures do not include time spent on child care, which if factored in would increase the gap. The UN (1995) has estimated that if all of the non-market work of women was accounted for, the official estimate of the size of the world economy would be $11 trillion higher. Findings like these have led Arlie Hochschild (1989) to call the state of relations between women and men a "stalled revolution." Why does housework remain women's work? This question has been the focus of a good deal of research in recent years.

Some sociologists have suggested that this phenomenon is best explained as a result of economic forces: Household work is exchanged for economic support. Because women earn less than men, they are more likely to remain economically dependent on their husbands and thus perform the bulk of the housework. Until the earnings gap is narrowed, women will likely remain in their dependent position. Hochschild suggests that women are thus doubly oppressed by men: once during the first shift and again during the second shift. But although this dependency model contributes to our understanding of the gendered aspects of housework, it breaks down when applied to situations in which the wife earns more than her husband. For instance, of the husbands that Hochschild studied who earned less than their wives, none shared in the housework.

Some sociologists have approached the problem from a symbolic interactionist perspective, asking how the performance or nonperformance of housework is related to the gender roles created by society. For example, through interviews and participant observation, Hochschild found that the assignment of household tasks falls clearly along gendered lines. Wives do most of the daily chores, such as cooking and routine cleaning, while husbands tend to take on more occasional tasks, such as mowing the lawn or doing home repairs. The major difference between these two types of tasks is the amount of control the individual has over when they do the work. The jobs women do in the home are those that tend to bind them to a fixed schedule, whereas men's household tasks are done less regularly and are more discretionary.

Sociologist Marjorie Devault looked at how the caring activities within a household are socially constructed as women's work in her book *Feeding the Family* (1991). She argues that women perform the bulk of the housework because the family "incorporates a strong and relatively enduring association of caring activity with the woman's position in the household." Even in households in which men contribute, an egalitarian division of household labor between spouses is greatly impeded when the couple have children—children require constant attention, and their care schedules are often unpredictable. Mothers overwhelmingly spend more time with child-rearing tasks than do fathers (Shelton 1992).

Sociologists argue that underlying this inequitable distribution of tasks is the implicit understanding that men and women are responsible for, and should operate in, different spheres. Men are expected to be providers, while women are expected to tend to their families—even if they are breadwinners as well as mothers. Expectations like this reinforce traditional gender roles learned during childhood socialization. By reproducing these roles in everyday life, men and women "do gender" and reinforce gender as a means for society to differentiate between men and women.

Education and Unequal Treatment in the Classroom

Sociologists have found that schools help foster gender differences in outlook and behavior. Although this has become less common today, regulations that compelled girls to wear dresses or skirts in school formed one of the most obvious ways in which gender typing occurred. The consequences went beyond mere appearance. As a result of the clothes they had to wear, girls lacked the freedom to sit casually, to join in rough-and-tumble games, or even run as fast as they were able. Although the strict enforcement of styles of school dress has become quite rare, differences in informal styles of dress still persist, influencing gender behavior in school. School reading texts also help perpetuate gender images. Although this too is changing, storybooks in elementary school often portray boys showing initiative and independence, while girls, if they appear at all, are portrayed as more passive and shown watching their brothers. Stories written especially for girls often have an element of adventure in them, but this usually takes the form of intrigues or mysteries in a domestic or school setting. Boys' adventure stories are more wide ranging, having heroes who travel off to distant places or who in other ways are sturdily independent (Statham 1986).

In general, people interact differently with men and women, and boys and girls (Lorber 1994). This is apparent even in the classrooms of elementary schools. Studies document that teachers interact differently—and often inequitably—with their male and female students. These interactions differ in at least two ways: the frequency of teacher–student interactions and the content of those interactions. Both of the patterns are based on—and perpetuate—traditional assumptions about male and female behavior and traits.

One study shows that regardless of the sex of the teacher, male students interact more with their teachers than female students do. Boys receive more teacher attention and instructional time than girls do. This is due in part to the fact that boys are more demanding than girls (American Association of University Women [AAUW] 1992). Another study reported that boys are eight times more likely to call out answers in class, thus grabbing their teachers' attention. This research also shows that even when boys do not voluntarily participate in class, teachers are more likely to solicit information from them than from girls. However, when girls try to bring attention to themselves by calling out in class without raising their hands, they were reprimanded by comments such as "In this class, we don't shout out answers, we raise our hands" (Sadker and Sadker 1994).

Sociologists have also found that the content of student-teacher interactions differs depending on the sex of the students.

After observing elementary school teachers and students over many years, researchers found that teachers provided boys with assistance in working out the correct answers, whereas they simply gave girls the correct answers and did not engage them in the problem-solving process. In addition, teachers posed more academic challenges to boys, encouraging them to think through their answers to arrive at the best possible response (Sadker and Sadker 1994).

Boys were also disadvantaged in several ways, however. Because of their rowdy behavior, they were more often scolded and punished than the girl students. Moreover, boys outnumber girls in special education programs by startling percentages. Sociologists have argued that school personnel may be mislabeling boys' behavioral problems as learning disabilities.

This differential treatment of boys and girls perpetuates stereotypic gender-role behavior. Girls are trained to be quiet and well behaved and to turn to others for answers, while boys are encouraged to be inquisitive, outspoken, active problem solvers. Female children from ethnic minorities are in some respects doubly disadvantaged. A study of what it was like to be a black female pupil in a white school reported that unlike the boys, the black girls were initially enthusiastic about school but altered their attitudes because of the difficulties they encountered. Even when the girls were quite small, aged seven or eight, teachers would disperse them if they were standing chatting in a group on the playground—in contrast to their treatment of the white children, whose similar behavior was tolerated. Once treated as "troublemakers," they rapidly became so (Bryan et al. 1987).

Gender Inequality in Politics

Women are playing an increasingly important role in U.S. politics, although they are still far from achieving full equality. Before 1993, there were only 2 women in the U.S. Senate (out of 100 Senate members), and 29 in the U.S. House of Representatives (out of 435). Less than a decade later—in 2001—there were a record 13 women in the Senate and 59 in the House. Currently, there are 14 women senators but 67 representatives (Center for American Women and Politics [CAWP] 2005). Women in 2005 held a little more than 22 percent of all seats in state legislatures, five times as many as they held in 1969, but only eight governorships (out of fifty) (CAWP 2005; National Governors Association [NGA] 2003). The U.S. Supreme Court had its first woman justice appointed in 1981, and its second twelve years later. It was not until 1984 that a woman was nominated as the vice presidential candidate of either major party, neither of which has ever nominated a woman for the presidency. Women politicians are overwhelm-

ingly affiliated with the Democratic party. In the U.S. Congress, 65 percent of women are Democrats and in state legislatures, almost 94 percent of women legislators are Democrats (CAWP 2005).

Typically, the more local the political office, the more likely it is to be occupied by a woman. Men outnumber women in politics at all levels, but women are often elected members of city and county governing boards and as mayors. In most states, women are less likely to be found as representatives to state government than as representatives at the local level, but even women elected at the state level are more common than women representatives to Congress. The reason is partly that local politics is often part-time work, particularly in smaller cities and towns. Local politics can thus be good "women's work," offering low pay, part-time employment, flexible hours, and the absence of a clear career path. The farther from home the political office, the more likely it is to be regarded as "man's work," providing a living wage, full-time employment, and a lifetime career.

Violence against Women

Violence directed against women is found in many societies, including the United States. One out of three women has been beaten, coerced into sex, or abused in some other way—most often by someone she knows, including her husband or a male relative (United Nations Population Fund [UNFPA] 2003). One in five worldwide will be a victim of rape or attempted rape in her lifetime (UNFPA 2005b). More women are injured as a result of beatings by spouses than by any other cause, a problem that is ignored by most governments (Human Rights Watch 1995). In Japan, three out of five women report having been sexually or physically abused by a partner. In India, an estimated twenty thousand brides were killed between 1990 and 1995—usually by being burned alive—for bringing an inadequate dowry to their husbands' families (Wright 1995). In 2004 alone, there were an estimated seven thousand deaths of women at the hands of husbands and relatives because the women brought an insufficient dowry. And the number of dowry deaths is on the rise, increasing by 3 percent from 2002 (Web India 2005). Between 100 and 140 million girls and women worldwide have been subjected to "genital mutilation"; and an equal number are "missing," partly as the result of female infanticide in cultures in which boys are more highly valued than girls (World Health Organization [WHO] 2000).

The trafficking of women for forced prostitution, which has been called "the largest slave trade in history," appears to be a growing problem (UNFPA 2005b). The United Nations estimates that each year 800,000 people—80 percent of which are women and 50 percent of which are minors—are moved across borders as a part of the worldwide sex trade. While victims of sex trafficking come from all regions of the world, nearly a quarter (250,000 per year) come from Asia, followed by the former Soviet Union and eastern Europe (275,000) (UNFPA 2005a). War, displacement, and economic and social inequities between and within countries, as well as the demand for low-wage labor and sex work, drive this illicit trade in women.

In the United States, many scholars argue that the increased depiction of violence in movies, on television, and elsewhere in American popular culture contributes to a climate in which women are often victimized. The most common manifestation of violence against women is rape, although stalking and sexual harassment increasingly are seen as a form of psychological (if not physical) violence as well.

RAPE

Rape can be sociologically defined as the forcing of nonconsensual vaginal, oral, or anal intercourse. Sociologists Paulene Bart and Patricia O'Brien (1985), who studied different forms of sexual relationships between men and women, offer the following classification (see also Brownmiller 1986):

- CONSENSUAL SEX: Intercourse that is desired equally by both partners.
- ALTRUISTIC SEX: One partner (usually female) "goes along" because she feels sorry for or guilty toward her partner.
- COMPLIANT SEX: One partner (usually female) goes along because she feels that the consequences of refusal would be worse than assenting to sex.
- RAPE: One partner (usually female) is forced, often by actual or threatened violence, to have sex against her will.

As one researcher observed, between consensual sex and rape lies "a continuum of pressure, threat, coercion, and force" (Kelly 1987). Common to all forms of rape is the lack of consent: At least in principle, *no* means "no" when it comes to sexual relations in most courts of law in the United States. Virtually all rapes are committed by men against women, although men rape other men in prisons and other all-male institutional environments.

Rape is an act of violence, rather than a purely sexual act. It is often carefully planned rather than performed on the spur of the moment to satisfy some uncontrollable sexual desire. Many rapes involve beatings, knifings, and even murder. Even when rape leaves no physical wounds, it is a highly traumatic violation of a woman's person that leaves long-lasting psychological scars.

It is difficult to know with accuracy how many rapes actually occur because most rapes go unreported. One comprehensive study of American sexual behavior found that 22 percent of the women surveyed reported having been forced into a sexual encounter. Yet the same study found that only 3 percent of the men admitted to having forced a woman into having sex, a discrepancy the study's authors attribute to different perceptions between men and women regarding what constitutes forced sex (Laumann et al. 1994). Based on its semiannual survey of nearly 100,000 Americans, the U.S. Department of Justice estimates that, in 2004, there were 95,420 sexual assaults on women, 43,440 attempted rapes, and 65,510 rapes. The total number of sexual assaults, attempted rapes, and rapes (204,370) was more than 21 percent lower than in 2002—part of an overall decrease in violent crimes since 1994. In fact, criminal victimizations, which include rape and sexual assault, were at their lowest point since 1973 (Catalano 2005).

Most rapes are committed by relatives (fathers or stepfathers, brothers, uncles), partners, or acquaintances. Among college students, most rapes are likely to be committed by boyfriends, former boyfriends, or classmates. The National College Women Sexual Victimization (NCWSV) study, a national survey of 4,446 women attending two- or four-year colleges or universities, presents a chilling picture of violence against women on campuses across the country (Fisher et al. 2000). The study, which was conducted during spring semester 1997, asked college women about their experience with rape, attempted rape, coerced sex, unwanted sexual contact, and stalking during the 1996–1997 school year. Overall, since the beginning of the school year, 1.7 percent had been the victim of a completed rape, and 1.1 percent of an attempted rape. Because students were typically interviewed seven months into the academic year, the authors estimate that over the entire academic year nearly 5 percent of the women in the sample would have fallen victim to a rape or attempted rape. Over the typical five years of a college career, this suggests that between a fifth and a quarter of all women attending college would fall victim to rape or attempted rape—some 2.2 million women.

Moreover, fully a tenth of the female students surveyed had been raped before the study period (which began in the fall of 1996), and a tenth had been the victims of attempted rape. The study also found that for both completed and attempted rapes, nine out of ten offenders were known to the victim. About 55 percent of rape victims used physical force in an effort to thwart the rape, as did 69 percent of attempted rape victims.

The incidence of other forms of victimization reported in the study was substantially higher than that of rape. Nearly one out of six female students reported being the target of attempted or completed sexual coercion or unwanted sexual contact during the current academic year, half involving the use or threat of physical force. More than a third reported that they had experienced a threatened, attempted, or completed unwanted sexual assault at some time during their lives. And about one out of every eight reported having been stalked at some time during the current year, almost always by someone they knew—typically a former boyfriend or classmate. Stalking, it was reported, was emotionally traumatizing and in 15 percent of the incidents involved actual or threatened physical harm.

The conclusions of the study are worth quoting at length:

> To summarize, the national-level survey of 4,446 college women suggests that many students will encounter sexist and harassing comments, will likely receive an obscene phone call, and will have a good chance of being stalked or of enduring some form of coerced sexual contact. During any given academic year, 2.8 percent of women will experience a completed and/or attempted rape.... Furthermore, the level of rape and other types of victimization found in the survey becomes an increasing concern when the victimization figures are projected over a full year, a full college career, and the full population of women at one college or at colleges across the nation.... Although exceptions exist, most sexual victimizations occur when college women are alone with a man they know, at night, and in the privacy of a residence. (Fisher et al. 2000)

WHY ARE WOMEN SO OFTEN THE TARGETS OF SEXUAL VIOLENCE?

Some scholars claim that men are socialized to regard women as sex objects and that this at least in part explains the high levels of victimization women reported to the NCWSV study (Dworkin 1981, 1987; Griffin 1979). Susan Brownmiller (1986), for example, claims that the constant threat of rape contributes to a "rape culture," one that is the result of male socialization that reinforces male domination by fostering a state of continual fear in women. One aspect of a "rape culture" is male socialization to a sense of sexual entitlement, which may encourage sexual conquest and promote insensitivity to the difference between consensual and nonconsensual sex (Scully 1990). From seemingly innocent high school locker-room jokes, to television commercials and magazine ads that depict women as sexually inviting, mindless bodies, to television and movie images equating masculinity with the conquest of women, many men grow up learning to believe that women exist for their pleasure. Under such circumstances, it is argued, rape is all too "normal" (Wolf 1992).

The fact that "acquaintance rapes" occur suggests that at least some men are likely to feel entitled to sexual access if they already know the woman. A survey of nearly 270,000 first-year

college students reported that 55 percent of male students agreed with the following statement: "If two people really like each other, it's all right for them to have sex even if they've known each other only for a very short time." Only 31 percent of female students were in agreement, suggesting a rather large gender gap concerning notions of sexual entitlement (American Council on Education [ACE] 2001). Another national study of first-year college students found that one out of five males felt they were entitled to have sex if the women "led them on" (Higher Education Research Institute [HERI] 1990), while a national survey reported that 43 percent of all men believed that a woman is partly to blame if she is raped after changing her mind about having sex (Yankelovich 1991). When

This sixteenth-century sculpture by Giambologna, titled *The Rape of the Sabines,* depicts the legend in which soldiers following Romulus, the mythical founder of Rome, captured and raped Sabine women to populate Rome.

a man goes out on a date with sexual conquest on his mind, he may force his attentions on an unwilling partner, overcoming her resistance through the use of alcohol, persistence, or both. While such an act may not be legally defined as rape, it would be experienced as such by many women.

Because men are socialized to feel a sense of sexual entitlement to women, rapes are most common when men believe that norms condemning rape somehow do not apply and so they are free to act as they choose. Rapes are thus common in times of war. Japanese soldiers raped as many as twenty thousand women when they conquered the city of Nanking in China in 1937 (Chang and Kirby 1997). Although this is one of the best-known modern cases of mass rape by conquering troops, war-related rapes are as old as human history. Followers of Rome's legendary founder, Romulus, were reputed to have captured and raped Sabine women to populate Rome—an act that was glamorized in the famous sixteenth-century sculpture *The Rape of the Sabines*. American soldiers committed rapes during the Civil War and the Vietnam War.

Rape is often an explicit military strategy: During World War II, for example, Japanese soldiers forced as many as two hundred thousand young women and girls to serve as "comfort women" for Japanese troops. These women—mainly Korean but also taken from other Asian countries conquered by the Japanese—were forced to work as sex slaves in military brothels throughout the Pacific. Many died in captivity, often of despair. A large number committed suicide (Stetz and Oh 2001). Rape was widely used as a Serbian strategy in the recent wars in Kosovo and Bosnia. By systematically raping and impregnating Muslim women, the Serbian forces hoped to humiliate the Muslim population into fleeing their homelands (Allen 1996).

Gender Inequality in Global Perspective

Women the world over experience economic and political inequality. Although the United States has made major strides during the past quarter century in achieving greater gender inequality, it is by no means the world's leader in this effort.

Economic Inequality

Worldwide, women now make up more than 40 percent of the world's paid workforce in all regions except northern Africa and western Asia (International Labor Organization [ILO] 2004a). Women around the world work in the lowest-wage jobs and are likely to make less than men doing similar work—although there is some evidence that the wage gap is slowly decreasing, at least in industrialized countries (ILO 1995). Because women work a second shift the world over, women also work longer hours than men in most countries. A recent United Nations report found that women in the United States worked on average 25 minutes each day more than men—a difference that was considerably smaller than that in Austria (45 minutes) or Italy (103 minutes). Because of persistent discrimination, higher unemployment, and lower wages, women represent 60 percent of the world's 550 million working poor (ILO 2004a).

Access to knowledge about birth control enables women to choose to exercise greater control over childbearing, so that many are able to work outside the home. Education also encourages women to seek financial independence from men. More women are getting college degrees and professional jobs than even before. Women make up about half of all college students in the economically developed countries of the industrial world and nearly half in Latin America, although in much of Africa and Asia, they are much less likely to go to college. Women's ability to achieve specialized education in science, engineering, business, and government has been limited, even with increased access to secondary and advanced education in much of the world.

Women remain in the poorest-paying industrial and service-sector jobs in all countries, and in the less industrialized nations, they are concentrated in the declining agricultural sector. The feminization of the global workforce has brought with it the increased exploitation of young, uneducated, largely rural women around the world. These women labor under conditions that are often unsafe and unhealthy, at low pay and with nonexistent job security.

Yet at the same time, even poor-paying factory jobs may enable some women to achieve a measure of economic independence and power. In China, for example, as many as forty to fifty million young women have left their home villages in search of factory jobs in large cities. Such "working sisters" earn and save more than their brothers, a fact that has raised their economic status in Chinese society, where women have traditionally been valued less than men. As one Chinese scholar explains, "A whole generation has learned that women have value and girls have choice. When they have a girl, they will feel differently toward her than their parents and grandparents did" (Farley 1998). There is some indication that women's changing economic role has changed their self-concept as well. More rural Chinese women are divorcing their husbands now that they can better afford to end unhappy marriages. And in a society where the oppressiveness of life as a woman contributes to one of the highest female suicide rates in the world, fewer women appear to be taking their own lives (Farley 1998; Rosenthal 1999).

The International Labor Organization (2004a) has found that, although the gap between the number of men and women in the labor force has been decreasing in all regions of the world since 1993, this decrease has varied widely. Women in the transition economies and East Asia—where the number of women working per one hundred men is ninety-one and eighty-three, respectively—have nearly closed the gap; but in other regions of the world, such as the Middle East, North Africa, and South Asia, only 40 percent of women work.

At the other end of the occupational spectrum, a recent study by the International Labor Organization concludes that women throughout the world still encounter a glass ceiling that restricts their movement into the top positions. Even though women have made progress in moving into managerial and professional positions, globally they still hold only 2 to 3 percent of the top corporate jobs, and those who do make it to the top typically earn less than men. In Japan, for example, women are especially likely to face barriers to upper-level positions: When college-educated Japanese women interview for managerial jobs, they are typically assigned to noncareer secretarial work. As many as 40 percent of Japanese companies hire no women college graduates for management-level positions (French 2001a). On the other hand, in Australia, Canada, Thailand, and the United States women own more than 30 percent of all businesses (ILO 2003a). Female participation in senior management has reached nearly 22 percent in the Netherlands, 21 percent in Canada, and over 36 percent in Hungary but remains low (13.6 percent) in the United States (ILO 2004b). In some developing countries, progress has been even greater: In Chile, for example, 27 percent of senior managers are women; in Singapore, 37 percent (ILO 1997, 2003a).

Women's share of professional jobs in 2002 was highest in eastern Europe and the former Soviet Union. Over 60 percent of professional jobs in Lithuania (70.2 percent), Latvia (67 percent), Estonia (66 per cent), Georgia (64.8 per cent), Ukraine (63.7 percent), Slovakia (63.1 percent), Poland (60.9 percent), and Moldova (60.3 percent) were held by women. The reason that these countries have a high proportion of women in professional jobs is due to long-standing policies supporting working mothers (ILO 2004b).

Political Inequality

Women play an increasing role in politics throughout the world. In Japan, for example, where women have traditionally faced significant barriers to achieving equality with men, five women were appointed to cabinet-level positions by Junichiro Koizumi, the reform-minded prime minister who took office in spring 2001—one in the key position of foreign minister (French 2001b). Yet of 188 countries that belong to the United Nations, only 9 are presently headed by women. Since World War II, 38 countries have been headed by women; the United States is not among them. Two countries—Monaco and Saudi Arabia—have never had a woman member of government (Worldwide Guide to Women in Leadership 2005).

As of 2005, women made up only 15.2 percent of the combined membership of the national legislatures throughout the world. Only in the Scandinavian countries of Sweden (45.3 percent), Finland (37.5 percent), Norway (38.2 percent), and Denmark (36.9 percent) do women make up a significant part of the parliament; in the Arab states, it is only 6.8 percent (Lopez-Claros and Zahidi 2005; United Nations Human Development Report [UNHDR] 2005a). It is interesting that Rwanda, which does not even receive a GEM (gender empowerment measure) rating (but rates very low on the UN's Human Development Index), ties with Sweden (45.3 percent) for the highest share of women in parliament (UNHDR 2005a). The U.S. Congress is 14.8 percent female, placing the United States 75th out of 168 countries for which data exist (UNHDR 2005a). Women are most likely to hold seats in national legislatures in countries in which women's rights are a strong cultural value. These are likely to be countries in which women have long had the right to vote and are well represented in the professions. They are also likely to be countries that have strong socialist parties that play a role in government (Kenworthy and Malami 1999).

The United Nations ranks countries according to a measure of "gender empowerment," which is based on such factors as seats in the national legislature held by women, female administrators and managers (as a percentage of total administrators and managers), female professional and technical workers (as a percentage of total professional and technical workers), and the ratio of women's to men's earned income. By this measure, the United States ranks twelfth—behind the Scandinavian and other northern European countries and Canada and New Zealand (Table 10.2).

Analyzing Gender Inequality

Sociologists have tried to explain why gender inequalities exist. One plausible explanation for gender inequality is relatively simple. Women give birth to and care for children. The helplessness of the human infant demands that such care be intensive and prolonged—hence the centrality of "mothering" to

TABLE 10.2

United Nations Gender Empowerment Rankings: The Top 12 Countries, 2005

RANK	COUNTRY	SEATS IN LEGISLATURE HELD BY WOMEN[a] (%)	FEMALE ADMINISTRATORS AND MANAGERS[b] (%)	FEMALE PROFESSIONAL AND TECHNICAL WORKERS[c] (%)
1	Norway	38.2	30	50
2	Denmark	36.9	26	51
3	Sweden	45.3	30	51
4	Iceland	30.2	29	55
5	Finland	37.5	28	53
6	Belgium	35.7	31	48
7	Australia	28.3[c]	36	55
8	Netherlands	34.2	26	48
9	Germany	31.3	36	50
10	Canada	24.7	35	54
11	Switzerland	24.8	28	45
12	United States	14.8	46	55

[a]Data are as of March 1, 2005. Where there are lower and upper houses, data refer to the weighted average of women's shares of seats in both houses.

[b]Data refer to the most recent year available during the period 1992–2003. Estimates for countries that have implemented the recent International Standard Classification of Occupations (ISCO-88) are not strictly comparable with those for countries using the previous classification (ISCO-68).

[c]The figure reflects the Senate composition until July 1, 2005.

SOURCE: UNHDR 2005.

women's experience (as emphasized by Chodorow; see Chapter 4). Because of their role as mothers, women are absorbed primarily in domestic activities. Women become what the French novelist and social critic Simone de Beauvoir (1974; orig. 1949) called "the second sex," because of their exclusion from the more public activities in which men are free to engage. Men are not dominant over women as a result of superior physical strength or any special intellectual powers but because before the development of birth control, women were at the mercy of their biological constitution. Constant childbirth and continuous caring for infants made them dependent on males for material provision (Firestone 1971; Mitchell 1975).

The prevailing division of labor between the sexes has led to men and women assuming unequal positions in terms of power, prestige, and wealth. Despite the advances that women have made in countries around the world, gender differences continue to serve as the basis for social inequalities. Investigating

and accounting for gender inequality has become a central concern of sociologists. Many theoretical perspectives have been advanced to explain men's enduring dominance over women—in the realm of economics, politics, the family, and elsewhere. In this section, we review the main theoretical approaches to explaining the nature of gender inequality at the level of society.

Functionalist Approaches

As we saw in Chapter 1, the functional approach sees society as a system of interlinked parts that, when in balance, operate smoothly to produce social solidarity. Thus functionalist and functionalist-inspired perspectives on gender seek to show that gender differences contribute to social stability and integration. Though such views once commanded great support, they have been heavily criticized for neglecting social tensions at the expense of consensus and for promulgating a conservative view of the social world.

Writers who subscribe to the natural differences school of thought tend to argue that the division of labor between men and women is biologically based. Women and men perform those tasks for which they are biologically best suited. Thus the anthropologist George Murdock (1949) saw it as both practical and convenient that women should concentrate on domestic and family responsibilities while men work outside the home. On the basis of a cross-cultural study of more than two hundred societies, Murdock concluded that the sexual division of labor is present in all cultures. Although this is not the result of biological programming, it is the most logical basis for the organization of society.

Talcott Parsons, a leading functionalist thinker, concerned himself with the role of the family in industrial societies (Parsons and Bales 1955). He was particularly interested in the socialization of children and believed that stable, supportive families are the key to successful socialization. In Parsons's view, the family operates most efficiently with a clear-cut sexual division of labor in which females act in *expressive* roles, providing care and security to children and offering them emotional support, and men perform *instrumental* roles—namely, being the breadwinner in the family. Because of the stressful nature of this role, women's expressive and nurturing tendencies should also be used to stabilize and comfort men. This complementary division of labor, springing from a biological distinction between the sexes, would ensure the solidarity of the family according to Parsons.

Another functionalist perspective on child rearing was advanced by John Bowlby (1953), who argued that the mother is crucial to the primary socialization of children. If the mother is absent or if a child is separated from the mother at a young age—a state referred to as *maternal deprivation*—the child runs a high risk of being inadequately socialized. This can lead to serious social and psychological difficulties later in life, including antisocial and psychopathic tendencies. Bowlby argued that a child's well-being and mental health can be best guaranteed through a close, personal and continuous relationship with his or her mother. He did concede that an absent mother can be replaced by a mother substitute, but suggested that such a substitute should also be a woman—leaving little doubt about his view that the mothering role is a distinctly female one. Bowlby's maternal deprivation thesis has been used by some to argue that working mothers are neglectful of their children.

Feminists have sharply criticized claims of a biological basis to the sexual division of labor, arguing that there is nothing natural or inevitable about the allocation of tasks in society. Women are not prevented from pursuing occupations on the basis of any biological features; rather humans are socialized into roles that are culturally expected of them.

There is a steady stream of evidence to suggest that the maternal deprivation thesis is questionable—studies have shown that children's educational performance and personal development are in fact enhanced when both parents are employed at least part of the time outside the home. Parsons's view on the "expressive" female has similarly been attacked by feminists and other sociologists who see his views as condoning the subordination of women in the home. There is no basis to the belief that the "expressive" female is necessary for the smooth operation of the family—rather it is a role that is promoted largely for the convenience of men.

In addition, cross-cultural studies show that even though most societies distinguish between men's and women's roles, the degree to which they differentiate tasks as exclusively male or female and assign different tasks and responsibilities to women and men can vary greatly (Coltrane 1992). The degree to which certain tasks can be shared between women and men, and even how open groups and societies are to women performing men's activities and roles, differs across cultures and across time. Finally, cultures and societies have assigned different values to women and men and differ in the degree to which men are seen as "naturally" dominant over women. Thus gender inequalities do not seem to be fixed or static. The division of labor based on gender and the devaluation of women relative to men have taken different forms and shapes throughout history.

Biological determinists see differences based on gender and gender inequalities as inevitable and unchangeable because they are consequences of biological necessities—not of social processes. Social constructionists disagree with biological determinists about where to find the sources of gender inequality and whether there is a potential for change: Sociological approaches look at society rather than at nature to explain why gender inequalities exist and how they can change. According to many sociologists, the key to understanding gender inequality is looking at a society's gendered division of labor and the value that society assigns to men's and women's roles (Baxter and Kane 1995; Chafetz 1997; Collins et al. 1993; Coltrane 1992; Dunn et al. 1993). It is also important to recognize that gender inequality is also tied to issues of race and class (Collins 1990).

Feminist Approaches

The feminist movement has given rise to a large body of **feminist theory** which attempts to explain gender inequalities and set forth agenda for overcoming those inequalities. Feminist theories in relation to gender inequality contrast markedly with one another. Feminist writers are all concerned with women's unequal position in society, but their explanations for it vary substantially. Competing schools of feminism have sought to explain gender inequalities through a variety of deeply embedded social processes, such as sexism, patriarchy, capitalism, and racism. In the following sections, we look at the arguments behind four main feminist perspectives—liberal, radical, black, and postmodern feminism.

LIBERAL FEMINISM

Liberal feminism looks for explanations of gender inequalities in social and cultural attitudes. Unlike radical feminists, liberal feminists do not see women's subordination as part of a larger system or structure. Instead, they draw attention to many separate factors that contribute to inequalities between men and women. For example, liberal feminists are concerned with sexism and discrimination against women in the workplace, educational institutions, and the media. They tend to focus their energies on establishing and protecting equal opportunities for women through legislation and other democratic means. Legal advances such as the Equal Pay Act and the Sex Discrimination Act were actively supported by liberal feminists, who argued that enshrining equality in law is important to eliminating discrimination against women. Liberal feminists seek to work through the existing system to bring about reforms in a gradual way. In this respect, they are more moderate in their aims and methods than radical feminists, who call for an overthrow of the existing system.

While liberal feminists have contributed greatly to the advancement of women over the past century, critics charge that they are unsuccessful in dealing with the root cause of gender inequality and do not acknowledge the systemic nature of women's oppression in society. They say that by focusing on the independent deprivations that women suffer—sexism, discrimination, the glass ceiling, unequal pay—liberal feminists draw only a partial picture of gender inequality. Radical feminists accuse liberal feminists of encouraging women to accept an unequal society and its competitive character.

RADICAL FEMINISM

At the heart of **radical feminism** is the belief that men are responsible for and benefit from the exploitation of women. The analysis of patriarchy—the systematic domination of females by males—is of central concern to this branch of feminism. Patriarchy is viewed as a universal phenomenon that has existed across time and cultures. Radical feminists often concentrate on the family as one of the primary sources of women's oppression in society. They argue that men exploit women by relying on the free domestic labor that women provide in the home and that as a group, men also deny women access to positions of power and influence in society.

Radical feminists differ in their interpretations of the basis of patriarchy, but most agree that it involves the appropriation of women's bodies and sexuality in some form. Shulamith Firestone (1971), an early radical feminist writer, argues that men control women's roles in reproduction and child rearing. Because women are biologically able to give birth to children, they become dependent materially on men for protection and livelihood. This "biological inequality" is socially organized in the nuclear family. Firestone speaks of a "sex class" to describe women's social position and argues that women can be emancipated only through the abolition of the family and the power relations that characterize it.

Other radical feminists point to male violence against women as central to male supremacy. According to such a view, domestic violence, rape, and sexual harassment are all part of the systematic oppression of women, rather than isolated cases with their own psychological or criminal roots. Even interactions in daily life—such as nonverbal communication, patterns of listening and interrupting, and women's sense of comfort in public—contribute to gender inequality. Moreover, the argument goes, popular conceptions of beauty and sexuality are imposed by men on women to produce a certain type of femininity. For example, social and cultural norms emphasizing a slim body and a caring, nurturing attitude toward men help perpetuate women's subordination. The objectification of women through the media, fashion, and advertising turns women into sexual objects whose main role is to please and entertain men.

Radical feminists do not believe that women can be liberated from sexual oppression through reforms or gradual change. Because patriarchy is a systemic phenomenon, they argue, gender equality can be attained only by overthrowing the patriarchal order.

The use of patriarchy as a concept for explaining gender inequality has been popular with many feminist theorists. In asserting that "the personal is political," radical feminists have drawn widespread attention to the many linked dimensions of women's oppression. Their emphasis on male violence and the objectification of women has brought these issues into the heart of mainstream debates about women's subordination.

Many objections can be raised, however, to radical feminist views. The main one, perhaps, is that the concept of patriarchy as it has been used is inadequate as a general explanation for women's oppression. Radical feminists have tended to claim that patriarchy has existed throughout history and across cultures—that it is a universal phenomenon. Critics argue, however, that such a conception of patriarchy does not leave room for historical or cultural variations. It also ignores the important influence that race, class, or ethnicity may have on the nature of women's subordination. In other words, it is not possible to see patriarchy as a universal phenomenon; doing so risks *biological reductionism*—attributing all the complexities of gender inequality to a simple distinction between men and women.

BLACK FEMINISM

Do the versions of feminism just outlined apply equally to the experiences of both white and nonwhite women? Many black feminists and feminists from developing countries claim they do not. They argue that ethnic divisions among women are not considered by the main feminist schools of thought, which are oriented to the dilemmas of white, predominantly middle-class women living in industrialized societies. It is not valid, they claim, to generalize theories about women's subordination as a whole from the experience of a specific group of women. Moreover, the very idea that there is a unified form of gender oppression that is experienced equally by all women is problematic.

Dissatisfaction with existing forms of feminism has led to the emergence of a **black feminism,** which concentrates on the particular problems facing black women. In the foreword to her personal memoirs, the African American feminist Bell Hooks (1996) argues:

> Many feminist thinkers writing and talking about girlhood right now like to suggest that black girls have better self-esteem than their white counterparts. The measurement of this difference is often that black girls are more assertive, speak more, appear more confident. Yet in traditional southern-based black life, it was and is expected of girls to be articulate, to hold ourselves with dignity.

Surrounded by minority women at the Houston Civic Center, Coretta Scott King speaks about the resolution on minority women's rights that won the support of the National Women's Conference in 1977. The minority resolution, proposed by representatives of many races, declared that minority women suffered discrimination based on both race and sex.

Our parents and teachers were always urging us to stand up right and speak clearly. These traits were meant to uplift the race. They were not necessarily traits associated with building female self-esteem. An outspoken girl might still feel that she was worthless because her skin was not light enough or her hair wasn't the right texture. These are the variables that white researchers often do not consider when they measure the self-esteem of black females with a yardstick that was designed based on values emerging from white experience.

Black feminist writings tend to emphasize history—aspects of the past that inform the current problems facing black women. The writings of African American feminists emphasize the influence of the powerful legacy of slavery, segregation, and the civil rights movement on gender inequalities in the black community. They point out that early black suffragettes supported the campaign for women's rights but realized that the question of race could not be ignored: Black women were discriminated against on the basis of their race *and* gender. In recent years, black women have not been central to the women's liberation movement in part because "womanhood" dominated their identities much less than concepts of race did.

Hooks has argued that explanatory frameworks favored by white feminists—for example, the view of the family as a mainstay of patriarchy—may not be applicable in black communities, where the family represents a main point of solidarity against racism. In other words, the oppression of black women may be found in different locations from that of white women.

Black feminists contend, therefore, that any theory of gender equality that does not take racism into account cannot be expected to explain black women's oppression adequately. Class dimensions are another factor that cannot be neglected in the case of many black women. Some black feminists have held that the strength of black feminist theory is its focus on the interplay among race, class, and gender concerns. Black women are multiply disadvantaged, they argue, on the basis of their color, their sex, *and* their class position. When these three factors interact, they reinforce and intensify each other (Brewer 1993).

POSTMODERN FEMINISM

Like black feminism, **postmodern feminism** challenges the idea that there is a unitary basis of identity and experience shared by all women. (Postmodern approaches in sociology were introduced in Chapter 1, and it may be helpful to review that section.) This strand of feminism draws on the cultural phenomenon of postmodernism in the arts, architecture, philosophy, and economics. Some of the roots of postmodern feminism are found in the work of continental theorists such as Derrida (1978, 1981), Lacan (1995), and de Beauvoir (1949). Postmodern feminists reject the claim that there is a grand theory that can explain the position of women in society or that there is any single, universal essence or category of "woman." Consequently, these feminists reject the accounts given by others to explain gender inequality—such as patriarchy, race, or class—as "essentialist" (Beasley 1999).

Instead, postmodernism encourages the acceptance of many different standpoints as equally valid. Rather than there existing an essential core to womanhood, there are many individuals and groups, all of whom have very different experiences (heterosexuals, lesbians, black women, working-class women, and so on). The "otherness" of different groups and individuals is celebrated in all its diverse forms. Emphasis on the positive side of otherness is a major theme in postmodern feminism and symbolizes plurality, diversity, difference, and openness: There are many truths, roles, and constructions of reality. Hence the recognition of difference (of sexuality, age, and race, for example) is central to postmodern feminism.

As well as the recognition of differences among groups and individuals, postmodern feminists have stressed the importance of deconstruction. In particular, they have sought to deconstruct male language and a masculine view of the world. In its place, postmodern feminists have attempted to create fluid, open terms and language that more closely reflect women's experiences. For many postmodern feminists, men see the world in terms of pairs or binary distinctions (good versus bad, right versus wrong, beautiful versus ugly). Men, they argue, have cast the male as normal, and female as a deviation from it. The founder of modern psychiatry, Sigmund Freud, for example, saw women as men who lacked a penis and argued that they envied males for possessing one. In this masculine worldview, the female is always cast in the role as the "other." Deconstruction involves attacking binary concepts and recasting their opposites in a new and positive manner.

Postmodern feminism is said to have the most difficult relationship with the previous strands of feminism discussed earlier (Carrington 1994, 1998). This is largely because of its belief that many feminists may be misconceived in assuming that it is possible to provide overarching explanations for women's oppression and to find steps toward its resolution.

Using Sociology to Understand Andrea's Life

We have reviewed how sociologists analyze gender inequality, but let us think about how these ideas might help us illuminate the life of Andrea Ellington, whom we met at the beginning of the chapter. Andrea, a young black woman working the night shift as a word processor at an elite law firm, grew up in a poor neighborhood on the South Side of Chicago and today has three children to raise on her own.

To Andrea and women in similar life circumstances, the difficult conditions in which they find themselves may seem natural because of their sex. In other words, people may think it is natural for Andrea to be responsible for her children or to work as a word processor because she is a woman. Others might be inclined to consider whether her life circumstances are all her own doing, the result of bad personal choices regarding childbearing and the decision not to be married. Part of the job of someone who thinks like a sociologist is to ask whether such explanations are convincing given what is known about gender inequality.

In conducting the exercise of thinking about Andrea's life, we also have a chance to employ one of the key insights of contemporary feminist theory in sociology: that gender does not operate by itself but comes together with race and class. This "coming together" is known as the intersection of gender, race, and class.

ANDREA'S JOB

The forms of gender inequality in the workplace, as discussed earlier, show that Andrea's experience as a clerical worker in the law firm is typical for women. Jobs for women have been created primarily in the service sector of the economy. Today, word processing and secretarial work are predominantly women's occupations, with the characteristics of lower pay, a high degree of sex segregation, and few possibilities for promotion. Typical of jobs that have been created since the 1970s, Andrea's job has nonstandard working hours—she works the night shift.

Although nothing about the biological differences between the sexes would lead more women than men to work as word processors, societal forces tend to encourage women to aspire to such jobs. To begin with, many business colleges in Chicago advertise their secretarial programs with photographs of women, and many firms would rather hire women for their secretarial and word processing positions. Such positions have traditionally been, after all, jobs that service the clerical needs of the upper class of workers, many of whom are still men. An analysis of gender inequality would look closely at the way that people learn roles associated with gender—both the word processors and the people who do the hiring at firms. But it would also look at how those perceptions of difference become part of the structure of the organization, thereby reinforcing even more inequality.

Andrea's problems as a low-wage worker are those of many other persons similarly situated. Women are usually found at the lower end of the job ladder. One reason is that unlike jobs in

Andrea's Dream

When journalists and sociologists seek to understand race relations, they seldom look closely at highly organized business offices. In trying to account for the disaffection, resistance and rebellious stances of the black poor, they think about the significance of Malcolm X caps, gangsta rap songs and the videotapes of Rodney King's struggles to rise from the pavement. When they want to understand urban poverty, they gravitate toward housing projects and street corners, carryouts and pool halls, and the vast arrays of institutions that comprise ghettos themselves.

Such an exclusive focus overlooks another less sensational story. During the [past few decades], while manufacturing declined, there was a rise in the financial and service sectors. A vast number of Chicago adults like Andrea Ellington participate in the larger society mainly through their work in the labor market that supports law firms, accounting firms and other high-level services.

Though in the past Andrea Ellington had worked overtime at [her law firm] when she needed extra money, recently there hadn't been much extra work in the Network Center, and the supervisor was allocating overtime more carefully. When Andrea could no longer get overtime assignments, she requested a number of cash advances from the personnel director at [the firm] so she could pay her bills on time. Then she wrote a memo to her supervisor, who worked the day shift, asking for more overtime:

"I don't know if the personnel director has brought this to your attention but in the past few weeks I have been requesting cash advances. The reasons are very personal but I did go over a few with him as to why I had been requesting the cash advances. He mentioned to me last Friday that he sympathizes with my situation but he also made very good and valuable sense that the firm is not a bank and should not be responsible for my management of money.

"One of the reasons I started requesting cash advances is because the Center no longer had overtime available because of budget reasons. I understand this, but I also recall you say-

ing that if anyone wants to work overtime he or she should come directly to you. Well, I really depended on the overtime that was available and if there is in any way possible that I can get overtime I would appreciate it greatly. . . . I want to apologize for any inconvenience that I have put upon the firm and especially toward the personnel director. My intent was not to abuse the privilege of cash advances. Please give me a call at home or respond with a memo so that maybe we can discuss this issue further."

The supervisor looked upon Andrea's letter as an act of "incredible conscientiousness." As she put it, "It seemed that she wanted to make sure she didn't overstep her bounds, yet she was coming to us with a problem and trying to solve it in a practical way. I felt that we had to try."

Later that day, the supervisor assigned Andrea to work an extra eight hours of overtime per week, on Sunday. Andrea came to work for the first two Sundays, and then began missing her weekend assignments when she couldn't find a baby-sitter for Lauren, Cubie, and Corey, her three children. When her supervisor learned of her absences, she canceled the overtime.

Andrea wrote again in response to that decision:

"This memo is in regards to the cancellation of overtime hours regarding the litigation project. I really counted on the overtime tremendously and it has been a big help in ways you can't imagine. I know my financial situation is not a priority or a concern of the firm's, but I really need to work the extra hours to get by for an everyday living. . . .

"This overtime has help me pay bills on time, buy cloths [*sic*] for my children, and buy food that I would normally have had to wait until each pay check to get. If the decision was made due to budget reasons by the firm then I have no choice but to try to do the best with what I have, but if you have any information on anyone looking for part-time help or know any agencies that hire for part-time, please inform me as soon as possible on anything you might know of." . . .

[Andrea is again given overtime, and again misses it because she cannot find reliable child care. She goes to see her supervisor.]

"Well, you cut out my overtime. I really need that overtime."

"I'm very sorry, Andrea," the supervisor responded.

"Maybe I can just come in an hour instead of the four hours I was coming in or whatever."

"No."

"Because it was really helping me out there."

The supervisor didn't know what to say. She looked up stonily from her desk.

Andrea says it took everything in her power not to break down and cry. "You know, I just don't make much money for what I do. I know I'm the lowest paid person in the Network Center."

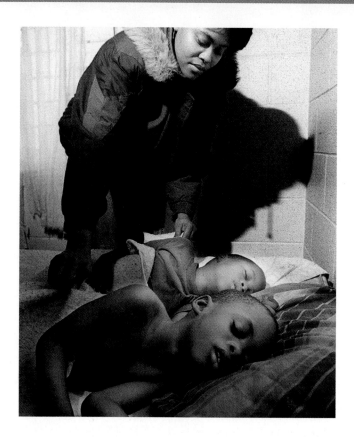

"How do you know?" the supervisor asked.

"That does not matter," Andrea answered. "I just need the money. Because I'm really not making what I should be making in the first place. So at least allow me to have the overtime."

"You're making a decent living," her supervisor said.

There was silence.

Andrea went on. "I might be a paycheck away from being homeless. Thank you."

SOURCE: Mitchell Duneier, "Andrea's Dream: A Single Parent's Fight for Independence," series, *Chicago Tribune*, December 1994, pp. 3–4, 13–15.

Questions

- Andrea belongs to several historically disadvantaged sociological groups: women, single mothers, African Americans, and the poor. In what ways might her problems at work and at home relate to her membership in these groups?
- Andrea is trying to raise a family and to keep her job. How and why do these two goals seem to contradict each other?

The International Women's Movement

Do you have any interest in joining the women's movement? Every year countless American college students are inspired by feminism and enlist in the fight for such causes as reproductive rights, equal pay, or the preservation of welfare benefits for poor women. In today's increasingly globalized world, there is a good chance that those who become active in the U.S. women's movement will come into contact with women pursuing other feminist struggles overseas.

The women's movement, of course, is not simply an American or western European phenomenon. In China, for example, women are working to secure "equal rights, employment, women's role in production, and women's participation in politics" (Zhang and Xu 1995). In South Africa, women played a pivotal role in the battle against apartheid and are fighting in the postapartheid era to improve "the material conditions of the oppressed majority; those who have been denied access to education, decent homes, health facilities, and jobs" (Kemp et al. 1995). In Peru, activists have been working for decades to give women a greater "opportunity to participate in public life" (Blondet 1995), while "in Russia, women's protest was responsible for blocking the passage of legislation that the Russian parliament

considered in 1992 that encouraged women to stay home and perform 'socially necessary labor'" (Basu 1995).

Although participants in women's movements have, for many years, cultivated ties to activists in other countries, the number and importance of such contacts has increased with

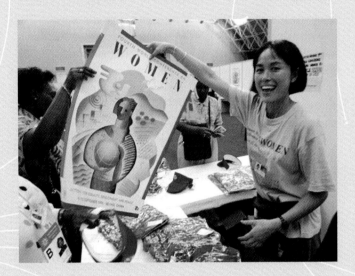

male-dominated areas, women's occupations tend to be dead-end jobs with fewer possibilities for promotion. Andrea's position on the lower end of the pay scale may be due to her age and her lower level of experience in the job, which would be equivalent to that of a poor, similarly undereducated white woman her age. However, another barrier she encounters is the result of her race. Within occupations dominated by women there can also be hierarchies according to class and/or race (Brewer 1993; Collins 1990). Thus someone studying gender inequality might look at the intersection of race, class, and gender to ask whether white women working as support staff at many law firms tend to have better-paying secretarial jobs, while black women might have word-processing positions with lower pay—a plausible possibility given the circumstances at the firm where Andrea works.

Finally, we need to examine broad global economic trends. We need to look at what kinds of jobs women can get in the present economy, which is influenced by processes of global-

ization and economic restructuring. Thus the mere integration of women into the labor market does not necessarily mean more gender equality in general. Differences based on class and race among women have increased because of specific economic processes (Brewer 1993).

ANDREA'S FAMILY

Contemporary political debates on welfare in the United States have heavily focused on marriage as the solution to the financial problems Andrea faces. The idea behind these political discussions is that if black single mothers would only get married, they would not be poor and would not need public assistance in the form of housing and health care.

It is further argued that women like Andrea must bear personal responsibility for having children out of wedlock.

A sociological analysis could begin by accepting the assumption that Andrea bears some personal responsibility for globalization. A prime forum for the establishment of cross-national contacts has been the United Nation's Conference on Women, held four times since 1975. Approximately thirty-five thousand people—of which more than two thirds were women—attended the most recent conference, held in Beijing, China, in 1995. Delegates from 180 nations were in attendance, along with representatives from thousands of nongovernmental organizations (*UN Chronicle* 1995). Seeking ways to "ensure women's equal access to economic resources including land, credit, science and technology, vocational training, information, communication and markets," conference participants spent ten days listening to presentations on the state of women worldwide, debating ways to improve their condition, and building professional and personal ties to one another. Mallika Dutt (1996), one of the attendees, wrote in the journal *Feminist Studies* that "for most women from the United States, Beijing was an eye-opening, humbling, and transformative experience. U.S. women were startled by the sophisticated analysis and well-organized and powerful voices of women from other parts of the world." At the same time, according to Dutt, many of the conference participants left Beijing with a "sense of global solidarity, pride, and affirmation."

The Platform for Action finally agreed to by the conference participants called on the countries of the world to address such issues as:

- The persistent and increasing burden of poverty on women
- Violence against women
- The effects of armed or other kinds of conflict on women
- Inequality between men and women in the sharing of power and decision making
- Stereotyping of women
- Gender inequalities in the management of natural resources
- Persistent discrimination against and violation of the rights of the girl child

Must women's movements have an international orientation to be effective? Are women's interests essentially the same throughout the world? What might feminism mean to women in the developing world? These and many other questions are being hotly debated as the process of globalization continues apace.

having children out of wedlock, while also trying to understand the societal conditions that lead so many poor women to make that choice. Here we can see again that there is a link between race, class, and gender. Studies of urban labor markets (Wilson 1987) have demonstrated that the loss of jobs for poor black men in the inner city has made marriage less attractive to many black women. Why, the reasoning goes, should women get married to men who don't have jobs? This increases women's independence from men to some degree, so that women do not necessarily have to marry the fathers of their children (Huber 1992).

In addition to the effect of this societal force on women like Andrea, there is likely also the influence of social norms. When many other women are influenced by the same structural barriers to meeting men with jobs, it comes to seem quite logical to those women to have children on their own. In these circumstances, we can begin to comprehend how women like Andrea make the choice to have children out of wedlock. The loss

of jobs that might make self-support for black men possible also makes it more difficult for them to fulfill their obligations to provide child support. One reason Andrea does not have enough money to pay her bills and to attain her dream to move out of the housing project she lives in is that she has not received enough money from the father of her children.

ANDREA'S CHALLENGES IN COMBINING WORK AND FAMILY

The most prominent example of how gender inequalities in the workplace are intertwined with inequalities arising from women's roles as mothers is seen in Andrea's negotiations with her employer about overtime.

Because Andrea did not earn enough money from her low-paying job, she asked her boss if she could work extra hours. When the boss scheduled these extra projects on a Sunday, Andrea was unable to find reliable child care. Because she missed work on several occasions, the boss canceled the extra projects. Subsequently, this boss assumed that Andrea wasn't able to work overtime and, therefore, refused to offer her extra projects. This, in turn, had an effect on how Andrea felt about her job, a process that lowers occupational aspirations (Huber 1990).

It is quite understandable how a reasonable employer would draw such a conclusion about Andrea. Yet a sociological approach would ask whether these incidents are due to a problem with Andrea or with the system of child care. If the system were different, is it possible that women like Andrea would appear much more responsible?

Someone aware of gender inequality would look at the way the gender division of labor in our society places the burden of child raising on mothers. In the United States, child care is not a public responsibility, nor is it seen as the responsibility of the employer. Andrea's boss feels that it is Andrea's task to find child care, even on a Sunday. And yet, because the wages of her job are low, she needs that overtime to earn enough money to support her children and to move out of the housing project.

The ways in which societies organize the care of children, elderly, and disabled people profoundly shape gender relations. For example, if there is little public support for child care, then parents have to find caregivers for their children when they are working outside the home. Moreover, in societies that view child care primarily as the task of women, yet attach little value to this task, mothers in the workplace are disadvantaged. In contrast, if society valued taking care of children as an important contribution for future generations, Andrea might get financial support for taking care of her children herself; or, if taking care of children was not a low-paying job but was supported by employers and government, Andrea might find a good-quality child-care center open on a Sunday.

Andrea's mother usually takes care of Andrea's daughter. We can see how child care can be informally organized across generations of women. Research on African American communities demonstrates that black women used to be tied into kinships, neighborhoods, and other networks of women who shared child raising responsibilities. But these structures of shared motherhood have been crumbling (Brewer 1993; Collins 1990; Glenn 1994).

Why Gender Inequality Matters

A Chinese saying holds that "women hold up half the sky." In fact, as we have seen in this chapter, women typically hold up far more than half: In the twenty-first century, women have become a central part of the world's paid workforce while, at the same time, maintaining their traditional responsibilities for home and family.

China was the site of the 1995 United Nations' Fourth World Conference on Women, where some thirty-five thousand people, representing 180 governments and seven thousand women's organizations, discussed the problems of women worldwide. The conference, held in Beijing, grappled with a central problem women face the world over: What happens when a country's traditional cultural beliefs conflict with modern notions of women's rights? Globalization not only has brought factories and television to nearly every place on the planet but has also exposed people throughout the world to ideas about equality and democracy. The modern women's movement has become a global champion of universal rights for women.

The Beijing women's conference's final action platform was clear: When cultural traditions conflict with women's rights, women's rights should take precedence. The platform called for women's right to control their own reproduction and sexuality as well as to inherit wealth and property—two rights that women are denied in many countries. It concluded that no society can truly hope to better the lives of its citizens until it fosters gender equality:

> The advancement of women and the achievement of equality between women and men are a matter of human rights and a condition for social justice and should not be seen in isolation as a women's issue. They are the only way to build a sustainable, just and developed society. Empowerment of women and equality between women and men are prerequisites for achieving political, social, economic, cultural and environmental security among all peoples. (Beijing Women's Conference 1995)

Five years after the Beijing conference, a special session of the United Nations General Assembly reaffirmed these principles, challenging the world's governments to realize the conference's goals. Noting that women occupied only 13 percent of parliament seats worldwide, the UN called for a global increase in women's political power. The Women's Environment and Development Organization, A New York–based women's advocacy group, was more specific in its statement to the UN: It pushed for equal representation of women in cabinet ministries and legislative bodies by 2005. The goal was set not only to benefit women but to benefit society as a whole. In the view of the organization's executive director, increased women's representation would help shift a country's policies to real-life concerns, as is seen in Scandinavia, where women are well represented in all levels of government: "Their commitment to the social safety net, to [an] expansive childcare system, to helping women and men balance work and family needs, I think, reflects women's experiences" (Hogan 2000). Clearly that goal has not been met. Had it been, the UN Human Development Report (2005b) notes, there would be "14 million more girls in primary school today, 6 million of them in India and Pakistan and another 4 million in Sub-Saharan Africa. Trend projections are not encouraging. By 2015 the shortfall from the gender parity target will be equivalent to 6 million girls out of school, the majority of them in Sub-Saharan Africa."

The feminization of labor has altered the world economy. Will the feminization of politics do the same for global governance? The shift to a greater role for women in economics and politics may well signal a shift to greater equality for all people —not only for women but also for minority people, including sexual minorities—the world over.

Study Outline

www.wwnorton.com/giddens

Gender Differences: Nature versus Nurture

- *Sex* in the sense of physical difference is distinct from *gender* (masculine and feminine), which concerns cultural and psychological differences. It is no simple matter to determine which observable differences are due to biology (sex) and which are socially constructed (gender). Arguments from animal behavior are usually ambiguous. Some researchers claim, for instance, that hormones explain such differences as greater male aggressiveness, but it may just as easily be the case that aggressive behavior causes changes in hormone levels. Studies of gender differences from a variety of human societies have shown no conclusive evidence that gender is biologically determined; rather biological differences seem to provide a means of marking or differentiating social roles.
- Studies of parent–infant interactions reveal that boys and girls are treated differently right from birth; the same features and behaviors are interpreted as either masculine or feminine, depending on the parents' expectations.

Forms of Gender Inequality

- *Patriarchy* refers to male dominance over women. There are few known societies that are not patriarchal, although the degree and character of inequalities between the sexes varies considerably across cultures. In the United States, women have made considerable progress yet are still unequal in many ways.
- Women's participation in the paid labor force has risen steadily, especially married women's and especially in expanding areas of the economy. Many women, however, are poorly paid and have dim career prospects. Even women who are successful in the corporate world face discrimination in the form of deeply held cultural expectations about the proper role of women in society.
- The increasing number of women in the labor force has had a big effect on family responsibilities like child care and housework. Though men are contributing more to these responsibilities, women still shoulder the bulk of the work. For working women, these household obligations constitute a second shift.
- The ways schools are organized and how classes are taught have tended to sustain *gender inequalities*. Rules specifying distinct dress for girls and boys encourages sex typing, as do the texts containing established gender images. There is evidence that teachers treat girls and boys differently, and there is a long history of specialized subjects for separate sexes.

Violence against Women

- Violence perpetrated by men against women is found in many societies—in the form of spousal abuse, rape, and sexual harassment, for example. The most common manifestation of violence against women is *rape*, which is the forcing of nonconsensual intercourse. Some scholars argue that women are often the targets of sexual violence because men are socialized to see women as sex objects and to feel a sense of sexual entitlement to women.

Gender Inequality throughout the World

- Women throughout the world work in the lowest-wage jobs and are likely to make less than men doing similar work—although there is some evidence that the wage gap is decreasing slowly, at least in industrialized countries. In developing countries, women are likely to experience exploitative job conditions. Yet at the same time, their enhanced economic role has sometimes resulted in increased economic independence and greater social status.
- Worldwide, women do not share the same political power as men, although thirty-eight countries have been headed by a woman since World War II. The United States is about average among countries in terms of women's representation in the national legislature, but has never had a woman president.
- *Gender* is one of the most important dimensions of inequality, although it was neglected in the study of stratification for a long time. Although there are few societies in which women have more wealth and status than men, there are significant variations in how women's and men's roles are valued within a society. Sociologists have argued that gender inequalities are not fixed. They have also

drawn attention to the links between gender inequality and race and class.

Theories of Gender Inequality

- In explaining gender inequality, functionalists have emphasized that gender differences and the sexual division of labor contribute to social stability and integration. Feminist approaches reject the idea that gender inequality is somehow natural. Liberal feminists have explained gender inequality in terms of social and cultural attitudes, such as sexism and discrimination. Radical feminists argue that men are responsible for the exploitation of women through patriarchy—the systematic domination of females by males. Black feminists have seen factors such as class and ethnicity, in addition to gender, as essential for understanding the oppression experienced by nonwhite women.

Key Concepts

black feminism (p. 318)
comparable worth (p. 305)
feminist theory (p. 316)
gender (p. 292)
gender inequality (p. 300)
gender socialization (p. 293)
gender typing (p. 301)
glass ceiling (p. 306)
glass escalator (p. 306)
human capital theory (p. 303)
liberal feminism (p. 317)
patriarchy (p. 300)
postmodern feminism (p. 318)
radical feminism (p. 317)
rape (p. 311)
sex (p. 292)
sexual harassment (p. 306)
social construction of gender (p. 295)

Review Questions

1. What's the difference between sex and gender?
   a. Sex refers to the physical differences in the body, whereas gender concerns the psychological, social, and cultural differences between males and females.
   b. Sex is what couples do to conceive, whereas gender is an attribute of their baby.
   c. A culture's understanding of gender determines what types of physical intimacy constitute sex.
   d. There is none. In sociology, as in everyday life, the terms are interchangeable.

2. What is the glass ceiling?
   a. It is the old-boy network in firms that helps men get ahead by making clear what management expects. Men can see through the glass ceiling but women cannot.
   b. It is an invisible barrier that prevents women from achieving the highest positions in a firm, usually because they do not have the sponsorship of a senior manager.
   c. It refers to the earnings gap between white women and women of color.
   d. It is an invisible barrier that prevents women from being hired in the first place because managers expect most women to leave the firm sooner or later to have a family.

3. What is patriarchy?
   a. The name given to societies in which property is passed down by the male lineage.
   b. The name given to societies in which Eastern Orthodoxy is the main religion.
   c. The name given to societies in which women are treated as property.
   d. The name given to male dominance in a society.

4. Which of the following passages best describes women's movement into the labor force?
   a. From 1940 until the middle to late 1960s, women's participation in the labor force was led by older women, past their childbearing years. From that point on, as women's educational achievements began to catch up with men's, labor force participation spread to younger women.
   b. From 1940 until the mid-1960s, women's participation in the labor force was led by men who wanted their wives to contribute to their household finances. From that point on, as women's educational achievements began to catch up with men's, labor force participation spread to young, unmarried women.
   c. From 1940 until the middle to late 1960s, women's participation in the labor force was led by younger women who were more willing to confront traditional conceptions of women's role in the home. From that point on, as the hold of traditional conceptions weakened, older women followed their younger sisters into the labor force.
   d. None of the above.

5. What is the second shift?
   a. The first shift was women's movement into the workforce. The second shift is women's movement into the professions.
   b. The first shift was the movement into the workforce of older women with grown-up children. The second shift was the movement into the workforce of younger women with small children.
   c. The first shift is overcoming traditional male conceptions that a woman's natural role is in the home. The second shift is overcoming male reluctance to treat women as equals in the workplace.

d. The first shift is a woman's day at work. The second shift is the extra responsibility she bears for housework when she gets home.

6. In which country has the women's movement played an important role in improving women's status?
   a. China
   b. Peru
   c. South Africa
   d. All of the above.

7. What does it mean for men and women to "do gender"?
   a. To do gender means to follow traditional conceptions of the responsibilities of men and women in everyday life and to reinforce the idea that gender is a natural means for society to differentiate itself.
   b. To do gender means to challenge traditional conceptions of the responsibilities of men and women in everyday life and to attack the idea that gender is a natural means for society to differentiate itself.
   c. To do gender means to take the traditional role of the opposite gender (men acting as women and women as men).
   d. To do gender refers to the process by which children learn about traditional conceptions of gender roles.

8. Paludi and Barickman found that most women who were abused by behavior that fits legal definitions of sexual harassment
   a. filed legal complaints.
   b. did not label what had happened to them as sexual harassment.
   c. filed legal complaints but withdrew their cases.
   d. got compensation from their offenders.

9. Most schoolteachers are women. In classroom discussions,
   a. female teachers are more likely to solicit information from boys than from girls.
   b. female teachers are more likely to solicit information from girls than from boys.
   c. female teachers are no more likely to solicit information from boys than from girls.
   d. this has not been studied.

10. According to Firestone and Mitchell, before the development of birth control, why were men dominant over women?
    a. Men have superior physical strength.
    b. Men controlled women's fertility.
    c. Women depended on men for material provision due to constant childbirth and continuous caring for infants.
    d. All of the above.

Thinking Sociologically Exercises

1. What does cross-cultural evidence from tribal societies in New Guinea, Africa, and North America suggest about the differences in gender roles? Explain.
2. Why are minority women likely to think very differently about gender inequality than white women? Explain.

Data Exercises

www.wwnorton.com/giddens
Keyword: Data10

While women in the United States still have a way to go before they can claim full equality, women in many other nations continue to face extreme disadvantages relative to men. Completing the data exercise for Chapter 10, you will learn more about women's lives in other countries and make global comparisons about women's social status.

Sharon Dawkins (*far right*) is pictured with her daughters Aisha, Tanika, Rhea, and Imani (on her lap). She has been married to their father, a Jamaican-British man, for more than twenty years. She has participated in a longitudinal ethnography conducted by France Winddance Twine. Photograph by Michael Smyth.

Race and Ethnicity: Key Concepts

Learn the cultural bases of race and ethnicity and how racial and ethnic differences create sharp divisions. Learn the leading psychological theories and sociological interpretations of prejudice and discrimination.

Ethnic Relations

Recognize the importance of the historical roots, particularly in the expansion of Western colonialism, of ethnic conflict. Understand the different models for a multiethnic society.

Global Migration

Understand global migration patterns and their effects.

Ethnic Relations in the United States

Familiarize yourself with the history and social dimensions of ethnic relations in America.

Racial and Ethnic Inequality

Learn the forms of inequality experienced by different racial and ethnic groups in the United States. See that the history of prejudice and discrimination against ethnic minorities has created conditions of hardship for many but that some have succeeded despite societal barriers.

CHAPTER ELEVEN

ETHNICITY AND RACE

maureen, a forty-five-year-old black woman who was born in the Caribbean, came to England at the age of twelve with her family. She is the social services manager for Home Care in Leicester, a city located ninety miles north of London in the East Midlands. She has three brothers and ten nieces and nephews. All of her brothers have established families with white English women. She describes six of her nieces and nephews as "dual heritage." Yet she also believes that these children of multiracial heritage will be classified as "black" by those outside the family. Here she sums her view of one of her white sisters-in-law whom she respects: "I feel—she very much wants the child to have a black identity. So, every Sunday she would bring [my niece] up to my mum's house so that she knows her black family. If you say 'Do this for her hair,' she'd be religiously doing it. And she's asked for advice about her hair. And you'd see her plaiting it. And her hair is always so pretty." Maureen and her other black Caribbean family members consider her niece to be "racially" black although she has a white birth mother. They recognize that in spite of having a white mother, this girl will be classified as black because of her physical appearance, and thus she should be trained to identify herself as a black. The labor required of Maureen's white sister-in-law demonstrates how "race," like ethnicity, is learned. They are "socially constructed."

In 1991, according to the U.K. census 50 percent of U.K.-born black men had selected a white partner (Modood et al. 1997). Sociologist France Winddance Twine found in her research among black–white multiracial families in the United States and the United Kingdom that some parents train their children to develop what she terms **"racial literacy"** skills to help them cope with racial hierarchies and to integrate multiple ethnic identities. Twine (2003) defines one dimension of racial literacy as a form of antiracist training that the parents of African-descent children employ to teach their children to recognize the forms of racism that they might encounter. Twine found that there were gaps among how parents viewed their children racially, their children's own racial self-identification, and how they were socially classified outside the home. For example, there were shifts and intense struggles among parents, extended family members, and teachers over a child's racial and ethnic classification (Twine, 1991, 1997, 2004). Twine's research, as well as that of others, illustrates how difficult it is to easily define the conditions of racial and ethnic group membership for some individuals of multiracial heritage. In recent decades a number of sociologists have turned their attention to this problem of multiracial identity and racial classification schemes. They have argued that a "static measure of race" is not useful for individuals of multiracial heritage who may assert different identities in different social contexts (Goldstein and Morning 2000; Harris 2003; Harris and Sim 2000).

Race and Ethnicity: Key Concepts

In your daily life, you have no doubt used the terms *race* and *ethnicity* many times, but do you know what they mean? In fact, defining these terms is very difficult, but what is most important is that you begin by dispensing with what you think you know. Do not think of race and ethnicity as completely different phenomena.

Ethnicity refers to cultural practices and outlooks of a given community that have emerged historically and tend to set people apart. Members of ethnic groups see themselves as culturally distinct from other groups in a society and are seen by those other groups to be so in return. Different characteristics may serve to distinguish ethnic groups from one another, but the most common are some combination of language, history, religious faith, and ancestry—real or imagined—and styles of dress or adornment. Some examples of ethnic groups in the United States are Irish Americans, Jewish Americans, Italian Americans, Cuban Americans, and Japanese Americans. Ethnic differences are learned.

The difference between race and ethnicity is not as clear-cut as some people think. When you think of it, everything that has been said here about ethnicity would apply very well to

Maureen's mixed-race nieces discussed earlier. Their black relatives and white mother are teaching them many cultural practices that people associate with being black—from how to braid their hair to how to respond to racism. So does this mean that race is really a kind of ethnicity?

In a way it is, but race has certain defining characteristics that make it different from ethnicity. At certain historical moments, ethnic differences take on two additional characteristics. First, some ethnic differences become the basis of stigmas that cannot be removed by conversion or assimilation. Second, these stigmas become the basis of extreme hierarchy.

The mixed-race children with white mothers and black relatives in the United Kingdom look black to many people. Some aspects of their blackness, such as learning to braid their hair from relatives and friends, are cultural practices akin to ethnicity. Yet what makes their blackness into race is the fact that in the United Kingdom, dark skin color has historically been stigmatized, as in the United States. And this stigma has laid the foundation for extreme hierarchy in England, as in the United States.

Race, then, can be understood as a classification system that assigns individuals and groups to categories that are ranked or hierarchical. But there are no clear-cut "races," only a range of physical variations among human beings. Differences in physical type among groups of human beings arise from population inbreeding, which varies according to the degree of contact among different social or cultural groups. Human population groups are a continuum. The genetic diversity *within* populations that share visible physical traits is as great as the diversity *between* them. Racial distinctions are more than ways of describing human differences—they are also important factors in the reproduction of patterns of power and inequality within society.

The process by which understandings of race are used to classify individuals or groups of people is called **racialization**. Historically, racialization meant that certain groups of people came to be labeled as constituting distinct biological groups on the basis of naturally occurring physical features. From the fifteenth century onward, as Europeans came into increased contact with people from different regions of the world, they attempted to systematize knowledge by categorizing and explaining both natural and social phenomena. Non-European populations were "racialized" in opposition to the European "white race." In some instances this racialization took on codified institutional forms, as in the case of slavery in the former British, French, and Spanish colonies in the Americas; slavery in the United States; and the establishment of apartheid in South Africa after World War II (in 1948). More commonly, however, everyday political, educational, legal, and other institutions become racialized through legislation. In the United States after the civil rights movement, de facto racial segrega-

Celebrating the Chinese New Year with performances and decorations is not just a picturesque event every year in Soho, but an important symbol of cultural continuity for London's Chinese community.

tion and racial hierarchies persisted even after state-sanctioned segregation was dismantled. Within a racialized system, an individual's social life and his or her life chances—including education, employment, incarceration, housing, health care, and legal representation are all shaped and constrained by the racial assignments and racial hierarchies in that system.

In recent years, sociologists who study ethnicity in the United States have come to understand that larger forces that give rise to ethnic-group collective consciousness have declined. For example, people who are Jewish or Irish no longer face the kind of housing discrimination that led them to cluster in particular neighborhoods before World War II. In addition, intermarriage between members of different religious groups and European and Asian groups has increased substantially. In the face of such changing conditions, sociologists have noted that ethnic identity, at least in the United States, has less of an effect on the everyday lives of the members of these social groups, unless they choose an ethnic label. As a result, ethnicity is now a choice of whether to be ethnic at all. More and more people must also make a choice about which ethnicity to be (Gans 1979; Waters 1990). Because of this phenomenon, sociologists refer to *situational ethnicity* and *symbolic ethnicity*.

Situational ethnicity is a concept that illustrates one of the ways in which ethnic and racial identification is socially constructed. Some people of multiracial ancestry may choose to assert or not to reveal a salient aspect of their identity or heritage in particular situations, such as applying for a job in which certain racial groups predominate. They may not report an identity at other times when it could lead to discrimination. This shows that larger political forces, such as the categories devised by governments, affect the identity people display.

Symbolic ethnicity occurs when members of an ethnic group assimilate into the larger culture, perhaps moving away from the old neighborhood to the suburbs where a smaller percentage of people are engaged in ethnic practices. Such people might participate in ethnic customs only on symbolic occasions such as Saint Patrick's Day, when they wear green, or at Passover, when they attend a seder. During the rest of the year, their ethnic identity might not be very salient at all.

Whereas ethnicity is primarily a symbolic option for white Americans, race is not always such a choice for non-whites. And, although it is sometimes a choice for people of "mixed race" whose racial characteristics are ambiguous, for members of many racial groups it is not a choice. One sociologist who studied how many Americans think about their ancestry and backgrounds wrote: "The social and political consequences of being Asian or Hispanic or black are not symbolic for the most part, or voluntary. They are real and often hurtful" (Waters 1990). Minority group status can have many negative consequences for its members. One such negative consequence is segregation (discussed later in this chapter).

Despite the increase in the number of people in the United States self-identifying as multiracial, many North Americans continue to believe, mistakenly, that race is a natural category and that human beings can be neatly separated into biologically distinct "races." This is a legacy of European colonialization and scientific racism. During the sixteenth century, Europeans began to classify animals, people, and the material culture that they collected as they explored the world. Racial classification schemes were invented during a period when Europeans were conquering territories and expanding. The Swedish botanist Carolus Linnaeus is considered the founder of

Four schoolboys represent the "racial scale" in South Africa: black, Indian, half-caste, and white.

scientific taxonomy. In 1735, he published what is recognized as the first version of a modern classification scheme of human populations. Linnaeus included humans in a larger classification scheme with relations to apes and monkeys. He grouped human beings into four basic varieties—Europaeus, Americanus, Asiaticus, and Africanus. At this time it was believed that human beings descended from a common original ancestor. Physical features, behaviors, and psychological traits were correlated. Linnaeus assumed that each species had qualities of behavior or temperament that were innate and could not be altered. He acquired much of his data from the writings, descriptions, commentaries, and beliefs of plantation owners, missionaries, slave traders, explorers, and travelers. Thus his scientific data were shaped by the prejudices and power that Europeans had over the people whom they conquered (Smedley 1993).

Racial Categories

Census categories today reflect political constituencies and power relations. The categories used on the census have not remained consistent over time and have changed. In 1970 the Hispanic category was added to the United States census. Other racial categories have been removed such as "mulatto," which last appeared on the 1920 census. The question of why some racial groups and ethnic groups appear and disappear from the census challenges the notion that racial groups are based on simple biological differences.

After a three-year study, a governmental task force proposed that the Office of Management and Budget (OMB) allow for the addition of a multiracial category to the 2000 U.S. Census. This recommendation came after a coalition of individuals of multiracial heritage and advocacy groups across the nation lobbied the OMB. For the first time the census allowed individuals to check more than one racial category if they desired. The debate surrounding the possible addition of a multiracial category reveals the degree to which Americans continue to hold beliefs that racial groups are "natural," even though in reality these groups reflect political relations among people descended from groups that were conquered and colonized. Racial and ethnic groups in the United States, as in other nations, are stratified. The U.S. Bureau of the Census distinguishes four races (American Indian/Alaska Native, Asian and Pacific Islander, black, and white), but too many exceptions and inconsistencies in the classifications have been found to make any of them workable without great controversy.

Racism and Antiracism

Both *racism* and *antiracism* are fairly new terms. Racism did not come into use until the 1930s and antiracism is a concept that emerged in the twentieth century but did not appear in regular usage until the 1960s. Both terms can be defined in many ways because there are different definitions of what constitutes racism in different national contexts.

RACISM

Some see **racism** as a system of domination that operates in social processes and social institutions; others see it as operating in the individual consciousness. Racism can refer to explicit beliefs in racial supremacy such as the systems established in Nazi Germany, before the civil rights movement in the United States, and in South Africa under apartheid.

Yet many have argued that racism is more than simply the ideas held by a small number of bigoted individuals. Rather, racism is embedded in the very structure and operation of society. The idea of **institutional racism** suggests that racism pervades all of society's structures in a systematic manner. According to this view, institutions such as the police, the health-care industry, and the educational system all promote policies that favor certain groups while discriminating against others.

The idea of institutional racism was developed in the United States in the late 1960s by black power activists (Stokeley Carmichael and Charles Hamilton) and taken up by civil rights campaigners who believed that white supremacy structured all social relations and that racism was the foundation of the very fabric of U.S. society, rather than merely representing the opinions of a small minority. In subsequent years, the existence of institutional racism came to be widely accepted and openly acknowledged in many settings. A 1990s investigation into the practices of the Los Angeles Police Department, in light of the beating of Rodney King, found that institutional racism is pervasive within the police force and the criminal justice system. A similar case occurred in 1999 in New York City, when police officers shot and killed an unarmed African man from Guinea, Amadou Diallo. In culture and the arts, institutional racism has been demonstrated to exist in Hollywood films, television broadcasting (negative or limited portrayals of racial and ethnic minorities in programming), and the international modeling industry (industrywide bias against fashion models who appear to be of non-European ancestry and/or mixed race).

FROM "OLD RACISM"
TO "NEW RACISM"

Just as the concept of biological race has been discredited, old-style "biological" racism based on differences in physical traits is rarely openly expressed in society today. The end of state-sanctioned segregation in the United States and the collapse of apartheid in South Africa in 1994 were important turning points in the rejection of biological racism. In both of these cases, racist attitudes were proclaimed by directly associating physical traits with biological inferiority. Such blatantly racist ideas are rarely heard today, except in the cases of violent hate crimes or the platforms of certain extremist groups. But racist attitudes have not disappeared from modern societies. Rather, as some scholars argue, they have been replaced by a more sophisticated "new racism" (or cultural racism), which uses the idea of cultural differences to exclude certain groups (Barker 1981).

Those who argue that a "new racism" has emerged claim that cultural arguments are now employed instead of biological ones to support discrimination against certain segments of the population. According to this view, hierarchies of superiority and inferiority are constructed according to the values of the majority culture. Those groups that stand apart from the majority can be marginalized or vilified for their refusal to assimilate. It is alleged that new racism has a clear political dimension. The fact that racism is increasingly based on cultural rather than biological grounds has led some scholars to suggest that we live in an age of "multiple racisms," where discrimination is experienced differently across segments of the population (Modood et al. 1997).

ANTIRACISM

Antiracism is a concept that emerged in the twentieth century but did not appear in regular usage until the 1960s. It has been defined by Alistair Bonnett (2000) as

> forms of thought and/or practice that seek to confront, eradicate and/or ameliorate racism. Antiracism implies the ability to identify a phenomenon—racism—and to do something about it. Different forms of antiracism exist because there are different definitions of what constitutes racism in different national contexts.

Opposition to racism has been embraced by some governments as a way to protect their political interests and prove themselves worthy of power. Affirmative-action programs, which are a form of antiracism, vary tremendously in different national contexts. In other national contexts, as in India and Malaysia, antiracism has been employed as a component of national identity and a symbol of national allegiance (Bonnett 2000). For example, in the aftermath of the race riots in Kuala Lumpur between Malays and Chinese in May 1969, the Malaysian government implemented affirmation-action programs. These affirmative action programs were introduced under the New Economic Policy (NEP) Act and established a quota in which 40 percent of jobs in most industries were set aside for Malays and a target of 30 percent was established for Malay ownership of commercial and industrial enterprises. Another measure, the Constitution Amendment Bill, gave the government the power to require universities to lower their qualification entrance requirements for Malay students (Nesiah 1997). Another example of antiracism is the affirmative-action program established in India to provide constitutional safeguards for what are known as the scheduled castes and tribes. Articles 330 and 332 of the Indian Constitution reserve a percentage of the legislative seats in the Lower Parliament for members of these groups. These quotas constitute a form of affirmative action that is much stronger and more radical in its goals than are programs in the United States.

Sociologists have only recently begun to place an analysis of antiracism, particularly white antiracism, at the center of analysis. Sociologist Becky Thompson (2001) interviewed white antiracists all over the United States to understand their political trajectories and how they formed an antiracist constituency and community after World War II. Many students of sociology today consider themselves to be antiracists, though many sociologists still believe that the science of society should be kept separate from personal politics.

Psychological Interpretations of Prejudice and Discrimination

Psychological theories can help us understand the nature of prejudiced and racist attitudes and also why ethnic differences matter so much to people.

PREJUDICE, DISCRIMINATION, AND RACISM

The concept of race is modern, but prejudice and discrimination have been widespread in human history, and we must first clearly distinguish between them. **Prejudice** refers to opinions or attitudes held by members of one group toward another. A prejudiced person's preconceived views are often based on hearsay rather than on direct evidence and are resistant to change even in the face of new information. People may harbor favorable prejudices about groups with which they identify and negative prejudices against others. Someone who is prejudiced against a particular group will refuse to give it a fair hearing.

Discrimination refers to *actual behavior* toward another group. It can be seen in activities that distribute rewards and benefits unequally based on membership in the dominant ethnic groups. It involves excluding or restricting members of specific racial or ethnic groups from opportunities that are available to other groups. For example, blacks have been excluded and continue to be underrepresented in entire job categories despite the increase of education among blacks and the emergence of an educated black middle class. Discrimination does not necessarily derive directly from prejudice. For example, white home buyers might steer away from purchasing properties in predominantly black neighborhoods, not because of attitudes of hostility they might feel toward African Americans, but because of worries about declining property values. Prejudiced attitudes in this case influence discrimination, but in an indirect fashion.

STEREOTYPES AND SCAPEGOATS

Prejudice operates mainly through the use of **stereotyping**, which means thinking in terms of fixed and inflexible categories. Stereotyping is often closely linked to the psychological mechanism of **displacement**, in which feelings of hostility or anger are directed against objects that are not the real origin of those feelings. People vent their antagonism against **scapegoats**, others who are blamed for problems that are not their fault. The term *scapegoat* originated with the ancient Hebrews, who each year ritually loaded all their sins onto a goat, which was then chased into the wilderness. Scapegoating is common when two deprived ethnic groups come into competition with one another for economic rewards. People who direct racial attacks against African Americans, for example, are often in a similar economic position to them. They blame blacks for grievances whose real causes lie elsewhere.

Scapegoating is normally directed against groups that are distinctive and relatively powerless, because they make an easy target. Protestants, Catholics, Jews, Italians, racial minorities, and others have played the unwilling role of scapegoat at various times throughout Western history. Scapegoating frequently involves *projection*, the unconscious attribution to others of one's own desires or characteristics. For example, research has consistently demonstrated that when the members of a dominant group practice violence against a minority and exploit it sexually, they are likely to believe that the minority group itself displays these traits of sexual violence. For instance, in the United States before the civil rights movement, some white men's bizarre ideas about the lustful nature of African American men probably originated in their own frustrations, since sexual access to white women was limited by the formal nature of courtship. Similarly, in apartheid South Africa, the belief that black males were exceptionally potent sexually and that black women were promiscuous was widespread among whites. Black males were thought to be sexually dangerous to white women— but in fact, virtually all criminal sexual contact was initiated by white men against black women (Simpson and Yinger 1986).

MINORITY GROUPS

The term *minority group* as used in everyday life can be quite confusing. This is because the term refers to political power and is not simply a numerical distinction. There are many minorities in a statistical sense, such as people having red hair or weighing more than two hundred fifty pounds, but these are not minorities according to the sociological concept. In sociology, members of a **minority group** are disadvantaged as compared with the dominant group (a group possessing more wealth, power, and prestige) and have some sense of group solidarity, of belonging together. The experience of being subject to prejudice and discrimination usually heightens feelings of common loyalty and interests.

Members of minority groups, such as Spanish speakers in the United States, often tend to see themselves as a people separated or distinct from the majority. Minority groups are sometimes, but not always, physically and socially isolated from the larger community. Although they tend to be concentrated in certain neighborhoods, cities, or regions of a country, their children may often intermarry with members of the dominant group. People who belong to minority groups sometimes (for example, Jews) actively promote endogamy (marriage within the group) to keep alive their cultural distinctiveness.

The idea of a minority group is more confusing today than ever before. Some groups that were once clearly identified as minorities, such as Asians and Jews, now have more resources, intermarry at greater rates, and experience less discrimination than they did when they were originally conceived of as minority groups. This highlights the fact that the concept of a minority group is really about disadvantage, rather than a numerical distinction. Perhaps in the future it would be more meaningful for sociologists to use the terms *dominant* and *disadvantaged* to avoid these misunderstandings, but these new terms would be fraught with their own problems! For now, sociologists continue to use the term *minority group*, so it is best for the student to be aware of its definitions and ambiguities as a concept.

Ethnic Relations

In an age of globalization and rapid social change, the rich benefits and complex challenges of ethnic diversity are confronting a growing number of states. International migration is accelerating with the further integration of the global economy; the movement and mixing of human populations seems sure to intensify in years to come. Meanwhile, ethnic tensions and conflicts continue to flare in societies around the world, threatening to lead to the disintegration of some multiethnic states and hinting at protracted violence in others. How can ethnic diversity be accommodated and the outbreak of ethnic conflict averted? Within multiethnic societies what should be the relation between ethnic minority groups and the majority population? There are four primary models of ethnic integration that have been adopted by multiethnic societies in relation to these challenges: assimilation, the "melting pot," pluralism, and multiculturalism. These will be discussed shortly.

To fully analyze ethnic relations in current times, we must first take a historical and comparative perspective. It is impossible to understand ethnic divisions today without giving prime place to the effect of the expansion of Western colonialism on the rest of the world (Global Map 11.1). Global migratory movements resulting from colonialism helped create ethnic divisions by placing different peoples in close proximity. We now delve into this history in more detail.

Ethnic Antagonism: A Historical Perspective

From the fifteenth century onward, Europeans began to venture into previously uncharted seas and unexplored land masses, pursuing the aims of exploration and trade but also conquering and subduing native peoples. They poured out by

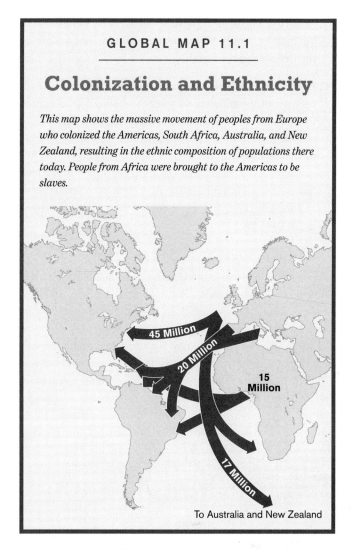

GLOBAL MAP 11.1

Colonization and Ethnicity

This map shows the massive movement of peoples from Europe who colonized the Americas, South Africa, Australia, and New Zealand, resulting in the ethnic composition of populations there today. People from Africa were brought to the Americas to be slaves.

45 Million

20 Million

15 Million

17 Million

To Australia and New Zealand

the millions from Europe to settle in these new areas. In the shape of the slave trade, they also occasioned a large-scale movement of people from Africa to the Americas. The following are the extraordinary shifts in population that have occurred over the past 350 years or so:

1. **Europe to North America.** From the seventeenth century to the present, some forty-five million people have emigrated from Europe to what is now the United States and Canada. About two hundred million people in North America today can trace their ancestry to this migration.

2. **Europe to Central and South America.** About twenty million people from Europe, mostly from Spain, Portugal, and Italy, migrated to Central and South America. Some fifty million people in these areas today are of European ancestry.

3. **Europe to Africa and Australasia.** Approximately seventeen million people in Africa and Australasia are of

European ancestry. In Africa, the majority emigrated to the state of South Africa, which was colonized mainly by the British and the Dutch.

4. **Africa to the Americas.** Starting in the sixteenth century, about 10 million blacks were unwillingly transported to the North and South American continents. Fewer than 1 million arrived in the sixteenth century; some 1.3 million, in the seventeenth century; 6 million, in the eighteenth century; and 2 million, in the nineteenth century. Black Africans were brought to the Americas in chains to serve as slaves; families and whole communities were destroyed in the process.

These population flows formed the basis of the current ethnic composition of the United States, Canada, the countries of Central and South America, South Africa, Australia, and New Zealand. In all of these societies, the indigenous populations were decimated by disease, war, and genocide and subjected to European rule. They are now impoverished ethnic minorities. Because the Europeans were from diverse national and ethnic origins, they transplanted various ethnic hierarchies and divisions to their new homelands. At the height of the colonial era, in the nineteenth and early twentieth centuries, Europeans also ruled over native populations in many other regions: South Asia, East Asia, the South Pacific, and the Middle East.

For most of the period of European expansion, ethnocentric attitudes were rife among the colonists, many of whom were convinced that, as Christians, they were on a civilizing mission to the rest of the world. Europeans of all political persuasions believed themselves to be superior to the peoples they colonized and conquered. The fact that many of those peoples possessed technologies, agricultural skills, and knowledge that the Europeans embraced and incorporated (for example, the civil service system in India) is not so relevant, because the Europeans possessed the power to institutionalize their interpretation. The early period of colonization coincided with the rise of scientific racism, and ever since then, the legacy of European colonization has generated ethnic divisions that have occupied a central place in regional and global conflicts. In particular, racist views distinguishing the descendants of Europeans from those of Africans became central to European racist attitudes.

The Rise of Racism

Why has racism flourished? There are several reasons. The first reason for the rise of modern racism lies in the exploitative relations that Europeans established with the peoples they encountered and conquered. The slave trade could not have

 been carried on had Europeans not constructed a belief system that allowed them to justify their actions by convincing themselves that Africans belonged to an inferior, even subhuman race. Racism helped justify colonial rule over nonwhite peoples and denied them the rights of political participation that were being won by whites in their European homelands. The relations between whites and nonwhites varied according to different patterns of colonial settlement—and were influenced as well by cultural differences among Europeans themselves.

Second, an opposition between the colors white and black as cultural symbols was deeply rooted in European culture. White had long been associated with purity, black with evil (there is nothing natural about this symbolism; in some other cultures, it is reversed). The symbol of blackness held negative meanings *before* the West came into extensive contact with black peoples. These symbolic meanings tended to infuse the Europeans' reactions to blacks when they were first encountered on African shores. The sense that there was a radical difference between black and white peoples combined with the "heathenism" of the Africans led many Europeans to regard blacks with disdain and fear. As a seventeenth-century observer expressed it, blacks "in color as in condition are little other than Devils incarnate" (quoted in Jordan 1968). Although the more extreme expressions of such attitudes have disappeared today, it is difficult not to believe that elements of this black–white cultural symbolism remain widespread.

A third important factor leading to modern racism was simply the invention and diffusion of the concept of race itself. Racist attitudes have been known to exist for hundreds of years. In China of 300 B.C.E., for example, we find recorded descriptions of barbarian peoples "who greatly resemble monkeys from whom they are descended." But the notion of race as a cluster of inherited characteristics comes from European thought of the eighteenth and nineteenth centuries. Count Joseph Arthur de Gobineau (1816–1882), who is sometimes called the father of modern racism, proposed ideas that became influential in many circles. According to de Gobineau, three races exist: white, black, and yellow. The white race possesses superior intelligence, morality, and will power, and these inherited qualities underlie the spread of Western influence across the world. The blacks are the least capable, marked by an animal nature, a lack of morality, and emotional instability.

The ideas of de Gobineau and others who proposed similar views were presented as supposedly scientific theories. The notion of the superiority of the white race, although completely without value factually, remains a key element of white racism. It is an explicit element, for example, in the ideology of the Ku Klux Klan, and it was the basis of **apartheid** (separate racial development) in South Africa.

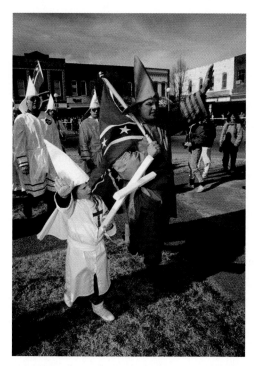

A young girl joins members of the Ku Klux Klan at a demonstration against the Martin Luther King Day holiday in Pulaski, Tennessee.

Ethnic Conflict

The most extreme and devastating form of group relations in human history involves **genocide**, the systematic, planned destruction of a racial, political, or cultural group. The most horrific recent instance of brutal destructiveness against such a group was the massacre of six million Jews in the German concentration camps during World War II. The Holocaust is not the only example of mass genocide in the twentieth century. Between 1915 and 1923 over a million Armenians were killed by the Ottoman Turkish government. In the late 1970s, two million Cambodians died in the Khmer Rouge's killing fields. During the 1990s, in the African country of Rwanda, hundreds of thousands of the minority Tutsis were massacred by the dominant Hutu group. In the former Yugoslavia, Bosnian and Kosovar Muslims were summarily executed by the Serb majority. And in the Darfur region of the Sudan, the conflict between the Arabic-speaking, nomadic *Janjawid* and the non-Arab Sudanese who speak African languages has escalated to genocide with hundreds of thousands of people being killed and approximately two million people being forced to flee their homes.

The conflicts in the former Yugoslavia have involved attempts at **ethnic cleansing**, the creation of ethnically homogeneous areas through the mass expulsion of other ethnic populations. Croatia, for example, has become an independent "monoethnic" state after a costly war in which thousands of Serbs were expelled from the country. The war—which broke out in Bosnia in 1992 among Serbs, Croats, and Muslims—involved the ethnic cleansing of the Bosnian Muslim population at the hands of the Serbs. Thousands of Muslim men were forced into internment camps and a campaign of systematic rape was carried out against Muslim women. The war in Kosovo in 1999 was prompted by charges that Serbian forces were ethnically cleansing the Kosovar Albanian (Muslim) population from the province.

In both Bosnia and Kosovo, ethnic conflict became internationalized. Hundreds of thousands of refugees spilled over into neighboring areas, further destabilizing the region. Western states intervened both diplomatically and militarily to protect the human rights of ethnic groups who had become targets of ethnic cleansing. In the short term, such interventions succeeded in quelling the systematic violence. Yet they have had unintended consequences as well. The fragile peace in Bosnia has been maintained, but only through the presence of peacekeeping troops and the partitioning of the country into separate ethnic enclaves. In Kosovo a process of reverse ethnic cleansing ensued after the North Atlantic Treaty Organization (NATO) bombing campaign. Ethnic Albanian Kosovars began to drive the local Serb population out of Kosovo; the presence of NATO-led Kosovo Force (KFOR) troops has been inadequate to prevent ethnic tensions from reigniting.

Ethnic cleansing involves the forced relocation of ethnic populations through targeted violence, harassment, threats, and campaigns of terror.

It has been noted that violent conflicts around the globe are increasingly based on ethnic divisions. Only a tiny proportion of wars now occur between states; the vast majority are civil wars with ethnic dimensions. In a world of increasing interdependence and competition, international factors become even more important in shaping ethnic relations, while the effects of internal ethnic conflicts are felt well outside national borders. As we have seen, ethnic conflicts attract international attention and have sometimes provoked physical intervention. International war crimes tribunals have been convened to investigate and try those responsible for the ethnic cleansing and genocide in the former Yugoslavia and Rwanda. Responding to and preventing ethnic conflict has become one of the key challenges facing both individual states and international political structures. Although ethnic tensions are often experienced, interpreted, and described at the local level, they are increasingly taking on national and international dimensions.

In other areas of the world, exploitation of minority groups has been an ugly part of many countries' histories. The concept of group closure has been institutionalized in the form of **segregation**, a practice whereby racial and ethnic groups are kept physically separate by law, thereby maintaining the superior position of the dominant group. For instance, in apartheid-era South Africa, laws forced blacks to live separately from whites and forbade sexual relations among races. In the United States, African Americans have also experienced legal forms of segregation. In 1967 the Supreme Court ruled in the case of *Loving v. Virginia* that the prohibition of interracial marriage violated the right to privacy. At that time racial intermarriage was still a crime in most southern states. Interracial marriage had been criminalized for more than 270 years in every state except Alaska and Hawaii. Economic and social segregation was enforced by law, for instance laws requiring blacks and whites to use separate public bathrooms. Even today, segregated residential areas still exist in many cities, leading some to claim that an American system of apartheid has developed (Massey and Denton 1993).

Conflict and Economic Power

Many commentators have argued that the best way to reduce ethnic conflicts, like those just discussed, is to establish democracy and a free market. They argue that this would promote peace by giving everyone a say in running the country and by giving all people access to the prosperity that comes from trading with others. In an influential book, *World on Fire: How Exporting Free Market Democracy Breeds Ethnic Hatred and Global Instability* (2003), Amy Chua, a professor at Yale University, contests this view.

Chua's starting point is that in many developing countries a small ethnic minority enjoys disproportionate economic power. One obvious example is the white minority that exploited the nonwhite ethnic groups in apartheid South Africa, as we saw in the introduction to this chapter. Chua argues that the massacre of Tutsis by Hutus in Rwanda in 1994 and the hatred felt by Serbs toward Croats in former Yugoslavia were also partly related to the economic advantage enjoyed by the Tutsis and the Croats in their respective countries.

Another example that Chua often uses concerns the Chinese ethnic minority in Indonesia. The free-market policies of the former Indonesian dictator General Suharto vastly enriched the country's tiny Chinese minority, who became the country's main beneficiaries of economic globalization. In turn Chinese-Indonesians tended to support the Suharto dictatorship. By 1998, the year that mass prodemocracy demonstrations forced Suharto to resign, Chinese Indonesians controlled 70 percent of Indonesia's private economy, but made up just 3 percent of its population. (The prodemocracy demonstrations in Indonesia are discussed in more detail in Chapter 23.) The end of Suharto's regime was accompanied by violent attacks against the Chinese minority. Chua (2003) writes: "The prevailing view among the pribumi [ethnic] majority was that

it was 'worthwhile to lose 10 years of growth to get rid of the Chinese problem once and for all.'"

As General Suharto's dictatorship collapsed, the United States and other Western countries called for the introduction of democratic elections. Yet, Chua argues that introducing democracy to countries with what she calls "market dominant minorities," such as the Chinese in Indonesia, is not likely to bring peace. Instead she argues that the competition for votes in a democracy is likely to lead to a backlash from the country's ethnic majority. Political leaders will emerge who seek to scapegoat the resented minority and encourage the ethnic majority to reclaim the country's wealth for the "true" owners of the nation, as the pribumi majority in Indonesia did against the Chinese minority.

Chua's account shows us that although democracy and the market economy are in principle beneficent forces, they must be grounded in an effective system of law and civil society. Where they are not, as in many parts of the developing world, new and acute ethnic conflicts can emerge.

Models of Ethnic Integration

For many years, the two most common positive models of political ethnic harmony in the United States were those of assimilation and the melting pot (Figure 11.1). **Assimilation** meant that new immigrant groups would assume the attitudes and language of the dominant white community. The idea of the **melting pot** was different—it meant merging different cultures and outlooks by stirring them all together. A newer model of ethnic relations is **pluralism**, in which ethnic cultures are given full validity to exist separately, yet participate in the larger society's economic and political life. A recent outgrowth of pluralism is **multiculturalism**, in which ethnic groups exist separately and *equally*. It does seem at least possible to create a society in which ethnic groups are separate but equal, as is demonstrated by Switzerland, where French, German, and Italian groups coexist in the same society. But this situation is unusual, and it seems unlikely that the United States could come close to mirroring this achievement in the near future.

Global Migration

Today floods of refugees and emigrants move restlessly across different regions of the globe, either trying to escape from conflicts or fleeing poverty in search of a better life. Often they reach a new country only to find they are resented by people who some generations ago were immigrants them-

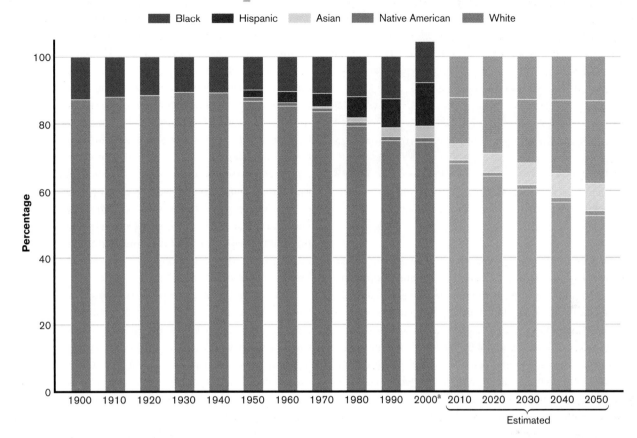

FIGURE 11.1

Racial and Ethnic Composition of the United States: 1900–2050

Black   Hispanic   Asian   Native American   White

Percentage

100

80

60

40

20

0

1900 1910 1920 1930 1940 1950 1960 1970 1980 1990 2000ᵃ 2010 2020 2030 2040 2050

Estimated

Why does the bar for the year 2000 go above 100 percent? This figure indicates that prior to 1950 there were only blacks and whites in the United States. Is this correct and if not, why? In what year does the figure predict that Hispanics will clearly become a greater percentage of the population than blacks? Which racial group(s) has been clearly declining as a percentage of the population since 1950? According to the reading, South Africa's former apartheid laws forced blacks and whites to live separately. Provide an example of legally enforced segregation in twentieth-century U.S. history.

ᵃTotal percentage exceeds 100 percent because starting in 2000, respondents were allowed to identify themselves as belonging to more than one race category.
SOURCE: U.S. Bureau of the Census, Factfinder, 2004a.

selves. Sometimes there are reversals, as has happened in southern California and other areas of the United States along the Mexican border. Much of what is now California was once part of Mexico. Today, some Mexican Americans might say the new waves of Mexican immigrants are reclaiming what used to be their heritage. Except that most of the existing groups in California don't quite see things this way.

Migratory Movements

Although migration is not a new phenomenon, it is one that seems to be accelerating as part of the process of global integration. Worldwide migration patterns can be seen as one reflection of the rapidly changing economic, political, and cultural ties among countries. It has been estimated that the world's migrant population in 1990 was more than eighty

Aborigines from all over Pitjabjantjaira Country gather to protest and protect their land from mining/mineral development.

million people, twenty million of whom were refugees. By 2005, the number of migrants was estimated at two hundred million (World Book 2006). This number appears likely to continue increasing in the twenty-first century, prompting some scholars to label this the "age of migration" (Castles and Miller 1993).

Immigration, the movement of people into a country to settle, and **emigration**, the process by which people leave a country to settle in another, combine to produce global migration patterns linking countries of origin and countries of destination. Migratory movements add to ethnic and cultural diversity in many societies and help shape demographic, economic, and social dynamics. The intensification of global migration since World War II, and particularly since the 1980s, has transformed immigration into an important political issue in many countries. Rising immigration rates in many Western societies have challenged commonly held notions of national identity and have forced a reexamination of concepts of citizenship.

Scholars have identified four models of migration to describe the main global population movements since 1945. The *classic model* of migration applies to countries such as Canada, the United States, and Australia, which have developed as nations of immigrants. In such cases, immigration has been largely encouraged and the promise of citizenship has been extended to newcomers, although restrictions and quotas help limit the annual intake of immigrants. The *colonial model* of immigration, pursued by countries such as France and the United Kingdom, tends to favor immigrants from former colonies over those from other countries. The large number of immigrants from former British colonies in Britain reflects this tendency.

Countries such as Germany, Switzerland, and Belgium have followed a third policy—the *guest workers model*. Under such a scheme, immigrants are admitted into the country on a temporary basis, often to fulfill demands within the labor market, but do not receive citizenship rights even after long periods of settlement. Finally, *illegal models* of immigration are becoming increasingly common due to tightening immigration laws in many industrialized countries. Immigrants who are able to gain entry into a country either secretly or under a nonimmigration pretense are often able to live illegally outside the realm of official society. Examples of this can be seen in the large number of Mexican illegal aliens in many southern U.S. states or in the growing international business of smuggling refugees across national borders.

What are the forces behind global migration and how are they changing as a result of globalization? Many early theories about migration focused on so-called push and pull factors. *Push factors* referred to dynamics within a country of origin that forced people to emigrate, such as war, famine, political oppression, or population pressures. *Pull factors*, by contrast, were those features of destination countries that attracted immigrants: prosperous labor markets, better overall living conditions, and lower population density, for example, could "pull" immigrants from other regions.

More recently, push and pull theories of migration have been criticized for offering overly simplistic explanations of a complex and multifaceted process. Instead scholars of migration are increasingly looking at global migration patterns as systems that are produced through interactions between macro-level and micro-level processes. This idea may sound complicated, but it is actually quite simple. Macro-level factors refer to overarching issues such as the political situation in an area, the laws and regulations controlling immigration and emigration, or changes in the international economy. Micro-level factors, on the other hand, are concerned with the resources, knowledge, and understandings that the migrant populations themselves possess.

The intersection of macro and micro processes can be seen in the case of Germany's large Turkish immigrant community. On the macro level are factors such as Germany's economic need for labor, its policy of accepting foreign "guest workers," and the state of the Turkish economy, which prevents many Turks from earning at the level they would wish. At the micro level are the informal networks and channels of mutual support within the Turkish community in Germany and the strong links to family and friends who have remained in Turkey. Among potential Turkish migrants, knowledge about Germany and "social capital"—human or community resources that can be drawn on—help make Germany one of the most popular destination countries. Supporters of the migration systems approach emphasize that no one factor can explain the process of migration. Rather, each particular migratory movement, like that between Turkey and Germany, is the product of an interaction of macro- and micro-level processes.

After examining late-twentieth-century trends in global migration, Stephen Castles and Mark Miller (1993) identified four tendencies that they claim will characterize migration patterns in the coming years:

- **Acceleration.** Migration across borders is occurring in greater numbers than ever before.
- **Diversification.** Most countries now receive immigrants of many different types, in contrast with earlier times when particular forms of immigration, such as labor immigration or refugees, were predominant.
- **Globalization.** Migration has become more global in nature, involving a greater number of countries as both senders and recipients (Global Maps 11.2 and 11.3).
- **Feminization.** A growing number of migrants are women, making contemporary migration much less male

dominated than in previous times. The increase in female migrants is closely related to changes in the global labor market, including the growing demand for domestic workers, the expansion of sex tourism and "trafficking" in women and the "mail-order brides" phenomenon.

Global Diasporas

Another way to understand global migration patterns is through the study of diasporas. The term **diaspora** refers to the dispersal of an ethnic population from an original homeland into foreign areas, often in a forced manner or under traumatic circumstances. References are often made to the Jewish and African diasporas to describe the way in which these populations have become redistributed

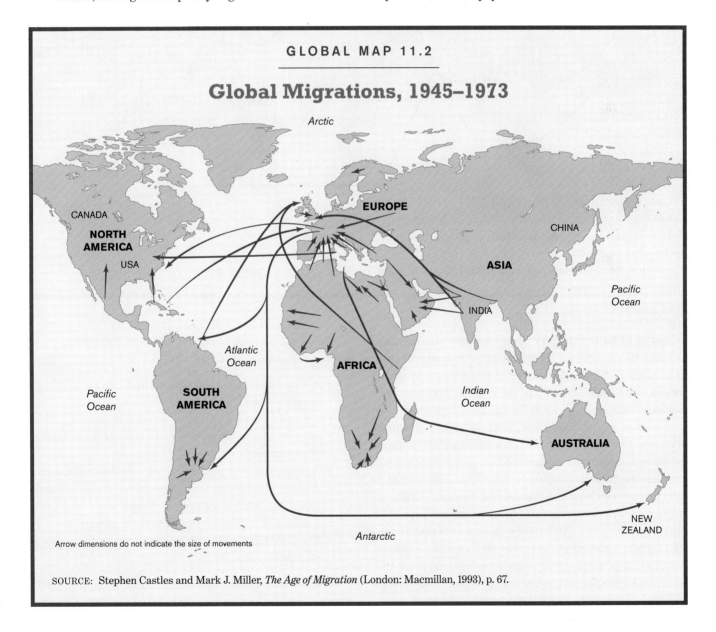

GLOBAL MAP 11.2

Global Migrations, 1945–1973

Arrow dimensions do not indicate the size of movements

SOURCE: Stephen Castles and Mark J. Miller, *The Age of Migration* (London: Macmillan, 1993), p. 67.

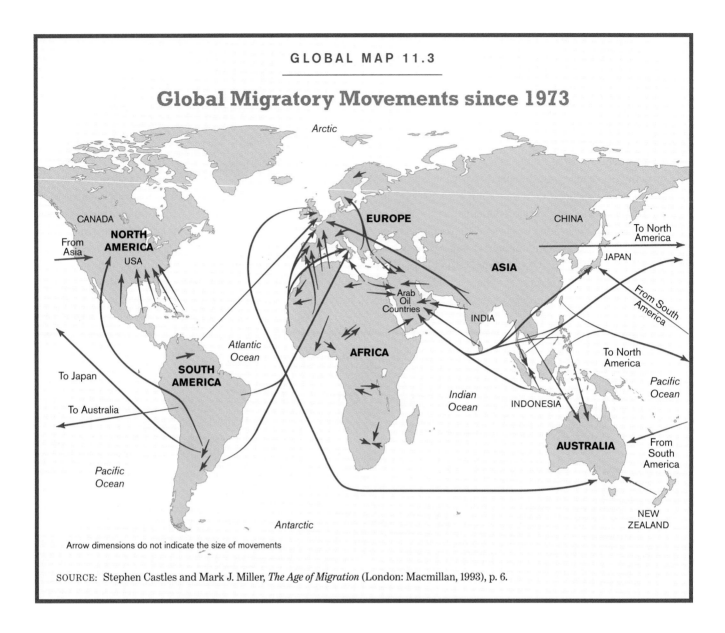

Global Migratory Movements since 1973

Arrow dimensions do not indicate the size of movements

SOURCE: Stephen Castles and Mark J. Miller, *The Age of Migration* (London: Macmillan, 1993), p. 6.

across the globe as a result of slavery and genocide. Although members of a diaspora are by definition scattered apart geographically, they are held together by factors such as shared history, a collective memory of the original homeland, or a common ethnic identity that is nurtured and preserved.

Robin Cohen has argued that diasporas occur in a number of diverse forms, although the most commonly cited examples are those that occurred involuntarily as a result of persecution and violence. In *Global Diasporas* (1997), Cohen adopts a historical approach and identifies five different categories of diasporas, according to the forces underlying the original population dispersion: *victim* (e.g., African, Jewish, and Armenian), *imperial* (British), *labor* (Indian), *trade* (Chinese), and *cultural* (Caribbean). In certain of these cases, such as that of the Chinese, large-scale population movements occurred on a voluntary basis, not as a result of a defining traumatic event.

Despite the diversity of forms, however, all diasporas share certain key features (R. Cohen 1997):

- A forced or voluntary movement from an original homeland to a new region or regions
- A shared memory about the original homeland, a commitment to its preservation, and a belief in the possibility of eventual return
- A strong ethnic identity sustained over time and distance
- A sense of solidarity with members of the same ethnic group also living in areas of the diaspora
- A degree of tension in relation to the host societies
- The potential for valuable and creative contributions to pluralistic host societies

Some scholars have accused Cohen of trying to simplify complex and distinctive migration experiences into a narrow typology, by associating categories of diasporas with particular ethnic groups. Others argue that his conceptualization of diaspora is not sufficiently precise for the analysis he undertakes. Yet despite these critiques, Cohen's study is valuable for demonstrating that diasporas are not static but instead are ongoing processes of maintaining collective identity and preserving ethnic culture in a rapidly globalizing world.

Ethnic Relations in the United States

We concentrate for the rest of the chapter on the origins and nature of ethnic diversity in the United States (Table 11.1)—and its consequences, which have often been highly contentious. More than most other societies in the world, this country is peopled almost entirely by immigrants. Only a tiny minority, less than 1 percent, of the population today are Native Americans, those whom Christopher Columbus, erroneously supposing he had arrived in India, called Indians.

Before the American Revolution, British, French, and Dutch settlers established colonies in what is now the United States. Some descendants of the French colonists are still to be found in parts of Louisiana. Millions of slaves were brought over from Africa to North America. Huge waves of European, Russian, Asian, and Latin American immigrants have washed across the country at different periods since then. The United States is one of the most *ethnically diverse* countries on the face of the globe. In this section we pay particular attention to the divisions that have separated whites and nonwhite minority groups, such as African Americans and Hispanic Americans. The emphasis is on *struggle*. Members of these groups have made repeated efforts to defend the integrity of their cultures and advance their social position in the face of persistent prejudice and discrimination from the wider social environment.

Early Colonization

The first European colonists in what was to become the United States were actually of quite homogeneous background. At the time of the Declaration of Independence, the majority of the colonial population was of British descent, and almost everyone was Protestant. Settlers from outside the British Isles were at first admitted only with reluctance, but the desire for economic expansion meant having to attract immigrants from other areas. Most came from countries in northwest Europe, such as Holland, Germany, and Sweden; such migration into

North America dates initially from around 1820. In the century following, about thirty-three million immigrants entered the United States. No migrant movement on such a scale has ever been documented before or since.

The early waves of immigrants came mostly from the same countries of origin as the groups already established in the United States. They left Europe to escape economic hardship and religious and political oppression, also seeking the opportunities to acquire land as the drive westward gained momentum. As a result of successive potato famines that had produced widespread starvation, 1.5 million people migrated from Ireland, settling for the most part in the coastal areas, in contrast to most other immigrants from rural backgrounds. The Irish were primarily from rural areas and accustomed to a life of hardship and despair, and most of them settled in urban industrial areas where they sought work.

A major new influx of immigrants arrived in the 1880s and 1890s, this time mainly from southern and eastern Europe—the Austro-Hungarian Empire, Russia, and Italy. Each successive group of immigrants was subject to considerable discrimination on the part of people previously established in the country. Negative views of the Irish, for example, emphasized their supposedly low level of intelligence and drunken behavior. Job vacancies often specifically stated, "No Irish need apply." But as they were concentrated within the cities, the Irish Americans were able to organize to protect their interests and gained a strong influence over political life. The Italians and Polish, when they reached America, were in turn discriminated against by the Irish.

Asian immigrants first arrived in the United States in large numbers in the late nineteenth century, encouraged by employers who needed cheap labor in the developing industries of the West. Some two hundred thousand Chinese emigrated in this period. Most were men, who came with the idea of saving money to send back to their families in China, anticipating that they would also later return there. Bitter conflicts broke out between white workers and the Chinese when employment opportunities diminished. The Chinese Exclusion Act, passed in 1882, cut down further immigration to a trickle until after World War II.

Japanese immigrants began to arrive not long after the ending of Chinese immigration. They were also subject to great hostility from whites. Opposition to Japanese immigration intensified in the early part of the twentieth century, leading to strict limits, or *quotas*, being placed on the numbers allowed to enter the United States.

Most immigrant groups in the early twentieth century settled in urban areas and engaged in the developing industrial economy. They also tended to cluster in ethnic neighborhoods of their own. Chinatowns, Little Italys, and other clearly defined areas became features of most large cities. The very size of the

TABLE 11.1

Racial and Ethnic Populations in the United States, 2004

RACE OR ETHNICITY	POPULATION	SHARE OF TOTAL POPULATION[a]
Total U.S. population	285,691,501	100.0
RACE		
One race	280,285,784	98.1
White (including Hispanics)	216,036,244	75.6
White alone (non-Hispanic)	192,362,875	67.3
Black or African American	34,772,381	12.2
American Indian and Alaska Native	2,151,322	0.8
Asian	12,097,281	4.2
Asian Indian	2,245,239	0.8
Chinese (except Taiwanese)	2,829,627	1.0
Filipino	2,148,227	0.8
Japanese	832,039	0.3
Korean	1,251,092	0.4
Vietnamese	1,267,510	0.4
Other Asian	1,523,547	0.5
Native Hawaiian and Other Pacific Islander	403,832	0.1
Native Hawaiian	154,666	0.1
Guamanian or Chamorro	68,336	0.0
Samoan	60,520	0.0
Other Pacific Islander	120,310	0.0
Hispanic or Latino (of any race)	40,459,196	14.2
Mexican	25,894,763	9.1
Puerto Rican	3,874,322	1.4
Cuban	1,437,828	0.5
Other Hispanic or Latino	9,252,283	3.2
Some other race	14,824,724	5.2
Two or more races	5,405,717	1.9

[a]Percentages do not total 100 percent because Hispanics or Latinos can be of any race.

SOURCE: U.S. Bureau of the Census, "General Demographic Characteristics: 2004," 2004b.

influx provoked backlash from the Anglo-Saxon sections of the population. During the 1920s, new immigration quotas were set up, which discriminated against new arrivals from southern and eastern Europe. Many immigrants found the conditions of life in their new land little better and sometimes worse than the areas from which they originated. Eva Morawska (1986), the author of a historical study of immigrants journeying from east central Europe to Johnstown, Pennsylvania, observes:

The ambivalence and heart-rending uncertainty that accompanied the immigrants when they made their decision to cross the ocean to try their luck in America became further sharpened in this country by feelings of bewilderment and nostalgia, and by disillusionment with the reality of the "Promised Land" as compared with the dreams they had harbored in Europe. To a number of East Central Europeans, the arrival in Johnstown was bitterly disappointing. The town was soiled and the air filled with soot and fumes from the furnace chimneys. "My disappointment was unspeakable," recalls an eighty-four-year-old Galician, "when after a twelve-day journey I saw the city of Johnstown: squalid and ugly, with those congested shabby houses, blackened with soot from the factory chimneys—this was the America I saw."

The immigrants may have gained greater religious and political freedom in their new home, but they met with prejudice and discrimination if their ways of life differed from those of the dominant Anglo-Saxon community. The large flow of immigration and competition for jobs allowed employers to compel workers to accept very long working days, low levels of pay, and unhealthy working conditions. Because new immigrants were commonly used as strike breakers (people hired to replace striking workers), conflicts between them and established groups were frequent. In spite of these conditions, the economy was rapidly growing, and a substantial proportion of immigrant workers in the end managed to improve their standards of living.

Immigration to the United States: The Sociological Debate

The United States is often euphemistically referred to as a melting pot, or a nation of immigrants. The cultural and social landscape of the United States is viewed as an amalgam of diverse cultures, due largely to our nation's history as a refuge for immigrants. Today, however, policy makers and social scientists are embroiled in a dispute over the social and economic costs of immigration. Do new immigrants help or hinder the United States' economy?

Before addressing both sides of this debate, it is important to understand the current state of immigration to the United States. It is estimated that there are nearly 33.5 million foreign-born individuals in the United States (U.S. Bureau of the Census 2003a). During the 1990s, the United States admitted on average more than 977,100 legal immigrants each year, and an additional 300,000 entered and stayed in the country illegally (U.S. Bureau of the Census 2006a). For the first five years of the twenty-first century, an average of more than 926,000 legal immigrants were admitted each year (U.S. Bureau of the Census 2006a). Unlike the major wave of immigration that occurred at the turn of the last century, fewer than 10 percent of immigrants admitted into the United States in the 1980s and 1990s were of European origin. In fact, between 1989 and 1993, more than half of all immigrants entering the United States came from just four countries: Mexico, the Philippines, Viet-

This nineteenth-century cartoon, *Where the Blame Lies,* offers an unflattering portrait of new immigrants and characterizes the discrimination that many new immigrants faced after arriving in the United States.

nam, and El Salvador. This change in the composition of immigrants is generally attributed to two government acts: the 1965 Immigration and Nationality Act Amendments, which abolished preference for northern and western European immigrants and gave preference to "family reunification"—rather than occupational skills—as a reason for accepting immigrants, and the 1986 Immigration Reform and Control Act, which provided amnesty for many illegal immigrants.

Consequently, many of the debates surrounding immigration focus on new immigrants' ability to secure employment and achieve economic self-sufficiency. In his 1994 essay "The Economics of Immigration," economist George Borjas argued that since the 1980s, the United States has attracted "lower-quality" immigrants, who have less education and few marketable job skills. Moreover, these new immigrants are less skilled than both natives (i.e., people born in the United States) and earlier migrants; thus they are more reliant on government assistance for survival. Borjas's estimates show that 21 percent of immigrant households participate in some means-tested social assistance program such as Medicaid or food stamps, as compared with 14 percent of native households. Because recent immigrants are often unable to find gainful employment in the short term, economic assimilation is quite slow; Borjas estimated that recent immigrants will likely earn 20 percent less than native-born Americans for most of their working lives.

Borjas also was concerned about the effect of immigrants on natives' economic prospects. He argued that large-scale migration of less-skilled workers has done harm to the economic opportunities of less-skilled natives—particularly African Americans. This occurs because immigrants increase the number of workers in the economy; they create additional competition in the labor market, and thus wages of the least skilled workers fall.

Immigrant America

If globalization is understood as the emergence of new patterns of interconnection among the world's peoples and cultures, then surely one of the most significant aspects of globalization is the changing racial and ethnic composition of Western societies. In the United States, shifting patterns of immigration since the end of World War II have altered the demographic structure of many regions, affecting social and cultural life in ways that can hardly be overstated. Although the United States has always been a nation of immigrants (with the obvious exception of Native Americans), most of those who arrived here before the early 1960s were European. Throughout the nineteenth and early twentieth centuries, vast numbers of people from Ireland, Italy, Germany, Russia, and other European and east European countries flocked to America in search of a new life, giving a distinctive European bent to American culture. (Of course, until 1808, another significant group of immigrants—Africans—came not because America was a land of opportunity, but because they had been enslaved.) In part because of changes in immigration policy, however, most of those admitted since 1965 have been Asian or Hispanic.

In the years 2000–2003, for example, of the approximately 4.5 million immigrants who were legally admitted to the United States, almost 1.2 million came from Asia and nearly 2.6 million were from Latin America (U.S. Bureau of the Census 2003a). There are also an estimated 7 to 11 million illegal immigrants living in the United States, about 70 percent of whom

are Mexican (CNN 2003; National Immigration Forum 2006). As a result, as of 2003, over 53 percent of U.S. residents who were foreign born were from Latin America, while 25 percent were from Asia (U.S. Bureau of the Census 2003b). In contrast, in 1900 almost 85 percent of the foreign born were European (Duignan and Gann 1998).

Although Borjas described a bleak scenario, other economists and policy analysts argue that recent immigration has either a positive effect or no influence on the U.S. economy. Economist Julian Simon has written several books, including *The Ultimate Resource* (1981) and *The Economic Consequences of Immigration* (1989), that argue that immigrants provide a windfall to the U.S. economy by joining the labor force and paying into the federal revenue system for their whole lives. By the time they retire and collect government benefits such as Social Security and Medicare, their children will be covering these costs by working and paying into the tax system. Simon's arguments, however, are based on the assumption that immigrants earn the same wages and are as employable as natives—an assumption refuted by Borjas's research.

Simon also argues that immigrants are a cultural asset to the United States. In fact, he claims that "the notion of wanting to keep out immigrants to keep our institutions and our values pure is prejudice" (quoted in Brimelow 1995). Moreover, Simon argues that human beings have the intelligence to adapt to their surroundings and that the more immigrants that come to the United States, the larger pool of potential innovators and problem solvers our nation will have.

Studies conducted by Simon and the Urban Institute, a nonprofit research organization, acknowledge that although some

Most of these new immigrants have settled in six "port-of-entry" states: California, New York, Texas, Illinois, New Jersey, and Massachusetts. These states are attractive to new immigrants not necessarily because of the job opportunities they afford, but because they house large immigrant communities into which newcomers are welcomed (Frey and Liaw 1998). As the flow of Asian and Hispanic immigration continues, and as some nonimmigrants respond by moving to regions of the country with smaller immigrant populations, the percentage of residents of port-of-entry states who are white will continue to drop. California was approximately 52 percent white in 1996; in 2004, this number dropped to 44.5 percent, and by 2010, it is expected to fall to 40 percent (Maharidge 1996; U.S. Bureau of the Census 2005). "Other states will follow," Dale Maharidge writes in the book *The Coming White Minority* (1996), "Texas sometime around 2015, and in later years Arizona, New York, Nevada, New Jersey, and Maryland. By 2050 the nation will be almost half nonwhite."

The effect of these demographic changes on everyday social life has been profound. Take California as an example. In California's urban centers, residents fully expect street scenes to be multiethnic in character and would be shocked to visit a state like Wisconsin, where the vast majority of public interactions take place between whites. In some California communities, store and street signs are printed in Spanish or Chinese or Vietnamese, as well as in English. Interracial marriages are on the rise, ethnic restaurants have proliferated, and the schools are filled with nonwhite children. In fact, nonwhites make up two thirds of the undergraduate population at the University of California, Berkeley, where Asian students are on the verge of predominating.

Unfortunately, these changes have exacerbated social tensions. Many white Californians have retreated into prosperous suburban enclaves and have grown resentful of immigrants and nonwhites. Because rates of voter turnout are higher for whites than for other racial groups in the state and because whites control a significant share of the state's wealth, they have managed to pass a number of laws that seek to preserve opportunities for the coming white minority. Proposition 187, for example, passed in 1994, denied vital public services to illegal immigrants. More recently, the regents of the University of California, in a highly controversial move, decided to abolish affirmative action for the entire nine-campus state university system. Were these decisions based on solid economic and philosophical rationales—the perception that California taxpayers were shouldering too much of the economic burden of illegal immigration or the sense that affirmative action constitutes "reverse discrimination" against whites—or were they motivated principally by xenophobia, the fear of those different from oneself? Whatever the answer, there can be little doubt but that immigration—an important aspect of globalization—is changing the face of American society.

recent immigrants may benefit from federally funded programs such as welfare, these costs are often quite short term. Immigrant children who benefit from the U.S. educational system go on to become productive, tax-paying workers.

The National Immigration Forum has estimated that, despite the costs of welfare, immigrant workers make a significant contribution to the national economy. Even though the majority of these work in low-wage and hard-labor jobs, without them the gross domestic product of the United States, which was approximately $10.4 trillion in 2005, would be $1 trillion less than it is (Rodriguez 2004). Assessing the fiscal costs of immigration proves difficult, however. Although much of the public debate focuses on the costs of providing services to illegal immigrants, actual statistics documenting the number of illegal immigrants are difficult to obtain and verify. Moreover, few policy analysts can predict whether U.S. immigration policy—or the characteristics of immigrants themselves—will change drastically in the future.

African Americans in the United States

By 1780, there were nearly 4 million slaves in the American South. Since there was little incentive for them to work, physical punishment was often resorted to. Slaves who ran away were hunted with dogs and on their capture were manacled, sometimes branded with their master's mark, and occasionally even castrated. Slaves had virtually no rights in law whatsoever. But they did not passively accept the conditions their masters imposed on them. The struggles of slaves against their oppressive conditions sometimes took the form of direct opposition or disobedience to orders, and occasionally outright rebellion (although collective slave revolts were more common in the Caribbean than in the United States). On a more subtle level, their response took the form of a cultural creativity—a mixing of aspects of African cultures, Christian ideals, and cultural threads woven from their new environments. Some of the art forms they developed, as in music—for example, the invention of jazz—were genuinely new.

Feelings of hostility toward blacks on the part of the white population were in some respects more strongly developed in states where slavery had never been known than in the South itself. The celebrated French political observer Alexis de Tocqueville (1969; orig. 1835) noted in 1835, "The prejudice of race appears to be stronger in the states that have abolished slavery than in those where it still exists; and nowhere is it so intolerant as in those states where servitude has never been known." Moral rejection of slavery seems to have been confined to a few more educated groups. The main factors underlying the Civil War were political and economic; most northern leaders were more interested in sustaining the Union than in abolishing slavery, although this was the eventual outcome of the conflict. The formal abolition of slavery changed the real conditions of life for African Americans in the South relatively little. The "black codes"—laws limiting the rights of blacks—placed restrictions on the behavior of the former slaves and punished their transgressions in much the same way as under slavery. Acts were also passed legalizing segregation of blacks from whites in public places. One kind of slavery was thus replaced by another, based on social, political, and economic discrimination.

INTERNAL MIGRATION FROM SOUTH TO NORTH

Industrial development in the North, combined with the mechanization of agriculture in the South, produced a progressive movement of African Americans northward from the turn of the century on. In 1900, more than 90 percent of African Americans lived in the South, mostly in rural areas. Today, less than half of the black population remains in the South; three quarters now live in northern urban areas. African Americans used to be farm laborers and domestic servants, but over a period of little more than two generations, they have become mainly urban, industrial, and service-economy workers. But African Americans have not become assimilated

Martin Luther King Jr. addresses a large crowd at a civil rights march on Washington in 1963. Born in 1929, King was a Baptist minister, civil rights leader, and winner of the 1964 Nobel Peace Prize. He was assassinated by James Earl Ray in 1968.

into the wider society in the way in which the successive groups of white immigrants were. They have for the most part been unable to break free from the conditions of neighborhood segregation and poverty that other immigrants faced on arrival. Together with those of Anglo-Saxon origin, African Americans have lived in the United States far longer than most other immigrant groups. What was a transitional experience for most of the later, white immigrants has become a seemingly permanent experience for blacks. In the majority of cities, both South and North, blacks and whites live in separate neighborhoods and are educated in different schools. It has been estimated that 80 percent of either blacks or whites would have to move to desegregate housing fully in the average American city.

THE CIVIL RIGHTS MOVEMENT

Struggles by minority groups to achieve equal rights and opportunities have for a long while been a part of the United States. In contrast to other racial and ethnic minorities, blacks and Native Americans have largely been denied opportunities for self-advancement. The National Association for the Advancement of Colored People (NAACP) and the National Urban League, founded in 1909 and 1910, respectively, fought for black civil rights but began to have some real effect only after World War II, when the NAACP instituted a campaign against segregated public education. This struggle came to a head when the organization sued five school boards, challenging the concept of separate but equal schooling that then prevailed. In 1954, in *Brown v. Board of Education of Topeka, Kansas,* the U.S. Supreme Court unanimously decided that "separate educational facilities are inherently unequal."

This decision became the platform for struggles for civil rights from the 1950s to the 1970s. The strength of the resistance from many whites persuaded black leaders that mass militancy was necessary to give civil rights any real substance. In 1955, a black woman, Rosa Parks, was arrested in Montgomery, Alabama, for declining to give up her seat on a bus to a white man. As a result, almost the entire African American population of the city, led by a Baptist minister, Martin Luther King Jr., boycotted the transportation system for 381 days. Eventually the city was forced to abolish segregation in public transportation.

Further boycotts and sit-ins followed, with the object of desegregating other public facilities. The marches and demonstrations began to achieve a mass following from blacks and white sympathizers. In 1963, a quarter of a million civil rights supporters staged a march on Washington and cheered as King announced, "We will not be satisfied until justice rolls down like the waters and righteousness like a mighty stream." In 1964, the Civil Rights Act was passed by Congress and signed into law by President Lyndon B. Johnson, comprehensively banning discrimination in public facilities, education, employment, and any agency receiving government funds. Further bills in following years were aimed at ensuring that African Americans became fully registered voters and outlawed discrimination in housing.

Attempts to implement the new civil rights legislation continued to meet with ferocious resistance from opponents. Civil rights marchers were insulted and beaten up, and some lost their lives. But in spite of barriers that hampered the full realization of its provisions, the Civil Rights Act proved to be fundamentally important. Its principles applied not just to African Americans but to anyone subject to discrimination, including other ethnic groups and women. It served as the starting point for a range of movements asserting the rights of oppressed groups.

How successful has the civil rights movement been? On one hand, a substantial black middle class has emerged over the last three to four decades. And many African Americans—such as the writer Toni Morrison, the literary scholar Henry Louis Gates, Secretary of State Condoleezza Rice, media mogul Oprah Winfrey, and basketball player Michael Jordan—have achieved positions of power and influence in the wider society. On the other hand, a large number of African Americans, making up an underclass, live trapped in the ghettos. Scholars have debated whether the existence of the black underclass has resulted primarily from economic disadvantage or dependency on the welfare system. We will examine the forms of inequality that African Americans and other minority groups continue to experience later in this chapter.

Latinos in the United States

The wars of conquest that created the boundaries of the contemporary United States were not only directed against the Native American population but also against Mexico. The territory that later became California, Nevada, Arizona, New Mexico, and Utah, along with a quarter of a million Mexicans—was taken by the United States in 1848 as a result of the American war with Mexico. The terms *Mexican American* and *Chicano* include the descendants of these people, together with subsequent immigrants from Mexico. The term *Latino* refers to anyone from Spanish-speaking regions living in the United States.

The three main groups of Latinos in the United States are Mexican Americans (around 26.6 million), Puerto Ricans (3.8 million), and Cubans (1.6 million). A further 8.3 million Spanish-speaking residents are from countries in Central and South America (U.S. Bureau of the Census 2004). The Latino population, as mentioned earlier, is increasing at an extraordinary rate—53 percent between 1980 and 1990, 58 percent between 1990 and 2000, and 17 percent in the first four years of the twenty-first century—mainly as a result of the large-scale flow of new immigrants from across the Mexican border (U.S. Bureau of the Census 2004). Latino residents now slightly outnumber African Americans.

MEXICAN AMERICANS

Mexican Americans continue to reside mainly in California, Texas, and the remaining southwestern states, although there are substantial groups in the midwest and in northern cities. The majority have come to work at low-paying jobs. In the post–World War II period up to the early 1960s, Mexican workers were admitted without much restriction. This was succeeded by a phase in which numbers were limited and efforts made to deport those who had entered illegally. Illegal immigrants today continue to flood across the border. Large numbers are intercepted and sent back each year by immigration officials, but most simply try again, and it is estimated that four times as many escape officials as are stopped.

Since Mexico is a relatively poor country existing alongside the much wealthier United States, it seems unlikely that this flow of people northward will diminish in the near future. Illegal immigrants can be employed more cheaply than indigenous workers, and they are prepared to perform jobs that most of the rest of the population would not accept. Legislation was passed by Congress in 1986 making it possible for illegal immigrants who had lived in the United States for at least five years to claim legal residence.

Many Mexican Americans resist assimilation into the dominant English-speaking culture and, in common with other

Closed Doors: Immigration, Politics, and Public Sociology

In the spring of 2004, Professor Douglas Massey received a troubling e-mail. Massey had recently been invited to author a chapter for the United Nations on international migration, a topic he has studied in depth for over two decades. As co-director of the Mexican Migration Project since 1982 (with Jorge Durand of the University of Guadalajara), Massey has visited countries throughout Central and Latin America over seventy times to learn about the causes and consequences of U.S. immigration policy at the grassroots level. His findings have been widely published in academic journals, books, and the popular press; and he is considered one of the foremost experts on immigration worldwide. When his name was vetted, however, Bush administration officials informed the United Nations that his participation was unacceptable. No explanation was provided. Massey had been blackballed by his own government (Massey 2006a).

"What Bush's people objected to," Massey (2006) learned through back channels, "was not my science, but a series of critical articles I had published on U.S. immigration policy" during the Clinton administration. In these articles, Massey argued that closed-door policies, advocating tighter border security, actually increase the problem of undocumented immigration to the United States by forcing migrants to cross in more remote areas and making it more difficult for them to return home. The result of tighter security, according to Massey (2006a), has been an unintended increase in the size of

Douglas Massey

the undocumented immigrant population in the United States "at great financial and human cost."

These conclusions are not simply Massey's personal opinions. They are derived from extensive data on international migration collected over twenty years in Mexico and Latin America. The Mexican Migration Project collects data on documented and undocumented migrants originating in both urban and rural communities throughout Mexico. As a sociol-

ethnic groups, have increasingly begun to display pride in their own cultural identity within the United States.

PUERTO RICANS AND CUBANS

Puerto Rico was acquired by the United States through war, and Puerto Ricans have been American citizens since 1917. The island is poor, and many of its inhabitants have migrated to the mainland United States to improve their conditions of life.

Puerto Ricans originally settled in New York City, but since the 1960s, they have moved elsewhere. A reverse migration of Puerto Ricans began in the 1970s; more have left the mainland than have arrived since that date. One of the most important issues facing Puerto Rican activists is the political destiny of their homeland. Puerto Rico is at present a commonwealth, not a full state within the United States. For years, Puerto Ricans have been divided about whether the island should retain its present status, opt for independence, or attempt to become the fifty-first state of the Union.

ogist, Massey is dedicated to the collection of facts about how immigration works, how people make decisions, and why they choose to leave their home countries for opportunities elsewhere. Letting the facts speak for themselves, Massey's data reveal that some common assumptions about immigration are actually false: Immigration from Mexico is not a one-way street—many migrants return home (and come back again) through a process of "circular migration." Migrants are not cut off financially from their families back home—they send money, called *remittances*, to family members on a regular basis. Immigrants are not socially isolated—they form social networks in the United States and in Mexico that yield social capital and increase the likelihood that migratory flows will continue into the future.

Massey believes that sociologists can make a difference only when acting as "objective scientists in possession of important facts about the social world" rather than as citizens with emotionally charged opinions. He is not naive enough to believe that facts automatically make a difference in the real world. "Policy is always about politics and politics is never straightforward," Massey admits. But during the 1990s, when the political climate was more receptive to scientific findings, Massey was able to successfully bridge the gap between science and policy. By looking closely at the U.S. Census, Massey documented, that two decades after the Fair Housing Act (1968), blacks in the United States remained more segregated from whites than any other racial or ethnic group. Racial segregation and poverty were interconnected, making the social, economic, and political isolation of urban African Americans more severe as jobs disappeared from inner-city neighborhoods. The nation's slow progress toward racial integration in housing, as revealed by Massey and his colleagues, became front-page news in the *New York Times*, the *Los Angeles Times*, the *Philadelphia Inquirer*, *USA Today*, and the *Washington Post*.

That was just the beginning. Massey and his colleagues continued their research over the following five years, pro-ducing a body of evidence suggesting that residential segregation not only separates people geographically but "represents a primary cause of racial inequality in the United States" (Massey and Denton 1993). By applying sociological thinking to real-life data, Massey demonstrated how segregation increases the severity of poverty and "perpetuates black disadvantage over time and across the generations" (Massey 2006b). The only other place on earth with comparable patterns of racial segregation was South Africa under apartheid, an official policy that promoted the separate development of racial groups.

Massey and Denton's award-winning book, *American Apartheid* (1993), produced further opportunities for public engagement. Throughout the 1990s, Massey was invited to address a variety of civic groups, fair housing organizations, governmental commissions, and academic audiences. Henry Cisneros, the secretary of Housing and Urban Development (HUD) under the Clinton administration assigned the book to be read by staff members at HUD, and invited Massey to Washington to educate politicians on issues relating to segregation and fair housing enforcement. Translating scientific findings for an audience of national policy makers, Massey helped pass the most important development in housing discrimination law since the late 1960s. The policy recommendations instituted by HUD further strengthened Fair Housing law and resulted in record settlements in discrimination cases (Massey 2006b).

Whether testifying before Congress, authoring articles, serving on government commissions, or lecturing before a classroom of students, Massey provides an excellent model of a public sociologist at work. For almost three decades and across multiple research topics, Massey has used his sociological understanding to suggest workable and humane solutions based on facts, not on slogans. His ability to translate those facts into more effective public policies, however, depends on political factors that remain largely outside of his control.

A third Latino group in the United States, the Cubans, differs from the two others in key respects. Half a million Cubans fled communism after the rise of Fidel Castro in 1959, and the majority settled in Florida. Unlike other Latino immigrants, they were mainly educated people from white-collar and professional backgrounds. They have managed to thrive within the United States, many finding positions comparable to those they abandoned in Cuba. As a group, Cubans have the highest family income of all Latinos.

A further wave of Cuban immigrants, from less affluent ori-gins, arrived in 1980. Lacking the qualifications held by the first wave, these people tend to live in circumstances closer to the rest of the Latino communities in the United States. Both sets of Cuban immigrants are mainly political refugees rather than economic migrants. The later immigrants to a large extent have become the "working class" for the earlier immigrants. They are paid low wages, but Cuban employers tend to take them on in preference to other ethnic groups. In Miami, nearly one third of all businesses are owned by Cubans, and 75 percent of the labor force in construction is Cuban.

Life on the Work Line

*Seven days a week—early mornings to mid-afternoons—men from south of the border, mostly from Mexico, hang out in work lines on Queens Boulevard or Roosevelt Avenue. They wait for cars, vans, or trucks belonging to small business owners, contractors, and construction companies who are looking for cheap day-labor. It took six years for Miguel to graduate from being one of the guys on the line to being one of the guys with the boss in the vehicle, picking who works and who doesn't. In between caring for their three kids, Miguel's wife, Marianna, practices aroma and herbal cleansings. They shared their story of *** migration and survival as undocumented "aliens" from their one-room basement apartment next to the Grand Central Expressway.*

***

MARIANNA: We went to Tijuana to get away from our mothers—but we ended up with his crazy cousin. A twenty-eight-year-old man married to a sixty-eight-year-old woman. Nothing but a liar and a thief, his cousin. I kept saying "Miguel, let's go north, to New York. We can stay with my father. Make enough to live good and send money home to our families." But Miguel was so macho about the United States.

MIGUEL: I always thought, why would I go to the United States? Just so they could humiliate me for cheap labor. *Never!* *** The high school I went to was a Socialist school. Always in my mind the United States was an evil place.

Miguel called a cousin who gave him the name of a coyote who could take them across the border.

***

MIGUEL: He takes us to a town closer to the border where he has other people waiting to cross. At one o'clock in the morning we leave in a Camaro with California plates. We were three men in a trunk big enough for only one man, *** I was curled up sideways in the trunk. Another guy was curled up the other way. The third one went across the two of us. ***

MARIANNA: I was in the backseat with the baby, three other women and two other little girls—all squashed together and a big cloth over everything. I was worried my baby was going to suffocate under the blanket. El Sabrás [the coyote] finally said "Okay, you can uncover the baby, but don't let him look up."

***

MIGUEL: The car stops and the trunk door opens. *** Two hours in the trunk and we could barely stand. Even if your whole body is numb, you have to make sure not to look suspicious because INS knows the look of people walking out of trunks.

***

MIGUEL: We spent whatever money we had left flying from L.A. to New York so Marianna could be near her father and sister. Everyone else in the airplane was white. They were staring at us with our nerves all at an end. Probably they were thinking, look, they are *mojaditos* [slang for Mexicans who cross; literally "the wet ones"]. My father-in-law forgot he was supposed to pick us up at JFK Airport. We're waiting in the cold for a long time, putting quarters in phone booths.

***

MIGUEL: Most of the jobs I've had here I got from the work line on Roosevelt Avenue. In the beginning they were day jobs, doing yard work, washing cars, passing out fliers, installing air conditioners. Sometimes the jobs are more steady: busboy, dishwasher, mechanic's assistant, selling carpets.

Work lines are like survival. The one who runs the fastest gets the job. We could be six or seven of us standing around, talking. When a van pulls up, you stop what you're doing and run. If they need two painters, you say you're a painter. If they need a mover, you're a mover. The guy working for the boss looking for people is an instant employment agency. *"You, you, and you come with me."* I'm that guy now. I'm working for a guy who's Turkish and it's easier for him to have me do it, because a lot of Mexican guys don't want to go with an Arab or a Chinese or a Greek.

We ask, "After everything that you've been through, was it worth it, coming to the United States?"

MARIANNA: I pray that my husband will get a job with better pay and that my children have a chance to study and have a good head so they don't become little bums. That's what they learn over here. Children are out by themselves without their parents' permission. Many of them are in gangs. They should be in their homes studying or with their family. Even if they are drawing on the walls, at least they're in their homes. More than anything I want my son, Lalo, to have the opportunity to study. It is better for him here in the U.S., even if it is not better for us.

SOURCE: Warren Lehrer and Judith Sloan, *Crossing the BLVD* (New York: W. W. Norton, 2003).

The Asian Connection

About 4.3 percent of the population of the United States is of Asian origin—12.3 million people (U.S. Bureau of the Census 2004b). Chinese, Japanese, and Filipinos (immigrants from the Philippines) form the largest groups; but now there are also significant numbers of Asian Indians, Pakistanis, Koreans, and Vietnamese living in America. And as a result of the war in Vietnam, some 350,000 refugees from that country entered the United States in the 1970s.

Most of the early Chinese immigrants settled in California, where they were employed mainly in heavy industries, such as mining and railroad construction. The retreat of the Chinese into distinct Chinatowns was not primarily their choice, but was made necessary by the hostility they faced. Since Chinese immigration was ended by law in 1882, the Chinese remained largely isolated from the wider society, at least until recently.

The early Japanese immigrants also settled in California and the other Pacific states. During World War II, after the attack on Pearl Harbor by Japan, all Japanese Americans in the United States were made to report to "relocation centers," which were effectively concentration camps, surrounded by barbed wire and gun turrets. In spite of the fact that most of these people were American citizens, they were compelled to live in the hastily established camps for the duration of the war. Paradoxically, this situation eventually led to their greater integration within the wider society because, after the war, Japanese Americans did not return to the separate neighborhoods in which they had previously lived. They have become extremely successful in reaching high levels of education and income, marginally outstripping whites. The rate of intermarriage of Japanese Americans with whites is now nearly 50 percent.

After the passing of a new immigration act in 1965, large-scale immigration of Asians into the United States again took place. Foreign-born Chinese Americans today outnumber those brought up in the United States. The newly arrived Chinese have avoided the Chinatowns in which the long-established Chinese have tended to remain, mostly moving into other neighborhoods.

Racial and Ethnic Inequality

A 1996 *New York Times* headline proclaimed "Quality of Life Is Up for Many Blacks" (Holmes 1996). The following year, the same paper ran this headline: "New Reports Say Minorities Benefit in Fiscal Recovery" (Holmes 1997). Since the civil rights movement of the 1960s, has real progress been made? On the one hand, an increasing number of blacks joined the middle class by acquiring college degrees, professional jobs, and new homes. On the other hand, blacks are far more likely than whites to live in poverty and be socially isolated from good schools and economic opportunity. Also, large numbers of immigrants came to the United States throughout the 1980s and 1990s to find new economic opportunity. Yet some of these groups, particularly immigrants from Mexico, have among the lowest levels of educational achievement and live in dire poverty. For the most part, sociologists agree on the facts about racial and ethnic inequality. There is, however, a disagreement among sociologists about how these facts should be interpreted. Are improving economic conditions for minority groups part of a long-term process or were they temporary reflections of the booming 1990s economy? Is racial and ethnic inequality primarily the result of a person's racial or ethnic background or does it reflect a person's class position? In other words, is a black American, for example, more likely to live in poverty because of racial discrimination or because of the lower-class status that many blacks hold? In this section, we first examine the facts: how racial and ethnic inequality is reflected in terms of educational and occupational attainment, income, health, residential segregation, and political power. We then look at the divergent social statuses found within the largest racial and ethnic groups. We conclude by looking at how sociologists have sought to explain racial inequality.

Educational Attainment

Differences between blacks and whites in levels of educational attainment have decreased, but these seem more the result of long-established trends rather than the direct outcome of the struggles of the 1960s. After steadily improving their levels of educational attainment, young African Americans are for the first time close to whites in terms of finishing high school. The number of blacks over the age of twenty-five with high school degrees has increased from about 20 percent in 1960 to 80.6 percent in 2004. By contrast, about 86 percent of whites have completed high school (Figure 11.2). Some analysts see this development as a positive sign and an indicator that young blacks need not live a life of hopelessness and despair. But not all signs have been positive. While more blacks are attending college now than in the 1960s, a much higher proportion of whites than blacks graduate from college today. In today's global economy and job market, which value college degrees, the result is a wide disparity in incomes between whites and blacks (see the next section). As sociologist Christopher Jencks remarked, "You have a situation where the black kids coming out of high school are better qualified, but the number

FIGURE 11.2

Educational Attainment (people 25 Years Old and Older)

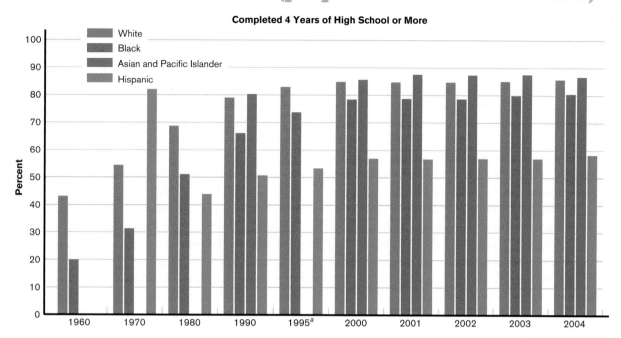

Completed 4 Years of High School or More

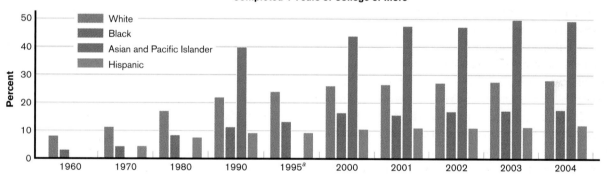

Completed 4 Years of College or More [b]

From 1980 to 2004, how did the percentage of blacks who graduated from college change compared to the change in the percentage of Hispanics who graduated from college? During which year did the percentage of whites who graduated from college match the percentage of Hispanics who graduated from college in 2004? What happens to the gap between the percentage of whites and the percentage of blacks who graduated from high school from 1960 to 2000? What happens to the gap between the percentage of whites and the percentage of blacks who graduated from college from 1960 to 2004? From 1980 to 2004, the percentage of blacks who completed four years of high school or more increased and came much closer to the percentage of whites who did so. How does this compare to the percentage of Hispanics during that same time period?

[a] High school graduates or more.
[b] B.A. degree or more.
SOURCE: U.S. Bureau of the Census, Table 215, Table 214, 2006b.

of jobs that they are qualified for is actually shrinking" (quoted in Holmes 1997).

Another negative trend with potentially far-reaching consequences is the large gap in educational attainment between Hispanics and both whites and blacks. Hispanics have by far the highest high school dropout rate of any group in the United States. While rates of college attendance and success in graduation have gradually improved for other groups, the rate for Hispanics has held relatively steady since the mid-1980s. Only about 12 percent hold a college degree (U.S. Bureau of the Census 2006b). It is possible that these poor results can be attributed to the large number of poorly educated immigrants from Latin America who have come to the United States since the 1980s. Many of these immigrants have poor English-language skills and their children encounter difficulties in schools. One study found, however, that even among Mexican Americans whose families have lived in the United States for three generations or more, there has been a decline in educational attainment (Bean et al. 1994). For Hispanics with low levels of education and poor language skills, living in the United States has been "the American nightmare, not the American dream" (Holmes 1997).

Employment and Income

As a result of the increase in educational attainment, blacks now hold a slightly higher proportion of managerial and professional jobs than in 1960, though still not in proportion to their overall numbers. In 2004, out of the approximately 45.6 million managerial or professional positions in the United States, whites held about 38.6 million (about 85.6 percent); African Americans, about 3.7 million (about 8 percent); and Hispanics, just under 3 million (about 8 percent) (U.S. Bureau of the Census 2006c). During that same year, black men were about twice as likely as whites to be service workers and about one and one half times as likely to hold a blue-collar job.

The unemployment rate of black and Hispanic men outstrips that of whites by the same degree today as was the case in the early 1960s. More than four times as many black and Hispanic men as white men are registered as unemployed (in 2005, 4.4 percent for whites versus about 10.4 percent for blacks and 6.4 percent for Hispanics) (Arthur 2005). There has also been some debate about whether employment opportunities for minorities have improved or worsened. Statistics on unemployment don't adequately measure economic opportunity because they measure only those known to be looking for work. A higher proportion of blacks and Hispanics have simply opted out of the occupational system, neither working nor looking for work. They have become disillusioned by the frus-

tration of searching for employment that is not there. Unemployment figures also do not reflect the increasing numbers of young men from minority groups who have been incarcerated (see also Chapter 7). Finally, although many new jobs were created during the economic boom of the 1990s, most of them available to those without a college degree were in lower-paying service occupations. As we just saw, blacks and Hispanics are underrepresented among college graduates.

Nevertheless, the disparities between the earnings of blacks and whites are gradually diminishing. As measured in terms of median weekly income, black men now earn 77.7 percent of the level of pay of whites (U.S. Bureau of Labor Statistics 2004). In 1959, the proportion was only 49 percent. In terms of household family income (adjusted for inflation), blacks are the only social group to have seen an improvement during the 1990s. By 2000, poverty rates for African Americans had fallen to their lowest rates since the government started tracking the figure in 1955. Milton Morris, who tracks trends among African Americans, claimed "I think that this is a short period of really very substantial and significant gains. . . . [V]ery few people have been paying serious attention. And yet when you do, you see that by virtually every measure of well-being, African Americans have been on a significant uptrend during the 90s" (quoted in Holmes 1996). These signs of improvement appear to be felt by African Americans across the country. One Jersey City resident said "In my area, I see things getting better all the time. It used to be like hell, groups always on the corner, cussing and fighting, ripping and raiding, shooting each other. It calmed down a whole hell of a lot" (quoted in Holmes 1996).

Some scholars have warned, however, that these gains could be reversed as the economy falters. They also pointed out that though there has been considerable improvement, large gaps between African Americans and whites still exist in terms of the attainment of college degrees, infant mortality, poverty rates, and household income (Figure 11.3). Finally, though the economic status of blacks appears to have improved, prospects for Hispanics have stagnated or worsened over the same time period. Between 1989 and 2000, Hispanic household incomes (adjusted for inflation) decreased significantly. Still, Hispanic household poverty remained very similar to that of blacks (in 2000–2003 the average poverty rate for Hispanics was 21.9 percent versus 23.7 percent for blacks). For the first time ever, the poverty rate of Hispanics surpassed that of African Americans. The large influx of immigrants, who tend to be poor, has caused some of the decline in average income, but even among Hispanics born in the United States, income levels declined as well. As one Latino group leader commented, "Most Hispanic residents are caught in jobs like gardener, nanny, and restaurant worker that will never pay well and from which they will never advance" (quoted in Goldberg 1997).

FIGURE 11.3

Median Household Income by Race, 1970–2003

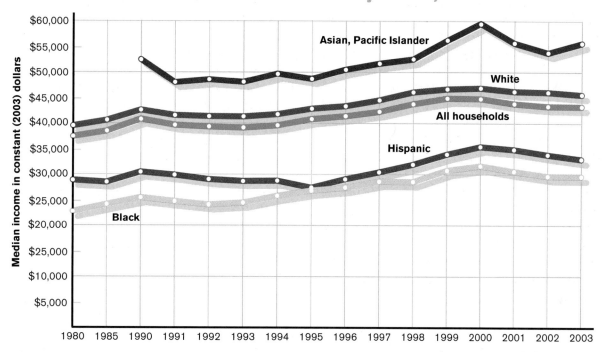

Which race or ethnic group has the highest median income through the 1990s and the early twenty-first century? What are the approximate differences between white median income and black median income in both 1970 and 2003? During what year did the Hispanic median income reach the 1970 level of white median income? What does the figure above indicate about the economic mobility of black and Hispanic racial groups as a whole in our society?

SOURCE: U.S. Bureau of the Census, 2001d, Table 662, 2006b, Table 674.

Health

Jake Najman (1993) surveyed the evidence linking health to racial and economic inequalities. He also considered what strategies might best be used to improve the health of the poorer groups in society. After studying data for a number of different countries, including the United States, he concluded that for people in the poorest 20 percent, as measured in terms of income, the death rates were 1.5–2.5 times those of the highest 20 percent of income earners. In the United States, the rate of infant mortality for the poorest 20 percent was four times higher than for the wealthiest 20 percent. When differences were measured between whites and African Americans in the United States, rather than only in terms of income, the contrast in infant mortality rates was

even higher—five times higher for blacks than for whites. The contrast between races is also seen in life expectancy—the average age to which individuals at birth can expect to live. In 2003, whites on average could expect to live 5.2 years longer than African Americans (National Center for Health Statistics 2005).

How might the influence of poverty and race on health be countered? Extensive programs of health education and disease prevention are one possibility. But such programs tend to work better among more prosperous, well-educated groups and in any case usually produce only small changes in behavior. Increased accessibility to health services would help, but probably to a limited degree. The only really effective policy option, it is argued, would be to attack poverty itself, so as to reduce the income gap between rich and poor (Najman 1993).

Residential Segregation

Neighborhood segregation seems to have declined little over the past quarter century. Studies show that discriminatory practices between black and white clients in the housing market continue (Lake 1981). Black and white children now attend the same schools in most rural areas of the South and in many of the smaller- and medium-size cities throughout the country. Most black college students now also go to the same colleges and universities as whites, instead of the traditional all-black institutions (Bullock 1984). Yet in the larger cities a high level of educational segregation persists as a result of the continuing movement of whites to suburbs or rural environs.

In *American Apartheid* (1993), Douglas Massey and Nancy A. Denton argue that the history of racial segregation and its specific urban form, the black ghetto, are responsible for the perpetuation of black poverty and the continued polarization of black and white.

The persistence of segregation, they say, is not a result of impersonal market forces. Even many middle-class blacks still find themselves segregated from the white society. For them, as for poor blacks, this becomes a self-perpetuating cycle. Affluent blacks who could afford to live in comfortable, predominantly white neighborhoods may deliberately choose not to, because of the struggle for acceptance they know they would face. The black ghetto, the authors conclude, was constructed through a series of well-defined institutional practices of racial discrimination—private behavior and public policies by which whites sought to contain growing urban black populations. Until policy makers, social scientists, and private citizens recognize the crucial role of such institutional discrimination in perpetuating urban poverty and racial injustice, the United States will remain a deeply divided and troubled society.

Political Power

Blacks have made some gains in holding local elective offices; the number of black public officials has increased from forty in 1960 to over eight thousand today. The numbers of black mayors and judges have increased appreciably. Blacks have been voted into every major political office, except president and vice president, including areas where white voters predominate. In 1992, after congressional districts were reshaped to give minority candidates more opportunity, a record number of African Americans and Latinos were elected to Congress. Yet these changes are still relatively small scale. In 2001, there were just over nine thousand black elected officials in the United States (Bositis 2001). This represents fewer than 2 percent of the elective offices in the country. Most of these individuals are in relatively minor local positions. The share of representation that

Latinos and African Americans have in Congress is not equal to their overall size in American society. Currently there are forty-two black members of the U.S. House of Representatives. But, after the defeat of Senator Carol Moseley-Braun in 1998, the U.S. Senate had no black members until Barack Obama was elected to represent Illinois in 2004. In addition, three Latinos—Ken Salazar from Colorado, Bob Menendez from New Jersey, and Mel Martinez from Florida—serve in the U.S. Senate. These were the first in three decades. And Martinez is the first Cuban American to be elected to the Senate in its history (National Association of Latino Elected Officials 2004).

Gender and Race

The status of minority women in the United States is especially plagued by inequalities (Figure 11.4). Gender and race discrimination combined make it particularly difficult for these women to escape conditions of poverty. They share the legacy of past discrimination against members of minority groups and women in general. Until about twenty-five years ago, most minority women worked in low-paying occupations such as household work or farmwork or low-wage manufacturing jobs. Changes in the law and gains in education have allowed for more minority women to enter white-collar professions, and their economic and occupational status has improved. By 1987, the average African American female college graduate over twenty-five years old working full-time earned roughly 90 percent of the average for white female college graduates; today, the figure is closer to 95 percent (U.S. Bureau of the Census 2004). But in general, female college graduates earn less than men with only high school educations. And white male high school dropouts, on average, earn more than black female college graduates (Higginbotham 1992; Rhode 1990).

Swearing in of the Congressional Black Caucus. Currently there are forty-two black members of the U.S. House of Representatives.

However unequal the status and pay of minority women, these women play a critical role in their communities. They are often the major or sole wage earners in their families. Yet their incomes are not always sufficient to maintain a family. About half of all families headed by African American or Latino women live at poverty levels.

Divergent Fortunes

When we survey the development and current position of the major ethnic groups in America, one conclusion that emerges is that they have achieved varying levels of success. Whereas successive waves of European immigrants managed to overcome most of the prejudice and discrimination they originally faced and become assimilated into the wider society, other groups have not. These latter groups include two minorities that have lived in North America for centuries, Native Americans and African Americans, as well as Mexicans, Puerto Ricans, and to some extent Chinese.

THE ECONOMIC DIVIDE WITHIN THE AFRICAN AMERICAN COMMUNITY

The situation of blacks is the most conspicuous case of divergent fortunes. After more than two centuries of continuous presence on the North American subcontinent, longer than any other group except for Native Americans and the European settlers, blacks are in the worst situation, with the sole exception of Native Americans, of any ethnic group in the United States. The reasons for this lie in the historical backdrop of slavery and its residue in the long years of struggle that it took to free African Americans from open prejudice and discrimination.

It seems probable that a division has opened up between the minority of blacks who have obtained white-collar, managerial, or professional jobs—who form a small black middle class—and the majority whose living conditions have not improved. In 1960, most of the nonmanual-labor jobs open to blacks were those serving the black community—a small proportion of blacks could work as teachers, social workers, or less often, lawyers or doctors. No more than some 13 percent of blacks held white-collar jobs, contrasted to 44 percent of whites. Since that date, however, there have been significant changes. Between 1960 and 1970, the percentage of blacks in white-collar occupations doubled—although this level of growth slowed markedly in the 1980s. This increase was greater than that for the half century previous to 1960.

Bart Landry (1988) carried out a systematic study of the growing black middle class. He surveyed white-collar blacks

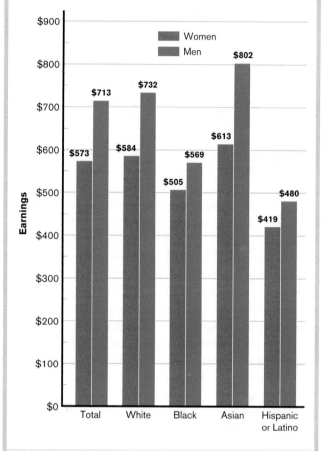

FIGURE 11.4

Median Weekly Income According to Gender and Race (2004)

According to the figure above, is the median weekly income of women from any of the three ethnic/racial groups reported to be more than their male counterparts? In 2004, what was the median weekly income of white males? Hispanic females? Which race/ethnic group has the greatest real discrepancy in median weekly income between its men and women? How much below the total male median weekly income is the median weekly income of black males? Think about what that would translate into for a year (fifty-two weeks). What two types of discrimination are illustrated in this figure?

SOURCE: U.S. Bureau of Labor Statistics, *Highlights of Women's Earnings in 2004*, 2005.

and whites in twenty-one metropolitan areas across the country and also analyzed government statistics from the early 1980s. Landry found that middle-class blacks were much better off, and much more numerous, than their predecessors twenty years before (see also Jacoby 1998). Opportunities have opened up partly through changes in legislation brought into being as a result of the civil rights movement. However, the population of blacks in middle-class jobs remains well below that of whites, and their average incomes are less.

THE ASIAN SUCCESS STORY

Unlike African Americans, other minority groups have outlasted the open prejudice and discrimination they once faced. The intense hostility once held toward the Irish, for instance, is now mostly a distant memory. Feelings of prejudice and antagonism still exist between people of Irish and Italian backgrounds in Boston and New York, and from both groups toward Jews. For the most part, however, such feelings are much less pronounced than in former times and are not widely expressed in practices of discrimination.

The changing fate of Asians in the United States is especially remarkable. Until about half a century ago, the level of prejudice and discrimination experienced by the Chinese and Japanese in North America was greater than for any other group of nonblack immigrants. Since that time, Asian Americans have achieved a steadily increasing prosperity and no longer face the same levels of antagonism from the white community. The median income of Asian Americans is now actually higher than that of whites.

This statistic conceals some big discrepancies between and within different Asian groups; there are still many Asian Americans, including those whose families have resided in the United States for generations, who live in poverty. However, the turnaround in the fortunes of Asian Americans, on the whole, is so impressive that some have referred to the Asian American success story as a prime example of what minorities can achieve in the United States.

LATINOS: A TALE OF TWO CITIES

Miami and Los Angeles both have large Latino populations. In Los Angeles, the large majority of Latinos are well down the ladder of privilege and power. But although both cities experience ethnic tensions, in Miami, Latinos have achieved a position of economic and political prominence not found elsewhere.

In *City on the Edge* (1993), Alejandro Portes and Alex Stepik describe the ethnic transformation of Miami over recent years. In 1980, whites were already in a minority in the city, at 48 percent of the population. African Americans made up 17 percent, and those of Spanish origin, 35 percent. In that year, as Portes

and Stepik (1993) put it, "the city abandoned, once and for all, the image of a sunny tourist destination and faced that of an uncertain bridge between two worlds." The reason was a large influx of Cuban immigrants. Struggles developed among the new immigrants, whites, and blacks; black leaders accused the Cubans of taking their jobs.

These struggles continue today. In Miami, those of Cuban origin have often moved into positions of considerable influence. Some Cubans have become very successful in business and have become more wealthy than the "old" white families that once ran the city. They haven't been assimilated into the white community but maintain their own customs, institutions, and language. Miami is now a place of "parallel structures" existing alongside one another, each including powerful and wealthy people, not integrated into one unified group. There is much tension, but some Anglo and Cuban politicians now speak of Miami as the capital of the Caribbean—a city that is

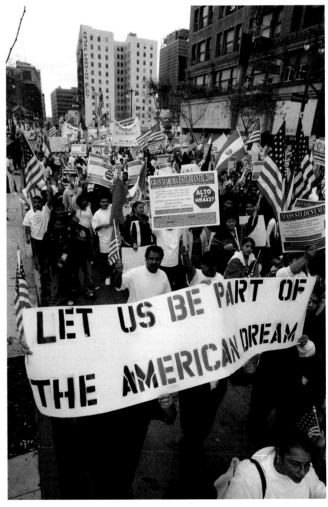

Hundreds of thousands of people marched in Los Angeles on May 1, 2006, to demand basic rights for immigrants.

not only part of the United States, but is also looking to the other societies, mostly developing countries, surrounding it.

Los Angeles points to the Pacific Rim—to what some analysts see as the future center of economic power, linking the West Coast of North America with Japan and the newly industrializing countries of Hong Kong, Taiwan, South Korea, and perhaps China. Immigrants from all of these countries have recently arrived in Los Angeles. At the same time, millions of Latinos have now settled in the city.

Los Angeles has been referred to as "the capital of the Third World" because of its large Latino and Asian populations. The city already contained the largest group of Mexicans in the United States in the 1920s. Then, as now, it was Mexicans who performed most of the menial jobs. Then, as now, most Anglos "were at once aware that this was the case," and "yet they would act as if these people, once they had finished working, went home not to the Old Plaza or, as now, to East L.A., but to another planet" (Rieff 1991).

Some optimistic observers have suggested that Los Angeles in the twenty-first century will combine Asian family loyalty, Hispanic industriousness, and Anglo-Saxon respect for individual liberty. Is such a vision possible? It would certainly take some profound social changes even to come close. Los Angeles is an ethnic mosaic that symbolizes the increasing diversity of American society as a whole. Will the Hispanic population of the city be able to achieve economic success similar to the Cubans in Miami? Will there exist separate but equal Hispanic communities in Los Angeles as well as in other U.S. cities in the future? How will such successes, if they happen, affect the black urban poor? These are all at the moment open questions, to which no one can give certain answers.

Understanding Racial Inequality

What distinguishes less fortunate groups such as African Americans and Mexican Americans is not just that they are nonwhite, but that they were originally present in America as *colonized peoples* rather than willing immigrants. In a classic analysis, Robert Blauner (1972) suggested that a sharp distinction should be drawn between groups who journeyed voluntarily to settle in the new land and those who were incorporated into the society through force or violence. Native Americans are part of American society as a result of military conquest; African Americans were transported in the slave trade; Puerto Rico was colonized as a result of war; and Mexicans were originally incorporated as a result of the conquest of the Southwest by the United States in the nineteenth century. These groups have consistently been the target of racism, which both reflects and perpetuates their separation from other ethnic communities.

But, given that this has been the case for most of American history, what explains the growth of the black middle class? William Julius Wilson (1978; see also Wilson et al. 1987) argues that race is of diminishing importance in explaining inequalities between whites and blacks. In his view, these inequalities are now based on class rather than skin color. The old racist barriers are crumbling. What remain are inequalities similar to those affecting all lower-class groups.

Wilson's work has proved controversial. His book was awarded a prize by the American Sociological Association, but the Association of Black Sociologists passed a resolution stating that the book "omits significant data regarding the continuing discrimination against blacks at all class levels." "It is the consensus of this organization," the resolution continues, "that this book denies the overwhelming evidence regarding the significance of race and the literature that speaks to the contrary" (quoted in Pinkney 1984). The resolution criticized the view that the circumstances of blacks have substantially improved or even that racism has declined significantly. Most of the changes, it was argued, have been relatively minor, and racism has only become less vocal since the 1964 Civil Rights Act, rather than diminishing in any substantial sense.

Yet Wilson made it clear in his book that the living conditions of poor blacks were deteriorating. In Wilson's view, his critics have almost completely ignored this aspect of his work. He has since extended his analysis of the most deprived sectors of the black population. Middle-class blacks today tend no longer to live in ghetto neighborhoods. Their exodus has led to an even higher concentration of the disadvantaged in these areas than previously was the case. Wilson recognizes that racism plays a part in this situation of the disadvantaged but points out that other class-related and economic factors are at least equally important—in particular, the very high rate of unemployment and welfare dependency characteristic of the poorest neighborhoods. Wilson's argument is not so much that racism as such has declined but that it has declined in its *significance* for blacks. Other forms of discrimination based more on economic and class-based disadvantages are as important.

Are racial inequalities to be explained primarily in terms of class? It is true that racial divisions provide a means of social closure, whereby economic resources can be monopolized by privileged class groups. But the argument that racial inequality should be explained primarily in terms of class domination, however, has never been a satisfactory one. Ethnic discrimination, particularly of a racial kind, is partly independent of class differences: the one cannot be separated from the other. This still seems to remain true in the United States today.

For instance, opinion surveys show a general decline in hostile attitudes toward blacks over the past thirty years among white Americans (Bobo and Kluegel 1991; Schuman et al. 1985). The overall level of prejudice seems to be diminishing fairly markedly. David Wellman (1987) argues, however, that the concept of prejudice captures only the more open and individual forms of hostile attitudes toward ethnic minorities. Racism can also be expressed in more subtle ways—in terms of beliefs that, regardless of the intentions involved, defend the position of privileged groups. Many sociologists, according to Wellman, have underestimated the true incidence of racism, because they have looked only at its more obvious manifestations. Most studies have investigated prejudice using surveys; but these do not get at the less obvious, complex aspects of people's views about such emotive topics as ethnicity and race.

Wellman sought to illuminate these complex aspects of racism by means of in-depth interviews with 105 white Americans of various backgrounds. Most of those he interviewed said that they believed that everyone is equal and that they held no hostility toward blacks. Their beliefs and attitudes did not show the rigidities characteristic of prejudice and stereotypical thinking. Yet their views about contexts of social life (such as education, housing, or jobs) in which black rights threatened their own position were effectively antiblack. Their opposition to change was expressed in ways that did not directly express racial antagonism. People would say, for instance, "I'm not opposed to blacks; but if they come into the neighborhood house prices will be affected"—or, as one individual put it, "I favor anything that doesn't affect me personally" (Wellman 1987).

These attitudes can still underlie quite rigid institutional patterns of discrimination. Ethnic inequalities are structured into existing social institutions, and patterns of behavior having no immediate connection to ethnicity can serve to reinforce them. Rights and opportunities are not the same thing. Even if it were true that every member of the population accepted that members of all ethnic groups have the same civil rights, major inequalities would persist. There are many examples that demonstrate this. A black person who wishes to obtain a bank loan to be able to make home improvements finds it hard to borrow money. The bank might use purely "objective" measures in reaching such decisions, based on the likelihood of the loan repayments being successfully made. Nevertheless, the effect of this institutional racism is the perpetuation of ethnic discrimination (Massey and Denton 1993).

In sum, although both individual and institutional racism seem to be declining in the United States, the differences between white and nonwhite ethnic groups are long enduring (Conley 1999; Ringer 1985). Moreover, the relative success of white ethnics has been to some degree purchased at the expense of nonwhites. A combination of continued white immigration and white racism, up to at least the World War II period, served to keep nonwhites out of the better-paid occupations, forcing them into the least-skilled, most marginal sectors of the economy. With the slowing down of white immigration, this situation is changing, although some newly arrived groups, like the Cubans in Miami, seem to be repeating the process.

Study Outline

www.wwnorton.com/giddens

Race and Ethnicity

- Ethnic groups have common cultural characteristics that separate them from others within a given population. Ethnic differences are wholly learned, although they are sometimes depicted as "natural."
- *Race* refers to physical characteristics, such as skin color, that are treated by members of a community or society as socially significant—as signaling distinct cultural characteristics. Many popular beliefs about race are mythical. There are no distinct characteristics by means of which human beings can be allocated to different races.
- *Racism* is prejudice based on socially significant physical distinctions. A racist is someone who believes that some individuals are superior, or inferior, to others as a result of racial differences.
- *Displacement* and *scapegoating* are psychological mechanisms associated with *prejudice* and *discrimination*. In displacement, feelings of hostility become directed against objects that are not the real origin of these anxieties. People project their anxieties and insecurities onto scapegoats. Prejudice involves holding preconceived views about an individual or group; discrimination refers to actual behavior that deprives members of a group of opportunities open to others. Prejudice usually involves *stereotypical thinking*—thinking in terms of fixed and inflexible categories.

Ethnic Relations

- Four models of possible future developments in race and ethnic relations can be distinguished—the first stressing Anglo-conformity, or *assimilation*, the second the *melting pot*, the third *pluralism*, and the fourth *multiculturalism*. In recent years there has been a tendency to emphasize the fourth of these avenues, whereby different ethnic identities are accepted as equal and separate within the context of the overall national culture.

Global Migration

- Beginning in the fifteenth century, global migratory movements resulting from exploration, colonialism, and slavery created multiethnic populations in various regions of the world and therefore ethnic and racial antagonism. Today, migration appears to be on the rise as part of the process of globalization.

Ethnic Relations in the United States

- A remarkable diversity of ethnic minorities is found in the United States today, each group having its own distinctive cultural characteristics. Some of the most important minority communities numerically, after blacks, are Native Americans, Mexican Americans, Puerto Ricans, Cubans, Chinese, and Japanese.

- An important distinction must be drawn between those minorities that came to America as willing immigrants and the colonized peoples who either were here already (Native Americans, Mexican Americans) or were brought by force (African Americans) and who were generally incorporated by violence. Racism targeted at these latter groups has been most persistent and most destructive. Gender discrimination compounds the difficulties facing women of color; about half of African American and Latino families that depend primarily on women's incomes live in poverty.

Key Concepts

antiracism (p. 333)
apartheid (p. 336)
assimilation (p. 338)
diaspora (p. 341)
discrimination (p. 334)
displacement (p. 334)
emigration (p. 340)
ethnic cleansing (p. 337)
ethnicity (p. 330)
genocide (p. 337)
immigration (p. 340)
institutional racism (p. 332)
melting pot (p. 338)
minority group (p. 334)
multiculturalism (p. 338)
pluralism (p. 338)
prejudice (p. 334)
race (p. 330)
racial literacy (p. 330)
racialization (p. 330)
racism (p. 332)
scapegoats (p. 334)
segregation (p. 337)
situational ethnicity (p. 331)
stereotyping (p. 334)
symbolic ethnicity (p. 331)

Review Questions

1. What is ethnicity?
   a. The physical manifestation of racial difference
   b. Any biologically grounded features of a group of people
   c. Any group outside the white, English-speaking majority
   d. The cultural practices and outlooks of a given community that have emerged historically and tend to set people apart

2. Why has racism flourished in modern societies?
   a. Because there was a symbolic distinction between white and black (denoting good and bad) in European cultures before European explorers went to Africa
   b. Because of the dissemination of the idea of race and the ideologies that developed around it
   c. Because of the relations of exploitation that Europeans established with Africans
   d. All of the above

3. What is the "master status"?
   a. A feature like skin color that dominates our perception, often overriding in our minds a person's other characteristics
   b. Our socioeconomic standing
   c. A feature such as skin color that dominates a person's perception of himself or herself, often overriding all other factors in the way a person sees himself or herself
   d. Our gender and/or sexual orientation

4. Which of the following is not one of the models of global population movements since 1945?
   a. Classic model
   b. Colonial model
   c. Guest worker model
   d. Refugee model

5. By the late 1990s, which of the following groups in U.S. society had the highest rate of poverty?
   a. Whites
   b. African Americans
   c. Hispanics
   d. Asian Americans

6. What's the difference between biological racism and cultural racism (new racism)?
   a. Biological racism is the belief that some groups are inferior because their members are biologically inferior, whereas cultural racism is the belief that some groups are inferior because they have a dysfunctional culture.
   b. Biological racism is the official ideology of a political party or social movement that supports the dominance of a majority group, such as white supremacist organizations; whereas cultural racism is a commonplace superstition, such as the widespread but ill-founded belief that the predominance of blacks in certain American sports reflects so-called racial advantages.
   c. Biological racism is the belief that there are absolute differences between groups, whereas cultural racism is the belief that there are only relative differences.

d. Biological racism is the belief that some groups are inferior because they have dysfunctional genes, whereas cultural racism is the belief that some groups are inferior because their members have inherently weaker cognitive abilities.

7. What is the difference between the assimilation and melting-pot models of integrating new ethnic groups into the dominant society?
   a. The assimilation model refers to the new group adopting the norms and values of the dominant society, whereas the melting-pot model refers to the merging and blending of dominant and ethnic cultures.
   b. The assimilation model refers to members of the new group becoming citizens of the host nation, whereas the melting-pot model refers to members of the new group remaining guest workers and having only the legal rights afforded to those on work visas.
   c. The assimilation model refers to members of the new group learning the language of the host nation and dispersing to the suburbs, whereas the melting-pot model refers to members of the new group sticking to their own language and concentrating in particular urban neighborhoods.
   d. The assimilation model refers to the experience of twentieth-century immigrants to the United States, whereas the melting-pot model refers to the experience of nineteenth-century immigrants.

8. Which of the following groups have *not* been the victim of scapegoating in Western history?
   a. Blacks
   b. Chinese
   c. White Protestants
   d. All have been victims at one time or another.

9. What is the difference between situational ethnicity and symbolic ethnicity?
   a. Situational ethnicity is secular, whereas symbolic ethnicity is religious.
   b. Situational ethnicity occurs when people choose to assert their ethnic background for social or economic advantage, whereas symbolic ethnicity occurs when people choose to participate in the most important religious holidays or parades of their ethnic group while ignoring their ethnicity for most of the year.
   c. Situational ethnicity is transitory, whereas symbolic ethnicity is permanent.
   d. Situational ethnicity occurs when people choose to participate in the most important religious holidays or parades of their ethnic group while ignoring their ethnicity for most of the year, whereas symbolic ethnicity occurs when people choose to assert their ethnic background for social or economic advantage.

10. How much difference did the formal abolition of slavery in the United States make to the condition of blacks?
    a. An enormous amount—they were no longer enslaved and were able to move in great numbers to seek manufacturing jobs in the northern cities.
    b. A good deal—their legal situation improved, and the formal rights they won formed the basis of the civil rights movement a century later.
    c. Relatively little—acts were soon passed legalizing the segregation of blacks and whites in public places.
    d. None—all of the conditions of slavery were replicated under sharecropping.

Thinking Sociologically Exercises

1. Review the discussion of the assimilation of different American minorities, then write a short essay comparing the different assimilation experiences of Asians and Latinos. In your essay identify the criteria for assimilation and discuss which group has assimilated most readily. Then explain the sociological reasons for the difference in assimilation between these two groups.

2. Does affirmative action still have a future in the United States? On the one hand, increasing numbers of African Americans have joined the middle class by earning college degrees, professional jobs, and new homes. Yet blacks are still far more likely than whites to live in poverty, to attend poor schools, and to lack economic opportunity. Given these differences and other contrasts mentioned in the text, do we still need affirmative action?

Data Exercises

www.wwnorton.com/giddens
Keyword: Data11

The American Indian and Alaska Native populations have often been described as the most disadvantaged racial minorities in the United States, and images of this population are often stereotypical. The data exercise for this chapter provides you with an opportunity to look beyond the stereotypes and learn more about the contemporary status of the American Indian and Alaska Native populations.

The Graying of U.S. Society

Learn some basic facts about the increase in the proportion of the U.S. population that is becoming elderly.

How Do People Age?

Understand that aging is a combination of biological, psychological, and sociological processes.

Growing Old: Competing Sociological Explanations

Consider the various theories of aging, particularly those that focus on how society shapes the social roles of the elderly and emphasize aspects of age stratification.

Aging in the United States

Evaluate the experience of growing old in the United States.

The Politics of Aging

Understand and analyze the politics of generational equity.

Globalization: The Graying of the World Population

Assess the social issues of graying on a global level.

CHAPTER TWELVE

AGING

W hen Fenya Crown decided to run the Los Angeles marathon, she was seventy years old. That was twenty-one years ago. Since that time, she has completed eight of the 26.2-mile races, most recently the Rome, Italy, marathon in March 2001. The ninety-one-year-old great-grandmother, who has recovered from three bouts with breast cancer during the past decade, has completed marathons from New York to Shanghai. Born in Ukraine in 1913, Crown emigrated to the United States, where she worked for many years as a dress designer in New York City's garment district.

Like Crown, Rose Freedman also worked as a young woman in the New York City garment industry. Although she never ran a marathon, she nonetheless possessed the endurance to work twelve- to fourteen-hour days as a seamstress in the city's garment factories. In 1911, at age eighteen, Freedman was working in the Triangle Shirtwaist Factory when fire swept through the building. She survived by racing up several floors to the factory's roof and then leaping to the safety of another building. Most of her co-workers—young female Jewish and Italian immigrants—were not so lucky: within thirty minutes, 500 were injured and 146 dead. The Triangle fire spurred the unionization of the garment industry and left Freedman with indelible memories of the disaster. She continued to speak out against abuses in the garment industry until her death in February 2001—at age 107.

John Glenn was seventy-seven years old when he completed a ten-day research mission in orbit aboard the space shuttle *Discovery* in the fall of 1998. This was not Glenn's first venture into space. Thirty-two years earlier, the longtime Democratic U.S. senator from Ohio was the first American astronaut in space, when he completed three orbits around the earth as part of America's fledgling space program. The purpose of Glenn's most recent trip was to study the effects of aging in the weightless environment of space. Glenn, who exercises daily and lifts weights, is in excellent shape. As expressed by National Aeronautics and Space Administration (NASA) administrator Daniel Goldin, Glenn was "poised to show the world that senior citizens have the right stuff."

More and more Americans are leading longer, healthier, and more productive lives than ever before. In 2004, there were nearly 36.3 million Americans sixty-five or older, including some 4.9 million over eighty-five years old (U.S. Bureau of the Census 2005a). Growing old can be a fulfilling and rewarding experience, as it was with the people just described. Or it can be filled with physical distress and social isolation. For most elderly Americans, the experience of aging lies somewhere in between.

In this chapter, we examine the nature of aging in U.S. society, exploring what it means to grow old in a world that is rapidly changing. We begin with a brief snapshot of how the American population is growing older, before examining biological, psychological, and social aspects of aging. We then look at the ways in which people adapt to growing old, at least in the eyes of sociologists. This will lead us to a discussion of aging in the United States, focusing on some of the special challenges and problems that the elderly face. We also discuss political issues surrounding the aging of the American population, issues that assume increasing importance given the growing numbers of elderly people. We conclude with a discussion of the graying of the world population and what it can mean for you.

The Graying of U.S. Society

The world's population is getting older. About two thousand years ago, the average newborn Roman baby could expect to live to the ripe old age of twenty-two. In fact, for most of human history the average life expectancy at birth was less than twenty years, with most people failing to survive the first few years of life. The average baby born into the world today can expect to live to be sixty-seven, although there is enormous variation, depending on where the baby is born—from an average life expectancy for women of eighty-five in Japan to one of thirty-two in Swaziland for both men and women (Weiss 1997; World Bank 2005). These changes are due to many factors. Modern agriculture, sanitation systems, epidemic control, and medicine have all contributed to a decline in mortality throughout the world. In most societies today, fewer children die in infancy, and more adults survive to become elderly.

The U.S. population, like other industrial societies, is aging even faster than the preindustrial societies of the world. Thanks to better nutrition and health care, people are living longer. They are also having fewer children. As a result, the median age of the population is rising. In 1850, half the population were younger than nineteen, and half were older. Today, half are over thirty-five; by the middle of the century, half will be over forty (Figure 12.1).

As a result, the United States and other industrial societies are said to be **graying**—that is, experiencing an increase in the proportion of the population becoming elderly. Graying is the result of two long-term trends in industrial societies: the tendency of families to have fewer children (discussed in Chapter 15) and the fact that people are living longer. The average life expectancy at birth for all Americans increased from forty-seven years for someone born in 1900 to seventy-seven years for someone born today (Figure 12.2). The average U.S. male born today can expect to live to about seventy-four; for females, the figure is nearly eighty. Most of these gains occurred in the first half of the twentieth century and were largely due to the improved chances for survival among the young. Although relatively few people made it to age sixty-five in the year 1900, most of those who did could expect to live to age seventy-seven, almost as long as most of those people who make it to sixty-five today, who can expect to live—to eighty-three (Centers for Disease Control and Prevention [CDC] 2004).

Because of the graying of the American population, there are today more than thirty-six million Americans older than sixty-five, a figure forecast to top seventy million people by the year 2030 (Treas 1995; U.S. Bureau of the Census 2004a). According to U.S. Bureau of the Census estimates, 25 percent of all people reaching age sixty-five today will live to be ninety. By the middle of this century, that figure is expected to rise to 42 percent. According to some projections, by that time there may be as many as two million living Americans who have celebrated their one-hundredth birthday (Healthful Life Project 2003; Weiss 1997).

These trends have enormous importance for the future of American society. In a culture that often worships eternal youth, what will happen when a quarter of the population is over sixty-five?

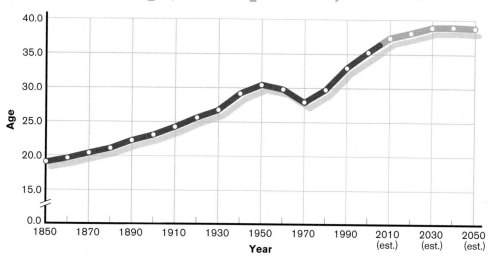

FIGURE 12.1

Median Age, U.S. Population, 1850–2050

How much did the median age of the U.S. population rise from 1910 to the estimate in 2010? Did the median age ever decline? If so, in what years and what could be the historical reason for this? How does the increase in median age in the forty years from 1910 to 1950 compare to the forty-year increase from 1970 to the estimate for 2010? What is the predicted trend for the median age of the population from 2030 to 2050? What are two long-term trends in the United States and other industrialized countries that account for the "graying" of these nations?

SOURCE: U.S. Bureau of the Census, 2002.

How Do People Age?

In examining the nature of aging we will draw on studies of **social gerontology**, a discipline concerned with the study of the social aspects of aging. Studying aging is a bit like examining a moving target: As people grow older, society itself changes at the same time, and so does the very meaning of being "old" (Riley et al. 1988). For Americans born in the first quarter of the twentieth century, a high school education was regarded as more than sufficient for most available jobs, and most people did not expect to live much past their mid-fifties—and then only at the cost of suffering a variety of disabilities. Today those very same people find themselves in their seventies and eighties; many are relatively healthy, unwilling to disengage from work and social life, and in need of more schooling than they ever dreamed would be necessary.

What does it mean to age? **Aging** can be sociologically defined as the combination of biological, psychological, and so-

cial processes that affect people as they grow older (Abeles and Riley 1987; Atchley 2000; Riley et al. 1988). These three processes suggest the metaphor of three different, although interrelated, developmental clocks: (1) a biological one, which refers to the physical body; (2) a psychological one, which refers to the mind and mental capabilities; and (3) a social one, which refers to cultural norms, values, and role expectations having to do with age. There is an enormous range of variation in all three of these processes, as we discuss next. Our notions about the meaning of age are rapidly changing, both because recent research is dispelling many myths about aging and because advances in nutrition and health have enabled many people to live longer, healthier lives than ever before.

Biological Aging

The biological effects of aging are well established, although the exact chronological age at which they occur varies greatly

How Do People Age? | **369**

FIGURE 12.2

Average Life Expectancy at Birth for Males and Females, 1900–2002 in the United States

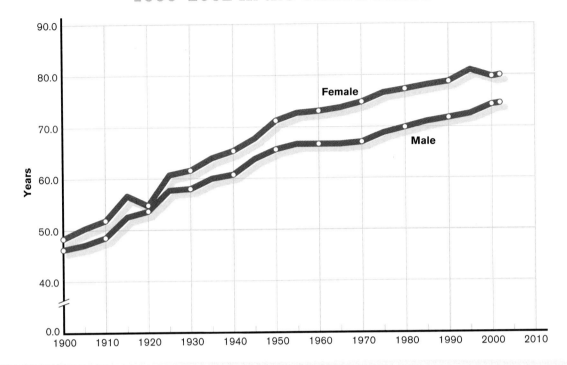

During which years in the last century was male life expectancy at birth greater than that of females? What is the difference in life expectancy at birth (in years) between men and women in 1900? In 1990? During the last century, which decade showed the smallest increase in male life expectancy? During what years did women's life expectancy at birth show a decline? How can age be socially constructed?

SOURCE: CDC 2002, Table 27, 2004, Table 27.

from individual to individual, depending on genetics, lifestyle, and luck. In general, for men and women alike, biological aging typically means:

- Declining vision, as the eye lens loses its elasticity (small print is the bane of most people over fifty)
- Hearing loss, first of higher-pitched tones, then of lower-pitched ones
- Wrinkles, as the skin's underlying structure becomes more and more brittle (billions of dollars invested in skin lotion and increasingly common surgical face lifts only delay the inevitable)
- A decline of muscle mass and an accompanying accumulation of fat, especially around the middle (eating habits

that were offset by exercise when you were twenty-five come back to haunt you when you are fifty)
- A drop in cardiovascular efficiency, as less oxygen can be inhaled and used during exercise (lifelong runners who ran six-minute miles at age thirty are happy to break eight-minute miles once they turn sixty)

The normal processes of aging cannot be avoided, but they can be partly compensated for and offset by good health, proper diet and nutrition, and a reasonable amount of exercise (John 1988). Lifestyle can make a significant health difference for people of all ages. For many people, the physical changes of aging do not significantly prevent them from leading active, independent lives well into their eighties. Some scientists have even argued that with a proper lifestyle and advances in medical technology, more and more people will be able to live relatively illness-free lives until they reach their biological maximum, experiencing only a brief period of sickness just before death (Fries 1980). Eventually, of course, the biological clock runs out for everyone. About ninety to one hundred years seems to be the upper end of the genetically determined age distribution for most human beings, although some have argued that it may be as high as 120 (Atchley 2000; Fries 1980; Rusting 1992; Treas 1995).

Even though the majority of older Americans suffer no significant physical impairment and remain physically active, unfortunate stereotypes about the "weak and frail elderly" continue to exist (Heise 1987). These stereotypes have more to do with the social than with the biological meaning of aging in U.S. culture, which is preoccupied with youthfulness and fears of growing old and dying.

Psychological Aging

The psychological effects of aging are much less well established than the physical effects. Even though such things as memory, learning, intelligence, skills, and motivation to learn are widely assumed to decline with age, research into the psychology of aging suggests a much more complicated process (Birren and Cunningham 1985; Schaie 1984). Memory and learning ability, for example, do not decline significantly until very late in life for most people, although the speed with which one recalls or analyzes information may slow somewhat, giving the false impression of mental impairment. For most elderly people whose lives are stimulating and rich, such mental abilities as motivation to learn, clarity of thought, and problem-solving capacity do not appear to decline significantly until the late eighties (Abeles and Riley 1987; Atchley 2000; Baltes and Schaie 1977; Cutler and Grams 1988; Schaie 1979; Schooler 1987).

Even **Alzheimer's disease**, the progressive deterioration of brain cells that is the primary cause of dementia in old age, is relatively rare in noninstitutionalized persons under seventy-five, although it may afflict as many as half of all people over eighty-five. Former president Ronald Reagan is perhaps the most famous example of someone who suffered from Alzheimer's (Treas 1995).

Social Aging

Social age consists of the norms, values, and roles that are culturally associated with a particular chronological age. Ideas about social age differ from one society to another and, at least in modern industrial societies, change over time as well. Societies such as Japan and China have traditionally revered elderly people, regarding them as a source of historical memory and wisdom. Societies such as the United States are more likely to dismiss them as nonproductive, dependent people who are out of step with the times—both because they are less likely to have the high-tech skills so valued by young people and because of American culture's obsession with youthfulness. In a country where the approximately seventy-five million once youthful baby boomers born in the decade after World War II are now turning sixty at the rate of one every seven seconds, a fortune is being spent on prescription drugs, plastic surgery, and home remedies that promise eternal youth. These include such things as tummy tucks and face lifts, antibaldness pills and lotions, and pills that claim to increase memory and concentration. Three weeks after it hit the market in 1998, the anti-impotence drug Viagra accounted for 94 percent of all prescription drug sales in the United States (Hotz 1998).

Role expectations are extremely important sources of one's personal identity. Some of the roles associated with aging in American society are positive: Supreme Court justice, senior adviser, doting grandparent, religious elder, wise spiritual teacher. Other roles may be damaging, leading to lowered self-esteem and isolation. Highly stigmatizing stereotypical roles for older people in American culture include grumpy old man (or woman), old-fashioned senior citizen, spinster, and mentally confused doddering old man. In fact, like all people, the elderly do not simply passively play out assigned social roles; they actively shape and redefine them (Riley et al. 1988).

Growing Old: Competing Sociological Explanations

Social gerontologists have offered a number of theories regarding the nature of aging in U.S. society. Some of the earliest theories emphasized individual adaptation to changing social roles as a person grows older. Later theories focused on how society shapes the social roles of the elderly, often in inequitable ways, and emphasized various aspects of age stratification. The most recent theories have been more multifaceted, focusing on the ways in which the elderly actively create their lives within specific institutional contexts (Hendricks 1992).

The First Generation of Theories: Functionalism

The earliest theories of aging reflected the functionalist approach that was dominant in sociology during the 1950s and

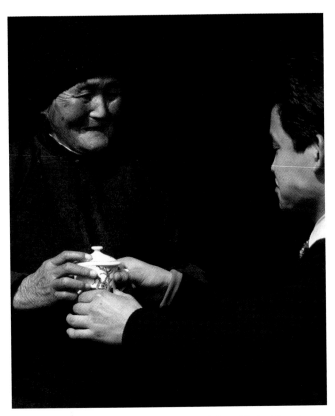

Some societies have traditionally revered the elderly. Here the young respect the old with an offering of tea, a traditional Chinese custom.

1960s. They emphasized how individuals adjusted to changing social roles as they aged and how those roles were useful to society. The earliest theories often assumed that aging brings with it physical and psychological decline and that changing social roles have to take this decline into account (Hendricks 1992).

Talcott Parsons (1960), one of the most influential functionalist theorists of the 1950s, argued that U.S. society needs to find roles for the elderly consistent with advanced age. He expressed concern that the United States, with its emphasis on youth and its avoidance of death, had failed to provide roles that adequately drew on the potential wisdom and maturity of its older citizens. Moreover, given the graying of U.S. society that was evident even in Parsons's time, he argued that this failure could well lead to older people's becoming discouraged and alienated from society. To achieve a "healthy maturity," Parsons (1960) argued, the elderly need to adjust psychologically to their changed circumstances, while society needs to redefine the social roles of the elderly. Old roles (such as work) have to be abandoned, while new forms of productive activity (such as volunteer service) need to be identified.

Parsons's ideas anticipated those of **disengagement theory**, the notion that it is functional for society to remove people

from their traditional roles when they become elderly, thereby freeing up those roles for others (Cumming and Henry 1961; Estes et al. 1992). According to this perspective, given the increasing frailty, illness, and dependency of elderly people, it becomes increasingly dysfunctional for them to occupy traditional social roles they are no longer capable of adequately fulfilling. The elderly therefore should retire from their jobs, pull back from civic life, and eventually withdraw from other activities as well. Disengagement is assumed to be functional for the larger society because it opens up roles formerly filled by the elderly for younger people, who presumably will carry them out with fresh energy and new skills. Disengagement is also assumed to be functional for the elderly, because it enables them to take on less taxing roles consistent with their advancing age and declining health. A number of studies of older adults indeed report that the large majority feel good about retiring, which they claim has improved their morale and increased their happiness (Atchley 2000; Crowley 1985; Howard et al. 1986; Palmore et al. 1985).

Although there is obviously some truth to disengagement theory, the idea that elderly people should completely disengage from the larger society takes for granted the prevailing stereotype that old age necessarily involves frailty and dependence. As a result, no sooner did the theory appear than these very assumptions were challenged, often by some of the theory's original proponents (Cumming 1963, 1975; Hendricks 1992; Henry 1965; Hochschild 1975; Maddox 1965, 1970). These challenges gave rise to another functionalist theory of aging, which drew conclusions quite opposite to those of disengagement theory: *activity theory*.

According to **activity theory**, elderly people who are busy and engaged, leading fulfilling and productive lives, can be functional for society. Activity theory regards aging as a normal part of human development and argues that elderly people can best serve society, as well as themselves, by remaining active as long as possible. Although there may come a time in most peoples' lives when disengagement will best serve their interests as well as society's, activity theory argues that an active individual is much more likely to remain healthy, alert, and socially useful. In this view, people should remain engaged in their work and other social roles as long as they are capable of doing so. If a time comes when a particular role becomes too difficult or taxing, then other roles can be sought—for example, volunteer work in the community.

Activity theory finds support in research showing that continued activity well into old age is associated with enhanced mental and physical health (Birren and Bengston 1988; Rowe and Kahn 1987; Schaie 1983). For example, there is some evidence that continued part- or full-time employment is associated with higher morale and happiness, possibly because of the expanded friendship networks that result from continued work

(Bosse et al. 1987; Conner et al. 1985; Mor-Barak et al. 1992; Riddick 1985; Soumerai and Avorn 1983).

Critics of functionalist theories of aging argue that these theories emphasize the need for the elderly to adapt to existing conditions, either by disengaging from socially useful roles or by actively pursuing them, but that they do not question whether or not the circumstances faced by the elderly are just. In reaction another group of theorists arose—those growing out of the social conflict tradition (Hendricks 1992).

The Second Generation of Theories: Social Conflict

Unlike their predecessors, whose emphasis was on how well the elderly could be integrated into the larger society, the second generation of theorists focused on sources of social conflict between the elderly and society (Hendricks 1992). Much like other theorists who were studying social conflict in U.S. society during the 1970s and early 1980s, these theorists stressed the ways in which the larger social structure helped shape the opportunities available to the elderly; unequal opportunities were seen as creating the potential for conflict.

According to this view, many of the problems of aging— such as poverty, inadequate health care, or lack of decent nursing homes—are systematically produced by the routine operation of social institutions. A capitalist society, the reasoning goes, favors those who are most economically powerful. While there are certainly some elderly people who have "made it" and are set for life, many have not—and these people must fight to get even a meager share of society's scarce resources.

Conflict theories of aging flourished during the 1980s, when a shrinking job base and cutbacks in federal spending threatened to pit different social groups against each other in the competition for scarce resources. The elderly were seen as competing with the young for increasingly scarce jobs and dwindling federal dollars. Conflict theorists further pointed out that even among the elderly, those who fared worst were women, low-income people, and minorities, in a cumulating spiral of social conflict (Atchley 2000; Estes 1986, 1991; Estes et al. 1982, 1984; Hendricks 1992; Hendricks and Hendricks 1986; McKinlay 1975).

The Third Generation of Theories: Self-Concept and Aging

The most recent theories reject what they regard as the one-sided emphases of both functionalism and conflict theory. They view the elderly as playing an active role in determining their own physical and mental well-being, rather than as merely adapting to the larger society (functionalism) or as victims of the stratification system (social conflict). Circumstances such as family, work, and living situation are important sources of one's self-concept, which in turn affects one's life satisfaction. The elderly are seen as playing a significant role in shaping those circumstances (Dannefer 1989; Hendricks 1992; Schaie and Hendricks 2000).

One research project, for example, involved a partnership between the Margaret Warner School of Education and Human Development at the University of Rochester (New York) and two local nursing homes. The project was set up to study how changes in the organizational culture of the homes— as seen in such things as architecture, physical layout, and programming—can affect resident satisfaction and well-being. The objective was to increase social interaction among residents, involving them in satisfying and useful activities. In the words of the gerontologist Dale Dannefer, who headed the project, "If we expect people in nursing homes to improve their health and thrive, to remain socially engaged and make contributions to

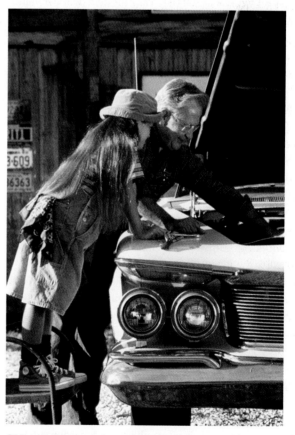

Older people are informed by experience and possess knowledge and skills that can be beneficial to young people. In turn, keeping active and maintaining close contact with young people can be vital in shaping a positive self-concept among the elderly.

the lives of others, it should show up in measurable gains in their health and functional status" (quoted in Dickman 1999). These recent theories also emphasize the increasing diversity among the elderly, showing how people age differently, depending on their circumstances (Nelson and Dannefer 1992). Many provide detailed ethnographic accounts of what it means to grow old in U.S. society, with concrete illustrations from elderly peoples' lives (Gubrium 1986, 1991, 1993; Gubrium and Sankar 1994).

Aging in the United States

The elderly make up a highly diverse category about whom few broad generalizations can be made. For one thing, the elderly reflect the diversity of U.S. society that we've made note of elsewhere in this textbook: They are rich, poor, and in between; they belong to all racial and ethnic groups; they live alone and in families of various sorts; they vary in their political values and preferences; and they are gay and lesbian as well as heterosexual. Furthermore, like other Americans, they are diverse with respect to health: Although some suffer from mental and physical disabilities, most lead active, independent lives.

There are significant racial differences among the elderly. Whites, on average, live five years longer than African Americans, largely because blacks have much higher rates of poverty and therefore are more likely to suffer from inadequate health care. As a result, a much higher percentage of whites are elderly than other racial groups (Table 12.1). The combined effect of race and sex is substantial—white women live, on average, twelve years longer than black men. Hispanics are graying the least, partly because this category includes many young immigrant workers with large families.

Currently, 3.7 million of the elderly population in the United States are foreign born (U.S. Bureau of the Census 2005c). In California, New York, Hawaii, and other states that receive large numbers of immigrants, as much as one fifth of the elderly population was born outside the United States (Treas 1995). Most elderly immigrants either do not speak English well or do not speak it at all. Integrating elderly immigrants into U.S. society poses special challenges: Some are highly educated, but most are not. Many require special education and training programs. Most lack a retirement income, so that they depend on their families or public assistance for support. Among those who arrived in the United States during the 1980s, 22 percent were living in poverty in 2003, over twice the rate of elderly people born in this country (U.S. Bureau of the Census 2005d). In 2003, approximately 570,000 (15.4 per-

TABLE 12.1

Percentage of Population over Sixty-Five and over Eighty-Five, in Different Racial Groups, 2004

Whites make up a higher percentage of the elderly than any other group. This is the result of lower fertility (whites have fewer children on average) and greater longevity (whites tend to live longer than most other racial and ethnic groups).

RACIAL GROUP	OVER AGE 65	OVER AGE 85
White	13.5	1.8
Black	8.1	0.9
Asian	8.5	0.8
American Indian	6.4	0.6
Native Hawaiian/ Other Pacific Islander	5.7	0.5
Hispanic (any race)	5.2	0.5
TOTAL	12.4	1.7

SOURCE: U.S. Bureau of the Census, 2005, Table 2.

cent) foreign-born elders were living below the poverty level in the United States (U.S. Bureau of the Census 2005e).

Finally, as people live to increasingly older ages, the elderly are becoming diverse in terms of age itself. It is useful to distinguish between different age categories of the elderly, such as the **young old** (ages sixty-five to seventy-four), the **old old** (ages seventy-five to eighty-four), and the **oldest old** (age eighty-five and older) (Figure 12.3). The "young old" are most likely to be economically independent, healthy, active, and engaged; the oldest old—the fastest-growing segment of the elderly population—are most likely to encounter difficulties such as poor health, financial insecurity, isolation, and loneliness. These differences are not necessarily due only to the effects of aging. The young old came of age during the post–World War II period of strong economic growth and benefited as a result: They are more likely to be educated; to have acquired wealth in the form of a home, savings, or investments; and to have had many years of stable employment. These advantages are much less likely to be enjoyed by the oldest old, partly because their education and careers began at an earlier time, when economic conditions were not so favorable (Treas 1995).

What is the experience of growing old in the United States? Although the elderly do face some special challenges, most elderly people lead relatively healthy, satisfying lives. Still, one national survey found a substantial discrepancy between what most Americans under sixty-five thought life would be like when they passed that milestone and the actual experiences of those who had (Figure 12.4, p. 376). In this section, we examine differences among the elderly in the United States, along with some of the common problems that they confront; in the next section, we look at their growing political ability to do something about these problems.

Poverty

Relatively few elderly people live in poverty, although some of the very poorest people are elderly, particularly among minorities. Because older people have for the most part retired from work, their income is based primarily on **Social Security** and private retirement programs. Social Security and **Medicare** have been especially important in lifting many elderly people out of poverty. Yet people who depend solely on these two programs for income and health-care coverage are likely to live modestly at best. Social Security accounts for only about 40 percent of the income of the typical retiree; most of the remainder comes from investments and private pension funds and sometimes earnings. Low-income

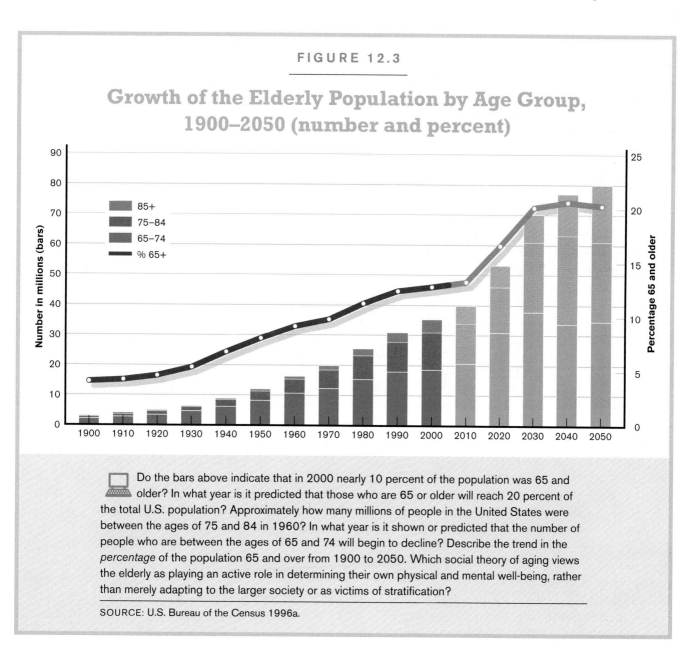

FIGURE 12.3

Growth of the Elderly Population by Age Group, 1900–2050 (number and percent)

Do the bars above indicate that in 2000 nearly 10 percent of the population was 65 and older? In what year is it predicted that those who are 65 or older will reach 20 percent of the total U.S. population? Approximately how many millions of people in the United States were between the ages of 75 and 84 in 1960? In what year is it shown or predicted that the number of people who are between the ages of 65 and 74 will begin to decline? Describe the trend in the *percentage* of the population 65 and over from 1900 to 2050. Which social theory of aging views the elderly as playing an active role in determining their own physical and mental well-being, rather than merely adapting to the larger society or as victims of stratification?

SOURCE: U.S. Bureau of the Census 1996a.

households in particular are likely to rely heavily on Social Security, which accounts for as much as three quarters of all income for retirees living on less than $10,000 a year (Atchley 2000). Yet even the combination of Social Security and private pensions results in modest retirement incomes for most people (Krueger 1995). Although almost all elderly are covered by Medicare, just over 60 percent of people over age sixty-five are covered by private health insurance as well (DeNavas-Walt et al. 2005).

The economic conditions of the elderly have improved steadily since the 1970s. As Figure 12.5 shows, in 1959, 35 percent of all people over sixty-five lived in poverty. That figure began to drop during President Lyndon B. Johnson's War on Poverty in the mid-1960s, when Medicare was enacted and Social Security benefits increased. By the early 1970s, poverty rates among the elderly had dropped to below 15 percent, and today they hover around 10 percent (9.8 percent in 2004). This is half the rate of poverty among children, 17.8 percent of whom were poor in 2004 (DeNavas-Walt et al. 2005). Race appears to be much more important than age in explaining poverty among the elderly (Figure 12.6). Among whites, only 7.5 percent of the elderly reported poverty-level incomes in 2004, compared with 23.9 percent of blacks, 13.4 percent of Asians, and 18.7 percent of Hispanics (DeNavas-Walt et al. 2005).

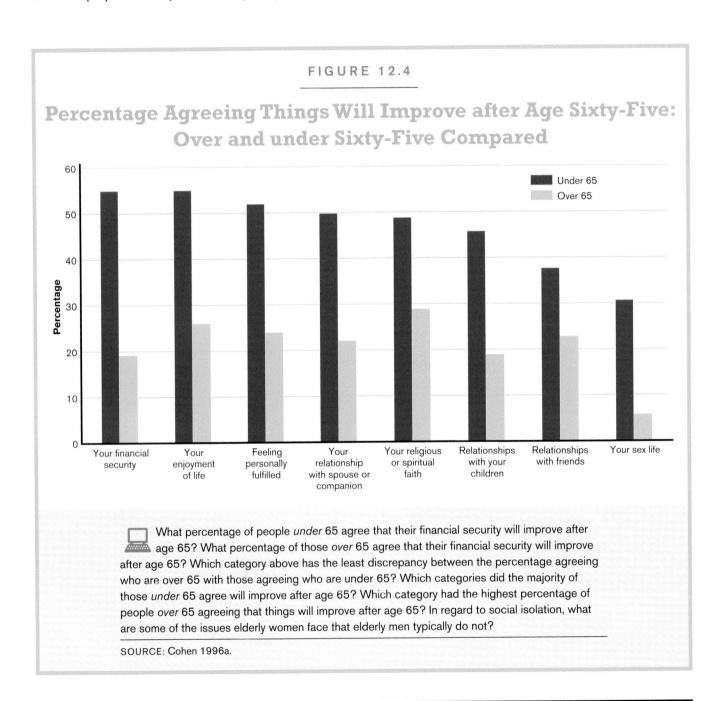

FIGURE 12.4

Percentage Agreeing Things Will Improve after Age Sixty-Five: Over and under Sixty-Five Compared

What percentage of people *under* 65 agree that their financial security will improve after age 65? What percentage of those *over* 65 agree that their financial security will improve after age 65? Which category above has the least discrepancy between the percentage agreeing who are over 65 with those agreeing who are under 65? Which categories did the majority of those *under* 65 agree will improve after age 65? Which category had the highest percentage of people *over* 65 agreeing that things will improve after age 65? In regard to social isolation, what are some of the issues elderly women face that elderly men typically do not?

SOURCE: Cohen 1996a.

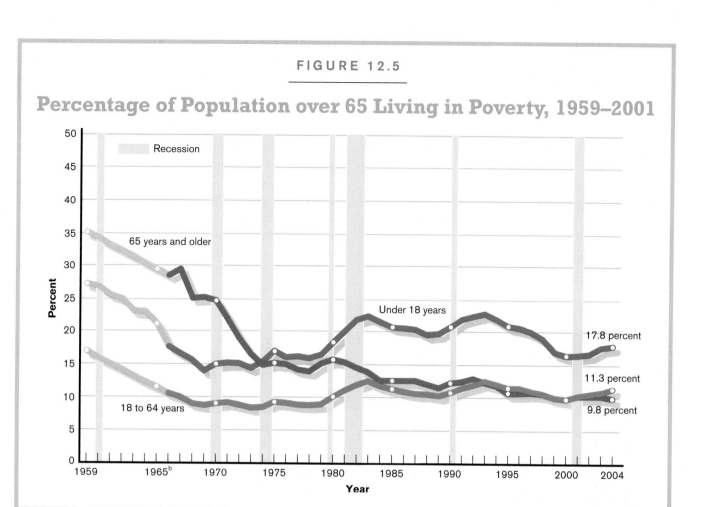

FIGURE 12.5

Percentage of Population over 65 Living in Poverty, 1959–2001

Recession

Percent

65 years and older

Under 18 years

18 to 64 years

17.8 percent

11.3 percent

9.8 percent

Year

1959   1965[b]   1970   1975   1980   1985   1990   1995   2000   2004

What is the general trend in the percentage of the population over 65 living in poverty from 1959–2004? Which ten-year period showed the biggest decrease in the percentage of the population over 65 living in poverty? What percentage of the typical retiree's income is provided by Social Security? What government programs were enacted or altered in the mid-1960s that led to the significant decline in elderly poverty?

SOURCE: Proctor and Dalaker 2002.

Social Isolation

One of the common stereotypes about the elderly is that they are isolated from human contact. This is not true of the majority of older people, however. Four out of five older people have living children, and the vast majority of them can rely on their children for support if necessary (American Association of Retired Persons [AARP] 1997). More than nine out of ten adult children report believing that maintaining parental contact is important to them, including the provision of financial support if it is needed (Finley et al. 1988). The reverse is also true: Many studies have found that elderly parents continue to provide support for their adult children, particularly during times of difficulty, such as divorce. Most elderly parents and

adult children report feeling that the amount of support they receive from the other is fair. In 2004, the U.S. Bureau of the Census (2004b) reported that there are over 25 million households with one or more persons 65 years or older. Being geographically distant from family members does not seem to be a problem either, since 85 percent of elderly people with children live close to at least one of them (Bankoff 1983; Bengston et al. 1990; Greenberg and Becker 1988; Martin et al. 2005; Moss et al. 1985; Peterson and Peterson 1988).

Future generations may suffer more from social isolation than do elderly people today. Changing patterns of gender relations, including increases in divorce and a decline in remarriage, may mean that an increasing proportion of elderly people will live alone (Goldscheider 1990). A majority of such

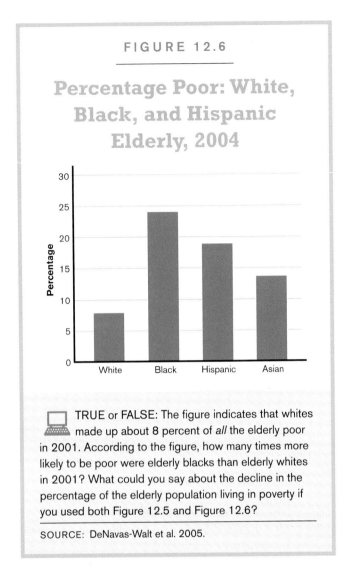

FIGURE 12.6

Percentage Poor: White, Black, and Hispanic Elderly, 2004

TRUE or FALSE: The figure indicates that whites made up about 8 percent of *all* the elderly poor in 2001. According to the figure, how many times more likely to be poor were elderly blacks than elderly whites in 2001? What could you say about the decline in the percentage of the elderly population living in poverty if you used both Figure 12.5 and Figure 12.6?

SOURCE: DeNavas-Walt et al. 2005.

women. In U.S. culture, youth and beauty are viewed as especially desirable qualities for women. Older men, on the other hand, are more likely to be valued for their material success: Graying at the temples is a sign of distinction for a man, rather than a call for a visit to the hairdresser. As a result, elderly divorced or widowed men are much more likely to find a mate than elderly women who are living alone, because the pool of eligible mates for elderly men is more likely to include potential partners who are many years younger. One study of fifty-nine elderly women who had lost their husbands found that some eventually managed to overcome their grief, while others never fully recovered from their husband's death (Hunter 1990). The widows who overcame their grief tended to be much more satisfied with their social support networks than those who did not.

Prejudice

Discrimination on the basis of age is now against federal law. Nonetheless, prejudices based on false stereotypes are common. **Ageism** is prejudice and/or discrimination based on age and, like all prejudices, is fueled in part by stereotypes. The elderly are frequently seen as perpetually lonely, sad, infirm, forgetful, dependent, senile, old-fashioned, inflexible, and embittered.

There are a number of reasons for such prejudice. The previously mentioned American obsession with youthfulness, reflected in popular entertainment and advertising, leads many younger people to disparage their elders, frequently dismissing them as irrelevant. The new information technology undoubtedly reinforces these prejudices, because youthfulness and computer abilities seem to go hand in hand. In the fast-paced world of MTV, the Web, and dot-com businesses that seem to flourish and perish overnight, young people may come to view the elderly as anachronistic. Associated with the emphasis of youthfulness is a fear-filled avoidance of reminders of death and dying. Such fear carries over into negative attitudes toward the elderly, who serve as a constant reminder of one's mortality (Fry 1980).

In one study (Levin 1988), college students were shown a photograph of the same man at ages twenty-five, fifty-two, and seventy-three and were asked to rate him in terms of a variety of personality characteristics. The ratings were significantly more negative for the man depicted at age seventy-three. When he looked old in his photograph, the students were more likely to perceive him negatively, even though they knew absolutely nothing about him. The mere fact of his being elderly was sufficient to trigger a negative cultural stereotype. Widely shared cultural stereotypes of grumpy old men can lead to private opinions that are hurtful to older people.

people will likely be women, given the fact that women on average outlive men. Among people over fifty-five years, there are only eighty-one men for every one hundred women; for those eighty-five or older, the number of men per one hundred women drops to forty-six. Partly because of the dearth of older men, only 56 percent of all women aged sixty-five to seventy-four live with a spouse or a mate, compared with over three quarters of men in that age range. Among those aged seventy-five to eighty-four, only 36 percent of all women live with a mate; the rate for men is 72 percent (Federal Interagency Forum on Aging-Related Statistics [FIFARS] 2004). Women are also more likely than men to be widowed. In 2002, 31 percent of women and only 9 percent of men aged fifty-five and older were widowed (Smith 2003).

The fact that women outlive men means that elderly women are more likely to experience problems of isolation and loneliness. These problems are compounded by cultural values that make growing old gracefully easier for men than for

Physical Abuse

The National Center on Elder Abuse (1999) defines seven types of elder abuse:

- Physical abuse—use of physical force that may result in bodily injury, physical pain, or impairment
- Sexual abuse—nonconsensual sexual contact of any kind with an elderly person
- Emotional abuse—infliction of anguish, pain, or distress through verbal or nonverbal acts
- Financial/material exploitation—illegal or improper use of an elder's funds, property, or assets
- Neglect—refusal, or failure, to fulfill any part of a person's obligations or duties to an elderly person
- Abandonment—desertion of an elderly person by an individual who has physical custody of the elder or by a person who has assumed responsibility for providing care to the elder
- Self-neglect—behaviors of an elderly person that threaten the elder's health or safety

Cases of elderly abuse certainly exist, but most research suggests that it is not so widespread as is commonly believed. Worldwide, it is estimated that between 4 and 6 percent of the elderly experience some form of abuse at home (Hood 2002). Nationwide it is estimated that between one and two million Americans over age sixty-five have been injured, exploited, or otherwise mistreated. Yet, particularly in cases of financial abuse, it is estimated that only one in twenty-five cases are reported (National Center on Elder Abuse 2005). One random survey among two thousand noninstitutionalized elderly people in the Boston area found that only about 2 percent had experienced physical violence, although these figures may be somewhat low because abuse rates may be higher among those who are unable to respond to surveys. Fewer than 1 percent reported being seriously neglected in terms of their daily needs, while about 1 percent claimed they were subject to chronic verbal aggression. These figures represent a small percentage of the elderly population. Still, they do represent eight to nine thousand cases in the Boston area alone. Although elderly men reported higher rates of abuse than did elderly women, 57 percent of the abused women (compared with 6 percent of the men) reported suffering injuries (Pillemer and Finkelhor 1988).

It is widely believed that abuse results from the anger and resentment that adult children feel when confronted with the need to care for their infirm parents (King 1984; Steinmetz 1983). Most studies, however, have found this to be a false stereotype. More than half of the abuse reported in the Boston study was perpetrated by a spouse; only a quarter of the cases occurred at the hands of an adult child (Pillemer and Finkelhor 1988). Furthermore, in cases when a child abused an elderly parent, it was found that he or she was more likely to be financially dependent on the parent, rather than the reverse. The child may feel resentment about being dependent, and the parent may be unwilling to terminate the abusive relationship because he or she feels obligated to help the child (Pillemer 1985).

Health Problems

The prevalence of chronic disabilities among the elderly has declined in recent years (Manton et al. 1993), and most elderly people rate their health as reasonably good and free of major disabilities. Still, elderly people obviously suffer from more health problems than most younger people, and health difficulties often increase with advancing age. In 2003, the elderly accounted for about one quarter of all U.S. health-care expenditures (Kaiser Family Foundation 2005). In 2002, over half of all noninstitutionalized persons over sixty-five reported having at least some problems with high blood pressure, whereas about a third reported suffering from such ailments as arthritis, heart disease, and hearing loss. One out of five elderly have had incidences of some type of cancer (FIFARS 2004b). One out of ten people diagnosed for the first time as having HIV/AIDS is over fifty and a quarter of these are over sixty; nearly three times as many people sixty and older died of AIDS in 1992 as did those under twenty (Bennet 1992; UNAIDS 2002). Age-related health conditions, such as osteoporosis, create complications for the treatment of the elderly living with AIDS and accelerates the progression from HIV to AIDS (UNAIDS 2002).

In 2002, nearly three quarters of noninstitutionalized people over age sixty-five considered their health to be "good" or "good to excellent," and more than two out of three people age eighty-five or older reported the same (FIFARS 2004c). It is not surprising that the percentage of people needing help with daily activities increases with age: Whereas only about one in ten people between the ages of sixty-five and seventy-five report needing daily assistance, the figure rises to one in five for people between seventy-five and seventy-nine and to one in three for people between eighty and eighty-four. Half of all people over age eighty-five require assistance (U.S. Bureau of the Census 1996a).

Paradoxically, there is some evidence that the fastest-growing group of elderly, the oldest old (those eighty-five and older), tend to enjoy relative robustness, which partially accounts for their having reached their advanced age. This is possibly one of the reasons that health-care costs for a person who dies at ninety are about a third of those for a person who dies at seventy (Angier 1995). Unlike many other Americans, the

Old and on Their Own

As a woman in my 90s, I have empathy for those who will come after me and live into their 100s and beyond. They will, I trust, include my grandchildren and great-grandchildren, of whom I have quite a few. I have some thoughts for those planning the quality of life to be enjoyed by this stunningly larger older population to come. The way things are going now, as I see it, the 21st century will be witness to two segments of society—the elderly and the rest of the human race. My word is: Please do not keep them apart. . . .

In a society that aims to be inclusive, why should older people be encouraged to live in a separate community? Most senior housing complexes are sterile—totally lacking the vitality that a generationally mixed community thrives on. Many people face old age just waiting to die, so society (and developers and the government) hand them a group of "activities" to keep them busy, to keep them occupied among people their own age, out of the sight of children, away from a flourishing community. Too often they have limited access to streets to walk on; shops to visit; churches, libraries, museums and other cultural centers. They are relegated to a life where they see only reflections of themselves, other old people.

Housing complexes ought to be designed for all ages, with some apartments appropriate for older people and others suited to the needs of younger people with families. Young mothers, as well as the elderly, can benefit from what is now offered in many senior complexes, like in-house restaurants, beauty parlors, libraries, and on-site nurses and doctors. And many planned "activities" can be enjoyed by all ages. A painting class, for example, is more fun when not limited to old people.

For sure, age-integrated housing will not cure the generation gap, but perhaps it is a way to help older people get over adopting judgmental attitudes toward the young—being horrified at dyed hair, baggy clothes, pierced bodies—without ever having a five-minute conversation with any of them. As for young people, it would do them no harm to live side by side with older people, to really see us day by day, recognize that we are still people, men and women who were once as young as they are, and that like us, if they are lucky, they will one day be old, too. We have a lot in common.

We are all just people, and we should be neighbors living on the same street.

SOURCE: Hila Colman, "Young and Old Thrive Side by Side," *New York Times*, August 15, 2001, p. A23.

[Robert Coles compiled his interviews with Americans over seventy-five in *Old and on Their Own* (1997). He described his book as "trying to catch sight of some people who manage, often with some difficulty, to *hold on*—to maintain considerably more than a semblance of their privacy, their independence, their personal sovereignty, their 'home rule,' one woman put it, delightfully, instructively. . . . Such affirmations, such declarations of determination, are no mere bombast, or frightened footnotes to the progression of disease, deformity, decay, disability, overall decline. Such spoken statements of intent as well as hope and wish cast a glow of light on lives inevitably darkened by all kinds of diminishment." Excerpts from his interviews follow.]

[A seventy-five-year-old Massachusetts man said of himself:]

"You know, that's what I do, every day," he remarked, and then the description: "I'll talk to myself—out loud. If one of you psychiatrists was here, listening, you'd fill out a legal form and have me sent away for observation. I know how you guys work—someone is behaving a little strange, so you check him off as nuts! Well, being old and being sick is being nuts, in a way. You're at the edge of life; you're hurting; you never do know if you'll see another day. . . . What I do—I talk to myself. I say, 'It's Tuesday today, and you've got this long desert to hike through, hours and hours of time. So, better make the best of it.' When I hear my voice, I feel I've got company. I'm alive, and that's something."

[When Anne was eighty-one, her husband of fifty years died. She struggled with alcoholism and grief for years, until ballroom dance lessons gave her a way to remember her happy moments and find meaning in her present life.]

Dancing had become her passion. She danced at the studio, of course, and at the social functions it sponsored, but more than anywhere else, she danced at home, alone. In the kitchen, especially, with its imitation tile floor, she glided here and there, mostly in a circle around the table

where she ate. She took to singing out loud, supplying her own music to her solo performances—all the while, in her mind, conjuring up a partner: the ever-available Fred Astaire, of course, her husband Carl, and some men she knew in the past, all husbands of her (four closest) friends, and all now "gone," the word that she used when speaking of someone's departure by virtue of death.

[Laura reconsiders old age while talking to her new friend Theresa:]

"Maybe, when you get old, you lose some of your perspective. You don't only forget people's names, and dates, and chores you're meant to do, but you forget what it was once like in the country; and since you're now old, and you're not in the middle of things, all you do is hear about the bad side, from radio and from television, and if your eyes hold out, from the papers. You're not seeing a lot of the good things that are happening, because you're cut off, more and more, from them. Theresa told me, 'Watch out, Laura—you'll get more and more scared of this world, the further off you are from it!'"

SOURCE: Robert Coles, *Old and on Their Own* (New York: Double-Take/W. W. Norton, 1997), pp. 4, 31–33, 72, 78–79, 84–85.

Questions

- How do these writings and images change your impression about the lives of older people?
- Compare the strategies used by these aging people to manage their pain and loneliness.
- Colman's article describes old people as isolated from mainstream society. How do the photographs and selections from *Old and on Their Own* argue for or against her point?

elderly are fortunate in having access to public health insurance (Medicare) and therefore medical services. The United States, however, stands virtually alone among the industrialized nations in failing to provide adequately for the complete health care of its most senior citizens (Hendricks and Hatch 1993; Hendricks and Rosenthal 1993).

Although nearly forty-six million Americans lacked health insurance in 2004 (about 16 percent of the population), less than 1 percent of the elderly lacked coverage (DeNavas-Walt et al. 2005). About 95 percent of the elderly are covered to some extent by Medicare. But because this program covers about half of the total health-care expenses of the elderly, nearly two out of three people supplement Medicare with their own private insurance (DeNavas-Walt et al. 2005; FIFARS 2004a). The rising costs of private insurance, unfortunately, have made this option impossible for a growing number of the elderly. Since 1977, the number of elderly with out-of-pocket health-care expenses increased from 83 to over 95 percent. Despite Medicare, today the elderly still spend on average over one fifth of their income on health care (FIFARS 2004a). At present, the rising costs of Medicare have made it a candidate for federal budget cuts.

When the elderly become physically unable to care for themselves, they may wind up in nursing homes. Only about one out of every twenty people over age sixty-five is in a nursing home, a figure that rises to about one out of every five among people over eighty-five (Atchley 2000). Medicaid, the government program that provides health insurance for the poor, covers long-term supervision and nursing costs, although only when most of one's assets (except for one's home) have been used up. About 7 percent of elderly people in nursing homes receive assistance from Medicaid (FIFARS 2004a). Because the average cost of a nursing home is now over $66,000 a year (*Chicago Tribune* 2003), the nonpoor elderly who require such institutionalization may find that their lifetime savings will be quickly depleted. Nursing homes have long had a reputation for austerity and loneliness. In fact, however, the quality of most has improved in recent years, both because federal programs such as Medicaid help cover the cost of care and because of federal quality regulations.

Still, living for many years in a nursing home was cited as a concern about growing old by over half of respondents, according to a recent national survey (Table 12.2). Perhaps that is why the average length of stay in nursing homes dropped from 1,026 days in 1985 to 876 days in 2003, as more elderly people seek home care (*Chicago Tribune* 2003; Dey 1997).

Lifelong Learning

As more and more people live well beyond the age of retirement, they enter a new stage of life for which there are few socially prescribed roles (Laslett 1991; Moen 1995). Many people can look forward to ten or twenty years of relatively healthy living, free from the obligations of paid work and raising a family. Furthermore, the elderly will be increasingly well educated, because young people today are much more likely to have gone to college than their parents—or grandparents. This is important for a number of reasons. Better-educated people tend to be economically comfortable in later life. They also tend to be healthier: They are better informed on health-related issues, more likely to choose a healthy lifestyle, and more likely to seek medical treatment when they require it (Treas 1995).

These trends suggest that the elderly are much more likely to remain a part of mainstream society, rather than to become isolated. As U.S. society continues to age, it will increasingly be forced to confront a growing elderly population that is unwilling to slip quietly into years of retirement and inactivity. It is important for elderly people to maintain a readiness to learn, stimulated by participation in a wide variety of learning activities. As noted earlier, this can contribute to mental alertness, a positive psychological attitude, and even improved physical health (Dychtwald 1990; Plett 1990; Plett and Lester 1991).

TABLE 12.2
What Is Your Biggest Fear about Growing Old?

When it comes to growing old, most Americans fear losing their health and independence far more than being alone or living in a nursing home.

Losing your health	73%
Losing ability to care for yourself	70%
Losing mental abilities	69%
Running out of money	60%
Not being able to drive/travel on own	59%
Being a burden on your family	54%
Winding up in a nursing home	52%
Not being able to work or volunteer	49%
Being alone	39%
Losing your looks	22%

SOURCE: Cohen and Langer 2005.

Some scholars have even argued that "adult education" will soon become as important as "youth education" (Brookfield 1986). Educators have coined the terms **andragogy** to refer to adult learning (literally, the "leading of adults") and **geragogy** (the "leading of the old") to refer to older-adult learning (John 1988). In contrast to conventional notions of teaching, adult learning methods emphasize building on the extensive life experience of older people, rather than providing them with information in a standard undergraduate-classroom format. Adult learning tends to be informal, combining the learners' concrete experience with more theoretical sorts of knowledge. It draws on the interests and concerns of adult learners, who may be unwilling to spend time studying things that seem unrelated to their central cares (John 1988; Plett 1990).

The Politics of Aging

Because of their growing numbers, the elderly are a potentially potent voice in Washington. The American Association of Retired People (**AARP**) has been one highly effective advocate for the elderly. It is a nonprofit organization that boasts a membership of over thirty-five million Americans over the age of fifty and which is reportedly the largest member-based organization in the world next to the Roman Catholic Church and over ten times larger than the National Rifle Association (Birnbaum 2005). Because of their high voter turnout rates—nearly 70 percent of those sixty-five and older voted in the 2004 election—the elderly account for as much as one fifth of all voters (Atchley 2000; Treas 1995; U.S. Bureau of the Census 2005f). This is not to suggest that the elderly all hold the same political views; on the contrary, they are as politically heterogeneous as the other groups in our society. But on issues they perceive as affecting their interests—such as retirement pensions and health-care benefits—they are likely to have strong opinions. Moreover, because cuts in programs for the elderly would shift the burden of supporting them to their families, opposition to significant reductions in these programs is likely to be widespread.

The two principal governmental programs that provide financial support for the elderly are Medicare, which was instituted in 1965, and Social Security, whose benefits were increased at about the same time (the program itself was begun in 1935). The full benefits of Medicare and Social Security are available at age sixty-five, although partial benefits are available to some people a few years earlier.

Social Security and Medicare are financed by workers' payroll deductions, employer contributions, and taxes on those who are self-employed. Working Americans pay into these programs today so they can be eligible for them when they are no longer able to earn a living. By providing a degree of economic support for the elderly, such programs also make it economically possible to retire; in the absence of the economic security such programs provide, elderly people would be under greater economic pressure to continue working as long as they are physically capable.

Medicare, which pays for acute medical costs for the elderly, reached more than 44.7 million people in 2004, and the estimated budget for 2005 is $489 billion, or about one eighth of the federal budget (U.S. Department of Health and Human Services [DHHS] 2005; White House 2005). It is the nation's largest health insurer, processing, in 2004, over one billion medical claims (DHHS 2005). Because it reaches so many people, Medicare has made an enormous difference in the elderly's access to adequate health care—although at a high cost. Controversial revisions to the Medicare program in 2003 provide government subsidies for the purchase of medicines by the elderly and provide special assistance to low-income elderly. AARP played an influential role in lobbying Congress during the debate over these changes.

Social Security provides retirement pay for all elderly persons who have worked a certain number of years during their lives and have contributed a portion of their paycheck (typically matched by their employer) into a government fund. The program disbursed $518 billion in 2005, and benefited 48 million individuals (U.S. Social Security Administration 2005a). Most of these were retirees over sixty-five, but some younger retirees and dependents of deceased workers received benefits as well. The amount of the monthly benefit one receives under Social Security depends in part on earnings before retirement. The average monthly benefit in June 2005 was $959 for retired workers, $897 for disabled workers, and $925 for nondisabled widows and widowers (U.S. Social Security Administration 2005a). Because retired women are less likely than men to have had continuous paid employment throughout their lives, their average retirement income is correspondingly lower. As these figures suggest, Social Security provides an extremely minimal level of support for the elderly—by itself, barely enough to keep recipients out of poverty (Belgrave 1988; Treas 1995; U.S. Social Security Administration 1997a).

The elderly are likely to be at the center of one of the major political debates of this century: the extent to which the government should continue funding programs that virtually eliminated poverty among the elderly since the 1970s. Programs such as Social Security and Medicare will become increasingly costly as more and more Americans retire. As people live longer, the first baby boomers retire, and the birth rate remains low, the share of the population funding Social Security shrinks. As a result the worker to beneficiary ratio has fallen from 16.5:1 in 1950 to 3.3:1 today. Within forty years it will be 2:1.

Redefining Retirement

Professor Phyllis Moen has testified before congressional and state legislative committees, appeared on television programs such as *60 Minutes,* and served on review panels for the National Academy of Sciences and the National Institutes of Health. She has given luncheon talks to Senate staffers in Washington, D.C.; provided interviews for national radio broadcasts, and advised nonprofit organizations. But for Moen, these public engagements are only part of her broader ambition as a sociologist: to help reframe the ways Americans—and especially American institutions—define and delimit life chances and life quality around age and gender.

Take the idea of a *career.* Conventional wisdom (left over from the 1950s) holds that life moves in a series of age-graded lock steps: After high school, you go to college, get a job, get married, get promoted, have kids, save money, and retire somewhere around age sixty-five. But for most Americans, this storyline is a myth, what Moen (2005) has called the "career mystique." "Lock-step arrangements around education, work, family, and retirement no longer fit the realities and risks of contemporary living," she explains. "Corporate restructuring, chronic job insecurity, and double demands at work and at home" are drastically changing the paths that both men and women take as they grow older. Focusing attention on how private troubles are actually public issues helps foster greater

Phyllis Moen

career and retirement flexibilities, such that there are possibilities for second acts and personal renewal at every age and every life stage.

This process of life-course reinvention will likely be driven by the seventy-eight million individuals who make up the baby boom generation, born between 1946 and 1964 in the years

At that point, there will not be enough workers to pay for the benefits required by retired persons (U.S. Social Security Administration 2005c). There is particular concern over whether the Social Security system will remain financially sound as retiring baby boomers collect their pensions. It is currently expected to have sufficient assets to pay full benefits until at least 2029, although if it is to avoid running out of money in the long run, changes will have to be made in the way the system is run (U.S. Social Security Administration 2005b). There have been calls to privatize at least part of Social Security—that is, to enable workers to invest part of their Social Security withholdings in the stock market, rather than simply paying it all into a government fund. The effectiveness of this approach depends,

of course, on how well the stock market performs in the future. Although it looked promising in the 1990s when stocks were soaring, today it does not look nearly so hopeful. And as of early 2006, proposals to privatize Social Security seemed unlikely to be adopted by Congress.

Do the Elderly Get an Unfair Amount of Government Support?

The costs of providing for the elderly come largely out of taxes paid by working people. In the United States, for example, the growing ratio of the elderly to the working-age population has after World War II. Starting in the year 2006, baby boomers turn sixty at the rate of one every seven seconds, a pace that will continue for the next two decades. These aging Americans will constitute the nation's largest group of retirement-age men and women, and their collective energy, good health, and productive activity will likely redefine what it means to be old or retired in America. For example, 82 percent of boomers plan to work beyond traditional retirement age (currently set at age sixty-two). Half plan to work their entire lives (Sturdevant 2006).

The concept of retirement is therefore one of those commonsense ideas in need of a twenty-first-century makeover. "We have these categories which become real—old, young, retirement age, etc.—and they're changing before our eyes," says Moen. "Let's think of these categories as socially *constructed* by rules and regulations. If they are constructed, then we can also *reconstruct* them." Baby boomers have already started. Moen's research reveals that many individuals in their fifties and sixties prefer to scale back work commitments or start second careers that are part-time or part-year instead of retiring cold turkey. "It is a mistake for policy makers to simply delay the official retirement age," she says. As Americans live longer and more productive lives, "people will agree to work longer, but on their own terms. Flexibility is key, as is the desire to do something meaningful, something worthwhile. These talented and experienced boomers constitute a potential windfall, a workforce for community building, a mentoring force for the next generation. But packaging matters; people will demand options that will change the way work is organized." Moen believes that we're on the cusp of rewriting what she calls "retirement scripts," the set of social expectations that guide perceptions of what's possible during the decades after middle age.

Those possibilities, however, will depend heavily on factors beyond the control of any single individual. If the current Social Security system remains unchanged, budgetary pressures will put at risk the government assistance millions of Americans currently depend on to survive. "Worries about the adequacy of personal income are already looming for boomers—and seem bound to get worse. A lot of moderate-income people who do not consider themselves poor today are going to find out that they are poor when they get old. This isn't on their radar screen at all" (Sturdevant 2006). Health care is another pressing issue for older Americans. More and more people work past the normal retirement age not because they are enthusiastic about their jobs but because work provides the only affordable way to secure health-care coverage. Add long-term care, increased life expectancy, pension liability, and housing shortages and a potential crisis seems to await seventy-eight million Americans for whom current public policies are not prepared.

Confronting these challenges will depend in part on changing stereotypes. "It may seem natural to regard what were formerly known as senior citizens as on the sidelines of society," Moen says, "but look at Mick Jagger and Tina Turner. They are definitely *not* senior citizens. Stereotypes are conventional ways of dividing up the world, but baby boomers will never be 'elderly,' never be 'senior citizens.' These labels and stereotypes don't fit anymore." For Moen, to change the world we must first recognize that the world is changing. Careers are changing. Retirement is changing. Aging is changing. And standing in the way of new workplace, retirement, and career flexibilities are cultural myths and institutional regimes that too narrowly define the process of growing old and staying young in America.

alarmed policy makers. They point out that for every one hundred people of working age (eighteen to sixty-four years old) in 1990, there were twenty people over sixty-five. By the year 2030, there will be thirty-six elderly people for every one hundred working-age people. A rapidly aging population will pose serious challenges to public policy throughout this century.

Do government programs adequately promote **generational equity**, the striking of a balance between the needs and interests of members of different generations? The issue of generational equity was first raised by an organization called Americans for Generational Equity (AGE), created in 1984 by Dave Durenberger, a U.S. senator from Minnesota, to challenge the notion that elderly people are entitled to Social Security

benefits (Quadagno 1989). AGE's chief criticisms were of the program's method of funding, which requires working people to contribute a portion of their earnings to a government-managed trust fund to pay for their retirement.

AGE argued that as the U.S. population grays, those who are working will bear an increasing burden for those who are not. AGE also argued that Social Security unfairly favors retirees over other needy groups in society. For example, AGE pointed out that retirees are sometimes wealthier than the working people whose taxes fund Social Security, and that there are nearly four times as many impoverished children under eighteen than impoverished people over sixty-five: 13 million versus 3.5 million (DeNavas-Walt et al. 2005). In the early 1990s, roughly a third of the total budget for Medicaid, the federal health insurance program for the poor, was used to provide long-term health care for the elderly. The elderly, blind, and disabled made up only a fifth of all Medicaid beneficiaries, yet required 70 percent of all Medicaid spending (Hudson 1995; Quadagno 1989).

The difficulty arises from the fact that there are fewer and fewer working-age people to shoulder the tax burden necessary to support more and more retirees. There may come a time when a predominantly white elderly retired population is supported by taxes paid by a predominantly nonwhite working population.

Globalization: The Graying of the World Population

An "elder explosion" is sweeping the world today. In 2002, the United Nations (2003) estimated that there were 629 million people over age sixty in the world. A 1998 report of the UN Population Fund (UNFPA) notes that the sixty-five and older population worldwide grew by about 9 million in 1998. By 2010, the elderly population will grow by 14.5 million; by 2050, 21 million. In 2050, the number of people over age sixty is expected to be 2 billion. The most rapid growth of the sixty-five and older group will take place in the industrialized nations of the world, where families have fewer children and people live longer than in poorer countries. By region, over half of the world's elderly live in Asia and a quarter live in Europe. In the industrialized countries, the percentage of the population that is elderly grew from 8 percent in 1950 to 15 percent in 2003, and it is projected to reach 25 percent by 2050 (FIFARS 2004a). After the middle of the century, the developing nations will follow suit, as they experience their own elder explosion, though only in the United States and other developed nations will the elderly continue to outnumber the population under fifteen (U.S. Bureau of the Census 1998).

The populations of most of the world's societies are aging as the result of a decline in both birth and death rates, although the populations of the poorer countries continue to have shorter life spans because of poverty, malnutrition, and disease (see Chapter 19). According to United Nations estimates (UNFPA 1998), the world's average life expectancy grew from forty-six in 1950 to fifty in 1985 and will reach seventy-one by 2025. At that time, some eight hundred million people will be over sixty-five, nearly a threefold increase in numbers from 1990. Among the very old (those over eighty-five), whose medical and service needs are the greatest, the number will increase by half in North America, while it will double in China and grow nearly one and a half times in West Africa (Sokolovsky 1990). This growth will place major demands on the resources of many countries that are already too poor to support their populations adequately.

This explosion has enormous implications for social policy. More than 150 nations currently provide public assistance for people who are elderly or disabled or for their survivors when they die. Elderly people are especially likely to require costly health-care services. Their rapid growth in numbers threatens to strain the medical systems in many industrial nations, where the cost of providing health care to the elderly threatens to overwhelm government budgets.

Countries vary widely in what they are doing to cope with their growing numbers of older people. As we have seen already, the United States relies primarily on Social Security and Medicare to serve the financial and health needs of the elderly. Other industrial nations provide a much broader array of services. In Japan, for example, men and women remain active well into old age because the Japanese culture encourages this activity and because business policies often support postretirement work with the same company one worked for before retirement. A number of national laws in Japan support the employment and training of older workers, and private businesses also support retraining.

Societies that have large extended families and practice ancestor worship are more likely to treasure their elders, honoring them at public events and seeking their counsel in political matters. In countries such as Thailand, China, and Japan, reverence for ancestors remains strong (Cowgill 1968; Falk et al. 1981; Glascock and Feinman 1981; Seefeldt and Keawkungwal 1985). Yet globalization has begun to change the treatment of the elderly throughout the world (Cowgill 1986; Foner 1984; Fry 1980; Homes 1983). As more and more people live to old age, respect for them has tended to decline. The reason is partly that their growing numbers result in a greater economic burden on their families. Additionally, as previously agrarian societies become a part of the emerging global economy, traditional ways of thinking and behaving are likely to change. When extended families are uprooted from farms and move into cities in search of factory work, their ability to support nonworking members is likely to decline. In those societies that are highly family oriented, the responsibility for supporting elderly parents and working for outside income often falls on young women. Research conducted in Taiwan, for example, has found that young girls often work a full day in a nearby factory, returning home during lunch and after work to care for infirm parents or grandparents (Cheng and Hsiung 1992).

The combination of graying and globalization will shape the lives of elderly people throughout the world well into this century. Traditional patterns of family care will be challenged, as family-based economies continue to give way to labor on the farms and in the offices and factories of global businesses. Like the industrial nations earlier in the twentieth century, all societies will be challenged to find roles for their aging citizens. This challenge will include identifying new means of economic support, often financed by government programs. It will also entail identifying ways to incorporate rather than isolate the elderly, by drawing on their considerable reserves of experience and talents.

Study Outline

www.wwnorton.com/giddens

Aging

- Biological, psychological, and social *aging* are not the same and may vary considerably within and across cultures. It is important not to confuse a person's *social age* with his or her chronological age.
- Physical aging is inevitable, but for most people, proper nutrition, diet, and exercise can preserve a high level of health well into old age.

The Graying of U.S. Society

- Because of low mortality and fertility rates, American society is rapidly graying, or aging. There are today some thirty-six million Americans older than sixty-five, a figure forecast to reach seventy million by the year 2030. The elderly are a large and rapidly growing category that is extremely diverse economically, socially, and politically.

Theories of Aging

- Functionalist theories of aging originally argued that the disengagement of the elderly from society was desirable. *Disengagement theory* held that the elderly should pull back from their traditional social roles as younger people move into them. *Activity theory*, on the other hand, soon came to emphasize the importance of being engaged and busy as a source of vitality.
- Conflict theorists of aging have focused on how the routine operation of social institutions produces various forms of inequality among the elderly.
- The most recent theories regard the elderly as capable of taking control over their own lives and playing an active role in politics and the economy.

Aging and Inequality

- Most of the elderly in U.S. society manage to lead independent lives that they report to be largely satisfying and fulfilling. Still, some suffer from poverty, social isolation, and costly medical problems, as well as from *ageism*, prejudice, and/or discrimination based on age.
- By providing the elderly with retirement income and critical health care insurance, Social Security and Medicare have helped raise a significant number of elderly people out of poverty. There is some debate over whether these programs are overly generous to the elderly and therefore threaten *generational equity*. In fact, however, the levels of support they offer are modest. Considerable debate nonetheless exists over whether their future funding is likely to be sound.

The Politics of Aging

- The elderly are as politically and socially diverse as any group in society. But on issues that affect their interest, they are capable of exerting a great deal of uniform political pressure. Their political influence is likely to increase as their numbers grow.

Lifelong Learning

- The elderly are capable of lifelong learning, and it seems likely that as their numbers increase, so will efforts to provide *andragogy* (adult-centered education) and *geragogy* (older-adult learning) for those who want it.

Globalization and Social Change

- Globalization threatens the traditional roles of the elderly in many societies. The role of the elderly throughout the world is in a rapid state of transition.

Key Concepts

Review Questions

1. For most of human history the average life expectancy at birth was
   a. more than sixty.
   b. more than forty.
   c. less than twenty.
   d. less than fifteen.

2. The graying of the population in the United States is the result of a
   a. lower fertility rate.
   b. longer life expectancy.
   c. lower mortality rate.
   d. lower fertility rate and longer life expectancy.

3. Aging can be sociologically defined as the combination of _____ processes that affect people as they grow older.
   a. biological, psychological, and social
   b. cultural, structural, and social
   c. biological, cultural, and social
   d. psychological, cultural, and social

4. Which of the following societies has or have traditionally revered elderly people?
   a. China
   b. Japan
   c. Both China and Japan
   d. United States

5. What is the effect of globalization on the status of the elderly in the less-developed world?
   a. It is likely to increase the status of the elderly.
   b. It is likely to decrease the status of the elderly.
   c. It is likely to have no effect on the status of the elderly.
   d. No definite answer.

6. What is the central argument of the functional theory in the analysis of aging?

a. An elderly person should never retreat from active social roles after he or she retires.
   b. Whether to retreat from one's active social roles depends on one's health condition.
   c. An elderly person should retreat from active social roles after he or she retires.
   d. An elderly person should retreat from active social roles even before he or she retires.

7. The second generation of aging theories emphasizes
   a. how well the elderly were integrated into the larger society.
   b. how an elderly person can play an active role in determining his or her own physical and mental well-being.
   c. how life style and exercise improve one's health.
   d. the sources of social conflict between the elderly and society.

8. The health-care costs for a person who dies at ninety are about _____ of those for a person who dies at seventy.
   a. three times
   b. one third
   c. five times
   d. the same

9. In the industrialized countries, the percentage of the population that is elderly is projected to reach _____ by 2050.
   a. 15 percent
   b. 25 percent
   c. 35 percent
   d. 45 percent

10. According to Cohen and Lenger (2005), what is the biggest fear about growing old among most Americans?
    a. Living for many years in a nursing home
    b. Losing your health
    c. Becoming a financial burden on others
    d. Being lonely

Thinking Sociologically Exercises

1. Briefly discuss the competing theories about growing old that are presented in this chapter. How do these theories compare with each other? Which theory do you feel is most appropriate to explain aging and why do you feel this way about it?

2. What do you think the United States could do socially and politically to alleviate the problems of aging for its elder citizens? How likely is it that your suggestions for alleviating the problems of age could be adopted into the American political process and why?

Data Exercises

www.wwnorton.com/giddens
Keyword: Data12

If you are a traditional-age student, you've probably not given much thought to aging, but our society is aging rapidly; we are experiencing *the graying of America*. The data exercise for this chapter provides you with an opportunity to learn more about what is happening in the United States and throughout the world, and what this demographic change means for society.

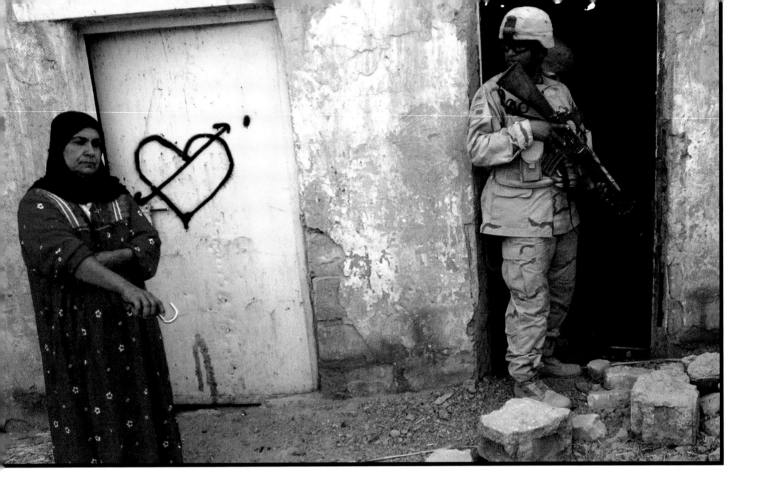

The Concept of the State

Learn the basic concepts underlying modern nation-states.

Democracy

Learn about different types of democracy, how this form of government has spread around the world, some theories about power in a democracy, and some of the problems associated with modern-day democracy.

Political and Social Change

Learn some basic theories about social movements and apply this understanding to the feminist movement in the United States. Assess the effect of globalization and technology on social movements today. Learn about nationalism and the importance of nationalist movements.

The Nation-State, National Identity, and Globalization

Evaluate whether or not globalization is weakening national identity.

Terrorism

Learn how social scientists define terrorism and the ways that new-style terrorism is different from the old.

CHAPTER THIRTEEN

GOVERNMENT, POLITICAL POWER, AND SOCIAL MOVEMENTS

n the early morning hours on March 20, 2003, the United States launched its "shock and awe" air campaign in Iraq. Intense bombing of strategic targets in the capital city of Baghdad and other Iraqi cities paved the way for the invasion of some 130,000 combat troops, mainly from the United States, with some from Britain and small numbers from a handful of other countries. Iraq's cities and oil fields were secured with a quickness that surprised many; and by the end of April, Iraq appeared to be securely in American hands. President George W. Bush, dressed in a flight suit, celebrated the seeming victory in dramatic fashion on May 2, aboard an aircraft carrier surrounded by sailors and with a banner fluttering in the background proclaiming "Mission Accomplished." It was a made-for-television moment. It also turned out to be badly mistaken.

Although the military objectives had been accomplished in record time, winning the war turned out not to be the same as winning on the battlefield. During the next three years, as Iraqis struggled to build a democracy under the tutelage (and military protection) of the United States, long-suppressed conflicts claimed the lives of over thirty thousand Iraqi citizens and about 3,000 American soldiers. Three years after President Bush's "mission accomplished" speech on board the *Abraham Lincoln,* nearly 140,000 U.S. soldiers (and another 15,000 British soldiers) remained in Iraq, training Iraqi security forces while fighting a growing insurgency. The reasons for the invasion of Iraq—and the causes of its bloody aftermath—reveal a great deal about the issues we discuss in this chapter.

391

One feature of modern politics is that in today's highly globalized world, even a country as powerful as the United States is under considerable pressure to act according to established international procedures before engaging in war. In the case of the Iraq War, one of the principal justifications for the invasion was that Iraq was said to have weapons of mass destruction (WMDs)—chemical, biological, and nuclear materials—that it was prepared to use against the West and possibly sell to terrorist organizations. The United States accordingly made its case to the United Nations Security Council, providing its best evidence that Iraq was violating the disarmament obligations it had agreed to after its 1991 defeat in the Persian Gulf War. At that time, Iraq had agreed to end production of WMDs and allow monitoring by UN inspectors. Saddam Hussein had stopped cooperating with the UN in 1998, and the inspections were ended.

In response to the U.S. presentation, the UN Security Council unanimously passed Resolution 1441, requiring Iraq to resume inspections and fully disclose its WMD program, threatening "serious consequences" if these conditions were not met. Although Iraq resumed inspections and issued a twelve-thousand-page declaration of its weapons program, the United States claimed that Iraq was still hiding its WMDs and then justified its invasion on the basis of the UN resolution. In modern times, for war to be regarded as fully legitimate, it requires some form of international authorization—in this case, that of the United Nations.

The buildup to the war illustrates another feature of modern politics: the importance of media, including the Internet. The Bush administration took its case to the American public, with frequent television appearances by the president and administration officials, emphasizing what they viewed as the threat posed by Iraq's WMDs, Saddam's possible connections to Osama bin Laden and al Qaeda, and the dire consequences of inaction—the "smoking gun that could come in the form of a mushroom cloud," as President Bush put it. The opponents of the U.S.-led invasion also used the media to great effect. They challenged the claims that Iraq had WMDs or posed an immediate threat to the United States, pointing out flaws in the U.S. intelligence reports on which the allegations were based. They also argued that contrary to the claims of the Bush administration, Saddam Hussein, who had long persecuted religious nationalists such as al Qaeda, was highly unlikely to cooperate with his former enemies. Critics' claims, which were widely circulated on the Internet, were supported by government leaks, former intelligence officials, and even UN inspectors—and turned out to be correct: neither WMDs nor Iraqi connections with Osama bin Laden were ever found. From activist blogs to Internet-based smart mobs (mobilizers) such as MoveOn.org, such information circulated around the globe. The largest antiwar demonstrations in world history were held on the weekend of February 15, 2003, involving simultanous protests by an estimated ten million people in eighty countries and eight hundred cities. Such well-coordinated global demonstrations resulted from an international network of nongovernmental organizations, an increasing force in global governance, as we shall see later in this chapter.

The violence that followed Saddam Hussein's defeat also illustrates another aspect of politics in the modern world: the challenges of building a democracy. One of the reasons given for the invasion, apart from ending the threat of WMDs, was the need to foster democracy in the Middle East, a region that is largely ruled by princes, military leaders, and corrupt government officials. Bush administration officials argued that toppling Saddam Hussein would not only remove a brutal dictator from power, effectively ending a major source of instability in the Middle East, but would also ripple throughout the region, showing others that democracy was possible. A parallel was often made with Eastern Europe, where, beginning in 1989, social movements had peacefully toppled communist dictatorships, leading to democratically elected governments in East Germany, Poland, Hungary, Czechoslovakia, Romania, Bulgaria, Albania, and other countries.

Unlike Eastern Europe, however—where democracy was generated by popular, widespread grassroots social movements—in Iraq, democracy came from above: an invasion by the U.S.-led coalition, followed by an occupying force whose purpose was to create democratic institutions, enforce elections, and keep the peace. Such an experiment in nation building proved to be fraught with difficulties. As we will see later in this chapter, a modern nation-state requires that citizens see themselves as one people under a single government. Previously ruled by Ottomans and the British, the "state of Iraq" is made up of many different tribal, ethnic, and religious groups, principal among which are the Sunni Kurds in the northern region; Sunni Arab Muslims in the central region (which includes the capital city of Baghdad); and Shiite Arab Muslims, the large majority, in the southern region. When they governed the region, the British had supported the Sunni Arab leadership; after the British were ousted in 1932, Sunni Arabs continued to rule the country, something they did with a vengeance under Saddam Hussein, a Sunni military leader who assumed power in 1979. Under Saddam's rule, Kurds and Shiite Muslims were often targets of persecution.

Many experts on the region predicted that the overthrow of Saddam Hussein might well lead to a civil war, in which Sunnis, Shiites, and Kurds fought bitterly over power and resources, while settling old scores. Sunni Arabs, who made up less than 15 percent of the total population, had enjoyed a disproportionate share of Iraqi wealth under Saddam, wealth that was largely generated by oil fields in the Kurdish north and the Shiite south. Moreover, the politics of creating a viable democracy were complicated by the presence of Islamists—religious nationalists, influenced (and perhaps supported) by Osama bin Laden, who sought to create a strict fundamentalist religious state and were willing to engage in widespread suicide bombing to achieve their goals. Furthermore, many Iraqis, whatever their ethnic identity or religious beliefs, resented the invasion itself, the continued presence of occupying forces, and the escalating violence associated with the occupation.

Democratization is one of the major political forces in the world; how best to achieve it is not quite so clear-cut. Like so many aspects of contemporary societies, the realm of government and politics is undergoing major changes. **Government** refers to the regular enactment of policies, decisions, and matters of state on the part of the officials within a political apparatus; as the example of Iraq shows, creating a stable and successful government can be a challenge in the modern world. **Politics** concerns the means whereby power is used to affect the scope and content of governmental activities. The sphere of the *political* may range well beyond that of government itself. As the example of Iraq shows, television and the Internet are among the means of exerting political influence; violence is another. In this chapter, we study the main factors affecting political life today. Many people find politics remote and uninteresting. Whether we like it or not, however, all of our lives are touched by what happens in the political sphere. Governments influence quite personal activities and, in times of war, can even order us to lay down our lives for aims they deem necessary. The sphere of government is the sphere of political power. All political life is about power: who holds it, how they achieve it, and what they do with it.

Power and Authority

As mentioned in Chapter 1, the study of power is of fundamental importance for sociology. **Power** is the ability of individuals or groups to make their own interests or concerns count, even when others resist. It sometimes involves the direct use of force, such as when the United States and the coalition forces invaded Iraq to overthrow Saddam Hussein and create a democracy. Power is an element in almost all social relationships, such as that between employer and employee. This chapter focuses on a narrower aspect of power, governmental power. In this form, it is almost always accompanied by ideologies, which are used to justify the actions of the powerful. For example, the U.S. government justified its invasion of Iraq partly on the basis of fostering the ideology of democracy; the escalating violence in that country is justified by its perpetrators in terms of such ideologies as Iraqi nationalism in the face of a foreign occupation and religious conviction.

Authority is a government's legitimate use of power: Those subject to a government's authority consent to it. Power is thus

different from authority. In Iraq, although power is increasingly in the hands of the newly created political institutions, the authority of those institutions remains in doubt. Contrary to what many believe, democracy is not the only type of government people consider legitimate. Dictatorships can have legitimacy as well, as can states governed by religious leaders. But as we shall see later, democracy is presently the most widespread form of government considered legitimate.

The Concept of the State

A **state** exists where there is a political apparatus of government (institutions like a parliament or congress, plus civil service officials) ruling over a given territory, whose authority is backed by a legal system and by the capacity to use military force to implement its policies. All modern states lay claim to specific territories, possess formalized codes of law, and are backed by the control of military force. **Nation-states** have come into existence at various times in different parts of the world (e.g., the United States in 1776 and the Czech Republic in 1993). Their main characteristics, however, contrast rather sharply with those of states in traditional civilizations.

Characteristics of the State

SOVEREIGNTY

The territories ruled by traditional states were always poorly defined, the level of control wielded by the central government being quite weak. The notion of **sovereignty**—that a government possesses authority over an area with clear-cut borders, within which it is the supreme power—had little relevance. All nation-states, by contrast, are sovereign states.

CITIZENSHIP

In traditional states, most of the population ruled by the king or emperor showed little awareness of, or interest in, those who governed them. Neither did they have any political rights or influence. Normally only the dominant classes or more affluent groups felt a sense of belonging to an overall political community. In modern societies, by contrast, most people living within the borders of the political system are **citizens,** having common rights and duties and knowing themselves to be members of a national community (Brubaker 1992). Although some people are political refugees or are "stateless," almost everyone in the world today is a member of a definite national political order.

NATIONALISM

Nation-states are associated with the rise of **nationalism,** which can be defined as a set of symbols and beliefs providing the sense of being part of a single political community. Thus individuals feel a sense of pride and belonging in being American, Canadian, or Russian. Probably people have always felt some kind of identity with social groups of one form or another—their family, village, or religious community. Nationalism, however, made its appearance only with the development of the modern state. It is the main expression of feelings of identity with a distinct sovereign community.

Nationalistic loyalties do not always fit the physical borders marking the territories of states in the world today. Virtually all nation-states were built from communities of diverse backgrounds. As a result, **local nationalisms** have frequently arisen in opposition to those fostered by the states. Thus, in Canada, for instance, nationalist feelings among the French-speaking population in Quebec present a challenge to the feeling of "Canadianness." Yet, while the relation between the nation-state and nationalism is a complicated one, the two have come into being as part of the same process. (We will return to nationalism later in the chapter as we look at its effect on international politics in the modern world.)

We can now offer a comprehensive definition of the nation-state: It is possessed of a government apparatus that is recognized to have sovereign rights within the borders of a territorial area, it is able to back its claims to sovereignty by the control of military power, and many of its citizens have positive feelings of commitment to its national identity.

Citizenship Rights

Most nation-states became centralized and effective political systems through the activities of monarchs who successfully concentrated more and more power in their own hands. Citizenship did not originally carry rights of political participation in these states. Such rights were achieved largely through struggles that limited the power of monarchs, as in Britain, or actively overthrew them—sometimes by a process of revolution, as in the cases of the United States and France, followed by a period of negotiation between the new ruling elites and their subjects (Tilly 1996).

Three types of rights are associated with the growth of citizenship (Marshall 1973). **Civil rights** refer to the rights of the individual in law. These include privileges many of us take for granted today but that took a long while to achieve (and are by no means fully recognized in all countries). Examples are the freedom of individuals to live where they choose, freedom of speech and religion, the right to own property, and the right to equal justice before the law. These rights were not fully established in most European countries until the early nineteenth century (Global Map 13.1). Even where these rights were generally achieved, some groups were not allowed the same privileges. Although the U.S. Constitution granted such rights to Americans well before most European states had them, African Americans were excluded. Even after the Civil War, when blacks were formally given these rights, they were not able to exercise them.

The second type of citizenship rights consists of **political rights,** especially the right to participate in elections and to run for public office. Again, these were not won easily or quickly. Except in the United States, the achievement of full voting rights even for all men is relatively recent and was gained only after a struggle in the face of governments reluctant to admit the principle of the universal vote. In most European countries, the vote was at first limited to male citizens owning a certain amount of property, which effectively limited voting rights to an affluent minority. Universal franchise for men was mostly won by the early years of the twentieth century. Women had to wait longer; in most Western countries, the vote for women was achieved partly as a result of the efforts of women's movements and partly as a consequence of the mobilization of women into the formal economy during World War I.

The third type is **social rights,** the right of every individual to enjoy a certain minimum standard of economic welfare and security. Social rights include such entitlements as sickness benefits, benefits in case of unemployment, and the guarantee of minimum levels of wages. Social rights, in other words, involve welfare provisions. Although in some countries, such as nineteenth-century Germany, welfare benefits were introduced before legal and political rights were fully established, in most societies social rights have been the last to develop. This is because the establishment of civil and particularly political rights has usually been the basis of the fight for social rights. Social rights have been won largely as a result of the political strength poorer groups were able to develop after obtaining the vote.

The broadening of social rights is closely connected with the **welfare state,** which has been firmly established in Western societies only since World War II. A welfare state exists when government organizations provide material benefits for those who are unable to support themselves adequately through paid employment—the unemployed, the sick, the disabled, and the elderly. All Western countries today provide extensive welfare benefits. In many poorer countries, these benefits are virtually nonexistent.

Although an extensive welfare state was seen as the culmination of the development of citizenship rights, in recent years welfare states have come under pressure from increasing global economic competition and the movement of people from poor,

Inmates wear orange jumpsuits in a holding center for illegal immigrants in Brownsville, Texas. The men are all OTMs (Other Than Mexicans) who have entered the United States through Mexico.

underdeveloped societies to richer, developed countries. As a result, the United States and some European countries have sought to reduce benefits to noncitizens and to prevent new immigrants from coming. For example, in 1994 voters in California passed Proposition 187, which denied social benefits to all illegal immigrants living there. At the national level, the welfare reform act of 1996 denied a wide range of benefits to *legal* immigrants. And for many years, the U. S. government has patrolled its border with Mexico and constructed walls of concrete and barbed wire in an attempt to keep illegal immigrants out of the country. Similar patterns of exclusion have occurred in Europe, particularly in Germany and Britain. In these ways, citizenship has served as a powerful instrument of social closure, whereby prosperous nation-states have attempted to exclude the migrant poor from the status and the benefits that citizenship confers (Brubaker 1992).

Having learned some of the important characteristics of modern states, we now consider the nature of democracy in modern societies.

Democracy

The word *democracy* has its roots in the Greek term *demokratia,* the individual parts of which are *demos* (people) and *kratos* (rule), and its basic meaning is, therefore, a political system in which the people, not monarchs (kings or queens) or aristocracies (people of noble birth like lords), rule. This sounds simple and straightforward, but it is not. What does it mean to be ruled by the people? As David Held (1987) has pointed out, questions can be raised about each part of that phrase. If we start with "the people":

1. Who are the people?
2. What kind of participation are they to be allowed?
3. What conditions are assumed to be conducive to participation?

Regarding "rule":

1. How broadly or narrowly should the scope of rule be? Should it be confined, for example, to the sphere of government or can there be democracy in other spheres, such as the economy?
2. Can rule cover the day-to-day administrative decisions governments must make or should it refer only to major policy decisions?

In the case of "rule by":

1. Must the rule of the people be obeyed? What is the place of obligation and dissent?
2. Should some of the people act outside the law if they believe existing laws to be unjust?
3. Under what circumstances, if any, should democratic governments use coercion against those who disagree with their policies?

Answers to these questions have taken contrasting forms, at various periods and in different societies. For example, "the

Freedom in Global Perspective

The level of freedom is based on the political rights and civil liberties individuals have in each country. According to Freedom House, the organization that produces the ratings, in 2004 about 44 percent of the world's population lived in free countries, 19 percent lived in partly free countries, and 37 percent lived in not-free countries.

SOURCE: Freedom House, 2006

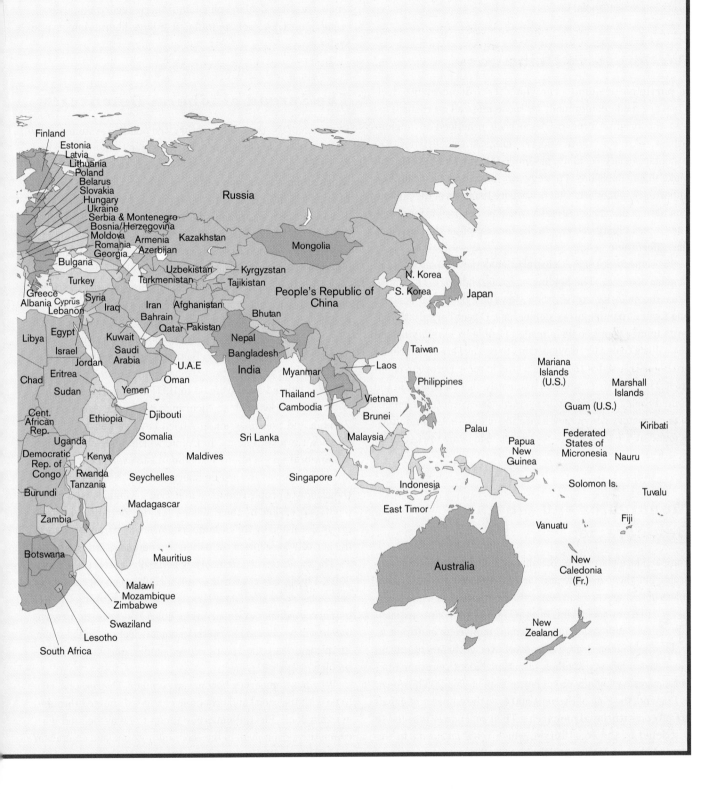

people" have been variously understood as owners of property, white men, educated men, men, and adult men and women. In some societies, the officially accepted version of **democracy** is limited to the political sphere, whereas in others, it is extended to other areas of social life.

Participatory Democracy

In **participatory democracy** (or **direct democracy**), decisions are made communally by those affected by them. This was the original type of democracy practiced in ancient Athens, in Greece. Those who were citizens, a small minority of Athenian society, regularly assembled to consider policies and make major decisions. Participatory democracy is of limited importance in modern societies, where the mass of the population have political rights, and it would be impossible for everyone to participate actively in the making of all the decisions that affect them.

Yet some facets of participatory democracy do play a part in modern societies. The holding of a referendum, for example, when the majority express their views on a particular issue, is one form of participatory democracy. Direct consultation of large numbers of people is made possible by simplifying the issue down to one or two questions to be answered. Referenda are regularly used at the national level in some European countries. They are also employed frequently on a state level in the United States to decide controversial issues. Another element of participatory democracy, a meeting of the whole community, is found at the local level—for example, in some townships in New England.

Monarchies and Liberal Democracies

Some modern states (e.g., Britain and Belgium) still have monarchs, but these are few and far between. Where traditional rulers of this sort are still found, their real power is usually limited or nonexistent. In a tiny number of countries, such as Saudi Arabia and Jordan, monarchs continue to hold some degree of control over government, but in most cases they are symbols of national identity rather than personages having any direct power in political life. The queen of England, the king of Sweden, and even the emperor of Japan are all **constitutional monarchs:** Their real power is severely restricted by the constitution, which vests authority in the elected representatives of the people. The vast majority of modern states are republican—there is no king or queen; almost every one, including constitutional monarchies, professes adherence to democracy.

Countries in which voters can choose between two or more parties and in which the mass of the adult population has the right to vote are usually called **liberal democracies**. The United States, the western European countries, Japan, Australia, and New Zealand all fall into this category. Some developing countries, such as India, also have liberal democratic systems.

The Spread of Liberal Democracy

For much of the twentieth century, the political systems of the world were divided primarily between liberal democracy and communism, as was found in the former Soviet Union (and which still exists in China, Cuba, and North Korea). **Communism** is essentially a system of one-party rule. Voters were given a choice not between different parties but between different candidates of the same party—the Communist party; sometimes only one candidate ran. There people had no real choice at all. The Communist party was easily the dominant power in Soviet-style societies: It controlled not just the political system but the economy as well.

Since 1989, when the hold of the Soviet Union over Eastern Europe was broken, processes of democratization have swept across the world in a sort of chain-reaction process. The number of democratic nations almost doubled between 1989 and 2005 from 66 to 119 (Freedom House 2005a). Countries such as Nicaragua in Central America and Zambia and South Africa in Africa have established liberal democratic governments. In China, which holds about a fifth of the world's population, the communist government is facing strong pressures toward democratization. During the 1990s, thousands of people remained in prison in China for the nonviolent expression of their desire for democracy. But some groups, resisted by the Communist government, are still working actively to secure a transition to a democratic system.

The trend toward democracy is hardly irreversible. Since 2004, Russia has returned to authoritarianism, according to some observers (Freedom House 2005a). Moreover, electoral democracy does not ensure that liberal democratic governments will be chosen by voters; in recent elections in Palestine, Egypt, and Iraq, the voters chose Islamist parties over more secular, democratic ones.

Why has democracy become so popular? The reasons have to do with the social and economic changes discussed throughout this book. First, democracy tends to be associated with competitive capitalism in the economic system, and capitalism has shown itself to be superior to communism as a wealth-generating system. Second, the more social activity becomes globalized and people's daily lives become influenced by events happening far away, the more they start to push for information about how they are ruled—and therefore for greater democracy (Huntington 1991).

Third is the influence of mass communication, particularly television. The chain reaction of the spread of democracy has probably been greatly affected by the visibility of events in the world today. With the coming of new television technologies, particularly satellite and cable, governments can't maintain control over what their citizens see.

THE INTERNET AND DEMOCRATIZATION

The Internet is another powerful democratizing force. It transcends national and cultural borders, facilitates the spread of ideas around the globe, and allows like-minded people to find one another in the realm of cyberspace. More and more people in countries around the world access the Internet regularly and consider it to be important to their lifestyles.

With the click of a mouse (and the miracle of Google), it is now possible to obtain, instantly and effortlessly, information on virtually any topic: The well-informed citizen need no longer depend on locally available newspapers, network news, cable television, or talk radio. During the 2003 Iraq war, those who tired of news reports by NBC or CNN or Fox could pick and choose from dozens of other news sources from around the world, from the official U.S. site military.com to the Web site of the Arab news service Aljazeera. Concerned citizens can e-mail their opinions to their elected representatives, while putting up a Web site to share their thoughts with anyone and everyone.

Whether Americans avail themselves of this technology to become better informed and more fully involved is another matter. While 68.7 percent of Americans report using the In-

ternet, those most likely to have access are well-to-do whites with college degrees, who live in urban or suburban (rather than rural) areas. And, it is not surprising, the young are much more likely to go online than the elderly (Horrigan et al. 2003; Internet World Stats 2005a).

One survey (Rainie 2003) of sixteen hundred adults, conducted about a week after the war in Iraq began, reported that among the country's adult Internet users (then estimated at 116 million), more than three quarters used the Internet to get information about the war, both through e-mail and by accessing Web sites. Of these, nearly a quarter went to the Internet seeking images that were deemed too gruesome or horrific for newspaper or television (Fallows and Rainie 2004). Still, the same survey found that only 17 percent of Internet users reported that the Internet was their main source of war news; nine out of ten relied primarily on television (roughly the same percentage as non-Internet users). In fact, the principal use of the Internet was to search U.S. television network, newspaper, and government Web sites for information. Only 6 percent reported viewing sites of groups that opposed the war, which is perhaps why the survey found that support for the war was even higher among Internet users than it was among nonusers (Rainie et al. 2003).

One prominent example of the political role of the Internet is provided by MoveOn.org, a liberal organization that was originally created to electronically mobilize opposition to the impeachment of then-President Bill Clinton. Led by twenty-two-year-old activist Eli Pariser and software entrepreneurs Wes Boyd and Joan Blades, MoveOn.org played a central role in the antiwar protest on February 15, 2003, when millions of people peacefully took to the streets in cities around the

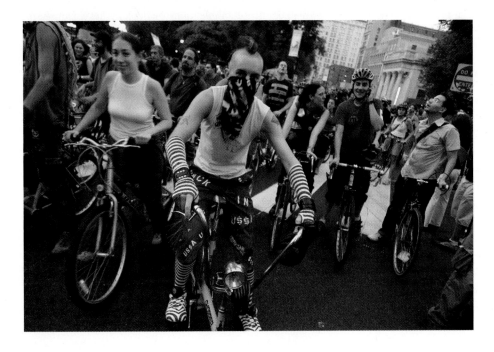

Movements like Critical Mass, which organizes bicycle rides to draw attention to alternative transportation, environmental, and urban issues, use the Internet, cell phones, and text messaging to coordinate their rallies.

The Wave of Democracy

When political sociologists of the future look back on the 1980s and 1990s, one historical development in particular is likely to stand out: the democratization of many of the world's nations. Since the early 1980s, a number of countries in Latin America, such as Chile, Bolivia, and Argentina, have undergone the transition from authoritarian military rule to democracy. Similarly, with the collapse of the Communist bloc in 1989, many East European states—Poland and the former Czechoslovakia, for example—have become democratic, adopting written constitutions, working to ensure that disputes will be resolved according to the rule of law, and, most important, holding popular elections. The resignation of the Indonesian dictator Suharto in 1998 following weeks of massive popular protest raised hopes that democratic forces will also come to prevail in that country, perhaps spurring the democratization of other Southeast Asian states. And in Africa, a number of previously undemocratic nations—including Benin, Ghana, Mozambique, and South Africa—have come to embrace democratic ideals. According to one recent estimate, 62 percent of the world's nations now rely on electoral processes to select their leaders (Freedom House 2005a).

Although a full explanation for these developments would require a detailed analysis of the social and political situations in each country that led up to the transition to democracy, there can be little doubt but that globalizing processes played an important role in this most recent wave of democratization.

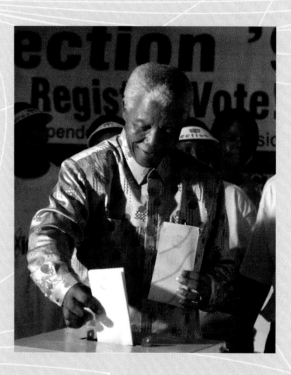

First, the growing number of cross-national cultural contacts that globalization has brought with it has invigorated democratic movements in many countries. Globalized media, along with advances in communications technology, have exposed inhabitants of many nondemocratic nations to democratic ideals, world to express their opposition to U.S. plans for military intervention in Iraq. The Web-based organization, with a paid staff of only four people, found out about the protest only a month before it was scheduled to occur. It effectively used its Web site to spread the word, enlist volunteers, and coordinate organization in numerous cities. The day after the demonstrations, MoveOn.org held a "virtual march on Washington," in which a million Americans e-mailed, faxed, and telephoned antiwar messages to their representatives. The ability to engage in such "smart mobbing"—gathering large masses of people electronically, often in only a few hours—

has been heralded as a new form of "Internet democracy" (Packer 2003).

Today MoveOn.org claims 3.3 million members. It has organized smart mobs around other issues, playing a key role in convincing Congress to defeat the proposed Terrorism Awareness Information Program, which would have enabled the government to collect extensive electronic information on private citizens. In December 2003, it organized some twenty-two hundred simultaneous "house parties" throughout the United States, at which a documentary opposed to the Iraq war was viewed by tens of thousands of people. The organizaincreasing internal pressure on political elites to hold elections. Of course, such pressure does not automatically result from the diffusion of the notion of popular sovereignty. More important is that with globalization, news of democratic revolutions and accounts of the mobilizing processes that lead to them are quickly spread on a regional level. News of the revolution in Poland in 1989, for example, took little time to travel to Hungary, providing prodemocracy activists there with a useful, regionally appropriate model around which to orient their work.

Second, international organizations such as the United Nations and the European Union—which, in a globalized world, come to play increasingly important roles—have put external pressure on nondemocratic states to move in democratic directions. In some cases, these organizations have been able to use trade embargoes, the conditional provision of loans for economic development and stabilization, and diplomatic maneuvers of various kinds to encourage the dismantling of authoritarian regimes.

Third, democratization has been facilitated by the expansion of world capitalism. Although transnational corporations are notorious for striking deals with dictators, corporations generally prefer to do business in democratic states—not because of an inherent philosophical preference for political freedom and equality, but because democracies tend to be more stable than other kinds of states, and stability and predictability are essential for maximizing profits. Because political, economic, and military elites, particularly in the developing world and in the former Soviet Union, are often anxious to increase levels of international trade and to encourage transnationals to set up shop in their countries, they have sometimes pursued a democratic agenda of their own, leading to what the political sociologist Barrington Moore Jr. once called "revolutions from above" (1966).

It is true that if globalization were the sole cause of the most recent wave of democratization, all countries today would be democratic. The persistence of authoritarian regimes in such countries as China, Cuba, and Nigeria suggests that globalizing forces are not always sufficient to force a transition to democracy. But democratic moves are afoot even in several of these countries, leading some sociologists to believe that under the influence of globalization, many more nations will become democratic in the years to come.

tion collects millions of dollars through its Web site in support of liberal causes and has attracted some big-money contributors as well: billionaires George Soros and Peter Lewis together gave the fledgling organization $5 million in late 2003 (Avins 2003; Brownstein 2003; Menn 2003; Neuman 2003).

MoveOn.org even sponsored a Democratic presidential electronic primary among its members, which was won by Howard Dean. Dean's run for the presidency was largely electronically based, at least at the beginning: The Democratic contender raised more than $10 million in small contributions (average: $200) during the first six months of his primary campaign. The primary vehicle for building his campaign was the Dean blog, which attracted thousands of youthful supporters, organized "meet ups" around the country, and fueled a highly effective grassroots effort.

Yet, as we shall see, political indifference and voter apathy are extremely high in the United States, and winning federal elections requires large sums of money that are unlikely to be raised through small online contributions. How Internet democracy plays itself out in the national political arena will depend not only on technology but also on the ability of grassroots efforts to make a real difference in political outcomes.

At the same time, the dynamic spread of the Internet is perceived as a threat by governments—especially authoritarian ones—that recognize the potential of online activity to subvert state authority. Although the Internet has been allowed to exist more or less freely in most countries, some states have begun to take steps to curb its use by citizens.

China, for example, saw the number of Internet users quadruple from 2.1 million to 8.9 million in 1999—and then explode to 103 million by 2005 (Internet World Stats 2005b). In July 2005, there were nearly 678 million Web sites in China, but the number is estimated to be doubling every six months (China Internet Network Information Center 2005; White 2003). In response to this rapid growth, the Chinese government has announced strict rules banning the publication of "state secrets" on the Internet, has blocked direct and indirect links between domestic Chinese and foreign Web sites, and has initiated a system of Web censors to monitor the context of news and information exchanged on the Internet.

In the eyes of the Chinese Communist leadership, the Internet presents a dangerous threat to state security by allowing political opposition groups to coordinate their activities. In April 1999, for example, thousands of supporters of Falun Gong—a spiritual movement whose members believe that breathing exercises prolong life—mobilized over the Internet and gathered in Beijing for a silent protest. Sensitive information on China's military and technological capacities has supposedly been published on Chinese Web sites. Such events confirm to the Chinese government that the Internet is a powerful medium of communication that must be controlled. The government requires Internet service providers (ISPs) to report detailed information on users and Internet activities, censoring all "subversive" content—which includes information on HIV/AIDS, as well as stories that feature information on democracy and Tibet. Much of the filtering is done with the help of U.S. companies that provide the software. Following a deadly fire in an Internet café in 2002, the Chinese government closed down thousands of such cafés, citing safety concerns as the reason (Reporters without Borders [RWB] 2003).

Other authoritarian governments have also concluded that the Internet can be a threat to their power. The Burmese government has announced a ban on the dissemination of information "detrimental to government" through the Internet or e-mail. The Malaysian authorities demanded that cyber cafés keep lists of all individuals who use their computers. In Russia, local ISPs are required to join an electronic monitoring scheme overseen by the federal security service. Reporters without Borders (2003) reports that (as of December 2003) fifty-three "cyberdissidents" are being held around the world

for their Internet activities, mainly in China, and firms such as Google, which are seeking to establish themselves in the lucrative Chinese Internet market, have agreed to some degree of government censorship. Moreover, the disclosure that the U.S. government has been engaged in secret monitoring of telephone conversations, e-mail, and Internet communication between U.S. citizens and suspected foreign terrorists has raised the question of whether such spying—without a warrant—violates U.S. laws and even the Constitution (Risen and Lichtblau 2005).

The U.S. government strongly stepped up its surveillance activities after the attacks of September 11, 2001. The FBI immediately requested all major ISPs to install Carnivore software, which would allow it to record, filter, and store e-mails on the basis of specific words. Internet surveillance was further strengthened by the USA Patriot Act, signed into law in October 2001, which expanded the types of Internet activity that could be obtained without the consent of a judge. The Pentagon's Information Awareness Office is working on software that can track Internet use, including credit-card and airline-ticket purchases, while the FBI is reportedly working on "magic lantern" software that can secretly record the keystrokes of an Internet user, enabling the agency to overcome the barriers to surveillance posed by encryption software (Hentoff 2002).

Democracy in the United States

POLITICAL PARTIES

A political party is an organization of individuals with broadly similar political aims, oriented toward achieving legitimate control of government through an electoral process. Two parties tend to dominate the political system where elections are based on the principle of winner take all, as in the United States. The candidate who gains the most votes wins the election, no matter what proportion of the overall vote he or she gains (Duverger 1954). The exceptions to this general rule in the United States involve presidential elections, which are actually decided by the electoral college. At three times in American history, one candidate won the majority of votes from citizens but still lost the electoral college vote. This occurred most recently in 2000, when Al Gore outpolled George W. Bush by about five hundred thousand votes but still lost the electoral vote by 271 to 267. Where elections are based on different principles, as in proportional representation (in which seats in a representative assembly are allocated according to the proportions of the vote attained), five or six different parties, or even more, may be represented in the assembly. When they lack an overall majority, some of the parties have to form a coalition—an alliance with each other to form a government.

In the United States, the system has become effectively a two-party one between the Republicans and the Democrats, although no formal restriction is placed on the number of political parties. The nation's founders made no mention of parties in the Constitution because they thought that party conflict might threaten the unity of the new republic.

Two-party systems such as that of the United States tend to lead to a concentration on the middle ground, where most votes are to be found, excluding more radical views. The parties often cultivate a moderate image and sometimes come to resemble one another so closely that the choice they offer is relatively slight. A plurality of interests may supposedly be represented by each party but can become blended into a bland program with few distinctive policies. Multiparty systems allow divergent interests and points of view to be expressed more directly and provide scope for the representation of radical alternatives. Green party representatives or representatives of far right parties, found in some European parliaments, are cases in point. On the other hand, no one party is likely to achieve an overall majority, and the government by coalition that results can lead to indecision and stalemate if compromises can't be worked out or to a rapid succession of elections and new governments, none able to stay in power for long.

Some writers have studied the connection between voting patterns and class differences: Liberal and leftist parties tend to gain most of their votes from those in lower-class groups, whereas conservative or rightist parties are more strongly supported by affluent groups (Lipset 1981). The party system in the United States is quite distinct from that of virtually all other Western societies because there is no large leftist party. Class-based voting is less pronounced than in other Western democracies. Although the Democratic party has tended to appeal more to lower-class groups, and the Republicans have drawn support from the more affluent sectors of the population, the connections are far from absolute. Each party has a conservative and a liberal wing; it is relatively common for conservative and liberal members of one party to align themselves with those holding parallel opinions in the other party on particular issues, such as free trade.

POLITICS AND VOTING

The founders of the American governmental system did not foresee a role for parties in the political order. George Washington recognized that interest groups would develop but spoke out forcefully against "the harmful effects of the spirit of party." Thomas Jefferson echoed these sentiments but in fact became the leader of one of the earliest party organizations, the Republicans—who were subsequently called the Democratic-Republicans, and in 1831, the Democrats. Policy disputes arose between Jefferson and Alexander Hamilton

during Washington's administration. Each had a group of followers: Hamilton's faction was called the Federalists. Jefferson's Republicans were the first to endorse candidates for Congress, leading the Federalists to do likewise. The national division of parties later spread to the state legislatures, and the parties soon developed into state organizations representing specific interests and points of view. A two-party system was well established by the 1830s, and although the parties themselves underwent subsequent changes, the fundamental nature of that system has not altered greatly to this day.

Building mass support for a party in the United States is difficult, because the country is so large and includes so many different regional, cultural, and ethnic groups. The parties have each tried to develop their electoral strength by forging broad regional bases of support and by campaigning for very general political ideals.

As measured by their levels of membership, party identification, and voting support, each of the major American parties is in decline (Wattenberg 1996). One study showed that the numbers declaring themselves to be "independent" of either party grew from 22 percent in 1952 to over 38 percent in 2004 (Pew Research Center 2004).

In recent years, Democrats have also lost ground to Republicans: Although Democrats held an edge in party identification during the Clinton years, by the end of 2003 roughly the same number of Americans (30–31 percent) identified with both parties. By July 2005, Democrats had regained a slight edge in voter identification, with 33 percent of Americans saying that they were Democrats versus 29 percent for Republicans (Pew Research Center 2004). Moreover, Democrats and Republicans have become increasingly polarized in the past few years. For example, Republicans are much more likely to favor an assertive national security strategy, whereas Democrats are increasingly critical of business and more likely to favor stronger government support for the poor (Pew Research Center 2003; Wattenberg 1996).

Since the early 1960s the proportion of the population that turns out to vote in the United States has steadily decreased, to the point at which today only slightly more than half the electorate votes in presidential elections. The turnout for congressional elections is lower still—around 40 percent (National Election Studies [NES] 2003). The presidential election of 2004 bucked this declining trend with voter turnout levels of nearly 59 percent, the highest since the election of 1968. The spike in the number of voters is attributed to campaigns by both parties to mobilize their core constituencies. Furthermore, there are significant differences in turnout by race and ethnicity, age, educational attainment, and income. Turnout is highest among whites and lowest among Hispanics, with blacks and Asian Americans in between. Generally, turnout increases directly with age: Only a little more than a third of all voters in the eighteen-to-twenty-four age group bothered to vote for president in 2000, compared with nearly three quarters of voters in their sixties. However, in the 2004 presidential election, the number of young voters swelled due to a highly organized voter mobilization campaign. Nearly 52 percent of voters under age thirty voted in the election. Education also makes a major difference in voting behavior: Fewer than two in five persons who lack a high school diploma voted in 2000, compared with four out of five with college degrees. Education is, of course, strongly related to income: Turnout was only about a third among individuals earning under $5,000, rising to three quarters among those earning over $75,000.

People give many reasons when asked why they don't bother to vote. In one study of the 2000 presidential election, two out of five nonvoters simply felt that voting was not worth the effort, given the electoral choices: 21 percent reported they were "too busy," while another 20 percent stated that they either didn't like the candidates or simply weren't interested. Many of the remaining nonvoters cited some difficulty that prevented them from going to the polls—an illness or other emergency, lack of transportation or some other inconvenience, bad weather, being out of town, forgetfulness. Only 7 percent cited problems in registering to vote, although this is likely to be a greater difficulty for lower-income voters (NES 2003). Clearly voting is not a high priority among many Americans.

Voter turnout in the United States is among the world's lowest. Sweden's International Institute for Democracy and Electoral Assistance tracked voter turnout in all countries that held national elections at any time during the period 1945–2002 by comparing the number of voters with the total voting-age population. According to their study, voter turnout in the United States averaged only 48 percent overall, earning it 138th place (out of 169 countries). By way of comparison, voter turnout in Europe over the same period averaged 74 percent; Asia, 70 percent; South America, 62 percent; Mexico, Central America, and the Caribbean, 60 percent; and Africa, 55 percent (Pintor and Gratschew 2002).

Why is voter turnout so low in the United States? Many studies have found that countries with high rates of literacy, high average incomes, and well-established political freedoms and civil liberties are likely to have high voter turnouts. Yet the United States ranks high on all of these measures, but still fails to motivate people to vote. Compulsory registration is common throughout Europe, and registration is often made easy. In the United States, where voters are required to register well in advance of elections, many fail to do so and are thus disqualified from voting. Not only is registration often compulsory elsewhere, but so too is compulsory voting, now practiced by thirty-three countries. Even though enforcement is often weak or nonexistent, voter turnout tends to be higher where voting is mandated by law (Pintor and Gratschew 2002).

Another possible reason is that because winner-take-all-type elections discourage the formation of third parties, voters may sometimes feel that they lack effective choices when it comes time to vote. A staunch environmentalist may decide there is no point in voting if the Green party candidate has no real chance of winning a seat in Congress; the strong antigovernment voter may draw the same conclusion in regard to the Libertarian party's chances. In many countries (including most European countries), some system of proportional representation is practiced, under which parties receive seats in proportion to the vote they get in electoral districts. Thus, for example, if a district has ten seats in Parliament, and the Conservative party gets 30 percent of the vote, that district would send three representatives to Parliament. Under this system, even small parties can often muster sufficient support to elect one or two representatives. When voters experience a wider range of choices, they are more likely to vote.

Finally, the range of elections is much more extensive in the United States than in other Western societies. In no other country is such a variety of offices at all levels—including sheriffs, judges, city treasurers, and many other posts—open to election. Americans are entitled to do about three or four times as much electing as citizens elsewhere. Low rates of voter turnout thus have to be balanced against the wider extent of voter choice.

INTEREST GROUPS

Interest groups and lobbying play a distinctive part in American politics. An **interest group** is any organization that attempts to influence elected officials to consider their aims when deciding on legislation. The American Medical Association, the National Organization for Women, and the National Rifle Association are but three examples. Interest groups vary in size; some are national; others statewide. Some are permanently organized; others are short lived. *Lobbying* is the act of contacting influential officials to present arguments to convince them to vote in favor of a cause or otherwise lend support to the aims of an interest group. The word *lobby* originated in the British parliamentary system. In days past, members of Parliament did not have offices, so their business was conducted in the lobbies of the Parliament buildings.

The U.S. Lobbying Disclosure Act of 1995 requires all organizations employing lobbyists to register with Congress and to disclose whom they represent, whom they lobby, what they are lobbying for, and how much they are paid. As of December 2005 nearly thirty-five thousand individual lobbyists were registered with the federal lobby director—more than fifty for each member of Congress (Birnbaum 2005; Center for Public Integrity 2003; Political Money Line 2003). To run as a candidate is enormously expensive, and interest groups provide much of the

Vice President Dick Cheney (center) accepts a rifle from the president (Kayne Robinson, right) and vice president (Wayne R. LaPierre, left) of the National Rifle Association after concluding his keynote address at the association's 2004 annual convention.

funding at all levels of political office. In the 2000 presidential election, for example, the Republican ticket (Bush-Cheney) raised nearly $200 million; the Democrats (Gore-Lieberman) nearly $135 million (Center for Responsive Politics [CRP] 2003). In 2004, the Bush-Cheney reelection campaign spent more than $367 million to retain the White House. The Kerry-Edwards ticket spent just over $326 million (Opensecrets.org 2005). Even to run for the House or Senate costs a small fortune. It cost about a half million dollars to run for the House of Representatives in 2004, and about $3 million to run for Senate. The most expensive congressional race in history, when Hillary Rodham Clinton (Democrat) beat Rick Lazio (Republican) in the battle to become a senator from New York in 2000, saw a total spending of $70.5 million. By 2002, total spending for all congressional races had reached nearly $1.4 billion (CRP 2003b; Federal Election Commission [FEC] 2003).

In the 2004 congressional election, 399 out of 407 incumbents running for reelection to the House of Representatives beat out their challengers—a stunning 98 percent success rate. Incumbents have an enormous advantage in soliciting money. In the 2004 race for the House, for example, they raised an average of six times as much money as their challengers (Opensecrets.org 2005). Incumbents are favored as fund-raisers partly because they can curry favor with special interests and other contributors, since they are in a position to ensure favorable votes on issues of importance to their funders, as well as obtain spending on pet projects and other pork for their districts. Incumbency also provides familiarity—a formidable obstacle for

most challengers to overcome. The cost of beating an incumbent has increased significantly in the last quarter century (Figure 13.1), which is perhaps why 43 percent of all newly elected congressional representatives in 2002 were millionaires—a distinction held by only 1 percent of the American public. (At least 40 percent of all senators are also millionaires.)

Corporations, which have a strong stake in getting favorable legislation and often government contracts, are by far the largest contributors to campaigns, accounting for nearly three quarters of the total in the 2002 election cycle (Figure 13.2). About three fifths of all corporate contributions go to Republican candidates. Labor unions overwhelmingly favor Democrats, who receive 93 percent of the contributions of organized labor. About a third of the funding in congressional or senatorial elections comes from political action committees (PACs), which are set up by interest groups to raise and distribute campaign funds. During the 1999–2000 election cycle, PACs made forty-five hundred contributions, totaling $579.4 million (FEC 2001). The National Rifle Association (NRA) tops the list of PAC spenders, contributing nearly $17 million—one of the reasons that gun-control legislation seldom makes headway in Congress, even though polls show that two thirds of all Americans favor stricter gun control laws (ABC 1999). Close behind is Emily's List ($15 million), an organization dedicated to electing women to Congress. Labor unions also weigh in heavily, accounting for nearly half of the largest contributors. Since 1989, The American Federation of State, County, and Municipal Employees has been the largest overall donor, giving nearly $37 million over fifteen years to various candidates for office (Opensecrets.org 2005a).

Interest groups and PACs not only help elect candidates—they also influence the outcome of votes in Congress. The Medicare Reform Act of 2003, which creates a $400 billion program to extend prescription drug benefits to the elderly, was heavily pushed by the pharmaceutical industry, which since 1996 has spent more than a half a billion dollars to lobby Congress, the White House, and federal regulators, as well as to launch advertising campaigns aimed at the general public (Common Cause 2003). Although the long-run benefit to the elderly was hotly debated by members of Congress, there is no question that drug companies will reap considerable benefit.

In 2002 Congress passed the McCain-Feingold campaign finance reform law, which severely restricted the ability to make unlimited campaign contributions. Under federal laws, some dating back a century, corporations and labor unions are prohibited from contributing to federal campaigns. Legal loopholes, however, permit unlimited "soft-money" contributions to be made to the political parties' "nonfederal accounts," supposedly destined for party-building activities unrelated to federal campaigns. In fact, almost all of the money finds its way back into presidential and congressional elections, reaching nearly a half a billion

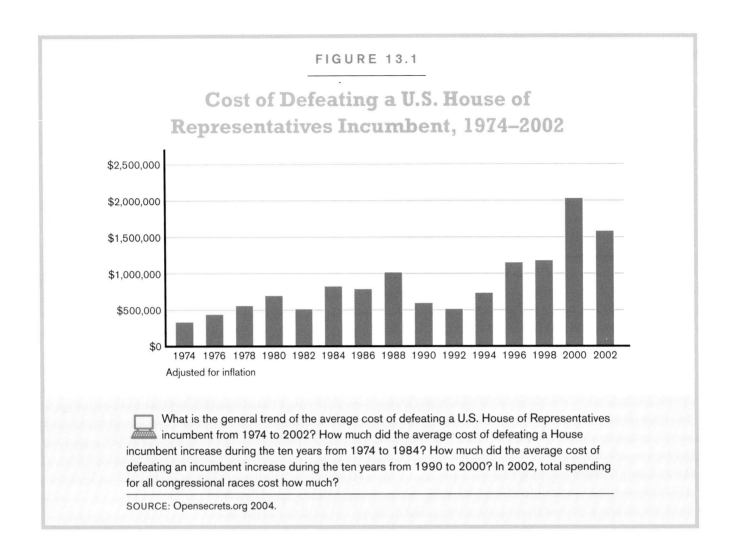

FIGURE 13.1

Cost of Defeating a U.S. House of Representatives Incumbent, 1974–2002

Adjusted for inflation

What is the general trend of the average cost of defeating a U.S. House of Representatives incumbent from 1974 to 2002? How much did the average cost of defeating a House incumbent increase during the ten years from 1974 to 1984? How much did the average cost of defeating an incumbent increase during the ten years from 1990 to 2000? In 2002, total spending for all congressional races cost how much?

SOURCE: Opensecrets.org 2004.

dollars in 2001–2002 (Common Cause 2002b). The McCain-Feingold law, which was upheld as constitutional in a landmark Supreme Court decision in December 2003, closes the loophole. Candidates for federal elections are once again restricted to raising money from individuals—$2,000 per candidate, $25,000 to political parties. However, campaigns have already found a loophole, 527 organizations. These groups are political organizations that typically engage in campaigning and lobbying for candidates and are funded by unlimited soft-money donations. They cannot coordinate their actions with any of the candidates, but they typically support one party or the other. In the 2004 presidential campaign, 527s like MoveOn.org and the Swift Vets and POWs for Truth spent a total of nearly $400 million.

The Political Participation of Women

Voting has a special meaning for women against the background of their long struggle to obtain universal suffrage. The members of the early women's movements saw the vote both as the symbol of political freedom and as the means of achieving greater economic and social equality. In the United States, where the attempts by women to gain voting rights were more active, and often provoked violence, women's leaders underwent considerable hardships to reach this end. Even today, in many countries, women do not have the same voting rights as men.

Women's obtaining the vote has not greatly altered the nature of politics. Women's voting patterns, like those of men, are shaped by party preferences, policy options, and the choice of available candidates. The influence of women on politics cannot be assessed solely through voting patterns, however. Feminist groups have made an impact on political life independently of the franchise, particularly in recent decades. Since the early 1960s, the National Organization for Women (NOW) and other women's groups in the United States have played a significant role in the passing of equal opportunity acts and have pressed for a range of issues directly affecting women to be placed on the political agenda. Such issues include equal rights at work, the availability of abortion, changes

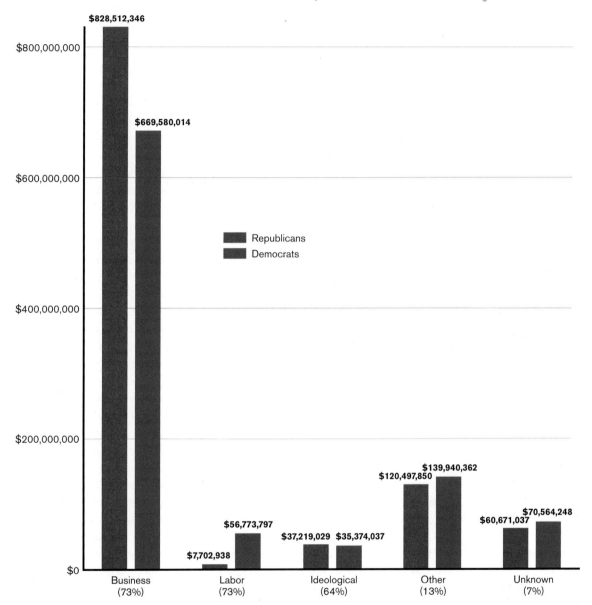

FIGURE 13.2

Business-Labor-Ideology Split in PAC, Soft, and Individual Donations to Candidates and Parties, 2002 Election Cycle

Which groups supported the Republican candidates and party in the 2002 election cycle more than the Democrats? "Business" donated what percentage of the total donations to both political parties and candidates during the 2002 election cycle? Which group most clearly favored one political party over the other with their donations, and which party do they favor?

SOURCE: Opensecrets.org 2004b.

in family and divorce laws, and lesbian rights. In 1973, women achieved a legal victory when the Supreme Court ruled in *Roe v. Wade* that women had a legal right to abortion. The 1989 Court ruling in *Webster v. Reproductive Health Services*, which placed restrictions on that right, resulted in a resurgence of involvement in the women's movement.

In most of the European countries, comparable national women's organizations have been lacking, but the "second wave" of feminism, characteristic of the 1960s and since, has brought the same issues to the center of the political stage. Although many of these matters—such as the question of whether abortion should be freely available—have proved highly controversial among women as well as men, it seems clear that many problems and concerns that particularly affect women, which previously had seemed to be outside politics, are now central to political debates.

Yet in general, as in so many other sectors of social life, women are poorly represented among political elites. After the 2006 midterm elections in the United States, there were seventy-one female members in the House of Representatives, making up just over 16 percent of the total membership. This number has almost tripled since the early 1970s, but it is still not representative of the number of female citizens. In 2006 there were only sixteen women in the Senate, representing 16 percent of those sitting in the upper chamber.

What is surprising about the figures on women's involvement at the higher levels of political organizations is not this lack of representation itself, but the slowness with which things seem to be changing. In the business sector, men still monopolize the top positions, but women are now making more inroads into the strongholds of male privilege than previously. As yet at least, this does not seem to be happening in the political sphere—even though nearly all political parties today are nominally committed to securing equal opportunities for women and men. Since 1990, female candidates for political office have been successful *when they have run for office*. The critical factor seems to be that political parties (which are largely run by men) have not recruited as many women to run for office.

The factors that present difficulties for women's advancement in the economy also exist in the realm of politics. Rising within a political organization requires a great deal of expenditure of effort and time, which women who have major domestic burdens can rarely generate. But there may be an additional influence in political life. A high level of power is concentrated in the political area: Perhaps men are especially reluctant to abandon their dominance in such a sphere.

From considering the position of women in politics, we now broaden our scope to look at some basic ideas of political power. First, we take up the issue of who actually holds the reins of power, drawing on comparative materials to help illuminate the discussion. We then consider whether democratic governments around the world are "in crisis."

Who Rules? Theories of Democracy

DEMOCRATIC ELITISM

One of the most influential views of the nature and limits of modern democracy was set out by Max Weber and, in rather modified form, by economist Joseph Schumpeter (1983; orig. 1942). The ideas they developed are sometimes referred to as the theory of **democratic elitism.**

Weber began from the assumption that direct democracy is impossible as a means of regular government in large-scale societies. This is not only for the obvious logistical reason that millions of people cannot meet to make political decisions but because running a complex society demands *expertise*. Participatory democracy, Weber believed, can succeed only in small organizations in which the work to be carried out is fairly simple and straightforward. When more complicated decisions have to be made, or policies worked out, even in modest-size groups—such as a small business firm—specialized knowledge and skills are necessary. Experts have to carry out their jobs on a continuous basis; positions that require expertise cannot be subject to the regular election of people who may have only a vague knowledge of the necessary skills and information. Although higher officials, responsible for overall policy decisions, are elected, there must be a large substratum of full-time bureaucratic officials who play a large part in running a country (Weber 1979; orig. 1921).

In Weber's view, the development of mass citizenship, which is so closely connected with the idea of general democratic participation, greatly expands the need for bureaucratic officialdom. For example, provision for welfare, health, and education demands permanent large-scale administrative systems. As Weber (1979; orig. 1921) expresses this, "It is obvious that technically the large modern state is absolutely dependent upon a bureaucratic basis. The larger the state, and the more it is a great power, the more unconditionally this is the case."

Representative multiparty democracy, according to Weber, helps defend against both arbitrary decision making on the part of political leaders, because they are subject to popular elections, and power being completely usurped by bureaucrats, because elected officials set overall policy. But under these circumstances, the contribution of democratic institutions is less than many advocates of a more pure democracy would hope. "Rule by the people" is possible in only a very limited sense. To achieve power, political parties themselves must become organized in a systematic way. In short, they, too, must become bureaucratized. "Party machines" develop, which threaten the autonomy of parliaments or congresses as places in which policies are discussed and formulated. If a party with a majority representation is able to dictate policy, and if that party is itself mainly run by officials who are permanently in control, the level of democracy that has been achieved is slim indeed.

For democratic systems to have some degree of effectiveness, Weber argued, two conditions have to be met. First, there must be parties that represent different interests and have different outlooks. If the policies of competing parties are more or less the same, voters are denied any effective choice. Weber rejected the idea that one-party systems can be democratic in any meaningful way. Second, there must be political leaders who have the imagination and courage necessary to escape the inertia of bureaucracy. Weber placed a great deal of emphasis on the importance of *leadership* in democracy—which is why his view is referred to as democratic elitism. He argued that rule by elites is inevitable; the best we can hope for is that those elites effectively represent our interests and that they do so in an innovative and insightful fashion. Parliaments and congresses provide a breeding ground for capable political leaders able to counter the influence of bureaucracy and to command mass support. Weber valued multiparty democracy more for the quality of leadership it generates than for the mass participation in politics it makes possible.

Joseph Schumpeter (1962) fully agreed with Weber about the limits of mass political participation. For Schumpeter, as for Weber, democracy is more important as a method of generating effective and responsible government than as a means of providing significant power for the majority. Democracy cannot offer more than the possibility of replacing a given political leader or party by another. Democracy, Schumpeter (1962) stated, is the rule of *the politician*, not *the people*. Politicians are "dealers in votes" much as brokers are dealers in shares on the stock exchange. To achieve voting support, however, politicians must be at least minimally responsive to the demands and interests of the electorate. Only if there is some degree of competition to secure votes can arbitrary rule effectively be avoided.

PLURALIST THEORIES

The ideas of Weber and Schumpeter influenced some of the **pluralist theories of modern democracy,** although the pluralists developed their ideas somewhat differently. Pluralists accept that individual citizens can have little or no *direct* influence on political decision making. But they argue that tendencies toward the centralization of power in the hands of government officials are limited by the presence of interest groups. Competing interest groups or factions are vital to democracy because they divide up power, reducing the exclusive influence of any one group or class (Truman 1981).

According to the pluralist view, government policies in a democracy are influenced by continual processes of bargaining among numerous groups representing different interests—business organizations, trade unions, ethnic groups, environmental organizations, religious groups, and so forth. A democratic political order is one in which there is a balance among competing interests, all having some effect on policy but none dominating the actual mechanisms of government. Elections are also influenced by this situation, for to achieve a broad enough base of support to lay claim to government, parties must be responsive to numerous diverse interest groups. The United States, it is held, is the most pluralistic of industrialized societies and, therefore, the most democratic. Competition between diverse interest groups occurs not only at the national level but within the states and in the politics of local communities.

THE POWER ELITE

The view suggested by C. Wright Mills in his celebrated work *The Power Elite* (1956) is quite different from pluralist theories. According to Mills, in earlier periods of its history, American society did show flexibility and diversity at all levels; however, this has since changed.

Mills argues that during the course of the twentieth century a process of institutional centralization occurred in the political order, the economy, and the sphere of the military. On the political side, individual state governments used to be very powerful and were only loosely coordinated by the federal government. Political power today, Mills argues, has become tightly coordinated at the federal level. Similarly, the economy was once made up of many small units, businesses, banks, and farms across the country, but has now become dominated by a cluster of very large corporations. Finally, since World War II, the military, once kept restricted in size, has grown to a giant establishment at the heart of the country's institutions.

Not only has each of these spheres become more centralized, according to Mills, but they have become increasingly merged with one another to form a unified system of power. Those who are in the highest positions in all three institutional areas come from similar social backgrounds, have parallel interests, and often know one another on a personal basis. They have become a single **power elite** that runs the country—and, given the international position of the United States, also influences a great deal of the rest of the world.

The power elite, in Mills's portrayal, is composed mainly of white Anglo-Saxon Protestants (WASPs). Many are from wealthy families, have been to the same prestigious universities, belong to the same clubs, and sit on government committees with one another. They have closely connected concerns. Business and political leaders work together, and both have close relationships with the military through weapons contracting and the supply of goods for the armed forces. There is a great deal of movement among top positions in the three spheres. Politicians have business interests; business leaders often run for public office; higher military personnel sit on the boards of the large companies.

In opposition to pluralist interpretations, Mills argues that there are three distinct levels of power in the United States. The power elite occupies the highest level, formally and informally making the most important policy decisions affecting both the domestic arena and foreign policy. Interest groups, on which the pluralists concentrate their attention, operate at the middle levels of power, together with local government agencies. Their influence over major policy decisions is limited. At the bottom is the large mass of the population, who have virtually no influence on the decisions at all, since these are made within the closed settings in which the members of the power elite come together. The power elite spans the top of both party organizations, each party being run by individuals with similar overall interests and outlooks. Thus the choices open to voters in presidential and congressional elections are so small as to be of little consequence.

Since Mills published his study, numerous other research investigations have analyzed the social background and interconnections of leading figures in the various spheres of American society (Dye 1986). All studies agree on the finding that the social backgrounds of those in leading positions are highly unrepresentative of the population as a whole (Domhoff 1971, 1979, 1983, 1998).

The main argument among sociologists about the distribution of power in the United States now focuses on the relative power of government officials and of the business leaders who run large corporations. One group of scholars argues that the government is where true power lies and that business leaders are not nearly as powerful as the experts and politicians who run the government (Amenta 1998; Orloff 1993; Skocpol 1992). An alternative view holds that corporate business executives and families of great wealth form a capitalist class, which has great influence over government officials and experts through lobbying, campaign contributions, the sponsorship of think tanks, and the appointment of top corporate leaders to important government positions (Domhoff 1998). Both sides agree, however, that it is not inevitable that business leaders or government officials will always be dominant. Although an elite class—whether elected, expert, or corporate—rules America, the power of groups can change over time, leaving open the possibility that those who are now powerless could be dominant sometime in the future.

THE ROLE OF THE MILITARY

Mills's argument that the military plays a central role in the power elite was buttressed by a well-known warning from a former military hero and U.S. president, Dwight David Eisenhower. In his farewell presidential speech in 1961, Eisenhower—who was the supreme commander of the Allied forces in Europe in World War II—warned of the dangers of what he termed the "military-industrial complex." As Eisenhower bluntly put it, "The conjunction of an immense military establishment and a large arms industry is new in the American experience. In the councils of government, we must guard against the acquisition of unwarranted influence, whether sought or unsought, by the military-industrial complex. The potential for the disastrous rise of misplaced power exists and will persist" (Eisenhower Library 1961).

With the collapse of the Soviet Union in 1991, the United States has emerged as the world's unrivaled military superpower, accounting for nearly half of total military spending—more than the next fifteen countries combined (Table 13.1). In 1989, at the end of the cold war, U.S. defense spending—which had reached $300 billion in that year—began to decline slightly. But the decline was short lived. There turned out to be no "peace dividend" to spend on improving schools, repairing highways, or other domestic needs. By 2001 military spending once again topped $300 billion. It reached $400 billion in 2004, and is projected at $500 billion in 2009, for a total of $2.3 trillion in military spending over the next five years—figures that do not include the cost of military operations in Afghanistan and Iraq (Center for Defense Information [CDI] 2003).

The global war on terrorism, discussed later in this chapter, has instead triggered yet another cycle of military spending. Eisenhower's dire warning seems no less true today than when he uttered it almost fifty years ago.

Democracy in Trouble?

As liberal democracy is becoming so widespread, we might expect it to be highly successful. Yet such is not the case. Democracy almost everywhere is in some difficulty. This is not only because it is proving difficult to set up a stable democratic order in Russia and other erstwhile communist societies. Democracy is in trouble in its main countries of origin—the United States is a good example. The numbers of people voting in presidential and other elections have been in decline for some time. In surveys, many people say they don't trust politicians and regard most of them as tricksters.

In 1964, confidence in government was fairly high: Nearly four out of five people answered *Most of the time* or *Just about always* when asked, "How much of the time do you trust the

TABLE 13.1

World's Fifteen Largest Military Budgets: 2004

RANK	COUNTRY	AMOUNT (BILLIONS)[a]	PERCENT WORLD SHARE
1	United States	$455.3	47
2	United Kingdom	$47.4	5
3	France	$46.2	5
4	Japan	$42.4	4
5	China[b]	$35.4	4
6	Germany	$33.9	3
7	Italy	$27.8	3
8	Russia[b]	$19.4	2
9	Saudi Arabia	$19.3	2
10	South Korea	$15.5	2
11	India	$15.1	2
12	Israel	$10.7	1
13	Canada	$10.6	1
14	Turkey	$10.1	1
15	Australia	$10.1	1
Subtotal (top 15)		$799.2	82
World		$975.0	100

[a]In U.S. dollars, at constant (2003) prices and exchange rates.

[b]Estimated figure.

SOURCE: Stockholm International Peace Research Institute, 2005.

tional forms of authority. Connected to this has been a shift in political values in democratic nations from "scarcity values" to "postmaterialist values" (Inglehart 1997). This means that after a certain level of economic prosperity has been reached, voters become concerned less with economic issues than with the quality of their individual (as opposed to collective) lifestyles, such as the desire for meaningful work. As a result, voters are generally less interested in national politics, except for areas involving personal liberty.

The last few decades have also been a period in which, in several Western countries, the welfare state has come under attack. Rights and benefits, fought for over long periods, have been contested and cut back. Rightist parties have attempted to reduce levels of welfare expenditure in their countries. Even in states led by socialist governments, such as Spain, commitment to government provision of public resources has been restricted. One reason for this governmental retrenchment is the declining revenues available to governments as a result of the general world recession that began in the early 1970s. Yet an increasing skepticism also seems to have developed, shared not only by some governments but by many of their citizens, about the effectiveness of relying on the state for the provision of many essential goods and services. This skepticism is based on the belief that the welfare state is bureaucratic, alienating, and inefficient, and that welfare benefits can create perverse consequences that undermine what they were designed to achieve (Giddens 1998).

Among the major industrial democracies, the United States spends the lowest portion of its total economy on government: roughly one third of its gross domestic product (GDP) goes for government spending at the federal, state, and local levels. By way of comparison, Sweden devotes more than half of its GDP to government spending; the European Union, 44 percent; and all industrial countries combined, 38 percent. Americans have relatively lower taxes than other industrial democracies, but they also received lower levels of support for health care, housing, education, unemployment compensation, and social services in general. This is arguably another reason for the low levels of confidence in government, and poor voter turnout: Americans simply expect less, and get less, from their government.

Why are so many people dissatisfied with the very political system that seems to be sweeping all before it across the world? The answers, curiously, are bound up with the factors that have helped spread democracy—the effect of capitalism and the globalizing of social life. For instance, while capitalist economies have proved to generate more wealth than any other type of economic system, that wealth is unevenly distributed (see Chapter 8). And economic inequalities influence who votes, joins parties, and gets elected. Wealthy individuals and corporations back interest groups that lobby for elected officials to support their aims when deciding on legislation. Not

government in Washington to do the right thing?" This level of confidence then dropped steadily for the following twenty years, rising somewhat in the 1980s, then dropping to a low of one in five in 1994. Following the terrorist attacks of September 11, 2001, a solid majority of Americans reported that they trust the government "most of the time" or "just about always." More recently, however, trust in the government has declined as scandals surrounding wiretapping, the war in Iraq, and indicted lobbyists have filled the news.

Of those expressing continuing trust in government, most vote in presidential elections; of those who lack trust, most do not vote. As we have seen, younger people have less interest in electoral politics than older generations have, although the young have a greater interest than their elders in issues like the environment (Nye 1997). Some have argued that trends like these indicate that people are increasingly skeptical of tradibeing subject to election, interest groups are not accountable to the majority of the electorate.

Economic inequalities also create an underclass of people living in poverty. About 20 percent of the population of liberal democracies lives below the poverty line. Most Western liberal democracies establish policies to reduce poverty levels, but they vary in how much they spend to achieve that aim. Societies that spend the most to implement a complex welfare system require a higher level of taxation and a larger nonelected government bureaucracy. The question arises, How much of an economic and political price is a society willing to pay to reduce poverty, and what is the effect of this cost?

Two theories have been put forward by different authors to account for this changing political situation. One is the theory of **state overload** (Britain 1975; Nordhaus 1975). According to this view, governments in the twentieth century acquired more responsibilities than they could capably fund and manage, from establishing public ownership of industries, utilities, and transportation to creating extensive welfare programs. One reason for this situation is that political parties tried to woo voters by promising to provide too many benefits and services. Governments were unable to deliver on these promises because the level of state expenditure rose beyond the resources provided by tax revenues: state responsibilities were overloaded (Etzioni-Halévy 1985).

Consequently, it is argued, voters have become skeptical about claims made by governments and political parties. The Democratic party in the United States and leftist parties elsewhere have lost some of their traditional support from lower-class groups, as it became apparent that states could no longer deliver the promised benefits. The rise of new right politics is explained as an attempt to cope with this situation by trimming back the state and encouraging private enterprise.

A rival theory, developed by Jürgen Habermas (1975), is known as the theory of **legitimation crisis** (Offe 1984, 1985). According to this theory, modern governments lack the legitimacy to carry out tasks they are required to undertake, such as providing highways, public housing, and health care. People who feel that they pay most for these services through higher taxes—the more affluent—are likely to believe that they gain least from them. On the one hand, governments are asked to take more and more responsibility for providing health care for those who cannot afford it; on the other, taxpayers resist any increases in taxation or even want tax payments reduced. Governments cannot cope with the contradictory demands of lower taxes and more responsibilities, leading to decreased public support and general disillusionment about government's capabilities. According to Habermas, legitimation crises could probably be overcome if the electorate were persuaded to accept high taxation in return for a wide range of government services.

As sociologist Daniel Bell (1976) has observed, national government is too small to respond to the big questions, such as the influence of global economic competition or the destruction of the world's environment, but it has become too big to deal with the small questions, issues that affect particular cities or regions. Governments have little power, for instance, over the activities of giant business corporations, the main actors within the global economy. A U.S. corporation may decide to shut down its production plants in America and set up a new factory in Mexico instead, to lower costs and compete more effectively with other corporations. The result is that thousands of American workers lose their jobs. They are likely to want the government to do something, but national governments are unable to control processes bound up with the world economy. All the government can do is try to soften the blow, for example, by providing unemployment benefits or job retraining.

At the same time that governments have shrunk in relation to global issues, they have also become more remote from the lives of most citizens. Many Americans resent that decisions affecting their lives are made by distant "power brokers" in Washington—party officials, interest groups, lobbyists, and bureaucratic officials. They believe that the government is unable to deal with important local issues as well, such as crime and homelessness. The result is that Americans' faith in government has dropped substantially. This in turn affects people's willingness to participate in the political process.

Political and Social Change

Political life is by no means carried on only within the orthodox framework of political parties, voting, and representation in legislative and governmental bodies. It often happens that groups find that their objectives or ideals cannot be achieved within, or are actively blocked by, this framework. Despite the spread of democracy described earlier, the persistence of authoritarian regimes in many countries—such as China, Cuba, and the former Yugoslavia—reminds us that effecting change within existing political structures is not always possible. Sometimes political and social change can be brought about only through recourse to unorthodox forms of political action.

The most dramatic and far-reaching example of unorthodox political action is **revolution**—the overthrow of an existing political order by means of a mass movement, using violence. Revolutions are tense, exciting, and fascinating events; understandably they attract great attention. Yet for all of their high drama, revolutions occur relatively infrequently. The most common type of unorthodox political activity takes place through **social movements**—collective attempts to further a common interest or secure a common goal through action outside the sphere of established institutions. A wide variety of social movements besides those leading to revolution—some enduring, some transient—have existed in modern societies. They are as evident a feature of the contemporary world as are the formal, bureaucratic organizations they often oppose. Many contemporary social movements are international in scope and rely heavily on the use of information technology in linking local campaigners to global issues.

Why Do Social Movements Occur?

Sociology arose in the late nineteenth century as part of an effort to come to grips with the massive political and economic transformations that Europe underwent on its way from the preindustrial to the modern world (Moore 1966). Perhaps because sociology was founded in this context, sociologists have never lost their fascination with these transformations.

Because mass social movements have been so important in world history over the past two centuries, it is not surprising that a diversity of theories exists to try to account for them. Some theories were formulated early in the history of the social sciences; the most important was that of Karl Marx. Marx, who lived well before any of the social movements undertaken in the name of his ideas took place, intended his views to be taken not just as an analysis of the conditions of revolutionary change, but as a means of furthering such change. Whatever their intrinsic validity, Marx's ideas had an immense practical effect on twentieth-century social change.

We shall look at four frameworks for the study of social movements, many of which were developed in the context of revolution: economic deprivation, resource mobilization, structural strain, and fields of action.

ECONOMIC DEPRIVATION

Marx's view of social movements is based on his interpretation of human history in general (see Chapter 1). According to Marx, the development of societies is marked by periodic class conflicts that, when they become acute, tend to end in a process of revolutionary change. Class struggles derive from the *contradictions*—unresolvable tensions—in societies. The main sources of contradiction can be traced to economic changes, or changes in the forces of production. In any stable society, there is a balance among the economic structure, social relationships, and the political system. As the forces of pro-

Deprivation of the peasantry compared to the elite in France led to the overthrow of the monarchy.

duction alter, contradiction is intensified, leading to open clashes between classes—and ultimately to revolution.

Marx applied this model both to the past development of feudalism and to what he saw as the probable future evolution of industrial capitalism. The traditional, feudal societies of Europe were based on peasant production; the producers were serfs ruled by a class of landed aristocrats and gentry. Economic changes within these societies gave rise to towns and cities, where trade and manufacture developed. This new economic system, created *within* feudal society, threatened its very basis. Rather than being founded on the traditional lord–serf relationship, the emerging economic order encouraged industrialists to produce goods for sale in open markets. The contradictions between the old feudal economy and the newly emerging capitalist one eventually became acute, taking the form of violent conflicts between the rising capitalist class and the feudal landowners. Revolution was the outcome of this process, the most important example being the French Revolution of 1789. Through such revolutions and revolutionary changes occurring in other European societies, Marx argued, the capitalist class managed to achieve dominance.

But the coming of industrial capitalism, according to Marx, set up new contradictions, which would eventually lead to a further series of revolutions prompted by ideals of socialism or communism. Industrial capitalism, an economic order based on the private pursuit of profit and on competition between firms to sell their products, creates a gulf between a rich minority who control the industrial resources and an impoverished majority of wage workers. Workers and capitalists come into more and more intense conflict with one another. Labor movements and political parties representing the mass of the working population eventually mount a challenge to the rule of the capitalist

Possibilities for Change in
American Communities

Teaching and learning sociology often involves finding ways to bring the outside world into the classroom. To more meaningfully connect students to the contexts within which social change efforts occur, I have developed the "Possibilities for Change in American Communities" program at Brandeis University. The yearlong program combines two semesters of in-class work with a month of bus travel around the eastern United States. In the classroom, our goal is to present theories of social change and introduce particular movements that we will experience firsthand during our travels. We then board a bus that serves as our home on wheels for a month, carrying us to a wide range of communities where we apply and test recently acquired ideas about social movements and social change.

The point of our travel is to connect students with activists and social movement organizations, and to the local communities in which these movements operate. Our route is designed to expose the group to a broad set of communities, consistent with our overall strategy of comparatively examining the contexts in which change occurs. Frequently, our students—typically raised in urban or suburban areas around Boston, New York, Chicago, or Los Angeles—learn enduring lessons in areas that diverge most sharply from their own backgrounds. Following a meeting with a local advocacy organization in rural North Carolina, for instance, the group's leader invited us to dinner at his truck-stop restaurant on the outskirts of town. We gladly accepted, and were treated not only to a delicious meal, but also to back-room political negotiations when our host and several of his colleagues held an impromptu meeting over barbeque with the local mayor and town planner. While readings and class discussions may focus on the tight-knit, highly interdependent nature of rural and small-town so-

David Cunningham

cial relations, such lessons have a lasting impact when we see these connections in action.

Our time spent on the road also provides an opportunity for students to engage in a range of community-based work. Our aim is not to passively study communities and organizations, but to integrate ourselves into their perspectives and activities. The groups we select are purposely wide-ranging, and include direct service, advocacy, and community organizing ventures. Over the course of a single month, we cooked and distributed meals with Food Not Bombs in Chapel Hill, North Carolina; spoke out for gun control legislation on CNN's *Talk Back Live* in Atlanta, Georgia; stuffed envelopes to support Sister Helen Prejean's Moratorium Campaign in New Orleans; helped restore a house with Habitat for Humanity in Baton Rouge, Louisiana; lobbied our congressional representatives in Washington, D.C.; and helped recruit participants in the Kensington Welfare Rights Union's battle for affordable housing

class and overthrow the existing political system. When the position of a dominant class is particularly entrenched, Marx believed, violence is necessary to bring about the required transition. In other circumstances, this process might happen peacefully through parliamentary action; a revolution (in the sense defined above) would not be necessary.

Contrary to Marx's expectations, revolutions failed to occur in the advanced industrialized societies of the West. Why? Sociologist James Davies (1962), a critic of Marx, pointed to periods of history when people lived in dire poverty but did not rise up in protest. Constant poverty or deprivation does not make people into revolutionaries; rather, and health care in Philadelphia. Alongside this work, we also met with participants in past and current activist efforts, spoke with several noted social movement scholars, and visited a number of historically important sites.

To many of the people we encounter along the way, our mode of travel seems at least as interesting as our educational mission. A sleeper bus is something used mostly by bands or touring theater groups—they stand out due to their large size, lack of windows, and airbrushed artwork. Considering the space constraints, the interior is really quite comfortable, providing living and sleeping space for fifteen. Importantly, the tight living arrangement provides plenty of opportunity for us to forge our own functioning community. And combining our accommodations with our mode of transportation is exceedingly efficient, as it allows us to travel at night while we sleep. We thus spend the vast majority of our waking hours at our destinations rather than in transit.

Quite literally, the bus provides a vehicle to understand the longer-term impacts of social movement activity, linking causes to effects and the past to the present. In Jackson, Mississippi, for instance, we visited with Bob Moses and Dave Dennis, both veterans of civil rights work with the Student Non-Violent Coordinating Committee during the 1960s. For the past twenty years, both have worked to develop the Algebra Project, a math literacy program that they view as key to students' future economic access in the same way that sharecroppers' ability to vote had determined their political access a generation earlier.

Just two days before our visit to Jackson, we spent time in Selma, Alabama, the site of the 1965 "Bloody Sunday" march in which several hundred civil rights marchers were brutally beaten by police officers seeking to prevent them from crossing the Edmund Pettus Bridge to begin their fifty-mile trek to the state capitol in Montgomery. In Selma, we were able to follow the aborted march route over the Pettus Bridge and hear firsthand accounts by local participants at the nearby National Voting Rights Museum and Institute. We also canvassed Selma neighborhoods to interview longtime residents about their lives since the 1960s, and met with current Mayor James Perkins, the first African American resident elected to that post in Selma.

By connecting to movement activists and directly experiencing the sites of social movement activity, we are able to explore more fully the long-term impact of specific events like the Selma-to-Montgomery march, and the larger civil rights movement. We also forge links to ongoing movements, gaining an on-the-ground understanding of their strategies, tactics, and day-to-day operations. These links are first put into action following our return, when students work on ambitious projects tied to our travels. From creating campus partnerships with community organizations to further their ongoing campaigns, to analyzing interview and archival data to formulate strategic plans to improve citizens' access to community resources, students continue to apply their experience and knowledge actively. Such activities provide a means to understand the dynamics of social movement activity, while creating long-term benefits both for our students and for the communities that they will be part of in the future.

DAVID CUNNINGHAM is an assistant professor in the Department of Sociology at Brandeis University. He is currently pursuing research on the political repression of protest groups and Ku Klux Klan mobilization in the civil rights–era South. He is the author of There's Something Happening Here: The New Left, the Klan, and FBI Counterintelligence *(University of California Press, 2004).*

they usually endure such conditions with resignation or mute despair. Social protest, and ultimately revolution, is more likely to occur, Davies argued, when there is an *improvement* in people's living conditions. Once standards of living have started to rise, people's levels of expectation also go up. If improvement in actual conditions subsequently slows down,

propensities to revolt are created because rising expectations are frustrated.

Thus it is not absolute deprivation that leads to protest but **relative deprivation**—the discrepancy between the lives people are forced to lead and what they think could realistically be achieved. Davies's theory is useful in understanding the connections between revolution and modern social and economic development. The influence of ideals of progress, together with expectations of economic growth, tend to induce rising hopes, which, if then frustrated, spark protest. Such protest gains further strength from the spread of ideas of equality and democratic political participation, ideas that played a basic role not only in the American Revolution of 1776 and the Russian Revolution of 1917 but also in the revolutions of 1989 in Europe.

As Charles Tilly (1978) has pointed out, however, Davies's theory does not show how and why different groups *mobilize* to seek revolutionary change. Protest might well often occur against a backdrop of rising expectations; to understand how it is transformed into a mass social movement, we need to identify how groups become collectively organized to make effective political challenges.

RESOURCE MOBILIZATION

In *From Mobilization to Revolution* (1978), Tilly analyzed processes of revolutionary change in the context of broader forms of protest and violence. He distinguished four main components of **collective action,** action taken to contest or overthrow an existing social order:

1. The *organization* of the group or groups involved. Protest movements are organized in many ways, varying from the spontaneous formation of crowds to tightly disciplined revolutionary groups. The Russian Revolution, for example, began as a small group of activists.
2. *Mobilization*, the ways in which a group acquires sufficient resources to make collective action possible. Such resources may include supplies of material goods, political support, and weaponry. Lenin was able to acquire material and moral support from a sympathetic peasantry, together with many townspeople.
3. The *common interests* of those engaging in collective action, what they see as the gains and losses likely to be achieved by their policies. Some common goals always underlie mobilization to collective action. Lenin managed to weld together a broad coalition of support because many people had a common interest in removing the existing government.
4. *Opportunity*. Chance events may occur that provide opportunities to pursue revolutionary aims. Numerous forms of collective action, including revolution, are greatly influenced by such incidental events. There was no inevitability to Lenin's success, which depended on a number of contingent factors—including success in

battle. If Lenin had been killed, would there have been a revolution?

Collective action itself can simply be defined as people acting together in pursuit of interests they share—for example, gathering to demonstrate in support of their cause. Some of these people may be intensely involved, others may lend more passive or irregular support. Effective collective action, such as action that culminates in revolution, usually moves through stages 1 to 4.

Social movements, in Tilly's view, tend to develop as means of mobilizing group resources either when people have no institutionalized means of making their voices heard or when their needs are directly repressed by the state authorities. Although collective action at some point involves open confrontation with the political authorities—"taking to the streets"—only when such activity is backed by groups who are systematically organized is confrontation likely to have much effect on established patterns of power.

Typical modes of collective action and protest vary with historical and cultural circumstances. In the United States today, for example, most people are familiar with forms of demonstration like mass marches, large assemblies, and street riots, whether or not they have participated in such activities. Other types of collective protest, however, have become less common or have disappeared altogether in most modern societies (such as fights between villages, machine breaking, or lynching). Protesters can also build on examples taken from elsewhere; for instance, guerrilla movements proliferated in various parts of the world once disaffected groups learned how successful guerrilla actions can be against regular armies. And, as discussed earlier, a new form of collective action may be emerging—smart-mobbing and other forms of social protest accomplished through the Internet.

When and why does collective action become violent? After studying a large number of incidents that have occurred in Western Europe since 1800, Tilly concluded that most collective violence develops from action that is not itself initially violent. Whether violence occurs depends not so much on the nature of the activity as on other factors—in particular, how the authorities respond. A good instance is the street demonstration. The vast majority of such demonstrations take place without damage either to people or to property. A minority lead to violence and are then labeled as riots. Sometimes the authorities step in when violence has already occurred; more often, the historical record shows, they are the originators of violence. In Tilly's (1978) words, "In the modern European experience repressive forces are themselves the most consistent initiators and performers of collective violence." Moreover, when violent confrontations do occur, the agents of authority are responsible for the largest share of deaths and injuries. This is not surprising given their special access to arms and military discipline. The groups they are attempting to control, conversely, do greater damage to objects or property.

Revolutionary movements, according to Tilly, are a type of collective action that occurs in situations of what he calls **multiple sovereignty**—these occur when a government for some reason lacks full control over the areas it is supposed to administer. Multiple sovereignty can arise as a result of external war, internal political clashes, or the two combined. Whether a revolutionary takeover of power is accomplished depends on how far the ruling authorities maintain control over the armed forces, the extent of conflicts within ruling groups, and the level of organization of the protest movements trying to seize power.

Tilly's work represents one of the most sophisticated attempts to analyze collective violence and revolutionary struggles. The concepts he develops seem to have wide application, and his use of them is sensitive to the variabilities of historical time and place. How social movements are organized, the resources they are able to mobilize, the common interests of groups contending for power, and chance opportunities are all important facets of social transformation.

Tilly says little, however, about the circumstances that lead to multiple sovereignty. This is such a fundamental part of explaining revolution that it represents a serious omission. According to Theda Skocpol (1979), Tilly assumes that social movements are guided by the conscious and deliberate pursuit of interests, and that successful processes of revolutionary change occur when people manage to realize these interests. Skocpol, by contrast, sees social movements as more ambiguous and indecisive in their objectives. Revolutions, she emphasizes, largely emerge as unintended consequences of more partial aims:

In fact, in historical revolutions, differently situated and motivated groups have become participants in complex unfoldings of multiple conflicts. These conflicts have been powerfully shaped and limited by existing social, economic and international conditions. And they have proceeded in different ways depending upon how each revolutionary situation emerged in the first place. (Skocpol 1979)

Skocpol's argument seems correct when we analyze the revolutionary changes that occurred in Eastern European societies in 1989, compared with earlier revolutionary episodes.

In addition to the theories just discussed, which seek to explain the collective behavior that leads to revolutions, other theoretical perspectives on more general forms of collective action are also important. We will now look at two of those theories, structural strain and fields of action.

STRUCTURAL STRAIN

Neil Smelser (1963) distinguished six conditions underlying the origins of collective action in general, and social movements in particular: the presence of structurally conducive conditions, the existence of structural strain in society, the spread of generalized beliefs, the presence of precipitating factors of effective leadership, and the nature of social control directed against the social movement.

1. *Structural conduciveness* refers to the general social conditions promoting or inhibiting the formation of social movements of different types. For example, in Smelser's view, the sociopolitical system of the United States leaves open certain avenues of mobilization for protest because of the relative absence of state regulation in those areas. For example, there is no official state-sponsored religion. People are free to exercise their religious beliefs. This makes for a conducive environment in which religious movements might compete for individuals, so long as they do not transgress criminal or civil law.

2. Just because the conditions are conducive to the development of a social movement does not mean those conditions will bring them into being. There must be **structural strain**—tensions (or, in Marx's terminology, contradictions) that produce conflicting interests within societies. Uncertainties, anxieties, ambiguities, and direct clashes of goals are expressions of such strains. Sources of strain may be quite general or specific to particular situations. Thus sustained inequalities among ethnic groups give rise to overall tensions; these may become focused in the shape of specific conflicts when, say, blacks begin to move into a previously all-white area.

3. The third condition Smelser outlined is the spread of *generalized beliefs*. Social movements do not develop simply as responses to vaguely felt anxieties or hostilities. They are shaped by the influence of definite ideologies, which crystallize grievances and suggest courses of action that might be pursued to remedy them. Revolutionary movements, for instance, are based on ideas about why injustice occurs and how it can be alleviated by political struggle.

4. *Precipitating factors* are events or incidents that actually trigger direct action by those who become involved in the movement. In 1955, when a black woman named Rosa Parks refused to give up her seat to a white man on a bus in Montgomery, Alabama, her action helped spark the civil rights movement (see Chapter 11).

Rosa Parks's refusal to give up her seat to a white man on a bus sparked the civil rights movement and is an example of a precipitating factor.

5. The first four conditions combined, Smelser argued, might occasionally lead to street disturbances or outbreaks of violence. But such incidents do not lead to the development of social movements unless there is a coordinated group that becomes mobilized for action. *Leadership* and some means of *regular communication* among participants, together with funding and material resources, are necessary for a social movement to exist.

6. Finally, the manner in which a social movement develops is strongly influenced by the *operation of social control.* The governing authorities may respond to initial protests by intervening in the conditions of conduciveness and strain that stimulated the emergence of the movement. For instance, in a situation of ethnic tension, steps might be taken to reduce ethnic inequality that generated resentment and conflict. Other important aspects of social control concern the responses of the police or armed forces. A harsh reaction might encourage further protest and help solidify the movement. Also, doubt and divisions within the police and military can be crucial in deciding the outcome of confrontations with revolutionary movements.

Smelser's model is useful for analyzing the sequences in the development of social movements and collective action in general. According to Smelser, each stage in the sequence "adds value" to the overall outcome; also, each stage is a condition for the occurrence of the next one. But some critical comments can be made about Smelser's theory. Some social movements become strong without any particular precipitating incidents. Conversely, a series of incidents might bring home the need to establish a movement to change the circumstances that gave rise to them. Also, a movement itself might create strains, rather than develop in response to them. For example, the women's movement has actively sought to identify and combat gender inequalities where previously those had gone unquestioned. Smelser's theory treats social movements as *responses* to situations, rather than allowing that their members might spontaneously organize to achieve desired social changes. In this respect his ideas contrast with the approach developed by Alain Touraine.

FIELDS OF ACTION

Alain Touraine (1977, 1981) developed his analysis of social movements on the basis of four main ideas. The first, which he called **historicity,** explains why there are so many more movements in the modern world than there were in earlier times. In modern societies, individuals and groups know that social activism can be used to achieve social goals and reshape society.

Second, Touraine focused on the *rational objectives* of social movements. Such movements do not just come about as irrational responses to social divisions or injustices; rather, they develop from specific views and rational strategies as to how injustices can be overcome.

Third, Touraine saw a process of *interaction* in the shaping of social movements. Movements do not develop in isolation; instead, they develop in deliberate antagonism with established organizations and sometimes with other rival social movements. All social movements have interests or aims that they are *for;* all have views and ideas they are *against.* According to Touraine, other theories of social movements (including that of Smelser) have given insufficient consideration to how the objectives of a social movement are shaped by encounters with others holding divergent positions as well as by the ways in which they themselves influence the outlooks and action of their opponents. For instance, the objectives and outlook of the women's movement have been shaped in opposition to the male-dominated institutions that it seeks to alter. The goals and outlook of the movement have shifted in relation to its successes and failures and have also influenced the perspectives of men. These changed perspectives in turn stimulated a reorientation in the women's movement, and so the process of shaping and reshaping continues.

Fourth, social movements and change occur in the context of what Touraine called "fields of action." A **field of action** refers to the connections between a social movement and the forces or influences against it. The process of mutual negotiation among antagonists in a field of action may lead to the social changes sought by the movement as well as to changes in the social movement itself and in its antagonists. In either circumstance, the movement may evaporate or become institutionalized as a permanent organization. For example, the labor-union movements became formal organizations when they achieved the right to strike and to engage in types of bargaining acceptable to both workers and employers. These changes in both the movement and the original worker–owner relationship were forged out of earlier processes involving widespread violent confrontation on both sides. Where there are continuing sources of conflict (as in the case of the relation between unions and employers), new movements still tend to reemerge.

Touraine's analysis can also be applied to movements concerned primarily with individual change even though Touraine himself has said little about them. For instance, Alcoholics Anonymous is a movement based on medical findings about the harmful effects of alcohol on people's health and social activities. The movement itself has been shaped by its own opposition to advertising designed to encourage alcoholic drinking and by its attempt to confront the outside pressures faced by alcoholics in a society in which drinking is easily tolerated.

Feminist Movements

As we just saw, theories of revolution inevitably tend to overlap with those of social movements. Charles Tilly's emphasis on resource mobilization, for example, has been applied to social movements such as the feminist movement.

The first groups actively organized to promote women's rights date from the period immediately following the American and French Revolutions (Evans 1977). In the 1790s, inspired by the ideals of freedom and equality for which the revolutions had been fought, several women's clubs were formed in Paris and major provincial cities. The clubs provided meeting places for women, but they also petitioned for equal rights in education, employment, and government. Marie Gouze, a leader of one of the clubs, drew up a statement titled "Declaration of the Rights of Women," based on the Declaration of the Rights of Man and the Citizen, the main constitutional document of the French Revolution. How could true equality be achieved, she argued, when half the population was excluded from the privileges that men share?

The response from the male revolutionary leaders was less than sympathetic—Gouze was executed in 1793, charged with "having forgotten the virtues which belong to her sex." The women's clubs were subsequently dissolved by government decree. Feminist groups and women's movements have been formed repeatedly in Western countries since that date, almost always encountering hostility, and sometimes provoking violence, from the established authorities. Gouze was by no means the only feminist to give her life to the cause of achieving equal rights for her sex.

In the nineteenth century, feminism became more advanced in the United States than elsewhere, and most leaders of women's movements in other countries looked to the struggles of American women as a model. In the 1840s and 1850s, American feminists were closely involved with groups devoted to the abolition of slavery. Yet, having no formal political rights (the Constitution did not give women the right to vote), women were excluded from the political lobbying through which reformers could pursue their objectives. No women were allowed to take part in a world antislavery convention held in London in 1840. This fact led the women's groups to turn more directly to considering gender inequalities. In 1848, just as their French counterparts had done a half century before, women leaders in the United States met to approve the "Declaration of Sentiments and Resolutions," modeled on the Declaration of Independence. "We hold these truths to be self-evident," it began, "that all men and women are created equal." The declaration set out a long list of the injustices to which women were subject (Hartman and Banner 1974). However, few real gains in improving the social or political position of women were made during this period. When slavery ended, Congress ruled that only freed *male* slaves should be given the vote.

Some African American women played a part in the early development of the women's movement in the United States, although they often had to contend with hostility and racism from their white sisters. One, Sojourner Truth, spoke out against both slavery and the disenfranchisement of women, linking the two issues closely. When she forcefully and passionately addressed an antislavery rally in Indiana in the 1850s and a white man yelled at her, "I don't believe you really are a woman," she publicly bared her breasts to prove him wrong. Although Truth played a prominent part in women's struggles of the period (Hooks 1981), other black women who tried to participate became disillusioned with the prejudice they encountered; African American feminists as a result were few in number.

One of the most important events in the early development of feminist movements in Europe was the presentation of a petition, signed by fifteen hundred women, to the British Parliament in 1866, demanding that the electoral reforms then being

Militant campaigner for female suffrage Emmeline Pankhurst and one of her daughters are welcomed to a meeting of fellow suffragettes with banners and flowers.

discussed include full voting rights for women. The petition was ignored; in response, its organizers set up the National Society for Women's Suffrage the following year. The members of the society became known as suffragettes, and throughout the remainder of the nineteenth century they continued to petition Parliament to extend voting rights to women. By the early twentieth century, the world influence of British feminism rivaled that of feminists in the United States. Frequent marches and street demonstrations were organized in both countries. An open-air meeting held in London in June 1908 attracted a crowd of half a million people. During this period, women's movements mushroomed in all the major European countries, together with Australia and New Zealand.

Emmeline Pankhurst, a leading suffragette, participated in several speaking tours of the United States, recounting the British struggles to large audiences. Two Americans who had become involved in the campaigns in Britain, Alice Paine and Harriet Stanton Blatch, organized massive marches and parades through New York and other eastern cities from 1910 onward.

By 1920, women had attained the right to vote in several Western countries (Table 13.2). After achieving that right, though, most feminist movements in the United States and elsewhere fell into decline. Radical women tended to be absorbed into other movements, such as those combating fascism, a political doctrine of the extreme right gaining ground in Germany, Italy, and elsewhere in the 1930s. Little was left of feminism as a distinct movement against male-dominated institutions. The achievement of equal political rights did little to extend equality to other spheres of women's lives.

In the late 1960s, women's movements again gained prominence (Chafe 1974, 1977). Since then, feminism has become a major influence in countries throughout the world, including many in the developing world. The resurgence began in the United States, influenced by the civil rights movement and by the student activism of the period. Women who were active in these causes often found themselves relegated by male activists to a traditionally subordinate role. Civil rights leaders were resistant to women's rights being included in their manifestos of equality. Hence women's groups began to establish independent organizations concerned primarily with feminist issues.

The women's movement today in fact involves a variety of interest groups and organizations. Among the most prominent in the United States is NOW, with more than half a million members (men as well as women, although the large majority are women). Another group is the National Women's Political Caucus (NWPC), with a membership about half that of NOW. Some organizations are concerned with single issues such as abortion, education, or pension rights. Yet other groups consist of women in various occupations, like the American Association of University Women (AAUW).

FEMINIST MOVEMENTS: AN INTERPRETATION

The rise of women's movements over the past century can easily be interpreted in terms of the concepts set out by Tilly. Social movements arise, Tilly argues, when people have no chance of making themselves heard or when they lack outlets for their aspirations. In the first phase of development of feminist movements, in the nineteenth and early twentieth centuries, feminist leaders sought above all to *gain a voice* for women in the political process—in other words, to obtain the right to vote. In the second phase, women's movements sought to extend the gains they had achieved, fighting for economic as well as political equality for women.

In both phases, the leaders of women's movements were able to *mobilize collective resources* to place effective pressure on the governing authorities. During the early period, women activists' chief resource was mass marches and demonstrations. Later on, organizations (such as NOW) were able to fight for women's rights in a more consistent and organized way. The *common interests* to which women's group leaders have been able to appeal include the concern that women should have a role in political decision making, be able to engage in paid work if they wish, and have equal rights in divorce proceedings.

TABLE 13.2

The Year in Which Women Achieved the Right to Vote on an Equal Basis with Men, by Country

1893	New Zealand	1946	Albania, Romania, Panama
1902	Australia	1947	Argentina, Venezuela
1906	Finland	1948	Israel, Korea
1913	Norway	1949	China, Chile
1915	Denmark, Iceland	1950	El Salvador, Ghana, India
1917	Soviet Union	1951	Nepal
1918	Canada	1952	Greece
1919	Austria, Germany, the Netherlands, Poland, Sweden, Luxembourg, Czechoslovakia	1953	Mexico
		1954	Colombia
1920	**United States**	1955	Nicaragua
1922	Ireland	1956	Egypt, Pakistan, Senegal
1928	Great Britain	1957	Lebanon
1929	Ecuador	1959	Morocco
1930	South Africa	1962	Algeria
1931	Spain, Sri Lanka, Portugal	1963	Iran, Kenya, Libya
1932	Thailand	1964	Sudan, Zambia
1934	Brazil, Cuba	1965	Afghanistan, Guatemala
1936	Costa Rica	1971	Switzerland
1937	Philippines	1977	Nigeria
1941	Indonesia	1979	Peru, Zimbabwe
1942	Dominican Republic, Uruguay		
1945	France, Hungary, Italy, Japan, Vietnam, Yugoslavia, Bolivia		

SOURCE: Tuttle 1986.

Finally, the *opportunity* of feminist activists to influence social change has been affected by a variety of factors. The outbreak of World War I, for example, helped in the aim of securing the vote: Governments fighting the war needed the support and active involvement of women in the war effort. In the second phase of the development of feminism, the civil rights movement was the spark that ignited a new wave of activism.

Social movements hold a double interest for sociologists. They provide subject matter for study, but more than this, they help shift the ways in which sociologists look at certain areas of behavior. The women's movement, for instance, is relevant to sociology not just because it provides material for research. It has identified weaknesses in established frameworks of sociological thought and developed concepts (such as that of patriarchy) that help us understand issues of gender and power. There is a continuing dialogue not only between social movements and the organizations, such as government, that they confront but also between social movements and sociology itself.

Globalization and Social Movements

Social movements come in all shapes and sizes. Some are very small, numbering no more than a few dozen members; others may include thousands or even millions of people. Although some social movements carry on their activities within the laws of the society in which they exist, others operate as illegal or underground groups. It is characteristic of protest movements, however, that they operate near the margins of what is defined as legally permissible by governments at any particular time or place.

Social movements often arise with the aim of bringing about change on a public issue, such as expanding civil rights for a segment of the population. In response to social movements, countermovements sometimes arise in defense of the status quo. The campaign for women's right to abortion, for example, has been vociferously challenged by antiabortion ("prolife") activists, who believe that abortion should be illegal.

Often, laws or policies are altered as a result of the action of social movements. These changes in legislation can have far-ranging effects. For example, it used to be illegal for groups of workers to call their members out on strike, and striking was punished with various degrees of severity in different countries. Eventually, however, the laws were amended, making the strike a permissible tactic of industrial conflict.

NEW SOCIAL MOVEMENTS

The last few decades have seen an explosion of social movements in countries around the globe. These various movements—ranging from the civil rights and feminist movements of the 1960s and 1970s to the antinuclear and ecological movements of the 1980s to the gay rights campaign of the 1990s—are often referred to by commentators as **new social movements.** This description seeks to differentiate contemporary social movements from those that preceded them. They are often concerned with the quality of private life as much as with political and economic issues, calling for large-scale changes in the way people think and act.

In other words, what makes new social movements "new" is that—unlike conventional social movements—they are not based on single-issue objectives that typically involve changes in the distribution of economic resources or power. Rather, they involve the creation of collective identities based around entire lifestyles, often calling for sweeping cultural changes. New social movements have emerged in recent years around issues such as ecology, peace, gender and sexual identity, gay and lesbian rights, women's rights, alternative medicine, and opposition to globalization.

Because new social movements involve new collective identities, they can provide a strong incentive for action. Social movements are always plagued by the free-rider problem—how can they motivate people to devote their time and resources when they will benefit from the movement's success regardless of their personal involvement? With new social movements, however, participation is viewed as a moral obligation (and even a pleasure), rather than a calculated effort to achieve some specific goal. Moreover, the forms of protest chosen by new social movements are a form of "expressive logic" whereby participants make a statement about who they are: Protest is an end in itself, a way of affirming one's identity as well as a means to achieving concrete objectives (Polletta and Jasper 2001).

Many observers believe that new social movements are a unique product of late modern society and are profoundly different in their methods, motivations, and orientations from forms of collective action in earlier times.

The rise of new social movements in recent years is a reflection of the changing risks facing human societies. The conditions are ripe for social movements—increasingly, traditional political institutions are unable to cope with the challenges before them. They find it impossible to respond creatively to the threats facing the natural environment, the potential dangers of nuclear energy and genetically modified organisms, and the powerful effects of information technology. Existing democratic political institutions cannot hope to fix these new problems. As a result, these unfolding challenges are frequently ignored or avoided until it is too late and a full-blown crisis is at hand.

The cumulative effect of these new challenges and risks is a sense that people are losing control of their lives in the midst of rapid change. Individuals feel less secure and more isolated—a combination that leads to a sense of powerlessness. By contrast, corporations, governments, and the media appear to be dominating more and more aspects of people's lives, heightening the sensation of a runaway world. There is a growing sense that left to its own logic, globalization will present ever-greater risks to citizens' lives.

Although faith in traditional politics seems to be waning, the growth of new social movements is evidence that citizens in late modern societies are not apathetic or uninterested in politics, as is sometimes claimed. Rather, there is a belief that direct action and participation is more useful than reliance on politicians and political systems. More than ever before, people are supporting social movements as a way of highlighting complex moral issues and putting them at the center of social life. In this respect, new social movements are helping revitalize democracy in many countries. They are at the heart of a strong civic culture or **civil society**—the sphere between the state and the marketplace occupied by family, community associations, and other noneconomic institutions.

Technology and Social Movements

In recent years, two of the most influential forces in late modern societies—information technology and social movements—have come together, with astonishing results. In our current information age, social movements around the globe are able to join together in huge regional and international networks including nongovernmental organizations, religious and humanitarian groups, human rights associations, consumer protection advocates, environmental activists, and others who campaign in the public interest. These electronic networks now have the unprecedented ability to respond immediately to events as they occur, to gain access to and share sources of information, and to put pressure on corporations, governments, and international bodies as part of their campaigning strategies. The enormous protests against the World Trade Organization (WTO) that took place in Seattle, Prague, and Genoa, for example, were organized in large part through Internet-based networks. And, as we saw earlier, Web-based organizations such as MoveOn.org played an influential role in the anti–Iraq War movement.

The Internet has been at the forefront of these changes, although mobile phones, fax machines, and satellite broadcasting have also hastened their evolution. With the press of a button, local stories are disseminated internationally. Grassroots activists from Japan to Bolivia can meet online to share informational resources, exchange experiences, and coordinate joint action.

This last dimension—the ability to coordinate international political campaigns—is the most worrisome for governments and the most inspiring to participants in social movements. In the last decade, the number of international social movements has grown steadily with the spread of the Internet. From global protests in favor of canceling Third World debt to the international campaign to ban land mines (which culminated in a Nobel Peace Prize), the Internet has proved its ability to unite campaigners across national and cultural borders. Some observers argue that the information

age is witnessing a migration of power away from nation-states into new nongovernmental alliances and coalitions.

There are reasons to think that social movements have indeed been radically transformed in recent years. Manuel Castells, in *The Power of Identity* (1997), examines the cases of three social movements that, although completely dissimilar in their concerns and objectives, have all attracted international attention to their cause through the effective use of information technology. The Mexican Zapatista rebels, the American militia movement, the Japanese Aum Shinrikyo cult, and al Qaeda have all used media skills to spread their message of opposition to the effects of globalization and to express their anger at losing control over their own destinies.

According to Castells, each of these movements relies on information technologies as its organizational infrastructure. Without the Internet, for example, the Zapatista rebels would remain an isolated guerrilla movement in southern Mexico. Instead, within hours of their armed uprising in January 1994, local, national, and international support groups had emerged online to promote the cause of the rebels and to condemn the Mexican government's brutal repression of the rebellion. The Zapatistas used telecommunications, videos, and media interviews to voice their objections to trade policies, such as the North American Free Trade Agreement (NAFTA), that further exclude impoverished Indians of the Oaxaca and Chiapas areas from the benefits of globalization. Because their cause was thrust to the forefront of the online networks of social campaigners, the Zapatistas were able to force negotiations with the Mexican government and to draw international intention to the harmful effects of free trade on indigenous populations.

Nationalist Movements

Some of the most important social movements in the contemporary world are nationalist movements. The sociological thinkers of the nineteenth and early twentieth centuries displayed little interest in or concern with nationalism. Marx and Durkheim saw nationalism as above all a destructive tendency and believed that the increasing economic integration produced by modern industry would cause its rapid decline. Only Max Weber spent much time analyzing nationalism or was prepared to declare himself a nationalist. But even Weber failed to estimate the importance that nationalism and the idea of the nation would have in the twentieth century.

At the start of the twenty-first century, nationalism is not only alive, but—in some parts of the world at least—flourishing. Although the world has become more interdependent, especially since the 1970s, this interdependence has not spelled the end of

The Antisweatshop Movement

"We have the university by the balls," said Nati Passow, a University of Pennsylvania junior, in a meeting with his fellow antisweatshop protestors. "Whatever way we twist them is going to hurt." Passow was one of thirteen Penn students—the group later grew to include forty—occupying the university president's office around the clock in early February [2000] to protest the sweatshop conditions under which clothing bearing the U-Penn logo is made. The Penn students, along with hundreds of other members of United Students Against Sweatshops nationwide, were demanding that their university withdraw from the Fair Labor Association (FLA), an industry-backed monitoring group, and instead join the Worker Rights Consortium (WRC), an organization independent of industry influence, founded by students in close cooperation with scholars, activists and workers'-rights organizations in the global south.

At first the administration met the students with barely polite condescension. In one meeting, President Judith Rodin was accompanied by U-Penn professor Larry Gross, an earring-wearing baby boomer well known on campus for his left-wing views, who urged the protesters to have more faith in the administration and mocked the sit-in strategy, claiming he'd "been there, done that." President Rodin assured them that a task force would review the problem by February 29, and there was no way she could speed up its decision. She admonished them to "respect the process."

Watching the Penn students negotiate with this university's president, it was clear they didn't believe any of her assurances. They knew there was no reason to trust that the administration would meet one more arbitrary deadline after missing so many others—so they stayed in the office. After eight days of torture by folk-singing, acoustic guitar, recorders, tambourines and ringing cell phones, as well as a flurry of international news coverage, Judith Rodin met the protesters halfway by withdrawing from the FLA. (To students' frustration, the task force decided in early April to postpone a decision about WRC membership until later [that] spring.)

The most remarkable thing about the Penn students' action was that it wasn't an isolated or spontaneous burst of idealism. Penn's was just the first antisweatshop sit-in of the year; by mid-April students at the universities of Michigan, Wisconsin, Oregon, Iowa and Kentucky, as well as SUNY-Albany, Tulane, Purdue and Macalester had followed suit. And the sit-in wasn't the protesters' only tactic: Purdue students held an eleven-day hunger strike. The protests were a coordinated effort; members of United Students Against Sweatshops (USAS), which was founded three years ago and now has chapters at more than 200 schools, work closely with one another, a process made easier by the many listservs and Web sites that the students use to publicize actions, distribute information and help fuel turnout.

Though the largest, most successful—and before Seattle, the most visible—thread of the movement has focused on improving work conditions in the $2.5 billion collegiate apparel industry, university licensing policies have not been the only targets of recent anticorporate agitation on campus. This year, from UC-Davis to the University of Vermont, students have held globalization teach-ins, planned civil disobedience for the April IMF/World Bank meetings, protested labor policies at the Gap and launched vigorous campaigns to drive Starbucks out of university dining services. Students at Johns Hopkins and at Wesleyan held sit-ins demanding better wages for university workers. And at the end of March hundreds of students, many bearing hideously deformed papier-mâché puppets to illustrate the potential horrors of biotechnology, joined Boston's carnivalesque protest against genetic engineering.

With a *joie de vivre* that the American economic left has probably lacked since before WWI, college students are increasingly engaged in well-organized, thoughtful and morally outraged resistance to corporate power. These activists, more than any student radicals in years, passionately denounce the wealth gap, globally and in the United States, as well as the lack of democratic accountability in a world dominated by corporations. While some attend traditionally political schools like Evergreen, Michigan and Wisconsin, this movement does not revolve around usual suspects; some of this winter's most dramatic actions took place at campuses that have always been conservative, like the University of Pennsylvania, Virginia Commonwealth and Johns Hopkins. . . . It is neither too soon, nor too naïvely optimistic, to call it a movement.

SOURCE: Liza Featherstone, "The New Student Movement," *The Nation*, May 15, 2000.

Questions

- Many antisweatshop activists view their protests as a political and moral crusade. Do you agree with them that morals and politics should influence economic behavior? How does this affect your understanding of the study of sociology?
- What techniques did the students use to present their point of view? How did media coverage influence their methods of political protest?
- The students involved in these protests attend prestigious schools, for the most part. How does their membership in an elite group complicate their response to the issue of globalization and its discontents?

nationalism. In some respects it has probably even helped intensify it. Recent thinkers have come up with contrasting ideas about why this is so. There are also disagreements about the stage of history at which nationalism, the nation, and the nation-state came into being. Some say they have much earlier origins than others.

NATIONALISM AND MODERN SOCIETY

Perhaps the leading theorist of nationalism is Ernest Gellner (1925–1995). Gellner (1983) argues that nationalism, the nation, and the nation-state are all products of modern civilization, whose origins lie in the industrial revolution of the late eighteenth century. He claims that nationalism and the feelings or sentiments associated with it do not have deep roots in human nature—they are the products of the new large-scale society that industrialism creates. According to Gellner, nationalism as such is unknown in traditional societies, as is the idea of the nation.

Several features of modern societies have led to the emergence of these phenomena. First, a modern industrial society is associated with rapid economic development and a complex division of labor. Gellner points out that modern industrialism creates the need for a much more effective system of state and government than existed before. Second, in the modern state, individuals must interact all the time with strangers, since the basis of society is no longer the local village or town, but a very much larger unit. Mass education, based on an official language taught in the schools, is the main means whereby a large-scale society can be organized and kept unified.

Gellner's theory has been criticized in more than one respect. It is a functionalist theory, critics say, that argues that education functions to produce social unity. As with the functionalist approach more generally, this view tends to underestimate the role of education in producing conflict and division. Gellner's theory does not really explain the passions that nationalism can, and often does, arouse. The power of nationalism is probably related not just to education but to its capacity to create an *identity* for people—something that individuals cannot live without.

The need for identity is certainly not just born with the emergence of modern industrial society. Critics therefore argue that Gellner is wrong to separate nationalism and the nation so strongly from premodern times. Nationalism is in some ways quite modern, but it also draws on sentiments and forms of symbolism that go back much further into the past. According to one of the best-known current scholars of nationalism, Anthony Smith (1988), nations tend to have direct lines of continuity with earlier ethnic communities, or what he calls "ethnies." An **ethnie** is a group that shares ideas of common ancestry, a common cultural identity, and a link with a specific homeland.

Many nations, Smith points out, do have premodern continuities, and at previous periods of history there have been ethnic communities that resemble nations. The Jews, for example, have formed a distinct ethnie for more than two thousand years. At certain periods, Jews clustered in communities that had some of the characteristics of nations. But only after World War II were all of these elements brought together in the form of the nation-state of Israel. Like most other nation-states, Israel was not formed from just a single ethnie. The Palestinian minority in Israel traces its origins to a quite different ethnic background and claims that the creation of the Israeli state has displaced the Palestinians from their ancient homelands—hence their persistent tensions with Jews in Israel, the tensions between Israel and most surrounding Arab states, and the tragic violence and fighting between Palestinians and Israelis that has escalated in the new years of the twenty-first century.

Different nations have followed divergent patterns of development in relation to ethnies. In some, including most of the nations of western Europe, a single ethnie expanded so as to push out earlier rivals. Thus, in France in the seventeenth century, several other languages were spoken and different ethnic histories were linked to them. As French became the dominant language, most of these rivals subsequently disappeared. Yet remnants of them persist in a few areas. One is the Basque country overlapping the French and Spanish frontiers. The Basque language is quite different from either French or Spanish, and the Basques claim a separate cultural history of their own. Some Basques want their own nation-state, completely separate from France and Spain. Although there has been nothing like the level of violence seen in other areas—such as East Timor, or Chechnya in southern Russia—separatist groups in the Basque country have sporadically used bombing campaigns to further their goal of independence.

NATIONS WITHOUT STATES

The persistence of well-defined ethnies within established nations leads to the phenomenon of **nations without states.** In these situations, many of the essential characteristics of the nation are present, but those who make up the nation lack an independent political community. Separatist movements such as those in Chechnya and the Basque country, as well as those in many other areas of the world—such as in Kashmir in northern India—are driven by the desire to set up an autonomous, self-governing state.

Several different types of nations without states can be recognized, depending on the relationship between the ethnie and the larger nation-state in which its exists (Guibernau 1999):

1. In some situations, a nation-state may accept the cultural differences among its minority or minorities and allow them a certain amount of active development. Thus in Great Britain, Scotland and Wales are recognized as having histories and cultural features partly divergent from the rest of the United Kingdom, and to some extent they have their own institutions. The majority of Scots, for instance, are Presbyterians, and Scotland has long had a separate educational system from that of England and Wales. Scotland and Wales achieved further autonomy within the United Kingdom as a whole with the setting up of a Scottish Parliament and a Welsh Assembly in 1999.

2. Some nations without states have a higher degree of autonomy. In Quebec (the French-speaking province of Canada) and Flanders (the Dutch-speaking area in the southwestern Netherlands), regional political bodies have the power to make major decisions, without actually being fully independent. As in the cases mentioned under the previous point, they also contain nationalist movements agitating for complete independence.

3. On the other hand, some nations more or less completely lack recognition from the state that contains them. In such cases, the larger nation-state uses force to deny recognition to the minority. The Palestinians are a clear example of such a group (although some would argue that their isolated acts of terrorism and violence against Israelis have encouraged the Israeli army's show of force). Others include the Tibetans in China and the Kurds, whose homeland overlaps parts of Turkey, Syria, Iran, and Iraq.

NATIONS AND NATIONALISM IN DEVELOPING COUNTRIES

In most of the countries of the developing world, the course followed by nationalism, the nation, and the nation-state has been different from that of industrial societies. Most less-developed countries were once colonized by Europeans and achieved independence at some point in the second half of the twentieth century. In many of these countries, boundaries between colonial administrations were agreed on arbitrarily in Europe and did not take into account existing economic, cultural, or ethnic divisions among the population. The colonial powers defeated or subjugated the kingdoms and tribal groupings existing on the African subcontinent, in India, and in other parts of Asia, and set up their own colonial administrations or protectorates. As a consequence, each colony was "a collection of peoples and old states, or fragments of these, brought together within the same

boundaries" (Akintoye 1976). Most colonized areas contained a mosaic of ethnies and other groups.

When former colonies achieved their independence, they often found it difficult to create a sense of nationhood and national belonging. Although nationalism played a great part in securing the independence of colonized areas, it was largely confined to small groups of activists. Nationalist ideas did not influence the majority of the population. Even today many postcolonial states are continually threatened by internal rivalries and competing claims to political authority.

The continent that was most completely colonized was Africa. Nationalist movements promoting independence in Africa following World War II sought to free the colonized areas from European domination. Once this had been achieved, the new leaders everywhere faced enormous problems in trying to create national unity. Many of the leaders in the 1950s and 1960s had been educated in Europe or the United States, and there was a vast gulf between them and their citizens, most of whom were illiterate, poor, and unfamiliar with the rights and obligations of democracy. Under colonialism, some ethnic groups had prospered more than others; these groups had different interests and goals and legitimately saw each other as enemies.

Civil wars broke out in a number of postcolonial states in Africa, such as Sudan, Zaire, and Nigeria, while ethnic rivalries and antagonisms characterized many others both in Africa and Asia. In the case of Sudan, about 40 percent of the population spoke Arabic and claimed Arabic ethnic origins. In other regions of the country, particularly in the south, Arabic was barely spoken at all. Once the nationalists took power, they set up a program for national integration based on Arabic as the national language. The attempt was only partly successful, and the stresses and strains it produced are still visible. The severe problems faced by much of the African continent are a direct result of difficulties like these.

The ongoing civil war in Sudan has displaced more than four million people. Some fled to southern cities, such as Juba; others trekked as far north as Khartoum and even into Ethiopia, Kenya, Uganda, Egypt, and other neighboring countries. These refugees were unable to grow food or earn money to feed themselves, and malnutrition and starvation became widespread. The lack of investment in the south also resulted in what international humanitarian organizations call a "lost generation," who lack educational opportunities, access to basic health-care services, and few prospects for productive employment in the small and weak economies of the south and the north.

In summary, most states in the developing world came into being as a result of different processes of nation formation from those that occurred in the industrialized world. States were imposed externally on areas that often had no prior cultural or ethnic unity. These problems are everywhere proving difficult to overcome. Modern nations have arisen most effectively either in areas that were never fully colonized or where there was already a great deal of cultural unity—such as Japan, Korea, and Thailand.

The Nation-State, National Identity, and Globalization

In some parts of Africa, nations and nation-states are not as yet fully formed. Yet in other areas of the world, some writers are already speaking of the "end of the nation-state" in the face of globalization. According to Japanese writer Kenichi Ohmae (1995), as a result of globalization we increasingly live in a borderless world in which national identity is becoming weaker.

How valid is this point of view? All states are certainly being affected by globalizing processes. The very rise of "nations without states" is probably bound up with globalization. As globalization progresses, people often react by reviving local identities in an effort to achieve security in a rapidly changing world. Nations have less economic power of their own than they used to have, as a result of the spread of the global marketplace.

Yet it wouldn't be accurate to say that we are witnessing the end of the nation-state. In some ways the opposite is the case. Today every country in the world is a nation-state or aspires to be one; the nation-state has become a universal political form. Until quite recently it still had rivals. For most of the twentieth century, colonized areas and empires existed alongside nation-states. It is arguable that the last empire only disappeared in 1990 with the collapse of Soviet communism. The Soviet Union was effectively at the center of an empire embracing satellite states in Eastern Europe. Now all of these have become independent nation-states, as have many areas inside what was formerly the Soviet Union. There are actually far more sovereign nations in the world today than there were twenty-five years ago.

Terrorism

The same forces that led to the emergence of nationalist movements in the nineteenth and twentieth centuries also led to the emergence of a new form of violence, terrorism. Social scientists disagree over whether the term *terrorism* can be a useful concept—that is, whether it can be used in a reasonably objective way—and terrorism is a notoriously difficult issue to define (Laqueur 2003). One issue concerns the shifting moral assessments people make of terrorism and terrorists. It's often said that "one person's terrorist is another person's freedom fighter." It is also well known that people who were once terrorists themselves can later come to condemn terror just as violently as they practiced it. It was only a few decades ago that the former South African leader Nelson Mandela was wildly reviled as potential terrorist, but he is now one of the most revered political figures of recent times. For *terrorism* to be a useful term it must be freed as far as possible from moral valuation that shifts across time or the perspective of the observer.

It is sensible to restrict the notion of terrorism to groups and organizations working outside of the state. Otherwise the concept becomes too close to that of *war* more generally. In spite of the problems just noted, a neutral definition can be found. We can define **terrorism** as "any action [by a non-state organization] . . . that is intended to cause death or serious bodily harm to civilians or non-combatants, when the purpose of such an act, by its nature or context, is to intimidate a population, or to compel a Government or an international organization to do or to abstain from doing any act" (Panyarachun et al. 2004). In other words, terrorism concerns attacks on civilians designed to persuade a government to alter its policies, or to damage its standing in the world.

Old- and New-Style Terrorism

Terrorism, as it was described earlier, is a specifically modern phenomenon and can be distinguished from acts of violence designed to terrorize in previous periods of history, such as the ancient razing of cities. As we described it, terrorism is connected to changes in communications technology. To terrorize populations on a fairly wide spectrum, information about the violence has to reach those populations affected quite quickly. It wasn't until the rise of modern communications in the late nineteenth century that this became possible. With the invention of the electronic telegraph, instantaneous communication became possible, which made possible the transcendence of time and space. Before the telegraph, information could take days or even months to spread.

A distinction can be drawn between old- and new-style terrorism. **Old-style terrorism** was dominant for most of the twentieth century and still exists today. This kind of terrorism is largely associated with the rise of nationalism and with the establishment of nations as sovereign, territorially bonded entities, which predominantly occurred from the late eighteenth

An example of an old-style terrorist movement, these Basque Nationalists are mostly concerned with territorial control and the formation of states.

century onward in Europe, as we discussed earlier. In all nations, boundaries are fixed somewhat arbitrarily, either as lines on a map, as they were by western colonizers in Africa and Asia, or through conquest, battle, and struggle. Ireland, for example, was brought into the United Kingdom in 1800, leading to independence struggles, which led to the partition of the country into north and south in the early 1920s.

A patchwork of nations mapped out by colonial administrators or founded on force has led in various cases to nations that do not have their own state—that is, nations with a claim to a common cultural identity but without the territorial and state apparatus that normally belongs to a nation. Most forms of old-style terrorism are linked to nations without states. The point of old-style terrorism is to establish states in areas where nations do not have control of the territory's state apparatus. This is true, for example, of Irish nationalists, such as the Irish Republican Army (IRA), and Basque nationalists, such as Euskadi ta Askatasuna (ETA; or Basque Homeland and Freedom), in Spain. The main issues are territorial integrity and identity in the formation of a state. Old-style terrorism is found where there are nations without states and where terrorists are prepared to use violence to achieve their ends. This type of terrorism is fundamentally local because its ambitions are local. It wants to establish a state in a specific national area.

NEW-STYLE TERRORISM

New-style terrorism is another matter (Tan and Ramakrishna 2002). New-style terrorism is made possible by the changes in communications technology that are driving globalization, and it has a global spread. This type of terrorism is most famously associated with the Islamic fundamentalism of al Qaeda, although it is no means limited to it. **New style terrorism** differs from old-style terrorism in several ways. First, they differ with respect of the scope of their claims. One of the distinguishing features of al Qaeda's view of the world, for example, is that it has global geopolitical aims; it seeks to restructure world society. Parts of the al Qaeda leadership have wanted to reconstruct an Islamic society stretching from the Indian subcontinent into Europe. This would involve establishing Islamic governments throughout the Middle East and recapturing northern Africa. Al Qaeda's supporters argue that over the last millennium the West has expelled Islamic groups from areas to which it has legitimate claim. Such areas include the Balkans and those parts of Spain that were previously ruled by the Moors (Muslims originally from North Africa who controlled much of Spain between the eighth and fifteenth centuries). Al Qaeda aims to reestablish the global role of Islam in these regions and areas. So, whereas old-style terrorism is local and linked to particular states—normally quite small states—new-style terrorism is global in its ambitions. It wants to reverse the tide of world power (Gray 2003).

Second, the two types of terrorism have different organizational structures. Although careful not to take this parallel too far, sociologist Mary Kaldor points out several similarities between the infrastructure of new terrorist groups, notably al Qaeda and international nongovernmental organizations (NGOs) such as Oxfam and Friends of the Earth. (NGOs are discussed in more detail in Chapter 6.) Both new terrorist organizations and NGOs are driven by a sense of mission and commitment. This sense of mission and commitment allows a fairly loose global organization to flourish (Anheier et al. 2002).

Both NGOs and new terrorist organizations are based on networks, of the kinds discussed by Manuel Castells (1996) and reviewed in Chapter 6 (page 147). They are highly decentralized structures. There is a lot of autonomy in the individual cells, which can reproduce without necessarily having any strong direction from the center. Furthermore, terrorist organizations and NGOs both have a global spread of supporters in many countries. Experts on terrorism disagree over the extent to which al Qaeda survived the American-led attack on Afghanistan in 2001, but it has been estimated that there are still al Qaeda cells in around sixty countries, drawing on approximately twenty thousand people who are willing to die violently for the cause; most of these cells exist semiautonomously from the center.

It can also be noted that new terrorist groups and NGOs both work with states. No NGO could flourish completely as a nonstate organization. They all have some contacts and support from states and this is true, Kaldor argues, of new-style terrorist organizations. The Libyan involvement in the bombing of a passenger plane that exploded over the Scottish village of Lockerbie in 1988 provides one example of this. Of course, the analogy between new terrorist organizations and NGOs cannot be taken too far; but in their organizational structures and shared sense of admittedly very different missions, al Qaeda could be seen as a malign kind of NGO.

Third, the two styles differ in terms of means. Old-style terrorism, as we saw, has relatively limited objectives; and as a result, the violence involved is normally fairly limited. The new-style terrorism seems much more ruthless in the means it is prepared to use. Al Qaeda Web sites, for example, talk in extremely destructive language of "the enemy," which is principally the United States but to some extent the West as a whole. These sites will often explicitly say that terrorist acts should be carried out to kill as many people as possible. This is very different from the more limited use of violent means characteristic of old style-terrorism. There are some cases in which the two overlap, as in Chechnya in the former Soviet Union, for example, which turned from a separatist struggle to a recruiting ground for newer forms of terrorism.

Terrorism and War

How should we respond to the threat of new-style terrorism? Terrorism of the kind seen on September 11 raises difficult questions for the political sociologists. Can terrorism be fought like conventional wars? The coalition that attacked Afghanistan in 2001 did destroy at least some of the al Qaeda terrorist networks. Yet, despite some successes against new-style terrorism through conventional warfare, critics are surely right to argue that in many cases the levels of violence, aims, and organizational structure of new-style terrorist groups differentiate them from conventional enemies, such as hostile nation-states. The debate about whether terrorism can be stopped through conventional warfare raises further difficult questions regarding the relationship between terrorism and the nation-states, like Afghanistan, that have supported it. In turn, this leads to questions about global governance. In a global age, what international support and proof are needed to respond to and prevent a perceived threat? And what are the best institutions to deal with a global terrorist threat?

Study Outline

www.wwnorton.com/giddens

Government and Power

- The term *government* refers to a political apparatus in which officials enact policies and make decisions. *Politics* refers to the use of power to affect government actions.
- *Power* is the capacity to achieve one's aims even against the resistance of others, and often involves the use of force. A government is said to have *authority* when its use of power is legitimate. Such legitimacy derives from the consent of those being governed. The most common form of legitimate government is democratic, but other legitimate forms are also possible.

The Concept of the State

- A *state* is characterized by a political apparatus (government institutions), including civil service officials, ruling over a geographically defined territory, and whose authority is backed by a legal system and that has the capacity to use force to implement policies.
- All modern states have certain additional features: *sovereignty*, the idea that government has authority over a given area; *citizenship*, the idea that people have common rights and duties and are aware of their part in the state; and *nationalism*, the sense of being part of a broader, unifying political community.

- Most nation-states became centralized through the activities of monarchs who concentrated social power. Citizens initially had few rights of political participation, or none at all; such rights were achieved only through a long process of struggle that continues to this day. *Civil rights* refer to the freedoms and privileges guaranteed to individuals by law. *Political rights* ensure that citizens may participate in politics (by voting, for example). *Social rights* guarantee every individual some minimum standard of living. Social rights are the basis for the *welfare state*, which supports citizens who are unable to support themselves.

Democracy

- The term *democracy* literally means rule by the people, but this phrase can be interpreted in various ways. For instance, "the people" has often really meant "adult male property owners," whereas "rule" might refer to government policies, administrative decisions, or both.
- Several different forms of democracy exist, including *participatory democracy*, also called *direct democracy*, which occurs when everyone is immediately involved in all decision making, although this can be cumbersome for larger groups; *liberal democracy*, which is a system in which citizens have a choice to vote between at least two political parties for representatives who will be entrusted with decision making; and *constitutional monarchy*, which includes a royal family whose powers are severely restricted by a constitution, which puts authority in the hands of democratically elected representatives.

Democracy in the United States

- A political party is an organization oriented toward achieving legitimate control of government through an electoral process. There is usually some connection between voting patterns and class differences. In many Western countries there has recently been a decline in allegiance to traditional parties and a growing disenchantment with the party system in general.
- Women achieved the right to vote much later than men in all countries and continue to be poorly represented among political elites. They have been influential on social and civil rights issues, and most Western countries have passed equal rights legislation over recent years.

Who Rules?

- According to Weber and Schumpeter, the level of democratic participation that can be achieved in a modern, large-scale society is limited. The rule of *power elites* is inevitable, but multiparty systems provide the possibility of choosing *who* exercises power. The *pluralist theorists* add the claim that the competition of *interest groups* limits the degree to which ruling elites are able to concentrate power in few hands.
- The number of countries with democratic governments has rapidly increased in recent years, due in large part to the effects of globalization and mass communication and to the spread of competitive capitalism. But democracy is not without its problems; people everywhere have begun to lose faith in the capacity of politicians and governments to solve problems and to manage economies, and many no longer vote.
- *Revolution* is the overthrow of an existing political order by means of a mass movement, using violence. *Social movements*, by contrast, involve a collective attempt to further common interests through collaborative action outside the sphere of established institutions. The term *new social movements* is applied to a set of social movements that have arisen in Western countries since the 1960s in response to the changing risks facing human societies. Unlike earlier social movements, new social movements are single-issue campaigns oriented to nonmaterial ends and draw support from across class lines. Information technology has become a powerful organizing tool for many new social movements.

Theories of Revolution and Social Movements

- Theories of social movements and revolutions overlap. Marx argued that class struggles deriving from the *contradictions*, or unresolvable tensions within society, lead to revolutionary changes. Davies argues that social movements occur from *relative deprivation*, a discrepancy between the lives people actually lead and what people believe to be possible. Tilly analyzes revolutionary change from a broader context of *collective action*, which refers to action taken to contest or overthrow an existing social order. Collective action culminating in social movements progresses from organization to mobilization, the perception of common interests, and finally the opportunity to act. For Tilly, social movements occur in circumstances of *multiple sovereignty*, a situation in which the government lacks full control.
- Smelser's theory treats social movements as responses to situations, which undergo a series of stages. Touraine argues that social movements rest on *historicity*, which is the idea that people know that social activism can shape history and affect society. Social movements occur in *fields of action*, which refers to the connection between a movement and the forces acting against it.
- Social movements not only provide a subject of study for sociologists but also challenge the established frameworks of thought of sociology (e.g., the effect of the women's movement on the study of gender).

Nationalism

- Nationalism refers to a set of symbols and beliefs that provide the sense of being part of a single political community. It emerged alongside the development of the modern state. Although the founders of sociology believed that nationalism would disappear in industrial societies, at the start of the twenty-first century it seems to be flourishing. *Nations without states* refer to cases in which a national group lacks political sovereignty over the area it claims as its own.

Terrorism

- Terrorism can be defined as tactics aimed at harming or killing civilians or noncombatants to compel a government or a population to act or stop acting in a particular way. The goal of old-style terrorism is used by nations to establish a state where no state previously existed. In contrast, new-style terrorism has much broader goals, such as reshaping global society, and has a decentralized organizational structure that relies on networks. These new terrorist groups frequently have contact with and get support from states, and they are willing to be more ruthless in the means of violence they use.

Key Concepts

authority (p. 393)
citizens (p. 393)
civil rights (p. 394)
civil society (p. 423)
collective action (p. 416)
communism (p. 398)
constitutional monarchs (p. 398)
democracy (p. 398)

Review Questions

1. What is the difference between politics and government?
   a. There is none.
   b. Politics involves the exercise of power in regard to the actions of government, whereas government is concerned with the enactment of policies, decisions, and matters of state.
   c. Politics involves the government's legitimate use of power, whereas government is concerned with the way power is used to influence the state's activities.
   d. Politics involves the enactment of policies, decisions, and matters of state, whereas government is concerned with the exercise of power in regard to the actions of government.

2. What is the difference between power and authority?
   a. Power is a Marxist concept, whereas authority is a Weberian concept.
   b. Power is the ability of individuals or groups to make their interests count, even in the face of opposition from others,

whereas authority is the use of power by government where the exercise of that power is seen as legitimate by those who are subject to it.
   c. Power is the ability to spend money to solve a problem, whereas authority is the respect a person is accorded by others.
   d. Power is the use of power by government where the exercise of that power is seen as legitimate by those who are subject to it, whereas authority is the ability of individuals or groups to make their interests count, even in the face of opposition from others.

3. What was Max Weber's theory of democracy?
   a. democratic elitism
   b. pluralism
   c. the power elite
   d. the "iron law of oligarchy"

4. What are the three rights associated with the growth of citizenship?
   a. civil, political, and social rights
   b. civil, voting, and welfare rights
   c. civil, social, and economic rights
   d. civil, human, and animal rights

5. When and why did women win the vote in most Western countries?
   a. The vote was given to women in the general wave of social reforms that followed World War II.
   b. The vote was won through the efforts of the suffragist movement and as a consequence of women's mobilization in World War I.
   c. Voting rights were accorded to women, as well as to blacks, in the Voting Rights Act of 1965.
   d. Women were allowed to vote as a result of their increased participation in the economy and their increasing economic independence from men.

6. In 1998 women made up 13 percent of the membership of the House of Representatives and 9 percent of the Senate. Why has women's participation in the higher echelons of the American political system remained so modest?
   a. Women are running for office in larger numbers than ever, but voters are not electing them to office because the majority still regard politics as a "man's game."
   b. The political parties (which are largely run by men) have not recruited many women to run for high political office.
   c. Women are being elected to lower offices, but more of them need to work their way up through the seniority system before they are given the chance to run for the House or Senate.
   d. Female candidates find it harder to raise money than male candidates.

7. In the 1990s, the United States and various governments in Europe passed immigration laws that attempt to use citizenship as a tool of social closure. What does this mean?
   a. Governments have set up immigration criteria in an effort to attract the most educated immigrants and exclude the least educated.

b. An increasing number of governments have tried to get all their citizens to register with a national identity-card system.

c. Governments have sought to exclude poor migrants from the status and benefits that full citizenship confers.

d. Conservative politicians have attempted to use immigration as a wedge to divide constituencies that would normally support their liberal or social democratic opponents.

8. What is liberal democracy and where can it be found in the modern world?

a. It is a nation-state where most adults have the right to vote and where two or more parties are involved in competitive elections. Generally, these conditions are found in the developed world, although some Third World countries have liberal democracies.

b. It is a political system that has a large established and competitive liberal or social democratic party that is in a position to affect the composition of government. Some nations—for example, Mexico and Ireland—have no liberal or social democratic party and are therefore not liberal democracies.

c. It is a nation-state whose constitution formally commits its government to the preservation of human rights. These conditions are found all over the world but are not always observed.

d. It is a political system in which there has been an alternation of power between parties. This is regarded as a crucial test of the robustness of a democracy and did not occur in some democracies in developed nations—such as Italy and Japan—before the 1980s.

9. What is the theory of relative deprivation?

a. Social movements go through four stages of collective action: organization, mobilization, dissemination of common interests, and seizing on opportunities to further the cause.

b. It is not absolute deprivation that leads to protest but comparison of present living standards with those of the upper class.

c. It is not absolute deprivation that leads to protest but relative deprivation—the discrepancy between the lives people are forced to lead and what they think could realistically be achieved.

d. It is not absolute deprivation that leads to protest but comparison of one's living standards with those of the more fortunate members of one's family.

10. Which two thinkers were responsible for the structural strain theory and the fields of action theory?

a. Neil Smelser and Alain Touraine

b. Mary Hartman and Lois Banner

c. Charles Tilly and Theda Skocpol

d. William Chafe and David Aberle

11. Kenichi Ohmae argues that as a result of globalization we increasingly live in a borderless world. What does he mean by *borderless world*?

a. The world has no geographic boundary.

b. National identity is becoming weaker.

c. The Internet makes it possible to travel across national boundaries.

d. Globalization reduces the need for obtaining visas when visiting other countries.

Thinking Sociologically Exercises

1. Discuss the differences between the pluralistic and the power elite theories of democratic political processes. Which theory do you find most appropriate to describe U.S. politics in recent years?

2. Your textbook offers a variety of explanations on the formation of social movements. Briefly review the predisposing conditions for social movements and then discuss their relevance in the development of the feminist social movement in the United States.

Data Exercises

www.wwnorton.com/giddens
Keyword: Data13

In the data exercise for this chapter you will learn more about the patterns of political participation. Did you know that more people are registered to vote today than thirty years ago, but fewer actually cast a ballot? As you work through the exercise, think about who is opting out of participation and why they are.

PART FOUR

SOCIAL INSTITUTIONS

Social institutions are the cement of social life. They are the basic living arrangements that human beings work out with one another, by means of which continuity is achieved across the generations.

We begin in Chapter 14 with work and economic life. Although the nature of work varies widely both within and between societies, it is one of the most pervasively important of all human pursuits.

In Chapter 15, we look at the institutions of kinship, marriage, and the family. Although the social obligations associated with kinship vary among different types of societies, the family is everywhere the context within which the young are provided with care and protection. Marriage is more or less universally connected to the family because it is a means of establishing new kin connections and forming a household in which children are brought up. In traditional cultures, much of the direct learning a child receives occurs within the family context. In modern societies, children spend many years of their lives in special places of instruction outside the family—schools and colleges. They also are constantly fed images and information from the mass media. Chapter 16 looks at the ways in which formal education is organized, concentrating particularly on how the educational system relates to the mass media.

The subject of Chapter 17 is religion. Although religious beliefs and practices are found in all cultures, the changes affecting religion in modern societies have been particularly acute. We analyze the nature of these changes, considering in what ways traditional types of religion still maintain their influence.

The Social Significance of Work

Assess the sociological ramifications of paid and unpaid work.

The Social Organization of Work

Understand that modern economies are based on the division of labor and economic interdependence. Learn Marx's theory of alienation. Familiarize yourself with modern systems of economic production.

The Modern Economy

See the importance of the rise of large corporations; consider particularly the global effect of transnational corporations.

The Changing Nature of Work

Learn about the effect of global economic competition on employment. Consider how work will change over the coming years.

CHAPTER FOURTEEN

WORK AND ECONOMIC LIFE

like many auto factories around the country, the GM assembly plant in Linden, New Jersey, confronted new challenges beginning in the 1980s (Milkman 1997). The plant, founded in 1937 to build Cadillacs, was a top-of-the-line operation that offered blue-collar workers salaries and benefits that were among the best in any industry. The emergence of a competitive auto industry, first in Japan and later in South Korea, threatened the GM system by producing high-quality cars at a lower cost than was possible in the United States. In the mid-1980s, GM responded to these pressures by reorganizing the plant in Linden and introducing robots and organizational innovations borrowed from the Japanese, such as "just-in-time" inventory systems. The plant also switched from producing luxury vehicles to producing small cars, a shift that resulted in significant numbers of job cuts in the plant. GM negotiated a plan with the United Auto Workers (UAW) union that offered cash payments to workers who voluntarily agreed to leave their jobs at GM.

Edward Salermo is a former GM employee who in 1987 accepted the company's offer to give up his job, after working at the plant for eight years. Salermo had grown up in Linden, and his father had worked at GM before him. He was never really happy with his job at GM—he had aspirations of finding a more challenging occupation—but was lured by the salary he could make on the production line when he was hired just out of high school. Consistent with these aspirations, Salermo took courses while he was laid off from GM during the year-long reorganization of the plant. He hoped that the electronics training he acquired would allow him to return to a spot in a more skilled position fixing the new robotics. After the plant reopened, however,

GM made it clear that they would rehire Salermo only as a production worker. Salermo decided to take the buyout offer, equivalent to a year's pay, about $30,000. Salermo used the money to go back to school to study computer programming. He was hired at a new job installing business telephone systems but was laid off after a few months. He then found his current job, working on payroll for a large insurance company. While he is happier at this current job than he was at GM—it is, he reports, a much less conflictual work environment—he is attempting to further improve his prospects by attending night school to obtain an associate's degree in computer science. "If something else came along, I would take it," he remarks (Milkman 1997).

Faced with a similar decision, Susan Roberts decided to keep her job at the newly reorganized GM plant in Linden. She was tempted to take GM's offer to leave, as she could have used the buyout money for the down payment on a house, but she did not have another job. Instead, along with three thousand of her co-workers, she returned to GM for a two-week retraining program. Much had changed in the organization of the plant. For one, workers were instructed to "build the car in the station," meaning that if they found a defect, they were to stop the line and correct the problem immediately, rather than just noting the defect for another worker to fix it somewhere down the line. For another, GM adopted the Japanese just-in-time inventory system, based on the tight coordination of parts delivered by suppliers just as they were needed, rather than stockpiling the parts in the factory. Finally, workers were encouraged to participate more in decision making and problem solving in the day-to-day operations of the plant.

Roberts was excited about many of these changes, as she felt that GM was finally taking the Japanese challenge seriously, giving the U.S. auto industry a chance of regaining its competitive edge. She was so enthusiastic about the new direction of the Linden plant that she even volunteered to take a leadership role in the newly introduced employee involvement groups (EIGs), an innovation that GM hoped would facilitate communication between workers and management about production and quality problems. But her enthusiasm soon waned. One reason is that Roberts discovered that stopping the line at each station to correct problems as they occurred created conflicts with workers farther down the line, who would immediately want to know why the line had stopped and become angry at the interruption. The EIG program was also a disappointment, as management was slow to implement suggestions made by workers (Milkman 1997).

The challenges faced by workers such as Edward Salermo and Susan Roberts illustrate dilemmas encountered by workers in many industries since the 1970s, as the organization of work and the economy has changed. In this chapter we examine these changes and try to place them in sociological perspective.

Work may be defined as carrying out tasks that require the expenditure of mental and physical effort, which has as its objective the production of goods and services that cater to human needs. An **occupation,** or job, is work that is done in exchange for a regular wage, or salary. In all cultures, work is the basis of the economic system, or economy. The **economy** consists of institutions that provide for the production and distribution of goods and services.

The study of economic institutions is of major importance in sociology, because the economy influences all segments of society and, therefore, social reproduction in general. Hunting and gathering, pastoralism, agriculture, industrialism—these different ways of gaining a livelihood have a fundamental influence on the lives people lead. The distribution of goods and variations in the economic position of those who produce them also strongly influence social inequalities of all kinds. Wealth and power do not inevitably go together, but in general the privileged in terms of wealth are also among the more powerful groups in a society.

In this chapter, we analyze the nature of work in modern societies and look at the major changes affecting economic life today. We investigate the changing nature of industrial production, the ownership structure of large business corporations, and the changing nature of work itself. Modern industry, as has been stressed in other parts of this book, differs in a fundamental way from premodern systems of production, which were based above all on agriculture. Most people worked in the fields or cared for livestock. In modern societies, by contrast, only a tiny proportion of the population works in agriculture, and farming itself has become industrialized—it is carried on largely by means of machines rather than by human hands.

Modern industry is itself always changing—technological change is one of its main features. **Technology** refers to the harnessing of science to machinery to achieve greater productive efficiency. The nature of industrial production also changes in relation to wider social and economic influences. In this chapter, we focus on both technological and economic change, showing how these are transforming industry today.

We also see that globalization makes a great deal of difference to our working lives; the nature of the work we do is being changed by forces of global economic competition.

The Social Significance of Work

To tackle these issues, we need to relate work to the broad contours of our society and to industrial organization as a whole. We often associate the notion of work with drudgery—with a set of tasks that we want to minimize and, if possible, escape from altogether. You may have this very thought in mind as you set out to read this chapter! Is this most people's attitude toward their work, and if so, why? We will try to find out in the following pages.

Work has more going for it than drudgery, or people would not feel so lost and disoriented when they become unemployed. How would you feel if you thought you would never get a job? In modern societies, having a job is important for maintaining self-esteem. Even where work conditions are relatively unpleasant, and the tasks involved dull, work tends to be a structuring element in people's psychological makeup and the cycle of their daily activities. Several characteristics of work are relevant here.

- *Money*. A wage or salary is the main resource many people depend on to meet their needs. Without such an income, anxieties about coping with day-to-day life tend to multiply.
- *Activity level*. Work often provides a basis for the acquisition and exercise of skills and capacities. Even where work is routine, it offers a structured environment in which a person's energies may be absorbed. Without it, the opportunity to exercise such skills and capacities may be reduced.
- *Variety*. Work provides access to contexts that contrast with domestic surroundings. In the working environment, even when the tasks are relatively dull, individuals may enjoy doing something different from home chores.
- *Temporal structure*. For people in regular employment, the day is usually organized around the rhythm of work. Although work may sometimes be oppressive, it provides a sense of direction in daily activities. Those who are out of work frequently find boredom a major problem and develop a sense of apathy about time. As one unemployed man remarked, "Time doesn't matter now as much as it used to. . . . There's so much of it" (Fryer and McKenna 1987).
- *Social contacts*. The work environment often provides friendships and opportunities to participate in shared activities with others. Separated from the work setting, a person's circle of possible friends and acquaintances is likely to dwindle.
- *Personal identity*. Work is usually valued for the sense of stable social identity it offers. For men in particular, self-esteem is often bound up with the economic contribution they make to the maintenance of the household. In addition, job conditions, such as the opportunity to work in jobs that are challenging, not routinized, and not subject to close supervision, are known to affect a person's sense of self-worth. (Kohn 1977)

Against the backdrop of this formidable list, it is not difficult to see why being without work may undermine individuals' confidence in their social value.

Unpaid Work

We often tend to think of work, as the notion of being "out of work" implies, as equivalent to having a paid job, but in fact this is an oversimplified view. Nonpaid labor (such as repairing one's own car or doing one's own housework) looms large in many people's lives. Many types of work do not conform to orthodox categories of paid employment. Much of the work done in the informal economy, for example, is not recorded in any direct way in the official employment statistics. The term **informal economy** refers to transactions outside the sphere of regular employment, sometimes involving the exchange of cash for services provided, but also often involving the direct exchange of goods or services.

Someone who comes to fix the television may be paid in cash, "off the books," without any receipt being given or details of the job recorded. People may exchange pilfered or stolen goods with friends or associates in return for other favors. The informal economy includes not only "hidden" cash transactions, but many forms of *self-provisioning* that people carry on inside and outside the home. Do-it-yourself activities and household appliances and tools, for instance, provide goods and services that would otherwise have to be purchased (Gershuny and Miles 1983).

Housework, which has traditionally mostly been carried out by women, is usually unpaid. But it is work, often very hard and exhausting work, nevertheless. Volunteer work, for charities or other organizations, has an important social role. Having a paid job is important for all the reasons listed earlier—but the category of "work" stretches more widely.

The Social Organization of Work

One of the most distinctive characteristics of the economic system of modern societies is the existence of a highly complex **division of labor:** Work has become divided into an enormous number of different occupations in which people specialize. In traditional societies, nonagricultural work entailed the mastery of a craft. Craft skills were learned through a lengthy period of apprenticeship, and the worker normally carried out all aspects of the production process from beginning to end. For example, a metalworker making a plow would forge the iron, shape it, and assemble the implement itself. With the rise of modern industrial production, most traditional crafts have disappeared altogether, replaced by skills that form part of more large-scale production processes. An electrician working in an industrial setting today, for instance, may inspect and repair only a few parts of one type of machine; different people will deal with the other parts and other machines.

The contrast in the division of labor between traditional and modern societies is truly extraordinary. Even in the largest traditional societies, there usually existed no more than twenty or thirty major craft trades, together with such specialized pursuits as merchant, soldier, and priest. In a modern industrial system, there are literally thousands of distinct occupations. The U.S. Bureau of the Census lists some twenty thousand distinct jobs in the American economy. In traditional communities, most of the population worked on farms and were economically self-sufficient. They produced their own food, clothes, and other necessities of life. One of the main features of modern societies, by contrast, is an enormous expansion of **economic interdependence.** We all depend on an immense number of other workers—today stretching right across the world—for the products and services that sustain our lives. With few exceptions, the vast majority of people in modern societies do not produce the food they eat, the houses in which they live, or the material goods they consume.

Taylorism and Fordism

Writing some two centuries ago, Adam Smith, one of the founders of modern economics, identified advantages that the division of labor provides in terms of increasing productivity. His most famous work, *The Wealth of Nations* (1776), opens with a description of the division of labor in a pin factory. A person working alone could perhaps make twenty pins per day. By breaking down that worker's task into a number of simple operations, however, ten workers carrying out specialized jobs in collaboration with one another could collectively produce forty-eight thousand pins per day. The rate of production per worker, in other words, is increased from twenty to forty-eight hundred pins, each specialist operator producing 240 times more than when working alone.

More than a century later, these ideas reached their most developed expression in the writings of Frederick Winslow Taylor, an American management consultant. Taylor's approach to what he called "scientific management" involved the detailed study of industrial processes to break them down into simple operations that could be precisely timed and organized. **Taylorism,** as scientific management came to be called, was not merely an academic study. It was a system of production designed to maximize industrial output, and it had a wide-spread effect not only on the organization of industrial production and technology but on workplace politics as well. In particular, Taylor's time and motion studies wrested control over knowledge of the production process from the worker and placed such knowledge firmly in the hands of management, eroding the basis on which craft workers maintained autonomy from their employers (Braverman 1974). As such, Taylorism has been widely associated with the deskilling and degradation of labor.

The principles of Taylorism were appropriated by the industrialist Henry Ford. In 1908, Ford designed his first auto plant at Highland Park, Michigan, to manufacture only one product—the Model T Ford—thereby allowing the introduction of specialized tools and machinery designed for speed, precision, and simplicity of operation. One of Ford's most significant innovations was the introduction of the assembly line, said to have been inspired by Chicago slaughterhouses, in which animals were disassembled section by section on a moving conveyor belt. Each worker on Ford's assembly line was assigned a specialized task, such as fitting the left-side door handles as the car bodies moved along the line. By 1929, when production of the Model T ceased, more than fifteen million cars had been assembled.

Ford was among the first to realize that mass production requires mass markets. Ford reasoned that if standardized commodities such as the automobile were to be produced on an ever greater scale, the presence of consumers who were able to buy those commodities must also be ensured. In 1914, Ford took the unprecedented step of unilaterally raising wages at his Dearborn, Michigan, plant to $5 for an eight-hour day—a very generous wage at the time and one that ensured a working-class lifestyle that included owning such an automobile. As Harvey (1989) remarks, "The purpose of the five dollar, eight hour day was only in part to secure worker compliance with the discipline required to work the highly productive assembly-line system. It was coincidentally meant to provide workers with sufficient income to consume the mass-produced products the corporations were about to turn out in ever vaster quantities." Ford also enlisted the services of a small army of social workers who were sent into the homes of workers to educate them in the proper habits of consumption.

Fordism is the name given to designate the system of mass production tied to the cultivation of mass markets. In certain contexts, the term has a more specific meaning, referring to a historical period in the development of post–World War II capitalism in which mass production was associated with stability in labor relations and a high degree of unionization. Under Fordism, firms made long-term commitments to workers, and wages were tightly linked to productivity growth. As such, *collective bargaining agreements*—formal agreements negotiated between firms and unions that specified working conditions

One of Henry Ford's most significant innovations was the introduction of the assembly line, which allowed for mass production of the Model T.

such as wages, seniority rights, benefits, and so on—closed a virtuous circle that ensured worker consent to automated work regimes *and* sufficient demand for mass-produced commodities. The system is generally understood to have broken down in the 1970s, giving rise to greater flexibility and insecurity in working conditions.

The reasons for the demise of Fordism are complex and intensely debated. As firms in a variety of industries adopted Fordist production methods, the system encountered certain limitations. Fordism was not suitable for all industries; it could only be applied successfully to industries that produced standardized commodities for large markets. At one time, it looked as though Fordism represented the likely future of industrial production as a whole. This has not proved to be the case. Setting up mechanized production lines is enormously expensive, and once a Fordist system is established, it is quite rigid; to alter a product, for example, substantial reinvestment is needed. Fordist production is easy to copy if sufficient funding is available to set up the plant. But firms in countries in which labor power is expensive find it difficult to compete with those where wages are cheaper. This was one of the factors originally leading to the rise of the Japanese car industry (although Japanese wage levels today are no longer low) and, more recently, that of South Korea.

Work and Alienation

Karl Marx was one of the first writers to grasp that the development of modern industry would reduce many people's work to dull, uninteresting tasks. According to Marx, the division of labor alienates human beings from their work. For Marx, **alienation** refers to feelings of indifference or hostility not only to work but to the overall framework of industrial production within a capitalist setting.

In traditional societies, he pointed out, work was often exhausting—peasant farmers sometimes had to toil from dawn to dusk. Yet peasants held a real measure of control over their work, which required much knowledge and skill. Many industrial workers, by contrast, have little control over their jobs, contribute only a fraction to the creation of the overall product, and have no influence over how or to whom it is eventually sold. Work thus appears as something alien, a task that the worker must carry out to earn an income but that is intrinsically unsatisfying.

Low-Trust and High-Trust Systems

Fordism and Taylorism are what some industrial sociologists call **low-trust systems.** Jobs are set by management and are geared to machines. Those who carry out the work tasks are closely supervised and are allowed little autonomy of action. Where there are many low-trust positions, the level of worker dissatisfaction and absenteeism is high, and industrial conflict is common. A **high-trust system** is one in which workers are permitted to control the pace and even the content of their work, within overall guidelines. Such systems are usually concentrated at the higher levels of industrial organizations.

Industrial Conflict

There have long been conflicts between workers and those in economic and political authority over them. Riots against conscription and high taxes and food riots at periods of harvest failure were common in urban areas of Europe in the eighteenth century. These "premodern" forms of labor conflict continued up to not much more than a century ago in some countries. For example, there were food riots in several large Italian towns in 1868 (Geary 1981). Such traditional forms of confrontation were not just sporadic, irrational outbursts of violence: The threat or use of violence had the effect of lowering the price of grain and other essential foodstuffs (Booth 1977; Rudé 1964; Thompson 1971).

Industrial conflict between workers and employers at first tended to follow these older patterns. In situations of confrontation, workers would quite often leave their places of employment and form crowds in the streets; they would make their grievances known through their unruly behavior or by engaging in acts of violence against the authorities. Workers in some parts of France in the late nineteenth century would threaten disliked employers with hanging (Holton 1978). Use of the *strike* as a weapon, today commonly associated with organized bargaining between workers and management, developed only slowly and sporadically.

STRIKES

We can define a **strike** as a temporary stoppage of work by a group of employees to express a grievance or enforce a demand (Hyman 1984). All the components of this definition are important in separating strikes from other forms of opposition and conflict. A strike is *temporary* because workers intend to return to the same job with the same employer; when workers quit altogether, the term *strike* is not appropriate. As a *stoppage of work*, a strike is distinguishable from an overtime ban or "slowdown." A *group* of workers has to be involved, because a strike is a collective action, not the response of one individual worker. That those involved are *employees* serves to separate strikes from protests such as may be conducted by tenants or students. Finally, a strike involves seeking to make known a grievance or press a demand; workers who miss work to go to a ball game could not be said to be on strike (Figure 14.1).

Strikes represent only one aspect or type of conflict in which workers and management may become involved. Other closely related expressions of organized conflict are lockouts (in which the employers rather than the workers bring about a stoppage of work), output restrictions, and clashes in contract negotiations. Less-organized expressions of conflict may include high labor turnover, absenteeism, and interference with production machinery.

Workers choose to go out on strike for many specific reasons. They may be seeking to gain higher wages, forestall a proposed reduction in their earnings, protest against technological changes that make their work duller or lead to layoffs, or obtain greater security of employment. However, in all these circumstances the strike is essentially a mechanism of power: a weapon of people who are relatively powerless in the workplace and whose working lives are affected by managerial decisions over which they have little or no control. It is usually a weapon of last resort, to be used when other negotiations have failed, because workers on strike either receive no income or depend on union funds, which might be limited.

Labor Unions

Although their levels of membership and the extent of their power vary widely, union organizations exist in all Western countries, which also all legally recognize the right of workers to strike in pursuit of economic objectives. Why have unions become a basic feature of Western societies? Why does union-management conflict seem to be a more or less ever-present possibility in industrial settings?

In the early development of modern industry, workers in most countries had no political rights and little influence over the conditions of work in which they found themselves. Unions developed as a means of redressing the imbalance of power between workers and employers. Whereas workers had virtually no power as individuals, through collective organization their influence was considerably increased. An employer can do without the labor of any particular worker but not without that of all or most of the workers in a factory or plant. Unions originally were mainly "defensive" organizations, providing the means whereby workers could counter the overwhelming power that employers wielded over their lives.

Workers today have voting rights in the political sphere, and there are established forms of negotiation with employers, by means of which economic benefits can be pressed for and grievances expressed. However, union influence, both at the level of the local plant and nationally, still remains primarily *veto power*. In other words, using the resources at their disposal, including the right to strike, unions can only *block* employers' policies or initiatives, not help formulate them in the first place. There are exceptions to this, for instance when unions and employers negotiate periodic contracts covering conditions of work.

The post–World War II period witnessed a dramatic reversal in the positions of unions in advanced industrial societies. In most developed countries, the period from 1950 to 1980 was a time of steady growth in **union density,** a statistic that represents the number of union members as a percentage of the number of people who could potentially be union members. Union density across the Western economies was highly variable, however. In the United States, for example, union density peaked in the late 1950s, much earlier than in Europe. Countries that reached the highest levels of union density—Belgium, Denmark, Finland, and Sweden, with more than 80 percent of all workers belonging to labor unions in 1985—shared three

FIGURE 14.1

Work Stoppages Involving 1,000 Workers or More, 1947–2004

During what year since the end of World War II did the greatest number of work stoppages involving 1,000 workers or more occur? Is it accurate to say that the number of work stoppages involving 1,000 workers or more has consistently declined since 1950? During what year did the decline in work stoppages involving 1,000 workers or more begin and fail to recover to any significant levels of the past? During which of the last twenty years has the number of work stoppages involving 1,000 workers or more come close to reaching the levels of the 1950s? What are some specific reasons that workers may go on strike? Name two causes of union decline that are consistent with the decline in union density within and among industries.

SOURCE: U.S. Bureau of the Census 2006a.

features in common (Western 1977). First, strong working-class political parties created favorable conditions for labor organizing. Second, bargaining between firms and labor unions was coordinated at the national level rather than occurring in decentralized fashion at sectoral or local levels. Third, unions rather than the state directly administered unemployment insurance, ensuring that workers who lost their jobs did not leave the labor movement. Countries in which some combination but not all three of these factors were present had lower rates of union density, ranging between two fifths and two thirds of the working population.

After 1980, unions suffered declines across the advanced industrial countries. In the United States, the share of the workforce belonging to unions declined from 23 percent in 1980 to 12.5 percent in 2004 (Hirsch and Macpherson 2004; U.S. Bureau of the Census 2006b). There are several prominent explanations for the difficulties confronted by unions since 1980. Perhaps the most common is the decline of the older manufacturing industries and the rise of the service sector. Traditionally, manufacturing has been a stronghold for labor, whereas jobs in services are resistant to unionization. However, this explanation has recently come under scrutiny. Sociologist Bruce

Dukes v. Wal-Mart Stores, Inc.

After six years of hard work and excellent performance reviews, Betty Dukes was finally promoted to management in 2000. Working at the customer-complaint desk, Dukes was given a raise to $6.45 an hour. In San Francisco, where she continues to work, that's below the poverty line.

In 2001, Dukes filed a lawsuit against Wal-Mart claiming that she had been systematically denied training and the opportunity for advancement. Dukes was frustrated, and she wasn't the only one. As more and more female employees came forward to tell their stories, the picture became clear: At stores across the country, women were being paid less and offered fewer promotions than men. Stephanie Odle, an assistant store manager in Riverside, California, was shocked to learn that a male assistant manager working at the same Wal-Mart store was making $60,000 a year, $23,000 more than she was earning. She said, "When I went to the district manager, he first goes, 'Stephanie, that assistant manager has a family and two children to support.' I told him, 'I'm a single mother and I have a 6-month-old child to support'" (Greenhouse and Hays 2004). Gina Espinoza, a Wal-Mart employee in northern California, recalled being sexually and even racially harassed by her boss on more than one occasion. "He used to call me the little Mexican princess," she said. Espinoza was fired from her job shortly after filing a sexual harassment complaint (Greenhouse and Hays 2004).

The suit *Dukes v. Wal-Mart Stores, Inc.*, was eventually expanded to represent 1.6 million current and former employees across the United States, making Dukes the lead plaintiff in the largest civil rights class-action lawsuit in history. The suit charged Wal-Mart with violating Title VII of the 1964 Civil Rights Act, which protects workers from sex discrimination in the workplace. Wal-Mart denied the allegations, claiming that women in the company have as many opportunities for advancement as men. And while anecdotes from individual em-

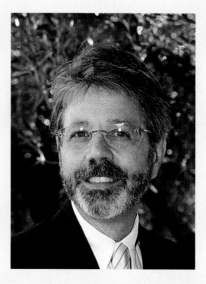

William Bielby

ployees like Stephanie Odle and Gina Espinoza may provide powerful storyline, evaluating the legal claim that women as a group—as a class of people—have endured discrimination takes sociological thinking.

Professor William Bielby, a sociologist at the University of Pennsylvania, has spent over fifteen years studying inequality in the workplace. His reputation for communicating complicated ideas to audiences not familiar with terms like *centralized coordination* and *personnel policy* qualified him to serve as an expert witness in the *Dukes* trial. In the trial, Bielby's main task was to look at Wal-Mart's policies and practices and compare them to scientific theories of how gender bias happens in organizations. At the heart of the case was whether Wal-Mart has a workplace culture that discriminates against women and whether those women as a group could force Wal-Mart to change the way they treat their female employees, both in the past (by providing back pay to women like Dukes) and in the

Western (1997) argues that such an explanation cannot account for the experience of the 1970s, which was generally (although not in the United States) a good period for unions and yet was also characterized by a structural shift from manufacturing to services. Similarly, a significant share of growth in service-

sector employment has occurred in social services—typically public-sector union jobs. Therefore, Western argues that declines in unionization *within* manufacturing may be more significant than declines across sectors. Explanations that are consistent with the fall in union density within as well as among future (by increasing the opportunities available to all employees regardless of their gender).

In his role as expert witness, Bielby reviewed hundreds of organizational charts, memos, reports, and presentation. He studied Wal-Mart's policies relating to personnel, diversity, and equal employment opportunity as well as documents describing the culture and history of the company. What evidence, if any, did Bielby find? He started by explaining that men and women making different amounts of money does not mean that the company is discriminating. How can that be?

It all comes down to the issue of qualifications. "There are many reasons why men and women can have different career trajectories," Bielby (2005) states in his report. "For example, jobs may have job-related skill and experience requirements that differ, on average, between men and women. Gender disparities arising from such factors would not be considered discriminatory, so long as the employer is not responsible for differences in men's and women's qualifications (e.g., by not providing equal access to training)."

Discrimination comes into play once people start making decisions about training, compensation, and promotion based on beliefs about a person's gender instead of on his or her qualifications or experience. Bielby says, "Employers also create gender barriers when they ignore (or encourage) an organizational climate that is hostile towards women and inhibits them from performing to their full potential." Bielby explained to the court that

> *gender stereotypes* are beliefs about traits and behaviors that differ between men and women. For example, men are believed to be competitive, aggressive, assertive, strong, and independent, while women are believed to be nurturing, cooperative, supportive, and understanding. Men are assumed to place a high priority on their careers, while women are assumed to be more strongly oriented towards family, even though research demonstrates that the commitments of men and women with similar job opportunities and family situations are virtually identical. These kinds of stereotypes are relevant to how men and women advance in careers with Wal-Mart. For example, if women are believed to be committed to and constrained by family circumstances, and men are

not, women will not be given the same consideration as men for management positions that are believed to interfere with family obligations.

In other testimony reviewed by Bielby, a male-centered, traditional culture was reinforced by those who made biblical references or noted the "long hours" to discourage female employees from pursuing promotions. Some women who had achieved senior management positions said that they were forced to go to strip bars and Hooters restaurants for office outings, and that senior management fostered a climate in which sexually demeaning comments and attitudes were the norm (Porter 2004).

Bielby supplemented his analysis of gender stereotypes with statistical evidence on job placements that was highly suggestive of gender discrimination. At Wal-Mart, women make up 89.5% of cashiers, 79% of department heads, 37.6% of assistant store managers, and 15.5% of store managers, compared to other discount stores like Target, Costco, and Home Depot, where women hold 57% of management positions (Bielby 2005). Bielby played an important role in bringing potential discrimination to light. In a 2003 ruling allowing the civil suit to proceed, Judge Jenkins, after reviewing Bielby's testimony, found that "women working at Wal-Mart stores are paid less than men in every region, that pay disparities exist in most job categories, that the salary gap widens over time, that women take longer to enter management positions, and that the higher one looks in the organization the lower the percentage of women" can be found (Ackman 2004).

Dukes still works at Wal-Mart. Since she filed the discrimination suit in 2001, she has received multiple raises and now makes over $12.00 an hour as a greeter at the same San Francisco store where she was originally hired. But she didn't file suit only for personal gain. As lead plaintiff, she believes that entrenched gender inequality within the nation's largest company is a violation of civil rights. For Bielby, who decided to become a professor in the 1960s to help "address issues that have to do with social change and social justice," the *Dukes* case provided him a rare opportunity to make a difference in the public realm (Dubilet 2005).

industries include the recession in world economic activity, associated with high levels of unemployment, which weakens the bargaining position of labor; the increasing intensity of international competition, particularly from Far Eastern countries where wages are often lower than in the West; and the rise to

power in many countries of rightist governments that launched an aggressive assault on unions in the 1980s.

In the United States, unions face a crisis of even greater dimensions than their counterparts in most European countries. Union-protected working conditions and wages have eroded in several major industries over the past twenty-five years. Workers in the trucking, steel, and car industries have all accepted lower wages than those previously negotiated. The unions came out second best in several major strikes, perhaps the most notable example being the crushing of the air traffic controllers' union in the early 1980s. At the same time, unions have made progress in organizing outside their traditional manufacturing base, including the successful unionization of janitors in Los Angeles; teaching assistants at the University of Massachusetts, the University of California, and other institutions; and attempts to organize doctors. These new fronts in attempts to organize labor reflect the changing conditions of work in the United States toward the provision of services.

Decline in union membership and influence is something of a general phenomenon in the industrialized countries and is not to be explained wholly in terms of political pressure applied by rightist governments against the unions. Unions usually become weakened during periods when unemployment is high, as has been the case for a considerable while in many Western countries. Trends toward more flexible production tend to diminish the force of unionism, which flourishes more extensively where many people are working together in large factories.

What Do Workers Want?

An individual's quality of life depends on his or her position in the labor market. Arguably this is more true in the United States than in any other comparably developed economy. Americans spend more time at work than do citizens of other advanced industrial countries. U.S. living standards also reflect income and employment-related benefits more directly than do living standards in other comparably developed countries where governments universally guarantee paid vacation, job training, and health insurance. There is also more variability in terms of pay and work conditions in the U.S. labor market than elsewhere. Yet, in spite of the overwhelming importance of the labor market for the life conditions of working Americans, there has been relatively little investigation of how workers view the framework through which the U.S. labor market is governed. For this reason, Richard Freeman of Harvard University and Joel Rogers of the University of Wisconsin set out to find out what workers want in regard to the conditions under which they labor. Freeman and Rogers (1999) designed the Worker Representation and Participation Survey (WRPS) to canvass workers systematically in a wide variety of professions for their opinions about their employment and how their workplaces could be improved.

Freeman and Rogers's findings are based on a national telephone survey of 2,400 workers in private-sector establish-

Members of the Service Employees International Union picketing outside city hall in Los Angeles. The county workers—who include nurses and medical staff; library workers; and staff workers at the civic center, beaches, and harbors—are demanding raises, improved job security, and better benefits.

ments that employ twenty-five or more people. They excluded top managers, the self-employed, owners of firms or their relatives, public-sector workers, and employees in small firms. Overall, the population from which survey respondents were selected covers approximately 75 percent of all private-sector workers. Freeman and Rogers's findings range across a wide variety of aspects of people's work lives, including causes of worker dissatisfaction, attitudes toward unionization, views of management, and worker knowledge of protective labor legislation. In-depth follow-up interviews were conducted with 801 workers, who were asked about their views of alternative institutional designs for American workplaces.

The overwhelming finding of Freeman and Rogers's study is that what workers want is more influence at work. American workers believe that if they had more say over how production is carried out, they would not only enjoy work more but their firms would be more competitive and problems would be solved more effectively. Furthermore, influence is associated with a broader range of attitudes about work: Workers satisfied with their degree of influence report that they enjoy going to work, grade employee–management relations as excellent, and trust their employer. In contrast, workers who are dissatisfied with their degree of influence tend to dislike going to work, report poor relations with management, and distrust their employers.

One of the most surprising findings of the WRPS concerns the kind of institutional arrangement that workers consider ideal for achieving greater say. Contrary to what Freeman and Rogers expected, workers prefer an organization run jointly by workers and management to one run by employees alone. Workers were also asked to choose between two hypothetical organizations, "one that management cooperated with in discussing issues, but had no power to make decisions," and "one that had more power but management opposed." Sixty-three percent of all employees chose the former organization, whereas only 22 percent stated that they would prefer the latter. These results—in which workers effectively indicated that they would prefer weaker to stronger organizations, in spite of the fact that they also reported wanting more say at work—make sense in light of another question on Freeman and Rogers's survey. When asked if they thought an organization could be effective without managerial support, three quarters of all respondents indicated that they believed an employee organization could function only with management cooperation.

The Modern Economy

Modern societies are, in Marx's term, capitalistic. **Capitalism** is a way of organizing economic life that is distinguished by the following important features: private ownership of the means of production; profit as incentive; free competition for markets to sell goods, acquire cheap materials, and use cheap labor; and restless expansion and investment to accumulate capital. Capitalism, which began to spread with the growth of the Industrial Revolution in the early nineteenth century, is a vastly more dynamic economic system than any other that preceded it in history. Although the system has had many critics, such as Marx, it is now the most widespread form of economic organization in the world.

So far in this chapter, we have been looking at industry mostly from the perspective of occupations and employees. We have studied how patterns of work have changed and the factors influencing the development of labor unions. But we have also to concern ourselves with the nature of the business firms in which the workforce is employed. (It should be recognized that many people today are employees of government organizations, although we will not consider these here.) What is happening to business corporations today, and how are they run?

Corporations and Corporate Power

Since the turn of the twentieth century, modern capitalist economies have been more and more influenced by the rise of large business **corporations.** The share of total manufacturing assets held by the two hundred largest *manufacturing* firms in the United States has increased by 0.5 percent each year from 1900 to the present day; these two hundred corporations now control over half of all manufacturing assets. The two hun-

dred largest *financial* organizations—banks, building societies, and insurance companies—account for more than half of all financial activity. There are numerous connections between large firms. For example, financial institutions hold well over 30 percent of the shares of the largest two hundred manufacturing firms.

Of course, there still exist thousands of smaller firms and enterprises within the American economy. In these companies, the image of the **entrepreneur**—the boss who owns and runs the firm—is by no means obsolete. The large corporations are a different matter. Ever since Adolf Berle and Gardiner Means published their celebrated study *The Modern Corporation and Private Property* (1982; orig. 1932) in the 1930s, it has been accepted that most of the largest firms are not run by those who own them. In theory, the large corporations are the property of their shareholders, who have the right to make all important decisions. But Berle and Means argue that because share ownership is so dispersed, actual control has passed into the hands of the managers who run firms on a day-to-day basis. *Ownership* of the corporations is thus separated from their *control.*

Whether they are run by owners or managers, the power of the major corporations is very extensive. When one or a handful of firms dominate in a given industry, they often cooperate in setting prices rather than freely competing with one another. Thus the giant oil companies normally follow one another's lead in the price charged for gasoline. When one firm occupies a commanding position in a given industry, it is said to be in a **monopoly** position. More common is a situation of **oligopoly,** in which a small group of giant corporations predominate. In situations of oligopoly, firms are able more or less to dictate the terms on which they buy goods and services from the smaller firms that are their suppliers.

The emergence of the global economy has contributed to a wave of mergers and acquisitions on an unprecedented scale, which have created oligopolies in industries such as communications and media. In 1998, the German automaker Daimler-Benz purchased Chrysler for $38 billion, and Exxon purchased the oil giant Mobil for $86 billion. In 1999, AT&T acquired the media corporation MediaOne for $5 billion to create the world's largest cable company. Also in 1999, CBS purchased Viacom for $35 billion. In 2000, Britian's Vodafone Airtouch took over Germany's Mannesmann for $130 billion in the world's largest hostile takeover. In that same year, Time Warner and the Internet service provider America Online announced the largest merger in history—worth over $166 billion (Public Broadcasting System [PBS] 2003). By 2004, the value of cross-border mergers and acquisitions had reached $380.6 trillion. Approximately 83% of these mergers and acquisitions occurred between companies in the developed world (United Nations Conference on Trade and Development [UNCTAD] 2005a). As the global market becomes increasingly integrated, we are likely to see more mergers and acquisitions on an even larger scale.

A number of factors have contributed to this trend, including technological advances, which have lowered global transportation and communications costs; a relaxation of regulation of corporate business activities; new and efficient ways of financing and pooling the large sums of capital needed to conduct a merger or acquisition. Yet over 70 percent of the mergers and acquisitions have been between businesses competing in the same industry (UNCTAD 2000). This suggests that the primary aim of the recent wave of business consolidations has been to eliminate direct competition and productive overcapacity. *Overcapacity* is a problem that occurs when businesses produce more goods than the market will consume. Following the logic of supply and demand, this leads to decline in the value of the goods that they produce and to a decline in profits. Consolidation of firms is an attempt to avoid this problem. Yet it doesn't always work. In response to the declining success of AOL, Time Warner dropped AOL from its name and posted a $99 billion dollar loss for 2002 (PBS 2003).

Types of Corporate Capitalism

There have been three general stages in the development of business corporations, although each overlaps with the others and all continue to coexist today. The first stage, characteristic of the nineteenth and early twentieth centuries, was dominated by **family capitalism.** Large firms were run either by individual entrepreneurs or by members of the same family and then passed on to their descendants. The famous corporate dynasties, such as the Rockefellers and Fords, belong in this category. These individuals and families did not just own a single large corporation but held a diversity of economic interests and stood at the apex of economic empires.

Most of the big firms founded by entrepreneurial families have since become public companies—that is, shares of their stock are traded on the open market—and have passed into managerial control. But important elements of family capitalism remain, even within some of the largest corporations, such as the Ford Motor Company, for which William Clay Ford Jr. serves as chair of the board. Among small firms, such as local shops run by their owners, small plumbing and house-painting businesses, and so forth, family capitalism continues to dominate. Some of these firms, such as shops that remain in the hands of the same family for two or more generations, are also dynasties on a minor scale. However, the small business sector is highly unstable, and economic failure is common; the proportion of firms that are owned by members of the same family for extended periods of time is minuscule.

In the large corporate sector, family capitalism was increasingly succeeded by **managerial capitalism.** As managers came to have more and more influence through the growth of very large firms, the entrepreneurial families were displaced. The result has been described as the replacement of the family in the company by the company itself. The corporation emerged as a more defined economic entity. In studying the two hundred largest manufacturing corporations in the United States, Michael Allen (1981) found that in cases in which profit showed a decline, family-controlled enterprises were unlikely to replace their chief executive, but manager-controlled firms did so rapidly.

There is no question that managerial capitalism has left an indelible imprint on modern society. The large corporation drives not only patterns of consumption but also the experience of employment in contemporary society—it is difficult to imagine how the work lives of many Americans would be different in the absence of large factories or corporate bureaucracies. Sociologists have identified another area in which the large corporation has left a mark on modern institutions. **Welfare capitalism** refers to a practice that sought to make the corporation—rather than the state or trade unions—the primary shelter from the uncertainties of the market in modern industrial life. Beginning at the end of the nineteenth century, large firms began to provide certain services to their employees, including child care, recreational facilities, profit-sharing plans, paid vacations, and group life and unemployment insurance. These programs often had a paternalistic bent, such as that sponsoring "home visits" for the "moral education" of employees. Viewed in less benevolent terms, a major objective of welfare capitalism was coercion, as employers deployed all manner of tactics—including violence—to avoid unionization. As such, conventional histories typically suggest that welfare capitalism met its demise in the depression years as labor unions achieved unprecedented levels of influence and as the New Deal administration began to guarantee many of the benefits provided by firms. In contrast to this standard interpretation, others argue that welfare capitalism did not die but instead went underground during the apex of the labor movement (Jacoby 1997). In firms that avoided unionization during the period between the 1930s and 1960s—such as Kodak, Sears, and Thompson Products—welfare capitalism was modernized, shedding blatantly paternalistic aspects and routinizing benefit programs. When the union movement began to weaken after 1970, these companies offered a model to many other firms, which were then able to press their advantage against flanking unions, reasserting the role of the firm as "industrial manor" and workers as "industrial serfs."

Despite the overwhelming importance of managerial capitalism in shaping the modern economy, many scholars now see the contours of a third, different phase emerging in the evolution of the corporation. They argue that managerial capitalism has today partly ceded place to **institutional capitalism.** This term refers to the emergence of a consolidated network of business leadership, concerned not only with decision making within single firms but also with the development of corporate power beyond them. Institutional capitalism is based on the practice of corporations holding shares in other firms. In effect, interlocking boards of directors exercise control over much of the corporate landscape. This reverses the process of increasing managerial control because the managers' shareholdings are dwarfed by the large blocks of shares owned by other corporations. One of the main reasons for the spread of institutional capitalism is the shift in patterns of investment that has occurred since the 1970s. Rather than investing directly by buying shares in a business, individuals now invest in money market, trust, insurance, and pension funds that are controlled by large financial organizations, which in turn invest these grouped savings in industrial corporations.

The Transnational Corporations

With the intensifying of globalization, most large corporations now operate in an international economic context. When they establish branches in two or several countries, they are referred to as **transnational,** or **multinational corporations.** *Transnational* is the preferred term, indicating that these companies operate across many different national boundaries. The United Nations Committee on Trade and Development (2006b) estimated that in 2004 over 69,720 transnational corporations controlled assets outside their home countries.

The largest transnationals are gigantic; their wealth outstrips that of many countries. Half of the hundred largest economic units in the world today are nations; the other half are transnational corporations. The scope of these companies' operations is staggering. The combined sales of the world's largest five hundred transnational corporations totaled $16.8 trillion in 2005—nearly half (41 percent) of the value of goods and services produced by the entire world (*Fortune* 2005; World Bank 2005). The revenues of the largest two hundred companies rose tenfold between the mid-1970s and the 1990s, reaching $9.5 trillion in 2001. By 2004, their revenues had grown by an additional 20 percent to $11.4 trillion (*Fortune* 2005). Over the past twenty years, the transnationals' activi-

ties have become increasingly global: In 1950 only three of the world's largest companies had manufacturing subsidiaries in more than twenty countries; some fifty do so today. These are still a small minority; most of the transnationals have subsidiaries in two to five countries. Altogether an estimated 69,000 affiliates of transnational corporations do business around the globe (UNCTAD 2005b).

Of the top 500 transnational corporations in the world, 176 are based in the United States, contributing about 37 percent of the total sales of all 500. The share of American companies has, however, fallen significantly since 1960, during which time Japanese companies have grown dramatically; only 5 Japanese corporations were included in the top 200 in 1960, compared to 28 in 2005. Of the 50 largest Asian corporations, 40 of them are Japanese (*Fortune* 2005).

Contrary to common belief, three quarters of all foreign direct investment occurs among the industrialized countries. Of the one hundred largest corporations, one is from Mexico and none is from Latin America, Africa, the Middle East, eastern Europe, or the former Soviet Union. The rest are all from North America, Europe, and Asia. Nevertheless, the involvements of transnationals in developing world countries are extensive, with Brazil, Mexico, and India showing the highest levels of foreign investment. The most rapid rate of increase in corporate investment by far has been in the Asian newly industrializing economies (NIEs) of Singapore, Taiwan, Hong Kong, South Korea, and Malaysia.

The reach of the transnationals since the mid-1970s would not have been possible without advances in transport and communications. Air travel now allows people to move around the world at a speed that would have seemed inconceivable even sixty years ago. Technological innovations, referred to together as "containerization," have permitted the rapid movement and distribution of bulk goods around the world. The best example of containerization is the development of extremely large ocean-going vessels (superfreighters) that carry tractor trailers full of goods. These trailers can be easily loaded and sealed at the point of manufacture, loaded onto ships and moved across an ocean, than transferred onto a train or truck and delivered to a store, where the trailers are finally opened and unloaded.

Telecommunications technologies now permit more or less instantaneous communication from one part of the world to another. Satellites have been used for commercial telecommunications since 1965, when the first satellite could carry 240 telephone conversations at once. Current satellites can carry 12,000 simultaneous conversations! The larger transnationals now have their own satellite-based communications systems. The Mitsubishi Corporation, for instance, has a massive network across which five million words are transmitted to and from its headquarters in Tokyo each day.

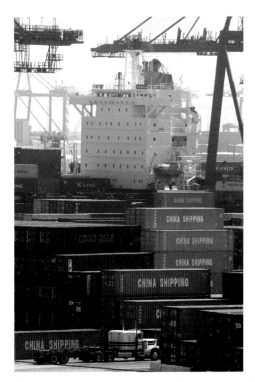

Container ships are cargo ships that carry all of their load in truck-size containers. As this technique greatly accelerates the speed by which goods can be transported to and from ports, these ships now carry the majority of the world's dry cargo.

TYPES OF TRANSNATIONAL CORPORATIONS

The transnationals have assumed an increasingly important place in the world economy over the course of this century. They are of key importance in the **international division of labor**—the specialization in producing goods for the world market that divides regions into zones of industrial or agricultural production or high- or low-skilled labor (Fröbel et al. 1979; McMichael 1996). Just as national economies have become increasingly *concentrated*—dominated by a limited number of very large companies—so has the world economy. In the case of the United States and several of the other leading industrialized countries, the firms that dominate nationally also have a wide-ranging international presence. Many sectors of world production (such as agribusiness) are oligopolies. Over the past two or three decades, international oligopolies have developed in the automobile, microprocessor, and electronics industries, and in the production of some other goods marketed worldwide.

H. V. Perlmutter (1972) divides transnational corporations into three types. One consists of **ethnocentric transnationals,** in which company policy is set and as far as possible put into practice from a headquarters in the country of origin. Companies and plants that the parent corporation owns around the world are cultural extensions of the originating company—its practices are standardized across the globe. A second category is that of **polycentric transnationals,** whose overseas subsidiaries are managed by local firms in each country. The headquarters in the country or countries of origin of the main company establish broad guidelines within which local companies manage their own affairs. Finally, there are **geocentric transnationals,** which are international in their management structure. Managerial systems are integrated on a global basis, and higher managers are very mobile, moving from country to country as needs dictate.

Planning on a World Scale

The global corporations have become the first organizations able to plan on a truly world scale. Coca-Cola ads reach billions. A few companies with developed global networks are able to shape the commercial activities of diverse nations. There are four webs of interconnecting commercial activity in the new world economy. These are what Richard Barnet and John Cavanagh (1994) call the Global Cultural Bazaar, the Global Shopping Mall, the Global Workplace, and the Global Financial Network.

The Global Cultural Bazaar is the newest of the four but already the most extensive. Global images and global dreams are diffused through movies, TV programs, music, videos, games, toys, and T-shirts, sold on a worldwide basis. All over the earth, even in the poorest developing countries, people use the same electronic devices to see or listen to the same commercially produced songs and shows.

The Global Shopping Mall is a "planetary supermarket with a dazzling spread of things to eat, drink, wear and enjoy," according to Barnet and Cavanagh. It is more exclusive than the Cultural Bazaar because the poor do not have the resources to participate—they only have the status of window shoppers. Of the 6 billion people who make up the world's population, 3.5 billion lack the cash or credit to purchase any consumer goods.

The third global web, the Global Workplace, is the increasingly complex global division of labor that affects all of us. It consists of the massive array of offices, factories, restaurants, and millions of other places where goods are produced and consumed or information is exchanged. This web is closely bound up with the Global Financial Network, which it fuels and is financed by. The Global Financial Network consists of billions of bits of information stored in computers and portrayed on computer screens. It entails almost endless currency exchanges, credit card transactions, insurance plans, and buying and selling of stocks and shares.

The Large Corporation:
The Same, but Different

There are big differences between the large corporation of the early twenty-first century and its mid-twentieth-century counterpart. Many of the names are the same—General Motors, Ford, IBM, AT&T—but these have been joined by other giant firms, largely unknown in the 1950s, such as Microsoft and Intel. They all wield great power, and their top executives still inhabit the large buildings that dominate so many city centers.

But below the surface similarities between today and half a century ago, some profound transformations have taken place. The origin of these transformations lies in that process we have encountered often in this book: globalization. Since the 1950s, the giant corporations have become more and more caught up in global competition; as a result, their internal composition, and in a way their very nature, has altered. The former U.S. Labor Secretary Robert Reich (1991) writes:

Underneath, all is changing. America's core corporation no longer plans and implements the production of a large volume of goods and services; it no longer invests in a vast array of factories, machinery, laboratories, inventories, and other tangible assets; it no longer employs armies of production workers and middle-level managers. . . . In fact, the core corporation is no longer even American. It is, increasingly, a facade, behind which teems an array of decentralized groups and subgroups continuously contracting with similarly diffuse working units all over the world.

The large corporation is less and less a big business than an "enterprise web"—a central organization that links smaller firms together. IBM, for example, which used to be one of the most jealously self-sufficient of all large corporations, in the 1980s and early 1990s joined with dozens of U.S.-based companies and more than eighty foreign-based firms to share strategic planning and cope with production problems.

Some corporations remain strongly bureaucratic and centered in the United States. However, most are no longer so clearly located anywhere. The old transnational corporation used to work mainly from its American headquarters, from where its overseas production plants and subsidiaries were controlled. Now, with the transformation of space and time noted earlier (Chapter 5), groups situated in any region of the world are able, via telecommunications and computer, to work with others. Nations still try to influence flows of information, resources, and money across their borders. But modern communications technologies make this more and more difficult, if not impossible. Knowledge and finances can be transferred across the world as electronic blips moving at the speed of light.

Even the production of the technology that makes the global activities of transnational corporations possible is spread out over the globe. The computer-chip manufacturer Intel has 86,200 employees; thirteen production sites; eleven assembly sites spread over seven countries; and 20,000 research and development employees in thirty countries, including China, India, and the Russian Federation. Two thirds of its workforce is located in the United States, while 11 percent is in Malaysia; 8 percent is in the Philippines; 4 percent is in Ireland; 3 percent is in Israel; 2 percent is in Costa Rica; and 1 percent is in China. Intel is the leading national exporter from Ireland, the Philippines, and Costa Rica, yet it is an "American" company (UNCTAD 2002).

The products of the transnational companies similarly have an international character. When is something "made in America," and when not? There is no longer any clear answer. What could be more American than a Ford? Today, the answer may be a Toyota or Honda. Automobiles contain over twenty thousand different parts, and the production and the manufacture of vehicles have become a truly globalized system (Figure 14.2). In 2005, Toyota employed over thirty-seven thousand people in North America and spent over $16.6 billion on American parts and accessories (Toyota 2005). The Toyota Avalon, for example, built at a production facility in Kentucky, is made up of 70 percent U.S. or Canadian parts. This is a higher percentage than the Chrysler-built PT Cruiser. And GM's use of a Honda-made engine in its Saturn cars actually increased the percentage of its parts and accessories made in the United States (*Charleston Business Journal* 2003). In fact, all of the Honda Accords sold in the United States contain 97 percent domestic parts and accessories and are assembled at one of its several North American production facilities (Honda Worldwide 2002).

On top of all of this, it is no longer clear what even constitutes an "American" car company. As mentioned earlier, in 1998, the German auto maker Daimler-Benz acquired Chrysler; Daimler-Benz also owns about 38 percent of Mitsubishi. General Motors owns 49 percent of Isuzu, 20 percent of the makers of Subaru, and 20 percent of Suzuki. Ford owns over 33 percent of Mazda and parts of Jaguar, Land Rover, and Volvo (*Charleston Business Journal* 2003).

The Changing Nature of Work

The globalizing of economic production, together with the spread of information technology, is altering the nature of the jobs most people do. As discussed in Chapter 8, the proportion

FIGURE 14.2

Where Does Your Car Come From?

Automobile parts are produced in several countries and then sent to a central plant for final production of the car.

France

Alternator, cylinder head, master cylinder, brakes, underbody coating, weather strips, clutch release bearings, steering shaft and joints, seat pads and frames, transmission cases, clutch cases, tires, suspension bushing, ventilation units, heater, hose clamps, sealers, hardware

Britain

Carburetor, rocker arm, clutch, ignition, exhaust, oil pump, distributor, cylinder bolt, cylinder head, flywheel ring gear, heater, speedometer, battery, rear wheel spindle, intake manifold, fuel tank, switches, lamps, front disc, steering wheel, steering column, glass, weather strips, locks

Germany

Locks, pistons, exhaust, ignition, switches, front disc, distributor, weather strips, rocker arm, speedometer, fuel tank, cylinder bolt, cylinder head gasket, front wheel knuckles, rear wheel spindle, transmission cases, clutch cases, clutch, steering column, battery, glass

The Netherlands

Tires, paints, hardware

Denmark

Fan belt

Canada

Glass, radio

Sweden

Hose clamps, cylinder bolt, exhaust pipes, hardware

Belgium

Tires, tubes, seat pads, brakes, trim

United States

EGR valves, wheel nuts, hydraulic tappet, glass

Austria

Tires, radiator and heater hoses

Spain

Wiring harness, radiator and heater hoses, fork clutch release, air filter, battery, mirrors

Italy

Cylinder head, carburetor, glass, lamps, defroster, grills

Switzerland

Underbody coating, speedometer, gears

Japan

Starter, alternator, cone and roller bearings, windshield-washer pump

Norway

Exhaust flanges, tires

The figure above demonstrates the globalization of manufacturing and corporations. Based on your reading, explain why we could call the Japanese Honda Accord an American automobile. What does the term "enterprise web" mean? Give an example other than a car.

of people working in blue-collar jobs in industrial countries has progressively fallen. Fewer people work in factories than before. New jobs have been created in offices and in service centers such as supermarkets and airports. Many of these new jobs are filled by women.

Work and Technology

The relationship between technology and work has long been of interest to sociologists. How is our experience of work affected by the type of technology that is involved? As industrialization has progressed, technology has assumed an ever greater role at the workplace—from factory automation to the computerization of office work. The current information technology revolution has attracted renewed interest in this question. Technology can lead to greater efficiency and productivity, but how does it affect the way work is experienced by those who carry it out? For sociologists, one of the main questions is how the move to more complex systems influences the nature of work and the institutions in which it is performed.

AUTOMATION AND THE SKILL DEBATE

The concept of **automation,** or programmable machinery, was introduced in the mid-1800s, when Christopher Spencer, an American, invented the Automat, a programmable lathe that made screws, nuts, and gears. Automation has thus far affected relatively few industries, but with advances in the design of industrial robots, its effect is certain to become greater. A robot is an automatic device that can perform functions ordinarily done by human workers. The term *robot* comes from the Czech word *robota*, or serf, popularized about fifty years ago by the playwright Karel Čapek.

The majority of the robots used in industry worldwide are to be found in automobile manufacture. The usefulness of robots in production thus far is relatively limited, because their capacity to recognize different objects and manipulate awkward shapes is still at a rudimentary level. Yet it is certain that automated production will spread rapidly in coming years; robots are becoming more sophisticated, while their costs are decreasing.

The spread of automation provoked a heated debate among sociologists and experts in industrial relations over the effect of the new technology on workers, their skills, and their level of commitment to their work. In his influential *Alienation and Freedom* (1964), Robert Blauner examined the experience of workers in four different industries with varying levels of technology. Using the ideas of Durkheim and Marx, Blauner operationalized the concept of *alienation* and measured the extent to which workers in each industry experienced it in the form of powerlessness, meaninglessness, isolation, and self-estrangement. He concluded that workers on assembly lines were the most alienated of all, but that levels of alienation were somewhat lower at workplaces using automation. In other words, Blauner argued that the introduction of automation to factories was responsible for *reversing* the otherwise steady trend toward increased worker alienation. Automation helped integrate the workforce and gave workers a sense of control over their work that had been lacking with other forms of technology.

A very different thesis was set forth by Harry Braverman in the famous *Labor and Monopoly Capital* (1974). In Braverman's eyes, automation was part of the overall "deskilling" of the industrial labor force. By imposing Taylorist organizational techniques and breaking up the labor process into specialized tasks, managers were able to exert control over the workforce. In both industrial settings and modern offices, the introduction of technology contributed to this overall degradation of work by limiting the need for creative human input. Instead, all that was required was an unthinking, unreflective body capable of endlessly carrying out the same unskilled task.

A newer study sheds some more light on this debate. Sociologist Richard Sennett (1998) studied the people who worked in a bakery that had been bought by a large food conglomerate and automated with the introduction of high-tech machinery. Computerized baking radically altered the way that bread was made. Instead of using their hands to mix the ingredients and knead the dough and their noses and eyes to judge when the bread was done baking, the bakery's workers had no physical contact with the materials or the loaves of bread. In fact, the entire process was controlled and monitored via computer screen. Computers decided the temperature and baking time of the ovens. Although at times the machines produced excellent-quality bread, at other times the results were burned, blackened loaves. The workers at this bakery (it would be erroneous to call them bakers) were hired because they were skilled with computers, not because they knew how to bake bread. Ironically, these workers used very few of their computer skills. The production process involved little more than pushing buttons on a computer. In fact, one time when the computerized machinery broke down, the entire production process was halted because none of the bakery's "skilled" workers was trained or empowered to repair the problem. The workers that Sennett (1998) observed wanted to be helpful, to make things work again, but they could not, because automation had diminished their autonomy. The introduction of computerized technology in the workplace has led to a general increase in all workers' skills, but has also led to a bifurcated workforce composed of a small group of highly skilled professionals with high degrees of flexibility and autonomy in their jobs and a larger group of clerical, service, and production workers who lack autonomy in their jobs.

The skill debate is very difficult to resolve, however. Both the conceptualization and measurement of skill are problematic. As feminist researchers have argued, what constitutes "skill" is socially constructed (Steinberg 1990). As such, conventional understandings of "skilled" work tend to reflect the social status of the typical incumbent of the job rather than the difficulty of the task in an objective sense. The history of occupations is rife with examples of jobs in which the very same task was assigned a different skill level (and even renamed!) once women entered the field (Reskin and Roos 1990). The same, of course, holds for other low-status workers, such as racial minorities. Even where gender and racial biases are not in operation, skill has multiple dimensions; the same job may be downgraded on one dimension while simultaneously upgraded on another (Block 1990). Thus opinions as to whether automation has deskilled work depend on which dimension of skill is examined. In his comprehensive review of the skill debate, Spenner (1983) notes that studies examining skill in terms of the substantive complexity of tasks have tended to support the "upskilling" position, whereas those that have examined skill in terms of the autonomy and/or control exercised by the worker have tended to find that work has in fact been "deskilled" through automation (Vallas and Beck 1996; c.f., Zuboff 1988).

INFORMATION TECHNOLOGY

Blauner's and Braverman's opposing perspectives on the effects of automation are echoed today in debates over the effect of information technology (IT) in the workplace. Certainly there is little question that the Internet, e-mail, teleconferencing, and e-commerce are changing the way in which companies do business. But they are also affecting the way in which employees work on a daily basis. Those who take an optimistic approach, as Blauner did, argue that information technology will revolutionize the world of work by allowing new, more flexible ways of working to emerge. These opportunities will permit us to move beyond the routine and alienating aspects of industrial work into a more liberating informational age giving workers greater control over and input into the work process. Enthusiastic advocates of technological advances are sometimes referred to as "technological determinists," because they believe in the power of technology to determine the nature and shape of work itself.

Others are not convinced that information technology will bring about an entirely positive transformation of work. As Shoshana Zuboff (1988) concluded in her research into the use of IT in firms, management can choose to use IT toward very different ends. When embraced as a creative, decentralizing force, information technology can help break down rigid hierarchies, engage more employees in decision making and involve workers more closely in the day-to-day affairs of the company. On the other hand, it can just as easily be used as a way to strengthen hierarchies and surveillance practices. The adoption of IT in the workplace can cut down on face-to-face interactions, block channels of accountability and transform an office into a network of self-contained and isolated modules. Such an approach sees the effect of information technology as influenced by the uses to which it is put and how those using the technology understand its role.

The spread of information technology will certainly produce exciting and heightened opportunities for some segments of the labor force. In the fields of media, advertising, and design, for example, IT both enhances creativity in the professional realm and introduces flexibility into personal work styles. It is qualified, valued employees in responsible positions for whom the vision of wired workers and telecommuting comes closest to being realized. Yet at the other end of the spectrum are thousands of low-paid, unskilled individuals working in call centers and data-entry companies. These positions, which are largely a product of the telecommunications explosion in recent years, are characterized by degrees of isolation and alienation that rival those of Braverman's deskilled workers. Employees at call centers that process travel bookings and financial transactions work according to strictly standardized formats with little or no room for employee discretion or creative input. Employees are closely monitored and their interactions with customers are tape recorded for "quality assurance." The information revolution seems to have produced a large number of routine, unskilled jobs on a par with those of the industrial economy.

Post-Fordism

Since the 1970s, flexible practices have been introduced in a number of spheres, including product development, production techniques, management style, the working environment, employee involvement, and marketing. Group production, problem-solving teams, multitasking, and niche marketing are just some of the strategies that have been adopted by companies attempting to restructure themselves under shifting conditions. Some commentators have suggested that, taken collectively, these changes represent a radical departure from the principles of Fordism; they contend that we are now operating in a period that can best be understood as post-Fordism. **Post-Fordism,** a phrase popularized by Michael Piore and Charles Sabel in *The Second Industrial Divide* (1984), describes a new era of capitalist economic production in which flexibility and innovation are maximized to meet market demands for diverse, customized products.

The idea of post-Fordism is somewhat problematic, however. The term is used to refer to a set of overlapping changes that are occurring not only in the realm of work and economic life but throughout society as a whole. Some writers argue that the tendency toward post-Fordism can be seen in spheres as diverse as party politics, welfare programs, and consumer and lifestyle choices. While observers of late modern societies often point to many of the same changes, there is no consensus about the precise meaning of post-Fordism or, indeed, if this is even the best way of understanding the phenomenon we are witnessing.

Despite the confusion surrounding the term *post-Fordism*, several distinctive trends within the world of work have emerged in recent decades that seem to represent a clear departure from earlier Fordist practices. These include the decentralization of work into nonhierarchical team groups, the idea of flexible production, the increase in mass customization as a result of technological advances, the spread of global production, and the introduction of more flexible working patterns. We now consider examples of the first four trends; the emergence of flexible working patterns is addressed later in the chapter.

GROUP PRODUCTION

Group production—collaborative work groups in place of assembly lines—has sometimes been used in conjunction with automation as a way of reorganizing work. The underlying idea is to increase worker motivation by letting groups of workers collaborate in team production processes rather than requiring each worker to spend the whole day doing a single repetitive task, such as inserting the screws in the door handle of a car.

An example of group production is **quality circles (QCs),** groups of between five and twenty workers who meet regularly to study and resolve production problems. Workers who belong to QCs receive extra training, enabling them to contribute technical knowledge to the discussion of production issues. QCs were initiated in the United States, taken up by a number of Japanese companies, then repopularized in the West in the 1980s. They represent a break from the assumptions of Taylorism, since they recognize that workers possess the expertise to contribute to the definition and method of the tasks they carry out.

The positive effects of group production on workers can include the acquisition of new skills, increased autonomy, reduced managerial supervision, and growing pride in the goods and services that they produce. However, studies have identified a number of negative consequences of team production. Although direct managerial authority is less apparent in a team process, other forms of monitoring exist, such as supervision by other team workers (Smith 1997). Sociologist Laurie Graham (1995) went to work on the assembly line at a Subaru-Isuzu factory and found that peer pressure from other workers to achieve greater productivity was relentless. One co-worker told her that after initially being enthusiastic about the team concept, she found that peer supervision was just a new means of management trying to work people "to death." Graham also found that Subaru-Isuzu used the group-production concept as a means to resist labor unions, their argument being that if management and workers were on the same "team," then there should be no conflict between the two. In other words, the good

"team player" doesn't complain. At the Subaru-Isuzu plant Graham worked in, demands for higher pay or reduced responsibilities were viewed as a lack of employee cooperativeness. Studies such as Graham's have led sociologists to conclude that although team-based production processes provide workers opportunities for less monotonous forms of work, systems of power and control remain the same in the workplace.

FLEXIBLE PRODUCTION

One of the most important changes in worldwide production processes over the past few years has been the introduction of computer-aided design and **flexible production.** Although Taylorism and Fordism were successful at producing mass products (that were all the same) for mass markets, they were completely unable to produce small orders of goods, let alone goods specifically made for an individual customer. Computer-aided designs, coupled to other types of computer-based technology, have altered this situation in a radical way. Stanley Davis (1987) speaks of the emergence of "mass customizing": The new technologies allow the large-scale production of items designed for particular customers. Five thousand shirts might be produced on an assembly line each day. It is now possible to customize every one of the shirts just as quickly as and at no greater expense than producing five thousand identical shirts.

Flexible production has produced benefits for consumers and the economy as a whole, but the effect on workers has not been wholly positive. Though workers do learn new skills and have less monotonous jobs, flexible production can create a whole new set of pressures for workers resulting from the need to coordinate carefully the complex production process and to quickly produce the results. Graham's study of the Subaru-Isuzu factory documented instances when workers were left waiting until the last minute for critical parts in the production process. As a result, employees were forced to work longer and more intensely to keep up with the production schedule, without additional compensation. And as we saw in Chapter 8, although the American economy was booming throughout most of the 1980s and 1990s, average pay for most workers remained quite steady. The profits of these companies mostly benefited upper management and shareholders.

TECHNOLOGY AND EVERYDAY LIFE: MASS CUSTOMIZATION

Technology such as the Internet can be used to solicit information about individual consumers and then manufacture products to their precise specifications. Enthusiastic proponents argue that mass customization offers nothing short of a

Deindustrialization

In 1929, sociologists Robert and Helen Lynd published a book about the effect of industrialization on a midwestern city they called "Middletown." The Lynds observed that as an increasing number of relatively high-wage factory jobs became available over the years in the city's glass and automobile-parts industries, the habits and values of Middletown workers began to change. Thriftiness, for example, which had been an important feature of the workers' Protestant value system, was replaced by a consumer culture emphasizing car ownership. Similarly, those who engaged in the standardized labor of factory work came to prefer passive and standardized forms of leisure such as listening to the radio and reading popular magazines. Almost every aspect of social life in the community, the Lynds argued, including child-rearing practices, housing patterns, and political beliefs, was somehow affected by the industrial boom that had taken place in Middletown since 1890.

Were the Lynds to conduct their study today, they would find that an opposite process—*deindustrialization*—has been under way in many American cities since the 1970s. Deindus-

trialization is defined as "a systematic decline in the industrial base" (Bluestone 1988), or as the process whereby the proportion of jobs in the manufacturing sector of the economy decreases over time. The consequences of deindustrialization are as significant as the changes noted by the Lynds almost seventy years ago.

Dell Computer has discovered a unique way to reconcile giving customers exactly what they want while maintaining a low production cost. By using the Internet to process orders, avoiding the expense of keeping a retail space, and producing only what is ordered and no more, Dell has succeeded in creating a system to rapidly produce custom-made products at an affordable price.

new industrial revolution, a development as momentous as the introduction of mass-production techniques in the previous century. Skeptics, however, are quick to point out that as currently practiced, mass customization only creates the illusion of choice—in reality, the options available to the Internet customer are no greater than those offered by a typical mail-order catalog (Collins 2000).

The manufacturer that has taken mass customization the farthest is Dell Computer. Consumers who want to purchase a computer from the manufacturer must go online—the company does not maintain retail outlets—and navigate Dell's Web site. Customers can select the precise mix of features they desire. After the order is placed, a computer is custom built according to specifications and then shipped—typically within days. In effect, Dell has turned traditional ways of doing business upside down: Firms used to build a product first, then worry about selling it; now, mass customizers like Dell sell first and build second. Such a shift has important consequences for industry. The need to hold stocks of parts on hand—a major cost for manufacturers—

It is estimated that factory, store, and office closings resulted in the loss of an astonishing thirty-eight million jobs in the United States in the 1970s (Bluestone and Harrison 1982), with job losses continuing into the present. Hardest hit are cities in the Northeast and Upper Midwest. Manufacturing employment in Allentown, Pennsylvania, for example, decreased by almost 28 percent between 1980 and 1987, and dropped a staggering 47 percent in Gary, Indiana, during the same period (Goe 1994). Similar changes are occurring in cities across Europe (Byrne 1995; Lash and Urry 1987).

Why is deindustrialization happening? Some sociologists argue that the economies of First World nations are increasingly oriented toward the production and consumption of services such as education and recreation rather than manufactured goods; this orientation may account for the relative decline of the manufacturing sector. Others attribute deindustrialization to the globalization of the economy. As manufacturing firms develop the capacity to do business overseas, they can relocate factories to countries where labor costs are low.

Whatever its causes, the effects of deindustrialization are readily apparent. First, although many laid-off industrial workers eventually find employment elsewhere, they typically wind up in low-wage service sector jobs. Deindustrialization may make downward mobility a common experience for blue-collar workers, with serious implications for their economic and psychological well-being as well as for the welfare of their families. Second, deindustrialization affects some groups of

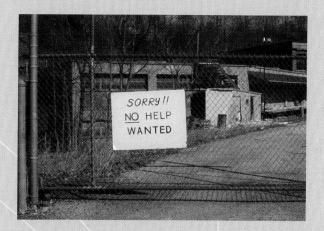

workers to a greater extent than others. Sociologist William Julius Wilson (1996), for example, argues that the decline in manufacturing jobs has had a particularly severe effect on African Americans, many of whom live in deindustrialized cities. The consequences of job loss for inner-city life are profound and include spiraling rates of poverty, crime, and drug use. Third, deindustrialization may undermine the strength of left-wing influence in political parties, inasmuch as the base of their working-class support narrows.

How serious has deindustrialization been in your community? If you were doing a study today like the one done by the Lynds in the 1920s, what aspects of social life would you expect to be affected by deindustrialization?

has been dramatically reduced. In addition, an increasing share of production is outsourced. Thus, the rapid transfer of information between manufacturers and suppliers—also facilitated by Internet technology—is essential to the successful implementation of mass customization.

GLOBAL PRODUCTION

Changes in industrial production include not only *how* products are manufactured, but, as we saw earlier with the example of an "American-made" car, *where* products are manufactured. For much of the twentieth century, the most important business organizations were large manufacturing firms that controlled both the making of goods and their final sales. Giant automobile companies such as Ford and General Motors typify this approach. Such companies employ tens of thousands of factory workers making everything from components to the final cars, which are then sold in the manufacturers' showrooms. Such manufacture-dominated production processes

are organized as large bureaucracies, often controlled by a single firm.

During the past quarter century, however, another form of production has become important—one that is controlled by giant retailers. In retailer-dominated production, firms such as Wal-Mart and Kmart buy products from manufacturers, who in turn arrange to have their products made by independently owned factories. Sociologists Edna Bonacich and Richard Appelbaum (2000), for example, show that in clothing manufacturing, most manufacturers actually employ no garment workers at all. Instead, they rely on thousands of factories around the world to make their apparel, which they then sell in department stores and other retail outlets. Clothing manufacturers do not own any of these factories and, therefore, are not responsible for the conditions under which the clothing is made.

Two thirds of all clothing sold in America is made in factories outside the United States, where workers are paid a fraction of U.S. wages. (In China, workers are lucky to make $40 a month.) Bonacich and Appelbaum argue that such competition has resulted in a global "race to the bottom," in which retailers and manufacturers will go anyplace on earth where they can pay the lowest wages possible. One result is that much of the clothing we buy today was likely made in sweatshops by young workers—most likely teenage girls—who get paid pennies for making clothing or athletic shoes that sell for $50, $100, or even more.

Trends in the Occupational Structure

The occupational structure in all industrialized countries has changed very substantially since the beginning of the twentieth century (Figure 14.3). In 1900, about three quarters of the employed population was in manual work, either farming or blue-collar work such as manufacturing. White-collar professional and service jobs were much fewer in number. By 1960, however, more people worked in white-collar professional and service jobs than in manual labor. By 1993, the occupational system had basically reversed its structure from 1900. Almost three quarters of the employed population worked in white-collar professional and service jobs, while the rest worked in blue-collar and farming jobs. In the period 2001–2004, the United States lost 2.6 million manufacturing jobs. By 2010, blue-collar work will have declined even further, with most of the increase in new jobs occurring in the service industries. As we saw in Chapter 10, over the course of the twentieth century, numerous women joined the paid labor force. In 1998, however, 42 percent of working women had service-based or clerical positions, while only 16 percent of men had these types of jobs. Likewise, 38 percent of men held blue-collar manual jobs, while only 10 percent of women were in such positions.

The reasons for the transformation of the occupational structure seem to be several. One is the continuous introduction of labor-saving machinery, culminating in the spread of information technology and computerization in industry in recent decades. Another is the rise of the manufacturing industry in other parts of the world, primarily Asia. The older industries in Western societies have experienced major job cutbacks because of their inability to compete with the more efficient Asian producers, whose labor costs are lower. As we have seen, this global economic transformation forced American companies to adopt new forms of production, which in turn forced employees to learn new skills and new occupations as manufacturing-related jobs moved to other countries. A final important trend is the decline of full-time paid employment with the same employer over a long period of time. Not only has the transformation of the global economy affected the

nature of day-to-day work but it has also changed the career patterns of many workers.

THE KNOWLEDGE ECONOMY

Taking these trends into account, some observers suggest that what is occurring today is a transition to a new type of society no longer based primarily on industrialism. We are entering,

---

FIGURE 14.3

The Changing Occupational Structure

The United States has lost a large number of manufacturing and other blue-collar jobs in the twentieth century. Many new professional/managerial and other white-collar jobs have been created. However, a large proportion entail work in the service industries, and although these can be classified as white-collar, they resemble blue-collar jobs in terms of pay.

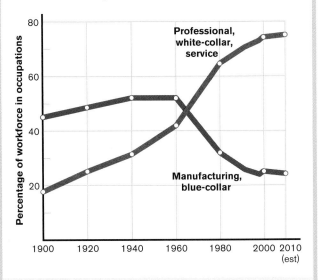

Until what year were manufacturing, blue-collar jobs a greater percentage of the workforce than professional, white-collar, and service jobs? In 1940, professional, white-collar, and service jobs made up what percentage of the workforce? During which twenty-year period did professional, white-collar, and service jobs increase the most? According to the reading, what is one of the reasons for the shift of the occupational structure?

SOURCE: U.S. Bureau of Labor Statistics 2000.

they claim, a phase of development beyond the industrial era altogether. A variety of terms have been coined to describe this new social order, such as the *postindustrial society*, the *information age*, and the *"new" economy*. The term that has come into most common usage, however, is the **knowledge economy.**

A precise definition of the knowledge economy is difficult to formulate, but in general terms, it refers to an economy in which ideas, information, and forms of knowledge underpin innovation and economic growth. In a knowledge economy, much of the workforce is involved not in the physical production or distribution of material goods, but in their design, development, technology, marketing, sale, and servicing. These employees can be termed "knowledge workers." The knowledge economy

is dominated by the constant flow of information and opinions and by the powerful potentials of science and technology.

How widespread is the knowledge economy at the start of the twenty-first century? A study by the Organization for Economic Cooperation and Development (1999) attempted to gauge the extent of the knowledge economy among developed nations by measuring the percentage of each country's overall business output that can be attributed to knowledge-based industries (Figure 14.4). Knowledge-based industries are understood broadly to include high technology, education and training, research and development, and the financial and investment sector. Among OECD countries as a whole, knowledge-based industries accounted for more than half of all

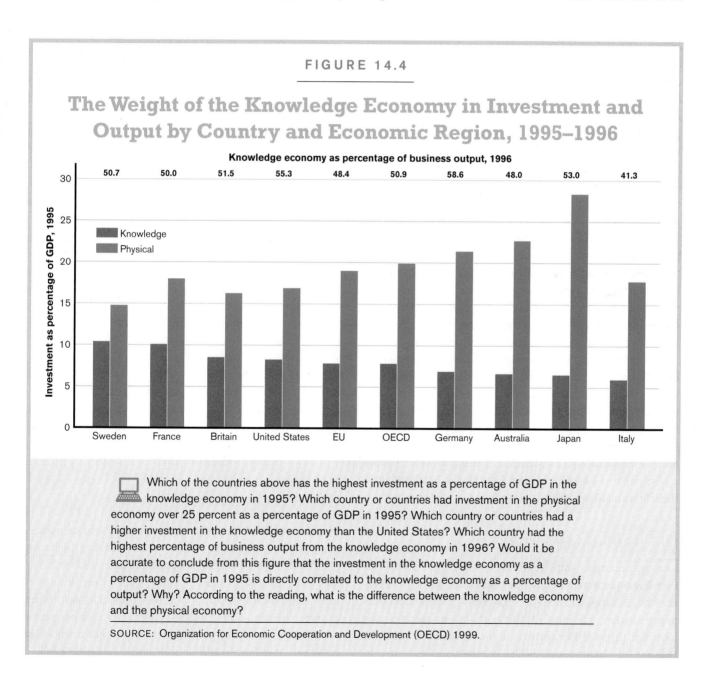

FIGURE 14.4

The Weight of the Knowledge Economy in Investment and Output by Country and Economic Region, 1995–1996

Knowledge economy as percentage of business output, 1996

Sweden	France	Britain	United States	EU	OECD	Germany	Australia	Japan	Italy
50.7	50.0	51.5	55.3	48.4	50.9	58.6	48.0	53.0	41.3

Legend: Knowledge / Physical

Investment as percentage of GDP, 1995

Which of the countries above has the highest investment as a percentage of GDP in the knowledge economy in 1995? Which country or countries had investment in the physical economy over 25 percent as a percentage of GDP in 1995? Which country or countries had a higher investment in the knowledge economy than the United States? Which country had the highest percentage of business output from the knowledge economy in 1996? Would it be accurate to conclude from this figure that the investment in the knowledge economy as a percentage of GDP in 1995 is directly correlated to the knowledge economy as a percentage of output? Why? According to the reading, what is the difference between the knowledge economy and the physical economy?

SOURCE: Organization for Economic Cooperation and Development (OECD) 1999.

business output in the mid-1990s. Germany had a high figure of 58.6 percent, and the United States, Japan, Britain, Sweden, and France were all at or over 50 percent.

Investments into the knowledge economy—in the form of public education, spending on software development, and research and development—now make up significant part of many countries' budgets. Sweden, for example, invested 10.6 percent of its overall gross domestic product in the knowledge economy in 1995. France was a close second because of its extensive spending on public education.

THE PORTFOLIO WORKER

In the light of the effect of the knowledge economy and the demand for a flexible labor force, some sociologists and economists have argued that more and more people in the future will become "portfolio workers." They will have a skill portfolio—a number of different job skills and credentials—that they will use to move between several jobs during the course of their working lives. Only a relatively small proportion of workers will have continuous careers in the current sense.

Some see this move to the **portfolio worker** in a positive light: Workers will not be stuck in the same job for years on end and will be able to plan their work lives in a creative way (Handy 1994). Others hold that flexibility in practice means that organizations can hire and fire more or less at will, undermining any sense of security their workers might have. Employers will have only a short-term commitment to their workforces and will be able to minimize the paying of extra benefits or pension rights.

A study of Silicon Valley, California, claims that the economic success of the area is already founded on the portfolio skills of its workforce. The failure rate of firms in Silicon Valley is very high: About three hundred new companies are established every year, but an equivalent number also go bust. The workforce, which has a high proportion of professional and technical workers, has learned to adjust to this. The result, the authors say, is that talents and skills migrate rapidly from one firm to another, becoming more adaptable on the way. Technical specialists become consultants, consultants become managers, employees become venture capitalists—and back again (Bahrami and Evans 1995).

THE CONTINGENT WORKFORCE

Another important employment trend of the past decade has been the replacement of full-time workers by part-time workers who are hired and fired on a contingency basis. Most temporary workers are hired for the least-skilled, lowest-paying jobs. But many of the portfolio workers whom we just discussed take jobs on a part-time basis as well. As a general rule,

part-time jobs do not include the benefits associated with full-time work, such as medical insurance, paid vacation time, or retirement benefits. Because employers can save on the costs of wages and benefits, the use of part-time workers has become increasingly common. Researchers estimate that contingency workers make up approximately 4 percent of the American workforce, or about 5.7 million people (U.S. Bureau of Labor Statistics 2005).

The temporary employment agency Manpower, Inc., founded in Milwaukee, Wisconsin, in 1948, has become a global leader in the provision of temporary workers. This company employed 2.5 million temps in seventy-two countries in 2005 and was the 140th largest corporation in the United States and 412th on *Fortune* list of the Global 500 (Manpower, Inc. 2006). Manpower provides labor on a flexible basis to 98 percent of *Fortune* 500 companies. Clearly, temporary labor has become a critical component of the worldwide organization of work and occupations.

There has been some debate over the psychological effects of part-time work on the workforce. Many temporary workers fulfill their assignments in a prompt and satisfactory manner, but others rebel against their tenuous positions by shirking their responsibilities or sabotaging their results. Some temporary workers have been observed trying to "look busy" or to work longer than necessary on rather simple tasks. Finally, contingency workers have tried to avoid emotionally intensive work that would require them to become psychologically committed to their employer.

However, some recent surveys of work indicate that part-time workers register higher levels of job satisfaction than those in full-time employment. This may be because most part-time workers are women, who have lower expectations for their careers than men or who are particularly relieved to escape from the monotony of domestic work. Yet many individuals seem to find reward precisely in the fact that they are able to balance paid work with other activities and enjoy a more varied life. Some people might choose to "peak" their lives, giving full commitment to paid work from their youth to their middle years, then perhaps changing to a second career, which would open up new interests.

Unemployment

The idea of work is actually a complex one. All of us work in many ways besides in paid employment. Cleaning the house, planting a garden, and going shopping are plainly all work. But for two centuries or more, Western society has been built around the central importance of paid work. The experience of unemployment—being unable to find a job when one wants it—is still a largely negative one. And unemployment does bring with it unfortunate effects including, sometimes, falling into poverty. Yet as we shall see, some today are arguing that we should think about the relation between being "in work" and "out of work" in a completely different way from the way we did in the recent past.

Rates of unemployment fluctuated considerably over the course of the twentieth century. In Western countries, unemployment reached a peak in the early 1930s, when some 20 percent of the workforce was out of work in the United States. Economist John Maynard Keynes, who strongly influenced public policy in Europe and the United States during the post–World War II period, believed that unemployment results from consumers' lacking sufficient resources to buy goods. Governments can intervene to increase the level of demand in an economy, leading to the creation of new jobs; and the newly employed then have the income with which to buy more goods, thus creating yet more jobs for people who produce them. State management of economic life, most people came to believe, meant that high rates of unemployment belonged to the past. Commitment to full employment became part of government policy in virtually all Western societies. Until the 1970s, these policies seemed successful, and economic growth was more or less continuous.

During the 1970s and 1980s, however, Keynesianism was largely abandoned. In the face of economic globalization, governments lost the capability to control economic life as they once did. One consequence was that unemployment rates shot up in many countries.

Several factors probably explain the increase in unemployment levels in Western countries at that time. One was the rise of international competition in industries on which Western prosperity used to be founded. In 1947, 60 percent of steel production in the world was carried out in the United States. Today, the figure is only about 9.4 percent, whereas steel production has risen by 300 percent in Japan, Singapore, Taiwan, and Hong Kong (Worldsteel.org 2005). A second factor was the worldwide economic recession of the late 1980s, which has still not fully abated. A third reason was the increasing use of microelectronics in industry, the net effect of which has been to reduce the need for labor power. Finally, beginning in the 1970s more women sought paid employment, meaning that more people were chasing a limited number of available jobs.

During this time, rates of unemployment tended to be lower in the United States, for example, than in some European nations. This is perhaps because the sheer economic strength of the country gives it more power in world markets than smaller, more fragile economies. Alternatively, it may be that the exceptionally large service sector in the United States provides a greater source of new jobs than in countries where more of the population has traditionally been employed in manufacturing. And within countries, unemployment is not equally distrib-

uted. It varies by race or ethnic background, by age, and by industry and geographic region (Figure 14.5). Ethnic minorities living in central cities in the United States have much higher rates of long-term unemployment than the rest of the population. A substantial proportion of young people are among the long-term unemployed, again especially among minority groups.

The Future of Work

Since the mid-1980s, in all the industrialized countries except the United States, the average length of the working week has become shorter. Workers still undertake long stretches of overtime, but some governments are beginning to introduce new limits on permissible working hours. In France, for example, annual overtime is restricted to a maximum of 130 hours a year. In most countries, there is a general tendency toward shortening the average working career. More people would probably quit the labor force at sixty or earlier if they could afford to do so.

If the amount of time given over to paid employment continues to shrink, and the need to have a job becomes less central, the nature of working careers might become substantially reorganized. Job sharing or flexible working hours, which arose primarily as a result of the increasing numbers of working parents trying to balance the commitments of workplace and family, for example, might become more common. Some work analysts have suggested that sabbaticals of the university type should be extended to workers in other spheres: People would be entitled to take a year off to study or pursue some form of self-improvement. Perhaps more individuals will engage in life planning, in which they arrange to work in different ways (paid, unpaid, full or part time, etc.) at different stages in their lives. Thus some people might choose to enter the labor force in their late thirties, having followed a period of formal education in their early twenties with time devoted to pursuits like travel. People might *opt* to work part time throughout their lives, rather than being forced to because of a lack of full-time employment opportunities.

French sociologist André Gorz (1982) has argued that in the future paid work will play a less and less important part in people's lives. Gorz bases his views on a critical assessment of Marx's writings. Marx believed that the working class—to which more and more people would supposedly belong—would lead a revolution that would bring about a more humane type of society, in which work would be central to the satisfactions life has to offer. Although writing as a leftist, Gorz rejects this view. Rather than the working class becoming the largest grouping in society (as Marx suggested) and leading a successful revolution, it is actually shrinking. Blue-collar workers have

Layoffs and Downsizing

When the last worker passed through the doors of White Furniture Company in May of 1993, hardly anyone beyond the city limits of Mebane, North Carolina, noticed. In national terms, it made little difference that 203 men and women were out of work or that a venerable, family-owned firm (the "South's oldest maker of fine furniture") had been sold to a conglomerate and now was being shut down. After all, what happened to White's is hardly unique. In the 1990s, in every walk of life and on all social levels, Americans have had to learn a new vocabulary of economic anxiety—layoff, outsourcing, buyout, offshoring, downsizing, closing. The statistics are mind-numbing: 70,000 people laid off from General Motors in 1991; 50,000 workers from Sears and 63,000 from IBM in 1993; 40,000 from AT&T in 1996. In these times, why should we care about the closing of one furniture factory in a small southern town?

There are many reasons to care, not least that the story of White Furniture Company is a study in miniature of work—what it means when you have it, what it means when you don't. Behind the grim headlines are real men and women who, like the White workers, are devastated not just by the lack of income but by the end of a way of life based on doing a job and doing it well. The wages at White Furniture may have been low; the equipment was antiquated and the working conditions

harsh—incessant noise, fumes pervading the air, the factory building cold in winter and sweltering in summer. Yet, looking back, White's workers mourn the closing of the plant and, mostly, they mourn the loss of their craft and their companions. Factory work—industrialization—had a high price tag. Now we are seeing, everywhere around us and on every social level, the dire cost of post-industrialism.

A closing doesn't happen in the melodramatic way one might expect: a door slamming shut and two hundred people out in the cold. It happens in bits and pieces, one worker at a time. At White's there was a grim logic to the layoffs. They followed production. The last piece of furniture came down the line, was worked on, and then the line closed down behind it, and the workers in that section would be let go. A few workers made one last walk-through of the plant, saying good-bye to their friends, but most just left.

The layoffs started in the kiln area where the lumber was brought in to the yard. After the lumber ran through the saws in the rough mill, those people would be let go. After the wood was glued together, the workers on the glue machine left. The piece was machined, and the next day the machine room was empty. The last piece of furniture was sanded, assembled, and then finished, with workers from each department leaving in turn. Finally, the piece went to rub and pack, where it was prepared for shipping and then boxed. The last piece on the line was ready to be sent away. And so were the last workers. You finished your job. You were called away from your department an hour or so before closing time. You sat in the personnel room and signed some papers. The personnel officer shook your hand. And then it was over.

There's a reason for laying off people in this way: it is the best way to ensure that a plant shutdown will be orderly, economical, and efficient. Yet, as many industrial psychologists have noted, people who leave their jobs like this typically feel despair, isolation, and shame. They feel oppressed by the enormity of what lies ahead for them, at the mercy of forces beyond their control. There is little sense of solidarity with other workers, either those who have gone before or those who will be laid off in the future. There is no opportunity for collective anger or organized protest. No one knows who is being laid off, when, how many, or who will be next.

***

Despite the fact that other companies paid better, workers stayed at White's out of some combination of job satisfaction,

friendship, loyalty, desire for security, and personal pride of craft. To use a formulation that is typically reserved for middle-class rather than for blue-collar workers, they chose to stay at White's because it was a career, not just a job. White's wasn't perfect, and none of the workers says it was. Yet metaphors of death run through the comments so many of the workers make about the closing precisely because people felt that something of themselves died when White Furniture closed.

***

[James Gilland worked at White Furniture Company from 1951 until 1992.] When you ask him about his job at White's, he answers with his philosophy of work: "Changing jobs is one of the worst things that anybody can do today as a young person. The best thing to do is to start looking when you're young and find a job that you're really interested in, one that you like, that you think you can work with. It's just like getting married. Somebody that you think you can live with the rest of your life. A job is the same way."

SOURCE: Bill Bamberger and Cathy N. Davidson, *Closing: The Life and Death of an American Factory* (New York: DoubleTake/W. W. Norton, 1998), pp. 17, 41, 72, 168.

Questions

- How is James Gilland's view of job loyalty outdated? How could it be revised to fit current hiring and firing patterns?
- Judging from the photographs, what do the impending layoffs and closing of the factory mean to the workers?
- Company buyouts and layoffs are more and more prevalent. Under these uncertain conditions, what can boost workers' morale and inspire pride in their work?

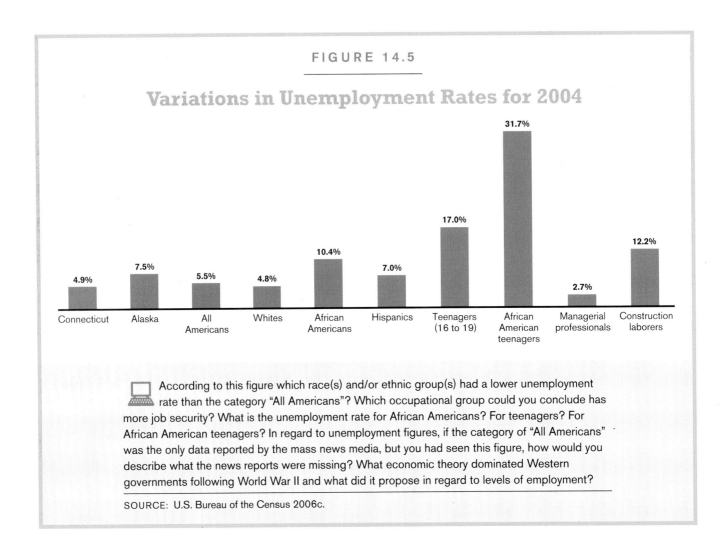

FIGURE 14.5

Variations in Unemployment Rates for 2004

Connecticut 4.9%
Alaska 7.5%
All Americans 5.5%
Whites 4.8%
African Americans 10.4%
Hispanics 7.0%
Teenagers (16 to 19) 17.0%
African American teenagers 31.7%
Managerial professionals 2.7%
Construction laborers 12.2%

According to this figure which race(s) and/or ethnic group(s) had a lower unemployment rate than the category "All Americans"? Which occupational group could you conclude has more job security? What is the unemployment rate for African Americans? For teenagers? For African American teenagers? In regard to unemployment figures, if the category of "All Americans" was the only data reported by the mass news media, but you had seen this figure, how would you describe what the news reports were missing? What economic theory dominated Western governments following World War II and what did it propose in regard to levels of employment?

SOURCE: U.S. Bureau of the Census 2006c.

now become a minority—and a declining minority—of the labor force.

It no longer makes much sense, in Gorz's view, to suppose that workers can take over the enterprises of which they are a part, let alone seize state power. There is no real hope of transforming the nature of paid work, because it is organized according to technical considerations that are unavoidable if an economy is to be efficient. "The point now," as Gorz (1982) puts it, "is to free oneself *from* work. . . ." This is particularly necessary where work is organized along Taylorist lines or is otherwise oppressive or dull.

Rising unemployment, together with the spread of part-time work, Gorz argues, has already created what he calls a "non-class of nonworkers," alongside those in stable employment. Most people, in fact, are in this non-class, because the proportion of the population in stable paid jobs at any one time is relatively small—if we exclude the young, the retired, the ill, and homemakers, together with people who are in part-time work or unemployed. The spread of microtechnology, Gorz believes, will further reduce the numbers of full-time jobs available. The

result is likely to be a swing toward rejecting the "productivist" outlook of Western society, with its emphasis on wealth, economic growth, and material goods. A diversity of lifestyles, followed outside the sphere of permanent, paid work, will be pursued by the majority of the population in coming years.

According to Gorz, we are moving toward a "dual society." In one sector, production and political administration will be organized to maximize efficiency. The other sector will be a sphere in which individuals occupy themselves with a variety of nonwork pursuits offering enjoyment or personal fulfillment.

How likely is all this to happen? It does seem possible that more and more people will become disenchanted with productivism—the stress on constant economic growth and the accumulation of material possessions. It is surely valuable to see unemployment not entirely in a negative light, but as offering opportunities for individuals to pursue their interests and develop their talents.

The nature of the work most people do and the role of work in our lives, like so many other aspects of the societies in which we live, are undergoing major changes. The chief reasons are global economic competition, the widespread introduction of information technology and computerization, and the large-scale entry of women into the work force.

How will work change in the future? It appears very likely that people will take a more active look at their lives than in the past, moving in and out of paid work at different points. These are only positive options, however, when they are deliberately chosen. The reality for most is that regular paid work remains the key to day-to-day survival and that unemployment is experienced as a hardship rather than an opportunity.

Study Outline

www.wwnorton.com/giddens

The Social Significance of Work

- *Work* is the carrying out of tasks that involve the expenditure of mental and physical effort and has as its objective the production of goods and services catering to human needs. An *occupation* is work that is done in exchange for a regular wage. In all cultures work is the basis of the *economy*.
- A distinctive characteristic of the economic system of modern societies is the development of a highly complex and diverse *division of labor*. The division of labor means that work is divided into different occupations requiring specialization. One result is *economic interdependence:* We are all dependent on each other to maintain our livelihoods.

Taylorism and Fordism

- One manifestation of this division is *Taylorism*, or scientific management. Taylorism divides work into simple tasks that can be timed and organized. *Fordism* extended the principles of scientific management to mass production tied to mass markets. Fordism and Taylorism can be seen as *low-trust systems* that maximize worker alienation. A *high-trust system* allows workers control over the pace and even content of their work.

Organizations and Economic Life

- Union organizations, together with recognition of the right to *strike*, are characteristic features of economic life in all Western countries. Unions emerged as defensive organizations, concerned to provide a measure of control for workers over their conditions of labor. Today, union leaders quite often play an important role in formulating national economic policies.
- The modern economy is dominated by large *corporations*. When one firm has a commanding influence in a given industry, it is in a *monopoly* position. When a cluster of firms wields such influence, a situation of *oligopoly* exists. Through their influence on government policy and on the consumption of goods, the giant corporations have a profound effect on people's lives.

Transnational Corporations

- Corporations have undergone profound transformations in recent years because of increasing world interdependence, or globalization. The modern corporation is increasingly an enterprise web of many smaller firms linked together, rather than a single big business.
- *Multinational* or *transnational corporations* operate across different national boundaries. The largest of them exercise tremendous economic power. Half of the one hundred largest economic units are not countries, but privately owned companies.

Automation and Group Production

- In recent years, computer-aided design and planning tools have provided the capability to develop *flexible production* systems. *Automation* involves the use of robots in the production process. *Group production*, often used with automation, establishes collaborative work groups such as the *quality circle*, in which workers actively participate in the design and implementation of production methods.

Work and Social Change

- Major changes have occurred in the occupational system during the course of the century. Particularly important has been the relative increase in non-manual occupations at the expense of manual ones. The interpretation of these changes, however, is disputed. Some speak of the arrival of the *portfolio worker*—the worker who has a portfolio of different skills and will be able to move readily from job to job. Such workers do exist, but for many people in the workforce flexibility is more likely to be associated with poorly paid jobs with few career prospects.
- Unemployment was a recurrent problem in the industrialized countries in the twentieth century. As work is a structuring element in a person's psychological makeup, the experience of unemployment is often disorienting. The effect of new technology seems likely to further increase unemployment rates.

- Major changes are currently occurring in the nature and organization of work. It seems certain that these will become even more important in the future. Nonetheless, work remains for many people the key basis of generating resources necessary to sustain a varied life.

Key Concepts

alienation (p. 441)
automation (p. 453)
capitalism (p. 447)
corporations (p. 447)
division of labor (p. 439)
economic interdependence (p. 440)
economy (p. 438)
entrepreneur (p. 447)
ethnocentric transnationals (p. 450)
family capitalism (p. 448)
flexible production (p. 455)
Fordism (p. 440)
geocentric transnationals (p. 450)
group production (p. 455)
high-trust system (p. 441)
informal economy (p. 439)
institutional capitalism (p. 449)
international division of labor (p. 450)
knowledge economy (p. 459)
low-trust systems (p. 441)
managerial capitalism (p. 448)
monopoly (p. 447)
multinational corporations (p. 449)
occupation (p. 438)
oligopoly (p. 447)
polycentric transnationals (p. 450)
post-Fordism (p. 454)
portfolio worker (p. 460)
quality circles (QCs) (p. 455)
strike (p. 442)
Taylorism (p. 440)
technology (p. 438)
transnational corporations (p. 449)
union density (p. 442)
welfare capitalism (p. 448)
work (p. 438)

Review Questions

1. What is the overwhelming finding of Freeman and Rogers's study on "what workers want"?

a. They want more vacation time.
b. They want more pay.
c. They want more influence.
d. They want fewer working hours.

2. From a sociological perspective, women who are housewives
a. don't have a job.
b. want a job.
c. do *work*, although they are not part of the paid labor force.
d. None of the above.

3. What is the informal economy?
a. It refers to domestic labor within the home.
b. It refers to transactions outside the sphere of regular employment, sometimes involving the exchange of cash for services provided, but also often involving the direct exchange of goods and services.
c. It refers to transactions between small businesses.
d. It refers to the economy in traditional societies.

4. What is the difference between high-trust and low-trust systems of production?
a. Low-trust systems, such as Taylorism and Fordism, are found in manufacturing and impose tough work regimes on workers. High-trust systems allow workers flexibility and autonomy in the way they perform their jobs.
b. Low-trust systems, which feature short-term contracts and high labor turnover, are more often found in the United States, whereas high-trust systems, which feature long-term contracts and low labor turnover, are more often found in Japan.
c. Low-trust systems are found in the employment of less-educated workers, whereas high-trust systems are found in the employment of better-educated workers.
d. In low-trust systems, most commonly found in large-scale public bureaucracies, workers and management are suspicious and resentful of one another. In high-trust systems, most commonly found in large corporations, workers and management have learned to cooperate and see that they are basically on the same side.

5. Which of the following types of transnational corporations has managerial systems integrated on a global basis?
a. ethnocentric
b. exocentric
c. geocentric
d. polycentric

6. What is Fordism?
a. The type of large corporation that manufactures and distributes its goods around the world.
b. The system of flexible production that allows goods to be customized on the assembly line.
c. The system of assembly-line mass production for mass-market consumption.
d. The type of credit plans Ford developed that allow consumers to pay back car loans at low monthly payments over a period of years.

7. What is the definition of a strike?
a. A spontaneous stoppage of work by a group of employees to

show their employers how angry they are at the company's actions.

   b. A temporary stoppage of work by a group of employees in order to express a grievance or enforce a demand.

   c. The culmination of a series of industrial actions that usually begin with increased absenteeism, which includes a slowdown and may involve a lockout.

   d. All of the above.

8. The decline in unionization can be attributed to

   a. the recession in world economic activity.

   b. the increasing intensity of international competition.

   c. the rise to power in many countries of rightist governments that launched an aggressive assault on unions in the 1980s.

   d. All of the above.

9. What is a portfolio worker?

   a. An artist or a graphic designer who brings a folder full of samples of work to job interviews

   b. A worker with a skill portfolio—a number of different job skills and credentials—that he or she will use to move between several different jobs during the course of a career

   c. A computer expert who specializes in a particular set of software applications

   d. An investment consultant who advises people on their retirement plans

10. The majority of the robots used in industry worldwide are to be found in

   a. computer production.

   b. electronic production.

   c. automobile production.

   d. furniture production.

Thinking Sociologically Exercises

1. Explain the meaning of globalization of the modern economy. Explain how this textbook sees globalization affecting workers in Third World countries and in advanced industrial societies.

2. Discuss some of the important ways that the nature of work will change for the contemporary worker as companies apply more automation and larger-scale production processes and as oligopolies become more pervasive. Explain each of these trends and how they affect workers, both now and in the future.

Data Exercises

www.wwnorton.com/giddens
Keyword: Data14

Approximately how many hours do you work each week? In what ways does the kind of job or even a worker's sex affect the number of hours worked? You may think that these social factors have nothing to do with structuring the workweek, but after completing the data exercise for this chapter you may be surprised by what you learn.

Theoretical Perspectives on the Family

Review the development of sociological thinking about the family and family life.

The Family in History

Learn how the family has changed over the last five hundred years.

Changes in Family Patterns Worldwide

See that although a diversity of family forms exist in different societies today, widespread changes are occurring that relate to the spread of globalization.

Marriage and the Family in the United States

Learn about patterns of marriage, childbearing, and divorce. Analyze how different these patterns are today compared with other periods.

The Dark Side of the Family

Learn about sexual abuse and violence within families.

Alternatives to Traditional Forms of Marriage and the Family

Learn some alternatives to traditional marriage and family patterns that are becoming more widespread.

CHAPTER FIFTEEN

FAMILIES AND INTIMATE RELATIONSHIPS

is the American family in a state of crisis? Or are family arrangements simply changing to keep pace with rapid economic, technological, and social changes in the United States? Sociologists David Popenoe and Judith Stacey offer very different perspectives on the future of the family. Popenoe (1993, 1996), a Rutgers University professor, argues that the family has changed for the worse since 1960. Since then, divorce, nonmarital births, and cohabitation rates have increased, while marriage and marital fertility rates have decreased. These trends, taken together, are at the root of countless social ills, including child poverty, adolescent pregnancy, substance abuse, and juvenile crime. Increasing rates of divorce and nonmarital births have created millions of female-headed households and have consequently removed men from the child-rearing process. Popenoe argues that this is harmful for children.

Stacey (1990, 1993, 1996), a professor at New York University, counters that the traditional American family of the 1950s—praised by Popenoe and conservative politicians as the panacea for all social problems—is a dated and oppressive institution. According to Stacey, the "breadwinner-father and child-rearing-mother" family, defined by Stacey as the "modern family," perpetuated the "segregation of the sexes by extracting men from, and consigning white married women to, an increasingly privatized domestic domain." The modern family has been replaced by many new family forms. These new forms, which Stacey has named the "postmodern family," include single mothers, blended families, cohabiting couples, lesbian and gay partners, communes, and two-worker families. The postmodern family is not inferior to the traditional two-parent family. To the contrary, it is well suited to meet the challenges of the current economy and is an appropriate setting for raising children: Children need capable, loving caretakers—regardless of their gender, marital status, or sexual orientation, argues Stacey.

Popenoe agrees with Stacey's claim that children need capable, loving caretakers, yet maintains that "on the whole, two parents—a father and a mother—are better for a child than one parent." Why? Popenoe claims that biological fathers make "distinctive, irreplaceable contributions" to their children's welfare. Fathers offer a strong male role model to sons, they play the role of disciplinarian for trouble-prone children, they provide their daughters with a male perspective on heterosexual relationships, and, through their unique play styles, they teach their children about teamwork, competition, independence, self-fulfillment, self-control, and regulation of one's emotions. Mothers, alternatively, teach their children about communion, or the feeling of being connected to others. Both needs must be met and can be achieved only through the gender-differentiated parenting of a mother and father, argues Popenoe.

Stacey retorts that the postmodern family is better suited to meet the challenges of the current postmodern economy. In the postmodern economy, employment has shifted from heavy industries to nonunionized clerical, service, and new industrial sectors. The loss of union-protected jobs means that men no longer earn enough to support a wife and children. At the same time, demand for clerical and service labor, escalating consumption standards, increases in women's educational attainment, and the persistence of high divorce rates has given more and more women reason to seek paid employment outside the home.

Stacey also takes issue with media rhetoric and claims by conservatives such as Popenoe, who elevate the married, two-parent family as the ideal family form. Their condemnation of other family forms is particularly harmful to the millions of children who live with gay or lesbian parents. Rather than condemning nontraditional family forms, Stacey reasons that family sociologists and policy makers should instead develop strategies to mitigate the harmful effects of divorce and single parenthood on children. She suggests that restructuring work schedules and benefit policies to accommodate familial responsibilities; redistributing work opportunities to reduce unemployment rates; enacting comparable-worth standards of pay equity to enable women as well as men to earn a family wage; providing universal health, prenatal, and child care, and sex education; and rectifying the economic inequities of divorce would be much more admirable efforts. These child-friendly efforts, she argues, are truly "pro-family."

Popenoe's policy recommendations are based on the claim that "marriage must be reestablished as a strong social institution." How? He argues that employers should reduce the practice of relocating married couples with children and should provide more generous parental leave. He also supports a two-tiered system of divorce law. Marriages without minor children would be relatively easy to dissolve, but marriages with young children would be dissolvable only by mutual agreement or on grounds that clearly involve a wrong by one party against the other. The proposal has been met by skepticism among feminist scholars who offer a perspective on the costs for kids and adults alike of reinstating grounds of fault for divorce.

The changes affecting the personal and emotional spheres go far beyond the borders of any particular country, even one as large as the United States. We find the same issues almost everywhere, differing only in degree and according to the cultural context in which they take place. In 2001, China, for example, made divorce more difficult to obtain and increased penalties for domestic abuse, bigamy, infidelity, and extramarital cohabitation. At the same time, the new laws better protect the privacy rights of couples wishing to divorce by no longer requiring the approval of their employers (China.org.cn 2001). In the late 1960s, very liberal marriage laws were passed. Marriage is a working contract that can be dissolved "when husband and wife both desire it." Even if one partner objects, divorce could be granted when "mutual affection" has gone from the marriage. Only a two-week wait is required, after which the couple pays $4 and are henceforth independent. The Chinese divorce rate is still low compared with that in Western countries; but it is rising rapidly, as is true in the other developing Asian societies. Despite the reforms, between 2003 and 2004 the number of divorces in China rose by over 21 percent to 1.6 million (Beach 2005). In Chinese cities, both divorce and cohabitation are becoming more frequent, a trend that the divorce law reforms were intended to counter. In the vast Chinese countryside, by contrast, everything is different. Marriage and the family are much more traditional—in spite of the official policy of limiting childbirth through a mixture of incentives and punishment. Marriage is an arrangement between two families, fixed by the parents rather than the individuals concerned. A recent study in the province of Gansu, which has only a low level of economic development, found that 60 percent of marriages are still arranged by parents. As a Chinese saying has it: "Meet once, nod your head and marry." There is a twist in the story in modernizing China. Many of those currently divorcing in the urban centers were married in the traditional manner in the country.

In China, there is much talk of protecting the "traditional" family. In many Western countries, the debate is even more intense and divisive. Defenders of the traditional family form argue that the emphasis on relationships comes at the expense of the family as a basic institution of society. Many of these critics now speak of the breakdown of the family. If such a break-

An extended family gathers for a photograph in Zimbabwe.

down is occurring, it is extremely significant. The family is the meeting point of a range of trends affecting society as a whole—increasing equality between the sexes, the widespread entry of women into the labor force, changes in sexual behavior and expectations, the changing relationship between home and work. Among all the changes going on today, none is more important than those happening in our personal lives—in sexuality, emotional life, marriage, and the family. There is a global revolution going on in how we think of ourselves and how we form ties and connections with others. It is a revolution advancing unevenly in different parts of the world, with much resistance.

Like much of sociology, studies of marriage and the family in the United States encompass a range of scholarship. Some researchers, such as Stacey and Popenoe, draw on their own and others' research to advocate for political, social, and/or economic change—albeit from different perspectives. But a vast majority of researchers restrict themselves to doing descriptive or scientific work that tries to solve some of the most interesting puzzles about marriage and family in the contemporary world. Much of this research is also quite fascinating, and demonstrates that sociology can give us insights that are by no means obvious. It's possible to understand what is going on in our personal lives and the family as a social institution today only if we know something about how people lived in the past and how people currently live in other societies. So in this chapter, after discussing several theoretical perspectives on the family, we look at the development of marriage and the family in earlier times, before analyzing the consequences of present-day changes both in the United States and elsewhere.

Basic Concepts

In light of the debates over the changing nature of families, let's define some basic concepts, particularly those of family, kin-

ship, and marriage. A **family** is a group of people directly linked by kin connections, the adult members of which assume responsibility for caring for children. **Kinship** ties are connections among individuals, established either through marriage or through the lines of descent that connect blood relatives (mothers, fathers, offspring, grandparents, etc.). **Marriage** can be defined as a socially acknowledged and approved sexual union between two adult individuals. When two people marry, they become kin to one another; the marriage bond also, however, connects together a wider range of kinspeople. Parents, brothers, sisters, and other blood relatives become relatives of the partner through marriage.

Family relationships are always recognized within wider kinship groups. In virtually all societies, we can identify what sociologists and anthropologists call the **nuclear family,** two adults living together in a household with their own or adopted children. In most traditional societies, the nuclear family was part of a larger kinship network of some type. When close relatives in addition to a married couple and children live either in the same household or in a close and continuous relationship with one another, we speak of an **extended family.** An extended family may include grandparents, brothers and their wives, sisters and their husbands, aunts, and nephews.

Whether nuclear or extended, so far as the experience of each individual is concerned, families can be divided into **families of orientation** and **families of procreation.** The first is the family into which a person is born; the second is the family into which one enters as an adult and within which a new generation of children is brought up. A further important distinction concerns place of residence. In the United States, when a couple marry, they are usually expected to set up a separate household. This can be in the same area in which the bride's or groom's parents live, but may be in some different town or city altogether. In some other societies, however, everyone who marries is expected to live close to or within the same dwelling as the parents of the bride or groom. When the couple live near or with the bride's parents, the arrangement is called **matrilocal.** In a **patrilocal** pattern, the couple live near or with the parents of the groom.

In Western societies, marriage, and therefore the family, is associated with **monogamy.** It is illegal for a man or woman to be married to more than one individual at any one time. But monogamy is not the most common type of marriage in the world as a whole. In a comparison of several hundred twentieth-century societies, George Murdock (1949) found that **polygamy,** a marriage that allows a husband or wife to have more than one spouse, was permitted in over 80 percent. There are two types of polygamy: **polygyny,** in which a man may be married to more than one woman at the same time, and **polyandry,** much less common, in which a woman may have two or more husbands simultaneously.

Theoretical Perspectives on the Family

The study of the family and family life has been taken up differently by sociologists with contrasting approaches. Many of the perspectives adopted even a few decades ago now seem much less convincing in the light of recent research and important changes in the social world. Nevertheless it is valuable to trace briefly the evolution of sociological thinking before turning to contemporary approaches to the study of the family.

Functionalism

The functionalist perspective sees society as a set of social institutions that perform specific functions to ensure continuity and consensus. According to this perspective, the family performs important tasks that contribute to society's basic needs and helps perpetuate social order. Sociologists working in the functionalist tradition have regarded the nuclear family as fulfilling certain specialized roles in modern societies. With the advent of industrialization, the family became less important as a unit of economic production and more focused on reproduction, child rearing, and socialization.

According to American sociologist Talcott Parsons, the family's two main functions are *primary socialization* and *personality stabilization* (Parsons and Bales 1955). **Primary socialization** is the process by which children learn the cultural norms of the society into which they are born. Because this happens during the early years of childhood, the family is the most important area for the development of the human personality. **Personality stabilization** refers to the role that the family plays in assisting adult family members emotionally. Marriage between adult men and women is the arrangement through which adult personalities are supported and kept healthy. In industrial society, the role of the family in stabilizing adult personalities is said to be critical. This is because the nuclear family is often distanced from its extended kin and is unable to draw on larger kinship ties as families could prior to industrialization.

Parsons regarded the nuclear family as the unit best equipped to handle the demands of industrial society. In the "conventional" family, one adult can work outside the home while the second adult cares for the home and children. In practical terms, this specialization of roles within the nuclear family involved the husband adopting the "instrumental" role as breadwinner and the wife assuming the "affective," emotional role in domestic settings.

In our present age, Parsons's view of the family comes across as inadequate and outdated. Functionalist theories of the family have come under heavy criticism for justifying the domestic division of labor between men and women as something natural and unproblematic. Yet viewed in their own historical context, the theories are somewhat more understandable. The immediate post–World War II years saw women returning to their traditional domestic roles and men reassuming positions as sole breadwinners. We can criticize functionalist views of the family on other grounds, however. In emphasizing the importance of the family in performing certain functions, both theorists neglect the role that other social institutions—such as government, media, and schools—play in socializing children. The theories also neglect variations in family forms that do not correspond to the model of the nuclear family. Families that did not conform to the white, suburban, middle-class ideal were seen as deviant.

Feminist Approaches

For many people, the family provides a vital source of solace and comfort, love and companionship. Yet it can also be a locus for exploitation, loneliness, and profound inequality. Feminism has had a great effect on sociology by challenging the vision of the family as a harmonious and egalitarian realm. In 1965, one of the first dissenting voices was that of the American feminist Betty Friedan, who wrote of "the problem with no name"—the isolation and boredom that gripped many suburban American housewives who felt relegated to an endless cycle of child care and housework. Others followed, exploring the phenomenon of the "captive wife" (Gavron 1966) and the damaging effects of "suffocating" family settings on interpersonal relationships (Laing 1971).

During the 1970s and 1980s, feminist perspectives dominated most debates and research on the family. If previously the sociology of the family had focused on family structures, the historical development of the nuclear and extended family, and the importance of kinship ties, feminism succeeded in directing attention inside families to examine the experiences of women in the domestic sphere. Many feminist writers have questioned the vision of the family as a cooperative unit based on common interests and mutual support. They have sought to show that the presence of unequal power relationships within the family means that certain family members tend to benefit more than others.

Feminist writings have emphasized a broad spectrum of topics, but three main themes are of particular importance. One of the central concerns is the *domestic division of labor—*the way in which tasks are allocated among members of a household. Among feminists, there are differing opinions about the historical emergence of this division. While some feminists see it as an outcome of industrial capitalism, others claim that it is linked to patriarchy and thus predates industrialization. There is reason to believe that a domestic division of labor existed before industrialization, but it seems clear that capitalist production brought about a much sharper distinction between the domestic and work realms. This process resulted in the crystallization of "male spheres" and "female spheres" and power relationships that are felt to this day. Until recently, the *male breadwinner* model has been widespread in most industrialized societies.

Feminist sociologists have undertaken studies on the way domestic tasks, such as child care and housework, are shared between men and women. They have investigated the validity of claims such as that of the "symmetrical family" (Young and Willmott 1973)—the belief that, over time, families are becoming more egalitarian in the distribution of roles and responsibilities. Findings have shown that women continue to bear the main responsibility for domestic tasks and enjoy less leisure time than men, despite the fact that more women are working in paid employment outside the home than ever before (Gershuny et al. 1994; Hochschild 1989; Sullivan 1997). Pursuing a related theme, some sociologists have examined the contrasting realms of paid and unpaid work, focusing on the contribution that women's unpaid domestic labor makes to the overall economy (Oakley 1974). Others have investigated the way in which resources are distributed among family members and the patterns of access to and control over household finances (Pahl 1989).

Second, feminists have drawn attention to the *unequal power relationships* that exist within many families. One topic that has received increased attention as a result of this is the phenomenon of domestic violence. Wife battering, marital rape, incest, and the sexual abuse of children have all received more public attention as a result of feminists' claims that the violent and abusive sides of family life have long been ignored in both academic contexts and legal and policy circles. Feminist sociologists have sought to understand how the family serves as an arena for gender oppression and even physical abuse.

The study of *caring activities* is a third area in which feminists have made important contributions. This is a broad realm that encompasses a variety of processes, from attending to a family member who is ill to looking after an elderly relative over a long period of time. Sometimes caring means simply being attuned to someone else's psychological well-being—several feminist writers have been interested in "emotion work" within relationships. Not only do women tend to shoulder concrete tasks such as cleaning and child care but they also invest large amounts of emotional labor in maintaining personal relationships (Duncombe and Marsden 1993). While caring activities are grounded in love and deep emotion, they are also a form of work that demands an ability to listen, perceive, negotiate, and act creatively.

New Perspectives in the Sociology of the Family

Theoretical and empirical studies conducted from a feminist perspective during the last few decades have generated increased interest in the family among both academics and the general population. Terms such as the *second shift*—referring to women's dual roles at work and at home—have entered our everyday vocabulary. But because they often focused on specific issues within the domestic realm, feminist studies of the family did not always reflect larger trends and influences taking place outside the home.

Since the 1990s, an important body of sociological literature on the family has emerged that draws on feminist perspectives but is not strictly informed by them. Of primary concern are the larger transformations that are taking place in family forms—the formation and dissolution of families and households and the evolving expectations within individuals' personal relationships. The rise in divorce and single parenting, the emergence of "reconstituted families" and gay families, and the popularity of cohabitation are all subjects of concern. Yet these transformations cannot be understood apart from the larger changes occurring in our late modern age. Attention must be paid to the shifts occurring at the societal, and even global, level if we are to grasp the link between personal transformations and larger patterns of change.

The Family in History

Sociologists once thought that before the modern period, the predominant form of family in western Europe was of the extended type. Research has shown this view to be mistaken. The nuclear family seems long to have been preeminent. Premodern household size was larger than it is today, but the difference is not especially great. In the United States, for example, throughout the seventeenth, eighteenth, and nineteenth centuries, the average household size was 4.75 persons. The current average is 2.57 (U.S. Bureau of the Census 2005a). Because the earlier figure includes domestic servants, the difference in family size is small. Extended family groups were more important in eastern Europe and Russia.

Balancing Family and Work

How many hours each week did your parents spend doing paid work when you were growing up? Did their commitment to work affect the way you or your siblings were raised? One of the ways globalization has affected family life in the United States is by increasing the amount of time that people spend each week at work. While there is some disagreement among researchers as to whether Americans, on average, are putting in more hours at work now than they did in the past, many sociologists give credence to the findings of economist Juliet Schor, author of the 1992 book *The Overworked American*. Schor argues that workers today spend on average 164 more hours each year at work than they did in the 1970s. Workers are also taking less vacation time than they did previously. Perhaps more significant, the percentage of mothers who are working full-time has increased dramatically since the end of World War II. In fact, in a comprehensive study of the multiple roles that modern women occupy, Daphne Spain and Suzanne Bianchi (1996) found that the group of women seeing the most dramatic increase in labor force participation in the United States was married women with young children. Taken together, these facts suggest that parents today have less time available to spend with their children than was the case in

Children in the premodern United States and Europe were often working—helping their parents on the farm—from seven or eight years of age. Those who did not remain in the family enterprise frequently left the parental household at an early age to do domestic work in the houses of others or to follow apprenticeships. Children who went away to work in other households would rarely see their parents again.

Other factors made family groups then even more impermanent than they are now, in spite of the high rates of divorce in current times. Rates of mortality (numbers of deaths per thousand of the population in any one year) for people of all ages were much higher. A quarter or more of all infants in early modern Europe did not survive beyond the first year of life (in contrast to well under 1 percent today), and women frequently died in childbirth. The death of children or of one or both spouses often dislocated or shattered family relations.

The Development of Family Life

Historical sociologist Lawrence Stone (1980) has charted some of the changes leading from premodern to modern forms of family life in Europe. Stone distinguishes three phases in the development of the family from the 1500s to the 1800s. In the early part of this period, the main family form was a type of nuclear family that lived in fairly small households but maintained deeply embedded relationships within the community, including with other kin. This family structure was not clearly separated from the community. According to Stone (although some historians have challenged this), the family at that time was not a major focus of emotional attachment or dependence for its members. People didn't experience, or look for, the emotional intimacies we associate with family life today. Sex within decades past. As a result, there has been a significant increase in the percentage of children enrolled in day-care programs—and, some would argue, a palpable increase in tension and stress within families as more of the day-to-day parental role is offloaded onto child-care providers.

In her book *The Time Bind* (1997), sociologist Arlie Hochschild suggests that these developments may be related to globalization. Globalization, of course, is not responsible for the gains women have made in securing positions in the paid labor force. Nevertheless, some corporations, according to Hochschild, have responded to the pressures of global competition by encouraging their salaried employees to put in longer hours at work, thus increasing levels of productivity. Why would employees willingly agree to spend so much time at their jobs—often considerably more than forty hours each week—when they are not paid to do so, when they know that such a commitment disrupts their family life, and in an age when computerization has greatly improved workplace efficiency? Shouldn't technological progress allow workers to spend more time with their families rather than less? Hochschild's answer to this question is that some corporations rely on the power of workplace norms to elicit a greater time commitment from their workers. New employees are socialized into a corporate culture in which working long hours is seen as a badge of dedication and professionalism. Employees, seeking status and the approval of their peers and supervisors, become motivated to put as much time into work as possible and to make sure that those around them know precisely how much time they spend working. In some cases, such a corporate culture has arisen unintentionally, as workers respond to the threat of corporate

downsizing by redoubling their commitment to the organization. In other cases—as with the corporation Hochschild studied—executives have consciously sought to shape the culture of the organization, reminding employees through handbooks, speeches, and newsletters that working more than forty hours a week is the mark of a "good" worker.

Although globalization has touched all the nations of the world, its effects on work time seem to vary by country. In France and Germany, for example, workers—sometimes acting through unions, sometimes making their power known at the voting booth—have rejected corporate calls for a longer workweek and are instead pressuring employers to reduce the workweek and to grant longer vacations. Do Europeans simply value family and leisure time more than Americans? Or would American workers be making the same demands if unions were stronger in this country?

marriage was not regarded as a source of pleasure but as a necessity to propagate children.

Individual freedom of choice in marriage and other matters of family life were subordinated to the interests of parents, other kin, or the community. Outside aristocratic circles, where it was sometimes actively encouraged, erotic or romantic love was regarded by moralists and theologians as a sickness. As Stone (1980) puts it, the family during this period "was an open-ended, low-keyed, unemotional, authoritarian institution. . . . It was also very short-lived, being frequently dissolved by the death of the husband or wife or the death or very early departure from the home of the children."

This type of family was succeeded by a transitional form that lasted from the early seventeenth century to the beginning of the eighteenth. This later type was largely confined to the upper reaches of society but was nevertheless very impor-

tant, because from it spread attitudes that have since become almost universal. The nuclear family became a more separate entity, distinct from ties to other kin and to the local community. There was a growing stress on the importance of marital and parental love, although there was also an increase in the authoritarian power of fathers.

In the third phase, the type of family system we are most familiar with in the West today gradually evolved. This family is a group tied by close emotional bonds, enjoying a high degree of domestic privacy and preoccupied with the rearing of children. It is marked by the rise of **affective individualism,** the formation of marriage ties on the basis of personal selection, guided by sexual attraction or romantic love. Sexual aspects of love began to be glorified within marriage instead of in extramarital relationships. The family became geared to consumption rather than production, as a result of the increasing

The family portrayed in the seventeenth-century painting on the left is an example of a premodern nuclear family, which emphasized work by all family members and did not focus on emotional intimacy. On the right is an example of an idealized nineteenth-century family, which became a more separate entity from the rest of the community and stressed emotional bonds and parental love.

spread of workplaces separate from the home. Women became associated with domesticity and men with being the bread-winners. Originating among more affluent groups, this family type became more or less universal in Western countries with the spread of industrialization.

In premodern Europe marriage usually began as a property arrangement, was in its middle mostly about raising children, and only in the end was about love. Few couples in fact married for love, but many grew to love each other in time as they jointly managed their household, reared their offspring, and shared life's experiences. Nearly all surviving epitaphs to spouses evince profound affection. By contrast, in most of the modern West, marriage *begins* with being in love; in its middle, it is still mostly about raising children (if there are children), and in the end, it is—often—about property, by which point love is absent or a distant memory (Boswell 1995).

"The Way We Never Were": Myths of the Traditional Family

Many people in current times feel that family life is being undermined. They contrast what they see as the decline of the family with more traditional forms of family life. Was the family of the past as peaceful and harmonious as many people recall it, or is this a simply idealized fiction? As Stephanie Coontz points out in her book *The Way We Never Were* (1992), as with other visions of a golden age of the past, the rosy light shed on the "traditional family" dissolves when we look back to previous times to see what things really were like.

Many admire the colonial family of early days as a disciplined, stable family. However, colonial families suffered from the same disintegrative forces as their counterparts in Europe. Especially high death rates meant that the average length of marriages was less than twelve years, and more than half of all children saw the death of at least one parent by the time they were twenty-one. The admired discipline of the colonial family was rooted in the strict authority of parents over their children. The way in which this authority was exercised would be considered exceedingly harsh by today's standards.

If we consider the Victorian family of the 1850s, the ideal family still eludes us. In this period, wives were more or less forcibly confined to the home. According to Victorian morality, women were supposed to be strictly virtuous, while men were sexually licentious: Many visited prostitutes and paid regular visits to brothels. In fact, wives and husbands often had little to do with one another, communicating only through their children. Moreover, domesticity wasn't even an option for poorer groups of this period. African American slaves in the South lived and worked frequently in the most appalling conditions. In the factories and workshops of the North, white families worked long hours with little time for home life. Child labor was also rampant in these groups.

Our most recent memory draws us to the 1950s as the time of the ideal American family. This was a period when women worked only in the home, while men were responsible for earning the family wage. Yet large numbers of women didn't actually *want* to retreat to a purely domestic role and felt miserable and trapped in it. Women had held paid jobs during World War II as part of the war effort. They lost these jobs when men returned from the war. Moreover, men were still emotionally removed from their wives and often observed a strong sexual double standard, seeking sexual adventures for themselves but setting strict codes for their spouses.

Betty Friedan's best-selling book *The Feminine Mystique* first appeared in 1963, but its research referred to the 1950s. Friedan struck a chord in the hearts of thousands of women when she spoke of the "problem with no name": the oppressive nature of a domestic life bound up with child care, domestic drudgery, and a husband who only occasionally put in an appearance and with whom little emotional communication was possible. Even more severe than the oppressive home life endured by many women was the alcoholism and violence suffered within many families during a time period when society was not prepared to fully confront these issues.

Let's now look directly at the changes affecting personal life, marriage, and the family in the world today. There is no doubt that some of these changes are profound and far-reaching. But interpreting their likely implications, particularly in the United States, means taking account of just how unrealistic it is to contrast what is happening now with a fictional or mythical view of the traditional family.

Changes in Family Patterns Worldwide

There is a diversity of family forms today in different societies across the world. In some areas, such as more remote regions in Asia, Africa, and the Pacific Rim, traditional family systems are little altered. In most developing countries, however, widespread changes are occurring. The origins of these changes are complex, but several factors can be picked out as especially important. One is the spread of Western culture. Western ideals of romantic love, for example, have spread to societies in which they were previously unknown. Another factor is the development of centralized government in areas previously composed of autonomous smaller societies. People's lives become influenced by their involvement in a national political system; moreover, governments make active attempts to alter traditional ways of behavior. Because of the problem of rapidly expanding population growth, states frequently introduce programs advocating smaller families, the use of contraception, and so forth.

A further influence is the large-scale migration from rural to urban areas. Often men go to work in towns or cities, leaving family members in the home village. Alternatively, a nuclear-family group will move as a unit to the city. In both cases, traditional family forms and kinship systems may become

weakened. Finally, and perhaps most important, employment opportunities away from the land and in such organizations as government bureaucracies, mines, plantations, and—where they exist—industrial firms tend to have disruptive consequences for family systems previously centered on landed production in the local community.

In general, these changes are creating a worldwide movement toward the predominance of the nuclear family, breaking down extended-family systems and other types of kinship groups. This was first documented by William J. Goode in his book *World Revolution in Family Patterns* (1963) and has been borne out by subsequent research.

Directions of Change

The most important changes occurring worldwide are the following:

1. Clans and other kin groups are declining in their influence.
2. There is a general trend toward the free choice of a spouse.
3. The rights of women are becoming more widely recognized, in respect to both the initiation of marriage and decision making within the family.
4. Kin marriages are becoming less common.
5. Higher levels of sexual freedom are developing in societies that were very restrictive.
6. There is a general trend toward the extension of children's rights.

In many countries, especially Western industrial societies, the nuclear family has been the preeminent family form. However, as mentioned earlier, in some societies extended families have been and still are the norm and traditional family practices continue. Moreover, there are differences in the speed at which change is occurring, and there are reversals and countertrends. A study in the Philippines, for example, found a higher proportion of extended families in urban areas than in surrounding rural regions. These had not just developed from traditional extended-family households but represented something new. Leaving the rural areas, cousins, nephews, and nieces went to live with their relatives in the cities to take advantage of the employment opportunities available there. Parallel examples have also been noted elsewhere in the world (Strinner 1979), including some industrialized nations. Certain regions of Poland, for instance, show evidence of a rejuvenation of the extended family. A good number of industrial workers in Poland have farms that they tend part time. In the cities, grandparents move in with their children's family, run the household, and bring up the grandchildren, while the younger generation is engaged in outside employment (Turowski 1977).

Given the ethnically diverse character of the United States, there are considerable variations in family and marriage within the country. Some of the most striking include differences between white and African American family patterns, and we need to consider why this is so. We will then move on to examine divorce, remarriage, and stepparenting in relation to contemporary patterns of family life.

Marriage and the Family in the United States

The United States has long been characterized by high marriage rates. Nearly every American adult eventually marries; over 90 percent of adults in their early fifties today are or have previously been married (U.S. Bureau of the Census 2005b). The age at which first marriages are contracted has risen, however, over the past twenty years (it was also high at the turn of the century, declining in the 1922–1950 period). There are several explanations for this trend in the last several decades toward later marriage. Some researchers contend that increases in cohabitation among younger people account for the decreases (or delays) in marriage among this group. Young people are cohabiting before or instead of marrying. Others argue that increases in postsecondary school enrollment, especially among women, are partially responsible for delays in marriage. Similarly, women's increased participation in the labor force often leads to delays in marriage as women work to establish their careers before marrying and starting a family (Oppenheimer 1988). Labor force participation also increases economic independence among women. By earning their own income, many women no longer need a male breadwinner in

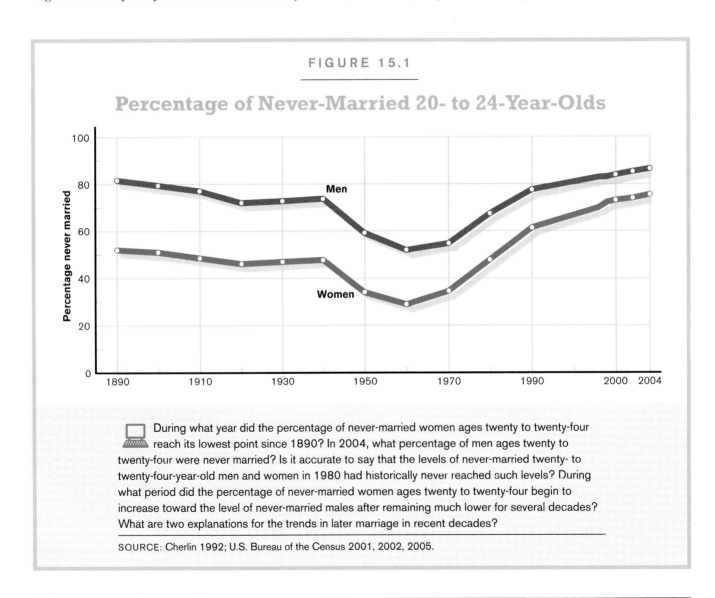

FIGURE 15.1

Percentage of Never-Married 20- to 24-Year-Olds

During what year did the percentage of never-married women ages twenty to twenty-four reach its lowest point since 1890? In 2004, what percentage of men ages twenty to twenty-four were never married? Is it accurate to say that the levels of never-married twenty- to twenty-four-year-old men and women in 1980 had historically never reached such levels? During what period did the percentage of never-married women ages twenty to twenty-four begin to increase toward the level of never-married males after remaining much lower for several decades? What are two explanations for the trends in later marriage in recent decades?

SOURCE: Cherlin 1992; U.S. Bureau of the Census 2001, 2002, 2005.

their home. The flip side of the economic independence argument is the idea that the deterioration of men's economic position since the late 1980s has made them less attractive mates and less ready to marry. Some researchers have used this idea—the marriageable men hypothesis—to explain the especially low marriage rates among blacks: Because black men have suffered the worst economic conditions in the last few decades, they might be viewed by black women as particularly poor marriage candidates. Finally, some researchers believe that modernization and a secular change in attitudes promote individualism and make marriage less important than it once was. The true reason for the decline in marriage is most likely some combination of the above explanations. But we must be careful how we make our comparisons. Although some have argued that the trend since 1970 toward later marriage is a break from tradition, it actually is close to the age of first marriage for the period 1890–1940. To say that people today are postponing marriage is true only if we compare ourselves with the 1950s generation. It might be more accurate to say that the 1950s generation married at an unusually young age.

In 1960, the average age of first marriages was 22.8 for men and 20.3 for women. The comparable ages in 2004 were 27 for men and 26 for women (National Marriage Project 2005a). Another way of measuring the relations between age and first marriage is to look at the numbers of people who remain unmarried before a certain age (Figure 15.1). Thus, in 1960, just 28 percent of women aged younger than 24 years had never married. In 2004, that proportion was 86.3 percent. The U.S. census now incorporates a category of "unmarried couples sharing the same household." As this practice of cohabitation is new, it is not easy to make direct comparisons with preceding years. Nonetheless, we can accurately estimate that the number of couples among younger age groups who have ever lived together without being married has risen steeply (Figure 15.2) from 11 percent around 1970 to 44 percent in the early 1980s and probably about 50 percent today (Cherlin 1999; National Center for Health Statistics 2005). By age thirty about 50 percent of women will have cohabited outside marriage (National Center for Health Statistics 2002). The U.S. Bureau of Census (2005c) estimated that in 2004 there were roughly 4.7 million heterosexual nonmarried couples, or about 8 percent, cohabiting, which is low by European standards; for example, in Sweden, about 28 percent of couples are cohabiting (National Marriage Project 2005).

No one knows for certain how the trend toward cohabitation will develop in the future. We can get some guidance from what has happened in other industrial countries. In France, cohabiting relationships are more widespread than in the United States and tend to be of longer duration. A survey in that country published in the late 1980s found that over half of cohabiting couples "did not think about marriage." Cohabitation, in

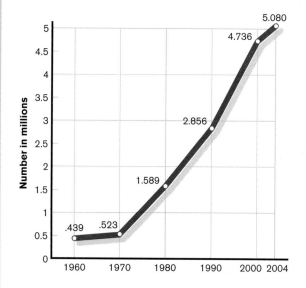

FIGURE 15.2

Changes in Cohabitation

Percentage cohabiting before first marriage, for persons marrying in 1965–1974, 1975–1979, and 1980–1984.

According to the reading, what can we predict about trends in cohabitation by looking at developments in other industrialized Western nations? Based on this figure, which decade had the steepest increase in the number of cohabitating couples? How do these changes in cohabitation in the United States compare to cohabitation in other parts of the world?

SOURCE: Bumpass and Sweet 1989.

other words, leads to marriage only for a minority; for most people, it is a phase of life in which partners want to leave their options open (Cherlin 1992; Sassler 2004). We return to the topic of cohabitation as an alternative to marriage later in this chapter.

An extraordinary increase in the proportion of people living alone in the United States has also taken place over recent years—a phenomenon that partly reflects the high levels of marital separation and divorce. More than one in every four households (26.4 percent) now consists of one person, a rise of 44 percent since 1960 (U.S. Bureau of the Census 2005d). There has been a particularly sharp rise in the proportion of individuals living alone in the twenty-four-to-forty-four age bracket.

Some people still suppose that the average American family is made up of a husband who works in paid employment and a

FIGURE 15.3

The Changing Structure of American Families with Children

Percentage of American children 17 and younger living in each of four types of families, 1790–1990.

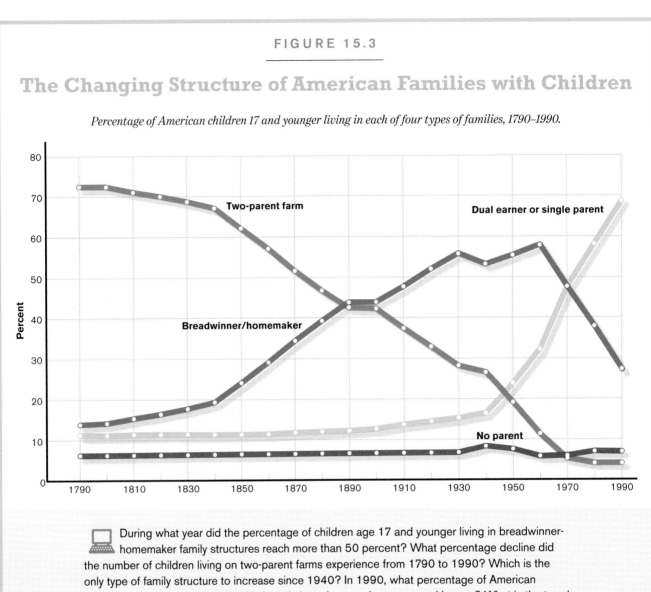

During what year did the percentage of children age 17 and younger living in breadwinner-homemaker family structures reach more than 50 percent? What percentage decline did the number of children living on two-parent farms experience from 1790 to 1990? Which is the only type of family structure to increase since 1940? In 1990, what percentage of American children under the age of 17 lived in breadwinner-homemaker structured homes? What is the trend in births to women over age 30 and the time between having children?

SOURCE: Hernandez 1993.

wife who looks after the home, living together with their two children. This is very different from the real situation: Only about 25 percent of children live in households that fit this picture. One reason is the rising rates of divorce: A substantial proportion of the population live either in single-parent households or in stepfamilies, or both. Another is the high proportion of women who work. Dual-career marriages and single-parent families are now the norm (Figure 15.3). The majority of married women working outside the home also care for a child or children. Although many working women are concentrated in

jobs with poor or nonexistent promotion prospects, the standard of living of many American couples depends on the income contributed by the wife, as well as on the unpaid work she undertakes in the home (see also Chapter 14).

There are also some large differences in patterns of childbearing between parents in the 1950s and later generations. The birthrate rose sharply just after World War II and again during the 1950s. Women in the 1950s had their first child earlier in their lives than has been true of the later generations, and subsequent children were born closer together. Since the late 1960s, the average age at which women have their first child has progressively risen. And women are leaving larger gaps between children. In 1976, only 20 percent of births were to women aged over thirty. By 2003, this proportion had grown to 38 percent despite an 8 percent decrease in the population of women aged thirty to thirty-four years. The number of births to women thirty-five to thirty-nine years old has increased even more dramatically—by 47 percent since 1990 (Centers for Disease Control and Prevention [CDC] 2005a).

Race, Ethnicity, and the American Family

ASIAN AMERICAN FAMILIES

One of the primary features of the Asian American family is that of dependence on the extended family. In many Asian cultures, family concerns are almost always a priority over individual concerns. Family interdependence also helps Asian Americans prosper financially. Asian American family and friend networks often pool money to help their members start a business or buy a house. This help is reciprocated as the recently endowed family member then contributes to the others. The result is a median family income for Asian Americans that is *higher* than that of the median for non-Hispanic whites.

There is a less detailed body of research on differences among Asian American subgroups than is the case with Hispanic subgroups. However, some fertility differences have been established. Chinese American and Japanese American women have much lower fertility rates than do any other racial/ethnic group. Chinese, Japanese, and Filipino families have lower levels of nonmarital fertility than all other racial/ethnic groups, including non-Hispanic whites. Low levels of nonmarital fertility combined with low levels of divorce for most Asian American groups demonstrate the emphasis on marriage as the appropriate forum for family formation and maintenance.

NATIVE AMERICAN FAMILIES

Kinship ties are very important in Native American families. As Cherlin (1999) notes, "kinship networks constitute tribal organization; kinship ties confer identity" for Native Americans. However, fewer than half of all Native Americans live on or near tribal lands, so for those who live in cities or away from reservations, kin ties may be less prominent. Furthermore, Native Americans have higher rates of intermarriage than any other racial/ethnic group. In fact, in 1990, less than half of all married Native Americans were married to other Native Americans (Sandefur and Liebler 1997).

The Native American fertility experience is similar to that of African Americans. Native American women have a high fertility rate and a high percentage of nonmarital fertility. Over 60 percent of all Native American women giving birth in 2003 were not married (CDC 2005c). Sandefur and Liebler (1997) also report a high divorce rate for Native Americans.

LATINO FAMILIES

As in many other areas, Hispanics are heterogeneous when it comes to family patterns. Mexicans, Puerto Ricans, and Cubans are the three largest Hispanic subgroups. In the U.S. census of 1990, Mexicans were the largest Hispanic group—more than 58 percent of the whole Hispanic population. Puerto Ricans constituted nearly 10 percent, down from 12 percent in 1990, and Cubans were just 3.5 percent; the rest of the Hispanic population was made up of much smaller groups from many Latin American nations (U.S. Bureau of the Census 2000a).

Mexican American families are characterized by multigenerational households and a high birthrate. Economically, Mexican American families are more well off than Puerto Rican families but less well off than Cuban families. Defying cultural stereotypes of a Mexican American home with a male breadwinner and female homemaker, more than half of all Mexican American women are in the labor force (Ortiz 1995). Still, ethnographic research indicates that this is due to necessity rather than desire. Many Mexican American families suggest that the breadwinner–homemaker model would be their preference, but that they are constrained by finances (Hurtado 1995).

Although Puerto Rico is a U.S. commonwealth, Puerto Ricans are still considered part of the umbrella category of Hispanics. However, because of their status as U.S. citizens, Puerto Ricans can and do move about freely between Puerto Rico and the mainland without the difficulties often encountered by immigrants. Researchers have shown that when barriers to immigration are high, only the most able (physically, financially, and so on) members of a society will be able to leave their homeland and move to another country. Because Puerto Ricans do not face as many barriers, even the least able can manage the migration process. The economic upshot of unrestricted migration for Puerto Ricans is that they are the most economically disadvantaged of all the major Hispanic groups. Puerto Rican families are also characterized by a higher percentage of children born to unmarried mothers than any other Hispanic group—59.8 percent in 2003 (CDC 2005b). Only African Americans (68.2 percent) and Native Americans (61.3 percent) had higher rates of births to unmarried women (CDC 2005c). However, consensual unions—cohabiting relationships in which couples consider themselves married but are not legally married—are often the context for births to unmarried mothers. Nancy Landale and Kelly Fennelly (1992) conducted a study of the marital experiences of Puerto Rican women and found that many of these women lived in consensual unions. They suggest that Puerto Ricans respond to tough economic times by forming consensual unions as the next best option to what is often a much more expensive legal marriage.

Cuban American families are the most prosperous of all the Hispanic groups but still less prosperous than whites. Most Cuban Americans have settled in the Miami area and have formed immigrant enclaves in which they rely on other Cubans for their business and social needs (such as banking, schools, and shopping). The relative wealth of Cuban Americans is driven largely by family business ownership. In terms of childbearing, Cuban Americans have lower levels of fertility than non-Hispanic whites and equally low levels of nonmarital fertility.

AFRICAN AMERICAN FAMILIES

As mentioned earlier, there are important differences in white and black family patterns. In particular, blacks have higher rates of childbearing outside of marriage, they are less likely to ever marry, and they are also less likely to marry after having a nonmarital birth. These differences are of particular interest to sociologists because single parenthood is associated with high rates of poverty in the United States (Harknett and McLanahan 2004).

More than forty years ago, Senator Daniel Patrick Moynihan (1965) described black families as "disorganized" and caught up in a "tangle of pathology." Moynihan, among others, looked back at the history of the black family for reasons. The early development of African American family patterns was largely governed by the conditions imposed by slavery. The circumstances of slavery prevented blacks from maintaining the cultural customs of their societies of origin. Members of similar African tribal groups were deliberately dispersed to different plantations. Some owners treated their slaves considerately, fostering the development of family life. Others, however, regarded their slaves as little better than livestock and inherently promiscuous and, therefore, believed marriage formalities to be unnecessary.

But slavery was not the only historical factor contributing to contemporary problems. After emancipation, new cultural experiences and structural factors came to wreak havoc on black families. Among these were continued yet new forms of discrimination against African Americans, changes in the economy such as the development of sharecropping in the South after the Civil War, and the migration of black families from the South to northern cities in the early decades of the twentieth century (Jones 1986).

The divergence between black and white family patterns has become much greater since the 1960s, when Moynihan's study was published, and it seems probable that we have to look mainly to present-day influences to explain them. In 2004, 78.2 percent of white families included a married couple, compared to 44.1 percent of black families (U.S. Bureau of the Census 2005e). In 1960, 21 percent of African American families were headed by females; among white families, the proportion was 8 percent. By 2004, the proportion for black families had risen to more than 47 percent, while that for white families was 16 percent (U.S. Bureau of the Census 2005e) (Figure 15.4). Female-headed families are more prominently represented among poorer blacks. One social condition from the current era that has exacerbated this situation is a shortage of black men. Marriage opportunities for women are constrained if there if there simply are not enough men employed in the for-

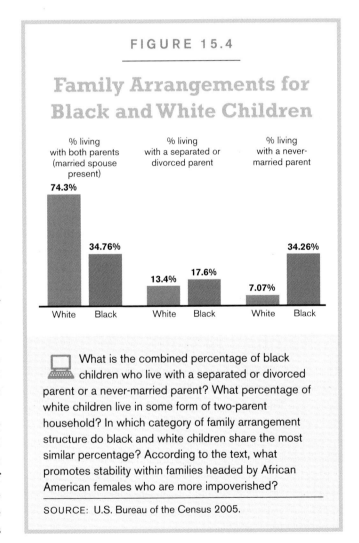

FIGURE 15.4

Family Arrangements for Black and White Children

% living with both parents (married spouse present)

% living with a separated or divorced parent

% living with a never-married parent

What is the combined percentage of black children who live with a separated or divorced parent or a never-married parent? What percentage of white children live in some form of two-parent household? In which category of family arrangement structure do black and white children share the most similar percentage? According to the text, what promotes stability within families headed by African American females who are more impoverished?

SOURCE: U.S. Bureau of the Census 2005.

mal labor market. Recent research further confirms that one of the best predictors of whether parents marry after a nonmarital birth is the marriage market characteristics—the availability of eligible partners—in a geographic area (Harknett and McLanahan 2004), demonstrating the continued importance of marriage markets even after the birth of a child.

But we should not see the situation of African American families purely in a negative light. When white anthropologist Carol Stack (1997) was a young doctoral student, she entered a black ghetto community in Illinois to study the support systems that poor black families form. Living in the community and getting to know the kinship system from the inside, she demonstrated that families adapted to poverty by forming large, complex support networks. Thus a mother heading a one-parent family is likely to have a close and supportive network of relatives to depend on. A far higher proportion of female-headed families among African Americans have other relatives living with them than do white families headed by females. This contradicts the idea that black single parents and their children form unstable families.

Class and the American Family

While Stack's arguments were specifically geared toward explaining racial differences in the organization of the extended family, contemporary researchers examining similar questions have concluded that "the differences between black and white extended family relationships are mainly due to contemporary differences in social and economic class positions of group members. Cultural differences are less significant" (Sarkisian and Gerstel 2004).

This leads to an interesting question: Are racial differences in family formation primarily due to economic or to cultural factors? A simple example may make this dilemma a bit more comprehensible. Consider four individuals, all women, who are the heads of their households: (1) a black doctor, (2) a white doctor, (3) a black nurse's aide, and (4) a white nurse's aide. The cultural argument suggests that blacks and whites are just different, which means that the black doctor and black nurse's aide should have family lives that are more similar to each other than they are to the family lives of the white doctor or white nurse's aide. The class argument argues the opposite, that the two nurse's aides and the two doctors will be much more similar to each other than they will be to people of the same race but from a different class position.

One of the problems with the culture–class debate is that there is a little research on middle-class black families or low-income white families, which makes it difficult to think about whether cultural factors or structural factors are driving racial

The number of children born out of wedlock is six times higher now than it was 50 years ago, and such births are increasingly occurring among the poor of all races. Often unable to afford other housing, many poor families pay rent by the month to live in motels like this one in downtown Las Vegas.

differences in terms of family formation. Despite the fact that there are no good empirical answers to this question, it does point toward the importance of considering how class differences could affect family life in America.

Nonmarital Childbearing

In recent years, researchers have been moving away from exclusively using race categories in analyzing family life. For example, the number of children born out of wedlock is six times higher now than in the 1950s and is increasingly occurring among the poor of all races. This suggests that examining the family by looking exclusively at race while ignoring class is too narrow.

One recent book by Katherine Edin and Maria Kefalas (2005) asks why low-income women continue to have children out of wedlock, when they can hardly afford to do so. Following in the tradition of scholars such as Stack and Anderson, Edin and Kefalas lived with their subjects—in this case among poor blacks, whites, and Puerto Ricans in Philadelphia, and Camden, New Jersey, getting to know them from the inside. The fascinating results of their interviews with 165 low-income single mothers in black and white neighborhoods lead them to argue that marriage has not lost its meaning in such communities and that we must look to other reasons for this trend. Women of all ethnicities who they interviewed actually valued marriage, even showing reverence for it. But these women believed that marriage commitments at that time would make things worse for them, either committing them to terrible relationships or leading to divorce. As one woman told Edin and

Kefalas, "I'd rather say I had a child out of wedlock than that I married this idiot." Or, as others said, a failed marriage would be worse than having children on their own. In an environment in which more men than ever were going to prison or were unemployed, these women felt they needed to be able to fend for themselves.

Two thirds of the pregnancies in the study were neither planned nor actively avoided. In these poor communities, Edin and Kefalas found that women tend to stop using contraception when the relationship becomes serious, even if they have not made an explicit plan to have children together. But why do women have children out of wedlock in the first place? The researchers find that young people in poor communities feel very confident about their ability to raise children, more so than most middle-class people do. This is because most of the pregnant mothers were themselves raised in social environments in which young people are typically involved in raising the other kids in a family or in a building. "I've always been a mom," one pregnant woman said.

A second reason women choose to have children, according to Edin and Kefalas, is that the poor place an extraordinary high value on children, perhaps even higher than that of middle-class families. Whereas middle-class people have more things to make their lives meaningful, the poor have less. For a person living in a low-income neighborhood, one of the worst things is to be childless. They view such a condition as one of the great tragedies of life. Finally, many women in the study reported that having a child actually saved their lives, bringing order to an otherwise chaotic life.

A third reason to "retreat from marriage" has to do with the changing meaning of marriage in low-income communities. Although it is true that low-income women value marriage highly (as shown earlier), what qualifies a man as a potential marital partner has changed over the last fifty years. Edin and Kefalas provide an insightful discussion of this, noting, "in the 1950s all but the most marginally employed men found women who were willing to marry them. Now, however, even men who are stably employed ar relatively good jobs at the time of the child's birth. . . . aren't automatically deemed marriageable by the women in their lives." This suggests that women have become pickier in terms of who meets the marriage bar. This shift in the meaning of marriage, when combined by the deteriorating economic position of low-income men, explains at least part of the reason more low-income women will be single for longer periods of their lives. When women who value motherhood highly also set the bar higher for marriage, higher rates of nonmarital fertility follow naturally.

Edin and Kefalas's (2005) research is in the best tradition of fieldwork in U.S. sociology. Through their work, we can understand the worldviews of black, white, and Puerto Rican young people who are having children out of wedlock. While it was beyond the scope of Edin and Kefalas's book to study of the outcome of these family formations for the children who are born into them, one issue American sociology must continue to grapple with is the fact that nonmarital childbearing leads to deleterious outcomes for children, including lower-than-average rates of high school graduation, higher rates of incarceration, and continued poverty. This is a topic we take up again in our consideration of single-parent families.

CLASS-BASED CULTURAL PRACTICES

The recognition that social class is crucial to understanding family life in the contemporary United States is central to the finding of another recent major work of field-based sociology. In *Unequal Childhoods* (2003), University of Maryland professor Annette Lareau closely observed the lives of twelve families—six white, five black, and one interracial—and came to some powerful insights about the nature of child-rearing practices in the United States. She found that middle-class and working class people have different cultural practices for raising children.

Middle-class parents tend to engage in "concerted cultivation," by which she means that they work especially hard to cultivate the talents of children through immersion in many non–school-based organized activities, as well as continuous linguistic interaction. Working-class and poor parents adopt a different style of child rearing, which Lareau calls the "accomplishment of natural growth." By this she means that in poorer homes, talk is brief and instrumental, children are taught to be more compliant with adult directives, and they have few organized activities outside of school. They learn to occupy themselves, often in play with neighborhood friends.

What is the result of these child-rearing strategies? According to Lareau, middle-class children end up with a sense of entitlement and place a high value on an individualized sense of self. They become comfortable questioning authority and making demands on adults and institutions. Lareau argues that the working-class culture of child rearing leads to an emerging sense of constraint on the part of working-class children. They end up being more cautious in dealing with adults, bureaucratic institutions, and authority. Like Stack, Lareau also finds that working-class and low-income parents are more likely to stress having close ties to kin, which means that these children end up having closer relationships on average with their siblings, cousins, and other relatives.

What are the implications of these differences for the outcomes of children from each background? Lareau argues that there are important signs of hidden advantages and disadvantages "being sown at early ages"; but because her research subjects were quite young, it was not possible or desirable to

According to Annette Lareau, middle-class parents tend to work especially hard to cultivate their children's talents through immersion in many non–school-based organized activities, while working-class children tend to have few organized activities and learn to occupy themselves, often by playing with neighborhood friends.

make claims about the way these child-rearing strategies affect adult outcomes. Further research, we hope, will test some of Lareau's hypotheses in large samples of children.

Like Edin and Kefalas, Lareau recognizes that social class is crucial to understanding the nature of family life in contemporary United States. Her work sets a new standard in showing how these differences emerge and operate in everyday life as well as their potential implications. She emphasizes that the differences between working-class and middle-class culture do not evolve because the different classes start out with radically different values and priorities but because parents' resources are vastly different in the two classes. It is the different levels of income and wealth between the working and middle classes that create the class differences in child rearing that Lareau notes. She found evidence to suggest that if poor and working-class people had more money, their child-rearing strategies would also change.

Divorce and Separation

Since the 1970s, we have seen major increases in rates of divorce, together with a relaxation of previously held attitudes of disapproval of divorce. For centuries in the West, marriage was regarded as virtually indissoluble. Divorces were granted only in limited situations, such as non-consummation of a marriage. Yet today most countries have moved rapidly toward making divorce more easily available.

Divorce rates, calculated by looking at the number of divorces per thousand married men or women per year, have fluctuated in the United States in different periods (Figure 15.5). They rose, for example, after World War II, then dropped off before climbing to much higher levels. The divorce rate increased steeply from the 1960s to the late 1970s, reaching a peak in 1980 (thereafter declining somewhat). It used to be common for divorced women to move back to their parents' homes after separation; today, most set up their own households.

Divorce exerts an enormous impact on the lives of children. Since 1970, more than 1 million American children per year have been affected by divorce. In one calculation, about one half of children born in 1980 became members of a one-parent family at some stage in their lives. Since two thirds of women and three fourths of men who are divorced eventually remarry, most of these children nonetheless grew up in a family environment. Only just over 2 percent of children under fourteen in the United States today are not living with either parent. The remarriage figures are substantially lower for African Americans. Only 32 percent of black women and 55 percent of black men who divorce remarry within ten years. Black children are half as likely as white children to be living with both parents or one parent and a stepparent (37 percent versus 76 percent) (Cherlin 1992).

Lenore Weitzman (1985) has argued that no-fault divorce laws have helped recast the psychological context of divorce positively (reducing some of the hostility it once generated), but they have had strong negative consequences for the economic position of women. Laws that were designed to be gender-neutral have had the unintended consequence of depriving divorced women of the financial protections that the old laws provided. Women are expected to be as capable as men of supporting themselves after divorce. Yet because most women's careers are still secondary to their work as homemakers, they may lack the qualifications and earning power of men. The living standards of divorced women and their children on average fell by 27 percent in the first year following the divorce settlement. The average standard of living of divorced men, by contrast, *rose* by 10 percent. Most court judgments left the former husband with a high proportion of his income intact; therefore, he had more to spend on his own needs than while he was married (Peterson 1996).

REASONS FOR DIVORCE

Divorce rates are obviously not a direct index of marital unhappiness. For one thing, they do not include people who are separated but have not been legally divorced. Moreover, people

FIGURE 15.5

Divorce Rates in the United States

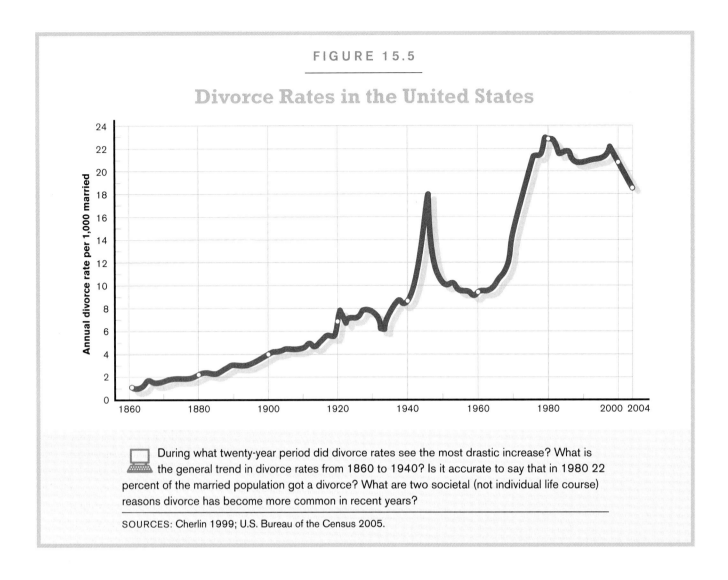

During what twenty-year period did divorce rates see the most drastic increase? What is the general trend in divorce rates from 1860 to 1940? Is it accurate to say that in 1980 22 percent of the married population got a divorce? What are two societal (not individual life course) reasons divorce has become more common in recent years?

SOURCES: Cherlin 1999; U.S. Bureau of the Census 2005.

who are unhappily married may choose to stay together—because they believe in the sanctity of marriage, they are wary about the consequences they will suffer in the case of a breakup, or they wish to remain with one another for the sake of the children.

Why has divorce become much more common over recent years? There are several reasons, which involve the wider changes going on in modern societies and in social institutions. As mentioned before, changes in the law have made divorce easier. In addition, except for a small proportion of wealthy people, marriage today no longer has much connection with the desire to perpetuate property and status from generation to generation. As women become more economically independent, marriage is less of a necessary economic partnership. Greater overall prosperity means that it is easier to establish a separate household in case of marital disaffection (Lee 1982). The fact that little stigma now attaches to divorce is in some part the result of these developments but adds momentum to them also. A further important factor is the growing tendency to evaluate marriage in terms of the levels of personal satisfaction it offers. Rising rates of divorce do not seem to indicate a deep dissatisfaction with marriage as such, but an increased determination to make it a rewarding and satisfying relationship (Cherlin 1990).

Other factors that show a positive correlation to the likelihood of divorce are related to an individual's life cycle. They include

- Parental divorce (people whose parents divorce are more likely to divorce)
- Premarital cohabitation (people who cohabitate before marriage have a higher divorce rate)
- Premarital childbearing (people who marry after having children are more likely to divorce)

- Marriage at an early age (people who marry as teenagers have a higher divorce rate)
- A childless marriage (couples without children are more likely to divorce)
- Low incomes (divorce is more likely among couples with low incomes) (White 1990)

THE EXPERIENCE OF DIVORCE

It is extremely difficult to draw up a balance sheet of the social advantages and costs of high levels of divorce. More tolerant attitudes toward divorce mean that couples can terminate an unrewarding relationship without incurring social ostracism. On the other hand, marriage breakup is almost always emotionally stressful and may create financial hardship, especially for women.

In her study *Uncoupling* (1986), Diane Vaughan carried out a series of interviews with 103 recently separated or divorced people (mainly from middle-class backgrounds) to chart the process of transition from living together to living apart. The notion of "uncoupling" refers to how people make the transition from intimate relationships to living alone. She found that in many cases, before the actual physical parting, there was a social separation—at least one of the partners developed a new life pattern, becoming interested in new pursuits and making new friends, in contexts in which the other was not included. This usually meant keeping secrets from the other—especially, of course, when a relationship with a lover was involved.

According to Vaughan's research, uncoupling is often unintentional in its beginnings. One individual—whom she calls the "initiator"—becomes more dissatisfied with the relationship than the other. The initiator creates a "territory" independent of the activities in which the couple engage together. For some time before this, the initiator may have been trying unsuccessfully to change the partner, to get him or her to behave in more acceptable ways, foster shared interests, and so forth. At some point, the initiator feels that this attempt has been a failure and that the relationship is fundamentally flawed. From then on, he or she becomes preoccupied with the ways in which the relationship or the partner is defective. Vaughan suggested that this is the opposite of the process of falling in love, when an individual focuses on the attractive features of the other and ignores those that may be more dubious.

DIVORCE AND CHILDREN

The effects of divorce on children are difficult to gauge. How contentious the relationship is between the parents before separation, the ages of the children at the time, whether there are brothers or sisters, the availability of grandparents and other relatives, the children's relationship with their individual parents, and how frequently they continue to see both parents can all affect the process of adjustment. Because children whose parents are unhappy with each other but stay together may also be affected, assessing the consequences of divorce for children is doubly problematic.

Research indicates that children often suffer a period of marked emotional anxiety after the separation of their parents. Judith Wallerstein and Joan Kelly (1980) studied 131 children of sixty families in Marin County, California, after the separation of the parents. They contacted the children at the time of the divorce, a year and a half after, and five years after. According to the authors, almost all the children experienced intense emotional disturbance at the time of the divorce. Preschool-age children were confused and frightened, tending to blame themselves for the separation. Older children were better able to understand their parents' motives for divorce but frequently worried about its effects on their future and expressed sharp feelings of anger. At the end of the five-year period, however, the researchers found that two thirds were coping reasonably well with their home lives and their commitments outside. A third remained dissatisfied with their lives, were subject to depression, and expressed feelings of loneliness, even in cases where the parent with whom they were living had remarried.

Wallerstein continued her study of this same group of children, following 116 of the original 131 into young adulthood with interviews at the end of ten-year and fifteen-year periods. The interviews revealed that these children brought memories and feelings of their parents' divorce into their own romantic relationships. Almost all felt that they had suffered in some way from their parents' mistakes. It is not surprising that most of them shared a hope for something their parents had failed to achieve—a good, committed marriage based on love and faithfulness. Nearly half the group entered adulthood as "worried, underachieving, self-deprecating, and sometimes angry young men and women." Although many of them got married themselves, the legacy of their parents' divorce lived with them. Those who appeared to manage the best were often helped by supportive relationships with one or both parents.

We cannot say, of course, how the children might have fared if their parents had stayed together. The parents and children studied all came from an affluent white area and might or might not be representative of the wider population. Moreover, the families were self-selected: They had approached counselors seeking help. Those who actively seek counseling might be less (or more) able to cope with separation than those who do not.

A more recent study found that the majority of people whose parents had divorced did not have serious mental health problems. The researchers did find small differences in

The American Family

Kansas

As divorce has increased, remarriage and stepparenting have become common family arrangements in both rural and urban America. For children and adults involved in "blended" families, the transition can be both challenging and rewarding. A family in rural Kansas has created friendships and connections that are extended to all of its family members. Six years ago two young girls participated in the wedding of their mother and new stepfather. Since then, the girls have helped to raise their half-brother and to support the family cattle and soybean business. The girls' biological father (a valued parent and friend) is also an active part of the family, visiting frequently, joining celebrations, and involving the girls with their paternal relatives.

"Living here in the Flint Hills country on a farm/ranch, we are involved in 4H, and all school activities. Grandparents, aunts, uncles, and cousins are also a big part of our lives. I feel very fortunate to be a part of this wonderful family. I guess we forget, or just don't think of ourselves as being 'blended,' just a family that enjoys, works, listens, and loves each other to the fullest. The girls are lucky that they have two dads that love and take care of them. I feel this has a great deal to do with our family doing so well together. The two dads do not compete to outdo the other or put the other down. They are both there for

the girls and the girls' needs. I think the girls enjoy having a little brother, although being the baby with two older sisters and old parents, he is as spoiled as we can get him, which means he can become a real pain from time to time. But we all love him so much, it's hard to be firm when his smile melts us all."

—Mom, Rural Kansas

South Dakota

Fostering children is a universally understood and commonly practiced Lakota Sioux custom. According to tradition, children in need of help are embraced as family members and foster families are highly regarded within the community. On the Rosebud Sioux Reservation in South Dakota, two sisters and a daughter have taken to heart the Lakota understanding of family and opened their doors to foster children for over twenty years. All of the children (placed by state and private foster agencies) are loved, provided for, celebrated and respected as precious members of the larger community circle.

"Being a 'foster' parent is something that came really naturally to me. Having grown up in a Lakota family, I have a large extended family. I saw so many people come and go through my grandmother's and my mother's house. It didn't matter if they were blood or not, their doors were always open. So I think this is why it was so easy for me to open my home to others. I never really thought about becoming a foster parent. Even before we were officially licensed, we cared for other kids in our home. I married my husband in 1987, when I was nineteen years old, and we got custody of his younger brothers and sisters in the next spring. So, I was nineteen taking care of a sixteen, thirteen, and eleven year old. It was hard, but I had my mom and family to help us. When the kids started to graduate and move on with their lives, the house felt empty, but there is always someone else who needs a family to love and support them. I don't like the word 'foster' because it puts separation between us and the kids. My own kids are happy to have more brothers and sisters. We are a family, and the kids are my kids. You know what they say; the more the merrier. Don't get me wrong; everything isn't always rosy, but you get

past the rough seas, and into calm waters. Even though the older ones are adults and have their own lives, they still come home when they need to or call when they are having a hard time. And we will always be there for all of them."

—Mom, Rosebud Sioux Reservation, South Dakota

Ohio

With the divorce rate estimated to be as high as 50 percent, single parent families are one of the largest and fastest growing family types in America. (In 1997, over one quarter of children lived with only one parent.) Raising the youngest three of his six adopted children, a single parent father in Cleveland cooks, cleans, and cares for his kids between working full-time shifts as an inner city police officer.

"Children are the heart of any family and mine are my heart. Most men think it's a woman's job to raise children, but it's not. I work, clean house, cook and help the kids with homework, and if one of the kids is sick, it's me that takes them to the hospital and sits at their bedside. Whether the times are good or bad, it's dad to the rescue."

—Dad, Cleveland, Ohio

SOURCE: Courteney Coolidge, "American Families: Beyond the White Picket Fence," 1999. A photo project, available at http://10families.com.

Questions

- How would you define *family*, based on these three examples?
- In terms of lifestyle and function, what are the differences between these families and the nuclear family?

mental health between those whose parents divorced and those whose parents stayed together (favoring those whose parents stayed together), but much of this difference in mental health had been identified in children at age seven, before any of the families experienced divorce (Cherlin et al. 1998). The most prominent sociologist of the family in the United States, Andrew Cherlin (1999), has argued that the general effects of divorce on children are

- Almost all children experience an initial period of intense emotional upset after their parents separate.
- Most resume normal development without serious problems within about two years after the separation.
- A minority of children experience some long-term problems as a result of the breakup that may persist into adulthood.

Remarriage and Stepparenting

Before 1900, the large majority of all marriages in the United States were first marriages. Most remarriages involved at least one widowed person. With the progressive rise in the divorce rate, the level of remarriage also began to climb, and in an increasing proportion of remarriages, at least one person was divorced.

Today, thirty-five out of every one hundred marriages involve at least one previously married person. Up to age thirty-five, the majority of remarriages are between divorced people. After that age, the proportion of remarriages with widows or widowers rises. By age fifty-five, the proportion of such remarriages is larger than those following divorce.

Odd though it might seem, the best way to maximize the chances of marriage, for both sexes, is to have been married previously. People who have been married and divorced are more likely to marry again than single people in similar age groups are to marry for the first time. At all age levels, divorced men are more likely to remarry than divorced women. Two in every three divorced women remarry, but three in every four divorced men eventually marry again. Many divorced individuals also choose to cohabitate instead of remarry. In statistical terms, at least, remarriages are less successful than first marriages: rates of divorce are higher.

This does not mean that second marriages are doomed to fail. People who have been divorced may have higher expectations of marriage than those who remain married to their first spouses. Hence they may be more ready to dissolve new marriages than those only married once. The second marriages that endure are usually more satisfying, on average, than the first.

A **stepfamily** may be defined as a family in which at least one of the adults is a stepparent. Many who remarry become

Thirty-five out of every one hundred marriages involve at least one previously married person. While most families don't look like the Bradys, they find their own ways to adjust to the relatively new circumstances in which they find themselves.

stepparents of children who regularly visit rather than live in the same household. By this definition, the number of stepfamilies is much greater than shown in available official statistics, because these usually refer only to families with whom stepchildren live. Stepfamilies bring into being kin ties that resemble those of some traditional societies but that are new in Western countries. Children may now have two "mothers" and two "fathers"—their natural parents and their stepparents. Some stepfamilies regard all the children and close relatives from previous marriages as part of the family. If we consider that at least some of the grandparents may be part of the family as well, the result is a situation of some complexity.

Certain particular difficulties tend to arise in stepfamilies. In the first place, there usually exists a biological parent living elsewhere whose influence over the child or children is likely to remain powerful. Cooperative relations between divorced individuals often become strained when one or both remarry. Take as an illustration the case of a woman with two children who marries a man also with two children, all six living together. If the "outside" parents demand the same times of visitation as previously, the tensions that arise from welding such a newly established family together are likely to be intense. It may prove impossible to have the new family all together on weekends.

Stepfamilies merge children from different backgrounds, who may have varying expectations in the family milieu. Since most stepchildren belong to two households, the possibilities of clashes of habits and outlooks are considerable. There are few established norms defining the relationship between stepparent and stepchild. Should a child call a new stepparent by name, or is "Dad" or "Mom" more appropriate? Should the stepparent play the same part in disciplining the children as the natural parent? How should a stepparent treat the new spouse of her previous partner when the children are picked up?

Research on family-structure effects on children shows that girls experience more detrimental outcomes from stepfamily living, whereas boys demonstrate more negative outcomes from single-parent family living. The more negative effects for boys may be because single-parent family living generally means living with a mother only, and thus the male role model is absent. Girls are more likely to bond with their mothers in this type of family. A remarriage that introduces a stepfather may cause girls to feel that their close relationship with their mother is threatened. It is speculated that this is why girls living in stepfamilies experience more negative outcomes.

Members of stepfamilies are finding their own ways of adjusting to the relatively uncharted circumstances in which they find themselves. Perhaps the most appropriate conclusion to be drawn is that while marriages are broken up by divorce, families on the whole are not. Especially when children are involved, ties persist.

Single-Parent Households

Single-parent households have become increasingly common. As a result of the increase in divorce rates and births before marriage, about one half of all children spend some time in their lives in a single-parent family (Furstenberg and Cherlin 1991). The vast majority are headed by women, since the mother usually obtains custody of the children after a divorce (in a small proportion of single-parent households, the individual, again almost always a woman, has never been married). There are over 12.6 million single-parent households in the

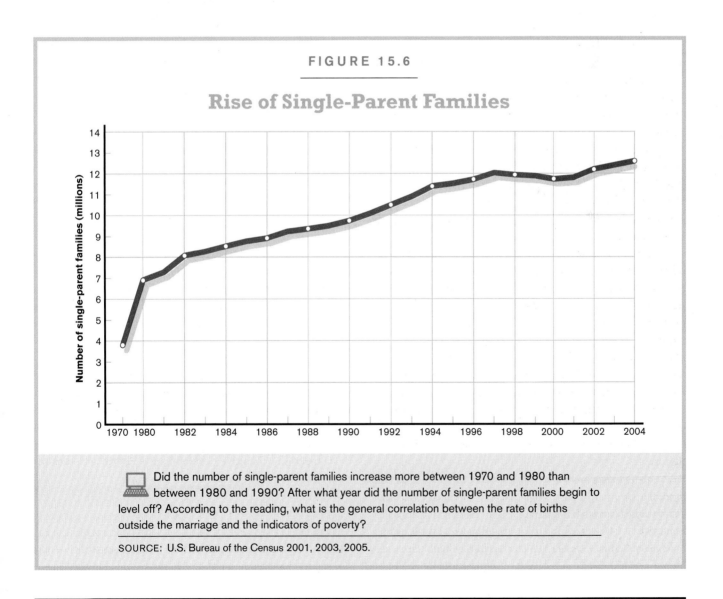

FIGURE 15.6

Rise of Single-Parent Families

Did the number of single-parent families increase more between 1970 and 1980 than between 1980 and 1990? After what year did the number of single-parent families begin to level off? According to the reading, what is the general correlation between the rate of births outside the marriage and the indicators of poverty?

SOURCE: U.S. Bureau of the Census 2001, 2003, 2005.

United States today, and the number may continue to increase (Figure 15.6). Such households make up nearly one in three (30.3 percent) of all families with dependent children (U.S. Bureau of the Census 2005g). On average, they are among the poorest groups in contemporary society. Many single parents, whether they have ever been married or not, still face social disapproval as well as economic insecurity. Earlier and more judgmental terms such as *deserted wives*, *fatherless families*, and *broken homes* are tending to disappear, however.

The category of single-parent household is an internally diverse one. For instance, more than half of widowed mothers are homeowners, but the vast majority of never-married single mothers live in rented accommodations. Single parenthood tends to be a changing state, and its boundaries are rather blurred. In the case of a person who is widowed, the break is obviously clear cut—although even here a person might have effectively been living on his or her own for some while if the partner was hospitalized before death. About 60 percent of single-parent households today, however, are brought about by separation or divorce. In such cases, individuals may live together sporadically over a quite lengthy period. As one single mother remarks:

> I think it takes a time to come to terms with being a single mother. In my case I've only accepted what I am in the past year. I suppose before I always thought that we might get back together but when he got married I had to give up. I felt very bad at the time, but now I think it was the best thing that could have happened because it made me come to terms with my life. (quoted in Crow and Hardey 1992)

Most people do not wish to be single parents, but a growing minority choose to become so—who set out to have a child or children without the support of a spouse or partner. "Single mothers by choice" is an apt description of some parents, normally those who possess sufficient resources to manage satisfactorily as a single-parent household. For the majority of unmarried or never-married mothers, however, the reality is different: There is a high correlation between the rate of births outside marriage and indicators of poverty and social deprivation. As we saw earlier, these influences are very important in explaining the high proportion of single-parent households among families of African American background in the United States.

A debate exists among sociologists about the effect on children of growing up with a single parent. The most exhaustive set of studies carried out to date, by Sara McLanahan and Gary Sandefur (1994), rejects the claim that children raised by only one parent do just as well as children raised by both parents. A large part of the reason is economic—the sudden drop in in-come associated with divorce. But about half of the disadvantage comes from inadequate parental attention and lack of social ties. Separation or divorce weakens the connection between child and father, as well as the link between the child and the father's network of friends and acquaintances. On the basis of wide empirical research, the authors conclude it is a myth that there are usually strong support networks or extended family ties available to single mothers. Others have also been quick to point out that although children who grow up in a single-parent home are on average disadvantaged, it is better for children's mental health if parents in extremely high-conflict marriages divorce rather than stay together (Amato et al. 1995). This suggests that divorce may benefit children growing up in high-conflict marriages while harming children whose parents have relatively low levels of marital conflict before divorcing.

The Dark Side of the Family

Since family or kin relations are part of almost everyone's experience, family life encompasses virtually the whole range of emotional experience. Family relationships—between wife and husband, parents and children, brothers and sisters, or more distant relatives—can be warm and fulfilling. But they can equally be full of the most extreme tension, driving people to despair or imbuing them with a deep sense of anxiety and guilt. The dark side of family life is extensive and belies the rosy images of family harmony frequently depicted in TV commercials and programs. It can take many forms. Among the most devastating in their consequences, however, are the incestuous abuse of children and domestic violence.

Family Violence

Violence within families is primarily a male domain. The two broad categories of family violence are child abuse and spousal abuse. Because of the sensitive and private nature of violence within families, it is difficult to obtain national data on levels of domestic violence. Data on child abuse is particularly sparse because of the cognitive development and ethical issues involved in studying child subjects.

CHILD ABUSE

Although there are many variations on what constitutes child abuse, the most common definition is serious physical harm (trauma, sexual abuse with injury, or willful malnutrition) with intent to injure. One national study of married or cohabiting adults indicates that about 3 percent of respondent adults abused their children in 1993, though cohabitating adults are no more or less likely to abuse their children than married couples (Brown 2004; Sedlak and Broadhurst 1996). More recent statistics are based on national surveys of child welfare professionals. These surveys miss children who are not seen by professionals or reported to state agencies. Researchers estimate that that as many as 50 to 60 percent of child deaths from abuse or neglect are not recorded (U.S. Department of Health and Human Services [DHHS] 2004). However, these surveys remain the most current source of information on child abuse. In the 1993 National Incidence Study (NIS) of Child Abuse and Neglect, almost half of all substantiated cases of child abuse and neglect fell into the neglect category (47 percent). Physical abuse was the next most common violation (25 percent), followed by sexual abuse (15 percent) (Sedlak and Broadhurst 1996). The most recent statistics based on the National Child Abuse and Neglect Reporting System indicate that in 2003 there were more than 906,000 reported child victims of abuse or neglect. Of these, 63.2 percent suffered neglect, 18.9 percent suffered physical abuse, and 9.9 percent were sexually abused (DHHS 2005). Almost 80 percent of child abuse or neglect is perpetrated by the child's parents and of those cases, more than 40 percent of perpetrators are mothers, nearly 19 percent are fathers, and 17 percent are mothers and fathers. Over half of all victims of child abuse or neglect are white and just over a quarter are black (DHHS 2005).

The number of reported cases of child abuse has stayed about the same since 1990 when there were 860,000 victims of child abuse or neglect. The number of victims rose to just over 1 million in 1994 before declining to 906,000 in 2003. At the same time, the overall child victimization rate has declined from 13.4 victims per 1,000 children in 1990 to 12.4 in 2003, reflecting an increase in the population of children in this country. Even while the overall rate of child victimization has declined, the rate of neglect has increased since 2000 by almost 6 percent, to 7.5 neglected children per 1,000 children. The rates of both physical and sexual abuse have remained constant (DHHS 2005). The highest child victimization rates were for the zero-to-three age group. These studies also show that child abuse is more likely to occur in low-income families and single-parent families.

SPOUSAL ABUSE

A 1985 study by Straus and his colleagues found that spousal violence has occurred at least once in the past year in 16 percent of all marriages and at some point in the marriage in 28 percent of all marriages. This does not, however, distinguish between severe acts, such as beating up and threatening with or using a gun or knife, and less severe acts of violence, such as slapping, pushing, grabbing, or shoving one's spouse. When the authors disaggregated this number, they found that approximately 3 percent of all husbands admitted to perpetrating at least one act of severe violence on their spouse in the last year, and this is likely to be an underestimate.

The national survey by Straus and his colleagues also uncovers a finding that is somewhat contrary to most people's beliefs about spousal violence: They find that women reported perpetrating about the same amount of violent acts as men. This lies in stark contrast to much of the literature based on crime statistics, hospital records, and shelter administrative records. These sources all indicate that spousal violence is almost exclusively man-on-woman violence.

Michael Johnson (1995) was able to untangle these inconsistencies. Johnson recognized that the data that were generating such conflicting findings were collected from two very different samples. In the shelter samples, respondents are generally women who were severely beaten by their husbands or partners. The severity of their situation drew them to a shelter. On the other hand, those responding to a national survey are generally living in their homes and have the time, energy, or wherewithal to complete a survey. It is unlikely that individuals who are experiencing extreme violence in the home would respond to a national survey. Furthermore, it is unlikely that those who experience less severe kinds of violence (e.g., slapping) will end up in a domestic violence shelter. Therefore, these are two very different groups of people.

Johnson argued that the spousal abuse in the two samples was also different in character. He referred to the extreme abuse experienced by many in the shelter samples as "patriarchal terrorism." This type of violence is perpetuated by feelings of power and control. The type of violence reported in national surveys is referred to as "common couple violence." This type of violence is generally reactionary to a specific incident and is not rooted in power or control.

Social Class Although no social class is immune to spousal abuse, several studies indicate that it is more common among low-income couples (Cherlin 1999). More than three decades ago, William Goode (1971) suggested that low-income men may be more prone to violence because they have few other means to control their wives, such as through having a higher income or education than their wives. In addition, the high levels of stress induced by poverty and unemployment may lead to more violence within families. In support of these assertions, Gelles and Cornell (1990) found that unemployed men are nearly twice as likely as employed men to assault their wives.

Improving Child Care Safety

As professor of sociology at the Graduate Center, City University of New York, Julia Wrigley researched relationships between parents and their children's child care providers. Caregivers often said they had more trouble dealing with parents—their employers—than with the children in their charge. Caregivers usually seemed to manage their relationships with children, but there were tragic exceptions. Wrigley heard about several cases in which nannies had injured or even killed the children in their care. One case involved a nine-month-old boy, Kieran Dunne, who pulled on his caregiver's long hair. The caregiver, Ann Franklin, violently threw him to the floor. He died six days later of a skull fracture. Another case dominated the national media for months. Nineteen-year-old British au pair Louise Woodward was convicted of second-degree murder after she shook eight-month-old Matthew Eappen and slammed his head into a table on February 5, 1997.

Wrigley wanted to know more about such rare, but devastating occasions. Did many children suffer harm in child care? Were the caregivers who harmed them mentally unstable, or were they ordinary people who snapped? The cases in the media usually involved caregivers in private homes. What about child-care centers? Were they safer or less safe?

Wrigley looked for data to answer these questions. She found none. No agency collected information on injuries or fatalities in child care. This was surprising because child care has become part of families' daily lives. The percentage of mothers working full-time has increased dramatically since World War II, causing an increase in the percentage of children enrolled in day-care programs nationwide. As more and more parents rely on childcare providers to successfully balance work and family responsibilities, new tensions have sur-

Julia Wrigley

faced about child rearing in the twenty-first century. Although many workers depend on child care, every parent who entrusts their child to outside care worries about safety.

Unsatisfied with reading about isolated cases, Wrigley decided to look for concrete answers. To gather information, Wrigley and her colleague and student Joanna Dreby analyzed reports of 1,362 fatalities from 1985 to 2003 by investigating media reports, legal cases, and state records. More than eight million children are in paid child care every day in America, but until recently little was known about their safety. The results caught Wrigley and Dreby by surprise. Deaths from violence in child care centers were almost nonexistent. Almost every fatality took place in a private home, whether that care was offered in the child's home by a nanny or in an arrangement called family day care, by which a provider looks after neighborhood children in her own home.

How could this be? Mothers and fathers across the country often believe that private care is a safer, more intimate, and educationally rich way for their child to spend the day. But Wrigley and Dreby (2005) conclude that *centers*, not private homes, are the safest form of child care, largely because centers afford children multiple forms of protection. Staff members at centers do not work alone, they cooperate with each other to maintain an environment of emotional control and are, therefore, less likely to experience unbearable frustration. In addition, center workers dedicate time and energy to professional training and watch for outsiders who may pose risks to children.

In other words, child-care centers have fundamentally different organizational environments than private homes. "The striking success of centers at controlling fatal violence against children—indeed, almost eliminating it—and their relative safety in terms of protection against accidents suggests the power of social organization in reducing risks" (Wrigley and Dreby 2005). When single *individuals* provide care without the protective influences of co-workers and constant supervision, children are at greater risk of violent abuse. "Not a single shaken baby fatality was found in a child care center, while 203 were reported in arrangements in private homes. The stress of infant crying, in particular, can drive caregivers to impulsive acts of violence. With little professional training, without supervisors or coworkers, and often paid very little for long hours of work, even some experienced caregivers can lose emotional control" (Wrigley and Dreby 2005). Although the tragic deaths caused by Ann Franklin and Louise Woodward may have been isolated incidents, they fit a general pattern. Both fatalities occurred in private homes at the hands of unsupervised individuals who lashed out in frustration. Although extremely rare, Wrigley and Dreby believe those deaths are preventable.

As a public sociologist, Wrigley helped spark a dialogue about how public policy might improve child welfare in organizational settings. "Child care is quite safe overall, but it could be made safer," says Wrigley. "We need to recognize what a stressful and demanding job it is to look after young children. Improved safety will only come with more resources and closer regulation of care." Wrigley notes that there are three main care options available: child-care centers, family day care, and

nannies working in the children's homes, each of which she believes would benefit from closer public attention. A major expansion of center care would be expensive, requiring a substantial social investment in the form of a federal or state subsidy, but research has consistently shown that centers can have a positive effect on child development (in terms of safety and intellectual stimulation). If this option is politically unfeasible, states could try to improve the safety of family day care by strengthening licensing requirements. Although many fatalities are unexpected, some deaths are attributable to child-care providers with long records of abuse. In addition to helping better identify facilities with poor records, increased regulation would also enable states to invest in improved training and certification of childcare workers, especially those who care for children alone.

Wrigley's overall goal is to help develop public policies that keep kids safe. In a recent op/ed piece for *Newsday*, Wrigley (2006) argues on the basis of her childcare findings that better regulation of day-care providers is necessary to ensure child safety. In New York and other states, many individuals who receive public money to provide informal child care remain unregulated by the state. No background checks are necessary. In New York, individuals are asked to voluntarily report to parents whether they have been convicted of a felony or have a history of child abuse. They also attest to the safety of the premises without inspection. In an act of almost willful blindness, "the state accepts these statements at face value." The result: "Very young children are being cared for by wholly unregulated providers who do not even have to undergo the most basic tests of fitness" (Wrigley 2006).

Many American families have luxuries of choice that are unavailable to other families. Some choose to raise children at home. Others choose services that provide a stimulating and healthy environment for children. But for families with little or no choice in childcare, Wrigley believes that part of government responsibility is to ensure that all children be provided their most basic rights of protection and all parents be spared the frantic phone call from a caregiver telling them that their baby is not breathing.

Alternatives to Traditional Forms of Marriage and the Family

Cohabitation

Cohabitation—in which a couple lives together in a sexual relationship without being married—has become increasingly widespread in most Western societies. Until a few decades ago, cohabitation was generally regarded as somewhat scandalous. As we saw earlier in the chapter, however, during the 1980s the number of unmarried men and women sharing a household went up sharply. Cohabitation has become widespread among college and university students, although they were not the initiators of this trend, as many people believe. Bumpass and co-workers (1991) found that the cohabitation phenomenon started with lower-educated groups in the 1950s. The college-educated population has always had and continues to have lower rates of cohabitation than those who do not go to college. The fact that those who are less educated were initiators in the trend toward cohabitation indicates that for this group, cohabitation may serve as a substitute for marriage, which may involve economic constraints.

While for some cohabitation may be a substitute for marriage, for many it is viewed as a stage in the process of relationship building that precedes marriage. Young people come to live together usually by drifting into it, rather than through calculated planning. A couple who are already having a sexual relationship spend more and more time together, eventually giving up one of their individual homes. The close connection between cohabitation and marriage for many is indicated in Figure 15.7, which shows that the most important reason for cohabiting for both women and men is so that "couples can be sure they are compatible before marriage."

Most cohabiting couples either marry or stop living together, although the chances of a cohabitating union transitioning to a first marriage is related to a number of socioeconomic factors. For instance, the probability that the first cohabitation will become a marriage within five years is 75 percent for white women, but only 61 percent for Hispanic women and 48 percent for black women. Similarly, the likelihood of a first marriage resulting from cohabitation is positively associated with higher education, the absence of children during cohabitation, and higher family income. It is also more likely in communities with low male unemployment rates (Bramlett and Mosher 2002). Although many view cohabitation as a precursor to marriage, for a large number of people, it does not end in marriage. Only about 35 percent of cohabitors married their partners within three years of starting to live together. Increasingly, we are seeing evidence that cohabitation is not necessarily a "stage in the process" between dating and marriage, but rather it may be an end in itself for an increasing number of cohabitors.

Evidence provided by Judith Seltzer (2002) cautions that although cohabitation is often viewed as a "trial marriage," an increasing proportion of cohabiting unions are not leading to marriage. Over the past decade, the rate of childbearing within cohabiting unions has increased by 25 percent (Seltzer 2000). At the same time, the percentage of all children born to unmarried parents has increased from about 18 percent in 1980 to just under 35 percent in 2004 (National Center for Health Statistics 2000a, 2004). Cohabiting couples are the source of much of this increase. In the early 1980s, 29 percent of all nonmarital births were to those in cohabiting unions. In 2004, this was up to nearly 45 percent (U.S. Bureau of the Census 2005c). Among first births to Hispanic women, one in five occurred within cohabiting unions, compared with one in ten of first births to white women and one in seven first births to black women (National Center for Health Statistics 2005b). Finally, in the past, couples who got pregnant before they were married often married before the birth of the baby. Currently, only 11 percent of single women who have a pregnancy that results in a live birth are married by the time the child is born. Although the percentage of those who marry before the birth of a child that was conceived while the couple was single has declined, there has been an increase in the rate at which unmarried women begin cohabiting with their partner once they find out they are pregnant. Currently, 11 percent of single women who have a pregnancy that results in a live birth begin cohabiting by the time the baby is born. Thus equal percentages of couples now marry and begin cohabiting to "legitimate" a pregnancy.

Does living together reduce the chances of divorce? Apparently not. People who live with their partner before marriage are more likely to divorce than those who do not cohabit before marriage.

FIGURE 15.7

Reasons for Cohabiting

Percentage of cohabiting women and men under thirty-five who agreed that each reason was the most important for "why someone might want to live with a person of the opposite sex without being married."

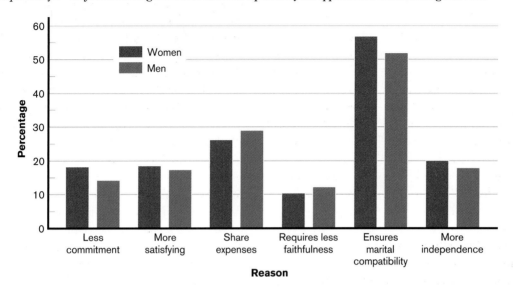

According to the figure, what did men identify as the most important reason for cohabitating without being married? What percentage agreed with this choice? Which reasons did more men than women identify as the most important? Which reason for cohabitating showed the largest difference between men and women? According to the text, are there differences among the rates of marriage within five years of the first cohabitation among different races? If so, what are they?

SOURCE: Bumpass et al. 1991.

Recent research, however, has shown that cohabitation is less stable than marriage. Where the likelihood of a first marriage ending in separation or divorce within five years is 20 percent, there is a 49 percent chance that a premarital cohabitation will break up within five years. Similarly, after ten years, the probability of a first marriage ending is 33 percent, compared with 62 percent for cohabitations (National Center for Health Statistics 2002).

The United States is certainly not alone in the increasing prevalence of cohabitation. Many European countries are experiencing similar, and in some cases much greater, proportions of unions beginning with cohabitation rather than marriage. The Nordic countries of Denmark, Sweden, and Finland, along with France, show particularly high rates of cohabita-

tion. However, unions in the southern European countries of Spain, Greece, and Italy—along with Ireland and Portugal—still largely begin with marriage.

As cohabitation becomes increasingly common as a first union and among those who have been married and now are divorced, children are spending more and more time in cohabiting unions. Recent research by Larry Bumpass and Hsien-Hen Lu (2000) finds that about two fifths of all children spend some time living with their mother and a cohabiting partner and that approximately one third of the time children spend with unmarried mothers is actually spent in cohabitation. Clearly, the lives of children are increasingly embedded in families formed by cohabitation. The effects of this alternative family form on children will become apparent only as these children age.

Many college students believe that if they live with a boyfriend or girlfriend, this will help them learn whether they are compatible, thus helping them decide whether they've picked the right partner for marriage. Since the countercultural revolution of the 1960s, scholars such as anthropologist Margaret Mead (1966) predicted that that living together would allow people to make better decisions about marriage. To some extent this might be true: The act of living together is a kind of trial marriage that can help poorly matched couples avoid a failed marriage (Elwert 2005).

Yet many people who think living together increases the likelihood of finding the right partner would be surprised to learn that it is well established that people who live with their partner before marrying them are *more* likely to divorce than are individuals who do not cohabit with their partner before marrying them. How could this be so?

The Selection Explanation One compelling explanation suggests that there is nothing about living together itself that promotes cohabitation. This explanation takes note of the fact that people who live together would be more likely to divorce whether or not they had lived together in the first place. At first this might not make a lot of sense, until we recognize that the condition of living together may not be the cause of more divorce. Instead, it could be the case that the very people who would choose to cohabit differ from those who don't. For example, the evidence shows that people who cohabit are less religious, and people who refuse to cohabit are more religious (Dush et al. 2003). People who are less religious would be less likely to stay married in any event, whereas people who are more religious would be more likely to stay married. So the cause of higher divorce among people who live together is that people who select to cohabit are the very people who are less religious and more likely to get divorced anyway.

The Experience of Living Together Explanation Although the selection explanation suggests that there is nothing about cohabitation in and of itself that promotes divorce, there is a competing explanation that suggests that living together is the kind of experience that erodes beliefs in the experience of marriage. Particularly as people go through their twenties living with various partners, they develop a sense that relationships can be started and ended more easily, and that they have many options for intimate relations outside of marriage (Teachman 2003).

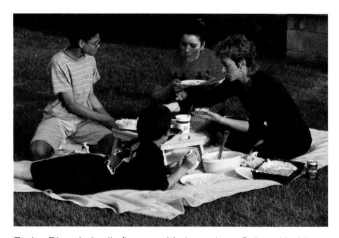

Evelyn Rivera's family (her son, Mark; nephew, Sal; and lesbian partner, Debbie Rodriguez) is just one example of the changing idea of the "typical" American family.

Which explanation is right? A tremendous amount of effort has gone into trying to determine the correct answer, and the best evidence seems to indicate that while the experience of cohabitation may slightly increase the probability of divorce, the vast majority of the divorces among those who cohabit are simply due to the fact that people who choose to live together before they marry have characteristics (such as low levels of religiosity) that would make divorce more likely for them in the first place. (This is not to suggest, of course, that if you are aren't religious you have no chance of staying married, just that your probability is lower.)

There is one other interesting fact that bears on everything that has been said here. People who cohabit only with the person they marry seem to have as low a divorce rate as people who never cohabit. Perhaps this is because such people don't live together with enough partners to get a sense that relationships can be started and ended at will. Or perhaps it is because the very kinds of people who would live with only one partner have characteristics, such as higher religiosity, that keep divorce down.

Gay-Parent Families

Many homosexual men and women now live in stable relationships as couples, and there is a movement afoot to legally recognize these unions as marriages. Four recent decisions, three in the United States and one in Canada, demonstrate the current pulse of this movement.

In November 1998, voters in Hawaii decided to approve a state constitutional amendment to limit legal marriages to one man and one woman. Before the issue was put to the elec-

Maria Castillo (left) and Georjina Graciano hold their marriage license at City Hall in San Francisco, California, on February 16, 2004. The mayor of San Francisco, Gavin Newsom, ignited a passionate nationwide debate by allowing 4,037 same-sex couples to wed over a four-week period before the California high court annulled the marriages.

torate, the Hawaii Supreme Court was closer than ever before to legalizing gay marriage. In fact, in 1993 the state's supreme court ruled that restricting marriage to heterosexual couples was sex discrimination, and the court asked the state of Hawaii to show a compelling reason for the restriction. Many legal observers believe the court would have ruled for gay marriage if not for the vote on the constitutional amendment.

In May 1999, the Supreme Court of Canada ruled that same-sex couples are entitled to equal legal treatment as married couples. That is, same-sex partners are entitled to the same benefits as married partners under Ontario's Family Law Act. The Canada case was initiated when a lesbian filed for spousal support from her ex-partner. Initially, the Family Law Act had permitted only partners of the opposite sex to make a claim for spousal support after a breakup. The court therefore decided to first resolve the constitutional issue of whether same-sex couples have a right to seek spousal support. The Supreme Court's decision was that the Family Law Act's restriction to opposite-sex partners was unconstitutional.

An even more recent decision on the issue of same-sex couples came in July 2000, when the Vermont legislature voted to allow same-sex partners to register their "civil unions" with town clerks. The move allows same-sex couples access to all the state-granted rights, privileges, and responsibilities of marriage. Though this was a big victory for gay and lesbian marriage advocates, the measure falls short of calling the partnerships "marriage" and instead opts for "civil unions." Also, it is still unclear if a civil union in Vermont will be recognized in other states.

Most recently, in November 2003, the Massachusetts Supreme Court ruled that the state constitution does not forbid gays and lesbians to marry and gave the Massachusetts State Legislature six months to rewrite the state's marriage laws to permit gay marriages. This decision in part encouraged the mayor of San Francisco, Gavin Newsom, to start issuing marriage licenses to gay and lesbian couples. Mayor Newsom has argued that the state referendum passed in 2000, which defined marriage as between a man and a woman, violates the state constitution, which prevents discrimination against any social group. This prompted an immediate response from California's governor, Arnold Schwarzenegger, to order the state attorney general to halt the action, and for President George W. Bush to publicly endorse a constitutional amendment "defining and protecting marriage as a union of a man and woman as husband and wife" (CNN 2004). (The president did not call for a ban on civil unions between homosexuals, which would be left up to the states to determine.)

Although the ultimate outcome—whether these marriages will be respected by state law—is yet to be determined, these events clearly demonstrate the growing social movement toward legalizing gay marriages.

Beyond civil unions or marriages, same-sex couples are forming families with children. Relaxation of previously intolerant attitudes toward homosexuality has been accompanied by a growing tendency for courts to allocate custody of children to mothers living in gay relationships. Techniques of artificial insemination mean that gay women may have children and become gay-parent families without any heterosexual contact. Moreover, only two of the fifty U.S. states—Florida and New Hampshire—have laws preventing lesbians and gay men from adopting children.

Staying Single

Several factors have combined to increase the numbers of people living alone in modern Western societies. One is a trend toward later marriages—people now marry on average about three years later than was the case in 1960; another is the rising rate of divorce. Yet another is the growing number of old people in the population whose partners have died. Being single means different things at different periods of the life cycle. A larger proportion of people in their twenties are unmarried than used to be the case. By their mid-thirties, however, only a small minority of men and women have never been married. The majority of single people aged thirty to fifty are divorced and "in between" marriages. Most single people over fifty are widowed.

More than ever before, young people are leaving home simply to start an independent life rather than to get married (which had been one of the most common paths out of the home in the past). Hence it seems that the trend of "staying single" or living on one's own may be part of the societal trend toward valuing independence at the expense of family life. Still, most people (over 90 percent) ultimately marry, so although independence or "staying single" may be an increasingly common path out of the parental home, a large majority of these people will eventually marry (Goldschneider and Goldschneider 1999).

Study Outline

www.wwnorton.com/giddens

Kinship, Family, and Marriage: Key Concepts

- *Kinship, family,* and *marriage* are closely related terms of key significance for sociology and anthropology. Kinship comprises either genetic ties or ties initiated by marriage. A family is a group of kin having responsibility for the upbringing of children. Marriage is a union of two persons living together in a socially approved sexual relationship.
- A *nuclear family* refers to a household in which a married couple or single parent lives with their own or adopted children. Where kin in addition to parents and children live in the same household or are involved in close and continuous relationships, we speak of the existence of an *extended family.*
- In Western societies, marriage, and therefore the family, is associated with *monogamy* (a culturally approved sexual relationship between one man and one woman). Many other cultures tolerate or encourage *polygamy,* in which an individual may be married to two or more spouses at the same time. *Polygyny,* in which a man may marry more than one wife, is far more common than *polyandry,* in which a woman may have more than one husband.

The Family in History

- The modern Western family, which features close emotional bonds, domestic privacy, and a preoccupation with child rearing, is also characterized by *affective individualism,* meaning that marriage partners are usually selected on the basis of romantic love. This is now the norm, but it was not always so. In premodern Europe, parents, extended family members, or even landlords decided on marriage partners, basing their choices largely on social or economic considerations.

- There are many types of families in the world, but there is a trend toward the Western norm of the nuclear family. Some reasons for this trend include the Western ideal of romantic love, the growth of urbanization and of centralized governments, and employment in organizations outside traditional family influence.

Changes in Family Patterns

- There have been major changes in patterns of family life in the United States during the post–World War II period: A high percentage of women are in the paid labor force, there are rising rates of divorce, and substantial proportions of the population are either in single-parent households or are living with stepfamilies. *Cohabitation* (in which a couple lives together in a sexual relationship outside of marriage) has become increasingly common in many industrial countries.
- Family life is by no means always a picture of harmony and happiness. The "dark side" of the family is found in the patterns of abuse and family violence that often occur within it. Although no social class is immune to spousal abuse, studies do indicate that it is more common among low-income couples.
- Cohabitation and homosexuality have become more common in recent years. It seems certain that alternative forms of social and sexual relationships to those prevalent in the past will flourish still further. Yet marriage and the family remain firmly established institutions.

Key Concepts

affective individualism (p. 475)
cohabitation (p. 496)
extended family (p. 471)
family (p. 471)
families of orientation (p. 471)

families of procreation (p. 471)

kinship (p. 471)

marriage (p. 471)

matrilocal (p. 471)

monogamy (p. 471)

nuclear family (p. 471)

patrilocal (p. 471)

personality stabilization (p. 472)

polyandry (p. 471)

polygamy (p. 471)

polygyny (p. 471)

primary socialization (p. 472)

stepfamily (p. 490)

Review Questions

1. The process by which children learn the cultural norms of the society in which they are born is called
   a. personality stabilization.
   b. primary socialization.
   c. secondary socialization.
   d. personality socialization.

2. Cherlin (1999) and Goode (1971) found that spousal abuse is more common among
   a. high-income couples.
   b. middle-income couples.
   c. low-income couples.
   d. both high- and middle-income couples.

3. What's the difference between families of orientation and families of procreation?
   a. Families of orientation are childless couples and families of procreation are couples with children.
   b. A family of orientation is the family into which a person is born, whereas a family of procreation is the family into which a person enters as an adult and within which their children are raised.
   c. Families of orientation are gay couples and families of procreation are straight couples.
   d. A family of orientation is the family into which a person enters as an adult and within which children are raised; whereas a family of procreation is the family into which a person is born.

4. According to Cherlin's research on the effects of divorce on children,
   a. almost all children experience an initial period of calmness.
   b. a majority of children experience some long-term problems as a result of the breakup that may persist into adulthood.
   c. most people whose parents divorced did not experience serious mental problems.
   d. most children resume normal development without serious problems within about six months of separation.

5. What is the "absent father"?
   a. The term refers to the period from the late 1930s through the 1940s when fathers rarely saw their children because of war service.
   b. The term refers to the period from the 1950s through the 1970s when fathers were the family's only breadwinner and would only see their children in the evening and on weekends.
   c. The term refers to the period from the 1970s until today and it refers to fathers who, as a result of separation and divorce, either have infrequent contact with their children or lose touch with them all together.
   d. All of the above.

6. About half the babies in Sweden are born to unmarried mothers. Nineteen out of twenty of these are born in households with a father, but many will grow up without their own fathers at home, as half of all Swedish marriages end in divorce and unmarried parents split up three times more often than married ones. What kind of social and economic problems are caused by these figures?
   a. Many. Sweden has exactly the same experience as the United States as a result of its high divorce rate.
   b. Some, but fewer than in the United States. There is a greater social taboo against becoming a "deadbeat dad" in the more socialistic climate of Sweden.
   c. Very few. In Sweden, generous welfare benefits mean that single-parent families do not slip into poverty.
   d. None whatsoever.

7. Which one of the following is *not* true regarding the important changes in families occurring worldwide?
   a. There is a general trend toward the free choice of a spouse.
   b. The rights of women are becoming more widely recognized.
   c. Kin marriages are becoming more common.
   d. Higher levels of sexual freedom are developing in societies that were very restrictive.

8. Which theoretical perspective is interested in the experience of women in the domestic sphere?
   a. functionalism
   b. symbolic interactionism
   c. feminism
   d. none of the above.

9. What percent of American families is made up of a husband who works in paid employment and a wife who looks after the home, living together with their two children?
   a. 15 percent
   b. 25 percent
   c. 35 percent
   d. 45 percent

10. Research on the effects of family structure on children shows that
    a. girls experience less detrimental outcomes from stepfamily living than boys.
    b. girls experience more detrimental outcomes from stepfamily living than boys.

c. both girls and boys experience the same detrimental outcomes from stepfamily living.

d. stepfamily living has no detrimental outcomes for either boys or girls.

marriage and the family remain firmly established institutions in our society. Explain the rising patterns of cohabitation and single-parent households and show how these seemingly paradoxical trends can be reconciled with the claims offered by this textbook.

Thinking Sociologically Exercises

1. Using this textbook's presentation, compare the structures and lifestyles between contemporary white non-Hispanic, Asian American, Latino, and African American families.

2. Increases in cohabitation and single-parent households suggest that marriage may be beginning to fall by the wayside in our contemporary society. However, this chapter claims that

Data Exercises

www.wwnorton.com/giddens
Keyword: Data15

The data exercise for Chapter 15 focuses on recent changes in marriage and family patterns within the United States. It is designed to give you an opportunity to analyze survey data and learn more about what's been happening with these important social institutions.

The Development of Schooling

Know how and why systems of mass education emerged in the United States.

Education and Inequality

Become familiar with the most important research on whether education reduces or perpetuates inequality. Learn the social and cultural influences on educational achievement.

Education and Literacy in the Developing World

Know some basic facts about the education system and literacy rates of developing countries.

Communication and the Mass Media

Recognize the important effect of the mass media on society and learn some important theories about that effect.

Technological Change, Media, and Education

See the ways in which technological change is transforming the mass media and education.

CHAPTER SIXTEEN

EDUCATION AND THE MASS MEDIA

imagine being in the shoes—or the wooden clogs—of Jean-Paul Didion, a peasant boy growing up in a French farming community two centuries ago. In 1750, Jean-Paul is fourteen years old. He cannot read or write, but this is not uncommon; only a few of the adults in his village have the ability to decipher more than the odd word or two of written texts. There are some schools in nearby districts run by monks and nuns, but these are completely removed from Jean-Paul's experience. He has never known anyone well who attended school, save the local priest. For eight or nine years, Jean-Paul has been spending most of his days helping with domestic tasks and working in the fields. The older he gets, the longer each day he is expected to share in the back-breaking chores demanded by the intensive tilling of his father's plot of land.

Jean-Paul is likely never to leave the area in which he was born and may spend virtually the whole of his life within the confines of the village and surrounding fields, only occasionally traveling to other local villages and towns. He may have to wait until he is in his late fifties before inheriting his father's plot of land, sharing control of it with his younger brothers. Jean-Paul is aware that he is "French," that his country is ruled over by Louis XV, and that there is a wider world beyond even France itself. But he only has a vague awareness even of "France" as a distinct political entity. There is no such thing as "news," nor any regular means by which information about events elsewhere reaches him. What he knows of the wider world comes from stories and tales he has heard told by adults and by visiting travelers. Like others in his community, he learns about major events—such as the death of the king—only days, weeks, or sometimes months after they have occurred.

Although in modern terms Jean-Paul is uneducated, he is far from ignorant. He has a sensitive and developed understanding of the family and children, having had to care for those younger than him since he was very young. He is already highly knowledgeable about the land, methods of crop production, and ways of preserving and storing food. His mastery of local customs and traditions is profound, and he can turn his hand to many different tasks over and above agricultural cultivation, such as weaving or basket making.

Jean-Paul is an invented figure, but the above description portrays the typical experience of a boy growing up in preindustrial Europe. Compare this with our situation today. In the industrialized countries, virtually everyone can read and write—that is, people are *literate*. We have all gone through a process of formal schooling. We are all aware of the common characteristics we share with other members of the same society and have at least some sort of knowledge of its geographical and political position in the world and of its past history. Our lives are influenced at all ages beyond infancy by information we pick up through books, newspapers, magazines, radio, and television, in short, the various *media*. We live in a media-saturated world. The printed word and electronic communication, combined with the formal teaching provided by schools and colleges, have become fundamental to our way of life. This being so, schooling and the media extend the process of socialization, which we took up earlier in Chapter 4. There, we focused on early influences, especially parent–infant interaction, but we touched only briefly on schooling and the media.

In this chapter, two themes dominate: education and media as socializing processes and education and media as sources of power. First, we show how present-day education developed and analyze its socializing influence, which at times complements, and at others competes with, the family. We also look at education in relation to social inequality and consider how far the educational system serves to encourage or to reduce such inequality. We then move to studying the nature of modern mass media.

The Development of Schooling

The term *school* has its origins in a Greek word meaning "leisure," or "recreation." In premodern societies, schooling existed for the few who had the time and resources available to pursue the cultivation of the arts and philosophy. For some,

their engagement with schooling was like taking up a hobby. For others, like religious leaders or priests, schooling was a way of gaining skills and thus increasing their ability to interpret sacred texts. But for the vast majority of people, growing up meant learning by example the same social habits and work skills as their elders. Learning was a family affair—there were no schools at all for the mass of the population. Because children often started to help with domestic duties and farming work at a very young age, they rapidly became full-fledged members of the community.

Education in its modern form, the instruction of pupils within specially constructed school premises, gradually emerged in the first few years of the nineteenth century, when primary schools began to be constructed in Europe and the United States. One main reason for the rise of large educational systems was the process of industrialization, with its ensuing expansion of cities.

Education and Industrialization

Until the first few decades of the nineteenth century, most of the world's population had no schooling whatsoever. But as the industrial economy rapidly expanded, there was a great demand for specialized schooling that could produce an educated, capable workforce. As occupations became more differentiated and were increasingly located away from the home, it was impossible for work skills to be passed on directly from parents to children.

As educational systems became universal, more and more people were exposed to abstract learning (of subjects like math, science, history, literature, and so on), rather than to the practical transmission of specific skills. In a modern society, people have to be furnished with basic skills—such as reading, writing, and calculating—and a general knowledge of their physical, social, and economic environment; but it is also important that they know how to learn, so that they are able to master new, sometimes very technical, forms of information. An advanced society also needs pure research and insights with no immediate practical value to push out the boundaries of knowledge.

In the modern age, education and qualifications became an important stepping-stone into job opportunities and careers. Schools and universities not only broaden people's minds and perspectives but are expected to prepare new generations of citizens for participation in economic life. The right balance between a generalist education and specific work skills is a difficult one at which to arrive. Specialized forms of technical, vocational, and professional training often supplement pupils' liberal education and facilitate the transition from school to work. Internships and work experience schemes, for example,

With the spread of industrialization, the demand for educated workers increased. The newly expanded education systems emphasized basic skills like reading, writing, and mathematics instead of specific skills for work.

allow young people to develop specific knowledge applicable to their future careers.

Although many teachers in schools and universities seek above all to provide a well-rounded education, policy makers and employers are concerned to ensure that education and training programs coincide with a country's economic profile and employment demands. Yet in times of rapid economic and technical change, there is not always a smooth match between the priorities of the educational system and the availability of professional opportunities. The rapid expansion of a country's health-care system, for example, would dramatically increase the demand for trained health professionals, laboratory technicians, capable administrators, and computer systems analysts familiar with public-health issues. Industrywide changes in factory-floor production technology would require a work force with a set of skills that might be in short supply.

Sociological Theories

Sociologists have debated why formal systems of schooling developed in modern societies by studying the social functions that schools provide. For example, some have argued that mass education promotes feelings of nationalism and aided the development of national societies, constituted of citizens from different regions who would know the same history and speak a common language (Ramirez and Boli 1987). Marxist sociologists have argued that the expansion of education was brought about by employer's need for certain personality characteristics in their workers—self-discipline, dependability, punctuality, obedience, and the like—which are all taught in schools (Bowles and Gintis 1976). Another influential perspective comes from the sociologist Randall Collins (1971, 1979), who has argued that the primary social function of mass education derives from the

need for diplomas and degrees to determine one's credentials for a job, even if the work involved has nothing to do with the education one has received. Over time, the practice of credentialism results in demands for higher credentials, which require higher levels of educational attainment. Jobs, such as sales representative, that thirty years ago would have required a high school diploma now require a college degree. Since educational attainment is closely related to class position, credentialism reinforces the class structure within a society.

Education and Inequality

The expansion of education has always been closely linked to the ideals of democracy. Reformers value education for its own sake—for the opportunity it provides for individuals to develop their capabilities. Yet education has also consistently been seen as a means of equalization. Access to universal education, it has been argued, could help reduce disparities of wealth and power. Are educational opportunities equal for everyone? Has education in fact proved to be a great equalizer? Much research has been devoted to answering these questions.

"Savage Inequalities"

Between 1988 and 1990, the journalist Jonathan Kozol studied schools in about thirty neighborhoods around the United States. There was no special logic to the way he chose the schools, except that he went where he happened to know teachers, principals, or ministers. What startled him most was the segregation within these schools and the inequalities among them. Kozol brought these terrible conditions to the attention of the American people in his book *Savage Inequalities* (1991), which became a best-seller.

In his passionate opening chapter, he first took readers to East St. Louis, Illinois, a city that is 98 percent black, had no regular trash collection, and few jobs. Three quarters of its residents were living on welfare at the time. City residents were forced to use their backyards as garbage dumps, which attracted a plague of flies and rats during the hot summer months. One resident told Kozol about "rats as big as puppies" that lived in his mother's yard. City residents also contended with pollution fumes from two major chemical plants in the city. Another public health problem resulted from raw sewage, which regularly backed up into people's homes. East St. Louis also had some of the sickest children in the United States, with extremely high rates of infant death, asthma, and poor nutrition and extremely low rates of immunization. Only 55 percent of the children had been fully immunized for polio, diphtheria, measles, and whooping cough. Among the city's other social problems were crime, dilapidated housing, poor health care, and lack of education.

Kozol showed how the problems of the city often spilled over into the schools, in this case literally. Over the course of two weeks, raw sewage backed up into the school on three occasions, each time requiring the evacuation of students and the cancellation of classes. But the city's problems also negatively affected the school on a daily basis. Teachers often had to hold classes without chalk or paper. One teacher commented on the school's poor conditions by saying, "Our problems are severe. I don't even know where to begin. I have no materials with the exception of a single textbook given to each child. If I bring in anything else—books or tapes or magazines—I bring it in myself. The high school has no VCRs. They are such a crucial tool. So many good things run on public television. I can't make use of anything I see unless I unhook my VCR and bring it into school. The AV equipment in the school is so old that we are pressured not to use it." Comments from students reflected the same concerns. "I don't go to physics class, because my lab has no equipment," said one student. Another added, "The typewriters in my typing class don't work." A third said, "I wanted to study Latin but we don't have Latin in this school." Only 55 percent of the students in this high school ultimately graduate, about one third of whom go on to college.

Kozol also wrote about the other end of the inequality spectrum, taking readers into a wealthy suburban school in Westchester County outside of New York City. This school had 96 computers for the 546 students. Most studied a foreign language (including Latin) for four or five years. Two thirds of the senior class were enrolled in an advanced placement (AP) class. Kozol visited an AP class to ask students about their perceptions of inequalities within the educational system. Students at this school were well aware of the economic advantages that they enjoyed at both home and school. In regard to their views about students less-well-off than themselves, the general consensus was that equal spending among schools was a worthy goal but it would probably make little difference since poor students lack motivation and would fail because of other problems. These students also realized that equalizing spending could have adverse affects on their school. As one student said, "If you equalize the money, someone's got to be shortchanged. I don't doubt that [poor] children are getting a bad deal. But do we want everyone to get a mediocre education?"

It is impossible to read these descriptions of life in East St. Louis and Westchester County without believing that the extremes of wealth and poverty in the public schools are being exposed. Yet, many sociologists have argued that although Kozol's book is a moving portrait, it provides an inaccurate

The problem of schools falling into disrepair is a chronic one in poverty-stricken areas all over the country. Dilapidated schools like this one in the South Bronx lack funding for even the most basic necessities and, once they have fallen into a state of ruin, there is no money to undertake necessary repairs.

view of educational inequality. Why would Kozol's research not be compelling? There are several reasons, including the unsystematic way that he chose the schools that he studied. But the most important criticism of his work is that sociological research has shown that student achievement varies much more within schools than among schools—the proportions are about 80 percent to 20 percent. This means that differences among schools are not the main sources of inequality in achievement, even though Kozol's study may provoke outrage over these inequalities. This fact does not mean that Kozol was wrong—there are schools at both extremes—but these are not the kinds of extremes that account for most educational inequality in America. Let's now look more closely at the work that sociologists have done to understand this complex relationship between education and inequality.

Sociological research addressing equal educational opportunities falls into two categories: research assessing between-school effects and research assessing within-school effects. Between-school effects refer to inequalities among children who go to different schools, asking—for example—whether students who attend schools with more resources end up ahead in the socioeconomic system. Within-school effects are differences among students in the same school, asking—for example—if dividing students into honors or remedial classes leads to later disparities in educational attainment, occupational prestige, and wealth.

Coleman's Study of Between-school Effects in American Education

The study of between-school effects has been the focus of sociological research on the educational system for the past several decades. One of the classic investigations of educational inequality was undertaken in the United States in the 1960s. As part of the Civil Rights Act of 1964, the commissioner of education was required to prepare a report on educational inequalities resulting from differences of ethnic background, religion, and national origin. James Coleman, a sociologist, was appointed director of the research program. The outcome was a study based on one of the most extensive research projects ever carried out in sociology (Coleman et al. 1966).

Information was collected on more than half a million pupils who were given a range of achievement tests assessing verbal and nonverbal abilities, reading levels, and mathematical skills. Sixty thousand teachers also completed forms providing data for about four thousand schools. The report found that a large majority of children went to schools that effectively segregated black from white. Almost 80 percent of schools attended by white students contained only 10 percent or less African American students. White and Asian American students scored higher on achievement tests than did blacks and other ethnic minority students. Coleman had supposed his results would also show mainly African American schools to have worse facilities, larger classes, and more inferior buildings than schools that were predominantly white. But it was surprising that the results showed far fewer differences of this type than had been anticipated.

Coleman, therefore, concluded that the material resources provided in schools made little difference to educational performance; the decisive influence was the children's backgrounds. The report stated, "Inequalities imposed on children by their home, neighborhood, and peer environment are carried along to become the inequalities with which they confront adult life at the end of school" (Coleman et al. 1966). There was, however, some evidence that students from deprived backgrounds who formed close friendships with those from more favorable circumstances were likely to be more successful educationally.

Not long after Coleman's study, Christopher Jencks and coworkers (1972) produced an equally celebrated work that reviewed empirical evidence accumulated on education and inequality up to the end of the 1960s. Jencks reaffirmed two of the earlier study's conclusions: (1) that educational and occupational attainment are governed mainly by family background and nonschool factors, and (2) that on their own, educational reforms can produce only minor effects on existing inequalities. Jencks's work has been criticized on methodological grounds, but the study's overall conclusions remain persuasive. Subsequent research has tended to confirm them.

Tracking and Within-school Effects

The practice of **tracking**—dividing students into groups that receive different instruction on the basis of assumed similarities in ability or attainment—is common in American schools. In some schools, students are tracked only for certain subjects; in others, for all subjects. Sociologists have long believed that tracking is entirely negative in its effects. The conventional wisdom has been that tracking partly explains why schooling seems to have little effect on existing social inequalities, since being placed in a particular track labels a student as either able or otherwise. As we have seen in the case of labeling and deviance, once attached, such labels are hard to break away from. Children from more privileged backgrounds, in which academic work is encouraged, are likely to find themselves in the higher tracks early on—and by and large stay there (Figure 16.1).

Jeannie Oakes (1985) studied tracking in twenty-five junior and senior high schools, both large and small and in both urban and rural areas. But she concentrated on differences *within* schools rather than between them. She found that although several schools claimed they did not track students, virtually all of them had mechanisms for sorting students into groups that seemed to be alike in ability and achievement, to make teaching easier. In other words, they employed tracking but did not choose to use the term *tracking* itself. Even where tracking existed only in this informal fashion, she found strong labels developing—high ability, low achieving, slow, average, and so on. Individual students in these groups came to be defined by teachers, other students, and themselves in terms of such labels. A student in a high-achieving group was considered a high-achieving *person*—smart and quick. Pupils in a

The Internationalization of Education

How many foreign students are enrolled in your sociology course? How many foreign students are there at your university? In 1943, approximately 8,000 foreign students were enrolled in American colleges and universities. By 2000, this number had skyrocketed to more than 537,000 (U.S. Bureau of the Census 2006a). Although the American university system as a whole grew considerably during this period, such that 573,000 students represented only 3.3 percent of total 2004 student enrollment, it is clear that foreign students are flocking to the United States in record numbers. Most foreign students today come from Asia—China, Japan, Taiwan, India, and South Korea all send sizeable contingents of students abroad. The

United States takes in more foreign students than any other country, and there are six times as many foreign students in the United States as there are American students overseas. What do foreign students in the United States study? At the undergraduate level, more than 18 percent focus on business and management, 16.5 percent study engineering, and 9 percent concentrate on math and computer science. Each of these fields, however, has declined slightly in popularity in recent years as foreign students increasingly study the physical and life sciences and well as health professions (Institute of International Education [IIE] 2005). More than 20 percent of foreign graduate students study engineering, and of those receiving a doctorate in engineering, 60 percent were foreign students (Lambert 1995; National Center for Education Statistics 2005).

Some scholars regard the exchange of international students as a vital component of globalization. Foreign students, in addition to serving as global "carriers" of specialized technical and scientific knowledge, have an important cultural role to play in the globalizing process. Cross-national understandings are enhanced and xenophobic and isolationist attitudes are minimized as native students in host countries develop social ties to their foreign classmates and as foreign students return to their country of origin with an appreciation for the cultural mores of the nation in which they have studied.

Yet there is considerable debate in the United States about what is sometimes called the "internationalization of education." On most college campuses, it is not hard to find disgrun-

low-achieving group came to be seen as slow, below average—or, in more forthright terms, as dummies, sweathogs, or yahoos. What is the effect of tracking on students in the low group? A subsequent study by Oakes (1990) found that these students received a poorer education in terms of the quality of courses, teachers, and textbooks made available to them. Moreover, the negative effect of tracking affected mostly African American, Latino, and poor students.

The usual reason given for tracking is that bright children learn more quickly and effectively in a group of others who are equally able and that clever students are held back if placed in

mixed groups. Surveying the evidence, Oakes attempted to show that these assumptions are wrong. The results of later research investigations are not wholly consistent, but a pathbreaking study by sociologist Adam Gamoran and his colleagues (1995) concluded that Oakes was partially correct in her arguments. They agreed with Oakes's conclusions that tracking reinforces previously existing inequalities for average or poor students but countered her argument by asserting that tracking does have positive benefits for "advanced" students. The debate about the effects of tracking is sure to continue as scholars continue to analyze more data.

tled students who complain that given the competitive nature of the U.S. higher education system, the influx of foreign students deprives deserving Americans of educational opportunities. Moreover, although more than two thirds of foreign students receive nothing in the way of scholarships, some top-notch foreign students *are* given financial inducements to attend American schools. The outcry against this practice has been loudest at public universities, which receive support from tax revenue. Critics charge that U.S. taxpayers should not shoulder the financial burden for educating foreign students whose families have not paid U.S. taxes and who are likely to return home after earning their degrees.

Supporters of international education find such arguments unconvincing. Some Americans may lose out to foreign students in the competition for slots at prestigious universities, but this is a small price to pay for the economic, political, and cultural benefits the United States receives from having educated millions of foreign business executives, policy makers, scientists, and professionals over the years—many of whom became sympathetically disposed to the United States as a result of their experiences here. And although some foreign students receive scholarships from American universities, most are supported by their parents. In fact, it is estimated that foreign students pump hundreds of millions of dollars each year into the U.S. economy—over $13 billion in 2005 (IIE 2005). Rather than curtail the number of foreign students admitted to American universities, supporters of international education suggest that even more should be done to encourage the exchange of students. On the one hand, greater effort should be made to recruit foreign students, to help them select the university and program that will best meet their needs and to provide them with a positive social and educational experience while they are in the United States. On the other hand, more Americans should be encouraged to study abroad. American students are notorious for having poor foreign-

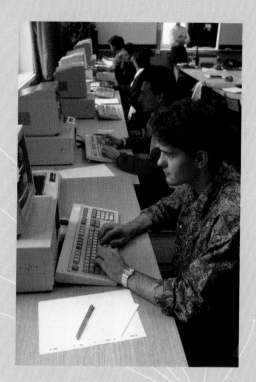

language skills and for knowing little about global geography, much less about the cultures of other nations. This ignorance puts the United States at a disadvantage relative to other countries as the world becomes increasingly globalized; encouraging Americans to study overseas may be the best way to inculcate a global worldview.

Should there be a greater focus on international education in American colleges and universities? Should the international exchange of students be expanded? These are among the issues that educational institutions are forced to confront in the context of globalization. Still, more and more U.S. students are studying abroad—191,321 in 2004–05, nearly a 10 percent increase over the year before (IIE 2005).

The Social Reproduction of Inequality

The educational system provides more than formal instruction: It socializes children to get along with each other, teaches basic skills, and transmits elements of culture such as language and values. Sociologists have looked at education as a form of social reproduction, a concept discussed in Chapter 1 and elsewhere. In the context of education, social reproduction refers to the ways in which schools help perpetuate social and economic inequalities across the generations. It also directs our

attention to the means whereby schools influence the learning of values, attitudes, and habits via the hidden curriculum.

The concept of the **hidden curriculum** addresses the fact that much of what is learned in school has nothing directly to do with the formal content of lessons. Schools, by the nature of the discipline and regimentation they entail, tend to teach students "passive consumption"—an uncritical acceptance of the existing social order. These lessons are not consciously taught; they are implicit in school procedures and organization. The hidden curriculum teaches children that their role in life is "to know their place and to sit still with it" (Illich 1983). Children

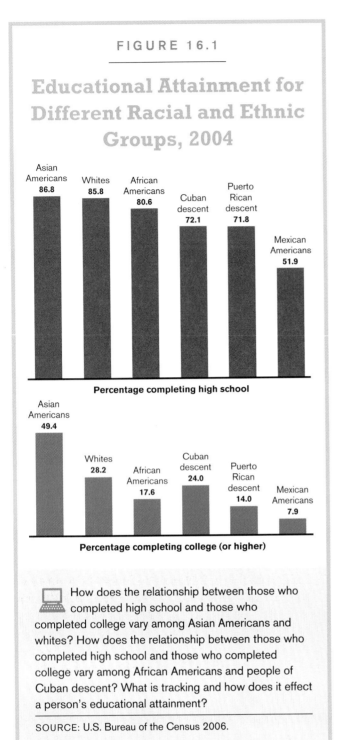

FIGURE 16.1

Educational Attainment for Different Racial and Ethnic Groups, 2004

Percentage completing high school

Asian Americans 86.8
Whites 85.8
African Americans 80.6
Cuban descent 72.1
Puerto Rican descent 71.8
Mexican Americans 51.9

Percentage completing college (or higher)

Asian Americans 49.4
Whites 28.2
African Americans 17.6
Cuban descent 24.0
Puerto Rican descent 14.0
Mexican Americans 7.9

How does the relationship between those who completed high school and those who completed college vary among Asian Americans and whites? How does the relationship between those who completed high school and those who completed college vary among African Americans and people of Cuban descent? What is tracking and how does it effect a person's educational attainment?

SOURCE: U.S. Bureau of the Census 2006.

Schools also reinforce variations in cultural values and outlooks picked up in early life. As we saw earlier in Chapter 8, French sociologist Pierre Bourdieu (1984, 1988) calls this process the transmission of **cultural capital,** whereby the cultural advantages that coming from a good home confers are capital, which succeeding generations inherit from one another, thus perpetuating inequalities.

Another influential theory on the question of how schools reproduce social inequality was introduced by Samuel Bowles and Herbert Gintis (1976). Modern education, they propose, is a response to the economic needs of industrial capitalism. Schools help provide the technical and social skills required by industrial enterprise, and they instill discipline and respect for authority into the labor force.

Authority relations in school, which are hierarchical and place strong emphasis on obedience, directly parallel those dominating the workplace. The rewards and punishments held out in school also replicate those found in the world of work. Schools help motivate some individuals toward "achievement" and "success," while discouraging others, who find their way into low-paying jobs.

Bowles and Gintis accept that the development of mass education has had many beneficial consequences. Illiteracy rates are low compared with premodern times, and schooling provides access to learning experiences that are intrinsically self-fulfilling. Yet because education has expanded mainly as a response to economic needs, the school system falls far short of what enlightened reformers had hoped from it. That is, schooling has not become the "great equalizer"; rather, schools merely produce for many the feelings of powerlessness that continue throughout their experience in industrial settings. The ideals of personal development central to education can be achieved only if people have the capability to control the conditions of their own life and to develop their talents and abilities of self-expression. Under the current system, schools "are destined to legitimate inequality, limit personal development to forms compatible with submission to arbitrary authority, and aid in the process whereby youth are resigned to their fate" (Bowles and Gintis 1976). If there were greater democracy in the workplace and more equality in society at large, Bowles and Gintis argue, a system of education could be developed that would provide for greater individual fulfillment.

spend long hours in school, and as Illich stresses, they learn a great deal more in the school context than is contained in the lessons they are actually taught. Children get an early taste of what the world of work will be like, learning that they are expected to be punctual and apply themselves diligently to the tasks that those in authority set for them.

Intelligence and Inequality

Suppose differences in educational attainment, and in subsequent occupations and incomes, directly reflected differential intelligence. In such circumstances, it might be argued, there is in fact equality of opportunity in the school system, for people find a level equivalent to their innate potential.

WHAT IS INTELLIGENCE?

For years, psychologists, geneticists, statisticians, and others have debated whether there exists a single human capability that can be called **intelligence** and, if so, whether it rests on innately determined differences. Intelligence is difficult to define because, as the term is usually employed, it covers qualities that may be unrelated to one another. We might suppose, for example, that the "purest" form of intelligence is the ability to solve abstract mathematical puzzles. However, people who are very good at such puzzles sometimes show low capabilities in other areas, such as history or art. Because the concept has proved so resistant to accepted definition, some psychologists have proposed (and many educators have by default accepted) that intelligence should simply be regarded as "what **IQ (intelligence quotient)** tests measure." Most IQ tests consist of a mixture of conceptual and computational problems. The tests are constructed so that the average score is 100 points: Anyone scoring below is thus labeled "below-average intelligence," and anyone scoring above is "above-average intelligence." In spite of the fundamental difficulty in measuring intelligence, IQ tests are widely used in research studies, as well as in schools and businesses.

IQ AND GENETIC FACTORS: THE SOCIOLOGICAL DEBATE

Scores on IQ tests do in fact correlate highly with academic performance (which is not surprising, since IQ tests were originally developed to predict success at school). They therefore also correlate closely with social, economic, and ethnic differences, because these are associated with variations in levels of educational attainment. White students score better, on average, than African Americans or members of other disadvantaged minorities. An article published by Arthur Jensen in 1967 caused a furor by attributing IQ differences between blacks and whites in part to genetic variations (see also Jensen 1979).

More recently, the psychologist Richard J. Herrnstein and the sociologist Charles Murray have reopened the debate about IQ and education in a controversial way. They argue in their book *The Bell Curve* (1994) that the accumulated evidence linking IQ to genetic inheritance has now become overwhelming. The significant differences in intelligence among various racial and ethnic groups, they say, must in part be explained in terms of heredity. According to Herrnstein and Murray, the available evidence strongly indicates that some ethnic groups on average have higher IQs than other groups. Asian Americans, particularly Japanese Americans and Chinese Americans, on average possess higher IQs than whites, although the difference is not large. The average IQs of Asians and whites, however, are substantially higher than those of blacks. Summarizing the findings of 156 studies, Herrnstein and Murray find an average difference of sixteen IQ points between these two racial groups. The authors argue that such differences in inherited intelligence contribute in an important way to social divisions in American society. The smarter an individual is, the greater the chance that he or she will rise in the social scale. Those at the top are there partly because they are smarter than the rest of the population—from which it follows that those at the bottom remain there because, on average, they are not as smart.

Herrnstein and Murray's claim created a great deal of controversy and raised the ire and indignation of countless liberals, social scientists, and members of the African American community. Although Herrnstein and Murray's claims may be seen as racist and reprehensible, is this sufficient reason to attack their work? Or are their conclusions based on faulty social research? The answer to both questions is a resounding yes. A team of sociologists at the University of California at Berkeley have reanalyzed much of the data that Herrnstein and Murray based their conclusions on and came up with quite different findings.

In the original analysis, Herrnstein and Murray analyzed data from the National Longitudinal Study of Youth (NLSY), a survey of more than ten thousand young Americans who were interviewed multiple times over more than a decade. As part of this study, subjects were given the Armed Forces Qualifying Test (AFQT), a short test that assesses IQ. Herrnstein and Murray then conducted statistical analyses, which used the AFQT score to predict a variety of outcomes. They concluded that having a high IQ was the best predictor of later economic success and that low IQ was the best predictor of poverty later in life.

The Berkeley sociologists, in their 1996 book *Inequality by Design* (Fischer et al. 1996), countered that the AFQT does not necessarily measure intelligence, but only how much a person has learned in school. Moreover, they found that intelligence is only one factor among several that predict how well people do in life. Social factors including education, gender, community conditions, marital status, current economic conditions, and—perhaps most important—parents' socioeconomic status better predict one's occupational and economic success. In the original analysis, Herrnstein and Murray measured parents' socioeconomic status by taking an average of mother's education, father's education, father's occupation, and family income.

The Berkeley sociologists recognized that each of these four factors matters differently in predicting a child's occupational outcomes and thus weighted the four components differently. Their analysis showed that the effects of socioeconomic background on a young adult's risk of later poverty were substantially greater than Herrnstein and Murray had originally found. The Berkeley sociologists also recognized that IQ is closely associated with one's level of education. They reanalyzed the NLSY data, taking into consideration the

What If We Ended Social Promotion?

[In 1998], I chaired a study of appropriate uses of testing for the National Research Council. The NRC panel was a diverse group of fifteen scholars from all over the country. We wrote our report, "High Stakes: Testing for Tracking, Promotion and Graduation," in response to a congressional mandate. The study was prompted by the Clinton administration's proposal, in 1997, for voluntary national tests of fourth grade reading and eighth grade math. The panel took no position about the value of voluntary national testing for its stated purposes—to tell American students, parents, and teachers how well they are doing relative to high national standards—but we recommended strongly against such tests' use for any high-stakes purpose. The report, published [in 1999], has a lot of useful information about proper test use, and I commend it to readers. One of the strongest recommendations is that "accountability for educational outcomes should be a shared responsibility of states, school districts, public officials, educators, parents, and students. High standards cannot be established and maintained merely by imposing them on students."

Early in its work, the NRC panel decided to consider whether good tests could serve bad purposes. Thus, we evaluated the consequences of high-stakes educational decisions that may be based, at least in part, on test scores. In particular, we found—as American schools presently operate—that decisions to place students in typical lower-level tracks and decisions to hold students back to repeat the same grade are not educationally sound. Those decisions hurt students, and good tests will not improve them. This is not to say that all forms of tracking are bad for students, or that all grade retention is necessarily bad for students. Our findings were based on the actual and typical, not the ideal. But research evidence based on actual experience should inform new policies.

Robert M. Hauser

***

We should know that a new policy works before we try it out on a large scale. In its plan to end social promotion, the administration appears to have mixed a number of fine and credible proposals for educational reform with an enforcement provision—flunking kids by the carload lot—about which the great mass of evidence is strongly negative. And this policy [would] hurt poor and minority children most of all.

***

Students who have been held back typically do not catch up; in fact, low-performing students learn more if they are promoted—even without remedial help—than if they are held

individuals' level of education, and found that Herrnstein and Murray drastically overestimated the effects of IQ on a person's later achievements.

The relationship between race and intelligence is also best explained by social rather than biological causes, according to the Berkeley sociologists. All societies have oppressed ethnic

groups. Low status, often coupled with discrimination and mistreatment, leads to socioeconomic deprivation, group segregation, and a stigma of inferiority. The combination of these forces often prevents racial minorities from obtaining education, and consequently, their scores on standardized intelligence tests are lower.

back. One reason for this is that the elementary and secondary school curriculum does not change radically from one grade to the next; there is a lot of review and overlap. Another is that it is simply boring to repeat exactly the same material.

Students who have been held back are much more likely to drop out before completing high school. That effect often occurs many years after a student is held back in grade and thus is invisible—without careful longitudinal study—to those who make the retention decision. The teachers and administrators who make decisions to hold children back do not have to live with the long-term consequences of their decisions.

***

There is one more critical point on which the National Research Council report provides strong evidence: We do not practice social promotion in the United States now, and we have not practiced it for many years. Our statistics are not very good; neither the federal government nor most states collect the right data, but we do know a few things.

Age at entry to first grade has increased since 1970. At that time, almost all six-year-olds were in the first grade (about 4 percent of six-year-old boys and 8 percent of six-year-old girls were enrolled below the first grade). In 1996, 18 percent of six-year-olds were enrolled below the first grade. Part of that change is due to holding children back in kindergarten.

Many students are held back during elementary and secondary school. Nationally, among children who entered school in the late 1980s, 21 percent were enrolled below the usual grade at ages six to eight; 28 percent were below the usual grade at ages nine to eleven; 31 percent at ages twelve to fourteen; and this rose to 36 percent at ages fifteen to seventeen. Not counting kindergarten and the later grades of high school, this means that at least 15 percent of children—and probably 20 percent—have been held back at some time in their childhood.

Worse yet, minorities and poor children are the most likely to be held back. Black, Hispanic, and white children enter first grade at just about the same ages, but between entry and adolescence, about 10 percent of white girls fall behind in grade, while 25 percent to 30 percent of minority children fall behind. By ages fifteen to seventeen, 45 percent to 50 percent of black

and Hispanic youths are below the expected grade levels for their ages.

Holding students back—flunking them—has a much greater impact on minority and poor youths than on majority, middle-class children. It decreases educational opportunity, and it makes opportunities less equal among groups. For thirty-five years, American education has aimed to reduce social inequality. While much remains to be done, we have made major gains—narrowing differences in test scores in the 1970s and 1980s and reducing the dropout difference between majority and minority children. If we start holding back ever larger numbers of children, we are likely to reverse the progress of the past four decades.

SOURCE: Robert M. Hauser, "What If We Ended Social Promotion?" *Education Week*, April 7, 1999.

ROBERT M. HAUSER is the Vilas research professor of sociology in the Center for Demography at the University of Wisconsin-Madison. He is the editor, with Jay P. Heubert, of the National Research Council's report "High Stakes: Testing for Tracking, Promotion, and Graduation" (National Academy Press, 1999).

The average lower IQ score of African Americans in the United States is remarkably similar to that of deprived ethnic minorities in other countries—such as the "untouchables" in India (who are at the very bottom of the caste system), the Maori in New Zealand, and the *burakumin* of Japan. Children in these groups score an average of 10 to 15

IQ points below children belonging to the ethnic majority. The *burakumin*—descendants of people who in the eighteenth century, as a result of local wars, were dispossessed from their land and became outcasts and vagrants—are a particularly interesting example. They are not in any way physically distinct from other Japanese, although they have suffered from prejudice and discrimination for centuries. In this case, the difference in average IQ results cannot derive from genetic variations since there are no genetic differences between them and the majority population; yet the IQ difference is as thoroughly fixed as that between blacks and whites. *Burakumin* children in America, where they are treated like other Japanese, do as well on IQ tests as other Japanese.

Such observations strongly suggest that the IQ variations between African Americans and whites in the United States result from social and cultural differences. This conclusion receives further support from a comparative study of fourteen nations (including the United States) showing that average IQ scores have risen substantially over the past half century for the population as a whole (Coleman 1987). IQ tests are regularly updated. When old and new versions of the tests are given to the same group of people, they score significantly higher on the old tests. Present-day children taking IQ tests from the 1930s outscored 1930s groups by an average of 15 points—just the kind of average difference that currently separates blacks and whites. Children today are not innately superior in intelligence to their parents or grandparents; the shift presumably derives from increasing prosperity and social advantages. The average social and economic gap between whites and African Americans is at least as great as that between the different generations and is sufficient to explain the variation in IQ scores. Although there may be genetic variations between individuals that influence scores on IQ tests, these have no overall connection to racial differences.

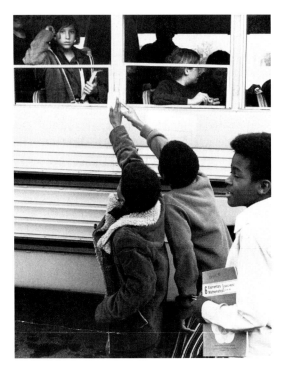

In 1970 a U.S. judge in North Carolina ordered that black students be bused to white schools and that white students be bused to black schools. It was hoped that this crosstown school busing would end the de facto segregation of public schools caused by white students living in predominantly white neighborhoods and black students living in predominantly black neighborhoods.

Educational Reform in the United States

Research done by sociologists has played a big role in reforming the educational system. The object of James Coleman's research, commissioned as part of the 1964 Civil Rights Act, was not solely academic; it was undertaken to influence policy. And influence policy it certainly did. On the basis of the act, it was decided in the courts that segregated schools violated the rights of minority pupils. But rather than attacking the origins of educational inequalities directly, as Christopher Jencks's later work suggested was necessary, the courts decided that the schools in each district should achieve a similar racial balance. Thus began the practice of busing students to other schools.

Busing provoked a great deal of opposition, particularly from parents and children in white areas, and led to episodes of violence at the gates of schools where the children were bused in from other neighborhoods. White children paraded with placards reading: "We don't want them!" Busing in fact

met with a good deal of success, reducing levels of school segregation quite steeply, particularly in the South. But busing has also produced a number of unintended consequences. Some white parents reacted to busing by either putting their children into private schools or moving to mainly white suburbs where busing wasn't practiced. As a result, in the cities, some schools are virtually as segregated as the old schools were in the past. Busing, however, was only one factor prompting the white flight to the suburbs. Whites also left as a reaction to urban decay: to escape city crowding, housing problems, and rising rates of crime.

While busing is less prominent today as an issue, another problem regarding the American educational system has become an important focus of research: functional illiteracy. Most of the population can read and write at a very basic level, but one in every five adults is functionally illiterate—when they leave school, they can't read or write at the fourth-grade level (U.S. Department of Education 1993). Of course, the United States is a country of immigrants, who when they arrive may not be able to read and write and who may also have trouble with English. But this doesn't explain why America lags behind most other industrial countries in terms of its level of functional illiteracy, because many people affected are not recent immigrants at all.

What is to be done? Some educationists have argued that the most important change that needs to be made is to improve the quality of teaching, either by increasing teachers' pay or by introducing performance-related pay scales, with higher salaries going to the teachers who are most effective in the classroom. Others have proposed giving schools more control over their budgets (a reform that has been carried out in Britain). The idea is that more responsibility for and control over budgeting decisions will create a greater drive to improve the school. Further proposals include the refunding of federal programs such as Head Start to ensure healthy early child development and thus save millions of dollars in later costs. Another proposal that has gained numerous supporters in recent years is that public education should be privatized.

PRIVATIZATION

Widespread concern about the crisis in education has opened the door for *public–private partnerships* aimed at injecting private sector know-how into failing public schools. In 1994, then President Bill Clinton signed into law the Goals 2000: Educate America Act, which authorized states to use federal funds for experiments with school privatization. Local school districts can choose to contract out specific educational services—or the entire school administration—to private companies without losing federal funding. In the past decade, a number of U.S. school districts—including large urban systems such as those in Hartford, Baltimore, and Minneapolis—have invited for-profit educational companies to run their school systems.

Supporters of school privatization argue that state and federal education authorities have shown that they are unable to improve the nation's schools. The educational system, they argue, is wasteful and bureaucratic; it spends a disproportionate amount of its funding on noninstructional administrative costs. Because of their top-heavy nature, it is nearly impossible for school systems to be flexible and innovative. Incompetent teachers are difficult to remove because of the strength of teacher unions.

What backers of school privatization claim can solve these problems is a strong dose of private-sector ideology: competition, experimentation, and incentive. For-profit companies can run school systems more efficiently and produce better outcomes by applying private sector logic. Good teachers would be attracted to teaching—and retained—by performance-based pay schemes, while underperforming teachers could be removed more easily. Competition within and between schools would lead to higher levels of innovation; privatized schools would have more liberty to institutionalize the results of successful experiments.

One of the leading players in the U.S. market for privatized education is the Edison Project, an educational company that manages a chain of eighty public schools in sixteen different states. The verdict on whether the Edison Project is improving educational outcomes in its schools is mixed, and the company itself has been heavily criticized on a number of fronts, including for poor financial management. Critics have been quick to point out that the Edison Project's vision for schools is little more than a slick repackaging of well-known practices from public education, such as cooperative learning and pupil-centered teaching (Molnar 1996). The company requires that all students in Edison schools have a computer at home—and assists those families that cannot afford them—but it is less clear how this enthusiasm for technology is linked into the curriculum in a meaningful way. Opponents of school privatization argue that companies such as the Edison Project are less serious about reforming education and reducing inequalities than about promoting education reform as a lucrative market for wealthy investors.

The crisis in American schools won't be solved in the short term, and it won't be solved by educational reforms alone, no matter how thoroughgoing. The lesson of sociological research is that inequalities and barriers in educational opportunity reflect wider social divisions and tensions. While the United States remains wracked by racial tensions and the polarization between decaying cities and affluent suburbs persists, the crisis in the school system is likely to prove difficult to turn around.

Education and Literacy in the Developing World

Literacy is the "baseline" of education. Without it, schooling cannot proceed. We take it for granted in the West that the majority of people are literate, but as has been mentioned, this is only a recent development in Western history, and in previous times no more than a tiny proportion of the population had any literacy skills.

Today, over 23 percent of the population of developing countries is still illiterate (Global Map 16.1). The Indian government has estimated the number of illiterate people in that country alone to be over 268 million (39 percent of the population), a number that almost equals the total population of the United States. Even if the provision of primary education increased to match the level of population growth, illiteracy would not be markedly reduced for years, because a high proportion of those who cannot read or write are adults. The absolute number of

Thomas Jefferson High School

The route to [New York City's] Thomas Jefferson High School for the students who commute on the L train is littered with broken glass and garbage. Jefferson High serves students from 53 different housing projects, which is notable because the violence is almost entirely territory related. There are only two white and no Asian students at the school, and the Hispanic students mix easily with the Caribbean and black students.

Of a senior class of about 400, that began with 600 freshmen, a mere 92 students were expected to graduate. Of those 92, 20 hopefuls didn't make it. But what became most fascinating to me was not the oppressive atmosphere but the unimaginable resilience of the students and faculty against what are truly horrendous odds. I photographed the self-esteem and leadership classes, the conflict resolution workshops, peer mediation sessions, and the range of support groups—the programs that combat the violent tendencies of the community.

Mr. Heath's bilingual class was silent as the students read their report cards. Jefferson falls short of what is considered a pitiful citywide average of seniors who graduate, 51.5 percent.

In the 1993–1994 school year, *** only 34.4 percent of the senior class graduated. Andre Hamilton, a senior, is about to get promoted to shift manager [at Taco Bell]. "Me and my friend we just get together every day and talk about how we can't wait to break out."

"You never know what the weekend might have brought," says one student. "You can't even be sure who'll come back to school after the weekend." In 1993 East New York had the highest homicide rate in the country—140 dead in the summer alone. The Seventy-fifth Precinct had T-shirts made that read, "You give us 22 minutes, we'll give you a homicide." With sixty-one surveillance monitors and twice the security officers of any other New York City high school, Jefferson, dubbed "Homicide High," at times feels more like a cell block than an academic institution. [Still,] Marion Johnson, like many students, stays after school rather than go home. "Someone actually wrote in my junior high yearbook, 'If you're going to Jeff, don't get shot.'"

Anyone will tell you racism is not the issue. Gangs assemble in the various housing projects. Eddy Denis worried about

Questions

- What aspects of education does Jefferson High fail to provide?
- What is the influence of race and class at Jefferson High?
- How does constant surveillance and police presence affect or interact with education?

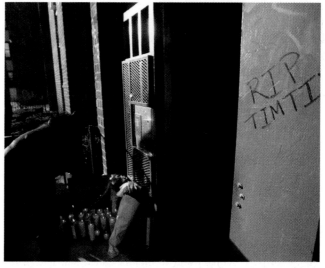

being jumped by the guys in the Alabama projects when he came to Jefferson as a freshman. But he has had no incidents to speak of, and told me, "Jefferson is just a school . . . not a bad school."

SOURCE: Alex Tehrani, "Thomas Jefferson High School," in *25 and Under*, ed. Alice Rose George (New York: DoubleTake/W. W. Norton, 1997).

illiterate people is actually rising (Coombs 1985). According to the United Nations Educational, Scientific, and Cultural Organization (UNESCO; 2003) estimates, the total grew from 569 million in 1970 to 625 million in 1980 to 826 million in 2003. The absolute number of illiterate people seems to have peaked in the 1990s. According to UNESCO (2006) estimates, the total grew from 569 million in 1970 to 625 million in 1980 to 871 million in 1990 and fell to 771 million in 2004. The number of illiterate people has decreased by 100 million since 1990. In large part, that reduction in global illiteracy figures was due to efforts made in China, where there are 94 million fewer illiterate people today than in 1990.

Although countries have instituted literacy programs, these have made only a small contribution to a problem of large-scale dimensions. Television, radio, and the other electronic media can be used, where they are available, to skip the stage of learning literacy skills and convey educational programs directly to adults. But educational programs are usually less popular than commercialized entertainment.

During the period of colonialism, colonial governments regarded education with some trepidation. Until the twentieth century, most believed indigenous populations to be too primitive to be worth educating. Later, education was seen as a way of making local elites responsive to European interests and ways of life. But to some extent, the result was to foment discontent and rebellion, since the majority of those who led anticolonial and nationalist movements were from educated elites who had attended schools or colleges in Europe. They were able to compare firsthand the democratic institutions of the European countries with the absence of democracy in their lands of origin.

The education that the colonizers introduced usually pertained to Europe, not the colonial areas themselves. Educated Africans in the British colonies knew about the kings and queens of England, read Shakespeare, Milton, and the English poets, but knew next to nothing about their own countries' histories or past cultural achievements. Policies of educational reform since the end of colonialism have not completely altered the situation even today.

Partly as a result of the legacy of colonial education, which was not directed toward the majority of the population, the educational system in many developing countries is top-heavy: Higher education is disproportionately developed, relative to primary and secondary education. The result is a correspondingly overqualified group who, having attended colleges and universities, cannot find white-collar or professional jobs. Given the low level of industrial development, most of the better-paid positions are in government, and there are not enough of those to go around.

In recent years, some developing countries, recognizing the shortcomings of the curricula inherited from colonialism, have tried to redirect their educational programs toward the rural poor. They have had limited success, because usually there is insufficient funding to pay for the scale of the necessary innovations. As a result, countries such as India have begun programs of self-help education. Communities draw on existing resources without creating demands for high levels of finance. Those who can read and write and who perhaps possess job skills are encouraged to take others on as apprentices, whom they coach in their spare time.

Communication and the Mass Media

The modern world depends on the continuous communication or interaction between people widely separated from one another. If we were not so dependent on "communication across distance," schooling would be less necessary. In traditional cultures—as that of Jean-Paul Didion in France, the example with which we opened the chapter—most knowledge was what anthropologist Clifford Geertz (1983) has called **local knowledge.** Traditions were passed on through the local community, and although general cultural ideas gradually spread across large areas, processes of cultural diffusion were long, drawn out, slow, and inconsistent. Today, we live in "the whole world" in a way that would have been quite inconceivable to Jean-Paul Didion, or anyone else living in cultures of the past.

We learn a great deal about the world from formal schooling. But we also learn much from the various communication media, which operate outside the context of schools. All of us are aware of situations and events that happen thousands of miles away—electronic communication makes such awareness almost instantaneous. Changes in the spread of information, and in information technologies, are as much a part of the development of modern societies as any aspect of industrial production (Kern 1983). During the twentieth century, rapid transportation and electronic communication such as the Internet greatly intensified the global diffusion of information.

The **mass media**—newspapers, magazines, movies, compact discs, digital video discs, TV, and the Internet—are often associated with entertainment and therefore are seen as rather marginal to most people's lives. Such a view is quite misleading. Mass communications enter our social activities at many different points. For instance, a bank account is no longer a pile of money kept in a safe, but is a series of digits printed on an account sheet and stored in a computer, and monetary transactions are now mainly performed through the exchange of information between computers. Anyone who uses a credit card is connected with a very complex system of electronically stored and transmitted information, which has now become the very basis of modern financial accounting. Today, many people use the Internet to buy CDs and books.

Even "recreational" media such as newspapers or TV have a wide-ranging influence over our experience. This is not just because they affect our attitudes in specific ways, but because they are the *means of access* to the knowledge on which many social activities depend. Voting in national elections, for example, would be quite different if information about current political events, candidates, and parties were not generally available. Even those who are largely uninterested in politics and have little knowledge of the personalities involved have some awareness of national and international events, such as former President Bill Clinton's impeachment trial. Only a complete hermit would be entirely detached from the "news events" that impinge to some degree on the consciousness of all of us—and we could suspect that a modern hermit might very well own a transistor radio!

The Sociological Study of the Mass Media

How do we go about studying the influence of the mass media on our lives? A basic concept needed here is that of **communication,** which means the transfer of information from one person, context, or group to another. We saw in Chapter 6 that the communication and storage of information has been fundamental to the development of modern societies. Sociologically speaking, therefore, we need to put the rise of the mass media and popular culture in the context of the basic trends analyzed earlier.

There are close connections between the rise of the media and the development of modern systems of mass education. The two can only be properly understood sociologically in relation to one another. German social thinker Jürgen Habermas (1962) offers a useful concept to describe this connection when he speaks of the emergence of a **public sphere** with the early development of the industrial societies. The public sphere is a sphere of communication, in which public opinion is formed and attitudes shaped. In earlier forms of society, most communication was local and simply carried through speech, the ordinary daily talk of neighbors and friends in village communities. A rudimentary public sphere developed in early civilizations, well before the emergence of industrial societies. But it was very restricted, because only small groups were literate—could read and write. Moreover, written documents had to be laboriously prepared by hand, so there weren't many in circulation. From about the sixteenth century onward in Eu-

New technologies like moveable type and the printing press led to the creation of the first newspapers in the 1700s. As literacy expanded, mass circulation of printed texts grew.

rope, as the new technology of printing spread and levels of literacy grew, the public sphere began to expand. The first local newspapers appeared in the mid-1700s. Mass-circulation newspapers followed about a century later, to be joined in our century by the electronic media of radio, TV, and other forms.

Learning to read and write and mastering other forms of knowledge is necessary for us to play a part in this developing wider society of communication. In the industrialized countries today, most people can read and write, but in historical terms, this is a recent development, dating back no more than a hundred years. The sorts of outlooks and knowledge acquired in school allow us to participate in the public sphere—to be able to read newspapers and magazines, for example. But the mass media might often also crosscut the goals of formal schooling. For instance, perhaps literacy and other educational skills are beginning to slump now that television and other forms of electronic media play such a large part in our lives. It isn't obvious, after all, that being able to do well at Nintendo games helps

GLOBAL MAP 16.1

Adult Literacy Rates Worldwide
(15 years and older)

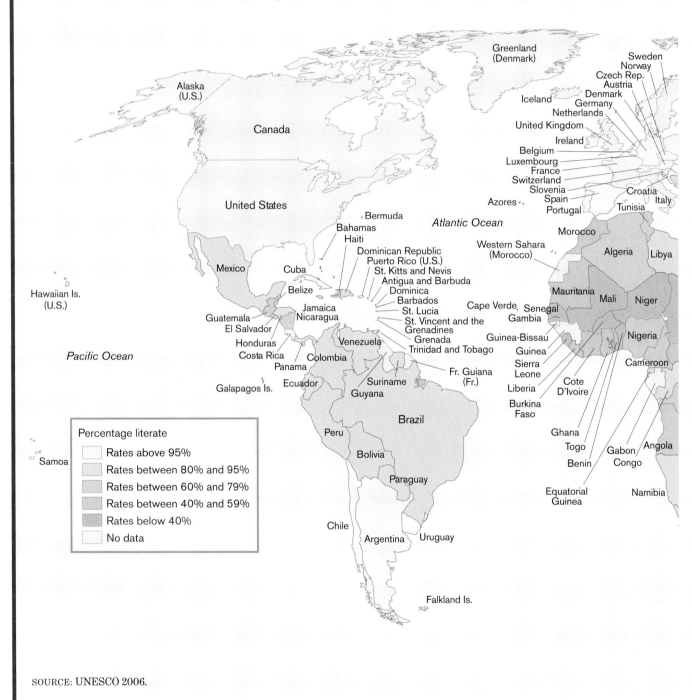

Percentage literate

- Rates above 95%
- Rates between 80% and 95%
- Rates between 60% and 79%
- Rates between 40% and 59%
- Rates below 40%
- No data

SOURCE: UNESCO 2006.

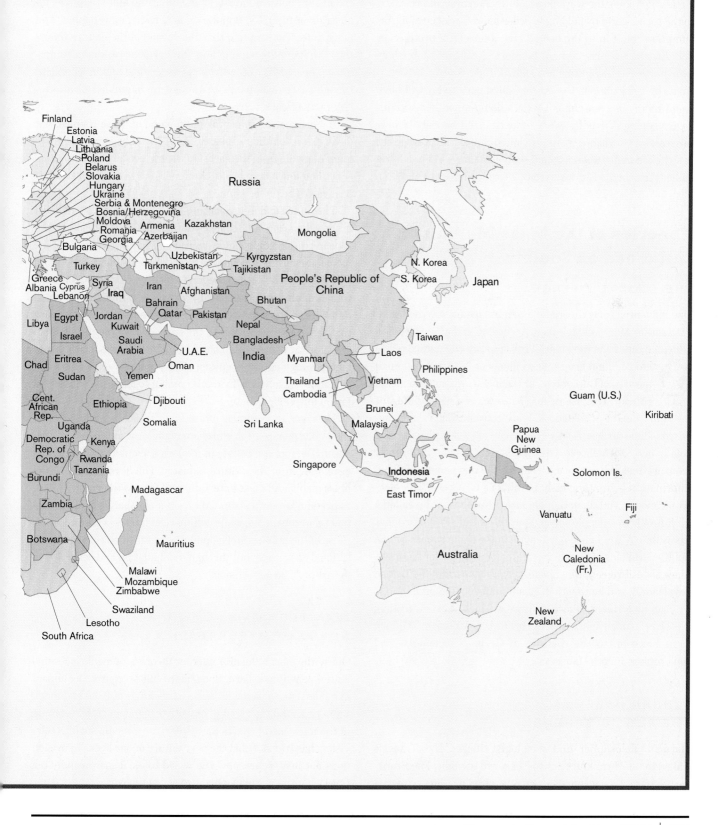

Finland
Estonia
Latvia
Lithuania
Poland
Belarus
Slovakia
Hungary
Ukraine
Serbia & Montenegro
Bosnia/Herzegovina
Moldova
Romania
Bulgaria
Greece
Albania
Cyprus
Lebanon
Turkey
Syria
Iran
Afghanistan
Iraq
Bahrain
Qatar
Jordan
Kuwait
Israel
Saudi Arabia
U.A.E.
Oman
Libya
Egypt
Chad
Eritrea
Sudan
Yemen
Djibouti
Cent. African Rep.
Ethiopia
Somalia
Uganda
Democratic Rep. of Congo
Kenya
Rwanda
Tanzania
Burundi
Madagascar
Zambia
Botswana
Mauritius
Malawi
Mozambique
Zimbabwe
Swaziland
Lesotho
South Africa

Russia
Kazakhstan
Mongolia
Armenia
Azerbaijan
Uzbekistan
Turkmenistan
Kyrgyzstan
Tajikistan
Georgia
People's Republic of China
N. Korea
S. Korea
Japan
Bhutan
Pakistan
Nepal
Bangladesh
India
Myanmar
Laos
Taiwan
Sri Lanka
Thailand
Cambodia
Vietnam
Philippines
Brunei
Malaysia
Singapore
Indonesia
East Timor

Guam (U.S.)
Kiribati
Papua New Guinea
Solomon Is.
Vanuatu
Fiji
New Caledonia (Fr.)
Australia
New Zealand

much with school achievement. The increasing influence of television is probably the single most important development in the media over the past forty years. Television is as important as books, magazines, and newspapers in the expansion of indirect forms of communication characteristic of modern societies. It frames the ways in which we interpret and respond to the social world by helping to order our experience of it. Assumptions built in to the overall character of TV production and distribution may perhaps be more significant than whatever particular programs are shown. If current trends continue, by age eighteen, the average child born today will have spent more time watching TV than doing any other activity save sleeping. Virtually every industrialized household now possesses a television set. In the United States, the average set is switched on between five and six hours a day, and much the same is true in the European countries (Goodhardt et al. 1987).

Theories of the Mass Media's Influence on Society

THE GLOBAL VILLAGE

One influential early theorist of the mass media was the Canadian author Marshall McLuhan. According to McLuhan (1964), "the medium is the message." That is to say, the nature of the media found in a society influences its structure much more than the content, or the messages, that the media convey. Television, for instance, is a very different medium from the printed book. It is electronic, visual, and composed of fluid images. A society in which television plays a basic role is one in which everyday life is experienced differently from one that only has print. Thus the TV news conveys global information instantaneously to millions of people. The electronic media, McLuhan thought, are creating what he called a **global village**—people throughout the world see major news items unfold and hence participate in the same events as one another. Millions of people in different countries, for example, knew about Princess Diana's life, her problems with the British royal family, and her death in an automobile accident in Paris.

Jean Baudrillard, whose ideas we will look at in this section, has been strongly influenced by the ideas of McLuhan. We turn first, however, to the theories of German sociologist and philosopher Jürgen Habermas.

JURGEN HABERMAS: THE PUBLIC SPHERE

German philosopher and sociologist Jürgen Habermas is linked to the "Frankfurt School" of social thought. The Frankfurt School was a group of authors inspired by Marx who nev-

ertheless believed that Marx's views needed radical revision to bring them up to date. Among other things, they believed that Marx had not given enough attention to the influence of culture in modern capitalist society.

The Frankfurt School made extensive study of what they called the "culture industry," meaning the entertainment industries of film, TV, popular music, radio, newspapers, and magazines. They argued that the spread of the culture industry, with its undemanding and standardized products, undermines the capacity of individuals for critical and independent thought. Art disappears, swamped by commercialization—"Mozart's Greatest Hits."

Habermas (1989) has taken up some of these themes, but developed them in a different way. He analyzes the development of media from the early eighteenth century up to the present moment, tracing out the emergence—and subsequent decay—of the public sphere.

The public sphere, according to Habermas, developed first in the salons and coffeehouses of London, Paris, and other European cities. People met in such salons to discuss issues of the moment, using as a means for such debate the news sheets and newspapers that had just begun to emerge. Political debate became a matter of particular importance. Although only small numbers of the population were involved, Habermas argues that the salons were vital to the early development of democracy, for they introduced the idea of resolving political problems through public discussion. The public sphere—at least in principle—involves individuals coming together as equals in a forum for public debate.

However, the promise offered by the early development of the public sphere, Habermas concludes, has not been fully realized. Democratic debate in modern societies is stifled by the development of the culture industry. The development of the mass media and mass entertainment causes the public sphere to become largely a sham. Politics is stage managed in government and the media, while commercial interests triumph over those of the public. Public opinion is not formed through open, rational discussion, but through manipulation and control—as, for example, in advertising.

JEAN BAUDRILLARD: THE WORLD OF HYPERREALITY

One of the most influential current theorists of media is French author Jean Baudrillard. Baudrillard (1988) regards the impact of modern mass media as being quite different from and much more profound than that of any other technology. The coming of the mass media, particularly electronic media such as television, has transformed the very nature of our lives. Television does not just "represent" the world to us, it increasingly defines what the world in which we live actually *is*.

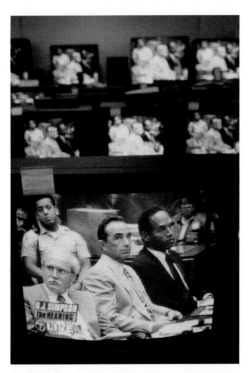

During the O. J. Simpson trial six television channels broadcast the court proceedings simultaneously. This excess of exposure, where televised events seem more real than the actual events, is an example of Baudrillard's concept of hyperreality.

Consider as an example the O. J. Simpson trial, a celebrated court case that unfolded in Los Angeles in 1994–95. Simpson originally became famous as an American football star, but later became known around the world as a result of appearing in several popular films, including the *Naked Gun* series. He was accused of the murder of his wife, Nicole, and after a very long trial was acquitted (although subsequently Simpson was found guilty in a civil suit filed by the families of Nicole Brown Simpson and the man who was murdered with her, Ronald Goldman). The criminal trial was televised live and was watched in many countries, including Britain. In America, six television channels covered the trial on a continuous basis.

The trial did not just happen in the courtroom. It was a televisual event linking millions of viewers and commentators in the media. The trial is an illustration of what Baudrillard calls **hyperreality.** There is no longer a "reality" (the events in the courtroom), which television allows us to see. The "reality" is actually the string of images on the TV screens of the world, which defined the trial as a global event.

Just before the outbreak of hostilities in the Persian Gulf in 1991, Baudrillard wrote a newspaper article titled "The Gulf War Cannot Happen." When war was declared and a bloody conflict took place it might seem obvious that Baudrillard had been wrong. Not a bit of it. After the end of the war, Baudrillard wrote a second article, "The Gulf War Did Not Happen." What did he mean? He meant that the war was not like other wars that have happened in history. It was a war of the media age, a televisual spectacle, in which, along with other viewers throughout the world, George Bush and Saddam Hussein watched the coverage by CNN to see what was actually "happening." Baudrillard argues that in an age where the mass media are everywhere, in effect a new reality—hyperreality—is created, composed of the intermingling of people's behavior and media images.

JOHN THOMPSON: THE MEDIA AND MODERN SOCIETY

Drawing in some part on the writings of Habermas, John Thompson (1990, 1995) has analyzed the relation between the media and the development of industrial societies. From early forms of print through to electronic communication, Thompson argues, the media have played a central role in the development of modern institutions. Thompson believes that the main founders of sociology—including Marx, Weber, and Durkheim—gave too little attention to the role of media in shaping even the early development of modern society.

Thompson's theory of the media depends on a distinction among three types of interactions. Face-to-face interaction, such as people talking at a party, is rich in clues that individuals use to make sense of what others say. **Mediated interaction** involves the use of a media technology—paper, electrical connections, electronic impulses. Characteristic of mediated interaction is that it is stretched out in time and space—it goes well beyond the contexts of ordinary face-to-face interaction. Mediated interaction takes place between individuals in a direct way—for instance, two people talking on the telephone—but there isn't the same variety of clues as when people are face to face.

A third type of interaction is **mediated quasi-interaction.** This refers to the sort of social relations created by the mass media. Such interaction is stretched across time and space, but it doesn't link individuals directly: hence the term *quasi-interaction.* The two previous types are "dialogical": Individuals communicate in a direct way. Mediated quasi-interaction is "monological": A TV program, for example, is a one-way form of communication. People watching the program may discuss it, and perhaps address some remarks to the TV set—but, of course, it doesn't answer back.

Thompson's point is not that the third type comes to dominate the other two—essentially the view taken by Baudrillard—but rather that all three types intermingle in our lives today. The mass media, Thompson suggests, change the balance between the public and the private in our lives. Contrary to what Habermas says, much more comes into the public domain than before, and this leads quite often to debate and controversy.

An example would be former President Bill Clinton's televised testimony about his affair with Monica Lewinsky. Viewers learned a great deal about the president's private business, perhaps more details than they cared to know. At the time, Clinton's affairs were widely discussed by many Americans. The media's reporting of the affair also sparked debate about the division between the private and public, not only in newspapers and on television, but in homes, bars, offices, and Internet chat rooms across the country.

GLOBALIZATION AND MEDIA IMPERIALISM

If today we all live in "one world," it is in large part a result of the international scope of the communications media. Anyone who switches on the TV set and watches the world news ordinarily gets what the description suggests: a presentation of events that occurred that day or shortly before in many different parts of the world. Television programs are sold to large international markets, and hundreds of millions of people watch them. Like other aspects of the global society, the development of a **world information order**—an international system for the production, distribution, and consumption of information—has been uneven and reflects the divisions between the developed societies and developing countries.

The paramount position of the industrialized countries, above all the United States, in the production and diffusion of media has led many observers to speak of *media imperialism.* A cultural empire, it is argued, has been established. Developing countries are held to be especially vulnerable, because they lack the resources to maintain their own cultural independence.

Via the electronic media, Western cultural products have certainly become widely diffused across the globe. Pico Iyer (1989) speaks of "video nights in Katmandu," of frequenting discos in Bali. American videos are commonplace in the Islamic republic of Iran, as are audiotapes of Western popular music, brought in on the black market (Sreberny-Mohammadi 1992). Not only more popular entertainment forms are at issue, however. Control of the world's news by the major Western agencies, it has been suggested, means the predominance of a First World outlook in the information conveyed. Thus it has been claimed that attention is given to the developing world in news broadcasts mainly in times of disaster, crisis, or military confrontation, and that the daily files of other types of news kept on the industrialized world are not maintained for developing world coverage.

Herbert Schiller (1989, 1991) has claimed that control of global communications by U.S. firms has to be seen in relation to various factors. He argues that American TV and radio networks have fallen increasingly under the influence of the federal government and particularly the Department of Defense. He points out that RCA, which until 1986 owned the NBC television and radio networks, is also a leading defense subcontractor to the Pentagon. American television exports, coupled with advertising, propagate a commercialized culture that corrodes local forms of cultural expression. Even where governments prohibit commercial broadcasting within their borders, radio and television from surrounding countries can often be directly received.

Schiller argues that although Americans were the first to be affected by the "corporate-message cocoon. . . . [W]hat is now happening is the creation and global extension of a new total corporate informational-cultural environment" (Schiller 1989). Because U.S. corporations and culture are globally dominant, they have "overwhelmed a good part of the world," such that "American cultural domination . . . sets the boundaries for national discourse" (Schiller 1991).

Technological Change, Media, and Education

Although we have concentrated so far on newspapers, television, and other parts of the "culture industry," we should not think of the media of communication only in those terms. Particularly as influenced by the computer, the media are affecting what we do in many other areas as well.

The Internet

By the early 1990s, many experts in the computer and technology industries were conceding that the reign of the personal computer was over. It was becoming increasingly clear to them that the future lay not with the individual computer but with a global system of interconnected computers—the *Internet*. Although many computer users may not have realized it at the time, the PC was quickly to become little more than a point of access to events happening elsewhere—events happening on a network stretching across the planet, a network that is not owned by any individual or company.

ORIGINS OF THE INTERNET

The Internet has come about in a spontaneous way. It is the product of an undivided world—a world after the fall of the Berlin Wall. Yet its first origins were in the cold war period that preceded 1989. The Internet had its beginnings in the Pentagon, the headquarters of the American military. It was established in 1969 and was first named the ARPA net, after the Pentagon's Advanced Research Projects Agency. The aim was limited. The ARPA sought to allow scientists working on military contracts in different parts of America to pool their resources and to share the expensive equipment they were using. Almost as an afterthought, its originators thought up a way of sending messages, too. Thus electronic mail—e-mail—was born.

Until the early 1980s, the Pentagon Internet consisted of five hundred computers, all located in military laboratories and university computer science departments. Other people in universities then started catching on and began using the system for their own purposes. By 1987 the Internet had expanded to include twenty-eight thousand host computers, at many different universities and research labs.

For several years, the Internet remained confined to universities. With the spread of home-based personal computers, however, it began to move outside—and then entered a period of explosive growth. By the year 2003, 61.8 percent of American households owned computers, and in 2005 more than 203 million adult Americans actively logged on to the Internet each month, with an average of 70 million using the Internet on any given day (Internet World Stats 2006; Pew Internet 2005; U.S. Bureau of the Census 2006b). The spread of commercial Internet service providers (ISPs) that offer dial-up access through modems and faster direct access through phone lines (DSL) and cable has fueled the growing proportion of households with online capabilities. Online services, electronic bulletin boards, chat rooms, and software libraries were uploaded onto the Internet by a bewildering variety of people, no longer situated just in North America, but all over the world. Corporations also got in on the act. In 1994, companies overtook universities as the dominant users of the network.

Access to the Internet is highly uneven. In 1998, 88 percent of the world's Internet users lived in the developed world. North America accounted for more than 50 percent of all users, although it contains only 5 percent of the total world population. By 2005, however, the share of Internet users located in North America had dropped to about 23 percent, indicating the rise of Internet usage worldwide (Internet World Stats 2006). The United States has the highest level of computer ownership and online access. More than 203 million Americans use the Internet; in Germany there are over 47 million Internet users, and Britain boasts more than 37 million. In Japan, a country where the Internet craze arrived somewhat late, nearly 61 percent of the population (78 million people) used the Internet in 2005 (Internet World Stats 2006). These numbers are expected to grow rapidly in the coming years.

THE EFFECT OF THE INTERNET

In a world of quite stunning technological change, no one can be sure what the future holds. Many see the Internet as exemplifying the new global order emerging at the close of the twentieth century. Users of the Internet live in "cyberspace." **Cyberspace** means the space of interaction formed by the global network of computers that compose the Internet. In cyberspace, much as Baudrillard might say, we are no longer people but instead are messages on each other's screens. Apart from e-mail, where users usually identify themselves, no one on the Internet can be sure of who anyone else really is, whether they are male or female, or where they are in the world.

The spread of the Internet across the globe has raised important questions for sociologists. The Internet is transforming the contours of daily life—blurring the boundaries between the global and the local, presenting new channels for communication and interaction, and allowing more and more everyday tasks to be carried out online. Yet at the same time as it provides exciting new opportunities to explore the social world, the Internet also threatens to undermine human relationships and communities. Although the information age is still in its early stages, many sociologists are already debating the complex implications of the Internet for late modern societies.

Opinions on the effects of the Internet on social interaction fall into two broad categories. On the one hand are those observers who see the online world as fostering new forms of electronic relationships that either enhance or supplement existing face-to-face interactions. While traveling or working abroad, individuals can use the Internet to communicate regularly with friends and relatives at home. Distance and separation become more tolerable. The Internet also allows the formation of new types of relationships: Anonymous online users can meet in chat rooms and discuss topics of mutual interest. These cyber contacts sometimes evolve into fully fledged electronic friendships or even result in face-to-face meetings. Many Internet users become part of lively online communities that are qualitatively different from those they inhabit in the physical world. Scholars who see the Internet as a positive addition to human interaction argue that it expands and enriches people's social networks.

Not everyone takes such an enthusiastic stance, however. As people spend more and more time communicating online and handling their daily tasks in cyberspace, it may be that they spend less time interacting with one another in the physical world. Some sociologists fear that the spread of Internet technology will lead to increased social isolation and atomization. They argue that one effect of increasing Internet access in households is that people are spending less quality time with their families and friends. The Internet is encroaching on domestic life as the lines between work and home are blurred: Many employees continue to work at home after hours—checking e-mail or finishing tasks that they were unable to complete during the day. Human contact is reduced, personal relationships suffer, traditional forms of entertainment such as the theater and books fall by the wayside, and the fabric of social life is weakened.

How are we to evaluate these contrasting positions? Most certainly there are elements of truth on both sides of the debate. The Internet is undoubtedly broadening our horizons and presents unprecedented opportunities for making contact with others. Yet the frenzied pace at which it is expanding also presents challenges and threats to traditional forms of human interaction. Will the Internet radically transform society into a fragmented, impersonal realm where humans rarely venture out of their homes and lose their ability to communicate? It seems unlikely. About fifty years ago very similar fears were expressed as television burst on the media scene. In *The Lonely Crowd* (1961), an influential sociological analysis of American society in the 1950s, David Riesman and his colleagues expressed concern about the effects of TV on family and community life. Some of their fears were justified, but television and the mass media have also enriched the social world in many ways.

Just like television before it, the Internet has aroused both hopes and fears. Will we lose our identities in cyberspace? Will computerized technology dominate us rather than the reverse? Will human beings retreat into an antisocial online world? The answer to each of these questions, fortunately, almost certainly

New technologies such as wireless Internet access and portable computers are blurring the boundaries between global and local and are reshaping everyday interactions in places like cafes and coffeeshops.

is no. For example, people don't use video conferencing if they can get together with others in an ordinary way. Business executives have far more forms of electronic communication available to them than ever before. At the same time, the number of face-to-face business conferences has shot up.

Education and New Communications Technology

The spread of information technology looks set to influence education in a number of different ways, some of which may perhaps be quite fundamental. The new technologies are affecting the nature of work, replacing some types of human work by machines. The sheer pace of technological change is creating a much more rapid turnover of jobs than once was the case. Education can no longer be regarded as a stage of preparation before an individual enters work. As technology changes, necessary skills change, and even if education is seen from a purely vocational point of view—as providing skills relevant to work—most observers agree that lifelong exposure to education will be needed in the future.

TECHNOLOGIES OF EDUCATION

The rise of education in its modern sense was connected with a number of other major changes happening in the nineteenth century. One was the development of the school. One might naively think that there was a demand for education and that schools and universities were set up to meet that demand. But that was not how things happened. Schools arose, as Michel Foucault has shown, as part of the administrative apparatus of the modern state. The hidden curriculum was about discipline and about the control of children.

A second influence was the development of printing and the arrival of "book culture." The mass distribution of books, newspapers, and other printed media was as distinctive a feature of the development of industrial society as were machines and factories. Education developed to provide skills of literacy and computation giving access to the world of printed media. Nothing is more characteristic of the school than the schoolbook or textbook.

In the eyes of many, all this is set to change with the growing use of computers and multimedia technologies in education. It has been said that "around 70–80 percent of telecommunications trials conducted in the emerging multimedia technologies around the world involve education or at least have an education component" (quoted in Kenway et al. 1995).

As in many other areas of contemporary social life, markets and information technology are major influences on educational change. The commercializing and marketizing of education also reflect such pressures. Schools are being reengineered in much the same way as business corporations.

Many of those likely to enter the education field will be organizations whose relation to schooling was previously marginal or nonexistent. They include cable companies, software houses, telecommunication groups, filmmakers, and equipment suppliers. Their influence will not be limited to schools or universities. They are already forming part of what has been called "edutainment"—a sort of parallel education industry linked to the software industry in general, to museums, science parks, and heritage areas.

EDUCATION AND THE TECHNOLOGY GAP

Whether the new technologies will have the radical implications for education that some claim is still an open question. Critics have pointed out that, even if they do have major effects, these may act to reinforce educational inequalities. **Information poverty** might be added to the material deprivations that currently have such an effect on schooling. The sheer pace of technological change and the demand of employers for computer-literate workers may mean that those who are technologically competent "leapfrog" over people who have little experience with computers.

Some already fear the emergence of a "computer underclass" within Western societies. Although developed countries have the highest levels of computer and Internet usage in the world, there are stark inequalities in computer use within those societies. Many schools and colleges are suffering from underfunding and long-standing neglect; even if these institutions become beneficiaries of schemes that distribute secondhand computer hardware to schools, they must gain the technical expertise and ability to teach information technology skills to pupils. Because the market for computer specialists is so strong, many schools are struggling to attract and keep information technology teachers, who can earn far greater incomes in the private sector.

Yet the technology gap within Western societies appears minor compared to the digital divide separating Western classrooms from their counterparts in the developing world. As the global economy becomes increasingly knowledge based, there is a real danger that poorer countries will become even more marginalized because of the gap between the information rich and the information poor.

Internet access has become a new line of demarcation between the rich and the poor. South Asia, with 23 percent of the world's total population, has less than 1 percent of world's Internet users. In Africa, there are a mere seven Internet hosts per one million people. Even though 14 percent of the world's population lives on the African continent, there are just under 24 million Internet users, or 2.5 percent of all Internet users (Internet World Stats 2006). About 20 percent of these individuals are located in South Africa, by far the most developed and prosperous African nation. In the Middle East, Internet usage has increased dramatically over the last five years—by over 325 percent. Yet the Middle East still represents only 1.7 percent (16,163,500) of the world's population of Internet users (Internet World Stats 2006).

Information technology enthusiasts argue that computers need not result in greater national and global inequalities—that their very strength lies in their ability to draw people together and to open up new opportunities. Schools in Asia and Africa that are lacking textbooks and qualified teachers can benefit from the Internet, it is claimed. Distance-learning programs and collaboration with colleagues overseas could be the key to overcoming poverty and disadvantage. When technology is put in the hands of smart, creative people, they argue, the potential is limitless.

Technology can be breathtaking and open important doors, but it has to be recognized that there is no such thing as an easy "techno-fix." Underdeveloped regions struggling with mass illiteracy and lacking telephone lines and electricity need an improved educational infrastructure before they can truly benefit from distance-learning programs. The Internet cannot be substituted for direct contact between teachers and pupils under these conditions.

Lifelong Learning

New technologies and the rise of the knowledge economy are transforming traditional ideas about work and education. The sheer pace of technological change is creating a much more rapid turnover of jobs than once was the case. Training and the attainment of qualifications are now occurring throughout people's lives, rather than just once early in life. Mid-career professionals are choosing to update their skills through continuing education programs and Internet-based learning. Many employers now allow workers to participate in on-the-job training as a way of enhancing loyalty and improving the company skills base.

As our society continues to transform, the traditional beliefs and institutions that underpin it are also undergoing change. The idea of education—implying the structured transmission of knowledge within a formal institution—is giving way to a broader notion of learning that takes place in a diversity of settings. The shift from education to learning is not an inconsequential one. Learners are active, curious social actors who can derive insights from a multiplicity of sources, not just within an institutional setting. Emphasis on learning acknowledges that skills and knowledge can be gained through all types of encounters—with friends and neighbors, at seminars and museums, in conversations at the local Starbucks, through the Internet and other media, and so forth.

The shift in emphasis toward *lifelong learning* can already be seen within schools themselves, where there are a growing number of opportunities for pupils to learn *outside* the confines of the classroom. The boundaries between schools and the outside world are breaking down, not only via cyberspace, but in the physical world as well. "Service learning," for example, has become a mainstay of many American secondary schools. As part of their graduation requirements, pupils devote a certain amount of time to volunteer work in the community. Partnerships with local businesses have also become commonplace in the United States, fostering interaction and mentor relationships between adult professionals and pupils.

Lifelong learning should and must play a role in the move toward a knowledge society. Not only is it essential to a well-trained, motivated workforce, but learning should also be seen in relation to wider human values. Learning is both a means and an end to the development of a rounded and autonomous self-education in the service of self-development and self-understanding. There is nothing utopian in this idea; indeed it reflects the humanistic ideals of education developed by educational philosophers. An example already in existence are lifelong learning programs for the elderly, which provide retired people with the opportunity to educate themselves as they choose, developing whatever interests they care to follow.

Study Outline

The Development of Schooling

- Education in its modern form, involving the instruction of pupils within specially designated school premises, began to emerge with the spread of printed materials and higher levels of literacy. Knowledge could be retained, reproduced, and consumed by more people in more places. With industrialization, work became more specialized, and knowledge was increasingly acquired in more abstract rather than practical ways—the skills of reading, writing, and calculating.

Education and Inequality

- The expansion of education in the twentieth century has been closely tied to perceived needs for a literate and disciplined workforce. Although reformers have seen education for all as a means of reducing inequalities, its effect in this respect is fairly limited.

Education tends to express and reaffirm existing inequalities more than it acts to change them.

- The formal school curriculum is only one part of a more general process of social reproduction influenced by many informal aspects of learning, education, and school settings. The *hidden curriculum* plays a significant role in such reproduction.

- Because *intelligence* is difficult to define, there has been a great deal of controversy about the subject. Some argue that genes determine one's *IQ;* others believe that social influences determine it. The weight of the evidence appears to be on the side of those arguing for social and cultural influences. A major controversy about IQ has developed as a result of the book *The Bell Curve.* The book claims that races differ in terms of their average level of inherited intelligence. Critics reject this thesis completely.

Communication and the Mass Media

- The *mass media* have come to play a fundamental role in modern society. The mass media are media of communication—newspapers, magazines, television, radio, movies, videos, CDs, DVDs, and other forms—that reach mass audiences. The influence of the mass media on our lives is profound. The media not only provide entertainment, but provide and shape much of the information that we utilize in our daily lives.

- A range of different theories of media and popular culture have been developed. McLuhan argued that media influence society more in terms of how they communicate than what they communicate. In McLuhan's words, "the medium is the message": TV, for example, influences people's behavior and attitudes because it is so different in nature from other media, such as newspapers or books.

- Other important theorists include Habermas, Baudrillard, and Thompson. Habermas points to the role of the media in creating a *public sphere*—a sphere of public opinion and public debate. Baudrillard has been strongly influenced by McLuhan. He believes that new media, particularly television, actually change the "reality" we experience. Thompson argues that the mass media have created a new form of social interaction—*mediated quasi-interaction*—that is more limited, narrow, and one-way than everyday social interaction.

Technological Change, Media, and Education

- The sense today of inhabiting one world is in large part a result of the international scope of media of communication. A *world information order*—an international system of the production, distribution, and consumption of informational goods—has come into being. Given the paramount position of the industrial countries in the world information order, many believe that the developing countries are subject to a new form of media imperialism.

- Recent years have seen the emergence of multimedia, linked to the development of the Internet. *Multimedia* refers to the combination on a single medium of what used to be different media needing different technologies, so that a CD-ROM, for example, can carry both visuals and sound and be played on a computer. Many claims have been made about the likely social effects of these developments, but it is still too early to judge how far these will be borne out.

Key Concepts

communication (p. 521)
cultural capital (p. 512)
cyberspace (p. 527)
global village (p. 524)
hidden curriculum (p. 511)
hyperreality (p. 525)
information poverty (p. 529)
intelligence (p. 513)
IQ (intelligence quotient) (p. 513)

local knowledge (p. 520)
mass media (p. 520)
mediated interaction (p. 525)
mediated quasi-interaction (p. 525)
public sphere (p. 521)
tracking (p. 509)
world information order (p. 526)

Review Questions

1. What is the "hidden curriculum"?
   a. The "tricks of the trade" that enable teachers to keep discipline in class, sustain student interest, and impart instruction.
   b. The effects of school procedures and organization on students. The hidden curriculum teaches students to know their place and to sit still.
   c. The strategies that students use to make otherwise dull classes interesting.
   d. The political agenda that is seen to animate education: for conservatives it is the liberal obsession with political correctness and multiculturalism; for liberals it is the conservative obsession with standardized testing and the moral character of education.

2. What is "social reproduction"?
   a. The way schools educate each succeeding generation.
   b. The ways schools help perpetuate social and economic inequalities across the generations.
   c. The combined effect of the formal and hidden curricula on student character.
   d. The ways schools handle sex education.

3. What is the main argument against the idea—popularized by Herrnstein and Murray's book *The Bell Curve*—that systematic differences in IQ test scores between whites and blacks are the result of genetic differences?
   a. White and Asian Americans are just better test takers.
   b. Ethnic minorities in many societies score lower on standardized intelligence tests than ethnic majorities because their subordinate position in society gives them fewer educational opportunities and results in their having less confidence and experiencing greater stress in testing situations.
   c. There is no such thing as the core intelligence that Herrnstein and Murray claim IQ tests measure.
   d. Blacks are steadily closing the IQ gap with whites.

4. What is "media imperialism"?
   a. The ability of the United States to disseminate Western values through the dominance of Hollywood and American television, and through the agenda of Western news organizations.
   b. The monopoly position of large media conglomerates such as Time Warner and Fox Communications.

c. The predominance of media—particularly television—in our private lives.

d. None of the above.

5. What was the main conclusion of the landmark studies of educational inequality carried out in the 1960s by James Coleman and Christopher Jencks?

a. Educational and occupational attainment are governed mainly by family background and nonschool factors.

b. Outside the poorest areas, black schools are often as well funded as white schools.

c. Reform of the educational system is essentially useless without reform of society.

d. Intelligence is largely a product not of heredity but of the environment and, in particular, the actions of parents.

6. What is shown by sociological research on the effect of tracking in schools?

a. Tracking does not benefit students, but it does make it easier for teachers to manage classes.

b. Tracking ameliorates previously existing inequalities for advanced students but has no benefit for average or poor students.

c. Tracking reinforces previously existing inequalities for average or poor students, but it does have benefits for advanced students.

d. Tracking works best where there is a proper system of promotion and relegation of good and bad students.

7. What is "cultural capital"?

a. The total monetary value of all the cultural artifacts—books, videos, CDs—in a home.

b. The cultural advantages conferred on children who come from a good home.

c. The city—not necessarily the political capital—with the most prestigious cultural institutions in a country, such as New York City for the United States.

d. The economic and political clout wielded by the cultural industries.

8. What did Baudrillard mean when he argued that the "Gulf War did not happen"?

a. There was no war as it is conventionally understood because the bombing campaign by the U.S. Air Force had obliterated the enemy before the army engaged them.

b. President George H. W. Bush made the whole thing up to increase his popularity.

c. The war was a hyperreal event and existed only in the public imagination and not on the ground in the Persian Gulf.

d. In an age where the mass media pervade our lives, a new reality—hyperreality—is created, composed of the intermingling of people's behavior and media images.

9. What does Thompson mean by "mediated quasi-interaction" and how is it related to face-to-face and mediated interaction?

a. It is the type of interaction created by the mass media: It is monological, or one-way, communication, from broadcaster to

viewer. Thompson argued that all three types of interaction intermingle in our lives today.

b. It is the type of interaction created by daytime chat shows that focus on issues in viewers' personal lives. It is that type of intimacy created by the public exposure of private troubles.

c. It is the type of interaction created by telephones and cell phones, where the voice is heard and communication takes place in real time, as opposed to the mediated type of interaction in letters and e-mail.

d. It is the type of interaction created by the mass media. Echoing Baudrillard, Thompson argued that it has come to predominate over mediated and face-to-face interactions in our private lives.

10. One main reason for the rise of large educational systems was the process of

a. medical innovation.

b. stock market expansion.

c. industrialization.

d. computer innovation.

Thinking Sociologically Exercises

1. From your reading of this chapter, describe what might be the principal advantages and disadvantages of having children go to private versus public schools in the United States at this time. Assess whether privatization of our public schools would help improve them.

2. Back in 1964, Marshall McLuhan argued that the developments of radio and television helped to produce a global village. Carefully explain what he meant by the term *global village* and its importance. Explain how the advent of the Internet and cell phones will be likely to extend the concept of the global village further and faster than ever before.

Data Exercises

www.wwnorton.com/giddens
Keyword: Data16

The data exercise for this chapter provides you with an opportunity to explore the link between a parent's educational attainment and that of his child. Before you begin, think about your own life. What are your own educational goals? In what ways did your parents' educational achievements influence your decisions about what kind of education and how much education to pursue?

The Sociological Study of Religion

Learn the elements that make up a religion.

Theories of Religion

Know the sociological approaches to religion developed by Marx, Durkheim, and Weber, as well as the contemporary debate over secularization and the religious economy approach.

Types of Religious Organizations

Learn the various ways religious communities are organized and how they have become institutionalized.

Gender and Religion

Recognize the changes taking place in the interrelationships between gender and religion.

World Religions

Familiarize yourself with the various forms religion takes in traditional and modern societies.

Religion in the United States

Learn about the sociological dimensions of religion in the United States, including the rise of fundamentalism and the electronic church.

Globalization and Religion

Recognize how the globalization of religion is reflected in religious activism in poor countries and the rise of religious nationalist movements.

CHAPTER SEVENTEEN

RELIGION IN MODERN SOCIETY

On September 11, 2001, a well-organized group of nineteen men, equipped with box cutters, a rudimentary knowledge of how to pilot commercial jet aircraft, and fervent religious conviction, forever changed our world. American Airlines Flight 11 and United Flight 175, both bound for Los Angeles from Boston, were hijacked shortly after takeoff and flown into the twin towers of New York City's World Trade Center. American Airlines Flight 77, en route from Washington's Dulles airport to Los Angeles was hijacked over Kansas and flown back to Washington, where it plummeted into the Pentagon. A fourth plane, United Airlines Flight 93, bound for San Francisco from Newark, crashed into a field in Pennsylvania, most likely because heroic passengers overpowered the hijackers before it could reach the White House or the Capitol.

The hijacking was organized by al Qaeda, a global network of religious extremists dedicated to restoring their version of traditional Islamic rule. Al Qaeda had already unleashed violent attacks before September 11. These included two 1998 car bombings of the U.S. embassies in Kenya and Tanzania that killed several hundred people and injured more than five thousand, and an attack on the U.S. destroyer *Cole* in 2000. The organization had also planned to blow up a dozen trans-Pacific U.S. commercial flights on a single day in 1995, a plot that was thwarted when one of the perpetrators was caught in the Philippines.

The September 11 attacks were unprecedented in U.S. history, claiming nearly three thousand lives. The images of passenger planes exploding into the twin skyscrapers, the buildings' fiery collapse, and the resulting human devastation were seared into the memories of countless people around the world who witnessed the event, over and over again, on television. As a result of the attacks, one of the largest governmental reorganizations in the past century occurred with the creation of the cabinet-level Department of Homeland Security. And a global "war on terrorism" was launched, first against the rulers of Afghanistan (where al Qaeda was headquartered), then against Iraq, whose repressive leader, Saddam Hussein, was said to pose a danger to global security.

Yet September 11 was not the first religiously motivated attack on U.S. soil. On April 19, 1995, a truck laden with two tons of explosive materials destroyed a government office building in Oklahoma City. One hundred sixty-eight people died, including nineteen children from the building's day-care center. More than five hundred were injured. The blast—at the time the worst terrorist attack in U.S. history—was immediately blamed on Islamic extremists. A number of men of Middle Eastern appearance were rounded up for questioning, until it became clear that the bombing was not the work of foreign terrorists. Rather, it was completely homegrown, planned and executed by American religious extremists who believed in a racially pure version of Protestantism. Timothy McVeigh, who was eventually convicted of the bombing and executed, was a twenty-seven-year-old ex-army sergeant who had served in the Gulf War. He was also connected with the Christian Identity movement, a loosely knit group of religious extremists who shared a hatred for racial minorities, Jews, and the U.S. government. Like al Qaeda, the Christian Identity movement claimed to base its beliefs in Scripture and was dedicated to the use of violence to achieve its objectives.

What explains the rise of militant, often violent religious movements in the modern world? Under what conditions does religion unite communities, and under what conditions does it divide them? To study these issues, we ask what religion actually is and look at some of the different forms that religious beliefs and practices take. We also analyze the various types of religious organizations. As in many of the other chapters in this book, the emphasis is on social change. Religious concerns today can be properly understood only in relation to social changes that have affected the position of religion in the wider world.

The study of religion is a challenging enterprise that places special demands on the sociological imagination. In analyzing religious practices, we must be sensitive to ideals that inspire profound conviction in believers, yet at the same time take a balanced view of them. We must confront ideas that seek the eternal while recognizing that religious groups also promote quite mundane goals, such as acquiring money or followers. We need to recognize the diversity of religious beliefs and modes of conduct, but also probe the nature of religion as a general phenomenon.

The Sociological Study of Religion

Religion is one of the oldest human institutions. Cave drawings suggest that religious beliefs and practices existed more than forty thousand years ago. According to anthropologists, there have probably been about one hundred thousand religions throughout human history (Hadden 1997a). Sociologists define **religion** as a cultural system of commonly shared beliefs and rituals that provides a sense of ultimate meaning and purpose by creating an idea of reality that is sacred, all-encompassing, and supernatural (Berger 1967; Durkheim 1965, orig. 1912; Wuthnow 1988). There are three key elements in this definition:

1. Religion is a form of culture. You will recall from Chapter 3 that *culture* consists of the shared beliefs, values, norms, and material conditions that create a common identity among a group of people. Religion shares all of these characteristics.
2. Religion involves beliefs that take the form of ritualized practices. All religions thus have a behavioral aspect—special activities in which believers take part and that identify them as members of the religious community.
3. Perhaps most important, religion provides a sense of purpose—a feeling that life is ultimately meaningful. It does so by explaining coherently and compellingly what transcends or overshadows everyday life, in ways that other aspects of culture (such as an educational system or a belief in democracy) typically cannot. (Geertz 1973; Wuthnow 1988)

What is absent from the sociological definition of religion is as important as what is included: Nowhere is there mention of God. We often think of **theism**—a belief in one or more supernatural deities (the term originates from the Greek word for god)—as basic to religion, but this is not necessarily the case. As we shall see later, some religions, such as Buddhism, believe in the existence of spiritual forces rather than a particular god.

How Sociologists Think about Religion

When sociologists study religion, they do so as sociologists and not as believers (or disbelievers) in any particular faith. This stance has several implications for the sociological study of religion:

1. **Sociologists are not concerned with whether religious beliefs are true or false.** From a sociological perspective, religions are regarded not as being decreed by God but as being socially constructed by human beings. As a result, sociologists put aside their personal beliefs when they study religion. They are concerned with the human rather than the divine aspects of religion. Sociologists ask: How is the religion organized? What are its principal beliefs and values? How is it related to the larger society? What explains its success or failure in recruiting and retaining believers? The question of whether a particular belief is "good" or "true," however important it may be to the believers of the religion under study, is not something that sociologists are able to address as sociologists. (As individuals, they may have strong opinions on the matter, but one hopes that as sociologists they can keep these opinions from biasing their research.)

2. **Sociologists are especially concerned with the social organization of religion.** Religions are among the most important institutions in society. They are a primary source of the deepest-seated norms and values. At the same time, religions are typically practiced through an enormous variety of social forms. Within Christianity and Judaism, for example, religious practice often occurs in formal organizations, such as churches or synagogues. Yet this is not necessarily true of such Asian religions as Hinduism and Buddhism, where religious practices are likely to occur in the home, as well as temples or some other natural setting. The sociology of religion is concerned with how different religious institutions and organizations actually function. The earliest European religions were often indistinguishable from the larger society, as religious beliefs and practices were incorporated into daily life. This is still true in many parts of the world today. In modern industrial society, however, religions have become established in separate, often bureaucratic, organizations, and so sociologists focus on the organizations through which religions must operate to survive (Hammond 1992). As we will see later, this institutionalization has even led some sociologists to view religions in the United States and Europe as similar to business organizations, competing with each other for members (Warner 1993).

3. **Sociologists often view religions as a major source of social solidarity.** To the extent that religions provide their believers with a common set of norms and values, they are an important source of social solidarity. Religious beliefs, rituals, and bonds help to create a "moral community" in which all members know how to behave toward one another (Wuthnow 1988). If a single reli-

gion dominates a society, the religion may be an important source of social stability. If a society's members adhere to numerous competing religions, however, religious differences may lead to destabilizing social conflicts. Recent examples of religious conflict within a society include struggles among Sikhs, Hindus, and Muslims in India; clashes between Muslims and Christians in Bosnia and other parts of the former Yugoslavia; and "hate crimes" against Jews, Muslims, and other religious minorities in the United States.

4. **Sociologists tend to explain the appeal of religion in terms of social forces rather than in terms of purely personal, spiritual, or psychological factors.** For many people, religious beliefs are a deeply personal experience, involving a deep sense of connection with forces that transcend everyday reality. Sociologists do not question the depth of such feelings and experiences, but they are unlikely to limit themselves to a purely spiritual explanation of religious commitment. A person may claim that he or she became religious when God suddenly appeared in a vision, but sociologists are likely to look for more earthly explanations. Some researchers argue that people often "get religion" when their fundamental sense of a social order is threatened by economic hardship, loneliness, loss or grief, physical suffering, or poor health (Berger 1967; Glock 1976; Schwartz 1970; Stark and Bainbridge 1980). In explaining the appeal of religious movements, sociologists are more likely to focus on the problems of the social order than on the psychological response of the individual.

What Do Sociologists of Religion Study?

Several types of social forces are likely to be of special interest to sociologists of religion. We discuss these in greater detail throughout this chapter.

First, sociologists sometimes focus on the ways in which religious fervor results from a crisis in prevailing beliefs. Such a crisis occurred in the United States during the 1960s, when the challenges to the status quo included opposition to the Vietnam War, the civil rights movement, social movements among racial and ethnic minorities, and the youth-oriented counterculture. As a result, unusually large numbers of people were attracted to religious teachers, ranging from Indian gurus to fundamentalist preachers, who offered everything from meditation and yoga to astrology and New Age religions (Wuthnow 1988).

Second, sociologists study how competition among religious organizations leads some to thrive and others to perish. This

"Living the Question"

As a young boy growing up in rural Kansas, the son of tenant farmers living twelve miles from the nearest town, Bob Wuthnow remembers contemplating questions he was too young to understand. Why had his father dropped out of school after eighth grade? How had the dogs found their way into the chicken coop again? He had particular trouble understanding why one day his friend, Harry Charles Kitchen, did not come home from the hospital, having passed away from something called an appendectomy. "This was the first time someone my own age actually died," Wuthnow remembers. "It hit my own mortality—all sixty-five pounds of it—like a ton of bricks. Suddenly all those sermons I'd heard at the little Baptist church where Harry Charles and I attended Sunday School together took on painful urgency" (Wuthnow 1990).

Although Wuthnow eventually left Kansas behind, he has never stopped wrestling with important questions, such as the role religion plays in our individual and collective lives. Especially in the wake of September 11, 2001, religious institutions, beliefs, trends, and differences have become central concerns to our national life. Increasing our knowledge of how religion functions in modern society is an important task for sociologists, and translating that knowledge for public audiences and policy makers is one of Wuthnow's main strengths as a scholar.

On multiple occasions Wuthnow has been invited to serve as a mediator to those serving on the front lines of religion and politics in the United States, helping clarify trends and navigate solutions. Early in his first term, President George W. Bush created the Office of Faith-Based and Community Initiatives, to help provide social services to those in need, and appointed John Dilulio Jr. director. To promote dialogue among religious leaders, the White House, and the press, Wuthnow invited Dilulio to Princeton to speak and field questions about how new initiatives would work on the ground. On another occasion, Wuthnow joined religious leaders from various denominations throughout the United States for their annual, off-the-record meeting to help them compare notes, build trust, and sort out differences.

Whereas many people are driven by the search for answers, Wuthnow believes in living the questions. "It's not so much whether stories can be verified by science," explains Wuthnow.

Robert Wuthnow

"Faith is a matter of living our stories—living the questions: Why are we here? Where did we come from? Where are we going? What is good? How should we live? . . . We make sense of our lives by telling stories," he says, but quickly points out that "those stories are *real*."

Questions line not only the path to faith. They constitute social inquiry, and social scientists like Wuthnow play an important role in asking and answering such questions. As a society, where did we come from? Where are we going? What directions might we take, and what might be the consequences? Living the questions provides a way for Wuthnow to connect the personal and the professional, to understand public issues in terms of personal experience. In the winter of 2005, Wuthnow delivered a public address at Yale University. His words are evidence of the sociological imagination at work, helping us better understand how religion relates to both individual experience and social change in American society. Sociology is not just a topic we study in school. To Wuthnow (2005),

Sociology is a way of relating to our humanity. I believe we need to understand that and affirm it, whether we are social scientists or theologians. Some sociologists have taken a rather different approach to the relationship between sociology and theology. Believing that theology is primarily about God, they have tried to imagine what a God-centered sociology would look like, and, especially, how it might be different from a humanistic one. They have argued, for instance, that Marxist approaches would not qualify because Marxism has no place for God. They favor theories in which human agency has a larger place than social structure because they believe in freewill. And so on. Their view is that social science cannot adequately speak of faith unless it is explicitly informed by faith and is thus distinctive. My view is rather different. I want a good physicist to respect and try to understand the physical universe. I want a good doctor to understand human physiology and anatomy. I want a good sociologist to understand social interaction and society. If these realities are understood as a created order, if they are understood as reality that is sacred in the broadest sense of that word, then the obligation of the researcher is to be true to them and pay attention to the truth within them. That is the first consideration in bringing responsible voices into the public arena.

In ordinary life, ordinary people experience the depths of their humanity in an extraordinary variety of ways. In the fears of our own mortality and the mortality of our loved ones, to the pain we observe in doing volunteer work or reading the morning newspaper, we experience the frailty of human life, and in laughter of children and the embraces of friends, we experience its joy. We have a remarkable capacity, though, to insulate ourselves from that which we do not want to experience. Especially in middle America, it is easy from day to day to remain oblivious—comfortably watching television that purports to be reality, but is not, and devoting our hours to acquiring what we do not need. Calling attention to that which we would just as soon ignore—engaging in the debunking of everyday assumptions, as Peter Berger, once wrote—should be high on the agenda of social research.

***

Conversations with social scientists, though, suggest that the idiosyncrasies of personal backgrounds often guide their research to a great extent. Immigrants study immigrants, single mothers study single mothers, and so on. If we are to understand the public role of social scientists, if we are interested in furthering that project and linking it with faith, we clearly must go behind the scenes, behind the public utterances and into the private realm, into the family, where fundamental convictions are shaped.

In my case, early childhood experiences, I have come to realize, provide the single best explanation for my lifelong interest in trying to understand social change. I grew up on a small farm in the middle of Kansas. I loved the farm, went to church in the community, and loved the community. I expected to grow up and live in that community. But the county in which I grew up was one of the poorest in the state. During the time I lived there, more farms went out of business than had during the Great Depression. My father died when I was eighteen. That summer, as I mourned his death and plowed his fields for the last time, I declared to myself that this was the end of an era, just as the era of horse-drawn farming had ended a generation earlier when my grandfather died. I moved on, struggled through college not knowing which way to turn, got married, gravitated toward the social sciences because it was something I felt I could do, and wound up as a graduate student in Berkeley at the height of the campus unrest. I was not interested in sociology of religion at the time, but took a course in it from Charles Glock. The only thing I remember from the course was a sloping line he drew on the chalkboard one day. I don't remember if it sloped up or down, but it represented social change. Glock was convinced we were living in a time of significant social change. Having recently driven from Kansas to Berkeley, I appreciated his point.

The connection of all this to theology, as I explained to another audience one time, is best expressed in an image Madeleine l'Engle has used. She writes of going out to a quiet place at night and looking up at the stars. When she does this, she sometimes hears music—the music of the universe, the music of God. I go back to Kansas once in a while to see what remains of the life I left behind. I go to the town where the Baptist church I attended as a child once stood. There is a small marker saying the church was torn down in 1978. I stop at the place where our farm buildings once stood—where my father came home from World War II, not in good health, and renovated an old ramshackle house, put a new roof on the barn, and planted a shelter belt of trees. Down in the ditch, under a clump of dead sunflowers, I find a small roll of rusted barbed wire. It is all that remains. I feel like a displaced person, a refugee. Like Madeleine l'Engle, I sometimes imagine the music of the universe. But it is music in a minor key.

study has led to an increased interest in the organizational dynamics of religious groups (Finke and Stark 1988, 1992; Hammond 1992; Roof and McKinney 1990; Stark and Bainbridge 1987).

Finally, sociologists are concerned with the relationship among religion, ethnic identity, and politics. This is seen in the resurgence of ethnically based religion in pluralist societies such as the United States as well as in the rise of religious nationalism throughout the world (Juergensmeyer 1993; Lawrence 1989; Merkyl and Smart 1983; Sahliyeh 1990; see the discussion below of religious nationalism).

Theories of Religion

Sociological approaches to religion are still strongly influenced by the ideas of Marx, Durkheim, and Weber. None of the three was religious himself, and all believed that religion would become less and less significant in modern times. Each argued that religion was fundamentally an illusion: The very diversity of religions and their obvious connection to different societies and regions of the world made the claims by their advocates inherently implausible. An individual born into an Australian society of hunters and gatherers would plainly hold different religious beliefs from someone born into the caste system of India or the Catholic Church of medieval Europe.

Marx: Religion and Inequality

In spite of the influence of his views on the subject, Karl Marx never studied religion in any detail. His thinking on religion was mostly derived from the writings of Ludwig Feuerbach, who believed that through a process he called **alienation,** human beings tend to attribute their own culturally created values and norms to alien, or separate, beings (i.e., divine forces or gods), because they do not understand their own history. Thus the story of the Ten Commandments given to Moses by God is a mythical version of the origins of the moral precepts that govern the lives of Jewish and Christian believers.

Marx accepted the view that religion represents human self-alienation. In a famous phrase, Marx declared that religion was the "opium of the people." Religion defers happiness and rewards to the afterlife, he said, teaching the resigned acceptance of existing conditions in the earthly life. Attention is thus diverted away from inequalities and injustices in this world by the promise of what is to come in the next. Religion contains a strong ideological element: Religious belief can often provide justifications for those in power. For example, "The meek shall inherit the earth" suggests attitudes of humility and nonresistance to oppression.

Durkheim: Religion and Functionalism

In contrast to Marx, Émile Durkheim spent a good part of his intellectual career studying religion, concentrating particularly on totemism as practiced by Australian aboriginal societies. *The Elementary Forms of the Religious Life,* first published in 1912, is perhaps the most influential single study in the sociology of religion. Durkheim connected religion not with social inequalities or power but with the overall nature of the institutions of a society. His argument was that totemism represented religion in its most "elementary" form—hence the title of his book.

Durkheim defined religion in terms of a distinction between the sacred and the profane. **Sacred** objects and symbols, he held, are treated as apart from the routine, utilitarian aspects of day-to-day existence—the realm of the **profane.** A totem (an animal or plant believed to have particular symbolic significance), Durkheim argued, is a sacred object, regarded with veneration and surrounded by ritual activities. These ceremonies and rituals, in Durkheim's view, are essential to binding the members of groups together.

Durkheim's theory of religion is a good example of the functionalist tradition of thought in sociology. To analyze the function of a social behavior or social institution like religion is to study the contribution it makes to the continuation of a group, community, or society. According to Durkheim, religion has the function of cohering a society by ensuring that people meet regularly to affirm common beliefs and values.

Weber: The World Religions and Social Change

Durkheim based his arguments on a restricted range of examples, even though he claimed his ideas applied to religion in general. Max Weber, by contrast, embarked on a massive study of religions worldwide. No scholar before or since has undertaken a task of the scope Weber attempted.

Weber's writings on religion differ from those of Durkheim because they concentrate on the connection between religion and social change, something to which Durkheim gave little direct attention. They also contrast with those of Marx, because Weber argued that religion was not necessarily a conservative force; on the contrary, religiously inspired movements have often produced dramatic social transformations. Thus Protestantism, particularly Puritanism, according to Weber, was the source of the capitalistic outlook found in the modern West. The early entrepreneurs were mostly Calvinists. Their drive to succeed, which helped initiate Western economic development, was originally prompted by a desire to serve God. Material success was a sign of divine favor.

Weber conceived of his research on the world religions as a single project. His discussion of the effect of Protestantism on the development of the West was connected to a comprehensive attempt to understand the influence of religion on social and economic life in various cultures. After analyzing the Eastern religions, Weber concluded that they provided insuperable barriers to the development of industrial capitalism such as took place in the West. This was not because the non-Western civilizations were backward; they were simply oriented toward different values, such as escape from the toils of the material world, from those that came to predominate in Europe.

In traditional China and India, Weber pointed out, there was at certain periods a significant development of commerce, manufacture, and urbanism. But these did not generate the radical patterns of social change involved in the rise of industrial capitalism in the West. Religion was a major influence inhibiting such change. Consider, for example, Hinduism. Hinduism is what Weber called an "other-worldly" religion. That is to say, its highest values stress escape from the toils of the material world to a higher plane of spiritual existence. The religious feelings and motivations produced by Hinduism do not focus on controlling or shaping the material world. On the contrary, Hinduism sees material reality as a veil hiding the

In his research on the social and economic influence of religions around the world, Max Weber categorized Eastern religions as "other-worldly" and Christianity as a "salvation religion." Weber believed that Hinduism stressed escaping material existence to locate a higher plane of being, which cultivated an attitude of passivity. In contrast, he argued that Christianity and its emphasis on salvation and constant struggle could stimulate revolt against the existing order.

true spiritual concerns to which humankind should be oriented. Confucianism also acts to direct activity away from economic "progress," as this came to be understood in the West. Confucianism emphasizes harmony with the world, rather than promoting an active mastery of it. Although China was for a long while the most powerful and culturally most developed civilization in the world, its dominant religious values acted as a brake on a stronger commitment to economic development.

Weber regarded Christianity as a *salvation religion.* According to such religions, human beings can be "saved" if they are converted to the beliefs of the religion and follow its moral tenets. The notions of sin and of being rescued from sinfulness by God's grace are important here. They generate a tension and an emotional dynamism essentially absent from the Eastern religions. Salvation religions have a "revolutionary" aspect. Whereas the religions of the East cultivate an attitude of passivity or acceptance within the believer, Christianity demands a constant struggle against sin and so can stimulate revolt against the existing order. Religious leaders—such as Luther or Calvin—have arisen who reinterpret existing doctrines in such a way as to challenge the extant power structure.

Critical Assessment of the Classical View

Marx, Durkheim, and Weber each identified some important general characteristics of religion, and in some ways their views complement one another. Marx was right to claim that religion often has ideological implications, serving to justify the interests of ruling groups at the expense of others. There are innumerable instances of this in history. For example, the European missionaries who sought to convert "heathen" peoples to Christian beliefs were no doubt sincere in their efforts. Yet their teachings in large part reinforced the destruction of traditional cultures and the imposition of white domination. Almost all Christian denominations tolerated, or endorsed, slavery in the United States and other parts of the world into the nineteenth century. Doctrines were developed proclaiming slavery to be based on divine law, disobedient slaves being guilty of an offense against God as well as their masters (Stampp 1956).

Yet Weber was certainly correct to emphasize the unsettling and often revolutionary effect of religious ideals on the established social order. In spite of the churches' early support for slavery in the United States, church leaders later played a key role in fighting to abolish the institution. Religious beliefs have prompted social movements seeking to overthrow unjust systems of authority; for instance, religious sentiments played a prominent part in the civil rights movements of the 1960s. Religion has also generated social change through wars fought for religious motives.

The Spread of New Age Religions

If you pick up a local newspaper in any U.S. city and turn to the classifieds section, you are likely to find a number of listings relating to spirituality and the New Age movement. You have no doubt seen advertisements like these before: "A course in miracles. Personal coaching by the hour." "Soul purpose, past lives, intuitive healing." "Under the guidance of a Living Spiritual Teacher, you can be guided to take the next step in your spiritual unfoldment." These ads appeal to those who feel strong spiritual yearnings, who have a sense that their lives are not going quite the way they should, and who have become disenchanted with well-established religions. While some of the advertisements are clearly attempts to profit from the willingness of some to believe anything they are told, most participants in the New Age movement see themselves as being on a sincere spiritual quest for self-enlightenment. Religious studies scholar Paul Heelas, in his 1996 book *The New Age Movement,* describes the New Age movement that has sprung up in response to this spiritual demand as having three essential characteristics: "It explains why life—as conventionally experienced—is not what it should be; it provides an account of what it is to find perfection; and it provides the means for obtaining salvation." By

most estimates, the number of people interested in such concerns is growing. Meditation groups, psychic fairs, spirituality discussion groups, training sessions designed to help participants reach their "true" spiritual potential, tarot card readings, books on spirituality and psychological self-help—all have proliferated since the 1960s.

These divisive influences of religion, so prominent in history, find little mention in Durkheim's work. Durkheim emphasized above all the role of religion in promoting social cohesion. Yet it is not difficult to redirect his ideas toward explaining religious division, conflict, and change as well as solidarity. After all, much of the strength of feeling that may be generated *against* other religious groups derives from the commitment to religious values generated *within* each community of believers.

Among the most valuable points of Durkheim's writings is his stress on ritual and ceremony. All religions hold regular assemblies of believers, at which ritual prescriptions are observed. As Durkheim rightly points out, ritual activities also mark the major transitions of life—birth, entry to adulthood (rituals associated with puberty are found in many cultures), marriage, and death (Van Gennep 1977).

Finally, Marx, Durkheim, and Weber's theories on religion were based on their studies of societies in which a single religion predominated. As a consequence, it seemed reasonable for them to examine the relationship between a predominant religion and the society as a whole. However, since the 1950s, this classical view has been challenged by some U.S. sociologists. Because of their own experience in a society that is highly tolerant of religious diversity, these theorists have focused on religious pluralism rather than on religious domination. It is not surprising that their conclusions differ substantially from the earlier views as advanced in different ways by Marx, Durkheim, and Weber, each of whom regarded religion as closely bound up with the larger society. Religion was believed to reflect and reinforce society's values, or at least the values of those who were most powerful; to provide an important source of solidarity and social stability; and to be an important engine

From the perspective of the sociology of religion, we can ask a number of questions about these developments. To what extent do these diverse phenomena form part of a coherent whole? What sociological factors account for the current popularity of the New Age movement? In what ways does the New Age movement differ from traditional forms of religiosity?

With respect to the last of these questions, one unique feature of the New Age movement is its eclecticism. Religions, of course, have always borrowed from one another. But most religions—no matter how much they adapt to current social and moral conditions—place a heavy emphasis on maintaining religious tradition. The faithful are often required by religious authorities to believe in the essential dogmas held by previous generations of worshipers. New Agers, however, tend to deny that there is much value in clinging to well defined religious traditions. Instead, they see it as important, that individuals pick and choose those spiritual beliefs and practices that suit them best. Heelas writes: "Much of the New Age would appear to be quite radically detraditionalized (rejecting voices of authority associated with established orders)." Individuals, New Agers believe, should learn to listen to their intuition or "inner voice" to help them select the spiritual practices and make the life choices that are right for them.

The social organization of the New Age movement is entirely consistent with this philosophy. The movement consists of thousands of different groups, varying tremendously in size, with each group oriented around a different eclectic appropriation of the world's spiritual traditions. Many groups borrow heavily from Eastern spirituality—from Tibetan Buddhism, for

example. Others incorporate certain Native American traditions. Still others combine these with elements of Christianity. There is an almost infinite number of permutations.

What does this have to do with globalization? New Agers insist that they should be free to borrow any spiritual practices that are right for them. Why, they ask, should Tibetan Buddhism be reserved for Tibetans, or Native American rituals for Native Americans? Without wishing to rob these groups of their rich cultural heritage, New Agers firmly believe that the geographic borders of nation-states are entirely irrelevant to spirituality. Their eclecticism is truly global, and, primarily through books and travel, they scour the world in search of meaningful forms of spirituality. If the differences between nation-states begin to fade in a globalized world, New Agers may well embody the growing penetration of globalization into the religious realm.

of social change. According to this view, religion is threatened by the rise of **secular thinking**—that is, worldly thinking, particularly as seen in the rise of science, technology, and rational thought in general.

The classical theories of religion argued that the key problem facing religions in the modern world is **secularization,** or a rise in worldly thinking and a simultaneous decline in the influence of religion. Secularization is typically accompanied by a decrease in religious belief and involvement and results in a weakening of the social and political power of religious organizations. Peter Berger (1967) has described religion in premodern societies as a "sacred canopy" that covers all aspects of life and is therefore seldom questioned. In modern society, however, the sacred canopy is more like a quilt, a patchwork of numerous different religious and secular belief systems. When beliefs are compared and contrasted, it becomes increasingly

difficult to sustain the idea that there is any single true faith. According to this view, secularization is the likely result.

Secularization: The Sociological Debate

The debate over secularization is one of the most complex areas in the sociology of religion. In the most basic terms, the disagreement is between supporters of the secularization thesis—who agree with sociology's founders and see religion as diminishing in power and importance in the modern world—and opponents of the concept, who argue that religion remains a significant force, albeit often in new and unfamiliar forms.

Secularization is a complex sociological concept in part because there is little consensus about how the process should be measured. Moreover, many sociologists employ definitions of religion that do not coincide: Whereas some argue that religion is best understood in terms of the traditional church, others argue that a much broader view must be taken to include dimensions such as personal spirituality and deep commitment to certain values. These differences in perception will necessarily influence arguments for or against secularization.

We can evaluate secularization according to a number of aspects or dimensions. Some of them are objective in nature, such as the *level of membership* of religious organizations. Statistics and official records can show how many people belong to a church or other religious body and are active in attending services or other ceremonies. As we will see, with the exception of the United States, the industrialized countries have all experienced considerable secularization according to this index. The pattern of religious decline seen in Britain is found in most of western Europe, including Catholic countries such as France or Italy. More Italians than French attend church regularly and participate in the major rituals (such as Easter Communion), but the overall pattern of declining religious observance is similar in both cases.

A second dimension of secularization concerns how far churches and other religious organizations maintain their *social influence, wealth,* and *prestige.* In earlier times, religious organizations could wield considerable influence over governments and social agencies and commanded high respect in the community. How much is this still the case? The answer to the question is clear. Even if we confine ourselves to the present century, we see that religious organizations have progressively lost much of the social and political influence they previously had, particularly in the advanced industrial nations, although there are some exceptions. Church leaders can no longer automatically expect to be influential with the powerful. Although some established churches remain very wealthy by any standards, and new religious movements may rapidly build up fortunes, the material circumstances of many long-standing religious organizations are insecure. Churches and temples have to be sold off or are in a state of disrepair, and entire dioceses have considered filing for bankruptcy.

The third dimension of secularization concerns beliefs and values. We can call this the dimension of *religiosity.* Levels of churchgoing and the degree of social influence of churches are obviously not necessarily a direct expression of the beliefs or ideals people hold. Many who have religious beliefs do not regularly attend services or take part in public ceremonies; conversely, regularity of such attendance or participation does not always imply the holding of strong religious views—people may attend out of habit or because it is expected of them in their community.

As in the other dimensions of secularization, we need an accurate understanding of the past to see how far religiosity has declined today. Supporters of the secularization thesis argue that in the past, religion was far more important to people's daily lives than it is today. The church was at the heart of local affairs and was a strong influence on family and personal life. Yet critics of the thesis contest this idea, arguing that just because people attended church more regularly does not necessarily prove that they were more religious. In many traditional societies, including medieval Europe, commitment to religious belief was less strong and less important in day-to-day life than might be supposed. Research into English history, for example, shows that lukewarm commitment to religious beliefs was common among the ordinary people. Religious skeptics seem to have been found in most cultures, particularly in the larger traditional societies (Ginzburg 1980).

Yet there can be no doubt at all that the hold of religious ideas today is weaker than was generally the case in the traditional world—particularly if we include under the term *religion* the whole range of the supernatural in which people believed. Most of us simply no longer experience our environment as permeated by divine or spiritual entities. Some of the major tensions in the world today—such as those afflicting the Middle East and the Balkans or the violence perpetrated by Osama bin Laden and the al Qaeda terrorist network—derive primarily, or in some part, from religious differences. But the majority of conflicts and wars are now mainly secular in nature—concerned with divergent political goals or material interests.

Contemporary Approaches: Religious Economy

One of the most recent and influential approaches to the sociology of religion is tailored to societies such as the United States, which offer many different faiths from which to pick and choose. Taking their cue from economic theory, sociologists who favor the **religious economy** approach argue that religions can be fruitfully understood as organizations in competition with each other for followers (Finke and Stark 1988, 1992; Hammond 1992; Moore 1994; Roof and McKinney 1990; Stark and Bainbridge 1987; Warner 1993).

Like contemporary economists who study businesses, these sociologists argue that competition is preferable to monopoly when it comes to ensuring religious vitality. This position is exactly opposite to those of the classical theorists. Marx, Durkheim, and Weber assumed that religion weakens when challenged by different religious or secular viewpoints, whereas the religious economists argue that competition increases the overall level of religious involvement in modern society. Religious economists believe this is true for two reasons. First, competition makes each religious group try that much harder

Religious economists believe that competition between religions leads to religious vitality. They also argue that successful religious groups have effective representatives spreading their beliefs and rituals. For example, the fall of communism in Mongolia brought religious freedom to this sparsely populated country located between China and Russia. It also brought foreigners eager for converts to Mongolia, like the Mormon missionaries pictured here, Korean Christians, and Catholics.

tributing to secularization. Rather, they argue that modern religion is constantly renewing itself through active marketing and recruitment. Although a growing body of research supports the notion that competition is good for religion (Finke and Stark 1992; Stark and Bainbridge 1980, 1985), not all research comes to this conclusion (Land et al. 1991).

The religious-economy approach overestimates the extent to which people rationally pick and choose among different religions, as if they were shopping around for a new car or a pair of shoes. Among deeply committed believers, particularly in societies that lack religious pluralism, it is not obvious that religion is a matter of rational choice. In such societies, even when people are allowed to choose among different religions, most are likely to practice their childhood religion without ever questioning whether or not there are more appealing alternatives. Even in the United States, where the religious-economy approach originated, sociologists may overlook the spiritual aspects of religion if they simply assume that religious buyers are always on spiritual shopping sprees. Wade Clark Roof's 1993 study of fourteen hundred baby boomers found that a third had remained loyal to their childhood faith, while another third had continued to profess their childhood beliefs although they no longer belonged to a religious organization. Thus only a third were actively looking around for a new religion, making the sorts of choices presumed by the religious economy approach.

to win followers. Second, the presence of numerous religions means that there is likely to be something for just about everyone. In a culturally diverse society such as the United States, a single religion will probably appeal to only a limited range of followers, whereas the presence of Indian gurus and fundamentalist preachers, in addition to mainline churches, is likely to encourage a high level of religious participation.

This analysis is adapted from the business world, in which competition presumably encourages the emergence of highly specialized products that appeal to the very specific markets. In fact, religious economists borrow the language of business in describing the conditions that lead to the success or failure of a particular religious organization. According to Roger Finke and Rodney Stark (1992), a successful religious group must be well organized for competition, have eloquent preachers who are effective "sales reps" in spreading the word, offer beliefs and rituals that are packaged as an appealing product, and develop effective marketing techniques. Religion, in this view, is a business much like any other. Television evangelists, whom we shall consider below, have been especially good businesspeople in selling their religious products.

Thus religious economists such as Finke and Stark do not see competition as undermining religious beliefs and con-

Types of Religious Organizations

The sociology of religion has concerned itself with non-European religions since its origins in the writings of Durkheim and Weber. Nonetheless, there has frequently been a tendency to view all religions through concepts and theories that grew out of the European experience. For example, notions such as *denomination* or *sect* presuppose the existence of formally organized religious institutions; they are of questionable utility in the study of religions that emphasize ongoing spiritual practice as a part of daily life or that pursue the complete integration of religion with civic and political life. In recent years, there has been an effort to create a more comparative sociology of religion, one that seeks to understand religious traditions from within their own frames of reference (Juergensmeyer 1993; Smart 1989; Van der Veer 1994; Wilson 1982).

Early theorists such as Max Weber (1963, orig. 1921), Ernst Troeltsch (1931), and Richard Niebuhr (1929) described religious organizations as falling along a continuum, based on the degree to which they are well established and conventional:

Megachurches as Minitowns

Patty Anderson and her husband, Gary, found faith where they least expected it—he on the free-throw line and she swathed in sweats in an aerobics class.

It happened at the 50,000-square-foot activities center of the Southeast Christian Church [in Louisville, Kentucky,] where pumping iron and praising the Lord go hand and hand. Amenities at the gym include 16 basketball courts and a Cybex health club, free to churchgoers, where the music is Christian and the rules ban cursing even during the crunch.

"I really had no intention of being part of a church," recalled Gary Anderson, a physiology professor at the University of Louisville School of Medicine. But hoops at this 22,000-member megachurch led him to the sanctuary. And after three years, he said, like a slam dunk, "the sermons sunk in."

Southeast Christian is an example of a new breed of megachurch—a full-service "24/7" sprawling village, which offers many of the conveniences and trappings of secular life wrapped around a spiritual core. It is possible to eat, shop, go to school, bank, work out, scale a rock-climbing wall and pray there, all without leaving the grounds.

These churches are becoming civic in a way unimaginable since the thirteenth century and its cathedral towns. No longer simply places to worship, they have become part resort, part mall, part extended family and part town square.

***

The churches reflect a desire by congregants for a "universe where everything from the temperature to the theology is safely controlled," [one professor] said. "They don't have to worry about finding schools, social networks or a place to eat. It's all prepackaged."

***

"People are looking at churches with a similar cost-benefit analysis they'd give to any other consumer purchase," [a megachurch consultant added]. "There is little brand loyalty. Many are looking for the newest and the greatest."

Dave Stone, the associate minister of Southeast, calls his church, which is open daily from 5:30 A.M. to 11 P.M., "a refueling station."

"If we can get people to come to our gym," he explained, "it's only a matter of time before we can get them to visit our sanctuary."

The church was deliberately designed like a mall. (The sanctuary is the anchor tenant.) Hallways 20 feet wide with curves enhance "people flow," said Jack Coffee, a church elder and chairman of the building committee. Preschoolers frolic at a Disneyesque play land, with mazes. There is an education wing for Bible classes, a concert-hall-size atrium with glass elevators, crisscrossing escalators and giant monitors that itemize the day's offerings: meetings to help smokers quit, a cross-trainers minimarathon and pat the Bible classes for six-month-olds.

Such amenities are typically paid for by the congregation with three-year capital campaigns, on top of the church's operating budget, which is often financed with tithes, said Malcolm P. Graham, president of Cargill Associates' church division, a fund-raising consultant. A study by the Hartford Institute for Religion Research at the Hartford Seminary finds the average annual income for a megachurch is $4.6 million a year. Annual contributions to Southeast Christian are more than $20 million.

Southeast Christian churchgoers speak of a 22,000-person family, and visitors are regaled with statistics: the coffeepot that serves 5,000 cups an hour, the 403 toilets. Southeast's size has spawned the invention of the Greenlee Communion Dispensing Machine, designed by Wilfred Greenlee, 79, a congregant. It can fill 40 communion cups in 2 seconds.

***

Not incidentally, it gives the congregants who flock to church for more than 80 activities each evening—like children's theater and adult computer classes—an excuse to stick around. "If you have to go home for dinner, you don't come back out," [a pastor said].

But some scholars and municipalities are troubled by the civic expansion of 24/7 churches. They are becoming "a parallel universe that's Christianized," in the words of Dr. Scott Thumma, a sociologist of religion at the Hartford Institute.

Dr. Wade Clark Roof, a professor of religion and society at the University of California at Santa Barbara, said he worried that full-service churches are "the religious version of the gated community."

"It's an attempt to create a world where you're dealing with like-minded people," he said. "You lose the dialogue with the larger culture."

***

SOURCE: Patricia Leigh Brown, "Megachurches as Minitowns," *New York Times,* May 9, 2002, pp. F1–F6.

Questions

- How might Marx, Durkheim, and Weber each analyze the development of megachurches?
- Are megachurches evidence in favor of the religious economy approach to the sociology of religion?
- In your view, what do megachurches reveal about American society? Are congregants seeking social solidarity or trying to isolate themselves from the rest of society?

Churches lie at one end (they are conventional and well established), cults lie at the other (they are neither), and sects fall somewhere in the middle. These distinctions were based on the study of European and U.S. religions. There is much debate over how well they apply to the non-Christian world.

Today, sociologists are aware that the terms *sect* and *cult* have negative connotations, something they wish to avoid. For this reason, contemporary sociologists of religion sometimes use the phrase *new religious movements* to characterize novel religious organizations that lack the respectability that comes with being well established for a long period of time (Hadden 1997b; Hexham and Poewe 1997).

Churches and Sects

Churches are large, established religious bodies; one example is the Roman Catholic Church. They normally have a formal, bureaucratic structure, with a hierarchy of religious officials. Churches often represent the conservative face of religion, since they are integrated within the existing institutional order. Most of their adherents are born into and grow up with the church.

Sects are smaller, less highly organized groups of committed believers, usually set up in protest against an established church, as Calvinism and Methodism were initially. Sects aim at discovering and following the "true way" and either try to change the surrounding society or withdraw from it into communities of their own, a process known as *revival*. The members of sects regard established churches as corrupt. Many sects have few or no officials, and all members are regarded as equal participants. For the most part, people are not born into sects, but actively join them to further commitments in which they believe.

Denominations and Cults

A **denomination** is a sect that has cooled down and become an institutionalized body rather than an activist protest group. Sects that survive over any period of time inevitably become denominations. Thus Calvinism and Methodism were sects during their early period of formation, when they generated great fervor among their members; but over the years, they have become more established. (Calvinists today are called Presbyterians.) Denominations are recognized as legitimate by churches and exist alongside them, often cooperating harmoniously with them.

Cults resemble sects, but their emphases are different. Cults are the most loosely knit and transient of all religious organizations. They are composed of individuals who reject what they see as the values of the outside society, unlike sects, which try to revive an established church. They are a form of religious innovation, rather than revival. Their focus is on individual experience, bringing like-minded people together. Like sects, cults often form around the influence of an inspirational leader.

Cults are likely to be in a high degree of tension with the larger society. A tragic example occurred in 1993 when eighty members of the Branch Davidian religious cult (including nineteen children) burned to death in their Waco, Texas, compound during an assault by federal officials that ended a lengthy armed standoff. Federal officials maintain that the cult members were virtual prisoners of their charismatic leader, David Koresh, who was allegedly stockpiling illegal weapons, practicing polygyny, and having sex with some of the children. Controversy remains over whether the fire was ordered by Koresh, who reportedly preferred mass suicide to surrender, or whether the actions of the federal authorities caused the tragedy (Tabor and Gallagher 1995). In 1997, thirty-nine members of Heaven's Gate, a cult whose members believed that they were destined for a "higher level," took their lives to ascend to a spaceship they believed lurked behind the Hale-Bopp comet.

Like sects, cults flourish when there is a breakdown in well-established and widespread societal belief systems. This is happening throughout the world today, in places as diverse as Japan, India, and the United States. When such a breakdown occurs, cults may originate within the society itself, or they may be "imported" from outside. In the United States, examples of homegrown, or indigenous, cults include New Age religions based on such things as spiritualism, astrology, and religious practices adapted from Asian or Native American cultures. Examples of imported cults include the Reverend Sun Myung Moon's Unification Church ("Moonies"), which originated in South Korea, and transcendental meditation.

It should be obvious that what is a cult in one country may well be an established religious practice in another. When Indian gurus (religious teachers) bring their beliefs into the United States, what might be considered an established religion in India is regarded as a cult in the United States. Christianity began as an indigenous cult in ancient Jerusalem, and in many Asian countries today Evangelical Protestantism is regarded as a cult imported from the United States. Thus cults should not be thought of as "weird." A leading sociologist of religion, Jeffrey K. Hadden (1997a), points out that all the approximately one hundred thousand religions that humans have devised were once new; most if not all were initially despised cults from the standpoint of respectable religious belief of the times. Jesus was crucified because his ideas were so threatening to the established order of the Roman-dominated religious establishment of ancient Judaea.

Religious Movements

Religious movements represent a subtype of social movement in general. A religious movement is an association of people who join together to spread a new religion or to promote a new interpretation of an existing religion. Religious movements are larger than sects and less exclusivist in their membership—although like churches and sects, movements and sects (or cults) are not always clearly distinct from each other. In fact, all sects and cults can be classified as religious movements. Examples of religious movements include the groups that originally founded and spread Christianity in the first century, the Lutheran movement that split Christianity in Europe about fifteen hundred years afterward, and the groups involved in the more recent Islamic revolution (discussed in more detail later in the chapter).

Religious movements tend to pass through certain definite phases of development. In the first phase, the movement usually derives its life and cohesion from a powerful leader. Max Weber classified such leaders as **charismatic**—that is, having inspirational qualities capable of capturing the imagination and devotion of a mass of followers. (Charismatic leaders in Weber's formulation could include political as well as religious figures—revolutionary China's Mao Zedong for example, as well as Jesus and Muhammad.) The leaders of religious movements are usually critical of the religious establishment and seek to proclaim a new message. In their early years, religious movements are fluid; they do not have an established authority system. Their members are normally in direct contact with the charismatic leader, and together they spread the new teachings.

The second phase of development occurs following the death of the leader. Rarely does a new charismatic leader arise from the masses, so this phase is crucial. The movement is now faced with what Weber termed the "routinization of charisma." To survive, it has to create formalized rules and procedures, since it can no longer depend on the central role of the leader in organizing the followers. Many movements fade away when their leaders die or lose their influence. A movement that survives and takes on a permanent character becomes a church. In other words, it becomes a formal organization of believers with an established authority system and established symbols and rituals. The church might itself at some later point become the origin of other movements that question its teachings and either set themselves up in opposition or break away completely.

New Religious Movements

Although traditional churches have been experiencing a decline in membership in recent decades, other forms of religious activity have been on the rise. Sociologists use the term **new religious movements** to refer collectively to the broad range of religious and spiritual groups, cults, and sects that have emerged in Western countries, including the United States, alongside mainstream religions. New religious movements encompass an enormous diversity of groups, from spiritual and self-help groups within the New Age movement to exclusive sects such as the Hare Krishnas (International Society for Krishna Consciousness).

Many new religious movements are derived from mainstream religious traditions, such as Hinduism, Christianity, and Buddhism, whereas others have emerged from traditions that were almost unknown in the West until recently. Some new religious movements are essentially new creations of the charismatic leaders who head their activities. This is the case with the Unification Church, led by the Reverend Sun Myung Moon. Membership in new religious movements mostly consists of converts rather than individuals brought up in a particular faith. Members more often than not are well educated and from middle-class backgrounds.

Since World War II, the United States has witnessed a far greater proliferation of religious movements than at any previous time in its history, including an unprecedented series of mergers of and divisions among denominations. Most have been short lived, but a few have achieved remarkable followings.

Various theories to explain the popularity of new religious movements have been advanced. Some observers argue that they should be seen as a response to the process of liberalization and secularization within society and even within traditional churches. People who feel that traditional religions have become ritualistic and devoid of spiritual meaning may find comfort and a greater sense of community in smaller, less impersonal new religious movements.

Others have pointed to new religious movements as an outcome of rapid social change (Wilson 1982). As traditional social norms are disrupted, people search for both explanations and reassurance. The rise of groups and sects that emphasize personal spirituality, for example, suggest that many individuals feel a need to reconnect with their own values of beliefs in the face of instability and uncertainty.

A further factor may be that new religious movements appeal to people who feel alienated from mainstream society. The collective, communal approaches of sects and cults, some authors argue, can offer support and a sense of belonging. For example, middle-class youth are not marginalized from society in a material sense, but they may feel isolated emotionally and spiritually. Membership in a cult can help overcome this feeling of alienation (Wallis 1984).

New religious movements can be understood as falling into three broad categories: *world-affirming, world-rejecting,* and *world-accommodating* movements. Each is based on the relationship of the individual group to the larger social world.

World-affirming movements are more akin to self-help or therapy groups than to conventional religious groups. These movements often lack rituals, churches, and formal theologies, turning their focus on members' spiritual well-being. As the name suggests, world-affirming movements do not reject the outside world or its values. Rather, they seek to enhance their followers' abilities to perform and succeed in that world by unlocking human potential.

The Church of Scientology is one such group. Founded by L. Ron Hubbard, the Church of Scientology has grown from its original base in California to include a large membership in countries around the world. Scientologists believe we are all spiritual beings but have neglected our spiritual nature. Through training that makes them aware of their real spiritual capacities, people can recover forgotten supernatural powers, clear their minds, and reveal their full potential.

Many strands of the so-called **New Age movement** fall under the category of world-affirming movements. The New Age movement emerged from the counterculture of the 1960s and 1970s and encompasses a broad spectrum of beliefs, practices, and ways of life. Pagan teachings (Celtic, Druidic, Native American, and others), shamanism, forms of Asian mysticism, Wiccan rituals, and Zen meditation are only a few of the activities that are thought of as New Age.

On the surface, the mysticism of the New Age movement appears to stand in stark contrast to the modern societies in

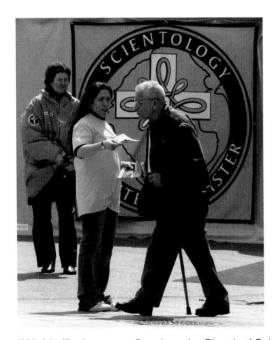

"World-affirming groups," such as the Church of Scientology, focus on members' spiritual well-being and do not reject the outside world's values. Science-fiction writer L. Ron Hubbard established scientology in 1954.

which it is favored. Followers of New Age movements seek out and develop alternative ways of life in order to cope with the challenges of modernity. Yet New Age activities should not be interpreted as simply a radical break with the present. They should also be seen as part of a larger cultural trajectory that *exemplifies* aspects of mainstream culture. In late modern societies, individuals possess unparalleled degrees of autonomy and freedom to chart their own lives. In this respect, the aims of the New Age movement coincide closely with the modern age: People are encouraged to move beyond traditional values and expectations and to live their lives actively and reflectively.

WORLD-REJECTING MOVEMENTS

As opposed to world-affirming groups, **world-rejecting movements** are highly critical of the outside world. They often demand significant lifestyle changes from their followers—members may be expected to live ascetically, to change their dress or hairstyle, or to follow a certain diet. World-rejecting movements are frequently exclusive, in contrast to world-affirming movements, which tend to be inclusive in nature. Some world-rejecting movements display characteristics of **total institutions;** members are expected to subsume their individual identities in that of the group, to adhere to strict ethical codes or rules, and to withdraw from activity in the outside world.

Most of the world-rejecting movements place far more demands on their members, in terms of time and commitment, than do older established religions. Some groups have been known to use the technique of "love bombing" to gain the individual's total adherence. A potential convert is overwhelmed by attention and constant displays of instant affection until he or she is drawn emotionally into the group. Some new movements, in fact, have been accused of brainwashing their adherents—seeking to control their minds in such a way as to rob them of the capacity for independent decision making.

Many world-rejecting cults and sects have come under the intense scrutiny of state authorities, the media, and the public. Certain extreme cases of world-rejecting cults have attracted much concern. For example, the Japanese group Aum Shinrikyo released deadly sarin gas into the Tokyo subway system in 1995, injuring thousands of morning commuters. In the United States, the Branch Davidian cult, based in Waco, Texas, became embroiled in a deadly confrontation with federal authorities in 1993 after accusations of child abuse and weapons stockpiling.

WORLD-ACCOMMODATING MOVEMENTS

The third type of new religious movement is the one most like traditional religions. **World-accommodating movements** tend to emphasize the importance of inner religious life over more worldly concerns. Members of such groups seek to reclaim the spiritual purity that they believe has been lost in traditional religious settings. Whereas followers of world-rejecting and world-affirming groups often alter their lifestyles in accordance with their religious activity, many adherents of world-accommodating movements carry on in their everyday lives and careers with little visible change. One example of a world-accommodating movement is Pentecostalism. Pentecostalists believe that the Holy Spirit can be heard through individuals who are granted the gift of "speaking in tongues."

NEW RELIGIOUS MOVEMENTS AND SECULARIZATION

The enduring popularity of new religious movements presents another challenge to the secularization thesis. Opponents of the thesis point to the diversity and dynamism of new religious movements and argue that religion and spirituality remain a central facet of modern life. As traditional religions lose their hold, religion is not disappearing, but is being channeled in new directions. Not all scholars agree, however. Proponents of the idea of secularization point out that these movements remain peripheral to society as a whole, even if they make a profound impact on the lives of their individual followers. New religious movements are fragmented and relatively unorganized; they also suffer from high turnover rates as people are attracted to a movement for some time and then move on to something new. Compared to a serious religious commitment, they argue, participation in a new religious movement appears little more than a hobby or lifestyle choice.

Gender and Religion

Churches and denominations resemble other institutions in social life in that women have been mostly excluded from power. This is clear in Christianity, but it is also characteristic of virtually all the major religions. In the following sections, we examine some of the interrelations of religion and gender. The issue is an important one, because this is an area in which significant changes are taking place.

Religious Images

In Christianity, although Mary, the mother of Jesus, is sometimes treated as if she had divine qualities, God is "the Father," a male figure, and Jesus took the human shape of a man. Genesis, the first book of the Bible, reveals that woman was created from a rib taken from man. These facts have not gone unnoticed by women's movements. A hundred years ago, Elizabeth Cady Stanton published a series of commentaries on the Scriptures, titled *The Woman's Bible*. In her view, the deity had created women and men as beings of equal value, and the Bible should fully reflect this fact. Its "masculinist" character, she believed, reflected not the authentic word of God, but the fact that the Bible was written by men. In 1870, the Church of England established a Revising Committee to revise and update the biblical texts; but as Stanton pointed out, the committee contained not a single woman. She asserted that there was no reason to suppose that God is a man, because it was clear in the Scriptures that all human beings were fashioned in the image of God. When a colleague opened a women's rights conference with a prayer to "God, our Mother," there was a virulent reaction from the church authorities. Yet Stanton pressed ahead, organizing the Women's Revising Committee in America, composed of twenty-three women, to advise her in preparing *The Woman's Bible,* which was published in 1895.

In some Buddhist orders, especially Mahayana Buddhism, women are represented in a favorable light. But on the whole, Buddhism, like Christianity, is "an overwhelmingly male-created institution dominated by a patriarchal power structure," in which the feminine is mostly "associated with the secular, powerless, profane, and imperfect" (Paul 1985). The contrasting pictures of women that appear in the Buddhist texts no doubt mirror the ambiguous attitudes of men toward women in the secular world: Women are portrayed as wise, maternal, and gentle yet also as mysterious, polluting, and destructive, threatening evil.

The Role of Women in Religious Organizations

In both Buddhism and (later) Christianity, women were allowed to express strong religious convictions by choosing to become nuns. The first orders for women were probably established as early as the twelfth century; their membership remained small until the 1800s. At that time, many women took religious vows to become teachers and nurses because these occupations were largely controlled by the religious orders. All along, however, female religious orders remained subject to a male hierarchy, and this subjugation was reinforced by some elaborate rituals. For example, all nuns were regarded as "brides of Christ." Until changes were made in some orders in the 1950s and 1960s, "marriage" ceremonies were carried out, during the course of which the novice would cut her hair,

Women are playing an increasingly important role as religious leaders today. Laura Geller is the senior rabbi at Temple Emanuel in Beverly Hills, one of the country's largest synagogues. When she was ordained in 1976, Geller was only the third female rabbi in the United States; she was the first to become the head rabbi at a major synagogue.

receive her religious name, and sometimes be given a wedding ring. After several years, a novice took a vow of perpetual profession, after which she was required to receive dispensation if she chose to leave.

Women's orders today show a considerable diversity in their beliefs and modes of life. In some convents, sisters still dress in full traditional habit and live together in communities removed from the secular world. In other convents, by contrast, the nuns wear ordinary dress and may live in apartments or houses. Traditional restrictions such as not talking to others at certain periods of the day or walking with the hands folded and hidden under the habit are rarely evident.

In spite of such liberalization, women have filled only inferior positions in religious organizations. This situation is changing, in line with changes affecting women in society generally. In recent years, women's groups have pressed to achieve equal status in religious orders. Increasingly, the Catholic and Episcopalian churches are under strong pressure to allow women an equal voice in their hierarchies. Yet in 1977, the Sacred Congregation for the Doctrine of the Faith in Rome declared formally that women could not be admitted to the Catholic priesthood; the reason given was that Jesus had not called a woman to be one of his disciples. Ten years later, 1987 was officially designated as the "Year of the Madonna," in which women were advised to recall their traditional role as wives and mothers. The barriers to Catholic women in the hierarchy of the church thus remain formidable. In a letter published in May 1994, Pope John Paul II reaffirmed the Roman Catholic Church's ban on the ordination of women. The letter stated: "Wherefore, in order that all doubt may be removed regarding a matter of great importance . . . I declare that the Church has no authority to confer priestly ordination on women and that this judgment is to be definitively held by all the Church's faithful."

The Episcopal Church has been more open and has allowed women into its priesthood since 1976. Altogether, women have been ordained as ministers in about half of the Protestant denominations in the United States, including the Presbyterian Church (U.S.A.), the Evangelical Lutheran Church in America, the African Methodist Episcopal Church, and the United Methodist Church. And except within Orthodox Judaism, women in the United States can become rabbis.

Women and Islam

Before a militant group of Islamic nationalists called the Taliban took over Afghanistan, Shafiqa Habibi's face was known throughout the country: She was Afghanistan's most popular television news anchor. But during the Taliban's rule, she spent her time at home doing chores, her face hidden from public view. When she dared to venture out of her house, none of her body was visible because it had to be covered by a tentlike garment with a screen sewn into the fabric over her face to hide her eyes but allow some ability to see out (Filkin 1998).

Shafiqa Habibi's experience was shared by all Afghan women. The Taliban's extreme Islamic beliefs, which were denounced by Iran and other neighboring Muslim nations, forbade women to work outside the home, attend school, or appear in public without covering their bodies from head to toe. Women who were seen in public with any man who was not their husband or relative were brutally beaten and sometimes killed. Since the overthrow of the Taliban in 2001, women have begun to regain their rights in Afghanistan, at least in the capital city of Kabul. But throughout much of the rest of the country, where there has been little effective U.S. military presence, local religious leaders, including the Taliban, have begun to make a comeback, and women are afraid to exercise their legal rights publicly, for fear of retribution—if not immediately, then when the U.S. military finally withdraws from the country.

World Religions

Although there are thousands of different religions throughout the world, three of them—Christianity, Islam, and Hinduism—are embraced by nearly three quarters of the people on earth (Table 17.1 and Global Map 17.1).

TABLE 17.1

Worldwide Adherents of All Religions, 2004

RELIGION	NORTH AMERICA	LATIN AMERICA	EUROPE	ASIA	AFRICA	OCEANIA	WORLDWIDE
Catholicism	24.1	86.5	38.1	3.1	16.5	26.0	17.3
Protestantism	20.0	9.7	9.8	1.5	13.3	23.6	5.8
Russian/Greek Orthodox	2.0	0.2	21.9	0.3	4.4	2.3	3.4
Other Christian	15.2	1.0	3.1	4.8	2.5	35.2	1.7
Judaism	1.9	0.2	0.3	0.1	0.0	0.3	0.2
Islam	1.6	0.3	4.6	23.1	40.3	1.3	20.1
Hinduism	0.4	0.1	0.2	21.8	0.3	1.3	13.3
Buddhism	0.9	0.1	0.2	9.5	0.0	1.5	5.9
Confucianism	0.0	0.0	0.0	0.2	0.0	0.2	0.1
Other religions	1.3	3.0	0.2	15.2	12.3	0.3	11.1
"New" religions	0.5	0.1	0.1	2.7	0.0	1.9	1.7
Nonreligious, atheism	10.1	3.4	18.0	18.7	0.8	13.1	14.4

SOURCE: Encyclopaedia Britannica Online 2006.

Christianity

With its estimated 2.1 billion followers—roughly a third of the world's population—Christianity encompasses enormously divergent denominations, sects, and cults. Common to all of these is the belief that Jesus of Nazareth was the Christ (Messiah, or "anointed one") foretold in the Hebrew Bible. Christianity is a form of **monotheism**—belief in a single all-knowing, all-powerful God—although in most Christian faiths God is also regarded as a trinity embracing a heavenly Father, His Son the Savior, and His sustaining Holy Spirit.

When Christianity originally emerged in Palestine some two thousand years ago, it was a persecuted sect outside mainstream Jewish and Roman religious practices. Yet, within four centuries, Christianity had become the official religion of the Roman Empire. In the eleventh century, Christianity divided into the Eastern Orthodox Church (based in Turkey) and the Catholic Church (based in Rome). A second great split occurred within the Catholic branch in the sixteenth century, when the Protestant Reformation gave rise to numerous divergent Protestant denominations, sects, and cults. Protestants tend to emphasize a direct relationship between the individual and God, each person being responsible for his or her own salvation. Catholics, on the other hand, emphasize the importance of the church hierarchy as the means to salvation, the pope in Rome being the highest earthly authority.

Christianity was spread through conquest and missionary work. The European colonization of much of Africa, Asia, and North and South America that began in the fifteenth century brought with it Christian teachings, churches, and large-scale conversion of native peoples. Today it has become the largest religion in the world, including over one billion Catholics and nearly half a billion Protestants. In some places, converts were marginal people from the impoverished classes, for whom Christianity was a means of social mobility. Only in Asia are Christians a small minority (9 percent), largely because countries like Japan and China successfully resisted most colonization and the Christianization that went along with it.

In recent years, there has been a substantial increase in the efforts of Protestant evangelical groups to convert people

Major Religions of the World

Missionaries and military force are two reasons that the majority of people in the world profess only a relative handful of religions today. Although Christianity (Catholicism and Protestantism) is the most widespread religion, it is rapidly being overtaken by Islam. Many of the predominantly Catholic countries of Central and South America have strong and, in some cases, growing Protestant minorities.

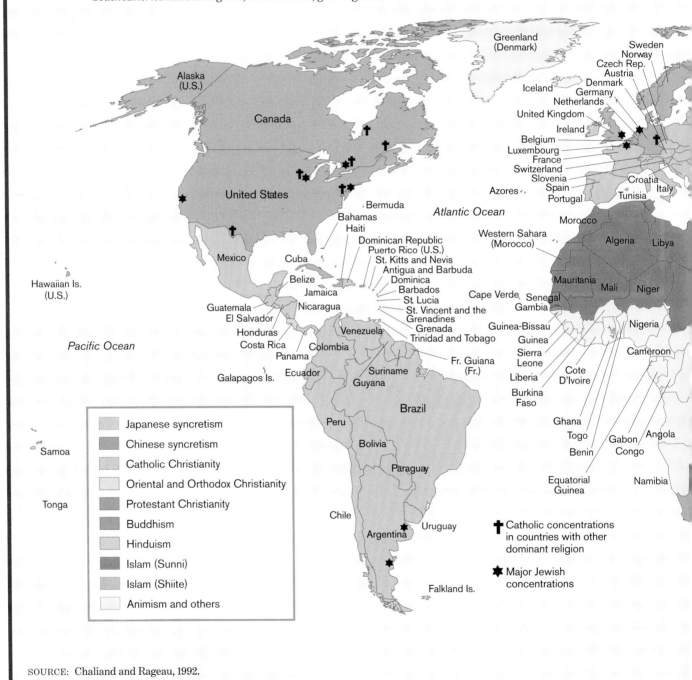

SOURCE: Chaliand and Rageau, 1992.

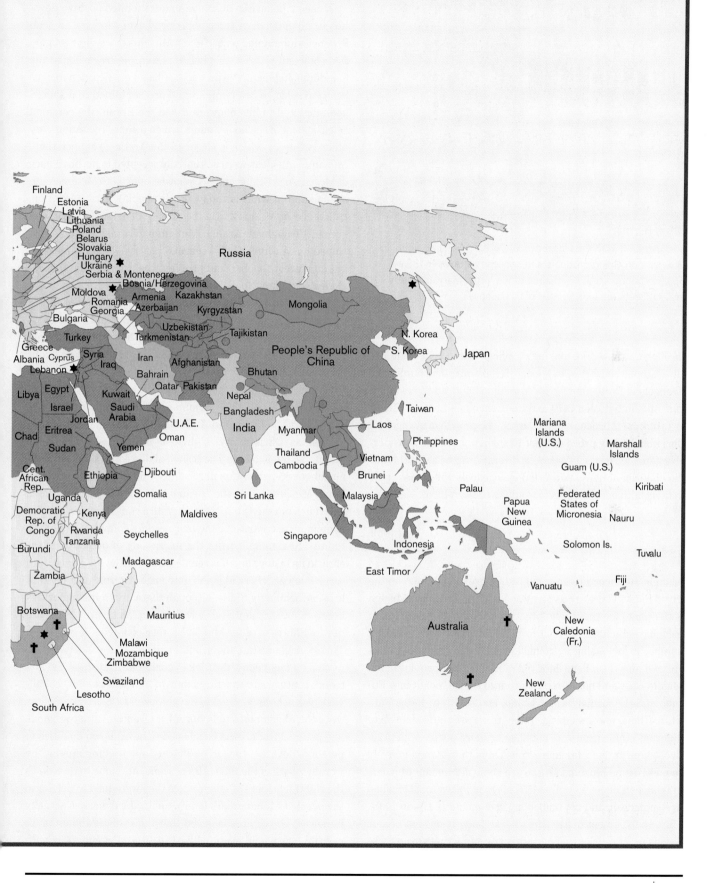

Finland
Estonia
Latvia
Lithuania
Poland
Belarus
Slovakia
Hungary
Ukraine
Serbia & Montenegro
Moldova
Romania
Bulgaria
Greece
Albania
Cyprus
Lebanon
Libya
Egypt
Israel
Jordan
Chad
Eritrea
Sudan
Cent.
African
Rep.
Uganda
Democratic
Rep. of
Congo
Burundi
Zambia
Botswana
South Africa
Lesotho
Swaziland
Malawi
Mozambique
Zimbabwe

Russia

Bosnia/Herzegovina
Armenia
Azerbaijan
Georgia
Turkey
Syria
Iraq
Bahrain
Qatar
Kuwait
Saudi
Arabia
U.A.E.
Oman
Yemen
Djibouti
Ethiopia
Somalia
Kenya
Rwanda
Tanzania
Seychelles
Madagascar
Mauritius

Kazakhstan
Kyrgyzstan
Uzbekistan
Turkmenistan
Tajikistan
Iran
Afghanistan
Pakistan
Nepal
India
Bhutan
Bangladesh
Myanmar
Sri Lanka
Maldives

Mongolia

People's Republic of
China

N. Korea
S. Korea
Japan
Taiwan

Laos
Thailand
Cambodia
Vietnam
Brunei
Malaysia
Singapore
Indonesia
East Timor
Philippines

Mariana
Islands
(U.S.)

Guam (U.S.)

Palau

Papua
New
Guinea

Federated
States of
Micronesia

Marshall
Islands

Kiribati

Nauru

Solomon Is.

Tuvalu

Vanuatu

Fiji

New
Caledonia
(Fr.)

Australia

New
Zealand

An illustration from the *Huexotzinco Codex* (1531) depicts Mexicans providing products and services as taxes to the Spanish conquerors. The banner of the Virgin Mary and baby Jesus reflects the early spread of Christianity.

throughout the world, making significant inroads in traditionally Catholic countries. In Mexico, for example, the number of Evangelical Protestants grew from nine hundred thousand to four million between 1970 and 1990, thanks largely to the efforts of local (Mexican) missionaries. The growth of evangelical Christianity may prove difficult to sustain. It makes considerable demands on its followers, so it remains to be seen whether the children of newly converted evangelicals will remain true to their faith once they become adults (Bowen 1996).

Islam

Islam is the second largest and fastest growing religion in the world today. There are as many as 1.3 billion Muslims (Muslim is the name for those who practice *al-islam,* an Arabic term meaning submission without reservation to God's will), and the number is increasing by 25 million each year. Islam began as and remains the official faith of Arabs and other peoples of the Middle East and has spread south into Africa, north into Europe and the former Soviet Union, and east into India, Pakistan, China, and Indonesia. Today there are more than sixty different ethnic groups of a million or more people who practice Islam. In fact, far more non-Arabs than Arabs identify themselves as Muslims. There are some 172 million Muslims in Indonesia alone, as well as 155 million in Pakistan, 133 million in Bangladesh, and 134 million in predominantly Hindu India. More than two out of five Africans, and nearly one out of four Asians practice Islam, along with many immigrants from these regions to the United States. A large number of African Americans are Muslim as well.

Muslims believe in absolute, unquestioning, positive devotion to Allah (God). Although modern Islam dates to the Arab Prophet Muhammad (c. 570–632), Muslims trace their religion to the ancient Hebrew prophet Abraham, also regarded as the founder of Judaism. The precepts of Islam are believed to have been revealed to Muhammad and are contained in a sacred book dictated to his followers called the Koran (the common English form of the book's name, which means "recitation"; another is Qur'ān, which is closer to the Arabic pronunciation). Muhammad's ideas were not initially accepted in his birthplace of Mecca, so in 622 he and his followers moved to Medina (both are located in what is today Saudi Arabia). This migration, called the *hijra,* marks the beginning of Islam, which soon spread throughout Arabia. Muhammad himself is not worshiped by Muslims. He is regarded not as a god or a messiah but as a great teacher and prophet, the last in a line that includes Abraham, Noah, Moses, and Jesus.

Islam is an all-encompassing religion. The sacred *sharia* (way)—which governs all aspects of personal and social life—includes prescriptions for worship, daily life, ethics, and even government. Although by U.S. standards Muslim beliefs might be judged extremely restrictive, Muslims frequently view American life as spiritually undisciplined, corrupt, and immoral (Abdul-Rauf 1975; Arjomand 1988; Esposito 1984; Kedouri 1992; MacEnoin and Al-Shahi 1983; Martin 1982).

Just as Christianity is divided into different religious groups, so too is Islam. The principal division is between Sunnis (about 85 percent of all Muslims) and Shiites (15 percent). Sunni Muslims follow the "Beaten Path," a series of traditions deriving from the Qur'ān that tolerate a considerable diversity of opinion, in contrast to the more rigidly defined views of the Shiites. Shiism split from the main body of orthodox Islam early in its history and has remained influential ever since. Iran (once known as Persia) is the only major Islamic country that is overwhelmingly Shiite, although there are Shiite majorities in several other countries, including Iraq. There are large numbers of Shiites in other Middle Eastern countries, as well as in Turkey, Afghanistan, India, and Pakistan.

Shiism has been the official religion of Iran since the sixteenth century and was the source of the ideas behind the religiously conservative Iranian Revolution of 1978–79. The Shiites trace their beginnings to Imam Ali, a seventh-century religious and political leader who is believed to have shown qualities of personal devotion to God and virtue outstanding among the worldly rulers of the time. Ali's descendants came to be seen as the rightful leaders of Islam, since they were held to belong to the prophet Muhammad's family, unlike the dynasties actually in power. The Shiites believed that the rule of Muhammad's rightful heir would eventually be instituted, doing away with

Every able-bodied Muslim who can afford to is obligated to make the pilgrimage to Mecca at least once in a lifetime. The pilgrims pictured here surround the *ka'aba*, a small cube-shaped building which houses the Hajar el Aswad (the Black Stone). Muslims believe that this stone fell from the sky during the time of Adam and that it has the power to cleanse worshipers of their sins by absorbing them into itself. The stone is believed to have originally been white, but it is said to have turned black because of the sins it has absorbed over the years.

the tyrannies and injustices associated with existing regimes. Muhammad's heir would be a leader directly guided by God, governing in accordance with the Qur'ān.

There is no separation of church and state in a few highly religious Islamic societies, such as Iran. In most Muslim countries, however, religious leaders live in a sometimes uneasy alliance with secular governments. Egypt, Algeria, Turkey, and Indonesia, for example, are all predominantly Muslim societies in which mosque and state are separate. In Algeria, religious groups that would have created an Islamic state won the popular vote, only to see the elections overturned by that country's military government. The result has been escalating violence and bloodshed (Juergensmeyer 1995).

Judaism

With just under 15 million followers worldwide, Judaism is by far the smallest of the world's major religions, yet it has exerted an influence greater than its limited numbers would sug-

gest. First, as we have already mentioned, it is the source of the world's two largest religions, Islam and Christianity. Second, in European and U.S. culture, Jews have played a role disproportionate to their numbers in such diverse fields as music, literature, science, education, and business. Third, the existence of Israel as a Jewish state since 1948 has given the Jewish faith international prominence. Israel has existed in a near constant state of tension with many of its neighboring Arab countries since its founding and has seldom been out of the news.

Jews have often suffered persecution at the hands of the surrounding society. From the twelfth century on, European and Russian Jews were often forced to live in special districts termed "ghettos," where they lacked full rights as citizens and were sometimes the target of harassment, attacks, and murders. Partly in reaction to these conditions, and partly because the Torah identifies the city of Jerusalem as the center of the Jewish homeland, some Jews embraced *Zionism,* a movement calling for the return of Jews to Palestine and the creation of a Jewish state. (Zion is a biblical name for the ancient city of Jerusalem.) Although secular Zionists viewed Israel as a country where persecuted Jews could seek refuge, religious Zionists saw it as the one Jewish homeland, returning to which would fulfill biblical prophecies. Zionists established settlements in Palestine early in the twentieth century, living peacefully with their Arab and Palestinian neighbors. After World War II and the Nazi extermination of six million Jews during the Holocaust, the state of Israel was created as a homeland for the survivors. This action, unfortunately, ended the once relatively peaceful relationship between Zionists and their neighbors.

Hinduism

Hinduism, which dates to about 2000 B.C.E., is one of the oldest religions in the world and is the source of Buddhism and Sikhism. It is not based on the teachings of any single individual, and its followers do not trace their national origins to a single god. Like other religions, Hinduism is an ethical religion that calls for an ideal way of life. Today nearly nine hundred million Hindus are found throughout the world, primarily in India, where Hindus make up the large majority of the population.

As we saw in Chapter 8, India's social structure is characterized by a caste system, in which people are believed to be born to a certain status that they must occupy for life. Although the caste system in India was officially abolished in 1949, it remains powerful to this day. The caste system has its origins in Hindu beliefs, which hold that an ideal life is partly achieved by performing the duties appropriate to one's caste.

Perhaps because Hinduism does not have a central organization or leader, its philosophy and practice are extremely diverse. Religious teachings direct all aspects of life but in a variety of ways, ranging from promoting the enjoyment of sensual pleasures to advising the stark renunciation of earthly pursuits. Mahatma Gandhi was a modern example of a man who led a virtuous life according to Hindu philosophy. Gandhi devoted his life to the Hindu virtues of "honesty, courage, service, faith, self-control, purity, and nonviolence" (Potter 1992).

Despite the teaching that life is *maya,* or illusion, Hindu religious beliefs have an earthly quality. For example, Hindu religious services do not have to occur in a special place of worship. Although there are sacred sites on which temples and pilgrimage centers are located, any location may be a place of devotion. Hindus believe in the godlike unity of all things, yet their religion also has aspects of **polytheism,** the belief that different gods represent various categories of natural forces. For example, Hindus worship gods representing aspects of the whole, such as the divine dimension of a spiritual teacher (Basham 1989; Kinsley 1982; Potter 1992; Schmidt 1980).

Religion in the United States

In comparison with the citizens of other industrial nations, Americans are unusually religious. With few exceptions, "the United States has been the most God-believing and religion-adhering, fundamentalist, and religiously traditional country in Christendom [where] more new religions have been born . . . than any other country" (Lipset 1991). Even though secularization may have weakened the power of religious institutions in the United States, it has not diminished the strength of religious beliefs.

More than half (55 percent) of all Americans surveyed in 1995–96 claimed to be "strong believers" in God or the sacred (Roof 1999). About 45 percent report having attended religious services in the past week (Bisna Group 2005), and slightly more than half (54 percent) live in a household where at least one person is a member of a church, mosque, or synagogue (Kosmin et al. 2001). According to public opinion polls, the overwhelming majority of Americans reportedly believe in God and claim they regularly pray, the majority one or more times a day (Bisna Group 2005; National Opinion Research Center 1998). More than eight out of ten Americans report that they believe in an afterlife, and a substantial majority claim to believe in the devil as well (Roof 1999).

Yet at the same time, one long-term measure of religiosity, based on indicators such as belief in God, religious membership, and attendance at religious services, found that the index reached its highest levels in the 1950s, and has declined ever since—in part because post–World War II baby boomers were less religious than their predecessors (Roof 1999). As Table 17.2 shows, in one national survey overwhelming majorities of Catholics, liberal Protestants, and conservative Protestants reported attending church on a weekly basis while they were children, although their attendance had dropped sharply by the time they had reached their early twenties. Among the three groups, attendance had declined the most among liberal Protestants, and least among conservative Protestants (Roof 1999).

One survey of more than 50,000 adults in 2001 and nearly 114,000 adults in 1990 found that religious identification had declined sharply during the eleven-year period. In 1990, 90 percent of all adults identified with some religious group; in 2001, the figure was only 81 percent. The principal decline was among self-identified Christians (from 86 percent to 77 percent). This decline was not because a growing proportion of adults identified with other religions; rather, it was because the number of adults identifying with no religion whatever had grown from 8 percent to 14 percent of the population. Membership in religious institutions showed a parallel decline (Kosmin et al. 2001).

Civil Religion in the United States

Although there is a constitutional separation of church and state in the United States, its presidents have all attended

TABLE 17.2

Weekly Attendance at Religious Services

GROUP	AGE 8–10	AGE EARLY 20s
Roman Catholics	95	28
Liberal Protestants	82	18
Conservative Protestants	91	40

SOURCE: Roof 1999.

church, and some—such as the current president, George W. Bush—have been deeply and publicly religious. In fact, sociologists have argued that the United States has a **civil religion,** a set of religious beliefs through which a society interprets its own history in light of some conception of ultimate reality (Bellah 1968, 1975). Civil religion usually consists of "god-language used in reference to the nation," including "historical myths about the society's divine origins, beliefs about its sacred historical purpose, and occasionally religious restrictions on societal membership" (Wuthnow 1988).

The importance of civil religion in the United States is seen in the Pledge of Allegiance. By referring to "one nation, under God," the pledge seeks to infuse civic life with a religious belief derived from the Judeo-Christian heritage. The Pledge of Allegiance has been used for over a century, but the phrase *under God* was added by Congress only in 1954, during the height of cold war fears about "godless communism." Even though the Bill of Rights of the U.S. Constitution clearly calls for a separation of church and state, in the pledge a theistic religious belief was seen as central to U.S. citizenship.

Trends in Religious Affiliation

Roof's (1993) study of baby boomers found that even though two out of three had dropped out of church or synagogue in their teens, for the most part they still remain *A Generation of Seekers* (the title of his book). Although less than a quarter had formally reaffiliated with a religious organization, three out of four claimed to "definitely" believe in God, while one third called themselves "born-again Christians." (For that matter, 70 percent also believed in "psychic powers.") Moreover, with many of the boomers raising families and approaching a midlife reexamination, Roof believes they were turning back to religion for themselves and their children. Increasingly, however, religious experience is being sought outside established religions, often in a highly personalized fashion.

It is difficult to estimate reliably the number of people belonging to churches because the U.S. government does not officially collect such data. Nonetheless, based on occasional government surveys, public-opinion polls, and church records, sociologists of religion have concluded that church membership has grown steadily since the United States was founded. About one in six Americans belonged to a religious organization at the time of the Revolutionary War. That number had grown to about one in three at the time of the Civil War, one in two at the turn of the nineteenth century, and two in three in the 1990s (Finke and Stark 1992).

One reason so many Americans are religiously affiliated is that religious organizations are an important source of social ties and friendship networks. Churches, synagogues, and mosques are communities of people who share the same beliefs and values, and who support one another during times of need. Religious communities thus often play a family-like role, offering help in times of emergency as well as more routine assistance such as child care.

Another reason so many people belong to religious organizations is simply that there are an enormous number of such organizations one can belong to. The United States is the most religiously diverse country in the world, with more than fifteen hundred distinct religions (Melton 1989). Yet the vast majority of people belong to a relatively small number of religious denominations (Figure 17.1). About 53 percent of Americans identify themselves as Protestants, 25 percent as Catholics, 2 percent as Jews, and 11 percent as "other," a category that includes Eastern Orthodox, Mormons, and Muslims. The remainder (9 percent) say they have no religious affiliation at all (U.S. Bureau of the Census 2003).

PROTESTANTS: THE GROWING STRENGTH OF CONSERVATIVE DENOMINATIONS

A somewhat clearer picture of recent trends in American religion can be obtained if we break down the large Protestant category into major subgroups. According to the American Religious Identification Survey of more than fifty thousand households in 2001, the largest number of households were Baptist, accounting for 31 percent of all Protestants—nearly two and a half times the percentage of the second largest group, Methodists (13 percent). There were far fewer Lutherans (9 percent), Presbyterians (5 percent), and Episcopalians (3 percent) (Kosmin et al. 2001). More than half of all Protestants today describe themselves as "born again" (*The Economist* 2003).

These figures are important because they indicate the growing strength of conservative Protestants in the United States. Conservative Protestants emphasize a literal interpretation of the Bible, morality in daily life, and conversion through evangelizing. They can be contrasted with the more historically established liberal Protestants, who tend to adopt a more flexible, humanistic approach to religious practice. Somewhere in between are moderate Protestants.

Although all groups of Protestants showed a growth in membership from the 1920s through the 1960s, a major reversal has occurred since that time. Both liberal and moderate churches have experienced a decline in membership, whereas the number of conservative Protestants has exploded. The conservative denominations inspire deep loyalty and commitment, and they are highly effective in recruiting new members, particularly young people. Today twice as many people belong to

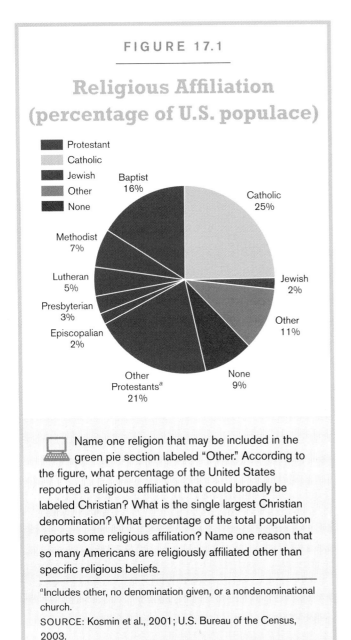

FIGURE 17.1

Religious Affiliation
(percentage of U.S. populace)

- Protestant
- Catholic
- Jewish
- Other
- None

Baptist 16%

Catholic 25%

Methodist 7%

Lutheran 5%

Presbyterian 3%

Episcopalian 2%

Jewish 2%

Other 11%

Other Protestants[a] 21%

None 9%

Name one religion that may be included in the green pie section labeled "Other." According to the figure, what percentage of the United States reported a religious affiliation that could broadly be labeled Christian? What is the single largest Christian denomination? What percentage of the total population reports some religious affiliation? Name one reason that so many Americans are religiously affiliated other than specific religious beliefs.

[a]Includes other, no denomination given, or a nondenominational church.
SOURCE: Kosmin et al., 2001; U.S. Bureau of the Census, 2003.

nearly twenty-three million members—almost the same number that was gained by such conservative Protestant denominations as the Southern Baptists, the Church of the Nazarene, the Seventh-Day Adventists, the Assemblies of God, the Church of God, and the Mormon Church. Black Protestant churches also continue to thrive in the United States, as their members move into the middle class and a degree of economic and political prominence (Finke and Stark 1992; Roof and McKinney 1990).

Since the 1960s, the fastest-growing religious group has been self-identified evangelicals. Moreover, although all religious groups lose some converts to other denominations or beliefs, the more conservative religions experienced a net gain in converts during the 1990s, whereas the more liberal religions experienced a net loss (Kosmin et al. 2001) (Table 17.3).

CATHOLICISM

Although Catholics continue to grow in number, church attendance has shown a sharp decline over the past few decades, beginning in the 1960s and leveling off in the mid-1970s. One of the main reasons was the papal encyclical of 1968 that reaffirmed the ban on the use of contraceptives by Catholics. The encyclical offered no leeway for people whose conscience allowed for the use of contraceptives. They were faced with disobeying the church, and many Catholics did just that. According to one study conducted by the Centers for Disease Control and Prevention (2005), 96 percent of all Catholic women who have had sexual relations report having used contraceptives at one time or another; the General Social Survey (Smith 1998) found that three out of five Catholics say that contraceptives should be available to teens even without parental approval.

The Catholic Church has shown by far the largest increase in membership, partly because of the immigration of Catholics from Mexico and Central and South America. Yet the growth in Catholic Church membership has also slowed in recent years, as some followers have drifted away, either ceasing to identify themselves as Catholics or shifting to Protestantism.

OTHER RELIGIOUS GROUPS

The number of Jews has declined in recent years as a result of low birthrates, intermarriage, and assimilation. Yet even assimilated Jews often identify themselves as Jewish, and in recent years, there has been a resurgence of interest among some younger American Jews in rediscovering orthodox practices (Bamberger 1992; Blech 1991; Danzger 1989; Davidman 1991; Eisen 1983; Goldberg and Rayner 1987).

Among other denominations, growing immigration from Asia and Africa may somewhat change the U.S. religious pro-

conservative Protestant groups as liberal ones, and conservative Protestants outnumber moderates as well (Green 2004; Roof and McKinney 1990). Liberal Protestantism in particular has suffered. The aging members of the liberal Protestant denominations have not been replaced by new, young followers, commitment is low, and some current members are switching to other faiths. As Figure 17.2 indicates, from 1965 to 1989, declines were substantial for such liberal and moderate denominations as Evangelical Lutherans, United Methodists, the United Church of Christ, Episcopalians, Presbyterians, and Disciples of Christ. Together these six denominations lost

FIGURE 17.2

Loss and Gain in Church Membership, 1965–1989, for Selected Moderate/Liberal and Conservative Protestant Churches

During the twenty-four-year period from 1965 to 1989, such mainstream denominations as the United Methodists, the United Church of Christ, the Episcopalians, the Presbyterians, and the Disciples of Christ lost between one fifth and one half of their membership. Conversely, such conservative Protestant churches as the Assemblies of God, the Mormons, and the Church of God more than doubled their membership.

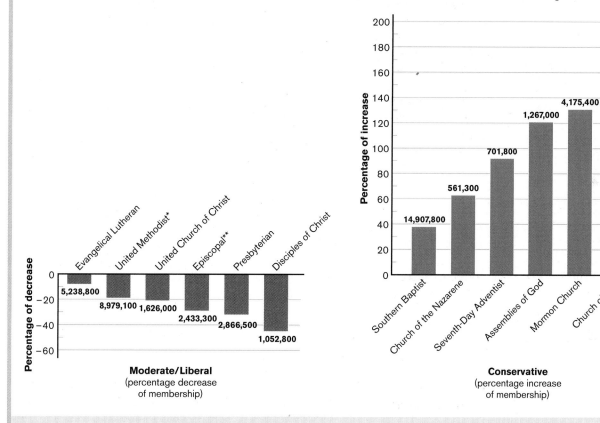

From 1965 to 1989, which moderate/liberal denominations increased their membership? From 1965 to 1989 which conservative denomination gained the most members in terms of numbers? From 1965 to 1989 which conservative denomination(s) experienced a more than 100% increase in their membership? What are the general trends that can be observed from this figure?

SOURCE: Ostling 1993.

file. For example, estimates of the number of Muslims in the United States run as high as three million; many come from Asia or are African refugees from countries like Somalia and Ethiopia (Finke and Stark 1992; Haddad 1979; Roof and McKinney 1990).

NEW CULTS

Since World War II, more religious movements have been founded in the United States than at any previous time in its history. Over this period, there has occurred an unprecedented series of mergers of and divisions between denominations.

Most have proved short lived, but a few have achieved notable followings.

An example is the Unification Church, founded by the Korean Sun Myung Moon. This movement was introduced into the United States at the beginning of the 1960s, and it appealed to many who at the time were rejecting traditional religion and looking for insight in Eastern religious teachings. The Unification Church mixed Eastern ideas with elements of fundamentalist Christianity and showed a strong bent toward anticommunism.

The cult boasts a membership of fifty thousand in the United States today and three million worldwide (Melton 1996). Its members are expected to fraternize only with each other, to donate their property to the cult, and to obey Moon's commands. Moon's doctrine of "heavenly deception" permits members to mislead the public when asking for money—for instance, by posing as a charity. Substantial funds were accumulated in this way.

Other examples of new religious movements include Scientology, Wiccan, Eckankar, Druid, Santería, and Rastafarianism. Their beliefs might seem unusual mixtures of traditional and modern religious ideas, but in fact all long-established religions

Unification Church leader Reverend Sun Myung Moon and his wife marry 2,075 pairs of his followers at Madison Square Garden on New Year's Day 1982.

mix elements taken from diverse cultural sources. The baby boomers studied by Wade Clark Roof, referred to earlier, are experimenting with a variety of mixed religious beliefs and practices.

Religious Affiliation and Socioeconomic Status

Substantial socioeconomic and regional differences exist among the principal religious groupings in the United States (see Table 17.4 for differences among Protestants). *Liberal Protestants* tend to be well educated, somewhat upper income, and middle or upper class. They are concentrated in the northeastern states, and, to a small extent, in the West as well. Ethnically, they tend to be white Anglo-Saxon Protestants (WASPs) of British or German origins. *Moderate Protestants* fall at a somewhat lower level than liberal Protestants in terms of education, income, and social class. In fact, they are typical of the national average on these measures. They tend to live in the Midwest, and, to some extent, in the West. Moderate Protestants are from a variety of European ethnic backgrounds, including British, German, Scandinavian, Irish, and Dutch. *Black Protestants* are, on average, the least educated, poorest, and least middle class of any of the religious groups listed in Table 17.4. *Conservative Protestants* have a similar profile, although they fall at a marginally higher level on all these measures. Like moderate Protestants, they include a diverse profile of European ethnicities, although some are African American as well.

Catholics strongly resemble moderate Protestants (which is to say, average Americans) in terms of their socioeconomic profile. They are largely concentrated in the Northeast, although many live in the West and the Southwest as well. The largest ethnic group is European in origin (primarily German,

TABLE 17.3

Changes in Religious Self-Identification in the United States, 1970–2005

RELIGIOUS SELF-IDENTIFICATION	NET GAIN OR LOSS
Evangelical/Born Again	12.8%
No religion	4.5%
Muslim	1.2%
Buddhist	0.8%
Atheist	0.4%
Hindu	0.3%
Catholic	−1%
Jewish	−1.3%
Protestant	−7.5%

SOURCE: Encyclopaedia Britannica Online 2006.

TABLE 17.4

Characteristics of Liberal, Moderate, Conservative, and Black Protestant Denominations

CHARACTERISTICS	LIBERAL	MODERATE	CONSERVATIVE	BLACK
Principal period of appearance	Historic "mainline" churches (pre–Revolutionary War)	Nineteenth century	Twentieth century	Nineteenth and twentieth centuries
Biblical interpretation	Humanistic, flexible	Fairly literal interpretation	Literal interpretation	Fairly literal interpretation, including emphasis on civil rights
Predominant income group	Middle and upper income	Middle income ("middle America")	Lower and middle income	Lower income
Higher education	Many college educated	Some college educated	Few college educated	Few college educated
Predominant region	Northeast, West	Midwest, West	South	South
Examples of denominations	Episcopalian, Presbyterian, United Church of Christ	Methodist, Lutheran, Disciples of Christ, Northern Baptist, Reformed churches	Southern Baptist Convention; Churches of Christ; Church of the Nazarene; Assemblies of God; Seventh-Day Adventist; Fundamentalist, Pentecostal and holiness groups	Black Methodist and Baptist churches

SOURCE: Adapted from Roof and McKinney 1990.

Italian, Slavic, and Irish, and to a lesser extent English and French), followed by Latinos from Mexico and Central and South America.

Finally, Jews have the most successful socioeconomic profile. Jews tend to be college graduates in middle- or upper-income categories. One study found that Jewish educational and occupational attainment was significantly higher than that of other whites (Hartman and Hartman 1996). Jews are largely European in origin, particularly Slavic and German, although some are from northern Africa (Roof and McKinney 1990). Whereas the large majority of Jews once lived in the northeastern states, today only half do, since many have moved throughout the United States. One recent study suggests that this high degree of geographical mobility is associated with lowered involvement in Jewish institutions. Jews who move across the country are less likely to belong to synagogues or temples, have Jewish friends, or be married to Jewish spouses (Goldstein and Goldstein 1996).

In sum, Jews and liberal Protestants are the most heavily middle and upper class; moderate Protestants and Catholics are somewhat in the middle (although the growing number of poor Catholic Latino immigrants may be changing this position); conservative and black Protestants are overwhelmingly lower class. These groupings correspond roughly to social and political liberalism and conservatism as well. In terms of civil liberties (such as the right of atheists to speak in public or homosexuals to teach), racial justice (such as support for interracial marriage), and women's rights (such as the right to have an abortion), Jews are by far the most tolerant. Liberal Protestants and Catholics are somewhat more tolerant than the average American, while moderate Protestants and black Protestants are somewhat less tolerant. Conservative Protestants are the least tolerant of all religious groupings (Roof and McKinney 1990).

There are political differences across religious groups as well. Jews tend to be the most heavily Democratic of any major religious groups; fundamentalist and evangelical Christians the most Republican. The more moderate Protestant denominations are somewhere in between (Kosmin et al. 2001).

Secularization or Religious Revival in America?

According to Phillip Hammond (1992), there have been three principal historical periods in the United States during which religion has undergone **disestablishment**—that is, a period during which the political influence of established religions is successfully challenged. The first such disestablishment occurred with the 1791 ratification of the Bill of Rights—the first ten amendments to the U.S. Constitution—which calls for a firm separation of church and state. Some sociologists have seen this separation as part of a larger trend characteristic of the industrial societies of Europe and North America, in which different institutions come to specialize in different functions— from economics to medicine and from education to politics. Religion is no exception to this process (Chaves 1993, 1994; Parsons 1951, 1960). The second disestablishment occurred between the 1890s and 1920s, fed by an influx of about seventeen million immigrants (mainly European), many of whom were Catholic. For the first time, the notion of a predominantly Protestant United States was challenged, and the mainstream Protestant churches never regained their influence in politics or in defining national values. The third disestablishment occurred during the 1960s and 1970s, when core religious beliefs and values were further eroded by the anti–Vietnam War movement, the fight for racial equality, and experimentation with alternative lifestyles. Fundamental challenges came in such basic areas as sexuality, family authority, sexual and lifestyle preferences, women's rights, and birth control (Glock and Bellah 1976; Hammond 1992; Hunter 1987; Roof and McKinney 1990; Wuthnow 1976, 1978).

The most recent disestablishment of religion resulted in a reduction in the political influence of religion. This does not mean, however, that religion is less important to individuals, or that secular influences are on the rise. On the contrary, the religious beliefs of many Americans appear to be stronger than ever (Roof et al. 1995). In fact, some sociologists of religion have argued that the absence of an official state religion has forced religious groups to compete with each other for followers, the result being religious practices that are more likely to be tailored to public tastes (Moore 1994). As we noted earlier, affiliations with conservative Protestant denominations have increased sharply in recent years. Furthermore, for many people, religious beliefs have become increasingly private as more and more people seek spiritual experiences outside established religious organizations. As mentioned in his study of baby boomers, Roof (1993) found that religion had become a highly personal (rather than public) experience for many people. From this he concluded that almost all Americans are religiously oriented, although often outside organized religion. Finally, counter to the overall trend toward religious disestablishment in the United States, some evidence indicates that in recent years conservative Protestant religious organizations have increasingly made their voices heard in U.S. politics.

In their 1992 book, *The Churching of America,* Roger Finke and Rodney Stark argue that disestablishment is a normal process through which mainstream groups become self-satisfied, losing followers to more aggressive sects and cults that promise to revitalize religious experience. In fact, Finke and Stark question whether the third disestablishment occurred at all, noting that cult formation in the 1960s was only slightly higher than in the 1950s. Some research (Kosmin 1991; Melton 1989) suggests that relatively minuscule numbers of people belong to groups such as the Unification Church (five thousand members), Krishna Consciousness (three thousand), Scientology (fifty-five thousand), or other New Age groups (twenty thousand) (Kosmin 1991; Melton 1989; U.S. Bureau of the Census 2003). What has happened, most scholars agree, is that the most liberal, intellectualized, and inclusive religious denominations have lost members, but the most conservative, traditional, and exclusive ones have thrived.

The Resurgence of Evangelicalism

Evangelicalism refers to a belief in spiritual rebirth (being "born again"). Evangelicalism can be seen in part as a response to growing secularism, religious diversity, and, in general, the decline of once-core Protestant values in American life (Wuthnow 1988). In recent years, there has been an enormous growth in Evangelical denominations, paralleled by a decline in the more mainstream Protestant religious affiliations. Many Protestants are clearly seeking the more direct, personal, and emotional religious experience promised by Evangelical denominations.

Evangelical organizations are good at mobilizing resources to help achieve their religious and political objectives. In the businesslike language used by religious economists, they have proved to be extremely competitive "spiritual entrepreneurs" in the "religious marketplace" (Hatch 1989). Radio and television have provided important new marketing technologies, used by some Evangelicals to reach a much wider audience than was previously possible. Called *televangelists* because they conduct their Evangelical ministries over television, these min-

Interior of the Crystal Cathedral in Garden Grove, California.

isters depart from many earlier Evangelicals in preaching a "gospel of prosperity": the belief that God wants the faithful to be financially prosperous and satisfied, rather than to sacrifice and suffer. This approach differs considerably from the austere emphasis on hard work and self-denial ordinarily associated with traditional conservative Protestant beliefs (Bruce 1970; Hadden and Shupe 1987). Luxurious houses of worship, epitomized by Robert H. Schuller's Crystal Cathedral in Garden Grove, California, provide the televised settings for electronic churches, whose geographically dispersed congregants are united primarily by means of electronic technology. Theology and fund-raising are the staples of televangelism, which must support not only the television ministries themselves but schools, universities, theme parks, and sometimes the lavish lifestyles of its preachers.

There is considerable debate over the number of people who watch such religious broadcasting. One of the most reliable studies (Bruce 1990), conducted in 1985 at the height of televangelism's popularity, estimated that the average audience for the top ten programs was about eight million people. During a typical month, at least thirty-four million *different* U.S. households—about 40 percent of all households—tuned in at least once. Yet, even at their peak, it is not clear that television ministries were actually bringing large numbers of new people "into the fold." Instead, they may have been merely providing an additional type of religious observation to those who were already well established in their local churches (Diekema 1991; Hadden 1990; Hadden and Shupe 1987; Hadden and Swann 1981).

During the late 1980s several prominent televangelists were involved in sexual and financial scandals. At the same time, the rising cost of television broadcasting made it more difficult to engage profitably in television ministries. Yet with the advent of cable and satellite television, it has been possible for televangelists to find a cost-effective market niche. The current

large number of religious television networks include the American Christian Television System, the Christian Broadcasting Network, the Eternal Word Broadcasting Network, and Family Net. It is difficult to estimate how many people draw inspiration from television (and radio) ministries today, but some scholars argue that these ministries are stronger today than ever before (Hadden 2004).

The electronic preaching of religion has become particularly prevalent in Latin America, where North American programs are shown. As a result, Protestant movements, most of them of the Pentecostal kind, have made a dramatic impact on such countries as Chile and Brazil, which are predominantly Catholic (Martin 1990).

Although some Evangelicals combine a thoroughly modern lifestyle with traditional religious beliefs, others strongly reject many contemporary beliefs and practices. **Fundamentalists** are Evangelicals who are antimodern in many of their beliefs, calling for strict codes of morality and conduct. These frequently include taboos against drinking, smoking, and other "worldly evils"; a belief in biblical infallibility; and a strong emphasis on Christ's impending return to earth (Balmer 1989). Their "old-time religion" clearly distinguishes good from evil and right from wrong (Roof and McKinney 1990).

Beginning with the Reverend Jerry Falwell's Moral Majority in the 1970s, some groups of fundamentalists have become increasingly involved in what has been termed the New Christian Right in national politics, particularly in the conservative wing of the Republican party (Kiecolt and Nelson 1991; Simpson 1985; Woodrum 1988). Groups such as the Christian Voice and the Religious Roundtable have advanced a political agenda that is compatible with fundamentalist beliefs. Antiabortion groups such as the Christian Action Council, Focus on the Family, and

On the campaign trail in 1999, presidential candidate George W. Bush addresses the Christian Coalition One Nation Under God Road to Victory Conference.

Prayers for Life were effective in getting the federal government to greatly restrict abortions between 1989 and 1992, despite public opinion polls showing that a majority of Americans believed abortion to be an acceptable alternative in some cases.

Fundamentalist religious organizations helped shape Republican party ideology and policies during the Reagan administration, as well as during both Bush administrations. White evangelical Protestants make up an estimated third of all registered voters, and they are overwhelmingly politically conservative. They have become a core constituency of the Republican party, contributing to its electoral success. The Republican party's program in turn reflects fundamentalist religious beliefs on such topics as opposition to gay marriage and abortion and a reduced role for government (*The Economist* 2003).

Globalization and Religion

Religion is one of the most truly global of all social institutions, affecting many aspects of life in the United States. As previously mentioned, nearly half of the world's population follow one of two faiths: Christianity or Islam, religions that have long been unconstrained by national borders. The current globalization of religion is reflected in religious activism in poor countries, particularly on the part of Catholic priests and missionaries, and in the rise of religious nationalist movements in opposition to the modern secular state.

Activist Religion and Social Change throughout the World

Religion has also played a particularly important role in global social changes of the past forty years. In Vietnam in the 1960s, Buddhist priests burned themselves alive to protest the policies of the South Vietnamese government. Their willingness to sacrifice their lives for their beliefs, seen on television sets around the world, contributed to growing U.S. opposition to the war. Buddhist monks in Thailand currently protest deforestation and care for victims of AIDS.

An activist form of Catholicism, termed **liberation theology,** combines Catholic beliefs with a passion for social justice for the poor, particularly in Central and South America and in Africa. Catholic priests and nuns organize farming cooperatives, build health clinics and schools, and challenge government policies that impoverish the peasantry. A similar role is played by Islamic socialists in Pakistan and Buddhist socialists in Sri Lanka (Berryman 1987; Juergensmeyer 1993; Sigmund 1990). Many religious leaders have paid with their lives for their activism, which government and military leaders often regard as subversive.

In some central and eastern European countries once dominated by the former Soviet Union, long-suppressed religious organizations provided an important basis for the overturning of socialist regimes during the early 1990s. In Poland, for example, the Catholic Church was closely allied with the Solidarity movement, which toppled the socialist government in 1989. Yet, as the socialist regimes have crumbled, religion has also all too often played a central role in reviving ancient ethnic and tribal hatreds. In Bosnia and elsewhere in the former Yugoslavia, to cite one example, religious differences have helped to justify "ethnic cleansing," with Christian Serbs and to a lesser extent Croatians engaging in the mass murder, rape, and deportation of Muslims from communities and farmlands where they had lived for centuries.

The Global Rise of Religious Nationalism

Perhaps the most important trend in global religion today is the rise of **religious nationalism,** the linking of strongly held religious convictions with beliefs about a people's social and political destiny. In numerous countries around the world, religious nationalist movements reject the notion that religion, government, and politics should be separate and call instead for a revival of traditional religious beliefs that are directly embodied in the nation and its leadership (Beyer 1994). These nationalist movements represent a strong reaction against the impact of technological and economic modernization on local religious beliefs. In particular, religious nationalists oppose what they see as the destructive aspects of "Western" influence on local culture and religion, ranging from U.S. television to the missionary efforts of foreign evangelicals. As one study notes, in the view of religious nationalists, "God's word is pure—not pluralist" (Marty and Appleby 1995).

Religious nationalist movements accept many aspects of modern life, including modern technology, politics, and economics. For example, Islamic fundamentalists fighting the Russian army in Chechnya have developed Web sites to help promulgate their views. Osama bin Laden used video and television to reach millions of Muslims around the world. However, at the same time they emphasize a strict interpretation of religious values and completely reject the notion of secularization (Juergensmeyer 1993, 2001). Nationalist movements do not simply revive ancient religious beliefs. Rather, nationalist movements partly "invent" the past, selectively drawing on different traditions and reinterpreting past events to serve their current beliefs and interests. Violent conflicts between religious groups sometimes result from their differing interpretations of the same historical event (Anderson 1991; Juergensmeyer 1993, 2001; Van der Veer 1994).

Religious nationalism is on the rise throughout the world because in times of rapid social change, unshakable ideas have strong appeal. The collapse of the Soviet Union, the end of the cold war, and today's sweeping global economic and political changes have led many nations to reject the secular solutions offered by the United States and its former socialist enemies, and to look instead to their own past and cultures for answers (Juergensmeyer 1995c). In the Middle East, many Palestinian Muslims as well as Israeli Orthodox Jews renounce the notion of a secular democratic state, arguing—often violently—for a religious nation purged of nonbelievers. In India, Hindus, Muslims, and Sikhs face off against each other. In India's nationwide elections held in early 1998, the religious nationalist Bharatiya Janata party (BJP) got more votes than the Congress party, which had dominated Indian politics since independence half a century earlier. (In 2004, the Congress party regained control of the government.)

Islamic nationalism has triumphed in Iran, Sudan, and until 2001, Afghanistan, where the United States overthrew the Islamist Taliban regime in response to its support for al Qaeda. Islamic nationalism has made significant inroads in Egypt, Algeria, Turkey, Pakistan, Palestine, Malaysia, and elsewhere (Global Map 17.2). Since the 1970s, Islamic nationalism has shaped the contours of both national and international politics. To understand this phenomenon, we have to look both to aspects of Islam as a traditional religion and to secular changes that have affected countries where its influence is pervasive.

Islamic Nationalism

Islam, like Christianity, has continually stimulated activism. The Qur'ān is full of instructions to believers to "struggle in the way of God." This struggle is against both unbelievers and those within the Muslim community who introduce corruption. Over the centuries there have been successive generations of Muslim reformers, and Islam has become as internally divided as Christianity.

ISLAM AND THE WEST

During the Middle Ages, there was a more or less constant struggle between Christian Europe and the Muslim states. During the height of Islamic power, the *caliphs* (Islamic rulers, believed to be successors of Muhammad) ruled over an area that extended from what later became Spain, Greece, the former Yugoslavia, Bulgaria, and Romania to India, Pakistan, and Bangladesh (Global Map 17.3). Most of the lands conquered by the Muslims were reclaimed by the Europeans, and many of their possessions in North Africa were in fact colonized as Western power grew in the eighteenth and nineteenth centuries. These reverses were catastrophic for Muslim religion and civilization, which Islamic believers held to be the highest and most advanced possible, transcending all others. In the late nineteenth century, the inability of the Muslim world effectively to resist the spread of Western culture led to reform movements seeking to restore Islam to its original purity and strength. A key idea was that Islam should respond to the Western challenge by affirming the identity of its own beliefs and practices.

This idea has been developed in various ways in the twentieth century and formed a backdrop to the Islamic revolution in Iran of 1978–1979. The revolution was fueled initially by internal opposition to the shah (the king), Mohammad Reza Pahlavi (1941–1979).

When the shah's premier, Mohammad Mossadeq, nationalized the oil industry in 1951, a conflict ensued between the pro-West shah and the supporters of the strongly nationalistic Mossadeq. The shah eventually fled the country but returned in 1953 when a U.S.- and British-led coup overthrew Mossadeq. The shah tried to promote forms of modernization modeled on the West—for example, land reform, extending the vote to women, and developing secular education. He also used the army and secret police brutally to repress those who opposed his regime. The fact that he had been installed by Western powers helped fuel nationalist sentiments that eventually led to the revolution that overthrew him. That revolution brought together people of diverse interests, not all of whom were attached to Islamic fundamentalism. A dominant figure, however, was Ayatollah Ruhollah Khomeini, a religious leader exiled in France during the shah's reign, who provided a radical reinterpretation of Shiite ideas.

Khomeini established a government in strict accordance with traditional Islamic law, calling that government the "Representative of All." The Islamic revolution fused religion and the state. It made Islam, as specified in the Qur'ān, the direct basis of all political and economic life in Iran. Under revived Islamic law, men and women were kept rigorously segregated, women were obliged to cover their heads in public, homosexuals faced the possibility of being shot by a firing squad, and women accused of adultery were stoned to death. The strict code was accompanied by a pronounced nationalistic outlook, strongly rejecting Western influences.

The aim of the Islamic Republic in Iran was to Islamize the state—to organize government and society so that Islamic

Islam in Power and in Opposition

Islamists in power

1 **Iran:** Ayatollah Khomeini overthrew the shah in 1979

2 **Sudan:** Ruled since 1989 by a military regime now led by General Umar Hassan al-Bashir and backed by National Congress party (formerly the National Islamic Front)

Islamists deposed

Afghanistan: The Taliban had consolidated their grip since 1996 and were deposed in 2001

Islamists in opposition

1 **Egypt:** The Muslim Brotherhood, with the Jamaat-e-Islam of Pakistan, was the fountainhead of "political Islam"

2 **Saudi Arabia:** An Islamic monarchy withstood an attempt by fanatics to overthrow it

3 **Turkey:** Western-style democracy has stripped its nonviolent Islamists of the power won by democratic means

4 **Iraq and Syria:** Totalitarian regimes have crushed Islamist uprisings savagely; Iraq regime overthrown by U.S.-led military invasion and occupation in 2003, constitutional democracy being introduced

5 **Palestine:** Hamas militants marry religious and patriotic zeal

6 **Pakistan:** "Moderate" Islamists have enjoyed more access to constitutional politics than those of any other Muslim country

7 **Chechnya:** A bitter struggle of independence from Moscow has provided a haven for Islamic extremists

8 **Nigeria and Malaysia:** Two of the "peripheral" countries of the Muslim world, where Islam is a growing force

SOURCE: Adapted and updated from *The Guardian* 2000.

The Global Extent of Islamic Power at Its Height

Islam, which originated in the sixth century and is based on the teachings of the prophet Muhammad, rapidly spread throughout much of the world. Under the leadership of powerful caliphs believed to be direct descendants of the Prophet, Islamic rule had reached what was to become France and Spain by the eighth century; it was to remain in southern Spain until the end of the fifteenth century, when Ferdinand and Isabella succeeded in uniting all of Spain under Catholic rule. Islamic rule in Spain was noted for its high degree of culture and religious tolerance, contributions to science and the arts, and advanced economy.

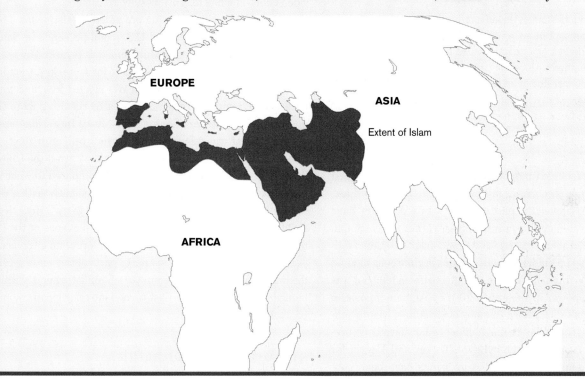

teachings would become dominant in all spheres. A twelve-member Guardian Council of religious leaders has the last say in determining whether or not laws, policies, and even candidates for Parliament conform to Islamic beliefs, even though Iran has a U.S.-style constitution providing for elected officials and the separation of powers.

Recent years have seen a growing movement to liberalize the country. Mohammed Khatami, the reform-minded president, and his allies recaptured control of the Parliament in the February 2000 elections. But that victory proved to be short-lived: the Guardian Council disqualified twenty-four hundred liberal candidates (nearly a third of all candidates) during the February 2004 elections and Mahmoud Ahmadinejad, a conservative candidate who is close to the religious leaders of Iran, won the presidency. The reformist movement—which had ef-fectively challenged the hard-liners in 2000—now controls less than a quarter of the seats in Parliament.

THE SPREAD OF ISLAMIC REVIVALISM

Although the ideas underlying the Iranian revolution were supposed to unite the whole of the Islamic world against the West, governments of countries where the Shiites are in a minority have not aligned themselves closely with the Islamic Revolution in Iran. Yet Islamic fundamentalism (often referred to as "Islamism," the complete adherence to Islamic law along with rejection of most non-Islamic influences) has achieved significant popularity in most of these states, and various forms of Islamic revivalism elsewhere have been stimulated by it.

In 1998 Osama bin Laden issued a *fatwa*, saying that any American, whether Muslim or not, should be killed. A *fatwa* is a religious decree or judgment issued by a recognized Islamic legal authority. Upon bin Laden's issuing of the *fatwa*, Mullah Omar (the head of the Taliban in Afghanistan) issued a statement saying that bin Laden was not qualified to give a *fatwa* because he "had not undergone the requisite Islamic schooling."

Although Islamic fundamentalist movements have gained influence in many countries in North Africa, the Middle East, and South Asia over the past ten to fifteen years, they have succeeded in coming to power in only two other states. Sudan has been ruled since 1989 by Hassan al-Turabi's National Salvation Front. The fundamentalist Taliban regime consolidated its hold on the fragmented state of Afghanistan in 1996 but was ousted from power at the end of 2001 by Afghan opposition forces and the U.S. military. In many other states, Islamic fundamentalist groups have gained influence but have been prevented from rising to power. In Egypt, Turkey, and Algeria, for example, Islamic fundamentalist uprisings have been suppressed by the state or the military.

Islamic opposition is building in states such as Malaysia and Indonesia. Several provinces in Nigeria have recently implemented *sharia* (strict Islamic law), and the war in Chechnya has attracted the participation of Islamic militants who support the establishment of an Islamic state in that region.

Al Qaeda is an example of a loosely knit transnational network of militant religious fundamentalists with a truly global vision. Founded by Osama bin Laden, al Qaeda seeks to overthrow what it regards as corrupt Muslim governments, drive Western influence from the Middle East, and eventually establish a religiously based government that would span half the globe, encompassing a billion Muslims in parts of Europe, Africa, and Asia. Its members envision a restoration of the original caliphates that controlled much of the world during the height of Islamic power. Islamic rule would be subject to strict religious discipline, much as it was during the rule of the Taliban in Afghanistan.

Such Islamic revivalism plainly cannot be understood wholly in religious terms. It represents in large part a reaction against what Iranian writer Jalal Al Ahmad (1997, orig. 1962) more than forty years ago called "Weststruckedness" or "Westoxification"—the seductive (and, in his view, corrupting) power of Western cultural beliefs and practices. In countries where as much as half the population is under fifteen, where poverty is widespread and growing, and where many well-educated young men and women face a life of marginal employment and uncertainty, such beliefs are bound to find fertile ground.

The strong Western presence in the Middle East has provided additional fuel for anti-Western sentiments. In his *fatwas* (opinions that he claimed to be grounded in Islamic law), bin Laden repeatedly condemned U.S. troop presence in Saudi Arabia (which, as the land of Muhammad, is regarded by Islam as its most sacred place), U.S. support for Israel in its conflict with the Palestinians, the first Gulf War against Iraq, and what bin Laden claimed were a million deaths resulting from the postwar economic sanctions against Iraq. In a videotaped statement that was televised around the world after the September 11 attacks, bin Laden also stated that "what the United States tastes today is a very small thing compared to what we have tasted for tens of years. Our nation has been tasting this humiliation and contempt for more than 80 years" (BBC News 2001b). What he was referring to was the collapse of the Ottoman Empire after World War I when more than a thousand years of Islamic rule—once spanning parts of Europe, the Middle East, Africa, and Asia—came to a humiliating end, with Islamic lands in the Middle East turned into European colonies (Global Map 17.3).

RELIGIOUS NATIONALISM AND VIOLENCE

To what extent are bin Laden's views shared in the Muslim world? In 2002 and 2003 the Pew Research Center (2003b) conducted public opinion polls that reached a total of fifty thousand people around the world. Large majorities of people, including Muslims, reported that such things as television, the Internet, and cellular phones were actually making their lives better. (Pakistan, one of the world's largest Islamic countries, was a notable exception.) Most people (including most Muslims) felt that foreign TV, movies, and music were on balance a "good thing" (again, except for Pakistan). This generally positive view of Western influence was shared despite the fact that large majorities of Muslims and others also believed that their traditional ways of life were being lost and needed to be protected against foreign influence. Although the overwhelming majority of Muslim respondents polled did express concern that "there are serious threats to Islam today," the vast majority also rejected suicide bombings and other forms of violence against civilians as a legitimate means of "defending Islam against its enemies."

Bin Laden's belief that "Westoxification" is a serious problem calling for a violent solution is clearly not widely shared among ordinary Muslims. Nonetheless, it is equally clear that he has a strong appeal among some Muslims—enough to make al Qaeda a serious threat. And his appeal appears to be strongest among Muslims whose religious convictions are sufficiently deep that they are willing to die for their beliefs.

How is it that Islamic religious views—or, for that matter, any religious views—could give rise to such a culture of violence? Sociologist Mark Juergensmeyer (2001), who has studied the relationship between violence and religion, has come to a startling conclusion: Even though virtually all major religious traditions call for compassion and understanding, violence and religion nonetheless go hand in hand. Juergensmeyer, who has studied religious violence among Muslims, Sikhs, Jews, Hindus, Christians, and Buddhists, argues that under the right conditions ordinary conflicts can become recast as religious "cosmic wars" between good and evil that must be won at all costs. Juergensmeyer (2001) argues that a violent conflict is most likely to seek religious justification as a cosmic war when (1) the conflict is regarded as decisive for defending one's basic identity and dignity—for example, when one's culture is seen as threatened, and (2) when losing the conflict is unthinkable, although (3) winning the conflict is unlikely in any realistic sense.

If any of these three conditions is present, Juergensmeyer argues, it is more likely that:

> a real-world struggle may be perceived in cosmic terms as a sacred war. The occurrence of all three simultaneously strongly suggests it. A struggle that begins on worldly terms may gradually take on the characteristics of a cosmic war as solutions become unlikely and awareness grows of how devastating it would be to lose.

In such instances, the proponents of cosmic warfare seek *Terror in the Mind of God* (the title of his book), justifying the loss of innocent lives as serving God's larger purpose. According to Juergensmeyer, bin Laden and al Qaeda exemplify such cosmic warfare. They are seeking to defend Islam against an all-engulfing Westernization. He also argues that responding to al Qaeda's violence with still greater violence runs the risk of showing the Islamic world that the conflict is indeed cosmic, particularly if the most powerful nations on earth become embroiled. Based on his interviews with proponents of terrorism around the world, Juergensmeyer concludes that this is just what al Qaeda wants—to be elevated from the status of a minor criminal terrorist organization to a worthy opponent in a global war against the West. This, in the view of some of his interviewees, will increase the appeal of al Qaeda to a wider group of young Islamic men who blame the West for the decline of Islamic influence and the current hardships faced by many Muslims around the world.

Conclusion

In the shape of fundamentalism and in the diversity of new groups and sects found in the United States and elsewhere, religion remains a vital force in society. It might appear strange, therefore, to suggest that the influence of religion in the modern world is actually declining. However, sociologists generally agree that such a decline has taken place, considered at least as a long-term trend.

Until the modern period, churches rivaled and frequently surpassed monarchs and governments in the political power they wielded and the wealth they managed to accumulate. The priesthood maintained control over the skills of literacy, scholarship, and learning. As in other areas of social life, much of this changed as industrialization took hold. Churches and religious organizations in Western countries lost most of their secular power. Governments took over tasks that the churches had previously controlled, including education.

Toward the end of the nineteenth century, German philosopher Friedrich Nietzsche announced, "God is dead." Religions, he argued, used to be a point of reference for our sense of purpose and meaning. Henceforth, we would have to live without this security, and indeed without any fixed moral reference points at all. Living in a world without God means creating our own values and getting used to what Nietzsche called "the loneliness of being"—understanding that our lives are without purpose and that no superior entities watch over our fate.

There can be little doubt that the hold of religious beliefs today is weaker than was generally the case in the past, particularly if we include under the term *religion* the whole range of supernatural phenomena in which people once believed. Most of us no longer see the world as permeated by spirits and demons.

Modern rationalist thought and religious outlook exist in an uneasy state of tension. A rationalist perspective permeates a good portion of our existence, and its hold in all probability will not become weakened in the foreseeable future. Yet there are bound to be reactions against rationalism, leading to periods of religious revivalism, as is happening today. Probably few individuals on the face of the earth have not been touched by religious sentiments at some time in their lives. Science and rationalist thinking remain silent on questions of the meaning and purpose of life, matters that have always been at the core of religion.

Study Outline

www.wwnorton.com/giddens

The Sociological Study of Religion

- There are no known societies that do not have some form of religion, although religious beliefs and practices vary from culture to culture. All religions involve a set of shared beliefs and rituals practiced by a community of believers.
- The sociology of religion is not concerned with whether a particular religion is true or false, but with how it operates as an organization and its relationship to the larger society. Religions are viewed as arising from social relationships and providing a sense of social solidarity to followers.

How Sociologists Think about Religion

- Sociological approaches to religion have been most influenced by the ideas of the three classical thinkers: Marx, Durkheim, and Weber. All believed that religion is fundamentally an illusion. They held that the "other" world that religion creates is *our* world, distorted through the lens of religious symbolism.
- To Marx, religion contains a strong ideological element: Religion provides justification for the inequalities of wealth and power found in society. To Durkheim, religion is important because of the cohesive functions it serves, especially in ensuring that people meet regularly to affirm common beliefs and values. To Weber, religion is important because of the role it plays in social change, particularly the development of Western capitalism.
- According to the classical view, religion in modern society is threatened by a long-term process of *secularization* in which the challenge of scientific thinking, as well as the coexistence of numerous competing religions, inevitably leads to the complete demise of religion.
- The more recent *religious economy* approach draws the opposite conclusion: that competition among religious groups and the challenges of secularization force religions to work harder to win followers, thereby strengthening the various groups and countering any trend toward secularization.

Types of Religious Organizations

- Several different types of religious organization can be distinguished. A *church* is a large, established religious body, having a bureaucratic structure. *Sects* are small and aim at restoring the original purity of doctrines that have become "corrupted" in the hands of official churches. A *denomination* is a sect that has become

institutionalized, having a permanent form. A *cult* is a loosely knit group of people who follow the same leader or pursue similar religious ideals.

- Although traditional churches have been experiencing a decline in membership in recent decades, many new religious movements have emerged alongside mainstream religions. New religious movements encompass a broad range of religious and spiritual groups, cults, and sects. They can be broadly divided into world-affirming movements, which are akin to self-help groups; world-rejecting movements, which withdraw from and criticize the outside world; and world-accommodating movements, which emphasize inner religious life over worldly concerns.
- The three most influential *monotheistic* religions (religions in which there is one God) in world history are Judaism, Christianity, and Islam. *Polytheism* (belief in several or many gods) is common in other religions, such as Hinduism.

Religion in the United States

- The United States is one of the most religious among the industrial nations. Although only about one quarter of all Americans report regularly attending church, the large majority claim to believe in God and to engage in regular prayer. Although church and state are legally separated by the U.S. Constitution, religious imagery and rituals pervade politics and civic life.
- Mainline liberal and moderate Protestant religious denominations in the United States have experienced declining membership recently, while more conservative or *evangelical* groups have seen an increase. These groups have sought to expand their direct influence in U.S. politics in recent years.

Religion as a Global Social Institution

- Religion has always been one of the most global of all social institutions. Fundamentalism has become common among some believers in different religious groups across the world. *Fundamentalists* are called this because they believe in returning to the fundamentals of their religious doctrines. Islamic fundamentalism has affected many countries in the Middle East following the 1979 Islamic revolution in Iran, which set up a religiously inspired government.
- Another important development is the role played by *liberation theologians* in fostering social justice and economic inequality, particularly in Latin America and Africa.

The Global Rise of Religious Nationalism

- Religious nationalism is an important force in the world today, existing in a precarious relationship with modern secular states. They often recast ordinary conflicts as religious cosmic wars between good and evil that must be won at all costs. This is especially likely to be the case when the conflict is seen as central to one's beliefs, losing it would be unthinkable, and winning it is unlikely.

Key Concepts

alienation (p. 540)
charismatic (p. 549)
churches (p. 548)
civil religion (p. 559)
cults (p. 548)
denomination (p. 548)
disestablishment (p. 564)
evangelicalism (p. 564)
fundamentalists (p. 565)
liberation theology (p. 566)
monotheism (p. 553)
New Age movement (p. 550)
new religious movements (p. 549)
polytheism (p. 558)
profane (p. 540)
religion (p. 536)
religious economy (p. 544)
religious movements (p. 549)
religious nationalism (p. 566)
sacred (p. 540)
sects (p. 548)
secularization (p. 543)
secular thinking (p. 543)
theism (p. 536)
total institutions (p. 550)
world-accommodating movements (p. 550)
world-affirming movements (p. 550)
world-rejecting movements (p. 550)

Review Quiz

1. The linking of strongly held religious convictions with beliefs about a people's social and political destiny is
   a. religious economy.
   b. religious nationalism.
   c. civil religion.
   d. ethical religion.
2. When sociologists study religion, they are concerned with
   a. whether religious beliefs are true or false.
   b. whether religious beliefs are good or bad.
   c. the social organization of religion.
   d. All of the above.
3. What is a millenarian movement?
   a. A social movement, typically religious, that attaches some particular spiritual significance to the passage of thousand-year periods.
   b. A group that anticipates immediate, collective salvation for believers, either because of some cataclysmic change in the present or through recovery of a golden age.
   c. A movement of landless peasants who believe in a prophet's promises of salvation and eternal good harvests.
   d. A type of ecstasy that is believed to overcome the body and soul at the movement of death and that represents the transition to a higher spiritual plane.
4. The classical theories of religion argued that the key problem facing religions in the modern world is
   a. animism.
   b. the electronic church.
   c. fundamentalism.
   d. secularization.
5. Secularization can be evaluated according to a number of aspects or dimensions. Which of the following is *not* one of them?
   a. level of industrialization
   b. social influence of churches
   c. level of membership
   d. level of religiosity
6. Which of the following religions is polytheistic?
   a. Catholicism
   b. Protestantism
   c. Hinduism
   d. Islam
7. Which is the fastest-growing religion in the world today?
   a. Christianity
   b. Islam
   c. Judaism
   d. Hinduism
8. Which of the following statements is *true* about Sunni Muslims?
   a. There is a large Sunni Muslim population in Iraq.
   b. They tolerate a considerable diversity of opinion.
   c. They are Muhammad's direct heirs.
   d. They trace their beginnings to Imam Ali.
9. What is the most important trend in global religion today?
   a. Islamic revivalism
   b. the creation of the Israeli state
   c. religious nationalism
   d. secularization
10. Which of the following is *not* a characteristic of evangelicalism?
   a. a commitment to spreading "the Word" to others
   b. admission of personal sin and salvation through acceptance of Christ
   c. a literal interpretation of the Bible
   d. an emphasis on collective (not personal) spiritual piety

Thinking Sociologically Exercises

1. Karl Marx, Émile Durkheim, and Max Weber each had different viewpoints on the nature of religion and its social significance. Briefly explain the viewpoints of each. Which theorist's views have the most to offer in explaining the rise of national and international fundamentalism today? Why?

2. Drawing on this textbook's discussion, summarize the role of religion for most Americans today and assess whether religion is increasing or decreasing in importance for most people. Explain what it means for people to become more secular or fundamentalist in their religious practices. Are Americans becoming more secular or fundamentalist in their religious observances?

Data Exercises

www.wwnorton.com/giddens
Keyword: Data17

In this chapter you have read about the patterns of religious practices in the United States. The data exercise for this chapter will give you a further opportunity to explore not only the differences in religious affiliation and worship among groups within our society, but more importantly, how these patterns are changing.

PART FIVE

SOCIAL CHANGE IN THE MODERN WORLD

For virtually the whole of human history, the pace of social change was relatively slow; most people followed ways of life similar to those of their forebears. By contrast, we live today in a world subject to dramatic and continuous transformation. In the remaining chapters, we look at some of the major areas of change.

One of the most far-reaching influences of globalization is the focus of the growing field known as sociology of the body. Chapter 18 examines how global processes affect our bodies, including our diets, our health, and our sexual behavior.

The globalizing of social life both influences and is influenced by changing patterns of urbanization, the subject of Chapter 19. This chapter also analyzes two of the most far-reaching changes occurring in modern times, the tremendous growth in world population and the increasing threat of environmental problems. Population growth has been greatly affected by the spread of Western techniques of hygiene and medicine. At the same time, threats to the global environment brought on by social change require global solutions if human societies are to continue to thrive in the future.

The concluding chapter looks directly at processes of change. In this chapter, we study some of the major processes of social change from the eighteenth century to the present day. We also consider general interpretations of the nature of social change. What is social change actually, and why has it become so profound and constant? We also consider where present-day patterns of global change are likely to lead us in the twenty-first century. In doing so, we explore the factors contributing to globalization, the causes of increasing globalization, the impact of globalization on our lives, and the debate over its consequences.

The Sociology of Health and Illness

Recognize that health and illness are culturally and socially determined. Learn the social and cultural differences in the distribution of disease. Learn more about HIV/AIDS as a sociological phenomenon.

Human Sexuality

Learn about the debate over the importance of biological versus social and cultural influences on human sexual behavior. Explore the cultural differences in sexual behavior and patterns of sexual behavior today.

CHAPTER EIGHTEEN

THE SOCIOLOGY OF THE BODY: HEALTH AND ILLNESS AND SEXUALITY

ook at the two photographs on the next page. The images of a sunken face and an emaciated body are almost identical. The young girl on the left is Somalian, dying from a simple lack of food. The young woman on the right is an American teenager, dying because, in a society with a superabundance of food, she chose not to eat or to eat so sparingly that her life was endangered.

The social dynamics involved in each case are utterly different. Starvation from lack of food is caused by factors outside people's control and affects only the very poor. The American teenager, living in the wealthiest country in the world, is suffering from anorexia, an illness with no known physical origin; obsessed with the ideal of achieving a slim body, she has eventually given up eating altogether. Anorexia and other eating disorders are illnesses of the affluent, not of those who have little or no food. It is completely unknown in the developing countries where food is scarce, such as Somalia.

Throughout much of human history, a few people such as saints or mystics have deliberately chosen to starve themselves for religious reasons. They were almost always men. Today, anorexia primarily affects women, and it has no specific connection to religious beliefs. It is an illness of the body, and thus we might think that we would have to look to biological or physical factors to explain it. But health and illness, like other topics we've studied, are also affected by social and cultural influences, such as the pressure to achieve a slim body.

Although it is an illness that expresses itself in physical symptoms, anorexia is closely related to the idea of being on a diet, which in turn is connected with changing views of physical

Take a look at the two women above: The first woman is painfully thin as a result of famine and malnutrition, sadly common problems in an area of the world plagued by frequent drought and crop failure. The second has become painfully thin by her own doing; people suffering from anorexia feel compelled by a variety of personal and social pressures to lose weight, and will often continue to view themselves as overweight even when they have reached a state of emaciation.

attractiveness, particularly of women, in modern society. In most premodern societies, the ideal female shape was a fleshy one. Thinness was not regarded as desirable at all—partly because it was associated with lack of food and therefore with poverty. Even in Europe in the 1600s and 1700s, the ideal female shape was well proportioned. Anyone who has seen paintings of the period, such as those by Rubens, will have noticed how curvaceous (even plump) the women depicted in them are. The notion of slimness as the desirable feminine shape originated among some middle-class groups in the late nineteenth century, but it has become generalized as an ideal for most women only recently.

Anorexia thus has its origins in the changing body image of women in the recent history of modern societies. It was first identified as a disorder in France in 1874, but it remained obscure until the past thirty or forty years (Brown and Jasper 1993). Since then, it has become increasingly common among young women. So has bulimia—bingeing on food, followed by self-induced vomiting. Anorexia and bulimia are often found together in the same individual. Someone may become extremely thin through a starvation diet and then enter a phase of eating enormous amounts and purging to maintain a normal weight, followed by a period of again becoming very thin. Today, somewhere between 2 and 6 percent of the total U.S. population is afflicted with these conditions; over 85 percent of those affected are under the age of twenty (Rader Programs 2003). About 90 percent of those who suffer from these dis-

orders are women. Anorexia has the highest mortality rate of any psychological disorder; 20 percent of those who suffer from anorexia will die from it (Eating Disorder Coalition [EDC] 2003).

Anorexia and other eating disorders are no longer obscure forms of illness in modern societies. The occurrence of eating disorders in the United States has doubled since 1960 (EDC 2003). On any given day 25 percent of men and 45 percent of women are dieting; Americans spend over $40 billion each year on dieting and dieting-related products (National Eating Disorders Association 2002). About 95 percent of U.S. college women say that they want to lose weight and up to 85 percent suffer serious problems with eating disorders at some point in their college careers. Around 25 percent experience bulimic episodes or anorexia. In American society, 60 percent of girls age thirteen have already begun to diet; this proportion rises to over 80 percent for young women of eighteen. College men also suffer similar experiences, though not in the same proportions. About 50 percent of American male college students claim that they want to lose weight, while about 30 percent are on diets (Hesse-Biber 1997). Over 80 percent of ten-year-old children are afraid of being fat (EDC 2003).

Nor is obsession with slenderness—and the resulting eating disorders—limited to women in the United States and Europe. As Western images of feminine beauty have spread to the rest of the world, so too have their associated illnesses. Eating disorders were first documented in Japan in the 1960s, a consequence of that county's rapid economic growth and incorporation into the global economy. Anorexia is now found among 2 percent of young Japanese women, and is occurring in younger and younger women (Curtin 2003). During the past several years, eating problems have surfaced among young, primarily affluent women in Hong Kong and Singapore, as well as in urban areas in Taiwan, China, the Philippines, India, and Pakistan (Efron 1997).

Once again, something that may seem to be a purely personal trouble—difficulties with food and despair over one's appearance—turns out to be a public issue. If we include not just life-threatening forms of anorexia but also obsessive concern with dieting and bodily appearance, eating disorders are now part of the lives of millions of people; they are found not only in the United States today but in all the industrial countries.

The astonishing spread of eating disorders brings home clearly the influence of social factors on our lives. The field known as **sociology of the body** investigates the ways in which our bodies are affected by these social influences. As human beings, we obviously all possess bodies. But the body isn't something we just have, and it isn't only something physical that exists outside of society. Our bodies are deeply affected by our social experiences, as well as by the norms and values of the groups to which we belong. It is only recently that sociologists have begun to recognize the profound nature of the interconnections between social life and the body. Therefore, this field is quite a new area, but it is one of the most exciting.

Sociology of the body draws together a number of basic themes, which we make use of throughout the chapter. One major theme is the effects of social change on the body. A second theme is the increasing separation of the body from "nature"—from our surrounding environment and our biological rhythms. Our bodies are being invaded by the influence of science and technology, ranging from machines to diets, and this is creating new dilemmas. The invention of a range of reproductive technologies, for example, has introduced new options but has also generated intense social controversies. We will look at two such controversies, over genetic engineering and abortion, later in the chapter.

The term *technology* should not be understood in too narrow a way here. In its most basic sense, it refers to material technologies such as those involved in modern medicine—for example, the scanning machine that allows a doctor to chart a baby's development prior to birth. But we must also take account of what Michel Foucault (1988) has called "social technologies" affecting the body. By this phrase, he means that the body is increasingly something we have to "create" rather than simply accept. A **social technology** is any kind of regular intervention we make into the functioning of our bodies in order to alter them in specific ways. An example is dieting, so central to anorexia.

In this chapter, we first analyze why eating disorders have become so common. From there, we study the social dimensions of health and illness. Then we turn to human sexuality, again by looking at the social and cultural influences on our sexual behavior.

The Sociology of Health and Illness

To understand why eating disorders have become so commonplace in current times, we should think back to the social changes analyzed earlier in the book. Anorexia actually reflects certain kinds of social change, including the effect of globalization.

The rise of eating disorders in Western societies coincides directly with the globalization of food production, which has increased greatly in the last three or four decades. The invention of new modes of refrigeration and container transportation have allowed food to be stored for long periods and to be delivered from one side of the world to the other. Since the 1950s, supermarket shelves have been abundant with foods from all parts of the world (for those who can afford it—now the majority of the population in Western societies). Most of them are available all the time, not just, as was true previously, when they are in season locally.

For the past decade or so, almost *everyone* in the United States and the other developed countries has been on a diet. This does not mean that everyone is desperately trying to get thin. Rather, when all foods are available more or less all the time, we must *decide* what to eat—in other words, construct a diet, where *diet* means the foods we habitually consume. First, we have to decide what to eat in relation to the many sorts of new medical information with which science now bombards us—for instance, that cholesterol levels are a factor in causing heart disease. Second, we can now worry about the calorie content of different foods. In a society in which food is abundant, we are able for the first time to design our bodies in relation to our lifestyle habits (such as jogging, bicycling, swimming, and yoga) and what we eat. Eating disorders have their origins in the opportunities, but also in the profound strains and tensions, this situation produces.

Why do eating disorders affect women in particular and young women most acutely? To begin with, it should be pointed out that not all those suffering from eating disorders are women; about 10 percent are men. But men don't suffer from anorexia or bulimia as often as women, partly because widely held social norms stress the importance of physical attractiveness more for women than for men and partly because desirable body images of men differ from those of women.

Anorexia and other eating disorders reflect a situation in which women play a much larger part in the wider society than they used to but are still judged as much by their appearance as by their attainments. Eating disorders are rooted in feelings of shame about the body. The individual feels herself to be inadequate and imperfect, and her anxieties about how others perceive her become focused through her feelings about her body. Ideals of slimness at that point become obsessive—shedding weight becomes the means of making everything all right in her world. Once she starts to diet and exercise compulsively, she can become locked into a pattern of refusing food altogether or of vomiting up what she has eaten. If the pattern is not broken (some forms of psychotherapy and medical treatment have proved effective), the sufferer can actually starve herself to death.

The spread of eating disorders reflects the influence of science and technology on our ways of life today: Calorie counting has been possible only with the advance of technology. But the effect of technology is always conditioned by social factors. We have much more autonomy over the body than ever before, a situation that creates new possibilities of a positive kind as well as new anxieties and problems. What is happening is part of

The Body Project

A century ago, American women were lacing themselves into corsets and teaching their adolescent daughters to do the same; today's teens shop for thong bikinis or midriff blouses on their own, and their middle-class mothers are likely to be uninvolved until the credit card bill arrives in the mail. These contrasting images might suggest a great deal of progress, but American girls at the end of the twentieth century actually suffer from body problems more pervasive and more dangerous than the constraints implied by the corset. Historical forces have made coming of age in a female body a different and more complex experience today than it was a century ago. Although sexual development—the onset of menstruation and the appearance of breasts—occurs in every generation, a girl's experience of these inevitable biological events is shaped by the world in which she lives, so much so, that each generation, at its own point in history, develops its own characteristic body problems and projects. Every girl suffers some kind of adolescent angst about her body; it is the historical moment that defines how she reacts to her changing flesh. From the perspective of history, adolescent self-consciousness is quite persistent, but its level is raised or lowered, like the water level in a pool, by the cultural and social setting. ***

In a New Year's resolution written in 1982, a girl wrote: "I will try to make myself better in any way I possibly can with the help of my budget and baby-sitting money. I will lose weight, get new lenses, already got new haircut, good makeup, new clothes and accessories." This concise declaration clearly captures how girls feel about themselves in the contemporary world. Like many adults in American society, girls today are concerned with the shape and appearance of their bodies as a primary expression of their individual identity. ***

Today, unlike in the Victorian era, commercial interests play directly to the body angst of young girls, a marketing strategy that results in enormous revenues for manufacturers of skin and hair products as well as diet foods. Although elevated body angst is a great boost to corporate profits, it saps the creativity of girls and threatens their mental and physical health. Progress for women is obviously filled with ambiguities. ***

Adolescent girls today face the issues girls have always faced—Who am I? Who do I want to be?—but their answers, more than ever before, revolve around the body. The increase in anorexia nervosa and bulimia in the past thirty years suggests that in some cases the body becomes an obsession, leading to recalcitrant eating behaviors that can result in death. But even among girls who never develop full-blown eating disorders, the body is so central to definitions of the self that psychologists sometimes use numerical scores of "body esteem" and "body dissatisfaction" to evaluate a girl's mental health. In the 1990s, tests that ask respondents to indicate levels of satisfaction or dissatisfaction with their own thighs or buttocks have become a useful key for unlocking the inner life of many American girls.

Why is the body still a girl's nemesis? Shouldn't today's sexually liberated girls feel better about themselves than their corseted sisters of a century ago? The historical evidence ***,

based on research that includes diaries written by American girls in the years between the 1830s and the 1990s, suggests that although young women today enjoy greater freedom and more options than their counterparts of a century ago, they are also under more pressure, and at greater risk, because of a unique combination of biological and cultural forces that have made the adolescent female body into a template for much of the social change of the twentieth century. I use the body as evidence to show how the mother-daughter connection has loosened, especially with regard to the experience of menstruation and sexuality; how doctors and marketers took over important educational functions that were once the special domain of female relatives and mentors; how scientific medicine, movies, and advertising created a new, more exacting ideal of physical perfection; and how changing standards of intimacy turned virginity into an outmoded ideal. The fact that American girls now make the body their central project is not an accident or a curiosity: it is a symptom of historical changes that are only now beginning to be understood.

SOURCE: Joan Jacobs Brumberg, *The Body Project* (New York: Vintage, 1997).

Questions

- What cultural and social factors may have driven girls to view their bodies as a primary source of their identities?
- How do the insecurities of adolescent girls affect the rest of the population, male and female?
- Can our culture avoid commodifying the body? Why are adolescent girls a primary target for marketers and manufacturers?

what sociologists call the **socialization of nature.** This phrase refers to the fact that phenomena that used to be "natural," or given in nature, have now become social—they depend on our own social decisions.

Sociological Perspectives on Health and Illness

One of the main concerns of sociologists is to examine the experience of illness—how being sick, chronically ill, or disabled is experienced and interpreted by sick persons and by those with whom they come in contact. If you have ever been ill, even for a short period of time, you know that patterns in everyday life are temporarily modified and your interactions with others become transformed. This is because the normal functioning of the body is a vital, but often unnoticed, part of our lives. We depend on our bodies to operate as they should; our very sense of self is predicated on the expectation that our bodies will facilitate, not impede, our social interactions and daily activities.

Illness has both personal and public dimensions. When we fall ill, not only do *we* experience pain, discomfort, confusion, and other challenges, but others are affected as well. People in close contact with us may extend sympathy, care, and support. They may struggle to make sense of the fact of our illness or to find ways to incorporate it into the patterns of their own lives. Others with whom we come into contact may also react to illness; these reactions in turn help shape our own interpretations and can pose challenges to our sense of self.

Two ways of understanding the experience of illness have been particularly influential in sociological thought. The first, associated with the functionalist school, sets forth the norms of behavior that individuals are thought to adopt when sick. The second view, favored by symbolic interactionists, is a broader attempt to reveal the interpretations that are ascribed to illness and how these meanings influence people's actions and behavior.

THE SICK ROLE

The prominent functionalist thinker Talcott Parsons (1951) advanced the notion of the **sick role** in order to describe the patterns of behavior that the sick person adopts in order to minimize the disruptive impact of illness. Functionalist thought holds that society usually operates in a smooth and consensual manner. Illness is, therefore, seen as a dysfunction that can disrupt the flow of this normal state of being. A sick individual, for example, might not be able to perform all of his or her standard responsibilities or might be less reliable and efficient than usual. Because sick people are not able to carry out their normal roles, the lives of people around them are disrupted: Assignments at work go unfinished and cause stress for coworkers, responsibilities at home are not fulfilled, and so forth.

According to Parsons, people learn the sick role through socialization and enact it—with the cooperation of others—when they fall ill. There are three pillars of the sick role:

1. **The sick person is not personally responsible for being sick.** Illness is seen as the result of physical causes beyond the individual's control. The onset of illness is unrelated to the individual's behavior or actions.

2. **The sick person is entitled to certain rights and privileges, including a withdrawal from normal responsibilities.** Since the sick person bears no responsibility for the illness, he or she is exempted from certain duties, roles, and behaviors that otherwise apply. For example, the sick person might be released from normal duties around the home. Behavior that is not as polite or thoughtful as usual might be excused. The sick person gains the right to stay in bed, for example, or to take time off from work.

3. **The sick person must work to regain health by consulting a medical expert and agreeing to become a patient.** The sick role is a temporary and conditional one that is contingent on the sick person's actively trying to get well. In order to occupy the sick role, the sick person must receive the sanction of a medical professional who legitimates the person's claim of illness. Confirmation of illness via an expert opinion allows those surrounding the sick person to accept the validity of his or her claims. The patient is expected to cooperate in his or her own recovery by following the doctor's orders. A sick person who refuses to consult a doctor or who does not heed the advice of a medical authority puts his or her sick-role status in jeopardy.

Parsons's sick-role idea has been refined by other sociologists, who suggest that all illnesses are not the same as far as the sick role is concerned. They argue that the experience of the sick role varies with the type of illness, since people's reactions to a sick person are influenced by the severity of the illness and by their perception of it. Thus everyone will not uniformly experience the added rights and privileges that are part of the sick role. Freidson (1970) has identified three versions of the sick role that correspond with different types and degrees of illness. The *conditional* sick role applies to individuals who are suffering from a temporary condition from which they can recover. The sick person is expected to get well and receives some rights and privileges according to the severity of the illness. For example, someone suffering from bronchitis would reap more benefits than the sufferer of a common cold. The *unconditionally legitimate* sick role refers to individuals who are suffering from incurable illnesses. Because the sick person cannot do anything to get well, he or she is automatically entitled to occupy the sick role. The unconditionally legitimate role might apply to individuals suffering from alopecia (total hair loss) or severe acne (in both cases there are no special privileges but rather an acknowledgment that the individual is not responsible for the illness), or from cancer or Parkinson's disease—which result in important privileges and the right to abandon many or most duties. The final sick role is the *illegitimate* role. The illegitimate role applies when an individual suffers from a disease or condition that is stigmatized by others. In such cases, there is a sense that the individual might somehow bear responsibility for the illness; additional rights and privileges are not necessarily granted. HIV/AIDS is perhaps the most vivid example of a stigmatized illness that affects a sufferer's right to assume the sick role.

A **stigma** is any characteristic that sets an individual or group apart from the majority of the population, with the result that the individual or group is treated with suspicion or hostility. As we have seen, most forms of illness arouse feelings of sympathy or compassion among nonsufferers, and the ill person receives special privileges. When an illness is seen as uncommonly infectious, however, or is perceived as somehow a mark of dishonor or shame, sufferers may be rejected by the healthy population. This was true in the Middle Ages of people afflicted with leprosy, who were popularly disowned and forced to live in separate leper colonies. HIV/AIDS often provokes such stigmatization today—in spite of the fact that, as with leprosy, the danger of contracting the disease in ordinary day-to-day situations is almost nil. For instance, the United Nations Joint Program with the World Health Organization on HIV/AIDS reports incidences in Kerala, India, when children infected with HIV have been barred from their schools and effectively denied any interaction with other children (UNAIDS 2003). Stigmas, however, are rarely based on valid understandings. They spring from stereotypes or perceptions that may be false or only partially correct.

EVALUATION

The sick role model has been an influential theory that reveals clearly how the ill person is an integral part of a larger social context. But a number of criticisms can be levied against it. Some writers have argued that the sick-role formula is unable to capture the *experience* of illness. Others point out that it cannot be applied universally. For example, the sick role theory does not account for instances when doctors and patients disagree about a diagnosis or have opposing interests. It also fails to explain those illnesses that do not necessarily lead to a sus-

pension of normal activity, such as alcoholism, certain disabilities, and some chronic diseases. Furthermore, assuming the sick role is not always a straightforward process. Some individuals suffer for years from chronic pain or from symptoms that are repeatedly misdiagnosed. They are denied the sick role until a clear diagnosis of their condition is made. In other cases, social factors such as race, class, and gender can affect whether and how readily the sick role is granted. The sick role cannot be divorced from the social, cultural, and economic influences that surround it.

The realities of life and illness are more complex than the sick role suggests. The increasing emphasis on lifestyle and health in our modern age means that individuals are seen as bearing ever greater responsibility for their own well-being. This contradicts the first premise of the sick role—that the individual is not to blame for his or her illness. Moreover, in modern societies the shift away from acute infectious disease toward chronic illness has made the sick role less applicable. Whereas the sick role might be useful in understanding acute illness, it is less useful in the case of chronic illness: There is no one formula for chronically ill or disabled people to follow. Living with illness is experienced and interpreted in a multiplicity of ways by sick people—and by those who surround them.

We now turn to some of the ways that sociologists of the symbolic interactionist school have attempted to understand the experience of illness.

ILLNESS AS "LIVED EXPERIENCE"

Symbolic interactionists are interested in the ways people interpret the social world and the meanings they ascribe to it. Many sociologists have applied this approach to the realm of health and illness to understand how people experience being ill or perceive the illness of others. How do people react and adjust to news about a serious illness? How does illness shape individuals' daily lives? How does living with a chronic illness affect an individual's self-identity?

We have seen that patterns of disease have been changing in modern societies. Rather than dying of acute, infectious diseases as was once the case, people in industrialized societies are now living longer and suffering later in life from chronic illnesses. Medicine is able to relieve the pain and discomfort associated with some of these conditions, but a growing number of people are faced with the prospect of living with illness over a long period of time. Sociologists are concerned with how illness in such cases becomes incorporated into an individual's personal biography.

One theme that sociologists have explored is how chronically ill individuals learn to cope with the practical and emotional implications of their illness. Certain illnesses demand regular treatments or maintenance that can affect people's daily routines. Undergoing dialysis or insulin injections, or taking large numbers of pills, demands that individuals adjust their schedules in response to illness. Other illnesses can have unpredictable effects on the body, such as the sudden loss of bowel or bladder control or violent nausea. Individuals suffering from such conditions often develop strategies for managing their illness in day-to-day life. These include both practical considerations—such as always noting the location of the toilet when in an unfamiliar place—as well as skills for managing interpersonal relations, both intimate and commonplace. Although the symptoms of the illness can be embarrassing and disruptive, people develop coping strategies to live life as normally as possible (Kelly 1992).

At the same time, the experience of illness can pose challenges to and bring about transformations in people's sense of self. These develop both through the actual reactions of others to the illness and through imagined or perceived reactions. For the chronically ill or disabled, social interactions that are routine for many people become tinged with risk or uncertainty. The shared understandings that underpin standard everyday interactions are not always present when illness or disability is a factor, and interpretations of common situations may differ substantially. An ill person may be in need of assistance but not want to appear dependent, for example. An individual may feel sympathy for someone who has been diagnosed with an illness but be unsure whether to address the subject directly. The changed context of social interactions can precipitate transformations in self-identity.

Some sociologists have investigated how chronically ill individuals manage their illnesses within the overall context of their lives (Jobling 1988; Williams 1993). Illness can place enormous demands on people's time, energy, strength, and emotional reserves. Corbin and Strauss (1985) studied the *regimes of health* that the chronically ill develop to organize their daily lives. They identified three types of "work" contained in people's everyday strategies. *Illness work* refers to those activities involved in managing their condition, such as treating pain, doing diagnostic tests, or undergoing physical therapy. *Everyday work* pertains to the management of daily life—maintaining relationships with others, running household affairs, and pursuing professional or personal interests. *Biographical work* involves those activities that the ill person does as part of building or reconstructing their personal narrative. In other words, it is the process of incorporating the illness into one's life, making sense of it, and developing ways of explaining it to others. Such a process can help people restore meaning and order to their lives after coming to terms with the knowledge of chronic illness.

The work of symbolic interactionists on living with illness is one of the most relevant dimensions of the sociology of the body. We are living in a society in which individuals are living longer and leading more active lives in their later years than ever before, but in some cases this also means living longer with illness and anxiety.

Changing Conceptions of Health and Illness

Cultures differ in what they consider healthy and normal, as the discussion of eating disorders showed. All cultures have known concepts of physical health and illness, but most of what we now recognize as medicine is a consequence of developments in Western society over the past three centuries. In premodern cultures, the family was the main institution coping with sickness or affliction. There have always been individuals who specialized as healers, using a mixture of physical and magical remedies, and many of these traditional systems of treatment survive today in non-Western cultures throughout the world. For instance, Ayurvedic medicine (traditional healing) has been practiced in India for nearly two thousand years. It is founded on a theory of the equilibrium of psychological and physical facets of the personality, imbalances of which are treated by nutritional and herbal remedies. Chinese folk medicine is similarly based on a conception of the overall harmony

Ayurvedic treatment: Ayurvedic physician Kumar Das uses a hot iron rod and fabric soaked in herbs to heal an arthritic hip.

of the personality, involving the use of herbs and acupuncture, a technique in which needles are strategically inserted into a patient's skin.

Modern medicine introduced a view of disease that sees its origins and treatment as physical and explicable in scientific terms. The application of science to medical diagnosis and cure was the major feature of the development of modern health care systems. Other, closely related features were the acceptance of the hospital as the setting within which serious illnesses were to be dealt with and the development of the medical profession as a body with recognized codes of ethics and significant social power. The scientific view of disease was linked to the requirement that medical training be systematic and long term; self-taught healers were excluded. Although professional medical practice is not limited to hospitals, the hospital provided an environment in which doctors for the first time were able to treat and study large numbers of patients, in circumstances permitting the concentration of medical technology.

In medieval times, the major illnesses were infectious diseases such as tuberculosis, cholera, malaria, and bubonic plague. The plague, or Black Death, epidemic of the fourteenth century (which was spread by fleas carried by rats) killed a quarter of the population of England and devastated large areas of Europe. Infectious diseases have now become a minor cause of death in industrialized countries, and several have been substantially eradicated. In industrialized countries, the most common causes of death are noninfectious diseases such as cancer and heart disease. Whereas in premodern societies the highest rates of death were among infants and young children, today death rates (the proportion of the population who die each year) rise with increasing age.

In spite of the prestige that modern medicine has acquired, improvements in medical care accounted for only a relatively minor part of the decline in death rates before the twentieth century. Effective sanitation, better nutrition, control of sewage, and improved hygiene were more consequential, particularly in reducing the infant mortality rate and the number of deaths of young children. Drugs, advances in surgery, and antibiotics did not significantly decrease death rates until well into the twentieth century. Antibiotics used to treat bacterial infections first became available in the 1930s and 1940s; most immunizations (against diseases such as polio) were developed later.

Alternative Medicine

Earlier in her life, Jan Mason enjoyed vibrant health. But when she began experiencing extreme fatigue and depression, she found that her regular doctor was unable to provide her much relief:

Before, I was a very fit person. I could swim, play squash, run, and suddenly I just keeled over. I went to the doctor but nobody could tell me what it was. My GP said it was glandular fever and gave me antibiotics which gave me terrible thrush. Then he kept saying that he did not know what it was either. . . . I went through all the tests. I was really very poorly. It went on for six months. I was still ill and they still did not know what it was. (quoted in Sharma 1992)

Mason's doctor suggested that she try antidepressants, concluding that she was suffering from the effects of stress. Mason knew that antidepressants were not the answer for her, even though she acknowledged that her undiagnosed condition had become a great stress in her life. After listening to a radio program, Mason suspected that her lethargy might be a result of postviral fatigue syndrome. On the advice of a friend, she sought out the assistance of a *homeopath*—an alternative medical practitioner who assesses the state of the whole body and then, using minuscule doses of substance, treats "like with like," on the assumption that the symptoms of a disease are part of a body's self-healing process. On finding a homeopath with whose approach she was comfortable, Mason was pleased with the treatment she received (Sharma 1992).

Did it work? Did she get better? Mason is one of a growing number of people who incorporate nonorthodox medical practices into their health routines. In many industrialized societies over the last decade, there has been a surge of interest in the potential of *alternative medicine*. The number of alternative medical practitioners is expanding, as are the forms of healing that are available. From herbal remedies to acupuncture, from reflexology to chiropractic treatments, modern society is witnessing an explosion of health-care alternatives that lie outside, or overlap with, the official medical system. It has been estimated that as many as one in ten Americans has consulted an alternative practitioner. The profile of the typical individual who seeks out alternative forms of healing is female, young to middle-aged, and middle class.

Industrialized countries have some of the best-developed, best-resourced medical facilities in the world. Why, then, are a growing number of people choosing to abandon the health-care system for unscientific treatments such as aromatherapy and hypnotherapy? First, it is important to stress that not everyone who uses alternative medicine does so as a substitute for orthodox treatment (although some alternative approaches, such as homeopathy, reject the basis of orthodox medicine entirely). Many people combine elements of both approaches. For this reason, some scholars prefer to call nonorthodox techniques *complementary* medicine, rather than alternative medicine (Saks 1992).

There are many reasons that individuals might seek the services of an alternative medicine practitioner. Some people perceive orthodox medicine to be deficient or incapable of relieving chronic, nagging pains or symptoms of stress and anxiety. Others are dissatisfied with the way modern health-care systems function—long waits, referrals through chains of specialists, financial restrictions, and so forth. Connected to this are concerns about the harmful side effects of medication and the intrusiveness of surgery—both techniques favored by modern health-care systems. The asymmetrical power relationship between doctors and patients is at the heart of some people's choice to avail themselves of alternative medicine. They feel that the role of the passive patient does not grant them enough input into their own treatment and healing. Finally, some individuals profess religious or philosophical objections to orthodox medicine, which tends to treat the mind and body separately. They believe that the spiritual and psychological dimensions of health and illness are often not taken into account in the practice of orthodox medicine. All these concerns are implicit or explicit critiques of the **biomedical model of health,** the foundation on which the Western medical establishment operates. The biomedical model of health defines disease in objective terms and believes that the healthy body can be restored through scientifically based medical treatment.

The growth of alternative medicine presents a number of interesting questions for sociologists to consider. First and foremost, it is a fascinating reflection of the transformations occurring within modern societies. We are living in an age where more and more information is available—from a variety of sources—to draw on in making choices about our lives. Health care is no exception in this regard. Individuals are increasingly becoming health consumers—adopting an active stance toward their own health and well-being. Not only are we able to make choices about the type of practitioners to consult but we are also demanding more involvement in our own care and treatment. In this way the growth of alternative medicine is linked to the expansion of the self-help movement, which involves support groups, learning circles, and self-help books. People are now more likely than ever before to seize control of their lives and actively reshape them, rather than to rely on the instructions or opinions of others.

Another issue of interest to sociologists relates to the changing nature of health and illness in the late modern period. Many of the conditions and illnesses for which individuals seek alternative medical treatment seem to be products of the modern age itself. Insomnia, anxiety, stress, depression, fatigue, and chronic pain (caused by arthritis, cancer, and other diseases) are all on the rise in industrialized societies. Although these conditions have long existed, they appear to be causing greater distress and disruption to people's health than ever before. Recent surveys have revealed that stress has now surpassed the common cold as the biggest cause of absence from work. The World Health Organization predicts that within twenty years, depression will be the most debilitating disease in the world. Ironically, it seems that these consequences of modernity are ones that orthodox medicine has great difficulty in addressing. Alternative medicine is unlikely to overtake mainstream health care altogether, but indications are that its role will continue to grow.

The Social Basis of Health

The twentieth century witnessed a significant overall rise in life expectancy for people who live in industrialized countries. Diseases such as polio, scarlet fever, and tuberculosis have virtually been eradicated. Compared with those in other parts of the world, standards of health and well-being are relatively high. Many of these advances in public health have been attributed to the power of modern medicine. It is a commonly held assumption that medical research has been—and will continue to be—successful in uncovering the biological causes of disease and in developing effective treatments to control them. As medical knowledge and expertise grow, the argument runs, we can expect to see sustained and steady improvements in public health.

Although this approach to health and disease has been extremely influential, it is somewhat unsatisfactory for sociologists. This is because it ignores the important role of social and environmental influences on patterns of health and illness. The improvements in overall public health over the past century cannot conceal the fact that health and illness are not distributed evenly throughout the population. Research has shown that certain groups of people tend to enjoy much better health than others. These *health inequalities* appear to be tied to larger socioeconomic patterns.

Sociologists and scientists in social **epidemiology**—the science that studies the distribution and incidence of disease and illness within the population—have attempted to explain the link between health and variables such as social class, gender, race, age, and geography. While most scholars acknowledge the correlation between health and social inequalities, there is no agreement about the nature of the connection or about how health inequalities should be addressed. One of the main areas of debate concentrates on the relative importance of individual variables (e.g., lifestyle, behavior, diet, and cultural patterns) versus environmental or structural factors (e.g., income distribution and poverty; Figure 18.1). In this section, we look at variations in health patterns in the United States according to social class, gender, race, and geography, and review some of the competing explanations for their persistence.

FIGURE 18.1

Cultural and Material Influences on Health

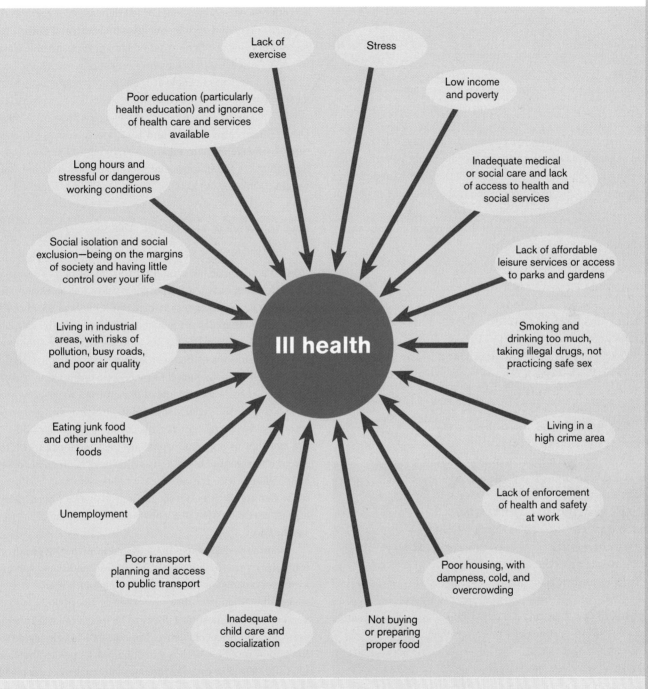

How might sociologists look at the spread of a virus differently from a medical doctor? Name three aspects of social class that affect health and how they do so. One of the contributions to ill health listed above is "Lack of affordable leisure services or access to parks and gardens." How might this affect one's health?

SOURCE: Reprinted with permission from Browne 1999. Crown copyright.

SOCIAL CLASS–BASED INEQUALITIES IN HEALTH

Think about the way that we defined "social class" in Chapter 8, as a concept that partakes of education, income, and occupation. In American society, people with better educations, higher incomes, and more prestigious occupations have better health. What is fascinating is that each of these dimensions of social class may be related to health and mortality for different reasons.

Income is the most obvious. In countries such as the United States, where medical care is expensive and many people are not covered by insurance, those with more financial resources have better access to physicians and medicine. But inequalities in health also persist in countries like Great Britain, which have national health insurance. One of the ways to understand this is to think beyond income about the other dimensions of social class, occupational status, and education.

Differences in occupational status may lead to inequalities in health and illness even when medical care is more or less evenly distributed. One study of health inequalities in Great Britain, *The Black Report* (Townsend and Davidson 1982), found that manual workers had substantially higher mortality rates than professional workers, even though Britain's health service had made great strides in equalizing the distribution of health care. Indeed, different occupations are associated with different levels of on-the-job health risks.

Those who work in offices or in domestic settings are at less risk of injury or exposure to hazardous materials. The extent of industrial-based disease is difficult to calculate, because it is

The number of people suffering from Type II diabetes, which is a chronic condition that typically develops in adults and disproportionally affects the poor and minority groups, is rapidly growing. Some research ties the onset of the disease to lifestyle choices like diet and exercise. How does the experience of diabetes patients challenge or support Parsons's three main tenets of the sick role?

not always possible to determine whether an illness is acquired from working conditions or from other sources. However, some work-related diseases are well documented: Lung disease is widespread in mining, as a result of dust inhalation; work with asbestos has been shown to produce certain types of cancer.

Differences in education, a third dimension of social class, also are correlated with inequalities in health and illness. Numerous studies document that education is positively related to preventative health behaviors. One set of researchers found that better-educated people are significantly more likely to engage in aerobic exercise and to know their blood pressure, and are less likely to smoke or be overweight (Shea et al. 1991). Other researchers have found that poorly educated people tend to engage in more cigarette smoking; they also tend to have more problems associated with cholesterol and body weight (Winkleby et al. 1992).

RACE-BASED INEQUALITIES IN HEALTH

Life expectancy at birth in 2003 was about eighty years for white females but just seventy-six years for black females. Likewise, life expectancy at birth in 2003 was seventy-five years for white males yet just sixty-nine years for black males (National Center for Health Statistics 2005a).

Health differences between blacks and whites are significant. When we note such differences, we are making use of a variable—race—that although different from social class, cannot be completely separated from it. One primary reason for inequalities of health between blacks and whites has to do with the fact that as a group blacks have less money than whites. About 58 percent of black households have no financial assets at all, almost twice the rate for white households (U.S. Bureau of the Census 2005a). And the median income of a black man is only 67 percent of that of a white man (U.S. Bureau of the Census 2005b).

Some of the differences in black and white health go beyond economic causes to differences in cultural conditions. Take, for example, racial gaps in mortality. Young black men are more susceptible to murder than any other group. In 2002, a black person was six times more likely to be murdered than a white person (U.S. Bureau of Justice Statistics 2004a). Homicide victimization rates for both whites and blacks peaked between 1993 and 1994. The murder rate for white males between eighteen and twenty-four years of age increased from 11.9 per 100,000 in 1984 to a high of 17.8 in 1994. By 2002, the murder rate for young white men had declined to 12.7 per 100,000. For young black males, the murder rate increased by over 270 percent between 1984 and 1994 (from 68 per 100,000 in 1984 to 183.5 in 1993). Since then the murder rate for blacks has declined to 102.3 per 100,000, which is 805 percent higher than for whites and still over 150 percent higher than the murder rate for young black men in 1984 (U.S. Bureau of Justice Statistics 2004b). This rise in violent crime has accompanied the rise of widespread crack cocaine addiction, a cultural condition of poor African American neighborhoods plagued by high levels of unemployment (Wilson 1996).

Besides the life expectancy and homicide rates, other race-based inequalities in health status are stark. There is a higher prevalence of hypertension among blacks—especially black men, a difference that may be biological. There are racial differences in cigarette smoking, with blacks smoking significantly more than whites. This may be due in some measure to cultural differences between blacks and whites, as well as the way in which the cigarette industry has deliberately targeted African Americans as a market.

But despite these depressing inequalities, it is important to note that some progress has been made in eradicating them. According to the National Center for Health Statistics (2005b), racial differences in cigarette smoking have decreased. In 1965, half of white men and 60 percent of black men age eighteen and over smoked cigarettes. By 2003, only 24 percent of white men and 26 percent of black men smoked. In 1965, roughly equal proportions of black and white women age eighteen and older smoked (33 to 34 percent). In 2003, a smaller proportion of black women (18 percent) smoked than did white women (20 percent).

Prevalence of hypertension among blacks has been greatly reduced. In the early 1970s, half of black adults suffered from hypertension. By 1994, however, roughly 36 percent of black adults between ages twenty and seventy-four suffered from hypertension (National Center for Health Statistics 2003). Yet, by 2002 the share of black women with hypertension had increased again to almost 40 percent (National Center for Health Statistics 2005c)

Patterns of physician visitation, hospitalization, and preventive medicine have also changed. In 1987, only 30 percent of white women and 24 percent of black women aged forty and older reported having a mammogram within the past two years. By 2003, the share of white and black women were equal at 71 percent (National Center for Health Statistics 2005d). Between 1983 and 2001, the proportion of blacks who had visited the dentist within the past year had increased from 39 percent to 58 percent, while the figure for whites increased from 57 percent to 68 percent (National Center for Health Statistics 2005e).

How might the influence of poverty on health be countered? Extensive programs of health education and disease prevention are one possibility. But such programs tend to work better among more prosperous, well-educated groups and in any case usually produce only small changes in behavior. Increased accessibility to health services would help, but probably to a lim-

There are significant racial differences in cigarette smoking, with blacks smoking more than whites. This may be due in some measure to cultural differences, as well as the way the cigarette industry has deliberately targeted African Americans as a market.

ited degree. The only really effective policy option is to attack poverty itself, so as to reduce the income gap between rich and poor (Najman 1993).

GENDER-BASED INEQUALITIES IN HEALTH

Women in the United States are likely to live longer than men. This gender gap is, it is interesting to note, a relatively recent phenomenon. In the United States, there was only a two-year difference in female and male life expectancies in 1900. By 1940, this gap increased to 4.4 years, and by 1970, the gap had widened to 7.7 years. The gender gap has since declined to 5.4 years in 2003 (Cleary 1987; National Center for Health Statistics 2005f).

How can we explain this changing gender gap? The main reason is that the leading cause of death has changed since the turn of the century. In 1900, the leading cause of death was infectious disease, which struck men, women, and children equally. Since mid-century, however, heart disease and cancer have been the leading causes of death for American adults. Heart disease and cancer are influenced by lifestyle, diet, and behavior—all of which are subject to gender differences.

Thus social explanations for women's mortality advantage tend to focus on behavioral differences between men and women, including smoking, drinking, and preventive health behaviors. Men are more likely to smoke cigarettes than are women, and smoking is associated with heart disease and various types of cancer. Likewise, higher proportions of men than women drink alcoholic beverages, admit to binge drinking, and smoke marijuana (National Center for Health Statistics 2005g).

Some researchers argue that male roles lead men to adopt the Coronary Prone Behavior Pattern, or Type A personality, and that Type A personalities (i.e., persons who are competitive, impatient, ambitious, and aggressive) are twice as likely as laid-back (Type B) personalities to suffer heart attacks (Spielberger et al. 1991). Indirect evidence for this hypothesis comes from examining gender differences in hypertension (i.e., elevated blood pressure or taking antihypertensive medication). In the early 1990s, 25 percent of men and 20 percent of women aged twenty to seventy-four reported having hypertension (National Center for Health Statistics 1996). By 2002, however, the differences between genders in the occurrence of hypertension had been reduced to less than 0.5 percent (National Center for Health Statistics 2005c). This may indicate that the gender gap in Type A personalities has declined, as more and more women enter the workforce and pursue careers. Other factors (such as diet) may contribute to the convergence of hypertension between men and women. More research will have to be done before any firm conclusions can be drawn.

Sociologists tend to focus on societal factors in explaining these differences, but biological arguments should also be considered. One study tested the hypothesis that higher male mortality rates are due to the greater stresses of the male role in the 1950s (competitiveness of the workforce, pressure for success and high earnings) compared with the "easy life" that wives and mothers were believed to have. The study was conducted on men and women who shared equal roles and equal stresses: nuns and monks. The nuns lived longer than the monks, and both had life expectancies essentially the same as the rest of the population. Because the environment was equalized for the two groups, lifestyle factors such as diet, drinking, and stress could be ruled out as explanatory factors (Madigan 1957). However, critics of this study note that the monks smoked more than the nuns did, so that lifestyle differences were not entirely accounted for.

Biologists have also cited the existence of genetic factors. Humans have twenty-three pairs of chromosomes, one of which determines sex. Males have XY sex chromosomes, while females have two X chromosomes. The X chromosome carries more genetic information than the Y, including some defects that can lead to physical abnormalities. Instead of making females more vulnerable to X-linked disorders, this seems to give females a genetic advantage. A female typically needs two defective X chromosomes for most genetically linked disorders to manifest themselves; otherwise, one healthy X chromosome can override the abnormal one. A male who has a defective X chromosome will have a genetically linked disease because there is no other X chromosome to cancel it out. This is thought to account for the higher number of miscarriages of male fetuses and for the greater ratio of male to female infant deaths and deaths at all ages due to congenital abnormalities (Hayflick 1994).

Despite the female advantage in mortality, most large surveys show women more often report poor health. Women have higher rates of illness from acute conditions and nonfatal chronic conditions, including arthritis, osteoporosis, and depressive and anxiety disorders. They are slightly more likely to report their health as fair to poor, they spend about 40 percent more days in bed each year, and their activities are restricted due to health problems about 25 percent more than men. In addition, they make more physician visits each year and have twice the number of surgical procedures performed on them as do men (National Center for Health Statistics 1996 2003e, 2003f).

There are two main explanations for women's poorer health, yet longer lives: (1) Greater life expectancy and age brings poorer health, and (2) women make greater use of medical services including preventive care (Centers for Disease Control and Prevention [CDC] 2003a). In 2000, the average number of visits to physician offices, hospital emergency rooms, and hospital outpatient departments was 25 percent higher for women than for men. Men may experience as many or more health symptoms as women, but men may ignore symptoms, may underestimate the extent of their illness, or may utilize preventive services less often (Waldron 1986).

Social Cohesion: The Key to Better Health?

In trying to unravel the causes of health inequalities, a growing number of sociologists are turning their attention to the role of social support and social cohesion in promoting good health. As you may recall from our discussion of Durkheim, social solidarity is one of the most important concepts in sociology. Durkheim saw the degree and type of solidarity within a culture as one of its most critical features. In his study of suicide, for example, he found that individuals and groups who were well integrated into society were less likely to take their own lives than were others.

In several articles and in his subsequent book, *Unhealthy Societies: The Afflictions of Inequality* (1996), Richard Wilkinson argues that the healthiest societies in the world are not the richest countries, but those in which income is distributed most evenly and levels of social integration are highest. High levels of national wealth, according to Wilkinson, do not necessarily translate into better health for the population. In surveying empirical data from countries around the world, Wilkinson notes a clear relationship between mortality rates and patterns of income distribution. Inhabitants of countries such as Japan and Sweden, which are regarded as some of the most egalitarian societies in the world, enjoy better levels of health on average than do citizens of countries where the gap between the rich and the poor is more pronounced, such as the United States.

In Wilkinson's view, the widening gap in income distribution undermines social cohesion and makes it more difficult for people to manage risks and challenges. Heightened social isolation and the failure to cope with stress is reflected in health indicators. Wilkinson argues that social factors—the strength of social contacts, ties within communities, availability of social support, a sense of security—are the main determinants of the relative health of a society.

Wilkinson's thesis has provoked energetic responses. Some claim that his work should become required reading for policy makers and politicians. They agree with Wilkinson that too much emphasis has been placed on market relations and the drive toward prosperity. This approach has failed many members of society, they argue; it is time to consider more humane and socially responsible policies to support those who are disadvantaged. Others criticize his study on methodological grounds and argue that he has failed to show a clear causal relationship between income inequality and poor health (Judge 1995). Illness, critics contend, could be caused by any number of other mediating factors. They argue that the empirical evidence for his claims remains suggestive at best.

Whereas Wilkinson investigates the links between social cohesion and health at the level of society as a whole, other sociologists have focused on particular segments of the population. Heather Graham (1987, 1994) has studied the effects of stress on the health of white working-class women. She has highlighted the fact that women at the lower socioeconomic end of the spectrum have less access to support networks in times of life crisis than do middle-class women. Working-class women, she notes, tend to encounter life crises (such as job loss, divorce, eviction from housing, or the death of a child) more often than other groups but generally have weaker coping skills and fewer outlets for anxiety. Not only is the resulting stress harmful both physically and psychologically, but some of the coping strategies these women turn to—such as smoking—are also damaging. Graham argues that smoking is a way of reducing tension when personal and material resources are stretched to the breaking point. Thus it occupies a paradoxical position in women's lives—increasing the health risk for women and their children while simultaneously allowing them to cope under difficult circumstances.

Ann Oakley and her colleagues (1994) studied the role of social support in the health of socially disadvantaged women and children in four English cities. They argue that the relationship

Dr. Regina Benjamin, a family physician dedicated to serving the working-class families in a small shrimping community on the Gulf Coast, visits one of her patients at home. Working-class women have less access to support networks in times of crisis than middle-class women. Social support—such as counseling services, hotlines, or home visits—can help patients cope with the effects of stress and illnesses.

between stress and health applies to both major life crises and smaller problems and that it is felt particularly acutely in the lives of working-class people. Oakley and co-workers note that social support—such as counseling services, hotlines, or home visits—can act as a buffer against the negative health consequences of stress commonly experienced by women. Other studies have shown that social support is an important factor that can help people in adjusting to disease and illness (Ell 1996).

The Developing World: Colonialism and the Spread of Disease

There is good evidence that the hunting and gathering communities of the Americas, before the arrival of the Europeans, were not as subject to infectious disease as the European societies of the period. Many infectious organisms only thrive when human populations are living above the density characteristic of hunting and gathering life. Permanently settled communities, particularly large cities, risk contamination of water supplies by waste products. Hunters and gatherers were less vulnerable in this respect because they moved continuously across the countryside.

The expansion of the West in the colonial era transmitted certain diseases into other parts of the world where they had not existed previously. Smallpox, measles, and typhus, among other major maladies, were unknown to the indigenous populations of Central and South America before the Spanish conquest in the early sixteenth century. The English and French colonists brought the same diseases to North America (Dubos 1959). Some of these illnesses produced epidemics so severe that they ravaged or completely wiped out native populations, which had little or no resistance to them.

In Africa and subtropical parts of Asia, infectious diseases have almost certainly been rife for a long period of time. Tropical and subtropical conditions are especially conducive to diseases such as malaria, carried by mosquitoes, and sleeping sickness, carried by the tsetse fly. Yet it seems probable that before contact with the Europeans, levels of risk from infectious diseases were lower. There was always the threat of epidemics, drought, or natural disaster, but colonialism led to major changes in the relation between populations and their environments, producing harmful effects on health patterns. The Europeans introduced new farming methods, upsetting the ecology of whole regions. For example, wide tracts of East Africa today are completely devoid of cattle as a result of the uncontrolled spread of the tsetse fly, which multiplied as a result of the changes the intruders introduced. (The tsetse fly carries illnesses which are fatal to both humans and livestock.) Before the arrival of the Europeans, Africans successfully maintained large herds in these same areas (Kjekshus 1977).

The most significant consequence of the colonial system was its effect on nutrition and therefore on levels of resistance to illness as a result of the changed economic conditions involved in producing for world markets. In many parts of Africa in particular, the nutritional quality of native diets became substantially depressed as cash-crop production supplanted the production of native foods.

This was not simply a one-way process, however, as the early development of colonialism also radically changed Western diets, having a paradoxical impact so far as health is concerned. On the one hand, Western diets were improved by the addition of a range of new foods either previously unknown or very rare, such as bananas, pineapples, and grapefruit. On the other hand, the importation of tobacco and coffee, together with raw sugar, which began increasingly to be used in all manner of foods, has had harmful consequences. Smoking tobacco, especially, has been linked to the prevalence of cancer and heart disease.

Infectious Diseases Today in the Developing World

Although major strides have been made in reducing, and in some cases virtually eliminating, infectious diseases in the developing world, they remain far more common there than in the West. The most important example of a disease that has almost completely disappeared from the world is smallpox, which, even as recently as the 1960s, was a scourge of Europe as well as many other parts of the world. Campaigns against malaria have been much less successful. When the insecticide DDT was first produced, it was hoped that the mosquito, the prime carrier of malaria, could be eradicated. At first, considerable progress was made, but this has slowed down because some strains of mosquito have become resistant to DDT.

HIV/AIDS

One devastating exception to the trend of eliminating infectious diseases in the developing world is HIV/AIDS, which has become a global epidemic. The true number of people infected with HIV is unknown, but estimates put the figure at between 37 and 45 million worldwide, with 40.3 million being the most frequently cited. In 2005 alone, over 3 million people worldwide died from AIDS-related illnesses (UNAIDS 2005a). Using middle-range estimates, about 720,000 people are living with HIV/AIDS in Europe, 1.2 million in North America, 2.1 million in Latin America and the Caribbean, and nearly 26 million in sub-Saharan Africa (Global Map 18.1). The main ef-

Looking AIDS in the Face: Anonymous (covering face) is a university student at Maputo University in Mozambique. Due to the extreme stigma he might face, he chose not to include any of his clothes in the photograph for fear of being identified. "I can't be identified because it may have a bad impact on my position as a university student. . . . Here in Mozambique there is discrimination promoted by the government. In one of his speeches the prime minister said Mozambique should not invest in educating people with AIDS as there is no hope for them. . . . If my faculty discovered my status there is real possibility that they would discriminate against me. Even if they don't expel me straight away, they would try all sorts of devious means to get rid of me."

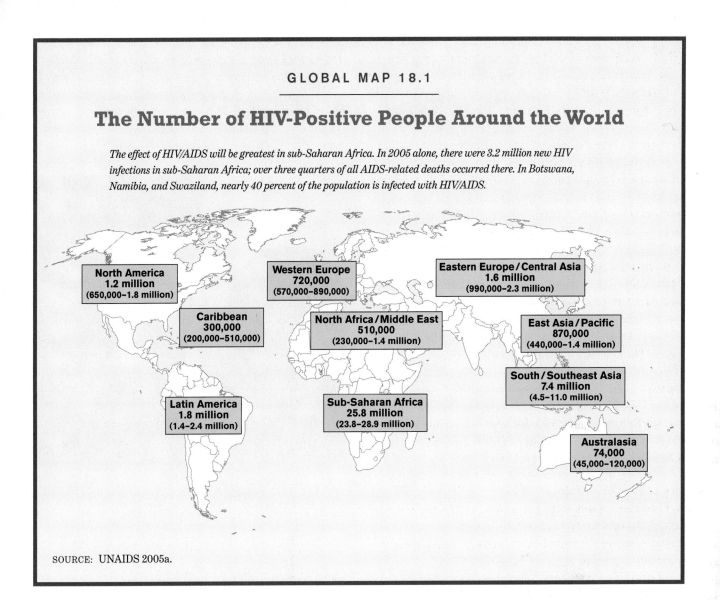

GLOBAL MAP 18.1

The Number of HIV-Positive People Around the World

The effect of HIV/AIDS will be greatest in sub-Saharan Africa. In 2005 alone, there were 3.2 million new HIV infections in sub-Saharan Africa; over three quarters of all AIDS-related deaths occurred there. In Botswana, Namibia, and Swaziland, nearly 40 percent of the population is infected with HIV/AIDS.

North America
1.2 million
(650,000–1.8 million)

Western Europe
720,000
(570,000–890,000)

Eastern Europe/Central Asia
1.6 million
(990,000–2.3 million)

Caribbean
300,000
(200,000–510,000)

North Africa/Middle East
510,000
(230,000–1.4 million)

East Asia/Pacific
870,000
(440,000–1.4 million)

Latin America
1.8 million
(1.4–2.4 million)

Sub-Saharan Africa
25.8 million
(23.8–28.9 million)

South/Southeast Asia
7.4 million
(4.5–11.0 million)

Australasia
74,000
(45,000–120,000)

SOURCE: UNAIDS 2005a.

fect of the epidemic is still to come, because of the time it takes for HIV infection to develop into full-blown AIDS. The majority of people affected in the world today are heterosexuals. As of 2005, about half are women. In sub-Saharan Africa, young women are more than 2.5 times more likely than men to be infected with HIV/AIDS. Worldwide, at least four HIV infections are contracted heterosexually for every instance of homosexual spread. In high-income countries the rate of new infections has been on the decline, yet the demographics of who is infected with HIV/AIDS are striking. In the United States, there were over 43,000 new infections in 2005 and nearly half of these were in southern states (National Center for Health Statistics 2005h; UNAIDS 2005a). Of these, nearly half were in African Americans, who constitute less than 12 percent of the total population. African American women are eight times more likely to be infected with HIV than white women, and HIV/AIDS is now the leading cause of death among African American women aged twenty-five to thirty-four in the United States (UNAIDS 2003, 2005b). Although there was a steep drop in the number AIDS-related deaths after the introduction of antiretroviral therapy, as these statistics demonstrate, African Americans are not benefiting from such life-prolonging treatments. The United Nations Joint Program on HIV and AIDS reports that African Americans are half as likely to be receiving antiretroviral treatment (UNAIDS 2005b).

Stigmatization of people with HIV/AIDS remains a major barrier to successful treatment programs. Stigma draws on preexisting prejudices to justify scapegoating and blaming in victimized people. The stigma that associates HIV positive status with sexual promiscuity and immorality results in an avoidance of HIV/AIDS prevention and treatment programs. Clearly, the statistics cited above demonstrate that HIV/AIDS is not a "gay disease."

The Spread of AIDS

There can be no question but that the threat of AIDS has significantly affected American sexual mores. Men and women, straight and gay, have come to realize the dangers posed by unprotected sex, and in many segments of the population, condom use has become the norm. As a result, the rate of transmission of HIV, the virus that causes AIDS, has dropped significantly in the United States. And although there remains no cure for the disease, the use of antiretroviral drugs has greatly increased the longevity of HIV-positive Americans.

The story is very different in the developing world. According to The Global Fund to Fight AIDS, Tuberculosis and Malaria (2005), which pools the money of governments and private business to fund disease-reduction programs, 95 percent of people with HIV live in developing nations, with the vast majority living in Africa. Because condom availability in the developing world is low, because most governments in the developing world offer little in the way of sex education, and

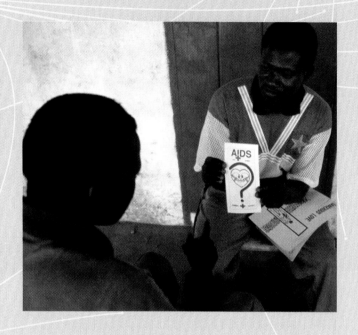

In the United States, it is estimated that a quarter of people living with HIV/AIDS do not know that they are infected (UNAIDS 2005b). Part of the reason why such a large group exists is the high level of fear and denial associated with being diagnosed as HIV positive. The stigma of having HIV/AIDS and the discrimination against people living with these infections are major barriers to the treatment of the epidemic worldwide. A 2002 survey found that one in ten doctors and nurses in Nigeria have refused treatment to a person because of his or her HIV/AIDS status. In India, 70 percent of people living with HIV/AIDS have reported discrimination by health-care workers (UNAIDS 2003).

Discrimination is also seen at the level of government health care planning (UNAIDS 2003). A case in point is South Africa, where President Thabo Mbeki, in a 2001 speech justifying his government's inaction on AIDS and unwillingness to spend government resources on AIDS prevention, declared that HIV did not cause AIDS and that, contrary to scientific opinion, antiretroviral medicines were ineffective (Forrest and Streek

2001). Such attitudes have slowed progress in confronting the rapid expansion of the AIDS epidemic in South Africa, where at the end of 2005, nearly 39 percent of the population was living with HIV/AIDS (UNAIDS 2005c).

Although the overall spread of AIDS in Western societies has slowed as the result of prevention programs, the opposite has been true in the developing world, where health education is limited and the medical establishment is poor.

In countries heavily affected by the HIV/AIDS epidemic, only 5 percent of pregnant women receive health-care services aimed at preventing mother-to-child HIV transmission (UNAIDS 2005d). Besides the devastation caused by HIV/AIDS to individuals who suffer from it, the AIDS epidemic is creating a range of severe social consequences, including the explosion in the number of orphaned children stemming from the deaths of HIV-infected parents. Worldwide, the parents of an estimated fifteen million children have died as a result of HIV/AIDS; twelve million of these are in sub-Saharan Africa alone (Global Map 18.1). In Uganda alone, 77 percent of the populabecause many mothers with HIV unknowingly pass the disease on to their children, in areas of Africa one in four adults is infected with HIV. With rates of transmission showing no signs of decreasing, AIDS threatens to reduce the average life expectancy drastically in many developing nations. One sign of hope is that antiretroviral therapies, which can cost thousands of dollars per patient per year and thus could be out of reach for all but the wealthy few, are now being supplied at little or no cost, thanks in part to protests and pressures placed on pharmaceutical companies by African governments and activists. Still, between 85 and 90 percent of people in southern Africa needing antiretroviral medications were not receiving them (UNAIDS 2005d).

The specter of AIDS in the developing world also poses a direct threat to the West—because of globalization. Westerners are traveling to the developing world in record numbers, either as tourists or on business. Although HIV cannot be transmitted through casual contact, it is certainly the case that many Americans or Europeans who travel to developing countries will have sexual contacts while they are there, some by using the services of prostitutes. Thailand, for example, has a flourishing sex-tourism business, with some major hotels and tour companies catering to foreigners who wish to take advantage of the country's semilegal prostitution industry (Truong 1990). Because many of these prostitutes are HIV positive,

American tourists, businesspeople, or military personnel who employ them and who fail to practice safe sex are at risk of contracting the virus and then spreading it on their return to the United States. Diseases, no less than people or goods, cross international borders more easily in a globalized world.

tion is under the age of eighteen; 30 percent of those are orphans (AIDS Orphans Educational Trust 2003). The decimated population of working adults combined with the surging populations of orphans sets the stage for massive social instability, as economies break down and governments are unable to provide for the social needs of orphans who become targets for recruitment into gangs and armies who train them to fight as soldiers.

In fact, basic medical resources are still lacking in the vast majority of developing countries. The hospitals that do exist, together with trained doctors, tend to be heavily concentrated in urban areas, where their services are mostly monopolized by the affluent minority. Most developing countries have introduced some form of national health service, organized by the central government, but the medical services available are usually very limited. The small section of the wealthy uses private health care, sometimes traveling to the West when sophisticated medical treatment is needed. Conditions in many developing world cities, particularly in the shantytowns, make

An eleven-year-old orphan girl sells her grandmother's brooms for 3¢ (U.S.) each in order to buy food in a shanty compound in Kitwe, Zambia. About 70 percent of the world's HIV-infected people live in sub-Saharan Africa and more than one million children in Zambia alone have been orphaned by parents who have succumbed to AIDS.

the control of infectious diseases very difficult: Many shanty-towns almost completely lack basic services such as water, sewage, and garbage disposal.

Studies carried out by the World Health Organization suggest that more than two thirds of people living in urban areas in developing countries draw their water from sources that fail to meet minimal safety standards. It has been estimated that seventeen out of the twenty-five common water-related diseases in developing nations could either be cut by half or eradicated altogether simply by the provision of ready supplies of safe water (Doyal and Pennell 1981). Only about a quarter of the city residents in developing countries have waterborne sewage facilities; some 30 percent have no sanitation at all. These conditions provide breeding grounds for diseases such as cholera (Dwyer 1975).

Human Sexuality

The global AIDS epidemic and attempts to halt its spread are further examples of the socialization of nature. As with the study of health and illness, scholars have also differed over the importance of biological versus social and cultural influences on human sexual behavior, another important facet of the sociology of the body.

Social Influences on Sexual Behavior

Judith Lorber (1994) distinguishes as many as ten different sexual identities: straight (heterosexual) woman, straight man, lesbian woman, gay man, bisexual woman, bisexual man, transvestite woman (a woman who regularly dresses as a man), transvestite man (a man who regularly dresses as a woman), transsexual woman (a man who becomes a woman), and transsexual man (a woman who becomes a man). Sexual practices themselves are even more diverse. Freud argued that human beings are born "polymorphously perverse." By this he meant that human beings are born with a wide range of sexual tastes that are ordinarily curbed through socialization—although some adults may follow these even when, in a given society, they are regarded as immoral or illegal. Freud first began his research during the Victorian period, when many people were sexually prudish; yet his patients still revealed to him an amazing diversity of sexual pursuits.

Among possible sexual practices are the following: A man or woman can have sexual relations with women, men, or both. This can happen with one partner at a time or with two or more partners participating. One can have sex with oneself (masturbation) or with no one (celibacy). Someone can have sexual relations with transsexuals or people who erotically cross-dress; use pornography or sexual devices; practice sadomasochism (the erotic use of bondage and the inflicting of pain); have sex with animals; and so on (Lorber 1994). In most societies, sexual norms encourage some practices and discourage or condemn others. Such norms, however, vary between different cultures. Homosexuality is a case in point. As will be discussed later, some cultures have either tolerated or actively encouraged homosexuality in certain contexts. Among the ancient Greeks, for instance, the love of men for boys was idealized as the highest form of sexual love.

Accepted types of sexual behavior also vary between different cultures, which is one way we know that most sexual responses are learned rather than innate. The most extensive study was carried out five decades ago by Clellan Ford and Frank Beach (1951), who surveyed anthropological evidence from more than two hundred societies. Striking variations were found in what is regarded as "natural" sexual behavior and in norms of sexual attractiveness. For example, in some cultures, extended foreplay, perhaps lasting hours, is thought desirable and even necessary before intercourse; in others, foreplay is virtually nonexistent. In some societies, it is believed that overly frequent intercourse leads to physical debilitation or illness. Among the Seniang of the South Pacific, advice on the desirability of spacing out lovemaking is given by the elders of the village—who also believe that a person with white hair may legitimately copulate every night!

In most cultures, norms of sexual attractiveness (held by both females and males) focus more on physical looks for women than for men, a situation that seems to be gradually changing in the West as women increasingly become active in spheres outside the home. The traits seen as most important in female beauty, however, differ greatly. In the modern West, a slim, small body build is admired, while in other cultures a much more generous shape is regarded as most attractive. Sometimes the breasts are not seen as a source of sexual stimulus, whereas in some societies great erotic significance is attached to them. Some societies place great store on the shape of the face, whereas others emphasize the shape and color of the eyes or the size and form of the nose and lips.

Sexuality in Western Culture

Western attitudes toward sexual behavior were for nearly two thousand years molded primarily by Christianity. Although different Christian sects and denominations have held divergent views about the proper place of sexuality in life, the dominant view of the Christian church was that all sexual behavior is suspect, except that needed for reproduction. During some periods, this view produced an extreme prudishness in society at large. But at other times, many people ignored or reacted against the church's teachings, commonly engaging in practices (such as adultery) forbidden by religious authorities. As was mentioned in Chapter 1, the idea that sexual fulfillment can and should be sought through marriage was rare.

In the nineteenth century, religious presumptions about sexuality became partly replaced by medical ones. Most of the early writings by doctors about sexual behavior, however, were as stern as the views of the church. Some argued that any type of sexual activity unconnected with reproduction causes serious physical harm. Masturbation was said to bring on blindness, insanity, heart disease, and other ailments, while oral sex was claimed to cause cancer. In Victorian times, sexual hypocrisy abounded. Virtuous women were believed to be indifferent to sexuality, accepting the attentions of their husbands only as a duty. Yet in the expanding towns and cities, prostitution was rife and often openly tolerated, "loose" women being seen as in an entirely different category from their respectable sisters.

Many Victorian men—who were on the face of things sober, well-behaved citizens, devoted to their wives—regularly visited prostitutes or kept mistresses. Such behavior was treated leniently, whereas "respectable" women who took lovers were

Sexual hypocrisy abounded in the Victorian era. Virtuous women were said to be indifferent to sexuality, while it was acceptable for their husbands to visit prostitutes or keep mistresses. This 1878 illustration of the St. Louis red-light district shows that prostitution was openly tolerated and "loose" women were not held to the same standards as their "respectable" sisters.

regarded as scandalous and shunned in polite society if their behavior came to light. The differing attitudes toward the sexual activities of men and women formed a double standard, which has long existed and whose residues still linger on today.

In current times, traditional attitudes exist alongside much more liberal attitudes toward sexuality, which developed particularly strongly in the 1960s. Some people, particularly those influenced by Christian teachings, believe that premarital sex is wrong and generally frown on all forms of sexual behavior except heterosexual activity within the confines of marriage—although it is now much more commonly accepted that sexual pleasure is a desirable and important feature of marriage. Others, by contrast, condone or actively approve of premarital sex and hold tolerant attitudes toward different sexual practices. Sexual attitudes have undoubtedly become more permissive over the past thirty years in most Western countries. In movies and plays, scenes are shown that previously would have been completely unacceptable, while pornographic material is readily available to most adults who want it. (Pornography is reportedly the predominant use for the World Wide Web.)

Sexual Behavior: Kinsey's Study

We can speak much more confidently about public values concerning sexuality in the past than we can about private practices, for by their nature such practices mostly go undocumented. When Alfred Kinsey began his research in the United States in the 1940s and 1950s, it was the first time a major investigation of actual sexual behavior had been undertaken. Kinsey and his co-researchers (1948, 1953) faced condemnation from religious organizations, and his work was denounced as immoral in the newspapers and in Congress. But he persisted, and eventually obtained sexual life histories of eighteen thousand people, a reasonably representative sample of the white American population.

Kinsey's results were surprising to most and shocking to many, because they revealed a great difference between the public expectations of sexual behavior prevailing at that time and actual sexual conduct. He found that almost 70 percent of men had visited a prostitute, and 84 percent had had premarital sexual experience. Yet, following the double standard, 40 percent of men expected their wives to be virgins at the time of marriage. More than 90 percent of males had engaged in masturbation and nearly 60 percent in some form of oral sexual activity. Among women, about 50 percent had had premarital sexual experience, although mostly with their prospective husbands. Some 60 percent had masturbated, and the same percentage had engaged in oral-genital contacts.

The gap between publicly accepted attitudes and actual behavior that Kinsey's findings demonstrated was probably especially great at that particular period, just after World War II. A phase of sexual liberalization had begun rather earlier, in the 1920s, when many younger people felt freed from the strict moral codes that had governed earlier generations. Sexual behavior probably changed a good deal, but issues concerning sexuality were not openly discussed in the way that has become familiar now. People participating in sexual activities that were still strongly disapproved of on a public level concealed them, not realizing the full extent to which others were engaging in similar practices. The more permissive era of the 1960s brought openly declared attitudes more into line with the realities of behavior.

Sexual Behavior Since Kinsey

In the 1960s, the social movements that challenged the existing order of things, like those associated with countercultural, or "hippie," lifestyles, also broke with existing sexual norms. These movements preached sexual freedom, and the invention of the contraceptive pill for women allowed sexual pleasure to be clearly separated from reproduction. Women's groups also started pressing for greater independence from male sexual values, the rejection of the double standard, and the need for women to achieve greater sexual satisfaction in their relationships. Until recently it was difficult to know with accuracy how much sexual behavior had changed since the time of Kinsey's research.

In the late 1980s, Lillian Rubin (1990) interviewed a thousand Americans between the ages of thirteen and forty-eight to try to discover what changes have occurred in sexual behavior and attitudes over the previous thirty years or so. According to her findings, there have indeed been significant changes. Sexual activity typically begins at a younger age than was true for the previous generation; moreover, the sexual practices of teenagers tend today to be as varied and comprehensive as those of adults. There is still a double standard, but it is not as powerful as it used to be. One of the most important changes is that women now expect, and actively pursue, sexual pleasure in relationships. They expect to receive, not only to provide, sexual satisfaction—a phenomenon that Rubin argues has major consequences for both sexes.

Women are more sexually available than once was the case; but along with this development, which most men applaud, has come a new assertiveness many men find difficult to accept. The men Rubin (1990) talked to often said they "felt inadequate," were afraid they could "never do anything right," and found it "impossible to satisfy women these days."

Men feel inadequate? Doesn't this contradict much of what we have learned in this textbook so far? For in modern society, men continue to dominate in most spheres, and they are in general much more violent toward women than the other way around. Such violence is substantially aimed at the control and continuing subordination of women. Yet a number of authors have begun to argue that masculinity is a burden as much as a source of reward. Much male sexuality, they add, is compulsive rather than satisfying. If men were to stop using sexuality as a means of control, not only women but they themselves would gain.

In 1994, a team of researchers, led by Edward Laumann, published *The Social Organization of Sexuality: Sexual Practices in the United States,* the most comprehensive study of sexual behavior since Kinsey. To the surprise of many, their findings reflect an essential sexual conservatism among Americans. For instance, 83 percent of their subjects had had only one partner (or no partner at all) in the preceding year, and among married people the figure rises to 96 percent. Fidelity to one's spouse is also quite common: Only 10 percent of women and less than 25 percent of men reported having an extramarital affair during their lifetime. According to the study, Americans average only three partners during their entire lifetime (Table 18.1). Despite the apparent ordinariness of sexual behavior, some distinct changes emerge from this study, the most significant being a progressive increase in the level of premarital sexual experience, particularly among women. In fact, over 95 percent of Americans getting married today are sexually experienced.

In addition, sexual experience is increasing among high school students. Sexual permissiveness among young people is much greater today than it was in the 1970s. According to the Centers for Disease Control and Prevention (2005), in 2003 nearly half (47 percent) of all high school students reported having had sexual intercourse; 14 percent reported having had four or more partners. Both of these figures represent declines from 1991, when more than 54 percent of high school students had ever had sex and nearly 19 percent had had four or more sex partners. U.S. rates are far higher than those in Japan and China, where only a small percentage of all young people report having had sexual relationships (Tang and Zuo 2000; Toufexis 1993). Considering that the General Social Survey in 1998 reported that over 70 percent of respondents believed that teenage sex is "always wrong" and another 16 percent believed it is "almost always wrong," parental beliefs and adolescent behavior are clearly in conflict. One study of the sexual behavior of tens of thousands of American middle and high school students concluded that early sexual activity was higher among students who were from single-parent families, from a lower socioeconomic status, who demonstrated lower school performance and intelligence, and had lower religiosity—and among students with high levels of "body pride" (Halpern et al. 2000; Lammers et al. 2000).

Sexual Behavior in the United States: The Sociological Debate

Sociologists frequently rely on responses to survey questionnaires as their main source of information on human behavior. However, obtaining detailed information on sexual behavior and attitudes is often particularly difficult. The two most comprehensive studies of sexuality in the United States—the Kinsey studies (1948, 1953) and the Laumann study (1994)—offer very different portraits of sexual preferences and behaviors. Do these conflicting results reflect historical changes in sexual mores, or are the observed differences an outcome of methodological approaches?

As we just saw, in stark contrast to Kinsey's results, which found that a high proportion of men had premarital or extramarital sex, the Laumann study revealed that 83 percent of survey respondents had only one or no sexual partners in the year prior to the study. Moreover, only 10 percent of women and fewer than 25 percent of men reported ever having had an extramarital affair during their lifetime. Certainly, it's possible that Americans have become more sexually conservative over time. Perhaps the fear of AIDS and sexually transmitted diseases has frightened men and women away from extramarital affairs and multiple sex partners.

An alternative explanation for the wildly discrepant findings is that the researchers adopted different methodological approaches. Kinsey, an evolutionary biologist, first gave a questionnaire about sexual practices to students in his zoology classes at Indiana University. Finding this method unsatisfactory, he next conducted face-to-face interviews and then focused his study on specific social groups. He and his colleagues eventually interviewed nearly eighteen thousand people.

Kinsey recognized that the ideal survey would select people at random and thus results would represent the general population. However, he did not believe it was possible to persuade a randomly selected group of Americans to answer deeply personal questions about their sexual behavior. Consequently, his survey respondents were primarily college students living in sorority and fraternity houses, prisoners, psychiatric patients, and friends. To make his data more credible, Kinsey made every effort to interview 100 percent of the members of each group, such as all students living in a given fraternity house. Because Kinsey's data are based on a convenience sample, they are not representative of the American public at large. Moreover, many of his survey respondents volunteered to participate in the study. Thus these people may be unique from nonvolunteers in that they have wider sexual experiences or a greater interest in sexuality.

The Laumann study, in contrast, is based on data from the National Health and Social Life Survey (NHSLS). The NHSLS data were obtained from a nationally representative random sample of more than three thousand American men and women aged eighteen to fifty-nine who spoke English. In addition, the Laumann research team purposely oversampled among blacks and Hispanics so that they would have enough members of these minority groups to analyze their survey responses separately with confidence that findings were statistically reliable and valid.

Recognizing that people are often hesitant to discuss sexuality, the Laumann team paid particular attention to choosing nonjudgmental language in their questionnaire. The team also built several "checks" into their questionnaire to ensure the veracity of responses. Several questions were redundant, but were asked in different ways throughout the interview to gauge whether respondents were truthful in their answers. The research team also included eleven questions that had been asked previously on another national random sample survey of Americans. Comparisons of responses to the two sets of questions provided the Laumann researchers with assurance that their results were consistent with other researchers' findings.

Although the Kinsey and Laumann studies are influential works on human sexuality, the studies taken together also demonstrate that the process through which sociological knowledge is obtained often is as important as the actual research findings.

Sexual Orientation

Another important aspect of sexuality concerns *sexual orientation,* the direction of one's sexual or romantic attraction. The term *sexual preference,* which is sometimes incorrectly used instead of *sexual orientation,* is misleading and is to be avoided

The term "lesbian" derives from the name of the Greek island, Lesbos, which was the birthplace of Sappho (pictured above), who taught poetry to a devoted group of young women.

TABLE 18.1

Sex in America: Social Influences on Sexual Behavior

TOTAL	SEX PARTNERS IN THE PAST 12 MONTHS				SEX PARTNERS SINCE AGE 18						MEDIAN NUMBER OF SEX PARTNERS SINCE AGE 18
	NONE	1	2–4	5+	NONE	1	2–4	5–10	11–20	21+	
	12%	71%	14%	3%	3%	26%	30%	22%	11%	9%	3
Men	10%	67%	18%	5%	3%	20%	21%	23%	16%	17%	6
Women	14	75	10	2	3	32	36	20	6	3	2
Ages 18–24	11%	57%	24%	9%	8%	32%	34%	15%	8%	3%	2
25–29	6	72	17	6	2	25	31	22	10	9	4
30–34	9	73	16	2	3	21	29	25	11	10	4
35–39	10	77	11	2	2	19	30	25	14	11	4
40–44	11	75	13	1	1	22	28	24	14	12	4
45–49	15	75	9	1	2	26	24	25	10	14	4
50–54	15	79	5	0	2	34	28	18	9	9	2
55–59	32	65	4	0	1	40	28	15	8	7	2
Never married, not living with someone	25%	38%	28%	9%	12%	15%	29%	21%	12%	12%	4
Never married, living with someone	1	75	20	5	0	25	37	16	10	13	3
Married	2	94	4	1	0	37	28	19	9	7	2
Divorced, separated, or widowed, not living with someone	31	41	26	3	0	11	33	29	15	12	5
Divorced, separated, or widowed, living with someone	1	80	16	3	0	0	32	44	12	12	6

because it implies that one's sexual or romantic attraction is entirely a matter of personal choice. As you will see below, sexual orientation results from a complex interplay of biological and social factors not yet fully understood.

The most commonly found sexual orientation in all cultures, including the United States, is *heterosexuality,* a sexual or ro-mantic attraction for persons of the opposite sex (*hetero* comes from the Greek word meaning "other" or "different"). Heterosexuals in the United States are also sometimes referred to as "straight." It is important to bear in mind that although heterosexuality may be the prevailing norm in most cultures, it is not "normal" in the more fundamental sense that it is some-

TOTAL	SEX PARTNERS IN THE PAST 12 MONTHS				SEX PARTNERS SINCE AGE 18						MEDIAN NUMBER OF SEX PARTNERS SINCE AGE 18
	NONE	1	2–4	5+	NONE	1	2–4	5–10	11–20	21+	
Less than high school degree	16%	67%	15%	3%	4%	27%	36%	19%	9%	6%	3
High school degree or equivalent	11	74	13	3	3	30	29	20	10	7	3
Some college or vocational school	11	71	14	4	2	24	29	23	12	9	4
College graduate	12	69	15	4	2	24	26	24	11	13	4
Advanced degree	13	74	10	3	4	25	26	23	10	13	4
No religion	11%	67%	17%	6%	3%	16%	29%	20%	16%	16%	5
Mainline Protestant	11	74	13	2	2	23	31	23	12	8	4
Conservative Protestant	13	70	14	3	3	30	30	20	10	7	3
Catholic	13	72	13	3	4	27	29	23	8	9	3
Jewish	4	78	15	4	0	24	13	30	17	17	6
Other religion	15	63	15	6	3	42	20	16	8	13	3
White	12%	73%	12%	3%	3%	26%	29%	22%	11%	9%	3
Black	13	60	21	6	2	18	34	24	11	11	4
Hispanic	11	70	17	3	3	36	27	17	8	9	2
Asian	15	77	8	0	6	46	25	14	6	3	1
Native American	12	76	10	2	5	28	35	23	5	5	3

SOURCE: Laumann et al., 1994.

how dictated by some universal moral or religious standard. Like all forms of behavior, heterosexual behavior is socially learned within a particular culture.

Homosexuality involves a sexual or romantic attraction for persons of one's own sex. Today, the term *gay* is used to refer to male homosexuals, *lesbian* for female homosexuals, and *bi* as a shorthand for *bisexuals,* people who experience sexual or romantic attraction for persons of either sex. (*Lesbian* derives from the name of the Greek island Lesbos, the birthplace of Sappho, the renowned ancient Greek poet who taught poetry to a devoted following of young women.) Although it is difficult to know for sure because of the stigma attached to homosexu-

ality, which may result in the underreporting of sexuality in demographic surveys, current estimates find that from 2 to 5 percent of all women and 3 to 10 percent of all men in the United States are homosexual or bisexual (Burr 1993; General Social Survey [GSS] 1997; Laumann et al. 1994).

The term *homosexual* was first used by the medical community in 1869 to characterize what was then regarded as a personality disorder. The American Psychiatric Association did not remove homosexuality from its list of mental illnesses until 1973 or from its highly influential *Diagnostic and Statistical Manual of Mental Disorders* (DSM) until 1980. These long-overdue steps were taken only after prolonged lobbying and

Sexuality and the Mass Media

What does it take to capture the imagination of the country? Information that surprises us. Information that comes from solid research and credible sources, and that bears on the way we live, our common humanity (or, more often, inhumanity), and our desire to know about how well we are doing as individuals, parents, partners, and citizens. That is why an article such as the one sociologist Diane Lye wrote on parenting gets picked up by reporters: It went beyond the intuitive and taught us something. It was news.

Lye found that there was a lower divorce rate among men who had sons. If the research had stopped there, the presumptive meaning likely would have been that men still prefer sons over daughters, and attachment to sons will keep them home. It would have been a story, but not one that hit most major newspapers in the country. But Lye went further. She had data to indicate that American men did not prefer sons over daughters, so she looked for other explanations. Her data allowed her to measure how much a father interacted with a child, and in what ways. She found that men interacted with sons more than with daughters—a fact she expected because men's traditional forms of leisure, spectator sports, and active participation in sports, might seem more appropriate for their sons than for their daughters. The next step: She decided to look at those fathers who broke the mold and did these activities with daughters and see what their rates of divorce were. She found that men who interacted with daughters in the same way as with sons also had lower divorce rates. She hypothesized that it is interaction that matters, and that men may feel they have fewer ways of interacting with a daughter, hence do less, and are thus less connected. If they do feel free to play with girl children in ways that are satisfying and comfortable, they will be equally attached to these children, creating an additional bond to support the marriage.

This finding was picked up by one reporter; again, wire services brought it to the attention of other newspapers and the story was repeated throughout the United States. It had a great deal of "play" in the various kinds of media (TV shows and magazine writers also crib from each other's stories) and showed an audience how children and sex role stereotypes about children might affect marital stability.

Pepper Schwartz

***

What does this tell us? That sociology not only needs to be the discoverer of truths and the corrector of politically expedient dogma or common myths, but it must be the framer of questions and the deliverer of memorable books and treatises of the journals and textbooks of academia. Right now, the common wisdom is skewing toward moral frames and explanations versus socioeconomic explanations, conflict theory, or cultural explanations. *** Television programs and magazine articles have interpreted romantic and sexual patterns of today as genetic and evolutionary strategies. *** Meanwhile, the public is buying millions of books by John Gray that tell us that men are from a different planet than women—and while sociologists feel that his assertions are easily torn apart, they do not choose a platform that reaches the same large audience that he does.

***

Why not? The answer to that involves, at least partly, the pretensions and customs of our discipline and, perhaps ironically, our ignorance about the way the world works. ***

In general, writing about contemporary issues as they unfold is akin to being an ambulance chaser in our profession—the word "popularizer" is not an accolade. ***

Yet, despite our attempts to ghettoize 95 percent of our work, journalists find us: Desperate for "fresh" information, they slog through our prose and latch on to our books and papers. They reduce research findings to two-minute segments and use us as talking heads in news clips or as part of their documentaries. ***

***

I am asking us to package our work and to have a purpose to our work—to put it in appropriate places, in language that is compelling, and to connect it to the important events of our day. ***

There is a huge emotional payoff in reaching the public with a sociological focus. I have had a couple of experiences where I felt that I was helping create a way of looking at things as well as supporting issues that meant a lot to me with evidence I believed in. I have worked as a journalist almost as much as I have worked as a sociologist. I have been on television in the Northwest for eighteen years in various capacities—as a "relationship expert," commentator, and as on-air support for news events. I write a column with sociologist Janet Lever for *Glamour* where each month 9 to 11 million women read what we feel is interesting and important about sex and health. In our two-page column, among other things, we comb books and the research literature looking for solid information for information-hungry readers. I have done this for several other media outlets as well—the most influential of which has been the *New York Times*—and I have found our journals crammed with good research upon which I could build a thesis and an article. I have also been an expert witness in a number of trials, the

most satisfying of which have been trials involving custody cases, the right to serve in the army, and the right to marriage for gay men and lesbians. Much of the data that I used in my testimony was part of a study conducted in the late 1970s and early 1980s with my dear friend and colleague, Philip Blumstein, now deceased from AIDS. ***

Was I the only one with this kind of information? No. But my work was still in the public eye because the book Phil and I wrote, *American Couples,* was published as a trade book, had been heavily promoted, and sold well. It had reached a number of publics, remained in the collective memory, not to mention Nexus and several rolodexes, and therefore was able to be put to good use. In the end, I felt that our ten years of work counted for something.

*** If we continue to ignore the media, we can be sure that others will claim their attentions. But I believe that we need to vie for their affections. I would like us to be good citizens as well as good scholars and enter—and be powerful in—the debates and policies of our time.

***

SOURCE: Pepper Schwartz, "Stage Fright or Death Wish: Sociology in the Mass Media," *Contemporary Sociology*, 27, no. 5 (September 1998): pp. 439–45.

PEPPER SCHWARTZ is Professor of Sociology at the University of Washington in Seattle. She is the author of fourteen books, including The Gender of Sexuality, Finding Your Perfect Match, The Great Sex Weekend, The Lifetime Love and Sex Quiz Book, American Couples *and* Everything You Know about Love and Sex is Wrong. *She is the past president of the Society for the Scientific Study of Sexuality, past president of the Pacific Sociological Association, and the 2005 recipient of the American Sociological Association's award for the Public Understanding of Sociology. She is currently the relationship expert for Perfectmatch.com and a columnist for* Seattle Metropolitan *magazine, among others. In the past she has been the sex and health columnist for* Glamour *magazine and for* American Baby *magazine. She lectures nationally and internationally on relationship issues, women's issues, parent and child issues, communication between men and women, and maintaining personal and family well-being in the modern world.*

pressure by homosexual rights organizations. The medical community was belatedly forced to acknowledge that no scientific research had ever found homosexuals as a group to be psychologically unhealthier than heterosexuals (Burr 1993).

In some cultures, same-sex relationships are the norm in certain contexts and do not necessarily signify what today is termed *homosexuality*. For example, the anthropologist Gilbert Herdt (1981, 1984, 1986) reported that among more than twenty tribes that he studied in Melanesia and New Guinea, ritually prescribed same-sex encounters among young men and boys were regarded as necessary for subsequent masculine virility (Herdt and Davidson 1988). Ritualized male–male sexual encounters also occurred among the Azande of Africa's Sudan and Congo (Evans-Pritchard 1970), Japanese samurai warriors in the nineteenth century (Leupp 1995), and highly educated Greek men and boys at the time of Plato (Rouselle 1999).

IS SEXUAL ORIENTATION INBORN OR LEARNED?

Most sociologists currently believe that sexual orientation—whether homosexual, heterosexual, or something else—results from a complex interplay among biological factors and social learning. Since heterosexuality is the norm for most people in U.S. culture, a great deal of research has focused on why some people become homosexual. Some scholars argue that biological influences are the most important, predisposing certain people to become homosexual from birth (Bell et al. 1981; Green 1987). Biological explanations for homosexuality have included differences in such things as brain characteristics of homosexuals (LeVay 1996; Maugh and Zamichow 1991) and the effect on fetal development of the mother's in utero hormone production during pregnancy (Blanchard and Bogaert 1996; Manning et al. 1997; McFadden and Champlin 2000). Such studies, which are based on small numbers of cases, give highly inconclusive (and highly controversial) results (Healy 2001). It is virtually impossible to separate biological from early social influences in determining a person's sexual orientation.

Studies of twins hold some promise for understanding if there is any genetic basis for homosexuality, since identical twins share identical genes. In two related studies, Bailey and Pillard (1991, 1993) examined 167 pairs of brothers and 143 pairs of sisters, with each pair of siblings raised in the same family, in which at least one sibling defined himself or herself as homosexual. Some of these pairs were identical twins (who share all genes), some were fraternal twins (who share some genes), and some were adoptive brothers or sisters (who share no genes). The researchers reasoned that if sexual orientation is determined entirely by biology, then all of the identical twins should be homosexual, since their genetic makeup is identical. Among the fraternal twins, some pairs would be homosexual, since

some genes are shared. The lowest rates of homosexuality were predicted for the adoptive brothers and sisters.

The results of this study seem to show that homosexuality, like heterosexuality, results from a combination of biological and social factors. Among both the men and the women studied, roughly one out of every two identical twins was homosexual, compared with one out of every five fraternal twins, and one out of every ten adoptive brothers and sisters (Bailey and Pillard 1991, 1993; see also Burr 1993; Maugh 1991, 1993). In other words, a woman or man is five times as likely to be lesbian or gay if her or his identical twin is lesbian or gay than if his or her sibling is lesbian or gay but related only through adoption. These results offer some support for the importance of biological factors, since the higher the percentage of shared genes, the greater the percentage of cases in which both siblings were homosexual. However, because approximately half of the identical twin brothers and sisters of homosexuals were not themselves homosexual, a great deal of social learning must also be involved; otherwise one would expect *all* identical twin siblings of homosexuals to be homosexual as well.

Its clear that even studies of identical twins cannot fully isolate biological from social factors. It is often the case that even in infancy, identical twins are treated more like one another by parents, peers, and teachers than are fraternal twins, who in turn are treated more like one another than are adoptive siblings. Thus identical twins may have more than genes in common: They may share a higher proportion of similar socializing experiences as well.

HOMOPHOBIA

Homosexuality has long been stigmatized in the United States. **Homophobia,** a term coined in the late 1960s, refers to an aversion or hatred of homosexuals and their lifestyles, along with behavior based on such aversion. It is a form of prejudice that is reflected not only in overt acts of hostility and violence toward lesbians and gays, but also in various forms of verbal abuse that are widespread in American culture: for example, using terms like *fag* or *homo* to insult heterosexual males, or using female-related offensive terms such as *sissy* or *pansy* to put down gay men.

One recent study of homophobia in U.S. schools concluded that the estimated two million lesbian, gay, and bisexual middle and high school students are frequently the targets of humiliating harassment and sometimes physical abuse. *Hatred in the Hallways,* which was based on interviews with lesbian, gay, and bisexual students as well as youth service providers, teachers, administrators, counselors, and parents in seven states, found harassment to be a common and painful experience among lesbian, gay, and bisexual students (Bochenek and Brown 2001). One gay student reported, "That's how you pick on someone, straight or gay. You call them a fag. I hear it a lot of times during the course of the day, a lot, at the very least ten to twenty times a day." A lesbian student reported getting threatening telephone calls at home, making her "hate every minute of school." The study cited a CBS poll reporting that a third of eleventh-grade students knew about incidents of sexual harassment of gays and lesbians, while more than a quarter admitted to engaging in harassment.

The study also found that verbal abuse often escalated into physical abuse. In one well-publicized incident, an openly gay Wisconsin student was verbally humiliated, spat and urinated on, hit, subjected to a mock rape conducted by classmates in a science lab, and finally brutally beaten and seriously injured. When he complained to the school principal after the mock rape, she reportedly told him that "boys will be boys" and that his open gayness was causing the problem (Bochenek and Brown 2001). This unhappy student twice attempted suicide—a tragically common occurrence because lesbian, gay, and bisexual youths are at a four times greater risk for suicide than their straight peers (Gibson 1989). Yet the vast majority of victims of antilesbian/gay violence never report the incident, for fear of being "outed" (New York City Gay and Lesbian Anti-Violence Project 1996).

Such homophobia is widespread in U.S. culture: According to public opinion polls, three out of five Americans report believing that homosexuality is "morally wrong" (Gallup 1998). Until 2003, when the Supreme Court ruled in *Lawrence v. Texas* that the state of Texas's prohibition on homosexual sex was a violation of the constitutional right to privacy, in many states homosexuality was still a legally punishable crime.

THE MOVEMENT FOR GAY AND LESBIAN CIVIL RIGHTS

Until recently, most gays and lesbians hid their sexual orientation, for fear that coming out of the closet would cost them their jobs, families, and friends and leave them open to verbal and physical abuse. Yet, since the late 1960s, many gays and lesbians have acknowledged their homosexuality openly, and in some cities the lives of lesbian and gay Americans has to a large extent been normalized (Seidman et al. 1999). New York City, San Francisco, London, and other large metropolitan areas around the world have thriving gay and lesbian communities. Coming out may be important not only for the person who does so but for others in the larger society: Previously closeted lesbians and gays come to realize they are not alone, while heterosexuals are forced to recognize that people whom they have admired and respected are homosexual.

The current global wave of gay and lesbian civil rights movements began partly as an outgrowth of the U.S. social movements of the 1960s, which emphasized pride in racial and

The Stonewall Inn nightclub raid is regarded as the first shot fired in the battle for gay rights in the United States. The twenty-fifth anniversary of the event was commemorated in New York City with a variety of celebrations as well as discussions on the evolution and future of gay rights.

ethnic identity. One pivotal event was the Stonewall riots in June 1969, when New York City's gay community—angered by continual police harassment—fought the New York Police Department for two days, a public action that for most people (gay or not) was practically unthinkable (D'Emilio 1983; Weeks 1977). The Stonewall riots became a symbol of gay pride, heralding the coming out of gays and lesbians, who insisted not only on equal treatment under the law but also on a complete end to the stigmatization their lifestyle. In 1994, on the twenty-fifth anniversary of the Stonewall riots, one hundred thousand people attended the International March on the United Nations to Affirm the Human Rights of Lesbian and Gay People. It is clear that significant strides have been made, although discrimination and outright homophobia remain serious problems for many lesbian, gay, and bisexual Americans.

There are enormous differences among countries in the degree to which homosexuality is legally punishable. Sixty-eight countries still outlaw sex between males, and twenty-six outlaw sex between women. In Africa, for example, male homosexual acts have been legalized in only a handful of countries, whereas female homosexuality is seldom mentioned in the law at all. In South Africa, the official policy of the former white government was to regard homosexuality as a psychiatric problem that threatened national security. Once it took power, however, the black government legislated full equality. In Asia and the Middle East, the situation is similar: Male homosexuality is banned in the vast majority of countries, including all those that are predominantly Islamic. On the other hand, Europe has some of the most liberal laws in the world: Homosexuality has been legalized in nearly all countries, and Denmark legally recognizes same-sex marriages.

Today there is a growing movement around the world for the civil rights of gays and lesbians. The International Lesbian and Gay Association (2005), which was founded in 1978, today has more than 450 member organizations in some ninety countries. It holds international conferences, supports lesbian and gay social movement organizations around the world, and lobbies international organizations. For example, it convinced the Council of Europe to require all of its member nations to repeal laws banning homosexuality. In general, active lesbian and gay social movements tend to thrive in countries that emphasize individual rights and liberal state policies (Frank and McEneaney 1999).

Sexuality and Procreative Technology

As with most of the topics in this chapter, the concept of "the socialization of nature" applies to a better sociological understanding of sexual behavior. An example is human reproduction. For hundreds of years, the lives of most women were dominated by childbirth and child rearing. In premodern times, contraception was ineffective or, in some societies, unknown. Even in Europe and the United States as late as the eighteenth century, it was common for women to experience as many as twenty pregnancies (often involving miscarriages and infant deaths). Improved methods of contraception have helped alter this situation in a fundamental way. Far from any longer being natural, it is almost unknown in the industrial countries for women to undergo so many pregnancies. Advances in contraceptive technology enable most women and men to control whether and when they choose to have children.

Contraception is only one example of a **procreative technology.** Some of the other areas in which natural processes have become social are described below.

CHILDBIRTH

Medical science has not always been involved with the major life transitions from birth to death. The medicalization of pregnancy and childbirth developed slowly, as local physicians and midwives were displaced by obstetric specialists. Today in industrialized societies, most births occur in a hospital with the help of a specialized medical team.

In the past, new parents had to wait until the day of birth to learn the sex of their baby and whether it would be healthy. Today, prenatal tests such as the sonogram (an image of the fetus produced by using ultrasonic waves) and amniocentesis (which draws off some of the amniotic fluid from around the fetus) can be used to discover structural or chromosomal ab-

normalities before birth. Such new technology presents couples and society with new ethical and legal decisions. When a disorder is detected, the couple is faced with the decision of whether or not to have the baby, knowing it may be seriously handicapped.

GENETIC ENGINEERING: DESIGNER BABIES

A great deal of scientific endeavor these days is being devoted to the expansion of genetic engineering—that is, intervening in the genetic makeup of the fetus so as to influence its subsequent development. The likely social effect of genetic engineering is starting to provoke debates almost as intense as those that surround the issue of abortion. According to its supporters, genetic engineering will bring us many benefits. It is possible, for example, to identify the genetic factors that make some people vulnerable to certain diseases. Genetic reprogramming will ensure that these illnesses are no longer passed on from generation to generation. It will be possible to "design" our bodies before birth in terms of skin color, color of hair and eyes, weight, and so forth.

There could be no better example of the mixture of opportunities and problems that the increasing socialization of nature creates for us. What choices will parents make if they can design their babies, and what limits should be placed on those choices? Genetic engineering is unlikely to be cheap. Will this mean that those who can afford to pay will be able to program out from their children any traits they see as socially undesirable? What will happen to the children of more deprived groups, who will continue to be born naturally?

Some sociologists have argued that differential access to genetic engineering might lead to the emergence of a "biological underclass." Those who don't have the physical advantages genetic engineering can bring might be subject to prejudice and discrimination by those who do enjoy these advantages. They might have difficulty finding employment and life or health insurance (Duster 1990).

THE ABORTION DEBATE

The most controversial ethical dilemma created by modern reproductive technologies in modern societies is this: Under what conditions should abortion be available to women? The abortion debate has become so intense precisely because it centers on basic ethical issues to which there are no easy solutions. Those who are "pro-life" believe that abortion is always wrong except in extreme circumstances, because it is equivalent to murder. For them, ethical issues are above all subject to the value that must be placed on human life. Those who are "pro-choice" argue that the mother's control over her own body—her own right to live a rewarding life—must be the primary consideration.

The debate has led to numerous episodes of violence. Can it ever be resolved? At least one prominent social and legal theorist, Ronald Dworkin (1993), has suggested that it can. The intense divisions between those who are prolife and those who are prochoice, he argues, hide deeper sources of agreement between the two sides, and in this there is a source of hope. At previous periods of history, life was often relatively cheap. In current times, however, we have come to place a high value on the sanctity of human life. Each side agrees with this value, but they interpret it differently, the one emphasizing the interests of the child, the other the interests of the mother. If the two sides can be persuaded that they share a common ethical value, Dworkin suggests, a more constructive dialogue may be possible.

Study Outline

www.wwnorton.com/giddens

The Sociology of the Body

- The field of the *sociology of the body* studies how the social world affects our bodies and is particularly concerned with processes of social change. Modern *social technologies* have managed, for instance, to separate the body from nature; an example is the notion of dieting, which involves planned interventions in the functioning of our bodies to modify or regulate them in various ways.
- Food production in the modern world has been globalized: Technologies of transportation and of storage (refrigeration) have meant that now everyone in the developed world is on a diet in some sense, having to *decide* what to eat every day. Such decisions are influenced by social relations. Women especially are judged by physical appearance, but feelings of shame about the body can lead anyone to compulsive dieting, exercising, or bodybuilding to make the body conform to social expectations.

The Experience of Health and Illness

- Sociologists are interested in the experience of illness—how being sick, chronically ill, or disabled is experienced by the sick person and by those nearby. The idea of the *sick role,* developed by Talcott Parsons, suggests that a sick person adopts certain forms of behavior to minimize the disruptive effect of illness. A sick individual is granted certain privileges, such as the right to withdraw from normal responsibilities, but in return must work actively to regain health by agreeing to follow medical advice.
- Symbolic interactionists have investigated how people cope with disease and chronic illness in their daily lives. The experience of illness can provoke changes in individuals' self-identity and in their daily routines. This dimension of the sociology of the body is becoming increasingly relevant for many societies; people are now living longer than ever before and tend to suffer more from chronic debilitating conditions than from acute illnesses.

Social Factors and Disease

- Health and illness are connected to population issues as well as being strongly affected by social factors such as class, race, and gender. Modern Western medicine, which arose in the past two or three centuries, views illness as having physical origins and hence as being explicable in scientific terms. In spite of modern medicine's importance, public health measures, such as better sanitation and nutrition, were more important in reducing infant mortality rates.
- The expansion of the West was accompanied by the spread of infectious diseases in what is now the developing world. Moreover, the colonial system, with its stress on cash crops, negatively affected the nutrition of developing-world people.

Status and Illness

- Susceptibility to the major illnesses is strongly influenced by socioeconomic status. For example, people in the industrialized world tend to live longer than those in the developing world; the richer tend to be healthier, taller, and stronger than those from less privileged backgrounds.

Human Sexuality

- Researchers have examined both biological and cultural influences on human sexual behavior, concluding that sexuality, like gender, is mostly socially constructed. There is an extremely wide range of possible sexual practices, but in any given society only some will be approved and reflected in social norms. Because these norms also vary widely, however, we can be quite certain that most sexual responses are learned rather than innate.

Key Concepts

biomedical model of health (p. 586)
epidemiology (p. 586)

homophobia (p. 604)
procreative technology (p. 606)
sick role (p. 582)
socialization of nature (p. 582)
social technology (p. 579)
sociology of the body (p. 578)
stigma (p. 583)

Review Questions

1. What are the "social technologies of the body"?
   a. the contents of the bathroom medicine cabinet
   b. any kind of regular intervention we make into the functioning of our bodies in order to alter them in specific ways
   c. anything we use to adorn our bodies, such as glasses, watches, and jewelry
   d. the increasing use of such devices as cell phones, pagers, and handheld computing devices that make it possible for people to communicate over large distances

2. Which of the following diseases was transmitted to other parts of the world as a result of the expansion of the West in the colonial era?
   a. smallpox
   b. measles
   c. typhus
   d. All of the above

3. Which of the following statements is true?
   a. About 95 percent of U.S. college women say that they want to lose weight.
   b. About 80 percent of U.S. college men say that they want to lose weight.
   c. About 50 percent of U.S. college women suffer serious problems with an eating disorder at some point in their college careers.
   d. About 50 percent of U.S. college men are on diets.

4. According to Talcott Parsons, which of the following is one of the three pillars of the sick role?
   a. The sick person is personally responsible for being sick.
   b. The sick person is not entitled to withdrawal from normal responsibilities.
   c. The patient should work to regain health by exercising and dieting.
   d. The sick person should consult a medical expert.

5. According to a recent study, how many lesbian, gay, and bisexual middle and high school students are frequently the targets of humiliating harassment, and sometimes physical abuse?
   a. a quarter million
   b. half a million
   c. one million
   d. two million

6. According to Frand and McEneancy, active lesbian and gay social movements tend to thrive in countries that emphasize

   a. polygamy.
   b. individual rights and liberal state policies.
   c. socialism.
   d. globalization.

7. According to Richard Wilkinson, the healthiest societies in the world are located in
   a. the richest countries.
   b. countries in which income is distributed most evenly.
   c. countries in which levels of social integration are lowest.
   d. the United States.

8. Kinsey's findings from the 1940s and 1950s showed Americans to be much more liberal about sexuality than Laumann's findings from the 1990s. What best explains the differences in their results?
   a. Sexually transmitted disease has made Americans much more cautious about whom they have sex with.
   b. In the 1930s and 1940s people were much more prudish when asked about sex than they are today, but much more experimental in private. Today people are much more open when talking about sex, but much more conservative in what they are actually prepared to engage in.
   c. XXX-rated videos—nowadays everyone's seen it all, and figured out that much of it is not for them.
   d. Differences in methodology—Kinsey went looking for people he felt would talk about sexuality, whereas Laumann based his study on survey data from a national study.

9. According to statistics released during the 1998 World AIDS Conference, 90 percent of those with HIV live in developing nations, with the vast majority living in
   a. Africa.
   b. America.
   c. Asia.
   d. Europe.

10. Which of the following statements is true about the decline of death rates before the twentieth century?
    a. Medical innovation was the most important factor in bringing down death rates.
    b. Effective sanitation, better nutrition, control of sewage, and improved hygiene were the most important factors in bringing down death rates.
    c. Both a and b are true.
    d. Immunization and antibiotics were the most important factors in bringing down death rates.

Thinking Sociologically Exercises

1. Statistical studies of our national health persistently show a gap in life expectancies between the rich and the poor. Review all the major factors that would explain why rich people on average live about eight years longer than poor people.

2. This text discusses the biological and sociocultural factors associated with sexual orientation. Why are twin studies the most promising type of research on the genetic basis of sexual orientation? Briefly summarize the analysis of these studies and show whether it presently appears that sexual orientation results from genetic differences and/or sociocultural practices and experiences.

Data Exercises

www.wwnorton.com/giddens
Keyword: Data18

This chapter addressed many issues related to health and human sexuality. Without question, these two topics come together in discussing the contemporary HIV/AIDS pandemic. In this chapter you learned that those nations that are most disadvantaged economically are the very nations that have been hardest hit by HIV/AIDS. This exercise will give you a chance to learn more about those countries and how they are coping with the enormous consequences of the disease.

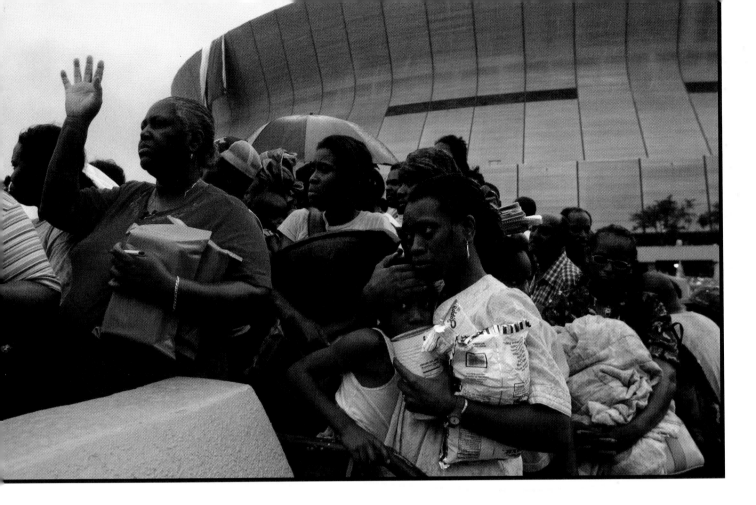

Living in Cities

Learn how cities have changed as a result of industrialization and urbanization.

Theories of Urbanism

Learn how theories of urbanism have placed increasing emphasis on the influence of socioeconomic factors on city life.

Urbanism in the United States

Learn about the recent key developments affecting American cities in the last several decades: suburbanization, urban decay, and gentrification.

Cities and Globalization

See that global economic competition has a profound impact on urbanization and urban life.

Urbanization in the Developing World

Recognize the challenges of urbanization in the developing world.

World Population Growth

Learn why the world population has increased dramatically and understand the main consequences of this growth.

Population Growth and the Environment

See that the environment is a sociological issue related to urbanization and population growth.

CHAPTER NINETEEN

URBANIZATION, POPULATION, AND THE ENVIRONMENT

O n August 29, 2005, Hurricane Katrina made landfall along the central Gulf Coast. The category-three storm was one of the strongest Atlantic hurricanes ever recorded, and it devastated the coastal towns and cities in Louisiana, Mississippi, and Alabama. In addition to wiping out many of the small communities in rural areas, the storm surge broke through the levees protecting New Orleans, which is below sea level, and flooded most of the city. Those who had vehicles or the resources to evacuate escaped the storm. However, thousands of people, mostly poor and black, were trapped in the city huddled on their roofs, in their attics, or in public facilities like the Louisiana SuperDome, which housed thousands of evacuees. Most of the survivors who remained in New Orleans waited days in dangerous conditions with little food or water until they could be evacuated to temporary housing in nearby cities and states. Hurricane Katrina displaced the entire population of New Orleans—approximately 1.5 million people, caused approximately $75 billion in damage, and took the lives of approximately 1,400 people.

As the effect of Hurricane Katrina on New Orleans recently demonstrated, cities continue to provide sociologists with a laboratory for studying the diversity of social life and conflict. As Americans watched the victims of Hurricane Katrina on their television screens, it became apparent that while an entire city was affected, some people were hurt much more than others. The extreme ghettoized poverty in New Orleans has long been recognized as among the worst in the United States, and for sociologists there was nothing surprising when the most vulnerable citizens were the most deeply hurt. Indeed, it is impossible to understand what went on in the United States in the aftermath of that disaster without a full consideration of urban sociology.

Cities are the capitals of civilization: They are culturally lively, commercially dynamic, and alluring. They are efficient in providing for a large number of the population in a small amount of space. However, an entire literature has been devoted to the problems of city life, including poverty, racial and ethnic exclusion and antagonism, and crime. In all modern societies, in contrast to the premodern era, most of the population live in urban areas, and even those who don't are affected by city life. In this chapter, we first of all study the origins of cities and the vast growth in the numbers of city dwellers that has occurred over the past century. From there, we review the most influential theories of urban life. We then move on to consider patterns of urban development in North America compared with cities in the developing world. Cities in the developing world are growing at an enormous rate. We consider why this is happening and at the same time look at changes now taking place in world population patterns. We conclude by assessing the connections among urbanization, world population growth, and environmental problems.

Traffic outside of the Bank of England in the financial district of London in 1896. In only one century, the population of London grew from over one million people to over seven million.

Living in Cities

Cities in Traditional Societies

The world's first cities appeared about 3500 B.C.E., in the river valleys of the Nile in Egypt, the Tigris and Euphrates in what is now Iraq, and the Indus in what is today Pakistan. Cities in traditional societies were very small by modern standards. Babylon, for example, one of the largest ancient Near Eastern cities, extended over an area of only 3.2 square miles and at its height, around 2000 B.C.E., probably numbered no more than fifteen to twenty thousand people. Rome under Emperor Augustus in the first century B.C.E. was easily the largest premodern city outside China, with some three hundred thousand inhabitants —the population of Birmingham, Alabama, or Tucson, Arizona, today.

Most cities of the ancient world shared certain features. They were usually surrounded by walls that served as a military defense and emphasized the separation of the urban community from the countryside. The central area of the city was almost always occupied by a religious temple, a royal palace, government and commercial buildings, and a public square. This ceremonial, commercial, and political center was some-

times enclosed within a second, inner wall and was usually too small to hold more than a minority of the citizens. Although it usually contained a market, the center was different from the business districts found at the core of modern cities, because the main buildings were nearly always religious and political (Fox 1964; Sjoberg 1960, 1963; Wheatley 1971).

The dwellings of the ruling class or elite tended to be concentrated in or near the center. The less privileged groups lived toward the perimeter of the city or outside the walls, moving inside if the city came under attack. Different ethnic and religious communities were often allocated to separate neighborhoods, where their members both lived and worked. Sometimes these neighborhoods were also surrounded by walls. Communication among city dwellers was erratic. Lacking any form of printing press, public officials had to shout at the tops of their voices to deliver pronouncements. "Streets" were usually strips of land on which no one had yet built. A few traditional civilizations boasted sophisticated road systems linking various cities, but these existed mainly for military purposes, and transportation for the most part was slow and limited. Merchants and soldiers were the only people who regularly traveled over long distances.

Although cities were the main centers for science, the arts, and cosmopolitan culture, their influence over the rest of the country was always weak. No more than a tiny proportion of the population lived in the cities, and the division between cities and countryside was pronounced. By far the majority of people lived in small rural communities and rarely came into contact with more than the occasional state official or merchant from the towns.

Industrialization and Urbanization

The contrast in size between the largest modern cities and those of premodern civilizations is extraordinary. The most populous cities in the industrialized countries number over twenty-six million inhabitants. A **conurbation**—a cluster of cities and towns forming a continuous network—may include even larger numbers of people. The peak of urban life today is represented by what is called the **megalopolis,** the "city of cities." The term was originally coined in ancient Greece to refer to a city-state that was planned to be the envy of all civilizations. The current megalopolis, though, bears little relation to that utopia. The term was first applied in modern times to refer to the Northeast Corridor of the United States, an area covering some 450 miles from north of Boston to south of Washington, D.C. In this region, about forty million people live at a density of over seven hundred persons per square mile. An urban population almost as large and dense is concentrated in the lower Great Lakes region.

Britain was the first society to undergo industrialization, beginning in the mid-eighteenth century. The process of industrialization generated increasing **urbanization**—the movement of the population into towns and cities, away from the land. In 1800, fewer than 20 percent of the British population lived in towns or cities with more than 10,000 inhabitants. By 1900, this proportion had risen to 74 percent. London held about 1.1 million people in 1800; by the beginning of the twentieth century, it had increased in size to a population of over 7 million, at that date the largest city ever seen in the world. It was a vast manufacturing, commercial, and financial center at the heart of the still-expanding British Empire.

The urbanization of most other European countries and the United States took place somewhat later. In 1800, the United States was more of a rural society than were the leading European countries. Fewer than 10 percent of Americans lived in communities with populations of more than 2,500 people. Today, well over three quarters of Americans are city dwellers. Between 1800 and 1900, as industrialization grew in the United States, the population of New York City leapt from 60,000 people to 4.8 million.

Urbanization in the twenty-first century is a global process, into which the developing world is being drawn more and more (Kasarda and Crenshaw 1991). From 1900 to 1950, world urbanization increased by 239 percent, compared with a global population growth of 49 percent. The past fifty plus years have seen a greater acceleration in the proportion of people living in cities. From 1950 to 1986, urban growth worldwide was 320 percent, while the population grew by 54 percent. Most of this growth has occurred in cities in developing world societies. In 1975, 39 percent of the world's population lived in urban areas; the figure was around 50 percent in 2000 and is predicted to be 63 percent in 2025. Eastern and southern Asia will be home to about half of the world's people in 2025. By that date, the urban populations of the developing countries will exceed those of Europe or the United States.

Along with this worldwide urbanization come the effects of globalization. For example, the rise of urban-industrial areas in developing countries has brought intensified economic competition to industries in U.S. cities. South Korea's shoe industry has led to the impoverishment of urban areas in Massachusetts that formerly relied on that industry for their prosperity. Similarly, Baltimore has had to adjust to losing much of the market for its steel industry to Japan. We will examine later in the chapter how the global economy has influenced forms of city life in recent years.

Theories of Urbanism

The Chicago School

A number of writers associated with the University of Chicago from the 1920s to the 1940s—especially Robert Park, Ernest Burgess, and Louis Wirth—developed ideas that were for many years the chief basis of theory and research in urban sociology. Two concepts developed by the "Chicago School" are worthy of special attention. One is the so-called **ecological approach** to urban analysis; the other, the characterization of urbanism as a *way of life,* developed by Wirth (Park 1952; Wirth 1938). It is important to understand these ideas as they were initially conceived by the Chicago School and to see how they have been revised and even supplanted by later sociologists.

URBAN ECOLOGY

Ecology is a term taken from a physical science: the study of the adaptation of plant and animal organisms to their environment. In the natural world, organisms tend to be distributed in systematic ways over the terrain, such that a balance or equilibrium between different species is achieved. The Chicago School believed that the siting of major urban settlements and the distribution of different types of neighborhoods within them can be understood in terms of similar principles. Cities do not grow up at random but grow in response to advantageous features of the environment. For example, large urban areas in modern societies tend to develop along the shores of rivers, in fertile plains, or at the intersection of trading routes or railways.

"Once set up," in Park's (1952) words, "a city is, it seems, a great sorting mechanism which . . . infallibly selects out of the population as a whole the individuals best suited to live in a particular region or a particular milieu." Cities become ordered into "natural areas," through processes of competition, invasion, and succession—all of which occur in biological ecology. If we look at the ecology of a lake in the natural environment, we find that competition among various species of fish, insects, and other organisms operates to reach a fairly stable distribution among them. This balance is disturbed if new species invade—try to make the lake their home. Some of the organisms that used to proliferate in the central area of the lake are driven out to eke out a more precarious existence around its fringes. The invading species are their successors in the central sections.

Patterns of location, movement, and relocation in cities, according to the ecological view, have a similar form. Different neighborhoods develop through the adjustments made by inhabitants as they struggle to gain their livelihoods. A city can be pictured as a map of areas with distinct and contrasting social characteristics. Cities can be seen as formed in concentric rings, broken up into segments. In the center are the **inner-city** areas, a mixture of big business prosperity and decaying private houses. Beyond these are older established neighborhoods, housing workers employed in stable manual occupations. Further out still are the suburbs in which higher-income groups tend to live. Processes of invasion and succession occur within the segments of the concentric rings. Thus as property decays in a central or near-central area, ethnic minority groups might start to move into it. As they do so, more of the preexisting population start to leave, precipitating a wholesale flight to neighborhoods elsewhere in the city or out to the suburbs.

Another aspect of the **urban ecology** approach emphasized the *interdependence* of different city areas. *Differentiation*—the specialization of groups and occupational roles—is the main way in which human beings adapt to their environment. Groups on which many others depend will have a dominant role, often reflected in their central geographical position. Business groups, for example, such as large banks or insurance companies, provide key services for many in a community and hence are usually to be found in the central areas of settlements (Hawley 1950, 1968).

Part of what it means to think like an urban sociologist today is to ask whether and how the conditions observed in cities are socially constructed or natural. We have seen that the early Chicago School leaned toward the idea that spatial patterns were natural outcomes. This all began to change when two black graduate students at the University of Chicago published the book *Black Metropolis* (Drake and Cayton 1945), which posed a challenge to the human-ecology framework.

Drake and Cayton's massive study, based on extensive historical and ethnographic data, showed that the black residential neighborhoods of Chicago were by no means the result of natural forces, but were constructed by unnatural, social forces. These areas were called *ghettos,* a term that has come to mean many things to many people but that can be most usefully defined as a residential area where a racial or ethnic group initially comes to live as a consequence of systematic exclusion from more desirable places. Drake and Cayton showed that the ghetto was not in such a poor state because the people living there were black, but because blacks were given no choice but to live in the worst areas of the city. There was nothing natural about this placement and it would not have occurred if not for social forces such as exclusion, violence, and restrictive covenants where neighborhood "improvement" associations passed laws making it illegal to sell land in a community to blacks. After Drake and Cayton's *Black Metropolis,* it was harder for sociologists to think of the distributions of populations in urban areas as natural.

URBANISM AS A WAY OF LIFE

Wirth's thesis of **urbanism** as a *way of life* (1938) is concerned less with whether cities are natural or socially constructed than with what urbanism *is* as a form of social existence. Urbanism is related to the focus, identified earlier in this chapter, with how life in cities is distinctive or different from life elsewhere. Wirth also asserted that the effects of life in cities can be felt outside of cities as well. For example, have you ever noticed that many young people today dress in garments that were once thought to be distinctive to urban minority youth? It is not uncommon to find some teenagers in suburban high schools all over America dressing in baggy pants, untucked T-shirts, and hightop sneakers. If Wirth were writing today he might cite this as an example for his claim that the cultural life that begins in cities draws in the outerlying population, so that urbanism is "a way of life" in many places outside cities as well.

Wirth's theory is important for its recognition that urbanism is not just *part* of a society but expresses and influences the nature of the wider social system. Aspects of the urban way of life are characteristic of social life in modern societies as a whole, not just the activities of those who happen to live in big cities.

But another aspect to Wirth's argument focused more on an aspect of life that he did think was distinctive to cities. In cities, Wirth points out, large numbers of people live in close proximity to each other, without knowing most others personally—a fundamental contrast to small, traditional villages. Most contacts between city dwellers are fleeting and partial and are means to other ends rather than being satisfying relationships in themselves. Interactions with sales clerks in stores, cashiers in banks, passengers or ticket collectors on trains are passing encounters, entered into not for their own sake but as means to other aims.

Because those who live in urban areas tend to be highly mobile, there are relatively weak bonds between them. People are involved in many different activities and situations each day—the pace of life is faster than in rural areas. Competition prevails over cooperation. Wirth accepts that the density of social life in cities leads to the formation of neighborhoods having distinct characteristics, some of which may preserve the characteristics of small communities. In immigrant areas, for example, traditional types of connections between families are found, with most people knowing most others on a personal basis. The more such areas are absorbed into wider patterns of city life, however, the less these characteristics survive.

Wirth was among the first to address the "urban interaction problem" (Duneier and Molotch 1999), the necessity for city dwellers to respect social boundaries when so many people are in close physical proximity all the time. Wirth elaborates that "the reserve, the indifference, and the blasé outlook that urbanites manifest in their relationships may thus be regarded as devices for immunizing themselves against the personal claims and expectations of others." Many people walk down the street in cities acting unconcerned about the others near them. Through such appearance of apathy they can avoid unwanted transgression of social boundaries.

Wirth's ideas have deservedly enjoyed **wide** currency. The impersonality of many day-to-day contacts in modern cities is undeniable—but to some degree this is true of social life in general in modern societies. Although one might assume that the "immunization" urban dwellers engage in to distance themselves from others is unique to city life, urban interaction may be only a subtype of the universal social condition. While the presence of strangers is more common in cities (Lofland 1973, 1998), all people must manage social boundaries in their face-to-face interactions with others—as has been found as far afield as Western Samoa (Duranti 1994) or among the African Poro people (Bellman 1984). It is always necessary to ask whether the problems one associates with cities are aspects of social life more generally. In assessing Wirth's ideas, we must also ask whether his generalizations about urban life hold true for all cities during all times.

We should also consider that neighborhoods involving close kinship and personal ties seem often to be actively *created* by city life; they are not just remnants of a preexisting way of life that survive for a period within the city. Claude Fischer (1984) has put forward an interpretation of why large-scale urbanism tends actually to promote diverse subcultures, rather than swamping everyone within an anonymous mass. Those who live in cities, he points out, are able to collaborate with others of like background or interests to develop local connections; and they can join distinctive religious, ethnic, political, and other subcultural groups. A small town or village does not allow the development of such subcultural diversity. Those who form ethnic communities within cities, for instance, might have had little or no knowledge of one another in their land of origin. When they arrive in a new country, they gravitate to areas where others from a similar linguistic and cultural background are living, and new subcommunity structures are formed. An artist might find few others in a village or small town with whom to associate, but in a large city, on the other hand, he or she might become part of a significant artistic and intellectual subculture.

A large city is a world of strangers, yet it supports and creates personal relationships. This is not paradoxical. We have to separate urban experience into the public sphere of encounters with strangers and the more private world of family, friends, and work colleagues. It may be difficult to meet people when one first moves to a large city. But anyone moving to a small, established rural community may find the friendliness of the inhabitants largely a matter of public politeness—it may take years to become accepted. This is not the case in the city. Although one finds a diversity of strangers, each is a potential friend. And once within a group or network, the possibilities for expanding one's personal connections increase considerably.

Wirth's ideas retain some validity, but in the light of subsequent contributions it is clear that they are overgeneralized. Modern cities frequently involve impersonal, anonymous social relationships, but they are also sources of diversity—and, sometimes, intimacy.

The "urban interaction problem" is the necessity for city dwellers to respect social boundaries when so many people are in close physical proximity all the time. Whether listening to music on portable devices or reading magazines or newspapers, many people have strategies for distancing themselves and managing social boundaries in busy urban environments.

JANE JACOBS: "EYES AND EARS UPON THE STREET"

Like most sociologists in the twentieth century, the Chicago School researchers were professors who saw their mission as contributing to a scholarly literature and advancing the field of social science.

At certain moments in the history of sociology, however, advances have also come from thinkers working outside universities without formal training in sociology. One such person was Jane Jacobs, who published *The Death and Life of Great American Cities* in 1961.

Jacobs was an architecture critic with a high school education, but through her own independent reading and research in the 1950s, she transformed herself into one of the most learned figures in the emerging field of urban studies. She is known as a public intellectual, because her main goal was to speak to the educated public, rather than to contribute to a scholarly literature. Nevertheless, her work has had an impact on scholarship in sociology as well.

Like sociologists such as Wirth of the Chicago School before her, Jacobs noted that "cities are, by definition, full of strangers," some of whom are dangerous. She tried to explain what makes it possible for cities to meet the challenge of "assimilating strangers" in such a way that strangers can feel comfortable together. She argued that cities are most habitable when they feature a diversity of uses, thereby ensuring that many people will be coming and going on the streets at any time. When enough people are out and about, Jacobs wrote, "respectable" eyes and ears dominate the street and are fixed on strangers, who will thus not get out of hand. Under-neath the seeming disorder of a busy street is the very basis for order in "the intricacy of sidewalk use, bringing with it a constant succession of eyes." The more people are out, or looking from their windows at the people who are out, the more their gazes will safeguard the street.

Although Jacobs's ideas seem to cover a broad range of urban situations, there have also been notable exceptions: Only three years after her book was published, for example, a young woman named Kitty Genovese was stabbed to death in Queens, New York, while thirty-eight people watched from their windows (A. M. Rosenthal 1999).

It is very common for people to make the mistake of believing that certain principles are natural to social life, only to discover later on that these principles only hold up under particular social conditions. The world has changed a great deal since Jacobs wrote *The Death and Life of Great American Cities*. Whereas when Jacobs was writing, most of the people on the sidewalks she discussed were similar in many respects, today homeless people, drug users, panhandlers, and others representing economic inequalities, cultural differences, and extremes of behavior can make sidewalk life unpredictable (Duneier 1999). Under these conditions, strangers do not necessarily feel the kind of solidarity and mutual assurance she described. Sociologists today must ask, What happens to urban life when "the eyes and ears upon the street" represent vast inequalities and cultural differences? Do the assumptions Jacobs made still hold up? In many cases the answer is yes, but in other cases the answer is no. More than four decades after her book was published, Jacobs's ideas remain extremely influential.

Urbanism and the Created Environment

Whereas the earlier Chicago School of sociology emphasized that the distribution of people in cities occurs naturally, we have seen that scholars such as Drake and Cayton showed this was not true with regard to the black population. They demonstrated that blacks often did not get to live where their incomes would naturally have led them to live, because of violence and restrictive covenants. More recent theories of the city have stressed that urbanism is not a natural process, but has to be analyzed in relation to major patterns of political and economic change.

According to this view, it is not the stranger on the sidewalk who is most threatening to many urban dwellers, especially the poor; instead, it is the stranger far away, working in a bank or real estate development company, who has the power to make decisions that transform whole blocks or neighborhoods (Logan and Molotch 1987). This focus on the political economy of cities, and on different kinds of strangers, represented a new direction for urban sociology.

Ida Robello and her friends in Brooklyn, New York, are examples of the "eyes and ears upon the street" described in *The Death and Life of Great American Cities* by Jane Jacobs. These women have lived on their block near the Gowanus Canal for over fifty years, and they spend nearly every afternoon chatting with each other on the stoop.

HARVEY: THE RESTRUCTURING OF SPACE

Urbanism, David Harvey (1973, 1982, 1985) emphasizes, is one aspect of the **created environment** brought about by the spread of industrial capitalism. In traditional societies, city and countryside were clearly differentiated. In the modern world, industry blurs the division between city and countryside. Agriculture becomes mechanized and is run according to considerations of price and profit, just like industrial work, and this process lessens the differences in modes of social life between urban and rural people.

In modern urbanism, Harvey points out, space is continually *restructured*. The process is determined by where large firms choose to place their factories, research and development centers, and so forth; the controls that governments operate over both land and industrial production; and the activities of private investors, buying and selling houses and land. Business firms, for example, are constantly weighing the relative advantages of new locations against existing ones. As production becomes cheaper in one area than another, or as the firm moves from one product to another, offices and factories will be closed down in one place and opened up elsewhere. Thus at one period, when there are considerable profits to be made, there may be a spate of office-block building in the center of large cities. Once the offices have been built and the central area redeveloped, investors look for the potential for further speculative building elsewhere. Often what is profitable in one period will not be so in another, when the financial climate changes.

The activities of private home buyers are strongly influenced by how far, and where, business interests buy up land, as well as by rates of loans and taxes fixed by local and central government. After World War II, for instance, there was vast expansion of suburban development outside major cities in the United States. This was partly due to ethnic discrimination and the tendency of whites to move away from inner-city areas. However, it was made possible, Harvey argues, only because of government decisions to provide tax concessions to home buyers and construction firms, and by the setting up of special credit arrangements by financial organizations. These provided the basis for the building and buying of new homes on the peripheries of cities and at the same time promoted demand for industrial products such as the automobile.

CASTELLS: URBANISM AND SOCIAL MOVEMENTS

Like Harvey, Manuel Castells (1977, 1983) stresses that the spatial form of a society is closely linked to the overall mechanisms of its development. But in contrast to the Chicago sociologists,

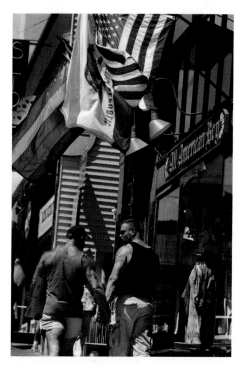

The Castro district in San Francisco is not only open but celebratory about its thriving gay and lesbian population.

Castells sees the city not only as a distinct *location*—the urban area—but as an integral part of processes of **collective consumption,** which in turn are an inherent aspect of industrial capitalism. Homes, schools, transport services, and leisure amenities are ways in which people consume the products of modern industry. The taxation system influences who is able to buy or rent where and who builds where. Large corporations, banks, and insurance companies, which provide capital for building projects, have a great deal of power over these processes. But government agencies also directly affect many aspects of city life, by building roads and public housing, planning parks, and so forth. The physical shape of cities is thus a product of both market forces and the power of government.

But the nature of the created environment is not just the result of the activities of wealthy and powerful people. Castells stresses the importance of the struggles of underprivileged groups to alter their living conditions. Urban problems stimulate a range of social movements, concerned with improving housing conditions, protesting against air pollution, defending parks, and combating building development that changes the nature of an area. For example, Castells has studied the gay movement in San Francisco, which succeeded in restructuring neighborhoods around its own cultural values—allowing many gay organizations, clubs, and bars to flourish—and gained a prominent position in local politics.

Cities, Harvey and Castells both emphasize, are almost wholly artificial environments, constructed by people. In

Joys in the Hood

In her book *The Death and Life of Great American Cities* (1961), the most influential American book ever written on urban planning, Jane Jacobs argued that the undesirable elements of city life—the noise, the energy, the crowding, the complexity—were precisely the elements that created healthy and vibrant communities. Born in Scranton, Pennsylvania, Jacobs managed to graduate high school before leaving for New York City during the Great Depression to become a writer. "Instead of listening in class, I always had something much more interesting I was reading under the desk," Jacobs recalls (Fulford 1997), betraying the rebellious streak that would characterize her future intellectual and professional life. Once in New York, she was so uninspired by coursework at Columbia University that she dropped out, devoting herself full-time to writing and social activism. Throughout her career, Jacobs has been an outspoken critic of urban policies, such as expressways and low-density housing, which speed suburban sprawl and rob communities of their vitality. For a *New York Times Magazine* issue dedicated in the spring of 2000 to exploring the rise of the "suburban nation" in America, Jacobs sat to speak with Mitchell Duneier, one of the authors of this text.

MD: The pioneering urban sociologist says the suburbs are an interesting case study, but she still wouldn't want to live there. You're known as one of the greatest champions of New York City neighborhood life. Why did you leave Greenwich Village for Toronto?

JJ: You know, I wasn't leaving Greenwich Village for Toronto. I was leaving the United States for Canada. And it was

Jane Jacobs

because of the Vietnam War, which neither Greenwich Village nor Toronto had anything to do with instigating. I'm glad I was brought up an American, but I'm not cut out to be a citizen of an empire. And I like it here. I like the civility and politeness. It's not a cruel city.

MD: Was it hard to make the adjustment after life in Greenwich Village?

JJ: It's remarkably like living in Greenwich Village. People think living in Greenwich Village is terribly exotic in some way, but actually, you raise children, you make meals, you feel very good if you can get new curtains for your windows. So the neighborhood I live in is very similar.

MD: It seems that some of the architects and developers in America today, inspired by the ideas in your book *The Death and Life of Great American Cities,* are now experi-

some ways, the views set out by Harvey and Castells and those of the Chicago School usefully complement each other and can be combined to give a comprehensive picture of urban processes. The contrasts between city areas described in the urban ecology approach do exist, as does the overall impersonality of city life. But these are more variable than the members of the Chicago School believed, and are primarily governed by the social and economic influences analyzed

by Harvey and Castells. John Logan and Harvey Molotch (1987) have suggested an approach that directly connects the perspectives of authors such as Harvey and Castells with some features of the ecological standpoint. They agree with Harvey and Castells that broad features of economic development, stretching nationally and internationally, affect urban life in a quite direct way. But these wide-ranging economic factors, they argue, are focused through local organimenting with new ways to build planned communities—communities that look pretty suburban—yet are patterned on mixed-use urban neighborhoods.

JJ: Yeah, I see those.

MD: Have you been to any of them, like Seaside, in Florida?

JJ: No. I've just seen the pictures of them. But where I think the New Urbanism will have the most difference is in in-filling suburbs, which we've been needing to do for a long time. Here we've got all these existing suburbs that—I don't want to say they're no good. There's a lot that they offer that is good. And people are ingenious about the way that they use them.

MD: Ingenious in what ways?

JJ: Lots of people who lost their jobs earlier in the 90s were very valuable, skilled people. And lots of people today have arranged to have home offices. And one thing that has heartened me is how many women in suburbs have their own businesses, performing useful operations that just didn't exist in suburbs before. Some didn't exist any-where. Some have to do with child care, some have to do with making houses better. Women have almost taken over the real estate business in the suburbs.

MD: And what did you mean by the in-filling of the suburbs?

JJ: There's a lot of underused land that's kind of a nuisance. For instance, all those malls. There are too many of them, and they're too boring. Really, buildings and other facilities could fit into those places. This happened in cities long ago: They had large backyards and side yards, and another house would be put into the backyard. You could get to it from the front yard with its own little walk. Some of the most charming places in Manhattan Island are like that and have been kept. It's a very old urban device. I think it will very likely become a suburban device.

MD: So you're in favor of these new suburban models?

JJ: Well, I'm in favor of lots of choices. There is no way that you can make things by one pattern and satisfy every-one's aspirations. And that's a good thing. Suburbs are among the choices, and there are people who want them. Their children may not want to stay there, but that's O.K. What I object to is that largely through the compul-sion of certain financing arrangements, mainly central-ized under the government, suburbs of a certain kind have taken way more than their share of choices and the market.

MD: In your new book, *The Nature of Economies*, you use the example of nature to show that diversity is an essential element of economic growth. So what do you make of the phenomenal suburban growth fueled by the relatively specialized new economy?

JJ: You mean like Silicon Valley? It really is a remarkably varied collection of services and suppliers. The busi-nesses that make up a place like Silicon Valley are terri-bly diverse. The place wouldn't work if it weren't. Everything from temporary workers when places are growing up rapidly to the venture capitalists that are fi-nancing the whole thing.

MD: What would you tell people who are concerned about the effects of suburban sprawl on the life of their community?

JJ: There's no reason why anyone should listen to me on suburbs, because I don't especially like suburbs and I don't understand them the way people who live in mod-ern suburbs understand them. And especially if I were to give any suggestions about what should be done with suburbs. That's one of the terrible things that happened to cities. People who not only didn't care about cities, but even hated them, began to prescribe for them. It was dis-astrous! No matter how well they meant or how much they thought they loved humankind.

SOURCE: Mitchell Duneier. "Questions for Jane Jacobs," *The New York Times Magazine*, April 9, 2000.

zations, including neighborhood businesses, banks, and gov-ernment agencies, together with the activities of individual house buyers.

Places—land and buildings—are bought and sold, accord-ing to Logan and Molotch, just like other goods in modern so-cieties, but the markets that structure city environments are influenced by how different groups of people want to *use* the property they buy and sell. Many tensions and conflicts arise

as a result of this process—and these are the key factors struc-turing city neighborhoods. For instance, an apartment house is seen as a home by its residents but as a source of income by its landlord. Businesses are most interested in buying and sell-ing property in an area to obtain the best production sites or to make profits in land speculation. Their interests and concerns are quite different from those of residents, for whom the neigh-borhood is a place to live.

Urbanism in the United States

What are the main trends that have affected city development in the United States over the past several decades? How can we explain the decay of central-city areas? These are questions we will take up in the following sections. One of the major changes in urban patterns in the period since World War II is the movement of large parts of city populations to newly constructed suburbs; this movement outward has been a particularly pronounced feature of American cities and is related directly to central-city decay. We therefore begin with a discussion of suburbia before moving on to look at the inner city.

Suburbanization

The word *suburb* has its origins in the Latin term *sub urbe,* or "under city control," an appropriate meaning throughout most of the history of urbanism. Suburbs were originally small pockets of dwellings dependent on urban centers for their amenities and livelihood. Today, they are any residential or commercial area adjoining a city, regardless of whether or not they are subject to central-city control. Many suburbs are effectively autonomous areas over which city administrations have little direct influence.

In the United States, **suburbanization,** the massive development and inhabiting of towns surrounding a city, rapidly increased during the 1950s and 1960s, a time of great economic growth. World War II had previously absorbed most industrial resources, and any development outside the war effort was restricted. But by the 1950s, war rationing had ended, automobiles instead of tanks were being mass produced, and people were encouraged to pursue at least one part of the "American dream"—owning a house and a piece of land. During that decade, the population in the cities increased by 10 percent, whereas in the suburban areas it grew by no less than 48 percent.

The prevailing economic scene also facilitated moving out of the city. The Federal Housing Administration (FHA) provided assistance in obtaining mortgage loans, making it possible in the early postwar period for families to buy housing in the suburbs for less than they would have paid for rent in the cities. The FHA did not offer financial assistance to improve older homes or to build new homes in the central areas of ethnically mixed cities; its large-scale aid went only to the builders and buyers of suburban housing. The FHA, together with the Veterans Administration, funded almost half of all suburban housing built during the 1950s and 1960s.

Early in the 1950s, lobbies promoting highway construction launched Project Adequate Roads, aimed at inducing the federal government to support the building of highways. President Eisenhower responded with a giant construction program for interstate roadways, and in 1956, the Highway Act was passed, authorizing $32 billion to be used for building such highways. This coincided with a period of expansion in the automobile industry such that families came to own more than one car; and the result was that previously out-of-the-way suburban areas, with lower property taxes, became accessible to places of work. At the same time, the highway program led to the establishment of industries and services in suburban areas themselves. Consequently, the movement of businesses from the cities to the suburbs took jobs in the manufacturing and service industries with them. Many suburban towns became essentially separate cities, connected by rapid highways to the other suburbs around them. From the 1960s on, the proportion of people commuting between suburbs increased more steadily than the proportion commuting to cities.

Although suburbia in the United States is white dominated, more and more members of racial and ethnic minorities are moving there. From 1980 to 1990, the suburban population of blacks grew by 34.4 percent, of Latinos by 69.3 percent, and of Asians by 125.9 percent. In contrast, the suburban white population grew by only 9.2 percent. In the following decade, from 1990 to 1999, the movement of racial and ethnic minority groups to the suburbs slowed, but remained diverse. The suburban population of blacks grew by 14.2 percent, Latinos by 40 percent, Asians by 45 percent, and whites by 7.6 percent (U.S. Bureau of the Census 1999). Members of minority groups move to the suburbs for reasons similar to those who preceded them: better housing, schools, and amenities. Like the people who began the exodus to suburbia in the 1950s, they are mostly middle-class professionals. According to the chairman of the Chicago Housing Authority, "Suburbanization isn't about race now; it's about class. Nobody wants to be around poor people because of all the problems that go along with poor people: poor schools, unsafe streets, gangs" (DeWitt 1994).

Nevertheless, the suburbs remain mostly white. Minority groups constituted only 18 percent of the total suburban population in 1999 (U.S. Bureau of the Census 1999). Three out of every four African Americans continue to live in the center cities, compared with one in every four whites. Most black suburban residents live in black-majority neighborhoods in towns bordering the city.

While the last several decades saw a movement from the cities to the suburbs, they also witnessed a shift in the regional distribution of the U.S. population from north to south and east to west. As a percentage of the nation's total population, the

This aerial photograph taken in 1948 shows a portion of Levittown, New York, shortly after the mass-produced suburb was completed. Located on Long Island farmland just twenty-five miles east of Manhattan, William Levitt's concept to resolve the postwar housing crisis represented the future of suburbia—an entirely new kind of home and nonurban culture.

Northeast dropped from 25 to 18.9 percent and the Midwest from 29 to 22.6 percent. Meanwhile the population of the South increased from 30.7 to 35.7 percent and that of the West from 15.6 to 22.8 percent (U.S. Bureau of the Census 2002).

Urban Problems

Inner-city decay is partially a consequence of the social and economic forces involved in the movement of businesses, jobs, and middle-class residents from major cities to the outlying suburbs since the 1950s. The manufacturing industries that provided employment for the urban blue-collar class largely vanished and were replaced by white-collar service industries. Millions of blue-collar jobs disappeared, and this affected in particular the poorly educated, drawn mostly from minority groups. Although the overall educational levels of minority groups improved over this period, the improvement was not sufficient to keep up with the demands of an information-based economy (Kasarda 1993). William Julius Wilson (1991, 1996) has argued that the problems of the urban underclass grew out of this economic transformation (see Chapter 8).

These economic changes also contributed to increased residential segregation of different racial and ethnic groups and social classes, as we saw in Chapter 11. Discriminatory practices by home sellers, real estate agents, and mortgage lending institutions further added to this pattern of segregation (Massey and Denton 1993). In the early 1990s, more than 90 percent of African Americans in the United States lived in neighborhoods, both urban and suburban, that were 60 percent or more black (Farley and Frey 1994). The social isolation of minority groups, particularly those in the underclass or "ghetto poor," can escalate urban problems such as crime, lack of economic opportunities, poor health, and family breakdown (Massey 1996).

Adding to these difficulties is the fact that city governments today operate against a background of almost continual financial crisis. As businesses and middle-class residents moved to the suburbs, the cities lost major sources of tax revenue. High rates of crime and unemployment in the city require it to spend more on welfare services, schools, police, and overall upkeep. Yet because of budget constraints, cities are forced to cut back many of these services. A cycle of deterioration develops, in which the more suburbia expands, the greater the problems faced by city dwellers become.

Explaining Urban Poverty: The Sociological Debate

The plight of the American inner city has grown bleak in recent times. According to U.S. Census data, the proportion of our nation's poor who live in central cities increased from 34 percent in 1970 to 43 percent in 1990. By 2002, the proportion of the poor living in central cities had dropped slightly to 41 percent (U.S. Bureau of the Census 2003). Not only are the poor increasingly concentrated in urban areas but the poor living in the inner city are clustered in neighborhoods overwhelmingly inhabited by other poor families. The consequences are that the urban poor—particularly the black urban poor—are living in very poor, socially isolated, racially homogeneous neighborhoods, which are increasingly plagued with troubles such as joblessness, crime, and poor quality of life.

How is it possible that the living conditions of inner-city blacks have taken such a turn for the worse—especially in the three decades that followed the civil rights movements of the 1960s and progressive public policies such as the Fair Housing Act of 1968? Two books on inner-city poverty posit distinct—yet complementary—explanations for the state of urban poverty today. In *When Work Disappears: The World of the New Urban Poor* (1996), sociologist William Julius Wilson argues, as we saw earlier in the chapter, that the loss of jobs is at the root of inner-city decline. Sociologists Douglas S. Massey and Nancy A. Denton, in their book *American Apartheid: Segregation and the Making of the Underclass* (1993), counter that the persistent poverty among urban blacks in the United States is due primarily to residential segregation.

Wilson's (1987, 1996) position can be described as the "economic restructuring" hypothesis. He argues that persistent

Americans on the Move

How many times did your parents move from one residence to another while you were growing up? America has a high rate of residential mobility. In 1999–2000, 16.1 percent of Americans changed their place of residence at least once. Of these, over half (56 percent) moved to another home within the same county (U.S. Bureau of the Census 2001). Although this number is no higher than the annual mobility rates of Canada, Australia, and New Zealand, Americans do tend to move more than residents of other industrially developed countries such as France, the United Kingdom, Japan, and Belgium. Yet except for a sharp increase in mobility in the mid-1980s, fueled by recovery from the recession of 1982–1983, mobility rates in the United States are in long-term decline. In the 1950s and 1960s, approximately twenty out of every hundred Americans moved

at least once every year. Mobility rates began to fall in the 1970s and, since the late 1980s, have consistently hovered around 17 percent.

Why do people move? According to a 1991 survey, the most commonly cited reason for moving was to improve one's housing situation: to buy a better home, to make the transition from renting to owning, and so on. Many respondents also cited employment factors as a reason for moving (Gober 1993).

Because many Americans move for job-related reasons, migration patterns tend to reflect regional patterns of economic development. For example, the Northeast and Midwest, long home to much of the nation's industrial manufacturing, have suffered what demographers call an "out-migration" as a result of the deindustrialization of the American economy. Much of the growth in service-sector work and high-tech production has occurred in the South and West, and millions of Americans have left the Northeast and Midwest in search of jobs in these areas. The Midwest has slowly been able to recover from this situation, shifting its economic base to more viable forms of production and thus attracting enough new residents from other regions to counter the out-migration to the South and West. But the Northeast continues to lose residents at a rapid pace. In 1994, the Northeast lost a total of 61,000 residents, while the West gained 379,000 and the South gained 827,000 (Hansen 1995). In 2000, the population of the Northeast continued to decline, with another 252,000 residents moving elsewhere. The South lost an additional 227,000, while the West also lost 57,000 residents. The Midwest received the only net gain of residents with

urban poverty stems primarily from the structural transformation of the inner-city economy. The decline of manufacturing industries, the "suburbanization" of employment, and the rise of a low-wage service sector have dramatically reduced the number of entry-level jobs that pay wages sufficient to support a family. The high rate of joblessness resulting from economic shifts has led to a shrinking pool of marriageable men (those financially able to support a family). Thus marriage has become less attractive to poor women, unwed childbearing has increased, and female-headed families have proliferated. New generations of children are born into poverty, and the vicious cycle is perpetuated. Wilson argues that blacks suffer disproportionately due to past discrimination and because they are concentrated in locations and occupations particularly affected by economic restructuring.

82,000 new people moving in (U.S. Bureau of the Census 2001).

It is all too easy to view these demographic shifts as the result of natural and inevitable long-term processes: High-tech and service sector work comes to account for a greater share of the gross national product (GNP), these industries naturally spring up in the South and West, making the regions attractive even for traditional manufacturing firms that wish to relocate, and the Northeast is depopulated.

A better explanation begins with—of all things—globalization. As globalization has proceeded, a number of important transformations have taken place in the economic sector. Changes in the financial infrastructure have made it easier for investors to put their money into enterprises anywhere on the globe, and corresponding improvements in communications technology, transportation, and managerial practices have made it more practical for businesses to move their production sites to wherever their costs will be minimized. Capital, economists and sociologists say, has become increasingly mobile under the influence of globalization.

Whereas the mobility of capital sometimes translates into American firms shifting the site of their production to the developing world, in other cases it means that firms will open in or relocate to regions of this country where their production costs will be low. All else being equal, if unions are strong in one region and weak in another, firms are more likely to do business in the region with the weak unions, because they will be able to get away with paying lower wages. Firms also prefer to operate in cities and states that are eager for new development and likely to grant substantial tax breaks. In general, state and local governments in the South and West have been more willing than governments in the Northeast to grant tax breaks to firms, and unions tend to be weaker in these regions than in the Northeast. These factors—in addition to cheaper land and energy—have helped pull some firms out of the Northeast and into the South and West, and have encouraged many startup firms to set up shop in the South and West. Al-

though the dynamics involved are clearly complex, globalization and the mobility of capital appear to lay behind recent trends in regional economic development and therefore underlie key patterns in regional migration.

Should attempts be made to halt these changes? What would migration patterns look like if unions were strong in all regions and if cities and states refused to grant generous tax breaks to corporate America? Is the depopulation of the Northeast a good or bad thing?

Wilson elaborated that these economic changes were accompanied by an increase in the spatial concentration of poverty within black neighborhoods. This new geography of poverty, he felt, was due in part to the civil rights movement of the 1960s, which provided middle-class blacks with new opportunities outside the ghetto. The out-migration of middle-class families from ghetto areas left behind a destitute community lacking the institutions, resources, and values necessary for success in postindustrial society. He also acknowledges that such neighborhoods lack locally available training and education and have suffered from the dissolution of government and private support of local organizations that once supplied job information as well as employment opportunities. Thus the urban underclass arose from a complex interplay of civil rights policy, economic restructuring, and a historical legacy of discrimination.

While Wilson emphasizes macro-level economic shifts as the cause underlying the concentration of urban poverty, Massey and Denton support the "racial residential segregation" hypothesis. This view holds that high levels of racial residential segregation may increase minority poverty by limiting access to employment opportunities. Segregation in ghettos exacerbates employment problems because it leads to weak informal employment networks and contributes to the social isolation of individuals and families, thereby reducing their chances of acquiring the skills, including adequate educational training, that facilitate mobility in a society. Because no other group in society experiences the degree of segregation, isolation, and poverty concentration that African Americans do, they are far more likely to be disadvantaged when they have to compete with other groups in society for resources and privileges.

Massey and Denton argue further that in the absence of residential segregation, the structural and economic changes observed by Wilson would not have produced the disastrous social and economic consequences observed in inner cities during the past thirty years. Although rates of black poverty were driven up by the economic dislocations Wilson identifies, it was segregation that confined the higher levels of deprivation to a small number of densely settled, tightly packed, and geographically isolated areas.

Massey and Denton (1993) also dispute Wilson's claim that concentrated poverty arose because the civil rights revolution allowed middle-class blacks to move out of the ghetto. Their principal objection to Wilson's focus on middle-class out-migration is that focusing on the flight of the black middle class deflects attention from the "real issue, which is the limitation of black residential options through segregation."

The debate between Wilson and Massey and Denton highlights an important aspect of sociology—namely that many of its leading practitioners are trying to think like scientists. Massey and Wilson are two of the leading sociologists of the past fifty years. From the standpoint of many Americans who would see both of their arguments as supporting the same progressive political agenda, it would not matter whether poverty was caused by segregation or joblessness. Either cause requires a major shift in political priorities and a significant role for the U.S. government in solving the problem. In their political sympathies, Wilson and Massey have a tremendous amount in common, so why has their debate been so fierce?

The answer is that one of their highest shared priorities is the scientific goal of explanation. Each of them is trying to explain the root causes of the contemporary ghetto. But ultimately, they have a great deal in common. Both of them agree that if you are poor, the neighborhood you live in has a major effect on your life chances, above and beyond other aspects of your life. These "neighborhood effects" must be addressed, regardless of how they came into being.

The Ghetto as a Sociohistorical Problem

Thus far, we have used the word *ghetto* without defining it. What are ghettos, and how did ghettoized poverty influence the results of the disaster in New Orleans? Many people mistakenly believe that ghettos are where African Americans or Latinos live, but the word *ghetto* derives from the Italian *ghet*, and the first ghettos were in Venice and Rome in the fourteenth century. Created by Pope Paul IV and later by Pope Pius V, as a way of isolating Jews from the mainstream Christian societies in which they lived, the first ghettos were associated with the Jews, and certainly not blacks or Latinos as is the case in the contemporary United States.

Sociologists originally drew a distinction between ghettos, on the one hand, and slums on the other. Ghettos were residential zones where particular groups were forced to live. The people who lived in these zones were not necessarily impoverished, but simply of a particular ethnic or racial group who were viewed as inferior and in need of being forceably cordoned off by the wider society. Slums were zones inhabited by poor people, including members of a dominant, nonstigmatized race such as poor whites in the United States. In recent years, many sociologists have started using the terms *ghettos* and *slums* interchangeably, but it is better to retain the analytical clarity inherent in the former distinction.

A crucial criterion for the definition of the ghetto is that the people who live there must have been forced to do so. Indeed, this was the situation of blacks in the United States and Jews in Rome. In the United States, blacks were forced to live in certain parts of the Northern cities due to restrictive covenants that made it illegal to sell them land in certain neighborhoods. Jews were forced to live in the *ghet*, due to a decree by various popes. During the fourteenth century, most Jews were also forced to wear insignias when they traveled outside the zone where they lived, to indicate that they were Jews.

Force or compulsion is a historical rather than a contemporary factor in defining the idea of a ghetto. In other words, whereas the inhabitants of the original ghettos were given but little choice as where they could live, inhabitants of today's ghettos may feel that they live in their highly segregated and impoverished neighborhoods by choice. Sociological studies have demonstrated over and again that when poor people have an opportunity to move they will often resist every chance to do so. This is not because they do not want to improve their life chances, but because they do not believe their lives would be better independent of the social networks and neighborhood institutions that sustain them.

Are ghettos necessarily zones for the economically marginalized and exploited populations of stigmatized people? Whereas the U.S. ghetto was used to warehouse a significant labor supply for growing factories during the two World Wars, the Jewish ghetto of Rome did not originally seem to have such a mission. Jews were very successful and they continued to have a significant economic ties to the wider society long after they were ghettoized (Stow 2000). Ultimately, laws were enacted that made it difficult for Jews to carry on their occupations, but these were not intrinsic to ghettoization.

There have been many ghettos in the history of the world, but there are no sociological studies that compare ghettos in more than a few societies. For this reason, there is still much to know about the characteristics that would define the ghetto concept. From what we know, it is a residential zone in which stigmatized racial or religious groups are compelled to live by the wider society.

This takes us back to the contemporary United States. The victims of the floods that ravaged New Orleans after Hurricane Katrina were mainly poor blacks who lived in the poorest ghettos of the city. Why were these poor people disproportionately affected by the extreme weather conditions? The answer has mainly to do with the social and political history of these particular residential zones, which were always given fewer resources for drainage and pumping systems after past storms. It also has to do with the limited resources that poor people have to evacuate, and the limited networks they have outside the zones where they live, especially consisting of people who have the resources to help them. By contrast with the poor blacks who were trapped inside the ghettos as they flooded, many middle-class whites had the resources and social connections to leave the city when warnings first appeared on the national news. The effect of Hurricane Katrina followed the fault lines of the larger urban problems associated with racial segregation and ghettoization in the inner cities today, a subject we return to later in this chapter.

Urban Renewal and Gentrification

Urban decay is not wholly a one-way process; it can stimulate countertrends, such as **urban renewal,** or **gentrification.** Dilapidated areas or buildings may become renovated as more affluent groups move back into cities. Such a renewal process is called gentrification because those areas or buildings become upgraded and return to the control of the urban "gentry"—high-income dwellers—rather than remaining in the hands of the poor.

Does gentrification of a run-down inner-city area necessarily result in the dispossession of the existing population, or do renewed interest and an infusion of money in such areas promote a revitalization that works to their advantage? Not long ago, Clinton Street was a graffiti-ridden streetscape (top), but it has evolved into a lively restaurant row on New York's Lower East Side (bottom).

In *Streetwise: Race, Class, and Change in an Urban Community* (1990), sociologist Elijah Anderson analyzed the effect of gentrification on cities. Although the renovation of a neighborhood generally increases its value, it rarely improves the living standards of its current low-income residents, who are usually forced to move out. In the Philadelphia neighborhood that Anderson studied, close to the ghetto, many black residences were condemned, forcing over one thousand people to leave. Although they were told that their property would be used to build low-cost housing that they would be given the first opportunity to buy, large businesses and a high school now stand there.

The poor residents who continued to live in the neighborhood received some benefits in the form of improved schools and police protection, but the resulting increase in taxes and rents also forced them to leave for a more affordable neighborhood, most often deeper into the ghetto. African American residents Anderson interviewed expressed resentment at the influx of "yuppies," whom they held responsible for the changes that drove the poorer people away.

The white newcomers had come to the city in search of cheap "antique" housing, closer access to their city-based jobs, and a trendy urban lifestyle. They professed to be "open minded" about racial and ethnic differences; in reality, however, little fraternizing took place between the new and old residents unless they were of the same social class. Because the African American residents were mostly poor and the white residents were middle class, class differences were compounded by racial ones. Though some middle-class blacks lived in the area, most chose to live far from the ghetto, fearing that otherwise they would receive the same treatment that whites reserved for the black underclass. Over time, the neighborhood was gradually transformed into a white middle-class enclave.

It is important to note that the process of gentrification parallels another trend discussed earlier: the transformation of the urban economy from a manufacturing to a service-industries base. Addressing the concerns of the victims of these economic changes is critical for the survival of the cities.

Cities and Globalization

In premodern times, cities were self-contained entities that stood apart from the predominantly rural areas in which they were located. Road systems sometimes linked major urban areas, but travel was a specialized affair for merchants, soldiers, and others who needed to cross distances with any regularity. Communication between cities was limited. The picture at the start of the twenty-first century could hardly be more different. Globalization has had a profound effect on cities by making them more interdependent and encouraging the proliferation of horizontal links between cities across national borders. Physical and virtual ties between cities now abound and global networks of cities are emerging.

Some people have predicted that globalization and new communications technology might lead to the demise of cities as we know them. This is because many of the traditional functions of cities can now be carried out in cyberspace rather than in dense and congested urban areas. For example, financial markets have gone electronic, e-commerce reduces the need for both producers and consumers to rely on city centers, and telecommuting permits a growing number of employees to work from home rather than in an office building.

Yet, thus far, such predictions have not been borne out. Rather than undermining cities, globalization is transforming

them into vital hubs within the global economy. Urban centers have become critical in coordinating information flows, managing business activities, and innovating new services and technologies. There has been a simultaneous *dispersion* and *concentration* of activity and power within a set of cities around the globe (Castells 1996).

Global Cities

The role of cities in the new global order has been attracting a great deal of attention from sociologists. Globalization is often thought of in terms of a duality between the national level and the global, yet it is the largest *cities* of the world that make up the main circuits through which globalization occurs (Sassen 1998). The functioning of the new global economy is dependent on a set of central locations with developed informational infrastructures and a hyperconcentration of facilities. It is in such points that the "work" of globalization is performed and directed. As business, production, advertising, and marketing assume a global scale, there is an enormous amount of organizational activity that must be done in order to maintain and develop these global networks.

Saskia Sassen has been one of the leading contributors to the debate on cities and globalization. She uses the term **global city** to refer to urban centers that are home to the headquarters of large, transnational corporations and a superabundance of financial, technological, and consulting services. In *The Global City* (1991), Sassen bases her work on the study of three such cities: New York, London, and Tokyo. The contemporary development of the world economy, she argues, has created a novel strategic role for major cities. Most such cities have long been centers of international trade, but they now have four new traits:

1. They have developed into command posts—centers of direction and policy making—for the global economy.
2. Such cities are the key locations for financial and specialized service firms, which have become more important in influencing economic development than is manufacturing.
3. They are the sites of production and innovation in these newly expanded industries.
4. These cities are markets on which the "products" of financial and service industries are bought, sold, or otherwise disposed of.

New York, London, and Tokyo have very different histories, yet we can trace comparable changes in their nature over the past two or three decades. Within the highly dispersed world economy of today, cities like these provide for central control of crucial operations. Global cities are much more than simply places of coordination, however; they are also contexts of production. What is important here is not the production of material goods, but the production of the specialized services required by business organizations for administering offices and factories scattered across the world, and the production of financial innovations and markets. Services and financial goods are the "things" the global city makes.

The downtown areas of global cities provide concentrated sites within which whole clusters of "producers" can work in close interaction, often including personal contact, with one another. In the global city, local firms mingle with national and multinational organizations, including a multiplicity of foreign companies. Thus 350 foreign banks have offices in New York City, plus 2,500 other foreign financial corporations; one out of every four bank employees in the city works for a foreign bank. Global cities compete with one another, but they also constitute an interdependent system, partly separate from the nations in which they are located.

Other authors have built on Sassen's work, noting that as globalization progresses, more and more cities are joining New York, London, and Tokyo in the ranks of the global cities. Castells has described the creation of a tiered hierarchy of world cities—with places such as Hong Kong, Singapore, Chicago, Frankfurt, Los Angeles, Milan, Zurich, and Osaka serving as major global centers for business and financial services. Beneath these, a new set of regional centers is developing as key nodes within the global economy. Cities such as Madrid, São Paulo, Moscow, Seoul, Jakarta, and Buenos Aires are becoming important hubs for activity within the so-called emerging markets.

Inequality and the Global City

The new global economy is highly problematic in many ways. Nowhere can this be seen more clearly than in the new dynamics of inequality visible within the global city. The central business district juxtaposed with impoverished inner-city areas in many global cities should be seen as interrelated phenomena, as Sassen and others remind us. The growth sectors of the new economy—financial services, marketing, high technology—are reaping profits far greater than any found within traditional economic sectors. As the salaries and bonuses of the very affluent continue to climb, the wages of those employed to clean and guard their offices are dropping. Sassen (1998) argues that we are witnessing the "valorization" of work located at the forefront of the new global economy and the "devalorization" of work that occurs behind the scenes.

The city of Los Angeles has taken steps to dissuade the homeless from sleeping in public places. Notice that the bench pictured here is not long enough for a person to stretch out on and that the shape and placement of the slats would make it quite uncomfortable for any extended period of time.

Disparities in profit-making capabilities are expected in market economies, but the magnitude of the disparities in the new global economy is having a negative effect on many aspects of the social world, from housing to the labor market. Those who work in finances and global services receive high salaries, and the areas where they live become gentrified. At the same time, orthodox manufacturing jobs are lost, and the very process of gentrification creates a vast supply of low-wage jobs—in restaurants, hotels, and boutiques. Affordable housing is scarce in gentrified areas, forcing an expansion of low-income neighborhoods. Whereas central business districts are the recipients of massive influxes of investment in real estate, development, and telecommunications, marginalized areas are left with few resources.

Within global cities, a geography of "centrality and marginality" is taking shape—as Mitch Duneier's (1999) study in New York's Greenwich Village revealed. Alongside resplendent affluence there is acute poverty. Yet although these two worlds coexist side by side, the actual contact between them can be surprisingly minimal. As Mike Davis (1990) noted in his study of Los Angeles, there has been a "conscious 'hardening' of the city surface against the poor." Accessible public spaces have been replaced by walled compounds, neighborhoods guarded by electronic surveillance, and "corporate citadels." In Davis's (1990) words:

To reduce contact with untouchables, urban redevelopment has converted once vital pedestrian streets into traffic sewers and transformed public parks into temporary receptacles for the homeless and wretched. The

American city . . . is being systematically turned inside out—or, rather, outside in. The valorized spaces of the new megastructures and super-malls are concentrated in the center, street frontage is denuded, public activity is sorted into strictly functional compartments, and circulation is internalized in corridors under the gaze of private police.

According to Davis, life is made as "unliveable" as possible for the poorest and most marginalized residents of Los Angeles. Benches at bus stops are short or barrel-shaped to prevent people from sleeping on them, the number of public toilets is fewer than in any other North American city, and sprinkler systems have been installed in many parks to deter the homeless from living in them. Police and city planners have attempted to contain the homeless population within certain regions of the city, but in periodically sweeping through and confiscating makeshift shelters, they have effectively created a population of "urban bedouins."

Urbanization in the Developing World

In 2000, 2.9 billion people, or 47 percent of the world's population, lived in cities. The world's urban population could reach 5 billion people, or over 60 percent of the world's population, by 2030. According to some estimates, 4 million of these urban dwellers will be residents of cities in the developing world. Currently, 40 percent of the populations of developing countries live in cities, but by 2030 urban dwellers are expected to account for 56 percent of the populations of developing countries. As Global Map 19.1 shows, most of the thirty-three cities projected to have more than 8 million residents in 2015 are located in the developing world. Most people in developed countries already live in cities. In 2000, 75 percent of the population of developed countries lived in cities, yet by 2030, 83 percent of people living in developed countries are anticipated to live in cities (UN Population Division 2002).

Manuel Castells (1996) refers to **megacities** as one of the main features of third millennium urbanization. They are defined not by their size alone—although they are vast agglomerations of people—but also by their role as connection points between enormous human populations and the global economy. Megacities are intensely concentrated pockets of activity through which politics, media, communications, finances, and production flow. According to Castells, megacities function as magnets for the countries or regions in which they are located.

People are drawn toward large urban areas for various reasons; within megacities are those who succeed in tapping into the global system and those who do not. Besides serving as nodes in the global economy, megacities also become "depositories of all these segments of the population who fight to survive."

Why is the rate of urban growth in the world's lesser developed regions so much higher than elsewhere? Two factors in particular must be taken into account. First, rates of population growth are higher in developing countries than they are in industrialized nations. Urban growth is fueled by *high fertility rates* among people already living in cities.

Second, there is widespread *internal migration* from rural areas to urban ones—as in the case of the developing Hong Kong–Guangdong megacity. People are drawn to cities in the developing world either because their traditional systems of rural production have disintegrated or because the urban areas offer superior job opportunities. Rural poverty prompts many people to try their hand at city life. They may intend to migrate to the city only for a relatively short time, aiming to return to their villages once they have earned enough money. Some actually do return, but most find themselves forced to stay, having for one reason or another lost their position in their previous communities.

Challenges of Urbanization in the Developing World

ECONOMIC IMPLICATIONS

As a growing number of unskilled and agricultural workers migrate to urban centers, the formal economy often struggles to absorb the influx into the workforce. In most cities in the developing world, it is the *informal economy* that allows those who cannot find formal work to make ends meet. From casual work in manufacturing and construction to small-scale trading activities, the unregulated informal sector offers earning opportunities to poor or unskilled workers.

Informal economic opportunities are important in helping thousands of families to survive in urban conditions, but they have problematic aspects as well. The informal economy is untaxed and unregulated. It is also less productive than the formal economy. Countries where economic activity is concentrated in this sector fail to collect much-needed revenue through taxation. The low level of productivity also hurts the general economy—the proportion of the gross domestic product (GDP) generated by informal economic activity is much lower than the percentage of the population involved in the sector.

The Organization for Economic Cooperation and Development (OECD) estimates that a billion new jobs will be needed by 2025 to sustain the estimated population growth in cities in

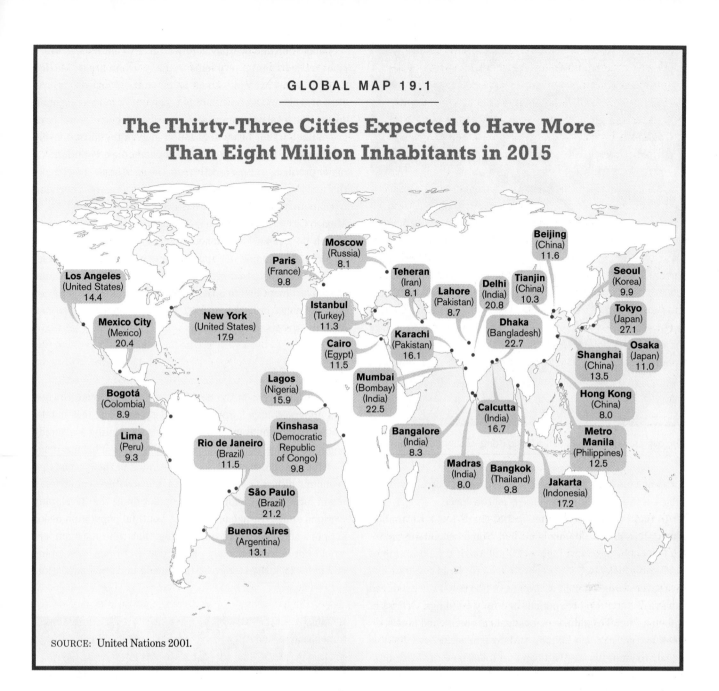

GLOBAL MAP 19.1

The Thirty-Three Cities Expected to Have More Than Eight Million Inhabitants in 2015

Los Angeles (United States) 14.4

Mexico City (Mexico) 20.4

New York (United States) 17.9

Moscow (Russia) 8.1

Paris (France) 9.8

Istanbul (Turkey) 11.3

Teheran (Iran) 8.1

Lahore (Pakistan) 8.7

Delhi (India) 20.8

Tianjin (China) 10.3

Beijing (China) 11.6

Seoul (Korea) 9.9

Tokyo (Japan) 27.1

Cairo (Egypt) 11.5

Karachi (Pakistan) 16.1

Dhaka (Bangladesh) 22.7

Osaka (Japan) 11.0

Shanghai (China) 13.5

Lagos (Nigeria) 15.9

Mumbai (Bombay) (India) 22.5

Calcutta (India) 16.7

Hong Kong (China) 8.0

Bogotá (Colombia) 8.9

Kinshasa (Democratic Republic of Congo) 9.8

Bangalore (India) 8.3

Metro Manila (Philippines) 12.5

Lima (Peru) 9.3

Rio de Janeiro (Brazil) 11.5

Madras (India) 8.0

Bangkok (Thailand) 9.8

Jakarta (Indonesia) 17.2

São Paulo (Brazil) 21.2

Buenos Aires (Argentina) 13.1

SOURCE: United Nations 2001.

the developing world. It is unlikely that all of these jobs will be created within the formal economy. Some development analysts argue that attention should be paid to formalizing or regulating the large informal economy, where much of the excess work force is likely to cluster in the years to come.

ENVIRONMENTAL CHALLENGES

The rapidly expanding urban areas in developing countries differ dramatically from cities in the industrialized world. Although cities everywhere are faced with environmental problems, those in developing countries are confronted by par-

ticularly severe risks. Pollution, housing shortages, inadequate sanitation, and unsafe water supplies are chronic problems for cities in less developed countries.

Housing is one of the most acute problems in many urban areas. Cities such as Calcutta and São Paulo are massively congested; the rate of internal migration is much too high for the provision of permanent housing. Migrants crowd into squatters' zones that mushroom around the edges of cities. In urban areas in the West, newcomers are most likely to settle close to the central parts of the city, but the reverse tends to happen in developing countries, where migrants populate what has been called the "septic fringe" of the urban areas. Shanty

The overcrowded streets of the Hong Kong–Guangdong megacity.

dwellings made of burlap or cardboard are set up around the edges of the city wherever there is a little space.

In São Paulo, it is estimated that there was a 5.4 million shortfall in habitable homes in 1996. Some scholars estimate that the shortage is as high as 20 million, if the definition of "habitable housing" is interpreted more strictly. Since the 1980s, the chronic deficit of housing in São Paulo has produced a wave of unofficial occupations of empty buildings. Groups of unhoused families initiate mass squats in abandoned hotels, offices, and government buildings. Many families believe that it is better to share limited kitchen and toilet facilities with hundreds of others than to live on the streets or in *favelas,* the makeshift shantytowns on the edges of the city. Still, 40 percent of the population live in *favelas* (Barcelona Field Studies Centre 2003).

City and regional governments in less developed countries are hard pressed to keep up with the spiraling demand for housing. In cities such as São Paulo there are disagreements among housing authorities and local governments about how to address the housing problem. Some argue that the most feasible route is to improve conditions within the *favelas*—to provide electricity and running water, pave the streets, and assign postal addresses. Others fear that makeshift shantytowns are fundamentally unhabitable and should be demolished to make way for proper housing for poor families.

Congestion and overdevelopment in city centers lead to serious environmental problems in many urban areas. Mexico City is a prime example. About 94 percent of Mexico City consists of built-up areas, with only 6 percent of land being open space. The level of green spaces—parks and open stretches of green land—is far below that found in even the most densely populated North American or European cities. Pollution is a major problem, coming mostly from the cars, buses, and trucks that pack the inadequate roads of the city, the rest deriving from industrial pollutants. It has been estimated that living in Mexico City is equivalent to smoking forty cigarettes a day. In March 1992, pollution reached its highest level ever. Whereas an ozone level of just under 100 points was deemed "satisfactory" for health, in that month the level climbed to 398 points. The government had to order factories to close down for a period, schools were shut, and 40 percent of cars were banned from the streets on any one day.

SOCIAL EFFECTS

Many urban areas in the developing world are overcrowded and underresourced. Poverty is widespread, and existing social services cannot meet the demands for health care, family planning advice, education, and training. The unbalanced age distribution in developing countries adds to their social and economic difficulties. Compared to industrialized countries, a much larger proportion of the population in the developing world is under the age of fifteen. A youthful population needs support and education, and during that time its members would not be economically productive. But many developing countries lack the resources to provide universal education.

Families sit on the sidewalk with their belongings after being evicted by police from a central São Paulo building. Hundreds of squatters had settled in São Paulo buildings until, facing forced eviction by riot police, they were compelled to leave.

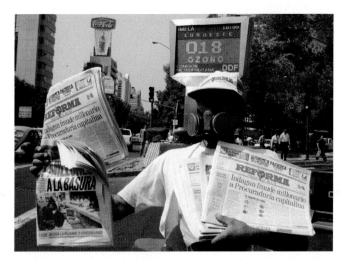

Newspaper salesman Alvarado uses mask to protect himself from air pollution as he sells papers at a busy crossroad in Mexico City. Behind him a screen indicates the day's pollution levels.

When their families are poor, many children must work full time, and others have to eke out a living as street children, begging for whatever they can. When the street children mature, most become unemployed, homeless, or both.

The Future of Urbanization in the Developing World

In considering the scope of the challenges facing urban areas in developing countries, it can be difficult to see prospects for change and development. Conditions of life in many of the world's largest cities seem likely to decline even further in the years to come. But the picture is not entirely negative.

First, although birthrates remain high in many countries, they are likely to drop in the years to come as urbanization proceeds. This in turn will feed into a gradual decrease in the rate of urbanization itself. In West Africa, for example, the rate of urbanization should drop to 3.4 percent per year by 2020, down from an annual rate of over 4.5 percent growth over the previous three decades (UN Population Division 2002).

Second, globalization is presenting important opportunities for urban areas in developing countries. With economic integration, cities around the world are able to enter international markets, to promote themselves as locations for investment and development, and to create economic links across the borders of nation-states. Globalization presents one of the most dynamic openings for growing urban centers to become major forces in economic development and innovation. Indeed, many cities in the developing world are already joining the ranks of the world's global cities.

World Population Growth

There are currently over 6 billion people in the world. It was estimated that "baby number 6 billion" was born on October 12, 1999, although of course no one can know when and where this event happened. Paul Ehrlich (Fremlin 1964) calculated in the 1960s that if the rate of population growth at that time continued, nine hundred years from now (not a long period in world history as a whole) there would be 60,000,000,000,000,000 (60 quadrillion) people on the face of the earth. There would be one hundred people for every square yard of the earth's surface, including both land and water. The physicist J. H. Fremlin (1964) worked out that housing such a population would require a continuous two-thousand-story building covering the entire planet. Even such a stupendous structure would have only three or four yards of floor space per person.

Such a picture, of course, is nothing more than nightmarish fiction designed to drive home how cataclysmic the consequences of continued population growth would be. The real issue is what will happen over the next thirty or forty years, by which time, if current trends are not reversed, the world's population will already have grown to intolerable levels. Partly because governments and other agencies heeded the warnings of Ehrlich and others twenty years ago by introducing population-control programs, there are grounds for supposing that world population growth is beginning to trail off. Estimates calculated in the 1960s of the likely world population by the year 2000 turned out to be inaccurate. The World Bank (2004) estimated the world population was just over 6 billion in 2000, compared with some earlier estimates of over 8 billion. Nevertheless, considering that a century ago there were only 1.5 billion people in the world, this still represents growth of staggering proportions. Moreover, the factors underlying population growth are by no means completely predictable, and all estimates have to be interpreted with caution.

Population Analysis: Demography

The study of population is referred to as **demography.** The term was invented about a century and a half ago, at a time when nations were beginning to keep official statistics on the nature and distribution of their populations. Demography is concerned with measuring the size of populations and explaining their rise or decline. Population patterns are governed by three factors: births, deaths, and migrations. Demography is customarily treated as a branch of sociology, because the fac-

Urbanization and Migration

Population Movements

Notable shifts in population movement today involve rapid urbanization, the movement of refugees and displaced persons, and international migration. Movements of people, which will continue and increase in the future, affect patterns of development. Much of this movement is forced by conditions such as poverty or environmental degradation.

Virtually all population growth in the next decades will be concentrated in the urban areas of the world. Urban growth has outpaced employment and services and is often accompanied by poverty, yet cities offer opportunities for social change and economic development.

Although accounting for only 2 percent of the global population, a growing number—now 125 million people—are living outside the countries of their birth (including refugees and undocumented migrants). International migration is projected to remain high during the twenty-first century. The more developed regions are expected to remain net receivers of international migrants, with an average gain of about 2 million per year over the next 50 years.

Half the World in Cities

- As of 2000, 2.9 billion people were living in urban areas, comprising 47 percent of the world population.
- By 2030, 4.9 billion are expected to live in urban areas, or 60 percent of the world population.

Most of this population increase will be absorbed by the urban areas of less developed regions, while their rural populations will grow very slowly. By 2007, the number of urban dwellers is also expected to exceed the number of rural dwellers for the first time in history.

Rapid urban growth on today's scale strains the capacity of local and national governments to provide even the most basic of services such as water, electricity and sewerage. The environment, natural resources, social cohesion, and individual rights are at risk. Squatter settlements and overcrowded slums are home to tens of millions, like the *favelas* that cling to the hillsides of Rio de Janeiro and the tombs used as homes by tens of thousands in Cairo's "City of the Dead." In some developing countries, notably in Africa, this growth reflects rural crisis rather than urban-based development.

But cities also speed up social transformation, opening new avenues for human development, especially for women. Cities can give women greater access to schooling, to reproductive health services including family planning and sexual health, and to work with fair wages.

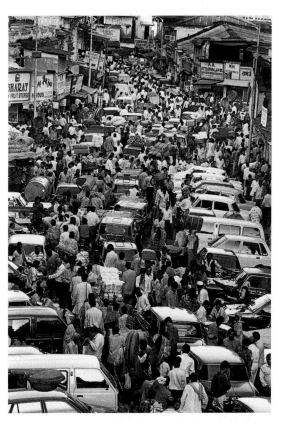

- "Brain drain," or the migration of more educated young people from developing countries to fill gaps in the work forces of industrialized countries.

SOURCE: United Nations Population Fund 2001.

Causes That Motivate International Migration

- The search for a better life for oneself and family;
- Income disparities among and within regions;
- The labor and migration policies of sending and receiving countries;
- Political conflict (which drives migration across borders as well as within countries);
- Environmental degradation, including the loss of farmland, forests, and pasture (most "environmental refugees" go to cities rather than abroad);

Questions

- What political or social changes might reduce the pressure to migrate?
- What is the connection between environmental problems and the shift toward urbanization?
- The article mentions certain benefits from living in a city rather than in rural areas. What are they, and why do you think migrants seek them in spite of the many negative aspects of city life?

tors that influence the level of births and deaths in a given group or society, as well as migrations of population, are largely social and cultural.

Much demographic work tends to be statistical. All the industrialized countries today gather and analyze basic statistics on their populations by carrying out censuses (systematic surveys designed to find out about the whole population of a given country). Rigorous as the modes of data collection now are, even in these nations demographic statistics are not wholly accurate. In the United States there is a comprehensive population census every ten years, and sample studies are regularly conducted. Yet for various reasons, many people are not registered in the official population statistics, including illegal immigrants, homeless people, transients, and others who for one reason or another avoided registration.

In many developing countries, particularly those with recent high rates of population growth, demographic statistics are much more unreliable. For instance, some demographers have estimated that registered births and deaths in India may represent only about three quarters of the actual totals (Cox 1976). The accuracy of official statistics is even lower in parts of central Africa.

Basic Demographic Concepts

Among the basic concepts used by demographers, the most important are crude birthrates, fertility, fecundity, and crude death rates. **Crude birthrates** are expressed as the number of live births per year per thousand of the population. They are called "crude" rates because of their very general character. Crude birthrates, for example, do not tell us what proportions of a population are male or female, or what the age distribution of a population is (the relative proportions of young and old people in the population). Where statistics are collected that relate birth or death rates to such categories, demographers speak of "specific" rather than "crude" rates. For instance, an age-specific birthrate might specify the number of births per thousand women in different age groups.

If we wish to understand population patterns in any detail, the information provided by specific birthrates is normally necessary. Crude birthrates, however, are useful for making overall comparisons between different groups, societies, and regions. Thus the crude birthrate in the United States is fifteen per thousand. Other industrialized countries have lower rates, such as nine per thousand in Germany, Russia, and Italy. In many other parts of the world, crude birthrates are much higher. In India, for instance, the crude birthrate is twenty-five per thousand; in Ethiopia it is forty-eight per thousand (World Bank 1998).

Birthrates are an expression of the fertility of women. **Fertility** refers to how many live-born children the average woman has. A fertility rate is usually calculated as the average number of births per thousand women of childbearing age.

Fertility is distinguished from **fecundity,** which means the potential number of children women are biologically capable of bearing. It is physically possible for a normal woman to bear a child every year during the period when she is capable of conception. There are variations in fecundity according to the age at which women reach puberty and menopause, both of which differ among countries as well as among individuals. Although there may be families in which a woman bears twenty or more children, fertility rates in practice are always much lower than fecundity rates, because social and cultural factors limit breeding.

Crude death rates (also called "mortality rates") are calculated in the same way as birthrates—the number of deaths per thousand of population per year. Again, there are major variations among countries, but death rates in many societies in the developing world are falling to levels comparable to those of the West. The death rate in the United States in 1996 was eight per thousand. In India it was nine per thousand; in Ethiopia it was seventeen per thousand. A few countries have much higher death rates. In Sierra Leone, for example, the death rate is twenty-seven per thousand. Like crude birthrates, crude death rates only provide a very general index of **mortality** (the number of deaths in a population). Specific death rates give more precise information. A particularly important specific death rate is the **infant mortality rate:** the number of babies per thousand births in any year who die before reaching age one. One of the key factors underlying the population explosion has been reductions in infant mortality rates.

Declining rates of infant mortality are the most important influence on increasing **life expectancy**—that is, the number of years the average person can expect to live. In 1900, life expectancy at birth in the United States was about forty years. Today it has increased to nearly seventy-four years. This does not mean, however, that most people at the turn of the century died when they were about forty years of age. When there is a high infant mortality rate, as there is in many developing nations, the average life expectancy—which is a statistical average—is brought down (Global Map 19.2). If we look at the life expectancy of only those people who survive the first year of life, we find that in 1900 the average person could expect to live to age fifty-eight. Illness, nutrition, and the influence of natural disasters are the other factors influencing life expectancy. Life expectancy has to be distinguished from **life span,** which is the maximum number of years that an individual could live. Although life expectancy has increased in most societies in the world, life span has remained unaltered. Only a small proportion of people live to be one hundred or more.

Dynamics of Population Change

Rates of population growth or decline are measured by subtracting the number of deaths per thousand over a given period from the number of births per thousand—this is usually calculated annually. Some European countries have negative growth rates—in other words, their populations are declining. Virtually all of the industrialized countries have growth rates of less than 0.5 percent. Rates of population growth were high in the eighteenth and nineteenth centuries in Europe and the United States but have since leveled off. Many developing countries today have rates of between 2 and 3 percent (Global Map 19.3). These may not seem very different from the rates of the industrialized countries, but in fact, the difference is enormous.

The reason is that growth in population is **exponential.** An ancient Persian myth helps illustrate this concept. A courtier asked a ruler to reward him for his services by giving him twice as many grains of rice for each service as he had the time before, starting with a single grain on the first square of a chess board. Believing himself to be on to a good thing, the king commanded grain to be brought up from his storehouse. By the twenty-first square, the storehouse was empty; the fortieth square required ten billion grains of rice (Meadows et al. 1972). In other words, starting with one item and doubling it, doubling the result, and so on, rapidly leads to huge figures: 1:2:4:8:16:32:64:128, and so on. In seven operations the figure has risen by 128 percent. Exactly the same principle applies to population growth. We can measure this effect by means of the **doubling time,** the period of time it takes for the population to double. A population growth of 1 percent will produce a doubling of numbers in seventy years. At 2 percent growth, a population will double in thirty-five years, while at 3 percent it will double in twenty-three years.

Malthusianism

In premodern societies, birthrates were very high by the standards of the industrialized world today. Nonetheless, population growth remained low until the eighteenth century because there was a rough overall balance between births and deaths. The general trend of numbers was upward, and there were sometimes periods of more marked population increase, but these were followed by increases in death rates. In medieval Europe, for example, when harvests were bad, marriages tended to be postponed and the number of conceptions fell, while deaths increased. These complementary trends reduced the number of mouths to be fed. No preindustrial society was able to escape from this self-regulating rhythm (Wrigley 1968).

During the period of the rise of industrialism, many looked forward to a new age in which scarcity would be a phenomenon of the past. The development of modern industry, it was widely supposed, would create a new era of abundance. In his celebrated work *Essay on the Principle of Population* (2003; orig. 1798), Thomas Malthus criticized these ideas and initiated a debate about the connection between population and food resources that continues to this day. At the time Malthus wrote, the population in Europe was growing rapidly. Malthus pointed out that whereas population increase is exponential, food supply depends on fixed resources that can be expanded only by developing new land for cultivation. Population growth therefore tends to outstrip the means of support available. The inevitable outcome is famine, which, combined with the influence of war and plagues, acts as a natural limit to population increase. Malthus predicted that human beings would always live in circumstances of misery and starvation, unless they practiced what he called "moral restraint." His cure for excessive population growth was for people to strictly limit their frequency of sexual intercourse. (The use of contraception he proclaimed to be a "vice.")

For a while, **Malthusianism** was ignored, since the population development of the Western countries followed a quite different pattern from that which he had anticipated—as we shall see below. Rates of population growth trailed off in the nineteenth and twentieth centuries. Indeed, in the 1930s there were major worries about population decline in many industrialized countries, including the United States. The upsurge in world population growth in the twentieth century has again lent some credence to Malthus's views, although few support them in their original version. Population expansion in developing countries seems to be outstripping the resources that those countries can generate to feed their citizenry.

The Demographic Transition

Demographers often refer to the changes in the ratio of births to deaths in the industrialized countries from the nineteenth century onward as the **demographic transition.** The notion was first worked out by Warren S. Thompson (1929), who described a three-stage process in which one type of population stability would be eventually replaced by another as a society reached an advanced level of economic development.

Stage one refers to the conditions characteristic of most traditional societies, in which both birth and death rates are high and the infant mortality rate is especially large. Population grows little if at all, as the high number of births is more or less balanced by the level of deaths. Stage two, which began in Europe and the United States in the early part of the nineteenth century—with wide regional variations—occurs when death

Life Expectancies in Global Perspective, 2002

The United States presently ranks eighteenth in the world in life-expectancy rates—low among Western nations, but considerably higher than most Second World and developing nations. How much of a correlation do you find between life expectancy and income level?

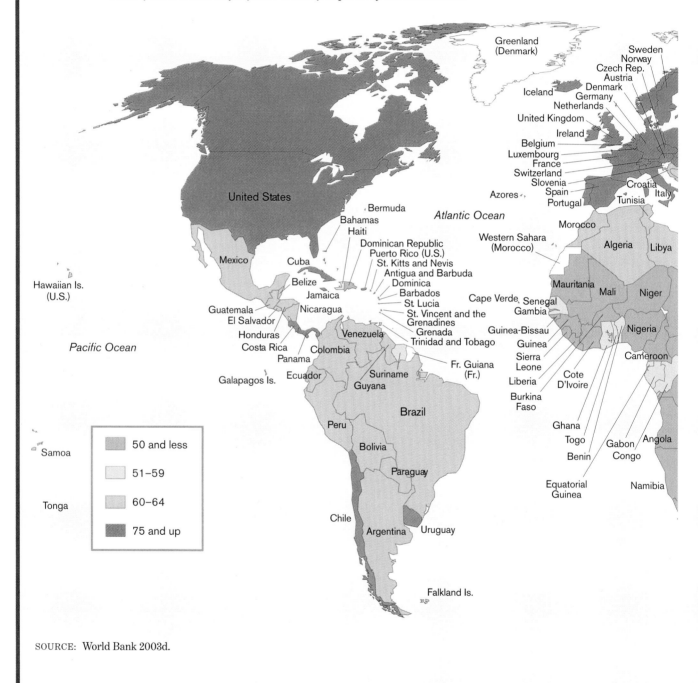

Greenland (Denmark)

Sweden
Norway
Czech Rep.
Austria
Denmark
Iceland   Germany
Netherlands
United Kingdom
Ireland
Belgium
Luxembourg
France
Switzerland
Slovenia   Croatia
Azores   Spain   Italy
Portugal   Tunisia

United States

Atlantic Ocean

Bermuda
Bahamas
Haiti
Dominican Republic
Puerto Rico (U.S.)
St. Kitts and Nevis
Antigua and Barbuda
Dominica
Barbados
St. Lucia
St. Vincent and the
Grenadines
Grenada
Trinidad and Tobago

Morocco

Western Sahara
(Morocco)   Algeria   Libya

Mexico   Cuba

Belize

Jamaica

Mauritania   Mali   Niger

Cape Verde Senegal
Gambia

Guatemala   Nicaragua
El Salvador

Guinea-Bissau   Nigeria

Venezuela

Guinea
Sierra   Cameroon
Leone

Honduras
Costa Rica   Colombia
Panama

Cote
D'Ivoire

Ecuador

Liberia

Galapagos Is.   Fr. Guiana
(Fr.)

Suriname
Guyana

Burkina
Faso

Pacific Ocean

Hawaiian Is.
(U.S.)

Peru

Brazil

Ghana
Togo   Gabon   Angola
Benin   Congo

Samoa

Bolivia

Equatorial   Namibia
Guinea

Tonga

Paraguay

Chile

Argentina   Uruguay

Falkland Is.

Legend	
	50 and less
	51–59
	60–64
	75 and up

SOURCE: World Bank 2003d.

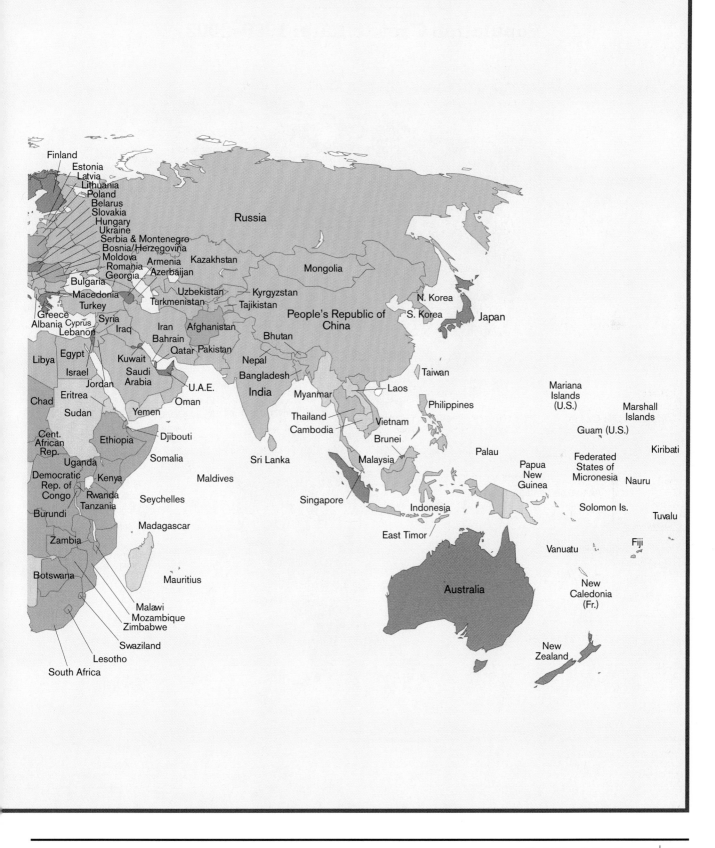

Population Growth Rate, 1980–2002

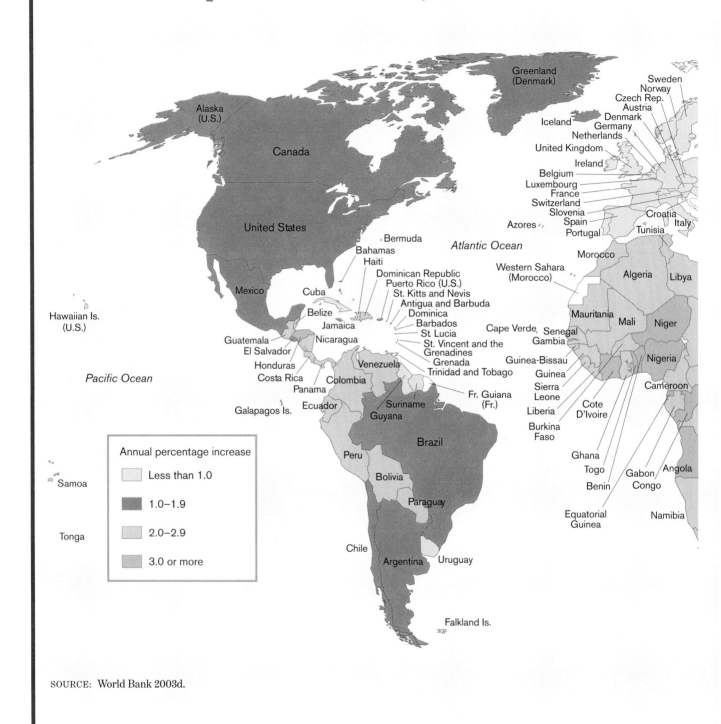

Annual percentage increase

- Less than 1.0
- 1.0–1.9
- 2.0–2.9
- 3.0 or more

SOURCE: World Bank 2003d.

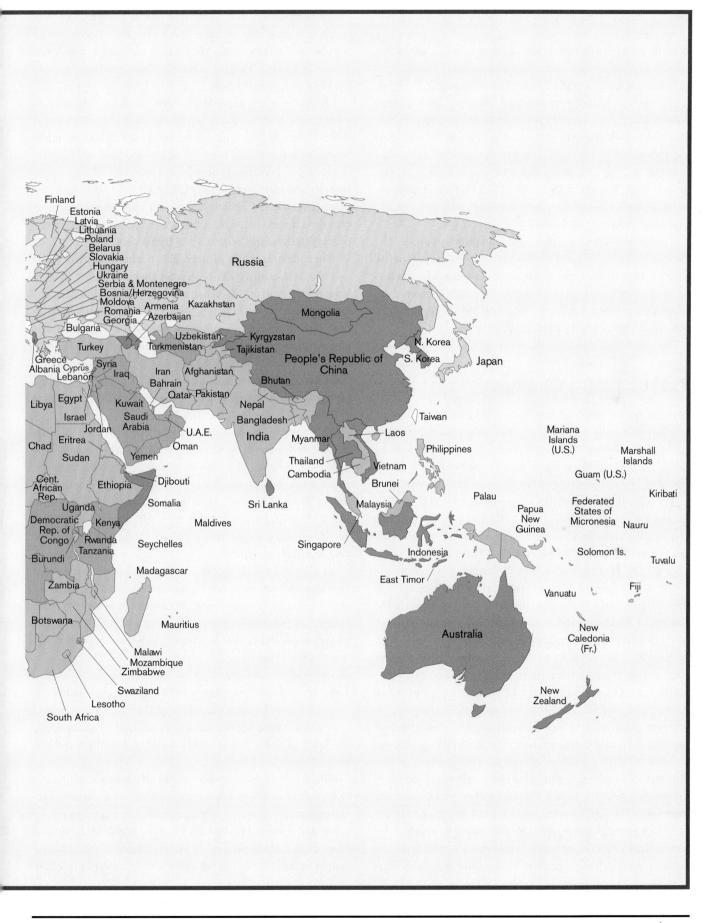

rates fall while fertility remains high. This is, therefore, a phase of marked population growth. It is subsequently replaced by stage three, in which, with industrial development, birthrates drop to a level such that population is again fairly stable.

Demographers do not fully agree about how this sequence of change should be interpreted, or how long lasting stage three is likely to be. Fertility in the Western countries has not been completely stable over the past century or so; considerable differences in fertility remain among the industrialized nations, as well as between classes or regions within them. Nevertheless, it is generally accepted that this sequence accurately describes a major transformation in the demographic character of modern societies.

The theory of demographic transition directly opposes the ideas of Malthus. Whereas for Malthus, increasing prosperity would automatically bring about population increase, the thesis of demographic transition emphasizes that economic development, generated by industrialism, would actually lead to a new equilibrium of population stability.

Prospects for Change

Fertility remains high in developing-world societies because traditional attitudes to family size have been maintained. Having large numbers of children is often still regarded as desirable, providing a source of labor on family-run farms. Some religions are either opposed to birth control or affirm the desirability of having many children. Contraception is opposed by Islamic leaders in several countries and by the Catholic Church, whose influence is especially marked in South and Central America. The motivation to reduce fertility has not always been forthcoming even from political authorities. In 1974, contraceptives were banned in Argentina as part of a program to double the population of the country as fast as possible; this was seen as a means of developing its economic and military strength.

Yet a decline in fertility levels has at last occurred in some large developing countries. An example is China, which currently has a population of about 1.3 billion people—almost a quarter of the world's population as a whole. The Chinese government established one of the most extensive programs of population control that any country has undertaken, with the object of stabilizing the country's numbers at close to their current level. The government instituted incentives (such as better housing and free health care and education) to promote single-child families, whereas families who have more than one child face special hardships (wages are cut for those who have a third child). As a response to this government program, some families went to the extreme of killing their female infants.

There is evidence that China's antinatal policies, however harsh they may appear, have had a substantial effect on its population (Mirsky 1982). Yet there is also much resistance within the country. People are reluctant to regard parents with one child as a proper family.

China's program demands a degree of centralized government control that is either unacceptable or unavailable in most other developing countries. In India, for instance, many schemes for promoting family planning and the use of contraceptives have been tried but with only relatively small success. India in 1988 had a population of 789 million. In 2000, its population just topped 1 billion. And even if its population-growth rate does diminish, by 2050, India will be the most populous country in the world, with over 1.5 billion people.

Some claim that the demographic changes that will occur over the next century will be greater than any before in all of human history. It is difficult to predict with any precision the rate at which the world population will rise, but the United Nations (UN) has several fertility scenarios. The "high" scenario places the world's population at more than 16 billion people by 2150! The "medium" fertility scenario, which the UN deems most likely, assumes that fertility levels will stabilize at just over two children per woman, resulting in a world population of 10.8 billion people in 2150 (UN 2003).

This overall population increase conceals two distinct trends. First, most developing countries will undergo the process of demographic transition described above. This will result in a substantial surge in the population, as death rates fall. India and China are each likely to see their populations reach 1.5 billion people. Areas in Asia, Africa, and Latin America will similarly experience rapid growth before the population eventually stabilizes.

The second trend concerns the developed countries that have already undergone the demographic transition. These societies will undergo very slight population growth, if any at all. Instead, a process of aging will occur in which the number of young people will decline in absolute terms and the older segment of the population will increase markedly. This will have widespread economic and social implications for developed countries: As the dependency ratio increases, pressure will mount on health and social services. Yet, as their numbers grow, older people will also have more political weight and may be able to push for higher expenditures on programs and services of importance to them.

What will be the consequences of these demographic changes? Some observers see the makings of widespread social upheaval—particularly in the developing countries undergoing demographic transition. Changes in the economy and labor markets may prompt widespread internal migration as people in rural areas search for work. The rapid growth of

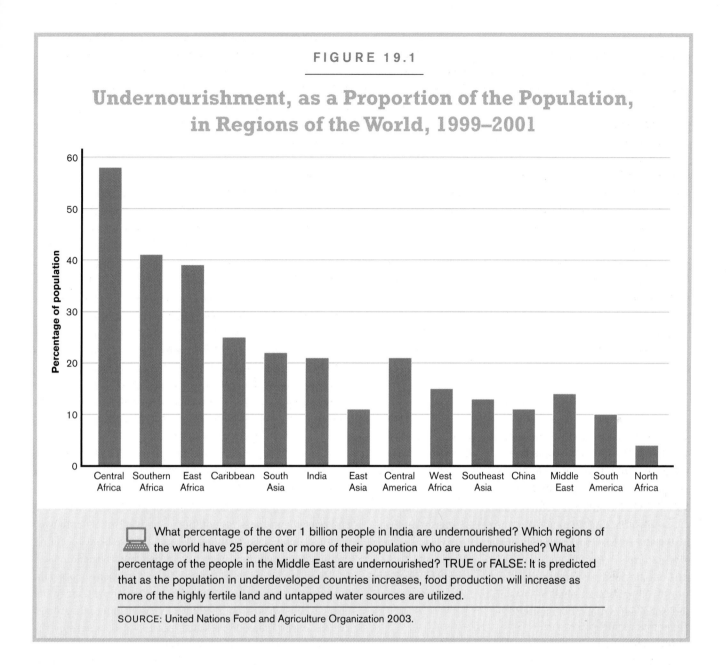

FIGURE 19.1

Undernourishment, as a Proportion of the Population, in Regions of the World, 1999–2001

What percentage of the over 1 billion people in India are undernourished? Which regions of the world have 25 percent or more of their population who are undernourished? What percentage of the people in the Middle East are undernourished? TRUE or FALSE: It is predicted that as the population in underdeveloped countries increases, food production will increase as more of the highly fertile land and untapped water sources are utilized.

SOURCE: United Nations Food and Agriculture Organization 2003.

cities will be likely to lead to environmental damage, new public-health risks, overloaded infrastructures, rising crime, and impoverished squatter settlements.

Famine and food shortages are another serious concern. There are already 842 million people in the world who suffer from hunger or undernourishment (United Nations Food and Agriculture Organization [UN FAO] 2003). In some parts of the world, more than a third of the population is undernourished (Figure 19.1). As the population rises, levels of food output will need to rise accordingly to avoid widespread scarcity. Yet this scenario is unlikely; many of the world's poorest areas are particularly affected by water shortages, shrinking farmland, and soil degradation—processes that reduce, rather than en-

hance, agricultural productivity. It is almost certain that food production will not occur at a level to ensure self-sufficiency. Large amounts of food and grain will need to be imported from areas where there are surpluses. According to the UN FAO (Nikos 1995), by 2010 industrialized countries will be producing 1,614 pounds of grain per person, compared to only 507 pounds per head in the developing world.

Technological advances in agriculture and industry are unpredictable, so no one can be sure how large a population the world might eventually be able to support. Yet even at current population levels, global resources may already be well below those required to create living standards in the less developed world comparable to those of the industrialized countries.

Population Growth and the Environment

Since the beginning of the practice of agriculture thousands of years ago, human beings have left an imprint on nature. Hunting and gathering societies mainly lived *from* nature; they existed on what the natural environment provided and made little attempt to change the world around them. With the coming of agriculture, this situation was altered. For crops to grow, land must be cleared, trees cut down, and encroaching weeds and wild foliage kept at bay. Even primitive farming methods can lead to soil erosion. Once natural forests are cut down and clearings made, the wind may blow away the topsoil. The farming community then clears some fresh plots of land, and so the process goes on. Some landscapes that we today think of as natural, such as the rocky areas and scrubland in southwestern Greece, are actually the result of soil erosion created by farmers five thousand years ago.

Yet before the development of modern industry, nature dominated human life far more than the other way around. Today the human onslaught on the environment is so intense that few natural processes are uninfluenced by human activity. Nearly all cultivable land is under agricultural production. What used to be almost inaccessible wildernesses are now often nature reserves, visited routinely by thousands of tourists. Modern industry, still expanding worldwide, has led to steeply climbing demands for sources of energy and raw materials. Yet the world's supply of such energy sources and raw materials is limited, and some key resources are bound to run out if global consumption is not restricted. Even the world's climate, as we shall see, has probably been affected by the global development of industry.

Global Environmental Threats

One problem we all face concerns **environmental ecology.** The spread of industrial production may already have done irreparable damage to the environment. Ecological questions concern not only how we can best cope with and contain environmental damage but also the very ways of life within industrialized societies. If the goal of continuous economic growth must be abandoned, new social institutions will probably be pioneered. Technological progress is unpredictable, and it may be that the earth will in fact yield sufficient resources for processes of industrialization. At the moment, however, this does not seem feasible, and if the developing countries are to achieve living standards comparable to those currently enjoyed in the West, global readjustments will be necessary.

Green movements and parties (such as Friends of the Earth or Greenpeace), which are themselves sometimes global organizations, have developed in response to the new environmental hazards. Although green philosophies are varied, a common thread concerns taking action to protect the world's environment, conserve rather than exhaust its resources, and protect the remaining animal species. Hundreds of animal species have become extinct even since the 1950s, and at the moment this is a continuing process.

Some environmental problems are particularly concentrated in specific areas. In the formerly communist societies of Eastern Europe and the Soviet Union, rivers, forests, and the air are highly polluted by industrial wastes. The consequences of such pollution, if it goes on unchecked, are potentially worldwide. As we have learned, the societies of the earth have become much more interdependent than ever before. As travelers on "spaceship earth," no matter where we live, we are all menaced by corrosion of the environment.

Global environmental threats are of several basic sorts: pollution, the creation of waste that cannot be disposed of in the short term or recycled, and the depletion of resources that cannot be replenished. The amount of domestic waste—what goes into our garbage cans—produced each day in the industrialized societies is staggering; these countries have sometimes been called the "throw-away societies" because the volume of items discarded as a matter of course is so large. For instance, food is mostly bought in packages that are thrown away at the end of the day. Some of these can be reprocessed and reused, but most cannot. Some kinds of widely employed plastics simply become unusable waste; there is no way of recycling them, and they have to be buried in garbage dumps.

When environmental analysts speak of waste materials, however, they mean not only goods that are thrown away, but also gaseous wastes pumped into the atmosphere. Examples are the carbon dioxide released into the atmosphere by the burning of fuels such as oil and coal in cars and power stations, and gases released into the air by the use of such things as aerosol cans, material for insulation, and air-conditioning units. Carbon dioxide is the main influence on the process of global warming that many scientists believe is occurring, while the other gases attack the ozone layer around the earth.

Global warming is thought to happen in the following way. The buildup of carbon dioxide in the earth's atmosphere functions like the glass of a greenhouse. It allows the sun's rays to pass through but acts as a barrier to prevent them from passing back. The effect is to heat up the earth; global warming is sometimes termed the "greenhouse effect" for this reason. If global warming is indeed taking place, the consequences are likely to be devastating. Among other things, sea levels will rise as the polar ice caps melt and the oceans will warm and expand. Cities that lie near the coasts or in low-lying areas will be flooded and

Greenpeace activists wearing targets protest outside the Brazilian Embassy in Hong Kong on October 18, 2001. The demonstrators urged the Brazilian government to guarantee the safety of environmentalists working to protect the Amazon following a telephoned death threat made against Greenpeace workers in Manaus, in the heart of the Amazon.

become uninhabitable. Large tracts of fertile land will become desert.

The ozone layer, which is high in the earth's atmosphere, forms a shield that protects against ultraviolet radiation. The gases used in aerosols and refrigerants produce particles that react with the ozone layer in such a way as to weaken it. It is thought that these chemicals have produced detectable holes in the ozone layer at both poles and thinning elsewhere. The radiation that is let into the earth's atmosphere produces a variety of potentially harmful effects, including an increase in cataracts of the eyes (which can cause blindness) and in levels of skin cancer.

Modern industry, still expanding worldwide, has led to steeply climbing demands for sources of energy and raw materials. Yet the world's supply of such energy sources and raw materials is limited. Even at current rates of use, for example, the known oil resources of the world will be completely consumed by the year 2050. New reserves of oil may be discovered, or alternative sources of cheap energy invented, but there plainly is a point at which some key resources will run out if global consumption is not limited.

Sustainable Development

Rather than calling for a reining back of economic growth, more recent developments turn on the notion of **sustainable development.** Sustainable development means that growth should, at least ideally, be carried on in such a way as to recycle physical resources rather than deplete them and to keep levels of pollution to a minimum. The term *sustainable development* was first introduced in a 1987 report commissioned by the United Nations, *Our Common Future.* This is also known as the Brundtland Report, since the organizing committee which produced the report was chaired by G. H. Brundtland, at that time the prime minister of Norway. Sustainable development was defined as the use of renewable resources to promote economic growth, the protection of animal species and biodiversity, and the commitment to maintaining clean air, water, and land. The Brundtland Commission regarded sustainable development as "meeting the needs of the present, without compromising the ability of future generations to meet their own needs."

After the publication of *Our Common Future,* the phrase *sustainable development* came to be widely used both by environmentalists and by governments. It was employed at the UN Earth Summit in Rio de Janeiro in 1992 and has subsequently appeared in other ecological summit meetings organized by the UN.

The Brundtland Report attracted much criticism. Critics see the notion of sustainable development as too vague and as neglecting the specific needs of poorer countries. According to the critics, the idea of sustainable development tends to focus attention only on the needs of richer countries; it does not consider the ways in which the high levels of consumption in the more affluent countries are satisfied at the expense of other people. For instance, demands on Indonesia to conserve its rain forests could be seen as unfair, because Indonesia has a greater need than the industrialized countries for the revenue it must forgo by accepting conservation.

Consumption, Poverty, and the Environment

Much of the debate surrounding the environment and economic development hinges on the issue of consumption patterns. *Consumption* refers to the goods, services, energy, and resources that are used up by people, institutions and societies. It is a phenomenon with both positive and negative dimensions. On the one hand, rising levels of consumption around the world mean that people are living under better conditions than in times past. Consumption is linked to economic development— as living standards rise, people are able to afford more food, clothing, personal items, leisure time, vacations, cars, and so forth. On the other hand, consumption can have negative impacts as well. Consumption patterns can damage the environmental resource base and exacerbate patterns of inequality.

The trends in world consumption over the course of the twentieth century are startling. According to the Human Development Report of the United Nations Development

Programme (UNDP 1998), private and public consumption expenditures in 1998 reached $24 trillion—twice the level of 1975 and six times that of 1950. In 1900, world consumption levels were just over $1.5 trillion. Consumption rates have been growing extremely rapidly since 1980. In industrialized countries, consumption per head has been growing at a rate of 2.3 percent annually; in East Asia growth has been even faster—6.1 percent annually. By contrast, the average African household consumes 20 percent *less* today than it did twenty-five years ago. There is widespread concern that the consumption explosion has passed by the poorest fifth of the world's population (UNDP 1998).

The inequalities in consumption between rich and poor are significant. The richest 20 percent of the world's population accounts for 86 percent of private consumption expenditures, whereas the poorest 20 percent accounts for only 1.3 percent (Figure 19.2). The richest 20 percent consumes 58 percent of total energy, 84 percent of all paper, 45 percent of all meat and fish, and owns 87 percent of all the vehicles.

Current consumption patterns are not only highly unequal, but they also are having a severe effect on the environment. For example, the consumption of fresh water has doubled since 1960, the burning of fossil fuels has almost quintupled in the past fifty years, and the consumption of wood is up by 40 per-

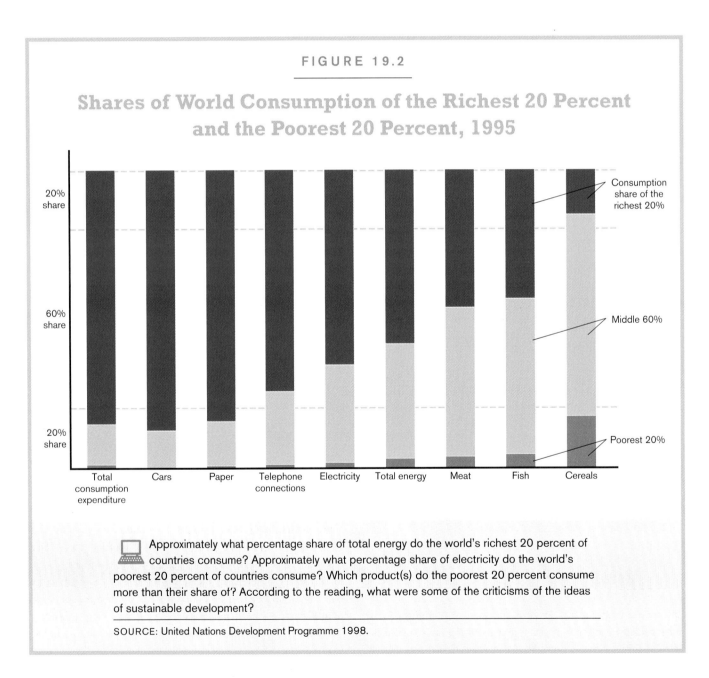

FIGURE 19.2

Shares of World Consumption of the Richest 20 Percent and the Poorest 20 Percent, 1995

Approximately what percentage share of total energy do the world's richest 20 percent of countries consume? Approximately what percentage share of electricity do the world's poorest 20 percent of countries consume? Which product(s) do the poorest 20 percent consume more than their share of? According to the reading, what were some of the criticisms of the ideas of sustainable development?

SOURCE: United Nations Development Programme 1998.

cent over twenty-five years ago. Fish stocks are declining, wild species are becoming extinct, water supplies are diminishing, and wooded areas are shrinking in size (UNDP 1998). Patterns of consumption are not only depleting existing natural elements, but are also contributing to its degradation through waste products and harmful emissions.

Finally, although the rich are the world's main consumers, the environmental damage that is caused by growing consumption has the heaviest effect on the poor. The wealthy are in a better position to enjoy the many benefits of consumption without having to deal with its negative effects. On a local level, affluent groups can usually afford to move away from problem areas, leaving the poor to bear most of the costs. Chemical plants, power stations, major roads, railways, and airports are often sited close to low-income areas. On a global level, we can see a similar process at work: Soil degradation, deforestation, water shortages, lead emissions, and air pollution are all concentrated within the developing world. Poverty also intensifies these environmental threats. People with few resources have little choice but to maximize the resources that are available to them. As a result, more and more pressures are put on a shrinking resource base as the human population increases.

The Environment:
A Sociological Issue?

Why should the environment be a concern for sociologists? Aren't we talking of issues that are the province purely of scientists or technologists? Isn't the effect of human beings on nature a physical one, created by modern technologies of industrial production? Yes, but modern industry and technology have come into being in relation to distinctive social institutions. The origins of our effect on the environment are social, and so are many of its consequences.

Rescuing the global environment will thus mean social as well as technological change. Given the vast global inequalities that exist, there is little chance that the poor developing countries will sacrifice their own economic growth because of environmental problems created largely by the rich ones. Yet the earth does not seem to possess sufficient resources for everyone on the planet to live at the standard of living most people in the industrialized societies take for granted. Hence if the impoverished sectors of the world are to catch up with the richer ones, the latter are likely to have to revise their expectations about constant economic growth. Some green authors argue that people in the rich countries must react against consumerism and return to more simple ways of life if global ecological disaster is to be avoided.

Prospects for Change

There can be no question but that global warming is a global problem. Greenhouse gases released in the atmosphere do not simply affect the climate of the country in which they were produced, but alter climatic patterns for the entire world. For this reason, many policy makers and scientists believe that any viable solution to the problem must also be global in scale. Yet the political difficulties in negotiating an international treaty to reduce greenhouse gases are enormous and suggest that although globalization has ushered in a new era of international cooperation, the world is still far from being able to speak decisively with a unified political voice about many of the issues that it confronts.

In December 1997, delegates from 166 nations gathered in Kyoto, Japan, in an effort to hammer out an agreement to reduce global warming. The summit was the culmination of two years of informal discussion among the countries. World leaders, faced with mounting scientific evidence that global warming is indeed occurring, and under pressure from voters to adopt environmentally friendly policies, clearly recognized that international action of some kind was needed. But faced as well with intense lobbying by industry, which fears it will bear the brunt of the cost for reducing fossil fuel emissions, world leaders felt compelled to balance safeguarding the environment against the threat of economic disruption.

As a result, the pollution reductions agreed to by the countries are meager. Thirty-eight of the advanced industrial nations represented at the conference agreed to reduce total emission levels by 2010 to approximately 5 percent below what they were in 1990. But different countries agreed to different specific targets: The United States agreed (upon ratification by the U.S. Congress) to reduce emission levels by 7 percent, the fifteen countries of the European Union pledged an 8 percent reduction, and Japan promised a 6 percent cut. The nations also tentatively agreed to establish an emissions "trading" system whereby a country that has reduced emissions levels beyond its target will be able to sell emissions "credits" to countries that have been unable to meet their goals. The agreement also includes commitments on behalf of the industrialized countries to assist developing countries by providing technology and funding to help overcome their limited capacity to respond to climate change.

To become an active and enforceable treaty, the Kyoto Protocol must receive support from countries that emit 55 percent of global greenhouse emissions. This finally happened in November 2004 when Russia ratified the agreement. This brought the total number of ratifying countries to 127, including China, India, Japan, New Zealand, and the European Union. Notably, Australia and the United States have refused to ratify the treaty even though the United States is responsible for the largest single share of global greenhouse gases of any country.

While politicians hailed the accord as an important first step in dealing with global warming, there are three serious problems with the Kyoto agreement. First, while many newly industrialized countries, such as China, India, and Russia, have now ratified the treaty, the terms of the agreement largely exempt them from making emission reductions. Because the reduction of greenhouse gas emissions requires expensive technology upgrades for factories and other industrial infrastructure, opponents of the agreement have argued that the exemption for developing countries gives them an unfair competitive advantage in the global market. Yet this critique fails to take into account that developed countries produce over five times more emissions per person than developing countries (UN 2004). This holds true even for China, which has the largest population and has been industrializing rapidly. The United States alone is responsible for over 25 percent of carbon dioxide emissions (BBC News 2001a). Second, many environmentalists warn that the reduction in greenhouse gases agreed to at Kyoto is not enough to reverse the trend toward global warming—only to slow its onset. Unless much greater emissions reductions are achieved, the world will still experience most of the disastrous consequences of global warming in the next century. Others, including President George W. Bush, have suggested that the science that supports the Kyoto Protocol is inconclusive and provides insufficient evidence that the measures adopted in the agreement would have their intended effect (White House Press Office 2001). This is contrary to the United Nations Intergovernmental Panel on Climate Change (IPCC), which reviewed all of the available scientific research on climate change and determined that, in fact, global warming is a result of human production of greenhouse gases and must be addressed immediately to avert a climatic disaster (UNIPCC 2001). In recent years, President Bush has started to accept the scientific evidence on global warming but has nevertheless resisted committing the United States to the treaty. Third, and most problematic, the Kyoto accord, which must be ratified by the legislative bodies of all the signatory countries, faces stiff political opposition. Industry leaders and conservative politicians in the United States, for example, claim that reaching even the 7 percent reduction agreed to by the U.S. delegation would be tremendously expensive and that the environmental regulations required to achieve even this modest goal would hamstring U.S. business and retard economic growth. The former House Speaker Newt Gingrich said the United States "surrendered" to pressure in Kyoto and called the proposed treaty an outrage that would cripple the American economy (Broder 1997). In 2001, in an attempt to satisfy American business interests, President Bush proposed an alternative strategy to lower greenhouse gas emissions through a system of government incentives for voluntary emission reductions by private businesses. Countries that ratified the treaty denounced the Bush plan as ineffective and openly criticized the unwillingness of the United States to ratify the Kyoto Protocol or seriously address the global problems created in no small part by American industrialism. In 2005, President Bush said that unless China and India (two of the largest emitters) would agree to be bound by the treaty, the United States would not do so.

It is clear that modern technology, science, and industry are not exclusively beneficial in their consequences. Sociologists perceive a responsibility to examine closely the social relations and institutions that brought about the current state of affairs, because rescuing the situation will require a profound consciousness of human authorship.

Study Outline

Traditional Cities

- Traditional cities differed in many ways from modern urban areas. They were mostly very small by modern standards, were surrounded by walls, and their centers were dominated by religious buildings and palaces.

Living in Cities

- In traditional societies, only a small minority of the population lived in urban areas. In the industrialized countries today, between 60 percent and 90 percent do so. Urbanism is also increasing very rapidly in developing countries.

Theories of Urbanism

- Early approaches to urban sociology were dominated by the work of the Chicago School. The members of this school saw urban processes in terms of ecological models derived from biology. Louis Wirth developed the conception of urbanism as a "way of life." These approaches have more recently been challenged, though without being discarded altogether.
- Later approaches to urban theory have placed more emphasis on the influence of broader socioeconomic factors—particularly those deriving from industrial capitalism—on city life.

Suburbanization

- The expansion of suburbs—*suburbanization*—has contributed to *inner-city* decay. Wealthier groups and businesses tend to move out of the central city to take advantage of lower tax rates. This begins a cycle of deterioration, in which the more suburbia expands, the greater the problems faced by those living in the central cities. *Urban renewal* (also called *gentrification*)—the refurbishing of old buildings to put them to new uses—has become common in many large cities.

Urban Development

- Urban analysis today must be prepared to link global and local issues. Factors that influence urban development locally are sometimes part of much more international processes. The structure of local neighborhoods and their patterns of growth and decline often reflect changes in industrial production internationally.
- Massive urban development is occurring in developing countries. Cities in these societies differ in major respects from those characteristic of the West. The majority of the population live in illegal makeshift housing, in conditions of extreme poverty.

- Population growth is one of the most significant global problems currently faced by humanity. About a quarter of the world's population suffers from malnutrition, and over ten million people die of starvation each year. This misery is concentrated in the developing countries.

Demography

- The study of population growth is called *demography*. Much demographic work is statistical, but demographers are also concerned with trying to explain why population patterns take the form they do. The most important concepts in population analysis are *birthrates, death rates, fertility,* and *mortality.*
- The changes in population patterns that have occurred in the industrialized societies are usually analyzed in terms of a process of *demographic transition.* Before industrialization, both birth and death rates were high. During the beginning of industrialization, there was population growth because death rates were reduced while birthrates took longer to decline. Finally a new equilibrium was reached with low birthrates balancing low death rates.
- World resources are finite, even if the limits of what can be produced are continually revised due to technological developments. Energy consumption and the consumption of raw materials and other goods are vastly higher in the Western countries than in other areas of the world. These consumption levels depend, moreover, on resources transferred from developing regions to the industrially developed nations. If resources were shared equally, there would be a significant drop in Western living standards.
- There are few aspects of the natural world that have not been affected by human activity. The industrialization of agriculture, the depletion of natural resources, the pollution of air and water, and the creation of vast mountains of unrecyclable waste are all sources of threat to the future survival of humanity. Addressing these issues will mean, among other things, that richer nations will have to revise their expectations of persistent economic growth.

Key Concepts

collective consumption (p. 617)
conurbation (p. 613)
created environment (p. 617)
crude birthrates (p. 634)
crude death rates (p. 634)
demographic transition (p. 635)
demography (p. 631)
doubling time (p. 635)
ecological approach (p. 613)
environmental ecology (p. 642)
exponential (p. 635)
fecundity (p. 634)
fertility (p. 634)

Study Guide | **647**

Review Questions

1. Most cities of the ancient world shared certain common features. Which one of the following is *not* one of those features?
   a. Cities were surrounded by walls.
   b. The central area of the city was occupied by a religious temple.
   c. The dwellings of the ruling class or elite tended to be concentrated in or near the center.
   d. Cities' influence over the rest of the countries was strong.

2. The inequalities in consumption between rich and poor are significant. The richest 20 percent of the world's population accounts for _____ percent of private consumption expenditures.
   a. 26
   b. 46
   c. 86
   d. 96

3. The Chicago School applied an ecological approach to the study of cities. What were the main concepts of this approach?
   a. Cities became ordered into "natural areas"—concentric rings—through processes of competition, invasion, and succession.
   b. The main concepts were differentiation and interdependence.
   c. Urbanism is a specific "way of life."
   d. Cities processed strangers by policing streets and pooling immigrants from the same backgrounds in their own neighborhoods.

4. What argument did Drake and Cayton make against the Chicago School with their book *Black Metropolis*?
   a. They showed how blacks were treated as a lower species in the competition with whites for space and employment.
   b. They demonstrated that the existence of black ghetto neighborhoods was the result not of natural competitive forces, but of segregation.
   c. They found that blacks were evenly distributed in

neighborhoods across the city when, according to the Chicago School's approach, they should have been specifically concentrated in ghettos.
   d. They argued from their study of street interactions in mixed neighborhoods, and a comparison with interactions in the South, that there was no distinctive urban way of life.

5. According to Wirth, what function do "the reserve, the indifference, and the blasé outlook of urbanites" have in everyday living?
   a. They are devices for immunizing urbanites against the personal claims and expectations of others.
   b. They are devices for demonstrating the sophistication and critical acumen of the urbanite.
   c. They are devices for reminding out-of-towners of their place as visitors.
   d. They are devices for getting about town in a hurry.

6. What's the difference between *fertility* and *fecundity*?
   a. *Fertility* refers to how many births the average woman has, whereas *fecundity* refers to how many of those births were of children who survived past one year of age.
   b. *Fertility* refers to a woman's ability to ovulate, whereas *fecundity* refers to a man's ability to produce healthy sperm.
   c. *Fertility* refers to how many live-born children the average woman has, whereas *fecundity* refers to the potential number of children women are biologically capable of having.
   d. *Fertility* is the rate of live births of individuals, whereas *fecundity* is the rate of live birth of twins.

7. What is the Malthusian perspective on population?
   a. Population growth will inevitably outstrip the food supply.
   b. Food supply and population growth will always be in balance.
   c. Agricultural technology will ensure enough food supply for the world's population.
   d. All of the above.

8. What role can sociologists play in helping society come to terms with global warming?
   a. Sociologists have a public duty to become actively engaged in the environmental movement and to put their unique perspective on social change to use for the public good.
   b. Sociologists can help educate politicians and the public to understand the complex interdependencies of globalization and to show everyone that we are all in this together.
   c. Sociologists can facilitate cross-cultural cooperation.
   d. Sociologists can help make members of the public conscious of the wasteful choices they make in consumption—for example, by lobbying the local supermarket to reduce the bulk of packaging and by picketing car lots that sell notoriously fuel-inefficient sport utility vehicles.

9. According to Saskia Sassen, an urban center that is home to the headquarters of large, transnational corporations and a superabundance of financial, technological, and consulting service is called a
   a. prime city.
   b. modern city.
   c. global city.
   d. developed city.

10. Why is the rate of urban growth in the world's less-developed regions so much higher than elsewhere?

   a. Rates of population growth are higher in developing countries than they are in industrialized nations.

   b. Rates of population growth are lower in developing countries than they are in industrialized nations.

   c. There is widespread internal migration from rural to urban areas.

   d. a and c.

Thinking Sociologically Exercises

1. Explain what makes the urbanization now occurring in developing countries, such as Brazil and India, different from and more problematic than the urbanization that took place a century ago in New York, London, Tokyo, and Berlin.

2. Following analysis presented in this chapter, concisely explain how the expanded quest for cheap energy and raw materials and present-day dangers of environmental pollution and resource depletion threaten not only the survival of people in developed countries, but also that of people in less developed countries.

Data Exercises

www.wwnorton.com/giddens
Keyword: Data19

One of the basic concerns of a society is the quality of life of its citizens. The overall quality of life is reflected in a society's measure of life expectancy or how long its citizens can expect to live, given current mortality levels. The data exercise for this chapter explores the association between life expectancy and national income.

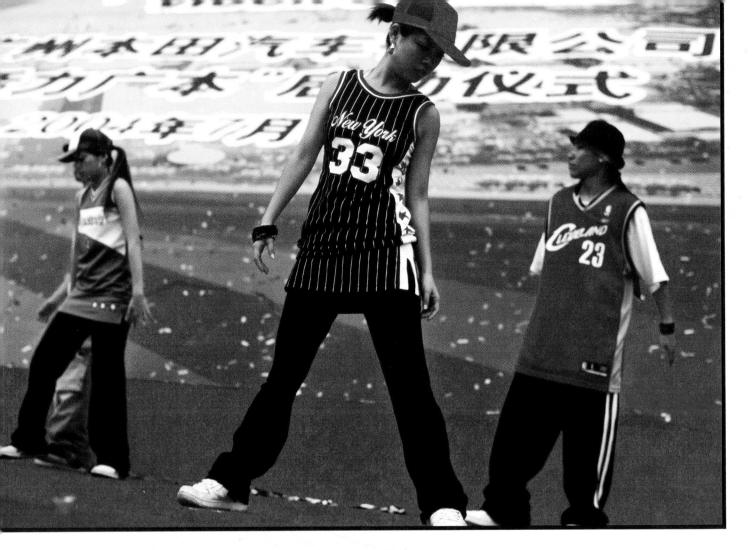

Social Change and Globalization

Recognize that a number of factors influence social change, including the physical environment, political organization, culture, and economic factors.

What Comes after Modern Industrial Society?

Be able to critically evaluate the notion that social change is leading us into a postindustrial or postmodern stage of social organization.

Factors Contributing to Globalization

Recognize the importance of information flows, political changes, and transnational corporations.

The Globalization Debate

Understand the theoretical debates among skeptics, hyperglobalizers, and transformationalists over whether globalization today is radically different from anything that has gone before in human history.

The Effect of Globalization on Our Lives

Appreciate how globalization has influenced the rise of individualism, changing work patterns, popular culture, risk, and inequality in modern society.

CHAPTER TWENTY

GLOBALIZATION IN A CHANGING WORLD

imagine you are standing before a clock that measures time on a cosmic scale, in which each second represents the passage of sixty thousand years. On such a clock it would take twenty-four hours for the five-billion-year history of our planet to unfold. Human-like apes would not even appear until the last two minutes, and human beings only in the last four seconds. Compared to us, even the dinosaurs would look like long-term residents of our planet—after all, they roamed the earth for nearly three quarters of an hour on our twenty-four-hour clock, before disappearing forever. Will human beings—whose great civilizations appeared only in the last quarter second—do nearly as well?

Human beings are very recent residents of planet earth. Yet during our brief time on this globe, we have unquestionably made our presence known. Our numbers have exploded to some 6.5 billion people and will probably increase by half again over the next fifty years. We have spread to every nook and cranny on the planet, crowding out all other forms of life—not to mention each other. Thanks to modern science and industry, each of us today uses up a vastly greater amount of the planet's limited resources than did our ape-like ancestors. Indeed, the combination of population explosion and modern industrial expansion today threatens both our planet and our human civilization.

Human beings have shown a unique ability to create massive problems—and then find ways to solve them. Today, more than ever before in the brief span of human history, our problems are global in nature, requiring global solutions. Globalization has contributed to such challenges as global warming, the worldwide spread of AIDS, conflict between nations, terrorism, and global poverty. Yet globalization can also contribute to their solution. All human beings share a common home and, therefore, a common interest in its preservation.

Globalization refers to the fact that we all increasingly live in one world, so that individuals, groups, and nations become more *interdependent*. Such interdependence is increasingly at a *global* scale—that is, what happens twelve thousand miles away is more likely then ever before to have enormous consequence for our daily lives. In this chapter we examine these global processes and see what leading sociologists and other social scientists have had to say about it.

Some of these ideas will already be familiar to you because much of this book has been about the consequences of globalization. In this chapter, we go beyond our earlier discussions, considering why the modern period is associated with especially profound and rapid social change. We see how globalization has contributed to such rapid social change and offer some thoughts on what the future is likely to bring.

Social Change and Globalization

The ways of living and social institutions characteristic of the modern world are radically different from those of even the recent past. During a period of only two or three centuries—a minute sliver of time in the context of human history—human social life has been wrenched away from the types of social order in which people lived for thousands of years.

Social change can be defined as the transformation over time of the institutions and culture of a society. Globalization has accelerated these processes of social change, bringing virtually all of humanity into the same turbulent seas. As a result, far more than any generation before us, we face an uncertain future. To be sure, conditions of life for previous generations were always insecure: People were at the mercy of natural disasters, plagues, and famines. Yet, although these problems still trouble much of the world, today we must also deal with the social forces that we ourselves have unleashed.

Social theorists have tried for the past two centuries to develop a single grand theory that explains the nature of social change. Marx, for example, emphasized the importance of economic factors in shaping all other aspects of social life, including politics and culture. But no single-factor theory has a chance of accounting for the diversity of human social development from hunting and gathering and pastoral societies to traditional civilizations and finally to the highly complex social systems of today. In analyzing social change, we can at most accomplish two tasks. We can identify a number of major factors that have consistently influenced social change, such as the physical environment, economics, political organization, and culture. We can also develop theories that account for particular periods of change, such as modern times.

The Physical Environment

The physical environment often has an effect on the development of human social organization. This is clearest in more extreme environmental conditions, where people must organize their ways of life in relation to weather conditions. People in polar regions necessarily develop different habits and practices from those living in subtropical areas. People who live in Alaska, where the winters are long and cold and the days very short, tend to follow different patterns of social life from people who live in the much warmer U.S. South. Most Alaskans spend more of their lives indoors and, except for the summer months, plan outdoor activities carefully, given the frequently inhospitable environment in which they live.

Less extreme physical conditions can also affect society. The native population of Australia has never stopped being hunters and gatherers because the continent contained hardly any indigenous plants suitable for regular cultivation or animals that could be domesticated to develop pastoral production. The world's early civilizations mostly originated in areas that contained rich agricultural land—for instance, in river deltas. The ease of communications across land and the availability of sea routes are also important: Societies cut off from others by mountain ranges, impassable jungles, or deserts often remain relatively unchanged over long periods of time.

A strong case for the importance of environment is made by Jared Diamond (2005) in his widely acclaimed book *Collapse: How Societies Choose to Fail or Succeed*. Diamond, a physiologist, biologist, and geographer, examines more than a dozen past and present societies, some of which collapsed (past examples include Easter Island and the Anasazi of Southwestern United States; more recent candidates include Rwanda and Haiti) and some of which overcame serious challenges to succeed. Diamond identifies five sets of factors that can contribute to a society's collapse. These are the presence of hostile neighbors, the absence (or collapse of) trading partners for essential goods, climate change, environmental problems, and an adequate response to environmental problems. Three of these five factors have to do with environmental conditions. The first four factors are often outside of a society's control and need not always result in collapse. The final factor, however, is always crucial: As the subtitle of his book suggests, success or failure depends on the choices made by a society and its leaders.

The collapse of Rwanda, for example, is typically attributed to ethnic rivalries between Hutu and Tutsi, fueled by Rwanda's colonial past. According to some explanations of the genocide that left more than eight hundred thousand Tutsi dead in the space of a few horrific months in 1994, a large part of the cause lay in the legacy of colonialism. During the first part of the twentieth century, Belgium ran Rwanda through Tutsi administrators because, according to the prevailing European racial theories of the time, the Tutsis—who tended on average to be somewhat taller and lighter skinned than the Hutus and, therefore, closer in resemblance to Europeans—were believed by the Belgians to be more "civilized." This led to resentments and hatred, which boiled over in 1994, fueled by Hutu demagogues urging the killing of all Tutsi.

Diamond does not reject this explanation but shows that it is only part of the story, which by itself could not account for the depth of the violence. Instead, through careful analysis of patterns of landholding, population, and killing, he argues that the root causes are found in overpopulation and resulting environmental destruction. Rwanda, he shows, was one of the fastest-growing places on earth, with disastrous consequences for its land and people, who had become one of the planet's most impoverished populations. Faced with starvation—and the absence of land to share among the growing number of (male) children—Rwanda was ripe for violence and collapse. Although ethnic rivalries may have fueled the fires of rage, Diamond also shows that in some hard-hit provinces Hutus killed other Hutus, as young men sought to acquire scarce farmland by any means.

Some have criticized Diamond for overemphasizing the importance of the environment, at the expense of other factors. By itself—except perhaps for extreme circumstances, such as the extended period of drought that doomed the Anasazi early in the fourteenth century—the environment does not necessarily determine how a society develops. Today especially, when humans can exert a high degree of control over their immediate living conditions, environment would seem to be less important: Modern cities have sprung up in the arctic cold and the harshest deserts.

Political Organization

A second factor strongly influencing social change is the type of political organization that operates in a society. In hunting and gathering societies, this influence is at a minimum because there are no political authorities capable of mobilizing the community. In all other types of society, however, the existence of distinct political agencies—chiefs, lords, monarchs, and governments—strongly affects the course of development a society takes. How a people respond to a crisis can play a decisive role in whether

Rwandan refugees trying to reach the United Nations camp in Tanzania. Over 800,000 Tutsis and moderate Hutus were killed during a period of 100 days. Hundreds of thousands of Rwandans fled to neighboring countries to escape the bloodshed.

they thrive or fail, and a society's leadership is obviously crucial to success or failure. A leader capable of pursuing dynamic policies and generating a mass following or radically altering preexisting modes of thought can overturn a previously established order. However, individuals can reach positions of leadership and become effective only if favorable social conditions exist. Mahatma Gandhi, the famous pacifist leader in India, was able to be effective in securing his country's independence from Britain because World War II and other events had unsettled the existing colonial institutions in India.

Japan provides one example of how effectively leadership was able to avert possible ecological and therefore economic collapse (Diamond 2005). Political and military stability under the Tokugawa *shoguns* (military rulers) ushered in a period of prosperity. (The Tokugawa Dynasty ruled Japan from 1603 to 1867.) This economic growth, however, contributed to the massive deforestation of the island country. Its leaders at the time (the celebrated *samurai* warriors) instituted programs of conservation and reforestation, and today—despite one of the highest population densities of any industrial country—nearly three quarters of Japan is covered with forests (Diamond 2005).

Seventh-century Japan was led by warriors, and military strength played a fundamental part in the establishment of most traditional states, influencing their subsequent survival or expansion in an equally basic way. But the connections between the level of production and military strength are again indirect. A ruler may choose to channel resources into building up the military, for example, even when this impoverishes most of the rest of the population—as happened in Iraq in the 1980s under the rule of Saddam Hussein or in North Korea during the 1990s under Kim Jong Il.

The most important political factor that has helped speed up patterns of change in the modern era is the emergence of the modern state, which has proved a vastly more efficient mechanism of government than the types that existed in pre-modern societies. Government plays a much bigger role in our lives, for better or worse, than it did before modern industrial societies came on the scene.

Globalization today may be challenging the ability of national governments to effectively exert leadership. For more then three centuries, governments have been the principal political actors on the world scene. Is political power in the world becoming increasingly uncoupled from geography? A number of theorists argue that this is exactly what is happening (Sassen 1996; Shaw 2000). Sociologist William Robinson (2001), for example, claims that as economic power has become increasingly deterritorialized, so too has political power: Just as transnational corporations operate across borders, with little or no national allegiances, transnational political organizations are becoming stronger even as national governments are becoming weaker. Groups such as the World Trade Organization (WTO) now have the power to punish countries that violate its principles of free trade (Conti 2003). European countries—some, like France and Germany, that have fought bitter wars against one another—have opened their borders to each other, established a common currency, and given up substantial political power to the European Union, a regional form of governance.

Will the twenty-first century see new forms of political organization better suited to a world in which people, products, knowledge, religious beliefs, pop culture, and pollution all cross borders with ever-greater ease? Although it is too soon to tell, it seems likely that the most important forms of political organization of this century will bear little resemblance to those of the twentieth.

Culture

The third main influence on social change consists of cultural factors, which include the effects of communication systems, religious and other belief systems, and popular culture.

A particularly important cultural influence that affects the character and pace of change is the nature of communication systems. The invention of writing, for instance, allowed for the keeping of records, making possible increased control of material resources and the development of large-scale organizations. In addition, writing altered people's perception of the relation between past, present, and future. Societies that write keep a record of past events, which then enables them to develop a sense of their society's overall line of evolution, which

members can then actively seek to promote (or thwart, if they wish to turn the clock back to earlier time). The existence of a written constitution and laws makes it possible for a country to have a legal system based on the interpretation of specific legal precedents—just as written scriptures enable religious leaders to justify their beliefs by citing chapter and verse from religious texts, like the Bible or Qur'ān.

We saw in Chapters 6, 13, and 16 how the Internet has helped change our personal relationships, the nature of politics and social movements, our forms of recreation, the ways in which we learn and work—in fact, almost every aspect of modern life. These changes have been among the most rapid in human history, resulting in what geographer David Harvey (1989) has aptly referred to as the compression of time and space. And they have all occurred within the last quarter century—a single generation.

Religion, as we have seen, may be either a conservative or an innovative force in social life. Some forms of religious belief and practice have acted as a brake on change, emphasizing above all the need to adhere to traditional values and rituals. Yet, as Max Weber emphasized, religious convictions frequently play a mobilizing role in pressures for social change. For instance, American church leaders promote attempts to lessen poverty or diminish inequalities in society. Religious leaders such as Dr. Martin Luther King Jr. were in the forefront of the American civil rights movement, and liberation theologists fought for better schools, water supplies, health services, and even democracy in Latin America—often at the cost of their lives.

Yet at the same time, as we saw in Chapter 17, religion today has become one of the driving forces against many of the cultural aspects of globalization. Islamists, fundamentalist Christians, and ultra-orthodox Jewish *haredim* all reject what they regard as the corrupting influences of modern secular culture, now rapidly spreading throughout the world thanks to mass media and the Internet (Juergensmeyer 1994, 2000). As we learned, Islamists call this "westoxification"—literally, getting drunk on the temptations of modern Western culture. While such religious communities are usually willing to embrace modern technology, which they often use effectively to disseminate their ideas, they reject what they view as the "McWorld" corruptions that go along with it.

Political scientist Samuel Huntington (1993, 1998) has advanced the controversial thesis that such differences are part of great seismic fault lines between entire civilizations. According to his "clash of civilization" thesis,

the fundamental source of conflict in this new world will not be primarily ideological or primarily economic. The great divisions among humankind and the dominating source of conflict will be cultural. Nation states will remain the most powerful actors in world affairs, but the principal conflicts of global politics will occur between nations and groups of different civilizations. The clash of civilizations will dominate global politics. The fault lines between civilizations will be the battle lines of the future. (1993)

Huntington identifies a half-dozen or so major civilizations as having great potential for future conflict: Christianity, subdivided into Western Christianity and Eastern Orthodox; Islam; Hindu; Chinese; African; Buddhist; and Japanese. Although Huntington's thesis seems especially plausible to many after September 11, 2001, it has been rightly criticized as overly simplistic. Each of his so-called civilizations embraces enormous differences in beliefs and practices, while old-fashioned geopolitical interests—for example, over scarce resources such as oil and water—are likely to shape international conflicts well into the twenty-first century. Moreover, to the extent that national policies are influenced by a belief in the clash of civilizations, Huntington's thesis may well become a self-fulfilling prophecy, as different sides square off for a cosmic war against what each believes to be the forces of unmitigated evil (Juergensmeyer 1994).

In fact, the principal cultural clashes of the 21st century will arguably *not* be between so-called civilizations, but rather between those who believe that truthful understanding is derived from religious faith, and those who argue that such understanding is grounded in science, critical thinking, and secular thought (Juergensmeyer 1994). Secular ideals, such self-betterment, freedom, equality, and democratic participation, are largely creations of the past two or three centuries.

German philosopher Friedrich Nietzsche first proclaimed the death of God in 1882. Nietzsche shared the belief, common among European intellectuals at the time, that absolute beliefs no longer could provide a guide to action in modern secular society. Secularism, Nietzsche believed, had won out over religious faith. It is no longer possible to make such a claim with any degree of confidence.

Economic Factors

Of economic influences, the farthest reaching is the effect of industrial capitalism. Capitalism differs in a fundamental way from preexisting production systems because it involves the constant expansion of production and the ever-increasing accumulation of wealth. In traditional production systems, levels of production were fairly unchanging as they were geared to habitual, customary needs. Capitalism requires the constant

revision of the technology of production, a process into which science is increasingly drawn. The rate of technological innovation fostered in modern industry is vastly greater than in any previous type of economic order. And such technological innovation, as we have seen, has helped create a truly global economy—one whose production lines draw on a worldwide workforce.

Economic changes help shape other changes as well. Science and technology, for example, are driven in part (often large part) by economic factors. Corporations, to remain competitive, must spend large sums of money on the research and development necessary to commercialize scientific insights. Governments often get into the act, spending far more money than individual businesses can afford in an effort to ensure their countries don't fall behind militarily or economically. For instance, when the Soviet Union launched the world's first satellite (*Sputnik*) into space in 1957, the United States responded with a massive and costly space program, inspired by fear that the Russians were winning the space race. During the 1960 presidential campaign, John F. Kennedy had effectively stoked that fear by repeatedly accusing the Republicans of being lax on Russian missile technology, suggesting that a growing "missile gap" made us vulnerable to a nuclear attack. The arms race, fueled by government contracts with corporations, has provided major economic support for scientific research as well as more general support for the U.S. economy.

Most recently, governments around the world are spending vast sums of money to win the next technological race—nanotechnology. Nanotechnology involves working with matter at the atomic, or "nano" scale, creating devices exhibiting properties that can exist only at such small sizes. (The nanoscale is defined as smaller than 100 nanometers; a nanometer is a billionth of a meter.) While much of this research remains in the early stages, nanotechnology has already produced such devices as:

- highly fluorescent nanocrystals ("quantum dots") that can penetrate into the tiniest of blood vessels, illuminating blockages that would otherwise be undetectable with current methods and holding promise for treating heart problems
- nanoscale sensors that can detect a single molecule of a chemical warfare agent, promising highly sensitive sensors that can be used in cities or battlefields
- nano-materials for explosives that have more than twice the energy of conventional explosives
- data storage devices based on nanoscale electronics that can store one hundred times as much data as the most powerful devices that are currently commercially available

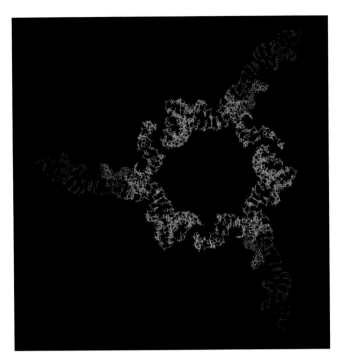

In the future, nanotechnology may be used for a range of activities, from medical applications to dealing with environmental issues. As an example, this triangular nanoparticle, developed by Purdue University, can carry anticancer treatments directly to infected cells.

- highly efficient nanoscale filtration devices that can remove major industrial contaminants from groundwater (National Nanotechnology Initiative [NNI] 2005)

A dozen countries are investing public funds to support research and development in this promising area, in hopes that they will be the first to profit from scientific breakthroughs. China, for example, is training some fifty thousand engineers in advanced chip design at universities in seven cities. The U.S. government launched the National Nanotechnology Initiative (NNI) in 2001; today it involves twenty-two federal agencies and spends more than $1 billion a year to foster nanoscale research and development.

What Comes after Modern Industrial Society?

Where is social change leading us today? Social theorists do not agree on the answers to these questions, which obviously involve a great deal of speculation. In this section, we examine two different perspectives: the notion that we are a postindustrial society and the idea that we have reached a postmodern period. In the final section of this chapter, we examine in some detail those theories that have focused on the dimensions, causes, and consequences of globalization.

Toward a Postindustrial Society?

Some observers have suggested that what is occurring today is a transition to a new society no longer primarily based on industrialism. We are entering, they claim, a phase of development beyond the industrial era altogether. A variety of terms have been coined to describe this new social order, such as **information society, service society,** and **knowledge society.** The term that has come into most common usage, however—first employed by Daniel Bell (1976) in the United States and Alain Touraine (1974) in France—is **postindustrial society,** the *post* (meaning "after") referring to the sense that we are moving beyond the old forms of industrial development.

The diversity of names is one indication of the countless ideas put forward to interpret current social changes. But one theme that appears consistently is the significance of *information* or *knowledge* in the society of the future. Our ways of life throughout the nineteenth and twentieth centuries, based in large part on machine power (the manufacture of material goods in factories), is being displaced by one in which information is the basis of the production system.

One of the earliest comprehensive portrayals of these changes is provided by Daniel Bell in his now-classic *The Coming of the Post-Industrial Society* (1976). The postindustrial order, Bell argues, is distinguished by a growth of service occupations at the expense of jobs that produce material goods. The blue-collar worker, employed in a factory or workshop, is no longer the most essential type of employee. White-collar (clerical and professional) workers outnumber blue-collar (factory) workers, with professional and technical occupations growing fastest of all.

People working in higher-level white-collar occupations specialize in the production of information and knowledge. The production and control of what Bell calls "codified knowledge"—systematic, coordinated information—is society's main productive resource. Those who create and distribute this knowledge—scientists, computer specialists, economists, engineers, and professionals of all kinds—increasingly become the leading social groups, replacing the industrialists and entrepreneurs of the old system. On the level of culture, there is a shift away from the work-ethic characteristic of industrialism; people are freer to innovate and enjoy themselves in both their work and their domestic lives.

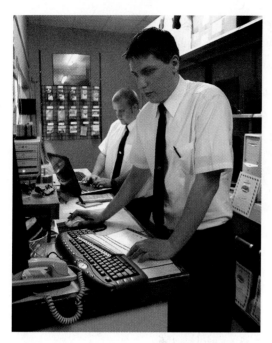

The "Geek Squad," a company founded by Robert Stephens in Minneapolis, Minnesota, and later purchased by the Best Buy retail chain, provides consumer computer support and technical repairs. They are an example of the new types of service-sector jobs emerging in a postindustrial society.

How valid is the view that the old industrial order is being replaced by a postindustrial society? Although the thesis has been widely accepted, the empirical assertions on which it depends are suspect in several ways.

1. The trend toward service occupations, accompanied by a decline in employment in other production sectors, dates back almost to the beginning of industrialism itself; it is not simply a recent phenomenon. From the early 1800s, manufacture and services both expanded at the expense of agriculture, with the service sector consistently showing a faster rate of increase than manufacture. The blue-collar worker never really was the most common type of employee; a higher proportion of paid employees has *always* worked in agriculture and services, with the service sector increasing proportionally as the numbers in agriculture dwindled. Easily the most important change has not been from industrial to service work but from farm employment to all other types of occupation.

2. Still, as we showed in Chapter 14, since the 1970s there has been a significant loss of factory jobs to low-wage countries, such as China, with a corresponding increase in service jobs (many of which pay far lower wages than the factory jobs that were lost). The most recent trends provide support for the postindustrial thesis that factory employment in the United States is declining while service sector employment is increasing.

3. The service sector is very diverse. Service occupations cannot be simply treated as identical to white-collar jobs; many service jobs (such as that of gas-station attendant) are blue collar, in the sense that they are manual. Most white-collar positions involve little specialized knowledge and have become substantially mechanized. This is true of much office work today. The notion that highly routinized factory work is being replaced by creative and challenging white-collar work is clearly incorrect; much service-sector employment today is as routinized and unsatisfying as factory work was in the past (and pays less).

4. Many service jobs contribute to a process that in the end produces material goods and, therefore, should really be counted as part of manufacture. Thus a computer programmer working for an industrial firm, designing and monitoring the operation of machine tools, is directly involved in a process of making material goods.

5. The postindustrial society thesis tends to exaggerate the importance of economic factors in producing social change. Such a society is described as the outcome of developments in the economy that lead to changes in other institutions. However, it is clear that the forces behind the changes going on today are political and cultural as well as economic—one simply has to look at the growing importance of religious beliefs as a force for social change to appreciate the fact that the production and consumption of goods and services is not the only driving force in history.

6. Finally, the very concept of *postindustrial* implies that we are somehow at the end of history—after all, what can come after "post"? Any attempt to divide history into clearly marked before-and-after stages is bound to be proven wrong over time, as new (and unanticipated) technological breakthroughs, and their associated social changes, occur. Will the postindustrial stage give way to a biosocial stage, in which genetic engineering results in new human capabilities and forms of society? A nanosocial stage, in which atomic devices solve all human problems, including the need to work at all? Such fanciful speculations may be the realm of science fiction, but they point out the dangers of predicting the future on the basis of the most recent technological trends.

Some of the developments cited by the postindustrial theorists are important features of the current era, but it is not obvious that the concept of the postindustrial society is the best way to come to terms with them.

Postmodernity

Some authors have recently gone as far as saying that the developments now occurring are even more profound than signaling the end of the era of industrialism. They claim that what is happening is nothing short of a movement beyond modernity—the attitudes and ways of life associated with modern societies, such as our belief in progress, the benefits of science, and our capability to control the modern world. A **postmodern** era is arriving, or has already arrived.

The advocates of postmodernity claim that modern societies took their inspiration from the idea that history has a shape—it "goes somewhere" and leads to progress—and that now this notion has collapsed. There are no longer any "grand narratives"—overall conceptions of history—that make any sense (Lyotard 1985). Not only is there no general notion of progress that can be defended but there is no such thing as history. The postmodern world is thus a highly pluralistic and diverse one. In countless films, videos, and TV programs, images circulate around the world. We come into contact with many ideas and values, but these have little connection with the history of the areas in which we live, or indeed with our own personal histories. Everything seems constantly in flux. As one group of authors expressed things:

> Our world is being remade. Mass production, the mass consumer, the big city, big-brother state, the sprawling housing estate, and the nation-state are in decline: flexibility, diversity, differentiation, and mobility, communication, decentralization and internationalization are in the ascendant. In the process our own identities, our sense of self, our own subjectivities are being transformed. We are in transition to a new era. (Hall et al. 1988)

Most contemporary social theorists accept that information technology and new communications systems, together with other technological changes, are producing major social transformations for all of us. However, the majority disagree with core ideas of the postmodernists, who argue that our attempts to understand general processes in the social world are doomed, as is the notion we can change the world for the better. Writers such as Ulrich Beck and one of the authors of this textbook, Anthony Giddens (2004), claim that we need as much as ever to develop general theories of the social world and that such theories can help us intervene to shape it in a

Fredric Jameson describes the Westin Bonaventure Hotel, located in downtown Los Angeles, as an original postmodern space. The architecture distorts viewers' sense of place—the glass exterior mirrors the building's surroundings rather than permitting a view inside.

positive way. Such theories have focused on how contemporary societies are becoming globalized, while everyday life is breaking free from the hold of tradition and custom. But these changes should not spell the end of attempts at social and political reform. Values, such as a belief in the importance of social community, equality, and caring for the weak and vulnerable, are still very much alive throughout the world.

Factors Contributing to Globalization

Globalization is often portrayed solely as an economic phenomenon. Some make much of the role of transnational corporations whose massive operations stretch across national borders, influencing global production processes and the international distribution of labor. Others point to the electronic integration of global financial markets and the enormous volume of global capital flows. Still others focus on the unprecedented scope of world trade, involving a much broader range of goods and services than ever before.

Although economic forces are an integral part of globalization, it would be wrong to suggest that they alone produce it. Globalization is created by the coming together of technological, political, and economic factors. It has been driven forward above all by the development of information and communication technologies that have intensified the speed and scope of interaction among people all over the world.

Information Flows

The explosion in global communications has been facilitated by some important advances in technology and the world's telecommunications infrastructure. In the post–World War II era, there has been a profound transformation in the scope and intensity of telecommunications flows. Traditional telephone communication, which depended on analog signals sent through wires and cables, has been replaced by integrated systems in which vast amounts of information are compressed and transferred digitally. Cable technology has become immensely more efficient and less expensive. The development of fiber-optic cables, for example, has dramatically expanded the number of channels that can be carried, and even this recent technology has achieved significant advances: while the first transoceanic fiber-optic cables could carry the equivalent of thirty-five thousand telephone circuits, the most recent have ten thousand times that capacity (Hecht 2003). The spread of communications satellites, beginning in the 1960s, has also been significant in expanding international communications. Today a network of more than two hundred satellites is in place to facilitate the transfer of information around the globe.

The effect of these communications systems has been staggering. In countries with highly developed telecommunications infrastructures, homes and offices now have multiple links to the outside world, including telephones (both land lines and mobile phones), fax machines, digital and cable television, electronic mail, and the Internet. The Internet has emerged as the fastest-growing communication tool ever developed—more than a billion people worldwide (one sixth of the world population) were estimated to be using the Internet in 2005, nearly twice the number of only five years earlier (Internet World Stats 2006).

As we noted earlier, these forms of technology facilitate the compression of time and space: Two individuals located on opposite sides of the planet—in Tokyo and London, for example—not only can hold a conversation in real time but can also send documents and images to one another with the help of satellite technology. Widespread use of the Internet and mobile phones is deepening and accelerating processes of globalization; more and more people are becoming interconnected through the use of these technologies and are doing so in places that have previously been isolated or poorly served by traditional communications (Figure 20.1). Although the telecommunications infrastructure is not evenly developed around the world (Table 20.1), a growing number of countries now have access to international communications networks in a way that was previously impossible.

Globalization is also being driven forward by the electronic integration of the world economy. The global economy is in-creasingly dominated by activity that is weightless and intangible (Quah 1999). This *weightless economy* is one in which products have their base in information, as is the case with computer software, media and entertainment products, and Internet-based services. This new economic context has been described using a variety of terms that we have already discussed, including *postindustrial society, information society,* and *knowledge society.* The emergence of the knowledge society has been linked to the development of a broad base of consumers who are technologically literate and eagerly integrate new advances in computing, entertainment, and telecommunications into their everyday lives.

The very operation of the global economy reflects the changes that have occurred in the information age. Many aspects of the economy now work through networks that cross national boundaries, rather than stopping at them (Castells 1996). To be competitive in globalizing conditions, businesses and corporations have restructured themselves to be more flexible and less hierarchical in nature. Production practices and organizational patterns have become more flexible, partnering arrangements with other firms have become commonplace, and participation in worldwide distribution networks has become essential for doing business in a rapidly changing global market.

Whether one works in a factory or a call center, the job can be done more cheaply in China, India, or some other developing country. The same is increasingly true for software engineers, graphic designers, and financial consultants. Of course, to the extent that global competition for labor reduces the cost of goods and services, it also provides for a wealth of cheaper products (Roach 2005). As consumers, we all benefit from low-cost flat-panel TVs made in China or inexpensive computer games programmed in India. It is an open question, however, whether the declining cost of consumption will balance out wage and job losses due to globalization.

Political Changes

A number of political changes are driving forces behind contemporary globalization. One of the most significant of these is the collapse of Soviet-style communism, which occurred in a series of dramatic revolutions in Eastern Europe in 1989 and culminated in the dissolution of the Soviet Union itself in 1991. Since the fall of Soviet-style Communism, countries in the former Soviet bloc—including Russia, Ukraine, Poland, Hungary, the Czech Republic, the Baltic states, and the states of the Caucasus and Central Asia—are moving toward Western-style political and economic systems. They are no longer isolated from the global community, but are becoming integrated within it. This development has meant the end to the system that existed during the cold war, when

FIGURE 20.1

The Multiplication of Television Sets and Telephones in Regions of the World, 1985–2003, and the Explosion in Online Communication

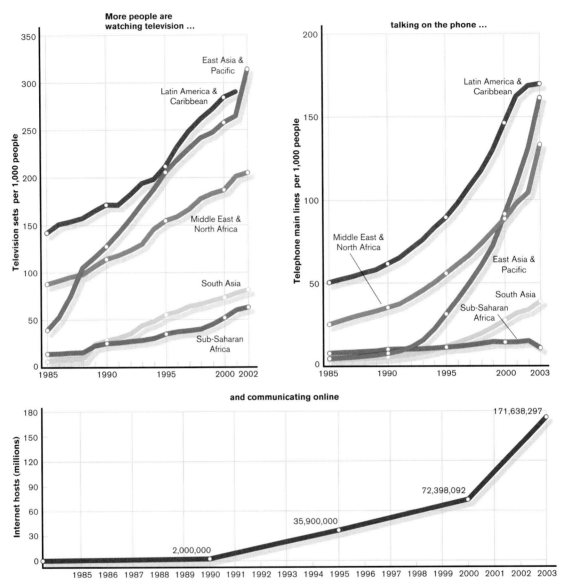

From 1985 to 2003, which region saw the greatest increase in television sets per 1,000 people? How would you describe the increase in main telephone lines per 1,000 people that Sub-Saharan Africa experienced from 1985 to 2003? What is the difference between East Asia/Pacific and South Asia in the number of main telephone lines per 1,000 people in 1985 and in 2003? What was the approximate increase in Internet hosts in the ten years from 1990 to 2003? In the three years from 2000 to 2003? What does Figure 20.1 have to do with globalization?

SOURCES: United Nations 2003; World Bank 1999, 2002, 2005.

TABLE 20.1

Global Unevenness of Telecommunications Infrastructure and Use

COUNTRY	POPULATION[a] (MILLIONS)	TELEPHONE MAINLINES (PER 1,000)[b]	CELLULAR SUBSCRIBERS (PER 1,000)[b]	PERSONAL COMPUTERS (PER 1,000)[b]
China	1,296.5	209.0	215	27.6
France	60.0	566.0	696	347.1
Germany	82.6	657.3	785	484.7
India	1,079.7	46.3	25	7.2
Japan	127.8	471.9	679	382.2
Sweden	9.0	735.7[c]	980	621.3
United Kingdom	59.4	590.6[c]	912	405.7
United States	293.5	621.3	546	658.9

[a] In 2004.

[b] In 2003.

[c] Data are for 2002.

SOURCES: United Nations, 2005; World Bank 2005.

capitalist countries stood apart from communist states. The collapse of communism has hastened processes of globalization but should also be seen as a result of globalization itself. The centrally planned communist economies and the ideological and cultural control of communist political authority were ultimately unable to survive in an era of global media and an electronically integrated world economy.

A second important political factor leading to intensifying globalization is the growth of international and regional mechanisms of government. The United Nations (UN) and the European Union (EU) are the two most prominent examples of international organizations that bring together nation-states into a common political forum. Whereas the UN does this as an association of individual nation-states, the EU is a more pioneering form of transnational governance in which a certain degree of national sovereignty is relinquished by its member states. The governments of individual EU states are bound by directives, regulations, and court judgments from common EU bodies, but they also reap economic, social, and political benefits from their participation in the regional union.

A third important political factor is the growing importance of international governmental organizations (IGOs) and in-

ternational nongovernmental organizations (INGOs; see also Chapter 6). An *international governmental organization* is a body that is established by participating governments and given responsibility for regulating or overseeing a particular domain of activity that is transnational in scope. The first such body, the International Telegraph Union, was founded in 1865. Since that time, a great number of similar bodies have been created to regulate issues ranging from civil aviation to broadcasting to the disposal of hazardous waste. In 1909, there were thirty-seven IGOs in existence to regulate transnational affairs; by 2005, there were estimated to be more than seven thousand (Union of International Organizations 2005). As the name suggests, INGOs differ from international governmental organizations in that they are not affiliated with government institutions. Rather, they are independent organizations that work alongside governmental bodies in making policy decisions and addressing international issues. Some of the best-known INGOs—such as Greenpeace, Médecins San Frontières (Doctors without Borders), the Red Cross, and Amnesty International—are involved in environmental protection and humanitarian relief efforts. But the activities of the nearly fifty-two thousand lesser-known groups also link together countries and communities (Figure 20.2).

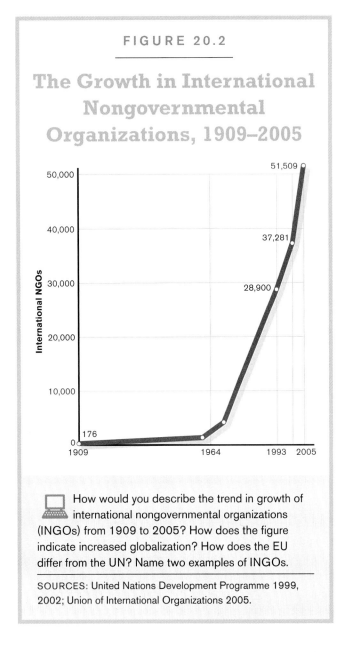

FIGURE 20.2

The Growth in International Nongovernmental Organizations, 1909–2005

How would you describe the trend in growth of international nongovernmental organizations (INGOs) from 1909 to 2005? How does the figure indicate increased globalization? How does the EU differ from the UN? Name two examples of INGOs.

SOURCES: United Nations Development Programme 1999, 2002; Union of International Organizations 2005.

edness with others and more likely to identify with global issues and processes than was the case in times past.

This shift to a global outlook has two significant dimensions. First, as members of a global community, people increasingly perceive that social responsibility does not stop at national borders but instead extends beyond them. Disasters and injustices facing people on the other side of the globe are not simply misfortunes that must be endured but are legitimate grounds for action and intervention. There is a growing assumption that the international community has an obligation to act in crisis situations to protect the physical well-being or human rights of people whose lives are under threat. In the case of natural disasters, such interventions take the form of humanitarian relief and technical assistance. In recent years, earthquakes in Armenia and Turkey, floods in Mozambique, famine in Africa, hurricanes in Central America, and the tsunami that hit Asia and Africa have been rallying points for global assistance.

There have also been stronger calls in recent years for interventions in the case of war, ethnic conflict, and the violation of human rights, although such mobilizations are more problematic than in the case of natural disasters. Yet in the case of the Gulf War in 1991 and the violent conflicts in the former Yugoslavia (Bosnia and Kosovo), military intervention was seen as justified by many people who believed that human rights and national sovereignty had to be defended.

Second, a global outlook means that people are increasingly looking to sources other than the nation-state in formulating their own sense of identity. This is a phenomenon that is both produced by and further accelerates processes of globalization. Local cultural identities in various parts of the world are experiencing powerful revivals at a time when the traditional hold of the nation-state is undergoing profound transformation. In Europe, for example, inhabitants of Scotland and the Basque region of Spain might be more likely to identify themselves as Scottish or Basque—or simply as Europeans—rather than as British or Spanish. The nation-state as a source of identity is waning in many areas as political shifts at the regional and global level loosen people's orientations toward the states in which they live.

Transnational Corporations

Among the many economic factors driving globalization, the role of **transnational corporations** is particularly important. Transnational corporations are companies that produce goods or market services in more than one country. These may be relatively small firms with one or two factories outside the country in which they are based or gigantic international ventures whose operations crisscross the globe. Some the biggest transnational corporations are companies known all around

Finally, the spread of information technology has expanded the possibilities for contact among people around the globe. It has also facilitated the flow of information about people and events in distant places. Every day, the global media bring news, images, and information into people's homes, linking them directly and continuously to the outside world. Some of the most gripping events of the past two decades—such as the fall of the Berlin Wall, the violent crackdown on democratic protesters in China's Tiananmen Square, and the terrorist attacks of September 11, 2001—have unfolded through the media before a truly global audience. Such events, along with thousands of less dramatic ones, have resulted in a reorientation in people's thinking from the level of the nation-state to the global stage. Individuals are now more aware of their interconnectthe world: ExxonMobil, Wal-Mart, Coca-Cola, Toyota, Ford, BMW, Nike, Disney, Google, Starbucks, McDonald's, and many others. Even when transnational corporations have a clear national base, they are oriented toward global markets and global profits.

Transnational corporations are at the heart of economic globalization: They account for two thirds of all world trade, they are instrumental in the diffusion of new technology around the globe, and they are major actors in international financial markets. As one group of writers has noted, they are "the linchpins of the contemporary world economy" (Held et al. 1999). Well over five hundred transnational corporations had annual sales of more than $10 billion in 2005, whereas only ninety *countries* (half of all countries in the world) could boast gross domestic products (GDPs) of at least that amount. In other words, the world's leading transnational corporations are larger economically than most of the world's countries (Table 20.2). In fact, the combined sales of the world's largest five hundred transnational corporations totaled nearly $17 trillion in 2005—more than two fifths (42 percent) of the value of goods and services produced by the entire world (*Fortune* 2005; World Bank 2006). Wal-Mart, the world's largest corporation, had revenues that surpassed the GDPs of all but twenty-one countries. Among the world's largest economies, fourteen are transnational corporations.

Transnational corporations became a global phenomenon in the years after World War II. Expansion in the initial postwar years came from firms based in the United States, but by the 1970s, European and Japanese firms also began to invest abroad. In the late 1980s and 1990s, transnational corporations expanded dramatically with the establishment of three powerful regional markets: Europe (the Single European Market), Asia-Pacific (the Osaka Declaration guaranteed free and open trade by 2010), and North America (the North American Free Trade Agreement). Since the early 1990s, countries in other areas of the world have also eased restrictions on foreign investment. By the turn of the twenty-first century, few economies in the world were beyond the reach of transnational corporations. Over the past decade, transnational corporations based in industrialized economies have been particularly active in expanding their operations in developing countries and in societies of the former Soviet Union and Eastern Europe.

The "electronic economy" is another factor that underpins economic globalization. Banks, corporations, fund managers, and individual investors are able to shift funds internationally with the click of a mouse. This new ability to move electronic money instantaneously carries with it great risks, however. Transfers of vast amounts of capital can destabilize economies, triggering international financial crises such as the ones that spread from the Asian "tiger economies" to Russia and beyond in 1998. As the global economy becomes increasingly integrated, a financial collapse in one part of the world can have an enormous effect on distant economies.

The political, economic, social, and technological factors described above are joining together to produce a phenomenon that lacks any earlier parallel in terms of its intensity and scope. The consequences of globalization are many and far reaching, as we will see later in this chapter. But first we turn our attention to the main views about globalization that have been expressed in recent years.

The Globalization Debate

In recent years, globalization has become a hotly debated topic. Most people accept that important transformations are occurring around us, but the extent to which it is valid to explain these as "globalization" is contested. This is not entirely surprising. As an unpredictable and turbulent process, globalization is seen and understood very differently by observers. David Held and his colleagues (1999) have surveyed the controversy and divided its participants into three schools of thought: *skeptics, hyperglobalizers,* and *transformationalists.* These three tendencies within the globalization debate are summarized in Table 20.3.

The Skeptics

Some thinkers argue that the idea of globalization is overrated —that the debate over globalization is a lot of talk about something that is not new. The skeptics in the globalization controversy believe that present levels of economic interdependence are not unprecedented. Pointing to nineteenth-century statistics on world trade and investment, they contend that modern globalization differs from the past only in the intensity of interaction between nations.

The skeptics agree that there may now be more contact among countries than in previous eras, but in their eyes the current world economy is not sufficiently integrated to constitute a truly globalized economy. This is because the bulk of trade occurs within three regional groups—Europe, Asia-Pacific, and North America. The countries of the European Union, for example, trade predominantly among themselves. The same is true of the other regional groups, thereby invalidating the notion of a single global economy (Hirst 1997).

Many skeptics focus on processes of *regionalization* within the world economy—such as the emergence of major financial and trading blocs. To skeptics, the growth of regionalization is evidence that the world economy has become less integrated

TABLE 20.2

Value of Sales of Top Corporations Compared with Gross Domestic Product (GDP) of Selected Countries, 2004–2005

ECONOMY RANK	ECONOMY	GDP OR TOTAL SALES ($ BILLIONS)
22	Wal-Mart	287,989
23	BP (British Petroleum)	285,059
24	ExxonMobil	270,772
25	Royal Dutch Shell Group	268,690
26	Indonesia	257,641
27	Saudi Arabia	250,557
28	Norway	250,168
29	Denmark	243,043
30	Poland	241,833
31	South Africa	212,777
32	Greece	203,401
33	General Motors	193,517
34	Finland	186,597
35	Ireland	183,560
36	DaimlerChrysler	176,688
37	Toyota Motor	172,616
38	Ford Motor	172,233
39	Portugal	168,281
40	Thailand	163,491
41	Hong Kong	163,005
42	Iran	162,005
43	General Electric	152,886
44	Total	152,610
45	Argentina	151,501
46	Chevron	147,967
47	ConocoPhillips	121,663
48	AXA	121,606
49	Allianz	118,937
50	Malaysia	117,776

SOURCES: Fortune 2005; World Bank 2006.

TABLE 20.3

Conceptualizing Globalization: Three Tendencies

CHARACTERISTIC	SKEPTICS	TRANSFORMATIONALISTS	HYPERGLOBALIZERS
What's new?	Trading blocs, weaker geogovernance than in earlier periods	Historically unprecedented levels of global interconnectedness	A global age
Dominant features	World less interdependent than in 1890s	"Thick" (intensive and extensive) globalization	Global capitalism, global governance, global civil society
Power of national governments	Reinforced or enhanced	Reconstituted, restructured	Declining or eroding
Driving forces of globalization	Governments and markets	Combined forces of modernity	Capitalism and technology
Pattern of stratification	Increased marginalization of global south	New architecture of world order	Erosion of old hierarchies
Dominant motif	National interest	Transformation of political community	McDonald's, Britney Spears, etc.
Conceptualization of globalization	As internationalization and regionalization	As the reordering of interregional relations and action at a distance	As a reordering of the framework of human action
Historical trajectory	Regional blocs/clash of civilizations	Indeterminate: global integration and fragmentation	Global civilization
Summary argument	Internationalization depends on government acquiescence and support	Globalization transforming government power and world politics	The end of the nation-state

SOURCE: Adapted from Held et al., 1999.

rather than more (Boyer and Drache 1996; Hirst and Thompson 1999). Compared with the patterns of trade that prevailed a century ago, they argue, the world economy is less global in its geographical scope and more concentrated on intense pockets of activity.

Skeptics reject the view held by some, such as the hyperglobalizers (see below), that globalization is fundamentally undermining the role of national governments and producing a world order in which they are less central. According to the skeptics, national governments continue to be key players because of their involvement in regulating and coordinating economic activity. Governments, for example, are the driving force behind many trade agreements and policies of economic liberalization.

The Hyperglobalizers

The hyperglobalizers take an opposing position to that of the skeptics. They argue that globalization is a very real phenomenon whose consequences can be felt almost everywhere. They see globalization as a process that is indifferent to national borders. It is producing a new global order, swept along by powerful flows of cross-border trade and production. Journalist Thomas Friedman has written two best-selling books, *The Lexus and the Olive Tree* (2000) and *The World Is Flat* (2005), that breathlessly paint a picture of globalization as a juggernaut that sweeps up everything in its path, sometimes with unfortunate short-term results, but ultimately with enormous benefits for everyone.

Sociologists without Borders

Misery for most sociologists is a topic of study, a research problem, set of data points abstracted from human experience and analyzed in offices and classrooms and computers far, far away from the everyday world. Dissatisfied with this level of detachment, Sociologists without Borders/*Sociólogos Sin Fronteras* (SSF) was founded in 2001 on the belief that poverty, disease, malnourishment, and torture are problems that sociologists should grapple with not only as analysts but as activists as well.

The "without borders" movement, according to Professor Judith Blau (2006), "was launched by professional groups from highly developed [countries] to assist peoples in poorer countries and to provide much needed services. The most famous such group is Doctors without Borders, and others include Reporters without Borders, Architects without Borders, and Engineers without Borders. As an academic INGO [international nongovernmental organization], Sociologists without Borders works to encourage collaborative teaching across international borders." In 2004, SSF began a partnership in Kibera, a dense urban settlement just outside of Kenya's capital city.

Judith Blau

The Kibera slums are located three miles southeast of Nairobi, Kenya, in East Africa. There are no roads in Kibera. Families rely on craftwork and small-scale vending of used clothing, vegetables, and cassettes to generate income—typically less than $1 a day. The average family home is nine feet by nine feet. Drinking water is pumped through plastic pipes alongside sewage trenches carrying refuse and human

Much of the analysis of globalization offered by hyperglobalizers focuses on the changing role of the nation-state. It is argued that individual countries no longer control their economies because of the vast growth in world trade. National governments and the politicians within them, it is said, are increasingly unable to exercise control over the issues that cross their borders—such as volatile financial markets and environmental threats. Citizens recognize that politicians are limited in their ability to address these problems and, as a result, lose faith in existing systems of governance. Some hyperglobalizers believe that the power of national governments is also being challenged from above—by new regional and international institutions, such as EU and WTO. Taken together, these shifts signal to the hyperglobalizers the dawning of a global age (Albrow 1997) in which national governments decline in importance and influence.

More scholarly (and less breathless) versions of a strong globalization position can be found in the writings of sociologists such as William Robinson (2001, 2004, 2005a, 2005b),

Leslie Sklair (2002a, 2000b, 2003), and Saskia Sassen (1996, 2005). These scholars do not see themselves as hyperglobalists. Nonetheless, like the hyperglobalists they argue that transnational economic actors and political institutions are challenging the dominance of national ones. Robinson, one of the stongest proponents of this position, has studied these changes throughout the world, with a special focus on Latin America. He argues that the most powerful economic actors on the world scene today are not bound by national boundaries; they are, instead, transnational in nature. For example, what he terms the "transnational capitalist class" is emerging out of (and is transforming) the capitalist classes of individual countries, since the transnational corporations they manage are global rather than national in nature. By the same token, he argues that nation-states are being transformed into "component elements" of a transnational state—exemplified, for example, by the WTO, whose purpose is to serve the interests of global businesses as a whole by ensuring that individual countries adhere to the principles of free trade. Robinson (2001) waste to a river at the base of the valley. Waterborne diseases like cholera, typhoid, and worm infestations are rampant. Health services and sexual education are minimal. An estimated 54 percent of people living in Kibera are either HIV positive or have AIDS.

In the United States, slums typically are found in just the poorest blocks of larger, thriving cities. But with a population of approximately eight hundred thousand, Kibera is a slum-city with more inhabitants than places like San Francisco, Detroit, or Boston all living in an area roughly the size of Central Park. Since Kibera is technically an illegal settlement, landlords are not obliged to provide any services—no toilets, no water, no electricity, no trash collection, no infrastructure, and no housing. Most Americans have no conception of what places like Kibera are really like, even though over one billion people throughout the world—about one sixth of the total human population—live in slums with similar conditions (Van Hove 2006).

In 2004, Sociologists without Borders partnered with an organization called Carolina for Kibera, an NGO originally founded to combat ethnic violence among young people in Kibera that has now expanded its commitments to include health, sports, women's outreach, and microfinance projects. Blau (2006), a sociologist at the University of North Carolina at Chapel Hill, stresses that "in contrast with the charity model, SSF works hand-in-hand with the residents of Kibera so that they set the priorities in their own terms, and SSF tries to provide resources. It is a variation on service-learning, and it is our intent that the residents and the NGO are steering us. They are the experts."

Each year, SSF and Carolina for Kibera select one college student to serve as a Nairobi Fellow in the Kibera slums. In her 2005 field report, Lynsey Farrell, a student at Boston University, describes some of the challenges she faced jumpstarting an income-generating newspaper project with local residents. Farrell's main goal was to help girls at the Binti Pamoja Centre who wanted to use writing as a tool to address the concerns of young women in Kibera. Drawing from their intimate knowledge of community life, the girls wrote articles about topics such as rape, relationships, and sexually transmitted diseases and distributed the newspaper throughout the slum.

After almost three months living in the community, Farrell submitted her final field report to SSF. Although Kibera was often a disheartening place, she found human strength and vitality amidst conditions of extreme poverty. "People in Kenya are resilient," Farrell (2005) writes. "I see in the girls at Binti Pamoja many strengths, and see in them determination to help their community. Given the opportunity, they laugh and gossip and flirt, just like teenagers across the world. *Maisha ni ngumu* (Life is hard), but it is not impossible. . . . Kiberans are not poor, although they lack the resources and property that we associate with wealth. Despite the reports and surveys and experts proclaiming the horror of this growing urban slum, after a couple months working there I came away with a positive impression of their resourcefulness and determination to maintain a sense of community and normalcy that those on the outside do not imagine they have."

concludes that "the nation-state is a historically-specific form of world social organization in the process of becoming transcended by globalization."

The Transformationalists

The transformationalists take more of a middle position. Writers such as David Held and Anthony G. McGrew (1999), as well as one of the authors of this textbook (Giddens 1990), see globalization as the central force behind a broad spectrum of changes that are currently shaping modern societies. According to them, the global order is being transformed, but many of the old patterns still remain. Governments, for instance, still retain a good deal of power in spite of the advance of global interdependence. These transformations are not restricted to economics alone but are equally prominent within the realms of politics, culture, and personal life. Transformationalists contend that the current level of globalization is breaking down

established boundaries between internal and external, international and domestic. In trying to adjust to this new order, societies, institutions, and individuals are being forced to navigate contexts where previous structures have been shaken up.

Unlike hyperglobalizers, transformationalists see globalization as a dynamic and open process that is subject to influence and change. It is developing in a contradictory fashion, encompassing tendencies that frequently operate in opposition to one another. Globalization is not a one-way process, as some claim, but a two-way flow of images, information, and influences. Global migration, media, and telecommunications are contributing to the diffusion of cultural influences. The world's vibrant "global cities" are thoroughly multicultural, with ethnic groups and cultures intersecting and living side by side. According to transformationalists, globalization is a decentered and self-aware process characterized by links and cultural flows that work in a multidirectional way. Because globalization is the product of numerous intertwined global networks, it cannot be seen as being driven from one particular part of the world.

Rather than losing sovereignty, as the hyperglobalizers argue, countries are seen by transformationalists as restructuring in response to new forms of economic and social organization that are nonterritorial in basis (e.g., corporations, social movements, and international bodies). They argue that we are no longer living in a state-centric world; governments are being forced to adopt a more active, outward-looking stance toward governance under the complex conditions of globalization (Rosenau 1997).

Whose view is most nearly correct? There are elements of truth in all three views, although those of the transformationalists are perhaps the most balanced. The skeptics are mistaken because they underestimate how far the world is changing; world finance markets, for example, are organized on a global level much more than they ever were before. Yet at the same time, the world has undergone periods of intense globalization before—only to withdraw into periods when countries sought to protect their markets and closed their borders to trade. Although the march of globalization today often seems inevitable, it is by no means certain that it will continue unabated: Countries that find themselves losing out may attempt to stem the tide. Many countries in Latin America, for example, have in recent years elected left-wing governments that rejected free trade, arguing instead for some system of protections that would protect their citizens.

The hyperglobalizers, on the other hand, are correct in pointing to the current strength of globalization as dissolving many national barriers, changing the nature of state power, and creating new and powerful transnational social classes. On the other hand, they often see globalization too much in economic terms, and as too much of a one-way process. In reality, globalization is much more complex. World-systems theorists such as Immanuel Wallerstein (2004) and Giovanni Arrighi (1994) argue that while countries remain important actors on the global field, so too are transnational corporations. National governments will neither dissolve under the weight of a globalized economy (as some hyperglobalizers argue) nor reassert themselves as the dominant political force (as some skeptics argue) but rather will seek to steer global capitalism to their own advantage. According to this argument, U.S. dominance of the world economy is being seriously challenged by the rise of East Asia, and particularly China, whose economy has been expanding at more than nine percent a year for nearly two decades.

The world economy of the future may be much more globalized than today's, with multinational corporations and global institutions such as the WTO playing increasingly important roles. But some countries in the world economy may still be more powerful than even the most powerful transnational actors. Clyde Prestowitz (2005), an expert on international trade, summarizes this position in his book on the rise of China and India as economic powers. In *Three Billion New Capitalists: The Great Shift of Wealth and Power to the East* (2005), Prestowitz concludes that

> Unless things go badly off track, the story of the next fifty years will be that of China recovering its historically central position as the Middle Kingdom [the world's center], with the world's largest population and economy. . . . Its GDP in 2050 will be $45 trillion versus about $35 trillion for the United States. China will be the world's largest market for virtually everything as well as the biggest recipient of investment from, and the largest investor in, most other countries . . . the [Chinese] yuan could well be the world's money, or at least one of its major currencies.

The Effect of Globalization on Our Lives

Although globalization is often associated with changes within big systems—such as the world financial markets, production and trade, and telecommunications—the effects of globalization are felt equally strongly in the private realm. Globalization is not something that is simply out there, operating on a distant plane and not intersecting with individual affairs. Globalization is an "in here" phenomenon that is affecting our intimate and personal lives in many diverse ways. Inevitably, our personal lives have been altered as globalizing forces enter into our local contexts, our homes, and our communities through impersonal sources—such as the media, the Internet, and popular culture—as well as through personal contact with individuals from other countries and cultures.

Globalization is fundamentally changing the nature of our everyday experiences. As the societies in which we live undergo profound transformations, the established institutions that used to underpin them have become out of place. This is forcing a redefinition of intimate and personal aspects of our lives, such as the family, gender roles, sexuality, personal identity, our interactions with others, and our relationships to work. The way we think of ourselves and our connections with other people is being profoundly altered through globalization.

The Rise of Individualism

In our current age, individuals have much more opportunity to shape their own lives than once was the case. At one time, tra-

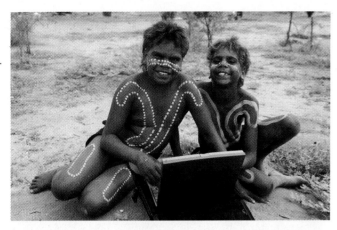

Advancements such as laptop computers and the Internet have allowed those in remote areas, such as these Aboriginal children in rural Australia, unprecedented access to technology and the ability to communicate easily with people all around the world.

dition and custom exercised a very strong influence on the path of people's lives. Factors such as social class, gender, ethnicity, and even religious affiliation could close off certain avenues for individuals or open up others. Being born the eldest son of a tailor, for example, would probably ensure that a young man would learn his father's craft and carry on practicing that craft throughout his lifetime. Tradition held that a woman's natural sphere was in the home; her life and identity were largely defined by those of her husband or father. In times past, individuals' personal identities were formed in the context of the community into which they were born. The values, lifestyles, and ethics prevailing in that community provided relatively fixed guidelines according to which people lived their lives.

Under conditions of globalization, however, we are faced with a move toward a new *individualism* in which people have actively to construct their own identities. The weight of tradition and established values is retreating as local communities interact with a new global order. The social codes that formerly guided people's choices and activities have significantly loosened. Today, for example, the eldest son of a tailor could choose any number of paths in constructing his future, women are no longer restricted to the domestic realm, and many of the other signposts that shaped people's lives have disappeared.

Traditional frameworks of identity are dissolving; new patterns of identity are emerging. Globalization is forcing people to live in a more open, self-aware way. This means that we are constantly responding and adjusting to the changing environment around us; as individuals, we evolve with and within the larger context in which we live. Even the small choices we make in our daily lives—what we wear, how we spend our leisure time, and how we take care of our health and our bodies—are part of an ongoing process of creating and re-creating our self-identities.

Work Patterns

Work is at the center of many people's lives—both on a day-to-day basis and in terms of larger life goals. Although we may regard work as a chore or a necessary evil, it is undeniable that work is a crucial element in our personal lives. We spend great amounts of time working or at work and find that many aspects of our existence—from our friends to our leisure pursuits—are shaped by our work patterns.

Globalization has unleashed profound transformations within the world of work. New patterns of international trade and the move to a knowledge economy have had a significant impact on long-standing employment patterns. Many traditional industries have been made obsolete by new technological advances or are losing their share of the market to competitors abroad whose labor costs are lower than in industrialized countries. Global trade and new forms of technology have had a strong effect on traditional manufacturing communities, where industrial workers have been left unemployed and without the types of skills needed to enter the new knowledge-based economy. These communities are facing a new set of social problems, including long-term unemployment and rising crime rates, as a result of economic globalization.

If at one time people's working lives were dominated by employment with one employer over the course of several decades—the so-called job-for-life framework—today many more individuals create their own career paths, pursuing individual goals and exercising choice in attaining them. Often this involves changing jobs several times over the course of a career, building up new skills and abilities, and transferring them to diverse work contexts. Standard patterns of full-time work are being dissolved into more flexible arrangements: working from home with the help of information technology, job sharing, short-term consulting projects, flextime, and so forth (Beck 1992). While this affords new opportunities for some, for most it means far greater uncertainty. Job security—and the health-care and retirement benefits that went with it—have largely become things of the past.

Women have entered the workforce in large numbers, a fact that has strongly affected the personal lives of people of both sexes. Expanded professional and educational opportunities have led many women to put off marriage and children until after they have begun a career. These changes have also meant that many working women return to work shortly after having children, instead of remaining at home with young children as was once the case. These shifts have required important adjustments within families, in the nature of the domestic division of labor, in the role of men in child rearing, and with the emergence of more family-friendly working policies to accommodate the needs of dual-earner couples.

Popular Culture

The cultural effects of globalization have received much attention. Images, ideas, goods, and styles are now disseminated around the world more rapidly than ever before. Trade, new information technologies, the international media, and global migration have all contributed to the free movement of culture across national borders. Many people believe that we now live in a single information order—a massive global network where information is shared quickly and in great volumes. A simple example should illustrate this point clearly.

Films like *King Kong, Harry Potter and the Goblet of Fire*, and *Star Wars: Revenge of the Sith* have enjoyed worldwide popularity. The film *Titanic*, the most popular film of all time, has grossed more than $1.8 billion in fifty-five countries since its release in 1997—two thirds of it outside of the United States. The film was popular with all age groups, but particularly with adolescent girls—many of whom paid to watch the film several times. The stars of *Titanic,* Leonardo DiCaprio and Kate Winslet, found their careers and futures utterly transformed; they had been elevated from little-known actors to global celebrities. *Titanic* is one of a handful of cultural products that has succeeded in cutting across national boundaries and creating a truly international phenomenon.

What can account for the enormous popularity of a film like *Titanic*? And what does its success tell us about globalization? At one level, *Titanic* was popular for very straightforward reasons: It combined a relatively simple plotline (a romance against the backdrop of tragedy) with a well-known historical event (the 1912 sinking of the *Titanic,* in which more than sixteen hundred people perished). The film was also lavishly produced, with great attention to detail, and included state-of-the-art special effects culminating in the spectacular sinking of the ocean liner. Romance, drama, raw fear—all played a role in the film's success.

But another reason for *Titanic*'s popularity is that it reflected a particular set of ideas and values that resonated with audiences worldwide. One of the film's central themes is the possibility of romantic love prevailing over class differences and family traditions. While such ideas are generally accepted in most Western countries, they are still taking hold in many other areas of the world. The success of a film like *Titanic* reflects the changing attitudes toward personal relationships and marriage, for example, in parts of the world where more traditional values have been favored. Yet *Titanic,* along with many other Western films, can also be said to *contribute* to this shift in values. Western-made films and television programs, which dominate the global media, tend to advance a set of political, social, and economic agendas that reflect specifically Western worldview. Some people worry that globalization is

A Chinese woman buys a ticket to see *Titanic* at a Beijing theater. *Titanic* is one of the most successful films ever made.

leading to the creation of a global culture in which the values of the most powerful and affluent—in this instance, Hollywood filmmakers—overwhelm the strength of local customs and tradition. According to this view, globalization is a form of cultural imperialism in which the values, styles, and outlooks of the Western world are being spread so aggressively that they smother individual national cultures.

Others, by contrast, have linked processes of globalization to a growing *differentiation* in cultural traditions and forms. Rather than cultural homogeneity, they claim that global society is now characterized by an enormous diversity of cultures existing side by side. Local traditions are joined by a host of additional cultural forms from abroad, presenting people with a bewildering array of lifestyle options from which to choose. Rather than a unified global culture, what we are witnessing is the fragmentation of cultural forms (Baudrillard 1988). Established identities and ways of life grounded in local communities and cultures are giving way to new forms of hybrid identity composed of elements from contrasting cultural sources (Hall 1992). Thus a black urban South African today might continue to be strongly influenced by the traditions and cultural outlooks of his tribal roots at the same time as he adopts cosmopolitan styles and tastes—in dress, leisure pursuits, hobbies, and so forth—that have been shaped by globalizing forces.

Globalization and Risk

The consequences of globalization are far reaching, affecting virtually all aspects of the social world. Yet because globalization is an open-ended and internally contradictory process, it produces outcomes that are difficult to predict and control.

Another way of thinking of this dynamic is in terms of *risk*. Many of the changes wrought by globalization are presenting us with new forms of risk that differ greatly from those that existed in previous eras. Unlike risks from the past, which had established causes and known effects, today's risks are incalculable in origin and indeterminate in their consequences.

THE SPREAD OF "MANUFACTURED RISK"

Humans have always had to face risks of one kind or another, but today's risks are qualitatively different from those that came in earlier times. Until quite recently, human societies were threatened by **external risk**—dangers such as drought, earthquakes, famines, and storms that spring from the natural world and are unrelated to the actions of humans. Today, however, we are increasingly confronted with various types of **manufactured risk**—risks that are created by the effect of our own knowledge and technology on the natural world. As we shall see, many environmental and health risks facing contemporary societies are instances of manufactured risk—they are the outcomes of our own interventions into nature.

Environmental Risks One of the clearest illustrations of manufactured risk can be found in threats currently posed by the natural environment (see Chapter 19). One of the consequences of accelerating industrial and technological development has been the steady spread of human intervention into nature. There are few aspects of the natural world that remain untouched by humans—urbanization, industrial production and pollution, large-scale agricultural projects, the construction of dams and hydroelectric plants, and nuclear power are just some of the ways in which human beings have had an effect on their natural surroundings. The collective outcome of such processes has been the creation of widespread environmental destruction whose precise cause is indeterminate and whose consequences are similarly difficult to calculate.

In our globalizing world, ecological risk confronts us in many guises. Concern over global warming has been mounting in the scientific community for some years; it is now generally accepted that the earth's temperature has been increasing from the buildup of harmful gases within the atmosphere. The potential consequences of global warming are devastating: If polar ice caps continue to melt as they currently are, sea levels will rise and may threaten low-lying land masses and their human populations. Changes in climate patterns have been cited as possible causes of the severe floods that afflicted parts of China in 1998 and Mozambique in 2000, or the record number of hurricanes (including the one that devastated New Orleans) that swept through the Atlantic and Gulf of Mexico in the fall of 1995.

Because environmental risks are diffuse in origin, it is unclear how they should be addressed or who bears responsibility for taking action to remedy them. A simple example demonstrates why this is so. Scientists have found that chemical pollution levels have had a harmful effect on certain Antarctic penguin colonies. But it is impossible to identify accurately either the exact origins of the pollution or its possible consequences for the penguins in the future. In such an instance—and in hundreds of similar cases—it is likely that effective action will not be taken to address the risk because the extent of both the cause and the outcome is unknown and unfixed (Beck 1995).

Health Risks In the past decade, the dangers posed to human health by manufactured risks have attracted great attention. In the media and public health campaigns, for example, people have been urged to limit their exposure to the harmful ultraviolet rays of the sun and to apply sunscreen to prevent burning. In recent years, sun exposure has been linked to a heightened risk of skin cancer in many parts of the world. This is thought to be related to the depletion of the ozone layer—the layer of the earth's atmosphere that normally filters out ultraviolet light. Due to the high volume of chemical emissions that are produced by human activities and industry, the concentration of ozone in the atmosphere has been diminishing and, in some cases, ozone holes have opened up.

There are many examples of manufactured risk that are linked to food. Modern farming and food production techniques have been heavily influenced by advances in science and technology. For example, chemical pesticides and herbicides are widely used in commercial agriculture, and many animals (such as chickens and pigs) are pumped full of hormones and antibiotics. Some people have suggested that farming techniques

There are many examples of manufactured risks associated with food. In recent years, avian flu has spread around the world. Fears about the disease spreading to humans have forced farms, like this one in Jordan, to contain outbreaks by killing all of their chickens or turkeys.

The Manufactured Risks of Electronic Viruses and World Climate Change

Globalization comes with many unfamiliar, manufactured risks. Among them are two that may have had a direct impact on you. On May 4, 2000, chaos engulfed the electronic world when a virus nicknamed the "love bug" succeeded in overloading computer systems worldwide. Launched from a personal computer in Manila, the capital of the Philippines, the love bug spread rapidly across the globe and forced almost a tenth of the world's e-mail servers to shut down. The virus was carried worldwide through an e-mail message with the subject heading "I Love You." When recipients opened the file that was attached to the message, they unknowingly activated the virus in their own computer. The love bug would then replicate itself and automatically send itself on to all the e-mail addresses listed in the computerized address book, before attacking information and files stored on the computer's hard drive. The virus spread westward around the globe as employees, first in Asia, then in Europe and North America, arrived to work in the morning and checked their e-mail. By the end of day, the love bug was estimated to have caused more than $1.5 billion of damage worldwide.

The love bug was a particularly fast-spreading virus, but it was not the first of its kind. Electronic viruses have become

such as these compromise food safety and could have an adverse effect on humans. In recent years, two particular controversies have raised widespread public concern over food safety and manufactured risk: the debate over genetically modified foods and mad cow disease.

The saga of genetically modified foods began only a few years ago when some of the world's leading chemical and agricultural firms decided that new knowledge about the workings of genes could transform the world's food supply. These companies had been making pesticides and herbicides, but wanted to move into what they saw as a major market for the future. The American firm Monsanto was the leader in developing much of the new technology. Monsanto bought up seed companies, sold off its chemical division, and devoted much of its energy to bringing the new crops to the market. Led by its chief executive, Robert Shapiro, Monsanto launched a gigantic advertising campaign promoting the benefits of its genetically modified crops to farmers and to consumers. The early responses were just as the company had confidently anticipated. By early 1999, 55 percent of the soybeans and 35 percent of the maize produced in the United States contained genetic alterations. It is currently estimated that between 60 and 70 percent of all produce sold in grocery stores contains some genetically modified components (Safe-food.org 2003). In addition to North America, genetically modified crops are being widely grown in China.

Since genetically modified crops are essentially quite new, no one can be certain about what their effects will be once they are introduced into the environment. Many ecological and consumer groups became concerned about the potential risks involved with the adoption of this largely untested technology.

Bovine spongiform encephalopathy (BSE), known popularly as mad cow disease, was first detected in British cattle in 1986. Scientists have linked BSE infection to the practice of raising cattle—normally herbivores—on feed containing traces of the parts of other animals. After the outbreak, the government more common—and more dangerous—as computers and electronic forms of communication have grown in importance and sophistication. Viruses such as the love bug demonstrate how interconnected the world has become with the advance of globalization. You might think that in this particular instance global interconnectedness proved to be quite a disadvantage, since a harmful virus was able to spread so rapidly around the globe. Yet many positive aspects of globalization are reflected in this case as well. As soon as the virus was detected, computer and security experts from around the world worked together to prevent its spread, protect national computer systems, and share intelligence about the virus's origins.

Another aspect of manufactured risk and one you likely have noticed—or been directly affected by—is the unusual weather in recent years. Scientists and disaster experts have pointed out that extreme weather events—such as unseasonably hot temperatures, droughts, floods, and cyclones—have been occurring with ever greater frequency. In 1998 alone, for example, eighty separate natural catastrophes were recorded at points around the globe, including devastating floods in China, hurricanes in Latin America, wildfires in Indonesia, and severe ice storms in North America. Since that time, drought has gripped regions as diverse as Ethiopia, southern Afghanistan, and the midwestern United States; floods have ravaged Venezuela and Mozambique; violent windstorms have battered parts of Europe; and a plague of locusts has swarmed through the Australian outback.

Although no one can be certain, many people believe that these natural disasters are caused in part by global warming (the heating up of the earth's atmosphere). If carbon dioxide emissions that contribute to global warming continue unchecked, it seems likely that the earth's climate will be irreversibly harmed. Who is to blame for global warming, and what can be done to slow its progress? As with so many aspects of our changing world, the risks associated with global warming are experienced worldwide, yet its precise causes are nearly impossible to pinpoint. In an age of globalization, we are constantly reminded of our interdependence with others: The actions of individuals or institutions in one part of the world can, and do, have significant consequences for people everywhere.

took steps to control the disease among cattle, but it claimed that eating beef was safe and posed no danger to humans. Only in the mid-1990s was it admitted that several human deaths from Creutzfeldt-Jakob disease, a degenerative brain condition, had been linked to the consumption of beef from infected cattle. Thousands of British cattle were killed and strict legislation was passed to regulate cattle farming and the sale of beef products. Most recently cattle infected with BSE have been discovered in Canada and the United States, sparking widespread fears about the safety of the food supply.

Although extensive scientific research has been launched to determine the risks to humans from BSE, the findings remain inconclusive. There is a risk that individuals who consumed British beef in the years preceding the discovery of BSE *may* have been exposed to infection. Yet as recently as December 1999 the European Union's Scientific Steering Committee declared that "the infectious dose to humans is currently not known." Calculating the risks humans run from BSE is an ex-

ample of the complexity of risk assessment in the contemporary world. It is necessary to know if and when infected cattle were part of a certain food chain, the level and distribution of the infection that was present in the cattle, the way in which the beef was processed, and many other details. The sheer quantity of unknown factors has complicated the task and made any precise analysis of risk challenging.

THE GLOBAL "RISK SOCIETY"

Global warming, the BSE crisis, the debate over genetically modified foods, and other manufactured risks have presented individuals with new choices and challenges in their everyday lives. Because there is no roadmap to these new dangers, individuals, countries, and transnational organizations must negotiate risks as they make choices about how lives are to be lived. Because there are no definitive answers about the causes and outcomes of such risks, each individual is forced

Global Health

An important aspect of the economic gap between developed and developing countries is the huge disparity in the health conditions experienced in the rich and poor parts of the world. The physical and economic burdens of diseases affect peoples in the developing world more significantly than they do those in developed countries. In its 1999 *World Health Report,* the World Health Organization (WHO) stated that "[d]espite the long list of success in health achieved globally during the 20th century, the balance sheet is indelibly stained by the avoidable burden of disease and malnutrition that the world's disadvantaged populations continue to bear." While WHO and other international organizations have tried to reduce the "health gap" between developed and developing countries, experts point to much evidence that the health gap still remains of daunting and, in some cases, worsening proportions. WHO argues that populations in developing countries now face not only continued threats from infectious diseases but also growing epidemics of non-communicable diseases, such as lung and heart disease. The continued presence of the global health gap becomes more worrisome when arguments that the processes of globalization are increasing, rather than narrowing, the gap are considered.

***

Not only has the "health gap" between developed and developing countries not disappeared, but it has also changed its nature. Previously, the gap was basically measured in terms of the burden of infectious diseases; countries were supposed to make the transition away from infectious diseases toward non-communicable diseases. Today and in the future, the gap is and will be measured in terms of the burdens of both infectious and non-communicable diseases. Any future "health transition" strategy now must aim to reduce the burdens of both infectious and non-communicable diseases—a public health undertaking of enormous proportions. The scale of the challenge can be glimpsed by briefly noting that it requires governments in developing countries (with international assistance) to improve basic sanitation and public health systems, making better use

These photos illustrate responses to health issues in India. (Left) Protesters, many of them prostitutes and health care workers, march in New Delhi's red light district, calling for job opportunities and medical facilities on World AIDS Day 1997. The UN estimates that India has between 3 and 5 million HIV-positive citizens, making it the country with the most cases in the world. (Above right) Members of the Socialist Unity Center of India (SUCI) tangle with police in front of the West Bengal Legislative Assembly House in Calcutta, India to protest price hikes in electricity and health services in this eastern Indian state. (Right) According to UNICEF more than 53 million children under the age of five suffer from chronic and moderate malnutrition. (Far right) Postal staff handling foreign mail take precautions against anthrax at the Mumbai airport in India.

of antimicrobial treatments to prevent the development of resistant pathogens, and alter individual behavior patterns that produce morbidity and mortality, such as tobacco consumption, promiscuous sexual behavior, illicit drug use, and poor dietary habits. Where the economic resources to undertake such massive and expensive public health endeavors will originate remains a mystery. The mystery becomes even more forbidding when we begin to factor in the public health and health care implications of the globalization of markets and culture.

***

Public health and health care in developed and developing countries have not escaped the impact of the processes of globalization. In fact, experts have identified the phenomenon of the "globalization of public health," under which states are losing the ability to protect the health of their publics from disease threats. The loss of the ability to provide for public health because of global forces is, of course, a matter of concern for

developed as well as developing countries. But as in other areas of globalization, the impact on developing countries is of a different magnitude in the health context because the health threats are greater and the financial, technological, and human resources to deal with them are smaller.

The relationship between globalization and health is complex; but it is necessary, even at the risk of oversimplification, to clarify how the processes of globalization adversely affect health in developing countries. From the broadest perspective, the adverse health effects from globalization in developing countries arise from structural imbalances in the international system that the processes of globalization exacerbate. The structural imbalances can be glimpsed through four features of globalization: (1) increases in international trade; (2) structural adjustment programs maintained by international financial organizations; (3) increases in international trade in services and in transnational investments in service industries; and (4) the international regime on intellectual property.

SOURCE: David P. Fidler, "Neither Science Nor Shamans: Globalization of Markets and Health in the Developing World," *Indiana Journal of Global Legal Studies* 7 (2001): 191.

Questions

- How might the economic and structural elements of international trade affect the society and health of a developing country?
- Name some ways that globalization can have a detrimental effect on health. How might we address and counteract these effects?
- Why might people participate in the globalizing trend, despite its negative aspects?

to make decisions about which risks he or she is prepared to take. This can be a bewildering endeavor! Should we use food and raw materials if their production or consumption might have a negative impact on our own health and on the natural environment? Even seemingly simple decisions about what to eat are now made in the context of conflicting information and opinions about the product's relative merits and drawbacks.

German sociologist Ulrich Beck (1992), who has written extensively about risk and globalization, sees these risks contributing to the formation of a global *risk society*. As technological change progresses more and more rapidly and produces new forms of risk, we must constantly respond and adjust to these changes. The risk society, he argues, is not limited to environmental and health risks alone; it includes a whole series of interrelated changes within contemporary social life: shifting employment patterns, heightened job insecurity, the declining influence of tradition and custom on self-identity, the erosion of traditional family patterns, and the democratization of personal relationships. Because personal futures are much less fixed than they were in traditional societies, decisions of all kinds present risks for individuals. Getting married, for example, is a riskier endeavor today than it was at a time when marriage was a lifelong institution. Decisions about educational qualifications and career paths can also feel risky: It is difficult to predict what skills will be valuable in an economy that is changing as rapidly as ours is.

According to Beck (1995), an important aspect of the risk society is that its hazards are not restricted spatially, temporally, or socially. Today's risks affect all countries and all social classes; they have global, not merely personal, consequences. Many forms of manufactured risk, such as those concerning human health and the environment, cross national boundaries. The explosion at the Chernobyl nuclear power plant in Ukraine in 1986 provides a clear illustration of this point. Everyone living in the immediate vicinity of Chernobyl—regardless of age, class, gender, or status—was exposed to dangerous levels of radiation. At the same time, the effects of the accident stretched far beyond Chernobyl itself—throughout Europe and beyond, abnormally high levels of radiation were detected long after the explosion.

Globalization and Inequality

Beck and other scholars have drawn attention to risk as one of the main outcomes of globalization and technological advance. New forms of risk present complex challenges for both individuals and whole societies that are forced to navigate through unknown terrain. Yet globalization is generating other important challenges as well.

Globalization is proceeding in an uneven way. The effect of globalization is experienced differentially, and some of its consequences are far from benign. Next to mounting ecological problems, the expansion of inequalities within and between societies is one of the most serious challenges facing the world at the start of the twenty-first century.

INEQUALITY AND GLOBAL DIVISIONS

As we learned in our discussion of types of society (Chapter 3) as well as global inequality (Chapter 8), the vast majority of the world's wealth is concentrated in the industrialized or developed countries of the world, whereas the nations of the developing world suffer from widespread poverty, overpopulation, inadequate educational and health care systems, and crippling foreign debt. The disparity between the developed and the developing world widened steadily over the course of the twentieth century and is now the largest it has ever been.

The 1999 *Human Development Report,* published by the United Nations Development Programme (UNDP), revealed that the average income of the fifth of the world's population living in the richest countries was seventy-four times greater than the average income of the fifth living in the poorest. In the late 1990s, more than one fifth of the world's population accounted for 86 percent of the world's overall consumption, 82 percent of export markets, and 74 percent of telephone lines. The combined income of the world's richest 500 people is greater than that of the poorest 416 million. The poorest 40 percent of the world's population, who live on less than $2 a day, account for 5 percent of global income; whereas the richest 10 percent, almost all of whom live high-income countries, account for 54 percent of global income (UNDP 2005). The UNDP estimates that if wealthy countries were to stop growing and poor countries were to continue growing at the rate that they are currently it would take over two hundred years for the poorest to catch up.

In much of the developing world, levels of economic growth and output over the past century have not kept up with the rate of population growth, whereas the level of economic development in industrialized countries has far outpaced it. These opposing tendencies have led to a marked divergence between the richest and poorest countries of the world. The distance between the world's richest and poorest country was approximately 3 to 1 in 1820, 11 to 1 in 1913, 35 to 1 in 1950, 72 to 1 in 1992, and 173 to 1 in 2001 (Figure 20.3). Over the past century, among the richest quarter of the world's population, income per head has increased almost sixfold, while among the poorest quarter, the increase has been less than threefold.

Globalization seems to be exacerbating these trends by further concentrating income, wealth, and resources within a small

FIGURE 20.3

The Widening of the Gaps between Richer and Poorer Countries between 1820 and 1992

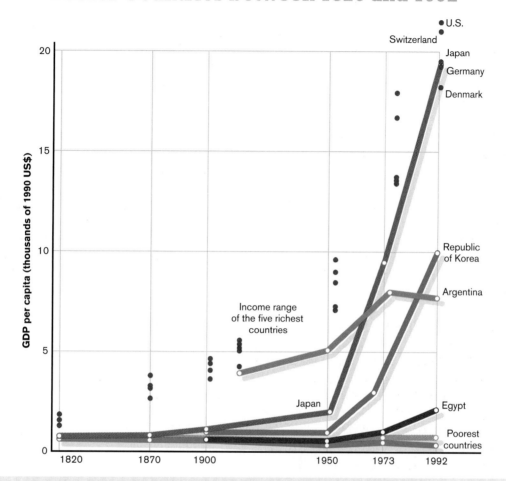

What is the approximate gap in GDP per capita between the cluster of wealthy countries and the poorest countries in 1900? What is the approximate gap in GDP per capita of the United States and poor countries in 1992? In what year was the income range of the five richest countries the most spread out? Which countries in the figure show a leveling off or decline in GDP per capita at any time since 1950? What is the general work of the World Trade Organization (WTO)?

SOURCES: UNDP 1999; World Bank 2003c.

core of countries (Figure 20.4). As we have seen in this chapter, the global economy is growing and integrating at an extremely rapid rate. The expansion of global trade has been central to this process—between 1990 and 1997, international trade grew by 6.5 percent. Since 2000, the volume of global trade has averaged an increase of about 5 percent a year (WTO 2006); only a

handful of developing countries have managed to benefit from that rapid growth, and the process of integration into the global economy has been uneven. Some countries—such as the East Asian economies, Chile, India, and Poland—have fared well, with growth in exports of over 5 percent. Other countries—such as Russia, Venezuela, and Algeria—have seen few benefits

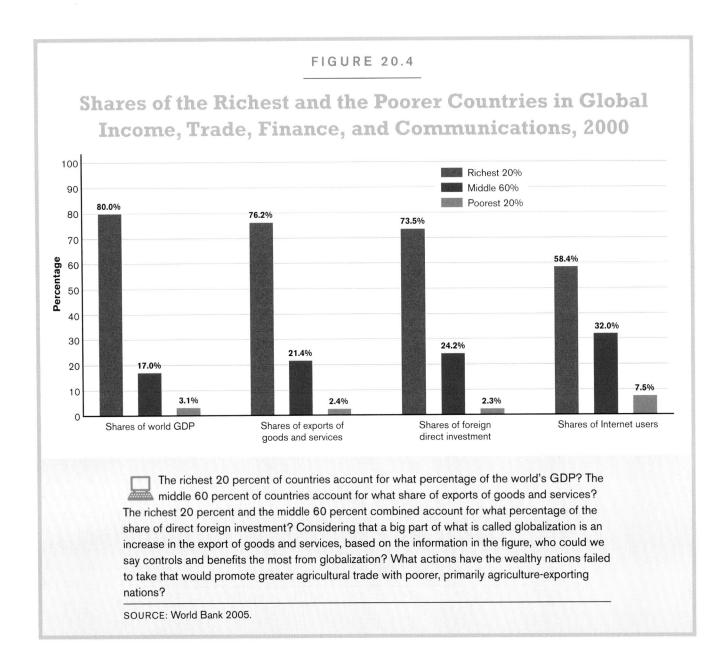

FIGURE 20.4

Shares of the Richest and the Poorer Countries in Global Income, Trade, Finance, and Communications, 2000

The richest 20 percent of countries account for what percentage of the world's GDP? The middle 60 percent of countries account for what share of exports of goods and services? The richest 20 percent and the middle 60 percent combined account for what percentage of the share of direct foreign investment? Considering that a big part of what is called globalization is an increase in the export of goods and services, based on the information in the figure, who could we say controls and benefits the most from globalization? What actions have the wealthy nations failed to take that would promote greater agricultural trade with poorer, primarily agriculture-exporting nations?

SOURCE: World Bank 2005.

from expanding trade and globalization (UNDP 1999). Findings from the World Bank (2000) support this picture: Among ninety-three nations in the developing world, only twenty-three can be said to be "rapid integrators." There is a danger that many of the countries most in need of economic growth will be left even further behind as globalization progresses.

Free trade is seen by many as the key to economic development and poverty relief. Organizations such as the WTO work to liberalize trade regulations and to reduce barriers to trade between the countries of the world. Free trade across borders is viewed as a win–win proposition for both developed and developing countries. While the industrialized economies are able to export their products to markets around the world, it is claimed that developing countries will also benefit by gaining

access to world markets. This, in turn, is supposed to improve their prospects for integration into the global economy.

THE CAMPAIGN FOR GLOBAL JUSTICE

Not everyone agrees that free trade is the solution to poverty and global inequality. In fact, many critics argue that free trade is a rather one-sided affair that benefits those who are already well off and exacerbates existing patterns of poverty and dependency within the developing world. Recently, much of this criticism has focused around the activities and policies of the WTO, which is at the forefront of efforts to increase global trade.

In December 1999, more than fifty thousand people from around the world took to the streets of Seattle to protest during the WTO's so-called Millennium Round of trade talks. For four days, Seattle was awash with colorful demonstrations, street theater, acts of civil disobedience, marches, workshops, and teach-ins. Trade unionists, environmentalists, human rights campaigners, antinuclear activists, farmers, and representatives from hundreds of local and international nongovernmental organizations joined forces to voice their frustration with the WTO—an organization seen by many as favoring economic imperatives over all other concerns, including human rights, labor rights, the environment, and sustainable development. The protests were mostly peaceful, but violent clashes did break out between protesters and the local police force, which used tear gas and rubber bullets to control the crowds that brought downtown Seattle to a halt.

Negotiators from the WTO's 134 member states (the number of members has since risen to 149) had come together to discuss and agree on measures to liberalize conditions for global trade and investment in agriculture and forest products, among other issues. Yet the talks broke off early with no agreements reached. The organizers of the protests were triumphant—not only had the demonstrations succeeded in disrupting the talks, but internal disputes among delegates had also risen to the surface. The Seattle protests were heralded as the biggest victory to date for campaigners for global justice. Since that time, every ministerial meeting of the WTO has been met by massive demonstrations by those excluded from the processes of setting the rules for global trade.

But what is this campaign about, and does it represent the emergence of a powerful antiglobalization movement, as some commentators have suggested? In the months following the Seattle protests, similar demonstrations were held in other cities around the world, such as London and Washington, D.C. These events were much smaller than those that took place in Seattle, but they were organized around similar themes. Protesters argued that free trade and economic globalization succeed in further concentrating wealth in the hands of a few, while increasing poverty for the majority of the world's population. Most of these activists agree that global trade is necessary and potentially beneficial for national economies, but they claim that it needs to be regulated by *different* rules from those favored by the WTO. They argue that trade rules should be oriented, first and foremost, to protecting human rights, the environment, labor rights, and local economies—not in ensuring larger profits for already rich corporations.

The protesters claim that the WTO is an undemocratic organization that is dominated by the interests of the world's richest nations—particularly the United States. Although the members of the WTO include many developing nations, many of them have virtually no practical influence over the organization's policies, because the agenda is set by the richest nations. Poorer nations have many fewer resources, in terms of

both money as well as trained personnel, to confront the many highly complex issues related to international trade. The president of the World Bank has pointed out that nineteen of the forty-two African states that are members of the WTO have little or no representation at its headquarters in Geneva (World Bank 2000). Such imbalances have very real consequences. For example, although the WTO has insisted that developing nations open their markets to imports from industrialized countries, it has allowed developed countries to maintain high barriers to agricultural imports and provide vast subsidies for their domestic agriculture production to protect their own agricultural sectors.

In 2005, the U.S. government spent $19 billion to boost the income of crop and livestock farmers, while European governments spent $80 billion to do the same (Walter and Palmer 2005). This has meant that the world's poorest countries, many of which remain predominantly agricultural, do not have access to the large markets for agricultural goods in developed countries. This issue has been at the heart of a protracted breakdown in negotiating the expansion of WTO rules covering trade in services, foreign investment, government procurement, and other trade issues. Beginning with the 2003 WTO ministerial meeting, in Cancún, Mexico, the "Group of 21" developing nations led by Brazil and India have refused to consider the expansion of WTO rules until the United States and the European Union eliminate subsidies for agriculture production and allow greater access to other agriculture markets, such as cotton. This led to the collapse of the Cancún ministerial meeting and derailed the progress of other trade deals, such as the Free Trade Area of the Americas (FTAA), which is a plan to make both North and South America a free trading zone. Still the issue of agriculture subsidies has not been resolved. A group of developing counties, again led by Brazil, won two major disputes at the WTO over subsidies for European sugar and American cotton. Despite these rulings by the highest international trade court at the WTO, the issue of illegal subsidies used by Europe and the United States to support their farmers led to the failure of another WTO ministerial meeting held at the end of 2005 in Hong Kong.

A similar divide exists over the protection of intellectual property rights—an issue monitored by a WTO multilateral agreement called TRIPS (Trade-Related Aspects of Intellectual Property Rights). Industrial countries own 97 percent of all patents worldwide, but the concept of intellectual property rights is alien to the developing world. There has been a significant increase in the number of patent claims over the past two decades as biotechnology companies and research institutes push to control and "own" more and more forms of knowledge, technology, and biodiversity. Many samples of plant material, for example, have been taken from biodiverse areas such as rain forests and developed by pharmaceutical companies into profitable—and patented—medicines. Local knowledge about the medicinal uses of the plants is often used in developing and marketing the medicines, yet the indigenous people of the area receive no compensation for their contribution. As industrialized countries within the WTO push to strengthen intellectual property laws, many people in developing countries argue that such a move works against the needs of their countries. Research agendas are dictated by profit interests, not human interests, and valuable forms of technology may end up out of the reach of poorer countries that could benefit greatly from their use.

Another criticism of the WTO is that it operates in secret and is not accountable to citizens who are directly affected by its decisions. In many ways, these criticisms are valid. Trade disputes between members of the WTO are decided behind closed doors by an unelected committee of "experts." When a decision is handed down, it is legally binding on all member states and enforceable through a mechanism that authorizes WTO member nations to enact punitive trade policies unless the losing nation complies with the decision. The WTO can also challenge or override laws in individual nations that are seen as barriers to trade. This includes national laws or bilateral agreements designed to protect the environment, conserve scarce resources, safeguard public health, or guarantee labor standards and human rights. For example, the WTO has ruled against the European Union, which refused to import U.S. hormone-treated beef because of its possible links to cancer, and has challenged a law passed in Massachusetts that prohibits companies from investing in Myanmar (Burma) because of its government's human rights violations. In another instance, the United States and the European Union have attempted to use the TRIPS provision to block the importation of inexpensive generic HIV/AIDS medication into countries in sub-Saharan Africa, whose populations are being devastated by this epidemic. This was met with worldwide public outrage, which forced the WTO to reconsider its rules that regulate patent rights when public health is at stake.

A final concern shared by many activists is the undue influence wielded by the United States over the activities of the WTO and other international bodies such as the World Bank and the International Monetary Fund. In the years after the collapse of the Soviet Union, the United States has often been described as the world's only remaining superpower. In some respects, this is certainly true. With its overwhelming economic, political, and military might, the United States is able to influence debates and decision making in many international institutions. The unevenness of globalization must be seen in part as a reflection of the fact that political and economic power is concentrated in the hands of a few core states. Even with the significant influence of the United States on the formation and operation of the WTO, it is also subject to the rules

At a rally in Geneva, Switzerland, Oxfam members protest the trade policies of the WTO. Many protesters claim that the WTO is an undemocratic organization that is dominated by the interests of the world's richest nations—particularly the United States. Although the members of the WTO include developing nations, many of them have almost no practical influence over the organization's policies, because the agenda is set by the richest nations.

and decisions of this organization. In fact, the United States almost always loses when it is forced to defend its trading practices before a WTO appellate panel (Conti 2003). For example, in 2003 the WTO determined that high tariffs placed on imports of steel into the United States violated the rights of WTO member nations. Under heavy pressure from its trading partners, the United States eventually rescinded the tariffs and came into compliance with WTO law. This example highlights a fundamental tension about the nature of power and the processes of globalization: Can we expect the world's sole superpower to always play by the rules when the rules go against the interests of the superpower? What effect will this tension have on the creation of a just and equitable global legal and political system?

Protesters against the WTO and other international financial institutions such as the World Bank and the International Monetary Fund argue that exuberance over global economic integration and free trade is forcing people to live in an economy rather than a society. Many are convinced that such moves will further weaken the economic position of poor societies by allowing transnational corporations to operate with few or no safety and environmental regulations. Commercial interests, they claim, are increasingly taking precedence over concern for human well-being. Not only within developing nations, but in industrialized ones as well, there needs to be more investment in "human capital"—public health, education, and training—if global divisions are not to deepen even further. The key challenge for the twenty-first century is to ensure that globalization works for people everywhere, not only for those who are already well placed to benefit from it.

Conclusion: The Need for Global Governance

As globalization progresses, existing political structures and models appear unequipped to manage a world full of risks, inequalities, and challenges that transcend national borders. It is not within the capacity of individual governments to control the spread of HIV/AIDS, to counter the effects of global warming, or to regulate volatile financial markets. Many of the processes affecting societies around the world elude the grasp of current governing mechanisms. In light of this governing deficit, some have called for new forms of global governance that could address global issues in a global way. As a growing number of challenges operate above the level of individual countries, it is argued that responses to them must also be transnational in scope.

Although it may seem unrealistic to speak of governance above the level of the nation-state, some steps have already been taken toward the creation of a global democratic structure, such as the formation of the United Nations and the European Union. The EU in particular can be seen as an innovative response to globalization and could well become a model for similar organizations in other parts of the world where regional ties are strong. New forms of global governance could help promote a cosmopolitan world order in which transparent rules and standards for international behavior, such as the defense of human rights, are established and observed.

The years that have passed since the end of the cold war have been marked by violence, internal conflict, and chaotic transformations in many areas of the world. Some have taken a pessimistic view, seeing globalization as accelerating crisis and chaos. Others see vital opportunities to harness globalizing forces in the pursuit of greater equality, democracy, and prosperity. The move toward global governance and more effective regulatory institutions is certainly not misplaced at a time when global interdependence and the rapid pace of change link all of us together more than ever before. It is not beyond our abilities to reassert our will on the social world. Indeed, such a task appears to be both the greatest necessity and the greatest challenge facing human societies at the start of the twenty-first century.

Study Outline

www.wwnorton.com/giddens

Influences on Social Change

- *Social change* may be defined as the transformation, over time, of the institutions and culture of a society. The modern period, although occupying only a small fraction of human history, has shown rapid and major changes, and the pace of change is accelerating.
- The development of social organization and institutions, from hunting and gathering to agrarian to modern industrial societies, is far too diverse to be accounted for by any single-factor theory of social change. At least three broad categories of influences can be identified: The physical environment includes such factors as climate or the availability of communication routes (rivers, mountain passes); these are important to consider, especially as they affect early economic development, but should not be overemphasized. Political organization (especially military power) affects all societies, traditional and modern, with the possible exception of hunting and gathering societies. Cultural factors include religion (which can act as a brake on change), communication systems (such as the invention of writing), and individual leadership.

Change in the Modern Period

- The most important economic influence on modern social change is industrial capitalism, which depends on and promotes constant innovation and revision of productive technology. Science and technology also affect (and are affected by) political factors, the most important of which is the emergence of the modern state with its relatively efficient forms of government. Cultural influences include another effect of science and technology, the critical and innovative character of modern thinking, which constantly challenges tradition and cultural habits.

Current Changes and Future Prospects

- Social theorists have speculated on where social change will lead us. One influential line of thinking about where modern society is headed holds that the industrial era is being superseded by a *post-industrial society* based on the importance of information and service, rather than on manufacturing and industrialization. Some authors go further and speak not only of the end of industrialism, but of the end of modernity itself. Our beliefs in progress, in the benefits of science, and in our ability to control the modern world are diminishing, say the *postmodernists;* and there is such a diversity and plurality of individual concerns and points of view that it is no longer possible to have any overarching conception of history or of where we are headed.

Globalization

- Globalization is often portrayed as an economic phenomenon, but this view is too simplified. Globalization is produced by the coming together of political, economic, cultural, and social factors. It is driven forward above all by advances in information and communication technologies that have intensified the speed and scope of interaction among people around the world.
- Several factors are contributing to increasing globalization. First, the end of the cold war, the collapse of Soviet-style communism, and the growth of international and regional forms of governance have drawn the countries of the world closer together. Second, the spread of information technology has facilitated the flow of information around the globe and has encouraged people to adopt a global outlook. Third, transnational corporations have grown in size and influence, building networks of production and consumption that span the globe and link economic markets.
- Globalization has become a hotly debated topic. Skeptics believe that the idea of globalization is overrated and that current levels of interconnectedness are not unprecedented. Some skeptics focus instead on processes of regionalization that are intensifying activity within major financial and trade groups. Hyperglobalizers take an opposing position, arguing that globalization is a real and powerful phenomenon that threatens to erode the role of national governments altogether. A third group, the transformationalists, believes that globalization is transforming many aspects of the current global order—including economics, politics, and social relations—but that old patterns still remain. According to this view, globalization is a contradictory process, involving a multidirectional flow of influences that sometimes work in opposition.
- Globalization is not restricted to large, global systems. Its impact is felt in our personal lives, in the way we think of ourselves and our connections with others. Globalizing forces enter our local contexts and our intimate lives both through impersonal sources such as the media and the Internet and through personal contacts with people from other countries and cultures.

Globalization and Risk

- Globalization is an open-ended, contradictory process—it produces outcomes that are difficult to control and predict. Globalization is presenting us with new forms of risk that differ from those that existed previously. *External risk* refers to dangers that spring from the natural world, such as earthquakes. *Manufactured risks* are risks that are created by the effect of human knowledge and technology on the natural world. Some believe that we are living in a global-risk society in which human societies everywhere are faced with risks (e.g., global warming) that have been produced by our own interventions into nature.

- Globalization is proceeding rapidly but unevenly. It has been marked by a growing divergence between the richest and poorest countries of the world. Wealth, income, resources, and consumption are concentrated among the developed societies, whereas much of the developing world struggles with poverty, malnutrition, disease, and foreign debt. Many of the countries most in need of the economic benefits of globalization are in danger of being marginalized.

World Trade Organization

- Barriers to international trade have been steadily reduced in recent decades, and many believe that free trade and open markets will allow developing countries to integrate more fully into the global economy. Opponents to this approach argue that international trade bodies, such as the WTO, are dominated by the interests of the richest countries and ignore the needs of the developing world. They claim that trade rules must, first and foremost, protect human rights, labor rights, the environment, and national economies, rather than simply ensuring larger profits for corporations.

Global Governance in the Future

- Globalization is producing risks, challenges, and inequalities that cross national borders and elude the reach of existing political structures. Because individual governments are unequipped to handle these transnational issues, there is a need for new forms of global governance that can address global problems in a global way. Reasserting our will on the rapidly changing social world may be the greatest challenge of the twenty-first century.

Key Concepts

external risk (p. 671)
information society (p. 656)
knowledge society (p. 656)
manufactured risk (p. 671)
postindustrial society (p. 656)
postmodern (p. 658)
service society (p. 656)
social change (p. 652)
transnational corporations (p. 662)

Review Questions

1. What is the sociology of social change?
   a. the study of revolution

b. the study of the transformation over time of the institutions and culture of society

c. the study of social movements

d. the study of collective behavior

2. According to hyperglobalizers, which one of the following statements is true?

a. Internationalization depends on government acquiescence and support.

b. Globalization is making national politics more powerful.

c. Globalization means the end of the nation-state.

d. Globalization has no impact on how nation-states or governments operate.

3. How do opponents of postindustrial theory refute the argument that the shift from manufacturing jobs to service jobs is a harbinger of postindustrialism?

a. Such a shift has been going on since the beginning of the Industrial Revolution. Manufacturing and service employment have expanded at the expense of agriculture.

b. Service jobs are not necessarily white-collar jobs. There are many blue-collar jobs in services.

c. White-collar work isn't necessarily service work. A lot of white-collar work supports manufacturing.

d. All of the above.

4. What is the argument of the "end of history" thesis?

a. The "end of history" is the end of the Industrial Revolution and the coming of postindustrial society.

b. The "end of history" is the end of the great ideological struggles that erupted in the wake of the Industrial Revolution: Capitalism has finally beaten socialism, and liberal democracy is unchallenged.

c. The "end of history" is the end of the belief that humanity can make progress, through the application of science and the development of technology, toward controlling its own destiny.

d. The "end of history" is the end of World War II.

5. Transnational corporations became a global phenomenon in the years following

a. World War I.

b. World War II.

c. the collapse of the Soviet Union.

d. the invention of the computer.

6. In 1992, the distance in terms of wealth between the world's richest and poorest countries was approximately

a. 3 to 1.

b. 11 to 1.

c. 35 to 1.

d. 72 to 1.

7. What is the relationship between science/technology and politics?

a. Science and technology influence changes in politics.

b. Politics influences how science and technology develop.

c. Science and technology both influence and are influenced by political factors.

d. Science and technology have no influence on politics.

8. According to Daniel Bell, what is postindustrial society's main strategic resource?

a. The production and control of computers

b. The production and control of nuclear weapons

c. The production and control of food

d. The production and control of codified knowledge

9. Which of the following can be controlled by individual governments?

a. the spread of HIV/AIDS

b. the effects of global warming

c. volatile financial markets

d. None of the above

10. The "unevenness" of globalization is in part due to the fact that political and economic power is concentrated in the hands of

a. the United States.

b. the United Nations.

c. a few core countries.

d. oil-rich countries.

Thinking Sociologically Exercises

1. Discuss the many influences on social change: environmental, political, and cultural factors. Summarize how each element can contribute to social change.

2. According to this chapter, we now live in a society where we are increasingly confronted by various types of manufactured risks. Briefly explain what these risks consist of. Do you think the last decade has brought us any closer to or further away from confronting the challenges of manufactured risks? Explain.

Data Exercises

www.wwnorton.com/giddens
Keyword: Data20

What role have transnational corporations played in the development of a global economy? In what ways do they adapt their products and operations to local markets and in what ways do they ignore cultural differences? The data exercise for this chapter will give you an opportunity to investigate the global operations of a selected number of transnational corporations.

HOW TO USE LIBRARIES

Libraries, especially large ones, can seem like daunting places. People can feel somewhat lost when confronted with the apparently innumerable sources of information that libraries contain. They may therefore end up using only a small proportion of what a library has to offer, perhaps with damaging effects on their academic work. It is a good idea to get to know—at the beginning of your course—the range of resources libraries have. If you do this early on, the "lost" feeling will not last long!

All the information available in the library is stored and cataloged systematically, in order to make finding things easy. Most smaller libraries operate with *open stacks*—the books can be visibly inspected on the shelves, and the user can select whichever volume she wants directly. Most larger collections keep only a proportion of their books on open shelves and store others in vaults, where less space is required to keep them. In these libraries, anyone who wishes to use or borrow a book must ask for it or fill in a request slip.

If you are looking for a particular book, you will be able to look it up under author or title in the index or catalog. This may be a computerized list, drawers of index cards, or microfiche—or all three. Once you find the book's catalog number you can then either order it from library staff by quoting that number or find it on the open shelves, which are always arranged by catalog number. All—or most—sociology books will be in one area. Any librarian will be able to explain how the cataloging system works. To find books on a particular topic when you don't know any names or titles, you need to use a subject index (again, this may be computerized or on cards). A subject index lists books by topics—such as "class," "bureaucracy," etc.

Many of the larger libraries today have computer-trace systems, which are very easy to operate and are normally available to all library users. You simply key in the area about which you require bibliographical information, and the computer will display a list of relevant titles.

Most libraries provide similar services, but different libraries have their own ways of doing things, and there are variations in cataloging systems. Never be afraid to ask the librarian or assistants for their help if there is any procedure that puzzles you. You should not be worried about bothering them; librarians are trained professionals, committed to making sure that the library resources are available to everyone who wants to make use of them. They are usually highly knowledgeable about the range of material the library contains and only too willing to provide guidance.

Sources of General Information in Sociology

If you are beginning the study of a particular topic in sociology and want to find some general information about it, there are a number of useful sources. Several dictionaries of sociology are available. These provide brief discussions of major concepts and accounts of the ideas of some of the leading contributors to the discipline. The major encyclopedias—like the *World Book Encyclopedia*—contain many entries relevant to sociological topics, such as "city," "crime," "family," "middle class," "prejudice," "research," and "statistics." The entries in dictionaries and encyclopedias virtually always provide short lists of books or articles as a guide to further reading.

There are other ways in which books and articles relevant to a given issue can be traced. The *International Bibliography of the Social Sciences*, published annually by UNESCO, offers a comprehensive listing of works that have appeared in different social science subjects over the course of any year. Thus, for example, you can look up the heading "Sociology of education" and find a range of up-to-date materials in that field. An equally useful source is *Sociological Abstracts*, which not only lists books and articles in the different areas of sociology, but gives a short description of the contents of each.

Sociological Journals

It is worth familiarizing yourself with the main journals in sociology. Journals usually appear three or four times a year. The information and debates they contain are often more up to date than those in books, which take longer to write and publish. Journal articles are sometimes quite technical, and a person new to sociology may not find them readily understandable. But all the leading journals regularly publish articles of general interest, accessible to those with only limited knowledge of the subject.

The most important sociology journals include the *American Sociological Review* and the *American Journal of Sociology*.

Writing Research Papers

On some occasions, you may wish to use the library to pursue a particular research project, perhaps in the course of writing a thesis. Such a task might involve carrying out a more in-depth search for relevant sources than is required for normal study.

If you need statistical information concerning the United States, a good place to start is *Statistical Abstract of the United States*, which is available from the Government Printing Office in Washington, D.C. This volume contains selected statistical information on many areas of American social life.

Newspaper articles provide a mine of valuable information for the sociological researcher. A few newspapers are what are sometimes called "journals of record." That is to say, they not only carry news stories, but also record sections from congressional speeches, government reports, and other official sources. The *New York Times*, the *Washington Post*, and the *Los Angeles Times* are the most important examples, and each produces an index of topics and names that have appeared in its pages.

Once you start using a library regularly, you are likely to find that it is more common to feel overwhelmed by the number of works available in a particular area than to experience difficulty in tracing relevant literature. One way of dealing with this problem is to base your selection of books or articles on reading lists provided by professors. Where such lists are not available, the best procedure to follow is to define the information you require as precisely as possible. This will allow you to narrow the range of choice to feasible limits. If your library is an open-stack one, it is worth looking through a number of potentially useful books or articles before selecting those you decide to work with. In making the decision, keep in mind *when* the book was written. New developments are constantly taking place in sociology and in the other social sciences, and obviously older books will not cover these.

GLOSSARY

Words in bold type within entries refer to terms found elsewhere in the glossary.

AARP: American Association of Retired Persons.

absolute poverty: The minimal requirements necessary to sustain a healthy existence.

achieved status: Social status based on an individual's effort.

activity theory: A functionalist theory of aging which holds that busy, engaged people are more likely to lead fulfilling and productive lives.

affective individualism: The belief in romantic attachment as a basis for contracting **marriage** ties.

age-grades: The system found in small traditional cultures by which people belonging to a similar age-group are categorized together and hold similar rights and obligations.

ageism: Discrimination or **prejudice** against a person on the grounds of age.

agents of socialization: Groups or social contexts within which processes of **socialization** take place.

aging: The combination of biological, psychological, and social processes that affect people as they grow older.

agrarian societies: Societies whose means of subsistence are based on agricultural production (crop growing).

alienation: The sense that our own abilities as human beings are taken over by other entities. The term was originally used by Marx to refer to the projection of human powers onto gods. Subsequently he used the term to refer to the loss of workers' control over the nature and products of their labor.

Alzheimer's disease: A degenerative disease of the brain resulting in progressive loss of mental capacity.

andragogy: Term coined by educators to refer to adult learning.

anomie: A concept first brought into wide usage in sociology by Durkheim, referring to a situation in which social **norms** lose their hold over individual behavior.

antiracism: Forms of thought and/or practice that seek to confront, eradicate and/or ameliorate racism.

apartheid: The system of racial **segregation** established in South Africa.

ascribed status: Social **status** based on biological factors such as **race, sex,** or age.

ascription: Placement in a particular social **status** based on characteristics such as family of origin, race, and gender.

assimilation The acceptance of a **minority group** by a majority population, in which the new group takes on the **values** and **norms** of the dominant **culture.**

authority: A **government**'s legitimate use of **power.**

automation: Production processes monitored and controlled by machines with only minimal supervision from people.

back regions: Areas apart from **front region** performances, as specified by Erving Goffman, in which individuals are able to relax and behave informally.

biomedical model of health: The set of principles underpinning Western medical systems and practices. The biomedical model of health defines diseases objectively, in accordance with the presence of recognized symptoms, and believes that the healthy body can be restored through scientifically based medical treatment. The human body is likened to a machine that can be returned to working order with the proper repairs.

black feminism: A strand of **feminist theory** that highlights the multiple disadvantages of **gender, class,** and **race** that shape the experiences of nonwhite women. Black feminists reject the idea of a single, unified gender oppression that is experienced evenly by all women and argue that early feminist analysis reflected the specific concerns of white, middle-class women.

bureaucracy: A type of **organization** marked by a clear hierarchy of authority and the existence of written rules of procedure and staffed by full-time, salaried officials.

capitalism: An economic system based on the private ownership of **wealth,** which is invested and reinvested in order to produce profit.

capitalists: People who own companies, land, or stocks (shares) and use these to generate economic returns.

caste societies: Societies in which different social levels are closed, so that all individuals must remain at the social level of their birth throughout life.

caste system: A social system in which one's social status is given for life.

causal relationship: A relationship in which one state of affairs (the effect) is brought about by another (the cause).

causation: The causal influence of one factor, or **variable,** upon another. A cause and effect relationship exists whenever a particular event or state of affairs (the effect) is produced by the existence of another (the cause). Causal factors in sociology include the reasons individuals give for what they do, as well as external influences on their behavior.

charismatic: The inspirational quality capable of capturing the imagination and devotion of a mass of followers.

churches: Large bodies of people belonging to an established religious organization. The term is also used to refer to the place in which religious ceremonies are carried out.

citizens: Members of a political community, having both rights and duties associated with that membership.

civil inattention: The process whereby individuals in the same physical setting demonstrate to one another that they are aware of each other's presence.

civil religion: A set of religious beliefs through which a society interprets its own history in light of some conception of ultimate reality.

civil rights: Legal rights held by all **citizens** in a given national community.

civil society: The realm of activity that lies between the **state** and the market, including the **family,** schools, community associations, and noneconomic institutions. Civil society, or civic culture, is essential to vibrant democratic societies.

class: Although it is one of the most frequently used concepts in **sociology,** there is no clear agreement about how the notion should be defined. Most sociologists use the term to refer to socioeconomic variations between groups of individuals that create variations in their material prosperity and power.

clock time: Time as measured by the clock, in terms of hours, minutes, and seconds. Before the invention of clocks, time reckoning was based on events in the natural world, such as the rising and setting of the sun.

cognition: Human thought processes involving perception, reasoning, and remembering.

cohabitation: Two people living together in a sexual relationship of some permanence, without being married to one another.

collective action: Action undertaken in a relatively spontaneous way by a large number of people assembled together.

collective consumption: A concept used by Manuel Castells to refer to processes of urban consumption—such as the buying and selling of property.

colonialism: The process whereby Western nations established their rule in parts of the world away from their home territories.

communication: The transmission of information from one individual or group to another. Communication is the necessary basis of all social interaction. In face-to-face **encounters,** communication is carried on by the use of **language** and by bodily cues that individuals interpret. With the development of writing and electronic media such as radio, television, and computers, communication becomes in some part detached from immediate face-to-face social relationships.

communism: A set of political ideas associated with Marx, as developed particularly by Lenin and institutionalized in the Soviet Union, Eastern Europe, and some Third World countries.

community policing: A renewed emphasis on crime prevention rather than law enforcement to reintegrate policing within the community.

comparable worth: Policies that attempt to remedy the gender pay gap by adjusting pay so that those in female-dominated jobs are not paid less for equivalent work.

comparative questions: Questions concerned with drawing comparisons between different human societies for the purposes of sociological **theory** or research.

comparative research: Research that compares one set of findings on one society with the same type of findings on other societies.

compulsion of proximity: People's need to interact with others in their presence.

concrete operational stage: A stage of cognitive development, as formulated by Piaget, in which the child's thinking is based primarily on physical perception of the world. In this phase, the child is not yet capable of dealing with abstract concepts or hypothetical situations.

conflict theory: Argument that deviance is deliberately chosen and often political in nature.

conflict theories of aging: Arguments that emphasize the ways in which the larger social structure helps to shape the opportunities available to the elderly. Unequal opportunities are seen as creating the potential for conflict.

constitutional monarchs: Kings or queens who are largely figureheads. Real power rests in the hands of other political **leaders.**

contradiction: A term used by Marx to refer to mutually antagonistic tendencies in a society.

contradictory class locations: Positions in the class structure, particularly routine white-collar and lower managerial jobs, that share characteristics of the class positions both above and below them.

controls: Statistical or experimental means of holding some **variables** constant in order to examine the causal influence of others.

control theory: A **theory** that views **crime** as the outcome of an imbalance between impulses toward criminal activity and controls that deter it. Control theorists hold that criminals are rational beings who will act to maximize their own reward unless they are rendered unable to do so through either social or physical controls.

conurbation: An agglomeration of towns or cities into an unbroken urban environment.

conversation analysis: The empirical study of conversations, employing techniques drawn from **ethnomethodology.** Conversation analysis examines details of naturally occurring conversations to reveal the organizational principles of talk and its role in the production and reproduction of social order.

core countries: According to **world-systems theory,** the most advanced industrial countries, which take the lion's share of profits in the world economic system.

corporate crime: Offenses committed by large corporations in society. Examples of corporate crime include pollution, false advertising, and violations of health and safety regulations.

corporate culture: An organizational culture involving rituals, events, or traditions that are unique to a specific company.

corporations: Business firms or companies.

correlation: The regular relationship between two **variables,** often expressed in statistical terms. Correlations may be positive or negative. A positive correlation between two variables exists when a high rank on one variable is associated with a high rank on the other. A negative correlation exists when a high rank on one variable is associated with a low rank on the other.

correlation coefficients: The measure of the degree of **correlation** between **variables.**

created environment: Constructions established by human beings to serve their needs, derived from the use of man-made **technology**—including, for example, roads, railways, factories, offices, private homes, and other buildings.

crimes: Any actions that contravene the **laws** established by a political authority. Although we may think of criminals as a distinct subsection of the population, there are few people who have not broken the law in one way or another during their lives. While laws are formulated by state authorities, it is not unknown for those authorities to engage in criminal behavior in certain situations.

crude birthrates: Statistical measures representing the number of births within a given population per year, normally calculated in terms of the number of births per thousand members. Although the crude birthrate is a useful index, it is only a general measure, because it does not specify numbers of births in relation to age distribution.

crude death rates: Statistical measures representing the number of deaths that occur annually in a given population per year, normally calculated as the ratio of deaths per thousand members. Crude death rates give a general indication of the **mortality** levels of a community or society, but are limited in their usefulness because they do not take into account the age distribution.

cults: Fragmentary religious groupings to which individuals are loosely affiliated, but which lack any permanent structure.

cultural capital: The advantages that well-to-do parents usually provide their children.

cultural relativism: The practice of judging a **society** by its own standards.

cultural turn: Sociology's recent emphasis on the importance of understanding the role of **culture** in daily life.

cultural universals: Values or modes of behavior shared by all human **cultures.**

culture: The **values, norms,** and **material goods** characteristic of a given group. Like the concept of **society,** the notion of culture is widely used in **sociology** and the other social sciences (particularly anthropology). Culture is one of the most distinctive properties of human social association.

culture of poverty: The thesis, popularized by Oscar Lewis, that poverty is not a result of individual inadequacies but is instead the outcome of a larger social and cultural atmosphere into which successive generations of children are socialized. The culture of poverty refers to the **values,** beliefs, lifestyles, habits, and traditions that are common among people living under conditions of material deprivation.

cybercrime: Criminal activities by means of electronic **networks** or involving the use of new information **technologies.** Electronic money laundering, personal identity theft, electronic vandalism, and monitoring electronic correspondence are all emergent forms of cybercrime.

cyberspace: Electronic networks of interaction between individuals at different computer terminals.

degree of dispersal: The range or distribution of a set of figures.

democracy: A political system that allows the **citizens** to participate in political decision making or to elect representatives to **government** bodies.

democratic elitism: A theory of the limits of **democracy,** which holds that in large-scale societies democratic participation is necessarily limited to the regular election of political **leaders.**

demographic transition: An interpretation of population change, which holds that a stable ratio of births to deaths is achieved once a certain level of economic prosperity has been reached. According to this notion, in preindustrial societies there is a rough balance between births and deaths, because population increase is kept in check by a lack of available food, by disease, or by war. In modern societies, by contrast, population equilibrium is achieved because **families** are moved by economic incentives to limit the number of children.

demography: The study of populations.

denomination: A religious **sect** that has lost its revivalist dynamism and become an institutionalized body, commanding the adherence of significant numbers of people.

dependency culture: A term popularized by Charles Murray to describe individuals who rely on state welfare provision rather than entering the labor market. The dependency culture is seen as the outcome of the "paternalistic" welfare state that undermines individual ambition and people's capacity for self-help.

dependency theories: Marxist theories of economic development arguing that the poverty of low-income countries stems directly from their exploitation by wealthy countries and the **multinational corporations** that are based in wealthy countries.

dependent development: The theory that poor countries can still develop economically, but only in ways shaped by their reliance on the wealthier countries.

dependent variable: A **variable,** or factor, causally influenced by another (the **independent variable**).

developing world: The less-developed societies, in which industrial production is either virtually nonexistent or only developed to a limited degree. The majority of the world's population live in less-developed countries.

developmental questions: Questions that sociologists pose when looking at the origins and path of development of **social institutions** from the past to the present.

deviance: Modes of action that do not conform to the **norms** or **values** held by most members of a group or **society.** What is regarded as deviant is as variable as the norms and values that distinguish different **cultures** and **subcultures** from one another. Forms of behavior that are highly esteemed by one group are regarded negatively by others.

deviant subculture: A **subculture** whose members hold values that differ substantially from those of the majority.

diaspora: The dispersal of an ethnic population from an original homeland into foreign areas, often in a forced manner or under traumatic circumstances.

differential association: An interpretation of the development of criminal behavior proposed by Edwin H. Sutherland, according to whom criminal behavior is learned through association with others who regularly engage in **crime.**

direct democracy: A form of **participatory democracy** that allows **citizens** to vote directly on **laws** and policies.

discrimination: Behavior that denies to the members of a particular group resources or rewards that can be obtained by others. Discrimination must be distinguished from **prejudice:** Individuals who are prejudiced against others may not engage in discriminatory practices against them; conversely, people may act in a discriminatory fashion toward a group even though they are not prejudiced against that group.

disengagement theory: A functionalist theory of **aging** which holds that it is functional for society to remove people from their traditional roles when they become elderly, thereby freeing up those roles for others.

disestablishment: A period during which the political influence of established religions is successfully challenged.

displacement: The transferring of ideas or emotions from their true source to another object.

division of labor: The specialization of **work** tasks, by means of which different **occupations** are combined within a production system. All **societies** have at least some rudimentary form of division of labor, especially between the tasks allocated to men and those performed by women. With the development of industrialism, the division of labor became vastly more complex than in any prior type of production system. In the modern world, the division of labor is international in scope.

doubling time: The time it takes for a particular level of population to double.

dyad: A group consisting of two persons.

ecological approach: A perspective on urban analysis emphasizing the "natural" distribution of city neighborhoods into areas having contrasting characteristics.

economic interdependence: The fact that in the **division of labor,** individuals depend on others to produce many or most of the goods they need to sustain their lives.

economy: The system of production and exchange that provides for the material needs of individuals living in a given **society.** Economic institutions are of key importance in all social orders. What goes on in the economy usually influences other areas in social life. Modern economies differ substantially from traditional ones, because the majority of the population is no longer engaged in agricultural production.

egocentric: According to Piaget, the characteristic quality of a child during the early years of her life. Egocentric thinking involves understanding objects and events in the environment solely in terms of the child's own position.

emigration: The movement of people out of one country in order to settle in another.

empirical investigations: Factual inquiries carried out in any area of sociological study.

encounter: A meeting between two or more people in a situation of face-to-face interaction. Our daily lives can be seen as a series of different encounters strung out across the course of the day. In modern societies, many of these encounters are with strangers rather than people we know.

endogamy: The forbidding of marriage or sexual relations outside one's **social group.**

entrepreneur: The owner/founder of a business firm.

epidemiology: The study of the distribution and incidence of disease and illness within a population.

ethnic cleansing: The creation of ethnically homogeneous territories through the mass expulsion of other ethnic populations.

ethnicity: Cultural **values** and **norms** that distinguish the members of a given group from others. An ethnic group is one whose members share a distinct awareness of a common cultural identity, separating them from other groups. In virtually all **societies,** ethnic differences are associated with variations in **power** and material **wealth.** Where ethnic differences are also racial, such divisions are sometimes especially pronounced.

ethnie: A term used to describe a group that shares ideas of common ancestry, a common cultural identity, and a link with a specific homeland.

ethnocentric transationals: Transnational corporations largely run directly from the headquarters of the parent company.

ethnocentrism: The tendency to look at other **cultures** through the eyes of one's own culture, and thereby misrepresent them.

ethnography: The firsthand study of people using **participant observation** or interviewing.

ethnomethodology: The study of how people make sense of what others say and do in the course of day-to-day social interaction. Ethnomethodology is concerned with the "ethnomethods" by which people sustain meaningful interchanges with one another.

evangelicalism: A form of Protestantism characterized by a belief in spiritual rebirth (being "born again").

exchange mobility: The exchange of positions on the socioeconomic scale such that talented people move up the economic hierarchy while the less talented move down.

experiment: A **research method** in which **variables** can be analyzed in a controlled and systematic way, either in an artificial situation constructed by the researcher or in naturally occurring settings.

exponential: A geometric, rather than linear, rate of progression, producing a fast rise in the numbers of a population experiencing such growth.

extended family: A **family** group consisting of more than two generations of relatives living either within the same household or very close to one another.

external risk: Dangers that spring from the natural world and are unrelated to the actions of humans. Examples of external risk include droughts, earthquakes, famines, and storms.

factual questions: Questions that raise issues concerning matters of fact (rather than theoretical or moral issues).

family: A group of individuals related to one another by blood ties, **marriage,** or adoption, who form an economic unit, the adult members of which are responsible for the upbringing of children. All known **societies** involve some form of family system, although the nature of family relationships varies widely. While in modern societies the main family form is the **nuclear family, extended family** relationships are also found.

family capitalism: Capitalistic enterprise owned and administered by entrepreneurial **families.**

families of orientation: The families into which individuals are born.

families of procreation: The families individuals initiate through **marriage** or by having children.

fecundity: A measure of the number of children that it is biologically possible for a woman to produce.

feminist theory: A sociological perspective that emphasizes the centrality of **gender** in analyzing the social world and particularly the uniqueness of the experience of women. There are many strands of feminist theory, but they all share the desire to explain **gender inequalities** in **society** and to work to overcome them.

feminization of poverty: An increase in the proportion of the poor who are female.

fertility: The average number of live-born children produced by women of childbearing age in a particular **society.**

field of action: The arena within which **social movements** interact with established **organizations,** the ideas and outlook of the members of both often becoming modified as a result.

First World: The group of **nation-states** that possesses mature industrialized economies based on capitalistic production.

flexible production: Process in which computers design customized products for a mass market.

focused interaction: Interaction between individuals engaged in a common activity or in direct conversation with one another.

Fordism: The system of production pioneered by Henry Ford, in which the assembly line was introduced.

formal operational stage: According to Piaget's theory, a stage of cognitive development at which the growing child becomes capable of handling abstract concepts and hypothetical situations.

formal organization: Means by which a group is rationally designed to achieve its objectives, often by means of explicit rules, regulations, and procedures.

formal relations: Relations that exist in groups and **organizations,** laid down by the **norms,** or rules, of the official system of authority.

front regions: Settings of social activity in which people seek to put on a definite "performance" for others.

functionalism: A theoretical perspective based on the notion that social events can best be explained in terms of the functions they perform—that is, the contributions they make to the continuity of a **society.**

fundamentalists: A group within **evangelicalism** that is highly antimodern in many of its beliefs, adhering to strict codes of morality and conduct.

gender: Social expectations about behavior regarded as appropriate for the members of each **sex.** Gender refers not to the physical attributes distinguishing men and women but to socially formed traits of masculinity and femininity. The study of gender relations has become one of the most important areas of **sociology** in recent years.

gender inequality: The inequality between men and women in terms of **wealth, income,** and **status.**

gender roles: Social roles assigned to each **sex** and labeled as masculine or feminine.

gender socialization: The learning of **gender roles** through social factors such as schooling, the media, and **family.**

gender typing: Women holding **occupations** of lower **status** and pay, such as secretarial and retail positions, and men holding **jobs** of higher status and pay, such as managerial and professional positions.

generalized other: A concept in the **theory** of George Herbert Mead, according to which the individual takes over the general **values** of a given group or **society** during the **socialization** process.

generational equity: The striking of a balance between the needs and interests of members of different generations.

genocide: The systematic, planned destruction of a racial, political, or cultural group.

gentrification: A process of **urban renewal** in which older, deteriorated housing is refurbished by affluent people moving into the area.

geocentric transnationals: Transnational corporations whose administrative structure is global, rather than organized from any particular country.

geragogy: Term coined by educators to refer to older-adult learning.

glass ceiling: A promotion barrier that prevents a woman's upward mobility within an **organization.**

glass escalator: The process by which men in traditionally female professions benefit from an unfair rapid rise within an **organization.**

global city: A city—such as London, New York, or Tokyo—that has become an organizing center of the new global economy.

global commodity chains: Worldwide **networks** of labor and production processes yielding a finished product.

global inequality: The systematic differences in **wealth** and **power** between countries.

globalization: The development of social and economic relationships stretching worldwide. In current times, we are all influenced by **organizations** and social **networks** located thousands of miles away. A key part of the study of globalization is the emergence of a **world system**—for some purposes, we need to regard the world as forming a single social order.

global village: A notion associated with Marshall McLuhan, who believed that the world has become like a small community as a result of the spread of electronic communication. For instance, people in many different parts of the world follow the same news events through television programming.

government: The enacting of policies and decisions on the part of officials within a political apparatus. We can speak of government as a process, or *the* government as the officialdom responsible for making binding political decisions. While in the past virtually all governments were headed by monarchs or emperors, in most modern **societies** governments are run by officials who do not inherit their positions of **power** but are elected or appointed on the basis of qualifications.

graying: A term used to indicate that an increasing proportion of a **society's** population is becoming elderly.

group production: Production organized by means of small groups rather than individuals.

groupthink: A process by which the members of a group ignore ways of thinking and plans of action that go against the group consensus.

hidden curriculum: Traits of behavior or attitudes that are learned at school but not included within the formal curriculum—for example, **gender** differences.

high-trust system: Organization or **work** setting in which individuals are permitted a great deal of autonomy and control over the work task.

historicity: The use of an understanding of history as a basis for trying to change history—that is, producing informed processes of **social change.**

homeless: People who have no place to sleep and either stay in free shelters or sleep in public places not meant for habitation.

homophobia: An irrational fear or disdain of homosexuals.

human capital theory: Argument that individuals make investments in their own "human capital" in order to increase their productivity and earnings.

human resource management: A style of management that regards a company's work force as vital to its economic competitiveness.

hunting and gathering societies: Societies whose mode of subsistence is gained from hunting animals, fishing, and gathering edible plants.

hyperreality: An idea associated with Jean Baudrillard, who argued that as a result of the spread of electronic communication, there is no longer a separate "reality" to which TV programs and other cultural products refer. Instead, what we take to be "reality" is structured by such communication itself. For instance, the items reported on the news are not just about a separate series of events, but actually define and construct what those events are.

hypotheses: Ideas or guesses about a given state of affairs, put forward as bases for empirical testing.

ideal type: A "pure type," constructed by emphasizing certain traits of a social item that do not necessarily exist in reality. An example is Max Weber's ideal type of bureaucratic organization.

identity: The distinctive characteristics of a person's or group's character that relate to who they are and what is meaningful to them. Some of the main sources of identity include **gender,** sexual orientation, nationality or **ethnicity,** and social **class.**

ideology: Shared ideas or beliefs that serve to justify the interests of **dominant groups.** Ideologies are found in all **societies** in which there are systematic and ingrained inequalities between groups. The concept of ideology connects closely with that of **power,** since ideological systems serve to legitimize the power that groups hold.

immigration: The movement of people into one country from another for the purpose of settlement.

impression management: Preparing for the presentation of one's **social role.**

income: Payment, usually derived from wages, salaries, or investments.

independent variable: A **variable,** or factor, that causally affects another (the **dependent variable**).

industrialism hypothesis: Theory that **societies** become more open to **social mobility** as they become more industrialized.

industrialization: The process of the machine production of goods. See also **industrialized societies.**

industrialized societies: Strongly developed **nation-states** in which the majority of the population work in factories or offices rather than in agriculture, and most people live in urban areas.

infant mortality rate: The number of infants who die during the first year of life, per thousand live births.

informal economy: Economic transactions carried on outside the sphere of orthodox paid employment.

informal relations: Relations that exist in groups and **organizations** developed on the basis of personal connections; ways of doing things that depart from formally recognized modes of procedure.

information poverty: The "information poor" are those people who have little or no access to information **technology,** such as computers.

information society: A **society** no longer based primarily on the production of **material goods** but on the production of knowledge. The notion of the information society is closely bound up with the rise of information technology.

information technology: Forms of **technology** based on information processing and requiring microelectronic circuitry.

in-groups: Groups toward which one feels particular loyalty and respect—the groups to which "we" belong.

inner city: The areas composing the central neighborhoods of a city, as distinct from the suburbs. In many modern urban settings in the **First World,** inner-city areas are subject to dilapidation and decay, the more affluent residents having moved to outlying areas.

instincts: Fixed patterns of behavior that have genetic origins and that appear in all normal animals within a given species.

institutional capitalism: Capitalistic enterprise organized on the basis of institutional shareholding.

institutional racism: Patterns of **discrimination** based on **ethnicity** that have become structured into existing social institutions.

intelligence: Level of intellectual ability, particularly as measured by **IQ (intelligence quotient)** tests.

interactional vandalism: The deliberate subversion of the tacit rules of conversation.

interest group: A group organized to pursue specific interests in the political arena, operating primarily by lobbying the members of legislative bodies.

intergenerational mobility: Movement up or down a social stratification hierarchy from one generation to another.

international division of labor: The interdependence of countries or regions that trade in global markets.

international governmental organization (IGO): An international organization established by treaties between **governments** for purposes of conducting business between the nations making up its membership.

international nongovernmental organization (INGO): An international organization established by agreements between the individuals or private **organizations** making up its membership.

intragenerational mobility: Movement up or down a **social stratification** hierarchy within the course of a personal career.

IQ (intelligence quotient): A score attained on tests of symbolic or reasoning abilities.

iron law of oligarchy: A term coined by Weber's student Robert Michels meaning that large **organizations** tend toward centralization of **power,** making **democracy** difficult.

job: See **occupation.**

kinship: A relation that links individuals through blood ties, **marriage,** or adoption. Kinship relations are by definition part of marriage and the **family,** but extend much more broadly. While in most modern societies few social obligations are involved in kinship relations extending beyond the immediate family, in other cultures kinship is of vital importance to social life.

knowledge economy: A **society** no longer based primarily on the production of **material goods** but based instead on the production of knowledge. Its emergence has been linked to the development of a broad base of consumers who are technologically literate and have made new advances in computing, entertainment, and telecommunications part of their lives.

knowledge society: Another common term for **information society**—a **society** based on the production and consumption of knowledge and information.

Kuznets curve: A formula showing that inequality increases during the early stages of capitalist development, then declines, and eventually stabilizes at a relatively low level; advanced by the economist Simon Kuznets.

labeling theory: An approach to the study of **deviance** that suggests that people become "deviant" because certain labels are attached to their behavior by political authorities and others.

language: The primary vehicle of meaning and communication in a society, language is a system of **symbols** that represent objects and abstract thoughts.

latent functions: Functional consequences that are not intended or recognized by the members of a social system in which they occur.

laws: Rules of behavior established by a political authority and backed by state **power.**

leader: A person who is able to influence the behavior of other members of a group.

legitimation crisis: The failure of a political order to generate a sufficient level of commitment and involvement on the part of its **citizens** to be able to govern properly.

liberal democracies: Systems of **democracy** based on parliamentary institutions, coupled to the free-market system in the area of economic production.

liberal feminism: Form of **feminist theory** that believes that **gender inequality** is produced by unequal access to **civil rights** and certain social resources, such as education and employment, based on **sex.** Liberal feminists tend to seek solutions through changes in legislation that ensure that the rights of individuals are protected.

liberation theology: An activist Catholic religious movement that combines Catholic beliefs with a passion for social justice for the poor.

life chances: A term introduced by Max Weber to signify a person's opportunities for achieving economic prosperity.

life course: The various transitions people experience during their lives.

life histories: Studies of the overall lives of individuals, often based on both self-reporting and documents such as letters.

life span: The maximum length of life that is biologically possible for a member of a given species.

linguistic relativity hypothesis: A **hypothesis,** based on the **theories** of Sapir and Whorf, that perceptions are relative to **language.**

local knowledge: Knowledge of a local community, possessed by individuals who spend long periods of their lives in it.

local nationalisms: The beliefs that communities that share a cultural identity should have political autonomy, even within smaller units of a **nation-states.**

lower class: A social class comprised of those who work part time or not at all and whose household income is typically lower than $17,000 a year.

low-trust systems: Organizational or **work** settings in which people are allowed little responsibility for, or control over, the work task.

macrosociology: The study of large-scale groups, **organizations,** or social systems.

Malthusianism: A doctrine about population dynamics developed by Thomas Malthus, according to which population increase comes up against "natural limits," represented by famine and war.

managerial capitalism: Capitalistic enterprises administered by managerial executives rather than by owners.

manifest functions: The functions of a type of social activity that are known to and intended by the individuals involved in the activity.

manufactured risk: Dangers that are created by the impact of human knowledge and **technology** on the natural world. Examples of manufactured risk include global warming and genetically modified foods.

market-oriented theories: Theories about economic development that assume that the best possible economic consequences will result if individuals are free to make their own economic decisions, uninhibited by governmental constraint.

marriage: A socially approved sexual relationship between two individuals. Marriage almost always involves two persons of opposite sexes, but in some cultures, types of homosexual marriage are tolerated. Marriage normally forms the basis of a **family of procreation—** that is, it is expected that the married couple will produce and bring up children. Some societies permit **polygamy,** in which an individual may have several spouses at the same time.

Marxism: A body of thought deriving its main elements from Marx's ideas.

mass media: Forms of communication, such as newspapers, magazines, radio, and television, designed to reach mass audiences.

master status: The **status**(es) that generally determine(s) a person's overall position in **society.**

material goods: The physical objects that a **society** creates, which influence the ways in which people live.

materialist conception of history: The view developed by Marx, according to which material, or economic, factors have a prime role in determining historical change.

matrilocal: A **family** system in which the husband is expected to live near the wife's parents.

mean: A statistical measure of central tendency, or average, based on dividing a total by the number of individual cases.

means of production: The means whereby the production of **material goods** is carried on in a **society,** including not just **technology** but the social relations between producers.

measures of central te[...] calculating averages.

median: The number that fa[...] range of numbers—a way o[...] central tendency that is somet[...] useful than calculating a **mean.**

mediated interaction: Interaction bet[...] individuals who are not physically in o[...] another's presence—for example, a telephone conversation.

mediated quasi-interaction: Interaction that is one-sided and partial—for example, a person watching a television program.

Medicare: A program under the U.S. Social Security Administration that reimburses hospitals and physicians for medical care provided to qualifying people over sixty-five years old.

megacities: A term favored by Manuel Castells to describe large, intensely concentrated urban spaces that serve as connection points for the global **economy.** It is projected that by 2015 there will be thirty-six megacities with populations of more than 8 million residents.

megalopolis: The "city of all cities" in ancient Greece—used in modern times to refer to very large **conurbations.**

melting pot: The idea that ethnic differences can be combined to create new patterns of behavior drawing on diverse cultural sources.

microsociology: The study of human behavior in contexts of face-to-face interaction.

middle class: A social **class** composed broadly of those working in white-collar and lower managerial occupations.

minority group (or **ethnic minority**): A group of people in a minority in a given **society** who, because of their distinct physical or cultural characteristics, find themselves in situations of inequality within that society.

mode: The number that appears most often in a given set of data. This can sometimes be a helpful way of portraying central tendency.

modernization theory: A version of market-oriented development theory that argues that low-income societies develop economically only if they give up their traditional ways and adopt modern economic institutions, **technologies,** and cultural **values** that emphasize savings and productive investment.

monogamy: A form of **marriage** in which each married partner is allowed only one spouse at any given time.

single firm

...dency: The ways of ...lls halfway in a ...e calculating ...mes more ...een ...e

...ist ...onomic ...s ...e

...on in which ...ingle sovereign **power** in a **society.**

nationalism: A set of beliefs and **symbols** expressing identification with a national community.

nation-states: Particular types of **states,** characteristic of the modern world, in which governments have sovereign **power** within defined territorial areas, and populations are **citizens** who know themselves to be part of single nations. Nation-states are closely associated with the rise of **nationalism,** although nationalist loyalties do not always conform to the boundaries of specific states. Nation-states developed as part of an emerging nation-state system, originating in Europe; in current times, they span the whole globe.

nations without states: Instances in which the members of a nation lack political **sovereignty** over the area they claim as their own.

neoliberalism: The economic belief that free market forces, achieved by minimizing government restrictions on business, provide the only route to economic growth.

networks: Sets of informal and formal social ties that link people to each other.

New Age movement: A general term to describe the diverse spectrum of beliefs and practices oriented on inner spirituality. Paganism, Eastern mysticism, shamanism, alternative forms of healing, and astrology are all examples of New Age activities.

new criminology: A branch of criminological thought, prominent in Britain in the 1970s, that regarded **deviance** as deliberately chosen and often political in nature. The new criminologists argued that **crime** and deviance could only be understood in the context of **power** and inequality within **society.**

newly industrializing economies (NIEs): Developing countries that over the past two or three decades have begun to develop a strong industrial base, such as Singapore and Hong Kong.

new religious movements: The broad range of religious and spiritual groups, **cults,** and **sects** that have emerged alongside mainstream **religions.** New religious movements range from spiritual and self-help groups within the **New Age movement** to exclusive sects such as the Hare Krishnas.

new social movements: A set of **social movements** that have arisen in Western **societies** since the 1960s in response to the changing risks facing human societies. New social movements such as **feminism,** environmentalism, the antinuclear movement, protests against genetically modified food, and antiglobalization demonstrations differ from earlier social movements in that they are single-issue campaigns oriented to nonmaterial ends and draw support from across class lines.

new-style terrorism: A recent form of **terrorism** characterized by global ambitions, loose global organizational ties, and a more ruthless attitude toward the violence the terrorists are willing to use.

nonverbal communication: Communication between individuals based on facial expression or bodily gesture rather than on **language.**

norms: Rules of conduct that specify appropriate behavior in a given range of social situations. A norm either prescribes a given type of behavior or forbids it. All human groups follow definite norms, which are always backed by **sanctions** of one kind or another—varying from informal disapproval to physical punishment.

nuclear family: A **family** group consisting of a wife, a husband (or one of these), and dependent children.

occupation: Any form of paid employment in which an individual regularly works.

old old: Sociological term for persons aged seventy-five to eighty-four.

oldest old: Sociological term for persons aged eighty-five and older.

old-style terrorism: A type of **terrorism** that is local and linked to particular states and has limited objectives, which means that the violence involved is fairly limited.

oligarchy: Rule by a small minority within an **organization** or **society.**

oligopoly: The domination of a small number of firms in a given industry.

oral history: Interviews with people about events they witnessed or experienced at some point earlier in their lives.

organic solidarity: According to Émile Durkheim, the social cohesion that results from the various parts of a **society** functioning as an integrated whole.

organization: A large group of individuals with a definite set of authority relations. Many types of organizations exist in **industrialized societies,** influencing most aspects of our lives. While not all organizations are bureaucratic, there are close links between the development of organizations and bureaucratic tendencies.

organized crime: Criminal activities carried out by **organizations** established as businesses.

out-groups: Groups toward which one feels antagonism and contempt—"those people."

pariah groups: Groups who suffer from negative **status discrimination**—they are looked down on by most other members of society. The Jews, for example, have been a pariah group throughout much of European history.

participant observation: A method of research widely used in **sociology** and anthropology, in which the researcher takes part in the activities of the group or community being studied.

participatory democracy: A system of **democracy** in which all members of a group or community participate collectively in making major decisions.

pastoral societies: Societies whose subsistence derives from the rearing of domesticated animals.

patriarchy: The dominance of men over women. All known **societies** are patriarchal, although there are variations in the degree and nature of the **power** men exercise, as compared with women. One of the prime objectives of women's movements in modern societies is to combat existing patriarchal institutions.

patrilocal: A **family** system in which the wife is expected to live near the husband's parents.

peer group: A friendship group composed of individuals of similar age and social **status.**

peripheral countries: Countries that have a marginal role in the world **economy** and are thus dependent on the core producing societies for their trading relationships.

personality stabilization: According to the theory of **functionalism,** the **family** plays a crucial role in assisting its adult members emotionally. **Marriage** between adult men and women is the arrangement through which adult personalities are supported and kept healthy.

personal space: The physical space individuals maintain between themselves and others.

pilot study: A trial run in **survey** research.

pluralism: A model for ethnic relations in which all ethnic groups in the United States retain their independent and separate identities, yet share equally in the rights and **powers** of **citizenship.**

pluralist theories of modern democracy: Theories that emphasize the role of diverse and competing **interest groups** in preventing too much **power** from being accumulated in the hands of political **leaders.**

political rights: Rights of political participation, such as the right to vote in local and national elections, held by **citizens** of a national community.

politics: The means by which **power** is employed to influence the nature and content of governmental activities. The sphere of the political includes the activities of those in **government,** but also the actions of others. There are many ways in which people outside the governmental apparatus seek to influence it.

polyandry: A form of **marriage** in which a woman may simultaneously have two or more husbands.

polycentric transnationals: Transnational **corporations** whose administrative structure is global but whose corporate practices are adapted according to local circumstances.

polygamy: A form of **marriage** in which a person may have two or more spouses simultaneously.

polygyny: A form of **marriage** in which a man may simultaneously have two or more wives.

polytheism: Belief in two or more gods.

population: The people who are the focus of social research.

portfolio worker: A worker who possesses a diversity of skills or qualifications and is therefore able to move easily from **job** to job.

post-Fordism: A general term used to describe the transition from mass industrial production, characterized by

Fordist methods, to more flexible forms of production favoring innovation and aimed at meeting market demands for customized products.

postindustrial society: A notion advocated by those who believe that processes of social change are taking us beyond the industrialized order. A postindustrial society is based on the production of information rather than **material goods.** According to postindustrialists, we are currently experiencing a series of social changes as profound as those that initiated the industrial era some two hundred years ago.

postmodernism: The belief that **society** is no longer governed by history or progress. Postmodern society is highly pluralistic and diverse, with no "grand narrative" guiding its development.

postmodern feminism: Feminist persepective that challenges the idea of a unitary basis of identity and experience shared by all women. Postmodern feminists reject the claim that there is a grand theory which can explain the position of women in society, or that there is any single, universal essence or category of "woman." Instead, postmodernism encourages the acceptance of many different standpoints as equally valid.

poverty line: An official **government** measure to define those living in poverty in the United States.

power: The ability of individuals or the members of a group to achieve aims or further the interests they hold. Power is a pervasive element in all human relationships. Many conflicts in **society** are struggles over power, because how much power an individual or group is able to achieve governs how far they are able to put their wishes into practice.

power elite: Small **networks** of individuals who, according to C. Wright Mills, hold concentrated **power** in modern **societies.**

prejudice: The holding of preconceived ideas about an individual or group, ideas that are resistant to change even in the face of new information. Prejudice may be either positive or negative.

preoperational stage: A stage of cognitive development, in Piaget's theory, in which the child has advanced sufficiently to master basic modes of logical thought.

primary deviation: According to Edwin Lemert, the actions that cause others to label one as a deviant.

primary groups: Groups that are characterized by intense emotional ties, face-to-face interaction, intimacy, and a strong, enduring sense of commitment.

primary socialization: The process by which children learn the cultural **norms** of the **society** into which they are born. Primary socialization occurs largely in the **family.**

procreative technology: Techniques of influencing the human reproductive process.

profane: That which belongs to the mundane, everyday world.

projection: Attributing to others feelings that a person actually has herself.

psychopaths: Specific personality types; such individuals lack the moral sense and concern for others held by most normal people.

public sphere: The means by which people communicate in modern **societies,** the most prominent component of which is the **mass media**—movies, television, radio, videos, records, magazines, and newspapers.

quality circles (QCs): Types of industrialized **group production,** where workers use their expertise to participate actively in decision making.

race: Differences in human physical characteristics used to categorize large numbers of individuals.

racialization: The process by which understandings of **race** are used to classify individuals or groups of people. Racial distinctions are more than ways of describing human differences; they are also important factors in the reproduction of patterns of **power** and inequality.

racial literacy: The skills taught to children of multiracial families to help them cope with racial hierarchies and to integrate multiple ethnic identities.

racism: The attribution of characteristics of superiority or inferiority to a population sharing certain physically inherited characteristics. Racism is one specific form of **prejudice,** focusing on physical variations between people. Racist attitudes became entrenched during the period of Western colonial expansion, but seem also to rest on mechanisms of **prejudice** and **discrimination** found in human **societies** today.

radical feminism: Form of **feminist theory** that believes that **gender inequality** is the result of male domination in all aspects of social and economic life.

random sample: Sampling method in which a sample is chosen so that every member of the **population** has the same probability of being included.

rape: The forcing of nonconsensual vaginal, oral, or anal intercourse.

rational choice approach: More broadly, the **theory** that an individual's behavior is purposive. Within the field of criminology, rational choice analysis argues that deviant behavior is a rational response to a specific social situation.

rationalization: A concept used by Max Weber to refer to the process by which modes of precise calculation and organization, involving abstract rules and procedures, increasingly come to dominate the social world.

reference group: A group that provides a standard for judging one's attitudes or behaviors.

reflexivity: This describes the connections between knowledge and social life. The knowledge we gain about **society** can affect the way in which we act in it. For instance, reading a **survey** about the high level of support for a political party might lead an individual to express support for that party too.

regionalization: The division of social life into different regional settings or zones.

relative deprivation: Feelings of deprivation a person feels by comparing himself with a group.

relative poverty: Poverty defined according to the living standards of the majority in any given society.

religion: A set of beliefs adhered to by the members of a community, incorporating **symbols** regarded with a sense of awe or wonder together with ritual practices. Religions do not universally involve a belief in supernatural entities.

religious economy: A theoretical framework within the sociology of **religion,** which argues that religions can be fruitfully understood as **organizations** in competition with one another for followers.

religious movements: Associations of people who join together to seek to spread a new **religion** or to promote a new interpretation of an existing religion.

religious nationalism: The linking of strongly held religious convictions with beliefs about a people's social and political destiny.

representative sample: A sample from a larger **population** that is statistically typical of that population.

research methods: The diverse methods of investigation used to gather empirical (factual) material. Different research methods exist in **sociology,** but the most commonly used are fieldwork (or **participant observation**) and **survey** methods. For many purposes, it is useful to combine two or more methods within a single research project.

response cries: Seemingly involuntary exclamations individuals make when, for example, being taken by surprise, dropping something inadvertently, or expressing pleasure.

revolution: A process of political change, involving the mobilizing of a mass **social movement,** which by the use of violence successfully overthrows an existing regime and forms a new **government.**

roles: The expected behaviors of people occupying particular **social positions.** The idea of **social role** originally comes from the theater, referring to the parts that actors play in a stage production. In every **society,** individuals play a number of social roles.

sacred: Describing something that inspires attitudes of awe or reverence among believers in a given set of religious ideas.

sample: A small proportion of a larger **population.**

sampling: Studying a proportion of individuals or cases from a larger **population** as representative of that population as a whole.

sanction: A mode of reward or punishment that reinforces socially expected forms of behavior.

scapegoats: Individuals or groups blamed for wrongs that were not of their doing.

science: In the sense of physical science, the systematic study of the physical world. Science involves the disciplined marshaling of empirical data, combined with **theoretical approaches** and **theories** that illuminate or explain those data. Scientific activity combines the creation of boldly new modes of thought with the careful testing of **hypotheses** and ideas. One major feature that helps distinguish science from other idea systems (such as **religion**) is the assumption that *all* scientific ideas are open to criticism and revision.

secondary deviation: According to Edwin Lemert, following the act of **primary deviation,** secondary deviation occurs when an individual accepts the label of deviant and acts accordingly.

secondary group: A group characterized by its large size and by impersonal, fleeting relationships.

Second World: Before the 1989 democracy movements, this included the industrialized Communist societies of Eastern Europe and the Soviet Union.

sect: A **religious movement** that breaks away from orthodoxy.

secularization: A process of decline in the influence of **religion.** Although modern **societies** have become increasingly secularized, tracing the extent of secularization is a complex matter. Secularization can refer to levels of involvement with religious organizations (such as rates of **church** attendance), the social and material influence wielded by religious organizations, and the degree to which people hold religious beliefs.

secular thinking: Worldly thinking, particularly as seen in the rise of **science, technology,** and rational thought in general.

segregation: The practices of keeping racial and ethnic groups physically separate, thereby maintaining the superior position of the **dominant group.**

self-consciousness: Awareness of one's distinct **social identity** as a person separate from others. Human beings are not born with self-consciousness but acquire an awareness of self as a result of early **socialization.** The learning of **language** is of vital importance to the processes by which the child learns to become a self-conscious being.

self-identity: The ongoing process of self-development and definition of our personal **identity** through which we formulate a unique sense of ourselves and our relationship to the world around us.

semiotics: The study of the ways in which nonlinguistic phenomena can generate meaning—as in the example of a traffic light.

semiperipheral countries: Countries that supply sources of labor and raw materials to the **core** industrial **countries** and the world economy but are not themselves fully **industrialized societies.**

sensorimotor stage: According to Piaget, a stage of human cognitive development in which the child's awareness of its environment is dominated by perception and touch.

service society: A concept related to the one of **postindustrial society,** it refers to a social order distinguished by the growth of service occupations at the expense of industrial jobs that produce **material goods.**

sex: The biological and anatomical differences distinguishing females from males.

sexual harassment: The making of unwanted sexual advances by one individual toward another, in which the first person persists even though it is clear that the other party is resistant.

shaming: A way of punishing criminal and deviant behavior based on rituals of public disapproval rather than incarceration. The goal of shaming is to maintain the ties of the offender to the community.

short-range downward mobility: Social mobility that occurs when an individual moves from one position in the **class** structure to another of nearly equal **status.**

sick role: A term associated with the functionalist Talcott Parsons to describe the patterns of behavior that a sick person adopts in order to minimize the disruptive impact of his or her illness on others.

signifier: Any vehicle of meaning and **communication.**

situational ethnicity: Ethnic identity that is chosen for the moment based on the social setting or situation.

slavery: A form of **social stratification** in which some people are literally owned by others as their property.

social age: The **norms, values,** and **roles** that are culturally associated with a particular chronological age.

social aggregate: A simple collection of people who happen to be together in a particular place but do not significantly interact or identify with one another.

social capital: The social knowledge and connections that enable people to accomplish their goals and extend their influence.

social category: People who share a common characteristic (such as **gender** or **occupation**) but do not necessarily interact or identify with one another.

social change: Alteration in basic structures of a **social group** or **society.** Social change is an ever-present

phenomenon in social life, but has become especially intense in the modern era. The origins of modern **sociology** can be traced to attempts to understand the dramatic changes shattering the traditional world and promoting new forms of social order.

social closure: Practices by which groups separate themselves off from other groups.

social constraint: The conditioning influence on our behavior of the groups and **societies** of which we are members. Social constraint was regarded by Émile Durkheim as one of the distinctive properties of **social facts.**

social constructionism: Theory that social reality is a creation of the interaction of individuals and groups.

social construction of gender: The learning of **gender roles** through **socialization** and interaction with others.

social exclusion: The outcome of multiple deprivations that prevent individuals or groups from participating fully in the economic, social, and political life of the **society** in which they live.

social facts: According to Émile Durkheim, the aspects of social life that shape our actions as individuals. Durkheim believed that social facts could be studied scientifically.

social gerontology: The study of **aging** and the elderly.

social group: A collection of people who regularly interact with one another on the basis of shared expectations concerning behavior and who share a sense of common **identity.**

social identity: The characteristics that are attributed to an individual by others.

social interaction: The process by which we act and react to those around us.

socialization: The social processes through which children develop an awareness of social **norms** and **values** and achieve a distinct sense of self. Although socialization processes are particularly significant in infancy and childhood, they continue to some degree throughout life. No individuals are immune from the reactions of others around them, which influence and modify their behavior at all phases of the **life course.**

socialization of nature: The process by which we control phenomena regarded as "natural," such as reproduction.

social mobility: Movement of individuals or groups between different **social positions.**

social movements: Large groups of people who seek to accomplish, or to block, a process of **social change.** Social movements normally exist in conflict with **organizations,** whose objectives and outlook they oppose. However, movements that successfully challenge **power,** once they become institutionalized, can develop into organizations.

social position: The **social identity** an individual has in a given group or **society.** Social positions may be general in nature (those associated with **gender roles**) or may be more specific (occupational positions).

social reproduction: The process of perpetuating **values, norms,** and social practices through **socialization,** which leads to structural continuity over time.

social rights: Rights of social and welfare provision held by all **citizens** in a national community, including, for example, the right to claim unemployment benefits and sickness payments provided by the **state.**

social roles: Socially defined expectations of an individual in a given **status,** or **social position.**

Social Security: A government program that provides economic assistance to persons faced with unemployment, disability, or agedness.

social self: The basis of **self-consciousness** in human individuals, according to the theory of G. H. Mead. The social self is the **identity** conferred upon an individual by the reactions of others. A person achieves self-consciousness by becoming aware of this **social identity.**

social stratification: The existence of **structured inequalities** between groups in **society,** in terms of their access to material or symbolic rewards. While all societies involve some forms of stratification, only with the development of state-based systems did wide differences in **wealth** and **power** arise. The most distinctive form of stratification in modern societies is **class** divisions.

social structure: The underlying regularities or patterns in how people behave and in their relationships with one another.

social technology: A means by which we try to alter our bodies in specific ways—for example, dieting.

society: A group of people who live in a particular territory, are subject to a common system of political **authority,**

and are aware of having a distinct **identity** from other groups. Some societies, like **hunting and gathering societies,** are small, numbering no more than a few dozen people. Others are large, numbering millions—modern Chinese society, for instance, has a population of more than a billion people.

sociobiology: An approach that attempts to explain the behavior of both animals and human beings in terms of biological principles.

sociological imagination: The application of imaginative thought to the asking and answering of sociological questions. Someone using the sociological imagination "thinks himself away" from the familiar routines of daily life.

sociology: The study of human groups and **societies,** giving particular emphasis to analysis of the industrialized world. Sociology is one of a group of social sciences, which include anthropology, economics, political science, and human geography. The divisions between the various social sciences are not clear-cut, and all share a certain range of common interests, concepts, and methods.

sociology of the body: Field that focuses on how our bodies are affected by social influences. Health and illness, for instance, are determined by social and cultural influences.

source: Origin of data used by a researcher, but gathered elsewhere.

sovereignty: The undisputed political rule of a **state** over a given territorial area.

standard deviation: A way of calculating the spread of a group of figures.

state: A political apparatus (**government** institutions plus civil service officials) ruling over a given territorial order, whose **authority** is backed by **law** and the ability to use force. Not all societies are characterized by the existence of a state. **Hunting and gathering societies** and smaller **agrarian societies** lack state institutions. The emergence of the state marked a distinctive transition in human history, because the centralization of political **power** involved in state formation introduced new dynamics into processes of **social change.**

state-centered theories: Development **theories** that argue that appropriate **government** policies do not interfere with economic development, but rather can play a key role in bringing it about.

state overload: A **theory** that holds that modern **states** face major difficulties as a result of being overburdened with complex administrative decisions.

status: The social honor or **prestige** that a particular group is accorded by other members of a **society.** Status groups normally display distinct styles of life—patterns of behavior that the members of a group follow. Status privilege may be positive or negative. **Pariah** status **groups** are regarded with disdain or treated as outcasts by the majority of the **population.**

status set: An individual's group of social **statuses.**

stepfamily: A **family** in which at least one partner has children from a previous **marriage,** living either in the home or nearby.

stereotyping: Thinking in terms of fixed and inflexible categories.

stigma: Any physical or social characteristic that is labeled by **society** as undesirable.

strike: A temporary stoppage of **work** by a group of employees in order to express a grievance or enforce a demand.

structural mobility: Mobility resulting from changes in the number and kinds of **jobs** available in a **society.**

structural strain: Tensions that produce conflicting interests within **societies.**

structuration: The two-way process by which we shape our social world through our individual actions and by which we are reshaped by **society.**

structured inequalities: Social inequalities that result from patterns in the **social structure.**

subcultures: Values and **norms** distinct from those of the majority, held by a group within a wider **society.**

suburbanization: The development of suburbia, areas of housing outside **inner cities.**

surplus value: The value of a worker's labor power, in **Marxist** theory, left over when an employer has repaid the cost of hiring the worker.

surveillance: The supervising of the activities of some individuals or groups by others in order to ensure compliant behavior.

surveillance society: Term referring to how information about our lives and activities is maintained by **organizations.**

survey: A method of sociological research in which questionnaires are administered to the **population** being studied.

sustainable development: The notion that economic growth should proceed only insofar as natural resources are recycled rather than depleted; biodiversity is maintained; and clean air, water, and land are protected.

symbol: One item used to stand for or represent another—as in the case of a flag, which symbolizes a nation.

symbolic ethnicity: Ethnic **identity** that is retained only for symbolic importance.

symbolic interactionism: A **theoretical approach** in **sociology** developed by George Herbert Mead, which emphasizes the role of **symbols** and **language** as core elements of all human interaction.

Taylorism: A set of ideas, also referred to as "scientific management," developed by Frederick Winslow Taylor, involving simple, coordinated operations in industry.

technology: The application of knowledge of the material world to production; the creation of material instruments (such as machines) used in human interaction with nature.

terrorism: Use of attacks on civilians designed to persuade a government to alter its policies, or to damage its standing in the world.

theism: A belief in one or more supernatural deities.

theoretical approach: A perspective on social life derived from a particular theoretical tradition. Some of the major theoretical traditions in **sociology** include **functionalism, symbolic interactionism,** and **Marxism.** Theoretical approaches supply overall perspectives within which sociologists work and influence the areas of their research as well as the modes in which research problems are identified and tackled.

theoretical questions: Questions posed by sociologists when seeking to explain a particular range of observed events. The asking of theoretical questions is crucial to allowing us to generalize about the nature of social life.

theory: An attempt to identify general properties that explain regularly observed events. Theories form an essential element of all sociological works. While theories tend to be linked to broader **theoretical approaches,** they are also strongly influenced by the research results they help generate.

Third World: A term used during the cold war to describe developing nations.

time-space: When and where events occur.

timetables: The means by which **organizations** regularize activities across time and space.

total institutions: Groups who exercise control over their members by making them subsume their individual **identities** in that of the group, compelling them to adhere to strict ethical codes or rules, and sometimes forcing them to withdraw from activity in the outside world.

tracking: Dividing students into groups according to ability.

transactional leaders: Leaders who are concerned with accomplishing the group's tasks, getting group members to do their **jobs,** and making certain that the group achieves its goals.

transformational leaders: Leaders who are able to instill in the members of a group a sense of mission or higher purpose, thereby changing the nature of the group itself.

transnational corporations: Business **corporations** located in two or more countries.

triad: A group consisting of three persons.

triangulation: The use of multiple **research methods** as a way of producing more reliable empirical data than is available from any single method.

underclass: A **class** of individuals situated at the bottom of the class system, normally composed of people from **ethnic minority** backgrounds.

unfocused interaction: Interaction occurring among people present in a particular setting but not engaged in direct face-to-face **communication.**

union density: A statistic that represents the number of union members as a percentage of the number of people who could potentially be union members.

upper class: A social **class** broadly composed of the more affluent members of **society,** especially those who have inherited **wealth,** own businesses, or hold large numbers of stocks (shares).

urban ecology: An approach to the study of urban life based on an analogy with the adjustment of plants and organisms to the physical environment. According to ecological theorists, the various neighborhoods and zones within cities are formed as a result of natural processes of adjustment on the part of **populations** as they compete for resources.

urbanism: A term used by Louis Wirth to denote distinctive characteristics of urban social life, such as its impersonality.

urbanization: The development of towns and cities.

urban renewal: The process of renovating deteriorating neighborhoods by encouraging the renewal of old buildings and the construction of new ones.

values: Ideas held by individuals or groups about what is desirable, proper, good, and bad. What individuals value is strongly influenced by the specific **culture** in which they happen to live.

variable: A dimension along which an object, individual, or group may be categorized, such as income or height.

vertical mobility: Movement up or down a hierarchy of positions in a **social stratification** system.

wealth: Money and material possessions held by an individual or group.

welfare capitalism: Practice in which large **corporations** protect their employees from the vicissitudes of the market.

welfare state: A political system that provides a wide range of welfare benefits for its **citizens.**

white-collar crime: Criminal activities carried out by those in white-collar, or professional, **jobs.**

work: The activity by which people produce from the natural world and so ensure their survival. Work should not be thought of exclusively as paid employment. In traditional cultures, there was only a rudimentary monetary system, and few people worked for money. In modern **societies,** there remain types of work that do not involve direct payment (e.g., **housework**).

working class: A social **class** broadly composed of people working in blue-collar, or manual, **occupations.**

working poor: People who work, but whose earnings are not enough to lift them above the **poverty line.**

world-accommodating movements: Religious movements that emphasize the importance of inner religious life and spiritual purity over worldly concerns.

world-affirming movements: Religious movements that seek to enhance followers' ability to succeed in the outside world by helping them to unlock their human potential.

world information order: A global system of **communication** operating through satellite links, radio and TV transmission, and telephone and computer links.

world-rejecting movements: Religious movements that are exclusive in nature, highly critical of the outside world, and demanding of their members.

world-systems theory: Pioneered by Immanuel Wallerstein, this **theory** emphasizes the interconnections among countries based on the expansion of a capitalist world **economy.** This economy is made up of **core countries, semiperipheral countries,** and **peripheral countries.**

young old: Sociological term for persons aged sixty-five to seventy-four.

ABC. 1999. "Support for Gun Control Stable," ABC News Poll (May 18). http://more. abcnews.go.com/sections/us/DailyNews/ guns_poll990518.html, accessed 5/18/99.

Abdul-Rauf, Muhammad. 1975. *Islam: Creed and Worship.* Washington, DC: Islamic Center.

Abeles, Ronald P.; and Riley, Matilda White. 1987. "Longevity, social structure, and cognitive aging," in Carmi Schooler and K. Warner Schaie, eds., *Cognitive Functioning and Social Structure over the Life Course.* Norwood, NJ: Ablex.

Accad, Evelyne. 1991. "Contradictions for contemporary women in the Middle East," in Chandra Talpade Mohanty, Ann Russo, and Lourdes Torres, eds., *Third World Women and the Politics of Feminism.* Bloomington: Indiana University Press.

Ackman, Dan. 2004. "Wal-Mart and Sex Discrimination by the Numbers." *Forbes,* June 23. www.forbes.com/2004/06/23/cx_ da_0623topnews.html, accessed 1/09/07.

AIDS Orphans Educational Trust. 2003. "AIDS Orphans Educational Trust– Uganda." www.orphanseducation.org, accessed 12/28/04.

Akerlof, George et al. 1996. "An Analysis of Out-of-Wedlock Childbearing in the U.S." *Quarterly Journal of Economics* 111:277–317.

Akintoye, Stephen. 1976. *Emergent African States: Topics in Twentieth Century African History.* London: Longman.

Al Ahmad, Jalal. 1997; orig. 1962. *Gharbzadegi: Weststruckedness.* Costa Mesa, CA: Mazda Publications.

Albrow, Martin. 1997. *The Global Age: State and Society beyond Modernity.* Stanford, CA: Stanford University Press.

Aldrich, Howard E.; and Marsden, Peter V. 1988. "Environments and organizations," in Neil J. Smelser, ed., *Handbook of Sociology.* Newbury Park, CA: Sage.

Ali, T. 2003. "Re-colonizing Iraq," *New Left Review,* 21 (May–June): 5–19.

Allen, Beverly. 1996. *Rape Warfare: The Hidden Genocide in Bosnia-Herzegovina and Croatia.* Minneapolis, MN: University of Minnesota Press.

Allen, Michael P. 1981. "Managerial power and tenure in the large corporation." *Social Forces,* vol. 60.

Alvarez, Rodolfo, et al. 1996. "Women in the professions: Assessing progress," in Paula J. Dubeck and Kathryn Borman, eds., *Women and Work: A Handbook.* New York: Garland.

Amato, Paul et al. 1995. "Parental Divorce, Marital Conflict, and Offspring Well-being during Early Adulthood." *Social Forces* 73:895–915.

Amenta, Edwin. 1998. *Bold Relief: Institutional Politics and the Origins of Modern American Social Policy.* Princeton, NJ: Princeton University Press.

American Association for the Advancement of Retired People (AARP). 1997. "Report of Social Security Advisory Council." www.aarp.org/focus/ssecure/part 2/ advisory.htm, accessed 11/24/03.

American Association of University Women (AAUW). 1992. *How Schools Shortchange Girls.* Washington, DC: American Association of University Women Educational Foundation.

American Council on Education, (ACE). 2001. *The American Freshman: National Norms for Fall 2000.* Los Angeles, California: UCLA Higher Education Research Institute and ACE. Results also published in "This year's freshmen at 4-year colleges: Their opinions, activities, and goals." *Chronicle of Higher Education,* January 26.

Amin, Samir. 1974. *Accumulation on a World Scale.* New York: Monthly Review Press.

Ammons, S. K. and Markham, W. T. 2004. "Working at home: Experiences of skilled white collar workers," *Sociological Spectrum,* 24(2): 191–238.

Amsden, Alice H. 1989. *Asia's Next Giant: South Korea and Late Industrialization.* New York: Oxford University Press.

_____; Kochanowicz, Jacek; and Taylor, Lance. 1994. *The Market Meets Its Match: Restructuring the Economies of Eastern Europe.* Cambridge, MA: Harvard University Press.

Anderson, Benedict. 1991. *Imagined Communities: Reflections on the Origin and Spread of Nationalism.* Revised ed. New York: Routledge.

Anderson, Elijah. 1990. *Streetwise: Race, Class, and Change in an Urban Community.* Chicago: University of Chicago Press.

_____. *Code of the Street.* 1999. New York: Norton.

Angier, Natalie. 1995. "If you're really ancient, you may be better off." *New York Times,* June 11.

Anheier, H., M. Glasius, et al., eds. 2002. *Global Civil Society 2002.* Oxford: Oxford University Press.

Anzaldua, Gloria. 1990. *Making Face, Making Soul: Haciendo Caras: Creative and Cultural Perspectives by Feminists of Color.* San Francisco: Aunt Lute Foundation.

Appadurai, Arjun. 1986. "Introduction: commodities and the politics of value," in A. Appadurai, ed., *The Social Life of Things.* Cambridge: Cambridge University Press.

Appelbaum, Richard P. 1990. "Counting the homeless," in J. A. Momeni, ed., *Homeless in the United States,* vol. 2. New York: Praeger.

_____; and Christerson, Brad. 1997. "Cheap labor strategies and export-oriented industrialization: Some lessons from the East Asia/Los Angeles apparel connection." *International Journal of Urban and Regional Research,* vol. 21, no. 2.

_____; and Henderson, Jeffrey. eds., 1992. *States and Development in the Asian Pacific Rim.* Newbury Park, CA: Sage.

Apter, Terri. 1994. *Working Women Don't Have Wives: Professional Success in the 1990s.* New York: St. Martin's Press.

Ariès, Philippe. 1965. *Centuries of Childhood.* New York: Random House.

Arjomand, Said Amir. 1988. *The Turban for the Crown: The Islamic Revolution in Iran.* New York: Oxford University Press.

Arrighi, Giovanni. 1994. *The Long Twentieth Century: Money, Power, and the Origin of Our Times.* New York: Verso.

Arthur, M.M.L. 2005. "Race in America." *Contexts,* vol. 4 (4):48–9.

Asch, Solomon. 1952. Social Psychology. Englewood Cliffs, NJ: Prentice-Hall.

Ashworth, Anthony E. 1980. *Trench Warfare: 1914–1918.* London: Macmillan.

Atchley, Robert C. 2000. *Social Forces and Aging: An Introduction to Social Gerontology.* 9th ed. Belmont, CA: Wadsworth.

Attaran, M. 2004. "Exploring the relationship between information technology and business process reengineering," *Information & Management,* 41(5): 585–596.

Avery, Robert B. and Glenn B. Canner. 2005. "New Information Reported under HMDA and Its Application in Fair Lending Enforcement." *Federal Reserve Bulletin.* Summer 2005. www.federalreserve.gov/pubs/bulletin/2005/3-05hmda.pdf, accessed spring 2006.

Avins, Mimi. 2003. "MoveOn redefines party politics," *Los Angeles Times* December 9, p. A-1.

Bahrami, Homa; and Evans, Stuart. 1995. "Flexible recycling and high-technology entrepreneurship." *California Management Review,* vol. 22.

Bailey, J. Michael. 1993. "Heritable factors influence sexual orientation in women." *Archives of General Psychiatry,* vol. 50.

———; and Pillard, Richard C. 1991. "A genetic study of male sexual orientation." *Archives of General Psychiatry,* vol. 48.

Bales, Kevin. 1999. *Disposable People: New Slavery in the Global Economy.* Berkeley, CA: University of California Press.

Bales, Robert F. 1953. "The egalitarian problem in small groups," in Talcott Parsons, ed., *Working Papers in the Theory of Action.* Glencoe, IL: Free Press.

———. 1970. *Personality and Interpersonal Behavior.* New York: Holt, Rinehart, and Winston.

Balmer, Randall. 1989. *Mine Eyes Have Seen the Glory: A Journey into the Evangelical Subculture in America.* New York: Oxford University Press.

Balswick, J. O. 1983. "Male inexpressiveness," in Kenneth Soloman and Norman B. Levy, eds., *Men in Transition: Theory and Therapy.* New York: Plenum Press.

Baltes, Paul B.; and Schaie, K. Warner. 1977. "The myth of the twilight years," in S. Zarit, ed., *Readings in Aging and Death: Contemporary Perspectives.* New York: Harper and Row.

Baltic 21 Secretariat, "Passenger Car Density," www.baltic21.org/reports/indicators/re08.hrm accessed spring 2006.

Bamberger, Bill; and Cathy M. Davidson. 1998. *Closing: The Life and Death of an American Factory.* New York: Norton.

Bankoff, Elizabeth A. 1983. "Aged parents and their widowed daughters: A support relationship." *Gerontologist,* vol. 38.

Barcelona Field Studies Centre. 2003. "Sao Paulo Growth and Management." www.geographyfieldwork.com/SaoPauloManagement.htm, accessed 12/28/04.

Barker, Martin. 1981. *The New Racism: Conservatives and the Ideology of the Tribe.* Frederick, MD: University Press of America.

Barna Group, Ltd. 2006. "Barna by Topic." www.barna.org/FlexPage.aspx?Page=Topics, accessed 1/23/06.

Barnet, Richard J.; and Cavanagh, John. 1994. *Global Dreams: Imperial Corporations and the New World Order.* New York: Simon and Schuster.

Bart, Pauline B.; and O'Brien, Patricia H. 1985. *Stopping Rape: Successful Survival Strategies.* New York: Pergamon Press.

Basham, A. L. 1989. *The Origins and Development of Classical Hinduism.* Boston: Beacon Press.

Basu, Amrita, ed. 1995. *The Challenge of Local Feminisms: Women's Movements in Global Perspective.* Boulder, CO: Westview.

Baudrillard, Jean. 1983. *Simulations.* New York: Semiotext(e).

———. 1988. *Jean Baudrillard: Selected Writings.* Stanford, CA: Stanford University Press.

Baxter, Jeanine; and Kane, Emily. 1995. "Dependence and independence: A cross national analysis." *Gender and Society,* vol. 9, no. 2.

BBC News. 2001. "Bin Laden's Warning: Full Text." http://news.bbc.co.uk/1/hi/world/south_asia/1585636.stm, accessed 1/10/05.

———. 2001a. "Anger at US Climate Retreat." http://news.bbc.co.uk/1/hi/sci/tech/1248278.stm, accessed 1/10/05.

Beach, Sophie. 2005. "China Witnesses Record Divorces in 2004—PTI." *China Digital Times.* August 19, 2005. http://chinadigitaltimes.net/2005/08/china_witnesses.php, accessed 1/13/06.

Bean, Frank D., et al. 1994. *Illegal Mexican Migration and the U.S./Mexico Border.* Washington, DC: U.S. Commission on Immigration Reform.

Beasley, Christine. 1999. *What Is Feminism?* Thousand Oaks, CA: Sage.

Beck, Ulrich. 1992. *Risk Society.* London: Sage.

———. 1995. *Ecological Politics in an Age of Risk.* Cambridge, UK: Polity Press.

———; Anthony Giddens; and Scott Lash. 1994. *Reflexive Modernization: Politics, Tradition, and Aesthetics in the Modern Social Order.* Cambridge, UK: Polity Press.

Becker, Gary. 1964. *Human Capital.* New York: National Bureau of Economic Research.

———. 1991. *A Treatise on the Family.* Cambridge, MA: Harvard University Press.

Becker, Howard S. 1963. *Outsiders: Studies in the Sociology of Deviance.* New York: Macmillan.

Beechey, Veronica; and Perkins, Tessa. 1987. *A Matter of Hours: Women, Part-Time Work, and the Labour Market.* Cambridge, UK: Polity Press.

Beijing Women's Conference. 1995. "Declaration and Platform for Action." *Critical Areas of Concern* No. 43. Fourth World Conference on Women: Action for Equality, Development, and Peace, Beijing, September 15, 1995.

Belgrave, Linda Liska. 1988. "The effects of race difference in work history, work attitudes, economic resources, and health in women's retirement." *Research on Aging,* vol. 10.

Belkin, Lisa. 2003. "The Opt-Out Revolution." *The New York Times Magazine* 26 October, p. 42.

Bell, A.; Weinberg, M.; and Hammersmith, S. 1981. *Sexual Preference: Its Development in Men and Women.* Bloomington: Indiana University Press.

Bell, Daniel. 1976. *The Coming of Post-Industrial Society: A Venture in Social Forecasting.* New York: Basic Books.

Bellah, Robert N. 1968. "Civil Religion in America," in William G. McLoughlin and Robert N. Bellah, eds., *Religion in America.* Boston: Houghton Mifflin.

———. 1975. *The Broken Covenant.* New York: Seabury Press.

———; Richard Madsen; William M. Sullivan; Ann Swidler; Steven M. Tipton. 1985. *Habits of the Heart: Individualism and Commitment in American Life.* New York: Harper & Row.

Bellman, Beryl. 1984. *The Language of Secrecy: Symbols and Metaphors in Poro Ritual.* New Brunswick, NJ: Rutgers University Press.

Bendick, Marc; Jackson, Charles; and Reinoso, Victor. 1993. "Measuring employment discrimination through controlled experiments," in *The Review of Black Political Economy.* Washington, DC: Fair Employment Council of Greater Washington.

Bengston, Vern L.; Rosenthal, Carolyn; and Burton, Linda. 1990. "Families and aging: Diversity and heterogeneity," in Robert H. Binstock and Linda K. George, eds., *Handbook of Aging and the Social Sciences.* 3rd ed. New York: Academic Press.

Bennet, James. 1992. "The old people sit and talk, about AIDS and secrecy." *New York Times,* September 21.

Bennett, John W. 1976. *The Ecological Transition: Cultural Anthropology and Human Adaptation.* New York: Pergamon Press.

Berger, Peter L. 1963. *Invitation to Sociology.* Garden City, NY: Anchor Books.

———. 1967. *The Sacred Canopy: Elements of a Sociological Theory of Religion.* Garden City, NY: Anchor Books.

———. 1986. *The Capitalist Revolution: Fifty Propositions about Prosperity, Equality, and Liberty.* New York: Basic Books.

———; and Hsiao, Hsin-Huang Michael. 1988. *In Search of an East Asian Development Model.* New Brunswick, NJ: Transaction.

———; and Luckmann, Thomas. 1966. *The Social Construction of Reality: A Treatise in the Sociology of Knowledge.* Garden City, NY: Doubleday.

Berle, Adolf; and Means, Gardiner C. 1982 (orig. 1932). *The Modern Corporation and Private Property.* Buffalo, NY: Heim.

Bernstein, Nina. 2001. "Homeless shelters in New York fill to highest levels since 80's." *New York Times,* February 7.

Berryman, Phillip. 1987. *Liberation Theology: Essential Facts About the Revolutionary Movement in Central America and Beyond.* Philadelphia: Temple University Press.

Bertram, Eva, et al. 1996. *Drug War Politics.* Berkeley, CA: University of California Press.

Beyer, Peter. 1994. *Religion and Globalization.* Thousand Oaks, CA: Sage.

Bielby, William. 2005."Applying Social Research on Stereotyping and Cognitive Bias to Employment Discrimination Litigation: The Case of Allegations of Systematic Gender Bias at Wal-Mart Stores," in Robert L. Nelson and Laura Beth Neilsen, eds., *Handbook on Employment Discrimination Research: Rights and Realities.* Norwell, MA: Kluwer Academic Press.

Birnbaum, Jeffrey H. 2005a. "AARP Leads With Wallet in Fight over Social Security." *The Washington Post* March 30. www.washingtonpost.com/wp-dyn/articles/A11076-2005Mar29.html, accessed 12/6/05.

———. 2005b. "The Road to Riches is called K Street." *The Washington Post.* June 22. www.washingtonpost.com/wpdyn/content/article/2005/06/21/AR2005062101632.html, accessed 1/9/06.

Birren, J. E.; and Bengston, V. L., eds. 1988. *Emerging Theories of Aging.* New York: Springer.

———; and Cunningham, W. 1985. "Research on the psychology of aging," in J. E. Birren and K. Warner Schaie, eds., *The Handbook of Aging.* 2nd ed. New York: Van Nostrand.

Blanchard, Ray; and Bogaert, A. F. 1996. "Homosexuality in men and number of older brothers." *American Journal of Psychiatry,* vol. 153.

Blau, Judith. 2004. "Internationalizing public sociologies," Sociologists Without Borders, www.sociologistswithout borders.org, accessed 12/27/04.

Blau, Peter. 1977. *Inequality and Heterogeneity: A Primitive Theory of Social Structure.* New York: Free Press.

———; and Duncan, Otis Dudley. 1967. *The American Occupational Structure.* New York: Wiley.

Blauner, Robert. 1964. *Alienation and Freedom.* Chicago: University of Chicago Press.

———. 1972. *Racial Oppression in America.* New York: Harper and Row.

Block, Fred. 1990. *Postindustrial Possibilities: A Critique of Economic Discourse.* Berkeley: University of California Press.

Blondet, Cecilia. 1995. "Out of the kitchen and onto the streets: Women's activism in Peru," in Amrita Basu, ed., *The Challenge of Local Feminisms.* Boulder, CO: Westview.

Bluestone, Barry. 1988. "Deindustrialization and unemployment in America." *Review of Black Political Economy,* vol. 17.

———; and Harrison, Bennett. 1982. *The Deindustrialization of America.* New York: Basic Books.

Blum, Linda M. 1991. *Between Feminism and Labor: The Significance of the Comparable Worth Movement.* Berkeley, CA: University of California Press.

Blumberg, Rae Lesser, ed. 1995. *Engendering Wealth and Well-Being: Empowerment for Global Change.* Boulder, CO: Westview.

Bobak, Laura. 1996. "India's Tiny Slaves," *Ottawa Sun,* October 23.

Bobo, Lawrence; and Kluegel, James R. 1991. "Modern American prejudice: Stereotypes, social distance, and perceptions of discrimination toward Blacks, Hispanics, and Asians." Paper presented at the 1991 meeting of the American Sociological Association.

Bochenek, Michael A.; and Brown, Widney. 2001. *Hatred in the Hallways: Violence and Discrimination against Lesbian, Gay, Bisexual, and Transgender Students in U.S. Schools.* New York: Human Rights Watch, www.hrw.org/reports/2001/uslgbt/toc.htm, May 30, accessed 12/28/04.

Boden, Deirdre; and Molotch, Harvey. 1994. "The compulsion of proximity," in Deirdre Boden and Roger Friedland, eds., *Nowhere: Space, Time, and Modernity.* Berkeley, CA: University of California Press.

Bohan, Suzanne. 1999. "Bohemian grove and global elite." *Sacramento Bee,* www.mt.net/watcher/bohemiangrove.html, August 2, accessed 12/28/04.

Bonacich, Edna; and Appelbaum, Richard P. 2000. *Behind the Label: Inequality in the Los Angeles Garment Industry.* Berkeley, CA: University of California Press.

Bonnell, Victoria E.; and Hunt, Lynn, eds. 1999. *Beyond the Cultural Turn.* Berkeley, CA: University of California Press.

Bonnett, Alastair. 2000. *Anti-Racism.* New York: Routledge.

Booth, Alan. 1977. "Food riots in the north-west of England, 1770–1801." *Past and Present,* no. 77.

Borjas, George J. 1994. "The economics of immigration." *Journal of Economic Literature,* vol. 32.

Bositis, David. 2001. "Black Elected Officials." Joint Center for Political and Economic Studies. www.jointcenter.org/publications1/publication-PDFs/BEO-pdfs/2001-BEO.pdf, accessed 1/27/06.

Bosse, R., et al. 1987. "Mental health differences among retirees and workers: Findings from the normative aging study." *Psychology and Aging,* vol. 2.

Boswell, John. 1995. The *Marriage of Likeness: Same-Sex Unions in Pre-Modern Europe.* London: Fontana.

Bouma et al. 2004. Conference on Human Factors in Computing Systems. CHI '04 extended abstracts on Human factors in computing systems. New York: ACM Press.

Bourdieu, Pierre. 1984. *Distinction: A Social Critique of Judgement of Taste.* Cambridge, MA: Harvard University Press.

———. 1988. *Language and Symbolic Power.* Cambridge, UK: Polity Press.

———. 1990. *The Logic of Practice.* Palo Alto, CA: Stanford University Press.

Bowen, Kurt. 1996. *Evangelism and Apostasy: The Evolution and Impact of Evangelicals in Modern Mexico.* Montreal: McGill-Queens University Press.

Bowlby, John. 1953. *Child Care and the Growth of Love.* Baltimore, MD: Penguin.

Bowles, Samuel; and Gintis, Herbert. 1976. *Schooling in Capitalist America.* New York: Basic Books.

Boyer, Robert; and Drache, Daniel. eds. 1996. *States against Markets: The Limits of Globalization.* New York: Routledge.

Braithwaite, John. 1996. "Crime, shame, and reintegration," in P. Cordella and L. Siegal, eds., *Readings in Contemporary Criminological Theory.* Boston: Northeastern University Press.

Bramlett, M.D.; and Mosher W.D. 2002. "Cohabitation, marriage, divorce, and remarriage in the United States." National Center for Health Statistics. *Vital Health Stat* vol. 23, no. 22.

Brass, Daniel J. 1985. "Men's and women's networks: A study of interaction patterns and influence in an organization." *Academy of Management Journal,* vol. 28.

Braverman, Harry. 1974. *Labor and Monopoly Capital.* New York: Monthly Review Press.

———. 1998. *Labor and Monopoly Capital: The Degradation of Work in the Twentieth Century.* New York: Monthly Review Press.

Brennan, Teresa. 1988. "Controversial discussions and feminist debate," in Naomi Segal and Edward Timms, eds., *The Origins and Evolution of Psychoanalysis.* New Haven, CT: Yale University Press.

Bresnahan, T.; Brynjolfsson, E.; and Hitt, L. 2002. "Information technology, workplace organization, and the demand for skilled labor: firm-level evidence," *Quarterly Journal of Economics,* vol. 117(1), pp. 339–76.

Brewer, Rose M. 1993. "Theorizing race, class and gender: The new scholarship of black feminist intellectuals and black women's labor," in Stanlie M. James and Abena P. A. Busia, eds., *Theorizing Black Feminisms: The Visionary Pragmatism of Black Women.* New York: Routledge.

Bricourt, J. C. 2004. "Using telework to enhance return to work outcomes for individuals with spinal cord injuries," *Neurorehabilitation,* 19(2): 147–159.

Brimelow, Peter. 1995. *Alien Nation: Common Sense About America's Immigration Disaster.* New York: Random House.

Britain, Samuel. 1975. "The economic contradictions of democracy." *British Journal of Political Science,* vol. 15.

Broder, John M. 1997. "The Climate Accord: The Overview; Clinton Adamant on 3rd World Role in Climate Accord" *New York Times,* December 12.

Brookfield, Stephen. 1986. *Understanding and Facilitating Adult Learning.* San Francisco: Jossey-Bass.

Brown, Catrina; and Jasper, Karin, eds. 1993. *Consuming Passions: Feminist Approaches to Eating Disorders and Weight Preoccupations.* Toronto: Second Story Press.

Brown, Donald E. 1991. *Human Universals.* New York: McGraw-Hill.

Brown, Judith K. 1977. "A note on the division of labor by sex," in Nona Glazer and Helen Y. Waehrer, eds., *Woman in a Man-Made World.* 2nd ed. Chicago: Rand McNally.

Browne, K. 1998. *An Introduction to Sociology* 2nd ed. From *Sociology Review* 9.2 (November 1999) p. 5 Crown Copyright.

Brown, Patricia Leigh. 2002. "Megachurches as Minitowns," *New York Times,* May 9, pp. F1–F6.

Brown, Susan L. 2004. "Family Structure and Child Well-being: the Significance of Parental cohabitation." *Journal of Marriage and Family* 66 (May): 351–367.

Brownmiller, Susan. 1975. *Against Our Will: Men, Women, and Rape.* New York: Simon and Schuster.

———. 1986. *Against Our Will: Men, Women, and Rape.* Rev. ed. New York: Bantam.

Brownstein, Ronald. 2003. "Liberal group flexes online muscle in its very own primary," *Los Angeles Times,* June 23, p. A-9.

Brubaker, Rogers. 1992. *The Politics of Citizenship.* Cambridge, MA: Harvard University Press.

Bruce, Steve. 1990. *Pray TV: Televangelism in America.* New York: Routledge.

Brumberg, Joan Jacobs. 1997. *The Body Project.* New York: Random House.

Bryan, Beverly; Dadzie, Stella; and Scafe, Suzanne. 1987. "Learning to resist: Black women and education," in Gaby Weiner and Madeleine Arnot, eds., *Gender under Scrutiny: New Inquiries in Education.* London: Hutchinson.

Bull, Peter. 1983. *Body Movement and Interpersonal Communication.* New York: Wiley.

Bullock, Charles, III. 1984. "Equal education opportunity," in Charles S. Bullock III and Charles M. Lamb, eds., *Implementation of Civil Rights Policy.* Monterey, CA: Brooks and Cole.

Bumpass, Larry; and Lu, Hsien-Hen. 2000. "Trends in cohabitation and implications for children's family context in the United States." *Population Studies,* vol. 54.

———; Sweet, James A.; and Cherlin, Andrew. 1991. "The role of cohabitation in declining rates of marriage." *Journal of Marriage and the Family,* vol. 53 (November).

Burawoy, Michael. 1972. *The Colour of Class.* Manchester, UK: Manchester University Press [for] the Institute for African Studies, University of Zambia.

———. 1979. *Manufacturing Consent.* Chicago: University of Chicago Press.

———. 1985. *The Politics of Production.* New York: Verso.

———. 2004. "For Public Sociology" Presidential Address, 2004 ASA Annual Meeting, San Francisco, California, August 17.

Burghart, D. Brian. 2003. "About a Man," *Reno News and Review,* September 4.

Burns, James MacGregor. 1978. *Leadership.* New York: Harper and Row.

Burns, Thomas; and Stalker, G. M. 1994. *The Management of Innovation.* Rev. ed. Oxford, UK: Oxford University Press.

Burr, Chandler. 1993. "Homosexuality and biology." *Atlantic Monthly,* March.

Burris, Beverly H. 1993. *Technocracy at Work.* Albany: State University of New York Press.

———. 1998. "Computerization of the workplace," in *Annual Review of Sociology,* vol. 24. Palo Alto, CA: Annual Reviews.

Burt, Martha R. 1992. *Over the Edge: The Growth of Homelessness in the 1980s.* New York: Russell Sage.

Business Journal. 2000. "Judge tosses insurer's bid to keep redlining data secret." http://sanjose.bizjournals.com/ sanjose/stories/2000/09/11/daily42.html, accessed 1/11/05.

Business Week. 1997. "Good News on Wage Inequality" December 15.

Butler, Judith. 1989. *Gender Trouble: Feminism and the Subversion of Identity.* New York: Routledge.

Butterfield, Fox. 1998. "Decline of violent crimes is linked to crack market." *New York Times,* December 28, p. A18.

Byles, Jeff. 2001. "Tales of the Kefir Furnaceman." *The Village Voice,* April 11–17.

Bynner, John, Elsa Ferri, and Peter Shepherd. 1997. *Twenty-Something in the 1990s: Getting On, Getting By, Getting Nowhere.* Brookfield, VT: Ashgate.

Byrne, David. 1995. "Deindustrialization and dispossession." *Sociology,* vol. 29.

Cairncross, Frances. 1997. *The Death of Distance: How the Communications Revolution Will Change Our Lives.* Boston: Harvard Business School Press.

Caplow, Theodore. 1956. "A theory of coalition in the triad." *American Sociological Review,* vol. 20.

———. 1959. "Further development of a theory of coalitions in triads." *American Journal of Sociology,* vol. 64.

———. 1969. *Two Against One: Coalitions in Triads.* Englewood Cliffs, NJ: Prentice Hall.

Cardoso, Fernando H.; and Faletto, Enzo. 1979. *Dependency and Development in Latin America.* Berkeley, CA: University of California Press.

Carnevale, Dan. 2000. "Brown U. and MCI WorldCom join to help colleges try to close the digital divide," *The Chronicle of Higher Education* (June 9).

Carr, Sarah. 1999. "U. of Nebraska's Class.com hooks up with a Kentucky school," *The Chronicle of Higher Education* (October 22).

———; and Young, Jeffrey R. 1999. "As distance-learning boom spreads, colleges help set up virtual high schools." *The Chronicle of Higher Education* (October 22).

Carrington, K. 1994. "Postmodern and feminist criminologies: disconnecting discourses?" *International Journal of the Sociology of Law* 22(3): 261–277.

———. 1998 (orig. 1994) "Essentialism and Feminist Criminologies." *The Critical Criminologist ,* M. Dragan, ed., Chicago: Northeastern Illinois University.

Castells, Manuel. 1977. *The Urban Question: A Marxist Approach.* Cambridge, MA: MIT Press.

———. 1983. *The City and the Grass Roots: A Cross-Cultural Theory of Urban Social Movements.* Berkeley, CA: University of California Press.

———. 1992. "Four Asian tigers with a dragon head: A comparative analysis of the state, economy, and society in the Asian Pacific Rim," in Richard P. Appelbaum and Jeffrey Henderson, eds., *States and Development in the Asian Pacific Rim.* Newbury Park, CA: Sage.

———. 1996. *The Rise of the Network Society.* Malden, MA: Blackwell.

———. 1997. *The Power of Identity.* Malden, MA: Blackwell.

———. 1998. *End of Millennium.* Malden, MA: Blackwell.

———. 2000. *The Rise of the Network Society.* Malden, MA: Blackwell.

———. 2001. *The Internet Galaxy.* Oxford: Oxford University Press.

Castles, Stephen; and Miller, Mark J. 1993. *The Age of Migration: International Population Movements in the Modern World.* London: Macmillan.

Catalano, Shannon M. 2005. "Criminal Victimization, 2004." www.ojp.usdoj.gov/bjs/pub/pdf/cv04.pdf, accessed 10/5/05.

Center for American Women and Politics (CAWP). 2005. "Women in Elected Office 2005 Fact Sheet Summaries." Eagleton Institute of Politics. www.cawp.rutgers.edu/Facts/Officeholders/cawpfs.html, accessed 12/3/05.

Center for Defense Information. 2003. "Highlights of the budget request," Washington, D.C.: Center for Defense Information (February 3). www.cdi.org/program/document.cfm?DocumentID=1041&StartRow=11&ListRows=10&appendURL=&Orderby=D.DateLast Updated&ProgramID=15&from_page=index.cfm, accessed 1/11/05.

Center for Public Integrity. 2003. "How the feds stack up," Washington, DC: The Center for Public Integrity (May 15), www.publicintegrity.org/hiredguns/report.aspx?aid=167, accessed 1/10/05.

Centers for Disease Control and Prevention (CDC). 2003. "National ambulatory care survey, 2001 summary." Advanced Data From *Vital and Health Statistics,* Number 337 (August 11), www.cdc.gov/nchs/data/ad/ad337.pdf, accessed 12/29/04.

———. 2004. "Health, United States, 2004." Table 27. www.cdc.gov/nchs/hus.htm, accessed 12/5/05.

———. 2005a. "Births: Final Data for 2003." *National Vital Statistics Reports.* www.cdc.gov/nchs/data/nvsr/nvsr54/nvsr54_02.pdf, accessed 1/12/06.

———. 2005b. "Births: Final Data for 2003." *National Vital Statistics Reports.* Table 14. www.cdc.gov/nchs/data/nvsr/nvsr54/nvsr54_02.pdf, accessed 1/12/06.

———. 2005c. "Births: Final Data for 2003." *National Vital Statistics Reports.* Table 13. www.cdc.gov/nchs/data/nvsr/nvsr54/nvsr54_02.pdf, accessed 1/12/06.

Central Intelligence Agency (CIA). 2000. CIA World Factbook. www.cia.gov/cia/publications/factbook/geos/rs.html#Econ, accessed 12/29/04.

Chafe, William H. 1974. *The American Woman: Her Changing Social, Economic, and Political Roles, 1920–1970.* New York: Oxford University Press.

———. 1977. *Women and Equality: Changing Patterns in American Culture.* New York: Oxford University Press.

Chafetz, Janet Saltzman. 1990. *Gender Equity: An Integrated Theory of Stability and Change.* Newbury Park, CA: Sage.

———. 1997. "Feminist theory and sociology: Underutilized contributions for mainstream theory." *Annual Review of Sociology,* vol. 23.

Chaliand, Gerard; and Ragu, Jean. 1992. *Strategic Atlas: A Comparative Geopolitics of the World's Powers.* New York: Harper & Row.

Chambliss, William J. 1973. "The saints and the roughnecks." *Society,* November.

———. 1988. *On the Take: From Petty Crooks to Presidents.* Bloomington: Indiana University Press.

Chandler, Mary Voelz. 1999. "Heartbreak, Mystery Shroud Shrine." *Rocky Mountain News,* May 2. Available from: Denver. rockymountainnews.com/shooting/0502shr51.shtml; accessed spring 2006.

Chaney, David. 1994. *The Cultural Turn: Scene-Setting Essays in Contemporary Cultural History.* New York: Routledge.

Chang, Iris; and Kirby, William C. 1997. *The Rape of Nanking: The Forgotten Holocaust of World War II.* New York: Basic Books.

Charleston Business Journal. 2003. "Are 'all-American cars' still made in America?" www.charlestonbusiness.com/pub/6_18/news/2930-1.html, accessed 1/11/05.

Chase-Dunn, Christopher. 1989. *Global Formation: Structures of the World Economy.* Cambridge, MA: Basil Blackwell.

Chaves, Mark. 1993. "Intraorganizational power and internal secularization in Protestant denominations." *American Journal of Sociology,* vol. 99 (July): 1–48.

———. 1994. "Secularization as declining religious authority." *Social Forces,* vol. 72.

Cheng, Lucie; and Hsiung, Ping-Chun. 1992. "Women, export-oriented growth, and the state: The case of Taiwan," in Richard P. Appelbaum and Jeffery Henderson, eds., *States and Development in the Asian Pacific Rim.* Newbury Park, CA: Sage.

Chepesiuk, Ron. 1998. *Hard Target: The United States War against International*

Drug Trafficking, 1982–1997. Jefferson, NC: McFarland and Company.

Cherlin, Andrew. 1990. "Recent changes in American fertility, marriage, and divorce." *Annals of the American Academy of Political and Social Science,* vol. 510 (July).

———. 1992. *Marriage, Divorce, Re-Marriage.* Rev. ed. Cambridge, MA: Harvard University Press.

———. 1999. *Public and Private Families: An Introduction.* 2nd ed. New York: McGraw Hill.

———, et al. 1998. "Effects of parental divorce on mental health throughout the life course." *American Sociological Review,* vol. 63.

Chicago Tribune. 2003. "Cost of a nursing home room jumps, study finds." www. chicagotribune.com/classified/realestate/over55/chi0308300022aug31,0,364422. story?coll5chi-classifiedover55-hed, accessed 12/29/04.

China Internet Network Information Center. 2005a. "Internet Statistics." www.cnnic. net.cn/en/index/0O/index.htm/, accessed 9/28/05.

———. 2005b. "16th Statistical Survey Report on the Internet Development in China." www.cnnic.net.cn/en/index/0O/index.htm, accessed spring 2006.

China.org.cn. 2001. "Privacy Key in Marriage Rule Revision." www.china.org.cn/english/PMD/13226.htm, accessed 1/13/06.

Chodorow, Nancy. 1978. *The Reproduction of Mothering.* Berkeley, CA: University of California Press.

———. 1988. *Psychoanalytic Theory and Feminism.* Cambridge, UK: Polity Press.

Christie, Les. 2005. "Number of Millionaires hits Record." *CNN/Money.* May 25. http://money.cnn.com/2005/05/25/pf/record_millionaires/, accessed spring 2006.

Chua, Amy. 2003. *World on Fire: How Exporting Free Market Democracy Breeds Ethnic Hatred and Global Instability.* New York: Doubleday.

Cleary, Paul D. 1987. "Gender differences in stress-related disorders," in Rosalind C. Barnett, ed., *Gender and Stress.* New York: Free Press.

Cleveland, Jeanette N. 1996. "Women in high-status nontraditional occupations," in Paula J. Dubeck and Kathryn Borman, eds., *Women and Work: A Handbook.* New York: Garland.

Cloward, Richard A.; and Ohlin, L. 1960. *Delinquency and Opportunity.* New York: Free Press.

CNN. 2003. "INS: 7 million Illegal Immigrants in United States." February 1.

www.cnn.com/2003/US/01/31/illegal. immigration, accessed 1/27/06.

———. 2004a. "Bush calls for ban on same-sex marriages." http://edition.cnn.com/2004/ALLPOLITICS/02/24/elec04.prez. bush.marriage/index.html (February 25), accessed 12/29/04.

———. 2004b. "The outspoken Bill Cosby." http://edition.cnn.com/2004/SHOWBIZ/TV/11/11/cosby/index.html, accessed spring 2006.

Coate, J. 1994. "Cyberspace innkeeping: Building online community." Online paper, www.well.com:70/0/Community/innkeeping, accessed 12/29/04.

Cohen, Albert. 1955. *Delinquent Boys: The Culture of the Gang.* Glencoe, IL: Free Press.

Cohen, Jon and Gary Langer. 2005. "Poll: Will You Live Longer and Better?" ABC News. October 24. http://abcnews.go.com/Health/PollVault/story?id=1232993&CMP=OTC-RSSFeeds0312, accessed 12/6/05.

Cohen, Lisa E.; Broschak, Joseph P.; and Haveman, Heather A. 1998. "And then there were more? The effect of organizational sex composition on the hiring and promotion of managers." *American Sociological Review,* vol. 63, no. 5.

Cohen, Robin. 1997. *Global Diasporas: An Introduction.* London: UCL Press.

Coleman, James S. 1987. "Families and schools." *Educational Researcher,* vol. 16, no. 6.

———. 1988. "Social capital in the creation of human capital." *American Journal of Sociology,* supplement, vol. 94.

———. 1990. *The Foundations of Social Theory.* Cambridge, MA: Harvard University Press.

———, et al. 1966. *Equality of Educational Opportunity.* Washington, DC: U.S. Government Printing Office.

Coles, Robert. 1997. *Old and on Their Own.* New York: DoubleTake/W. W. Norton.

Collins, Jane. 2000. "Quality by other means." Unpublished manuscript, Department of Sociology, University of Wisconsin–Madison.

Collins, Patricia Hill. 1990. *Black Feminist Thought: Knowledge, Consciousness, and the Politics of Empowerment.* Boston: Unwin Hyman.

Collins, Randall. 1971. "Functional and conflict theories of educational stratification." *American Sociological Review,* vol. 36.

———. 1979. *The Credential Society: An Historical Sociology of Education.* New York: Academic Press.

———. 1985. *Weberian Sociological Theory.* Cambridge, MA.: Cambridge University Press.

———, et al. 1993. "Toward an integrated theory of gender stratification." *Sociological Perspectives,* vol. 36.

Colman, Hila. 2001, "Young and Old Thrive Side by Side," *New York Times,* August 15, p. A23.

Coltrane, Scott. 1992. "The micropolitics of gender in non-industrial societies." *Gender and Society,* vol. 6.

Combat 18. 1998. www.combat18.org, accessed 1/10/05.

Common Cause. 2002. "Campaign finance reform: Election 2002—incumbent advantage," www.commoncause.org/news/default.cfm?ArtID538, accessed 11/6/02.

———. 2003. "Spending more than a half billion on political contributions, lobbying and ad campaigns, Pharma wins big on Medicare," www.commoncause.org/action/070103_phrma_report.pdf, accessed 7/1/03.

Computer Security Institute and FBI. 2005. "2005 CSI/FBI Computer Crime and Security Survey." http://i.cmpnet.com/gocsi/db_area/pdfs/fbi/FBI2005.pdf, accessed 10/5/05.

Computer World. 2002. "The Best Places to Work in IT: United States," www. computerworld.com/departments/surveys/bestplaces/bestplaces_us_region_sort/0, 10984,,00.html, accessed 1/20/05.

Conley, Dalton. 1999. *Being Black, Living in the Red: Race, Wealth, and Social Policy in America.* Berkeley and Los Angeles: University of California Press.

———. 2003. "The cost of slavery," *New York Times,* February 15.

Connell, R. W. 1987. *Gender and Power: Society, the Person, and Sexual Politics.* Boston: Allen and Unwin.

Conner, K. A.; Dorfman, L. T.; and Tompkins, J. B. 1985. "Life satisfaction of retired professors: The contribution of work, health, income, and length of retirement." *Educational Gerontology,* vol. 11.

Conti, Joseph A. 2003. "Trade, power, and law: Dispute resolution in the World Trade Organization, 1995–2002." Masters Thesis. University of California, Santa Barbara.

Cooley, Charles Horton. 1964 (orig. 1902). *Human Nature and the Social Order.* New York: Schocken Books.

Coolidge, Courteney. 1999. "American Families: Beyond the White Picket

Fence," A photo project, available at http://10families.com.

Coontz, Stephanie. 1992. *The Way We Never Were: American Families and the Nostalgia Trap.* New York: Basic Books.

Corbin, Juliet; and Strauss, Anselm. 1985. "Managing chronic illness at home: Three lines of work." *Qualitative Sociology,* vol. 8.

Corsaro, William. 1997. The Sociology of Childhood. Thousand Oaks, CA: Pine Forge Press.

Cosmides, Leda; and Tooby, John. 1997. "Evolutionary psychology: A primer." University of California at Santa Barbara: Institute for Social, Behavioral, and Economic Research Center for Evolutionary Psychology, available at www.psych.ucsb.edu/research/cep/primer.htm, accessed 1/11/05.

Coward, Rosalind. 1984. *Female Desire: Women's Sexuality Today.* London: Paladin.

Cowgill, Donald O. 1968. "The social life of the aged in Thailand." *Gerontologist,* vol. 8.

———. 1986. *Aging around the World.* Belmont, CA: Wadsworth.

Cox, W. Michael; and Alm, Richard. 1999. *Myths of Rich and Poor: Why We're Better Off Than We Think.* New York: Basic Books.

Crompton, Rosemary. 1998. *Class and Stratification: An Introduction to Current Debates.* 2nd ed. Cambridge, UK: Polity Press.

Crow, Graham; and Hardey, Michael. 1992. "Diversity and ambiguity among lone-parent households in modern Britain," in Catherine Marsh and Sara Arber, eds., *Families and Households: Divisions and Change.* London: Macmillan.

Crowley, J. E. 1985. "Longitudinal Effects of Retirement on Men's Psychological and Physical Well-Being," in H. S. Parnes, J. E. Crowley, R. J. Haurin, L. J. Less, W. R. Morgan, F. L. Mott and G. Nestel (Eds.), *Retirement Among American Men,* Lexington, MA: Lexington Books, pp. 147–173.

CRP. 2003a. "2000 Presidential Race: Total Raised and Spent," Center for Responsive Politics. www.opensecrets.org/2000elect/index/AllCands.htm, accessed 12/29/04.

———. 2003b. "Election overview 2002 cycle: Business-labor-ideology split in PAC, soft & individual donations to candidates and parties" Center for Responsive Politics, based on data released by the FEC on Monday, June 9, 2003. www.opensecrets.org/overview/blio.asp?cycle52002, accessed 12/29/04.

Cumings, Bruce. 1987. "The origins and development of the northeast Asian political economy: Industrial sectors, product cycles, and political consequences," in F. C. Deyo, ed., *The Political Economy of the New Asian Industrialism.* Ithaca, NY: Cornell University Press.

———. 1997. *Korea's Place in the Sun: A Modern History.* New York: Norton.

Cumming, Elaine. 1963. "Further thoughts on the theory of disengagement." *International Social Science Journal,* vol. 15.

———. 1975. "Engagement with an old theory." *International Journal of Aging and Human Development,* vol. 6.

———; and Henry, William E. 1961. *Growing Old: The Process of Disengagement.* New York: Basic.

Currie, Elliott. 1998. *Crime and Punishment in America.* New York: Henry Holt.

Curtin, J. Sean. 2003. "Youth trends in Japan: Part four—anorexia and other teenage eating disorders on the rise." Japanese Institute of Global Communications. www.glocom.org/special_topics/social_trends/20030701_trends_s46, accessed 12/29/04.

Cutler, Stephen J.; and Grams, Armin E. 1988. "Correlates of everyday self-reported memory problems." *Journal of Gerontology,* vol. 43.

Dahlburg, John-Thor. 1995. "Sweatshop case dismays few in Thailand." *Los Angeles Times,* August 27, p. A-4.

D'Andrade, Roy. 1995. *The Development of Cognitive Anthropology.* New York: Cambridge University Press.

Dannefer, Dale. 1989. "Human action and its place in theories of aging." *Journal of Aging Studies,* vol. 3.

Danzger, M. Herbert. 1989. *Returning to Tradition.* New Haven, CT: Yale University Press.

Danziger, Sheldon H.; and Gottschalk, Peter. 1995. *America Unequal.* Cambridge, MA: Harvard University Press.

Davidman, Joy. 1991. *Tradition in a Rootless World: Women Turn to Orthodox Judaism.* Berkeley: University of California Press.

Davies, Bronwyn. 1991. *Frogs and Snails and Feminist Tales.* Sydney: Allen and Unwin.

Davies, James C. 1962. "Towards a theory of revolution." *American Sociological Review,* vol. 27.

Davis, Donald; and Polonko, Karen. 2001. "Telework America 2001 Summary," International Telework Association &

Council, www.telecommute.org/telework/twa2001.htm, accessed 1/20/05.

Davis, Kingsley; and Moore, Wilbert E. 1945. "Some principles of stratification." *American Sociological Review,* vol. 10 (April).

Davis, Mike. 1990. *City of Quartz: Excavating the Future in Los Angeles.* New York: Verso.

Davis, Stanley M. 1987. *Future Perfect.* Reading, MA: Addison-Wesley.

———. 1988. *2001 Management: Managing the Future Now.* New York: Simon and Schuster.

Deacon, Terrance W. 1998. *The Symbolic Species: The Co-Evolution of Language and the Brain.* New York: Norton.

de Beauvoir, Simone. 1974 (orig. 1949). *The Second Sex.* New York: Random House.

Delany, Samuel R. 1999. *Times Square Red, Times Square Blue.* New York: New York University Press.

D'Emilio, John. 1983. *Sexual Politics, Sexual Communities: The Making of a Homosexual Minority in the United States, 1940–1970.* Chicago: University of Chicago Press.

DeNavas-Walt, Carmen, Bernadette D. Proctor, and Cheryl Hill Lee. 2005. U.S. Census Bureau, Current Population Reports, P60-229, *Income, Poverty, and Health Insurance Coverage in the United States: 2004,* U.S. Government Printing Office, Washington, DC. www.census.gov/prod/2005pubs/p60-229.pdf, accessed spring 2006.

DeParle, Jason. 2005. "What Happens to a Race Deferred." *New York Times,* September 4.

de Tocqueville, Alexis. 1969 (orig. 1835). *Democracy in America.* New York: Doubleday.

Derrida, Jacques. 1978. *Writing and Difference.* Chicago: University of Chicago Press.

———. 1981. *Positions.* London: Athlone.

Devault, Marjorie L. 1991. *Feeding the Family: The Social Organization of Caring as Gendered Work.* Chicago: University of Chicago Press.

de Witt, Karen. 1994. "Wave of suburban growth is being fed by minorities." *New York Times,* August 15, pp. A1, B6.

Dey, Achintya N. 1997. "Characteristics of elderly nursing home residents: Data from the 1995 national nursing home survey." *Advance Data,* vol. 289 (July 2).

Deyo, Fred C. 1987. *The Political Economy of the New Asian Industrialism.* Ithaca, NY: Cornell University Press.

———. 1989. *Beneath the Miracle: Labor Subordination in the New Asian*

Industrialism. Berkeley, CA: University of California Press.

Diamond, Jared. 2005. *Collapse: How Societies Choose to Fail or Succeed.* New York: Penguin.

Dickman, Sharon. 1999. "Can life in nursing homes by meaningful?" University of Rochester press release, June 23.

Dicum, Gregory; and Luttinger, Nina. 1999. *The Coffee Book: Anatomy of an Industry from Crop to the Last Drop.* New York: New Press.

Diekema, David A. 1991. "Televangelism and the mediated charismatic relationship," *Social Science Journal,* vol. 28, no. 2: 143–62.

DiMaggio, Paul. 1997. "Culture and cognition." *Annual Review of Sociology,* vol. 23.

Dimitrova, D. 2003. "Controlling teleworkers: supervision and flexibility revisited," *New Technology Work and Employment,* 18(3): 181–195.

DiPrete, Thomas A.; and Nonnemaker, K. Lynn. 1997. "Structural change, labor market turbulence, and labor market outcomes." *American Sociological Review,* vol. 62.

_____; and Soule, Whitman T. 1988. "Gender and promotion in segmented job ladder systems." *American Sociological Review,* vol. 53.

Dobash, R. Emerson; and Dobash, Russell P. 1992. *Women, Violence, and Social Change.* New York: Routledge.

Dolbeare, Cushing. 1995. *Out of Reach: Why Everyday People Can't Find Affordable Housing.* Washington, DC: Low Income Housing Information.

Domhoff, G. William. 2005. "Power in America: Wealth, Income, and Power." http://sociology.ucsc.edu/whorules america/power/wealth.html, accessed spring 2006.

_____. 1998. *Who Rules America?: Power and Politics in the Year 2000.* Belmont, CA: Mayfield.

_____. 1983. *Who Rules America Now?* A View for the '80s New York: Prentice-Hall.

_____. 1979 .*The Powers That Be: Processes of Ruling Class Domination in America.* New York: Vintage Books

_____. 1974. *The Bohemian Grove and Other Retreats.* New York: Harper & Row.

_____. 1971. *The Higher Circles: The Governing Class in America.* New York: Vintage Books.

Dore, Ronald. 1980. *British Factory, Japanese Factory: The Origins of National Diversity*

in Industrial Relations. Berkeley, CA: University of California Press.

Doyal, Lesley; and Pennell, Imogen. 1981. *The Political Economy of Health.* Boston: South End Press.

Drake, St. Clair; and Cayton, Horace R. 1945. *Black Metropolis: A Study of Negro Life in a Northern City.* New York: Harcourt, Brace.

Draper, P. 1975. "!Kung women: Contrasts in sexual egalitarianism in foraging and sedentary contexts," in R. R. Reiter, ed., *Toward an Anthropology of Women.* New York: Monthly Review Press.

Dreier, Peter; and Appelbaum, Richard P. 1992. "The housing crisis enters the 1990s." *New England Journal of Public Policy,* spring–summer.

Drentea, Patricia. 1998. "Consequences of women's formal and informal job search methods for employment in female-dominated jobs." *Gender and Society,* vol. 12.

DrugWarFacts.org. 2005. "Drug War Facts: Economics." www.drugwarfacts.org/ economi.htm, accessed spring 2006.

Du Bois, W. E. B. 1903. *The Souls of Black Folk.* New York: Dover.

Dubos, René. 1959. *Mirage of Health.* New York: Doubleday/Anchor.

Duignan, Peter; and Gann, L. H., eds. 1998. *The Debate in the United States over Immigration.* Stanford, CA: Hoover Institution Press.

Duncan, Greg J.; Brooks-Gunn, Jeanne; Yeung, W. Jean; Smith, Judith R. 1998. "How much does childhood poverty affect the life chances of children?" *American Sociological Review,* vol. 63, no. 3 (June): 406–23.

Duncombe, Jean; and Marsden, Dennis. 1993. "Love and intimacy: The gender division of emotion and emotion work: A neglected aspect of sociological discussion of heterosexual relationships." *Sociology,* vol. 27.

Duneier, Mitchell. 1994., "Andrea's Dream: A Single Parent's Fight for Independence," series, *Chicago Tribune,* December 1994, pp. 3–4, 13–15.

_____. 1999. *Sidewalk.* New York: Farrar, Straus, and Giroux.

_____. 2000. "Questions for Jane Jacobs" *New York Times* April 9.

_____; and Molotch, Harvey. 1999. "Talking city trouble: Interactional vandalism, social inequality, and the urban interaction problem." *American Journal of Sociology,* vol. 104.

Dunn, Dana; Almquist, Elizabeth M.; and Saltzman Chafetz, Janet. 1993.

"Macrostructural perspectives on gender inequality," in Paula England, ed., *Theory on Gender, Feminism on Theory.* New York: Aldine DeGrutyer.

Duranti, Alessandro. 1994. *From Grammar to Politics: Linguistic Anthropology in a Western Samoan Village.* Berkeley, CA: University of California Press.

Durkheim, Émile. 1964. *The Division of Labor in Society.* Originally published 1893. New York: Free Press.

_____. 1965. *The Elementary Forms of the Religious Life.* Originally published 1912. New York: Free Press.

_____. 1966. *Suicide.* Originally published 1897. New York: Free Press.

Duster, Troy. 1990. *Backdoor to Eugenics.* New York: Routledge.

Dutt, Mallika. 1996. "Some reflections on U.S. women of color and the United Nations fourth world conference on women and NGO forum in Beijing, China." *Feminist Studies,* vol. 22.

Duverger, Maurice. 1954. *Political Parties.* London: Methuen.

Dworkin, Andrea. 1981. *Pornography: Men Possessing Women.* New York: Pedigree.

_____. 1987. *Intercourse.* New York: Free Press.

Dworkin, R. M. 1993. *Life's Dominion: An Argument About Abortion, Euthanasia, and Individual Freedom.* New York: Knopf.

Dwyer, D. J. 1975. *People and Housing in Third World Cities.* London: Longman.

Dychtwald, K. 1990. *Age Wave: How the Most Important Trend of Our Time Will Change Your Future.* New York: Bantam Books.

Dye, Thomas R. 1986. *Who's Running America?* 4th ed. Englewood Cliffs, NJ: Prentice Hall.

E-Crime Watch. 2004. "2004 E-Crime Watch Survey: Summary of Findings." www.cert.org/archive/pdf/2004eCrime WatchSummary.pdf, accessed spring 2006.

Earth Trends. 2003. "Agriculture Inputs, 2003," http://earthtrends.wri.org/pdf_ library/data_tables/agr2_2003.pdf, accessed fall 2005.

Eating Disorder Coalition (EDC). 2003. "Statistics." www.eatingdisorders coalition. org/reports/statistics.html, accessed 12/29/04.

Ebomoyi, Ehigie. 1987. "The prevalence of female circumcision in two Nigerian communities." *Sex Roles,* vol. 17, nos. 3–4.

The Economist. 1996. *Pocket World in Figures.* London: Profile Books.

_____. 2003. "A Nation Apart," May 6, www. economist.com/surveys/showsurvey.cfm? issue520031108, accessed 12/29/04.

Edin, K.; and Lein, L. 1997. "Work, welfare, and single mothers' economic survival strategies." *American Sociological Review,* vol. 62, no. 2.

_____; and Maria Kefalas. 2005. *Promises I Can Keep: Why Poor Women Put Motherhood before Marriage.* Berkeley: University of California Press.

Efron, Sonni. 1997. "Eating disorders go global," Los Angeles Times, October 18, p. A-1.

Ehrlich, Paul. 1968. *The Population Bomb.* New York: Ballantine Books.

Eibl-Eibesfeldt, I. 1972. "Similarities and differences between cultures in expressive movements," in Robert A. Hinde, ed., *Nonverbal Communication.* New York: Cambridge University Press.

Eisen, Arnold M. 1983. *The Chosen People in America: A Study in Jewish Religious Ideology.* Bloomington, IN: Indiana University Press.

Eisenhower Library. 1961. "Farewell Address," Abilene, Kansas: The Dwight D. Eisenhower Presidential Library. www. eisenhower.utexas.edu/farewell.htm, accessed 12/29/04.

Ekman, Paul; and Friesen, W. V. 1978. *Facial Action Coding System.* New York: Consulting Psychologists Press.

el Dareer, Asma. 1982. *Woman, Why Do You Weep? Circumcision and Its Consequences.* Westport, CT: Zed.

Elias, Norbert. 1987. *Involvement and Detachment.* London: Oxford University Press.

_____; and Dunning, E. 1987. *Quest for Excitement: Sport and Leisure in the Civilizing Process.* Oxford, UK: Blackwell.

Ell, Kathleen. 1996. "Social networks, social support, and coping with serious illness: The family connection." *Social Science and Medicine,* vol. 42.

Ellsworth American. 2001. "Laptop Computers for Students," editorial, *Ellsworth American,* www. ellsworthamerican.com/archive/ edit2001/02_01/ea_edit2-02-08-01.html, accessed 1/10/05.

Ellwood, David; and Christopher Jencks. 2004. "The Uneven Spread of Single-Parent Families: What Do We Know? Where Do We Look for Answers?" in *Social Inequality,* edited by Kathryn M. Neckerman. New York: Russell Sage Foundation.

Elshtain, Jean Bethke. 1981. *Public Man: Private Woman.* Princeton, NJ: Princeton University Press.

Elwert, Felix. 2005. "How Cohabitation Does—and Does Not—Reduce the Risk of Divorce." Unpublished Manuscript.

Emmanuel, Arghiri. 1972. *Unequal Exchange: A Study of the Imperialism of Trade.* New York: Monthly Review Press.

Encyclopedia Britannica. 2006. "Religion" *Britannica Book of the Year,* 2005. Retrieved January 23, 2006, from Encyclopædia Britannica Online http:// search.eb.com/eb/article-9398490

England, Paula. 1992. *Comparable Worth: Theories and Evidence.* New York: Aldine de Gruyter.

Epstein, Gene. 2003. "More women advance, but sexism persists," *Barron's.* Available at www.collegejournal.com/successwork/ workplacediversity/20030605=Epstein. html, accessed spring 2006.

Equal Employment Opportunity Commission (EEOC). 1993. "National database fiscal year 1983 to fiscal year 1992." Washington, DC: Equal Employment Opportunity Commission.

Ericson, Richard; and Haggerty, Kevin. 1997. *Policing the Risk Society.* Toronto: University of Toronto Press.

Erikson, Kai. 1966. *Wayward Puritans: A Study in the Sociology of Deviance.* New York: Wiley.

Erikson, R.; and Goldthorpe, J. H. 1992. *The Constant Flux: A Study of Class Mobility in Industrial Societies.* Oxford, UK: Oxford University Press.

Estes, Carol L. 1986. "The politics of aging in America." *Aging and Society,* vol. 6.

_____. 1991. "The Reagan legacy: Privatization, the welfare state, and aging," in J. Myles and J. Quadagno, eds., *States, Labor Markets, and the Future of Old Age Policy.* Philadelphia: Temple University Press.

_____; Binney, Elizabeth A.; and Culbertson, Richard A. 1992. "The gerontological imagination: Social influences on the development of gerontology, 1945–present." *Aging and Human Development,* vol. 35.

_____; Swan, J.; and Gerard, L. 1982. "Dominant and competing paradigms in gerontology: Toward a political economy of aging." *Aging and Society,* vol. 2.

_____, et al. 1984. *Political Economy, Health, and Aging.* Boston: Little, Brown.

Estrich, Susan. 1987. *Real Rape.* Cambridge, MA: Harvard University Press.

Etzioni-Halévy, Eva. 1985. *Bureaucracy and Democracy: A Political Dilemma.* New York: Routledge, Chapman and Hall.

Europa: Gateway to the European Union. 2000. "European enlargement: A historical opportunity." http://europa.eu. int/comm/enlargement/docs/newsletter/ weekly_070700.htm, accessed 1/10/05.

_____. 2004. http://europa.eu/abc/history/ index_en.htm, accessed spring 2006.

Evans, Peter. 1979. *Dependent Development.* Princeton, NJ: Princeton University Press.

_____. 1987. "Class, state, and dependence in East Asia: Some lessons for Latin Americanists," in F. C. Deyo, ed., *The Political Economy of the New Asian Industrialism.* Ithaca, NY: Cornell University Press.

_____. 1995. *Embedded Autonomy: States and Industrial Transformation.* Princeton, NJ: Princeton University Press.

Evans, Richard J. 1977. *The Feminists: Women's Emancipation Movements in Europe, America, and Australasia, 1840–1920.* New York: Barnes & Noble.

Evans-Pritchard, E. E. 1956. *Nuer Religion.* New York: Oxford University Press.

_____. 1970. "Sexual inversion among the Azande." *American Anthropologist,* vol. 72.

Falk, G.; Falk, U.; and Tomashevich, V. 1981. *Aging in America and Other Cultures.* Saratoga, CA: Century Twenty-One.

Fallows, Deborah and Leed Rainic. 2005. "The Internet as a Unique News Source." Pew Internet & American Life Project. www.pewinternet.org/pdfs/PIP_News_ Images_July04.pdf, accessed 1/9/06.

Farley, Maggie. 1998. "Women in the new China." *Los Angeles Times,* November 22.

Farley, Reynolds; and Frey, William H. 1994. "Change in the segregation of whites from blacks during the 1980s: Small steps toward a more integrated society." *American Sociological Review,* vol. 59, no. 1.

Farrell, Lynsey. 2005. Sociologists Without Borders Field Report www.sociologists withoutborders.org/essays/SSF%20 Report.pdf, accessed spring 2006.

Featherman, David L.; and Hauser, Robert M. 1978. *Opportunity and Change.* New York: Academic Press.

Featherstone, Liza.2000. "The New Student Movement." *The Nation,* May 15.

FEC. 2001. "PAC activity increases in 2000 election cycle," Federal Election Commission, News releases, Media Advisories (May 31), www.fec.gov/press/

press2001/053101pacfund/053101pacfund. html, accessed 1/11/05.

Federal Bureau of Investigation. 2005a. "Crime in the United States, 2004." The Uniform Crime Report. Table 41. www.fbi. gov/ucr/cius_04/persons_arrested/table_ 38-43.html#table41.

——. 2005b. "Uniform Crime Report." Table 1. www.fbi.gov/ucr/cius_04/ offenses_reported/offense_tabulations/ table_01-01a.html. Accessed October 17, 2005.

——. 2005c. "Crime in the United States, 2004." The Uniform Crime Report. Table 42. www.fbi.gov/ucr/cius_04/index.html.

——. 2005d. "Crime in the United States, 2004." The Uniform Crime Report. Table 38. www.fbi.gov/ucr/cius_04/persons_ arrested/table_38-43.html.

Federal Interagency Forum on Aging-Related Statistics. 2004a. "Older Americans 2004: Key Indicators of Well-Being." Federal Interagency Forum on Aging-Related Statistics, Washington, DC: U.S. Government Printing Office. November.

——. 2004b. "Older Americans 2004: Key Indicators of Well-Being." Indicator 15. Federal Interagency Forum on Aging-Related Statistics, Washington, DC: U.S. Government Printing Office. November.

——. 2004c. "Older Americans 2004: Key Indicators of Well-Being." Indicator 20. Federal Interagency Forum on Aging-Related Statistics, Washington, DC: U.S. Government Printing Office. November.

Federal Register. 2005. Vol. 70, No. 33, February 18, pp. 8373-8375. http:// frwebgate3.access.gpo.gov/cgibin/ waisgate.cgi?WAISdocID= 66100220387+0+0+0&WAISaction= retrieve, accessed spring 2006.

Ferguson, Kathy E. 1984. The Feminist Case against Bureaucracy. Philadelphia: Temple University Press.

Fernandez Kelly, Maria Particia. 1987. "Women and International Development: Issues for a Feminist Agenda," Women's Studies Quarterly XIV 3/4:2-6.

Fidler, David P. 2001. "Neither Science Nor Shamans: Globalization of Markets and Health in the Developing World," Indiana Journal of Global Legal Studies 7 (2001): 191.

Filkins, Dexter. 1998. "Afghans pay dearly for peace." Los Angeles Times, October 22, p. A-1.

Finke, Roger; and Stark, Rodney. 1988. "Religious economies and sacred canopies: Religious mobilization in American cities, 1906." American Sociological Review, vol. 53.

——. 1992. The Churching of America, 1776-1990: Winners and Losers in Our Religious Economy. New Brunswick, NJ: Rutgers University Press.

Finley, Nancy J.; Diane Roberts; and Benjamin F. Banahan. 1988. "Motivators and Inhibitors of Attitudes of Filial Obligation Toward Aging Parents." The Gerontologist 28:73-78.

Firestone, Shulamith. 1971. The Dialectic of Sex. London: Paladin.

Fischer, Claude S. 1984. The Urban Experience. 2nd ed. New York: Harcourt Brace Jovanovich.

——, et al. 1996. Inequality by Design: Cracking the Bell Curve Myth. Princeton, NJ: Princeton University Press.

Fisher, Bonnie S.; Cullen, Francis T.; and Turner, Michael G. 2000. The Sexual Victimization of College Women. Washington, DC: U.S. Department of Justice, National Institute of Justice, Bureau of Justice Statistics (December), NJJ 182369, www.ncjrs.org/pdffiles1/nij/ 182369.pdf, accessed 12/29/04.

Foner, Nancy. 1984. Ages in Conflict: A Cross-Cultural Perspective on Inequality between Old and Young. New York: Columbia University Press.

Forbes. 2005. "The Forbes 400." www.forbes. com/free_forbes/2005/1010/089.html, accessed spring 2006.

Ford, Clellan S.; and Beach, Frank A. 1951. Patterns of Sexual Behavior. New York: Harper and Row.

Forrest, Drew; and Streek, Barry. 2001. "Mbeki in bizarre AIDS outburst" Daily Mail and Guardian (Johannesburg) October 26. www.aegis.com/news/dmg/ 2001/MG011021.html, accessed 12/29/04.

Fortune. 2005. "Global 500." http://money. cnn.com/magazines/fortune/global500, accessed 1/10/06.

Foucault, Michel. 1971. The Order of Things: An Archaeology of the Human Sciences. New York: Pantheon.

——. 1979. Discipline and Punish: The Birth of the Prison. New York: Random House.

——. 1987. The Use of Pleasure. Harmondsworth, UK: Penguin.

——. 1988. "Technologies of the self," in Luther H. Martin, Huck Gutman, and Patrick H. Hutton, eds., Technologies of the Self: A Seminar with Michel Foucault. Amherst, MA: University of Massachusetts Press.

Fox, Oliver C. 1964. "The pre-industrial city reconsidered." Sociological Quarterly, vol. 5.

Frank, Andre Gundar. 1966. "The development of underdevelopment." Monthly Review, vol. 18.

——. 1969a. Latin America: Underdevelopment or Revolution. New York: Monthly Review Press.

——. 1969b. Capitalism and Underdevelopment in Latin America: Historical Studies of Chile and Brazil. New York: Monthly Review Press.

——. 1979. Dependent Accumulation and Underdevelopment. London: Macmillan.

Frank, David John; and McEneaney, Elizabeth H. 1999. "The individualization of society and the liberalization of state policies on same-sex sexual relations, 1984-1995." Social Forces, vol. 7, no. 3.

Free the Children. 1998. www.freethe children.org, accessed 12/29/04.

Freedom House. 2005a. "Electoral Democracies, 2005" www.freedomhouse. org/template.cfm?page=205&year=2005, accessed 1/9/06.

——. 2005b. "Map of Freedom, 2005" www.freedomhouse.org/template.cfm? page=20&year=2005, accessed 1/9/06.

Freeman, Richard B. 1999. The New Inequality: Creating Solutions for Poor America. Boston: Beacon Press.

——; and Rogers, Joel. 1999. What Workers Want. Ithaca, NY: ILR Press and Russell Sage Foundation.

Freidson, Eliot. 1970. Profession of Medicine: A Study of the Sociology of Applied Knowledge. New York: Dodd, Mead.

Fremlin, J. H. 1964. "How many people can the world support?" New Scientist, (October 19).

French, Howard W. 2001a. "Diploma at hand, Japanese women find glass ceiling reinforced with iron." New York Times, January 1, p. A1.

——. 2001b. "Japan's new premier picks precedent-setting cabinet." New York Times, April 27, p. A1.

Frey, William; and Liaw, Kao-Lee. 1998. "The impact of recent immigration on population redistribution in the United States," in James Smith and Barry Edmonston, eds., The Immigration Debate. Washington, DC: National Academy Press.

Friedan, Betty. 1963. The Feminine Mystique. New York: Norton.

Friedlander, Daniel; and Burtless, Gary. 1994. Five Years After: The Long-Term Effects of

Welfare-to-Work Programs. New York: Russell Sage.

Friedman, R.A.; and Currall, S.C. 2003. "Conflict Escalation: Dispute Exacerbating Elements of E-mail Communication." *Human Relations* 56(11): 1325–1347.

Friedman, Thomas. 2000. *The Lexus and the Olive Tree: Understanding Globalization.* New York: Anchor.

———. 2005. *The World is Flat: A Brief History of the Twenty-First Century.* New York: Farrar, Straus and Giroux.

Fries, James F. 1980. "Aging, natural death, and the compression of morbidity." *New England Journal of Medicine,* vol. 303.

Frobel, Folker; Heinrichs, Jurgen; and Kreye, Otto. 1979. *The New International Division of Labor.* New York: Cambridge University Press.

Fry, C. L. 1980. *Aging in Culture and Society.* New York: Bergin.

Fryer, David; and McKenna, Stephen. 1987. "The laying off of hands—unemployment and the experience of time," in Stephen Fineman, ed., *Unemployment: Personal and Social Consequences.* London: Tavistock.

Fulford, Robert. 1997. "Radical Dreamer: Jane Jacobs on the streets of Toronto" *Azure,* October–November.

Furstenberg, Frank F., Jr.; and Cherlin, Andrew J. 1991. *Divided Families.* Cambridge, MA: Harvard University Press.

Gallup Organization. 2005. "The Death Penalty." http://poll.gallup.com/content/default.aspx?ci=1606, accessed 10/17/05.

———. 1998. Gallup/CNN/USA Today Poll, July 21.

Gamoran, Adam, et al. 1995. "An organizational analysis of the effects of ability grouping." *American Educational Research Journal,* vol. 32, no. 4.

Gans, Herbert J. 1979. "Symbolic ethnicity: The future of ethnic groups and cultures in America." *Ethnic and Racial Studies,* vol. 2 (January).

Ganzeboom, H. B. G.; Luijkx, R.; and Treiman, D. 1989. "Intergenerational class mobility in comparative perspective." *Research in Social Stratification and Mobility,* vol. 8.

Gardner, Carol Brooks. 1995. *Passing By: Gender and Public Harassment.* Berkeley and Los Angeles: University of California Press.

Garfinkel, Harold. 1963. "A conception of, and experiments with, 'trust' as a condition of stable concerted actions," in O. J. Harvey,

ed., *Motivation and Social Interaction.* New York: Ronald Press.

Garland, D. 2002. *The Culture of Control: Crime and Social Order in Contemporary Society.* Chicago: University of Chicago Press.

Gavron, Hannah. 1966. *The Captive Wife: Conflicts of Housebound Mothers.* London: Routledge and Kegan Paul.

Geary, Dick. 1981. *European Labor Protest, 1848–1939.* New York: St. Martin's Press.

Geertz, Clifford. 1973. *The Interpretation of Cultures.* New York: Basic Books.

———. 1983. *Local Knowledge: Further Essays in Interpretative Anthropology.* New York: Basic Books.

Gelb, I. J. 1952. *A Study of Writing.* Chicago: University of Chicago Press.

Gelles, Richard; and Cornell, C. P. 1990. *Intimate Violence in Families.* 2nd ed. Newbury Park, CA: Sage.

Gellner, Ernest. 1983. *Nations and Nationalism.* Ithaca, NY: Cornell University Press.

General Social Survey (GSS). 1997. "General Social Surveys, 1972–1994: [Cumulative File]." Accessed and Analyzed online through the University of Michigan Interuniversity Consortium for Political and Social Research (ICPSR), http://webapp.icpsr.umich.edu/cocoon/ICPSR-STUDY/03728.xml, accessed 1/10/05.

Gereffi, Gary. 1995. "Contending paradigms for cross-regional comparison: Development strategies and commodity chains in East Asia and Latin America," in Peter II. Smith, ed., *Latin America in Comparative Perspective: New Approaches to Methods and Analysis.* Boulder, CO: Westview Press.

———. 1996. "Commodity chains and regional divisions of labor in East Asia." *Journal of Asian Business,* vol. 12, no. 1.

Gershuny, Jonathan, et al., 1994. "The domestic labor revolution: A process of lagged adaptation," in Michael Anderson, Frank Bechofer, and Jonathan Gershuny, eds., *The Social and Political Economy of the Household.* Oxford, UK: Oxford University Press.

———; and Miles, I. D. 1983. *The New Service Economy: The Transformation of Employment in Industrial Societies.* London: Francis Pinter.

Gerth, Ulrika G. 2005. "Video Game Violence a 'Risk Factor' for Children," *Foster's Daily Democrat,* January 16.

Gibbs, Nancy. 2005. "A Female Midlife Crisis?" *Time,* May 16.

Gibson, P. 1989. "Gay male and lesbian youth suicide." Report of the Secretary's Task

Force on Youth Suicide. Washington, D.C.: U.S. Department of Health and Human Services.

Giddens, Anthony. 1984. *The Constitution of Society.* Cambridge, UK: Polity Press.

———. 1990. *The Consequences of Modernity.* Cambridge, UK: Polity Press.

———. 1998. *The Third Way: The Renewal of Social Democracy.* Cambridge, UK: Polity Press.

Gilligan, Carol. 1982. *In a Different Voice: Psychological Theory and Women's Development.* Cambridge, MA: Harvard University Press.

Ginzburg, Carlo. 1980. *The Cheese and the Worms.* London: Routledge and Kegan Paul.

Gitlin, Todd. 2000. "C. Wright Mills, Free Radical" in *The Intellectuals and the Flag.* New York: Columbia University Press, 2006.

Giuffre, Patti A.; and Williams, Christine L. 1994. "Boundary lines: Labeling sexual harassment in restaurants." *Gender and Society,* vol. 8.

Gladwell, Malcolm. 2000. "Designs for Working," *New Yorker,* December 11.

Glascock, A.; and Feinman, S. 1981. "Social asset or social burden: An analysis of the treatment for the aged in non-industrial societies," in C. L. Fry, ed., *Dimensions: Aging, Culture, and Health.* New York: Praeger.

Glasius, M.; M. Kaldor; and H. Anheier, eds. 2002. *Global Civil Society.* Oxford, UK: Oxford University Press.

Glassner, Barry. 1999. *The Culture of Fear: Why Americans Are Afraid of the Wrong Things.* New York: Basic Books.

Glenn, Evelyn Nakano. 1994. "Introduction," in Grace Change, Linda Rennie Forcey, and Evelyn Nakano Glenn, eds., *Mothering: Ideology, Experience, and Agency.* New York: Routledge.

The Global Fund. 2005. "Fighting AIDS." www.theglobalfund.org/en/about/aids/default.asp, accessed 1/19/06.

Glock, Charles Y. 1976. "On the origin and evolution of religious groups," in Charles Y. Glock and Robert N. Bellah, eds., *The New Religious Consciousness.* Berkeley, CA: University of California Press.

Glueck, Sheldon W.; and Glueck, Eleanor. 1956. *Physique and Delinquency.* New York: Harper and Row.

Gober, Patricia. 1993. *Americans on the Move.* Washington, DC: Population Reference Bureau.

Goe, W. Richard. 1994. "The producer services sector and development within the deindustrializing urban community." *Social Forces,* vol. 72.

Goffman, Erving. 1967. *Interaction Ritual.* New York: Doubleday/Anchor.

_____. 1971. *Relations in Public: Microstudies of the Public Order.* New York: Basic Books.

_____. 1973. *The Presentation of Self in Everyday Life.* New York: Overlook Press.

_____. 1981. *Forms of Talk.* Philadelphia: University of Pennsylvania Press.

Gold, T. 1986. *State and Society in the Taiwan Miracle.* Armonk, NY: M. E. Sharpe.

Goldberg, Carey. 1997. "Hispanic households struggle amid broad decline in income." *New York Times,* January 30, pp. A1, A16.

_____. 2001. "School computer money approved," *New York Times,* July 27.

Goldberg, David J.; and John D. Rayner. 1987. *The Jewish People: Their History and Their Religion.* New York: Penguin Books.

Goldin, Claudia Dale. 1990. *Understanding the Gender Gap: An Economic History of American Women.* New York: Oxford University Press.

Goldscheider, Frances K. 1990. "The aging of the gender revolution: What do we know and what do we need to know?" *Research on Aging,* vol. 12.

_____; and Goldscheider, Calvin. 1999. *The Changing Transition to Adulthood: Leaving and Returning Home.* Thousand Oaks, CA: Sage.

_____; and Waite, Linda J. 1991. *New Families, No Families? The Transformation of the American Home.* Berkeley, CA: University of California Press.

Goldstein, Joshua, and Ann Morning. 2000. "The Multiple-Race Population of the United States: Issues and Estimates." *Proceedings of the National Academy of Sciences* 97(11): 6230–6235.

Goldstein, Sidney; and Goldstein, Alice. 1996. *Jews on the Move: Implications for Jewish Identity.* Albany, NY: SUNY Press.

Gonnerman, J. 2004. *Life on the Outside: The Prison Odyssey of Elaine Bartlett.* New York: Farrar Straus and Giroux.

Goode, William J. 1963. *World Revolution in Family Patterns.* New York: Free Press.

_____. 1971. "Force and violence in the family," *Journal of Marriage and the Family,* vol. 33.

Goodhardt, G. J.; Ehrenberg, A. S. C.; and Collins, M. A. 1987. *The Television Audience: Patterns of Voting.* 2nd ed. London: Gower.

Gorz, Andre. 1982. *Farewell to the Working Class.* London: Pluto.

Gottfredson, Michael R.; and Hirschi, Travis. 1990. *A General Theory of Crime.* Stanford, CA: Stanford University Press.

Graham, Heather. 1987. "Women's smoking and family health." *Social Science and Medicine,* vol. 25.

_____. 1994. "Gender and class as dimensions of smoking behavior: Insights from a survey of mothers." *Social Science and Medicine,* vol. 38.

Graham, Laurie. 1995. *On the Line at Subaru-Isuzu.* Ithaca, NY: Cornell University Press.

Granovetter, Mark. 1973. "The strength of weak ties." *American Journal of Sociology,* vol. 78.

Grasmuck, Sherri. 2005. *Protecting Home: Class, Race, and Masculinity in Boys' Baseball.* New Brunswick: Rutgers University Press.

Grassroots. 1989. "Why Did They Kill David Webster?" Vol 10 No 2 http://disa.nu.ac.za/articledisplaypage.asp?filename=GRMay89&articletitle=Why+did+they+kill+David+Webster%3F, accessed spring 2006.

Gray, J. 2003. *Al Qaeda and What It Means to be Modern.* Chatham, UK: Faber and Faber.

Greeley, Andrew. 1989. *Religious Change in America.* Cambridge, MA: Harvard University Press.

Green, F. 1987. *The "Sissy Boy" Syndrome and the Development of Homosexuality.* New Haven, CT: Yale University Press.

Green, John C. 2004. "The American Religious Landscape and Political Attitudes: A Baseline for 2004." The Pew Forum on Religion & Public Life. Table 1 http://pewforum.org/publications/surveys/green-full.pdf, accessed 1/23/06.

Greenberg, Jan S.; and Becker, Marion. 1988. "Aging parents as family resources." *Gerontologist,* vol. 28.

Greenhouse, Steven; and Constance L. Hays. 2004. "Wal-Mart Sex-Bias Suit Given Class-Action Status," *New York Times,* June 23.

Griffin, Susan. 1979. *Rape, the Power of Consciousness.* New York: Harper and Row.

Grint, Keith. 1991. *The Sociology of Work.* Cambridge, UK: Polity Press.

Gross, Jane. 1992. "Suffering in silence no more: Fighting sexual harassment." *New York Times,* July 13, p. A1.

Grusky, David B.; and Sorensen, J. B. 1998. "Can class analysis be salvaged?" *American Journal of Sociology,* vol. 103, no. 5.

The Guardian. 2002. "Top 1% earn as much as the poorest 57%" www.guardian.co.uk/business/story/0,,635292,00.html, accessed 1/10/05.

Gubrium, Jabber F. 1986. *Oldtimers and Alzheimer's: The Descriptive Organization of Senility.* Greenwich, CT: JAI Press.

_____. 1991. *The Mosaic of Care: Frail Elderly and Their Families in the Real World.* New York: Springer.

_____. 1993. *Speaking of Life: Horizons of Meaning for Nursing Home Residents.* Hawthorne, NY: Aldine de Gruyter.

_____; and Sankar, Andrea, eds. 1994. *Qualitative Methods in Aging Research.* Newbury Park, CA: Sage.

Guibernau, Montserrat. 1999. *Nations without States: Political Communities in a Global Age.* Cambridge, MA: Blackwell.

Guynup, Sharon. 2004. "Scarification: Ancient Body Art Leaving New Marks." National Geographic Channel, July 28. http://news.nationalgeographic.com/news/2004/07/0728_040728_tvtabooscars.html, accessed spring 2006.

Habermas, Jürgen. 1975. *Legitimation Crisis.* Trans. Thomas McCarthy. Boston: Beacon Press.

_____. 1989. *The Structural Transformation of the Public Sphere: An Inquiry into a Category of Bourgeois Society.* Cambridge, UK: Polity Press.

Haddad, Yvonne Y. 1979. "The Muslim Experience in the United States." *The Link,* September–October, Volume 12, Issue 4.

Hadden, Jeffrey. 1990. "Precursors to the globalization of American televangelism," *Social Compass,* vol. 37 (March): 161–67.

_____. 1997a. "The concepts 'cult' and 'sect' in scholarly research and public discourse." New Religious Movements website, http://religiousmovements.lib.virginia.edu/cultsect/concult.htm, accessed 1/10/05.

_____. 1997b. "New religious movements mission statement." New Religious Movements website, http://religousmovements.lib.virginia.edu/welcome/mission.htm, accessed 1/10/05.

_____; and Shupe, Anson. 1987. "Televangelism in America," *Social Compass,* vol. 34, no. 1: 61–75.

_____. 2004. Religious Broadcasting website, "Televangelism." http://religiousbroadcasting.lib.virginia.edu/televangelism.html, accessed 1/3/05.

Hagan, John; and McCarthy, Bill. 1992. "Mean streets: The theoretical significance of situational delinquency among homeless youth." *American Sociological Review,* vol. 98.

Haggard, Stephan. 1990. *Pathways from the Periphery: The Politics of Growth in Newly Industrializing Countries.* Ithaca, NY: Cornell University Press.

Hall, Edward T. 1969. *The Hidden Dimension.* New York: Doubleday.

_____. 1973. *The Silent Language.* New York: Doubleday.

Hall, Stuart. 1992. "The question of cultural identity," in Stuart Hall, David Held, and Tony McGrew, eds., *Modernity and Its Futures.* Cambridge, UK: Polity Press.

_____, et al. 1988. "New times." *Marxism Today,* October.

Halpern, Carolyn Tucker, et al. 2000. "Smart teens don't have sex (or kiss much either)." *Journal of Adolescent Health,* vol. 26, no. 3.

Hamel, G. 1991. "Competition for competence and inter-partner learning within international strategic alliances." *Strategic Management Journal,* summer supplement, vol. 12.

Hamilton, Martha M. 2000. "Web retailer Kozmo accused of redlining; Exclusion of D.C. minority areas cited." *Washington Post,* April 14.

Hammond, Phillip E. 1992. *Religion and Personal Autonomy: The Third Disestablishment in America.* Columbia, SC: University of South Carolina Press.

Handy, Charles. 1994. *The Empty Raincoat: Making Sense of the Future.* London: Hutchinson.

Hansen, Kristin A. 1995. "Geographical mobility: March 1993 to March 1994," in U.S. Bureau of the Census, Current Population Reports, P20–485. Washington, DC: U.S. Government Printing Office.

Hare, A. Paul; Borgatta, Edgar F.; and Bales, Robert F. 1965. *Small Groups: Studies in Social Interaction.* New York: Knopf.

Harknett, Kristen; and Sara McLanahan. 2004. "Racial and Ethnic Differences in Marriage after the Birth of a Child." *American Sociological Review* 69:790–811.

Harris, D. 2003."Racial classification and the 2000 census." Commissioned paper, Panel to Review the 2000 Census, Committee on National Statistics. University of Michigan, Ann Arbor.

Harris, David R. and Jeremiah Joseph Sim. 2000. "An Empirical Look at the Social Construction of Race: The Case of Mixed-Race Adolescents." Population Studies Center Research Report 00-452, University of Michigan.

Harris, Judith Rich. 1998. *The Nurture Assumption: Why Children Turn Out the Way They Do.* New York: Free Press.

Harris, Marvin. 1975. *Cows, Pigs, Wars, and Riches: The Riddles of Culture.* New York: Random House.

_____. 1978. *Cannibals and Kings: The Origins of Cultures.* New York: Random House.

_____. 1980. *Cultural Materialism: The Struggle for a Science of Culture.* New York: Vintage Books.

Hartig, Terry; Gunn Johansson; Camilla Kylin. 2003. "Residence in the Social Ecology of Stress and Restoration," *Journal of Social Issues* 59 (3), 611–636.

Hartman, Chris. 2000. "Facts and figures on wealth." Inequality.org, www.inequality. org/factsfr.html, accessed 1/3/05.

Hartman, Mary; and Banner, Lois, eds. 1974. *Clio's Consciousness Raised: New Perspectives on the History of Women.* New York: Norton.

Hartman, Moshe; and Hartman, Harriet. 1996. *Gender Equality and American Jews.* Albany: SUNY Press.

_____; and Swann, Charles. 1981. *Prime Time Preachers: The Rising Tide of Televangelism.* Reading, MA: Addison-Wesley.

Hartmann, Heidi I., et al. 1985. "An agenda for basic research on comparable worth," in H. I. Hartmann et al., eds., *Comparable Worth: New Directions for Research.* Washington, DC: National Academy Press.

Harvard Magazine. 2000. "The world's poor: A Harvard Magazine roundtable." Vol. 103, no. 2. www.harvard-magazine.com/ on-line/1100134.html, accessed 1/11/03.

Harvey, David. 1973. *Social Justice and the City.* Oxford, UK: Blackwell.

_____. 1982. *The Limits to Capital.* Oxford, UK: Blackwell.

_____. 1985. *Consciousness and the Urban Experience: Studies in the History and Theory of Capitalist Urbanization.* Oxford, UK: Blackwell.

_____. 1989. *The Condition of Postmodernity.* Cambridge, MA: Blackwell.

Hatch, Nathan O. 1989. *The Democratization of American Christianity.* New Haven, CT: Yale University Press.

Hathaway. 1997. "Marijuana and tolerance: Revisiting Becker's sources of control." *Deviant Behavior,* vol. 18, no. 2.

Haugen, Einar. 1977. "Linguistic relativity: Myths and methods," in William C. McCormack and Stephen A. Wurm, eds., *Language and Thought: Anthropological Issues.* The Hague: Mouton.

Hauser, Robert M. 1999. "What if we ended social promotion?" *Education Week* (April 7).

Hawkes, Terence. 1977. *Structuralism and Semiotics.* Berkeley, CA: University of California Press.

Hawley, Amos H. 1950. *Human Ecology: A Theory of Community Structure.* New York: Ronald Press Company.

_____. 1968. "Human ecology," in *International Encyclopedia of Social Science,* vol. 4. New York: Free Press.

Hayflick, Leonard. 1994. *How and Why We Age.* New York: Ballantine Books.

Hays, Sharon. 2000. "Constructing the centrality of culture—and deconstructing sociology?" *Contemporary Sociology,* vol. 29, no. 4.

Healthful Life Project. 2003. "The World's Ageing Population and Scientific Attempts to Make it an Even Greater Problem." http://healthfullife.umdnj.edu/ archives/aging_pop%20_archive.htm, accessed 12/7/05.

Healy, Melissa. 2001. "Pieces of the puzzle." *Los Angeles Times,* http://pqasb. pqarchiver.com/latimes/results.html? RQT=511&sid=1&firstIndex= 460& PQACnt=1, accessed 1/10/05.

Hecht, Jeff. 2003. "New Life for Undersea Fiber," *Technology Review,* Massachusetts Institute of Technology, May 16. www. techreview.com/NanoTech/wtr_13185, 318,p1.html, accessed spring 2006.

Hecker, Daniel. 2004. "Occupational Employment Projections to 2012." *Monthly Labor Review Online.* February, vol. 127 (2) pp. 80–105. www.bls.gov/opub/ mlr/2004/02/art5full.pdf, accessed spring 2006.

Heelas, Paul. 1996. *The New Age Movement.* Oxford: Blackwell.

Heidensohn, Frances. 1985. *Women and Crime.* London: Macmillan.

Heise, David R. 1987. "Sociocultural determination of mental aging," in Carmi Schooler and K. Warner Schaie, eds., *Cognitive Functioning and Social Structure Over the Life Course.* Norwood, NJ: Ablex.

Held, David. 1987. *Models of Democracy.* Stanford, CA: Stanford University Press.

_____, et al. 1999. *Global Transformations: Politics, Economics, and Culture.* Cambridge, UK: Polity Press.

Helm, Leslie. 1992. "Debt puts squeeze on Japanese." *Los Angeles Times,* November 21.

Henderson, Jeffrey. 1989. *The Globalization of High Technology Production: Society, Space, and Semiconductors in the Restructuring of the Modern World.* London: Routledge.

———; and Appelbaum, Richard P. 1992. "Situating the state in the Asian development process," in Richard P. Appelbaum and Jeffrey Henderson, eds., *States and Development in the Asian Pacific Rim.* Newbury Park, CA: Sage.

Hendricks, J.; and Hatch, L. R. 1993. "Federal policy and family life of older Americans." In J. Hendricks & C.J. Rosenthal (Eds.) *The Remainder of Their Days: Impact of Public Policy on Older Families.* New York: Greenwood.

Hendricks, Jon. 1992. "Generation and the generation of theory in social gerontology." *Aging and Human Development,* vol. 35.

———; and Hendricks, C. Davis. 1986. *Aging in Mass Society: Myths and Realities.* Boston: Little, Brown.

Henry, William E. 1965. *Growing Older: The Process of Disengagement.* New York: Basic Books.

Henslin, James M.; and Biggs, Mae A. 1971. "Dramaturgical desexualization: The sociology of the vaginal examination," in James M. Henslin, ed., *Studies in the Sociology of Sex.* New York: Appleton-Century-Crofts.

———. 1997. "Behavior in public places: The sociology of the vaginal examination," in James M. Henslin, ed., *Down to Earth Sociology: Introductory Readings.* 9th ed. New York: Free Press.

Hentoff, Nat. 2002. "The FBI's magic lantern: Ashcroft can be in your computer," *The Village Voice,* May 24.

Herdt, Gilbert. 1981. *Guardians of the Flutes: Idioms of Masculinity.* New York: McGraw-Hill.

———. 1984. *Ritualized Homosexuality in Melanesia.* Berkeley, CA: University of California Press.

———. 1986. *The Sambia: Ritual and Gender in New Guinea.* New York: Holt, Rinehart and Winston.

———; and Davidson, J. 1988. "The Sambia 'urnim-man': Sociocultural and clinical aspects of gender formation in Papua, New Guinea." *Archives of Sexual Behavior,* vol. 17.

Heritage, John. 1985. *Garfinkel and Ethnomethodology.* New York: Basil Blackwell.

Hernandez, D. J. 1993. *America's Children: Resources from Family, Government, and Economy.* New York: Russell Sage Foundation.

Herrnstein, Richard J.; and Murray, Charles. 1994. *The Bell Curve: Intelligence and Class Structure in American Life.* New York: Free Press.

Hesse-Biber, Sharlene. 1997. *Am I Thin Enough Yet?: The Cult of Thinness and the Commercialization of Identity.* New York: Oxford University Press.

Hexham, Irvine; and Poewe, Karla. 1997. *New Religions as Global Cultures.* Boulder, CO: Westview Press.

Higginbotham, Elizabeth. 1992. "Making up with kin and community: Upward social mobility for black and white women." *Gender and Society,* vol. 6, no. 3.

Higher Education Research Institute (HERI). 1990. "The American freshman." Los Angeles: University of California.

Hirshci, Travis. 1969. *Causes of Delinquency.* Berkeley, CA: University of California Press.

Hirst, Paul. 1997. "The global economy: Myths and realities." *International Affairs,* vol. 73.

———; and Thompson, Grahame. 1992. "The problem of 'globalization': International economic relations, national economic management, and the formation of trading blocs." *Economy and Society,* vol. 24.

———. 1999. *Globalization in Question: The International Economy and the Possibilities of Governance.* Rev. ed. Cambridge, UK: Polity Press.

Ho, S. Y. 1990. *Taiwan: After a Long Silence.* Hong Kong: Asia Monitor Resource Center.

Hochschild, Arlie Russell. 1975. "Disengagement theory: A critique and proposal." *American Sociological Review,* vol. 40.

———. 1997. *The Time Bind.* New York: Metropolitan Books.

———; with Machung, Anne. 1989. *The Second Shift: Working Parents and the Revolution at Home.* New York: Viking.

Hodge, Robert; and Tripp, David. 1986. *Children and Television: A Semiotic Approach.* Cambridge, UK: Polity Press.

Hogan, Beatrice. 2000. "U.N.: Women's conference presses for political parity." Radio Free Europe, June.

Holmes, Steven A. 1996. "Quality of life is up for many blacks, data say." *New York Times,* November 18, p. A1.

———. 1997. "New reports say minorities benefit in fiscal recovery." *New York Times,* September 30, p. A1.

Holton, Robert J. 1978. "The crowds in history: Some problems of theory and method." *Social History,* vol. 3.

Homans, George. 1950. *The Human Group.* New York: Harcourt, Brace.

Homans, Hilary. 1987. "Man-made myth: The reality of being a woman scientist in the NHS," in Anne Spencer and David Podmore, eds., *In a Man's World: Essays on Women in Male-Dominated Professions.* London: Tavistock.

Honda Worldwide. 2002. "Honda Accord best-selling car in 2001 regains title after a decade." http://world.honda.com/news/2002/c020103_2.html, accessed 1/3/05.

Hood, James R. 2002. "More Abuse Seen as Elder Population Grows." *Caregiver USA News.* December 16. www.andthoushalt honor.org/news/abuse.html, accessed 12/7/05.

Hooks, Bell. 1981. *Ain't I a Woman: Black Women and Feminism.* Boston: South End Press.

———. 1996. *Bone Black: Memories of Girlhood.* New York: Henry Holt.

Hopkins, Terence K.; and Wallerstein, Immanuel. 1996. *The Age of Transition: Trajectory of the World-System, 1945–2025.* London: Zed Books.

Horrigan, John, et al. 2003. *The Ever-Shifting Internet Population: A New Look at Internet Access and the Digital Divide.* Washington, D.C.: The PEW Internet and American Life Project (April 16). www.pewinternet. org/ppt/PIP_Ever_Shifting_Internet_ Pop_NCI_NIH%206.25.03nn2.ppt, accessed 1/10/05.

Hotz, Robert Lee. 1998. "Boomers firing magic bullets at signs of aging." *Los Angeles Times,* May 4.

Hout, Michael. 1988. "More universalism, less structural mobility: The American occupational structure in the 1980s." *American Journal of Sociology,* vol. 93.

———. 1997. "Inequality at the margins: The effects of welfare, the minimum wage, and tax credits on low-wage labor markets." *Politics and Society* vol. 25 (December): 513–24.

———; and Lucas, Samuel R. 1996. "Education's role in reducing income disparities." *The Education Digest,* vol. 62, no. 3.

Howard, John H., et al. 1986. "Change in Type A behavior a year after retirement." *Gerontologist,* vol. 26.

Huber, Joan. 1990. "Macro-micro link in gender stratification," *American Sociological Review,* vol. 55.

———, ed. 1992. *Micro-Macro Linkages in Sociology.* Newbury Park, CA: Sage.

Hudson, Terese. 1995. "Medicaid's new crisis: Are we pitting the elderly against the poor?" *Hospitals and Health Networks,* May 20.

Hughes, Donna M. 2001. "The 'Natasha' Trade: Transnational Sex Trafficking." *National Institute of Justice Journal.* January, pps. 9–15.

Hughes, Everett C. 1945. "Dilemmas and contradictions of status." *American Journal of Sociology,* vol. 50.

Human Rights Watch. 1995. "The global report on women's human rights," www.hrw.org/about/projects/womrep/, accessed 1/3/05.

Humphreys, Laud. 1970. *Tearoom Trade: Impersonal Sex in Public Places.* Chicago: Aldine.

Hunter, James Davison. 1987. *Evangelism: The Coming Generation.* Chicago: University of Chicago Press.

Hunter, Lisa. 1990. *After Bereavement: A Study of Change in Attitudes about Life among Older Widows.* Ph.D. diss., The Fielding Institute, Santa Barbara, CA.

Huntington, Samuel P. 1991. *The Third Wave: Democratization in the Late Twentieth Century.* Norman, OK: University of Oklahoma Press.

———. 1993. "The Clash of Civilizations?" *Foreign Affairs* 72: 3 (summer): 22–49.

———. 1998. *The Clash of Civilizations and the Remaking of World Order.* New York: Simon & Schuster.

Hurtado, A. 1995. "Variation, combinations, and evolutions: Latino families in the United States," in R. Zambrana, ed., *Understanding Latino Families.* Thousand Oaks, CA: Sage.

Hyman, Herbert H.; and Singer, Eleanor. 1968. *Readings in Reference Group Theory and Research.* New York: Free Press.

Hyman, Richard. 1984. *Strikes.* 2nd ed. London: Fontana.

Illegems, V.; and Verbeke, A. 2004. "Telework: What does it mean for management?" *Long Range Planning,* 37(4): 319–334.

Illich, Ivan D. 1983. *Deschooling Society.* New York: Harper & Row.

InflationData.com. 2006. InflationCalculator. http://inflationdata.com/inflation/Inflation_Rate/InflationCalculator.asp, accessed spring 2006.

Inglehart, Ronald. 1997. *Modernization and Postmodernization: Cultural, Economic and Political Change in 43 Societies.* Princeton, NJ: Princeton University Press.

Institution for International Education (IIE). 2005. "U.S. Study Abroad Increases by 9.6%, Continues Record Growth," November 14. www.iie.org/Content/ NavigationMenu/Pressroom/Press Releases/U_S__STUDY_ABROAD_ INCREASES_BY_9_6_CONTINUES_ RECORD_GROWTH.htm, accessed spring 2006.

———. 2005. "Open Doors Online: Report on International Educational Exchange." http://opendoors.iienetwork.org/?p= 69736, accessed 1/20/06.

Intelligence Report. 2001. "Reevaluating the Net." Summer, no. 102. Montgomery, AL: The Southern Poverty Law Center.

International Campaign to Ban Land Mines (ICBL). 2001. www.icbl.org, accessed 1/3/05.

———. 2005. "Treaty Members." www.icbl. org, accessed 9/25/05.

International Centre for Prison Studies. 2005. "Entire World: Prison Population rates per 100,000 of National Population." www.prisonstudies.org/ accessed 10/5/05.

International Labor Organization (ILO). 2004a. "More Women are Entering the Global Labor Force Than Ever Before, But Job Equality, Poverty Reduction Remain Elusive." www.ilo.org/public/ english/bureau/inf/pr/2004/9.htm, accessed 12/4/05.

———. 2004b. "Breaking the Glass Ceiling: Women in Management." www.ilo.org/ dyn/gender/docs/RES/292/F267981337/ Breaking%20Glass%20PDF%20English. pdf, accessed 12/4/05.

———. 2000. "Statistical information and monitoring programme on child labour (SIMPOC): Overview and strategic plan 2000–2002." Prepared by the International Program on the Elimination of Child Labour (IPEC) and Bureau of Statistics (STAT), January.

———. 1999. C182 Worst Forms of Child Labour Convention, www.ilo.org/public/ english/standards/ipec/ratification/ convention/text.htm, accessed 1/11/05.

———. 1995. "Women work more, but are still paid less." Press release. www.ilo.org/ public/english/bureau/pr/1995/22.htm, accessed 1/11/05.

International Lesbian and Gay Association (ILGA). 2001. www.ilga.org, accessed 1/3/05.

———. 2005. "Working to Achieve Equal Rights on a Global Scale Since 1978." www.ilga.org/aboutilga.asp, accessed 1/29/06.

International Money Fund. 2005. *World Economic Lookout.* www.imf.org/external/ pubs/ft/weo/2005/01/pdf/chapter4.pdf, accessed spring 2006.

International Road Federation. 1987. *United Nations Annual Bulletin of Transport Statistics,* cited in *Social Trends* London: HMSO.

International Telework Association & Council (ITAC). 2004. "Telework Facts and Figures," www.telecommute.org/ resources/abouttelework.htm, accessed 1/20/05.

Internet Society (ISOC). 1997. "Web Languages Hit Parade," http://alis.isoc. org/palmares.en.html, accessed 1/11/05.

Internet World Stats. 2005. "Internet Usage Statistics—The Big Picture." www. internetworldstats.com/stats.htm, accessed 9/10/05.

———. 2005b. "Internet Users by Language." www.internetworldstats.com/ stats7.htm, accessed 9/10/05.

———. 2005c. "North America Internet Usage and Population." www.internet worldstats.com/stats2.htm#north, accessed 9/25/05.

———. 2005d. "Internet Usage Statistics for the Americas." www.internetworldstats. com/stats2.htm#north, accessed 1/9/06.

———. 2005e. "China." www.internetworld stats.com/asia/cn.htm, accessed 1/9/06.

———. 2006. "North American Internet Usage and Population." www.internet worldstats.com/stats2.htm#north, accessed spring 2006.

Iyer, Pico. 1989. *Video Night in Kathmandu.* New York: Vintage.

Jacobs, Jane. 1961. *The Death and Life of Great American Cities.* New York: Random House.

Jacoby, Sanford. 1997. *Modern Manors: Welfare Capitalism since the New Deal.* Princeton, NJ: Princeton University Press.

Jaher, Frederic Cople, ed. 1973. *The Rich, the Well Born, and the Powerful.* Urbana, IL: University of Illinois Press.

Janis, Irving L. 1972. *Victims of Groupthink.* Boston: Houghton Mifflin.

———. 1989. *Crucial Decisions: Leadership in Policy Making and Crisis Management.* New York: Free Press.

———; and Mann, Leon. 1977. *Decision Making: A Psychological Analysis of Conflict, Choice, and Commitment.* New York: Free Press.

Jencks, Christopher. 1994. *The Homeless.* Cambridge, MA: Harvard University Press.

———, et al. 1972. *Inequality: A Reassessment of the Effects of Family and School in America.* New York: Basic Books.

Jensen, Arthur. 1967. "How much can we boost IQ and scholastic achievement?" *Harvard Educational Review,* vol. 29.

———. 1979. *Bias in Mental Testing.* New York: Free Press.

Jobling, Ray. 1988. "The experience of psoriasis under treatment," in Michael Bury and Robert Anderson, eds., *Living with Chronic Illness: The Experience of Patients and Their Families.* London: Unwin Hyman.

John, M. T. 1988. *Geragogy: A Theory for Teaching the Elderly.* New York: Haworth.

Johnson, Mark; and Morton, J. 1991. *Biology and Cognitive Development: The Case of Face Recognition.* Oxford, UK: Blackwell.

Johnson, Michael P. 1995. "Patriarchal terrorism and common couple violence: Two forms of violence against women in U.S. families." *Journal of Marriage and the Family,* vol. 57.

Johnson-Odim, Cheryl. 1991. "Common themes, different contexts: Third World women and feminism," in Chandra Mohanty, et al., eds., *Third World Women and the Politics of Feminism.* Bloomington, IN: Indiana University Press.

Joint Center for Housing Studies. 2005. www.jchs.harvard.edu/publications/markets/son2005/son2005.pdf, accessed spring 2006.

———. 1994. *The State of the Nation's Housing.* Cambridge, MA: Harvard University Press.

Jones, Eric. 1998. "Globalism and the American tide." *National Interest,* vol. 53 (fall).

Jones, Jacqueline. 1986. *Labor of Love, Labor of Sorrow: Black Women, Work, and the Family from Slavery to the Present.* New York: Random House.

Jones, S. G. 1995. "Understanding community in the information age." in S. G. Jones, ed., *CyberSociety: Computer-Mediated Communication and Community.* Thousand Oaks, CA: Sage.

Jordan, Winthrop. 1968. *White over Black.* Chapel Hill: University of North Carolina Press.

Judge, Ken. 1995. "Income distribution and life expectancy: A critical appraisal." *British Medical Journal,* vol. 311.

Juergensmeyer, Mark. 1993. *The New Cold War? Religious Nationalism Confronts the Secular State.* Berkeley, CA: University of California Press.

———. 1994. *The New Cold War? Religious Nationalism Confronts the Secular State* (Comparative Studies in Religion and Society). Berkeley: University of California Press.

———. 1995a. *Radhasoami Reality: The Logic of a Modern Faith.* Princeton, NJ: Princeton University Press.

———. 1995b. "The New Religious State" *Comparative Politics,* Vol. 27, No. 4 July, pp. 379–391.

———. 2001. *Terror in the Mind of God: The Global Rise of Religious Violence.* Berkeley, CA: University of California Press.

Kaiser Family Foundation. 2005. "Trends and Indicators in the Changing Health Care Marketplace." www.kff.org/insurance/7031/print-sec1.cfm, accessed 12/7/05.

Kamp Dush, Claire et al. 2003. "The Relationship between Cohabitation and Marital Quality and Stability: Change across Cohorts?" *Journal of Marriage and the Family* 65:539–549.

Kanter, Rosabeth Moss. 1977. *Men and Women of the Corporation.* New York: Basic Books.

———. 1983. *The Change Masters: Innovation for Productivity in the American Corporation.* New York: Simon and Schuster.

———. 1991. "The future of bureaucracy and hierarchy in organizational theory," in Pierre Bourdieu and James Coleman, eds., *Social Theory for a Changing Society.* Boulder, CO: Westview.

Kasarda, John. 1993. "Urban industrial transition and the underclass," in William Julius Wilson, ed., *The Ghetto Underclass.* Newbury Park, CA: Sage.

———; and Crenshaw, Edward M. 1991. "Third World urbanization: Dimensions, theories, and determinants," in *Annual Review of Sociology 1991.* Vol. 17. Palo Alto, CA: Annual Reviews.

Karatnycky, Adrian. 2005. "Civic Power and Electoral Politics." Freedom House. www.freedomhouse.org/template.cfm?page=130&year=2005, accessed 1/9/06.

Katz, Jack. 1999. *How Emotions Work.* Chicago: University of Chicago Press.

Kedouri, Elie. 1992. *Politics in the Middle East.* New York: Oxford University Press.

Keister, Lisa A. 2000. *Wealth in America: Trends in Wealth Inequality.* New York: Cambridge University Press.

Kelling, George L.; and Coles, Catherine M. 1997. *Fixing Broken Windows: Restoring Order and Reducing Crime in Our Communities.* New York: The Free Press.

Kelley, Jonathan; and Evans, M. D. R. 1995. "Class and class conflict in six western nations." *American Review of Sociology,* vol. 60, no. 2.

Kelly, Liz. 1987. "The continuum of sexual violence," in Jala Hanmer and Mary Maynard, eds., *Women, Violence, and Social Control.* Atlantic Highlands, NJ: Humanities Press.

Kelly, Michael P. 1992. *Colitis: The Experience of Illness.* London: Routledge.

Kemp, Amanda, et al. 1995. "The dawn of a new day: Redefining South African feminism," in Amrita Basu, ed., *The Challenge of Local Feminisms.* Boulder, CO: Westview.

Kenway, Jane, et al. 1995. "Pulp fictions?: Education, markets, and the information superhighway." *Australian Educational Researcher,* vol. 22.

Kenworthy, Lane; and Malami, Melissa. 1999. "Gender inequality in political representation: A worldwide comparative analysis." *Social Forces,* vol. 78, no. 1.

Kern, Steven. 1983. *The Culture of Time and Space: 1880–1918.* Cambridge, MA: Harvard University Press.

Kerr, Clark, et al. 1960. *Industrialism and Industrial Man: The Problems of Labor and Management in Economic Growth.* Cambridge, MA: Harvard University Press.

Kiecolt, K. Jill; and Nelson, Hart M. 1991. "Evangelicals and party realignment, 1976–1988," *Social Science Quarterly,* vol. 72 (September).

Kinder, Marsha. 1993. *Playing with Power in Movies, Television, and Video Games.* Berkeley: University of California Press.

King, Nancy R. 1984. "Exploitation and abuse of older family members: An overview of the problem," in J. J. Cosa, ed., *Abuse of the Elderly.* Lexington, MA: Lexington Books.

Kinsey, Alfred C., et al. 1948. *Sexual Behavior in the Human Male.* Philadelphia: Saunders.

———. 1953. *Sexual Behavior in the Human Female.* Philadelphia: Saunders.

Kinsley, David. 1982. *Hinduism: A Cultural Perspective.* Englewood Cliffs, NJ: Prentice Hall.

Kjekshus, H. 1977. *Ecology, Control, and Economic Development in East African History.* Berkeley, CA: University of California Press.

Kling, Robert. 1996. "Computerization at work," in R. Kling, ed., *Computers and Controversy.* 2nd ed. New York: Academic Press.

Kluckhohn, Clyde. 1949. *Mirror for Man.* Tucson: University of Arizona Press.

Knoke, David. 1990. *Political Networks: The Structural Perspective.* New York: Cambridge University Press.

Knorr-Cetina, Karen; and Cicourel, Aaron V., eds. 1981. *Advances in Social Theory and Methodology: Towards an Integration of Micro- and Macro-Sociologies.* Boston: Routledge and Kegan Paul.

Kobrin, Stephen J. 1997. "Electronic Cash and the End of National Markets," *Foreign Policy* 107.

Kohli, Martin, Harald Künemund & Jörg Lüdicke. 2005. "Family, Structure, Proximity and Contact." January 24. www.iue.it/SPS/People/Faculty/Current Professors/PDFFiles/KohliPDFfiles/ FamilyStructure.pdf, accessed 12/6/05.

Kohn, Melvin. 1977. *Class and Conformity,* 2nd ed. Homewood, IL: Dorsey Press.

Kollock, P.; and Smith, M. A. 1996. "Managing the virtual commons: Cooperation and conflict in computer communities," in S. Herring, ed., *Computer-Mediated Communication.* Amsterdam: John Benjamins.

Kosmin, Barry A. 1991. *Research Report: The National Survey of Religious Identification.* New York: City University of New York Graduate Center.

_____; Mayer, Egon; and Keysar, Ariela. 2001. American Religious Identification Survey (ARIS). New York: CUNY Graduate Center (December 19). www.gc. cuny.edu/studies/aris.pdf, accessed 1/3/05.

Kozol, Jonathan. 1991. *Savage Inequalities: Children in America's Schools.* New York: Crown.

Kroeger, Brooke. 2004. "When a dissertation makes a difference," *New York Times,* March 20.

Krueger, Colleen. 1995. "Retirees with company heath plans on decline." *Los Angeles Times,* September 22.

Kuznets, Simon. 1955. "Economic growth and income inequality." *Economic Review,* vol. XLV, no. 1.

Lacan, Jacques. 1995 (orig. 1977). *Écrits: A Selection,* transl. by Alan Sheridan, New York: Norton.

Lacayo, Richard. 1994. "Lock 'em up!" *Time,* February 7.

Laing, R. D. 1971. *Self and Others.* London: Tavistock.

Lake, R. 1981. *The New Suburbanites: Race and Housing in the Suburbs.* New Brunswick, NJ: Center for Urban Policy Research, Rutgers University Press.

Lambert, Richard. 1995. "Foreign student flows and the internationalization of higher education," in Katharine Hanson and Joel Meyerson, eds., *International Challenges to American Colleges and Universities.* Phoenix: Oryx Press.

Lammers, Cristina, et al. 2000. "Influences on adolescents' decision to postpone onset of sexual intercourse: A survival analysis of virginity among youths aged 13 to 18 years." *Journal of Adolescent Health,* vol. 26, no. 1.

Land, Kenneth C.; Deane, Glenn; and Blau, Judith R. 1991. "Religious pluralism and church membership." *American Sociological Review,* vol. 56.

Landale, N., and Fennelly, K. 1992. "Informal unions among mainland Puerto Ricans: Cohabitation or an alternative to legal marriage?" *Journal of Marriage and the Family,* vol. 54.

Landry, Bart. 1988. *The New Black Middle Class.* Berkeley, CA: University of California Press.

Lane, Harlan. 1976. *The Wild Boy of Aveyron.* Cambridge, MA: Harvard University Press.

Lappe, France Moore, et al. 1998. *World Hunger: 12 Myths.* 2nd ed. New York: Grove Press.

Laquer, Walter. 2003. *No End to War: Terrorism in the 21st Century.* New York & London: Continuum.

Lareau, Annette. 2003. *Unequal Childhoods: Class, Race, and Family Life.* Berkeley: University of California Press.

Lash, Scott; and Urry, John. 1987. *The End of Organized Capitalism.* Madison, WI: University of Wisconsin Press.

Lashbrook, Jeff. 1996. "Promotional timetables: An exploratory investigation of age norms for promotional expectations and their association with job well-being." *Gerontologist,* vol. 36, no. 2.

Laslett, P. 1991. *A Fresh Map of Life.* Cambridge, MA: Harvard University Press.

Laumann, Edward O., et al. 1994. *The Social Organization of Sexuality: Sexual Practices in the United States.* Chicago: University of Chicago Press.

Lawrence, Bruce B. 1989. *Defenders of God: The Fundamentalist Revolt Against the Modern Age.* San Francisco: Harper & Row.

Lazarsfeld, Paul F.; Berelson, Bernard; and Gaudet, Hazel. 1948. *The People's Choice.* New York: Columbia University Press.

Leach, Edmund. 1976. Culture *and Communication: The Logic by Which Symbols Are Connected.* New York: Cambridge University Press.

Lee, Gary. 1982. *Family Structure and Interaction: A Comparative Analysis.* 2nd ed. Minneapolis: University of Minnesota Press.

Lee, Richard B. 1968. "What hunters do for a living, or how to make out on scarce resources," in Richard B. Lee and Irven DeVore, eds., *Man the Hunter.* Chicago: Aldine.

_____. 1969. "!Kung bushman subsistence: An input-output analysis," in A. P. Vayda, ed., *Environment and Cultural Behavior.* New York: Natural History Press.

Lehrer, Warren; and Sloan, Judith. 2003. *Crossing the BLVD: Strangers, Neighbors, Aliens in a New America.* New York: Norton.

Lemert, Edwin. 1972. *Human Deviance, Social Problems, and Social Control.* Englewood Cliffs, NJ: Prentice-Hall.

Leonhardt, David. 2001. "Belt tightening seen as threat to the economy." *New York Times,* July 15, p. 1.

Lepkowsky, M. 1990. "Gender in an egalitarian society: A case study from the Coral Sea," in P. R. Sandy and R. G. Goodenough, eds., *Beyond the Second Sex.* Philadelphia: University of Pennsylvania Press.

Leupp, Gary P. 1995. *Male Colors, the Construction of Homosexuality in Tokugawa Japan.* Berkeley, CA: University of California Press.

Levay, Simon. 1996. *Queer Science: The Uses and Abuses of Research into Homosexuality.* Cambridge, MA: MIT Press.

Levin, William C. 1988. "Age stereotyping: College student evaluations." *Research on Aging,* vol. 10.

Lewis, Oscar. 1968. "The culture of poverty," in Daniel P. Moyhihan, ed., *On Understanding Poverty: Perspectives from the Social Sciences.* New York: Basic Books.

Liebow, Elliot. 1993. *Tell Them Who I Am: The Lives of Homeless Women.* New York: Free Press.

Lightfoot-Klein, Hanny. 1989. *Prisoners of Ritual: An Odyssey into Female Genital Circumcision in Africa.* New York: Haworth.

Lipset, Seymour Martin, ed. 1981. *Party Coalitions in the 1980s.* San Francisco: Institute for Contemporary Affairs.

_____. 1991. "Comments on Luckmann," in Pierre Bourdieu and James S. Coleman, eds., *Social Theory in a Changing Society.* Boulder, CO: Westview.

_____; and Bendix, Reinhard. 1959. *Social Mobility in Industrial Society.* Berkeley, CA: University of California Press.

Lipsky, David. 2003a. *Absolutely American: Four Years at West Point.* Boston, MA: Houghton Mifflin.

_____. 2003b. "After Four Years at West Point, David Lipsky Still Wants More," Powell's Author Interviews, August 6. www.powells.com/authors/lipsky.html, accessed spring 2006.

Locke, John. 2000. "Can a sense of community flourish in cyberspace?" *The Guardian,* March 11.

Lofland, Lyn H. 1973. *A World of Strangers.* New York: Basic Books.

_____. 1998. *The Public Realm: Exploring the City's Quintessential Social Territory.* New York: Aldine de Gruyter.

Logan, John R.; and Molotch, Harvey L. 1987. *Urban Fortunes: The Political Economy of Place.* Berkeley, CA: University of California Press.

Long, Elizabeth, ed. 1997. *From Sociology to Cultural Studies: New Perspectives.* Malden, MA: Blackwell.

Lopez-Claros, Augusto; and Zahidi, Saadia. 2005. "Women's Empowerment: Measuring the Global Gender Gap." http://ncwo-online.org/data/images/WorldEconomicForum.pdf, accessed spring 2006.

Loprest, Pamela. 1999. "Families who left welfare: Who are they and how are they doing?" Washington, DC: Urban Institute, www.urban.org/Template.cfm?NavMenuID=24&template=/TaggedContent/ViewPublication.cfm&PublicationID=7297, accessed 1/3/05.

Lorber, Judith. 1994. *Paradoxes of Gender.* New Haven, CT: Yale University Press.

Loury, Glenn. 1987. "Why should we care about group inequality?" *Social Philosophy and Policy,* vol. 5.

Lowe, Graham S. 1987. *Women in the Administrative Revolution: The Feminization of Clerical Work.* Toronto: University of Toronto Press.

Lynd, Robert; and Lynd, Helen. 1929. *Middletown: A Study in Contemporary American Culture.* New York: Harcourt, Brace, and Co.

Lyon, David. 1994. *The Electronic Eye: The Rise of Surveillance Society.* Minneapolis: University of Minnesota Press.

Lyotard, Jean-François. 1985. *The Post-Modern Condition: A Report on Knowledge.* Minneapolis: University of Minnesota Press.

Macenoin, Deni; and al-Shahi, Ahmed, eds., 1983. *Islam in the Modern World.* New York: St. Martin's Press.

Maddox, G. L. 1965. "Fact and artifact: Evidence bearing on disengagement from the Duke Geriatrics Project." *Human Development,* vol. 8.

_____. 1970. "Themes and issues in sociological theories of human aging." *Human Development,* vol. 13.

Madigan, F. C. 1957. "Are sex mortality differentials biologically caused?" *Millbank Memorial Fund Quarterly,* vol. 25.

Magnier, Mark. 2005. "China Clamps Down on Internet News, Blogs." *Los Angeles Times,* September 27.

Maharidge, Dale. 1996. *The Coming White Minority.* New York: Times Books.

Malotki, Ekkehart. 1983. *Hopi Time: A Linguistic Analysis of the Temporal Concepts in the Hopi Language.* Berlin: Mouton.

Malthus, Thomas. 2003. *Essay on the Principle of Population: A Norton Critical Edition,* Revised Edition. Ed. Philip Appleman. Originally published 1798. New York: Norton.

Manning, John T.; Koukourakis, K.; and Brodie, D. A. 1997. "Fluctuating asymmetry, metabolic rate and sexual selection in human males." *Evolution and Human Behavior,* vol. 18, no. 1.

Manpower, Inc. 2006. "Company Overview." www.manpower.com/mpcom/content.jsp?articleid=33, accessed 1/10/06.

Manton, Kenneth G.; Corder, Larry S.; and Stallard, Eric. 1993. "Estimates of change in chronic disability and institutional incidence and prevalence rates in the U.S. elderly population from the 1982, 1984, and 1989 national long term care survey." *Journal of Gerontology,* vol. 48, no. 466.

Mare, Robert D. 1991. "Five decades of educational assortative mating." *American Sociological Review,* vol. 56, no. 1.

Marsden, Peter. 1987. "Core discussion networks of Americans." *American Sociological Review,* vol. 52.

_____; and Lin, Nan. 1982. *Social Structure and Network Analysis.* Beverly Hills, CA: Sage.

Marshall, T. H. 1973. *Class, Citizenship, and Social Development: Essays by T. H. Marshall.* Westport, CT: Greenwood Press.

Martin, David. 1990. *Tongues of Fire: The Explosion of Protestantism in Latin America.* Cambridge, UK: Blackwell.

Martin, Richard C. 1982. *Islam: A Cultural Perspective.* Englewood Cliffs, NJ: Prentice Hall.

Martineau, Harriet. 1962. *Society in America.* Originally published 1837. Garden City, NY: Doubleday.

Marty, Martin E.; and Appleby, R. Scott, eds. 1995. *Fundamentalisms Comprehended.* Chicago, IL: University of Chicago Press.

Marx, Karl. 1977. *Capital: A Critique of Political Economy.* Vol. 1. Originally published 1864. New York: Random House.

Massey, Douglas S. 1996. "The age of extremes: Concentrated affluence and poverty in the twenty-first century." *Demography,* vol. 33, no. 4.

_____; and Denton, Nancy A. 1993. *American Apartheid: Segregation and the Making of the Underclass.* Cambridge, MA: Harvard University Press.

Matsueda, Ross L. 1992. "Reflected appraisals, parental labeling, and delinquency: Specifying a symbolic interactionist theory." *American Journal of Sociology,* vol. 97.

Mauer, Marc. 2004. *Hispanic Prisoners in the United States.* The Sentencing Project www.sentencingproject.org/Admin%5CDocuments%5Cpublications%5Cinc_hispanicprisoners.pdf, accessed spring 2006.

Maugh, Thomas H., II. 1991. "Survey of identical twins links biological factors with being gay." *Los Angeles Times,* December 15.

_____. 1993. "Genetic compound found in lesbianism, study says." *Los Angeles Times,* March 12.

Mayer, Susan; and Jencks, Christopher. 1994. "Trends in the economic well-being of children." Unpublished manuscript, cited in David Whitman, "The poor aren't poorer." *U.S. News and World Report* (July 25).

McDonald, Michael P. 2004. "Up, Up and Away! Voter Participation in the 2004 Presidential Election," *The Forum,* Vol. 2: No. 4, Article 4. www.bepress.com/forum/vol2/iss4/art4, accessed spring 2006.

McDonough, Siobhan. 2005. "U.S. Prison Population Soars in 2003, '04." ABCNews.com. April 25. http://abcnews.go.com/US/LegalCenter/wireStory?id=699808&CMP=OTC-RSSFeeds0312, accessed spring 2006.

McFadden, Dennis; and Champlin, C. A. 2000. "Comparison of auditory evoked potentials in heterosexual, homosexual, and bisexual males and females." *Journal of the Association for Research in Otolaryngology,* vol. 1.

McGeehan, Patrick, Lowell Bergman, Robin Stein and Marlena Telvick. 2004. "The

Plastic Trap: Debt that Binds." November 21, 2005. http://proquest.umi.com/pqdweb?did=739826521&sid=2&Fmt=3&clientId=1563&RQT=309&VName=PQD, accessed spring 2006.

McGrew, A. and D. Held. 1999. *Global Transformations: Politics, Culture and Economics.* Cambridge, UK: Polity Press.

McKinlay, J. B. 1975. "A case for refocusing downstream: The political economy of illness," in P. Conrad and R. Kern, eds., *The Sociology of Health and Illness: Critical Perspectives.* New York: St. Martin's Press.

McLanahan, Sara; and Sandefur, Gary. 1994. *Growing Up with a Single Parent: What Hurts, What Helps.* Cambridge, MA: Harvard University Press.

————. 2004. "Diverging Destinies: How Children Are Faring under the Second Demographic Transition." *Demography* 41:607–627.

McLuhan, Marshall. 1964. *Understanding Media.* London: Routledge and Kegan Paul.

McMichael, Philip. 1996. *Development and Social Change: A Global Perspective.* Thousand Oaks, CA: Pine Forge.

McNeely, Connie L. 1995. *Constructing the Nation-State: International Organization and Prescriptive Action.* Westport, CT: Greenwood.

Mead, Margaret. 1963. *Sex and Temperament in Three Primitive Societies.* Originally published 1935. New York: William Morrow.

————. 1966. "Marriage in Two Steps." *Redbook Magazine* (July):48–49,84–86.

————. 1972. *Blackberry Winter: My Earlier Years.* New York: William Morrow.

Meadows, Donnella H., et al. 1972. *The Limits to Growth.* New York: Universe Books.

Meatto, Keith. 2000. "Real reformers, real results: Our seventh annual roundup of student protest." *Mojo Wire* Magazine, September–October, www.mojones.com/mother_jones/SO00/activist_campuses.html, accessed 1/3/05.

Melton, J. Gordon. 1989. *The Encyclopedia of American Religions,* 3rd ed. Detroit, MI: Gale Research Co.

————. 1996. *The Encyclopedia of American Religions,* 5th ed. Detroit, MI: Gale Research Co.

Menn, Joseph. 2003. "The 'geeks' who once shunned activism amid the digital revolution are using their money and savvy to influence public policy," *Los Angeles Times,* August 11, p. A-1.

Merkyl, Peter H.; and Smart, Ninian, eds. 1983. *Religion and Politics in the Modern World.* New York: New York University Press.

Merton, Robert K. 1957. *Social Theory and Social Structure.* Rev. ed. New York: Free Press.

————. 1968. "Social structure and anomie." Originally published 1938. *American Sociological Review,* vol. 3.

————; and Rossi, Alice Kitt. 1968. "Contributions to the theory of reference group behavior," in Robert K. Merton, ed., *Social Theory and Social Structure.* Originally published 1949. Glencoe, IL: Free Press.

Meyer, John W.; and Rowan, Brian. 1977. "Institutionalized organizations: Formal structure as myth and ceremony." *American Journal of Sociology,* vol. 83.

Michels, Robert. 1967. *Political Parties.* Originally published 1911. New York: Free Press.

Milgram, Stanley. 1963. "Behavioral studies in obedience." *Journal of Abnormal Psychology,* vol. 67.

Milkman, Ruth. 1997. *Farewell to the Factory: Auto Workers in the Late Twentieth Century.* Berkeley, CA: University of California Press.

Mills, C. Wright. 1948. *The New Men of Power.* New York: Harcourt Brace.

————. 1951. *White Collar.* New York: Oxford University Press.

————. 1956. *The Power Elite.* New York: Oxford University Press.

————. 1959. *The Sociological Imagination.* New York: Oxford University Press.

————. 1960. *Listen, Yankee.* New York: McGraw Hill.

————. 2000 (orig. 1959). *The Sociological Imagination.* New York: Oxford University Press.

Mills, Theodore J. 1967. *The Sociology of Small Groups.* Englewood, NJ: Prentice-Hall.

Milner Jr., Murray. 2004. *Freaks, Geeks, and Cool Kids: American Teenagers, Schools, and the Culture of Consumption.* New York: Routledge.

Miner, Horace. 1956. "Body ritual among the Nacirema." *American Anthropologist,* vol. 58.

Mirsky, Jonathan. 1982. "China and the one child family." *New Society* (February 18), no. 59.

Mirza, H. 1986. *Multinationals and the Growth of the Singapore Economy.* New York: St. Martin's Press.

Mitchell, Juliet. 1975. *Psychoanalysis and Feminism.* New York: Random House.

Mitnick, Kevin. 2000. "They call me a criminal." *The Guardian* (February 22).

Modood, Tariq, et al. 1997. *Ethnic Minorities in Britain: Diversity and Disadvantage.* London: Policy Studies Institute.

Moen, Phyllis. 1995. "A life course approach to postretirement roles and well-being," in Lynne A. Bond, Stephen J. Cutler, and Armin Grams, eds., *Promoting Successful and Productive Aging.* Newbury Park: Sage.

————. 2005. *The Career Mystique: Cracks in the American Dream,* with Patricia Roehling. Boulder, CO: Rowman & Littlefield.

Moffitt, Terrie E. 1996. "The neuropsychology of conduct disorder," in P. Cordella and L. Siegel, eds., *Readings in Contemporary Criminological Theory.* Boston: Northeastern University Press.

Mohanty, Chandra Talpade. 1991. "Under Western eyes: Feminist scholarship and colonial discourse," in Chandra Talpade Mohanty, Ann Russo, and Lourdes Torres, eds., *Third World Women and the Politics of Feminism.* Bloomington, IN: Indiana University Press.

Molnar, Alex. 1996. *Giving Kids the Business: The Commercialization of America's Schools.* Boulder, CO: Westview.

Moore, Barrington, Jr. 1966. *Social Origins of Dictatorship and Democracy: Lord and Peasant in the Making of the Modern World.* Boston: Beacon Press.

Moore, Gwen. 1990. "Structural determinants of men's and women's personal networks." *American Sociological Review,* vol. 55.

Moore, Laurence R. 1994. *Selling God: American Religion in the Marketplace of Culture.* New York: Oxford University Press.

Morawska, Eva. 1986. *For Bread with Butter: Life Worlds of East-Central Europeans in Johnstown, Pennsylvania, 1890–1940.* New York: Cambridge University Press.

Mor-Barak, Michal E., et al. 1992. "Employment, social networks, and health in the retirement years." *International Journal of Aging and Human Development,* vol. 35.

Morris, Jan. 1974. *Conundrum.* New York: Harcourt Brace Jovanovich.

Moss, Miriam S.; Moss, Sidney Z.; and Moles, Elizabeth L. 1985. "The quality of relationships between elderly parents and their out-of-town children." *Gerontologist,* vol. 25.

Moynihan, Daniel Patrick. 1965. *The Negro Family: A Case for National Action.* Washington, DC: U.S. Government Printing Office.

_____. 1993. "Defining deviancy down." *American Scholar,* vol. 62, no. 1.

Mumford, Lewis. 1973. *Interpretations and Forecasts.* New York: Harcourt Brace Jovanovich.

Muncie, John. 1999. *Youth and Crime: A Critical Introduction.* London: Sage.

Murdock, George Peter. 1949. *Social Structure.* New York: Macmillan.

Murray, Charles A. 1984. *Losing Ground: American Social Policy, 1950–1980.* New York: Basic Books.

Najman, Jake M. 1993. "Health and poverty: past, present, and prospects for the future." *Social Science and Medicine,* vol. 36, no. 2.

Narayan, Deepa. 1999. *Can Anyone Hear Us? Voices From 47 Countries.* Washington, DC: World Bank Poverty Group, PREM, December.

National Association of Latino Elected Officials (NALEO). 2004. "Latinos Win Big On Election Night." www.naleo.org/press_releases/PR_NALEO_EDay_Win_110304.pdf, accessed 1/27/06.

National Bureau of Economic Research (NBER). 2005. "Changing Work Behavior of Married Women," NBER Digest OnLine, www.nber.org/digest/nov05/w11230.html, accessed spring 2006.

National Center for Education Statistics. 2005. "Digest of Education Statistics, 2004." http://nces.ed.gov/programs/digest/d04/tables/dt04_298.asp, accessed 1/20/06.

National Center for Health Statistics. 2000. Health, United States 2001/2000 with Adolescent Chartbook. Hyattsville, MD: NCHS.

_____. 2001. Health—United States 2001/2000 Washington, DC: U.S. Government Printing Office.

_____. 2002. Bramlett, Matthew; and Mosher William D. "Cohabitation, Marriage, Divorce, and Remarriage in the United States." *Vital and Health Statistics, Series 23, No. 22.* Washington, D.C.: National Center for Health Statistics, www.cdc.gov/nchs/data/series/sr_23/sr23_022.pdf, accessed 1/9/07.

_____. 2003a. "Women's health." www.cdc.gov/nchs/fastats/womens_health.htm, accessed 1/11/05.

_____. 2003b. "Men's Health." www.cdc.gov/nchs/fastats/men.htm, accessed 1/3/05.

_____. 2004a. "Health, United States, 2004." With Chartbook on Trends in the Health of Americans. Table 160. Hyattsville, Maryland. www.cdc.gov/nchs/hus.htm, accessed 9/10/05.

_____. 2004b. "Birth Rate for Women Aged 40-44 Years Rose in 2003, New Report Finds." www.cdc.gov/nchs/pressroom/04facts/birthrates.htm, accessed spring 2006.

_____. 2005a. "Deaths: Preliminary Data for 2003." Table A. National Vital Statistics Report, Vol. 53, No. 15, February 28, 2005. www.cdc.gov/nchs/data/nvsr/nvsr53/nvsr53_15.pdf, accessed spring 2006.

_____. 2005b. "Health, United States, 2005" Table 63. www.cdc.gov/nchs/data/hus/hus05.pdf, accessed spring 2006.

_____. 2005c. "Health, United States, 2005" Table 69. www.cdc.gov/nchs/data/hus/hus05.pdf, accessed spring 2006.

_____. 2005d. "Health, United States, 2005" Table 86. www.cdc.gov/nchs/data/hus/hus05.pdf, accessed spring 2006.

_____. 2005e. "Health, United States, 2005" Table 84 www.cdc.gov/nchs/data/hus/hus05.pdf, accessed spring 2006.

_____. 2005f. "Deaths: Preliminary Data for 2003." Table A. National Vital Statistics Report, Vol. 53, No. 15, February 28, 2005. www.cdc.gov/nchs/data/nvsr/nvsr53/nvsr53_15.pdf, accessed spring 2006.

_____. 2005g. "Health, United States, 2005" Table 66. www.cdc.gov/nchs/data/hus/hus05.pdf, accessed spring 2006.

_____. 2005h. "Health, United States, 2005" Table 52. www.cdc.gov/nchs/data/hus/hus05.pdf, accessed spring 2006.

_____. 2005i. "Fertility, Family Planning and Reproductive Health of U.S. Women: Data from the 2002 National Survey of Family Growth." *U.S. Department of Health and Human Services.* www.cdc.gov/nchs/pressroom/02news/div_mar_cohab.htm, accessed spring 2006.

National Center on Elder Abuse. 1997. "Types of Elder Abuse in Domestic Settings." *Elder Abuse Information Series* No. 2. www.elderabusecenter.org/pdf/basics/fact2.pdf, accessed 12/7/05.

_____. 1999. "Types of Elder Abuse in Domestic Settings." *Elder Abuse Information Series* No. 1. www.elderabusecenter.org/pdf/basics/fact1.pdf, accessed 12/7/05.

_____. 2005. "Fact Sheet: Elder Abuse Prevalence and Incidence." www.elderabusecenter.org/pdf/publication/FinalStatistics050331.pdf, accessed 12/7/05.

National Coalition for the Homeless. 2005. "How Many People Experience Homelessness?" June. www.nationalhomeless.org/publications/facts/How_Many.pdf, accessed spring 2006.

National Eating Disorders Association. 2002. "Statistics: Eating Disorders and their Precursors." www.nationaleatingdisorders.org/p.asp?WebPage_ID=286&Profile_ID=41138, accessed 1/29/06.

National Governors Association (NGA). 2003. "Trivia." www.nga.org/governors/1,1169,C_TRIVIA^D_2117,00.html, accessed 1/3/05.

National High-Tech Crime Unit (NHTCU) 2005. "High-Tech Crime: The Impact on UK Business 2005." www.nhtcu.org/media/documents/publications/8817_Survey.pdf, accessed 10/5/05.

National Immigration Forum. 2006. "Facts on Immigration." January 26. www.immigrationforum.org/DesktopDefault.aspx?tabid=790, accessed 1/27/06.

National Interfaith Committee for Worker Justice (NICWJ). 1998. "Cross border blues: A call for justice for Maquiladora workers in Tehuacán." (July) Chicago, IL: NICWJ.

National Law Center on Homelessness and Poverty. 2004. "Key Data Concerning Homeless Persons in America." July. www.nlchp.org/FA_HAPIA/HomelessPersonsinAmerica.pdf, accessed spring 2006.

National Low Income Housing Coalition (NLIHC). 2000. *Out of Reach: The Growing Gap between Housing Costs and Income of Poor People in the United States.* (September) Washington, DC: The National Low Income Housing Coalition/Low Income Housing Information Service, www.nlihc.org/oor2000/index.htm, accessed 1/3/05.

National Marriage Project. 2005a. "The State of Our Unions: The Social health of Marriage in America." http://marriage.rutgers.edu/Publications/SOOU/SOOU2005.pdf, accessed 1/13/06.

National Nanotechnology Initiative (NNI). 2005. "About the NNI," www.nano.gov/html/about/home_about.html, accessed spring 2006.

National Public Radio (NPR). 2001. "Poverty in America." www.npr.org/programs/specials/poll/poverty/staticresults.html, accessed spring 2006.

National Research Council. 1994. *Information Technology in the Service Society.* Washington, DC: National Academy Press.

NCES. 2000. *Teachers' Tools for the 21st Century: A Report on Teachers' Use of Technology.* National Center for Education

Statistics, Office of Educational Research and Improvement, U.S. Department of Education. NCES 2000-102 (September) http://nces.ed.gov/pubs2000/2000102.pdf, accessed 1/3/05.

Nellie May. 2005. "Undergraduate Students and Cards in 2004: An Analysis of Usage Rates and Trends." Braintree, MA: Nellie Mae www.nelliemae.com/library/ccstudy_2005.pdf, accessed spring 2006.

Nelson, E. Anne; and Dannefer, Dale. 1992. "Aged heterogeneity: Fact or fiction? The fate of diversity in gerontological research." *Gerontologist,* vol. 32.

NES. 2003. "The NES Guide to Public Opinion and Electoral Behavior, The National Election Studies, Graph 5A.1.2," Center for Political Studies, University of Michigan. Ann Arbor, MI: University of Michigan, Center for Political Studies. www.umich.edu/,nes/nesguide/graphs/g5a_1_2.htm, accessed 1/3/05.

———. 2003. The National Election Studies, "The NES Guide to Public Opinion and Electoral Behavior—Voter Turnout 1948–2002," Table 6A.2. www.umich.edu/,nes/nesguide/toptable/tab6a_2.htm, accessed 1/3/05.

Nesiah, Devanesan. 1997. *Discrimination with Reason?: The Policy of Reservations in the United States, India and Malaysia.* New York: Oxford University Press.

Neuman, Johanna. 2003. "Liberals take a cue from Republicans and turn to big donors to set up think tanks and media outlets to counter the conservative message," *Los Angeles Times,* November 30, p. A-20.

Newman, Katherine S. 2000. *No Shame in My Game: The Working Poor in the Inner City.* New York: Vintage.

New York City Gay and Lesbian Anti-Violence Project. 1996. Project Annual Report. www.avp.org, accessed 1/3/05.

Nie, Norman; and Lutz Ebring. 2000. "Internet and Society—a Preliminary Report." Stanford Institute for the Quantitative Study of Society (SIQSS). www.stanford.edu/group/siqss/Press_Release/Preliminary_Report.pdf, accessed 9/23/05.

———; Alberto Simpser; Irena Stepanikova; and Lu Zheng. 2004. "Ten Years After the Birth of the Internet, How do Americans use the Internet in their Daily Lives?" Draft Report. Stanford University. www.stanford.edu/group/siqss/SIQSS_Time_Study_04.pdf, accessed 9/23/05.

Niebuhr, H. Richard. 1929. *The Social Sources of Denominationalism.* New York: Holt.

Nielsen Media Research. 2001b. "Internet access for blue collar workers spikes 52 percent, according to Nielsen/Net-ratings," http://209.249.142.22/press_releases/ PDF/pr_010412.pdf, accessed 5/3/01.

———. 2001c. "Lower income surfers are the fastest growing group on the web, according to Nielsen/Netratings." http://209.249.142.22/press_releases/PDF/pr_010313.pdf, accessed 5/3/01.

Nielson, Francois. 1994. "Income inequality and industrial development: Dualism revisited." *American Sociological Review,* vol. 59 (October).

Nordhaus, W. D. 1975. "The political business cycle." *Review of Economic Studies,* vol. 42.

Nua.com. 2000. www.nua.ie/surveys/how_many_online/ index.html, accessed 1/3/05.

Nye, Joseph. 1997. "In government we don't trust." *Foreign Affairs* (fall).

Oakes, Jeannie. 1985. *Keeping Track: How Schools Structure Inequality.* New Haven, CT: Yale University Press.

———. 1990. *Multiplying Inequalities: The Effects of Race, Social Class, and Tracking on Opportunities to Learn Mathematics and Science.* Santa Monica, CA: Rand.

Oakley, Ann. 1974. *The Sociology of Housework.* New York: Pantheon.

———, et al. 1994. "Life stress, support, and class inequality: Explaining the health of women and children." *European Journal of Public Health,* vol. 4.

Offe, Claus. 1984. *Contradictions of the Welfare State.* Cambridge, MA: MIT Press.

———. 1985. *Disorganized Capitalism.* Cambridge, MA: MIT Press.

Office of National Drug Control Policy. 2005. "Drug Control Funding Tables." The White House. www.whitehousedrugpolicy.gov/publications/policy/06budget/funding_tbls.pdf, accessed spring 2006.

Ohmae, Kenichi. 1990. *The Borderless World: Power and Strategy in the Industrial Economy.* New York: HarperCollins.

Oliver, Melvin L.; and Shapiro, Thomas M. 1995. *Black Wealth/White Wealth: A New Perspective on Racial Inequality.* New York: Routledge.

Olson, M. H. 1989. "Work at home for computer professionals." *ACM Trans. Inf. Sys.,* vol. 7, no. 4.

———; and Primps, S. B. 1984. "Working at home with computers." *Journal of Social Issues,* vol. 40, no. 3.

Omi, Michael; and Winant, Howard. 1994. *Racial Formation in the United States: From the 1960s to the 1990s.* 2nd ed. New York: Routledge.

Opensecrets.org. 2005a. "2004 Presidential Election." The Center for Responsive Politics. www.opensecrets.org/presidential/index.asp, accessed 1/9/06.

———. 2005b. "Blue Chip Investors." Center for Responsive Politics. www.opensecrets.org/orgs/index.asp, accessed 1/9/06.

———. 2005c. "Business-Labor-Ideology Split in PAC and Individual Donations to Candidates and Parties." Center for Responsive Politics. www.opensecrets.org/overview/blio.asp?cycle=2004, accessed 1/9/06.

Oppenheimer, Valerie K. 1970. *The Female Labor Force in the United States.* Westport, CT: Greenwood Press.

———. 1988. "A theory of marriage timing." *American Journal of Sociology,* vol. 94.

Organization for Economic Co-operation and Development (OECD). 2005a. *Factbook: Economic, Environmental, and Social Statistics.* www.oecd.org/site/0,2865,en_21571361_34374092_1_1_1_1,00/html, accessed spring 2006.

———. 2005b. "OECD Science, Technology, and Industry Scoreboard 2005—Towards a Knowledge-based Economy." Section C. 11. http://lysander.sourceoecd.org/vl=11306884/cl=28/nw=1/rpsv/scoreboard/c11.htm, accessed 12/1/05.

Orloff, Ann Shola. 1993. *The Politics of Pensions: A Comparative Analysis of Britain, Canada, and the United States, 1880–1940.* Madison, WI: University of Wisconsin Press.

Ortiz, V. 1995. "The diversity of Latino families," in R. Zambrana, ed., *Understanding Latino Families.* Thousand Oaks, CA: Sage.

Ostling, Richard. 1993. "The Church Search." *Time,* April 5.

Ouchi, William G. 1979. "A conceptual framework for the design of organizational control mechanisms." *Management Science,* vol. 25.

———. 1982. *Theory Z: How American Business Can Meet the Japanese Challenge.* New York: Avon.

Packer, George. 2003. "Smart-mobbing the war," *New York Times,* May 9.

Pager, Devah. 2003. "The mark of a criminal record," *American Journal of Psychology* vol. 108, no. 5: 937–75.

Pahl, Jan. 1989. *Money and Marriage.* London: Macmillan.

Palmore, Erdman B., et al. 1985. *Retirement: Causes and Consequences.* New York: Springer.

Paludi, Michele A., and Barickman, Richard B. 1991. *Academic and Workplace Sexual Harassment: A Resource Manual.* Albany, NY: SUNY Press.

Panyarachun, Anand et al. 2004. *A More Secure World: Our Shared Responsibility: report of the high-level panel on threats, challenges and change.* New York: United Nations. www.un.org/secureworld, accessed spring 2006.

Park, Robert E. 1952. *Human Communities: The City and Human Ecology.* New York: Free Press.

Parkin, Frank. 1971. *Class Inequality and Political Order: Social Stratification in Capitalist and Communist Societies.* New York: Praeger.

_____. 1979. *Marxism and Class Theory: A Bourgeois Critique.* London: Tavistock.

Parry, Noel; and Jose Parry. 1976. *The Rise of the Medical Profession.* London: Croom Helm.

Parsons, Talcott. 1951. *The Social System.* Glencoe, IL: Free Press.

_____. 1960. "Towards a healthy maturity." *Journal of Health and Social Behavior,* vol. 1.

_____. 1964. *The Social System.* New York: Free Press.

_____; and Bales, Robert F. 1955. *Family, Socialization, and Interaction Process.* Glencoe, IL: Free Press.

Pascoe, Eva. 2000. "Can a sense of community flourish in cyberspace?" *The Guardian* (March 11).

Patillo-McCoy, Mary. 1999. *Black Picket Fences: Privilege and Peril among the Black Middle Class.* Chicago: University of Chicago Press.

Patterson, Orlando. 1999. "When 'they' are 'us.'" *New York Times,* April 30, p. A31.

Paul, Diana Y. 1985. *Women in Buddhism: Images of the Feminine in the Mahayana Tradition.* Berkeley, CA: University of California Press.

Pearce, Frank. 1976. *Crimes of the Powerful: Marxism, Crime, and Deviance.* London: Pluto Press.

Perlmutter, Howard V. 1972. "Towards research on and development of nations, unions, and firms as worldwide institutions," in H. Gunter, ed., *Transnational Industrial Relations.* New York: St. Martin's Press.

Peterson, Candida C.; and Peterson, James L. 1988. "Older men's and women's relationships with adult kin: How equitable are they?" *International Journal of Aging and Human Development,* vol. 27.

Peterson, Richard. 1996. "A re-evaluation of the economic consequences of divorce." *American Sociological Review,* vol. 61.

Pew Internet. 2005. "Internet: The Mainstreaming of Online Life." Pew Internet & American Life Project. www. pewinternet.org/pdfs/Internet_Status_ 2005.pdf, accessed spring 2006.

Pew Research Center for the People and the Press. 2002. "Public Opinion Six Months Later." March 7. http://people-press.org/ commentary/display.php3?AnalysisID=44, accessed 9/25/05.

_____. 2003. "The 2004 political landscape: evenly divided and increasingly polarized," The PEW Research Center for the People and the Press (November 5). http://people-press.org/reports/display. php3?ReportID5196, accessed 1/3/05.

_____. 2004. "Democrats Gain Edge in Party Identification." http://people-press. org/commentary/display.php3? AnalysisID=95, accessed 1/9/06.

_____. 2005. "Internet: The Mainstreaming of On-line Life." www.pewinternet.org/ pdfs/Internet_Status_2005.pdf, accessed 9/25/05.

Pfizer. 2005. "Research & Development." www.pfizer.com/pfizer/help/index.jsp, accessed 12/1/05.

Pillemer, Karl. 1985. "The dangers of dependency: New findings in domestic violence against the elderly." *Social Problems,* vol. 33.

_____; and Finkelhor, David. 1988. "The prevalence of elder abuse: A random sample survey." *Gerontologist,* vol. 28.

Pinkney, A. 1984. *The Myth of Black Progress.* New York: Cambridge University Press.

Pintor, Rafael López; and Gratschew, Maria. 2002. *Voter Turnout Since 1945: A Global Report.* Stockholm, Sweden: International Institute for Democracy and Electoral Assistance (International IDEA). www. idea.int/publications/turnout/VT_ screenopt_2002.pdf, accessed 1/3/05.

Piore, Michael J.; and Sabel, Charles F. 1984. *The Second Industrial Divide: Possibilities for Prosperity.* New York: Basic Books.

Pitts, Victoria. 2004. "Debating body projects: Reading *Tattooed,*" *Health: An Interdisciplinary Journal for the Social Study of Health, Illness and Medicine,* Vol. 8, No. 4, 533–535.

Plett, P. C. 1990. *Training Report: Training of Older Workers in Industrialized Countries.* Geneva: International Labor Organization.

_____; and Lester, B. T. 1991. *Training for Older People: A Handbook.* Geneva: International Labor Organization.

Political Money Line. 2003. "Federal Lobby Directory" (December 14) www.tray.com, accessed 1/3/05.

Pollak, Otto. 1950. *The Criminality of Women.* Philadelphia: University of Pennsylvania Press.

Polletta, Francesca; and Jasper, James M. 2001. "Collective Identity and Social Movements," *Annual Review of Sociology* vol. 27: 283–305.

Popenoe, David. 1993. "American family decline, 1960–1990: A review and appraisal." *Journal of Marriage and Family,* vol. 55.

_____. 1996. *Life without Father: Compelling New Evidence That Fatherhood and Marriage Are Indispensable for the Good of Children and Society.* New York: Martin Kessler Books.

Portes, Alejandro; and Stepik, Alex. 1993. *City on the Edge: The Transformation of Miami.* Berkeley, CA: University of California Press.

Potter, Karl H. 1992. "Hinduism," in the *American Academic Encyclopedia* (online edition). Danbury, CT: Grolier Electronic.

Powell, W. W.; and Brantley, P. 1992. "Competitive cooperation in biotechnology: Learning through networks?" in N. Nohria and R. Eccles, eds., *Networks and Organizations: Structure, Form and Action.* Boston: Harvard Business School Press.

_____; Koput, K. W.; and Smith-Doerr, L. 1996. "Interorganizational collaboration and the locus of innovation: Networks of learning in biotechnology." *Administration Science Quarterly,* vol. 41.

Pratt, Joanne H. 2003. Teleworking Comes of Age with Broadband. International Telework Association & Council, www. telecommute.org/pdf/TWA2003_ Executive_Summary.pdf, accessed 1/20/05.

Prebisch, Raul. 1967. *Hacia una dinamica del desarollo Latinoamericano.* Montevideo, Uruguay: Ediciones de la Banda Oriental.

_____. 1971. *Change and Development—Latin America's Great Task: Report Submitted to the Inter-American Bank.* New York: Praeger.

President's Commission on Organized Crime. 1986. Records of Hearings, June 24–26, 1985. Washington, DC: U.S. Government Printing Office.

Prestowitz, Clyde. 2005. *Three Billion New Capitalists: The Global Shift of Wealth and Power to the East.* New York: Basic Books.

Provenzo, Eugene F., Jr. 1991. *Video Kids: Making Sense of Nintendo.* Cambridge, MA: Harvard University Press.

Putnam, Robert. 1993. "The prosperous community: Social capital and public life." *American Prospect,* vol. 13.

_____. 1995. "Bowling alone: America's declining social capital." *Journal of Democracy,* vol. 6.

_____. 2000. *Bowling Alone: The Collapse and Revival of American Community.* New York: Simon and Schuster.

Quadagno, Jill. 1989. "Generational equity and the politics of the welfare state." *Politics and Society,* vol. 17.

Quah, Danny. 1999. *The Weightless Economy in Economic Development.* London: Centre for Economic Performance.

Quinn, Joseph F.; and Burkhauser, Richard V. 1994. "Retirement and labor force behavior of the elderly," in Linda G. Martin and Samuel H. Preston, eds., *Demography of Aging.* Washington, DC: National Academy Press.

Rader Programs. 2003. "Prevalence and Outcome." www.raderprograms.com/prevalen.htm, accessed 1/3/05.

Raghuram, S. and Wiesenfeld, B. 2004. "Work-nonwork conflict and job stress among virtual workers," *Human Resource Management,* 43(2–3): 259–277.

Raines, Pat; and Leathers, Charles G. 2001. "Telecommuting: The New Wave of Workplace Technology Will Create a Flood of Change in Social Institutions," *Journal of Economic Issues,* vol. 35.

Rainie, Lee; Fox, Susannah; and Fallows, Deborah. 2003. *The Internet and the Iraq War: How Online Americans Have Used the Internet to Learn War News, Understand Events, and Promote Their Views.* Washington, D.C.: The PEW Internet and American Life Project. www.pewinternet.org/PPF/r/87/report_display.asp, accessed 1/10/05.

Ramirez, Francisco O.; and Boli, John. 1987. "The political construction of mass schooling: European origins and worldwide institutionalism." *Sociology of Education,* vol. 60.

Ranis, Gustav. 1996. "Will Latin America now put a stop to 'stop-and-go?'" New Haven, CT: Yale University, Economic Growth Center.

_____; and Mahmood, Syed Akhtar. 1992. *The Political Economy of Development Policy Change.* Cambridge, MA: Blackwell.

Redding, S. G. 1990. *The Spirit of Chinese Capitalism.* Berlin: De Gruyter.

Reich, Robert. 1991. *The Work of Nations: Preparing Ourselves for 21st-Century Capitalism.* New York: Knopf.

Renzetti, Claire; and Daniel Curran. 2000. *Social Problems: Society in Crisis.* 5th ed. Needham Heights, MA: Allyn & Bacon.

_____. 1995. *Women, Men, and Society.* 3rd ed. Needham Heights, MA: Allyn and Bacon.

Reskin, Barbara; and Padavic, Irene. 1994. *Women and Men at Work.* Thousand Oaks, CA: Pine Forge Press.

_____; and Roos, Patricia A. 1990. *Job Queues, Gender Queues: Explaining Women's Inroads into Male Occupations.* Philadelphia: Temple University Press.

Rheingold, Howard. 1999. "Look Who's Talking," *Wired* 7.01, January.

Rhode, Deborah L. 1990. "Gender equality and employment policy," in Sara E. Rix, ed., *The American Woman, 1990–1991: A Status Report.* New York: Norton.

Richardson, Diane; and May, Hazel. 1999. "Deserving victims? Sexual status and the social construction of violence." *Sociological Review,* vol. 47.

Riddick, C. C. 1985. "Life satisfaction for older female homemakers, retirees, and workers." *Research on Aging,* vol. 7.

Rieff, David. 1991. *Los Angeles: Capital of the Third World.* New York: Simon and Schuster.

Riesman, David. 1961. *The Lonely Crowd: A Study of the Changing American Character.* New Haven, CT: Yale University Press.

Riley, Matilda White; Foner, Anne; and Waring, Joan. 1988. "Sociology of age," in Neil J. Smelser, ed., *Handbook of Sociology.* Newbury Park, CA: Sage.

Ringer, Benjamin B. 1985. *"We the People" and Others: Duality and America's Treatment of Its Racial Minorities.* New York: Tavistock.

Risen, James; and Eric Lichtblau. 2005. "Bush Lets U.S. Spy on Callers Without Courts." *New York Times.* December 16.

Ritzer, George. 1993. *The McDonaldization of Society.* Newbury Park, CA: Pine Forge Press.

Roach, Steven S. 2005. "The New Macro of Globalization," *Global: Daily Economic Comment,* June 6.

Roberts, Sam. 2005. "In Manhattan, Poor Make 2¢ for Each Dollar to the Rich." *New York Times,* September 4.

_____. 1995. "Women's Work: What's New, What Isn't." *New York Times,* April 27, p. B6.

Robinson, William I. 2001. "Social Theory and Globalization: The Rise of a transnational State," *Theory and Society* 30:2 (April): 157–200.

_____. 2004. *A Theory of Global Capitalism: Production, Class and State in a Transnational World.* Baltimore: Johns Hopkins University Press.

_____. 2005a. "Gramsci and Globalisation: From Nation-State to Transnational Hegemony," *Critical Review of International Social and Political Philosophy* 8: 4 (December): 1–16.

_____. 2005b. "Global Capitalism: The New Transnationalism and the Folly of Conventional Thinking," *Science and Society* 69: 3 (July): 316–328.

Rodriguez, Ciro D. 2004. "The Immigrant Contribution." *La Prensa San Diego.* June 11. www.laprensa-sandiego.org/archieve/june11-04/imigrant.htm, accessed spring 2006.

Roof, Wade Clark. 1993. *A Generation of Seekers: The Spiritual Journeys of the Baby Boom Generation.* San Francisco: Harper San Francisco.

_____. 1999. *Spiritual Marketplace: Baby Boomers and the Remaking of American Religion.* Princeton, NJ: Princeton University Press.

_____; Carroll, Jackson W.; and Roozen, David A., eds. 1995. *The Post-War Generation and Establishment Religion: Cross-Cultural Perspectives.* Boulder, CO: Westview Press.

_____; and McKinney, William. 1990. *American Mainline Religion: Its Changing Shape and Future Prospects.* New Brunswick, NJ: Rutgers University Press.

Roscoe, W. 1991. *The Zuni Man-Woman.* Albuquerque, NM: University of New Mexico Press.

Rosenau, James N. 1997. *Along the Domestic-Foreign Frontier: Exploring Governance in a Turbulent World.* Cambridge, UK: Cambridge University Press.

Rosenbaum, James E. 1979. "Organizational career mobility: Promotion chances in a corporation during periods of growth and contraction." *American Journal of Sociology,* vol. 85.

Rosener, Judy B. 1997. *America's Competitive Secret: Women Managers.* New York: Oxford University Press.

Rosenthal, A. M. 1999. *Thirty-Eight Witnesses: The Kitty Genovese Case.* Berkeley, CA: University of California Press.

Ross, Patricia; and Reskin, Barbara. 1992. "Occupational desegregation in the 1970s—integration and economic equity." *Sociological Perspectives,* vol. 35.

Rossi, Alice. 1973. "The first woman sociologist: Harriett Martineau," in *The Feminist Papers: From Adams to de Beauvoir.* New York: Columbia University Press.

Rostow, W. W. 1961. *The Stages of Economic Growth.* Cambridge, UK: Cambridge University Press.

Rousselle, Robert. 1999. "Defining ancient Greek sexuality." *Digital Archives of Psychohistory,* vol. 26, no. 4, www. geocities.com/kidhistory/ja/defining.htm, accessed 1/11/05.

Rowe, R. H.; and Kahn, R. L. 1987. "Human aging: Usual and successful." *Science* (July 10).

Rowling, J. K. 1998. *Harry Potter and the Sorcerer's Stone.* New York: Scholastic.

Rubin, Lillian B. 1990. *Erotic Wars: What Happened to the Sexual Revolution?* New York: Farrar, Straus, and Giroux.

Rubinstein, W. D. 1986. *Wealth and Inequality in Britain.* Winchester, MA: Faber and Faber.

Rudé, George. 1964. *The Crowd in History: A Study of Popular Disturbances in France and England, 1730–1848.* New York: Wiley.

Ruggles, Patricia. 1990. *Drawing the Line: Alternative Poverty Measures and Their Implications for Public Policy.* Washington, DC: Urban Institute Press.

_____. 1992. "Measuring poverty." *Focus,* vol. 14. University of Wisconsin-Madison, Institute for Research on Poverty.

Rusting, Ricki L. 1992. "Why do we age?" *Scientific American,* vol. 267.

Rutter, M.; and Giller, H. 1984. *Juvenile Delinquency: Trends and Perspectives.* New York: Guilford Press.

RWB. 2003. *The Internet Under Surveillance: 2003 Report.* Paris, France: Reporters Without Borders. www.rsf.org/IMG/pdf/ doc-2236.pdf, accessed 1/3/05.

Ryan, Tom. 1985. "The roots of masculinity," in Andy Metcalf and Martin Humphries, eds., *Sexuality of Men.* London: Pluto.

Sabel, Charles F. 1982. *Work and Politics: The Division of Labor in Industry.* New York: Cambridge University Press.

Sachs, Jeffrey. 2000. "A new map of the world." *The Economist* (June 22).

Sadker, Myra; and Sadker, David. 1994. *Failing at Fairness.* New York: Scribner.

Safe-food.org. 2003. "You are eating genetically engineered food. Is it good for you? Do you have a choice?" www.safe-food.org, accessed 1/3/05.

Sahliyeh, Emile, ed. 1990. *Religious Resurgence and Politics in the Contemporary World.* Albany, NY: SUNY Press.

Saks, Mike, ed. 1992. *Alternative Medicine in Britain.* Oxford, UK: Clarendon.

Salter, Howard. 1998. "Making a world of difference: Celebrating 30 years of development progress." U.S. AID press release, June 25.

Sampson, Robert J.; and Cohen, Jacqueline. 1988. "Deterrent effects of the police on crime: A replication and theoretical extension." *Law and Society Review,* vol. 22, no. 1.

Sandefur, Gary; and Libeler, Carolyn. 1997. "The demography of American Indian families." *Population Research and Policy Review,* vol. 16.

Sarkisian, Natalia, and Naomi Gerstel. 2004. "Kin Support among Blacks and Whites: Race and Family Organization." *American Sociological Review* 69:812–837.

Sartre, Jean-Paul. 1965. *Anti-Semite and Jew.* Originally published 1948. New York: Schocken Books.

Sassen, Saskia. 1991. *The Global City: New York, London, Tokyo.* Princeton, NJ: Princeton University Press.

_____. 1996. *Losing Control: Sovereignty in the Age of Globalization.* New York: Columbia University Press.

_____. 1998. *Globalization and Its Discontents.* New York: New Press.

_____. 2005. *Denationalization: Territory, Authority and Rights.* Princeton, NJ: Princeton University Press.

Sassler, Sharon. 2004. "The Process of entering in Cohabitating Unions." *Journal of Marriage and Family.* 66: 491–505.

Savage, David G. 1998. "Same-sex harassment illegal, says high court." *Los Angeles Times,* March 5.

Sawhill, Isabel V. 1989. "The underclass: An overview." *Public Interest,* vol. 96.

Sax, L. J.; Lindholm, J. A.; Astin, A. W.; Korn, W. S.; and Mahoney, K. M. 2001. "The American freshman: National norms for fall 2001." Higher Education Research Institute, UCLA Graduate School of Education & Information Studies. www. gseis.ucla.edu/heri/norms_pr_01.html, accessed 1/3/05.

Sayers, Janet. 1986. *Sexual Contradiction: Psychology, Psychoanalysis, and Feminism.* New York: Methuen.

Schaie, K. Warner. 1979. "The primary mental abilities in adulthood: An exploration in the development of psychometric intelligence," in Paul B. Baltes and O. G. Brim, eds., *Lifespan Development and Behavior.* Vol. 2. New York: Academic Press.

_____. 1983. *Longitudinal Studies of Adult Psychological Development.* New York: Guilford Press.

_____. 1984. "Midlife influences upon intellectual functioning in old age." *International Journal of Behavioral Development,* vol. 7.

_____; and Hendricks, Jon, eds. 2000. *The Evolution of the Aging Self: The Societal Impact on the Aging Process.* New York: Springer.

Scheff, Thomas. 1966. *Being Mentally Ill.* Chicago: Aldine.

Schiller, Herbert I. 1989. *Culture Inc.: The Corporate Takeover of Public Expression.* New York: Oxford University Press.

_____. 1991. "Not yet the post-imperialist era." *Critical Studies in Mass Communication,* vol. 8.

Schmidt, Roger. 1980. *Exploring Religion.* Belmont, CA: Wadsworth.

Schooler, Carmi. 1987. "Cognitive effects of complex environments during the life span: A review and theory," in Carmi Schooler and K. Warner Schaie, eds., *Cognitive Functioning and Social Structure over the Life Course.* Norwood, NJ: Ablex.

Schor, Juliet. 1992. *The Overworked American.* New York: Basic Books.

Schuman, Howard; Steel, Charlotte; and Bobo, Lawrence. 1985. *Racial Attitudes in America: Trends and Interpretations.* Cambridge, MA: Harvard University Press.

Schumpeter, Joseph. 1983. *Capitalism, Socialism, and Democracy.* Originally published 1942. Magnolia, MA: Peter Smith.

Schwartz, Pepper. 1998. "Stage fright or death wish: Sociology in the mass media," *Contemporary Sociology,* vol. 27, no. 5 (September): 439–45.

Schwarz, John E.; and Volgy, Thomas J. 1992. *The Forgotten Americans.* New York: Norton.

Scott, Catherine V. 1995. *Gender and Development: Rethinking Modernization and Dependency Theory.* London: Lynne Rienner Publishers.

Scott, Sue; and Morgan, David. 1993. "Bodies in a social landscape," in Sue Scott and David Morgan, eds., *Body Matters: Essays* on the Sociology of the Body. Washington, DC: Falmer Press.

Scott, W. Richard; and Meyer, John W. 1994. *Institutional Environments and Organizations: Structural Complexity and Individualism.* Thousand Oaks, CA: Sage.

Scully, Diana. 1990. *Understanding Sexual Violence: A Study of Convicted Rapists.* Boston: Unwin Hyman.

Sedlak, Andrea; and Broadhurst, Diane. 1996. *Third National Incidence Study of Child Abuse and Neglect.* Washington, DC: U.S. Department of Health and Human Services.

Seefeldt, C.; and Keawkungwal, S. 1985. "Children's attitudes toward the elderly in Thailand and the United States." *International Journal of Comparative Sociology,* vol. 26.

Segura, Denise A.; and Pierce, Jennifer L. 1993. "Chicana/o family structure and gender personality: Chodorow, familism, and psychoanalytic sociology revisited." *Signs,* vol. 19.

Seidman, Steven. 1997b. "Relativizing sociology: The challenge of cultural studies," in Elizabeth Long, ed., *From Sociology to Cultural Studies: New Perspectives.* Malden, MA: Blackwell.

———; Meeks, Chet; and Traschen, Francie. 1999. "Beyond the closet? The changing social meaning of homosexuality in the United States." *Sexualities,* vol. 2, no. 1.

Seltzer, Judith. 2000. "Families formed outside of marriage." *Journal of Marriage and the Family* (November).

Senior Journal.com. 2004. "Retiring in the Red: A New reality for Older Americans," March 29. www.seniorjournal.com/ NEWS/Money/4-03-29Retiringinred.htm, accessed spring 2006.

Sennett, Richard. 1998. *The Corrosion of Character: The Personal Consequences of Work in the New Capitalism.* New York: Norton.

The Sentencing Project. 2004. "New Incarceration Figures: Growth in Population Continues." www.sentencing project.org/pdfs/1044.pdf, accessed spring 2006.

"Seville Statement on Violence." 1990. American Psychologist, vol. 45, no. 10, www.lrainc.com/swtaboo/taboos/seville1. html, accessed 1/3/05.

Sewell, William H., Jr. 1992. "A theory of structure: Duality, agency, and transformation." *American Journal of Sociology,* vol. 98.

———. 1999. "The concept of culture," in Victoria E. Bonnell and Lynn Hunt, eds., *Beyond the Cultural Turn.* Berkeley, CA: University of California Press.

———; Sewell, William H.; and Hauser, Robert M. 1980. "The Wisconsin longitudinal study of social and psychological factors in aspirations and achievements." *Research in Sociology of Education and Socialization,* vol. 1.

Sharma, Ursula. 1992. *Complementary Medicine Today: Practitioners and Patients.* London: Routledge.

Shattuck, Roger. 1980. *The Forbidden Experiment: The Story of the Wild Boy of Aveyron.* New York: Farrar, Straus, and Giroux.

Shaw, Martin. 2000. *Theory of the Global State: Globality as an Unfinished Revolution.* Cambridge: Cambridge University Press.

Shea, S.; Stein, A. D.; Basch, C. E.; Lantigua, R.; Maylahn, C.; Strogatz, D.; and Novick, L. 1991. "Independent associations of educational attainment and ethnicity with behavioral risk factors for cardiovascular disease." *American Journal of Epidemiology,* vol. 134, no. 6.

Sheldon, William A., et al. 1949. *Varieties of Delinquent Youth.* New York: Harper and Row.

Shelton, Beth Anne. 1992. *Women, Men, and Time: Gender Differences in Paid Work, Housework, and Leisure.* Westport, CT: Greenwood.

———; and John, Daphne. 1993. "Does marital status make a difference?: Housework among married and cohabiting men and women." *Journal of Family Issues,* vol. 14, no. 3.

Siegel, Jacob. 1993. *A Generation of Change: A Profile of America's Older Population.* New York: Russell Sage Foundation.

Sigle-Rushton, Wendy; and Sara McLanahan. 2004. "Father Absence and Child Well-Being: A Critical Review," in Daniel Moynihan et al., eds., *The Future of the Family.* New York: Russell Sage.

Sigmund, Paul E. 1990. *Liberation Theology at the Crossroads: Democracy or Revolution?* New York: Oxford University Press.

Simmel, Georg. 1955. *Conflict and the Web of Group Affiliations.* Trans. Kurt Wolff. Glencoe, IL: Free Press.

Simon, Julian. 1981. *The Ultimate Resource.* Princeton, NJ: Princeton University Press.

———. 1989. *The Economic Consequences of Immigration.* Cambridge, MA: Basil Blackwell.

Simpson, George Eaton; and Yinger, J. Milton. 1986. *Racial and Cultural Minorities: An Analysis of Prejudice and Discrimination.* New York: Plenum Press.

Simpson, Ida H.; Stark, David; and Jackson, Robert A. 1988. "Class identification processes." *American Sociological Review,* vol. 53.

Simpson, John H. 1985. "Socio-moral issues and recent presidential elections," *Review of Religious Research,* vol. 27: 115–23.

Sjoberg, Gideon. 1960. *The Pre-Industrial City: Past and Present.* New York: Free Press.

———. 1963. "The rise and fall of cities: A theoretical perspective." *International Journal of Comparative Sociology,* vol. 4.

Sklair, Leslie 2002a. "Democracy and the Transnational Capitalist Class," *Annals of the American Academy of Political and Social Science* 581: 144–157

———. 2002b. *Globalization: Capitalism and its Alternatives.* 3rd edition. New York: Oxford University Press.

———. 2003. "Transnational Practices And The Analysis Of The Global System," pp. 15–32 in Axel Hulsemeyer, *Globalization in the Twenty-First Century.* New York: Palgrave Macmillan.

Sklar, Holly. 1999. "Brother, can you spare a billion?" *Z Magazine* (December), www. zmag.org/ZNET.htm, accessed 1/3/05.

Skocpol, Theda. 1979. *States and Social Revolutions: A Comparative Analysis of France, Russia, and China.* New York: Cambridge University Press.

———. 1992. *Protecting Soldiers and Mothers: The Political Origins of Social Policy in the United States.* Cambridge, MA: Harvard University Press.

Slapper, Gary; and Tombs, Steve. 1999. *Corporate Crime.* Essex, UK: Longman.

Slevin, Peter. 2005. "Prison Experts See Opportunity for Improvement." *Washington Post.* July 26, 2005. www. washingtonpost.com/wpdyn/content/ article/2005/07/25/AR2005072501484. html, accessed spring 2006.

Smart, Ninian. 1989. *The World Religions.* Englewood Cliffs, NJ: Prentice Hall.

Smedley, Audrey. 1993. *Race in North America: Origin and Evolution of a World View.* Boulder: Westview Press.

Smeeding, Timothy M. 2000. "Changing income inequality in OECD countries: Updated results from the Luxembourg income study (LIS)." Luxembourg Income Study Working Paper #252, March. Syracuse, New York: Maxwell School of Citizenship and Public Affairs, Syracuse University, www.lisproject.org/ publications/liswps/252.pdf, accessed 1/11/05.

_____; Rainwater, Lee; and Burtless, Gary. 2000. "United States poverty in a cross-national context." Luxembourg Income Study Working Paper #244, September. Syracuse, New York: Maxwell School of Citizenship and Public Affairs, Syracuse University, www.lisproject.org/publications/liswps/244.pdf, accessed 1/11/05.

Smelser, Neil J. 1963. *Theory of Collective Behavior.* New York: Free Press.

Smith, Anthony. 1988. *The Ethnic Origins of Nations.* Boston: Blackwell.

Smith, Denise. 2003. *The Older Population in the United States: March 2002.* U.S. Census Bureau Current Population Reports, P20-546. Washington, DC. www.census.gov/prod/2003pubs/p20-546.pdf, accessed spring 2006.

Smith, Philip; and West, Brad. 2000. "Cultural studies," in *Encyclopedia of Naturalism.* Vol. 1. San Diego, CA: Academic Press.

Smith, Vicki. 1997. "New forms of work organization." *Annual Review of Sociology,* vol. 23.

Smolowe, Jill. 1994. ". . . And throw away the key." *Time* (February 7).

Snyder, Mitch. 1984. Appearance on *Nightline,* November.

So, Alvin. 1990. *Social Change and Development: Modernization, Dependency, and World-Systems Theories.* Newbury Park, CA: Sage.

_____; and Chiu, Stephen W. K. 1995. *East Asia and the World Economy.* Thousand Oaks, CA: Sage.

Social Security Administration. 2005a. "Social Security Basic Facts." www.ssa.gov/pressoffice/basicfact.htm, accessed 12/7/05.

_____. 2005b. *"2005 Annual Report of the Board of Trustees of the Federal Old-Age and Survivors Insurance and Disability Insurance Trust Funds"* March 23. www.ssa.gov/OACT/TR/TR05/index.html, accessed 12/6/05.

_____. 2005c. "Frequently Asked Questions About Social Security's Future." www.ssa.gov/qa.htm, accessed 12/7/05.

Sokolovsky, J., ed. 1990. *The Cultural Context of Aging: Worldwide Perspectives.* New York: Bergin and Garvey.

Sorokin, Pitirim A. 1927. *Social Mobility.* New York: Harper.

Soumerai, S. B.; and Avorn, J. 1983. "Perceived health, life satisfaction, and activity in urban elderly: A controlled study of the impact of part-time work." *Journal of Gerontology,* vol. 38.

Southwick, S. 1996. Liszt: Searchable Directory of E-Mail Discussion Groups. www.liszt.com, accessed 1/3/05.

Spain, Daphne; and Bianchi, Suzanne M. 1996. *Balancing Act: Motherhood, Marriage, and Employment among American Women.* New York: Russell Sage Foundation.

Spenner, Kenneth. 1983. "Deciphering Prometheus: Temporal change in the skill level of work." *American Sociological Review,* vol. 48.

Spielberger, C. D.; Crane, R. S.; Kearns, W. D.; Pellegrin, K. L.; Rickman, R. L.; and Johnson, E. H. 1991. "Anger and anxiety in essential hypertension." In C. D. Spielberger, I. G. Sarason, Z. Kulcs, and G. L. Van Heck, eds., *Stress and Emotion.* Vol. 14. New York: Hemisphere/Taylor & Francis.

Spilerman, Seymour. 1977. "Careers, labor market structure, and socioeconomic achievement." *American Journal of Sociology,* vol. 83.

Spinks, W. A.; and Wood J. 1996. "Office-Based Telecommuting: An International Comparison of Satellite Offices in Japan and North America," in *Proceedings of SIGCPR/SIGMIS '96.* Denver, CO: ACM.

Sreberny-Mohammadi, Annabelle. 1992. "Media integration in the third world," in B. Gronbeck et al., eds., *Media, Consciousness, and Culture.* London: Sage.

Stacey, Judith. 1990. *Brave New Families: Stories of Domestic Upheaval in Late Twentieth Century America.* New York: Basic Books.

_____. 1993. "Good riddance to 'the family': A response to David Popenoe." *Journal of Marriage and Family,* vol. 55.

_____. 1996. *In the Name of the Family: Rethinking Family Values in a Postmodern Age.* Boston: Beacon Press.

Stack, Carole B. 1975. *All Our Kin: Strategies For Survival In A Black Community.* New York: Harper Calophon.

Stampp, Kenneth. 1956. *The Peculiar Institution.* New York: Knopf.

Stark, Rodney; and Bainbridge, William Sims. 1980. "Towards a theory of religious commitment." *Journal for the Scientific Study of Religion,* vol. 19.

_____. 1987. *A Theory of Religion.* New Brunswick, NJ: Rutgers University Press.

Starrs, Paul F. 1997. "The sacred, the regional, and the digital." *Geographical Review,* vol. 87, no. 2.

Statham, June. 1986. *Daughters and Sons: Experiences of Non-Sexist Childraising.* New York: Basil Blackwell.

Statistical Office of the European Communities. 1991. *Basic Statistics of the Community.* Luxembourg: European Union.

Steinberg, Ronnie J. 1990. "Social construction of skill: Gender, power, and comparable worth." *Work and Occupations,* vol. 17.

Steinmetz, Suzanne K. 1983. "Family violence toward elders," in Susan Saunders, Ann Anderson, and Cynthia Hart, eds., *Violent Individuals and Families: A Practitioner's Handbook.* Springfield, IL: Charles C. Thomas.

Stephen, James J. 2004. "State Prison Expenditures, 2001." Bureau of Justice Special Reports. June 2004. www.ojp.usdoj.gov/bjs/pub/pdf/spe01.pdf, accessed spring 2006.

Sterling, Bruce. 1996. "Greetings from Burning Man," *Wired* 4.11, November.

Stetz, Margaret; and Oh, Bonnie, eds. 2001. *Legacies of the Comfort Women of World War II.* Armonk, NY: M. E. Sharpe.

Stillwagon, Ellen. 2001. "AIDS and poverty in Africa." *The Nation* (May 21).

Stockholm International Peace Research Institute. 2005. *SIPRI 2005 Yearbook,* www.sipri.org, accessed spring 2006.

Stone, Lawrence. 1980. *The Family, Sex, and Marriage in England, 1500–1800.* New York: Harper and Row.

Stone, Michael. 1993. *Shelter Poverty: New Ideas on Affordable Housing.* Philadelphia: Temple University Press.

Stouffer, Samuel A., et al. 1949. *The American Soldier: Adjustment during Army Life.* Princeton, NJ: Princeton University Press.

Stow, Kennedy. 2000. *Theater of Acculturation: The Roman Ghetto in the Sixteenth Century.* Seattle: University of Washington Press.

Strinner, William F. 1979. "Modernization and the family extension in the Philippines: A social-demographic analysis." *Journal of Marriage and the Family,* vol. 41.

Stryker, Robin. 1996. "Comparable worth and the labor market," in Paula J. Dubeck and Kathryn Borman, eds., *Women and Work: A Handbook.* New York: Garland.

Sullivan, Oriel. 1997. "Time waits for no (wo)man: An investigation of the gendered experience of domestic time." *Sociology,* vol. 31.

Sutherland, Edwin H. 1949. *Principles of Criminology.* Chicago: Lippincott.

Swidler, Ann. 1986. "Culture in action: Symbols and strategies." *American Sociological Review,* vol. 51.

_____. 2001. *Talk of Love: How Culture Matters.* Chicago: University of Chicago Press.

Tabor, James D.; and Gallagher, Eugene V. 1995. *Why Waco? Cults and the Battle for Religious Freedom in America.* Berkeley, CA: University of California Press.

Tan, A. and K. Ramakrishna, eds. 2002. *The New Terrorism.* Singapore: Eastern Universities Press.

Tang, Shengming; and Zuo, Jiping. 2000. "Dating attitudes and behaviors of American and Chinese college students." *Social Science Journal,* vol. 37, no. 1.

Taylor, Verta, and Leila J. Rupp. 2003. *Drag Queens at the 801 Cabaret.* Chicago: University of Chicago Press.

Teachman, Jay. 2003. "Premarital Sex, Premarital Cohabitation, and the Risk of Subsequent Marital Dissolution among Women." *Journal of Marriage and the Family* 65:444–455.

Tehrani, Alex. 1997. "Thomas Jefferson High School," in *25 and Under,* ed. Alice Rose George New York: DoubleTake/W. W. Norton.

Telework Coalition. 2004. "Telework Facts." www.telcoa.org/id33.htm, accessed 9/23/05.

Tempest, Rone. 1996. "Barbie and the world economy." *Los Angeles Times,* September 22.

Tétreault, Mary Ann. ed. 1994. *Women and Revolution in Africa, Asia, and the New World.* Columbia, SC: University of South Carolina Press.

Thomas, G. M., et al. 1987. *Institutional Structure: Constituting State, Society and the Individual.* Newbury Park, CA: Sage.

Thomas, W. I.; and Znaniecki, Florian. 1966. *The Polish Peasant in Europe and America: Monograph of Our Immigrant Group.* 5 vols. Originally published 1918–20. New York: Dover.

Thompson, Becky. 2001. *A Promise and a Way of Life.* Minneapolis: University of Minnesota Press.

Thompson, E. P. 1971. "The moral economy of the English crowd in the eighteenth century." *Past and Present,* vol. 50.

Thompson, John B. 1990. *Ideology and Modern Culture.* Cambridge, UK: Polity Press.

_____. 1995. *The Media and Modernity: A Social Theory of the Media.* Cambridge, UK: Polity Press.

Thompson, Warren S. 1929. "Population." *American Journal of Sociology,* vol. 34.

Thorne, Barrie. 1993. *Gender Play: Girls and Boys in School.* New Brunswick, NJ: Rutgers University Press.

Tiano, Susan. 1994. *Patriarchy on the Line: Labor, Gender, and Ideology in the Mexican Maquila Industry.* Philadelphia: Temple University Press.

Tilly, Charles. 1978. *From Mobilization to Revolution.* Reading, MA: Addison-Wesley.

_____. 1992. "How to detect, describe, and explain repertoires of contention." Working Paper No. 150. Center for the Study of Social Change. New York: New School for Social Research.

_____. 1995. "Globalization threatens labor's rights." *International Labor and Working Class History,* vol. 47.

_____. 1996. "The emergence of citizenship in France and elsewhere," in Charles Tilly, ed., *Citizenship, Identity, and Social History.* Cambridge, UK: Cambridge University Press.

Time, Asia Edition. 2004. "The Respect They Deserve." November, 29.

TimesDispatch.com. 2005. Profile: H. Lee Scott Jr., President and CEO, Wal-Mart Stores Inc. Updated 6-12-05. *Richmond Times-Herald* www.timesdispatch.com/servlet/Satellite?pagename=RTD/HTML Page/RTD_HTMLPage&c=HTMLPage& cid=1031775880716, accessed spring 2006.

Totti, Xavier F. 1987. "The making of a Latino ethnic identity." *Dissent,* vol. 34 (fall).

Toufexis, Anastasia. 1993. "Sex has many accents." *Time* (May 24).

Touraine, Alain. 1974. *The Post-Industrial Society.* London: Wildwood.

_____. 1977. *The Self-Production of Society.* Chicago: University of Chicago Press.

_____. 1981. *The Voice and the Eye: An Analysis of Social Movements.* New York: Cambridge University Press.

Townsend, Eric. 2002. "E-activism Connects Protest Groups." *The Hartford Courant,* December 4. Reposted at www.globalpolicy.org/ngos/advocacy/protest/iraq/2002/1204activism.htm, accessed 9/23/05.

Townsend, Peter; and Davidson, Nick, eds. 1982. *Inequalities in Health: The Black Report.* Harmondsworth, UK: Penguin.

Toyota Corporation. 2001. "2001 Number and Diffusion Rate for Motor Vehicles in Major Countries," www.toyota.co.jp/IRweb/corp_info/and_the_word/pdf/2003_c07.pdf, accessed spring 2006.

_____. 2004. "Toyota by the numbers." www.toyota.com/about/operations/numbers/index.html#, accessed 1/3/05.

_____. 2005. "By the Numbers." www.toyota.com/about/operations/numbers/factsfigures04/by_numbers.html, accessed 1/10/06.

Treas, Judy. 1995. "Older Americans in the 1990s and beyond." *Population Bulletin,* vol. 5.

Treiman, Donald. 1977. *Occupational Prestige in Comparative Perspective.* New York: Academic Press.

Troeltsch, Ernst. 1931. *The Social Teaching of the Christian Churches.* 2 vols. New York: Macmillan.

Truman, David B. 1981. *The Governmental Process.* Westport, CT: Greenwood Press.

Truong, Tranh-Dam. 1990. *Sex, Money, and Morality.* London: Zed Books.

Tumin, Melvin M. 1953. "Some principles of stratification: A critical analysis." *American Sociological Review,* vol. 18 (August).

Turnbull, Colin. 1983. *The Human Cycle.* New York: Simon and Schuster.

Turowski, Jan. 1977. "Inadequacy of the theory of the nuclear family: The Polish experience," in Luis Lenero Otero, ed., *Beyond the Nuclear Family Model: Cross-Cultural Perspectives.* Beverly Hills, CA: Sage.

Tuttle, Lisa. 1986. *Encyclopedia of Feminism.* New York: Facts on File.

Twine, France Winddance 1991. *Just Black? Multiracial Identity.* color, 57 minutes. New York: Filmmakers Library.

_____. 1997. *Racism in a Racial Democracy: The Maintenance of White Supremacy in Brazil.* New Brunswick, NJ: Rutgers University Press.

_____. 2003. "Racial Literacy in Britain: Antiracist Projects, Black Children, White Parents." *Contours: A Journal of the African Diaspora,* vol. 1, no. 2 (Fall 2003): 129–153.

_____. 2004 "A White Side of Black Britain: The Concept of Racial Literacy." *Ethnic and Racial Studies,* (a special issue on racial hierarchy), vol. 27, no. 6 (November): 1–30.

UNAIDS. 2002. "Impact of AIDS on older populations." www.unaids.org/html/pub/publications/fact_shhets02/fs_older_en_pdf.htm, accessed 1/10/05.

_____. 2003. "AIDS Epidemic Update, December 2003." Joint United Nations Program on HIV/AIDS. www.unaids.org/html/pub/publications/irc_pubOb/jc948-epiupdate2003_en_pdf.htm, accessed 1/10/05.

_____. 2005a. "Press Release: HIV Infection Rates Decreasing in Several Countries But Global Number of People Living with HIV Continues to Rise." United Nations Programme on HIV/AIDS. www.unaids.

org/epi2005/doc/docs/PR_EpiUpdate_
Nov05_en.pdf, accessed 12/1/05.

———. 2005b. "Global Summary of the
AIDS epidemic, December 2005." www.
unaids.org/epi/2005/doc/EPIupdate2005_
pdf_en/Epi05_02_en.pdf, accessed
spring 2006.

———. 2005c. "AIDS Epidemic Update,
December 2005: North American,
Western and Central Europe." www.
unaids.org/epi/2005/doc/EPIupdate2005_
pdf_en/Epi05_10_en.pdf, accessed
spring, 2006.

———. 2005d. "AIDS Epidemic Update,
December 2005: Sub-Saharan Africa."
www.unaids.org/epi/2005/doc/EPIupdate
2005_pdf_en/Epi05_05_en.pdf, accessed
spring, 2006.

UN Chronicle. 1995. vol. 32, no. 4: 29.

UNICEF. 1997. *The State of the World's
Children, 1997.* New York: Oxford
University Press.

———. 2000. *State of the World's Children,
2000.* New York: United Nations
Children's Fund.

Union of International Associations. 1996–
1997. "International organizations by year
and by type, 1909–1996," in *Yearbook of
International Organizations, 1996/97.*
Statistics obtained from UIA Web site,
www.uia.org/statistics/organizations-
stybv296.php, accessed 1/3/05.

Union of International Organizations. 2005.
*Yearbook of International Organizations—
Guide to Global Civil Society.* 42nd edition.
Vol. 1B. Appendix 3, Table 1. Munich: K.G.
Saur.

United Nations (UN). 1995. "Human
Development Report, Gender and Human
Development—Overview" http://hdr.
undp.org/reports/global/1995/en/pdf/hdr_
1995_overview.pdf, accessed 1/3/05.

———. 2003. Table 26. United Nations
Human Development Report, 2003. www.
undp.org/hdr2003/pdf/hdr03_HDI.pdf,
accessed 1/3/05.

United Nations Conference on Trade
and Development (UNCTAD). 2002.
World Investment Report 2002:
Transnational Corporations and Export
Competitiveness. New York: United
Nations.

———. 2004. "UN Report says World Urban
Population of 3 billion Today Expected to
Reach 5 billion by 2030." Press Release,
24 March. www.un.org/esa/population/
publications/wup2003/pop899_English.
doc, accessed 9/25/05.

———. 2005a. "World Investment Report,
2005" pp. 325 Annex table B4.

———. 2005b. "World Investment Report,
2005" Table Annex A.I.8.

United Nations Development Programme
(UNDP). 1998. Human Development
Report 1998. New York: Oxford University
Press.

———. 1999. Human Development Report
1999. New York: Oxford University Press.

———. 2002. Human Development Report
2002. http://hdr.undp.org/reports/global/
2002/en/default.cfm, accessed 1/3/05.

———. 2005. "Human Development Report,
2005." http://hdr.undp.org/reports/global/
2005/, accessed 9/28/05.

United Nations Economic Commission for
Europe. 2003. "Ireland," www.unece.org/
stats/trend/irl.pdf, accessed spring 2006.

United Nations Educational, Scientific, and
Cultural Organization (UNESCO). 2003.
"Institute for statistics." www.uis.unesco.
org/ev.php?URL_ID54926&URL_
DO5DO_TOPIC&URL_SECTION5201,
accessed 1/3/05.

———. 2006. "Education For All: Global
Monitoring Report, 2006." Paris, France:
United Nations Educational, Scientific
and Cultural Organization. www.unesco.
org/education/GMR2006/full/chapt2_eng.
pdf, accessed spring 2006.

United Nations Food and Agriculture
Organization (UN FAO). 2001. "The
impact of HIV/AIDS on food security."
United Nations Food and Agriculture
Organization, Conference on World Food
Security, May 28–June 1.

———. 2003. "The state of food insecurity
in the world, 2003." www.fao.org/docrep/
006/j0083e/j0083e00.htm, accessed
1/3/05.

———. 2004. "The State of Food Insecurity,
2004." United Nations Food and
Agriculture Organization. www.fao.org/
documents/show_cdr.asp?url_file=/
docrep/007/y5650e/y5650e00.htm,
accessed 11/30/05.

———. 2005. "Armed Conflicts Leading
Cause of World Hunger Emergencies."
United Nations Food and Agriculture
Organization. www.fao.org/newsroom/en/
news/2005/102562/index.html, accessed
12/1/05.

United Nations Intergovernmental Panel on
Climate Change (UN IPCC). 2001. *Climate
Change 2001: The Scientific Basis.*
Cambridge, UK: Cambridge University
Press.

United Nations Office on Drugs and Crime.
2005. "World Drug Report, 2005" www.
unodc.org/unodc/en/world_drug_report.
html, accessed spring 2006.

United Nations Population Division. 2001.
*World Urbanization Prospects: The 2001
Revision,.* www.un.org/esa/population/
publications/wup2001/wup2001dh.pdf,
accessed spring 2006.

———. 2002. "World urbanization prospects,
2001 revision—Data tables and
highlights." www.un.org/esa/population/
publications/wup2001/wup2001dh.pdf,
accessed 1/3/05.

United Nations Population Fund (UNFPA).
1998. The State of World Population, 1998.
New York: United Nations.

———. 2003. "Ending widespread violence
against women." www.unfpa.org/gender/
violence.htm, accessed 1/3/05.

———. 2005a. "Violence Against Women
Fact Sheet." www.unfpa.org/swp/2005/
presskit/factsheets/facts_vaw.htm,
accessed 12/4/05.

———. 2005b. "Gender-Based Violence:
A Price too High." *State of the World
Population, 2005.* www.unfpa.org/swp/
2005/english/ch7/index.htm, accessed
12/4/05.

United Nations World Food Program (UN
WFP). 2001. "News release: WFP head
releases world hunger map and warns of
hunger 'hot spots' in 2001." (January 8)
New York: UNWFP.

———. 2004. "Paying the Price of Hunger:
The Impact of Malnutrition on Women
and Children." United Nations World
Food Program. http://documents.wfp.org/
stellent/groups/public/documents/
newsroom/wfp076313.pdf, accessed
12/1/05.

Urban Institute. 2005. "Low-Income Working
Families: Facts and Figures." August 25.
www.urban.org/UploadedPDF/900832.
pdf, accessed spring 2006.

———. 2000. "America's homeless II:
Populations and services." www.urban.
org/template.cfm?Template=/Tagged
Content/VicesPublication.cfm&
PublicationID=6846&NavMenuID=95,
accessed 1/10/05.

Urry, John. 1990. *The Tourist Gaze.* London:
Sage.

U.S. Bureau of Justice Statistics. 2002a.
"Justice Expenditure and Employment
Extracts, 2002" Table 1 Percent
distribution of expenditure for the justice
system by type of government, fiscal 2002
www.ojp.usdoj.gov/bjs/eande.htm#
selected, accessed spring 2006.

———. 2002b. "Justice Expenditure and
Employment Extracts, 2002" Table 2.
Percent distribution of employment and
payrolls for the justice system by level of

government, March 2002. www.ojp.usdoj. gov/bjs/eande.htm#selected, accessed spring 2006.

———. 2003a. "Key facts at a Glance: Prisoners on Death Row." www.ojp.usdoj. gov/bjs/glance/tables/drtab.htm, accessed spring 2006.

———. 2003b. "Capital Punishment, 2003." www.ojp.usdoj.gov/bjs/pub/pdf/cp03.pdf, accessed spring 2006.

———. 2004a. National Crime Victimization Survey (NCVS). Table 2 and Figure 8. www.ojp.usdoj.gov/bjs/pub/pdf/cv04.pdf, accessed spring 2006.

———. 2004b. National Crime Victimization Survey (NCVS). Table 9. www.ojp.usdoj. gov/bjs/pub/pdf/cv04.pdf, accessed spring 2006.

———. 2004c. "Prison and Jail Inmates at Midyear 2004" NCJ 208801 www.ojp. usdoj.gov/bjs/abstract/pjim04.htm, accessed spring 2006.

———. 2004d. "National Crime Victimization Survey, 2004." Table 7 and 8. www.ojp.usdoj.gov/bjs/abstract/cv04. htm, accessed spring 2006.

———. 2004e. National Crime Victimization Survey: Violent Crime Trends, 1973–2004." www.ojp.usdoj.gov/bjs/glance/tables/viortrdtab.htm, accessed spring 2006.

———. 2004f. "Racial Differences Exist, with Blacks Disproportionately Represented among Homicide Victims and Offenders." www.ojp.usdoj.gov/bjs/homicide/race.htm, accessed spring 2006.

———. 2004g. "Homicide Trends in the United States." www.ojp.usdoj.gov/bjs/homicide/tables/varstab.htm, accessed spring 2006.

U.S. Bureau of Labor Statistics. 2003a. "Household data annual averages" Table 11. www.bls.gov/cps/ cpsaat11.pdf, accessed 1/3/05.

———. 2003b. "Household data annual averages" Table 37. www.bls.gov/cps/cpsaat37.pdf, accessed 1/3/05.

———. 2003c. "Women's earnings up relative to men's in 2002." www.bls.gov/opub/ted/2003/apr/wk3/art03.htm, accessed 1/3/05.

———. 2004. "Highlights of Women's Earnings in 2003." Current Population Survey. Table 9. www.bls.gov/cps/cpswom2003.pdf, accessed 12/3/05

———. 2005a. "Women in the Labor Force: a Databook." Table 6. www.bls.gov/cps/wlf-databook2005.htm, accessed 12/2/05.

———. 2005b. "Women in the Labor Force: a Databook." Table 19. www.bls.gov/cps/wlf-table19-2005.pdf, accessed 12/3/05.

———. 2005c. "Women in the Labor Force: a Databook." Table 2. www.bls.gov/cps/wlf-databook2005.htm, accessed 12/2/05.

———. 2005d. "Families with Own Children: Employment Status of Parents by age and family type, 2003-2004." Table 4. www.bls. gov/news.release/famee.t04.htm, accessed 12/3/05.

———. 2005e. "Women in the Labor Force: a Databook." Table 11. www.bls.gov/cps/wlf-table11-2005.pdf, accessed 12/3/05.

———. 2005f. "Household Data Annual Averages" Table 37, "Median weekly earnings of full-time wage and salary workers by selected characteristics," www.bls.gov/cps/cpsaat37.pdf, accessed spring 2006.

———. 2005g. "National Compensation Survey: Occupation Wages in the United States, July 2004." p. 4 www.bls.gov/ncs/ocs/sp/ncbl0757.pdf, accessed spring 2006.

———. 2005h. "A Profile of the Working Poor, 2003." www.bls.gov/cps/cpswp2003. pdf, accessed spring 2006.

———. 2005i. "Contingent and Alternative Employment Arrangements" www.bls. gov/news.release/conemp.toc.htm, accessed 3/13/06.

———. 2005j. "Highlights of Women's Earnings in 2004." Report 987. Table 13. www.bls.gov/cps/cpswom2004.pdf, accessed spring 2006.

U.S. Bureau of the Census. 1996. P23-190 Current Population Reports: Special Studies—651 in the United States, by Frank B. Hobbs with Bonnie L. Damon. Washington, DC: U.S. Government Printing Office.

———. 1998. "World population profile, 1998—Highlights." www.census.gov/ipc/www.wp98001.html, accessed 1/3/05.

———. 1999. "Population profile of the United States, chapter 2" www.census. gov/population/pop-profile/1999/ chap02. pdf, accessed 1/4/05.

———. 2000. "The changing shape of the nation's income distribution." www. census.gov/prod/2000pubs/p60-204.pdf, accessed 1/4/05.

———. 2001a. "Asset ownership of households: 1995." www.census.gov/hhes/ www.wealth/1995/wlth95-1.html, accessed 1/4/05.

———. 2001b. Statistical Abstract of the United States. Washington, DC: U.S. Government Printing Office.

———. 2002. "Geographical mobility, population characteristics" Current Population Reports, PS20-538. www. census.gov/prod/2001pubs/p20-538.pdf, accessed 1/4/05.

———. 2003a. "Asset ownership of households: 2000." www.census.gov/hhes/www.wealth/1998_2000/wlth00-1.html, accessed 1/4/05.

———. 2003b. "Number in poverty and poverty rate by race and Hispanic origin: 2001 and 2002" www.census.gov/hhes/poverty/poverty02/table1.pdf, accessed 1/4/05.

———. 2003d. "People and families by selected characteristics: 2001 and 2002." www.census.gov/hhes/poverty/poverty02/table2.pdf, accessed 1/4/05.

———. 2003e. "Table 4. Poverty status: Status of families, by type of family, presence of related children, race, and Hispanic origin: 1959 to 2002." www. census.gov/hhes/poverty/histpov/hstpov4. html, accessed 1/4/05.

———. 2003h. Statistical Abstract of the United States 2000. Washington, D.C.: U.S. Government Printing Office. www. census.gov/prod/2004pubs/03statab/pop. pdf, accessed 1/4/05.

———. 2003i. "Characteristics of the Foreign Born by World Region of Birth." Table 3.6. www.census.gov/population/www.socdemo/foreign/ppl-174.html#reg, accessed spring 2006.

———. 2003j. "Characteristics of the Foreign Born by World Region of Birth." Table 3.1. www.census.gov/population/www.socdemo/foreign/ppl-174.html#reg, accessed spring 2006.

———. 2004a. Current Population Survey, Annual Social and Economic Supplement, 2004, Ethnicity and Ancestry Statistics Branch, Population Division. Table 1.2. www.census.gov/population/socdemo/hispanic/ASEC2004/2004CPS_tab1.2a. html, accessed spring 2006.

———. 2004b. "Race and Hispanic Origin in 2004." *Population Profile of the United States: Dynamic Version.* Table 1 www. census.gov/population/pop-profile/dynamic/RACEHO.pdf, accessed spring 2006.

———. 2004c. From table 8: www.census. gov/population/socdemo/education/cps2004/tab08-3.pdf, accessed spring 2006.

———. 2004d. American Community Survey: Selected Social Characteristics, 2004" Table DP-2. http://factfinder.

census.gov/servlet/ADPTable?_bm=y&-geo_id=01000US&-qr_name=ACS_2004_EST_G00_DP2&-ds_name=ACS_2004_EST_G00_&-redoLog=false&-_scrollToRow=46&-format, accessed 12/7/05.

_____. 2004e. "Projected Population of the United States, By Age and Sex, 2000-2050." www.census.gov/ipc/www.usinterimproj/natprojtab02a.pdf, accessed spring 2006.12/7/05.

_____. 2004f. American Community Survey: Selected Social Characteristics, 2004" Table DP-2. http://factfinder.census.gov/servlet/ADPTable?_bm=y&-geo_id=01000US&-qr_name=ACS_2004_EST_G00_DP2&-ds_name=ACS_2004_EST_G00_&-redoLog=false&-_scrollToRow=46&-format Accessed 12/7/05.

_____. 2004g. "Educational Attainment in the United States, 2004". Table 1. www.census.gov/population/www.socdemo/education/cps2004.html, accessed spring 2006.

_____. 2004h. "Table P-16. Educational Attainment—People 25 years Old and Over by Median Income and Sex, 1991 to 2003." www.census.gov/hhes/www.income/histinc/p16.html, accessed spring 2006.

_____. 2005a. "Number, Timing, and Duration of Marriages and Divorces: 2001." Current Population Reports (P70-97) by Rose Krieder. www.census.gov/prod/2005pubs/p70-97.pdf, accessed 9/5/2005.

_____. 2005b. "Statistical Abstract of the United States, 2004–2005." Table No. 297. Homicide Victims by Race and Sex: 1980 to 2001. www.census.gov/prod/2004pubs/04statab/law.pdf, accessed spring 2006.

_____. 2005c. "Historical Income Table H-2: Share of Aggregate Income Received by Each Fifth and Top Five Percent of Households, All Races. 1967-2004." www.census.gov/hhes/www.income/histinc/h02ar.html, accessed spring 2006.

_____. 2005d. "Historical Income Table H-1: Income Limits for Each Fifth and Top 5 Percent of Households, All Races, 1967 to 2004." www.census.gov/hhes/www.income/histinc/h01ar.html, accessed spring 2006.

_____. 2005e. "Table H-9. Race of Head of household by Median and Mean Income, 1980-2004." www.census.gov/hhes/www.income/histinc/h09w.html, accessed spring 2006.

_____. 2005f. "Table 4. Poverty Status of Families, by Type of Family, Presence of Related Children, Race and Hispanic Origin, 1959–2004." www.census.gov/hhes/www.poverty/histpov/hstpov4.html, accessed spring 2006.

_____. 2005g. "Table H-3. Mean Household Income Received by Each Fifth and Top 5 Percent, All Races, 1967 to 2004." www.census.gov/hhes/www.income/histinc/h03ar.html, accessed spring 2006.

_____. 2005h. "Table H-13. Educational Attainment of Householder Households with Householder 25 years Old and Over by Median and Mean Income, 1991 to 2004." www.census.gov/hhes/www.income/histinc/h13.html, accessed spring 2006.

_____. 2005i. "No. 573. Civilian Labor Force and Participation Rates by Educational Attainment, Sex, Race, and Hispanic Origin: 1992 to 2003" Statistical Abstract of the United States, 2004-2005. www.census.gov/prod/www.statistical-abstract-04.html, accessed spring 2006.

_____. 2005j. "Hispanic Population Passes 40 Million, Census Bureau Reports." Table 2. www.census.gov/Press-Release/www.releases/archives/population/005164.html, accessed 12/6/05.

_____. 2005k. "Older Americans Month Celebrated in May." www.census.gov/Press-Release/www.releases/archives/facts_for_features_special_editions/004210.html, accessed 12/7/05.

_____. 2005l. "Table 1.11 Poverty Status of the Population by Sex, Age, and U.S. Citizenship Status: 2003" www.census.gov/population/socdemo/foreign/ppl-176/tab01-11.pdf, accessed 12/7/05

_____. 2005m. "Table 2.11. Poverty Status of the Foreign-born Population by Sex, Age, and year of Entry: 2003." www.census.gov/population/socdemo/foreign/ppl-176/tab02-11.pdf, accessed 12/7/05.

_____. 2005n. "Voting and Registration in the Election of November 2004." Table 4b. www.census.gov/population/www.socdemo/voting/cps2004.html, accessed 12/6/05.

_____. 2005o. "America's Families Living Arrangements: 2004." Current Population Survey. Table AVG1. www.census.gov/population/www.socdemo/hh-fam/cps2004.html, accessed 1/12/06.

_____. 2005p. "America's Families Living Arrangements: 2004." Current Population Survey. Table A1. www.census.gov/population/www.socdemo/hh-fam/cps2004.html, accessed 1/12/06.

_____. 2005q. "America's Families Living Arrangements: 2004." Current Population Survey. Table UC1. www.census.gov/population/www.socdemo/hh-fam/cps2004.html, accessed 1/12/06.

_____. 2005r. "America's Families Living Arrangements: 2004." Current Population Survey. Table H2. www.census.gov/population/www.socdemo/hh-fam/cps2004.html, accessed 1/12/06.

_____. 2005s. "America's Families Living Arrangements: 2004." Current Population Survey. Table FG7. www.census.gov/population/www.socdemo/hh-fam/cps2004.html, accessed 1/12/06.

_____. 2005t. "America's Families Living Arrangements: 2004." Current Population Survey. Table C2. www.census.gov/population/www.socdemo/hh-fam/cps2004.html, accessed 1/12/06.

_____. 2005u. "America's Families Living Arrangements: 2004." Current Population Survey. Table FG6. www.census.gov/population/www.socdemo/hh-fam/cps2004.html, accessed 1/12/06.

_____. 2005v. "Asset Ownership Rates for Households, by Selected Characteristics: 2000." Table 2. www.census.gov/hhes/www.wealth/1998_2000/wlth00-2.html Accessed January 29, 2006.

_____. 2005w. "Race and Hispanic Origin of People by Median Income and Sex: 1947 to 2004" Table P-2. www.census.gov/hhes/www.income/histinc/p02.html Accessed January 29, 2006.

_____. 2005x. "Race and Hispanic Origin in 2004." Population Profile of the United States: Dynamic Version. www.census.gov/population/pop-profile/dynamic/RACEHO.pdf, accessed spring 2006.

_____. 2006a. "Statistical Abstract of the United States." Table 646. 125th edition. www.census.gov/statab/www. accessed 1/9/06.

_____. 2006b. "Statistical Abstract of the United States." Table 647. 125th edition. www.census.gov/statab/www. accessed 1/9/06.

_____. 2006c. "Statistical Abstracts of the United States, 2006." Tables 206 and 269. Washington, D.C.: U.S. Government Printing Office. www.census.gov/prod/2005pubs/06statab/educ.pdf, accessed spring 2006.

_____. 2006d. "Statistical Abstracts of the United States, 2006." Table 1149. Washington, D.C.: U.S. Government Printing Office. www.census.gov/prod/

2005pubs/06statab/infocomm.pdf, accessed spring 2006.

———. 2006e. "Statistical Abstract of the United States, 2006." Table 5. www.census.gov/prod/2005pubs/06statab/pop.pdf, accessed spring 2006.

———. 2006f. "Statisitical Abstract of the United States, 2006." Table 214. www.census.gov/prod/2005pubs/06statab/pop.pdf, accessed spring 2006.

———. 2006g. "Statisitical Abstract of the United States, 2006." Table 607. www.census.gov/prod/2005pubs/06statab/pop.pdf, accessed spring 2006.

U.S. Department of Education, National Center for Education Statistics. 1993. *Adult Literacy in America: A First Look at the Results of the National Adult Literacy Survey.* Washington, DC: U.S. Government Printing Office.

U. S. Department of Health and Human Services. 2004a. *Indicators of Welfare Dependence: Annual Report to Congress,* 2004, Table 2, aspe.hhs.gov/hsp/indicators04, accessed spring 2006.

———. 2004b. "Child Abuse and Neglect Fatalities: Statistics and Interventions." National Clearinghouse on Child Abuse and Neglect Information. http://nccanch.acf.hhs.gov/pubs/factsheets/fatality.cfm, accessed spring 2006.

———. 2005a. "National Survey of Drug Use and Health, 2004." Department of Health and Human Services, Substance Abuse and Mental Health Services. Tables A. 3 and A. 8 www.drugabusestatistics.samhsa.gov/nsduh/2k4nsduh/2k4overview/2k4overview.htm#toc, accessed spring 2006

———. 2005b. "Child Maltreatment, 2003" Washington, DC: U.S. Government Printing Office. www.acf.hhs.gov/programs/cb/pubs/cm03/cm2003.pdf, accessed spring 2006.

U.S. Department of Labor, "History of Federal Minimum Wage Rates under the Fair Labor Standards Act, 1938–1996," n.d., www.dol.gov/esa/minwage/chart.htm, accessed spring 2006.

———. 2005c. "HHS: What We Do." www.hhs.gov/about/whatwedo.html, accessed 12/7/05.

U.S. Equal Employment Opportunity Commission. 2005. "Sexual Harassment Charges EEOC & FEPAs Combined: FY 1992–FY 2004" www.eeoc.gov/stats/harass.html, accessed 12/2/05.

U.S. Federal Reserve Board. 2000. "Credit cards: Use and consumer attitudes, 1970 to 1998." *Federal Reserve Bulletin,* www.federalreserve.gov/pubs/bulletin/2000/0900lead.pdf, accessed 1/4/05.

U.S. Patent and Trade Office. 2005. "Performance and Accountability Report: Fiscal Year 2005." www.uspto.gov/web/offices/com/annual/2005/2005annualreport.pdf, accessed 12/1/05.

U.S. Social Security Administration. 1997a. "Highlights of Social Security data, October 1997," SSA website, www.ssa.gov/statistics/highlite.html, accessed 10/28/97.

U.S. Surgeon General. 1964. "Smoking and Health." Washington, DC: Public Health Service. Office of the Surgeon General.

Vallas, S.; and Beck, J. 1996. "The transformation of work revisited: The limits of flexibility in American manufacturing." *Social Problems,* vol. 43, no. 3.

van der Veer, Peter. 1994. *Religious Nationalism: Hindus and Muslims in India.* Berkeley, CA: University of California Press.

van Gennep, Arnold. 1977. *The Rites of Passage.* Originally published 1908. London: Routledge and Kegan Paul.

Vanneman, Reeve D.; and Cannon, Lynn W. 1987. *The American Perception of Class.* Philadelphia: Temple University Press.

Vaughan, Diane. 1986. *Uncoupling: Turning Points in Intimate Relationships.* New York: Oxford University Press.

———. 1996. *The Challenger Launch Decision: Risky Technology, Culture, and Deviance at NASA.* Chicago: University of Chicago Press.

———. 2003. "How theory travels: A most public public sociology," Public Sociology in Action, *ASA Footnotes* (Nov/Dec).

Viorst, Judith. 1986. "And the prince knelt down and tried to put the glass slipper on Cinderella's foot," in Jack Zipes, ed., *Don't Bet on the Prince: Contemporary Feminist Fairy Tales in North America and England.* New York: Methuen.

Vogel, Ezra F. 1979. *Japan as Number One: Lessons for America.* New York: Harper Colophon.

Wacquant, Loic J. D. 1993. "Redrawing the urban color line: The state of the ghetto in the 1980s," in Craig Calhoun and George Ritzer, eds., *Social Problems.* New York: McGraw-Hill.

———. 1996. "The rise of advanced marginality: Notes on its nature and implications." *Acta Sociologica,* vol. 39, no. 2.

———. 2002. "Scrutinizing the street: poverty, morality, and the pitfalls of urban ethnography," *American Journal of Sociology,* vol. 107 (May): 1468–1532.

———; and Wilson, William Julius. 1993. "The cost of racial and class exclusion in the inner city," in William Julius Wilson, ed., *The Ghetto Underclass: Social Science Perspectives.* Newbury Park, CA: Sage.

Wagar, Warren. 1992. *A Short History of the Future.* Chicago: University of Chicago Press.

Wajcman, Judy. 1998. *Managing Like a Man: Women and Men in Corporate Management.* Cambridge, UK: Polity Press.

Waldron, Ingrid. 1986. "Why do women live longer than men?" in Peter Conrad and Rachelle Kern, eds., *The Sociology of Health and Illness.* New York: St. Martin's.

Walker, Sophie; and Doug Palmer. 2005. "Update 1—U.S. Prepared to Cut its Farm Subsidies by 60 Percent." *Reuters.* October 9.

Wallerstein, Immanuel. 1974a. *Capitalist Agriculture and the Origins of the European World-Economy in the Sixteenth Century.* New York: Academic Press.

———. 1974b. *The Modern World-System.* New York: Academic Press.

———. 1979. *The Capitalist World Economy.* Cambridge, UK: Cambridge University Press.

———. 1990. *The Modern World-System II.* New York: Academic Press.

———. 1996a. *Historical Capitalism with Capitalist Civilization.* New York: Norton.

———, ed. 1996b. *World Inequality.* St. Paul, MN: Consortium Books.

———. 2004. *World-System Analysis: An Introduction.* Durham, NC: Duke University Press.

Wallerstein, Judith S.; and Kelly, Joan Berlin. 1980. *Surviving the Break-Up: How Children and Parents Cope with Divorce.* New York: Basic Books.

Wallis, Roy. 1984. *The Elementary Forms of New Religious Life.* London: Routledge and Kegan Paul.

Wallraff, Barbara. 2000. "What global language?" *Atlantic Monthly* (November).

Walmart Class. 2005. "Case Developments." www.walmartclass.com/public home.html, accessed 12/4/05.

Walum, Laurel Richardson. 1977. *The Dynamics of Sex and Gender: A Sociological Perspective.* Chicago: Rand McNally.

Warner, Stephen. 1993. "Work in progress toward a new paradigm for the sociological study of religion in the

United States." *American Journal of Sociology,* vol. 98.

Warren, B. 1980. *Imperialism: Pioneer of Capitalism.* London: Verso.

Waters, Mary C. 1990. *Ethnic Options: Choosing Identities in America.* Berkeley, CA: University of California Press.

Wattenberg, Martin P. 1996. *The Decline of American Political Parties, 1952–1994.* Rev. ed. Cambridge, MA: Harvard University Press.

Waxman, Laura; and Hinderliter, Sharon. 1996. *A Status Report on Hunger and Homelessness in America's Cities.* Washington, DC: U.S. Conference of Mayors.

Weber, Max. 1947. *The Theory of Social and Economic Organization.* New York: Free Press.

———. 1963 (orig. 1921). *The Sociology of Religion.* Boston: Beacon Press.

———. 1977 (orig. 1904). *The Protestant Ethic and the Spirit of Capitalism.* New York: Macmillan.

———. 1979 (orig. 1921). *Economy and Society: An Outline of Interpretive Sociology.* 2 vols. Berkeley, CA: University of California Press.

WebIndia. 2005. "One in Five Married Women Subjected to Violence, Survey." November 28. http://news.webindia123.com/news/showdetails.asp?id=175075&cat=India, accessed 12/4/05.

Weeks, Jeffrey. 1977. *Coming Out: Homosexual Politics in Britain, from the Nineteenth Century to the Present.* New York: Quartet.

———. 1986. *Sexuality.* New York: Routledge, Chapman and Hall.

Weiss, Rick. 1997. "Aging: New answers to old questions." *National Geographic,* vol. 192, no. 5.

Weitzman, Lenore. 1985. *Divorce Revolution: The Unexpected Social and Economic Consequences for Women and Children in America.* New York: Free Press.

———, et al. 1972. "Sexual socialization in picture books for preschool children." *American Journal of Sociology,* vol. 77.

Wellman, Barry S. 1994. "I was a teenage network analyst: The route from the Bronx to the information highway." *Connections,* vol. 17, no. 2.

———; Carrington, Peter J.; and Hall, Alan. 1988. "Networks as personal communities," in Barry Wellman and S. D. Berkowitz, eds., *Social Structures: A Network Approach.* New York: Cambridge University Press.

Wellman, Barry, et al. 1996. "Computer networks as social networks: Collaborative work, telework, and virtual community." *Annual Review of Sociology,* vol. 22.

Wellman, David T., ed. 1977. *Portraits of White Racism.* New York: Cambridge University Press.

———. 1987. *Portraits of White Racism.* New York: Cambridge University Press.

West, Candace; and Fenstermaker, Sarah. 1995. "Doing difference." *Gender and Society,* vol. 9, no. 1.

———; and Zimmerman, Don. 1987. "Doing gender." *Gender and Society,* vol. 1 (June).

Western, Bruce. 1997. *Between Class and Market: Postwar Unionization in the Capitalist Democracies.* Princeton, NJ: Princeton University Press.

———; and Beckett, Katherine. 1999. "How unregulated is the U.S. labor market?: The penal system as a labor market institution." *American Journal of Sociology,* vol. 104, no. 4.

Wheatley, Paul. 1971. *The Pivot of the Four Quarters.* Edinburgh: Edinburgh University Press.

Wheeler, Deborah L. 1998. "Global culture or culture clash: New information technologies in the Islamic world—a view from Kuwait." *Communication Research,* vol. 25, no. 4.

White, Caroline. 2003. "China is top of the gaggers," *Dot Journalism* (June 27). www.journalism.co.uk/news/story673.html, accessed 1/4/05.

White House Press Office. 2001. "President Bush discusses global climate change," press release, June 11.

White House. 2005. "Where the Money Comes From – and Where it Goes." Table 2.2. Office of Management and Budget. www.whitehouse.gov/omb/budget/fy2002/guide02.html, accessed 12/7/05.

White, Lynn K. 1990. "Determinants of divorce: A review of research in the eighties." *Journal of Marriage and the Family,* vol. 52 (November).

White, Merry I. 1993. *The Material Child: Coming of Age in Japan and America.* New York: Free Press.

White, Michael; and Trevor, Malcolm. 1983. *Under Japanese Management: The Experience of British Workers.* New York: Gower.

Widom, Cathy Spatz; and Newman, Joseph P. 1985. "Characteristics of non-institutionalized psychopaths," in David P. Farrington and John Gunn, eds., *Aggression and Dangerousness.* Chichester, UK: Wiley.

Wilkinson, Richard. 1996. *Unhealthy Societies: The Afflictions of Inequality.* New York: Routledge.

Will, J.; Self, P.; and Datan, N. 1976. "Maternal behavior and perceived sex of infant." *American Journal of Orthopsychiatry,* vol. 46.

Williams, Christine L. 1992. "The glass escalator: Hidden advantages for men in the 'female' professions." *Social Problems,* vol. 39.

Williams, Simon J. 1993. *Chronic Respiratory Illness.* London: Routledge.

Wilson, Bryan. 1982. *Religion in Sociological Perspective.* New York: Oxford University Press.

Wilson, Edward O. 1975. *Sociobiology: The New Synthesis.* Cambridge, MA: Harvard University Press.

———. 1978. *On Human Nature.* Cambridge, MA: Harvard University Press.

Wilson, James Q.; and Kelling, George. 1982. "Broken windows," *Atlantic Monthly* (March).

Wilson, William Julius. 1978. *The Declining Significance of Race: Blacks and Changing American Institutions.* Chicago: University of Chicago Press.

———. 1987. *The Truly Disadvantaged: The Inner City, the Underclass, and Public Policy.* Chicago: University of Chicago Press.

———. 1991. "Studying inner-city social dislocations: The challenge of public agenda research." *American Sociological Review,* vol. 56 (February).

———. 1996. *When Work Disappears: The World of the New Urban Poor.* New York: Knopf.

———, et al. 1987. "The changing structure of urban poverty." Paper presented at the annual meeting of the American Sociological Association.

Winkleby, Marilynn A., et al. 1992. "Socioeconomic status and health: How education, income, and occupation contribute to risk factors for cardiovascular disease." *American Journal of Public Health,* vol. 82.

Wirth, Louis. 1938. "Urbanism as a way of life." *American Sociological Review,* vol. 44 (July).

Witkowski, Stanley R.; and Brown, Cecil H. 1982. "Whorf and universals of number nomenclature." *Journal of Anthropological Research,* vol. 38.

Wolf, Naomi. 1992. *The Beauty Myth: How Images of Beauty Have Been Used against Women.* New York: Anchor Books.

Wolff, Edward N. 2000. "Recent trends in wealth ownership, 1983–1998." Tables 8 and 9. Jerome Levy Economic Institute, www.levy.org/default.asp?view5 publications_view&pubIDƒ73a204517, accessed 1/4/05.

Wong, Siu-Lun. 1986. "Modernization and Chinese culture in Hong Kong." *Chinese Quarterly,* vol. 106.

Woodrum, Eric. 1988. "Moral conservatism and the 1984 presidential election," *Journal for the Scientific Study of Religion,* vol. 27: 192–210.

Woolgar, Steve; and Pawluch, Dorothy. 1985. "Ontological gerrymandering: The anatomy of social problems explanations." *Social Problems,* vol. 32, no. 3.

World Bank. 1997. *World Development Report 1997: The State in a Changing World.* New York: Oxford University Press.

———. 1998. *World Development Indicators.* Washington, DC: World Bank.

———. 1999. International Bank for Reconstruction and Development, *World Development Indicators 1999.* Washington, DC: World Bank.

———. 2000. *World Development Report.* New York: Oxford University Press.

———. 2000–2001. "World development indicators," in *World Development Report 2000–2001: Attacking Poverty.* http://poverty.worldbank.org/library/topic/3389/ accessed 1/4/05.

———. 2001. "PovertyNet: Topics relevant to social capital."

———. 2003a. "World development indicators 2003" www.worldbank.org/data/onlinedatabases/onlinedatabases.html, accessed 1/4/05.

———. 2003b. World Development Indicators. www.worldbank.org/poverty/scapital/topic/index.htm, accessed 1/4/05.

———. 2004. *World Development Indicators.* http://devdata.worldbank.org/data-query/, accessed spring 2006.

———. 2005. *World Development Indicators 2005.* http://devdata.worldbank.org/wdi2005/cover.ht, accessed spring 2006.

———. 2006. "Migration can Deliver Welfare Gaines, Reduce Poverty, says Global Economic Prospects 2006." http://web.worldbank.org/WBSITE/EXTERNAL/TOPICS/EXTPOVERTY/0,,contentMDK:20724214-menuPK:336998-pagePK:64020865-piPK:149114-theSitePK:336992,00.html, accessed spring 2006.

World Health Organization. 2000. "What is Female Genital Mutilation?" www.who.int/mediacentre/factsheets/fs241/en/print.html, accessed 12/4/05.

Worldsteel.org. 2005. "World Steel in Figures 2005." www.worldsteel.org/wsif.php, accessed 1/9/06.

World Tourism Organization. 2004. "Tourism Highlights, 2004." Madrid: World Tourism Organization.

World Trade Organization (WTO). 2005. "International Trade Statistics, 2005." Table IV.22. Geneva: The World Trade Organization.

World Wide Guide to Women in Leadership. 2005. "Worldwide Guide to Women in Leadership." www.guide2womenleaders.com, accessed 12/4/05.

Worrall, Anne. 1990. *Offending Women: Female Lawbreakers and the Criminal Justice System.* London: Routledge.

Wright, Erik Olin. 1978. *Class, Crisis, and the State.* London: New Left Books.

———. 1985. *Classes.* New York: Shocken.

———. 1997. *Class Counts: Comparative Studies in Class Analysis.* New York: Cambridge University Press.

———. 2000. *Class Counts: Student Edition.* New York: Cambridge University Press.

Wrigley, E. A. 1968. *Population and History.* New York: McGraw-Hill.

Wrigley, Julia; and Joanna Dreby. 2005. "Fatalities and the Organization of U.S. Child Care 1985–2003." *American Sociological Review* 70: 729–757.

———. 2006. "Keeping kids safe, To prevent more Nixzmary Brown cases, the state must regulate informal day care." *Newsday* Jan 29, p. A.42.

Wuthnow, Robert. 1976. *The Consciousness Reformation.* Berkeley, CA: University of California Press.

———. 1978. *Experimentation in American Religion.* Berkeley, CA: University of California Press.

———. 1988. "Sociology of religion," in Neil J. Smelser, ed., *Handbook of Sociology.* Newbury Park, CA: Sage.

———. 1990. "Improving Our Understanding of Religion and Giving: Key Issues for Research," in Robert Wuthnow and Virginia A. Hodgkinson, eds., *Faith and Philanthropy in America.* San Francisco: Jossey-Bass, 1990, pp. 271–83.

———. 2005. "Hanging in the Balance: Sociology and Theology." Lecture Recorded on Friday, February 4.

Yankelovich, Claney Shulman. 1991. "What's OK on a date." Survey for Time and CNN, May 8.

Young, I. M. 1990. *Throwing Like a Girl and Other Essays in Feminist Philosophy and Social Theory.* Bloomington: Indiana University Press.

Young, Jock. 1998. "Breaking windows: Situating the new criminology," in Paul Walton and Jock Young, eds., *The New Criminology Revisited.* London: Macmillan.

———. 1999. *The Exclusive Society: Social Exclusion, Crime, and Difference in Late Modernity.* London: Sage.

Young, Michael; and Willmott, Peter. 1973. *The Symmetrical Family: A Study of Work and Leisure in the London Region.* London: Routledge and Kegan Paul.

Zammuner, Vanda Lucia. 1986. "Children's sex-role stereotypes: A cross-cultural analysis," in Phillip Shaver and Clyde Hendrick, eds., *Sex and Gender.* Beverly Hills, CA: Sage.

Zerubavel, Eviatar. 1979. *Patterns of Time in Hospital Life.* Chicago: University of Chicago Press.

———. 1982. "The standardization of time: A sociohistorical perspective." *American Journal of Sociology,* vol. 88.

Zhang, Naihu; and Xu, Wu. 1995. "Discovering the positive within the negative: The women's movement in a changing China," in Amrita Basu, ed., *The Challenge of Local Feminisms.* Boulder, CO: Westview.

Zimbardo, Philip G. 1969. "The human choice: Individuation, reason, and order versus deindividuation, impulse, and chaos," in W. J. Arnold and D. Levine, eds., *Nebraska Symposium on Motivation.* Vol. 17. Lincoln, NE: University of Nebraska Press.

———. 1972. "Pathology of imprisonment." *Society,* vol. 9.

———; Ebbesen, Ebbe B.; and Maslach, Christina. 1977. *Influencing Attitudes and Changing Behavior.* Reading, MA: Addison-Wesley.

Zuboff, Shoshana. 1988. *In the Age of the Smart Machine: The Future of Work and Power.* New York: Basic Books.

CREDITS

Text

Bill Bamberger and Cathy M. Davidson: From *Closing: The Life and Death of an American Factory* by Bill Bamberger and Cathy N. Davidson. Copyright © 1998 by Cathy N. Davidson. Used by permission of W. W. Norton and Company.

Patricia Leigh Brown: "Megachurches as Minitowns" by Patricia Leigh Brown. Copyright © 2002 by The New York Times Company. Reprinted by permission.

Joan Jacobs Brumberg: From *The Body Project* by Joan Jacobs Brumberg, copyright © 1997 by Joan Jacobs Brumberg. Used by permission of Random House, Inc.

Brian Burghart: "About a Man" by Brian Burghart from *Reno News and Review,* September 4, 2003. Reprinted by permission of the author.

M.V. Chandler: "Heartbreak, Mystery Shroud Shrine" by M.V. Chandler from *Rocky Mountain News,* May 2, 1999. Reprinted by permission.

Robert Coles: From *Old and On Their Own* by Robert Coles. Copyright © 1997 by Robert Coles. Used by permission of W. W. Norton and Company.

Hila Colman: "Young and Old Thrive Side by Side" by Hila Colman. Copyright © 2001 by the New York Times. Reprinted by permission.

Courtney Coolidge: "American Families: Beyond the White Picket Fence" from www.10 families.com. Reprinted by permission of the author.

Gregory Dicum and Nina Luttinger, © 2006 by Nina Luttinger and Gregory Dicum. This piece originally appears in *The Coffee Book: Anatomy of an Industry from Crop to the Last Drop* by Nina Luttinger and Gregory Dicum. Reprinted by permission of The New Press.

Mitchell Duneier: "Questions for Jane Jacobs" by Mitchell Duneier. Copyright © 2000 by Mitchell Duneier. Reprinted by permission. "Using Your Sociological Imagination: Andrea's Dream" as excerpted from the *Chicago Tribune* article series "Andrea's Dream" by Mitchell Duneier. Copyright © 12/1994, Chicago Tribune Company. All rights reserved. Used by permission. Excerpts from "Talking to Women" from *Sidewalk* by Mitchell Duneier. Copyright © 1999 by Mitchell Duneier. Reprinted by permission of Farrar, Straus and Giroux, LLC.

Liza Featherstone: "The New Student Movement" by Liza Featherstone. Reprinted by permission from the May 15, 2000 issue of *The Nation.*

David P. Fidler: "Neither Science Nor Shamans" by David P. Fidler from the *Journal of Global Legal Studies.* Reprinted by permission of the Indiana University Press.

Ulrika Gerth: "Video Games Violence a 'Risk Factor' for Children" by Ulrika Gerth. Reprinted courtesy of *Foster's Daily Democrat,* Dover, NH.

Robert Hauser: "What If We End Social Promotion?" by Robert Hauser from *Education Week,* April 7, 1999. Reprinted by permission of the author.

Brooke Kroeger: Excerpts from "When a Dissertation Makes a Difference" by Brooke Kroeger. Copyright © 2004 by The New York Times Company. Reprinted with permission.

Warren Lehrer and Judith Sloan, from *Crossing the BLVD: Strangers, Neighbors, Aliens in New America* by Warren Lehrer and Judith Sloan. Copyright © 2003 by Warren Lehrer and Judith Sloan. Used by permission of W. W. Norton and Company, Inc.

Howard Rheingold: Excerpt from "Look Who's Talking" by Howard Rheingold, *Wired,* Issue 7.10, January 1999. Reprinted by permission of the author.

Pepper Schwartz: "Stage Fright or Death Wish: Sociology in Mass Media" by Pepper Schwartz from *Contemporary Sociology,* Vol. 27, No. 5 (Sept., 1998), pp. 439–445. Reprinted by permission of the author and the American Sociological Association.

Bruce Sterling: Excerpts from "Greetings from Burning Man" by Bruce Sterling. Originally published in *Wired.* Reprinted by permission of the author.

Alex Tehrani: "Thomas Jefferson High School" by Alex Tehrani, from *25 & Under: Fiction* by Susan Ketchin and Neil Giordano. Copyright © 1997 by Susan Ketchin and Neil Giordano. Used by permission of W. W. Norton and Company.

United Nations Population Fund: Excerpts from the UNFPA Population Issues Briefing Kit 2001. Reprinted by permission.

Diane Vaughan: "How Theory Travels: A Most Public Public Sociology" by Diane Vaughan from *ASA Footnotes, Nov. 2003.* Reprinted by permission of the author and the American Sociological Association.

Robert Wuthnow: Reprinted by permission of the author.

Photos

Chapter One: p. 1: (from left to right): Reuters/Corbis; Rodolfo Gonzalez/Rocky Mountain News/Polaris; Steve Prezant/Corbis; Bettmann/Corbis; Philip G. Zimbardo/Stanford Prison Experiment; Joseph Rodriguez/Black Star; p. 2: Reuters/Corbis; p. 5: Reuters/Corbis; p. 6: (left): Bo Zaunders/Corbis; (right): Bettmann/Corbis; p. 7: © The New Yorker Collection, 1969 Dana Fradon, www.cartoonbank.com, All Rights Reserved.; p. 8: Pablo Corral V/Corbis; p. 9: Thomas Hoeker/Magnum/PNI; p. 10: Rodolfo Gonzalez/Rocky Mountain News/Polaris; p. 11: (top left): Rocky Mountain News/Polaris; (top right): George Kochaniec Jr./Rocky Mountain News/Polaris; (bottom right): Steve Liss/Corbis Sygma; p. 13:

Masterfile; p. 476: (left): Giraudon/Bridgeman Art Library: (right): © Museum of the City of New York/Bridgeman Art Library; p. 483: David Butow/Corbis Saba; p. 485: Getty Images; pp. 488–489: (all): Photos by Courteney Coolidge from *American Families: Beyond the White Picket Fence,* www.10families.com; p. 490: Everett Collection; p. 494: Courtesy of Julia Wrigley; p. 496: Corbis; p. 498: Najlah Feanny/Corbis Saba; p. 499: Kimberly White/Reuters/Corbis.

Chapter Sixteen: p. 504: Ed Kashi/Corbis; p. 507: Bettmann/Corbis; p. 508: J.A. Giordano/Corbis; p. 510: Gary Connor/PhotoEdit/PNI; p. 511: Greg Meadors/Stock Boston/PNI; p. 514: Courtesy of Robert Hauser; p. 515: Will & Deni McIntyre/Corbis; p. 516: Ted Streshinsky/Corbis; p. 518: (left): Karen Stallwood/Dallas Morning News/KRT; (right): Camilio Vergara/AP Images; p. 519: (top left): Najlah Feanny/Corbis; (top right): Corbis; (bottom right): Gregory Bull/AP Images; p. 521: Granger Collection; p. 525: Bill Nation/Corbis; p. 526: © 1997, Lloyd Dangle; p. 528: Getty Images.

Chapter Seventeen: p. 534: Scott Nelson/Getty Images; p. 538: Courtesy of Robert Wuthnow; p. 541: Bennett Dean/Eye Ubiquitous/Corbis; p. 542: Joseph Sohm: ChromoSohm Inc./Corbis; p. 543: © 1999 Joel Gordon; p. 545: Elizabeth Dalziel/AP Images;

pp. 546–547: (all): Rob Carr/New York Times; p. 550: Siewert Falko/dpa/Corbis; p. 552: Raffi Alexander/Spiderbox; p. 556: Library of Congress, *Huexotzinco Codex,* Painting V, Manuscript 1531; p. 557: World Religions Photo Library/Photos12.com; p. 562: Bettmann/Corbis; p. 565: (top): Catherine Karnow/Corbis; (bottom): Susan Walsh/AP Images; p. 570: Reuters/Landov.

Chapter Eighteen: p. 575: (from left to right): © Howard Schatz/IPN Stock; Gideon Mendel/Corbis; Michael Ainsworth/Dallas Morning News/Corbis; Guillermo Gutierrez/AP Images; David Butow/Redux; Reprinted with permission from *Nano Letters* Vol. 5, No. 9, pg. 1798. Copyright 2005 American Chemical Society. Permission granted by author Peixuan Guo; p. 576: © Howard Schatz/IPN Stock; p. 578: (left): C. Steele Perkins/Magnum Photos; (right): Ed Quinn/Corbis; p. 580: (left): Reuters/Corbis; (right): Image Courtesy of www.adbusters.org; p. 581: (left): Corbis; (right): Rachel Royse/Corbis; p. 584: Lindsay Hebberd/Corbis; p. 588: Vincent Laforet/New York Times; p. 589: Getty Images; p. 591: Jeffery Allan Salter/Corbis; p. 592: Gideon Mendel/Corbis; 594: Liba Taylor/Corbis; p. 595: (top): Eye Ubiquitous/Corbis; (bottom) Louise Gubb/Corbis Saba; p. 597: Granger Collection; p. 599: Mimmo Jodice/Corbis; p. 602: Courtesy of Pepper Schwartz; p. 605: New York Daily News.

Chapter Nineteen: p. 610: Michael Ainsworth/Dallas Morning News/Corbis; p. 612: Getty Images; p. 615: David Brabyn/Sipa; p. 616: Andrew Lichtenstein/Corbis; p. 617: Kat Wade/Corbis; p. 618: Aaron Harris/AP Images; p. 621: Levittown Public Library/AP Images; p. 622: Philippa Lewis/Edifice/Corbis; p. 623: AP Images; p. 625: (top): Arlene Gottfried/The Image Works; (bottom): Nicole Bengiveno/New York Times; p. 627: Dvir Bar-Gal/Zuma Press; p. 630: (top): Giry Daniel/Corbis Sygma; (bottom): Ormuzd Alves/AP Images; p. 631: Guillermo Gutierrez/AP Images; pp. 632–633: (all): Sebastiao Salgado/Contact Press Images; p. 643: Reuters/Corbis.

Chapter Twenty: p. 650: David Butow/Redux; p. 653: Getty Images; p. 656: Reprinted with permission from *Nano Letters* Vol. 5, No. 9, pg. 1798. Copyright 2005 American Chemical Society. Permission granted by author Peixuan Guo; p. 657: Getty Images; p. 658: Carl & Ann Purcell/Corbis; p. 666: Courtesy of Judith Blau; p. 669: Robert Essel NYC/Corbis; p. 670: Greg Baker/AP Images; p. 671: Ammar Awad/Reuters/Corbis; p. 672: Getty Images; p. 673: Greg Baker/AP Images; p. 674: R.J. Kumar/AP Images; p. 675: (top left): Bikas Das/AP Images; (top right): AP Images; (bottom left): Saurabh Das/AP Images; p. 680: Martial Trezzini/epa/Corbis.

INDEX

AARP (American Association of Retired Persons), 172, 383
abortion
  anti-abortion activists, 422, 565–66
  debate over, 606–7
  right to, 406, 408, 422
absolute poverty, 239
abstract learning, 506
achieved status, 125
acquaintance rape, 195, 312–13
acquisitions and mergers, corporate, 447–48
activity theory of aging, 372–73
Addams, Jane, 22
adolescents, *see* teenagers
adoption, 499
advertising, 104
  imaginary reference groups, 142
affective individualism, 475
affirmative action, 333, 347
Afghanistan
  Taliban rule of, 4, 86, 552, 567, 570
  U.S. invasion of, 536
Africa
  civil wars in, 427
  famine and hunger in, 270
  HIV/AIDS in, 267, 270, 592–95
  homosexuality in, 605
  nationalism in, 427
  poverty in, 81
African Americans, 347–49
  black feminism, 318, 419
  caste in the United States, 218–19
  civil rights movement, 348–49, 415, 417
  civil rights of, 396
  with criminal records, effect on employment of, 203, 204–205
  deindustrialization and, 457
  discrimination against, 218–19, 232–33

double consciousness of, 17
economic divide among, 359–60, 361
families, 482–83, 492
gender inequality and, 322–24
ghettos in urban areas, 132–33, 614, 624, 625
health status inequalities, 588–89
homicide victimization rates, 588–89
income inequality, 232–34, 356–57
internal migration from South to North, 348
IQ and race, 513–16
marriage and, 21, 322–23, 479, 482–83
political power of, 358
poverty among, 83, 244
prison population, 177, 203
Protestant churches and, 559, 562, 563
remarriage by, 485
residential segregation of, 621, 624
segregation, 218, 338, 358, 614
sexual stereotyping, 334
slavery, *see* slavery
social interaction on urban streets between whites and, 134–35
street culture of the ghetto, 132–33
urban poverty and, 621–24
as victims of crime, 191
wealth gap between whites and, 232–33, 236, 237
  see also race
African Methodist Church, 552
African National Congress (ANC), 144, 218
age, wealth and, 221, 223
age-grades, 96, 108, 109, 111
ageism, 378

agents of socialization
  the family, 95–96
  mass media, 97–100
  peer relationships, 96–97
  schools, 96
aging, 367–87
  biological, 369–71
  categories of the elderly, 374–75
  credit card debt and, 224
  defining, 369
  graying of industrial societies, 368, 386–87
  median age of U.S. population, 1850-2050, 369
  politics of, 383–86
  psychological, 371
  social, 371
  sociological explanations of, 371–74
  stereotypes, 371
  in the U.S.
    fears about growing old, 382
    graying of the population, 368
    growth of the elderly population, 375
    health problems, 379–82
    lifelong learning, 382–83
    physical abuse, 379
    politics of, 383–86
    poverty and, 375–77, 378
    prejudice and, 378
    race and, 374, 378
    social isolation and, 377–78
agrarian societies, 12, 438
  social stratification in, 217
agriculture
  environmental impact of, 642
  global population growth and, 641
  manufactured risk from, 671–73
  subsidies, 679
  see also agrarian societies

Al Ahmad, Jalal, 570
Ahmadinejad, Mahmoud, 569
AIDS, 267, 270, 566, 583, 592–96, 674, 680
Aid to Families with Dependent Children, 247
air pollution, 630
air traffic controllers' union, 446
Alabama state constitution, 219
alcohol consumption, health and, 589
alcoholism, homelessness and, 251
Algebra Project, 415
Algeria, religion in, 557, 567, 570
alienation
  religion and, 540
  of workers, 441, 453
Alienation and Freedom (Blauner), 453
Allen, Michael, 448
Alomari, Abdulaziz, 5
al Qaeda, 392, 423, 429, 430, 535, 536, 567, 570, 571
Alsaud, Prince Alwaleed Bin Talal, 260
alternative medicine, 585–86
altruistic sex, 311
Alzheimer's disease, 371
American Academy of Child and Adolescent Psychiatry, 98
American Academy of Pediatrics, 98
American Apartheid: Segregation and the Making of the Underclass (Massey and Denton), 351, 358, 621
American Association of Retired Persons (AARP), 172, 383
American Association of University Women (AAUW), 420
American Christian Television System, 565

Ford Motor Company, 448, 451, 457
formal operational stage of child development, 95
formal organizations, 150
formal relations within organizations, 152
formal sanctions, 181
"For Public Sociology," 22
fossil fuel emissions, *see* global warming
foster parenting, 488–89
Foucault, Michel, 154–55, 156, 157
France
　American "cultural imperialism" and, 55–56
　cohabitation in, 479
　cultural diversity and ethnocentrism in, 70
　ethnies in, 426
　workweek in, 475
Frankfurt School of social thought, 524
Franklin, Ann, 494, 495
Freaks, Geeks, and Cool Kids (Milner), 215–16
Freedman, Rose, 367
Freedom House, 396
Freeman, Richard, 446–47
free markets, ethnic conflict and, 338
free-rider problem, 422
free trade, *see* trade, international
Free Trade Area of the Americas (FTAA), 679
Fremlin, J. H., 631
French Revolution, 413, 419
Freud, Sigmund
　gender socialization, theory of, 105–6
　on human sexuality, 596
Friedan, Betty, 477
Friedlander, Daniel, 247
Friedman, Thomas, 665
Friedson, Eliot, 582
Friends of the Earth, 642
Friesen, W. V., 117, 118
From Mobilization to Revolution (Tilly), 416
front regions, 125
functional illiteracy, 516–17
functionalism, 19–20, 32, 426
　aging theories, 371–73
　deviance and crime, theories of, 185–87
　family, perspectives on, 472
　gender inequality theories, 315–16

gender socialization and, 294
sick role, 582–83
fundamentalist Christians, 564, 565–66

Gallup polls, 241
Gamoran, Adam, 510
Gandhi, Mahatma, 216, 558, 653
Gangi, Robert, 203
gangs, 186
　see also crime; juvenile delinquency; police and policing; prisons
gangsta rap, 67
Gap, 9
Gardner, Carol Brooks, 134
gated communities, 249
Gates, Bill, 228, 259
Gates, Henry Louis, 349
gays and lesbians
　civil rights movements for, 605–6
　as crime victims, 196
　drag, 298–99
　gay-parent families, 498–99
　gay rights movement, 33
　homophobia, 604–5
　Humphreys' study of the "tearoom trade," 31–33, 44–45, 48–50
　marriage by, 498–99
　origin of term "lesbian," 599, 601
　restructuring of urban neighborhoods, 617
　see also homosexuality
"Geek Squad," 657
Geertz, Clifford, 520
Gehman, Admiral Harold, 154, 155
Geller, Laura, 552
Gelles, Richard, 493
Gellner, Ernest, 426
gender
　crime and, 193–96
　defined, 292
　distinguished from sex, 292
　eating disorders and, 578, 579
　health and illness and, 589–90
　life expectancy and, 378
　multiple genders, 297
　nature/nurture, 292–95
　　biology's role, 292–93
　　socialization's role, *see* gender socialization
　nonverbal communication and, 118–19

religion and, 551–52
as social construction, 295
　evidence from other cultures, 296–97
　social mobility and, 235, 238, 239
　　downward mobility, 238–39
　stereotypes, 445
gender contract, 194
gender identity, 295–96
gender inequality, 300–325
　analysis of, 314–24
　　feminist approaches, 316–19
　　functional approaches, 315–16
　defined, 300
　in education, 309–10, 313
　global perspective on, 82
　in politics, 310, 314, 315, 324–25
　race and, 322–23, 358–59
　relevance of, 324–25
　street talk and, 123, 134
　violence against women, 195–96, 310–13
　in the workplace, *see* women, in the workplace
Gender Play (Thorne), 96–97
gender socialization, 101–7, 293–95
　Chodorow's theory of, 106–7
　debate about, 105–7
　defined, 101, 293
　Freud's theory of, 105–6
　gender learning, 104
　Gilligan's theory of, 107
　nonsexist child rearing, difficulty of, 105
　parents and adults, reactions of, 101, 294–95
　peer groups and, 96–97
　from storybooks, 104, 105, 309
　from television, 104
gender typing in the workplace, 301–2, 303, 313, 319–22
generalized other, 94
General Motors (GM), 437–38, 451, 457, 462
General Social Survey, 559
generational equity, 385
Generation of Seekers, A (Roof), 559
genetically modified foods, 673
genetic engineering, 606
Genie (unsocialized child), 92–93
"genital mutilation," 69–70, 310
genocide, 337, 338, 653

Genovese, Kitty, 616
Gentile, Douglas, 98, 99
gentrification, 625–26, 627
geocentric transnationals, 450
geragogy, 383
Gerbner, George, 97
Germany, 420
　American culture in, 56
　Turkish immigrant community, 340
　welfare benefits in, 394, 395
　workweek in, 475
gestures, 118
　cultural norms for, 58
Ghana, 400
ghettos, 217, 614, 624
　African Americans in urban areas, 132–33, 614, 624, 625
　Jewish ghettos in Europe, 217, 557, 624, 625
　as sociohistorical problem, 624–25
Giddens, Anthony, 658
Gilland, James, 462–63
Gilligan, Carol, 107
Gingrich, Newt, 147, 646
Gintis, Herbert, 512
Giuliani, Rudy, 190
glass ceiling, 306, 314
glass escalator, 306
Glenn, John, 368
global cities, 626–27
　inequality and, 627–28
global citizens, 83
Global City, The (Sassen), 626
global commodity chains, 278–79
Global Diasporas (Cohen), 342
Global Fund to Fight AIDS, Tuberculosis and Malaria, 594
global inequality, 224, 259–86, 676–81
　consumption patterns, and the environment, 643–45
　defined, 260
　differences among countries, 260–67
　　high-income countries, 262, 264–67
　　low-income countries, 262–63, 264–67
　　middle-income countries, 262, 264–65, 266
　in education and literacy, 271
　gap between the rich and poor, 259, 411
　global cities and, 627–28
　globalization and, 260

culture of, 246
economic deprivation and social movements, 413–16
global, 81–82, 84, 224, 267
see also global inequality
relative, 239
in the U.S., 239–47
attitudes toward the poor, 241, 245–46
children, 245
explanations of, 245–46
feminization of, 244–45
measuring, 239–41
race and ethnicity, 83, 244, 245
urban, explanations for, 621–24
welfare systems to combat, 246–47
working poor, 241–44
poverty line, 239–40
Powell, Colin, 147
power
crimes of the powerful, 197–200
defined, 20, 393
governmental, 393
power elite, 409–10
Power Elite, The (Mills), 48, 409
Power of Identity, The (Castells), 423
POWs for Truth, 406
Prayers for Life, 566
prejudice, 334, 361–62
ageism, 378
premodern societies, 74–78
agrarian, 75, 77
hunting and gathering, 75–77
pastoral, 75, 77
traditional societies or civilizations, 75, 78
preoperational stage of child development, 95
Presbyterians, 548, 552, 559, 560
presidential elections, voter turnout in, 172
Prestowitz, Clyde, 668
primary deviation, 188
primary social groups, 141, 142
primary socialization, 472
"primitive" cultures, 56
printing press, 521
prison-industrial complex, 202
prisons, 201
costs of prison system, 201, 202

criminal record, impact on employment of, 179, 203, 204–25
incarceration rates in industrialized countries, 177, 178
nonviolent drug-related crimes, sentences for, 203
privatization of, 202
recidivism, 179
release from, preparation for, 178, 179, 204
as schools for crime, 203
statistics, 201–2
gender, 193
U.S., 177
surveillance in, 156–57
privatization of education, 517
privilege, 224
procreative technology, 606–7
productivity, 220
profane, the, 540
Project Adequate Roads, 620
projection, 334
proportional representation, 404
prostitution, forced, *see* sex trafficking
Protestant Ethic and the Spirit of Capitalism, The (Weber), 18
Protestantism, 553
"born again" Christians, *see* evangelical Christians
capitalism and, 18, 540–41
in the U.S., 559–60, 561, 562–64
worldwide, 553–56
see also individual denominations, sects, and cults
Protestant Reformation, 553
Prozac, 197
psychopaths, 184
Public Enemy, 67, 68
public-private partnerships in education, 517
public sociology, 22–23, 48–49, 102–3, 154–55, 236–37, 284–85, 350–51
public sphere, 521, 524
Puerto Ricans, 349, 350, 361
families, 481–82
Puff Daddy (Sean "Puffy" Combs), 68
pull factors of migration, 340
punishment
shaming as, 208

social control through, 62
see also crime; police and policing; prisons
Purdue University, 425, 656
Puritanism, 541
push factors of migration, 340
Putnam, Robert, 171

quality circles (QCs), 455
quality of life, global changes in, 263, 267–71
Quebec separatism, 72, 394, 427
questionnaires, 35, 38
open-ended, 39
pilot studies for, 40
respondents, considering characteristics of, 39–40
standardized, 39
questions, sociological, 32–33, 34

race, 354–62
aging and, 374, 378
criminal record, effect on employment of, 203, 204–205
defined, 330
discrimination, 218–19, 230
Du Bois's focus on, 17
education and, 224, 354–56
ethnicity distinguished from, 330
gender inequality and, 322–23, 358–59
health and, 357, 588–89
income inequality and, 232–34, 356–57
intelligence and, 513–16
interactional vandalism, 123
intermarriage, 338
multiple racial identities, 329–30, 332
poverty in the U.S. and, 83, 244, 245
segregation, 218, 330–31, 333, 337–38, 351, 358
social interaction on urban streets between races, 134–35
understanding racial inequality, 361–62
wealth and, 221–22, 224, 232–34
see also ethnicity; minority groups; *individual races*
racial categories, 332

racialization, 330
history of, 330–31, 332–33, 336
racial literacy, 330
racism, 332–33
antiracism, 333
factors leading to rise of, 336
institutional, 332–33, 362
"old" and "new," 333
scientific, 331–32, 336
radical feminism, 317–18
random sampling, 40
rape, 195–96, 310, 311–13
Rape of the Sabines, The, 312, 313
Rastafarianism, 71, 562
rational choice theory, 20–21, 32
rationalization, 16, 18
Reagan, Ronald, 230, 371, 566
real income, 220
reality, social construction of, 131–34
Red Cross, 661
reference groups, 142
referendum, 398
reflexivity, 50
reggae music, 70–71
regionalization, 127, 663–65
Reich, Robert, 165, 451
reintegrative shaming, 208
relative deprivation, theory of, 23–24, 415–16
relative poverty, 239
religion, 535–73
activist, and social change, 566
as cultural universal, 71
defined, 536
Durkheim's views on, 14, 540, 542
fertility rates and, 640
gender and, 551–52
globalization and, 566–71
"living the question," 538–39
Marx's view of, 540, 541, 542
New Age religions, 538, 542–43, 564
organizations
types of, 545–51
women in, 551–52
"other-worldly" religions, 541
religious economy approach to, 544–45
religious pluralism, 542
ritual and, 542
salvation religions, 541
secularization
debate over, 543–44
new religious movements and, 551

theories of, 613–19
traditional societies, cities in, 612
underclass and, 230, 621, 623–24
urban renewal, or gentrification, 625–26
in the U.S., 613, 620–26
  explanations for urban poverty, 621–24
  suburbanization, 619, 620–21
  urban problems, 621
urban renewal, 625–26, 627
Urry, John, 129
USA Patriot Act, 402

values, 56–57
variables, 36
  dependent, 37
  independent, 37
Vaughan, Diane, 487
Vermont, same-sex couples in, 499
vertical mobility, 235
Veterans Administration, 620
Viacom, 447
Victorian sexual values and behavior, 597
video games
  social and intellectual development of children and, 97–100
  violent, as "risk factor" for children, 98–99
Video Kids (Provenzo), 97
Vietnam, 280, 283, 566
Vietnam War, 280, 566
violence
  collective action that becomes, 416–17
  crime, *see* crime, violent
  race and, 588–89
  religious nationalism and, 570–71
  school shootings, 5, 10–11
  television, 97
  terrorism, *see* terrorism
  video game, 98–99
  against women, 195–96, 310–13, 473
Vodafone Airtouch, 447
volunteer work, 439
Volvo, 451
voting
  class-based, 403
  politics and, 403–4
  voter registration, 404

voter turnout, 172, 403–4, 410, 411
voting rights, 394, 406, 419, 420, 421

Wajcman, Judy, 159–61
Wales, 427
Wallerstein, Immanuel, 277–79, 668
Wallerstein, Judith, 487
Wal-Mart, 232, 305, 444–45, 457, 663
warfare
  -related rapes, 313
  religious motives for, 541, 566, 571
  terrorism and, 430
  trench, historical analysis of, 44
war on terrorism, 4–5, 410, 536
Washington, George, 403
waste materials, environmental threat of, 642
water-related diseases, 596
Wayward Puritans (Erikson), 181
Way We Never Were, The (Coontz), 476
wealth, 221–24
  age and, 221, 223
  defined, 221
  education and, 221, 223, 224
  global inequality, 224
  inherited, 221
  privilege and, 224
  race and, 221–22, 224, 232–34, 237
  in the U.S., concentration of, 221, 222–24, 228, 230–34
Wealth of Nations, The (Smith), 440
weapons trafficking, 199
Weber, Max, 15–16, 22, 219
  bureaucracy and organizations, study of, 15–16, 18, 150–52, 157, 161, 168, 408–9
  on capitalism, 18, 272–73, 541
  on class and status, 252
  democratic elitism theory, 408
  nationalism and, 423
  on religion, 18, 540–41, 542, 549, 654
Webster, David, 284–85
Webster v. Reproduction Health Services, 408

weightless economy, 659
Weitzman, Lenore, 485
welfare capitalism, 448
welfare reform, 230
welfare state, 394–95, 411
welfare systems, 246–47, 248
Wellman, David, 362
Wesleyan University, 9
Western, Bruce, 443–44
West Point, 139–40
Wheeler, Deborah, 84–85
When Work Disappears: The World of the New Urban Poor (Wilson), 621
Where the Blame Lies (cartoon), 345
White, Merry, 108–9
White Collar (Mills), 48
white-collar crime, 197–98
White Furniture Company, 462–63
Whorf, Benjamin Lee, 72
"Wild Boy of Aveyron," 92
Wilkinson, Reginald, 205
Wilkinson, Richard, 590–91
Williams, Christine, 306
Williams, Jody, 170, 171
Wilson, Edward O., 64–65
Wilson, William Julius, 361, 457, 621–24
Winfrey, Oprah, 349
Wirth, Louis, 613, 614–15
Woman's Bible, The (Stanton), 551
women
  child care, responsibility for, 307–8
  crime and, 193–96
    crimes against women, 195–96
  eating disorders among, 577–78, 579
  family and, *see* family
  feminism, *see* feminism and feminist theory
  health and illness and, 589–90
  housework and, 308–9
  interactional vandalism, 120–21, 122–23
  in management, 159–61, 408
  Martineau's sociologic focus on, 17
  "new mid-life," 102–3
  political participation of, 310, 314, 405, 406–8, 419
  poverty, feminization of, 244–45
  religious images and, 551

religious organizations, role in, 551–52
  sexuality of, *see* sexuality
  social mobility and, 235, 238
    downward mobility, 238–39
  violence against, 195–96, 310–13, 473, 493
  voting rights of, 394, 406, 419, 420, 421
  in the workplace, 238, 300–307, 319–24, 480, 669
    age at first marriage and, 478–79
    balancing family and work, 474–75, 669
    child care and, 307–8, 320–21, 324
    comparable-worth policies, 303, 305–6
    dual-career couples, 480
    exploitation of, 280–81
    gender pay gap, 302–5, 313, 314
    gender typing or sex segregation, 301–2, 303, 313, 319–22
    glass ceiling, 306, 314
    glass escalator, 306
    global perspective, 313–14
    in management, 159–61, 408
    midlife, women at, 102–3
    networking and, 147–48
    as percentage of total force, 300, 301
    sexual harassment, 306–7
    societal changes, 102, 103
    as support staff, 300–302, 319–22
    telecommuting, 163
    trends in, 300
Women's Environment and Development Organization, 324
women's movement
  international, 322–23
Woodward, Louise, 494, 495
Woolgar, Steve, 133
work and the workplace, 437–65
  alienation, 441, 453
  balancing family and, 474–75
  changing nature of, 451–65, 669
  children in the, 109–10, 274–76, 631
  contingent workforce, 460
  criminal record, impact on employment of, 179, 203, 204–205

ANSWER KEY

Chapter 1
1. C
2. A
3. A
4. A
5. C
6. D
7. D
8. D
9. B
10. C

Chapter 2
1. B
2. B
3. C
4. A
5. A
6. C
7. D
8. C
9. D
10. A

Chapter 3
1. B
2. B
3. A
4. A
5. C
6. D
7. C
8. B
9. D
10. C

Chapter 4
1. B
2. D
3. A
4. B
5. B
6. B
7. B
8. D
9. A
10. C

Chapter 5
1. B
2. C
3. D
4. B
5. C
6. B
7. C
8. B
9. B
10. C

Chapter 6
1. C
2. D
3. B
4. B
5. D
6. A
7. C
8. C
9. C
10. B

Chapter 7
1. A
2. B
3. C
4. B
5. B
6. C
7. A
8. C
9. A
10. A

Chapter 8
1. A
2. B
3. C
4. C
5. C
6. A
7. B
8. C
9. B
10. A

Chapter 9
1. D
2. A
3. D
4. C
5. D
6. C
7. D
8. B
9. C
10. B

Chapter 10
1. A
2. B
3. D
4. D
5. D
6. D
7. A
8. B
9. A
10. C

Chapter 11
1. D
2. D
3. A
4. D
5. C
6. A
7. A
8. D
9. B
10. C

Chapter 12
1. C
2. D
3. A
4. C
5. B
6. C
7. D
8. B
9. B
10. A

Chapter 13
1. B
2. B
3. A
4. A
5. B
6. B
7. C
8. A
9. C
10. A
11. B

Chapter 14
1. C
2. C
3. B
4. A
5. C
6. C
7. B
8. D
9. B
10. C

Chapter 15
1. B
2. C
3. B
4. C
5. D
6. C
7. C
8. C
9. B
10. B

Chapter 16
1. B
2. B
3. B
4. A
5. A
6. C
7. B
8. D
9. A
10. C

Chapter 17
1. B
2. C
3. B
4. D
5. A
6. C
7. B
8. B
9. C
10. D

Chapter 18
1. B
2. D
3. A
4. D
5. D
6. B
7. B
8. D
9. A
10. B

Chapter 19
1. D
2. C
3. A
4. B
5. A
6. C
7. A
8. B
9. C
10. D

Chapter 20
1. B
2. C
3. D
4. B
5. B
6. D
7. C
8. D
9. D
10. C